Introduction to Sociology

Sixth Edition

To Sue, from George: With much love for enduring, mostly with her usual good humor intact, all the years I was often unavailable while writing this book

To mom, my best friend, from Michael: With much love for always believing in me and supporting me in all of my whirlwind adventures

Sara Miller McCune founded SAGE Publishing in 1965 to support the dissemination of usable knowledge and educate a global community. SAGE publishes more than 1000 journals and over 600 new books each year, spanning a wide range of subject areas. Our growing selection of library products includes archives, data, case studies and video. SAGE remains majority owned by our founder and after her lifetime will become owned by a charitable trust that secures the company's continued independence.

Los Angeles | London | New Delhi | Singapore | Washington DC | Melbourne

Introduction to Sociology

Sixth Edition

George Ritzer
University of Maryland

J. Michael Ryan
Pontificia Universidad Católica del Perú

FOR INFORMATION:

2455 Teller Road
Thousand Oaks, California 91320
E-mail: order@sagepub.com

1 Oliver's Yard
55 City Road
London EC1Y 1SP
United Kingdom

Unit No 323-333, Third Floor, F-Block
International Trade Tower
Nehru Place, New Delhi – 110 019
India

18 Cross Street #10-10/11/12
China Square Central
Singapore 048423

Acquisitions Editors: Erica DeLuca and Jeff Lasser
Content Development Editor: Cassie Carey
Production Editor: Veronica Stapleton Hooper
Copy Editor: Diana Breti
Typesetter: diacriTech
Cover Designer: Gail Buschman
Marketing Manager: Jennifer Haldeman

Copyright © 2024 by Sage.

All rights reserved. Except as permitted by U.S. copyright law, no part of this work may be reproduced or distributed in any form or by any means, or stored in a database or retrieval system, without permission in writing from the publisher.

All third party trademarks referenced or depicted herein are included solely for the purpose of illustration and are the property of their respective owners. Reference to these trademarks in no way indicates any relationship with, or endorsement by, the trademark owner.

Printed in the United States of America

Library of Congress Cataloging-in-Publication Data

Names: Ritzer, George, author. | Ryan, J. Michael, author.
Title: Introduction to sociology / George Ritzer, University of Maryland, J. Michael Ryan, Pontificia Universidad Católica del Perú.
Description: Sixth Edition. | Thousand Oaks, California : SAGE, [2024] | Revised edition of Introduction to sociology, [2020] | Includes bibliographical references and index.
Identifiers: LCCN 2023037100 (print) | LCCN 2023037101 (ebook) | ISBN 9781071875179 (paperback) | ISBN 9781071875162 (epub)
Subjects: LCSH: Sociology.
Classification: LCC HM585 .R568 2024 (print) | LCC HM585 (ebook) | DDC 301--dc23/eng/20230810
LC record available at https://lccn.loc.gov/2023037100
LC ebook record available at https://lccn.loc.gov/2023037101

This book is printed on acid-free paper.

23 24 25 26 27 10 9 8 7 6 5 4 3 2 1

BRIEF CONTENTS

Letter from the Authors — xix
Acknowledgments — xxi
About the Authors — xxiii

Chapter 1	An Introduction to Sociology in the Global Age	1
Chapter 2	Thinking Sociologically	31
Chapter 3	Researching the Social World	59
Chapter 4	Culture	91
Chapter 5	Socialization and Interaction	113
Chapter 6	Organizations, Societies, and Global Relationships	139
Chapter 7	Deviance and Crime	169
Chapter 8	Social Stratification	193
Chapter 9	Race and Ethnicity	223
Chapter 10	Genders and Sexualities	249
Chapter 11	Families	277
Chapter 12	Education and Religion	301
Chapter 13	Politics and the Economy	337
Chapter 14	The Body, Medicine, Health, and Health Care	363
Chapter 15	Population, Urbanization, and the Environment	391
Chapter 16	Social Change, Social Movements, and Collective Action	423

Glossary — 449
References — 461
Index — 501

DETAILED CONTENTS

Letter from the Authors	xix
Acknowledgments	xxi
About the Authors	xxiii

Chapter 1 An Introduction to Sociology in the Global Age — 1

Why Study Sociology?	2
What Is Sociology?	2
Becoming a Good Sociologist	5
Tips for Critical Thinking	9
The Sociological Imagination	9
The Micro–Macro Relationship	11
The Agency–Structure Relationship	12
The Social Construction of Reality	12
Understanding Social Constructionism	13
Social Structures and Processes	14
Sociology's Purpose: Science or Social Reform? Or Both?	15
Sociology, the Other Social Sciences, and Common Sense	15
Central Concerns for a Twenty-First-Century Sociology	17
Globalization	17
The COVID-19 Pandemic	20
Consumption	20
Critiquing Consumption	22
McDonaldization	23
The Digital World	25
Digital Living: Blogging and Tweeting about Sociology	27
Summary	28
Key Terms	28
Review Questions	29

Chapter 2 Thinking Sociologically — 31

How Do Theories Help Us Understand Politics and Other Social Institutions?	32
The Giants of Classical Sociological Theory	34
Early Sociological Theorists	34
Karl Marx	35
Max Weber	37
Émile Durkheim	38
Other Important Early Theorists	40
Georg Simmel	40
W. E. B. Du Bois	40
Thorstein Veblen	41
Contemporary Sociological Theory	42
Structural/Functional Theories	43
Structural-Functionalism	43
Structuralism	44

Conflict/Critical Theories	45
Conflict Theory	45
Critical Theory	46
Feminist Theory	47
Queer Theory	48
Critical Theories of Race and Racism	49
Postmodern Theory	50
Inter/Actionist Theories	52
Symbolic Interactionism	52
Ethnomethodology	53
Exchange Theory	54
Rational Choice Theory	54
Summary	55
Key Terms	56
Review Questions	56

Chapter 3 Researching the Social World — 59

Sociology as a Science	60
The Scientific Method	61
The Development of Scientific Knowledge	63
Sociological Research	65
Qualitative and Quantitative Research	66
Observational Research	67
Participant and Nonparticipant Observation	68
Ethnography	69
Netnography	70
Interviews	70
The Interview Process	72
Survey Research	73
Types of Surveys	73
Sampling	74
Experiments	75
Secondary Data Analysis	77
Historical-Comparative Method	79
Content Analysis	79
Issues in Social Research	80
Reliability and Validity	80
Research Ethics	80
Physical and Psychological Harm	81
Illegal Acts	83
The Violation of Trust	84
Informed Consent and Institutional Review Boards	85
Objectivity, or "Value-Free" Sociology	87
Summary	88
Key Terms	88
Review Questions	89

Chapter 4 Culture — 91

Culture and the COVID-19 Pandemic	92
Defining Culture	92
The Basic Elements of Culture	94
Values	94
Norms	95

Symbolic Culture and Language	97
Material Culture	99
Cultural Differences	**99**
Ideal and Real Culture	99
Ideology	100
Subcultures	100
Countercultures	101
Culture Jamming	102
Culture Wars	103
Multiculturalism and Assimilation	104
Cultural Relativism and Ethnocentrism	107
Global Culture	**107**
The Globalization of Values	107
Cultural Imperialism	108
Cyberculture	109
Digital Living: Netiquette	109
Summary	**110**
Key Terms	**110**
Review Questions	**110**

Chapter 5 Socialization and Interaction — 113

The Nature vs. Nurture Debate	**114**
The Individual and the Self	**115**
Symbolic Interaction and Development of the Self	115
Humans and Nonhumans	116
Symbolic Interaction	117
Mind and Self	117
The Generalized Other	118
The "I" and the "Me"	119
The Individual as Performer	**120**
Impression Management	120
Front and Back Stage	120
Socialization	**122**
Childhood Socialization	122
Family	122
Peers	123
Gender	124
Mass Media and New Media	125
Digital Living: Cyberbullying	126
Consumer Culture	126
Adult Socialization	127
Workplaces	127
Total Institutions	128
Other Aspects of Adult Socialization	128
Interaction	**129**
Superordinate–Subordinate Interactions	129
Reciprocity and Exchange	129
"Doing" Interaction	130
Interaction Order	131
Status and Role	131
Micro-Level Social Structures	**132**
Interpersonal Relationships	132
Social Networks	133
Groups	134

Types of Groups	134
Conformity to the Group	135
Summary	136
Key Terms	137
Review Questions	137

Chapter 6 Organizations, Societies, and Global Relationships — 139

Questioning Governmental Authority	140
Organizations	141
Bureaucracies	141
Authority Structures and Bureaucracy	143
Rationality and Irrationality	144
The Informal Organization	146
Contemporary Organizational Realities	147
Gender Inequalities	147
Racialized Organizations	148
Other Issues	150
Contemporary Changes	151
Globalization	153
McDonaldization and Bureaucratic Organizations	154
Network Organizations	155
Characteristics of the Network Organization	155
Informationalism	157
Societies	157
Global Relationships	159
Controlling Global Flows and Mobilities	160
Other Global Flows	161
Landscapes	161
Digital Living: Digital Currency	162
Global Barriers	163
Are Global Barriers Effective?	164
Organizational Barriers	164
More Open Organizations?	165
Summary	165
Key Terms	166
Review Questions	166

Chapter 7 Deviance and Crime — 169

Norms, Labels, and Judgment	170
Deviance	170
Shifting Definitions of Deviance	171
Deviance and Consumption	173
Deviance and Morality	174
Theories of Deviance	174
Structural/Functional Theories	175
Strain	175
Conflict/Critical Theories	177
Deviance and the Poor	177
Deviance and the Elite	177
Inter/Actionist Theories	179
Labeling	179
Primary and Secondary Deviance	180

Key Ideas in the Labeling Process	180
Moral Panics	180
Stigmas	181
Crime	182
The Criminal Justice System	183
Types of Crimes	185
Globalization and Crime	187
Global Crime Control	188
COVID-19, Deviance, and Crime	189
Summary	190
Key Terms	190
Review Questions	191

Chapter 8 Social Stratification — 193

Stratification and Life Saving Vaccines	194
Dimensions of Social Stratification	194
Social Class	195
Status	195
Power	195
Achievement and Ascription	196
Distribution of Rewards vs. Distribution of Opportunities for Rewards	197
Economic Inequality	198
Income Inequality	198
Digital Living: Income Inequality in the New Sharing Economy	199
Wealth Inequality	201
Growing Wealth Disparities	201
Status, Power, and Wealth	202
The Perpetuation of Wealth	203
The Decline of the Middle Class	203
Poverty	204
Analyzing Poverty	204
Poverty in the United States	205
The Feminization of Poverty	206
Social Mobility	208
Types of Social Mobility	208
Theories of Social Stratification	208
Structural/Functional Theories	209
Conflict/Critical Theories	209
Social Rewards and Status	209
Women and the Workplace	210
Inter/Actionist Theories	210
Global Stratification	211
The Global North and Global South	211
High-, Middle-, and Low-Income Countries	211
The Richest People in the World: The Global Concentration of Wealth	213
The Poorest People in the World: The Bottom Billion	213
Theories of Global Stratification	214
Structural/Functional Theories	214
Conflict/Critical Theories	214
Other Global Inequalities	215
The Global Digital Divide	215
Global Health Inequality	216
Global Gender Stratification	217

Inequality in Employment, Occupations, and Wealth	218
Women and Informal Employment	218
Women in Global Care Chains	219
Changing Positions in Global Stratification	219
Race to the Bottom	219
Foreign Aid and Development	220
Summary	221
Key Terms	222
Review Questions	222
Endnote	222

Chapter 9   Race and Ethnicity   223

Minorities Acquire Political Power	224
The Concepts of Race and Ethnicity	224
Historical Thinking about Race and Ethnicity	225
"Scientific" Explanations	225
Cultural Explanations	226
The Fluidity of Racial and Ethnic Categories	227
Measuring Race and Ethnicity	228
Majority–Minority Relations	230
Stereotypes, Prejudice, and Discrimination	230
Intersectionality	232
Patterns of Interaction	233
Racism	233
Foundations of Racism	234
Institutional Racism	236
The "Invisibility" of Institutional Racism	236
Race, Ethnicity, and COVID-19	237
Social Movements and Race	237
Hate Groups	237
The Civil Rights Movement	238
Collective Identity and "Power" Movements	239
Black Lives Matter Movement	240
Race and Ethnicity in a Global Context	240
Ethnic Identity and Globalization	241
Global Prejudice and Discrimination	241
Global Flows Based on Race and Ethnicity	242
Ethnic Conflict within Nation-States	243
Expulsion	244
Ethnic Cleansing	245
Genocide	245
Summary	246
Key Terms	247
Review Questions	247

Chapter 10   Genders and Sexualities   249

Challenging Gender Stereotypes	250
Sex and Gender	250
Femininities and Masculinities	251
Gender Diversity	253
Gendered Inequalities	254
Gender and Education	255
Gender, Work, and Family	258

Separate Spheres	258
Dual-Earner Households and the Stalled Revolution	259
Gender Inequality at Work	260
Gender and Consumer Culture	261
Consumption, Work, and Family	261
Women and Girls as Consumers	261
Men and Boys as Consumers	262
The Sociology of Sexualities	263
Sexual Selves	263
Sexual Identities and Orientations	263
Sexual Double Standards	264
Social Constraints on Sexuality	266
Culture and Consent	267
Sex and Consumption	268
Sexuality, Gender, and Globalization	269
Social Change and the Globalization of Sexuality	269
Global Flows Related to Sex and Sexuality	270
Lesbian, Gay, Bisexual, Transgender, and Queer Sexualities in a Global Context	270
The Global Sex Industry	270
Global Flows Related to Gender	271
The Feminization of Migration	272
The Feminization of Labor	272
The Feminization of Poverty and Female Proletarianization	273
Gender, War, and Violence	273
The Global Women's Movement	274
Summary	275
Key Terms	275
Review Questions	275

Chapter 11 Families — 277

Fictional Families Get Real	278
Family, Marriage, and Intimate Relationships	279
Marriage	279
Intimate Relationships	279
Love	280
Broad Changes in Marriage and the Family	280
Decline in Marriage	280
Perspectives on the Decline in Marriage	282
The Deinstitutionalization of Marriage	282
Pure Relationships	283
Digital Living: Online Dating	284
Nonfamily Households	284
Other Family Forms and Structures	285
Cohabitation	285
Living Apart Together	285
Arranged Marriages	286
Single-Parent Families	286
Nonresident Parents	286
Stepfamilies and Blended Families	287
Adoption	287
Same-Sex Families	287
Families of Choice	288

Theorizing the Family	288
Structural/Functional Theories	288
Conflict/Critical Theories	289
Feminist Theory	289
Inter/Actionist Theories	290
Symbolic Interactionism	290
Exchange Theory	290
Family Issues	290
Family Conflict	290
Abuse and Violence within the Family	290
Child Abuse	291
Intimate Partner Violence	291
Elder Abuse	292
Poverty and the Family	293
Gender Inequalities	293
Divorce	294
COVID-19 and the Family	296
Global Families	296
Global Flows That Involve the Family	297
Global Flows That Affect the Family	297
Global Economic Flows	298
Global Migration	298
Global Trafficking	298
Global Conflict	298
Summary	299
Key Terms	299
Review Questions	300

Chapter 12 Education and Religion — 301

Science versus Religion in the Public Schools	302
Education	302
Inequality in Education	303
Who Succeeds in School?	305
The Coleman Report: How Much Do Schools Matter?	305
Intelligence and School Success	306
Class Differences in Early Childhood	307
Preschool	308
Inequality within Schools: Tracking and Student Outcomes	309
Alternatives to Traditional Public Schools	309
Vouchers	310
Homeschooling	310
Charter Schools	311
Who Goes to College?	313
Education and the COVID-19 Pandemic	314
Learning Outcomes During the Pandemic	315
Pandemic Impact on Minority Students	316
Globalization and Education	317
PISA Rankings	317
German, Japanese, and U.S. Education Systems	317
Religion	320
Components of Religion	320
Belief	320
Ritual	320
Experience	322

Secularization	323
Civil Religion	324
Religion as a Form of Consumption	324
Digital Living: Practicing Virtual Faith	326
Types of Religious Institutions	326
Sects	327
Churches	327
Denominations	328
Cults and New Religious Movements	328
Religion and Globalization	329
The Most Prominent Global Religions	330
Judaism	330
Hinduism	331
Buddhism	331
Islam	332
Christianity	332
Mormonism	333
Fundamentalism	333
Faith on the Move	334
Summary	335
Key Terms	335
Review Questions	336

Chapter 13 Politics and the Economy — 337

The COVID-19 Pandemic and Politics and Economies	338
Politics: Democracy or Dictatorship	339
Democracy: Citizenship as a Radical Idea	339
Characteristics of Democracies	339
The Rise of Illiberal Democracy, or Is It Fascism?	340
Dictatorship: The Seizure of Power	341
Who Rules the World?	342
The Structural/Functional Perspective: Pluralism	342
The Conflict/Critical Perspective: The Power Elite	342
Global Politics	343
Geopolitics	344
The Nation and the Nation-State	344
The Economy: From Industrial to Postindustrial	345
The Industrial Revolution	345
From Fordism to Post-Fordism	346
Other Industrial Revolutions	346
Socialism, Communism, and Capitalism	346
Socialism and Communism	347
Welfare States	347
Capitalism	348
Deindustrialization	349
Factors in Deindustrialization	349
Decline of Labor Unions	350
The Postindustrial Society	351
Work, Consumption, and Leisure	352
Employment, Unemployment, and Underemployment	352
Consumption and Consumer Culture	354
Children in a Consumer Culture	354
Consumer Settings	355

Other Types of Consumer Settings	356
A Postconsumer Culture?	357
Leisure	357
Globalization and the Economy	358
Globalization and Consumption	359
Local and Regional Differences	359
Global Brands	360
Summary	361
Key Terms	361
Review Questions	361

Chapter 14 The Body, Medicine, Health, and Health Care — 363

The Opioid Crisis	364
The Sociology of Health	364
The Body	366
The Healthy Body: Lifestyle, Beauty, and Fitness	366
Beauty: Cultural Contexts	367
The Quest for the Ideal, the Consumption of Beauty, and the Fit Body	368
Fitness and the Healthy Body	369
Body Modifications	370
Risky Behavior	371
The Sociology of Medicine	373
The Medical Profession	373
Weaknesses in the U.S. Health Care System	375
Inequalities in U.S. Health Care	376
Health Care Reform in the United States	379
Consumerism and Health Care	379
The Internet and the Consumption of Health Care	380
Telemedicine	381
Globalization and Health	382
Growing Global Inequality	382
Disease	382
Malnutrition	383
Smoking	384
Borderless Diseases	384
HIV/AIDS	385
Superbugs	386
COVID-19	386
Globalization and Improvements in Health and Health Care	387
Summary	389
Key Terms	389
Review Questions	389

Chapter 15 Population, Urbanization, and the Environment — 391

The Paris Agreement	392
Population	392
Basic Population Processes	392
Fertility	393
Mortality	394
The Demographic Transition	396
Migration	397
Population Growth	401
Population Decline	402

Urbanization	403
Ever-Larger Urban Areas	403
Suburbanization	404
The Changing Nature of Major Cities	405
Cities and Globalization	406
Global Cities	406
Megacities (and Beyond)	407
The Center of Culture and Consumption	407
Digital Living: Smart Cities	408
The Environment	409
Perspectives on the Environment and Its Problems	409
Globalization and the Environment	410
The Leading Environmental Problems	411
Destruction of Natural Habitats	411
Adverse Effects on Marine Life	412
The Decline in Fresh Water	412
Global Warming	413
Global Responses	416
Environmental Activism	416
Sustainable Development	418
Technological Fixes	419
COVID-19 and the Environment	419
Summary	420
Key Terms	420
Review Questions	420

Chapter 16   Social Change, Social Movements, and Collective Action   423

Workers' Rights, Consumer Activism, and Social Change	424
Social Movements	425
The Civil Rights Movement	425
Feminist Movements	426
The Women's Movement in the United States	427
The Global Women's Movement	430
Digital Living: #MeToo Movement	430
LGBTQ Movements	431
World War II and the Lavender Scare	431
The U.S.-Based Homophile Movement	432
Stonewall	432
Lesbian Herstory	433
HIV/AIDS, ACT UP, and Queer Nation	433
The Ongoing Fight for Marriage Equality	433
Trans Rights	434
COVID-19 and Social Movements	434
Emergence, Mobilization, and Impact of Social Movements	435
Factors in the Emergence of a Social Movement	435
Resources and Mobilization of Social Movements	436
Participation	436
Goals, Strategies, and Tactics	436
Factors in Success	437
The Impact of Social Movements	438
The Internet, Globalization, and Social Movements	438

Collective Action		439
Crowds		439
Riots		440
Negative Views of Riots		440
Disasters		440
Human Involvement in Disasters		441
The Effects of Disasters		442
Social Change: Globalization and the Internet		442
Globalization as Social Change		443
Global "Liquids"		443
Global "Flows"		443
Globalization and the Internet		444
Cyberactivism		445
Summary		446
Key Terms		446
Review Questions		446
Endnote		447

Glossary   449

References   461

Index   501

LETTER FROM THE AUTHORS

An Introduction to Learning Sociology in the Twenty-First Century (and to Our Textbook)

This edition of *Introduction to Sociology* brings on a new co-author. The relationship between George Ritzer and J. Michael Ryan goes back more than two decades. In this letter, the two authors talk more about their relationship, how they came to work together on this text, and hopefully, to inspire students to see how sociology, and sociologists, work "behind the scenes."

George:

"Michael was first a student in one of my classes at the University of Maryland. He went on to take every class I offered, and even co-taught a class with me. He also became a research assistant serving as managing editor of a scholarly journal I edited, the *Journal of Consumer Culture*. Michael also contributed several updates to another book of mine, *The McDonaldization of Society*, and will be co-author on future editions. Most recently, he has been my co-editor (also with Chris Rojek) on *The Wiley-Blackwell Encyclopedia of Sociology*, 2nd edition (the largest major reference work in the field today). In between all of that, we have published several academic articles together, had a few quarrels, and more than a few laughs. Michael has emerged as a leading global scholar in his own right, providing fresh perspectives on many of the classical issues I write about. Significantly, he has held academic positions across five continents. In a world where understanding the importance of globalization has perhaps never been so important, this standpoint has served to significantly enhance this edition."

Michael:

"It goes without saying that George is one of the leading sociologists in the world today. His contributions to the discipline have spanned nearly five decades and have had a significant influence within the discipline of sociology, as well as beyond it. One of the many strengths of this new edition is that it represents a more rounded vision of sociology. Despite being frequent collaborators, we often have very different perspectives and, while frequently overlapping, our individual areas of expertise are often quite different. George, for example, is an expert in theory, consumption, and globalization, while my scholarly work focuses more on genders and sexualities, the COVID-19 pandemic and health issues, and social inequalities. As we think you will find in this textbook, these "differences" are, in fact, interdependent and complementary."

Both:

"Sociology is more than just a major; it can also become a way of life. That is certainly the case for us. Sociology is about facts. And about opinions. And about trends. And about each of us, our families and friends, social networks, and the worlds in which we live. In sum, sociology is about how all of these things blend together and allow us to develop a social scientific understanding of our contemporary world and our own individual places within it.

"This textbook is not intended to persuade but, rather, to inform. Like the societies we live in, it is made stronger by complementary knowledges. We present it to readers as a living testament to the idea that society can be rooted in differences (a growing reality, especially in recent years) yet still grow through mutual understandings based in science, reason, and the many tools that the exciting field of sociology can provide."

"We do believe that, though imperfect, our text represents the most comprehensive, academic base for gaining an introduction into the exciting field of sociology in the world today. We hope that you will feel the same."

"Welcome to sociology!"

George Ritzer, Distinguished University Professor Emeritus, University of Maryland, USA
J. Michael Ryan, Associate Professor of Sociology, Pontificia Universidad Católica del Perú

ACKNOWLEDGMENTS

George: I need to begin with my friends for decades, and coauthors of a previous introductory textbook, Kenneth C. W. Kammeyer and Norman R. Yetman. That book went through seven editions, the last of which was published in 1997. It was most useful to me in this text in helping define various sociological concepts that have changed little over the years. I have also been able to build on discussions of many issues covered in that text. However, because of the passage of nearly three decades in sociology and in the social world (an eternity in both), as well as the innumerable changes in them, this text has little in common with the earlier one. Nonetheless, my perspective on sociology was strongly shaped by that book and the many insights and ideas provided by my friends and coauthors before, during, and in the many years after the writing of that book.

Professor Rebecca Plante played a key role in the second edition of this book. She offered useful comments and suggestions throughout, and she was especially central in the revision of Chapter 10, on gender and sexuality. These are her areas of expertise, and the chapter is much improved because of her contributions to it. I would also like to thank Professor Paul Dean, coauthor of the second edition of my book *Globalization: A Basic Text*, for his numerous and important contributions to Chapter 8, on social stratification.

Thanks also to P. J. Rey, William Yagatich, Jillet Sam, Zeynep Tufekci, and Margaret Austin Smith for their contributions. Also to be thanked for writing first drafts of parts of earlier versions of chapters are Professors William Carbonaro (Chapter 12, on education), Deric Shannon (Chapter 13, on politics), and Lester Kurtz (Chapter 12, on religion). Professor Peter Kivisto made particularly important and numerous contributions to the second edition of this book. I'm especially thankful for his work on the religion and education chapters.

At SAGE Publications, I am especially grateful for Senior Vice President Michele Sordi's confidence in, and support for, the project. She agreed from the beginning to do and spend whatever was necessary to make this a first-class introductory sociology text. As you can see from the finished project, she was true to her word. Michele also worked closely with me in an editorial capacity on the first edition to help get the project through some of its most difficult periods. Michele was a positive force and upbeat presence throughout the writing of this book, and I am deeply grateful for who she is and what she has done. Late in the process Brenda Carter took over Michele's role and performed it with the same level of expertise, good humor, and good sense (plus she got me prime seats to a game in New York involving my beloved Yankees). Jeff Lasser came on board at SAGE as sociology publisher during production of the first edition, in which he played a key role, and he has played a much more important role in subsequent editions. Jeff has proven to be not only easy to work with but a sage (pun intended) adviser on many aspects of the book and its publication. Unfortunately, he is a Boston Red Sox fan, but nobody is perfect.

Michael: I first want to thank George for bringing me on to this project. Sociology is my passion, and teaching it even more so, so the opportunity to work on an introductory textbook helped fulfill a longtime dream of mine. I also never (or at least rarely) turn down an opportunity to work with George.

We (George and myself) also want to thank Kimberly Krane for her great work on helping to update figures and tables throughout this edition. Cassie Carey of Graphic World and Veronica Stapleton Hooper of SAGE were both instrumental in helping with production issues. Diana Breti was a brilliant copy editor who also went far above and beyond to provide a number of very useful content suggestions. Her insights were truly appreciated. Last, but certainly not least, I also want to thank Jeff Lasser. His patience, insights, and invaluable expertise have been the oil that has kept this machine running smoothly.

PUBLISHER'S ACKNOWLEDGMENTS

SAGE wishes to acknowledge the valuable contributions of the following reviewers who assisted us in preparing the Sixth Edition:

Billy Brocato, University of Maryland, Eastern Shore
Cecilia Casarotti, Hillsborough College
Jessica Anna Cebulak, Kent State University
Kristen Connolly, SUNY Buffalo
Kevin Early, University of Michigan, Dearborn
Donna Miller, University of Texas–San Antonio
Lori Park-Smith, Ridgewater College
Julie Pelton, University of Nebraska-Omaha
Laurie Wood, Vanderbilt University

ABOUT THE AUTHORS

George Ritzer

George Ritzer is Distinguished University Professor Emeritus at the University of Maryland. Among his awards are an honorary doctorate from La Trobe University, Melbourne, Australia; honorary patron, University Philosophical Society, Trinity College, Dublin; American Sociological Association's Distinguished Contribution to Teaching Award; and being named the Eastern Sociological Society's Robin Williams Lecturer. He has chaired four sections of the American Sociological Association: Theoretical Sociology, Organizations and Occupations, Global and Transnational Sociology, and the History of Sociology. In the application of social theory to the social world, his books include *The McDonaldization of Society* (10th ed., 2020; 11th ed., forthcoming with J. Michael Ryan), *Enchanting a Disenchanted World* (3rd ed., 2010), and *The Globalization of Nothing* (2nd ed., 2007). He is the author of *Globalization: A Basic Text* (2010; 2nd ed., 2015, with Paul Dean). He edited *The Wiley-Blackwell Companion to Sociology* (2012) and *The Blackwell Companion to Globalization* (2008) and co-edited (with Jeff Stepnisky) *The Wiley-Blackwell Companions to Classical and Contemporary Major Social Theorists* (2012) and the *Handbook of Social Theory* (2001). He was founding editor of the *Journal of Consumer Culture*. He also edited the 11-volume *Encyclopedia of Sociology* (2007; 2nd ed., forthcoming, with Chris Rojek and J. Michael Ryan), the five-volume *Encyclopedia of Globalization* (2012), and the two-volume *Encyclopedia of Social Theory* (2005). His books have been translated into more than 20 languages, with more than 15 translations of *The McDonaldization of Society* alone. In a 2019 article in the *Journal of Consumer Culture* (coauthored with Steve Miles), "The Changing Nature of Consumption and the Intensification of McDonaldization in the Digital Age," Ritzer deals with at least three of the distinctive concerns (consumption, the digital world, and McDonaldization) in *Introduction to Sociology*, 6th edition.

J. Michael Ryan

J. Michael Ryan is professor-researcher (docente-investigador) at Pontificia Universidad Católica del Perú. After receiving his PhD in sociology from the University of Maryland (where he worked closely with Ritzer), he has gone on to become an award-winning teacher who has held academic positions across five continents. He was previously an associate professor of sociology at Nazarbayev University (Kazakhstan), a researcher for the TransRights Project at The University of Lisbon (Portugal) and has taught courses at The American University in Cairo (Egypt), Facultad Latinoamericana de Ciencias Sociales (FLACSO; Ecuador) and the University of Maryland (USA). Before returning to academia, Michael worked as a research methodologist at the National Center for Health Statistics (which is part of the Centers for Disease Control and Prevention) in Washington, D.C., where he led multiple projects aimed at improving national statistical survey methodology. In addition to this textbook, Michael

will be co-authoring (with Ritzer) the next editions of *The McDonaldization of Society* and also (with Ritzer and Chris Rojek) *The Wiley-Blackwell Encyclopedia of Sociology*, 2nd edition. He is also the co-author (with Serena Nanda) of *COVID-19: Social Inequalities and Human Possibilities* (2022). Michael has edited or co-edited more than 15 volumes, including *The Wiley-Blackwell Encyclopedia of Health, Illness, Behavior, and Society*, 2nd edition (with William Cockerham et. al., forthcoming); *Pandemic Pedagogies: Teaching and Learning during the COVID-19 Pandemic* (2023); *COVID-19: Global Pandemic, Societal Responses, Ideological Solutions* (2021); *COVID-19: Social Consequences and Cultural Adaptations* (2021); *Trans Lives in a Globalizing World: Rights, Identities, and Politics* (2020); *Gender in the Middle East and North Africa: Contemporary Issues and Challenges* (with Helen Rizzo; 2020); *Essential Concepts in Sociology* (2019); and *The Wiley-Blackwell Encyclopedia of Social Theory* (with Bryan Turner et al., 2017). He has also served as advisory editor on *The Wiley-Blackwell Encyclopedia of Gender and Sexuality Studies* and is the founding editor of Routledge's *The COVID-19 Pandemic* series.

Future Publishing/Getty Images

1 AN INTRODUCTION TO SOCIOLOGY IN THE GLOBAL AGE

> **LEARNING OBJECTIVES**
>
> **1.1** Identify the purpose of sociology.
>
> **1.2** Discuss ways to become a good sociologist.
>
> **1.3** Describe how sociologists understand continuity and change, particularly in the context of the sociological imagination and the social construction of reality.
>
> **1.4** Evaluate how sociology relates to other social sciences and how sociological knowledge differs from common sense.
>
> **1.5** Explain why sociologists today focus on globalization, consumption, McDonaldization, and the digital world.

WHY STUDY SOCIOLOGY?

Ask yourself the following questions:

- How do we know social rules? And why do we know (or not) when we have broken them?
- Why are certain identities praised while others are treated so poorly?
- How are race and ethnicity understood, and understood differently, in different societies?
- What does it mean when we say that gender and sexuality are social constructs?
- What does the institution of religion mean for society?
- How does the educational level of our parents impact our own socialization into the world?
- How do medical issues intersect with social issues, especially during the age of COVID-19?
- How does what we buy shape how others see us?
- Does capitalism really work better than socialism or communism?
- What is the relationship between media and politics?
- Why is Taylor Swift so popular around the world?
- Why are so many people poor and so few people rich?
- What have the last several years of the global COVID-19 pandemic meant for how we understand our social world?

Sociology can help us answer all of these questions, and more! Sociology can help us better understand the world around us, how it works, why it works that way, and even to better understand who we are and why we think the way we do, act the way we do, and live the way we do. This textbook will help you better understand sociology, the world around you, and also, hopefully, yourself.

WHAT IS SOCIOLOGY?

Sociology can be defined as the systematic study of the ways in which people are affected by and affect the social structures and social processes associated with the groups, organizations, cultures, societies, and world in which they exist. If that definition sounds a bit complicated for now, don't worry. In this textbook we will be exploring what all of those concepts mean.

One of the most important lessons you will learn in your study of sociology is that what you think and do as an individual is affected by what is happening in groups, organizations, cultures, societies, and the world. This is especially true of social changes, even those that are global in scope and seem at first glance to be remote from you. At the same time, you are not only affected by larger events but also capable, to some degree, of having an impact on large-scale structures and processes. This is an example of the **butterfly effect** (Lorenz 1995). Although this concept is generally applied to physical phenomena, it also applies to social phenomena. The idea is that a relatively small change in a specific location can have far-ranging, even global, effects over both time and distance. For example, when countries change their trade or labor policies, it can be a trigger for corporations to move in, or out, of those countries. This can affect employment opportunities in both the receiving and the host country. Wars, invasions, and civil conflict can also spark global impacts. For example, Russia's invasion of Ukraine has led to a change in energy and food prices in many countries. It has also impacted the way resources have been distributed within countries, most notably political attention and military funding. Celebrities and influencers also exert a great deal of power. For example, when Oprah recommends a book it tends to become an overnight best seller, and when videos go viral on social media, especially TikTok, it can lead to changes in fashion, behavior, and even eating habits by individuals around the world. Perhaps the trajectory of your own life and career will be affected by one of these examples. More important, it is very possible that actions you take in your lifetime will have wide-ranging, perhaps global, effects.

Will our highways be safer and injury rates lower because of the sensors in self-driving cars like this one? Or will we have more air pollution and therefore more illness because there will be so many self-driving cars on the road? Sociologists assess the so-called butterfly effects of changes like driverless cars.

ROSLAN RAHMAN/AFP/Getty Images

Sociology certainly deals with contemporary phenomena, but its deep historical roots have led to many longer-term interests. In the fourteenth century, the Muslim scholar Abdel Rahman Ibn Khaldun studied various social relationships, including those between politics and economics. He was arguably one of the world's first widely influential sociologists. Of special importance to the founding of sociology as a formal academic discipline was the eighteenth- and nineteenth-century Industrial Revolution. During this industrial age, many early sociologists concentrated on factories, the production that took place in those settings, and those who worked there, especially blue-collar, manual-labor workers. Sociologists also came to focus on the relationship between industry and the rest of society, including, for example, the state and the family.

By the middle of the twentieth century, manufacturing in the United States and many other countries was in the early stages of a long decline that continues to this day. (However, manufacturing in other parts of the world, most notably in China, is booming.) Those countries had moved from the industrial age to the "postindustrial age" (Bell 1973; Leicht and Fitzgerald 2006). In the United States, as well as in the Western world more generally, the center of the economy and the attention of many sociologists shifted from the factory to the office. That is, the focus moved from blue-collar, manual-labor work to white-collar office work (Mills 1951) as well as to the bureaucracies in which many people worked (Clegg and Lounsbury 2009; Weber [1921] 1968). Another change in the postindustrial age was the growth of the service sector of the economy, involving everyone from high-status service providers such as physicians and lawyers to lower-status workers behind the counters of fast-food restaurants and now those who drive for Uber or Lyft.

The more recent rise of the "information age" (Castells 2010; Kline 2015) can be seen as a part, or an extension, of the postindustrial age. Knowledge and information are critical in today's world. So, too, are the technologies—computers, smartphones, the internet—that have greatly increased the productivity of individual workers and altered the nature of their work. Rather than designers drawing designs by hand, computer-assisted technologies are now used to create designs for everything from electric power grids to patterned fabrics. The widespread use of smartphones has enabled, among many other things, the rise of companies such as Uber and Lyft, the success of which is threatening the rental car industry and especially the taxicab industry and the livelihoods of many taxi drivers (who are also threatened by driverless cars). Some of the drivers work a few hours a day for these services in search of a little extra money, while others work full-time for the services. Their willingness to do this work has reduced the need for taxicabs and full-time taxi drivers.

More generally, less and less work occurs in the office because the computer and the internet now allow many people, at least those with access to such technologies, to work from anywhere. The COVID-19 pandemic has greatly accelerated this trend (Ryan and Nanda 2023c). Many are also increasingly part of the "gig economy" meaning that they are temporary workers handling a number of short-term jobs ("gigs") rather than working fulltime for an organization.

However, it is not just work that has been affected by new technologies. Uber is part of the growing "sharing economy" (Sundararajan 2016), in which people share (for a fee) many things; most notably, some share their homes through websites such as Airbnb.com. One key component of this new technological world, Google, is so powerful that a 2011 book is titled *The Googlization of Everything* (Vaidhyanathan 2011). Thus, much sociological attention has shifted to computers and the internet, including social media, as well as those who work with them (Lynch 2016; Scholz 2013).

From his home in Israel, this wine expert is giving a presentation on the Israeli wine industry to a group of British journalists via Zoom. In the information age, much work can be performed anywhere, using a computer and the internet.

David Silverman/Getty Images

The transition from the industrial to the postindustrial and now to the information age has important personal implications. Had you been a man who lived in the industrial age, you would have worked (if you could find a job) for money (pay). You would have done so to be able to buy what you needed and wanted. Women working in the private sphere were largely uncompensated or compensated at a lower rate, as is often still the case. However, in the postindustrial age, it is increasingly likely that nearly all people will be willing, or forced, to work part time or even for free (Anderson 2009; Dusi 2017; Ritzer and Jurgenson 2010), as in the case of many interns, bloggers, and contributors to YouTube, TikTok, and Wikipedia.

You may be willing to perform free labor because you enjoy it and because much of what is important in your life is, in any case, available for free on the internet. There is no need for you to buy newspapers when blogs are free. Similarly, there is no need buy CDs when music is streamed free on various internet sites or inexpensively by Spotify. Why buy or rent DVDs when movies can be downloaded, or viewed, at no cost or inexpensively from the internet (from Netflix, for example)? However, although all of this, and much else, is available for free (or at very low cost), the problem is that the essentials of life—food, shelter, clothing—still cost money, lots of money.

Many hope that the labor they currently perform for free will eventually have an economic payoff. One person (known as PewDiePie) played video games on YouTube. By early 2023, he had garnered more than 110 million subscribers and 29 billion views. He has earned millions of dollars for essentially just playing video games. In fact, playing video games has become big business—one tournament drew 11,000 fans to a stadium and offered $11 million in prize money. Many hope that their work as bloggers or on YouTube will lead to full-time jobs, although that happens for very, very few.

These are a few of the many social changes to be discussed in this book. The essential point is that the social world (people, groups, organizations, and so on)—*your* social world—is continually changing. Sociology is a field that is, and must be, constantly attuned to and involved in studying those changes.

BECOMING A GOOD SOCIOLOGIST

A common complaint of many sociologists is that everyone thinks they are a sociologist. To some extent, that is true. Everyone is capable of observing the social world around them and analyzing it. That said, studying sociology is about gaining certain knowledge (as you will do in this book) and, most important, about gaining certain skills in observation and analysis of the social world. A **professional sociologist** is someone who has a deep body of knowledge about the social world and a refined skill set to better analyze that world. This text will be an introduction to helping you start building that knowledge and developing those skills.

It is important to understand the difference between a fact and an opinion. A **fact** is a piece of knowledge about the world that can be proven by scientific methods. For example, that the earth is round is a scientific fact. An **opinion** is a perspective of a particular individual or group that is based on feelings or beliefs with or without any scientific evidence to support it. For example, that Taylor Swift is the greatest singer of all time is an opinion. Opinions make for interesting conversations on a first date or at a party but do little to help us understand how the world "really" is. And here enters sociology.

Sociologists all have opinions. We are, after all, also people and have our own individual set of experiences, beliefs, and individual viewpoints. That said, a professional sociologist attempts to put those personalized individual things aside in order to better understand how *society* works. There are more than 8 billion human beings on the planet, with an incredible variety of languages, religions, politics, and beliefs. Sociologists value each of those individuals, but they are most interested in the society, that is, the broader collective of individuals and how they relate to one another.

Sociologists also understand that facts can change. An immediate question, then, should be how can something that is scientifically proven change? The simple answer is that as our means of better understanding the world improve, so can, and likely will, what we know about. For example, during most of recorded human history it was considered a fact that the earth is flat. There was no way to conceive of it being a big sphere (wouldn't we all fall off?). But as scientific methods improved, we came to understand that the world is, in fact, round. Many things that human beings have long assumed to be facts have been altered as knowledge improves. For example, the invention of the microscope allowed us to see viruses and bacteria, a discovery that radically changed how we think about our bodies and our health and revolutionized the field of medicine.

Sociologists face a particular challenge in that the social world, unlike the physical universe, does not really operate on "facts." We cannot invent a device that can prove that capitalism is better or worse than socialism. There is no machine that can show us which political system is best. There is no one "right" answer to questions of abortion, gun control, or immigration. Instead, sociologists rely on using scientific methods to collect evidence about the social world to arrive at conclusions that are scientifically informed. For example, a sociologist could look at rates of gun ownership in a given country and compare them to homicide rates, suicide rates, and gun deaths caused by accident. They could then compare those rates between different countries and come to reasonable conclusions about the impact of gun ownership on number of deaths caused by guns. Further, they could then examine different social and cultural phenomena that might help to explain expected (and even *un*expected) differences in rates.

One major challenge for a sociologist is finding ways to provide evidence that do not rely on personal opinions or beliefs. A good sociologist wants to understand the social world, not just their own personal world. The word "sociology," after all, has its roots in the word "social." One way to do this is to work to overcome limitations of everyday thinking, to find ways to not let our personal beliefs influence our findings and observations. Below are some common limitations of everyday thinking and some strategies to overcome them.

- *Relying on "common sense."* We have probably all questioned something that we didn't understand and been told that the answer is just "common sense." For example, that you are supposed to act in a certain way, or go to college to "get ahead," or sleep at certain hours are all considered "common sense." But what exactly does that mean? Who's sense is it that gets made "common"? A sociologist seeks to question "common sense" and understand if there is any evidence to support it. For example, is college really the best way to "get ahead"? Well, evidence shows that salaries do, in fact, increase up to the level of having a master's degree and then they commonly decline after getting a PhD. Why? Again, evidence suggests that many MAs work in the private sector (which is generally better paid), but many PhDs work in the academic sector (which is relatively poorer paid in terms of education level required to get the job). We also see that many of the world's richest people, like Bill Gates or Mark Zuckerberg, never graduated from college. And many people who have graduated from college are very poor. Why is this the case if "common sense" tells us that education is the best way to "get ahead"? A sociologists will seek out evidence, including why there are exceptions to that evidence (like Gates or Zuckerberg), to better understand the value of education as it relates to economic prosperity. In this way, evidence can be used to better understand why a certain idea is considered "common sense," but also to provide nuance to it.

- *Assuming "our" world is "the" world.* We all live in bubbles. We cannot be in all places with all people at all times. And so, generally speaking, we tend to live in bubbles of people like ourselves. We likely live in neighborhoods with people who are close to us in terms of how much money they have. We probably have friends with similar education levels (it is likely that many of your friends are also students). We are likely to more frequently associate with people of the same religion and, often, political beliefs. That said, the way we live, however that is, is not the way most people live. More important, we are rarely exposed in any meaningful way to people who do not live the way we do. Most college students spend most of their time around professors and other college students, and most (statistically speaking) have parents who also went to college. They might, therefore, assume that most people go to college or have college degrees. Yet only about 7 percent of the world's population has a college degree. Our personal experience, whatever that is, is not usually the "reality" for most people. That said, a sociologist does not discount personal experience, but rather seeks to collect a lot of personal experiences to get a better understanding of the *social* (there's that word again!) experience.

- *Believing that the way things are now is the way they always have been, and always will be.* We often assume that the world has always been the way it is now. It might be difficult for many college students to imagine that their professors most likely spent their childhoods without the internet, or even a computer. There was no widespread social media in the twentieth century. Most people in their 40s have listened to cassette tapes, watched VHS tapes, and used a card catalogue at the library. We can go back even further (but not by much) to say that if you had been born 100 years earlier, you would not have had a television in your house (such a thing didn't exist). You would not have been able to fly anywhere (there were no commercial planes). You couldn't have taken an antibiotic (also not invented yet). And nearly 20 percent of all the earth's land would have been controlled by Great Britain. That's a lot of change in a short period of time! And although 100 years might sound like a long time, your parents knew people who were alive then.

  We can safely say that society is changing, as it always has. Some even argue that society is changing faster now than ever and that changes are happening at speeds that we can barely keep up with. The internet revolution has certainly transformed society in ways that we still do not understand. As has air travel. As have antibiotics. As have light bulbs (which are not even 150 years old yet). The world changes.

  On the other side, some scientists believe that the first person who will live to be 200 years old has already been born. It is likely that many of you will live to see human beings on Mars, while many of your grandparents remember when we first landed on the moon. The world has changed. It is changing. And it will continue to change. We cannot assume that the way things are is the way they always have been, or always will be. A good sociologist will understand that and seek to understand why these changes are happening, and, more important, what they mean for society.

- *Accepting authority without question.* Most of us are taught from a young age to accept what we are told and not to ask too many questions. We are told that our parents, our religious leaders, our political leaders, even our professors should never be questioned. Such unconditional acceptance of what authority figures say limits our ability to better understand the world around us. And for every authority figure you find who says one thing, you can certainly find many more who will say something completely different. So what is a person to do?

Many of us live in our own "bubbles," and associate frequently with people who share similar backgrounds, beliefs, and life experiences. Thinking sociologically requires that we look beyond personal experience to gain a broader understanding of the larger social world.

Julian J Rossig/ iStock Photos

It is important to emphasize that sociology does not teach that we should always question every single thing that we are told by every single person who tells it to us, or to assume that everyone is lying or trying to manipulate us. This is not what sociology is about. It is, however, about learning skills to be able to critically think for ourselves and to evaluate evidence (including what others claim to be "true" or "common sense"). It is unlikely that your parents are purposefully lying to you. Or that your college professor is trying to teach you to think in only one certain way. That said, a good sociologist will question what gives someone the authority to speak and, more important, to be able to evaluate for themselves whether what they are being told is based in evidence or reason. Sociology is not about indoctrination. It is about learning critical thinking skills. If you are expected to believe something, then there should be evidence to do so. Otherwise, why believe one thing and not another?

- *Biased and selective observation.* The internet can be a valuable tool to help us do research. It is a great, fast, way to help us find information. That said, the internet is uncontrolled and full of as much bad information as it is good (probably more!). Whatever answer you want to find, you can certainly find on the internet. There are a number of websites that will tell you that the earth is flat. There are perhaps just as many that will tell you that COVID-19 is a hoax. Neither of these things is true according to the material world in which we all live. So with all of the information out there, how can we know what is true?

  We need to be able to develop our own critical thinking skills and to rely on evidence rather than opinion. To paraphrase a popular saying, when someone has a hammer, the world looks full of nails. In other words, we often find the answers that we are looking for because we lack the skills to differentiate between what is "good" information (i.e., based in science and reason) and what is "bad" information (i.e., based in opinion, bias, or discrimination). Sociology can help you learn how to become less biased and better observers.

- *Thinking in definitive terms.* We have a tendency in everyday thinking and conversation to use words like "never" and "always," or "of course," "proves," and "should." Sociologists generally try to avoid these kinds of terms as there are few things that fit those categories. For example, there are few things that never happen (people still die of the Black Plague every year!) or that always happen (not even taxes!). It is also difficult to prove that anything happens 100 percent of the time for 100 percent of people in 100 percent of places (the social sciences, like sociology, work different than the physical sciences, like physics—more on that below). We should also avoid using terms like "of course." That implies that something is understood to be the same for all people in all places under all circumstances and, again, that rarely happens. We might say that "of course" some people will be poor while others are rich, and yet we have bountiful examples of when that hasn't been the case and no reason to assume that it has to be that way or that it always will be. Similarly, the word "should" implies a moral judgment. That one has the right, and only, answer. Sociologists generally try to avoid making such moral judgments (although that is debated among sociologists, as we will see) or implying that one person knows what is best for everyone else.

  Instead, as good sociologists, we can use the following:
  - Instead of "never" or "always," try using "under these circumstances."
  - Instead of "proves," try using "suggests" or "indicates."
  - Instead of "should," try using "could."
  - Instead of "all" or "every," try using "most" or "a majority."
  - Instead of "of course," try using "according to" or "as evidence suggests."

  The above said, there will be times when definitive terms are perhaps the most appropriate. For example, it is true (at least for now) that human beings "always" die. The question for sociologists in that case isn't so much the "always" as the why, when, how, and especially the inequalities in those answers.

Tips for Critical Thinking

One of the most important skills of becoming a good sociologist is to fine tune our critical thinking skills. We have already outlined several ways that we can improve our critical thinking skills, but let's add a couple of more to the list:

- *Don't assume; ask questions!* The task of any scientist, including a social scientist like a sociologist, is to investigate the world. Rather than make assumptions about how the world operates, we want to rely on observation, evidence, and analysis. In order to do that, a good sociologist will find as much joy in questions as they do in answers.

- *Be prepared to be wrong and to have your understanding of the world, and yourself, challenged.* The main point of education is to learn. The reason we seek to learn is so that we know more. Nobody knows everything but by educating ourselves we can start to learn more than we did. In order to learn, however, we must be prepared to have been wrong about what we thought we already knew. For example, many children around the world are taught that there is a fairy princess who will collect our teeth when they fall out and exchange them for money or gifts. The "tooth fairy" is a common mythology in many societies. As we grow older, we learn that such a person does not exist. As adults, we must be open to having our beliefs challenged in a similar kind of way. It can be quite challenging to have our assumptions and beliefs about the world questioned. At the same time, it can also be quite liberating as it allows us to think in different ways, and, perhaps more important, to better understand why we think the way we do.

- *Question the "ordinary."* Some of the most profound sociological insights have come from questioning, or examining, everyday situations. For example, great sociological insights have been gained by carefully analyzing such everyday events as conversations between friends at dinner or even just riding an elevator. By questioning everyday interactions, we can learn more about why they are considered so ordinary.

- *Ask questions!* This repeats the first point, but is worth repeating. Ask questions! As sociologists, it is our job to try to better understand the world around us. In order to better understand something, we first need to question it. If someone tells you something but cannot tell you why what they told you is "true," then you should begin to question that. We can also question why certain reasons are given, if there are motivations of the person telling us things to do so, and to think outside the box about the way the world could be (and whether we even want it to be that way).

The Sociological Imagination

The systematic study of the social world has always required imagination on the part of sociologists. There are various ways to look at the social world. For example, instead of looking at the world from the point of view of an insider, one can, at least psychologically, place oneself outside that world. The political (and sometimes even physical) attacks against immigrants might make sense to some, but if you imagine yourself in the place of an innocent child whose parents brought them to a different country seeking a better life, you might see things differently. As another example, the sanctions being placed against Russia as a country might make sense from a global state perspective, but it is having horrendous impacts on innocent Russians, many of whom are also opposed to the invasion of Ukraine, but who are nonetheless being cut off from many essential supplies because of global sanctions.

The phenomenon of being able to look at the social world from different, imaginative perspectives attracted the attention of the famous sociologist C. Wright Mills, who in 1959 wrote a very important book titled *The Sociological Imagination*. He argued that sociologists have a unique perspective—the **sociological imagination**—that gives them a distinctive way of looking at data or reflecting on the world around them (Selwyn 2015).

The sociological imagination may be most useful in helping sociologists see the linkage between private troubles and public issues. For example, ADHD—attention-deficit/hyperactivity disorder—can easily be seen as a private trouble. For years there was little public awareness of ADHD, and those who had it were likely to suffer alone. But since the 1980s, it has become clear that ADHD is also a public issue, and it is becoming an increasingly important one in many societies. It is clear that many people suffer from ADHD: The number of children in the United States alone ages 3 to 17 ever diagnosed with ADHD increased from 4.4 million in 2003 to more than 6 million in 2019 (Centers for Disease Control and Prevention [CDC] 2022), which creates a number of larger issues for schools, employers, and society as a whole. The fact that it has become a public issue may make ADHD less of a private trouble for some, as there is now greater public understanding of the problem and many more support groups are available.

Another example of the relationship between private troubles and public issues relates to the fact that women are more likely than men to be concentrated in lower-paying jobs (see Figure 1.1; Field 2018). For example, women are much more likely to be comparatively poorly paid dental hygienists than dentists or legal assistants rather than lawyers. Being limited occupationally creates personal troubles for many women, such as inadequate income and job dissatisfaction. This is also a public issue, not only because the discrepancy between the genders is unfair to women as a whole but also because society is not benefiting from the many contributions women could be making.

C. Wright Mills (1916–1962) was a prominent post–World War II sociologist who urged the use of the "sociological imagination" to study issues of concern to sociology . . . and to you.

Archive Photos/Getty Images

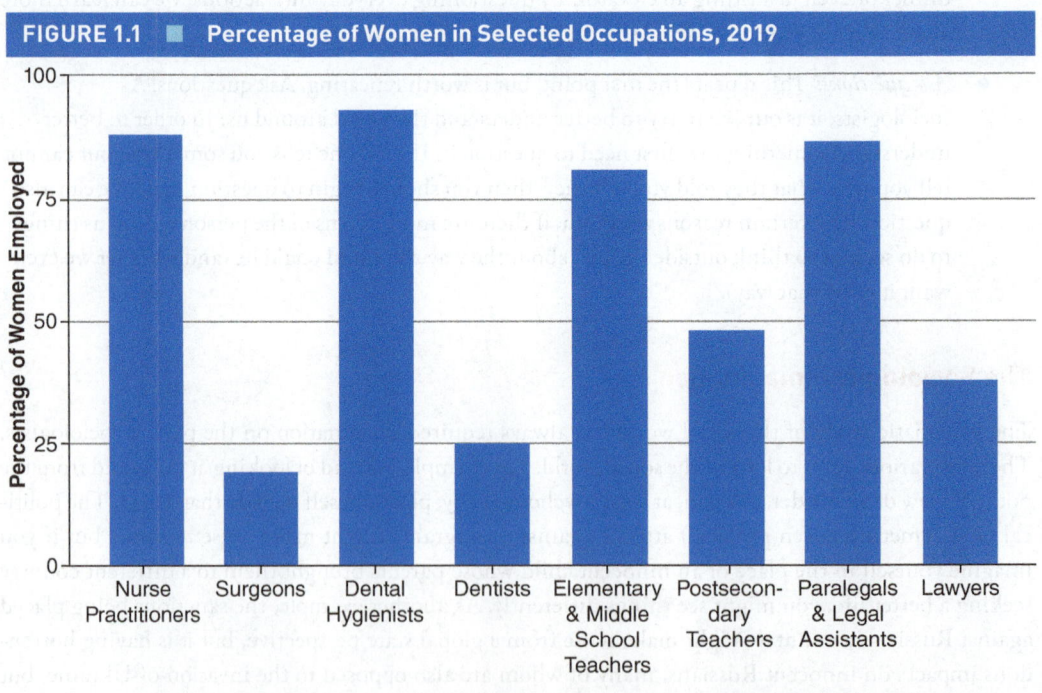

FIGURE 1.1 ■ Percentage of Women in Selected Occupations, 2019

Source: U.S. Census Bureau, 2019.

The decision to pursue one college major or career path over another could become a private trouble if a student makes a poor choice or has one forced on him or her. Sociologists have also shown that such choices are very much related to larger public issues. If many people make poor choices, or are forced into them—as women and other minorities often are—this will lead to public issues such as widespread job dissatisfaction and poor performance on the job. Culturally based ideas about gender often shape personal preferences in choosing a college major, and gendered beliefs about career competence steer women and men toward some types of jobs and away from others (Speer 2017). Being in a poorly paid and unsatisfying job is a personal trouble for an individual, but it is a public issue when large numbers of people find themselves in this situation.

The Micro–Macro Relationship

The interest in personal troubles and public issues is a specific example of a larger and more basic sociological concern with the relationship between small-scale (**micro**) social phenomena, such as individuals and their thoughts and actions, and large-scale (**macro**) social phenomena, such as groups, organizations, cultures, society, and the world, as well as the relationships among them. Karl Marx, often considered one of the earliest and most important sociologists, was interested in the relationship between what workers do and think (micro issues) and the capitalist economic system in which the workers exist (a macro issue). To take a more contemporary example, Randall Collins (2009) has sought to develop a theory of violence that deals with everything from individuals skilled in violent interactions, such as attacking those who are weak, to the material resources needed by violent organizations to cause the destruction of other violent organizations. An example of the former type of violent organization is the well-equipped U.S. Navy SEALs team that killed Osama bin Laden in 2011 and through that act helped hasten the decline of al-Qaeda. However, the decline of al-Qaeda helped lead to the rise of a new, even more violent, organization, the Islamic State.

In fact, a continuum runs from the most microscopic to the most macroscopic of social realities, with phenomena at roughly the midpoint of this continuum best thought of as **meso** (middle or intermediate) realities. The definition of sociology presented at the beginning of this chapter fits this continuum quite well. Individual actions and thoughts lie on the micro end of the continuum; groups, organizations, cultures, and societies fall more toward the macro end; and worldwide structures and processes are at the end point on the macro side of the continuum. Although in their own work the vast majority of individual sociologists focus on only very limited segments of this continuum, the field as a whole is concerned with the continuum in its entirety, as well as with the interrelationships among its various components.

Members of Patriot Front, a White supremacist group, clash with protesters during a march in Boston. Sociologists study violence by examining the thoughts and motivations of violent individuals, as well as the larger social forces that support them.

MediaNews Group / Boston Herald via Getty Images

The Agency–Structure Relationship

Many sociologists tend to think in terms of the micro–macro relationship. The agency–structure continuum is another complex set of relationships, but for our purposes we can think of agency as resembling the micro level and structure as resembling the macro level.

The utility of the agency–structure terminology is that it highlights several important social realities and aspects of the field of sociology. Of greatest significance is the fact that the term *agency* gives great importance to the individual—the "agent"—as having power and a capacity for creativity (Giddens 1984). In sociological work on agency, great emphasis is placed on the individual's mental abilities and the ways in which these abilities are used to create important, if not decisive, actions.

However, individual agents are seen as enmeshed in macro-level social and cultural structures that they create and by which they are constrained (King 2004). For example, as a student, you help create the universities you attend, but you are also constrained by them and the power they have over you. Your university can require you to do certain things (such as take specific courses in order to earn your degree) and prevent you from doing other things (such as taking courses that might be of greater interest or even taking no courses at all). On the other hand, you as a student can act to change or overthrow those structures. You might organize student-run groups on topics of interest, such as religious rights or manga cartoons, attract many participants to the groups, and eventually prompt the university to add courses on those topics. Or perhaps you might organize students to stop enrolling in an elective course that seems irrelevant to their lives, causing that elective to be dropped from the course catalog.

Agents (you as a student, in this case) have great power. In the words of another important sociologist, Erving Goffman (1961b), individuals are **dangerous giants**. That is, they have the potential to disrupt and destroy the structures in which they find themselves. Yet often agents do not realize the power they possess. As a result, social structures such as the university and the class you are currently taking function for long periods of time with little or no disruption by individual agents.

Students across the world have organized to challenge the social and political structures seen as abetting the process of global climate change.
Erik McGregor/Getty Images

However, there are times, such as during the Vietnam War protests of the late 1960s and early 1970s, when students come to realize that they are dangerous giants and act to change not only the university but also the larger society (Gitlin 1993). For example, students at some universities are protesting against the possible deportation of undocumented immigrants by pressuring school administrators to create "sanctuary campuses" that protect faculty, students, and staff from federal immigration authorities. Another example is the recent rise in protests, especially organized walk outs, to protest environmental issues.

There are far more minor, everyday actions that reflect the fact that people can be dangerous giants. Examples involving students include questioning a professor's argument or going to the dean to protest the excessive absences of an instructor. However, most people most of the time do not realize that they are dangerous giants—that they have the capacity to alter greatly the social structures that surround them and in which they are enmeshed.

THE SOCIAL CONSTRUCTION OF REALITY

The discussion of agency and structure leads to another basic concept in sociology: the **social construction of reality** (Berger and Luckmann 1967; Knoblauch and Wilke 2016). People at the agency end of the continuum are seen as creating social reality, basically macro-level phenomena, through their thoughts and actions. That reality then comes to have a life of its own. That is, it becomes a structure that is partly or wholly separate from the people who created it and exist in it. Once macro phenomena have lives of their own, they constrain and even control what people do. Of course, people can refuse to accept these constraints and controls and create new social realities. This process of individual creation of structural realities, constraints, and coercion then begins anew, in a continuing loop. It is this continuous loop that is the heart of agency–structure and micro–macro relationships, the social world, and the field of sociology.

For example, in the realm of consumption, it is people—as designers, manufacturers, consumers, and bloggers—who create the world of fashion (Entwhistle 2015; Mair 2018). However, once the fashion world comes into existence, that world has a great deal of influence over the social constructions, especially the tastes, of individuals who purchase the fashions it produces. Famous fashion houses such as Dior and Givenchy dominate the industry and perpetuate their existence through continual fashion changes. These companies—and, more important, the "fast-fashion" companies that copy and mass-produce their products, such as H&M, Forever 21, and Zara—control people's tastes in fashion and thereby the nature of the clothing they buy and wear. Changing fashions are highly profitable for the companies involved. Consumers are led to be eager to buy the latest fashions, although most often in the form of relatively inexpensive fast-fashion knockoffs.

Of course, many people do not accept such social constructions; they do not go along with the constraints of the fashion industry. They do not wear what the industry wants them to wear, and they do not change the way they dress because of changes in fashion induced by the fashion industry. Many people have their own sense of fashion and create their own way of dressing. Others ignore fashion altogether. Of greatest importance from this perspective is the fact that the idea of what is in fashion often comes not from the fashion industry but rather from the ways of dressing that people put together themselves. These people, in a real sense, construct their own social reality. In fact, in a process known as "cool hunting" (Gloor and Cooper 2007), scouts for the fashion industry seek out new and interesting ways of dressing, often focusing on what young people in the suburbs and the inner cities are wearing. They bring those innovative ideas back to the fashion industry, and some of them are turned into next year's fashions.

Understanding Social Constructionism

Let's have a pop quiz (sorry!).

Which of the following is true?

a. The world is flat.

b. There are seven continents on Earth.

c. Chewing gum in public is a crime.

d. There are eight planets in our solar system.

The answer? All of the above. And none of the above! How is that possible? The answer lies in the fundamental sociological concept of social constructionism.

The world actually isn't flat. We know that thanks to advances in science and technology. That said, for most of recorded human history, most people thought that it was flat. So whether (a) is true depends on *when you are asking the question.*

Many in the United States are taught that there are seven continents (North America, South America, Europe, Africa, Asia, Australia, Antarctica). For many in South America, there are six continents (North America and South America are simply known as "Americas"). The same is true for many in Central Asia, although they learn a different set of continents (North America and South America are different, but Europe and Asia are combined into "Eurasia"). So whether (b) is true depends on *who you are asking.*

Chewing gum in public is probably not a crime where you live, but it is a crime in Singapore. Understanding of crime and deviance and socially acceptable behavior varies. So whether (c) is true depends on *where you are.*

Scientists today agree that there are eight planets in our solar system. Many of you were probably taught that. But when Pluto was first discovered in 1930, it was considered the ninth planet and didn't lose that title until scientists reclassified how we define a planet in 2006. Thus, for 76 years there were nine planets. Now there are eight. So whether (d) is true depends on *scientific classification.*

All of the above should lead us to wonder why we should believe anything at all. Does science mean anything? The answer is yes! And, paradoxically, what makes science so valuable is that it can change and be questioned. That is what sociology is all about! However, there are better, and worse, ways to find answers to our questions. Sociology is also about learning that difference.

Social Structures and Processes

A nineteenth-century sociologist, Auguste Comte, was the first person to formally use the term *sociology* in 1839. Crucial for our purposes here is his early distinction between what he called "social statics" and "social dynamics." In his social statics, Comte looked at the various "parts" (structures) of society, such as the manufacturers and retailers of clothing fashions, and the ways in which they relate to one another as well as to the whole of society. In examining such relationships, Comte investigated social processes among and between parts of society as well as in society as a whole. However, under the heading of social dynamics, his main focus was on a specific social process—social change—and how the various parts of society change.

It is important to emphasize that **social structures** are enduring and regular social arrangements, such as the family and the state. Although social structures do change, they are generally not very dynamic; they change very slowly. **Social processes** are the dynamic and ever-changing aspects of the social world.

Auguste Comte (1798–1857) invented the term *sociology*, argued that the discipline should be a science, and created a general theory of the social world.

Granger, NYC—All rights reserved.

The elements of globalization can be divided between structures (e.g., the United Nations) and a variety of more specific social processes (e.g., the migration of people across national borders). In terms of consumption, we can think of the shopping mall (or Amazon) as a structure and the shopping (or consumption) that takes place in it as a process. Finally, the internet as a whole and social networking sites in particular are structures, while the communication and the social interaction that take place in them can be viewed as processes.

Needless to say, neither the shopping mall nor the internet existed in Comte's day. Once again, we see that the social world is constantly changing and that sociologists, as well as students of sociology, must be sensitive to those changes. However, some of sociology's earliest concepts continue to be applicable, and usefully applied, to the social world.

Sociology's Purpose: Science or Social Reform? Or Both?

Comte was famous not only for examining the relationship between structure and process but also for arguing that such study ought to be scientific. He believed that the social world was dominated by laws and that sociology's task was to uncover those laws. As those laws were uncovered, the science of sociology would develop. But Comte was also concerned about the problems of his day and interested in solving them through social reform. In fact, to Comte, science and reform should not be separated from one another. A number of classical sociologists—Karl Marx, Émile Durkheim, Jane Addams, and others—shared this view. Marx and Engels's *Communist Manifesto* (1848) was not only a commentary on the social ills of the capitalist economy but also a rallying cry to workers to organize and abolish capitalism.

Many of today's sociologists study social problems of all sorts, such as poverty and crime. They use a variety of scientific methods to collect large amounts of data on such problems. Many also seek to use what they learn about those problems to suggest ways of reforming society. They believe that these two activities—scientific research and social reform—are not necessarily distinct; they can and should be mutually enriching. Although many contemporary sociologists accept this position, a division has developed over time, with some sociologists focusing more on scientific research and others more engaged in activities designed to reform society and address social problems.

The sociologists who engage in "pure science" operate with the conviction that we need to have a better understanding of how the social world operates before we can change it, if that's what we want to do. The knowledge gained through social research may ultimately be used by those who want to change society, or to keep it as it is, but that is not the immediate concern of these researchers.

Other sociologists take the opposite position. C. Wright Mills, for example, was little interested in doing scientific research. He was mostly interested in such social reforms as limiting or eliminating the unwholesome and worrisome ties between the military and industry in the United States. He was also critical of many of the most prominent sociologists of his day for their orientation toward being pure scientists, their lack of concern for the pressing problems of the day, and their unwillingness to do anything about those problems. Feminist sociologists have extended the argument, pointing out that the topics and methods of objective, scientific sociology themselves sometimes reflect, and ultimately reinforce, social inequality along the lines of race, gender, and class because they are based on the assumptions of society's elite.

SOCIOLOGY, THE OTHER SOCIAL SCIENCES, AND COMMON SENSE

Sociology is one of the social sciences; that is, it is one of the fields that studies various aspects of the social world. Among others are anthropology, communication studies, economics, geography, political science, and psychology. Generally speaking, sociology is the broadest of these fields; social scientists in other fields are more likely than sociologists to delve into specific aspects of the social world in much greater depth. Sociological study touches on the culture of concern to anthropologists, the nation-state of interest to political scientists, and the mental processes that are the focus of psychologists. However, that does not mean that sociology is in any sense "better" than—or, conversely, not as good as—the other social sciences.

Rather than comparing and contrasting these fields in general terms, we can look at the different ways in which these fields approach one of this book's signature concerns: globalization.

- *Anthropology:* Focuses on cultural aspects of societies around the world, such as the foods people eat and how they eat them, as well as the differences among cultures around the globe.
- *Communication studies:* Examines communications across the globe, with the internet and digital technologies of growing concern.
- *Economics:* Investigates the production, distribution, and consumption of resources through markets and other structures that span much of the globe, especially those based on and involving money.

- *Geography:* Studies spatial relationships on a global scale and maps those spaces.
- *Political science:* Studies nation-states and political actors, especially the ways in which they relate to one another around the world as well as how they have grown increasingly unable to control global flows of migrants, viruses, recreational drugs, internet scams, and the like.
- *Psychology:* Examines the ways in which individual identities are shaped by increased awareness of the rest of the world and tensions associated with globalization (e.g., job loss), which may lead to individual psychological problems such as depression (Lemert and Elliott 2006).

Sociology encompasses all these concerns, and many others, in its approach to globalization. It studies globe-straddling cultures (such as consumer or fast-food culture), relationships between political systems (e.g., the European Union and its member nations), communication networks (e.g., CNN, Telemundo, and Al Jazeera or Twitter and Facebook), and markets (e.g., for labor or stocks and bonds) that cover vast expanses of the globe. Sociology maps all of these, and even their impacts (both good and bad) on individuals. You might want to study the other fields to get a sense of the depth of what they have to offer on specific aspects of globalization. However, if you are looking for the field that gives you the broadest possible view of all of these things as well as the ways in which they interrelate, that field is sociology.

Although sociology and the other social sciences differ in important ways, they are all quite different from commonsense understandings of the social world. Everyone participates in globalization in one way or another. However, few if any people research these phenomena in the same rigorous way and to the same degree that social scientists examine them. That research leads, among other things, to a greater understanding of the nature of globalization. For example, you probably have a sense that globalization has changed society—perhaps even an impression that it is changing your life. What you are unlikely to spend much time thinking about are globalization's causes, effects, and linkages to other social phenomena, or its largely invisible effects on society and the world. Research on the topic is also likely to yield much more insight into the pros and cons of globalization on personal, societal, and global levels. Such detailed knowledge and insight will help you, and others, to navigate more successfully the accompanying changes in social processes and structures.

One example of the gap between common sense and social scientific knowledge relates to perceptions of the causes of climate change. There is strong consensus in the scientific community that global warming is occurring and that it is caused primarily by human activities, especially the burning of fossil fuels. However, data from a recent survey, illustrated in Figure 1.2, show that belief

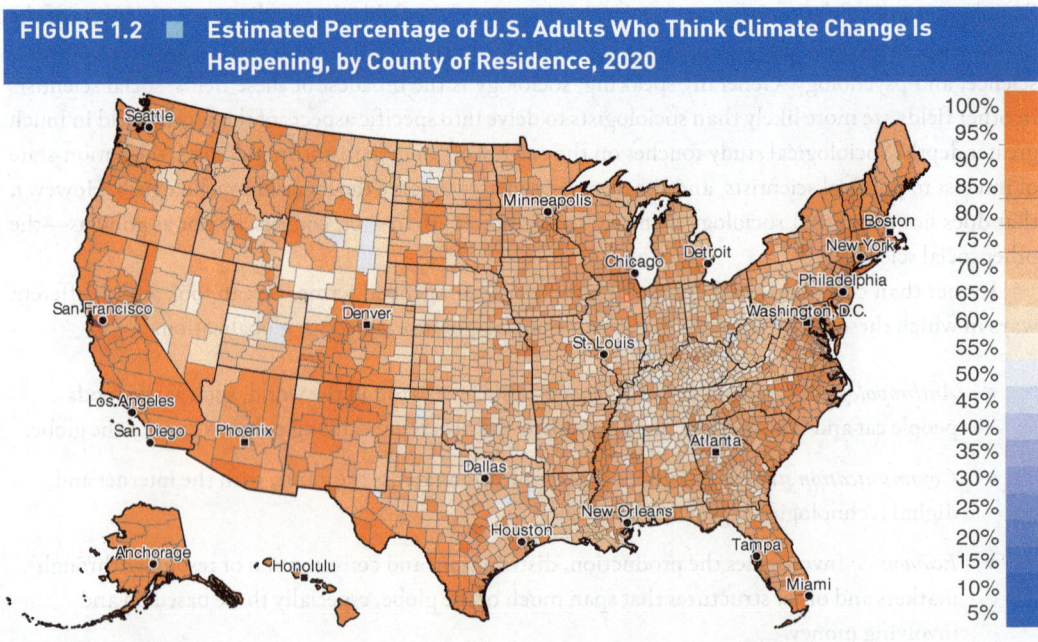

FIGURE 1.2 ■ Estimated Percentage of U.S. Adults Who Think Climate Change Is Happening, by County of Residence, 2020

Source: Yale Program on Climate Change Communication: "Yale Climate Opinion Maps 2020."

in climate change varies widely from place to place in the United States. Overall, only 72 percent of people in the United States believe that global warming is happening and just 57 percent believe that it is caused by human activity. Furthermore, 43 percent believe that most scientists don't think global warming is happening.

Although common sense is important, even to sociologists, there is no substitute for the systematic study of the social world in both its minutest detail and its broadest manifestations.

CENTRAL CONCERNS FOR A TWENTY-FIRST-CENTURY SOCIOLOGY

Although the social world has been changing dramatically over the last two centuries or so and sociology has adapted to those changes, sociology has continued to focus on many of its traditional concerns. We have already mentioned industry, production, and work as long-term sociological interests; others include deviance and crime (see Chapter 7), the family (see Chapter 11), and the city (see Chapter 15). Of particular concern to many sociologists has been, and continues to be, the issue of inequality as it affects the poor, particularly racial and ethnic groups, women, and gender and sexual minorities (see Chapters 9 and 10). The bulk of this book is devoted to these basic sociological topics and concerns, but the discussion also encompasses the very contemporary issues of globalization, consumption, McDonaldization, and the digital world.

Globalization

Arguably, no social change is as important today as globalization because it is continually affecting all aspects of the social world everywhere on the globe. A date marking the beginning of globalization cannot be given with any precision, and in fact, it is in great dispute (Ritzer 2012b; Ritzer and Dean 2019; Steger 2017). However, the concept of globalization first began to appear in the popular and academic literature around 1990. Today, globalization is a central issue in the social world as a whole as well as in sociology; globalization and talk about it are all around us. In fact, we can be said to be living in the "global age" (Albrow 1996). However, this fact as well as the advantages of globalization have become increasingly questioned by some. Such questioning has led to talk of "deglobalization" (however, see the blog post "Deglobalization? Not a Chance" [Ritzer 2016]). Deglobalization was also behind the vote in the United Kingdom to exit the European Union (called Brexit), as well as actions taken by other European nations to create border restrictions. However, none of these actions are going to have much impact on globalization as a whole or in such areas as the internet, the media, and culture.

A major component of any past or present definition of sociology is society. **Society** is a complex pattern of social relationships that is bounded in space and persists over time. Society has traditionally been the largest unit of analysis in sociology. However, in the global age, societies are seen as declining in importance. This is the case, in part, because larger transnational and global social structures are growing in importance. These include the United Nations (UN); the European Union (EU); the Organization of the Petroleum Exporting Countries (OPEC); multinational corporations (MNCs), such as Google and ExxonMobil; and multinational nongovernmental organizations (NGOs), such as Amnesty International. In at least some cases, these transnational structures are becoming more important than individual societies. OPEC is more important to the rest of the world's well-being than are the organization's key member societies, such as Abu Dhabi or even Saudi Arabia. However, this emphasis on the transnational and global has led to a counterreaction in which the focus has shifted back to one's own society (e.g., "America First").

Social processes, like social structures, exist not only at the societal level but also at the global level, and these global processes are increasing in importance. Consider migration (see Chapter 15). People move about, or migrate, within and between societies. For example, many people have moved from the northeastern United States to the West and the South. However, in the global age, people are increasingly moving between societies, some halfway around the world. (For example, one of the co-authors of this textbook, J. Michael Ryan, has held professional academic positions on five continents). The United States now has a higher percentage of immigrants than it has had in almost a century (see Figure 1.3). Many have migrated from and through Mexico to the United States (Massey 2003; Ortmeyer and

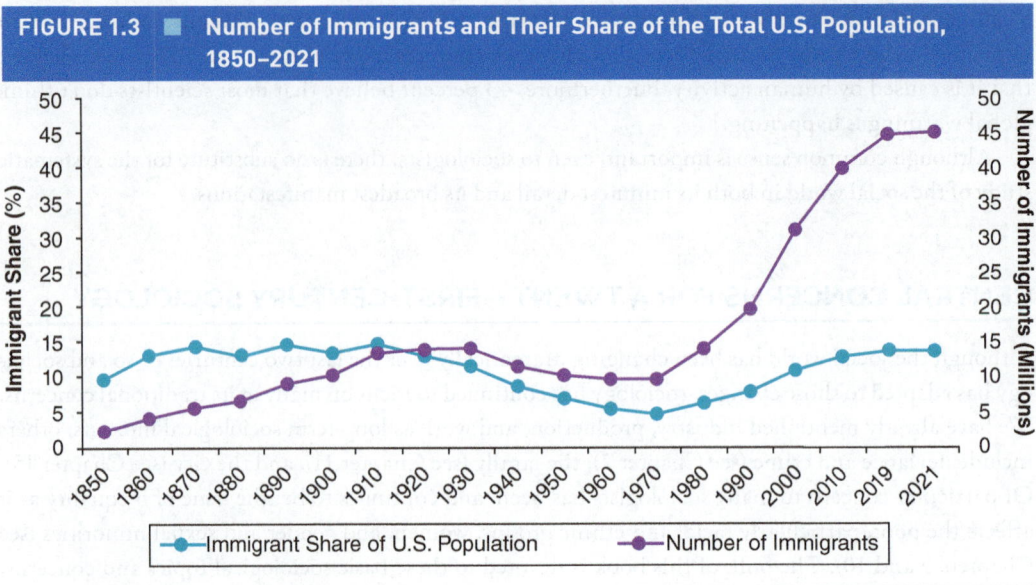

FIGURE 1.3 ■ Number of Immigrants and Their Share of the Total U.S. Population, 1850–2021

Source: Migration Policy Institute (MPI), 2021.

Quinn 2012). More generally, large numbers of people are migrating from a number of predominantly Islamic societies in the Middle East and Africa to the West (Voas and Fleischmann 2012). In many cases, they were fleeing from war-torn countries such as Syria, Iraq, and Libya (Yeginsu and Hartocollis 2015). In addition, the movement of thousands of people from the West to join radical Islamist organizations (such as the Islamic State), especially in Syria and Iraq, has been of major concern to Western governments. Some fear that at least some of those involved in radical Islamist activities there will migrate back to the West and engage in terrorist acts.

There have always been large-scale population movements. However, in the global age, and even with recent restrictions, people generally move around the world far more freely and travel much greater distances than ever before. Another way of saying this is that people—and much else—are more "fluid." That is, they move farther, more easily, and more quickly than ever before. Younger people, especially millennials (or Generation Y, those born from the early 1980s through the late 1990s, as well as the following Generation Z), are likely to be especially mobile, including globally. Their greater fluidity is reflected in, among many other things, the fact that they are more likely to book airline tickets and to check in for flights online and to use boarding passes sent directly to their smartphones.

The movement of products of all types is also more fluid as a result of massive container ships, jet cargo planes, and package delivery services such as FedEx and UPS. Even more fluid is the digital "stuff" you buy on the internet when you download music, videos, movies, and so on. And in the realm of the family, tasks once confined to the home, such as caregiving and housework, have become increasingly fluid, as those who can afford to do so often outsource domestic labor (van der Lippe, Frey, and Tsvetkova 2012; Yeates 2009). More generally that greater fluidity is manifested in the information that flows throughout the world in the blink of an eye as a result of the internet, texting, e-mail, and social networking sites such as Facebook, Instagram, Snapchat, TikTok, and Twitter.

These flows can be expedited by structures of various types.

- Air cargo delivery will increasingly be facilitated by the development of the "aerotropolis" (Kasarda and Lindsay 2011), a planned "city of the future" developed because of proximity and access to a large, modern airport (Kasarda 2016). The "smart city" of New Songdo, South Korea, was built because such an airport (Incheon) is nearby and easily reached via a 12-mile-long bridge. This is in contrast to the usual situation in which the airport (e.g., Reagan National in Washington, D.C.; LAX in Los Angeles; Heathrow in London) is built within or very close to a city center. Traditional airports are typically too small and too difficult to reach, create too much noise for city residents, and cannot expand much beyond their current confines.

- The European Union (EU), founded in 1993, is an example of a social structure that serves to ease the flow of citizens among member nations (but not of people living outside the EU). Border restrictions were reduced or eliminated among the 27 EU member nations, although some of them have been reinstituted in recent years because of concern about the flow of undocumented immigrants. Similarly, the launch of the euro in 1999 greatly simplified economic transactions among the 20 EU countries that accept it as their currency.

- The continuing free flow of information on the internet is made possible by an organization called ICANN (Internet Corporation for Assigned Names and Numbers). It handles the internet's underlying infrastructure.

There are also structures that impede various kinds of global flows. National borders, passports and passport controls, security checks, and customs controls limit the movement of people throughout the world (some more than others). Such restrictions were greatly increased in many parts of the world after the terrorist attacks on New York City and Washington, D.C., on September 11, 2001. This made global travel and border crossing more difficult and time-consuming. Then there are the even more obvious structures designed to limit the movement of people across borders. Examples include the fences between Israel and the West Bank, as well as one between Israel and Egypt completed in 2013. Even more recent are border fences under construction or completed in several European countries (e.g., Hungary, Slovenia), which are designed to limit, direct, or stop the flow of migrants from Syria and elsewhere (Surk 2015). During his presidential campaign, Donald Trump promised to turn the existing barriers between the United States and Mexico into a wall, at least for part of the length of the border. In the early days of his presidency, Trump encountered opposition to the wall because of its high cost and environmental concerns (among other reasons). From late 2018 to early 2019, the U.S. government endured a partial shutdown because of Trump's insistence on building the wall and congressional resistance to funding it. To date, the entire wall has not (yet) been completed.

The existing fences across the Mexican border, and increased border police and patrols, have already led unauthorized migrants to take longer and riskier routes into the United States. There are more than 100 immigration detention centers in the United States (see Figure 1.4). A crisis arose at the Mexican border in mid-2014 when tens of thousands of children from Central America flooded the area and overwhelmed detention centers (Archibold 2014). Another occurred in late 2018 when Trump exaggerated the risks posed by a "caravan" of immigrants from Central America and sought to counter it by sending thousands of U.S. troops to guard the border. There are, of course, many other structural barriers in the world, most notably trade barriers and tariffs, which limit the free movement of goods and services of many kinds.

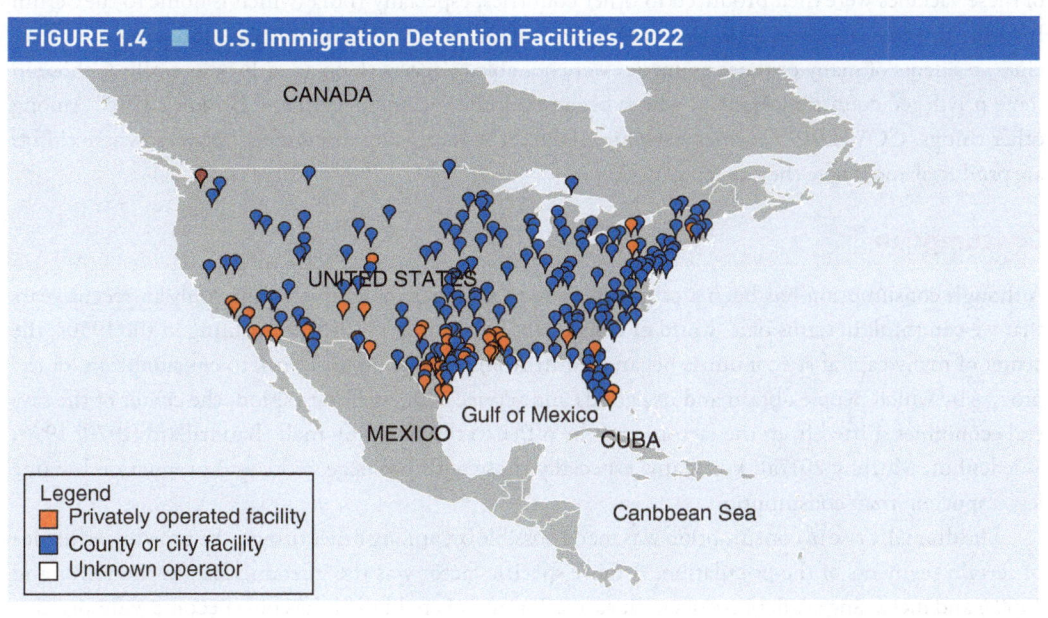

FIGURE 1.4 ■ U.S. Immigration Detention Facilities, 2022

Legend
- Privately operated facility
- County or city facility
- Unknown operator

Source: Freedom for Immigrants, "Mapping U.S. Immigration Detention," 2022.

In sum, **globalization** is defined by increasingly fluid global flows and the structures that expedite and impede those flows. Globalization is certainly increasing, and it brings with it a variety of both positive and negative developments (Ritzer and Dean 2021). On one side, most people throughout the world now have far greater access to goods, services, and information from around the globe than did people during the industrial age (especially thanks to the internet). On the other side, a variety of highly undesirable things also flow more easily around the world, including diseases such as COVID-19, Zika, HIV/AIDS, and Ebola, and pollution released primarily by industrialized countries that worsens the adverse effects of climate change (including global warming). Also on the negative side are the flows of such forms of "deviant globalization" as terrorism, sex trafficking, and the black markets for human organs and drugs (Gilman, Goldhammer, and Weber 2011; Marmo and Chazel 2016).

The COVID-19 Pandemic

The COVID-19 pandemic is an example of a global phenomenon that has had a significant impact on nearly every aspect of our daily lives (Ryan 2021). The SARS-CoV-2 virus responsible for causing COVID-19 moves around the world without concern for national borders, passport controls, or who it infects (although some are certainly more susceptible than others; see Ryan and Nanda 2023c). As of January 2023, Turkmenistan is the only country in the world to have not reported a single case of the virus, although nearly every scientist (and many others) believes that it does exist there as well. The virus has been confirmed to have infected hundreds of millions (though billions is a more likely estimate) and killed many millions around the world. And although some countries have had higher reported rates of infection and death than others, the virus has no doubt been a truly global phenomenon.

One reason the virus was able to spread so quickly is exactly because of globalization and the increase in travel around the world. One can now go almost anywhere else in the world within 24 hours (depending on flight times, of course), and a growing number of people do indeed travel great distances, and more regularly than before. The global movement of people has also meant a global movement of viruses.

Globalization also contributed to the breadth and depth of the impact of the pandemic. As countries went into lockdown, global travel, especially tourism, was significantly reduced. The movement of goods around the world also slowed considerably. The economic fallout of the pandemic sent shockwaves through the global economic system. The growing number of migrant workers were hit particularly hard as they were often caught between the policies of their host countries and their home countries.

The global availability of vaccines represents another example of globalization. Although many of the first global vaccines were invented (or discovered) in the UK and the United States, a larger number of these vaccines were then produced in other countries, especially India (which is home to the Serum Institute of India, the world's largest vaccine manufacturer). That said, despite producing these vaccines, residents of many of those countries were not able to access them as early or as easily as those in more privileged countries, many of whom began to horde vaccines (Ryan and Nanda 2023c). Among other things, COVID-19 vaccines have highlighted the increasing disconnect between where things are produced and where they are consumed.

Consumption

Although consumption has been a central feature of societies for centuries, it is only in recent years that we can think in terms of a "world of consumers" (Trentmann 2016). Beginning in the 1950s, the center of many capitalist economies began to shift from production and work to **consumption**, or the process by which people obtain and use goods and services. During that period, the center of the several economies shifted from the factory and the office to the shopping mall (Baudrillard [1970] 1998; Wiedenhoft Murphy 2017a). For many, especially those with privilege, work and production became less important than consumption.

The dramatic rise in consumption was made possible by, among other things, the growing affluence of certain segments of the population. A more specific factor was the introduction (in the 1950s and 1960s) and increasing availability of credit cards. The use of credit cards has now become widespread at shopping malls, on the internet, and in many other settings. One indicator of the increase in consumption in the United States is the increase in credit card debt. As you can see in Figure 1.5, credit card debt per household grew astronomically in the early years of credit card use (the figure begins with $37 in 1969). Credit card debt reached its high point, $8,729, in 2008 and steadily declined after the Great Recession to an average of $5,525 per household in 2021.

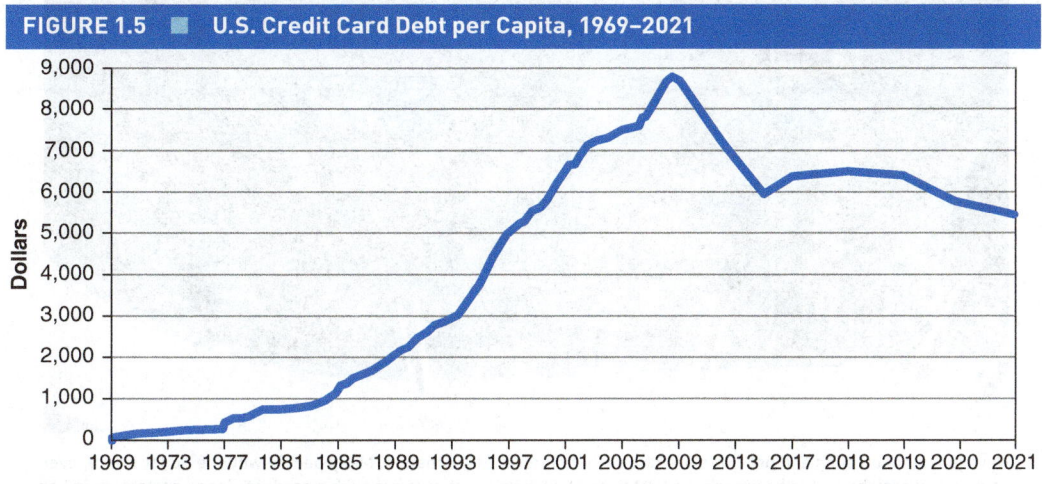

FIGURE 1.5 ■ U.S. Credit Card Debt per Capita, 1969–2021

Source: Data from the U.S. Federal Reserve, U.S. Census Bureau, and Experian Credit Reporting

Consumption is certainly significant economically, but it is significant in other ways as well. For example, culture is very much shaped by consumption, and various aspects of consumption become cultural phenomena. A good example is the iPhone, which is used in many ways to consume but more generally has revolutionized culture in innumerable ways. Billions of people have bought iPhones and similar smartphones as well as the ever-increasing number of apps associated with them. These phones have altered how and where people meet to socialize and the ways in which they socialize. In addition, the media and people in general spend so much time discussing the implications of the latest iPhone and similar products that these devices have become central to the larger culture in which we live. Rumors about the characteristics and release date of the next version of the iPhone continually add to the excitement.

Consumption and globalization are also deeply intertwined. Much of what we consume in the developed world comes from other countries. In 2022 alone, the United States imported more than $575 billion worth of goods from China; the comparable figure in 1985 was only $4 million in goods (Trading Economics 2023). Furthermore, the speed and convenience of internet commerce tend to make global realities and distances irrelevant to consumers. Finally, travel to other parts of the world—a form of consumption itself—is increasingly affordable and common. A major objective of tourists is often the sampling of the foods of foreign lands, as well as the purchasing of souvenirs (Chambers 2010; Gmelch 2010; Mak, Lumbers, and Eves 2012). Medical tourism is also becoming more common, with some estimating that it is a $100-billion-per-year industry (Fetscherin and Stephano 2016). Growing numbers of people are traveling great distances for such services as cosmetic procedures and even open heart surgery. They do so largely because the costs are much lower elsewhere in the world. For example, many U.S. women who have difficulty conceiving travel to developing countries such as India in order to hire surrogates, "rent" their uteruses and ovaries, and exploit their eggs (Pfeffer 2011).

Sociologists are understandably interested in these developments in the realm of consumption. Early sociologists completed many studies of work, production, factories, and factory workers. Today's sociologists continue to study work-related issues, but they are devoting increasing attention to consumption in general (Warde 2017) and more specifically to such phenomena as online shopping, done increasingly through the use of smartphones (Kim et al. 2017); the behavior of shoppers in more material locales such as department stores (Miller 1998) and lifestyle centers (Ryan 2013); and the

New consumption sites and products are often a hot cultural phenomenon. Many people will line up for hours, even camp out overnight, just to be among the first to be at such an event or to get such a product. These customers in Los Angeles are waiting to purchase the latest iPhone or Apple Watch.

Associated Press

development of more recent consumption sites, such as fast-food restaurants (Ritzer 2021) and shopping malls (Ritzer 2010b). All these have become increasingly global phenomena. The most popular destination for visitors to Barcelona is *not* one of Antoni Gaudí's amazing architectural creations (such as Sagrada Familia, the symbol of the city) but rather a new outlet mall on the outskirts of the city (Mount 2014). Online shopping is increasingly popular in many places, including in India and especially in China (Bearak 2014; Wang and Pfanner 2013). The growth of online shopping in developed countries, and even more in less-developed countries, has been made possible by the massive expansion and growing popularity of smartphones.

Critiquing Consumption

The sociological study of consumption sites involves, among many other things, a critical look at the ways in which they are structured. These sites may be set up to lead people to consume certain things and not others, to consume more than they might have intended, and to go into debt (Brubaker, Lawless, and Tabb 2012; Manning 2001; Marron 2009; Ritzer 1995). Consider Shoedazzle (www.shoedazzle.com), a website that uses commercials and "style quizzes" to recruit new members. Shoedazzle highlights an "exclusive" VIP membership status on its webpage, which anyone can join. Making its members feel special through seemingly personalized style quizzes and VIP memberships are intended to lure consumers into buying more shoes (and other products) than they really need.

Sociologists are also interested in how consumers use shopping malls and e-tailers in ways that were not anticipated by their designers. For example, people often wander through shopping malls and their many shops, which have been designed to spur consumption, without buying anything. Defunct malls are serving as impromptu skate parks. Students are using Amazon as a source for term-paper bibliographies rather than buying the books. Travelers are using internet sites such as Expedia and KAYAK to compare prices but then buying airplane tickets on the airlines' own websites.

Social change continues. The Great Recession and its aftermath altered many things, including the degree to which society is dominated by consumption. Even today, long after the onset of the recession in 2007 and its supposed end, many consumers remain reluctant to spend money, or at least as much as they did in the past, on consumption (Kurtz 2014). As a result, many consumption sites have experienced great difficulties. Many outdoor strip malls and some indoor malls have emptied; they have become "dead malls" (as documented on the site http://deadmalls.com). Many of the malls that continue to exist have numerous vacant stores, including abandoned large department stores. Casinos in Atlantic City, New Jersey, are being shuttered, and there are those who want to see the city become more like the simpler beach community it once was (Hurdle 2014). It seems possible, although highly unlikely, that even though we entered the consumption age only about half a century ago, we now may be on the verge of what could be called the "postconsumption age." Although excessive consumption and the related high level of debt were key factors in causing the Great Recession, a postconsumption age would bring with it problems of its own, such as fewer jobs and a declining standard of living for many.

McDonaldization

Ritzer's study of a major site for consuming food—the fast-food restaurant—led to the development of the concept of **McDonaldization**, or the process by which the rational principles of the fast-food restaurant are coming to dominate more and more sectors of society and more societies throughout the world (Ritzer 2021; Ritzer and Miles, 2019; for a number of critical essays on this perspective, see Ritzer 2010c). This process leads to the creation of rational systems—not only fast-food restaurants, but also, among others, online shopping sites—that have four defining characteristics:

- *Efficiency.* The emphasis is on the use of the quickest and least costly means to whatever end is desired. It is clear that employees of fast-food restaurants work efficiently: Burgers are cooked and assembled as if on an assembly line, with no wasted movements or ingredients. Similarly, customers are expected to spend as little time as possible in the fast-food restaurant. Perhaps the best example of efficiency is the drive-through window, a highly organized means for employees to dole out meals in a matter of seconds.

- *Calculability.* You hear a lot at McDonald's about quantities: how large the food portions are—the Big Mac—and how low the prices are—the dollar breakfast. You don't hear as much, however, about the quality of the restaurant's ingredients or its products. Similarly, you may hear about how many burgers are served per hour or how quickly they are served, but you don't hear much about the skill of employees. A focus on quantity also means that tasks are often done under great pressure. This means that they are often done in a slipshod manner.

- *Predictability.* McDonaldization ensures that the entire experience of patronizing a fast-food chain is nearly identical from one geographic setting to another—even globally—and from one time to another. When customers enter a McDonald's restaurant, employees ask what they wish to order, following scripts created by the corporation. For their part, customers can expect to find most of the usual menu items. Employees, following another script, can be counted on to thank customers for their order. Thus, a highly predictable ritual is played out in the fast-food restaurant.

- *Control.* In McDonaldized systems, technology exerts a good deal of control over people, processes, and products. French fry machines limit what employees can do and control any remaining tasks. They buzz when the fries are done and even automatically lift them out of the hot oil when they've reached just the right amount of crispiness. Workers must load fry baskets with uncooked fries and unload them when the baskets emerge from the oil. The automatic fry machine may save time and prevent accidents, but it limits and dictates employee actions and leaves them with little meaningful work. Similarly, the drive-through window can be seen as a technology that ensures that customers dispose of their own garbage, if only by dumping it in the backseats of their cars or on the roadside.

Paradoxically, rationality often seems to lead to its exact opposite—irrationality. Just consider the problems of meaningless work, roadside litter due to drive-through services at fast-food restaurants, or the societal problems associated with childhood obesity, which has been blamed, in part, on the ubiquity of fast food. Another of the irrationalities of rationality is dehumanization. Fast-food employees are forced to work in dehumanizing jobs, which can lead to job dissatisfaction, alienation, and high turnover rates. Fast-food customers are forced to eat in dehumanizing settings, such as in the cold and impersonal atmosphere of the fast-food restaurant, in their cars, or on the move as they walk down the street. As more of the world succumbs to McDonaldization, dehumanization becomes increasingly pervasive.

Sociologist George Ritzer theorized that the rational principles of fast food are coming to dominate many aspects of our social lives. The same defining characteristics of this Lotteria fast food restaurant in Vietnam—efficiency, predictability, calculability, and control—can be observed across a range of contemporary organizations and institutions.

David R. Frazier Photolibrary, Inc. / Alamy Stock Photo

It is clear that the internet has become increasingly important to many and for more things and that Amazon is a dominant force on the internet, especially in consumption (representing nearly 38 percent of all e-commerce in the United States in 2022), but it is also increasingly a force in bricks-and-clicks with the opening in recent years of conventional bookstores and convenience stores and with its purchase in 2017 of the Whole Foods chain of supermarkets. These "brick" sites complement in various ways the "clicks" on Amazon, and they are increasingly likely to do so in the future as Amazon creates a more seamless system.

Comparisons between McDonald's and Amazon from the point of view of the McDonaldization thesis demonstrate that Amazon is far more McDonaldized than McDonald's.

- Amazon makes obtaining a wide array of products highly *efficient* by eliminating lengthy and perhaps fruitless trips to department stores, big-box stores (such as Walmart), and the mall. What could be more efficient than sitting at home, ordering products online, and having your order delivered in a day or two? Although McDonald's made obtaining a meal in a restaurant more efficient through the drive-through window, it still has the inefficiency of requiring consumers to drive (or walk) to the restaurant to get their food.

- Shopping on Amazon involves a highly predictable series of online steps that lead to the completion of an order. McDonald's brought great *predictability* to eating in a restaurant. There are well-defined steps in obtaining a meal there: join the line, scan the marquee to know what to order when you (finally) get to the counter, order, pay, take the tray of food to a table, eat it, and dispose of the debris on completion of the "meal." However, there are a series of unpredictabilities at McDonald's, absent at Amazon, such as those associated with inattentive, surly, or incompetent counter people.

- There is great *calculability* involved in shopping on Amazon. Prices are clearly marked and consumers know exactly what the total cost of an order is. Before finalizing a purchase customers are able to delete items, thereby reducing the final cost. The marquee at McDonald's offers preset prices and similar calculability, although unless customers are able to do the math in their heads, the final price is not known until the purchase is completed.

- Shopping on Amazon is tightly controlled by the nature of the site and its reliance on nonhuman technologies. Consumers can only order what is on the site and cannot ask (there is no one to ask) for products to be modified. In addition, there are no crowds, to say nothing of unreliable and intrusive salespeople, on Amazon. Great *control* is exerted over customers at McDonald's, but they are able to request some modifications in at least some of the food they order. This is one of the reasons that lines can be long at counters and drive-throughs. Counter people, as well as those who staff the drive-through windows, can adversely affect the process in various ways (e.g., food may not be modified as requested; it is not unusual to drive or walk some distance only to find that one's sack of food does not include exactly what was ordered).

The main *irrationality of rationality* associated with Amazon is its tendency to lead to excessive consumption, while that is not possible at McDonald's given its limited menu and low prices. However, it is possible, even likely, to consume too many calories, too much fat, and too much sugar at McDonald's (Spurlock 2005).

The Digital World

Sociology has always concerned itself with the social aspects and implications of **technology**, or the interplay of machines, tools, skills, and procedures for the accomplishment of tasks. One example is the assembly line, a defining feature of early twentieth-century factories. Later, sociologists became interested in the automated technologies that came to define factories. However, technologies have continued to evolve considerably since then. Sociologists are now devoting an increasing amount of attention to the digital world that has emerged as a result of new technologies already mentioned in this chapter, such as computers, smartphones, the internet, and social media sites such as TikTok, Facebook and Twitter (Mukherjee 2018).

Although we discuss life in the digital world throughout this book, living digitally is not separate from living in the social world. In fact, the two forms of living are increasingly intersecting and creating an augmented world (Jurgenson 2012). The widespread use of smartphones allows people to text many others to let them know they are going to be at a local club. This can lead to a spontaneous social gathering at the club that would not have occurred were it not for this new technology. One of the most dramatic examples of the effect of smartphones on the social world are seen in their use in mobilizing, especially through Twitter, large numbers of people to become involved, and stay involved, in social movements such as the revolutions in Egypt (2011) and Ukraine (2014).

The networking sites on the internet that involve social interaction are the most obviously sociological in character (Aleman and Wartman 2008; Patchin and Hinduja 2010). For example, Hodkinson (2015) has pointed out the similarities between teenagers' bedrooms and their social networking sites in terms of privacy issues. Both are intimate personal spaces where teenagers socialize and individualize in ways that express their identities. Social networking sites are especially important in North America (Europe is not far behind), where the percentage of those with access to the internet is highest (see Figure 1.6). However, their importance is increasing elsewhere, especially in the Middle East and North Africa, as reflected in the role they played there in recent social revolutions. Protesters used cell phones and the internet to inform each other, and the world, about the evolving scene. To take another example, Facebook.com/yalaYL has become a key site where Israelis, Palestinians, and other Arabs communicate with each other about both everyday concerns and big issues such as the prospect for peace in the Middle East. This social networking takes place online, while peaceful face-to-face interaction between such people, and between their leaders, is difficult or nonexistent, especially in light of continuing violence in and around Israel (Bronner 2011).

Although social networking sites can bring about greater interaction, they also come between people and affect the nature of interaction. Twitter limits each message to 280 characters (though premium subscribers have up to 4,000 characters), but face-to-face communication has no such limits. On the other hand, face-to-face communication is limited to a shared physical space, whereas communication via Twitter travels anywhere there is a device connected to the internet. Sociologists are interested in getting a better handle on the nature of the differences, as well as the similarities, between mediated

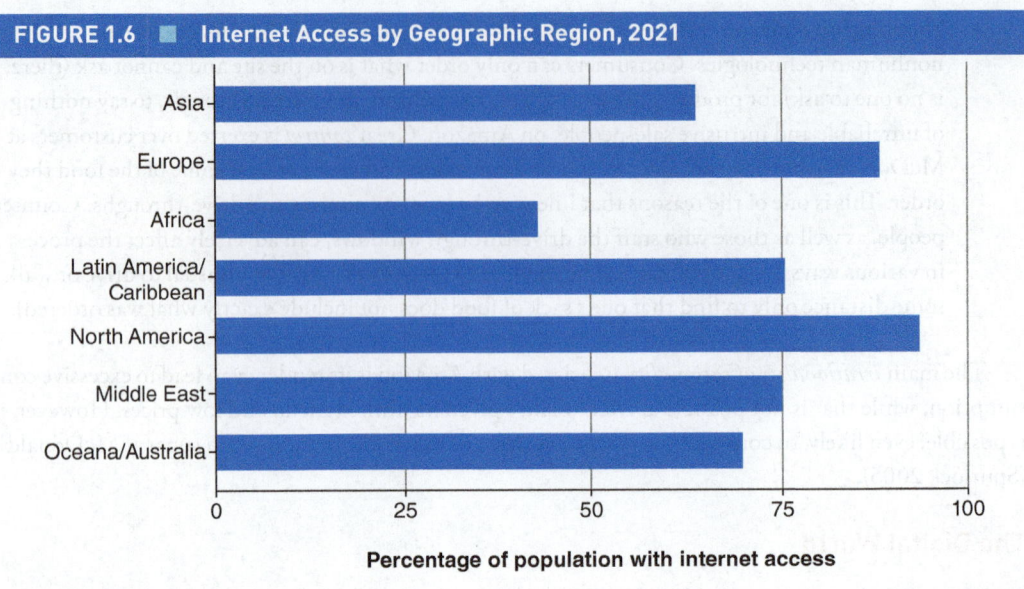

FIGURE 1.6 ■ Internet Access by Geographic Region, 2021

Source: Internet World Stats. 2021. "Internet Users Distribution in the World—2021."

and nonmediated (e.g., face-to-face) interaction. In technologically **mediated interaction**, technology such as the internet and the smartphone comes between the people who are communicating, while there is no such interference in nonmediated interaction. People who are shy and insecure when it comes to dating or sex, for example, may be much more comfortable relating to others on mediated websites such as Hinge, Match.com, OkCupid, and Tinder.

Another sociological issue related to the internet is the impact on our lives of spending so much time interacting on social networking sites. For example, are you more likely to write term papers for your college classes using shorter sentences and more abbreviations because of your experience on Twitter or with texting? Consider also the impact of the nearly 7.5 hours per day that kids aged 15–18 in the United States spend in front of a screen using entertainment media (CDC 2023). In some cases, little time remains for other activities (e.g., schoolwork, face-to-face interaction). Increasing the ability of children to spend time on screen media is the growing availability of mobile devices such as smartphones and tablets. In 2017, 98 percent of children in the United States under 8 years of age lived in homes with mobile devices, compared to 52 percent just two years earlier. They were also more than 30 percent more likely in 2017 to use such devices than they were in 2013 (Common Sense Media 2017a). The pandemic has no doubt seen those numbers rise although it will be some time before we know how stable such a rise might become. A study of parents and children in fast-food restaurants found that a significant majority of the parents were more absorbed in their mobile devices than they were in relating to their children (Radesky et al. 2014).

We may also multitask among several online and offline interactions simultaneously, such as in class or while doing homework. You may think you do a great job of multitasking, but dividing focus in this way can actually reduce your ability to comprehend and remember and thus lower your performance on tests and other assignments (PBS 2010).

Internet technology also affects the nature of consumption. More of it is taking place on such sites as eBay and Amazon, and that trend has definitely been accelerated by the COVID-19 pandemic. Globally, consumers spent a record $5.7 trillion shopping online in 2022 (Pasquali 2023). It is also easier for people to spend money on consumption on internet sites than it is in the material world. It is worth noting that these sites, as well as the internet in general, are global in scope. The ease with which global interactions and transactions occur on the internet is a powerful indicator of, and spur to, the process of globalization.

Smartphones are also having a variety of effects on consumption. For example, on the one hand, they are making it easier for people to find particular kinds of restaurants and to get to them quickly and efficiently. On the other hand, when people are eating in those restaurants, smartphones tend to slow down service because diners take time photographing the meal, taking selfies, and asking waitstaff to take photos of them (Griswold 2014). Many shoppers use their smartphones in stores to look

Social changes brought about by the thorough integration of the internet in most areas of our lives have been enormously influential—and the changes are far from over. Teenagers and even very young children take our constant connectivity for granted, suggesting that most of the changes we are witnessing will become ever more pervasive.

Hill Street Studios/Blend Images/Getty Images

up product information, compare prices, and download coupons (Skrovan 2017). Target now uses Bluetooth beacon technology to locate shoppers in its stores via a Target app on their smartphone and to direct them to products on their shopping lists (Perez 2017).

Digital Living: Blogging and Tweeting about Sociology

Blogging and tweeting are two popular ways to transmit and acquire information today. Current events are often posted in real time, sometimes by individuals who are witnessing them. The Arab Spring was referred to as the Twitter Revolution because people around the world were able to follow these political uprisings through tweets posted by protestors. Sports fans can follow their favorite teams and on game day receive instantaneous alerts when their team scores a touchdown or scores a run. Individuals who want to find alternative perspectives on social issues from the mainstream press can follow a variety of alternative online sites (e.g., the far-right-wing Breitbart News) and blogs (e.g., the left-leaning Mother Jones). Blogging and tweeting encourage individual agency. They offer the opportunity for those of us with access to participate in the social construction of reality and can be used as platforms to promote social reforms, such as #BlackLivesMatter. But there are a few structural constraints attached to these methods of communication. Twitter limits tweets to 280 characters unless you are a paid subscriber. Many popular blogs and Twitter accounts are written and maintained by celebrities, professional experts, and representatives of formal organizations (some of which are highly politicized), who have more power to shape reality than the average person does. Especially notable in this regard is the use of Twitter by Donald Trump, both as presidential candidate and as president, to reach directly his supporters and thereby bypass the traditional media. Trump's Twitter account (@RealDonaldTrump) has almost 90 million followers.

Sociologists and organizations devoted to sociological theory and research use blogs and tweets to expose others to the sociological imagination, helping individuals at the micro level realize that their private troubles are connected to larger public issues. Popular sociologists who blog include one of the authors of this book, George Ritzer (https://georgeritzer.wordpress.com), who discusses the themes addressed in this book, such as McDonaldization, globalization, and consumption, and Philip Cohen, who writes about family inequality (https://familyinequality.wordpress.com). The Society Pages blog (https://thesocietypages.org) includes a set of sociology blogs such as The Color Line (https://thesocietypages.org/colorline) and Sociology Lens (www.sociologylens.net) that keep readers current on issues pertaining to inequality, race, gender, crime, and health. The American Sociology Association's blog (speak4sociology.org) offers a forum for its followers to debate sociological issues. A variety of Twitter accounts regularly post comments about and links to relevant sociological topics, including @Soc_Imagination, @SociologyLens, @DiscoverSoc, @SocWomen, and @SocImages. In addition, professional sociologists, such as Michael Burawoy (@burawoy), Matthew Desmond (@just_shelter), Zeynep Tufekci (@zeynep), and Sudhir Venkatesh (@avsudhir), tweet to promote awareness about social problems and publicize their research and social activism.

SUMMARY

Sociology is the systematic examination of the ways in which people are affected by and affect the social structures and social processes associated with the groups, organizations, cultures, societies, and world in which they exist. Social changes in the last few centuries, including the Industrial Revolution, the growth of the service sector, and the arrival of the information age, have strongly influenced the field of sociology. This book deals with innumerable social issues, but it focuses especially on the powerful structural forces in the social world that have drawn the attention of contemporary sociologists: globalization, consumption, McDonaldization and digital technology.

As the world has become more globalized, it has become more fluid as people, products, and information flow more quickly and easily across national borders. The role of consumption in our daily lives over the past few decades has resulted in the increasing use of credit cards and the growing popularity of online shopping. Digital technology is changing how and when we interact with others, including the near ubiquitous use of smartphones and social media. The process of McDonaldization, or an emphasis on efficiency, calculability, predictability, and technological control, characterizes many aspects of globalization, consumption, and digital technology.

Social changes such as globalization, consumption, and digital technology can be understood using C. Wright Mills's "sociological imagination," which calls on us to look at social phenomena not just from a personal perspective but also from the outside, from a distinctively sociological perspective. In addition, recognizing that much of our reality is socially constructed can help us comprehend how the agency of individuals can bring about social change; at the same time, these changes become structures that both enable and constrain social action. These social structures become enduring and slow to change, while social processes represent the more dynamic aspects of society.

Sociologists study many issues, sometimes to understand them through scientific research and sometimes to help generate change and reform. The goal of sociology as a pure science is to collect large quantities of data about the social world to build knowledge, while the goal of sociology as a means of social reform aims to use this knowledge for social change.

Sociology, like other social sciences, distinguishes itself from commonsense opinions about the social world by developing rigorous theories and engaging in systematic research to study social phenomena. Sociology, the least specialized of the social sciences, encompasses aspects of anthropology, political science, psychology, economics, and communications.

KEY TERMS

butterfly effect
consumption
dangerous giants
fact
globalization
macro

McDonaldization
mediated interaction
meso
micro
opinion
professional sociologist

social construction of reality
social processes
social sciences
social structures

society
sociological imagination
sociology
technology

REVIEW QUESTIONS

1. How is the projected impact of the driverless car an example of the butterfly effect? Use your sociological imagination to think of ways in which your individual choices and actions will be influenced by this development.

2. Your social world is continually changing. What are some examples of new technologies that have been developed during your lifetime? How have they changed the way you interact with and relate to others?

3. How do shopping malls reflect increasing globalization? Do you think shopping malls lead to a sameness of culture around the world, or do they allow local areas to retain their differences?

4. What items are you most likely to buy using the internet? How do social networking sites (e.g., Facebook, Twitter, Instagram, TikTok) influence what you consume?

5. What social structures have impeded the flow of information in the past? How have the internet and social networking sites made it easier to get around these structural barriers?

6. According to C. Wright Mills, how are private troubles different from public issues? How can we use the micro/macro distinction to show how private troubles are related to public issues?

7. What is the difference between structure and agency? Within your classroom, could you be a "dangerous giant"? In what ways does your school prevent you from becoming a dangerous giant?

8. What do sociologists mean by the social construction of reality? How can you apply this perspective to better understand trends in the fashion industry?

9. Can you think of ways in which we can use "pure science" to better understand the process of McDonaldization? What do you believe should be the goal of research?

10. How is sociology's approach to globalization different from that of other social sciences? What are the advantages of using a sociological approach to understand globalization?

iStock Images/vitomirov

2 THINKING SOCIOLOGICALLY

> **LEARNING OBJECTIVES**
>
> **2.1** Identify the most important classical sociologists and their major contributions to the field.
>
> **2.2** Identify other influential early figures in classical sociology.
>
> **2.3** Compare and contrast structural/functional, conflict/critical, and inter/actionist theories.

HOW DO THEORIES HELP US UNDERSTAND POLITICS AND OTHER SOCIAL INSTITUTIONS?

The election of a number of highly polarizing political figures in recent years (Donald Trump in the United States, Jair Bolsonaro in Brazil, Viktor Orbán in Hungary) has arguably led to increased levels of political maneuvering, fiery rhetoric, and intense partisanship, including after such people have been voted out of office. Many countries have witnessed increasing divergence between political parties on a range of social issues and, to paraphrase a popular saying, politics no longer seems as usual.

How would a sociologist explain such highly partisan political action and mutual antagonism? The answer depends to a large extent on which sociologist you ask. Like other scientists, sociologists use theories to make sense of the phenomena they study. A sociologist's perspective on any given issue is therefore framed by the particular explanatory theories to which they subscribe.

Some sociologists suggest that partisan political maneuvering and debate, even if impassioned, are a normal aspect of stable government, necessary to resolve issues and move society forward. Others believe that factions fighting to promote their own interests are enacting a simple, if large-scale, power struggle. Still others might explain the partisanship as a reflection of the deep ideological divide that exists within the population as a whole. In this view, politicians' actions represent nothing more than the dominant ideas, beliefs, and feelings of their constituents.

In this chapter, we identify the particular sociological theories that frame each of these perspectives—and many more. Each is the product of decades (and sometimes centuries) of development, and each has undergone testing, modification, and critique by some of sociology's greatest minds. As you learn about the notable sociological thinkers—both classical and contemporary—and the theories they developed, consider the sociopolitical events that shaped them during their lives. Consider, too, the events that have shaped, and are shaping, you and your own perspectives on the world.

This chapter is devoted to the ways in which sociologists think, or theorize. All sociologists theorize. While some stay very close to their data, others feel free to depart from the data and offer very broad and general theories—"grand theories"—of the social world (Hoffman 2013; Skinner 1985; Vidal, Adler, and Delbridge 2015). Most of this chapter is devoted to grand theories and to the people who produced them.

Theories are sets of interrelated ideas that have a wide range of applications, deal with centrally important issues, and have stood the test of time (Ritzer and Stepnisky 2018). Theories have stood the test of time when they continue to be applicable to the changing social world and have withstood challenges from those who accept other theories. Sociological theories are necessary to make sense of both the innumerable social phenomena and the many highly detailed findings of sociological research. Without such theories, we would have little more than knowledge of isolated bits of the social world. However, once those theories have been created, they can be applied broadly to such areas as the economy, organizations, religion, society as a whole, and even the globe. The theories to be discussed in this chapter deal with very important social issues that have affected the social world for centuries and will likely continue to affect it. Among these issues are violence, suicide, alienation and exploitation in the work world, and revolution.

Consider, for example, a recent theory of violence developed by Randall Collins (2008; Ferret and Collins 2018), which was mentioned briefly in Chapter 1. In line with the definition of theory offered previously, violence is clearly an important social issue, and Collins's theory promises to stand the test of time. Collins seeks to contradict the idea that violence is inherent in people and emphasizes the social contexts and causes of violence instead. He is developing a broad theory of violence that encompasses everything from a slap in the face to war, a quarrel to mass murder in gas chambers, drunken carousing to serial killing, a rape to systematic rape as a war crime, and the murder of someone with a different ethnicity to ethnic cleansing. Beyond being a very wide-ranging social phenomenon, violence usually generates powerful reactions among those who commit it, its victims, and those who witness it or read about it. As Collins puts it, violence is "horrible and heroic, disgusting and exciting, the most condemned and glorified of human acts" (2008, 1). But the details of Collins's theory are not the concern here. Rather, it is the fact that he is seeking to develop a perspective that meets our definition of theory. In the coming years we will need to see whether Collins's specific theory actually stands the test of time. However, it is clear that violence is an important social phenomenon worth theorizing about (and studying). Collins has taken an important step in developing such a theory.

Officials exhume the bodies of unidentified civilians killed in 2022 during the Russian invasion of Ukraine. Sociologists construct theories to explain violence of all kinds, including war crimes.

Getty Images/Sergei Supinsky

Violence is not only important in itself as a social phenomenon; it also raises important issues for other aspects of the social world. For example, the mass media are constantly confronted with decisions about how much violence—and the resulting carnage—they should show to the public. The wrenching choices that such depictions (often readily and permanently available on internet sites such as YouTube and Twitter) pose for the mass media, to say nothing about the families and friends of the victims, continue.

Theorizing about the social world is not restricted to sociologists such as Randall Collins; everyone theorizes. What, then, distinguishes the theorizing of sociologists from the typical person on the street? One difference is that whereas the typical person on the street might theorize casually, sociologists go about their theorizing systematically by, among other things, making the social world their laboratory. For example, someone might notice two people together. Drawing on their observations of how those people are interacting (including what they are wearing and their nonverbal communication) and your ideas of romantic relationships and behaviors, they may conclude that they are dating (Weigel 2016). They have a (perhaps unconscious) theory about dating, and they use it to interpret their actions and predict how they might interact next. In contrast, sociologists are likely to be conscious of their theory of dating. With that theory as background, they might study behaviors among many pairs of people, carefully analyze the similarities and differences among them, compare those behaviors to those of people in other societies, and then conclude that a particular style of interaction characterizes dating couples. More concretely, a study of 144 college students used a classical theory of deviance to demonstrate that academic and interpersonal stress increased dating violence (Mason and Smithey 2012).

Using another (social learning) theory, Giordano and colleagues (2015) interviewed nearly 1,000 students in 32 schools and found that the level of violence in a school was a significant predictor of whether a student would perpetrate a violent act. To some degree, perpetrators "learn" to commit violent acts in the context of schools characterized by violence. At some level, we are all theorists, but professional sociologists consciously use theories to analyze scientific data systematically in order to make better sense of their results and of the social world.

Sociologists not only work directly with, and read the work of, other contemporary sociologists; they also base their theories on the work of many important thinkers in the field who have come before them. As the great physicist Sir Isaac Newton ([1687] 2005) put it, "If I have seen further, it is only by standing on the shoulders of giants." Many of today's sociologists theorize because they are able to build on the thoughts of the classical "grand theorists" to be discussed in this chapter.

THE GIANTS OF CLASSICAL SOCIOLOGICAL THEORY

The roots of professional academic sociology lie primarily in early nineteenth-century Europe. However, there were much earlier thinkers whose ideas are relevant to sociology. Examples from the third and fourth centuries BCE are Plato and Aristotle. Centuries later, Ibn Khaldun (1332–1406) developed sociological theories that dealt with such issues as the scientific study of society, the interrelationship between politics and the economy, and the relationship between primitive societies and the medieval societies of his time (Alatas 2011, 2013). Such topics were also of interest to nineteenth-century theorists and continue to be of interest today. For example, Alatas (2014) has applied Khaldun's thinking to such modern Arab states as Syria and its prospects in light of the war raging there.

The emergence of professional academic sociological theory was closely related to intellectual and social developments throughout the nineteenth century in Europe. It is important to recognize that sociological theory did not develop in isolation or come of age in a social vacuum. In Chapter 1, we briefly mentioned the impact of the Industrial Revolution. Other changes that profoundly affected sociological theorizing were the political revolutions that wracked European society (especially the French Revolution, 1789–1799), the rise of socialism, the women's rights movement, the urbanization occurring throughout Europe, ferment in the religious realm, and the growth of science.

Early Sociological Theorists

Among the most important early sociological theorists are Auguste Comte, Harriet Martineau, and Herbert Spencer.

- *Auguste Comte* (1798–1857) is noted, as pointed out in Chapter 1, for the invention of the term *sociology*, development of a general theory of the social world, and interest in developing a science of sociology (Pickering 2011).

- *Harriet Martineau* (1802–1876), like Comte, developed a scientific and general theory, although she is best known today for her feminist, women-centered sociology (Hoecker-Drysdale 2011).

- *Herbert Spencer* (1820–1903) also developed a general, scientific theory of society, but his overriding theoretical interest was in social change, specifically evolution in not only the physical domain but also the intellectual and social domains (Francis 2011).

Although Comte, Martineau, and Spencer were important predecessors, the three theorists to be discussed in this section—Karl Marx, Max Weber, and Émile Durkheim—are arguably the most significant of the classical era's social theorists and of the greatest continuing contemporary relevance to sociology (and other fields). Their relevance to you lies in the fact that, among many other points, they analyzed the negative effects of too much (Marx and Weber) and too little (Durkheim) social control on people. Their analyses were connected to their major fears about the modern world—that capitalist systems alienate and exploit us (Marx), that rational systems trap and limit us (Weber), and that a weak shared culture exerts too little external control and leads us to run wild in the endless pursuit of that which ultimately proves unsatisfying, if not disastrous (Durkheim).

Karl Marx

Marx (1818–1883) is often dismissed as an ideologue. In recent years, he has been disparaged because of the supposed failure of a social system—communism—that is generally considered to be his brainchild. In fact, the communism that came to be practiced in the Soviet Union and other countries had little relationship to Marx's abstract sense of communism. He would have been as critical of it as he was of capitalism. However, there is an important sociological theory in Marx's work (Antonio 2011; Holt 2015). Its importance is reflected in the fact that many theorists have built on it and many others have created theories in opposition to Marx's perspective (Sitton 2010).

Marx was mainly a macro theorist who focused most of his attention on the structure of capitalist society, a relatively new phenomenon in his day. Marx defined **capitalism** as an economic system based on the fact that one group of people—the **capitalists**—owns what is needed for production, including factories, machines, and tools. A second group—the **proletariat**, or workers—owns little or nothing except their capacity for work and labor. In order to work and survive, the workers must sell their labor to the capitalists in exchange for wages. In Marx's view, the capitalist system is marked by **exploitation** (Carver 2018). The proletariat produces virtually everything but gets only a small portion of the income derived from the sale of the products. The capitalists, who do little productive work, reap the vast majority of the rewards. In other words, the capitalists *exploit* the workers. Furthermore, driven by the desire to generate larger and larger profits, the capitalists seek to keep costs, including wages, as low as possible. As a result, the proletariat barely subsists, often working long hours but still barely, or not at all, able to survive.

Though Herbert Spencer never earned an academic degree, his work contributed greatly to the field of scientific sociology, especially in the study of evolutionary change.

Granger, NYC—All rights reserved.

In addition, the workers experience **alienation** on the job and in the workplace (Carver 2018; Mészáros 2006). They are alienated because

- The work they do—for example, repetitively and mechanically inserting wicks into candles or attaching hubcaps to cars—is not a natural expression of human skills, abilities, and creativity.
- They have little or no connection to the finished product.
- Instead of working harmoniously with their fellow workers, they may have little or no contact with them. In fact, they are likely to be in competition or outright conflict with them over, for example, who keeps and who loses their jobs or who gets promotions and raises.

Thus, what defines people as human beings—their ability to think, to act on the basis of that thought, to be creative, to interact with other human beings—is denied to the workers in capitalism. As capitalists adopt new technologies to make their companies more competitive and seek to continually extract more and more profit, alienation among the workers increases. For example, faster, more mechanized assembly lines make it even more difficult for coworkers to relate to one another.

Over time, Marx believed, the workers' situation would grow much worse as the capitalists increased the level of exploitation and restructured the work so that the proletariat became even more alienated. The gap between these two social classes would grow wider and increasingly visible in terms of the two groups' economic position and the nature of their work (or lack thereof). Once workers understood how capitalism "really" worked, especially the ways in which it worked to their detriment, they would rise up and overthrow that system in what Marx called a proletarian revolution.

According to Marx, the outcome of the proletarian revolution would be the creation of a communist society. Interestingly, Marx had very little to say explicitly about what a communist society would look like. In fact, he was highly critical of utopian thinkers who wasted their time drawing beautiful portraits of an imaginary future state. Marx was too much the sociologist and concentrated instead on trying to better understand the structures of the ongoing capitalist society. He was particularly interested in the ways in which they operated, especially to the advantage of the capitalists and to the disadvantage of the proletariat.

Marx believed that his work was needed because the capitalist class tried hard to make sure that the proletariat did not truly understand the nature of capitalism. One of the ways in which the capitalists did this was to produce a set of ideas, an ideology, which distorted the reality of capitalism and concealed the ways in which it really operated. As a result, the proletariat suffered from **false consciousness**—the workers did not truly understand capitalism and may have even believed, erroneously, that the system operated fairly and perhaps even to their benefit. Marx's work was devoted to providing the members of the proletariat with the knowledge they needed to see through these false ideas and achieve a truer understanding of the workings of capitalism.

Marx hypothesized that the workers could develop **class consciousness**, and such a collective consciousness would lead them to truly understand capitalism, their role in it, and their relationship to one another as well as to the capitalists. Class consciousness was a prerequisite of the revolutionary actions to be undertaken by the proletariat. In contrast, the capitalists could never achieve class consciousness because, in Marx's view, they were too deeply involved in capitalism to be able to see how it truly operated.

Marx's theories about capitalism are relevant to contemporary society. For example, in the United States, a capitalist country, the income gap that Marx predicted between those at the top of the economic system and the rest of the population is huge and growing. In 2020, the top 20 percent of the population in terms of household income had a greater average income than the rest of the population combined (U.S. Census 2020). As you can see in Figure 2.1, those at the top have greatly increased their average income since 1967; this is especially true of the top 5 percent of the population. Furthermore, the top 1 percent controlled almost 40 percent of the nation's wealth in 2020.

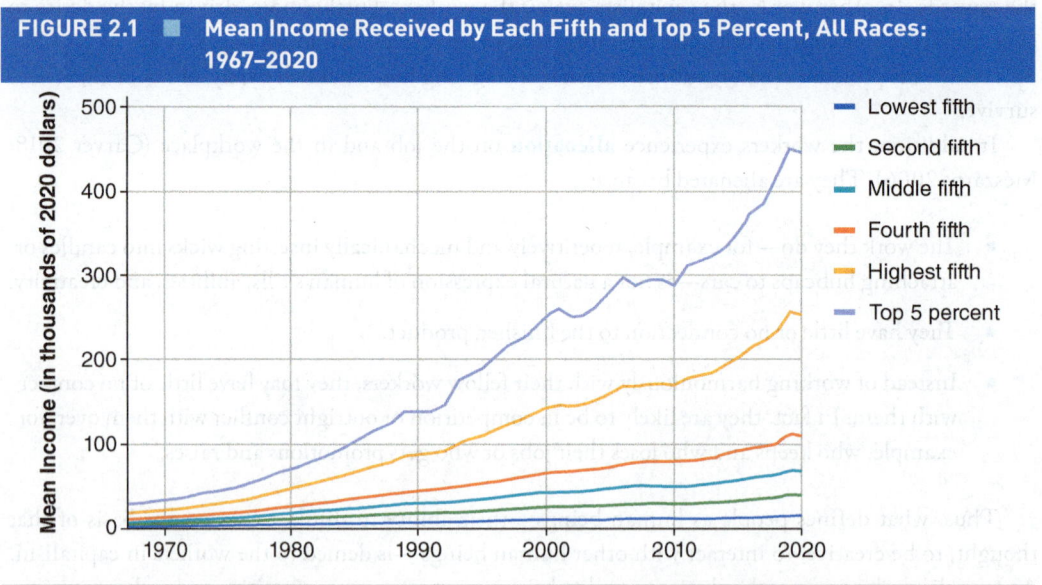

FIGURE 2.1 ■ Mean Income Received by Each Fifth and Top 5 Percent, All Races: 1967–2020

Source: U.S. Census Bureau. 2020. "Table H3. Mean Household Income Received by Each Fifth and Top 5 Percent." Retrieved January, 04, 2022 (https://www.census.gov/data/tables/time-series/demo/income-poverty/historical-income-households.html).

Marx also theorized that capitalism would force the capitalists to find the cheapest sources of labor and resources wherever they existed in the world. As Marx predicted, corporations continue to scour the globe for workers willing (or forced) to work for lower wages, driving down pay closer to home and reaping as much profit as possible from lower labor costs (among other things, including environmental controls and tax rates).

However, history has yet to bear out much of Marx's thinking about the demise of capitalism. For example, there has not yet been a widescale global proletarian revolution. This is the case, among other reasons, because of the increasing ability of capitalism to put off such a revolution. Despite the threats to the proletariat, capitalism continues to exist, and Marx's ways of thinking about it, and the concepts he developed for that analysis, continue to be useful and highly influential throughout much of the world.

Max Weber

Although Karl Marx was an important social theorist, he developed most of his ideas outside the formal academic world. It took time for those ideas to gain recognition from scholars. In contrast, Max Weber (1864–1920; pronounced VAY-ber) was a leading professional academic of his day (Kalberg 2011, 2017). Weber, like Marx, devoted great attention to the economy. Many of Marx's ideas informed Weber's thinking, in large part because those ideas were finding a wide public audience at the time that Weber was active. Furthermore, Weber south to understand the dramatic changes, inspired at least in part by Marx's ideas, taking place in Europe and elsewhere. Nevertheless, Weber rarely discussed Marx's theories explicitly. Thus, observers have characterized much of Weber's work as a debate with Marx's "ghost."

Weber's best-known work—*The Protestant Ethic and the Spirit of Capitalism* ([1904–1905] 1958)—is part of his historical-comparative study of religion in various societies throughout the world. One of his main objectives was to analyze the relationship between the economy and religion. This is a good example of his debate with Marx. Marx had argued that religion is a force that serves to distract the masses from the problems caused by capitalism. In Marx's ([1843] 1970) famous words, religion "is the opium of the people." In comparison, Weber focused more explicitly on his argument of the central role religion had played in the Western world's economic development.

Weber argued that beginning in the seventeenth century, it was Protestantism in general, and especially Calvinism, that led to the rise of capitalism in the West and not in other areas of the world. Calvinists believed that people were predestined to go to heaven or hell; that is, they would end up in heaven or hell no matter what they did or did not do. Although they could not affect their destiny, they could uncover "signs" that indicated whether they were "saved" and going to heaven. Economic success was a particularly important sign that one was saved. However, isolated successful economic successes were not sufficient. Calvinists had to devote their lives to hard work and economic success, as well as to other "good works." At the same time, the Calvinists were quite frugal. All of this was central to the distinctive ethical system of the Calvinists, and more generally Protestants, that Weber referred to as the **Protestant ethic**.

Weber was interested not only in the Protestant ethic but also in the "spirit of capitalism" it helped spawn. The Protestant ethic was a system of ideas closely associated with religion, while the spirit of capitalism involved a transformation of those ideas into a perspective linked directly to the economy. As the economy came to be infused with the spirit of capitalism, it was transformed into a capitalist economic system. Eventually, however, the spirit of capitalism, and later capitalism itself, grew apart from its roots in Calvinism and the Protestant ethic. Capitalist thinking eventually could not accommodate such seemingly irrational forms of thought as ethics and religion.

Despite his attention to it, Weber was *not* interested in capitalism per se. He was more interested in the broader phenomenon of **rationalization**, or the process by which social structures are increasingly characterized by the most direct and efficient means to their ends. In Weber's view, this process was becoming more and more common in many sectors of society, including the economy, especially in bureaucracies and in the most rational economic system—capitalism. Capitalism is rational because of, for example, its continual efforts to find ways to produce more profitable products efficiently, with fewer inputs and simpler processes. A specific and early example of rationalization in capitalism is the assembly line, in which raw materials enter the line and finished products emerge at the end. Fewer workers performed very simple tasks in order to allow the assembly line to function efficiently. More recently, manufacturers have added more rational, "lean" production methods, such as the just-in-time inventory system (Janoski 2015). Instead of storing extra components in case they are needed, the just-in-time system relies on the delivery of materials just when they are needed in the production process. This makes for highly efficient use of storage space and the funds needed to purchase materials.

Weber saw rationalization as leading to an "iron cage" of rationalized systems. Such a cage makes it increasingly difficult for people to escape the process. This gives a clear sense of his negative opinion of rationalization. In this light, consider what he has to say about the cage-like character of capitalism:

> Capitalism is today an immense cosmos into which the individual is born, and which presents itself to him, at least as an individual, as an unalterable order of things in which he must live. It forces the individual, in so far as he is involved in the system of market relationships, to conform to capitalist rules of action. (Weber [1904–1905] 1958, 54)

Such a negative view of rationalization and its constraints and socially harmful effects has persisted. It is frequently portrayed in popular entertainment, including George Orwell's novel, and later movie, *1984* (1949), as well as movies such as *Brazil* (1985), *V for Vendetta* (2005), the *Hunger Games* series (2012–2015), and television programs like *The Handmaid's Tale* (2017–present) and *Black Mirror* (2011–present).

In sum, while for Marx the key problems in the modern world were the exploitation and alienation that are part of the capitalist economy, for Weber the central problem was the control that rationalized structures such as capitalism exercise over us in virtually all aspects of our lives. Furthermore, while Marx was optimistic and had great hope for socialism and communism, Weber was a pessimist about most things. Socialism and communism, he felt, would not eliminate or prevent the iron cage from enveloping us: "Not summer's bloom lies ahead of us, but rather a polar night of icy darkness and hardness, no matter which group may triumph externally now" (Weber [1919] 1958, 128).

Émile Durkheim

Émile Durkheim (1858–1917) developed a theoretical orientation very different from those of his peers (Fournier 2013; Milibrandt and Pearce 2011). Like Marx and Weber, Durkheim focused on the macro end of the social continuum. However, while Marx and Weber were critical of the macro structures of prime concern to them—capitalism (Marx) and rationalized structures (Weber)—Durkheim generally had a positive view of macro structures.

For Durkheim, the major concern of the science of sociology was **social facts**. These are macro-level phenomena, such as social structures and cultural norms and values, that stand apart from people and, more important, impose themselves on people. Examples of social facts that impose themselves on you include the structures of your university and the national government. They are Durkheimian social facts because they have an independent existence and are able to force people to do things. Durkheim felt that such structures and their constraints were not only necessary but also highly desirable (at least to a point).

The differences among Marx, Weber, and Durkheim can be traced to each theorist's sense of the essential character of human beings (see Figure 2.2). Both Marx and Weber had a generally positive sense of people as thoughtful, creative, and naturally social. They criticized social structures for stifling and distorting people's innate characteristics. In contrast, Durkheim had a largely negative view of people as being slaves to their passions, such as lust and gluttony. Left to their own devices, he believed, people would seek to satisfy those passions. However, the satisfaction of one passion would simply lead to the need to satisfy other passions. This endless succession of passions could never be satisfied. In Durkheim's view, passions should be limited, but people are unable to exercise this control themselves. They need social facts that are capable of limiting and controlling their passions.

The most important of these social facts is the **collective conscience**, or the set of beliefs shared by people throughout society (Bowring 2016). In Durkheim's view, the collective conscience is highly desirable not only for society but also for individuals. For example, it is good for both society and individuals that we share the belief that we are not supposed to kill one another. Without a collective conscience, murderous passions would be left to run wild. Individuals would be destroyed, of course, and eventually so would society.

This leads us to Durkheim's *Suicide* ([1897] 1951), one of the most famous research studies in the history of sociology. Because he was a sociologist, Durkheim did not focus on why any given individual committed suicide. Rather, he dealt with the more collective issue of suicide rates and why one group of people had a higher rate of suicide than another. The study was, in many ways, an ideal example of the power of sociological research. Using publicly available data, Durkheim found, for example, that

> **FIGURE 2.2 ■ Karl Marx, Émile Durkheim, and Max Weber**
>
> Marx, Durkheim, and Weber were three of the most significant social theorists of their era. Though their theories were very different in many ways, all three were interested in the effect of social control on people.

Getty Images/Roger Viollet; Getty Images/Bettman; Getty Images/ullstein bild

suicide rates were not related to psychological and biological factors such as alcoholism or race and heredity. The causes of differences in suicide rates were *not* to be found within individuals. Rather, suicide rates were related to social factors that exert negative pressure on the individual. These include collective feelings of rootlessness and normlessness. Suicide literally destroys individuals. The tendency to emulate celebrity suicides, such as those of designer Kate Spade and food celebrity Anthony Bourdain in 2018, led to greater interest in contagion as another social factor in increasing suicides (Keller 2018). Suicide also constitutes a threat to society because those who commit suicide are rejecting a key aspect of the collective conscience—that one should not kill oneself.

Suicide has at least two important characteristics. First, the study was designed, like much sociological research today, to contribute to the public understanding of an important sociological problem or issue. Second, and more important for the purposes of this introduction to sociology, it demonstrated the power of sociology to explain one of the most private and personal of acts. Suicide had previously been seen as the province of the field of psychology, and responsibility for the act was most often accorded to the individual. Durkheim believed that if sociology could be shown to be applicable to suicide, it could deal with any and all social phenomena.

Durkheim differentiated among four types of suicide. The most important one for our purposes is *anomic suicide*. **Anomie** is defined as people's feeling that they do not know what is expected of them in society—the feeling of being adrift in society without any clear or secure moorings. According to Durkheim, the risk of anomic suicide increases when people do not know what is expected of them, when society's regulation over them is low, and when their passions are allowed to run wild.

More generally, Durkheim believed that anomie is the defining problem of the modern world. In contrast to Marx and Weber, who worried about too much external control over people, Durkheim, at least in his thinking on anomie, worried about too little control, especially over passions. This broad view appeared in another famous work by Durkheim, *The Division of Labor in Society* ([1893] 1964). He began by describing an early form of society with little division of labor. People there were held together by a type of solidarity—**mechanical solidarity**—stemming from the fact that they all did pretty much the same kinds of work, including hunting, gathering, and cooking. More important, people in this type of society had a strong collective conscience.

However, as Durkheim demonstrated, an increasing division of labor took place over time. Instead of continuing to do the same sorts of things, people began to specialize. Some became hunters, others farmers, and still others cooks. What held them together was not their similarities but their differences. That is, they had become more dependent on one another; people needed what others did and produced in order to survive. Durkheim called this later form of social organization **organic solidarity**. This can be a powerful form of solidarity, but it is accompanied by a decline in the power of the collective conscience. Because people were doing such different things, they no longer necessarily believed as strongly in the same set of ideas. This weakened collective conscience was a problem, Durkheim argued, because it progressively lost the power to control people's passions. Further, because of the weakened collective conscience, people were more likely to feel anomic and, among other things, were more likely to commit anomic suicide.

OTHER IMPORTANT EARLY THEORISTS

Although Marx, Weber, and Durkheim are the classical sociologists whose theories have most shaped contemporary sociology, several others made important contributions as well. Georg Simmel, W. E. B. Du Bois, and Thorstein Veblen all had grand theories of society, and you will see references to their ideas throughout this book.

Georg Simmel

Georg Simmel (1858–1918) offered an important grand theory that parallels those of the thinkers discussed previously (Helle 2015), but his major importance in contemporary sociology lies in his contributions to micro theory. Simmel believed that sociologists should focus on the way in which conscious individuals interact and associate with one another (Scaff 2011).

Simmel was interested in the *forms* taken by social interaction. One such form involves the interaction between superiors and subordinates. An example would be the interaction between the managers at IKEA and those who stock the shelves at that chain. Simmel was also interested in the *types* of people who engage in interaction. For example, one type is the poor person and another is the rich person. For Simmel, it was the nature of the interaction between these two types of people and not the nature of the people themselves that was of greatest importance. Therefore, poverty is not about the nature of the poor person but about the kind of interaction that takes place between the poor and the rich. A poor person is defined, then, not as someone who lacks money but rather as someone who receives aid from a rich person.

There is great detail in Simmel's analyses of forms of interaction and types of interactants, as there is in his larger macro theory. But for our purposes here, the main point is that Simmel was of greatest importance to the microinteractionist theories to be discussed in this chapter and at other points in this book.

Georg Simmel's interest in the forms taken by social interaction contributed to his influential theory that interaction defines people and society.

INTERFOTO/Alamy Stock Photo

W. E. B. Du Bois

Just as Harriet Martineau was a pioneer in bringing gender to the forefront in sociology, W. E. B. Du Bois (1868–1963) was crucial to the later focus of sociology on race (see Figure 2.3). Although Du Bois lived long into the modern era, his most important theoretical work was completed in the early twentieth century (Taylor 2011).

Du Bois is best known in sociology for his theoretical ideas but was also, like Durkheim and Weber, a pioneering researcher. In *The Philadelphia Negro* ([1899] 1996), Du Bois reported on his studies of the residents of the Seventh Ward in Philadelphia. He used a variety of social scientific methods, including field research, observation, and interviews. He dealt with such basic concerns in sociology as marriage and the family, education, work, the church, housing, and politics, as well as such social problems as illiteracy and crime. Du Bois placed most of the blame for the problems experienced by Black Philadelphians on Whites, racism, and discrimination. However, he did not ignore the role played by Blacks themselves in these problems. One example was their tendency to visit White physicians, thereby adversely affecting the livelihood of Black physicians.

As for his theoretical contributions, Du Bois saw what he called the "race idea" as central. He saw a "color line" existing between Whites and Blacks in the United States. (He ultimately came to recognize that such a divide existed globally.) He argued that this barrier was physical in the sense that Blacks could be distinguished visually, through their darker skin color, from White Americans. The barrier was also political in that much of the White population did not see Blacks as "true" Americans. As a result, they denied Blacks many political rights, such as the right to vote. And the barrier was psychological because, among other things, Blacks found it difficult to see themselves in ways other than the ways in which White society saw them.

FIGURE 2.3 ■ W. E. B. Du Bois and Harriet Martineau

Du Bois and Martineau were essential to efforts to bring a focus on race and gender, respectively, to the field of sociology.

Getty Images/Bettman

One of Du Bois's goals, especially in *The Souls of Black Folk* ([1903] 1966), was to lift the veil of race and give Whites a glimpse of "Negroes" in America. He also wanted to show Blacks that they could see themselves in a different way, especially outside the view that White society had prescribed for them. Politically, he hoped for the day when the veil would be lifted forever, thereby freeing Blacks. However, he did understand that destroying the veil of race would require a great deal of time and effort.

Another of Du Bois's important ideas is **double consciousness**. By this he meant that Black Americans have a sense of "two-ness," of being American and of being Black. Black Americans want to tear down the barriers that confront them but do not want to give up their identity, traditions, knowledge, and experience. That is, Black Americans are both inside and outside dominant, White American society. Double consciousness results in a sense among Black Americans that they are characterized by "two souls, two thoughts, two unreconciled strivings; two warring ideals" (Du Bois [1903] 1966, 5).

Double consciousness obviously produces great tension for Black Americans, much greater than the tensions felt by White Americans in regard to their race. However, it also gives Black Americans unusual insights into themselves, White Americans, and American society in general. Du Bois urged Black Americans to reach full maturity as a social group by reconciling and integrating these two conflicting aspects of their selves.

The idea of double consciousness has much broader applicability than just to Black Americans. Other racial and ethnic minorities can be seen as having such a double consciousness—for example, of being Hispanic and American. Similarly, women likely see themselves as both females and Americans. This leads us to wonder: Who does *not* have double consciousness? It also leads to the view that Du Bois did not go nearly far enough with this idea. There may be more, perhaps many more, than two consciousnesses. Consider, for example, the quadruple consciousness of a *female* immigrant from *Guatemala* who is *Hispanic* and has become a *U.S. citizen*.

Thorstein Veblen

Like many of the other figures discussed in this chapter, Thorstein Veblen (1857–1929) had a broader theory (McCormick 2011), but given that one of our focuses in this book is on consumption, we address here only the ideas associated with his most famous book, *The Theory of the Leisure Class* (Veblen [1899] 1994).

One of Thorstein Veblen's major concerns is the ways in which the upper classes demonstrate their wealth. One way to show off wealth is through *conspicuous leisure,* or doing things that demonstrate quite publicly that one does not need to do what most people consider to be work. Veblen believed that the wealthy want to demonstrate to all that they can afford to waste time, often a great deal of time. Sitting on one's porch sipping margaritas, perhaps in "Margaritaville," having workers tend to one's lawn, and frequently playing golf at expensive golf clubs would be examples of conspicuous leisure. However, the problem with conspicuous leisure is that it is often difficult for very many others to witness these displays (though in contemporary times, increasingly easier through the use of social media).

Thus, over time the focus for the wealthy shifts from publicly demonstrating a waste of time to publicly demonstrating a waste of money. (Compare this set of values to the frugality of the Calvinists studied by Weber.) The waste of money is central to Veblen's most famous idea, conspicuous consumption. It is much easier for others to see conspicuous consumption than it is for them to see conspicuous leisure. Examples include building extravagant homes, such as David and Jackie Siegel's 90,000-squarefoot mansion (named Versailles) in Orlando, Florida; driving around one's neighborhood in a Porsche; and wearing Dolce & Gabbana clothing with the D&G logo visible to all. The well-to-do, Veblen's "leisure class," stand at the top of a society's social class system. Many in the social classes below the wealthy, the middle and lower classes, copy the leisure class. For example, people in lower social classes might build relatively inexpensive McMansions or buy cheap knockoffs of D&G clothing.

Veblen is important because he focused on consumption at a time when it was largely ignored by other social theorists. Furthermore, his specific ideas, especially conspicuous consumption, continue to be applied to the social world.

Thorstein Veblen theorized that conspicuous consumption is a way for the wealthy to show off their wealth by purchasing expensive, highly visible houses, cars, jewelry, and clothing, among many other things.

Getty Images/Bettman

CONTEMPORARY SOCIOLOGICAL THEORY

As sociology has developed and grown as a discipline, the grand theories of earlier sociologists have evolved and branched out into dozens of newer theories. The work of the classical theorists has influenced each of these theories. For example, Marx's thinking on the relationship between capitalists and the proletariat strongly affected conflict/critical theory, and Simmel's micro-sociological ideas on forms and types of interaction helped shape inter/actionist theories. As Table 2.1 shows, these contemporary theories and the others reviewed in the rest of this chapter can be categorized under three broad headings: structural/functional, conflict/critical, and inter/actionist theories.

TABLE 2.1 ■ Major Sociological Theories		
Structural/Functional Theories	**Conflict/Critical Theories**	**Inter/Actionist Theories**
Structural-functionalism	Conflict theory Critical theory	Symbolic interactionism
Structuralism	Feminist theory Queer theory Critical theories of race and racism Postmodern theory	Ethnomethodology Exchange theory Rational choice theory

Structural/Functional Theories

Structural/functional theories have evolved out of the observation and analysis of large-scale social phenomena. These phenomena include the state and the culture, the latter encompassing the ideas and objects that allow people to carry out their collective lives. The two major theories under the broad heading of structural/functional theories are *structural-functionalism*, which looks at both social structures and their functions, and *structuralism*, which concerns itself solely with social structures, without concern for their functions. Note that while the names sound the same, structural-functionalism is one theory under the broader heading of structural/functional theories.

Structural-Functionalism

Structural-functionalism focuses on social structures as well as the functions that such structures perform. Structural-functionalists are influenced by the work of, among others, Émile Durkheim, who discussed, for example, the functions of and structural limits placed on deviance. Structural-functional theorists start out with a positive view of social structures. In the case of the sociology of deviance, those structures might include the military, the police, and the prison system. Structural-functional theorists also assert that those structures are desirable, necessary, and even impossible to do without. However, as you will see later, not all sociologists view social structures as completely positive.

Structural-functionalism tends to be a "conservative" theory. The dominant view is that if given structures exist and are functional—and it is often assumed that if they exist, they are functional—they ought to be retained and conserved.

A series of well-known and useful concepts have been developed by structural-functionalists, especially Robert Merton ([1949] 1968). These concepts are easily explained in the context of globalization. Specifically, they can be applied to issues such as border controls and the passports needed to pass through them, customs charges such as tariffs, and even the physical barriers at borders, such as the highly debated "wall" between many parts of the United States and Mexico.

One central concept in Merton's version of structural-functionalism is function. Functions are the observable, positive consequences of a structure that help it survive, adapt, and adjust. National borders are functional in various ways. For example, the passport controls at borders allow a country to monitor who is entering the country and to refuse entry to those it considers undesirable or dangerous. This function has become increasingly important in the era of global terrorism. Some of the individuals who perpetrated the 9/11 attacks on the United States entered the country by passing without notice through passport controls. Obviously, those controls were deficient. Now, however, more stringent passport and border controls serve the function of keeping out most other potential foreign terrorists. However, they are of no help with domestic terrorists, or those already living within a country's borders.

Structural-functionalism is greatly enriched when we add the concept of dysfunctions, which are observable consequences that negatively affect the ability of a given system to survive, adapt, or adjust. Although border and passport controls clearly have functions, they also have dysfunctions. After 9/11, Congress passed many immigration-related acts. As a result, it has become much more difficult for everyone to enter the United States (Kurzban 2006). This is true not only for potential terrorists but also for legitimate workers, businesspeople, tourists, and family members. As a result, many talented workers and businesspeople (and tourists) from other countries have decided to go elsewhere in the world, where there are fewer restrictions on their ability to come and go. However, large numbers of students continue to flock to the United States. Table 2.2 lists the top 10 countries of origin of international students attending school in the United States. Note the dominance of students from China.

The fact that both functions and dysfunctions are associated with structures raises the issue of the relative weight of the functions and the dysfunctions. How can we determine whether a given structure is predominantly functional or dysfunctional? In terms of the tightening of border controls, we would need to weigh the benefits of keeping out potential terrorists against the losses in international business transactions and university enrollments by overseas students. Such weightings are never easy.

TABLE 2.2 ■ Top 10 Countries of Origin of International Students in the United States, 2019–2020

Rank	Country of Origin	Number of Students	Percentage of Total
1	China	373,000	34.6
2	India	193,000	18.0
3	South Korea	50,000	4.6
4	Saudi Arabia	31,000	2.9
5	Canada	26,000	2.4
6	Vietnam	24,000	2.2
7	Taiwan	24,000	2.2
8	Japan	18,000	1.6
9	Brazil	17,000	1.6
10	Mexico	14,000	1.3

Source: Migration Policy Institute. 2021. "International Students in the United States." (https://www.migrationpolicy.org/article/international-students-united-states-2020).

Merton further elaborated on his basic theory by differentiating between two types of functions. The first encompasses **manifest functions**, or positive consequences brought about consciously and purposely. For example, taxes (tariffs) are imposed on goods imported into a given country from elsewhere in the world in order to make the prices of those goods higher compared with domestic-made goods and thus protect domestic producers. That is a manifest function of tariffs. However, such actions often have **latent functions**, or unintended positive consequences. For example, when foreign products become more expensive and therefore less desirable, domestic manufacturers may produce more and perhaps better goods in their own country. In addition, more jobs for local citizens may be created. Note that in these examples, both manifest and latent functions, like all functions within the structural-functionalist perspective, are positive.

One more concept of note is the idea of **unanticipated consequences**, or consequences that are unexpected and can be either positive or, more importantly, negative. A negative unanticipated consequence of increased tariffs is a trade war. China, for example, has responded to an increase in U.S. tariffs by raising its own tariffs on U.S. imports. As the United States retaliates with new and still higher tariffs, we could be in the midst of an unanticipated, and probably undesirable, trade war involving the United States, China, and perhaps other nations.

Structuralism

A second structural/functional theory, **structuralism**, focuses on structures but is not concerned with their functions. In addition, while structural-functionalism focuses on quite visible structures, such as border fences, structuralism is more interested in the social impacts of hidden or underlying structures, such as the global economic order or gender relations. It adopts the view that these hidden structures determine what transpires on the surface of the social world. This perspective comes from the field of linguistics, which has largely adopted the view that the surface, the way we speak and express ourselves, is determined by an underlying grammatical system (Saussure [1916] 1966). A sociological example would be that behind-the-scenes actions of capitalists and the capitalist system determine the public positions taken by political leaders.

Marx can be seen as a structuralist because he was interested in the hidden structures that determine how capitalism works. So, for example, on the surface capitalism seems to operate to the benefit of all. However, hidden below the surface is a structure that operates mostly for the benefit of the capitalists, who exploit the workers and often pay them subsistence wages. Similarly, capitalists argue that the value of products is determined by supply and demand in the market. In contrast, Marx argued that hidden beneath the surface is the fact that value comes from the labor that goes into the products, and this labor comes entirely from the workers.

Marx's frequent collaborator Friedrich Engels ([1884] 1970) looked at relationships between women and men and theorized that the structures of capitalism and patriarchy kept women subordinated to men. Engels assumed, as most writers of his time did, that family structure followed an evolutionary path from primitive to modern. In the early communistic society, members had multiple sexual pairings, and the uncertainty about who had fathered a child gave women power in the family and in society. Property passed from mother to child, and women were held in high esteem. However, as wealth began to accumulate and men gained control of agricultural production, men claimed more status. To guarantee the fidelity of the wife and therefore the paternity of the children, the social system evolved so that the wife was subjugated to male power and men sought to claim women as their own property. Monogamy eventually led to the even more restrictive marriage bond. Engels believed that with the advent of "marriage begins the abduction and purchase of women" ([1884] 1970, 735).

Engels believed that female oppression was rooted in the hidden and underlying structure of private property rights in capitalism. As a result, he thought that the key to ending that oppression was to abolish private property. Engels was arguably mistaken, however, in his conception of history. The period he describes as "primitive communism" arguably never really existed. Nevertheless, the connections he drew between gender inequality and the underlying structure of society have proved to be enduring, and many contemporary feminist theorists have built more sophisticated analyses on them (Chae 2014).

A structuralist approach is useful because it leads sociologists to look beyond the surface for underlying structures and realities, which determine what transpires on the surface. Thus, for example, military threats made by North Korea, and its test-firing of missiles, may not really be about military matters at all but instead about that country's failing economic system. North Korea may hope that the symbolic expression of military power will distract its citizens, strengthen its global prestige, frighten others, and perhaps coerce other countries, into providing economic aid. A very useful sociological idea in this context is debunking (Berger 1963). **Debunking** plays off the idea that visible social structures such as the state are mere facades. It is the task of the sociologist to debunk, or to look beneath and beyond, such facades. This is very similar to the approach taken by many structuralists, although there is an important difference. The goal of many structuralists is merely to understand the underlying structure of, for example, the state, language, or family systems. In contrast, debunking not only seeks such understanding but also critically analyzes the underlying reality and its impact on visible social structures. Sociologists accomplish debunking by questioning societally accepted goals and the accounts provided by those in positions of authority. For example, although the United States seems to emphasize peace, sociologists have pointed out that it has a hidden and powerful military-industrial complex with a vested interest in war, or at least in preparations for war (Ledbetter 2011). Many sociologists see debunking as going to the very heart of the field of sociology (Baehr and Gordon 2012).

Conflict/Critical Theories

The idea of debunking is clearly critical in nature and therefore a perfect lead-in to a discussion of conflict/critical theories. Several theories are discussed under this heading: conflict theory, critical theory, feminist theory, queer theory, critical theories of race and racism, and postmodern theory. They all tend to emphasize stresses, strains, and conflicts in society. They are critical of society in a variety of different ways, especially of the power exercised over less powerful members of society.

Conflict Theory

Perhaps the best known of these theories is **conflict theory**. It has roots in Marx's theory, and much of it can be seen as an inversion of structural-functionalism, which conflict theory was designed to compete with and to counteract. While structural-functionalism emphasizes what is positive about society, conflict theory focuses on its negative aspects. To the structural-functionalist, society is held together by consensus; virtually everyone accepts the social structure, its legitimacy, and its benefits. To the conflict theorist, in contrast, society is held together by coercion. Those adversely affected by society, especially economically, would rebel were it not for coercive forces such as the police, the courts, and the military.

A good example of conflict theory is to be found in the work of Ralf Dahrendorf (1959). Although he was strongly influenced by Marx, he was more strongly motivated by a desire to develop a viable alternative to structural-functionalism. For example, while structural-functionalists tend to see society as static, conflict theorists like Dahrendorf emphasize the ever-present possibility of change. Where structural-functionalists see the orderliness of society, conflict theorists see dissension and conflict everywhere. Finally, structural-functionalists focus on the sources of cohesion internal to society, while conflict theorists stress the coercion and power that holds together an otherwise fractious society.

Overall, conflict theorists like Dahrendorf see two basic sides to society—consensus and conflict—and believe that both are needed. Sociology therefore needs, at least in this view, two different theories: conflict theory and "consensus" (or structural-functional) theory.

Dahrendorf offered a very sociological view of authority, arguing that it resides not in individuals (e.g., Joe Biden) but in positions (e.g., the presidency of the United States) and in various associations of people. In his view, those associations are controlled by a hierarchy of authority positions and the people who occupy them. However, there are many such associations in any society. Thus, a person may be in authority in one type of association but be subordinate in many others. For example, your professor might have authority in the classroom, but be subordinate to the head of the university, or perhaps to their parents or spouse.

What most interested Dahrendorf was the potential for conflict between those in positions of authority and those in subordinate positions. They usually have very different interests. Like authority, those interests are not characteristics of individuals but rather are linked to the positions they hold. Thus, the top management of a retail or fast-food corporation such as Walmart or McDonald's is interested in making the corporation more profitable by keeping wages low. In contrast, those who hold such low-level jobs as cashier or stock clerk are interested in increasing their wages to meet basic needs. Because of this inherent tension and conflict, authority within associations is always tenuous.

In general, the interests of those involved in associations are unconscious, but at times they become conscious and therefore more likely to lead to overt conflict. *Conflict groups* may form, as when a group of baristas goes on strike against Starbucks. The coalitions formed out of resistance efforts often increase cohesion among group members, further uniting them and bolstering the strength of the movement (Coser 1956). The actions of conflict groups can change society, as well as elements of society such as the Starbucks corporation, sometimes quite radically.

Critical Theory

While Marx's work was critical of the capitalist economy, **critical theory** shifts the focus to culture. Marx believed that culture is shaped by the economic system. In contrast, the critical school has argued that by the early twentieth century, and at an ever-accelerating rate to this day, culture has succeeded in becoming important in its own right. Furthermore, in many ways it has come to be more important than the economic system. Instead of being controlled by the capitalist economy, more of us are controlled—and controlled more often—by culture in general, specifically by the culture industry.

The **culture industry**, in Weber's sense, consists of the rationalized and bureaucratized structures that control modern culture. In their early years, the 1920s and 1930s, critical theorists focused on radio, magazines, and movies. Today, movies remain important, but the focus has shifted to television and various aspects of the internet, especially social media. These are critiqued for producing, or serving as an outlet for, **mass culture**, or cultural elements that are administered by organizations, lack spontaneity, and are phony. Two features of mass culture and its dissemination by the culture industry are of particular concern to critical theorists:

- *Falseness*. True culture should emanate from the people, but mass culture involves prepackaged sets of ideas that falsify reality. The so-called reality shows (e.g., *Survivor*) are a contemporary example of mass culture. These programs are also highly formulaic. They are presented as if they are authentic, but in fact they are scripted, highly controlled, and selectively edited—although in a different way than fictional dramas, comedies, and soap operas are. They are also false in the sense that they give consumers of mass culture the sense that there is a quick and easy route to fame and fortune.

- *Repressiveness*. Like Marx, the critical theorists feel that the masses need to be informed about things such as the falseness of culture so that they can develop a clear sense of society's failings and the need to rebel against them.

However, the effect of mass culture is to pacify, stupefy, and repress the masses so that they are far less likely to demand social change. Those who rush home nightly to catch up on their favorite reality TV shows are unlikely to have much interest in, or time for, revolutionary activities, or even civic activities and reforms. Additionally, according to some theorists, the culture industry has succeeded in creating a class of corporate brands (e.g., Facebook, TikTok) that are globally recognized and sought after as cultural symbols (Lash and Lury 2007). Instead of engaging in revolutionary activities, many people are striving to keep up with and acquire the latest and hottest brands.

Critical theory can be applied to some of the newest media forms, such as YouTube, Twitter, Instagram, TikTok, and especially Facebook (Denegri-Knott and Zwick 2012). Despite there being plenty of false and stupefying content on these sites, along with all the educational material, the sites are not totally controlled by large rationalized bureaucracies—at least not yet. Almost all the content that appears on sites such as YouTube, Facebook, and Twitter is provided by those who also consume material on the sites. The sites exercise little control over original content (an issue that is becoming increasingly heavily debated); that content is arguably spontaneously produced by those who use the sites. It's tempting to conclude that these new aspects of the culture industry are not assailable from a traditional critical theory perspective. Sites such as Facebook structure what is to be found there, especially through the use of algorithms. In addition, at least some of that which is to be found there is false. Seemingly relevant here is the idea of "fake news" made famous by Donald Trump and now employed by politicians in many other countries. However, the label of fake news was mainly applied by Trump to the mainstream media (e.g., *New York Times*, CNN), and it arguably was created to further stupefy people by demeaning the importance of news from relatively balanced sources.

Yet even if the content is not produced by the culture industry, the content is disseminated by it. So although many websites have yet to become profitable, they have come to be worth many billions of dollars each because of investors' belief in their future profitability. More important, the masses are pacified, repressed, and stupefied by spending endless hours buying and selling on eBay, watching YouTube videos, updating their Facebook pages, creating TikTok videos, and following day-to-day, even minute-by-minute, developments in the lives of others. Similar things could be said about Twitter's tweets, which inform us instantaneously that, among other things, one of our friends has gotten a haircut or a manicure. Although people do find friends, learn useful things, and perhaps even foment revolutions on Twitter (as in the case of the Arab Spring uprisings in 2011 and, briefly, the quickly aborted coup d'état in Turkey in mid-2016), they also may spend, and likely waste, endless amounts of time on it. Not infrequently, they also may find that corporations are using increasingly sophisticated online techniques to target them and to get them to consume their products.

Feminist Theory

Historically, male social theorists have received the most attention (one exception, mentioned previously, is Harriet Martineau), and to a large (though decreasing) extent, that is still the case today. Not surprisingly, then, social theories in the main have downplayed or ignored women and the distinctive problems they face (one exception is the work of Engels discussed previously). Many social theories have also tended to ignore gender more generally. Specifically, they have neglected to critically examine how femininity (and masculinity) are part of everything from social structures and institutions to everyday interactions. Feminist theorists point up and attempt to rectify the masculine bias built into most social theories. Similar to the broad range of sociological theories you have already encountered is a large and growing number of feminist theories that deal with a wide range of social issues (Adichie 2015; Bromley 2012; Lengermann and Niebrugge-Brantley 2014; see also the journal *Feminist Theory*). A central aspect of **feminist theory** in general is the critique of patriarchy (male dominance) and the problems it poses not only for women but also for men. Feminist theory also offers ideas on how everyone's (women's *and* men's) situation can be bettered, if not revolutionized.

One fundamental debate within feminist theory is whether gender inequality causes or results from gender differences. A few feminist theorists (e.g., Rossi 1983) believe that there are *essential* (or biologically determined) differences between men's and women's behavior and that gender inequality is a result of the social devaluing of female characteristics (such as nurturing). But the majority of feminist scholars argue that gender differences are *socially constructed*. In other words, the differences we see in behavior between men and women are not biologically determined but rather created socially.

Even feminist theorists who agree that gender differences are socially constructed disagree on the underlying causes. One view is that men, as the dominant group in society, have defined gender in such a way as to purposely restrain and subordinate women. Another view holds that social structures such as capitalist organizations and patriarchal families have evolved to favor men and traditionally male roles. Both structures benefit from the uncompensated labor of women, so there is little incentive for men as a dominant group to change the status quo. Clearly these perspectives all involve a critical orientation.

Despite the many global and individual changes in women's lives over the almost two centuries since professional academic sociology came into existence, there is also a broad consensus among feminist theorists that women continue to face extraordinary problems related directly to gender inequality. As you will learn about more in Chapter 10, these problems include, among innumerable others, a persistent wage gap between men and women in most countries and in most fields and systematic and widespread rape by invading forces in wartime. These extraordinary problems require extraordinary solutions. However, feminist theories vary in the degree to which they support dramatic, even revolutionary, changes in women's (and men's) situation. Some feminist theories suggest that the solution to gender inequality is to change social structures and institutions so that they are more inclusive of women and allow more gender diversity. Other feminist theories argue that because those very structures and institutions create gender difference and inequality, we must first deconstruct and then rebuild them in a wholly different way.

Women of color (and others) have sometimes been dissatisfied with feminist theory for not representing their interests very well. Several scholars argue that feminist theory generally reflects the perspective of White women while ignoring the unique experiences and viewpoints of women of color (Collins 2000; hooks 2000; Moraga and Anzaldua 2015; Zinn 2012). Similarly, studies related to race tend to focus largely (or wholly) on the position of men. Thus, many contemporary feminists have advocated for scholarship that takes into account not just gender but also how it intersects with race and ethnicity, social class, and sexuality. The upcoming discussion of critical theories of race and racism provides more detail on this view.

Queer Theory

The term *queer* was originally used as a negative term for gay men. Contemporary gay men, lesbians, bisexuals, trans, and others whose identities fall outside the gender and sexual mainstream have reclaimed the label *queer*, but now with a positive connotation. However, queer theory is *not* a theory of queer folks. As Ryan (2020) notes, "While the term 'queer' has also become a shorthand for those lying outside the dominant sex/gender/sexuality paradigm, in the sense of queer theory it is meant more to imply 'queering' something, that is to say questioning it, turning it inside out, and decentering it from the norm" (79).

Queer theory is based on the argument that there are no fixed and stable identities that determine who we are (McCann 2016; Fikry and Ryan 2015). The theory also unsettles identities that have long been thought to be fixed, stable, or natural, especially those formed through binaries (like man/woman, or gay/straight). Among others, it unsettles *queers* as a noun, as well as gender identities in general (Butler 1990). It seeks to question what it means to have an identity. In another sense, queer theory also seeks to decenter the core and to problematize that which is usually considered "normal." It leaves everything up for question and puts even our base assumptions under investigation.

As mentioned, queer theory does not focus exclusively on homosexuality. Instead it is willing to look at different aspects of social life through a sexual lens and to investigate the ways in which sexuality is embodied in those social institutions. This can even include areas of social life that are not typically seen as sexual, like archaeology (Dowson 2009), or even accounting (Rumens 2016). The aim is to show how sexuality, rather than being a distinct component of the social, is inextricably intertwined with the social. Thus, queer theory sees the sexual as a part of every aspect of our social lives and not just a distinct area of our personal lives.

Critical Theories of Race and Racism

As we saw earlier, W. E. B. Du Bois was a pioneer in the study of race and racism. In recent years, this perspective has blossomed in sociology under the heading of **critical theories of race and racism** (Delgado and Stefancic 2017; Slatton and Feagin 2019). Theorists who adopt this perspective argue that race continues to matter globally and that racism continues to have adverse effects on people of color. Given its history of slavery and racism, the United States has often been singled out for analysis using this theory.

Some commentators have argued that racism today is of little more than historical interest because White Americans have become "color blind." Those who adopt this point of view argue that we have come to ignore skin color when discussing social groups and that skin color is no longer being used in hiring or admissions policies. However, critical theorists of race and racism (as well as most empirical evidence) disagree. They argue that although skin color has nothing to do with a person's physical or intellectual abilities, color blindness ignores the past and present realities facing racial minorities, including the social consequences of years of racial discrimination. As a result, critics of the claim of color blindness argue that it is little more than a "new racism," a smoke screen that allows Whites to practice and perpetuate racial discrimination (Bonilla-Silva 2009, 2015). See the differing perceptions about employment opportunities illustrated in Figure 2.4, for example. The vast majority of White Americans believe that there is equal employment opportunity, but only a minority of Black Americans subscribe to that view. The White belief in the smoke screen of equal opportunity serves to rationalize continued discrimination against Blacks.

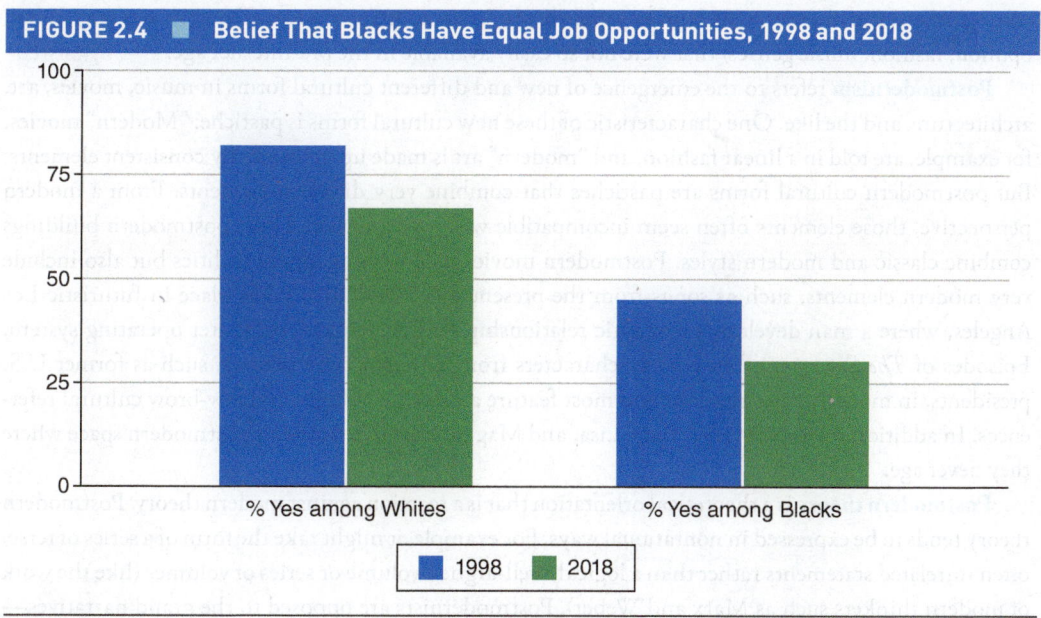

FIGURE 2.4 ■ Belief That Blacks Have Equal Job Opportunities, 1998 and 2018

Source: Gallup. 2019. "Fewer See Equal Opportunity for Blacks in Jobs, Housing." (https://news.gallup.com/opinion/gallup/246137/fewer-equal-opportunity-blacks-jobs-housing.aspx). https://docs.google.com/spreadsheets/d/e/2PACX-1vSEZXT30gNj3B86zm58tdM4pJIBIoQJK61nQvzaPuve KtQULfJ53DBayIKZRbqw3Z2CZtxMTVGf8KnB/pubhtml

The idea that racism continues has been very much in the news in recent years, especially with the murder of many people of color by White police officers. It has also become an issue associated with a number of politicians, most notably Donald Trump. It began haunting Trump in 2016 (and since) as he emerged victorious in the presidential campaign to replace a Black president, Barack Obama. During the campaign, Trump was accused of using "dog whistles" to appeal to White racists and others opposed to Obama and his designated successor, Hillary Clinton. *Dog whistles* are old-fashioned biased statements repackaged to make them more acceptable and to hide the true message from all but those with such biases. For example, at least initially, Trump refused to disavow the Ku Klux Klan and one of its most public figures, David Duke. He has since gone on to have strong associations with a number of proclaimed White Nationalists (both individuals and groups). That refusal, and those associations, could be considered dog whistles to White racists and other White supporters of his candidacy.

Of particular importance to recent work in this area is the idea of **intersectionality** (Collins and Bilge 2016), which points to the fact that people are affected, often adversely, not only by their race but also by their gender, sexual orientation, class, age, global location, and a variety of other demographic factors. The confluence, or intersection, of these various statuses and the inequality and oppression associated with combinations of them are what matter most. Not only are we unable to deal with race, gender, class, and so on separately; we also cannot gain an understanding of oppression by simply adding them together. For example, we cannot understand the position of a poor, Black, disabled lesbian simply by considering the situation of being poor, Black, disabled, or lesbian on their own. It is the combination of those identities that makes the oppression unique.

Postmodern Theory

Postmodern theory has many elements that fit well under the heading of critical theory, although there is more to it than critique. The term *postmodern* is used in various ways in relation to social theory. **Postmodernity**, for instance, is the state of society beyond the "modern era," which was the era analyzed by the classical social theorists. Among the characteristics of the modern world is rationality, as discussed in Weber's work. The postmodern world is less rational, nonrational, or even irrational. For example, although in the modern world groups such as the proletariat can plan in a rational manner to overthrow capitalism, in the postmodern world such changes come about accidentally or are simply fated to occur (Baudrillard [1983] 1990; Kellner 2011). Although modernity is characterized by a highly consistent lifestyle, postmodernity is characterized by eclecticism in what we eat, how we dress, and what sorts of music we listen to (Lyotard [1979] 1984). This eclecticism has been fostered by, among others, the internet, which gives people ready access to many more different things (e.g., news, opinion, fashion, music genres) that were not so easily available in the pre-internet age.

Postmodernism refers to the emergence of new and different cultural forms in music, movies, art, architecture, and the like. One characteristic of these new cultural forms is pastiche. "Modern" movies, for example, are told in a linear fashion, and "modern" art is made up of internally consistent elements. But postmodern cultural forms are pastiches that combine very different elements. From a modern perspective, those elements often seem incompatible with one another. Thus, postmodern buildings combine classic and modern styles. Postmodern movies deal with historical realities but also include very modern elements, such as songs from the present day. *Her* (2013) takes place in futuristic Los Angeles, where a man develops a romantic relationship with a "female" computer operating system. Episodes of *The Simpsons* often portray characters from different time periods, such as former U.S. presidents, in modern-day situations and most feature a pastiche of high- and low-brow cultural references. In addition, Homer, Marge, Bart, Lisa, and Maggie exist in a timeless, postmodern space where they never age.

Postmodern theory is a theoretical orientation that is a reaction against modern theory. Postmodern theory tends to be expressed in nonrational ways. For example, it might take the form of a series of terse, often unrelated statements rather than a logical, well-argued volume or series of volumes (like the work of modern thinkers such as Marx and Weber). Postmodernists are opposed to the grand narratives—the broad depictions of history and society—offered by modern theorists (Ryan 2017). An example of such a narrative is Weber's theory of the increasing rationalization of the world and the rise of an "iron cage" constraining our thoughts and activities. Instead, postmodernists tend to offer more limited, often unrelated, snapshots of the social world. In fact, postmodernists often deconstruct, or take apart, modern grand narratives. Postmodernists are also opposed to the scientific pretensions of much modern social theory. They adopt instead a nonscientific or even antiscientific approach to the social world. Feminist postmodernists reject the very language used by modern feminist scholars because words like *lesbian* have been constructed out of modern, male-centered thought. To some observers, the sociological study of deviance has all but disappeared because of postmodern conclusions that deviance is a purely relative phenomenon, dependent strictly on the definitions of those who have the power to define what is deviant (Sumner 1994).

In spite of, or perhaps because of, these differences, postmodern theory offers a new and important way of theorizing. Postmodern social theorists look at familiar social phenomena in different ways or adopt very different focuses for their work. For example, in his study of the history of prisons, Michel Foucault ([1975] 1979) was critical of the modernist view that criminal justice had grown progressively liberal. He contended that prisons had, in fact, grown increasingly oppressive through the use of techniques such as constant, enhanced surveillance of prisoners. Similarly, he argued against the traditional view that in the Victorian era people were sexually repressed; he found instead an explosion of sexuality in the Victorian era (Foucault 1978).

The most important postmodernist, Jean Baudrillard, argued that we are now living in a consumer society where much of our lives is defined not by our productive work but by what we consume and how we consume it. The postmodern world is, in fact, characterized by **hyperconsumption**, which involves consuming more than we need, more than we really want, and more than we can afford. The generally rising level of credit card debt around the world in recent decades is a sign of the hyperconsumption noted by Baudrillard. A more recent sign is found in "haul videos" posted online, mainly by young women, showing their "hauls" from given shopping trips accompanied by commentary on the products obtained.

This is not New York City but the hotel-casino called New York–New York in Las Vegas, Nevada. One hypothesis of postmodern theory is that we live in a world characterized by an increasing number of simulations of reality. How many others can you think of?

iStock Images/santirf

Another of Baudrillard's critical ideas that demonstrates the nature of postmodern social theory is simulation. A **simulation** is an inauthentic or fake version of something. Baudrillard saw the world as increasingly dominated by simulations. For example, when we eat at McDonald's, we consume Chicken McNuggets, or simulated chicken. It is fake in the sense that it is often not meat from one chicken but bits of meat that come from many different chickens. When we go to Disney World, we enter via Main Street, a simulation of early America that is really a shopping mall. We also go on simulated submarine rides to see simulated sea life rather than going to a nearby aquarium to see "real" sea life. When we go to Las Vegas, we stay in hotel-casinos that are simulations of New York of the early to mid-twentieth century (New York–New York), Venice (the Venetian), and ancient Egypt (the Luxor). The idea that we increasingly consume simulations and live a simulated life is a powerful critique of consumer society and, more generally, of the contemporary world. That is, not only are we consuming more; also, much of what we consume is fake.

Inter/Actionist Theories

The slash between *inter* and *action(ist)* in the heading to this section is meant to communicate the fact that we will deal with two closely related sets of theories here. The first consists of those theories that deal mainly with the interaction of two or more people (symbolic interactionism, ethnomethodology, and exchange theory). The second consists of those that focus more on the actions of individuals (rational choice theory). A common factor among these theories is that they tend to focus on the micro level of individuals and groups. This is in contrast to the theories discussed previously that tend focus more on the macro structures of society.

Symbolic Interactionism

As the name suggests, **symbolic interactionism** is concerned with the interaction of two or more people through the use of symbols (Quist-Adade 2018). We all engage in mutual action—interaction—with many others on a daily basis, whether it be face-to-face or more indirectly via cell phone, e-mail, or social media. But interaction could not take place without symbols: words, gestures, internet memes (Benaim 2018; Fikry et. al. 2021), and even objects that stand for things. Symbols allow the communication of meaning among a group of people.

Although we can interact with one another without words, such as through physical gestures like the shrug of a shoulder, in the vast majority of cases we need and use words to interact. And words make many other symbols possible. For example, the Harley-Davidson brand has meaning because it symbolizes a particular type of motorcycle. Both the brand name and the motorcycle are further symbolized by nicknames such as "Harley" and "hog."

Symbolic interactionism has several basic principles:

- Human beings have a great capacity for thought, which differentiates them from other animals (an idea that is heavily debated by others, including some sociologists). That innate capacity for thought is greatly shaped by social interaction. It is during social interaction that people acquire the symbolic meanings that allow them to exercise their distinctive ability to think. Those symbolic meanings in turn allow people to act and interact in ways that other animals arguably cannot.

- Symbolic meanings are not set in stone. People are able to modify them based on a given situation and their interpretation of it. A flag composed of the colors red, blue, yellow, orange, green, and purple, for example, is a symbol whose meaning can vary. For many, when in a particular order, it symbolizes the LGBTQ+ community. For some indigenous tribes in South America, it symbolizes their cultural heritage without reference to sexuality.

- People are able to modify symbolic meanings because of their unique ability to think. Symbolic interactionists frame *thinking* as people's ability to interact with themselves. In that interaction with themselves, people are able to alter symbolic meanings. They are also able to examine various courses of action open to them in given situations, to assess the relative advantages and disadvantages of each, and then to choose among them.

- It is the pattern of those choices of individual action and interaction that is the basis of groups, larger structures such as bureaucracies, and society as a whole. Most generally, in this theoretical perspective, symbolic interaction is the basis of everything else in the social world.

Symbolic interactionists are interested in how various aspects of identity are created and sustained in social interaction. For example, symbolic interactionists argue that gender (like ethnicity or career identity) is something that we "do" or perform (West and Zimmerman 1987). For example, a male may take pains to act in a masculine way so that he will be seen as a man by both himself and others. In some respects, his behavior (which is socially determined) can be considered symbolic of attributes commonly associated with the male sex (which is largely biologically determined). People who see his behavior can then simply relate to him as a man, according to the meaning of the symbolic behavior that has developed over time through innumerable interactions. Gender (i.e., masculinity and femininity) is thus both a result and a cause of social interaction.

Ethnomethodology

Although symbolic interactionism deals primarily with people's interactions, it is also concerned with the mental processes, such as mind and self, that are deeply implicated in these interactions. **Ethnomethodology** is another inter/actionist theory, but it focuses on what people *do* rather than on what they think (Liu 2012). The Greek root of the term *ethnomethodology* refers to people (*ethno*) and the everyday methods through which they accomplish their daily lives. In other words, ethnomethodologists study the ways in which people organize everyday life.

Ethnomethodologists regard people's lives and social worlds as practical accomplishments that are really quite extraordinary. For example, one ethnomethodological study of coffee drinkers attempted to understand their participation in a subculture of coffee connoisseurship (Manzo 2010). Learning to enjoy coffee is something of an accomplishment itself; taking that enjoyment to the next level and becoming a connoisseur requires even more doing.

Ethnomethodologists take a different view of largescale social structures than do structural-functionalists, who tend to see people and their actions as being highly constrained by those structures. Ethnomethodologists argue that this view tells us very little about what really goes on within structures such as courtrooms, hospitals, and police departments. Rather than being constrained, people act within these structures and go about much of their business using common sense rather than official procedures. They may even adapt those structures and rules to accomplish their goals. For example, an employee at Wal-Mart might violate the rules about handling returns in order to please a customer and make the process easier or less stressful. Police departments have rules about categorizing a death as a homicide or manslaughter. However, police officers often apply their own commonsense rules rather than organizational rules when interpreting the evidence.

Many ethnomethodologists study conversations and focus on three basic issues (Zimmerman 1988):

- *Vocal cues as an element of conversation.* Conversation involves not only words but also vocal cues, such as pauses, throat clearings, and silences. These nonverbal vocal behaviors can be important methods in making conversation. For example, one person may sit silently in order to force the other to speak. Or clearing one's throat may be meant to express disapproval of what the other person is saying.

- *Stable and orderly properties of conversations.* The people in conversation generally take turns speaking and know when it is their turn to talk. Ethnomethodologists might examine how those properties change when two strangers converse rather than two friends. One of their findings has been that a higher-status person is more likely to interrupt a lower-status person.

- *Actions necessary to maintain conversations.* The properties of conversation are not carved in stone. Those involved in a conversation can observe them, enforce them, or upset them. For example, turn taking is a stable and orderly property of a conversation, but in an actual conversation you need to act in order to get your turn to speak. Turn taking does not occur automatically.

The best-known example of an ethnomethodological approach relates to gender (O'Brien 2016; Stokoe 2006). Ethnomethodologists point out that people often erroneously think of gender as being biologically based. It is generally assumed that we do not have to do or say anything in order to be considered masculine or feminine; we are born that way. But, in fact, there are things we all do (e.g., the way we dress) and say (e.g., the tone of our voice) that allow us to accomplish being masculine or feminine. That is, being masculine or feminine is based on what people do on a regular basis. This is clearest in the case of those who are defined as being male or female at birth (based on biological characteristics) but then later do and say things that lead others to see them as belonging to another gender (based on social characteristics) other than the one most commonly associated with their assigned sex.

For example, the Dutch painter Einar Wegener enjoyed wearing feminine attire, which his wife, also a painter, discovered after he filled in for one of her models. With his wife's support he became the first man to undergo a sex reassignment operation, becoming the female Lili Elbe. In reality, we all say and do things that allow us to accomplish our gender (and, in certain ways, the "opposite" gender). If this is the case for gender, a great many other facts of our everyday lives can be analyzed as accomplishments.

Exchange Theory

Like ethnomethodologists, exchange theorists are not concerned with what goes on in people's minds and how that affects behavior. Instead, they are interested in the behavior itself and the rewards and costs associated with it (Molm, Whithama, and Melameda 2012). The key figure in **exchange theory**, George Homans (1910–1989), argued that instead of studying large-scale structures, sociologists should study the "elementary forms of social life" (Homans 1961, 13).

Exchange theorists are particularly interested in social behavior that usually involves two or more people and a variety of tangible and intangible exchanges. For example, you can reward someone who does you a favor with a tangible gift or with more intangible words of praise. Those exchanges are not always rewarding; they also can be punitive. You could, for example, punish someone who wrongs you by slapping them or complaining about them to mutual acquaintances.

In their actions and interactions, people are seen as rational profit seekers. Basically, people will continue on courses of action, or in interactions, in which the rewards are greater than the costs. Conversely, they will discontinue those in which the costs exceed the rewards. For example, people in search of a mate, especially a marriage partner, often choose to live in the city, even though the cost of living is higher, because there are more potential partners there. However, once they are married, they are more likely to move out of the city to where the costs are lower (Gautier, Svarer, and Teulings 2010). Although exchange theory retains an interest in the elementary forms of social behavior, over the years it has grown more concerned with how those forms lead to more complex social situations. That is, individual exchanges can become stable over time and develop into persistent **exchange relationships**. One particular type of exchange relationship is "hooking up," or forming sexual relationships that are also sometimes called "friends with benefits." For example, because you and another person find your initial sexual interactions rewarding, you may develop a pattern of repeat sexual interactions.

Exchange relationships, including hookups, rarely develop in isolation from other exchange relationships. Sociologists study how hooking up is not an isolated occurrence—for example, one place where it often happens is on college campuses, where it has been normalized (Kuperberg and Padgett 2015). All these exchange relationships may become so highly interconnected that they become a single network structure (Cook et al. 1983).

Key issues in such network structures, and in exchange relationships more generally, are the power that some members have over others and the dependency of some members (Molm 2007; Molm and Cook 1995). Exchange theorists are interested in studying the causes and effects of these status differences within exchange relationships and networks. For example, variations in the wealth, status, and power of individuals and their families affect the position they come to occupy in a social network and influence their ability to succeed educationally, financially, and occupationally (Lin 1999).

Rational Choice Theory

In **rational choice theory**, as in exchange theory, people are regarded as rational, but the focus is not on exchange, rewards, and costs. Rather, the basic principle in rational choice theory is that people act intentionally in order to achieve goals. People are seen as having purposes, as intending to do certain things. To achieve their goals, people have a variety of means available to them and choose among the available means on a rational basis. They choose the means that are likely to best satisfy their needs and wants; in other words, they choose on the basis of "utility" (Kroneberg and Kalter 2012). In the case of hookups, for example, we can easily imagine a series of potential purposes for hooking up, such as engaging in sexual exploration, having fun, and doing something sexual (presumably) without the risk of getting deeply involved emotionally.

There are two important constraints on the ability to act rationally (Friedman and Hechter 1988):

- *Access to scarce resources.* It is relatively easy for those with access to lots of resources to act rationally and reach their goals. Those who lack access to such resources are less likely to be able to act rationally in order to achieve their goals. A simple example: If you have access to money, you can rationally pursue the goal of purchasing food for dinner. However, without access to money, you will have a much harder time taking rational actions that will lead to the acquisition of food. Those with ample resources may be able to pursue two or more goals simultaneously (obtaining the money needed for dinner and for club hopping afterward with friends). However, those with few resources may have to forgo one goal (socializing with friends) in order to attain the other (getting enough money to eat).

- *Requirements of social structures.* The structures in which people find themselves—businesses, schools, hospitals—often have rules that restrict the actions available to those within the structures. For example, the need to work overtime or on weekends may restrict a person's ability to socialize. Similarly, being a full-time student may limit one's ability to earn enough money to always be able to obtain the kind of food one prefers to eat.

Rational choice theorists understand that people do not always act rationally. They argue, however, that their predictions will generally hold despite these occasional deviations (Coleman 1990; Zafirovski 2013). The degree to which people act rationally is one of the many topics that can be, and has been, researched by sociologists. It is to the general topic of sociological research that we turn in the next chapter.

SUMMARY

Karl Marx, Max Weber, and Émile Durkheim are arguably the most important classical sociological theorists.

Marx focused the majority of his attention on macro issues, particularly the structure of capitalist society. Unlike Marx, Weber was most interested in bureaucracy and the process of rationalization. Durkheim believed that social structures and cultural norms and values exert control over individuals that is not only necessary but also desirable.

Among other early sociological theorists, Georg Simmel focused on micro-level issues, specifically interactions among individuals. W. E. B. Du Bois was a pioneering researcher of race in America at the beginning of the twentieth century. Thorstein Veblen studied consumption, particularly the ways in which the rich show off their wealth through conspicuous consumption.

Three main schools of theory inform contemporary sociological theory: structural/functional, conflict/critical, and inter/actionist theories. Structural-functionalists such as Robert Merton are concerned with both social structures and the functions and dysfunctions the structures perform. They believe that society is held together by consensus. In contrast, structuralism studies the social impact of hidden or underlying structures.

Conflict/critical theories tend to emphasize societal struggles and inequality. Conflict theorists believe that society is held together by power and coercion. Critical theorists critically analyze culture and how it is used to pacify opposition. Feminist theory critiques the social situation confronting women and offers ideas on how women's situation can be bettered, if not revolutionized. Queer theory stresses the broader idea that there are no fixed and stable identities. Critical theories of race and racism argue that race continues to matter and raise the issue of oppression at the intersection of gender, race, sexual orientation, and other social statuses. Postmodern theory is similarly critical of society for, among other things, coming to be dominated by simulations.

Inter/actionist theories deal with micro-level interactions among people. Symbolic interactionism, for instance, studies the effect of symbols, including words, on the interaction between two or more people. Ethnomethodology focuses on what people do rather than on what they think and often analyzes conversations. Exchange theory looks not at what people think but at their behavior. Rational choice theory considers behavior to be based on rational evaluations of goals and the means to achieve them.

KEY TERMS

alienation
anomie
capitalism
capitalists
class consciousness
collective conscience
conflict theory
critical theories of race and racism
critical theory
culture industry
debunking
double consciousness
dysfunctions
ethnomethodology
exchange relationships
exchange theory
exploitation
false consciousness
feminist theory
functions
hyperconsumption

intersectionality
latent functions
manifest functions
mass culture
mechanical solidarity
organic solidarity
postmodernism
postmodernity
postmodern theory
proletariat
Protestant ethic
queer theory
rational choice theory
rationalization
simulation
social facts
structural-functionalism
structuralism
symbolic interactionism
theories
unanticipated consequences

REVIEW QUESTIONS

1. What are theories, and how do sociologists use theories to make sense of the social world? In what ways are theories developed by sociologists better than your own theorizing?

2. According to Karl Marx, what are the differences between capitalists and the proletariat? How are workers alienated on the job and in the workplace? Do you think workers are alienated today? Why or why not?

3. Max Weber said that the world is becoming increasingly rationalized. What are the benefits and disadvantages of rationality? In what ways is McDonaldization (from Chapter 1) the same as, or different from, rationalization?

4. Why has our collective conscience weakened over time, according to Émile Durkheim? Do you think that globalization continues to weaken our collective conscience? Why or why not?

5. You live in a world increasingly dominated by consumption. How are the goods and services you consume reflective of Thorstein Veblen's concept of "conspicuous consumption"?

6. What are the functions and dysfunctions of using the internet to consume goods and services? On balance, do you think that consumption through the internet is positive or negative?

7. What is mass culture, and why are critical theorists concerned about the dissemination of mass culture? Do you think the internet and social networking sites contain elements of mass culture and are part of the "culture industry"?

8. Why is feminist theory considered to be a critical theory?

9. What would proponents of the critical theories of race and racism outlined in this chapter think of the racial "dog whistles" used by Donald Trump in the 2016 (and 2020) presidential campaign and throughout his presidency? Would they see this as an advance over the more overt racism evident in the past?

10. According to symbolic interactionist theory, why are symbols so important to our interactions? In what ways has language changed because of the development of the internet?

Getty Images/Kaveh Kazemi

 RESEARCHING THE SOCIAL WORLD

> **LEARNING OBJECTIVES**
>
> **3.1** Describe the scientific method.
>
> **3.2** Explain how scientific knowledge develops over time.
>
> **3.3** Identify the various methods of sociological research.
>
> **3.4** Explain how sociologists engage in secondary data analysis.
>
> **3.5** Discuss five key issues in social research.

SOCIOLOGY AS A SCIENCE

Humankind has made amazing advances during its short existence on Earth. From the development of agriculture to the Industrial Revolution to the advent of the digital and the global ages, each generation has pushed further into an unknown future. Many, especially the world's privileged, enjoy longer lives, improved standards of living, a plethora of inexpensive manufactured goods, affordable and readily available food, quick and effortless communication, and the ability to travel, even around the world. But many of these luxuries have come at a significant ecological price.

Climate change, marked by long-term fluctuations in Earth's intricate and interwoven weather patterns, has occurred since the formation of the planet. Some fluctuations affect only specific regions, while others affect the entire world. Some span decades; others occur over millions of years. Although gradual climate change is a natural process, a growing body of careful research suggests that significant recent changes, including fossil fuel combustion and deforestation, are directly attributable to human activities.

Despite this scientific consensus, our impact on climate change remains a hotly debated issue. If the available geological, atmospheric, and oceanographic evidence is solid enough to convince the scientific community, why do so many people remain fiercely unconvinced? Who is opposed to the notion that human actions are a major cause of climate change, and how have institutional forces influenced their personal beliefs over time?

Physical science can help us understand and explain climate change, but to understand the motivations, beliefs, and actions that affect our response to it (or lack thereof), we need sociologists and their research methods. There are many types of social research; each can uncover unknown or even unsuspected truths about the relationship between people and climate change, as well as many other social issues. Thus, sociology is a science, like—but also unlike—any other.

Like all scientists, passionate sociologists may unintentionally let their personal feelings or drive to succeed affect their research. Although all sociologists—indeed all scientists—make occasional errors, the research methods they use must be ethical, reliable, and valid for the results they yield to have a chance of being widely accepted. This is especially important because contemporary sociological research often deals with controversial, red-hot issues, such as the role of people and society in climate change.

As you learn about the major types and purposes of sociological research, consider the issues and phenomena that you yourself might like to research. You may someday have an opportunity to do so.

Sociology is a science of the social world, and research is absolutely central to such a science. All sociologists study others' research, and most do research of their own. Sociologists may theorize, speculate, and even rely on their imaginations for answers to questions about society. However, they almost always do so on the basis of data or information derived from research. Put another way, sociologists practice **empiricism**, which means that they gather information and evidence using their senses, especially their eyes and ears. Because we all do that in order to experience the world, what makes sociology different? In addition to using their senses, sociologists adopt the scientific method, or a similarly *systematic* approach, in search of a thorough understanding of the social world. They have a variety of methods at their disposal in researching and analyzing society, but they also experience a few significant constraints on their ability to conduct such research.

THE SCIENTIFIC METHOD

The **scientific method** is a structured way of finding answers to questions about the world (Carey 2011). The scientific method employed by sociologists is much the same as that used in other sciences (see Table 3.1). The basic scientific method tends to adhere to the following steps:

1. A sociologist uncovers questions in need of answers. These questions can be inspired by key issues in the larger society, personal experiences, or topics of concern specifically in sociology. The best and most durable research and findings often stem from issues that the researcher connects with personally. Karl Marx, for example, detested the exploitation of workers that characterized capitalism; Max Weber feared the depersonalizing impact of bureaucracies (see Chapter 2). Thus, powerful motivations spurred both Marx and Weber to do research on, and eventually to come up with key insights into, these monumentally important aspects of social life.

2. Sociologists review the relevant literature on the questions of interest to them. This is because others have likely done similar or related research in the past. After more than a century of doing scientific research, sociologists have learned a great deal about many things. It would make no sense to start over from the beginning. For example, Ritzer's (2021) work on McDonaldization is based on the study of the work on rationalization by Max Weber ([1921] 1968), his successors (such as Kalberg 1980), and more contemporary researchers. He concluded that the fast-food restaurant is an apt, current example of the rationalization process. Other scholars have since reviewed his work and that of other scholars of McDonaldization (for a collection of this work, see Ritzer 2010c). They have amplified the concept and applied it to domains such as religion (Drane 2008), higher education (Hayes 2017; Hayes and Wynyard 2002), social work (Dustin 2007), psychotherapy (Goodman 2016), and Disney World (Bryman 2004; Huddleston, Garlen, and Sandlin 2016). The ideas associated with McDonaldization have also been used as a way of teaching Max Weber's complex theories to undergraduates (Aldrich and Lippmann 2018).

3. Researchers often develop hypotheses, or educated guesses, about how social phenomena can be expected to relate to one another. Uri Ram (2007) hypothesized that Israeli society would grow increasingly McDonaldized, and he found evidence to support that idea. As another example, Marx hypothesized that the conflict between capitalists and workers would ultimately lead to the collapse of capitalism. Over the years, conflict between capitalists and workers has increased in some areas of the world, but it has decreased in others. Capitalism has not collapsed (at least not yet), although it came close in 1929 at the beginning of the Great Depression and maybe in 2008 at the onset of the Great Recession. Hypotheses are simply hypotheses. They may not be confirmed by research or borne out by social developments, but such speculation is important to the scientific method.

4. Researchers must choose research methods that will help them answer their research questions. Sociology offers diverse methodological tools; some are more appropriate than others for answering certain kinds of questions. For example, some sociologists are interested in how a person's social class shapes their opinions about social issues. Surveys and other quantitative tools may be best to evaluate the relationship between class and attitudes. Other sociologists want to know how people interpret and make sense of their social world, and how this meaning-making shapes social action. Qualitative methods, such as observations and interviews, may be helpful for studying these issues. The researcher might observe two individuals flirting at a party. The researcher may interview the individuals to see how each of them interprets gestures, body language, clothing, and other nonverbal cues that might suggest romantic or sexual interest. Sociologists select from among these and other methods to best answer their research questions.

5. Researchers use their chosen methods to collect data that can confirm—or fail to confirm—their hypotheses. Many classical sociologists conducted their research in libraries, and some

contemporary sociologists do as well, analyzing secondary sources, such as reports based on data collected by others. But many contemporary sociologists venture into the field to collect original data through observations, interviews, questionnaires, and other means.

6. Researchers analyze the data collected, assessing their meaning in light of the hypotheses that guided the research. For example, as you learned in Chapter 2, Émile Durkheim hypothesized that those who were involved with other people would be less likely to commit suicide than those who lived more isolated existences and were experiencing what he called anomie. (For a more recent study showing the relationship between isolation—and other social breakdowns—and the risk of dying in an extreme heat wave, see Klinenberg 2015.) That is, being integrated with other people would, in a way, "protect" an individual from suicide. Analyzing data from several nineteenth-century European countries, Durkheim ([1897] 1951) found that the suicide rates were, in fact, higher for widowed or divorced people than for those who were married and therefore presumably better integrated socially.

TABLE 3.1	■ Steps in the Research Process
1	Uncover a question in need of an answer.
2	Review the relevant literature.
3	Develop hypotheses.
4	Identify an appropriate method for answering the research question.
5	Collect data.
6	Analyze the data.

The research process may begin again if a researcher discovers additional questions when analyzing the existing data. For example, Robert Putnam, in his famous book *Bowling Alone* (2001), addresses the applicability of Durkheim's concept of anomie in the contemporary world. As the title of his book suggests, he found that people are now less likely to bowl in leagues and more likely to bowl alone. More generally, people are increasingly doing many things alone (e.g., shopping online, socializing through Facebook and Twitter) that in the past they did with other people. Further analysis of Durkheim's work—or a new application of it—might lead to the hypothesis that people who "bowl alone" are more likely to commit suicide.

A study of the social world concluded that people today are increasingly likely to undertake many activities—including bowling—alone. Does this conclusion apply to you and your life?

KENA BETANCUR/AFP/Getty Images

Here's an even more current example. Imagine that you are wondering how relying on social networks like Facebook might affect a person's susceptibility to suicide. Having read this far in the book, you already know something about Durkheim's work on suicide. However, as a professional sociologist, you would, of course, conduct a much more thorough review of the relevant theory and research on this issue. You would find some work that argues that social networking can prevent suicide (Luxton, June, and Kinn 2011). From this, and from what you now know about Durkheim's thinking, you might hypothesize that those who have many Facebook friends are more socially integrated and therefore less likely to commit suicide than those who have few Facebook friends, "likes," or are not on Facebook at all. An alternative hypothesis would be that no matter how many friends (or likes) one has on Facebook, those who have few, if any, friends in the "real world" are more likely to commit suicide.

How would you collect data to test your hypotheses? You'd probably need to get some data about a group's Facebook friends, their friends in the real world, and their suicide rates. You would then analyze the patterns in these data. And then, if all went well, you could determine whether either of these hypotheses is supported by the evidence. That would be a scientific approach to answering your questions.

THE DEVELOPMENT OF SCIENTIFIC KNOWLEDGE

Scientific knowledge develops gradually and cumulatively as one set of empirical findings builds on another. Some studies fail to confirm earlier findings and come to be seen as dead ends. Other studies confirm previous findings. Confidence in those findings grows as they are confirmed by additional research, and eventually some of them begin to be treated as scientific facts. All sciences are built on such facts. Over time and with additional research, however, some widely accepted facts may be found to be erroneous. For example, early scientists who studied the brain believed that female's relatively smaller brain size in comparison to male's was evidence of mental inferiority. Later research demonstrated that brain size does not determine intelligence, so those earlier ideas are no longer accepted (Gould 1981; Van Valen 1974). But some facts do survive empirical tests; these facts come to form the basis of what we think of as a science. For example, as you learned in this chapter's opening vignette, an accumulation of data from research on climate patterns leads most scientists to treat the idea of climate change as a scientific fact. The National Aeronautics and Space Agency reports that 97 percent or more of climate scientists actively working in the field believe the evidence that the global warming (see Figure 3.1) we have witnessed over the last century is traceable to human actions. The Intergovernmental Panel on Climate Change (IPCC 2007), the most authoritative group of global scientists studying climate change, reviewed past research findings and confirmed both that global warming is a scientific fact *and* that human activity is its main cause. This gradual and orderly pattern of scientific development is what we would expect from the systematic use of the scientific method and the evolution of a science.

Thomas Kuhn ([1962] 1970), a philosopher of science, proposed a different model of scientific development that focuses on the role of abrupt and dramatic scientific breakthroughs. According to Kuhn, what defines a science is the existence of a **paradigm**, a general model of the world accepted by most practitioners in the field. One such paradigm today is that humans are the main cause of climate change. Other long held examples include the idea in astronomy that Earth and the other planets revolve around the sun and in biology that "germs" cause most infectious diseases. With a generally agreed-on paradigm, scientists need not squabble among themselves over their general orientation and their most basic premises. They are free to do research within the confines and safety of that paradigm. As research expands on the paradigm, it is "fleshed out" in a series of tiny steps. Its fundamentals remain unaltered, at least for a time.

But some research does not support the dominant paradigm, and serious questions arise. If those questions are not answered and new ones continue to be raised, the old paradigm eventually collapses and is replaced by a new paradigm; a scientific revolution occurs. Kuhn argues that it is in those revolutions—the death of an old paradigm and the birth of a new one—that science takes great leaps forward. For centuries scientists believed that Earth was at the center of the universe, with the sun orbiting it (a geocentric model). It was not until the sixteenth century, when better research methods

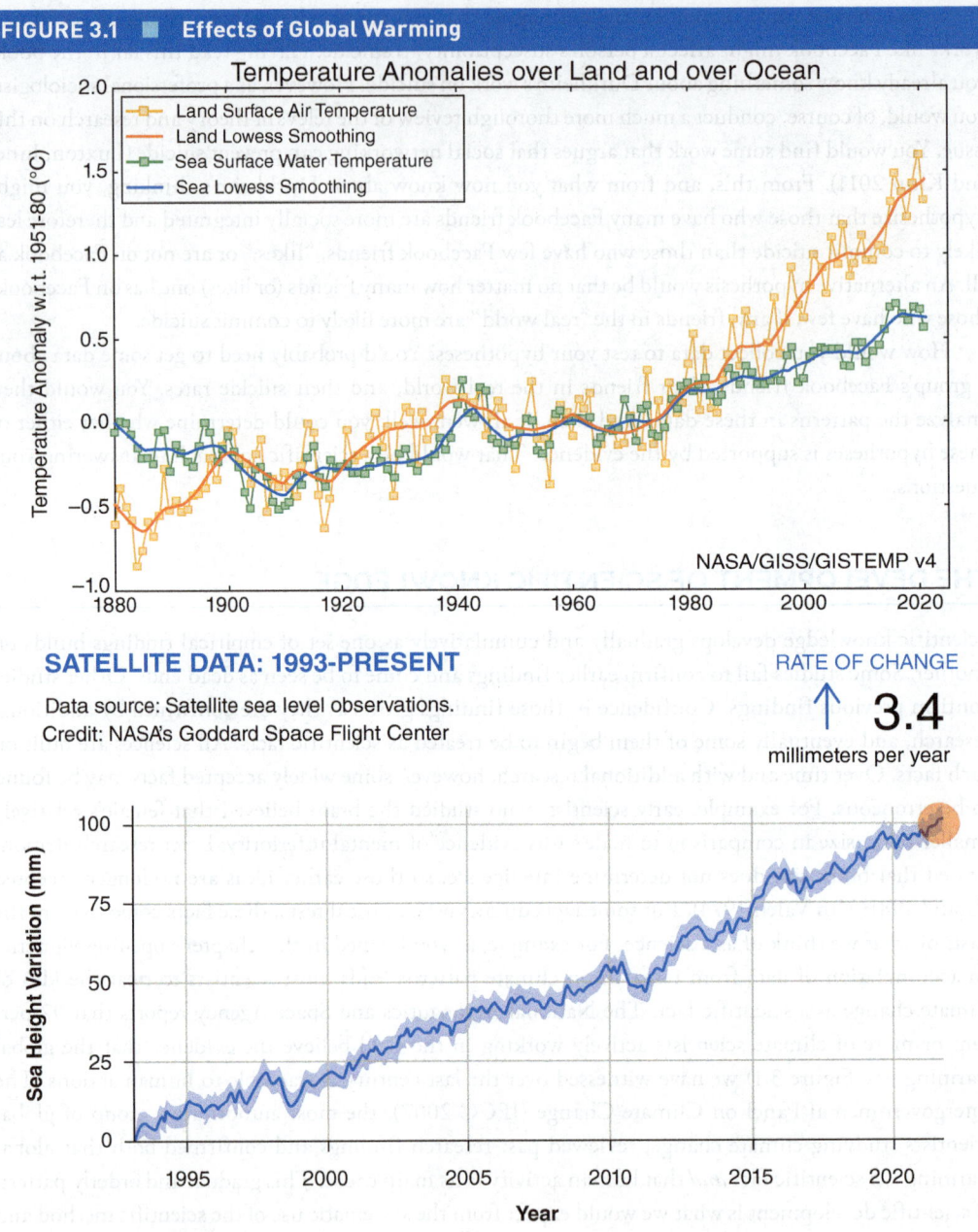

FIGURE 3.1 ■ Effects of Global Warming

Source: NASA, Global Climate Change: Vital Signs of the Planet. http://climate.nasa.gov

became available, that the geocentric paradigm began to be supplanted by a paradigm that saw Earth as orbiting the sun (a heliocentric model). This was a revolution in astronomical thought. In the centuries that followed, other astronomers built on that knowledge and came to the consensus that Earth and the sun are in fact parts of one solar system within one galaxy of many in the universe. Heliocentrism remains the dominant paradigm for explaining the relationship between Earth and the sun. However, the nature of paradigms means that new ones are always developing, leading to new explanations of the role of both bodies in the universe as it is currently understood.

Kuhn's single-paradigm approach fits very well with the history of the physical sciences, such as astronomy and physics, but sociology and the other social sciences (e.g., geography; see Malik 2014) can perhaps better be seen as "multiple paradigm sciences" (Bills 2013; Friedrichs 1970; Ritzer 1975). The social world, social phenomena, and individuals—to say nothing of the interrelationships among them—are highly complex. No single paradigm is powerful enough to deal with all of them and able to unify the discipline. So research tends to occur *within* each sociological paradigm, expanding each over time but not contributing to a consensus in the discipline as a whole. Furthermore, some of the research stemming from one paradigm may be in conflict with research stemming from other paradigms. Because of these differences and conflicts, the development of sociology as a whole tends to be slower and more sporadic than the development of the physical sciences. And because there has never been a single dominant paradigm in sociology, the field has never experienced any dramatic paradigm revolutions. Rather, the fortunes of various paradigms have risen and fallen over time.

In a multiple-paradigm science, it is more difficult to accumulate knowledge that is accepted by practically everyone in the field. Sociologists do not operate safely within the confines of a single dominant, broadly agreed-on paradigm. The most basic assumptions of a given sociologist or group of sociologists are constantly open to question and attack by those who operate on the basis of other paradigms. There is a much less settled, universally agreed-on knowledge base in sociology than there is in, say, biology or astronomy. Nonetheless, there *is* a substantial body of knowledge in sociology, some of which is summarized throughout this book. The lack of a dominant paradigm means that there are also many more controversies in sociology than there are in some other fields. As a result, you will find sociology to be characterized by many interesting, stimulating, and exciting debates, as well as many facts.

SOCIOLOGICAL RESEARCH

Sociological knowledge is derived from research that may use a variety of different methods. Typically, the method chosen is and should be driven by the nature of the research question. Imagine that you are a sociologist interested in studying differences in the behavior of people who visit Las Vegas. You might start by observing, perhaps by watching people gamble. You might look for variations: Are men and women equally represented at the slot machines? Are they equally likely to play craps or blackjack? Do people of different ages play different games? You could do much the same thing by looking for differences among those who attend the shows and musical events at the casinos. Are there gender differences between the Las Vegas audiences of, say, Cirque du Soleil's *Mystère* or *Zumanity* and the audiences of the music of Barry Manilow or a Penn & Teller magic show? Are there age differences between the audience members at a Carrot Top show and those at a Mariah Carey concert? To better understand such differences, you might be inspired to participate, to become a *participant observer*, by gambling or being entertained alongside those you are studying.

You may realize that your specific research questions are better answered through use of the interview method. You might interview those who have come to Las Vegas to gamble, asking about their expectations for having fun or winning a lot of money. This could be a more efficient use of your time because it would not entail waiting around for gamblers to do or say something relevant to your research question. But in interviews, people might not be willing to talk to you about their gambling experiences, especially if they have been losing money—and most gamblers lose most of the time! Furthermore, even if they are willing to talk to you, they might not give you totally honest answers.

In this case, perhaps administering an anonymous questionnaire or survey would be better. You could hand the questionnaires out to people leaving the casino, and the respondents might feel protected by the anonymity of the process. Unfortunately, survey questions are not easy to word in just the right way. And many people might not be willing to take your survey, especially if they have stayed up late gambling or have lost money. Even if they do take a questionnaire from you, they might not answer the questions or mail the questionnaire back to you. You could also develop an anonymous online survey and provide people with the link; this would be perhaps the most efficient way to administer a survey, but the response rate may still remain low.

Instead of randomly distributing questionnaires or an online survey link, you could be more systematic and scientific by obtaining a list of guests at a given hotel-casino. However, it is highly unlikely that you would be given such private information. You could use a random number table to generate a random sample of people drawn from the phone book in your hometown and mail each person in the sample your questionnaire or survey link, but it is unlikely that many of them would have visited

Las Vegas recently. Among the relatively few who have, it is likely that only a very small number would return the completed questionnaires to you. And your phone book would not include the many people who have abandoned landlines and have only cell phones. In the age of the cell phone, phone books are declining in importance—in many areas they're disappearing altogether.

You could also create an experiment. Using a social science lab at your university, you could set up a Las Vegas–style poker table and recruit students as participants. You could tell them that the typical player loses 90 percent of the time and that previous research has shown that *most* players lose *most of the time*. You could then ask whether, in spite of that information, they still want to gamble at your poker table. Of greatest interest would be those who say yes. You could interview them before they start "gambling" at your table, observe them as they gamble, and interview them again after they finish gambling. Did they start out believing, despite all the evidence to the contrary, that they would win? How could they have retained such a belief in spite of all the counterevidence? What are their feelings after gambling at your table? Did those feelings seem to be related to whether they won or lost? How likely are they to gamble again? Are there important differences between women and men in terms of their answers to these questions?

Observation is a primary method of sociological research. Do you think people behave differently when they are being observed?

Laura Dwight/Alamy Stock Photo

Observation, interviews, surveys, experiments, and other research methods are all useful and important to sociologists. All have strengths but also limitations. Before we examine these methods and their strengths and limitations in more detail, there is an important distinction between two basic types of research methods that should be clarified.

Qualitative and Quantitative Research

Each of the research methods in the wide variety available to sociologists can be classified as either qualitative or quantitative.

Qualitative research consists of studies done in natural settings that produce in-depth, descriptive information (e.g., in respondents' own words) about the social world (Denzin 2018; Silverman 2016). Such research does not necessarily require statistical methods for collecting and reporting data (Marshall and Rossman 2010). Observation—watching, listening, and taking detailed notes—and open-ended interviews are just two of the qualitative methods used by sociologists. These methods are used to capture descriptive information about an incredibly wide range of social phenomena, ranging from social movements to cultural practices, to people's lived experiences and feelings, to the ways in which organizations function, to interactions between nations. By gathering information from often small numbers of groups and individuals, studies employing qualitative methods produce rich data about the social world and in-depth understanding of particular social processes. Sometimes they help provide insights about new areas where little research has been done. However, because qualitative methods usually rely on small sample sizes, the findings cannot be generalized to the broader population; for this, we use quantitative methods.

Quantitative research involves the analysis of numerical data, usually derived from surveys and experiments (Schutt, 2019). The analysis of quantitative data on or from groups of people can help us describe and better understand important observable (empirical) social realities. In his analysis of social mobility in the United States, Gilbert (2018) analyzed previously collected General Social Survey (GSS) data on the relationship between the occupational status of fathers and the occupations achieved by their sons. (GSS data come from surveys that use random, representative samples drawn from the adult population of the United States.) Among Gilbert's findings is the fact that 42 percent of the sons of fathers who held upper-level white-collar occupations ultimately attained similarly high-level jobs, while only 15 percent of these sons went into lower-level manual work. At the other end of the occupational hierarchy, 36 percent of the sons of fathers who held lower-level manual occupations came to hold same-level occupations, while 20 percent moved into upper-white-collar occupations. It is clear that if your father has a higher-level position in the occupational structure, you are more likely to reach a similar level in your lifetime. Such survey data provide great insights into the process of social mobility in the United States—and much else.

The mathematical method used to analyze numerical data is **statistics**. It is a powerful tool, and most sociological researchers learn statistical methods. Statistics can aid researchers in two ways:

- When researchers want to see trends over time or compare differences between groups, they use **descriptive statistics**. The purpose of such statistics is to *describe* some particular body of data that is based on a phenomenon in the real world. For example, researchers can use survey data to track trends in occupational mobility over time and then use statistical analysis to describe how occupational mobility varies by race, gender, and age.

- To test hypotheses, researchers use **inferential statistics**. Such statistics allow researchers to use data from a relatively small group to speculate with some level of certainty about a larger group. For example, researchers might conduct research on racial discrimination in higher education by examining the acceptance rate of Black and Latinx students at a sample of select schools. They can draw generalizations about the broader population of applicants based on their findings from this sample. Each method has its own set of strengths and limitations in terms of what it can do to help a researcher answer a specific question.

Sociologists often debate the relative merits of quantitative versus qualitative methods, but they generally recognize that each method has value. There is a broad consensus that quantitative and qualitative research methods can complement one another (Creswell and Creswell 2018). In practice, sociologists (and other social scientists) may conduct **mixed-methods research** by combining both quantitative and qualitative research methods in a single study. For example, Reich and Bearman (2018) combined oral histories, participant observations, and big data in their recent study of the unjust labor conditions experienced by workers at Walmart.

Observational Research

As mentioned earlier, one of the primary qualitative methods is **observation**. It consists of systematically watching, listening to, and recording what takes place in a natural social setting over some, usually extended, period of time. Though the observational techniques of sociologists are similar to those used by investigative journalists, sociological techniques may be much more systematic and in-depth. The two primary observational methods are participant and nonparticipant observation.

There are several key dimensions to any type of observation in sociology:

- *The degree to which those being observed are aware that they are being observed.* This dimension can vary, from everyone involved being fully informed about the research to participants being observed from afar or through hidden cameras, one-way mirrors, and the like. In 2014 the National Geographic Channel produced a documentary film titled *Inside: Undercover in North Korea* that used covert research methods. The film's camera crew was ostensibly in North Korea to document a medical team helping the blind. However, its real purpose was to observe and record what life is like in this secretive and difficult-to-penetrate country. The reality TV series *Undercover Boss* (*Celebrity Undercover Boss* debuted in 2018) also employs covert observational research. Top-level executives work incognito at lower levels in their own firms to learn more about the work and the workers. Although the boss might have ulterior motives, such as uncovering and firing incompetent employees, sociologists who do this kind of research are not supposed to have such motives. A desire to understand the complex facets of a setting or environment is their main motivation.

- *The degree to which the presence of the observer affects the actions of those being observed.* When people are aware that they are being observed, they often present themselves in the way they think the observer expects or will accept. For instance, North Koreans might behave differently toward outsiders if they notice they are being observed. Similarly, gang members might not engage in illegal activities in the presence of a researcher.
  - The **Hawthorne Effect** refers to the degree to which individuals change their behaviors when they are know they are being observed. The name comes from a study that was conducted at the Hawthorne Works plant in Illinois in the 1920s. During the study, lighting changes were made to see if that impacted the productivity of the workers in the plant. As it turns out, no matter how much the lighting changed, worker productivity increased. It also turned out that worker productivity slumped once the study was over. The conclusion drawn by some sociologists was that worker productivity increased not because of the changes in lighting, but because the workers knew they were being observed.

- *The degree to which the process is structured.* Highly structured observational research might use preset categories, codes, or a checklist to guide observations, but some observation studies are intended to seek the widest possible range of data. Researchers thus attempt to take note of as much as possible in the field setting; their method is totally open and unstructured.

Participant and Nonparticipant Observation

There are two major types of observational methods. One is **participant observation**, in which the researcher actually plays a role, even a minor one, in the group or setting being observed. A participant observer might become a hostess or bartender to study the sex industry in Ho Chi Minh City, Vietnam (Hoang 2015), sell books on the sidewalk to watch what happens on a busy city street (Duneier 1999), or live in a trailer park to witness how individuals cope with poverty (Desmond 2016). In one classic example of participant observation, a sociologist with tuberculosis methodically studied the hospital he was in, as well as the actions of doctors, nurses, and other patients (Roth 1963). In another, Barbara Ehrenreich (2001) worked in low-wage jobs (including as a waitress, hotel maid, housecleaner, nursing home aide, and Walmart associate) to study the experiences of low-wage workers. She found that many of the women she studied, despite working extra hours, were unable to meet the basic living expenses of housing, transportation, and food. Aasha Abdill (2018) spent four years studying black fathers in a low-income area of Brooklyn, discovering that they are present in their children's daily lives despite high rates of unemployment and incarceration.

The second observational method is **nonparticipant observation**, in which the sociologist plays little or no role in what is being observed. Sociologists Clare L. Stacey and Lindsay L. Ayers (2012) spent six months observing (and interviewing) 16 people who provide home care for the elderly or the disabled, as well as nurses and social workers who visit the elderly or disabled in their homes. The home care workers are paid (although poorly, $9 to $11 per hour) for their work. However, the care work they do is normally provided for free by family members or friends of those in need of care. How do the care workers rationalize receiving pay for their work? For one thing, they emphasize the technical and emotional skills required to do the work. For another, they see themselves as providing a service that is of help to the larger society by, for example, saving taxpayers money. Because the recipients are poor, the state would have to pay a great deal more money to keep them in institutions than the sums paid to home care workers. One of sociology's most prolific observational researchers, Gary Fine, has done nonparticipant observation research on Little League baseball (Fine 1987), restaurant kitchens (Fine 2008), meteorologists (Fine 2010), and chess players involved in a chess tournament (Fine 2015).

Big Brother, a reality show that began on Dutch TV in 1999 and is now franchised in many television markets around the world, is another example of nonparticipant observation. Of course, sociologists are not involved in this show, and the observation is not as systematic as it would be if it were a sociological study. The show's premise is simple: Select a group of young people who have never met, have them live together in a "house" (stage set) that is cut off from the outside world, and see what happens. Although cameras record much of the group's activities (including in the bathroom), no outsiders are present in the house to participate in those activities. The "observers" are the viewing audience, who can be seen as amateur nonparticipant observers in the sense that they "study" interaction patterns and other sociological aspects of what goes on among the residents.

In reality, there are no firm dividing lines between participant and nonparticipant observation, and at times the two blend imperceptibly into one another. The participant often becomes simply an observer. An example is the sociologist who begins with participant observation of a gang, hanging out with members in casual settings, but becomes a nonparticipant when illegal activities such as drug deals take place. And the nonparticipant observer sometimes becomes a participant. An example is the sociologist who is unable to avoid being asked to take sides or share opinions in squabbles among members of a Little League team or, more likely, among their parents.

Ethnography

At times, sociologists pose research questions that require an observational method traditionally associated with anthropology. **Ethnography** is the creation of a detailed account of what a group of people do and the way they live, usually entailing much more intensive, immersive, and lengthy periods of observation (sometimes participant) than traditional sociological observation requires. Researchers may live for years with the groups, tribes, or subcultures (such as gamblers) being studied.

Sociologists interested in a variety of topics advocate the use of ethnographic methods. This is especially true of those interested in studying women, because such methods can reveal much about the experiences of traditionally understudied and marginalized groups of women—for example, Latina girls (Garcia 2012), lap dancers (Colosi 2010), and gang members (Ward 2012). Some suggest that the personal relationships that develop between researchers and subjects in ethnographic studies make it less likely that the power researchers exert over subjects will distort the results (Bourdieu 1992). Researchers who employ feminist methods are especially intent on ensuring that study participants are not coerced or exploited in the research process.

Normally ethnographies are small in scale, micro, and local. Researchers observe people, talk to them, hang out with them, sometimes live with them, and conduct formal and informal interviews with them over an extended period of time. Nevertheless, the ethnographic method has now been extended to the global level. Michael Burawoy (2000; see also Kenway and McCarthy 2016; Tsuda, Tapias, and Escandell 2014) argues that a **global ethnography** is the best way to understand globalization. This type of ethnography is grounded in various parts of the world and seeks to understand globalization as it exists in people's social lives. Burawoy and his colleagues "set out from real experiences . . . of welfare clients, homeless recyclers, mobilized feminists, migrant nurses, union organizers, software engineers, poisoned villagers, redundant boilermakers, and breast cancer activists in order to explore *their* global contexts" (Burawoy 2000, 341).

Three interconnected phenomena are central to the global ethnographies undertaken by Burawoy and others:

- Do people experience globalization as an external force? If so, is it a force to be combatted or accepted?
- In what ways, if at all, do people participate in creating and furthering global connections?
- Do people work for or against processes that are global in scope?

Burawoy and his colleagues have sought to answer these questions wherever in the world they traditionally have undertaken their studies.

For example, a global ethnography by George (2000) looked at nurses in Chicago who were originally from India and examined their place in the transnational community of nurses. Concerns here might be U.S.-born nurses who have lost their jobs as a result of the availability of qualified nurses from all over the world or who are unable to find jobs because the positions are being occupied by Indian nurses. There is also the issue of the communication linkages between Indian nurses in the United States and those back home in India, as well as the degree to which those linkages are used to bring still more Indian nurses to the United States.

Netnography

The basic concerns of sociology—communications, relationships, and groups—are key elements of the internet, especially social media sites such as Facebook, Twitter, TikTok and Instagram. Online discussions, digital networking, and posting photos and videos are how many of us connect virtually with each other every day. Not surprisingly, netnography, or an account of what transpires online, has become an important method of sociological research (Kozinets 2015; Quinton 2018). Netnographers are digital ethnographers who are able to observe thousands of phenomena online. For example, they might follow the Twitter account of a celebrity or sports star to learn about their fans or play an online video game such as World of Warcraft to understand how individuals engage in virtual role-playing and collaboration. One recent study used netnography to examine the blogs of female Chinese tourists in Macao, discovering how crossing the border influenced perceptions of their self-identity and enhanced their personal relationships (Zhang and Hitchcock 2014). Outside of academia, netnography is used by web designers, marketers, and advertisers to observe, record, and analyze our digital behaviors. The virtual data we create when shopping on Amazon or streaming music on Spotify offer these professionals valuable information that they can use to entice us to buy more products or visit new websites.

Netnography, like other social research, raises ethical questions. Researchers who join an internet community to observe its ongoing communications might not inform other members that they have joined with the objective of studying the group. The issue of informed consent is especially ambiguous when conducting online research because so much of what transpires in virtual reality is public. Although we can take steps to protect our privacy online, many of us do not. For some internet users, the whole point of posting a video on YouTube or writing a blog is to attract as many views and followers as possible. Revealing personal information about ourselves, family, and friends is common on popular social media sites. This makes it easy for anyone, including social researchers, to investigate our relationships and identities.

Interviews

Although observers often interview those they are studying, they usually do so very informally and on the spur of the moment. Other sociologists rely mainly, or exclusively, on interviews in which they seek information from participants (respondents) by asking a series of questions that have been formulated, at least to some degree, before the research is conducted (Gubrium et al. 2012). Interviews are usually conducted face-to-face, although they can be done by phone and are increasingly being done via the internet (James 2016). In addition, large-scale national surveys are increasingly including interviews. For example, the Centers for Disease Control and Prevention is known for its national surveys, but it

Interviews can take many forms and be more or less structured depending on the researcher's needs. Here, a field researcher in Thailand interviews a passenger on a boat about a local dam building project.

Getty Images/Thierry Falise

also uses interviews in its National Health Interview Survey, which has been conducted continuously since 1957 (Sirkin et al. 2011; see http://www.cdc.gov/nchs/nhis/about_nhis.htm).

The use of interviews has a long history in sociology. One very early example is W. E. B. Du Bois's ([1899] 1996) study of the "Philadelphia Negro." A watershed in the history of interviewing in sociology was reached during World War II, when large-scale interview studies of members of the U.S. military were conducted. Some of the data from those studies were reported in a landmark study, *The American Soldier* (Stouffer et al. 1949). More recently, Robert Wuthnow (2018) and his research assistants conducted over 1,000 in-depth interviews with individuals residing in rural communities to learn about how their norms, values, and local experiences are changing.

The questions asked in an interview may be preselected and prestructured so that respondents must choose from sets of preselected answers such as *agree* and *disagree.* Or an interview may be more spontaneous, unstructured, and completely open-ended. The latter form is used by those who do observational research. An unstructured interview offers no preset answers; respondents are free to say anything they want.

Prestructured interviews are attractive when the researcher wants to avoid any unanticipated reactions or responses from those being studied. In a prestructured interview, the interviewer attempts to

- Behave in the same way in each interview
- Ask the same questions, using the same exact words, and in the same sequence
- Ask closed-ended questions that the participant must answer by choosing from a set of preselected responses
- Offer the same explanations when they are requested by respondents
- Not show any kind of reaction to the answers, no matter what they might be

Interviews conducted in this way often yield information that, like data obtained from questionnaires, can be coded numerically and then analyzed statistically.

There are problems associated with prestructured interviews. First, interviewers often find it difficult to live up to the guidelines for such interviews:

- They are frequently unable to avoid reacting to answers (especially unexpected or outrageous ones).
- They may use different intonation from one interview to another.
- They may change the wording, and even the order, of the questions asked (which can affect respondents' answers).

Second, respondents may not respond accurately or truthfully. For example, they may want to conceal things or give answers they believe the interviewer wants to hear. Third, and most important, closed-ended questions limit the responses, possibly cutting off useful unanticipated information that might be provided in a more free-flowing interview.

The last problem is solved by the use of open-ended or *unstructured interviews*. The interviewer begins with only a general idea of the topics to be covered and the direction to be taken in the interview. The answers in unstructured interviews offer a good understanding of the respondents and what the issues under study mean to them. Such understandings and meanings are generally not obtained through structured interviews. However, unstructured interviews create problems of their own. For example, they may yield so much diverse information that it is hard to offer a coherent summary and interpretation of the results.

The Interview Process

Conducting interviews, especially those that are prestructured, usually involves several steps. The researcher does not simply make a list of questions and start asking them. Rather,

1. The interviewer must *gain access* to the setting being studied. This is relatively easy in some cases, such as when interviewing one's friends in the student union or at a local bar. However, access would likely be much more difficult if one wanted to interview one's friends in a sorority house or on the job. People might be less eager to talk to a researcher—to any outsider—in such settings. Some groups, such as the top executives of major corporations or the extremely wealthy, have the resources to insulate, or even isolate, themselves. They can be quite difficult for researchers to gain access to and thus may be underrepresented in sociological research.

2. The interviewer must often seek to *locate a **key informant*** (Rieger 2007). This is a person who has intimate knowledge of the group being studied and is willing to talk openly to the researcher about the group. A key informant can help the researcher gain access to the larger group of respondents and verify information being provided by them. The latter is useful because interviewees may well provide erroneous, perhaps purposely erroneous, information. For example, in William F. Whyte's (1943) famous study of "street corner society," a leader of the group, "Doc," served as Whyte's key informant. In Sudhir Venkatesh's (2008) study of a Chicago housing project and its gangs, his key informant was the gang leader "J. T." Of this relationship, Venkatesh said, "In the course of my fieldwork I became dependent on the continual support of J. T." (1994, 322). J. T. not only corrected Venkatesh's misinformation and misinterpretations but also retained the right to delete information from published reports on the study that might disclose his identity or that of his gang.

3. The interviewer must seek to *understand the language and culture* of the people being interviewed. In some cases this is very easy. For example, it is in many ways easier for an academic interviewer to understand the language and culture of college students. However, it is more difficult if the academician interviews people with their own, very different language and culture. Examples might include interviews with members of motorcycle gangs or prostitutes (assuming the academic is not also a member of one of these groups). In these kinds of cases, it is all too easy for the researcher to misunderstand or to impose incorrect meanings on the words of respondents.

4. The researcher must *gain the trust of the respondents and develop a rapport* with them. Establishing trust and rapport can be easy or difficult, depending on the characteristics of

the researcher and the respondents. Well-educated and relatively powerful male researchers may intimidate less privileged female respondents. Older researchers may have trouble interviewing traditional-age college students. Depending on the field site, a researcher's point of view and (perceived) similarities with the respondents may increase rapport.

In a few cases, trust and rapport need to be earned only once, but in many cases they need to be earned over and over. And trust can easily be lost. Venkatesh (2008) had to work constantly on his rapport with J. T., gang members, and many others who lived in the urban areas he studied. In fact, J. T. thought at first that Venkatesh might be a cop, and he later confessed that he was never 100 percent sure that Venkatesh was not a police officer. Venkatesh was also in constant danger of losing the very tenuous trust his participants had in him and what he was doing. There was ever-present fear on the part of those he studied that he was in league with a rival gang or would inform on them to the police.

Survey Research

Survey research involves the collection of information from a population, or more usually a representative portion of a population, through the use of interviews and, most important, questionnaires. Although some sociologists do their own surveys, most rely on data derived from surveys done by others, such as a government agency (a national census, for example) or a survey firm (such as Pew or Gallup).

Interviews, as we know, involve questions asked by the researcher in person, on the telephone, or via the internet. In contrast, **questionnaires** are (most often) self-administered, written sets of questions. Questions can be presented to respondents face-to-face, but they are more often delivered to them by mail, asked over the telephone, or presented in a web-based format.

Types of Surveys

There are two broad types of surveys. The first is the **descriptive survey**, which is designed to gather accurate information about, for example, members of a certain group, people in a given geographic area, or people in a particular organization. A descriptive survey might gather data on the level of sexual activity among college students, the employment status of people in a certain industry, or the way in which former manufacturing employees are coping with job loss. The best-known descriptive surveys are those conducted by organizations such as Gallup to gather information on the preferences, beliefs, and attitudes of given samples of people.

In one example of descriptive survey research using the internet, a survey was placed on a website designed to allow married people to find extramarital sexual partners. Based on a sample of more than 5,000 respondents, the data showed that females were more likely than males to engage in "sexting" and that males and females involved in serious real-life relationships were about equally likely to engage in cheating on their partners, both online and in real life (Wysocki and Childers 2011).

For many years, the Institute for Social Research at the University of Michigan has conducted a descriptive survey of high school seniors in the United States. One of the subjects has been marijuana use. As you can see in Figure 3.2, the prevalence of marijuana use among high school seniors has risen and fallen, as if in waves. Marijuana use in this group peaked in 1979 (with more than half of students admitting use of the drug), reached a low of 22 percent in 1992, and then increased again, although it has never again approached the 1979 level. In 2021, 30 percent of twelfth graders reported having used marijuana in the previous year, a 5 percent decline from the previous year.

The data in Figure 3.2 are derived from descriptive surveys, but what if we wanted to explain, and not just statistically describe, changes in marijuana use among high school seniors? To get at this, we would need to do an **explanatory survey**, which seeks to uncover potential causes of, in this case, changes in marijuana use (including, perhaps because of the increasing legalization of marijuana in several states). For example, having discovered variations in marijuana use by high school students over the years, we might hypothesize that the variation is linked to students' (and perhaps the general public's) changing perceptions about the riskiness of marijuana use. Specifically, we might hypothesize that as students (and the public) increasingly come to see marijuana as less risky, marijuana use among students will go up. In this case, we would use the survey to learn more about respondents' attitudes toward and beliefs about the riskiness of marijuana use and not simply measure student use of marijuana.

FIGURE 3.2 ■ Marijuana Use Among U.S. High School Seniors, 1976–2021

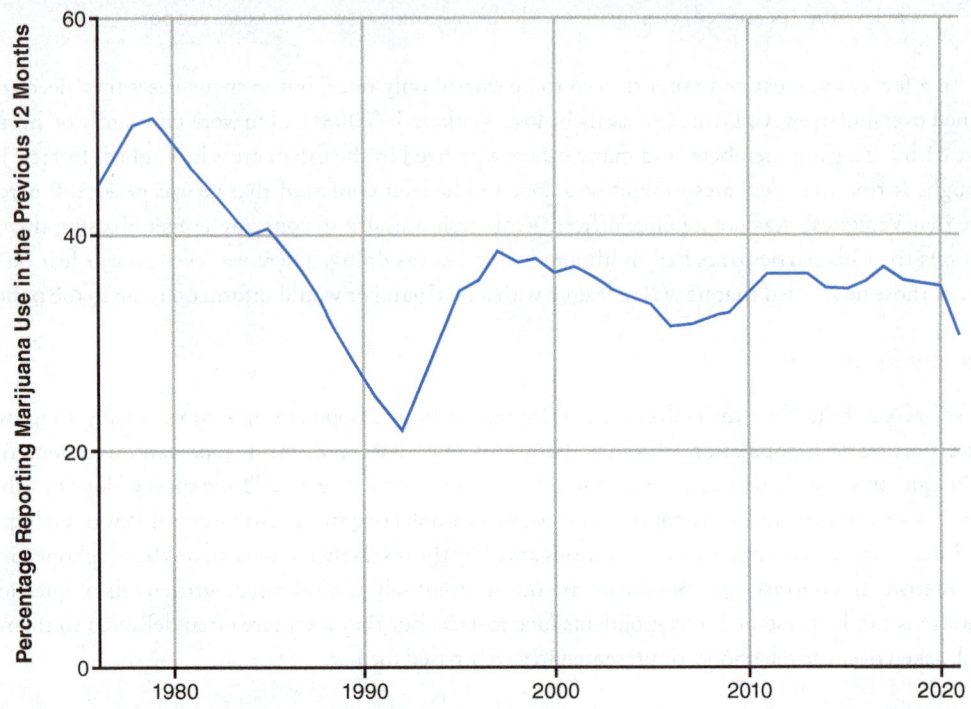

Source: Data from The University of Michigan Institute for Social Research. 2021. *Monitoring the Future: National Survey Results on Drug Use 1975–2021*. "Marijuana: Trends in 12 Month Prevalence of Use in 8th, 10th, and 12th Grade." Retrieved January 05, 2022.

Sampling

It is almost never possible to survey an entire population, such as all people living in an entire country, all students at your college or university, or even all sorority members at that university. Thus, survey researchers usually need to construct a **sample**, or a representative portion of the overall population. The more careful the researcher is in avoiding biases in selecting the sample, the more likely the findings are to be representative of the whole group.

The most common way to avoid bias is to create a **random sample**, a sample in which every member of the group has an equal chance of being included. One way of obtaining a random sample is by using a list—for example, a list of the names of all the professors at your university. A coin is tossed for each name on the list, and those professors for whom the toss results in heads are included in the sample. More typical and efficient is the use of random number tables, found in most statistics textbooks, to select those in the sample (Kirk 2007). In our example, each professor is assigned a number, and those whose numbers come up in the random number table are included in the sample. More recently, use is being made of computer-generated random numbers. Other sampling techniques are used in survey research as well. For example, the researcher might create a **stratified sample** in which a larger group is divided into a series of subgroups (e.g., assistant, associate, and full professors) and then random samples are taken within each of these groups. This ensures representation from each group in the final sample, something that might not occur if one simply does a random sample of the larger group. Thus, random and stratified sampling are the safest ways of drawing accurate conclusions about a population as a whole. However, there is an element of chance in all sampling, especially random sampling, with the result that findings can vary from one sample to another. Even though sampling is the safest way to reach conclusions about a population, errors are possible. Random and stratified sampling are depicted in Figure 3.3.

Sometimes researchers use **convenience samples**, which avoid systematic sampling and simply include those who are conveniently available to participate in a research project. An example of

FIGURE 3.3 ■ Random Samples and Stratified Samples

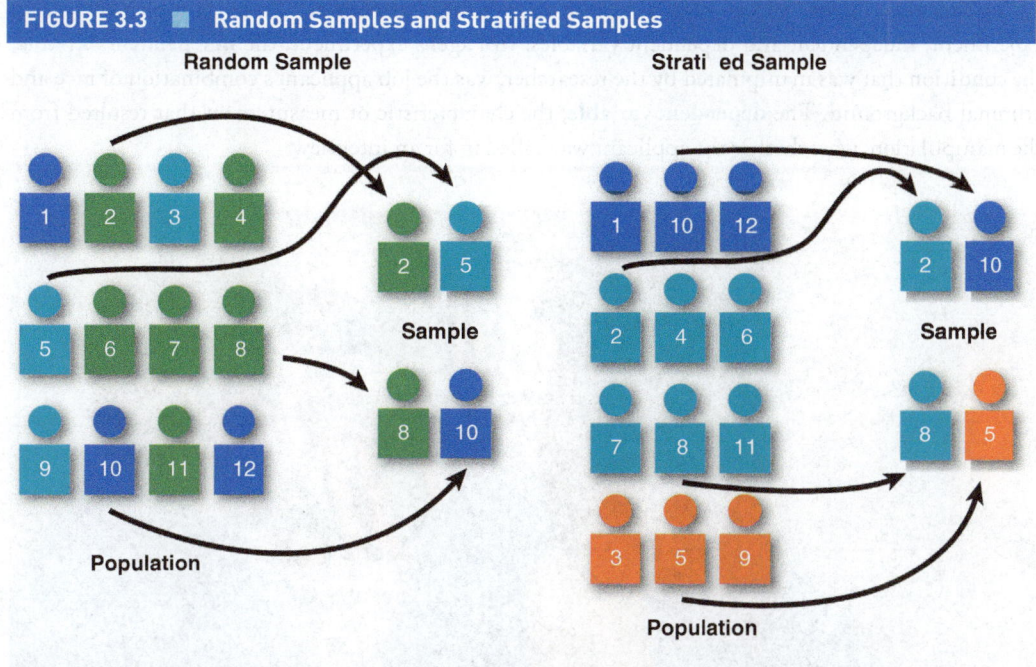

Source: Random Samples and Stratified Samples is reprinted with permission of Dan Kernler, associate professor of mathematics, Elgin Community College, Elgin, IL.

a convenience sample might involve researchers passing out surveys to the students in their classes (Lunneborg 2007). These nonrandom samples are rarely ever representative of the larger population whose opinions the researcher is interested in knowing. Nonrandom samples therefore may create a substantial bias in researchers' results. Many surveys that pop up on the internet are suspect because the respondents are the people who happened to be at a certain website (which is likely to reflect their interests) and who felt strongly enough about the topic of the survey to answer the questions.

Research using convenience samples is usually only exploratory. It is almost impossible to draw any definitive conclusions from such research. There are, however, some cases in which convenience sampling is not only justified but also useful. For researchers trying to study elite social networks (such as political leaders or the wealthy), simply gaining access to the group can be a difficult task in itself. Convenience sampling—surveying anyone in the group to whom one is introduced—may be the only way to proceed (Tansey 2006). Convenience sampling also sometimes leads to larger, more scientific projects that rely on random or stratified samples.

Experiments

Sociologists do not do nearly as many experiments as do researchers in hard sciences such as chemistry, or even researchers in other social sciences such as psychology. However, some sociologists do perform experiments, and experimentation is one of the fundamental methods in the field (Jackson and Cox 2013). An **experiment** involves the manipulation of one or more characteristics in order to examine the effect of that manipulation (Kirk 2007).

A study by Devah Pager (2009) provides a good example of a sociological experiment. Pager was interested in how the background of a job applicant affects the likelihood of that individual's being called back for an interview. Pager randomly assigned fake criminal records to pairs of similar young men, one in each pair Black and one White. Thus, in each pair, one person had a criminal record and one did not, and one was White and one was not. These young men then sent résumés to companies in Milwaukee, seeking entry level jobs. One major finding of this experiment was that the young men believed to have criminal records received callbacks less than half as often as did those of the same race believed not to have criminal records. A second was that Black men without criminal records received callbacks at about the same rate as White men with criminal records.

In this experiment, we can clearly see the relationship between two important elements of an experiment: independent and dependent variables. In Pager's experiment, the **independent variable**, the condition that was manipulated by the researcher, was the job applicant's combination of race and criminal background. The **dependent variable**, the characteristic or measurement that resulted from the manipulation, was whether the applicant was called in for an interview.

Sociologist Devah Pager designed an experiment to investigate the role of race and criminal background in hiring for entry level jobs. She discovered that White applicants with apparent criminal records were called back for interviews as often as Black applicants with no criminal records.

Daniel Ernst/Alamy Stock Photo

There are several types of experiments (Walker and Willer 2007):

- *Laboratory experiments*. **Laboratory experiments** take place in controlled settings. The "laboratory" may be, for example, a classroom or a simulated environment. The setting offers the researcher great control over the selection of the participants as well as the independent variables—the conditions to which the participants are exposed (Lucas, Graif, and Lovaglia 2008). The famous experiments by Solomon Asch on conformity (see Chapter 6) were laboratory experiments. This type of experiment can be difficult to organize and sometimes yields artificial results. However, it allows for more accurate tests of research hypotheses.

- *Natural experiments*. **Natural experiments** are those in which researchers take advantage of a naturally occurring event to study its effect on one or more dependent variables. Such experiments offer the experimenter little or no control over independent variables (De Silva et al. 2010). For example, a recent natural experiment at Harvard University assigned first-year students from different races as roommates. Among the findings was that breakups among the roommates were more likely when an East Asian student lived with two White students (Chakravarti, Menon, and Winship 2014).

- *Field experiments*. In some natural situations, researchers are able to exert at least some control over who participates and what happens during experiments (Bertrand and Mullainathan 2004; Pager and Western 2012). These are called **field experiments**. One of the most famous studies in the history of sociology is the "Robbers Cave" field experiment (Sherif et al. [1954] 1961), so called because it took place in Robbers Cave State Park in Oklahoma. The researchers controlled important aspects of what took place at the site. For example, they were able to assign the 22 boys in the study into two groups, called the Rattlers and the Eagles. The researchers were also able to create various situations that led to rivalry, bickering, and hostility between the groups. At the end of the experiment, they had each group rate the other: 53 percent of ratings of the Eagles were unfavorable, while nearly 77 percent of ratings of the Rattlers were unfavorable. Later, the researchers introduced conditions they hoped would reduce bad feelings and friction between the groups. In fact, greater harmony between the groups was created by having them work together on tasks such as securing needed water and paying collectively and equitably for a movie that everyone wanted to see. By the end of the latter part of the experiment, just 5 percent of the ratings of the Eagles were unfavorable, and unfavorable ratings of the Rattlers had dropped to 23 percent. A more recent field experiment in Sweden dealt, in part, with hiring discrimination against ethnic groups (Bursell 2014). Pairs of equally qualified applicants were sent to interview for open jobs. Those with Arabic or North African names were less likely to be called back for additional consideration.

Some observers see a bright future for experimentation in sociology, in part because of its growth in neighboring fields such as psychology and especially in fields such as economics and political science, which in the past did not do much experimentation. Another reason is the potential for using the internet as a site for sociological experiments (Hanson and Hawley 2010; Parigi, Santana, and Cook 2017). In one internet-based experiment, male respondents were asked to evaluate the attractiveness of digitally altered pictures of females based on their perception of the women's body mass index (BMI)—in other words, on how overweight the women appeared to be. One finding was that respondents who were overweight were less likely to report differences in the attractiveness of the women based on the women's BMI (Conley and McCabe 2011). In another internet study in the Netherlands, similar to the field study discussed previously using résumés with White- and Black-sounding names, fictitious résumés with Arabic and Dutch names were posted on online résumé databases. The résumés of those with Arabic names were requested less often than were those with Dutch names (Blommaert and Coenders 2014).

SECONDARY DATA ANALYSIS

All of the methods discussed thus far involve the collection of new and original data, but many sociologists engage in **secondary data analysis**, in which they (re)analyze data collected by others. Secondary analysis can involve a wide variety of different types of data, from censuses and other surveys to historical records and old transcripts of interviews and focus groups. Until recently, obtaining and using some of these secondary data sets was laborious and time-consuming. Today, however, thousands of data sets are available online, and they can be accessed with a few keystrokes. A number of websites provide both the data sets and statistical software for looking at them in different ways (Quinton 2018).

Secondary data analysis very often involves statistical analysis of government surveys and census data. The technique has a long history in sociology, extending back to Karl Marx's analyzing government statistics at the British Library. U.S. census data, which are collected every 10 years (last collected in 2020), are a gold mine for sociologists both in the United States and abroad. It is not unusual for one body of data to lead to hundreds of secondary analyses. For example, the World Values Survey (WVS; http://www.worldvaluessurvey.org) is conducted in nearly 100 countries containing almost 90 percent of the world's population. Its seven waves (the eighth is planned to begin in 2023) have been used to produce more than 1,000 research publications in more than 20 languages. Some of this research has used the WVS to examine which social, cultural, and economic factors contribute to an individual's happiness. Another study examined data from 1981 to 2007 and found that perceptions of freedom of choice are more likely to lead to higher levels of happiness (Inglehart et al. 2008). However, subsequent research may look differently at the data and describe new parts of the puzzle. Using similar data from the WVS, another study looking at individual cases within countries demonstrated that inequalities in health quality, among other factors, also shape happiness (Ovaska and Takashima 2010). A study focusing on migration found that emigration rates were high in countries with both high and low levels of happiness, but the rates were low for countries in the middle (Polgreen and Simpson 2011). Yet another study that looked at the impact of different welfare systems concluded that people who live in liberal and conservative countries are at least twice as likely to be unhappy as people living in social democratic welfare states (Deeming and Hayes 2012). Figure 3.4 shows levels of happiness among the citizens of various countries included in the WVS surveys from 2020–2022.

FIGURE 3.4 ■ World Happiness Rankings, 2020–2022

Source: World Happiness Report, 2023. https://worldhappiness.report/

Note: Happiness scores consider such factors as GDP per capita, social support, healthy life expectancy, freedom to make life choices, and perceptions of corruption.

Although secondary analysis is far easier and far less expensive to carry out than collecting one's own data is, especially for large amounts of data, it has distinct problems. For one thing, secondary researchers cannot refine their methods on the basis of preliminary research. For another, because others have chosen the methods of data collection, the data may not be ideal for the secondary researcher's needs. It is possible that the research may have to be abandoned until an appropriate data set is available or created. In some cases, researchers who find the data set inadequate for a study of their original interest may find that other relevant issues are covered better by the data. Another type of problem with using government data sets is political: Certain types of sensitive data may not have been collected. Or social or political changes may end the collection of certain types of data or change the ways in which the data are reported or categorized. For instance, the collection and reporting of U.S. census data on race have changed over the years to accommodate changing demographics and sensitivities. The resulting inconsistencies in the data set over time can pose great difficulties for the secondary researcher.

Historical-Comparative Method

The goal of **historical-comparative research** is to contrast how different historical events and conditions in various societies have led to different societal outcomes. The hyphenation of *historical-comparative* makes it clear that two separable methods are being combined. The historical component involves the study of the history of societies as well as of the major components of society, such as the state, religious system, and economy. The addition of the comparative element, comparing the histories of two or more societies, or of components of societies, makes this method more distinctively sociological.

One of the things that differentiates the discipline of history from historical-comparative sociology is the level of historical detail. Historians go into much more detail, and collect far more original historical data, than do sociologists. In contrast, sociologists are much more interested in generalizing about society than are historians. Perhaps the best way to exemplify the difference between a historical-comparative sociologist and a historian is in the concept of the ideal type (Weber [1921] 1968). An **ideal type**, as defined by Max Weber ([1903–1917] 1949, 90), is a "one-sided *accentuation*" of social reality. Unlike the goal of the historian, an ideal type is not meant to be an accurate depiction of reality. Rather, it is designed to help us better understand social reality. It is a sort of measuring rod. Thus, for example, Weber developed an ideal type of bureaucracy that accentuated its rational elements. He then used that ideal type to compare organizations in different societies and time periods in terms of their degree of rationality.

Recent instances of historical-comparative research have covered a wide range of issues, but one of the most popular topics has been examining the relationship between the state and war. Theda Skocpol's (1979) pivotal study of revolutions in France (1789), China (1911), and Russia (1917) found that they were not simply political revolutions that changed the structure of the state but also social revolutions that changed the social structure, especially class relations. Rodriguez-Franco (2016) used historical-comparative research to examine whether internal wars could lead to state formation. Using the ability to collect taxes as a key factor, internal wars were found to strengthen states if solidarity existed among the elite.

Some scholars have combined the use of other methods with historical-comparative analysis to generate important theoretical insights about more contemporary issues. For example, Piketty (2014) examined a variety of statistical data to uncover the historical changes of income and wealth inequality in Europe and the United States. He found that inequality has been produced and reproduced over time due to the concentration of wealth in the upper class. The concentration of wealth was quite high in Europe during the eighteenth and nineteenth centuries and in the United States in the decades before the Great Depression but leveled off during and after World War II due to inflation, higher taxes, and the policies of the modern welfare state. However, near the end of the twentieth century the concentration of wealth (and income) started to increase dramatically when inherited wealth, in particular, began to grow faster than economic output and income (Piketty 2014). If we aspire to a more egalitarian society, Piketty suggests that states implement a global tax on wealth.

Content Analysis

Another type of secondary analysis, called **content analysis**, relies on the systematic and objective analysis of the content of cultural artifacts in print, visual, audio, and/or digital media, including photographs, movies, advertisements, speeches, newspaper articles, or blog posts. The goal is to use qualitative and especially quantitative methods to understand the content of messages. In one well-known study, Herbert Gans (1979) did a quantitative and qualitative content analysis of news on television and in news magazines to identify patterns in the reporting of news. For example, he found that well-known people were dealt with much more frequently than were unknowns. Among non-war-related stories, government conflicts and disagreements were more likely to be dealt with than were government decisions. Gans supplemented the powerful insights that derived from his content analysis with additional participant observation research among journalists working at NBC and CBS News and *Time* and *Newsweek* magazines. This additional work enabled him to produce an incredibly rich and detailed account of the various political, commercial, and other forces that produce the values and informal rules that guide journalism.

Gans's content analysis took as its focus the overt content of the news, but it is also possible to use content analysis to analyze other issues, such as gender inequality. For example, researchers performed a content analysis of 1,245 characters on 89 prime-time television programs, finding that though some gender stereotypes have declined, others, such as dominant men and sexually provocative women, persist (Sink and Mastro 2016). Content analysis is moving beyond traditional media and is now also being conducted on social media. For example, Pilkington and Rominov (2017) researched fathers' worries during their partners' pregnancies by analyzing the content of their posts on Reddit. They found that most fathers-to-be are worried about infant well-being and the potential for prenatal loss.

ISSUES IN SOCIAL RESEARCH

The research conducted by sociologists raises a number of issues of great importance. Some of these issues concern how we should interpret the data sociologists collect. Some involve the obligations sociologists have to research participants and to society as a whole. Other issues are raised by sociologists themselves. As mentioned earlier, sociology is a multiple-paradigm science—with a full range of debates not only on various sociological perspectives but also on whether sociology can truly be as objective as a science is presumed to be.

Reliability and Validity

A key issue with sociological data relates to one's ability to trust the findings. As a sociologist, you would want to be reassured that the data you might use to further your own research, to formulate hypotheses, or to tell colleagues and the public about your research represent the social world as accurately as possible. As a consumer of sociological research, you would do well to evaluate the methods used in order to assess their trustworthiness. This issue is frequently raised in regard to reports of political and social surveys, but it affects every form of sociological research.

Scientists talk about two dimensions of trustworthiness: reliability and validity. **Reliability** involves the degree to which a given question, or another kind of measure, produces the same results time after time. In other words, would the same question asked one day get the same response from the participants or the same measurement on the scale the following day, or week, or month? For instance, do those involved in your hypothetical study of Las Vegas gamblers give the same answers at various points in time to questions about whether they routinely lose money when gambling?

The other dimension of trustworthiness is **validity**, or the degree to which a question, or another kind of measure, gets an accurate response. In other words, does the question measure what it is supposed to measure? For example, suppose you asked gamblers, "When you leave Las Vegas, do you consider yourself a 'winner'?" You may be asking this question to find out whether they left Las Vegas with more money than the amount they had when they arrived there. However, they may interpret the question more broadly as asking about the total experience of being in Las Vegas. Thus, even though they have lost money, they might answer yes to the question because they had a great time and consider their losses as part of the price for having such an experience. A more valid question might be, "On balance, do you win more money than you lose while gambling in Las Vegas?"

Research Ethics

Ethics is concerned with issues of right and wrong, the choices that people make, and how people justify those choices (Hedgecoe 2016). World War II and the behavior of the Nazis helped make ethics a central issue in research. The Nazis engaged in horrendous medical experiments on inmates in concentration camps. They used them as human guinea pigs to study such things as the effects of hypothermia, high altitudes, low altitudes, hemorrhages, and the drinking of saltwater. In some studies, inmates were infected with such diseases as typhus, malaria, and hepatitis to test various vaccines and drugs. Acting on the pseudoscience of Nazi race ideology, yet other doctors tried to develop efficient methods of mass sterilization of what the regime defined as inferior races (Korda 2006; Spitz 2005). This is perhaps one of the most outrageous examples of a violation of the ethical code in the conduct of research, but it is certainly not the only one. Another well-known example is the research conducted between 1932 and 1972 at Tuskegee Institute in Alabama on 399 poor Black men suffering from syphilis. The researchers were interested in studying the natural progression of the disease over time, but they never told the participants that they were suffering from syphilis. Despite regular visits to collect data from and about the participants, the researchers did not treat them for the disease and allowed them to suffer over long periods of time before they died painfully (Reverby 2009).

A more recent example of questionable research ethics is the case of Henrietta Lacks (Skloot 2011; see also the 2017 HBO movie *The Immortal Life of Henrietta Lacks*). Lacks was a poor Black woman who died of cervical cancer in 1951. Without her knowledge or consent, some of her tumor was removed. Cancer cells from that tumor live on today and have spawned much research and even highly successful industries. Although those cells have led to a variety of medical advances, a number of ethical issues are raised by what happened to Lacks and subsequently to her family. For example, should the tumor have been removed and its cancer cells reproduced without Lacks and her family knowing about, and approving of, what was intended? Would the same procedures have taken place if Lacks were a well-to-do White woman? Finally, should Lacks's descendants get a portion of the earnings of the industries that have developed on the basis of her cancer cells?

No research undertaken by sociologists has caused the kind of suffering and death experienced by the people studied in Nazi Germany or at Tuskegee Institute, or even generated an ethical firestorm like the one raging around the Lacks case. Nonetheless, such research is the context and background for ethical concerns about the harmful or negative effects of research on participants in sociological research (the code of ethics of the American Sociological Association can be found online at https://www.asanet.org/about/ethics/). There are three main areas of concern: physical and psychological harm to participants, illegal acts by researchers, and deception and violation of participants' trust. A final issue discussed here is the structure established to safeguard participants from these kinds of negative actions.

Henrietta Lacks was responsible for major advances in medical science, all without her knowledge or consent. Cells taken during testing while she was undergoing treatment for cervical cancer in 1951 are still used today. Lacks's cells continue to be invaluable to researchers, but should the manner in which they were obtained affect how they are used?

Photo Researchers, Inc /Alamy Stock Photo

Physical and Psychological Harm

The first issue, following from the Nazi experiments and Tuskegee studies, is concern over whether research can actually cause participants physical harm. Most sociological research is not likely to cause such harm. However, physical harm may be an unintended consequence. In the Robbers Cave research, discussed earlier as an example of a natural experiment, competition and conflict were engendered between two groups of 12-year-old boys. The hostility reached such a peak that the boys engaged in apple-throwing fights and in raids on one another's compounds.

A much greater issue in sociological research is the possibility of psychological harm to those being studied. Even questionnaire or interview studies can cause psychological harm merely by asking people about sensitive issues such as criminal activity, drug use, and experience with abortion. This risk is greatly increased when, unbeknownst to the researcher, a participant is hypersensitive to these issues because of a difficult or traumatic personal experience.

Some of the more extreme risks of psychological harm have occurred in experiments. The most famous example is Stanley Milgram's (1974) laboratory study of how far people will go when they are given orders by those in positions of authority. This study was inspired by the discovery after World War II that Nazi subordinates went so far as to torture and kill innocent citizens if ordered to do so by their superiors. In the Milgram experiment, one group, the "learners," were secretly paid to pretend that painful shocks were being applied to them by the other group of participants, the "teachers," who were led to believe that the shocks they thought they were applying were real (see Figure 3.5). The

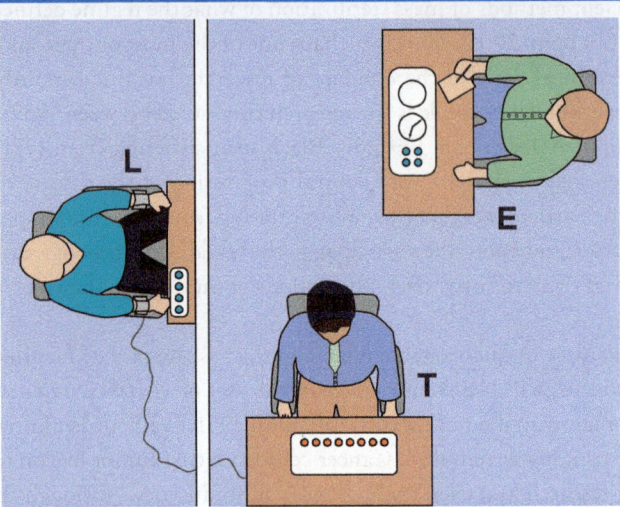

FIGURE 3.5 ■ The Teacher (T), Learner (L), and Experimenter (E) in the Milgram Experiment

researcher, dressed officially in a white coat and projecting an aura of scientific respectability, ordered the teachers to apply shocks that appeared to be potentially lethal. The teachers did so even though the learners, who were in another room and not visible, were screaming with increasing intensity. The research clearly showed that if they were ordered to do so by authority figures, people would violate the social norms against inflicting pain on, and even possibly endangering the lives of, others.

The 2015 movie *Experimenter* deals in a fictionalized way with Milgram and his research. The lead character in the 2018 Netflix series *Maniac*, Owen Milgrim, is the subject of a series of experiments and drug trials. *Compliance* is a 2012 movie based explicitly on Milgram's work. It deals with a real life case in which a caller spoke to a McDonald's restaurant manager and identified himself as a police officer investigating a theft. The caller was able to convince the manager of the restaurant that a young girl working there was a suspect in the theft. The caller eventually persuaded the manager to, among other things, allow the girl to be taken to a back room, where she was strip-searched and left with nothing on but an apron. The manager needed to return to her work in the busy front of the store, but the caller insisted that others be brought in to watch the girl. Eventually, the manager's fiancé was brought in and, under pressure from the caller, had the girl do nude jumping jacks, spanked her for not following directions, and eventually coerced her into performing oral sex on him. When the fiancé left, he was replaced by a male custodian who saw through the caller's requests. The police were called and discovered that similar incidents had occurred elsewhere (the movie claims that more than 70 such incidents had occurred throughout the United States). The real case on which *Compliance* was based took place in a small town in Kentucky in 2004; the caller, a telemarketer and family man, was apprehended, but he was acquitted of all charges in 2006 ("Acquittal in Hoax" 2006). Like the Milgram experiment, *Compliance* shows how far people are willing to go, even to the extent of committing a crime, when ordered to do so by someone they believe to be in an authority position.

The results of the Milgram experiment (as well as events depicted in *Compliance*) are important in many senses. We are concerned here with what the study did to the psyches of the people involved. For one thing, the "teachers" came to know that they were very responsive to the dictates of authority figures, even if they were ordered to commit immoral acts. Some of them certainly realized that their behavior indicated they were perfectly capable in such circumstances of harming, if not killing, other human beings. Such realizations had the possibility of adversely affecting the way participants viewed, and felt about, themselves. But the research has had several benefits as well, for both participants and others who have read about the Milgram studies. For example, those in powerful positions can better understand, and therefore limit, the potential impact of their orders to subordinates, and subordinates can more successfully limit how far they are willing to go in carrying out the orders of their superiors.

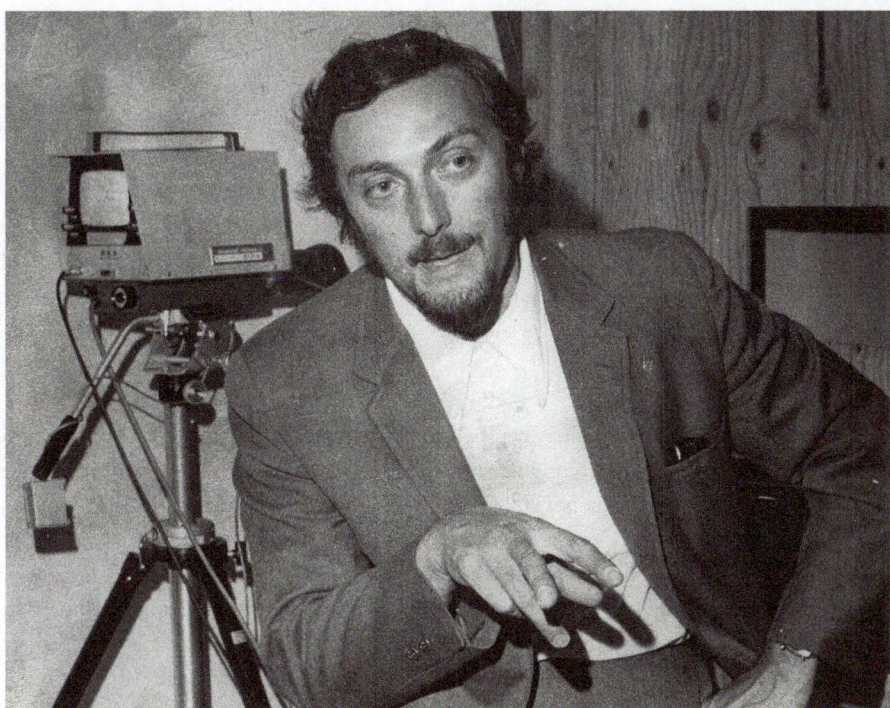

Phillip Zimbardo's experimental recreation of prison conditions was so realistic, and the participants were so severely affected by their involvement in it, that the experiment had to be cut short by several weeks. Could this early cutoff have invalidated the research?

San Francisco Chronicle/Hearst Newspapers via Getty Images

Another famous study that raises similar ethical issues was conducted by Philip Zimbardo (1973). (The 2010 movie *The Experiment* and the 2015 movie *The Stanford Prison Experiment* are both fictionalized depictions of this experiment.) Zimbardo set up a prisonlike structure called "Stanford County Prison" as a setting in which to conduct his experiment. Participants were recruited to serve as either prisoners or guards. The "prison" was very realistic, with windowless cells, minimal toilet facilities, and strict regulations imposed on the inmates. The guards had uniforms, badges, keys, and clubs. They were also trained in the methods of managing prisoners.

The experiment was supposed to last six weeks, but it was ended after only six days when the researchers grew fearful about the health and sanity of the prisoners, whom some of the guards insulted, degraded, and dehumanized. Only a few guards were helpful and supportive. However, even the helpful guards refused to intervene when prisoners were being abused. The prisoners could have left, but they tended to go along with the situation, accepting both the authority of the guards and their own lowly and abused position. The ethical issues in this case are similar to those raised by the Milgram research. Some of the guards experienced psychological distress, but it was worse for the prisoners when they realized how much they had contributed to their own difficulties. Social researchers learned that a real or perceived imbalance of power between researcher and participant may lead the participant to comply with a researcher's demands even though they cause distress. However, like Milgram's research, the Zimbardo experiment yielded positive by-products, such as a greater understanding of how those put in guard positions may lose their humanity and how submissive prisoners can become.

Illegal Acts

In the course of ethnographic fieldwork, a researcher might witness or even become entangled in illegal acts. This problem confronted Randol Contreras in his research on a group of Dominican men who robbed upper-level drug dealers in the South Bronx (Contreras 2017). These "stickup kids" engaged in brutal acts of violence and possessed illegal drugs and cash. Contreras, himself a former—though admittedly unsuccessful—drug dealer, had to be careful to avoid participating in illegal activities that the stickup kids were describing to him, particularly because some of them were childhood friends.

In other cases, researchers must weigh sticky legal and ethical ramifications for participants. In one study of children in a nursery, the researchers witnessed an illegal act (Anspach and Mizrachi 2006). They had to decide whether to report it. They had to juggle concerns about the criminality of the act with a desire to protect their research participants and the trust they had extended. Other concerns lingered in the background. Publishing an account of such a dramatic act might help the researchers' careers, but it might also send the perpetrator of the illegal act to jail. It was also possible that not informing the police, or refusing to turn over field notes, could lead to imprisonment for the researchers (Emerson 2001; Van Maanen 1983).

The Violation of Trust

There are several ways in which researchers can betray participants' trust in the research enterprise. For instance, the researcher might inadvertently divulge the identity of respondents even though they were promised anonymity. There is also the possibility of exploitative relationships, especially with key informants. Exploitation is of special concern in cases where there is a real or perceived imbalance of power—often related to race, class, or gender—between researcher and participant. In the Tuskegee case, for example, Black men suffered the adverse effects of the research even though syphilis is distributed throughout the larger population. Although this research should not have occurred under any circumstances, a more equitable research design would have meant that most of the participants were White males.

It is also a betrayal of trust for the researcher to develop inappropriate relationships with participants. One noteworthy example of this is a study conducted by Erich Goode (2002) to better understand the stigma of obesity. Goode has publicly acknowledged that he had sexual relations with some of his female informants. He argues that because of this, he was able to obtain information that may not have been obtainable by any other means. However, one must ask about the cost to participants of his obtaining the knowledge in this way. One can only imagine how his participants felt when some of them discovered that Goode had an ulterior motive in having intimate relations with them. Many of his participants were already very sensitive about their body image and their relationships with men. Because Goode's participants did not have full knowledge of his motives, they were unable to make informed choices about engaging in sexual relations with him. In this case, the power imbalance between researcher and participant led to exploitation.

The best-known example of sociological research involving deception and intrusion into people's lives is Laud Humphreys's (1970) study of the homosexual activities of men in public restrooms ("tearooms"). Humphreys (1930–1988) acted as a lookout outside tearooms and signaled men engaged in anonymous acts of fellatio when members of the public or the police were approaching. He interviewed some of the men with full disclosure. However, he also noted the license plate numbers of some of those he observed and tracked down their addresses. Humphreys appeared at their homes a year or so later, in disguise, to interview them under false pretenses. In this way he uncovered one of the most important findings of his study: More than half the men were married, with wives and families. Humphreys deceived these men by not telling them from the outset that he was doing research on them and, with those he interviewed under false pretenses, by not revealing the true nature of the research. His research had at least the potential of revealing something that most of the participants wanted to conceal. He later admitted that if he had the chance to do the research over again, he would tell the participants about his true role and goal. But the research itself is not without merit. It helped distinguish between homosexual acts and homosexual identity. Many of these men also experienced considerable stress in trying to live as married men while simultaneously engaging in impersonal homosexual activity with strangers. Humphreys's research, though ethically flawed and harmful to the unwitting participants, did have some benefit: It provided much-needed insight into the social construction of sexuality and the difficulties involved in understanding how people develop their sexual selves.

For 40 years researchers studied the progression of syphilis in hundreds of poor black men in Tuskegee, Alabama. Unethically, they did not tell them they had the disease, nor did they treat them for it. Worse, they simply watched them suffer and eventually die painfully.

A survivor of the Tuskegee Syphilis Study. For 40 years researchers studied the progression of syphilis in hundreds of poor black men in Tuskegee, Alabama. Unethically, they did not tell them they had the disease, nor did they treat them for it.
Associated Press/National Archives

Informed Consent and Institutional Review Boards

Various ethical codes have been devised to protect people from overzealous or malicious researchers. The Hippocratic oath taken by medical doctors offers helpful guidelines for dealing with human participants. The Nuremberg Code was developed in 1947 to protect biomedical research subjects after the Nazi experiments on concentration camp inmates were revealed (see Table 3.2). Codes like these were later broadened to a concern for all research involving human participants. Such ethical codes have helped protect research participants, but it is important to realize that they are only codes of conduct and not enforceable laws or regulations.

Following revelations of the Tuskegee experiments, the U.S. Congress passed the 1974 National Research Act, requiring ethical oversight for research funded by the federal government. Since then, the U.S. Department of Health and Human Services has required that all research in the United States receiving federal funding be approved by an institutional review board (IRB; Cameron 2015). (In the United Kingdom and Australia, research ethics committees, or RECs, serve a similar purpose.) IRBs are designed to deal with the issue of deception in social research and the harm that social research can do to participants. Universities have their own IRBs, and board committee members are typically faculty members from a wide variety of disciplines, along with members of the community. IRBs generally protect three broad ethical principles:

- *Respect for persons.* Participants—especially those with diminished capacities, such as physical or mental disabilities—are to be treated with dignity and respect.

- *Beneficence.* As little harm as possible is to be done to participants, and every effort is to be made to be of benefit to them. However, there are exceptions where the benefits of the research are overwhelming and the harm to be done is unavoidable.

- *Justice.* Research should operate on the principle of justice, so that burdens and rewards are distributed equitably.

TABLE 3.2	The Nuremberg Code
	Directives for Human Experimentation
1	The voluntary consent of the human subject is absolutely essential.
2	The experiment should be such as to yield fruitful results for the good of society.
3	The experiment should be so designed and based on the results of animal experimentation and a knowledge of the natural history of the disease.
4	The experiment should be so conducted as to avoid all unnecessary physical and mental suffering and injury.
5	No experiment should be conducted where there is an a priori reason to believe that death or disabling injury will occur.
6	The degree of risk to be taken should never exceed that determined by the humanitarian importance of the problem to be solved by the experiment.
7	Proper preparations should be made and adequate facilities provided to protect the experimental subject against even remote possibilities of injury, disability, or death.
8	The experiment should be conducted only by scientifically qualified persons.
9	During the course of the experiment, the human subject should be at liberty to bring the experiment to an end.
10	During the course of the experiment, the scientist in charge must be prepared to terminate the experiment at any stage, if he has probable cause to believe, in the exercise of the good faith, superior skill, and careful judgment required of him, that a continuation of the experiment is likely to result in injury, disability, or death to the experimental subject.

Source: U.S. Department of Health and Human Services. https://ori.hhs.gov/chapter-3-The-Protection-of-Human-Subjects-nuremberg-codedirectives-human-experimentation.

Of particular importance is that most IRBs require evidence of written **informed consent** of those being studied. Typically, researchers present a statement for participants to sign that ensures informed consent. It includes such details as

- What the study entails and why it is being conducted
- How and why research participants have been recruited to participate
- What participation involves
- The risks and benefits associated with participation
- The degree to which participants' privacy and confidentiality will be protected
- How the study safeguards vulnerable populations (such as children, prisoners, and the impaired)
- Whom the participants can contact at the university if they have further questions

Participants have a right not only to be aware that they are being studied but also to know about the potential harms and benefits they might experience in the course of the research. Research that does not include obtaining such consent or, more important, that poses dangers to participants is likely to be turned down by the IRB unless it is justified by extraordinary reasons.

In addition to the statement for participants, researchers submit to the IRB a research protocol that provides an overview of the way in which the research will be conducted. For example, if the research is interview based, the protocol might specify that the interviewer will first provide the participant with an introduction to the research and a review of the participant's role in the research, show him or her the informed consent form that will be signed by participants, and provide a basic script of the questions that will be asked during the interview. The IRB committee then reviews these materials and decides whether the proposed research plan should be approved, modified, or disapproved.

Objectivity, or "Value-Free" Sociology

Another issue relating to sociological research is whether researchers are, or can be, objective. That is, do they allow personal preferences and judgments to bias their research? Many argue that value-laden research jeopardizes the entire field of sociology. The publication of such research—and public revelations about researcher biases—erodes and could destroy the credibility of the field as a whole. In the history of sociology, this discussion is traceable, once again, to the work of Max Weber (Black 2013). Taken to its extreme, *value-free sociology* means preventing all personal values from affecting any phase of the research process. However, this is not what Weber intended in his work on values, and it is instructive to take a brief look at what he actually meant.

Weber was most concerned with the need for teachers, especially professors, to be value-free in their lectures. Weber was opposed to using the classroom to express any values. He took this position because he felt that young students were neither mature nor sophisticated enough to see through such arguments. He believed that they were also likely to be too intimidated by the position of their professors, especially in the authoritarian Germany of his day, to be able to evaluate their ideas critically. The idea of, and the need for, value-free teaching seems clear and uncontestable. However, we must realize that all professors, like all other human beings, have values. Therefore, the best we can hope for is for them to strive to be as objective as possible in the classroom.

Weber did *not* take the same position with reference to research. In fact, he saw at least two roles for values in social research. The first is in the selection of a question to be researched. In that case, it is perfectly appropriate for researchers to be guided by their personal values, or the values that predominate in the society of the day. The second is in the analysis of the results of a research study. In that analysis, sociologists can, and should, use personal and social values to help them make sense of their findings. These values are an aid in interpretation and understanding. However, they are not to be used purposely to distort the findings or mislead the reader of a report on the study.

In Weber's opinion, the only place in research to be value free is in the collection of research data. This is a rather unexceptional argument, meaning that researchers should do everything they can to prevent bias in the data collection process. Few, if any, scientists would accept the opposing position that it is perfectly acceptable to engage in such distortions. Such a position would undermine all research and the scientific status and aspirations of sociology.

Some sociologists, especially feminist and critical scholars (Reid 2004), question whether even this limited attempt to conduct value-free research is possible. In a famous essay, Alvin Gouldner (1962) argued that value-free sociology is a myth. Even when researchers strive to be completely objective, they carry with them their own experiences, assumptions about the world, and personal biases that inevitably shape the ways in which they approach their research and collect their data. The fact that women and people of color were largely overlooked by social researchers until relatively recently is an example of how an unquestioned assumption—the belief that the experiences of men and women or of people of color and Whites are all the same—can be problematic. For this reason, many scholars (such as Bourdieu 1992) argue that researchers should be extremely reflective and explicit about their own social positions and how those might influence the research process.

In contemporary terms, what Weber argued for was an attitude of objectivity during the research process. But there is another kind of objectivity, *procedural objectivity*, that entails reporting the research in such a way that any reader will understand how the research was conducted. Researchers should report as many details as possible to allow for outside assessment of the research. Among other things, details about sampling, the questions asked in interviews or on questionnaires, the statistical procedures employed, and known limitations of the research should be made available in research reports. Other researchers can then, if they choose, repeat (or replicate) the study to see if they get the same results. The ability to replicate research is a hallmark of any science.

SUMMARY

Sociologists apply the scientific method. First, the sociologist finds a question that needs to be answered and then reviews the literature to see what has already been found. Next, the sociologist develops a hypothesis, chooses a research method, and collects data that can confirm, or fail to confirm, the hypothesis. Finally, the researcher analyzes the data in relation to the initial hypothesis. Sociology is a multiple-paradigm science, which means that no one model unifies all sociologists.

Sociologists use different research methods, depending on the research questions they are studying. Quantitative research yields data in the form of numbers, usually derived from surveys and experiments. Qualitative research is conducted in natural settings and yields descriptive information. Observation consists of systematically watching, listening to, and recording what takes place in a natural social setting over some period of time. Researchers may choose to participate and play a role in what they are observing or engage in nonparticipant observation. Ethnographic research is more likely to be based on participant observation over an extended length of time. In interviews, respondents are asked a series of questions, usually face-to-face. Survey research collects data through interviews and questionnaires.

Experimentation manipulates one or more independent variables to examine their effect on one or more dependent variables.

Sociologists also often engage in secondary data analysis, in which they reanalyze data collected by others. Secondary data may consist of statistical information, historical documents and analyses, or the content of cultural artifacts and messages.

Reliability is the degree to which a given measure produces the same results time after time, and validity is the degree to which a measure is accurate. Past problems with questionable research ethics have led to the development of institutional review boards (IRBs). A key requirement is that researchers obtain informed consent from participants by explaining the purpose of the study and any sensitive or dangerous aspects of the research.

It is difficult to avoid bias altogether. However, clear and objective descriptions of research procedures will enable other researchers to evaluate and perhaps replicate those procedures.

KEY TERMS

content analysis
convenience samples
dependent variable
descriptive statistics
descriptive survey
empiricism
ethics
ethnography
experiment
explanatory survey
field experiments
global ethnography
Hawthorne Effect
historical-comparative research
ideal type
independent variable
inferential statistics

informed consent
interviews
key informant
laboratory experiments
mixed methods research
natural experiments
netnography
nonparticipant observation
observation
paradigm
participant observation
qualitative research
quantitative research
questionnaires
random sample
reliability
sample

scientific method
secondary data analysis
statistics

stratified sample
survey research
validity

REVIEW QUESTIONS

1. What steps do researchers take when applying the scientific method? How would you apply the scientific method to get answers to a question you have about the social world?

2. What does it mean to say that sociology is a multiple-paradigm science? What are the benefits and disadvantages of a multiple-paradigm science?

3. What are the differences between participant and nonparticipant observational methods? How do sociologists ensure that their observations are systematic using both approaches?

4. What is the key value of conducting ethnographic research? How would a global ethnography help you make sense of your own place in the world?

5. Researchers use interviews to gather data by asking individuals a series of questions. How do researchers choose between prestructured and unstructured interviews? What are the advantages and disadvantages of each type of interview?

6. Why do sociologists who conduct surveys rely on samples? What techniques do researchers use to avoid biases in their samples?

7. A researcher uses the World Values Survey to examine the relationship between people's religious beliefs and their level of happiness. In this study, what is the independent variable, and what is the dependent variable? What reliability and validity issues could arise in conducting this survey across countries?

8. Some experiments allow researchers to take advantage of a naturally occurring event to study its effect on one or more dependent variables. Can you think of any recent events that might have been conducive to natural experiments? What would be the dependent variable or variables in your example?

9. What are some of the ethical concerns raised by sociological research? Use specific examples from research discussed in this chapter to describe these ethical concerns. How do IRBs help keep research ethical?

10. What role do values play in the research process? According to Weber, when is objectivity most important?

TOLGA AKMEN / Contributor

4 CULTURE

> **LEARNING OBJECTIVES**
>
> 4.1 Define culture.
>
> 4.2 Identify the basic elements of culture.
>
> 4.3 Discuss cultural differences.
>
> 4.4 Describe global culture, consumer culture, and cyberculture.

CULTURE AND THE COVID-19 PANDEMIC

The spread of deadly diseases, such as the COVID-19 pandemic, can reveal a lot about how different societies operate and even about the belief systems of individuals. The COVID-19 pandemic, for example, has brought a lot of individual and societal differences to the forefront of the media and led to protests, political shifts, and fights around the family dinner table.

It is clear that different government responses to the pandemic, the unequal distribution of access to healthcare resources, beliefs about vaccinations and the use of masks, and the influence of politicized media, especially social media, have all influenced how the COVID-19 virus has spread, or not, in different places and among different populations. Especially relevant to the spread of disease has been people's (un)willingness to adhere to effective safety measures, like wearing masks, physical distancing, and avoiding crowded events. These elements vary both within and between different societies. For example, in many Asian countries wearing masks is a common culturally accepted practice, in heavy contrast to the more anti–mask wearing culture of many Western nations, which was a central reason COVID-19 infections in the United States and the UK, for example, spread so much faster than in Asia.

In the early days of the pandemic, countries like Singapore and Taiwan effectively contained the virus while the United States and Brazil had among the world's highest rates. This can be attributed, in large part, to cultural norms surrounding health and safety practices. Research has suggested that cultures that place the collective good above individual "rights" tended to fare better in terms of infection rates and vaccination rates (Ryan and Nanda 2022).

It is worth noting that similar government responses to the pandemic have occurred in culturally different societies. The use of extreme surveillance, for example, has been used by President Vladimir Putin in the autocratic state of Russia but was also used by Benjamin Netanyahu, leader of the democratic state of Israel, as well as in the democratic states of South Korea and Taiwan. The use of digital technologies as forms of disease surveillance has been effective in helping to contain the pandemic in many Asian countries, while in Israel and Russia there has been widespread resistance to the use of digital tracking because it is seen as an invasion of privacy and there is a fear that such surveillance will expand government control even when the pandemic ends (Ryan and Nanda 2022). This fear is less widespread in many Asian nations.

DEFINING CULTURE

Culture refers to the collection of ideas, values, norms, beliefs, practices, and material objects that are shared by a group of people. Although there are innumerable ideas, values, practices, and material objects associated with most cultures, most people know at least the most basic and important elements of their own culture and often even elements of other cultures. Participation in a shared culture often leads members of that culture to behave in similar ways and to adopt similar ways of looking at the world. However, it is important to remember that there are differences within, as well as between, cultures. For example, we could think of Muslims as a cultural group, but there are also important differences between different sects of Islam, and even within the same sect. Thus, although culture is a useful tool for thinking about a collective, it is also very difficult to put hard and fast boundaries around what defines any particular culture.

Cultures also change over time. This is especially true when certain technologies are introduced into the culture. For example, most students today cannot imagine a world without cell phones. We use them to communicate with one other, to play games, to order food, to pay for things, to listen to music. In fact, it seems we use them for just about everything except talking on the phone! And yet, most students' parents grew up in an age when there were no cell phones. The rapid transition to such a high dependence on cell phones to manage our daily lives is one example of a cultural change.

Cultures also vary significantly based on their core principles. One example of this is the difference between individualist versus collectivist cultures. **Individualist cultures** tend to place the rights and freedoms of individuals above larger collective concerns. For example, many individualist cultures resisted mask mandates, claiming they infringed on individual rights, even though they are a proven method to protect community health (Ryan 2023). **Collectivist cultures,** on the other hand, tend to place greater value on the community good. In collectivist cultures, mask mandates are not only more easily enforced, but also more widely accepted as there is an understanding that the individual must sometimes do things they do not want to do for the greater good of society. This is not to say that cultures are entirely individualistic or entirely collectivist. In fact, most cultures fall somewhere in the middle, with more individualist views on certain issues and more collectivist views on others. For example, even many individualistic societies have banned smoking inside public places due to the concern for communal public health.

Andy Warhol's art is both high culture and popular culture.
AFP/Stringer/Getty Images

Another dimension along which culture can vary is between **high culture** and **popular culture**. High culture refers to those cultural elements typically associated with the elites—things like art museums, opera, and classical literature. Elements of high culture typically require a certain amount of money and education to appreciate. Popular culture, on the other hand, refers to cultural elements that typically have broader appeal within a society—like blue jeans, Hollywood blockbusters, and songs by Taylor Swift. Elements of popular culture are typically less expensive and more easily appreciated by most people. It is important to note, however, that there are no hard and fast dividing lines between what is high culture and what is popular culture. For example, the Andy Warhol Museum is indeed an art museum, but one that showcases pop art. On the other hand, Lady Gaga's fashion is often considered high culture even if her music is more often thought of as popular culture.

Lady Gaga is known for her fashion almost as much as her music.
Dimitrios Kambouris/Staff/Getty Images

THE BASIC ELEMENTS OF CULTURE

As pointed out earlier, every group and society has a culture. Culture surrounds such diverse social phenomena as sports, cooking, funeral ceremonies, dating, medicine, marriage, sex, body piercings, dancing, games, hairstyles, religion, and even people's names! Cultures differ from one another mainly because each represents a unique mix of values, norms, objects, and language inherited from the past, derived from other groups, and created anew by each group.

Values

The broadest element of culture is **values**, the general and abstract standards defining what a group or society as a whole considers good, desirable, right, or important. Values also express what a group or society as a whole considers bad, undesirable, wrong, or unimportant. In short, values express the ideals and beliefs of society.

In his classic work *Democracy in America* ([1835–1840] 1969), the French scholar Alexis de Tocqueville detailed what he perceived to be America's values. According to de Tocqueville, among the things Americans valued in the early nineteenth century were democracy, equality, individualism, "taste for physical comfort," spirituality, and economic prosperity. Although de Tocqueville wrote about his impressions of the United States almost 200 years ago, the vast majority of Americans today would accept most, if not all, of the values he described (Crothers 2018).

At this point, it is important to point out that the values associated with a society, or that people in a society claim to find important, are not necessarily reflective of how that society operates. For example, although de Tocqueville claimed that Americans in the 1830s valued democracy, it was also the case that women and non-White men could not vote. Americans at that time also claimed to value equality, and yet many owned slaves. Thus, it is important to remember that the values associated with a particular society, or that members of that society claim to find desirable, are not necessarily reflective of how that society actually operates. Values should not be confused with practice.

Despite the above argument, that a given society expresses a belief that certain values are desirable (or not) is itself an element of culture. For example, many contemporary societies express capitalist values, that is, a belief that the individual should be responsible for themselves and not depend on social "handouts." In fact, many, like the United States, hold such values at the core of their identities. That said, even the most capitalist of societies still contain highly socialist elements, that is, those things to which everyone contributes even if not everyone uses. For example, public schools, libraries, parks, roadways, and fire departments are generally funded by taxes that everybody pays, even if not everybody will make use of those services. The fact that those elements exist, however, does not change the fact that the society itself expresses a belief in capitalist values.

In short, values are a complicated component of culture. There are the values that are expressed, those that are seen as desirable or not, and the values that are actually lived. But what are the consequences of values? Where do they come from? How are they expressed? In the next section, we will explore some of these questions by looking at another element of culture: norms.

Norms

Norms are the rules that guide what people do and how they live. Norms tell us what we should and should not do in a given situation. Many norms are informal. That is, they are not formally written down in any one place. They are often seen as "common sense." For example, that one should not pick their nose in public is a commonly accepted norm in most cultures. On the other hand, **laws** are norms that *have* been written down and that are formally enforced through institutions like the police and the legal system. For example, people under the age of 21 are not allowed to purchase alcohol in the United States (though the age is lower in many other countries). Someone under 21 purchasing alcohol is at risk of running into trouble with the police.

The consequences of failing to follow norms are usually very different from those of disobeying laws. Cyclists are expected to obey the laws of the road.

Design Sensation/iStock Photo

You are expected to follow norms and obey laws, but the consequences of failing to do so are usually very different in the two cases. If you violate the law against murdering someone, you can expect to be arrested, sent to prison, and perhaps even executed. But if you fail to follow the norm of not burping loudly at the family dinner table, you can expect merely a few raised eyebrows and perhaps a cross word from your mother. However, reactions to violating norms are not always so gentle. For example, a gang member's violation of a norm against fleeing a fight with another gang may lead to physical violence, death, and other not-so-subtle outcomes.

Norms are reinforced through **sanctions,** which can take the form of punishments (negative sanctions) or rewards (positive sanctions). In general, when norms have been violated, punishments are used, but when norms are followed, rewards might be given. For example, your mother might frown

Have you ever deliberately broken a social norm?
ajr_images/Getty Images

when you burp at the family dinner but might grin approvingly when you put your napkin in your lap before eating. In other words, sanctions may be applied when norms are observed as well as when they are violated. Sometimes either positive or negative sanctions are enough to enforce norms. However, enforcement is generally more effective when positive and negative sanctions are used together—when *both* the "carrot" (reward) and the "stick" (punishment) are applied.

Not all norms are the same, are equally important, or carry the same penalties if violated. On the one hand, there are **folkways**, or relatively unimportant norms. Whether they are observed or violated, they carry with them few, if any, sanctions (Sumner [1906] 1940). For example, talking loudly on your cell phone in a crowded restaurant might get you a few dirty looks, but it is not likely to result in severe punishments.

In contrast, **mores** (pronounced MOR-ays) are more important norms whose violation is likely to be met with severe negative sanctions. For example, talking loudly on your cell phone during class is likely to anger your classmates (and your teacher!) and could get you thrown out of the classroom. Although a clear distinction is often made between folkways and mores, in fact they exist along a continuum; it is often hard to distinguish where folkways end and mores begin.

But how do we know when something is a norm and when it is not? And how do others react when someone doesn't seem to know what a norm is? Sociologist Harold Garfinkel set out to understand these questions with his idea of a **breaching experiment**, or a purposeful violation of a norm to see how others will react. For example, it is expected that when one enters an elevator with strangers that one will face forward and not engage in conversation. A breaching experiment might involve entering an elevator, facing the back of the elevator, and asking very personal questions of other people in the elevator. By examining how others react in that situation, we can begin to understand the norm of facing forward and remaining silent and how important that norm is, or is not, to others.

Sharing an armrest on a train can be a fraught experience. How do you react if someone violates what you see as an established social norm?
BE&W agencja fotograficzna Sp. z o.o./Alamy Stock Photo

Symbolic Culture and Language

Symbolic culture includes the various symbols that we use to represent key values and norms. For example, a national flag is a symbol of belonging to, or pride in, a given country. By wearing a shirt with a particular national flag, we are expressing that we value the country that flag represents. Not all symbols mean the same thing in every country, however. For example, a flag striped with the colors of the rainbow is a symbol of gay pride in many cultures. In the Andean cultures of Peru, however, a very similar flag represents the city of Cusco as well as Incan culture in general (see Figure 4.1).

FIGURE 4.1 ■ Similar Symbols can Have Different Meanings in Different Contexts

Mixmike/Getty Images; FG Trade/Getty Images

One important aspect of symbolic culture is **language**, a set of meaningful symbols that enables communication. Language, especially in its written form, allows for the storage, transmission, and development of culture. Cultures with largely oral traditions do manage to accumulate culture and transmit it from one generation or group to another, though written language is often a far more effective way of retaining and transmitting a culture between generations.

Perhaps more important, language facilitates communication within a culture. Our words reflect the ways in which we think about and see the world. They also shape and influence culture. It was this idea that inspired Edward Sapir and Benjamin Whorf to advance their **Sapir-Whorf hypothesis**, or the idea that our ability to understand and experience the world around us is shaped by our knowledge of language. For example, in English one can "like" something or "love" something, but we have no word for a feeling between like and love. Of course, you can like something a lot, or really love something, but there is no single word that captures a middle ground. However, in Spanish one can "gustar" (roughly, like), "amar" (roughly, love), or "querer" (a word that is difficult to directly translate into English but that falls somewhere between like and love). Another example would be the difference between "snow" and "ice." In English, those two words mean very different things. In Arabic, the same word is used to represent both. And in many Inuit languages, there are more than a dozen words to clearly represent different kinds of snow.

The contemporary world has given nearly all languages a wealth of new words. For example, in the world of social networking, a "tweet" refers to a message sent on Twitter. A "selfie" refers to a picture taken of oneself. And a "bot" refers to an automated computer program that attempts to interact with other users. The meaning of words can also change with time, and especially with the introduction of technology. For example, the word *hashtag* once simply referred to the symbol "#"; now, it most commonly refers to a label on Twitter that helps us search tweets. And the term *troll*, which originally described a fairy-tale monster, now most commonly refers to someone who instigates arguments or anonymously insults others on social media forums.

The consumption-oriented nature of our society has also led to the creation of many new words, a large number of them brand names. For example, the now nearly extinct iPod was the leading portable music device for some time; it led to the development of iTunes. The iPhone is the leading smartphone (another new word), and it has replaced the iPod as well as led to a booming industry in apps (applications) of all sorts. Similarly, globalization has led to new words, including *globalization* itself, which was virtually unused prior to 1990 (Ritzer and Dean 2019). The boom in sending work to be performed in another country or countries has given us the term *outsourcing* (Ritzer and Lair 2007).

Words like these are shared by people all over the world and allow them to communicate with one another. Communication among people of different cultures is also easier if they share a mother tongue. As you can see in the simplified map of world languages in Figure 4.2, African cultures use a variety of official and national languages. People in countries where French is the official language, such as Burkina Faso and Niger, can transact their business more easily with one another than they can with nations where Arabic or Portuguese is the primary language, such as Mauritania and Cape Verde.

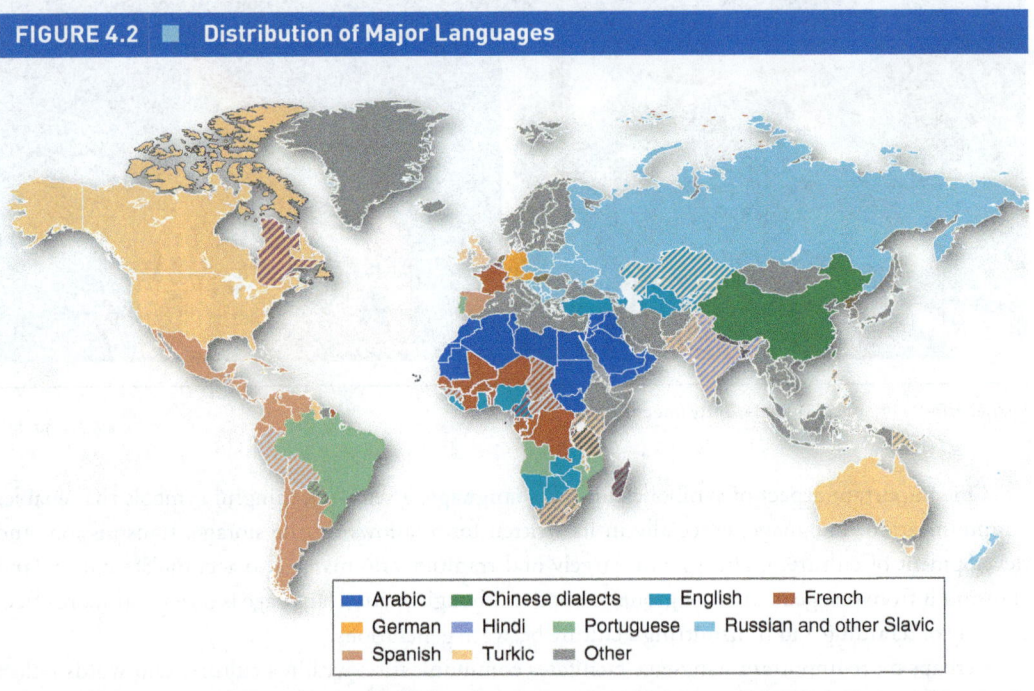

FIGURE 4.2 ■ Distribution of Major Languages

Source: Data from Languages of the World, One World, Nations Online Project. https://www.nationsonline.org/oneworld/languages.htm

Communication between cultures is often not as easy or as clear as is communication within a given culture. For example, in the 2017 movie *The Big Sick*, Pakistan-born comedian Kumail Nanjiani and his American girlfriend experience numerous clashes over their cultural differences. After she becomes seriously ill, Kumail faces cultural entanglements not only with her parents but also with his own parents, who wish to find him a spouse that conforms to their cultural expectations.

In a world dominated by consumption, communication between cultures also takes place through the viewing of common brands. However, brand names well known in some cultures may not translate well in other cultures. As a result, brands are often renamed to better reflect the cultures in which they are being sold. The following list shows the names of some well-known brands in the United States and elsewhere and the way in which they are translated into Chinese.

Brand	Chinese Translation
Nike	Enduring and Persevering
BMW	Precious Horse
Heineken	Happiness Power
Coca-Cola	Tasty Fun
Marriott	10,000 Wealthy Elites

Although such name changes are common, some brand names are simply phonetically translated into Chinese. For example, Cadillac is translated "Ka di la ke." Although this name means nothing to the Chinese, the fact that it is foreign gives it an aura of status and respectability to many. However, if Microsoft had used a phonetic Chinese translation of the name of its search engine, Bing, it would have been in big trouble. In Chinese, the word *bing* means "disease" or "virus." To avoid being seen as disease-ridden or a carrier of a virus, Microsoft changed the search engine's Chinese name to "Bi ying." This has the far more appealing meaning of "responding without fail" (Wines 2011).

Material Culture

In the next section we will look more closely at some of the key elements of culture, but we first want to distinguish between **material culture** and **nonmaterial culture**. Nonmaterial culture refers to things that we cannot necessarily see or touch, such as values, beliefs, norms, symbols, and language. On the other hand, material culture refers to the things that we can typically see and touch, for example, buildings, household items, clothing, and cars. These elements can, and often do, overlap and influence one another. For example, a headscarf is itself an item of material culture, but wearing a headscarf is often seen as a cultural symbol identifying the wearer with a certain set of beliefs and values.

Culture shapes many of the objects around us. For instance, the value that many place on economic prosperity is reflected in the board game Monopoly. This game was first patented in the mid-1930s (ironically, as a reaction to the Great Depression), and its icon is a well-dressed, economically successful tycoon with a monocle. The goal of the game is to accumulate the most property and money. There are now also nonmaterial games (such as Fortnite and Pokémon Go) that are not only enjoyed by millions of people online but are also played by thousands in material sports arenas for millions of dollars in real and material prize money (Wingfield 2014b, 2014c).

Material culture also shapes the larger culture in various ways. For example, when playing Monopoly, children are learning about, helping support, and furthering a culture that values wealth and material success. To take a different example, the centuries-old value of individual freedom and individualism has been greatly enhanced by the widespread adoption of such material objects as the automobile, the single-family home, and the smartphone.

CULTURAL DIFFERENCES

As you have seen so far, we can think in terms of the culture of a society as a whole, and later in this chapter we will even conceive of the possibility of a global culture. But you have also seen that there is great diversity within cultures, from gang culture to internet culture and many other culture variants as well. Studying and understanding culture becomes easier, however, with the aid of a few key ideas: ideal and real culture, ideology, subculture and counterculture, culture war, and multiculturalism.

Ideal and Real Culture

As we mentioned before, there is often a very large gap between **ideal culture**, or what the norms and values of society lead us to think people should believe and do, and **real culture**, or what people actually think and do in their everyday lives. For example, we have discussed how democracy is seen as a central part of American culture (and many others). However, barely a majority of Americans bother to vote in presidential elections—barely 2/3 voted in the 2020 election, and that was considered a record setting turnout. An even smaller percentage of those who are eligible make the effort to vote in state and local elections. Worse, very few Americans are active in politics in other ways, such as canvassing on behalf of a political party or working to get people out to vote.

In another example, the cultural ideal that mothers should be completely devoted to their children (Hays 1998) often comes into conflict with lived reality for many women who work outside the home and must balance their time between job and family. This contradiction is apparent in the incidence of breastfeeding, which at least for some women is once again a norm of motherhood (Avishai 2007; Stearns 2009). Breastfeeding is often difficult for many mothers because it is labor- and time-intensive, and given work and all the other constraints women face in their lives, it is difficult for them to find the time and energy to do it. Despite its health benefits for baby and mother, under such circumstances breastfeeding can have adverse social and economic consequences for women. One study demonstrated that women who breastfed for more than six months suffered greater economic losses than those who did so for less time or not at all (Rippeyoug and Noonan 2012). Though some women who do not breastfeed can feel that they have failed to live up to cultural standards of being a "good mom," others have developed resistance strategies to maintain a positive maternal identity, such as recognizing that the use of formula is not always an individual choice (Holcomb 2017).

Ideology

An **ideology** is a set of shared beliefs that explains the social world and guides people's actions. There are many ideologies in any society, and some of them become dominant. For example, in many societies, **meritocracy** is a dominant ideology involving the widely shared belief that all people have an equal chance of succeeding economically based on their hard work and skills. Many people act on the basis of that belief and, among other things, seek the education and training they think they need to succeed.

However, even with dedication and adequate education and training, not everyone succeeds economically. For example, not all professions pay the same amount and there is not a guaranteed relationship between more education and higher pay. In fact, for many professions, average salaries actually decrease between having a master's degree and having a PhD. Also important is the difference in costs, especially debts, associated with getting an education. One's economic origin, even more so than their level of education or training, is most often what determines their economic position later in life. This reflects the key fact that not all ideologies are true. For one thing, they may come from, and be true for, some groups of people (such as those in the upper classes) and not for others (those in the lower classes). For another, they may be outright distortions used by one group to hide reality from another group (Marx [1857–1858] 1964). In this sense, it could be argued that meritocracy is an ideology created by the upper classes to hide the fact that those in the lower classes have little or no chance of succeeding. This fact is hidden from them to prevent them from becoming dissatisfied and rebellious. If the lower classes accept the ideology of meritocracy, they may be more likely to blame themselves for failing rather than the upper classes or the capitalist economic system as a whole.

Subcultures

Within any culture there are **subcultures**, or groups of people who accept much of the dominant culture but are set apart from it by one or more culturally significant characteristics. Major subcultures in some countries include the LGBTQ+ community (lesbian, gay, bisexual, transgender, and queer people), Hispanics, Hasidic Jews, hip-hop fans, and youth. Of course, whether a given identity is part of the larger culture or is a subculture depends on where it is located. For example, Muslims are the dominant culture in many countries in the Middle East, but they are a subculture in the United States and much of Europe.

Subcultures arise in the realm of consumption as well. For example, "brand communities" develop around particular brand name products (Todd and Soule 2018). Harley-Davidson motorcycle riders are one such subculture (called HOGs, for Harley Owners Group), with distinctive clothing, events, and norms. Brand communities have formed around a number of Apple products, such as the Macintosh computer (the "Mac") and the iPad. The members of these communities share a number of cultural elements, including norms. In the case of the Mac, for example, some community members positively sanction "jailbreaking," a method for hacking into Apple's software to get around its restrictions and limitations.

Most societies include many subcultures, such as hackers or those devoted to fishing, that develop around particular styles of life and whose members share special vocabularies. A great deal of attention has been devoted to "deviant" subcultures, such as punks, goths, and the like (Barmaki 2016). In Great Britain and elsewhere, "football hooligans," those who often engage in violence at or in regard to soccer matches, constitute another example of a deviant subculture (Ayres and Treadwell 2012;

Dunning, Murphy, and Williams 1988). Another example of a subculture is the world of skateboarders. The majority of skateboarders accept most of the larger society's culture, norms, values, and language, but they also differ in some ways. Many are more willing than most members of society to take physical risks, for example, by participating in the sport known as parkour, which involves using the body to overcome urban obstacles such as walls and ledges (Kidder 2012; Thorpe and Ahmad 2015). Skateboarders in general, as well as those who practice parkour, see such obstacles as enhancing the thrill of their activity.

Skateboarding has developed a subculture with its own norms, values, language, and environments. Do you belong to any similar subcultures?

fcscafeine/iStock Photo

Countercultures

Countercultures are groups that not only differ from the dominant culture but also adhere to norms and values that may be incompatible with those of the dominant culture. They may, in fact, consciously and overtly act in opposition to the dominant culture. The term *counterculture* was introduced by Theodore Roszak ([1968] 1995) in the late 1960s in reference to hippies, antiwar activists, and radical students.

Computer hackers are a contemporary example of a counterculture. Many hackers simply seek to show their technical mastery of computers through relatively benign actions, such as writing free computer software, but a minority are devoted to subverting authority and disrupting the internet, and some are involved in stealing personal identification data (identity theft) and money (Alleyne 2018). They may write malicious code in order to interrupt or even shut down the normal operations of computers. In one famous case in 1988, Robert Tappan Morris unleashed what was thought to be the first worm that slowed down thousands of computers, making many of them unusable. Since then, many attempted and successful breaches have threatened government and corporate computer systems (e.g., the Equifax data breach of 2017); the hackers' goal has been to steal secret or personal information (like consumer credit data, in the case of Equifax). A rash of hacks of corporate computers was aimed at stealing credit card numbers and account information. For example, in 2021 the account information of more than 500 million Facebook users was compromised. That same year more than 700 million users of LinkedIn also had their accounts compromised. In another incident, hackers exposed the names of 30 million people who had accounts with Ashley Madison. This was particularly troublesome to the account holders because those who participated on the Ashley Madison website were interested in having adulterous affairs. The site's slogan was "Life is short; have an affair" (McPhate 2016). Personal accounts have also been hacked and locked until the account holders paid ransom demanded by the hackers (Simone 2015).

In the realm of consumption, an important contemporary counterculture is associated with or sympathetic to the "voluntary simplicity" movement (Elgin 2010; Pelikán, Galcanova, and Kala, 2017). Sociologist Juliet Schor (1993, 1998) has critiqued the dominant American culture's emphasis on what she calls "work and spend." That is, we are willing to work long hours so that we can spend a great deal on consumption and live an ever-more elaborate lifestyle. In addition, Schor (2005) points out the ways in which our consumer culture has led to the commercialization of childhood, with advertising pervading all aspects of children's lives. As a countercultural alternative, she suggests that we both work less and spend less and instead devote ourselves to more meaningful activities. Living a simpler life means avoiding overconsumption, minimizing the work needed to pay for consumption, and doing less harm to the environment.

Globalization, especially economic globalization, has also spawned a number of very active countercultural groups. They are not necessarily antiglobalization, but they favor alternative forms of globalization (Kahn and Kellner 2007; Obara-Minnitt 2014; Pleyers 2010). In fact, many of them are part of the process of globalization. The World Social Forum (WSF) was created in 2001 following a series of antiglobalization protests, particularly one in Seattle in 1999. Its members come from all over the world. The WSF's slogan is "Another world is possible." That other world would be less capitalistic. It would also allow for more democratic decision making on matters that affect large portions of the world's population. Those who accept this kind of perspective are clearly part of a counterculture. They oppose the global spread of the dominant capitalist culture that prioritizes maximizing profits over democratic decision making, human labor rights, and the environment.

Culture Jamming

Culture jamming radically transforms mass media messages, often turning them on their heads completely (Kuehn 2015; Lasn 2000). It is a form of social protest aimed at revealing underlying realities of which consumers may be unaware. The hope is that once people are made aware of these realities through culture jamming, they will change their behaviors or perhaps even band together to change those underlying realities.

The best examples of culture jamming are to be found in the magazine *Adbusters* and the media campaigns it sponsors. The magazine's main targets are in the realm of consumption, especially web and magazine advertisements and billboards. The idea is to transform a corporation's ads into anticorporate, anticonsumption advertisements (Handelman and Kozinets 2007).

The following are some examples of the ways in which culture jamming turns commercial messages inside out:

- "Tommy Sheep" is a spoof of a Tommy Hilfiger ad, with sheep (presumably representing the conformists who buy such clothing) pictured in front of a huge American flag.

- "Absolute on Ice," spoofing an Absolut vodka ad, depicts the foot of a corpse (presumably someone killed by excessive alcohol consumption) with a toe tag.

- People for the Ethical Treatment of Animals (PETA) used the Burger King logo with the phrase "Murder King" to raise awareness of animal brutality in the beef industry.

- FORCE, a feminist organization, culture jammed Victoria Secret's "Pink Loves Consent" advertising campaign by using social media to troll the company's online brand community with the goal of starting a meaningful conversation about sexual consent (Madden et al. 2018).

- Brandalism, an activist artist movement, subverted advertisements with art at bus stops during the 2015 United Nations climate conference in Paris to promote environmental sustainability (Lekakis 2017).

These examples show the hidden realities (sickness, death, sexism, environmental problems, and other miseries) and goals (conformist consumers, obscene profits) of corporations. A broader objective is to show viewers the folly of **consumer culture**, which encourages the consumption of numerous harmful substances (e.g., cigarettes, alcohol) and wasteful goods and services (e.g., expensive clothing). In addition to advertisements, culture jammers create memes to spread ideas and information that challenge the status quo (Lasn 2012). For example, one meme designed by culture jammers depicts a photo of Walmart with the following words: "One of the biggest companies in the world owned by one of the richest families in America . . . holds food drive for needy employees instead of paying them a living wage" (CursedByTheDiceGods 2017). In this way, culture jamming can also be used as a form of activism.

Culture jamming often takes an iconic media message and turns it on its head for shock value, as in this anti-smoking campaign from the California Department of Health Services.

Alamy/Retro AdArchives

Culture Wars

In the 1960s, the hippies, student radicals, and Vietnam War activists vocally, visibly, and sometimes violently rejected traditional norms and values. Among other things, they rejected unthinking patriotism and taboos against recreational drugs and sexual freedom. The term *culture war* was used to describe the social upheaval that ensued. More generally, a **culture war** is a conflict pitting a subculture or counterculture against the dominant culture (e.g., those who are anti-vax versus the dominant cultural norm to get vaccinated; see Blum, Smith, and Sanford 2021), or a conflict between dominant groups within a society. Culture wars sometimes lead to the disruption of the social, economic, and political status quo (Hunter 1992; Luker 1984).

In the United States today, the major culture war being fought is between those who place themselves on the conservative end of the sociopolitical spectrum and those who place themselves on the liberal end. It is largely viewed as a political battle over such things as abortion, immigration, government spending, taxes, social services, national defense, and environmental measures. Conservatives generally favor less government spending, lower taxes for the wealthy, fewer entitlements for the poor, aggressive national defense, and minimal environmental regulations. Liberals usually support higher government spending on education, health care, and services for the poor; less spending on national defense; and stricter environmental regulations. Today, this battle is epitomized by struggles between former President Donald Trump and his conservative allies in the Republican Party and liberal Democrats in the Congress.

There are important differences in fundamental values between these groups. Consider, for example, the long-running battle over abortion. The political battle is over legal limits to abortion and contraception. However, the underlying values have to do with differing definitions of life and attitudes toward women's role in society. Similarly, much heat is generated over "family values," with conservatives worrying about the decline in the traditional nuclear family, the increasing prevalence of cohabitation and single parenthood, and marriage equality for couples of the same sex. They place more emphasis on strict moral codes (at least on their own moral codes) and individualism, whereas liberals, in contrast, place more significance on empathy, openness, and fairness. Liberals tend to see the developments in the family as signs of greater acceptance of people's differences and circumstances

(Lakoff 2016; Wuthnow 2018). Within the field of sociology, in fact, there is intense debate between family scholars who argue that the family is in decline and those who feel that the concept of the family needs to be broadened to embrace the many ways in which people experience kin connections (Popenoe 1993; see Chapter 12).

The conservative–liberal culture war is debated endlessly in the popular media. The media themselves tend to be increasingly divided along conservative (Fox News) and liberal (MSNBC) lines. News reports on these stations are often wildly different, taking contrasting or conflicting positions and even featuring completely different stories or takes on the same stories. The leading media pundits (e.g., former Fox News conservative Tucker Carlson and MSNBC's liberal Rachel Maddow) are often at war with one another.

Another example of a culture war that is taking place in many countries around the world is between those who are taking scientifically proven measures to prevent the spread of COVID-19 (wearing masks, physical distancing, vaccinations) and those who are refusing to do so. As we saw in the introduction to this chapter, wearing a mask has been a commonly accepted cultural practice in many societies around the world for a long time. Those societies have tended to see less of a culture war around mask mandates to prevent the spread of COVID-19. In societies like the United States and Europe, however, wearing a mask has historically been seen as something "foreign" and suspicious. In those societies, a minority, albeit a highly vocal one, has rejected mask wearing, claiming that it infringes on their individual rights. In this way, we can see how the rapid introduction of a "foreign" cultural practice, even one aimed at preventing disease and death, can lead to a culture war.

Examples of culture wars are also to be found in the digital world. For example, open-source advocates believe that the internet, or at least large portions of it, should be protected from control by governments or corporations. They support free open-source software (e.g., Linux, Firefox, OpenOffice, GNU Image Manipulation Program) as well as free access to information. One of their models is nonprofit Wikipedia, where anyone can create entries and modify them. They oppose the dominant profit-oriented players on the internet, including Microsoft, Google, Apple, and internet service providers. These large corporations are seen as carving up the digital world and controlling access to generate huge profits. There is a constant low-level conflict going on between members of these two cultures and the groups that support them. More recently, a culture war broke out between those who want to give some corporations (such as Comcast and Verizon) control over the internet and those who favor "net neutrality," in which the internet is free and open to all. The issue seemed settled when in mid-2016 a federal court ruled in favor of net neutrality, but it is far from dead. In late 2017, the Federal Communications Commission (FCC) voted to eliminate at least some of the rules that made net neutrality possible. As a result, it is likely that large corporations will gain an even greater presence in, and control over, the internet.

Multiculturalism and Assimilation

A great deal of attention has been paid in recent years to another aspect of cultural diversity—**multiculturalism**, or an environment in which cultural differences are accepted and appreciated both by the state and by the majority group (Pakulski 2014). The cultural groups may be based on race, ethnicity, nationality, language, or other factors. People in many societies, for example, generally accept that young and old people have their own cultural preferences.

When it comes to ethnicity and national origin, however, multiculturalism has not always been celebrated in many countries. Dominant cultures have often been interested primarily in **assimilation**, or the process of fully integrating the minority group into the mainstream, rather than **acculturation**, or the process whereby minority groups take on aspects of the dominant culture but still retain distinctive elements of their own culture. As a so-called nation of immigrants, the United States has always had to resolve issues of cultural diversity. Until late in the twentieth century, most immigrants to the United States were from Europe, especially eastern and southern Europe. Many of these groups did assimilate to a large degree, even if their assimilation occurred over a couple of generations. Today we do not think twice about whether Polish Americans or Italian Americans, for instance, are "regular" Americans.

But immigrants from the next large wave, in the 1990s and 2000s, have often acculturated rather than assimilated. Figure 4.3 demonstrates that the largest flow of immigrants is now from the Americas, with another large—and growing—group from Asia. These immigrants, especially those from Mexico, Cuba, and China, often live in largely separate enclaves and often speak their native languages (see Figure 4.4 for a graph depicting the percentage of the population speaking a language other than English at home). They also often retain their basic cultures, such as their tastes in food. It remains to be seen whether, and to what degree, these groups will be assimilated into mainstream culture or their cultures will be able to retain their own distinctive elements.

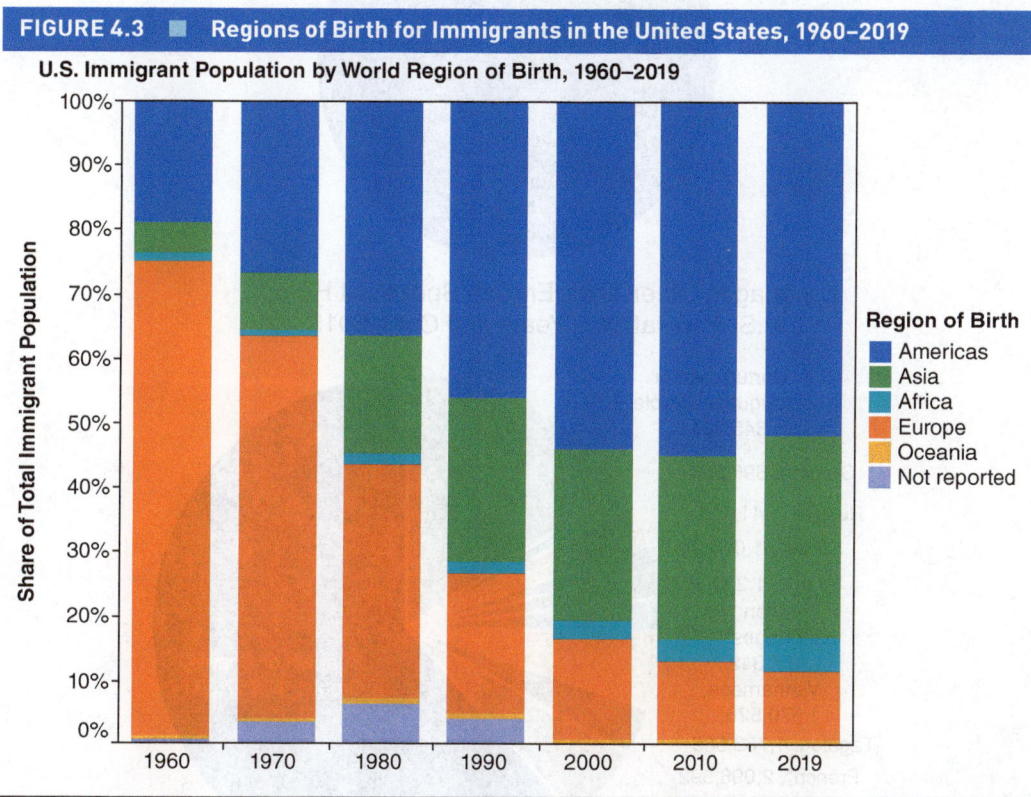

FIGURE 4.3 ■ Regions of Birth for Immigrants in the United States, 1960–2019

Source: Migration Policy Institute (MPI) tabulation of data from U.S. Census Bureau, 2010, 2019, and 2021 American Community Surveys (ACS), and 2000 Decennial Census; data for 1960 to 1990 were from Campbell J. Gibson and Emily Lennon, "Historical Census Statistics on the Foreign-Born Population of the United States: 1850–1990" (Working Paper No. 29, U.S. Census Bureau, Washington, D.C., February 1999).

In the past, Muslims have generally assimilated well in the United States (Freedman 2016). The future of their assimilation, however, is in doubt (Bulut 2016). This is a result of the current widespread hostility toward Muslims because of their perceived association with 9/11 and terrorism in the United States and many other parts of the world. This hostility increased greatly during the 2016 presidential campaign and throughout Trump's presidency when he suggested, and then implemented, a temporary ban on Muslim immigration to the United States. In mid-2018 the Supreme Court upheld the ban on immigrants, but only from five primarily Muslim countries. Muslims, as well as members and supporters of the rights of all minority groups, have every reason to be alarmed.

Multiculturalism is a relatively recent issue for many European societies, particularly the Scandinavian countries and the Netherlands, which have traditionally been almost monocultures. However, beginning in the 1950s, many European countries began to experience labor shortages (Fassmann and Munz 1992; Fielding 1989). Large numbers of people from poorer southern European countries, such as Spain and Italy,

FIGURE 4.4 ■ Languages Spoken at Home in the United States

A: Languages Spoken at Home by the U.S. Population, 5 Years and Over, 2021; B: Languages Other Than English Spoken at Home by the U.S. Population, 5 Years and Over, 2019

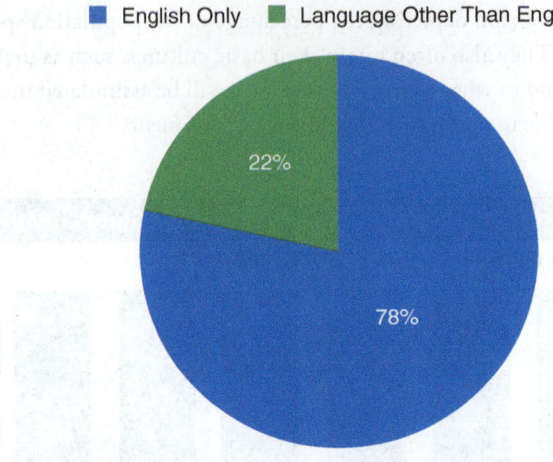

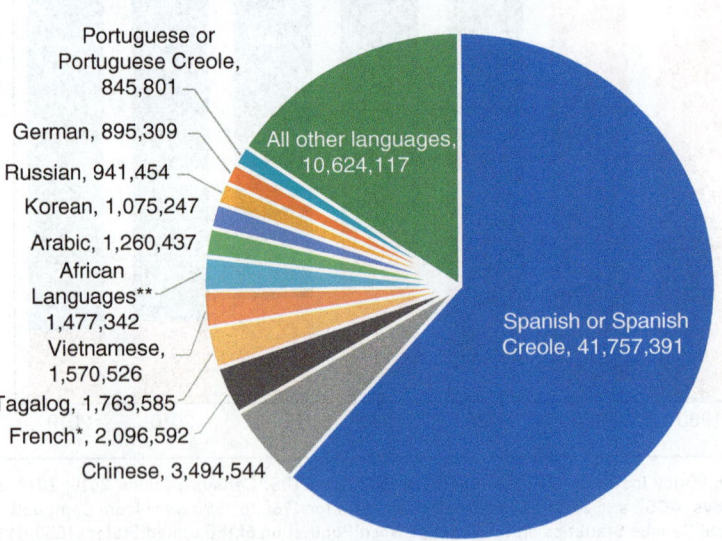

Based on a total U.S. population of 308,834,688, 5 years and over.

*Includes Patois, Creole, Cajun, Haitian

**Includes Amharic, Somali, Yoruba, Twi, Igbo, Swahili

Source: American Community Survey, 5-Year Estimates Data Profiles, 2021 (https://data.census.gov/table?tid=ACSDP5Y2021.DP02&hidePreview=true); American Community Survey Report, Language Use in the United States: 2019, 2023.

migrated to northern European countries. Later, migration flowed from less developed countries outside Europe, such as China, a number of largely Islamic countries, and many African countries. The fall of the Soviet Union in 1991 brought additional eastern Europeans from places such as Romania. Many northern European governments had intended for these immigrant workers to stay only a short time. However, the immigrants built lives for themselves, brought their families, and chose to remain. The result is that European countries today are far more multicultural than they were several decades ago.

Southern Europeans, especially in Italy and the Canary Islands in Spain, are increasingly having difficulty in dealing with waves of immigrants from North Africa. In fact, many would-be immigrants are dying in accidents at sea before they even get to Italy as they seek to navigate the Mediterranean Sea in overcrowded and rickety boats. For years Italy and other countries sought to prevent migrants from leaving North Africa, especially the failed state of Libya. However, a 2012 ruling by the European Court of Human Rights stopped them from doing so. The resistance of Italy, Spain, and other southern European countries to such immigration, like that in northern Europe, is motivated in part by economics and the fear that immigrants will cost natives their jobs. However, it is also cultural in the sense that the different cultures of these immigrants are seen as a threat to Italian, Spanish, and other European cultures. There are also concerns that the waves of immigrants will hurt the tourism industry, which is a major component of the Italian and Spanish economies.

In short, European countries today have more cultural diversity than ever. However, the situation is fraught with tension, conflict, and danger as people from very different cultures, religions, and languages struggle to find a way to live side by side. Given these recent developments in Europe, the United States, and elsewhere in the world, some are declaring multiculturalism a failure. States, and especially majority groups, are growing less appreciative of, and less willing to accept, groups that represent different cultures (Gozdecka, Ercan, and Kmak 2014).

Cultural Relativism and Ethnocentrism

Multiculturalism and **identity politics** are closely related to **cultural relativism**, which is the idea that aspects of a culture such as norms and values need to be understood within the context of that culture; there are no cultural universals or universally accepted norms and values. In this view, different cultures simply have different norms and values. There is no basis for saying that one set of norms and values is better than another. Thus, for example, those in Western countries should not judge Islamic women's use of headscarves. Conversely, those in the Islamic world should not judge Western women who bare their midriffs.

Cultural relativism runs counter to the tendency in many cultures toward **ethnocentrism,** or the belief that the norms, values, traditions, and material and symbolic aspects of one's own culture are better than those of other cultures. The tendency toward ethnocentrism both among subcultures and in cultures throughout the world represents a huge barrier to greater cultural understanding. However, to be fair, a belief in one's own culture can be of great value to that culture. It gives the people of that culture a sense of pride and identity. Problems arise when ethnocentrism serves as a barrier to understanding other cultures, a source of conflict among cultures, or an excuse for one culture to deny rights or privileges to another.

GLOBAL CULTURE

There are certainly major differences within cultures, such as those that exist among subcultures. Yet few would dispute the idea that it is possible to talk about, for example, American or European culture in general. However, discussing a global culture, a culture common to the world as a whole, is not as easy. Some elements of material culture, including hamburgers, cell phones, cars, and coffee shops, have spread widely around the world. However, the global diffusion of nonmaterial culture—values, norms, and symbolic culture—is somewhat more problematic.

The Globalization of Values

We have already discussed how values differ, sometimes greatly, from one society to another. How, then, can we discuss global values—values shared throughout the world? Some scholars argue that global values exist because all people share a biological structure that produces universal tendencies, including common values. Others contend that although particular values vary from country to country, the underlying structure of values is much the same across societies. However, the most persuasive argument for the existence of global values is traceable to the process of globalization. Global flows of all sorts of things—information, ideas, products, and people—produce realities in most parts of the world more similar than ever before. If these realities are increasingly similar, it seems likely that what people value will also come to be increasingly similar throughout the world.

Cultural Imperialism

Many have the strong view that what affects global culture most of all is **cultural imperialism**, or the imposition of at least some aspects of one dominant culture on other cultures (Inglis 2017; Tomlinson 1999). Cultural imperialism tends to undermine, even destroy, local cultures. For example, drinking tea is a cultural practice that existed, and to some degree still does exist, as a dominant practice in many cultures. However, with the onset of globalization, a growing number of tea-drinking cultures are switching to coffee. This practice is being further accelerated with the spread of Starbucks, which now has more than 32,000 stores across 80 countries, especially as that brand is coming to be associated with status and "being cool" in many places.

There is certainly a great deal of cultural imperialism in the world today, much of it associated with the United States (Crothers 2018; Kuisel 1993). The process of **Americanization** includes the importation by other countries of a variety of cultural elements—products, images, technologies, practices, norms, values, and behaviors—closely associated with the United States (Ritzer and Ryan 2004). One example is the American movie industry: The popularity of American movies around the world has decimated the film industries of many countries, including Great Britain and France. (India is one exception, with its thriving Bollywood productions, including the 2009 Academy Award winner for Best Picture, *Slumdog Millionaire* [Rizvi 2012].) Another successful U.S. cultural export is Americans' taste for food, especially fast food and the way in which it is eaten (quickly, with one's hands, standing up or in the car). Starbucks has also had an influence here, especially in exporting its model of large, slowly consumed cups of coffee. In contrast, in France and Italy and other countries, the historic preference has been for tiny cups of espresso quickly consumed (although the first Starbucks opened in Italy in 2018). In this way, Starbucks has not only changed the drink of choice for many (from tea to coffee), but also how that drink is consumed.

Cultural imperialism certainly exists, but it would be wrong to overestimate its power. Local cultures can be quite resilient. Not all cultures suffer the fate of French movie producers and local tea shops. Consider the following:

- The powerful process of Americanization is often countered by **anti-Americanism**, which is an aversion to the United States in general, as well as to the influence of its culture abroad (Huntington 1996; O'Connor and Griffiths 2005).

- Many cultures—Chinese and Islamic cultures, for example—have long, even ancient, histories. These cultures have resisted at least some impositions from other cultures for centuries. They are likely to continue to resist changes that threaten their basic values and beliefs.

- Local cultures modify inputs and impositions from other cultures by integrating them with local realities and in the process produce cultural hybrids that combine elements of both (Nederveen Pieterse 2015). Hybridization occurs when, for instance, British people watch Asian rap performed by a South American in a London club owned by a Saudi Arabian; another example is the Dutch watching Moroccan women engage in Thai boxing. In the fast food realm, McDonald's sells such hybrid foods as McChicken Korma Naan, which caters to those in Great Britain who have developed a taste for Indian food (including the many Indians who live there); McLaks, a grilled salmon sandwich served in Norway; and McHuevos, a hamburger with a poached egg served in Uruguay.

Thus, cultural imperialism needs to be examined in the context of the counterreactions to it, counterflows from elsewhere in the world, and the combination of global and local influences that produce unique cultural elements.

Cyberculture

The internet is one of the most important sites for the proliferation of consumer culture and perhaps postconsumer culture. It is also the site of a relatively new culture—**cyberculture** (Turner 2008). That is, the internet as a whole (as well as the individual websites on it) has the characteristics of all cultures, including distinctive values and norms.

Some of the distinctive values within cyberculture are openness, knowledge sharing, and access. These values have their roots in the open-source software that emerged before computing became an attractive commercial opportunity. They are also rooted in the knowledge sharing and continuous improvement that were the practice when early computer professionals survived through reciprocity (Bergquist 2003). These roots have been maintained through the open-source movement, through actions against censorship, and through organizations such as the Free Software Foundation and the "copyleft" movement. In line with the values of a postconsumer society, these "cyber-libertarians" favor user control of information and applications and free products (Dahlberg 2010; Himanen 2001). They are in conflict with the more dominant values of profit maximization and control of the internet by large corporations. This conflict of values, a culture war by the definition offered earlier in this chapter, goes a long way toward defining the internet today.

Various norms have also come to be a part of cyberculture. Internet users are not supposed to hack into websites, create and disseminate spam, unleash destructive worms and viruses, maliciously and erroneously edit user-generated sites such as Wikipedia, and so on. Many norms relate to desirable behavior on the internet. For example, creating and editing entries on Wikipedia is supposed to be taken seriously and done to the best of one's ability. Once an entry exists, the many people who offer additions and deletions are expected to do so in a similar spirit. Those who purposely add erroneous information on Wikipedia will suffer the stern disapproval of other contributors to, and users of, the site. They may even be banned from the site by those who manage it.

There is, of course, much more to the culture of the internet. For example, in addition to a general cyberculture, there are a number of cybercultures that vary from nation to nation. But the point is that cyberculture, like all culture, is emerging and evolving as other changes take place within and around it. The biggest difference between cyberculture and other cultures is that, because the internet is relatively new and the changes in it are so rapid, cyberculture is far more fluid than culture in general.

Digital Living: Netiquette

Social media websites are developing faster than the norms that can help guide and regulate the behavior of their users (McLaughlin and Vitak 2011). Online etiquette, or netiquette, tends to be implicit—there are few, if any, formal rules on how to use TikTok, Snapchat, or Instagram. Norms for these sites often emerge when users directly sanction the behavior of each other and content they feel is inappropriate. They may flag a sexually explicit photograph or hide a person from their Facebook feed who posts too many status updates. Our understanding and practice of online norms typically reflects the habits of our close friends, whom we are more likely to confront with norm violations. For example, if our friends are discreet about the photos they post of us, then we will likely reproduce this norm of being considerate when we post photos that include them (McLaughlin and Vitak 2011).

Netiquette can be complicated, considering the diversity of our online audience—what might be appropriate for our close friends to read or see might not be acceptable to our teachers or bosses. Furthermore, some sites might encourage people to behave in ways online that might not be acceptable in the real world. Snapchat can automatically delete photos, which might encourage users to post inappropriate or unflattering pictures of themselves or their friends. The legality of such practices has become an issue with teenagers when they send sexual images of themselves to each other. In some states this is considered to be the distribution of child pornography. In addition, cyberbullying occurs on a variety of social media sites, such as Tumblr, Twitter, Instagram, and Facebook, prompting some people to question whether these digital means of communication are making cruelty more normative.

SUMMARY

Culture encompasses the ideas, values, norms, practices, and objects that allow a group of people, or even an entire society, to carry out their collective lives with a minimum of friction. Values are the general, abstract standards defining what a group or society as a whole considers to be good, right, or important. Norms are the rules that guide what people do and how they live. Culture has material and symbolic elements. Material culture encompasses all the objects and technologies that are manifestations of a culture. Symbolic culture, the nonmaterial side of culture, is best represented by language.

We are surrounded by cultural differences. Subcultures include people who may accept much of the dominant culture but are set apart from it by one or more culturally significant characteristics. Countercultures are groups of people who differ in certain ways from the dominant culture and whose norms and values may be incompatible with it. Culture wars pit one subculture or counterculture against another or against the dominant culture.

Many societies tend to be ethnocentric—those living in them believe that their own culture's norms, values, and traditions are better than those of other cultures. In many cases, newcomers are expected to assimilate, or to replace elements of their own culture with elements of the dominant culture. A society that values multiculturalism accepts and even embraces the cultures of many different groups and encourages cultural diversity. Multicultural societies often embrace cultural relativism, or the belief that there are no cultural universals.

Global culture is the source of many debates, including whether it even exists. Cultural imperialism can be found in processes like Americanization. Cyberculture is a relatively new type of culture that is quickly developing its own set of norms and values.

KEY TERMS

acculturation	ideal culture
Americanization	identity politics
anti-Americanism	ideology
assimilation	language
breaching experiment	laws
collectivist culture	material culture
consumer culture	meritocracy
countercultures	mores
cultural imperialism	multiculturalism
cultural relativism	nonmaterial culture
culture	norms
culture jamming	popular culture
culture war	real culture
cyberculture	sanctions
ethnocentrism	Sapir-Whorf hypothesis
folkways	subcultures
high culture	symbolic culture
individualist culture	values

REVIEW QUESTIONS

1. How has the COVID-19 pandemic impacted culture in the society in which you live?
2. How and why might the value of democracy have created tensions in Iraq and Afghanistan?

3. As part of our material culture, what values do smartphones reflect? In what ways have "brand communities" or other subcultures formed around smartphones and their use?

4. Consider the terminology that has developed around the internet. How does this language reflect changes in the world around us? In what ways does it shape the world around us?

5. Skateboarders constitute a subculture because they have certain cultural differences (in language, dress, values) that set them apart from other groups in society. What is another example of a subculture, and what elements of that culture (both material and symbolic) make it unique?

6. How does a counterculture differ from a subculture? Is it reasonable to say that computer hackers are part of a counterculture? Can you think of other examples of countercultures?

7. How does culture jamming work? What are some examples of culture jamming that you have encountered?

8. What is the difference between assimilation and multiculturalism? Would you say that your country is an assimilationist or a multiculturalist society? Would you say that multiculturalism is more a part of the ideal culture or the real culture in your country? Why?

9. What are some of today's important culture wars? In what ways and to what degree are you engaged in them? Even if you are not active in them, how is your life affected by them?

10. What do we mean by the term *global culture?* Do you think the evolution of popular social networking sites such as Facebook and Twitter is related more to the evolution of a global culture or to Americanization? In what ways are these sites reflective of cultural hybridization?

iStock Images/Hispanolistic

SOCIALIZATION AND INTERACTION

113

> **LEARNING OBJECTIVES**
>
> 5.1 Describe the development of the self.
>
> 5.2 Discuss the concept of the individual as performer.
>
> 5.3 Explain the significance of socialization in childhood and adulthood.
>
> 5.4 Describe the key aspects of interaction with others.
>
> 5.5 Identify micro-level social structures.

THE NATURE VS. NURTURE DEBATE

Questions around why we are who we are have interested philosophers, medical doctors, and sociologists, among others, for millennia. One simplified way of thinking about this question is commonly expressed as the nature vs. nurture debate. Nature, or something related to our inherent biology and genetics, is seen in contrast to nurture, or what we learn from our surroundings. The most likely reality is that we are who we are due to a combination of both nature and nurture.

That said, sociologists are particularly interested in the nurture side of the argument. Although there is no denying that our genes play a significant role in things like our eye and hair color; likelihood of certain medical conditions; and maybe even, more controversially, intelligence level, there is also no denying that social factors also heavily influence those aspects of our lives. For example, we can buy colored contacts at most pharmacies; our health choices, like smoking, can heavily impact our chances of disease; and attending college (and taking a course in sociology!) can increase our intelligence.

The nature vs. nurture debate has also been used to frame issues related to social and civil rights. For example, are people born gay? Or do they choose to be gay? The answer to that question has heavy political implications because it is more difficult to justify denying someone equal rights because of something they did not choose (and although nearly all gay people agree it is not a choice, many report that they would have chosen to be gay even if it were).

As sociologists, we cannot definitively solve this, or many other, debates. What we can do is to better understand the ways in which our social surroundings, including how we were raised, the friends we have, and the lifestyles we lead, all influence who we are.

We can safely say that behavior and experiences are as influential as biology. You are who you are because of the people, institutions, and social structures that have surrounded you since birth (and that were in play even before then). You have been socialized to look, think, act, and interact in ways that allow you to live harmoniously, at least most of the time, with those around you. However, at times you may come into contact with those who socialize you into ways at variance with the dominant culture. Discovering how socialization and social interaction shape who we are and how we act, as we do in this chapter, is the most basic level of sociological analysis. But, in fact, sociologists are concerned with everything along the **micro–macro continuum**, which was introduced in Chapter 1. That includes the individual's mind and self; interactions among individuals; and interactions within and between groups, formally structured organizations, entire societies, and the world as a whole, as well as all the new global relationships of the "global age."

Sociology's micro–macro continuum means that rather than being clearly distinct, social phenomena tend to blend into one another, often without our noticing. For example, the interaction that takes place in a group is difficult to distinguish from the group itself. The relationships between countries are difficult to distinguish from their regional and even global connections. Everything in the social world, and on the micro–macro continuum, interpenetrates.

This chapter and the next introduce you, at least briefly, to the full range of sociological concerns along the micro–macro continuum. We start with the smallest-scale social phenomena and work our way to ever larger ones as these two chapters progress.

THE INDIVIDUAL AND THE SELF

Sociologists study individuals in general but rarely concern themselves with any particular individual. A primary sociological question is what, if anything, distinguishes humans as individuals from other animals. Some argue it stems from characteristics such as a larger brain or an opposable thumb. However, most sociologists believe the essential difference between humans and other animals is the human capability of having distinctive interaction with other humans.

An important source of this view is data about individuals who grew up in social isolation and did not experience human interaction during their development. For instance, we have information on cases in which children have been locked in closets or in single rooms for much or all of their childhoods (Curtiss 1977; Davis 1940, 1947). More recently, five children, ages 2 through 13, were discovered by authorities in York, Pennsylvania. They had lived their entire lives with their parents in a single room in a private home without any functioning utilities; their water source was rain dripping through the roof. The children had no birth certificates and had received no formal schooling, and there was no evidence that they had ever received any medical care, including vaccinations. They suffered from physical and mental health problems and were below average in terms of educational level ("Police Discover Five Children" 2010).

Of related interest is the existence of feral, or wild, children—that is, children who have been raised by animals in the wilderness (Benzaquen 2006; Dombrowski, Gischlar, and Mrazik 2011; Friedmann and Rusou 2015; Newton 2002). Oxana Malaya is from a small village in Ukraine (Grice 2006). In 1986, after being abandoned by her parents at age three, she crawled into a hovel that housed dogs. The "Dog Girl" lived there for five years before a neighbor reported her existence. When she emerged, she could hardly speak. Like the dogs she lived with, she barked, ate with her tongue, and ran about on all fours. Years later, when she was living in a home for the mentally disabled, Oxana was found to have the mental capacity of a six year old. She could not spell her name or read. She was able to communicate like other humans and talk because she had acquired some speech before she began living with dogs. She had also learned to eat with her hands and to walk upright.

The concept of feral children relates to the fundamental question of the relationship between nature and nurture. The "nature" argument is that we are born to be the kinds of human beings that we ultimately become; it is built into our "human nature." The "nurture" argument is that we are human beings because of the way we are nurtured—that is, the way we are raised by, and interact with, other human beings who teach us what it is to be human. The cases of feral children indicate that nurture is in many ways more important than nature in determining the human beings we become.

Symbolic Interaction and Development of the Self

As the example of feral and isolated children suggests, development as a human presupposes the existence of other humans and interaction with and among them. This brings us into the domain of symbolic interactionism, which developed many ideas of great relevance to this view of humans. In general, the interaction that takes place between people is loaded with symbols and symbolic meaning.

Symbolic interactionism is concerned with the interaction of two or more people through the use of symbols (Quist-Adade 2018). We all engage in interaction with many others on a daily basis, whether it be face-to-face or more indirectly via cell phone, e-mail, or social media. But interaction could not take place without symbols: words, gestures, internet memes (Benaim 2018), and even objects that stand for things. Symbols allow the communication of meaning among a group of people.

Although we can interact with one another without words, such as by using physical gestures like the shrug of a shoulder, in the vast majority of cases we need and use words to interact.

Symbolic interactionism has several basic principles:

- Human beings have a great capacity for thought, which differentiates them from lower animals. That innate capacity for thought is greatly shaped by social interaction. It is during social interaction that people acquire the symbolic meanings that enable them to exercise their distinctive ability to think. Those symbolic meanings, in turn, enable people to act and interact in ways that lower animals cannot.

- Symbolic meanings are not set in stone. People are able to modify them based on a given situation and their interpretation of it. For example, the rainbow flag is associated with LGBTQ+ culture in many places. The official flag of Cusco, Peru appears very similar (it does, in fact, have one extra stripe) and has often caused confusion about its meaning among tourists.

- People are able to modify symbolic meanings because of their unique ability to think. Symbolic interactionists frame *thinking* as people's ability to interact with themselves. In that interaction with themselves, people are able to alter symbolic meanings. They are also able to examine various courses of action open to them in given situations, to assess the relative advantages and disadvantages of each, and then to choose among them.

- It is the pattern of those choices of individual action and interaction that is the basis of groups, larger structures such as bureaucracies, and society as a whole. Most generally, in this theoretical perspective, symbolic interaction is the basis of everything else in the social world. Although symbolic interactionists deal primarily with interaction, they are also concerned with mental processes, such as mind and self, that are deeply implicated in those processes.

One early symbolic interactionist, Charles Horton Cooley (1864–1929), explained how parents help children develop the ability to interact with others with his famous concept of the **looking-glass self**. This is the idea that as humans we develop a self-image that reflects how others see and respond to us. We imagine how we appear to others and how they evaluate our appearance. Based on that, we develop some sort of self-feeling, such as pride or embarrassment. Because children's earliest interactions are typically with those who are raising them, it is that interaction that is most important in the formation of a self-image. This helps explain why feral children and others who spend their formative years in prolonged social isolation are unlikely to form a fully developed self-image: There are no others to respond to them. It is as we interact with others, especially when we are young, that we develop a sense of our selves.

The major thinker associated with symbolic interactionism is one of Cooley's contemporaries, George Herbert Mead (1863–1931). Mead ([1934] 1962) was very concerned with the micro level (the individual, the mind, the self). He prioritized the social relationship, including interaction, and the importance of symbols in social interaction. In fact, it is this prioritization of the social that distinguishes sociologists from psychologists in their studies of individuals and interaction.

Humans and Nonhumans

Mead distinguished between humans and nonhumans. However, both are capable of making gestures (e.g., by raising a limb). By **gestures**, Mead meant the movements of one individual that elicit automatic and appropriate responses from another individual.

Both animals and humans are capable of not only gestures but also **conversations of gestures**, whereby they use a series of gestures to relate to one another. Thus, the snarl of one dog may lead a second dog to snarl in return. That second snarl might lead the first dog to become physically ready to attack or be attacked. In terms of humans, Mead gave the example of a boxing match, where the cocking of one boxer's arm may cause the other boxer to raise an arm to block the anticipated blow. That raised arm might cause the first boxer to throw a different punch or even to hold back on the punch. As in the case of nonhuman animals, the gestures of boxers are often instantaneous and involve few, if any, conscious thought processes.

George Herbert Mead's ideas strongly influenced the development of sociological theory, especially symbolic interactionism. His most famous work, *Mind, Self, and Society*, originated as lectures from his teachings at the University of Chicago.

Granger, NYC—All rights reserved.

In addition to physical gestures, animals and humans are both capable of vocal gestures. The bark of a dog and the grunt of a human (boxer) are both vocal gestures. In both cases, a conversation of vocal gestures is possible, as the bark of one dog (or the grunt of a boxer) elicits the bark (or grunt) of another. However, when humans (and nonhuman animals) make facial gestures (such as originating eye contact in an effort to flirt), they cannot *see* their own facial gestures. In contrast, both animals and humans can *hear* their own vocal gestures. As a result, misunderstanding is more likely when people rely on facial rather than vocal gestures.

It is the vocal gesture that truly begins to separate humans from animals. In humans, but not other animals, the vocal gesture can affect the speaker as much and in the same way it does the hearer. Thus, humans react to and interpret their own vocal gestures and, more important, their words. Furthermore, humans have a far greater ability to control their vocal gestures. We can stop ourselves from uttering sounds or saying various things, and we can alter what we say as we are saying it. Nonhuman animals do not possess this capacity. In short, only humans are able to develop a language out of vocal gestures; nonhuman animals remain restricted to isolated vocal gestures.

It is important to note that many sociologists have come to reject the clear distinction between the abilities of nonhuman animals and those of humans (Greenebaum and Sanders 2015). Some sociological work has examined symbolic interaction between humans and nonhuman animals (Alger and Alger 1997; Irvine 2004).

Symbolic Interaction

Of greatest importance in distinguishing humans from animals is a kind of gesture that can be made *only* by humans. Mead calls such a gesture a **significant symbol**: a gesture that arouses in the individual making it a response of the same kind as the one it is supposed to elicit from those to whom it is addressed. It is only with significant symbols, especially those that are vocal, that we can have communication in the full sense of the term. In Mead's view—although more and more research on animals tends to contradict it (Gerhardt and Huber 2002; Gillespie-Lynch et al. 2013)—ants, bees, dogs, and apes are unable to communicate by means of such symbols.

Over time, humans develop a set of vocal significant symbols, or language. According to Mead, language involves significant symbols that call out the same meaning in the person to whom an utterance is aimed as they do in the person making the utterance. The utterances have meaning to all parties involved. In a conversation of gestures, only the gestures are communicated. With language, both the (vocal) gestures and the meanings are communicated. One of the key functions of language is that it makes the mind and mental processes possible. To Mead, thinking (and the mind; see the following section) is nothing more than internalized conversations individual humans have with themselves. It is little different from talking to other people.

Symbols also make possible **symbolic interaction**, or interaction based on significant symbols. This allows for much more complex interaction patterns than those that occur when interaction is based only on gestures. Because people can think about and interpret significant symbols, they can interact with large numbers of people and make complex plans for future undertakings. They can interpret the symbolic meaning of what others say and do and understand, for example, that some of them are acting in accord with their own plans. Nonhuman animals arguably lack the ability to make and understand complex plans.

Mind and Self

Central to Mead's ideas about the development of human beings, and the differences between humans and nonhumans, are the concepts of mind and self. The **mind** is an internal conversation using words (and also images). That internal conversation arises, is related to, and is continuous with interactions, especially conversations one has with others in the social world. Thus, the social world and its relationships and interactions precede the mind and not vice versa. This perspective stands in contrast to the conventional view that prioritizes the brain and argues that we think first and then engage in social relationships. It also differs from the view that the mind and the brain are one and the same thing. The brain is a physiological organ that exists within us, but the mind is a social phenomenon. It is part of, and would not exist without, the social world.

The **self** is the ability to take oneself as an object. The self develops over time. Key to the development of self is the ability to imagine being in the place of others and looking at one's self as they do. In other words, people need to take the role of others to get a sense of their own selves. There are two key stages in Mead's theory of how the self develops over time, the **play stage** and the **game stage**.

1. *Play stage.* Babies are not born with the ability to think of themselves as having a self. However, as they develop, children learn to take on the attitudes of specific others toward themselves. Thus, young children play at being Mommy and Daddy, adopt Mommy's and Daddy's attitudes toward the child, and evaluate themselves as do Mommy and Daddy. However, the result is a very fragmented sense of the self. It varies depending on the specific other (e.g., Mommy *or* Daddy) being taken into consideration. Young children lack a more general and organized sense of themselves.

2. *Game stage.* Children begin to develop a self in the full sense of the term when they take on the roles of a group of people simultaneously rather than the roles of discrete individuals. Each of those different roles comes to be seen as having a definite relationship to all the others. Children develop organized personalities because of their ability to take on multiple roles—indeed, the entirety of roles in a given group. The developed personality does not vary with the individual role (Mommy, Daddy) a child happens to be taking. This development allows children to function in organized groups. Most important, it greatly affects what they do within specific groups.

Mead offers the example of a baseball game (or what he calls "ball nine") to illustrate his point about the game stage of development. It is not enough in a baseball game for you to know what you are supposed to do in your position on the field. To play your position, you must know what those who play the other eight positions on the team are going to do. In other words, a player, every player, must take on the roles of all the other players. A player need not have all of those roles in mind all of the time; three or four of them will suffice on most occasions. For example, a shortstop must know that the center fielder is going to catch a particular fly ball; that he is going to be backed up by the left fielder; that because the runner on second is going to "tag up," the center fielder is going to throw the ball to third base; and that it is his job as shortstop to back up the third baseman. This ability to take on multiple roles obviously applies in a baseball game, but it applies as well in a playgroup, a work setting, and every other social setting.

The Generalized Other

Mead also developed the concept of the generalized other, or the attitude of the entire group or community. The **generalized other** includes the roles, prescriptions, and proscriptions individuals use to develop their own behaviors, attitudes, and so forth. Individuals take the role of the generalized other. That is, they look at themselves and what they do from the perspective of the group or community. "What would people think if I . . ." is a question that demonstrates the role of the generalized other.

The generalized other becomes central to the development of self during the game stage. In the classroom, the generalized other is the attitude of a group working on a collaborative project. In the family, to take still another example, it is the attitude of all family members. In taking on the perspectives of the generalized other, children begin developing more fully rounded and complete selves. They can view and evaluate themselves from the perspective of a group or community and not merely from the viewpoints of discrete others. To have a coherent self, in the full sense of the term, as an adult one must become a member of a group or community. An adult must also be sensitive to the attitudes common to the community. Having members who can take the role of the generalized other is also essential to the development of the group, especially in its organized activities. The group can function more effectively and efficiently because it is highly likely that individual members will understand and do what is expected of them. In turn, individuals can operate more efficiently within the group because they can better anticipate what others will do.

This discussion might lead you to think that the demands of the generalized other produce conformists. However, Mead argues that although selves within a group share some commonalities, each

In Mead's game stage of the development of the self, we learn how to work with others by understanding their roles as well as our own. Do you think this learning process is ever complete?
iStock Images/BraunS

self is different because each has a unique biographical history and experience. Furthermore, there are many groups and communities in society and therefore many generalized others. Your generalized other in a baseball game is different from your generalized other in a classroom or in the family.

The "I" and the "Me"

Critical to understanding the difference between conformity and creative thinking and acting is Mead's distinction between two aspects, or phases, of the self—the "I" and the "me." The "I" and the "me" are subprocesses involved in the larger thinking process.

The **"I"** is the immediate response of an individual to others. It is that part of the self that is unconscious, incalculable, unpredictable, and creative. Neither the person nor the members of the group know in advance what that response of the "I" is going to be. As a result of the "I," people often surprise themselves, and certainly others, with the unexpected things they say and do. Mead greatly values the "I" for various reasons, including the fact that it is the source of new and original responses.

The **"me"** is the organized set of others' attitudes and behaviors adopted by the individual. In other words, the "me" involves the acceptance and internalization by the individual of the generalized other. To Mead, the "me" involves a conscious understanding of what a person's responsibilities are to the larger group. The behaviors associated with the "me" also tend to be habitual and conventional. We all have a "me," but conformists have an overly powerful "me." It is through the "me" that society is able to dominate the individual. In fact, Mead defines "social control" as the dominance of the "I" by the "me."

An individual sometimes displays more of the "I" aspect of the self and sometimes more of the "me" aspect. In any given instance, the relative mix of "I" and "me" determines the degree to which an individual acts creatively (more "I") or more as a conformist (more "me"). Nevertheless, people and society as a whole need both "I" and "me." For the individual, the "me" allows for a comfortable existence within various social groupings. The "I" lends some spice to what might otherwise be a boring existence. For society, the "me" provides the conformity needed for stable and orderly interaction. The "I" is the source of changes in society as it develops and adapts to the shifting environment.

THE INDIVIDUAL AS PERFORMER

Erving Goffman (1922–1982) is another important contributor to the symbolic interactionists' understanding of the self and how it develops (Jacobsen and Kristiansen 2015). Goffman's work on the self was deeply influenced by Mead's thinking, especially the tension between the "I" and the "me." In Goffman's work, this distinction takes the form of the tension between what we want to do spontaneously and what people expect us to do (Goffman 1959).

Goffman developed the notion of **dramaturgy**, which views an individual's social life as a series of dramatic performances akin to those that take place on a theatrical stage. To Goffman, the self is not a thing possessed by the individual but the dramatic product of the interaction between people and their audiences (Manning 2007). Although many performances of the self are successful, there is always the possibility that performances can be disrupted by the actions of audiences. For example, audiences can jeer at performances or even walk out on them. Goffman focuses on these possibilities and what people can do to prevent them by improving their dramatic performances or to deal with disruptions once they occur.

Impression Management

When people interact with others, they use a variety of techniques to control the images of themselves they want to project during their social performances. They seek to maintain these impressions even when they encounter problems in their performances (Manning 2005). Goffman (1959) called these efforts to maintain certain images **impression management**.

For example, in your sociology class you might typically project an image of a serious, well-prepared student. One night you might stay up late partying instead of completing your required reading. When the instructor asks a question in class, you might try to maintain your image by pretending to take notes rather than raising your hand. Called on nonetheless, you struggle, in vain, to give a well-thought-out, serious answer to the question. The smiles and snickers of fellow students who know that you were out partying late the night before might disrupt the performance you are trying to put on. To deflect attention from you to them, you might suggest that they try to answer the question.

Impression management relates directly to the plots of many movies. In many romantic comedies, for example, the humor is often found by having one of the characters fail to maintain their desired impression. This can be through having food stuck in their teeth, passing gas, or looking less than presentable first thing in the morning. Biographical documentaries are fascinating when they dig beyond the ability of their subjects to maintain their desired impression.

In some cases, failure at impression management can have dire consequences (e.g., Jews trying to pass as non-Jews in Nazi Germany). Thus, more than simply a desire to "look one's best," impression management can also be a survival strategy for people whose physical safety can be in danger because of their identities.

Although the idea of impression management is generally associated with face-to-face social interaction, it also applies to interaction on social networking sites. For instance, many people constantly change the pictures on their Instagram pages to alter the images of themselves (sometimes, quite literally, with Photoshop) being conveyed to others. Others use social media platforms like Twitter or Instagram to create personal brands, marketing their presentations of self to become popular or newsworthy (Brems et al. 2017).

Front and Back Stage

Continuing the theatrical analogy, Goffman (1959) argued that in every performance there is a **front stage**, where the social performance tends to be idealized and designed to define the situation for those who are observing it. When you are in class, as in the previous example, you are typically performing on your front stage. Your audience is the teacher and perhaps other students. As a rule, people feel they must present an idealized sense of themselves when they are front stage (e.g., by giving that seemingly well-thought-out answer). Because this performance is idealized, things that do not fit the image must be hidden (such as the fact that you were partying the night before and are now unprepared to answer questions).

Also of concern to Goffman is the back stage. In the **back stage**, people feel free to express themselves in ways that are suppressed in the front (Cahill et al. 1985). Thus, after class you might well confess to your friends in the cafeteria that you had been partying and faked your answer to a question asked in class. If somehow your front-stage audience—the instructor, in this case—sees your back-stage performance, your ability to maintain the impression you are trying to project in the classroom, in the front stage, is likely to become difficult or impossible in the future. The existence of two stages, front and back, causes us all sorts of tensions and problems. We are always afraid that those in the front stage will find out about our back stage or that elements of the back stage will intrude on the front stage.

The popular use of Zoom (and other video conferencing programs) during COVID-19 made questions of the front stage and back stage even more relevant for many students and instructors (Smith, Sanford, and Blum 2021). Whereas before, students and teachers most often interacted face-to-face in the more neutral setting of a classroom, Zoom found many connecting from their own homes, including often from their bedrooms. When individuals had to turn on their cameras, their audience had an often unwelcome insight into their private home lives, their back stages. Various viral media moments of the unexpected appearance of children, pets, and family members speak to the ways in which impression management became disrupted with these intrusions into our back stages.

Couples on a first date are likely to perform impression management by presenting an idealized sense of themselves to each other.

iStock Images/kazuma seki

Although the distinction between front and back stage is important, bear in mind that these are not "real" places, nor are they rigidly separated from one another. That is, what is the front stage at one point can become the back stage at another. For example, hosting friends for a dinner party makes the dining room a front stage but attending a class via Zoom from the same table now makes it a back stage. Nevertheless, in general, people are most likely to perform in an idealized manner on their front stage when they are most concerned about making positive impressions. They are likely to perform more freely back stage, among those who are more accepting of less-than-ideal behavior and attitudes.

SOCIALIZATION

Socialization is the process by which an individual learns and generally comes to accept the ways of a group or a society of which they are a part. During the socialization process, children develop a self as they learn the need, for example, to take on the role of the generalized other. Socialization almost always involves a process of interaction, as those with knowledge and experience teach those with a need to acquire that knowledge or to learn from others' experiences (Grusee and Hastings 2015).

Although socialization occurs throughout an individual's lifetime, it can generally be divided into two parts: childhood and adulthood. Socialization during childhood sets the course for a lifetime and has been a central focus for researchers. However, researchers have increasingly pointed to a variety of ways in which adults continue to learn how to function within their society.

Childhood Socialization

A central concern in the study of socialization is those who do the socializing, or the **agents of socialization**. The first and often most effective agents of socialization are the child's caretakers, as well as family members and friends. These are defined as primary agents of socialization. In addition, broader, less personal influences, such as the educational system, the media (Prot et al. 2015), and consumer culture, are important in socialization. These are defined as secondary agents of socialization. All play a part in creating an individual who can effectively operate within and shape culture. Except for education, which is discussed in Chapter 11, we examine each of these various agents of socialization in the following sections.

Family

In a process known as **primary socialization**, newborns, infants, and young children acquire language, identities, cultural routines, norms, and values as they interact with caretakers and family members (Laible, Thompson, and Froimson 2015). This socialization lays the foundation for later personality development. Early socialization performs various functions for society, such as equipping the young to fit better into society and perpetuating the culture from one generation to the next.

In addition to a great deal of primary socialization, parents provide **anticipatory socialization**—that is, they teach children what will be expected of them in the future. Anticipatory socialization is how parents prepare children for the important developmental changes (puberty, for example) they will experience. Among the many other things that must be anticipated in family socialization are entrance into grade school, high school, college, the work world, and life as an independent adult. Anticipatory socialization is especially important in societies and during time periods undergoing a great deal of change. Children need to be prepared not only for changes within society but also for changes within the family and changes that will affect them more directly.

Many assumptions about primary and anticipatory socialization are changing dramatically as the nature of families and the way in which they are understood culturally undergo major transformations. The socialization process was thought to be rather straightforward when the ideal of the nuclear family, composed of a mother, a father, and two or more children all living in the same home, predominated, as it did throughout much of the twentieth century. The lesson children were required to learn, at least as far as the family was concerned, was that when they became adults, they would go on to reproduce the same kind of nuclear family as the one in which they grew up. However, assumptions about the goodness and inevitability of the nuclear family and the ease of the socialization process are now impossible to accept (McLanahan 1999). This is the case because of increasing public awareness of the many problems associated with the nuclear family, such as divorce, abuse, and unhappiness (see Chapter 10).

Then there is the expansion of what were at one time called "alternative family forms" (e.g., single parent households, grandparents as primary caregivers, same-sex households) and the increasing centrality of day care centers and their workers to the socialization process (Patterson, Farr, and Hastings 2015). The agencies doing the socializing today are much more complex and varied than they were in the era of the predominance of the nuclear family. As a result, socialization is not as straightforward as it once was thought to be. In addition, it is no longer possible to think of a seamless relationship between the agencies of socialization and the socialization process. For example, the family may be socializing its children in one way, but the day care center may be doing it very differently.

At one time socialization was seen as one-directional, for example, from parent to child. Current thinking sees such socialization among intimates as two-directional, even multidirectional, with parents socializing children and children socializing parents, other adults, and families (Gentina and Muratore 2012). For example, children tend to be far more familiar with the latest advances in digital technology than their elders are, and they teach their parents much about both the technology itself and the digital culture. Another example is found in the large number of immigrant families in the United States and elsewhere. Children in these families are more likely than their parents to learn the language and culture of their new country (often in school). As a result, they are frequently the ones to teach, or at least try to teach, that knowledge to their parents (Mather 2009). This is **reverse socialization**, in which those who are normally being socialized are instead doing the socializing.

Peers

A good deal of socialization in school takes place informally, through children's interaction with fellow students (see Chapter 11 for a discussion of the role of schools and teachers in the process of socialization). Here primary agents of socialization (peers) compete with secondary agents of socialization (teachers and other employees of the school system; Bukowski et al. 2015). Such informal socialization grows increasingly important as students progress through the school years, especially high school. Peers are also important sources of socialization in contexts outside of school, such as scouting groups and athletic teams (Bennett and Fraser 2000; Corsaro 2018; Fine 1987). For example, researchers have found that children involved in contact sports, such as football and wrestling, are socialized to be more physically aggressive in everyday life (Kreager 2007). Male students (and their friends) who participate in contact sports such as football are more likely to get into serious fights than are nonathletic males or males involved in noncontact sports such as baseball, basketball, and tennis.

As the child matures and spends an increasing amount of time in the company of friends, peer socialization is increasingly likely to conflict with what is being taught at home and in school. Peer involvement in risky and delinquent behavior exerts an influence that is often at odds with the goals set forth by parents and educators (Gardner and Steinberg 2005; Haynie 2001). In *Peer Pressure, Peer Prevention*, Barbara Costello and Trina Hope (2016) examined the role of friends in

Peers are highly influential in the socialization process, especially during adolescence and early adulthood. What role do you think fellow students play in your socialization? Which ones will most influence you?

iStock Images/master1305

both encouraging and preventing deviant or criminal behavior by investigating a variety of peer influence mechanisms that had either negative or positive effects. For example, the emulation of an admired role model could have a positive peer influence if they set a good example or a negative one if they encourage deviant behavior. Coercive tactics such as appeals to peer loyalty operated in a similar manner—if their peers were all drinking (or abstaining from drinking), study participants stated that they were likely to conform to demonstrate the strength of their friendships. Interestingly, several peer influence mechanisms were more prevalent in affecting deviant behaviors, such as the fear of the loss of status and the presence of onlookers. Costello and Hope emphasize that whether it was negative or positive, the informal social control exerted by peer groups is important when examining childhood socialization.

Peer socialization continues to be important throughout the life course. For example, peers help us learn what we are expected to do at college (Brimeyer, Miller, and Perrucci 2006), at work (Montoya 2005), in social settings (Friedkin 2001), and in civic arenas (Dey 1997), as well as how to be sports fans (Melnick and Wann 2011).

Gender

Sociologists devote a great deal of attention to gender socialization, or the transmission of norms and values about what boys and girls can and should do (Leaper and Farkas 2015; McHale, Crouter, and Whiteman 2003).

Even before babies are born, their parents (and many others) start to "gender" them (Kane 2018). In the United States they do so by frequently buying blue clothing for males and pink for females (interestingly, it was the opposite—blue for females and pink for males—until around the 1950s). Parents often dress females in frilly dresses and affix bows to their bald heads to signal to others that the babies are female. These gender differences are often reinforced by the toys children are given by parents—trucks and soldiers for males, dolls and dollhouses for females. Male children may get toys and games organized around action, activity, and role-playing thought to be appropriate for boys. Female children may get toys and games focused on interactions, relationships, and less active play thought to be appropriate for girls. Sociologist Emily Kane (2012) found that although parents often want to challenge gender assumptions about what constitute appropriate toys and clothing for children, they are constrained by traditionally gendered structures and social institutions.

As children grow up, they learn from their parents and other significant others (as well as from the generalized other) what behaviors are considered appropriate and inappropriate for their gender. They also learn the consequences, or sanctions, for deviating from these expectations. For example, parents may give a female child a great deal of sympathy when she cries, whereas they may tell a male child to "be a man" and not cry after an injury. Males may be expected to have an interest in sports, to play roughly with each other, and to be unable to sit still. Females, in contrast, are expected to display more "ladylike" behaviors, such as sitting quietly and sharing. Many children come to see these traditional gender expectations as "natural" expressions of being male or female. Parents trying to raise male children are more likely to socialize them into narrow gender roles. They often cite biology, or "nature," as the reason for doing so. Parents also do so because they fear social sanctions if they socialize them differently.

Beginning in the 1970s, the feminist movement challenged traditional notions about the socialization of male and female children (Lorber 2000). Today, some parents pride themselves on their "gender-neutral" child rearing (Auster 2016). They socialize their children without rigid adherence to traditional binary gender roles, rejecting the ideas that male and female children are completely different (Martin 2005). Yet many parents continue to strongly discourage males from expressing an interest in activities stereotyped as "for girls" (Kane 2006).

Historically, traditional socialization for gender roles has been reinforced in schools, sports, and the mass media. In schools, teachers and curricula once tended to support traditional gender norms, and peer groups were likely to be segregated by sex (Thorne 1993). In sports, males and females were channeled into different sports; for example, females tended to play softball, while males played baseball (Coakley 2007). When females did play "male" sports, their efforts were often labeled differently; for instance, female football competitions might be called "powderpuff" football. The passage in 1972 of Title IX of the U.S. Education Amendments, which bars discrimination on the basis of gender in educationally based sporting activities receiving federal funding, has changed such views dramatically. Since the passage of Title IX, females' athletic activities in college and even in high school have become increasingly visible and, in some cases, more highly regarded as "real" sports. One of the best examples is women's basketball at the collegiate level.

The media, especially movies, TV, and video games, have also tended to reinforce children's traditional gender role socialization. However, that, too, is changing. Television programs are increasingly featuring strong female characters (*Game of Thrones, Big Little Lies, Veep*), and numerous shows have featured female cops and police chiefs (*CSI, Elementary, The Fall*). Other TV shows featuring strong female leads in recent years include *She's Gotta Have It* and *The Handmaid's Tale*. Female action stars (Sigourney Weaver in the *Alien* movies, Angelina Jolie in most of her films, Michelle Rodriguez in *The Fast and the Furious* series) are increasingly likely to play strong and aggressive characters. Young-adult novels and the movies based on them often also have strong female leading characters, such as the extremely smart Hermione Granger in the *Harry Potter* series, or Katniss Everdeen in the *Hunger Games* series.

Change is less obvious in other settings. Malls reinforce traditional gender roles by offering separate shops, or at least separate sections within the same shop, for boys and girls and for men and women. The Disney theme parks offer highly differentiated attractions aimed at boys (Pirates of the Caribbean) and girls (It's a Small World). Modern advertisements, both in print and on television, continue to feature men and women in their "traditional" roles—men are often shown fixing things around the house or doing hard labor, while women are shown cooking, cleaning, and taking care of the kids. Most video games are targeted at boys, while girls are offered computer games focused on facial makeovers and shopping. This media emphasis on female appearance is not new. Movies, television programming, and advertisements have been widely critiqued for decades for their unrealistic portrayal of women's bodies (Cole and Daniel 2005; Milkie 1999; Neuendorf et al. 2009). Magazines such as *Rolling Stone* have featured sexualized images of men on their covers, but they still use many more such images of women. More striking is the fact that the images of women have become increasingly sexualized over time (Hatton and Trautner 2011). Many of the action heroines (e.g., those in James Bond and X-Men movies) continue to embody traditional male preferences for female bodies: young, attractive, and slender. Young women comparing themselves with these versions of adult Barbie dolls become anxious about their own bodies. Media images of women may also reaffirm racial stereotypes, with young women of color often being sexualized or portrayed as poor and irresponsible (Collins 2004).

Mass Media and New Media

Until recently, much of the emphasis on the role of the mass media in socialization has been on the effects of television and the enormous number of hours per week children spend in front of their screens. TV remains an important socialization agent, especially for young children. However, it is clear that as children mature, especially in the middle and upper classes, more of their socialization is taking place via the computer, smartphones, tablets, video games, and other recent and emerging technologies. This trend increased dramatically during the COVID-19 pandemic.

Of course, a world of wonderful information is available to children via the internet. However, there are also lots of worrying things online that children can easily find or stumble upon. In addition, access to computers has changed the viewing experience considerably. Watching TV programs or movies is a passive activity. Even when "adult themes" are presented, the child is an observer, not a participant. However, on computers and other new digital media, the child can play video games such as *Slime Rancher, Fortnite,*

What do you think the impact will be of the increasing amount of time young children are spending looking at devices' screens?

iStock Images/LordRunar

Red Dead Redemption 2, and *Call of Duty: Infinite Warfare*. Some of these games engage children in simulations of antisocial activities, such as stealing cars, evading police chases, and engaging in shootouts. Clearly, the nature of the socialization implicit in such games is at odds with the lessons parents and teachers wish to impart.

Smartphones and social media sites play a role in socialization as well, mostly through the influence of peers (Ibáñez-Cubillas, Díaz-Martín, and Díaz-Martín 2017). A great deal of peer socialization also takes place via sites such as Facebook, Twitter, Instagram, and TikTok. On average, 1.5 billion people log onto Facebook daily, and among 18- to 24-year-olds, 94 percent watch videos shared on YouTube and 78 percent use Snapchat, often more than once a day (Smith and Anderson 2018). All of this is so new, and new forms of media are emerging so rapidly, that it is hard to know exactly what role the new media will play in socialization in the future, but its role is likely to be increasingly powerful and pervasive.

Digital Living: Cyberbullying

Cyberbullying is the "willful and repeated harm inflicted through the use of computers, cell phones, and other electronic devices" (cited in Simmons 2011, 104). Although cyberbullying involves both genders, teenage girls are more likely to be the targets and (to a lesser degree) the perpetrators of cyberbullying. This is true, in part, because girls are more likely to be online, especially to use social media such as Instagram and Twitter. The cyberworld, especially social media, is very much about relationships, and girls are particularly likely to engage in them on the internet. They are also more likely to wreck online relationships by being cyberbullies or have them wrecked by comments or images created by other cyberbullies. On Instagram, for example, they can easily find out who has the most followers or "likes" and use that information to humiliate the victim. Most instances of cyberbullying involve those known to the victim (e.g., a friend, a former boyfriend); few involve total strangers.

Cyberbullying has advantages (at least, to the bully) in comparison to face-to-face bullying. Cyberbullying is faster and simpler and involves fewer complications than a physical assault. A click by a cyberbully will do the job and excludes eye contact, raised voices, and immediate material consequences. In addition, it leaves a near-permanent trail that others can follow later. The internet also offers a wide range of weapons to the cyberbully, such as attacking physical appearance, undermining romantic or social relationships, tagging humiliating or embarrassing photos, leaving vicious comments, and even suggesting that the target might want to kill herself or himself. Inhibitions are reduced or eliminated on the internet, and there are few deterrents to cyberbullying. More people can gang up on the target than is possible in face-to-face situations. Victims of cyberbullying "are more likely to experience anxiety, depression, school violence, academic trouble, suicidal ideation, and suicide attempts" (Simmons 2011, 109). Although bullying occurs online, it usually has roots in, and repercussions for, the social world and lives of those involved.

Consumer Culture

Consistent with the emphasis on consumption in the contemporary world, it is important to understand that children need to be socialized to consume, especially to devote a significant portion of their lives to consumption. Like many other types of socialization, much of this takes place early on in the family (Meuleman and Lubbers 2016), in schools, and in peer groups. Children readily learn the nuts and bolts of how to consume. They also learn various norms and values of consumption, especially to value the processes of consumption and shopping and the goods and services acquired through those processes. Of course, we must not ignore the role of marketing, especially to children, in how people learn to consume (Schor 2005).

There is a toy line produced by Moose Toys called Shopkins, which are small plastic figures shaped like food and household items with a face (see www.shopkinsworld.com). They also produce miniatures of actual brand-name products, called Real Littles, and the playset to keep them in is a mini convenience store! These products promote unbridled consumption (the Shopkins slogan is "Once you shop . . . you can't stop!") both in the present and implicitly throughout the lifespan of those who first play with the toys as children. The immediate goal is to entice children into collecting as many Shopkins and as much associated paraphernalia as possible. A broader goal is implicit in the fact that the figurines are characters associated with a wide array of items that can be purchased in stores. Among them are Kooky Cookie (a chocolate chip cookie), Polly Polish (a bottle of nail polish), and Lippy Lips (a tube of lipstick). Most broadly, the goal is to encourage a lifetime of "hyperconsumption" (Ritzer 2012a).

Online consumption and shopping sites (such as Amazon and eBay) are also socializing agents. Navigation and buying strategies are learned at digital retailers, and those have an effect on consumption in the brick-and-mortar world. For instance, many younger people who have grown up with online shopping are adept comparison shoppers. They are likely to compare products online and to search out the best possible deals before making purchases. Some storefront retailers have gone out of business as a result of online competition and, more recently, the COVID-19 pandemic, further reinforcing the use of online retailers. Other largely storefront retailers (e.g., Walmart) have developed new hybrids of online and storefront retailing. They offer consumers the ability to buy online and then pick up their items at local outlets. The hope is that visits to local stores will lead consumers to make unplanned purchases. These new forms of retailing offer new ways of socializing young people into our culture of consumption.

The "influencers" on social media also play a role in socializing children (and adults) into consuming. Many leading influencers use their status to market products, often either getting paid to do so or getting products for free. Their followers are then encouraged to purchase the same items; links in the media posts make it easy to do so.

Adult Socialization

A great deal of adult socialization takes place in later life as people enter the work world (Ellis, Bauer, and Erdogan 2015), become independent of their birth families, and start families of their own.

Workplaces

At one time, socialization into a workplace was a fairly simple and straightforward process. Many workers were hired for jobs in large corporations (e.g., General Motors, U.S. Steel) and remained there until they reached retirement age. Especially for those who held jobs in the lower reaches of the corporate hierarchy, socialization occurred, for the most part, in the early stages of a career. Today, however, relatively few workers can look forward to, or even report a desire to have, a career in a single position within a single company. Increasing numbers of workers are changing employers, jobs, and even careers with some frequency. Each time workers change jobs, they are likely to need **resocialization** to unlearn old behaviors, norms, and values and to learn new ones associated with their new employer.

Consider the findings of one study of U.S. workers' experiences in the job market. The researchers found that the generation of workers who entered the labor market in the late 1980s were 43 percent more likely to change jobs during their lifetimes than the generation that began in the early 1960s (Bernhardt et al. 2001). Today, workers will hold an average of 12 jobs during their lifetime and average just 4.2 years per job (Doyle 2018). Millennials, in particular, tend to "job hop," or work less than two years in a job position (Chatzky 2018). Clearly, workers are changing jobs more frequently and performing more different jobs over a lifetime.

Allison Pugh (2015) argues that this change in work has helped create a culture of insecurity—a "tumbleweed society"—that affects not just the economy and our jobs but also our personal relationships and self-identity. She discovered through her interviews with 80 mothers and fathers that this culture of insecurity profoundly shapes their expectations of commitment, loyalty, and obligation. Flexibility in the workplace has weakened employer commitment but not the work ethic of the labor force. Some workers value flexibility because it gives them more freedom and mobility. This is especially true for well-educated professionals, who are better positioned financially to relocate for a new job. But others, particularly unskilled males, feel angry that their hard work does not guarantee stable employment. Interestingly, this anger is directed not against their bosses but at themselves for being too dependent on their jobs. Pugh describes this as a "one-way honor system" that holds individual workers, not their employers, responsible for their job successes and failures.

Total Institutions

At some point in their lives, many adults find themselves in some type of total institution (Gambino 2013; Goffman 1961a). A **total institution** is a closed, all-encompassing place of residence and work set off from the rest of society that meets all the needs of those enclosed in it.

A noteworthy example of a total institution is the prison. In 2022, more than 2 million people in the United States were housed in prisons and jails of various types (including, among others, military prisons and detention centers for immigrants). On entry into prison, inmates undergo formal resocialization when they are told the rules and procedures they must follow. However, of far greater importance is the informal socialization that occurs over time through their interactions with guards and especially with other inmates. In fact, other inmates often socialize relatively inexperienced criminals into becoming more expert criminals; prisons are often "schools for crime" (Lopez-Aguado 2016; Sykes [1958] 2007).

Another total institution is the military. Members generally live in military housing. They often eat together, share living quarters, and have access to all necessary services on the military base. They must follow strict rules of dress, conduct, physical appearance, and organization of their time.

Other Aspects of Adult Socialization

Adult socialization and resocialization take place in many other ways and in many other settings. For example, medical schools, law schools, and graduate schools of various types socialize their students to be doctors, lawyers, nurses, and members of other professions (Becker and Geer 1958; Granfield 1992; Hafferty 2009). Students have to learn the norms that govern their appearance; conduct; and interactions with others in their professions, their patients or clients, and the public at large. Medical residents, for example, need to learn how to present their diagnoses to patients with sensitivity and confidence.

Life in a total institution, like this Marine Corps basic training facility, is cut off from the rest of society.
iStock Images/Joel Carillet

A number of other situations lead to the need for adult socialization or resocialization (Brim 1968; Lutfey and Mortimer 2006; Wilson 1984):

- *Changes in societal values and norms.* As a result of the COVID-19 pandemic, many aspects of culture are experiencing rapid change, and people need to be socialized into the new cultural realities (e.g., the increasing use of video conferencing technologies or wearing a mask; Ryan and Nanda 2023).

- *Family changes.* Separation, divorce, death of a spouse, and remarriage involve particularly important transitions for the adults involved (as well as for the children, if there are any). They require considerable adult resocialization into new relationships, new household organization, and new public images.

- *Geographic mobility.* Job change, retirement, and migration are becoming increasingly likely. People undergoing any of these transitions must be resocialized into not only new physical environments but also new subcultures.

- *Changes associated with aging.* As people age, they often gradually become disengaged from work, which has implications for relationships and financial well-being. A retired person must become resocialized into this new status.

INTERACTION

In the first part of the chapter, we focused on the socialization of individuals. However, socialization generally involves **interaction**, or social engagement involving two or more individuals who perceive, and orient their actions to, one another. Interaction has generally been seen as involving face-to-face relationships between people, but in the twenty-first century, and especially during the COVID-19 pandemic, interaction is increasingly taking place using digital technologies. Interaction is an important topic of study in itself because of its important influence on individuals. It is also a key building block for more large-scale social phenomena, such as networks and groups as well as larger organizations, societies, and the global domain, which is explored more deeply in the next chapter.

Personal interaction occurs throughout our lifetimes: between parents and children, between children and their siblings, between teachers and students, between coworkers, between spouses, and between medical personnel and patients. Interactions early in the life cycle, especially in the family and in schools, tend to be long-term and intense. Later in life, many interactions tend to be more fleeting (a quick hello on the street or a brief conversation at a cocktail party), although interactions with those we consider to be family tend to remain intense.

Superordinate–Subordinate Interactions

Georg Simmel saw society as being defined by interaction. Moreover, he differentiated between the forms interaction takes and the types of people who engage in interaction. For example, one "form" of interaction is the relationship between a *superordinate* and a *subordinate* (Simmel [1908] 1971a). This type of relationship is found in many settings, for example, between teacher and student in the classroom, between judge and defendant in the courtroom, and between guard and prisoner in the jail. We tend to think of this relationship as eliminating the subordinate's independence. However, a relationship between the two cannot exist unless the subordinate has at least some freedom to be an active party to the interaction. The relationship between employee and supervisor is a good example. If the employee cannot react to the supervisor's direction, there is no interaction—only one-way communication from the supervisor to the employee. Furthermore, experimental research has demonstrated that the greater the equality in an employee–manager relationship, the greater the amount of two-way communication. In such a situation, the subordinate feels less resentment, anger, and worry when conflict arises with the manager (Johnson, Ford, and Kaufman 2000).

Reciprocity and Exchange

To sociologists who theorize about exchange, interaction is a rational process in which those involved seek to maximize rewards and minimize costs. Exchange theorists are not concerned with what goes on in people's minds and how that affects behavior. Instead, they are interested in the behavior itself and the rewards and costs associated with it (Molm, Whithama, and Melameda 2012). Interaction is likely to persist as long as those involved find it rewarding, and it is likely to wind down or end when one or more of the parties no longer finds it rewarding. An important idea in this context is the social norm of **reciprocity**, which means that those engaged in interaction expect to give and receive rewards of roughly equal value (Gouldner 1960; Mazelis 2015; Molm 2010). When one party feels that the other is no longer adhering to this norm—that is, not giving about as much as he or she is receiving—the relationship is likely to end.

Exchange theorists are particularly interested in social behavior that usually involves two or more people and a variety of tangible and intangible exchanges. For example, you can reward someone who does you a favor with a tangible gift or with more intangible words of praise. Those exchanges are not always rewarding; they also can be punitive. You could, for example, punish someone who wrongs you by slapping them or complaining about them to mutual acquaintances.

Although exchange theory retains an interest in the elementary forms of social behavior, over the years it has grown more concerned with how those forms lead to more complex social situations. That is, individual exchanges can become stable over time and develop into persistent **exchange relationships**. One particular type of exchange relationship is "friends with benefits." For example, because you and another person find your initial sexual interactions rewarding, you may develop a pattern of repeat interactions. Exchange relationships, including hookups, rarely develop in isolation from other exchange relationships. Sociologists study how hooking up is not an isolated occurrence—it happens within the context of college campuses, for example, where it has been normalized (Kuperberg and Padgett 2015).

Studies of exchange relationships, like much else in sociology, are now being challenged to find ways of dealing with new forms of virtual interaction: e-mail, social networking, and interaction on Twitter, Instagram, and Facebook. One researcher who has explored the effects of virtual reality on interaction in the "real" world, and vice versa, concludes that "the constantly evolving avatar [or digital representation of oneself] influences the 'real' self, who now also orients toward virtual, yet all-too-real others" (Gottschalk 2010, 522). In other words, interactions in the digital realm and those in the physical realm both influence the self. Additional research questions come to mind readily. For example, are people compelled to cooperate to the same extent in the digital realm (such as when using e-mail communication) as they are in the material world (such as during in-person communication; Naquin, Kurtzberg, and Belkin 2008)? However, it is important to remember that the digital and material worlds are not separate from one another but, rather, are often interrelated. An important issue, then, is the connection between, for example, collaborative relationships online and offline (Ritzer 2013).

"Doing" Interaction

Another interactionist theory of great relevance here is **ethnomethodology**, which focuses on people's everyday practices, especially those that involve interaction. Ethnomethodology focuses on what people *do* rather than on what they think. For example, the simple act of two people walking together can be considered a form of interaction. Engaging in certain practices makes it clear that you are walking with a particular someone and not with someone else (Pantzar and Shove 2010; Ryave and Schenkein 1974). You are likely to walk close to, or perhaps lean toward, a close friend. When you find yourself walking in step with a total stranger, you probably behave differently. You might separate yourself, lean away, and say, "Excuse me," to make it clear that you are not walking with that stranger and are not engaged in interaction with them. More complex forms of interaction require much more sophisticated practices. In the process of interacting, people create durable forms of interaction, such as those that relate to gender (West and Zimmerman 1987) and the family.

Ethnomethodologists regard people's lives and social worlds as practical accomplishments that are really quite extraordinary. For example, one ethnomethodological study of coffee drinkers attempted to understand their participation in a subculture of coffee connoisseurship (Manzo 2010). Learning to enjoy coffee is something of an accomplishment itself; taking that enjoyment to the next level and becoming a connoisseur requires even more doing.

Their view of large-scale social structures differs from that of structural-functionalists, who tend to see people and their actions as being highly constrained by those structures. Ethnomethodologists argue that this view tells us very little about what really goes on within structures such as courtrooms, hospitals, and police departments. Rather than being constrained, people act within these structures and go about much of their business using common sense rather than official procedures.

Some of the best-known examples of an ethnomethodological approach relate to gender (O'Brien 2016; Stokoe 2006). Ethnomethodologists point out that people often erroneously think of gender as being biologically based. It is generally assumed that we do not have to do or say anything in order to be considered masculine or feminine; we are born that way. But, in fact, there are things we all do (e.g., the way we walk) and say (e.g., the tone of our voice) that allow us to accomplish being masculine or feminine. That is, being masculine or feminine is based on what people do on a regular basis. This is clearest in the case of those who are defined as being male or female at birth (based on biological characteristics) but then later do and say things that lead others to see them as belonging to another gender than that typically associated with their medically assigned sex at birth (based on social characteristics).

Ethnomethodology also spawned **conversation analysis**, which is concerned with how people do, or accomplish, conversations (Heritage and Stivers 2012). For example, you must know and use certain practices to carry on a successful conversation: You must know when it is your turn to talk and when it is appropriate to laugh at a comment made by someone else. Conversation analysts have taken the lead in studying conversations, and interaction more generally, in great depth. They typically record conversations using audio or video devices so that they can study them in detail. Later, they transcribe the conversations to create written records of them and perform detailed analysis of how conversations unfold including noting things like frequency of interrupting someone, the use of particular phrases, and even where, and for how long, pauses appear in conversations.

Interaction Order

Although every instance of interaction may seem isolated and independent of others, each is part of what Erving Goffman (2000) called the **interaction order** (Rawls 2015). This is a social domain that is organized and orderly. The order is created informally and governed by those involved in the interaction rather than by some formal structure, such as a bureaucracy and its constraints (Fine 2012). One example of an interaction order is a group of students who form a clique and develop their own norms to govern their interaction. In this thinking, Goffman was following Simmel's view that society is based, in a real sense, on interaction. In many ways, society *is* interaction. Some sociologists have suggested that human interaction with animals is another area in which we can observe the interaction order (Jerolmack 2009, 2013).

Status and Role

Status and role are key elements in the interaction order, as well as in the larger structures in which such interactions often exist. A **status** is a position within a social system occupied by people. Within the university, for example, key statuses are professor and student. A **role** is what is generally expected of a person who occupies a given status. Thus, a professor is expected to show up for class, to be well prepared, to teach in an engaging manner, and so on. For their part, students are also expected to attend class, to listen and sometimes to participate, to avoid texting and checking their social media during class, to complete the required assignments, and to take and pass examinations.

The concept of status can be broken down further into ascribed and achieved status. An **ascribed status** is one that is not chosen; it is beyond the individual's control. It involves a position into which the individual is placed or to which they move, regardless of what that person does or the nature of their capacities or accomplishments. In some cases, individuals are born into an ascribed status—for example, the status associated with race, ethnicity, social class, or sex. In contrast, an **achieved status** is a position a person acquires based on accomplishment or the nature of the individual's capacities. It may be based on merit, earned, given, or the person may choose it—for example, by seeking out and finding someone who will be a mate for life. Spouse, parent, and career as a "successful" entrepreneur are all achieved statuses. In addition, adults can achieve improvement in their social class or socioeconomic status (children's social class is almost always ascribed).

There are also a number of ascribed statuses that can change to achieved statuses. For example, although one's social class is ascribed when one is born, adults can achieve improvement in their social class or socioeconomic status. Legal sex is another example. Although we are medically assigned a sex at birth, we can change our sex during our lifetimes (including legally, in a growing number of countries).

Whether ascribed or achieved, a status can become a **master status**, or a position that is (or becomes) more important than any other status, both for the person in the position and for all others involved. A master status will become central to a person's identity, roles, behaviors, and interactions. Primary examples of master statuses are those associated with race, disability, gender, and even sexuality. It is important to note that our master status can, and does, change depending on our context. For example, someone born in the UK living in London will most likely be considered a "local," but if they move to Peru, the status of "foreigner" is likely to become a master status in certain situations. A gay person enjoying drinks with friends in a gay bar isn't likely to think of their sexuality as a master status in that situation, but if they go to a homophobic setting, their sexuality is likely to become a master status.

The social roles connected with any statuses can be congruent; that is, the expectations attached to a given status can be consistent. Student status (achieved) may have role expectations of attending class and doing homework outside of class. But roles can also come into conflict—for example, going to class and keeping up with your social life. **Role conflict** can be defined as conflicting expectations associated with a given position or multiple positions (Merton 1957; Schmidt et al. 2014). A professor who is expected to excel at both teaching and research can be seen as having role conflict. Devoting a lot of time to research can mean that a professor is ill prepared to teach their classes. Or a professor may be torn between the expectations of being a teacher (preparing for class) and those of being a parent (playing with their children). A student may need to deal with the role conflict between being a student and studying and being a friend who spends the evening helping a close acquaintance deal with a personal problem.

Much research has been done on the role conflicts experienced by workers with domestic obligations. Each role often interferes with the individual's ability to satisfactorily meet the expectations associated with the other role (Moore 1995). Research has supported this idea. For example, women who work outside the home, who still tend to be responsible for the care of children and the home, experience higher levels of stress and poorer physical health than do working men (Gove and Hughes 1979; Pearlin 1989; Roehling, Hernandez Jarvis, and Swope 2005). The heavy burden of the female caretaking role often complicates women's ability to fulfill their role as caretakers of themselves.

Another role-related problem is **role overload,** in which people are confronted with more expectations than they can possibly handle (Mathews, Winkel, and Wayne 2014). Students during final exams week are often confronted with role overload in trying to satisfy the expectations of several professors and courses. One study of the "time crunch" and mental health suggests that feeling under time pressure is likely the active ingredient in role overload, which in turn affects people's psychological well-being (Roxburgh 2004).

There is a tendency to see roles as fixed, unchanging, and constraining. However, people do have the ability to engage in **role making**. That is, they have the ability to modify their roles, at least to some degree (Turner 1978). Thus, the professor in the previous example might take their child to the office so that they can perform parent and teacher roles simultaneously. Researchers have noted that parents adopt a variety of strategies to reduce work–family conflict (Kelly et al. 2014; Minnotte and Minnotte 2018). Such strategies include reducing work hours, turning down promotions, and negotiating trade-offs with one's partner.

MICRO-LEVEL SOCIAL STRUCTURES

Through an accumulation of persistent patterns of interaction and social relationships, individuals contribute to the creation of **social structures**, which are enduring and regular social arrangements. Social structures include everything from the face-to-face interaction that is characteristic of the interaction order to networks, groups, organizations, societies, and the globe. This chapter focuses on micro-level social structures—interpersonal relationships, social networks, and groups. Chapter 6 covers larger-scale social structures.

Interpersonal Relationships

A good place to start a discussion of social structures is with another famous set of concepts created by Georg Simmel (1950) to describe the structures common to interpersonal relationships. A **dyad** is a two-person group, and a **triad** is a three-person group.

Dyads are the most basic of interpersonal relationships, but they often evolve into triads—as when a couple welcomes a new child. It would appear on the surface that the addition of one person to a dyad, creating a triad, would be of minimal importance sociologically. After all, how important can the addition of one person be? Simmel demonstrated that no further addition of members to a group, no matter how many that might be, is as important as the addition of a single person to a dyad. A good example is the dramatic change in the spousal relationship caused by the arrival of a first child. Another is the powerful impact of a new lover on an intimate dyadic relationship. In cases like these, social possibilities exist in the triad that do not exist in a dyad. For example, in a triad, two of the parties can form a coalition against the third: A parent and child can form a coalition against the other parent. Or one member of the triad—say, the child—can take on the role of mediator or arbitrator in disputes involving the other members.

The most important point to be made about Simmel's ideas on the triad is that it is the group structure that matters, *not* the people involved in the triad or the nature of their personalities. Different people with different personalities will make one triad different from another, but it is not the nature of the people or their personalities that make the triad itself possible.

Social Networks

Simmel's work also informs the study of social networks (Erikson and Occhiuto 2017). The most basic social networks involve two or more individuals, but social networks also include groups, organizations, and societies; there can even be global social networks.

Network analysts are interested in how networks are organized and the implications of that organization for social life. They look at the nodes, or positions, occupied by individuals (and other entities) in a network, the linkages between nodes, and the importance of central nodes to other nodes in the network. Figure 5.1 shows a network with low centrality and one with high centrality. In the low-centrality network, one node appears in the center, but it is actually linked to only two other nodes. The central node in the high-centrality example is far more influential. Every other node is connected to it, and there is only one link that is independent of the central node. Those who occupy positions that are central in any network have access to a great many resources and therefore have a considerable ability to gain and to exercise power in a network.

FIGURE 5.1 ■ Social Network Centrality

Opposite Degrees of Network Centrality

Low Network Centrality   High Network Centrality

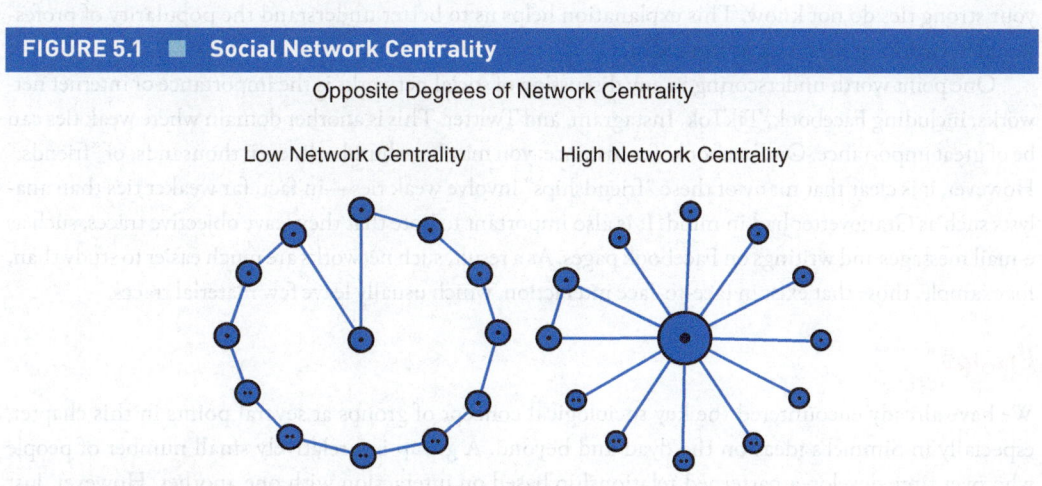

Source: Social Network Centrality is reprinted by permission of S. Joshua Mendelsohn.

A key idea in network theory is the **strength of weak ties**. We are all aware of the power of strong ties between, for example, family members, or among those who belong to close-knit social groups such as gangs. However, as Mark Granovetter (1973) has demonstrated, those who have only weak ties with others (i.e., they are just acquaintances) can have great power. Although those with strong ties tend to remain within given groups, those with weak ties can more easily move between groups and thus provide important linkages among and between group members (see Figure 5.2). Those with weak ties are the ones who hold together disparate groups that are themselves linked internally by strong ties.

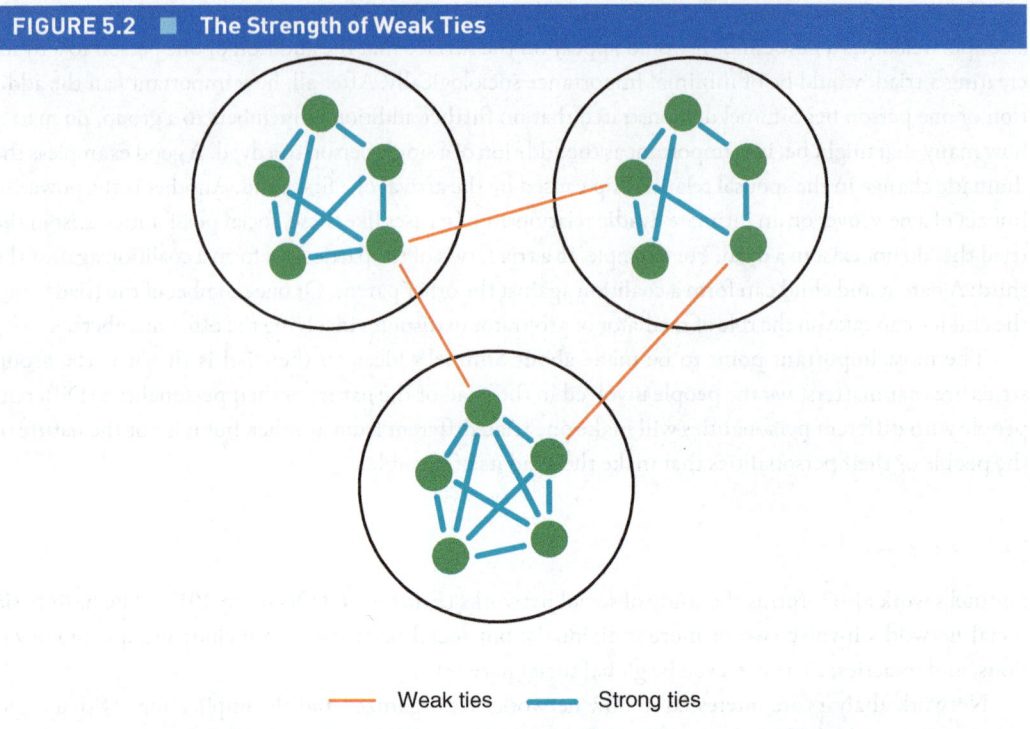

FIGURE 5.2 ■ The Strength of Weak Ties

— Weak ties   — Strong ties

Source: The Strength of Weak Ties is adapted from Weak Ties in Social Networks, Bokardo, a blog about interface and product design, Joshua Porter.

Many workers have obtained their jobs through informal means, meaning referrals, rather than formal job postings (Marsden and Gorman 2001; Pfeffer and Parra 2009). It makes sense, then, to understand the strength of weak ties. If you are looking for a job, you may want to seek out the help of friends and acquaintances who have weak ties to many groups. This is because they are likely to have many diverse and potentially useful contacts at a number of different employers with people you *and* your strong ties do not know. This explanation helps us to better understand the popularity of professional networking sites such as LinkedIn.

One point worth underscoring in any discussion of social networks is the importance of internet networks, including Facebook, TikTok, Instagram, and Twitter. This is another domain where weak ties can be of great importance. On Facebook, for instance, you may have hundreds, even thousands, of "friends." However, it is clear that many of these "friendships" involve weak ties—in fact, far weaker ties than analysts such as Granovetter had in mind. It is also important to note that they leave objective traces, such as e-mail messages and writings on Facebook pages. As a result, such networks are much easier to study than, for example, those that exist in face-to-face interaction, which usually leave few material traces.

Groups

We have already encountered the key sociological concept of groups at several points in this chapter, especially in Simmel's ideas on the dyad and beyond. A **group** is a relatively small number of people who over time develop a patterned relationship based on interaction with one another. However, just because we see a small number of people who appear to be together—say, in a queue waiting to board a plane—that does not mean they necessarily constitute a group. Most people in a queue are not likely to interact with one another, to have the time or inclination to develop patterned relationships with one another, or, if they do interact, to do so beyond the time it takes to board the plane and find their seats.

Types of Groups

Several key concepts in sociology relate to groups. Consider the traditional distinction between the primary group and the secondary group (Cooley 1909). **Primary groups** are small, are close-knit, and have intimate face-to-face interaction. Relationships in primary groups are personal, and people identify strongly with the groups. Members of your household would be an example of what is typically a primary group. In contrast, **secondary groups** are generally large and impersonal; ties are relatively weak, members do not know one another very well, and members' impacts on one another are typically not very powerful. Members of a local parent–teacher association would be a good example of a secondary group.

Reference groups are those that you consider in evaluating yourself. Your reference group can be one to which you belong, or it can be another group to which you do not belong but nevertheless often relate (Merton and Kitt 1950). People often have many reference groups, and those groups can and do change over time. Knowing people's reference groups and how they change tells us a great deal about their behavior, attitudes, and values. We often think of reference groups in positive terms. An example would be a group of people whose success you would like to emulate. They also can be negative if they represent values or ways of life that you reject (say, neo-Nazis). The reference group to which one belongs is not necessarily the most powerful group in one's life.

Reference groups can be illustrated by the case of immigrants. Newly arrived immigrants are more likely to take those belonging to the immigrant culture, or even those in the country from which they came, as their reference group. In contrast, their children, second-generation immigrants, are much more likely to take as their reference group those associated with the new culture in the country to which they have immigrated (Kosic et al. 2004).

One final set of concepts that can help us understand the sociological importance of groups is the distinction between in-groups and out-groups (Sumner [1906] 1940). An **in-group** is one to which people belong and with which they identify, perhaps strongly. An **out-group** is one to which outsiders, at least from the perspective of the in-group, belong. Thus, from your perspective, the group you sit with at your regular table in the college dining hall or fast-food court would be the in-group, while other groups at other tables might be the out-groups. The differences between these groups may be insignificant (e.g., whether they get their food in the food court from McDonald's or Pizza Hut). However, they can also come to be so important ("jocks" versus "geeks") that each group not only accepts its own ways but also rejects those of the others. In extreme cases this can lead to conflict between the in-group and the out-group. Research suggests that hostility often arises when members of the in-group perceive the out-group as constituting a threat to their self-interest (Rosenstein 2008). This is particularly evident in research on immigration (Schlueter and Scheepers 2010; Schneider 2008). In that case, native-born individuals (representing the in-group) may maintain discriminatory attitudes toward a growing population of foreign-born individuals (representing the out-group).

Conformity to the Group

We have seen that group members generally conform to certain aspects of the group with which they prefer to identify. Some conformity is clearly necessary for a group to survive. If everyone did their own thing or went their own way, there would be no group. But too much conformity can have disastrous consequences. A central issue in the sociological study of groups has been the degree to which members conform to the expectations and demands of the group, despite their own misgivings.

A series of experiments, conducted by Solomon Asch (1952), showed the power of the group to promote conformity. Asch demonstrated that its power is so great that it may override an individual's own judgments and perceptions. In one of the experiments, groups of seven to nine students were assembled. All but one (the subject) were confederates of the researcher. All but the subject knew the details of the experiment. Only the subject believed that the experiment was investigating vision. Each group was shown two cards, one with one vertical line on it and a second with three such lines (see Figure 5.3). One of the lines on the second card was the same length as the line on the first card. The other two lines were clearly different. All the students were asked to choose the line on the comparison card that matched the single line on the reference card. As they had been instructed, each of the confederates chose, out loud, one of the wrong lines. The subjects were always positioned last in their groups. When the subjects' turns came, about a third of them conformed to their group's erroneous choice and selected the same wrong line. They made the wrong choice even though they apparently knew it was the wrong choice.

There is no question that some people conform to group demands at least some of the time. Conformity is especially likely when the demands come from someone in authority in the group. However, it is important to remember that about two-thirds of the choices made by subjects in the Asch conformity experiments indicated independence from the group.

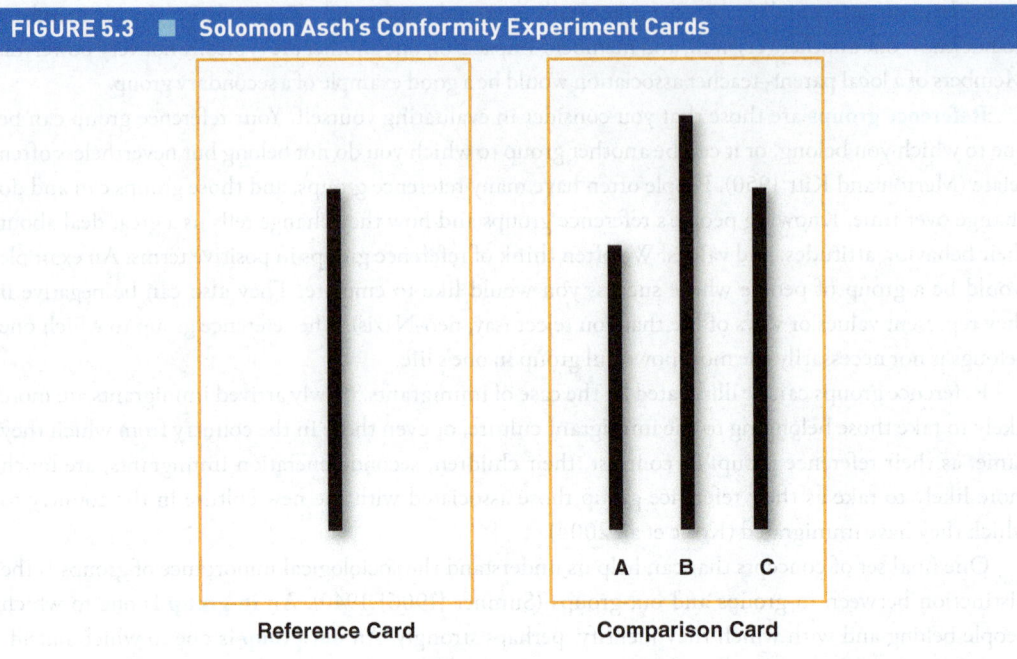

FIGURE 5.3 ■ Solomon Asch's Conformity Experiment Cards

Source: Solomon Asch's Conformity Experiment Cards is adapted from Solomon E. Asch, *Opinions and Social Pressure, Scientific American,* 193 (1955), pp. 31–35.

This chapter has focused largely on such micro-level phenomena as individuals, interaction, and groups. In Chapter 6, we turn to the progressively more macro-level phenomena of organizations, societies, and the globe as a whole.

SUMMARY

The sociological perspective on the individual and the self focuses on the social interactions humans are capable of having with each other. Cooley's concept of the looking-glass self, the idea that humans develop self-images reflecting the way in which others respond to them, is fundamental to sociology.

Symbolic interactionism posits that humans use significant symbols, such as gestures and language, to develop a sense of self. George Herbert Mead defined the self as the ability to take oneself as an object. Once individuals are able to internalize the perspective of a group or community, they come to possess a sense of the generalized other. According to Mead, the self is composed of two parts, the "I" that is impulsive and the "me" that is conformist.

Erving Goffman believed that in every interaction, or performance, individuals attempt to manage projections of themselves. On a front stage, they operate in an idealized manner, but on a back stage, they can more freely express themselves.

Socialization is the process by which a person learns and generally comes to accept the ways of a group or of a society as a whole. Primary socialization begins with newborns and infants and continues over the course of their childhood during anticipatory socialization. Socialization does not end with childhood—adults continue to be socialized throughout their lives. Our families, peers, workplaces, and the media are important agents of socialization.

Socialization involves interaction, or social engagement, between two or more individuals. Some interaction involves reciprocity, or the expectation that those involved in it will give and receive equally, while other interactions transpire between those with power and their subordinates. Interaction is deeply involved in people's statuses and their related roles.

Patterns of interaction and social relationships that occur regularly and persist over time become social structures. A group is one type of social structure that develops when individuals interact over time and develop a patterned relationship. A small, closely knit group with intimate face-to-face interactions is a primary group. A secondary group is larger and more impersonal; its members do not know each other very well.

KEY TERMS

achieved status	micro–macro continuum
agents of socialization	mind
anticipatory socialization	out-group
ascribed status	play stage
back stage	primary groups
conversation analysis	primary socialization
conversation of gestures	reciprocity
cyberbullying	reference groups
dramaturgy	resocialization
dyad	reverse socialization
ethnomethodology	role
exchange relationships	role conflict
front stage	role making
game stage	role overload
generalized other	secondary groups
gestures	self
group	significant symbol
"I"	social structures
impression management	socialization
in-group	status
interaction	strength of weak ties
interaction order	symbolic interaction
looking-glass self	symbolic interactionism
master status	total institution
"me"	triad

REVIEW QUESTIONS

1. How can we use the literature on feral children to explain the importance of interaction to human development? In what ways does this relate to the "nature versus nurture" debate?

2. According to Mead, what distinguishes humans from nonhumans?

3. How does the socialization process help individuals develop their sense of self? Why are games so important to the socialization process?

4. What is the difference between the "I" and the "me"? Why do people and society as a whole need both the "I" and the "me"?

5. According to Goffman, in what ways do we use impression management in our front-stage performances?

6. Why are families important agents of socialization? How do families from higher social classes socialize their children differently than families from lower social classes do? What effects might these differences in socialization have on children?

7. How are we socialized to be consumers? In what ways has the internet resocialized us as consumers?

8. Is being a fifth grader in the United States an ascribed or an achieved status? Or is it both? What does this suggest about the differences between roles attached to ascribed statuses versus those attached to achieved statuses?

9. In the realm of social networks, why are "weak ties" helpful to those looking for jobs? What effect has the internet had on the development of weak ties and strong ties?

10. In what ways do we use images in the mass media as reference groups? How do the mass media help to define in-groups and out-groups?

MediaNews Group/Orange County Register via Getty Images / Contributor

6 ORGANIZATIONS, SOCIETIES, AND GLOBAL RELATIONSHIPS

LEARNING OBJECTIVES

6.1 Describe the features of bureaucracies and informal organizations.

6.2 Discuss challenges that arise in contemporary organizations.

6.3 Contrast *gemeinschaft* and *gesellschaft* societies.

6.4 Describe global social organization and global flows.

QUESTIONING GOVERNMENTAL AUTHORITY

Famous movie director Oliver Stone's biopic *Snowden* gave renewed life to the controversy surrounding U.S. Central Intelligence Agency contractor Edward Snowden and his leak of thousands of classified government documents. The clamor in the United States became especially loud—and it has not died away to this day—when Snowden told the world that the U.S. government, through its National Security Agency, had been attempting to prevent terrorist acts by spying on ordinary citizens. This was being done through the systematic accumulation of bulk data (or metadata) on routine phone calls. Public reaction was swift and divided, with some arguing that Snowden was a hero for revealing this fact and that the government had gone to unwarranted lengths in breaching its citizens' privacy. This view was upheld by a federal appeals court ruling that such data collection was illegal. Others continue to argue that any and all steps necessary to uncover terrorist plots, including spying on everyday citizens, are defensible. Snowden eventually fled to Russia, where he long received asylum until obtaining Russian citizenship in 2022. Snowden's revelations continue to have impacts. Some terrorist groups have altered the way in which they communicate because some of the documents Snowden released revealed information about U.S. surveillance techniques. The leaks also led to great changes in the way in which the government protects secret documents.

The events surrounding Snowden's leaks reveal the relationship between us as individuals and the organizations and institutions that frame our lives, such as our local and national governments. These organizations cannot exist, at least for very long, without willing members. When groups of individuals begin to question the authority and rationality of the bureaucracies that govern them, they may voice concern about, seek to change, or even rebel against those bureaucracies. Social order cannot be maintained if citizens refuse to adhere to society's shared laws and norms. How do governments, as institutions, react? Some believe that governments and institutions often overreact. Snowden is still wanted by the U.S. government for violating the Espionage Act.

We have seen how technology and globalization facilitate the global flow of information, fundamentally altering the way in which we communicate. But this nearly instantaneous dissemination of ideas has become a bonanza for everyone, including whistleblowers, revolutionaries, rioters, potential terrorists, and even elected governments. For instance, revelations that swiftly followed Snowden's initial leak suggested that the United States had also been secretly conducting extensive monitoring of the communications of its European Union allies (including the prime minister of Germany). Some governments (e.g., the United Kingdom) have considered shutting down digital communication during public disturbances. Other countries, such as China, Syria, Turkey, Egypt, and Iran, routinely censor their citizens' use of the internet. Such barriers to the flow of information, as well as efforts such as Snowden's to overcome them, are of profound interest to sociologists, public figures, and social activists alike.

Picking up where the previous chapter left off with groups, this chapter moves on to the more macro levels of interest to sociologists: organizations, societies, and global relationships. These social structures are discussed here as if they were clearly distinct from one another. However, the fact is that they tend to blend together in many clear-cut ways, as well as in other almost imperceptible ones.

The individuals, interaction, and groups of focal concern in Chapter 5 all exist within, affect, and are affected by the various macro phenomena of concern here. In fact, neither micro nor macro social phenomena make much sense without the other level. Individuals, interaction, and groups do not exist in isolation from macro-level phenomena, and organizations, societies, and global social relationships cannot exist without individuals, interaction, and groups. What is new in recent years is the emergence, largely because of the explosive growth of digital communication, of an increasingly networked social world where both micro-level and macro-level phenomena are ever more closely intertwined. And this contributes to the dramatic expansion of globalization as a process and of the growth of global relationships at every point in the continuum that runs from the most micro to the most macro social phenomena. You are, of course, deeply implicated in all of this. In fact, if you are a young person, you are the most likely to participate in, and be affected by, these recent developments, especially those involving digitized interrelationships. For example, through our (micro-level) smartphones, we are able to access, participate in, and even influence everything from the most micro (our close friends) to the most macro (global) levels of the social world.

ORGANIZATIONS

The social world is awash in **organizations**, collectives purposely constructed to achieve particular ends. Examples include your college or university, which has the objective of educating you as well as your fellow students; corporations, such as Apple, Google, IKEA, Amazon, and Walmart, whose objective is to earn profits; the International Monetary Fund (IMF), which seeks to stabilize currency exchanges throughout the world; and Greenpeace, which works to protect and conserve the global environment. Of course, some organizations can serve more than one purpose. In fact, many do. So, for example, if you are attending a for-profit college or university, then their objective is both to educate students as well as to earn a profit.

A particularly long and deep body of work in sociology deals with organizations, much of it traceable to the thinking of Max Weber on a particular kind of organization, the bureaucracy. As you may recall, a **bureaucracy** is a highly rational organization, especially one that is very efficient. However, both Weber's own thinking and later sociological research (see the following section) make it clear that bureaucracies are *not* always so rational and are even as irrational as you undoubtedly sometimes find them to be. Nevertheless, the bureaucracy is a key element of Weber's theory of rationalization. In fact, along with capitalism, the bureaucracy best exemplifies what Weber meant by rationalization. For decades, the concept of bureaucracy dominated sociological thinking about organizations, and it led to many important insights about the social world.

Bureaucracies

Throughout his work, Weber created and used many "ideal types" as methodological tools with which to study the real world and conduct historical-comparative analysis. An **ideal type** greatly exaggerates the characteristics of a social phenomenon such as a bureaucracy. It is a model of how the social phenomenon is supposed to operate in some optimal sense (though they rarely do). Once the model has been created, we can compare it to the characteristics of any specific example of the social phenomenon anywhere in the world. It serves to identify the ways in which the ideal type differs from the way in which the social phenomenon actually operates. In short, it is a type of yardstick against which we can measure real world phenomenon against a sort of perfect stereotyped image of what they "should" be.

For example, we can think of an ideal type house as having four walls and a slanted roof. Maybe also with a door in the middle and symmetrical windows on each side. Think of the image that many of us learned to draw as children of what a house looks like. Now think about different kinds of houses, most of which have more than four walls, different kinds of roofs, and are not often symmetrical. The way we understand what is "unique" about a given house (perhaps it has a flat roof and six sides) is by comparing it to the ideal type of what a house "should" look like (our childhood drawing; see Figure 6.1).

FIGURE 6.1 ■ Two Houses: An Ideal Type and a Unique Variation

iStock/Ekaterina79
iStock/tulcarion

One of Weber's most famous ideal types was the bureaucracy. The ideal type of bureaucracy is primarily a methodological tool used to study real-life bureaucracies. However, it also gives us a good sense of the advantages and disadvantages of bureaucracies over other types of organizations. The ideal-typical bureaucracy is a model of what most large-scale organizations throughout much of the twentieth century looked like or at least tried to resemble. Figure 6.2 is an organization chart for a typical bureaucracy. A bureaucracy has the following characteristics:

FIGURE 6.2 ■ Organization Chart for a Typical Bureaucracy

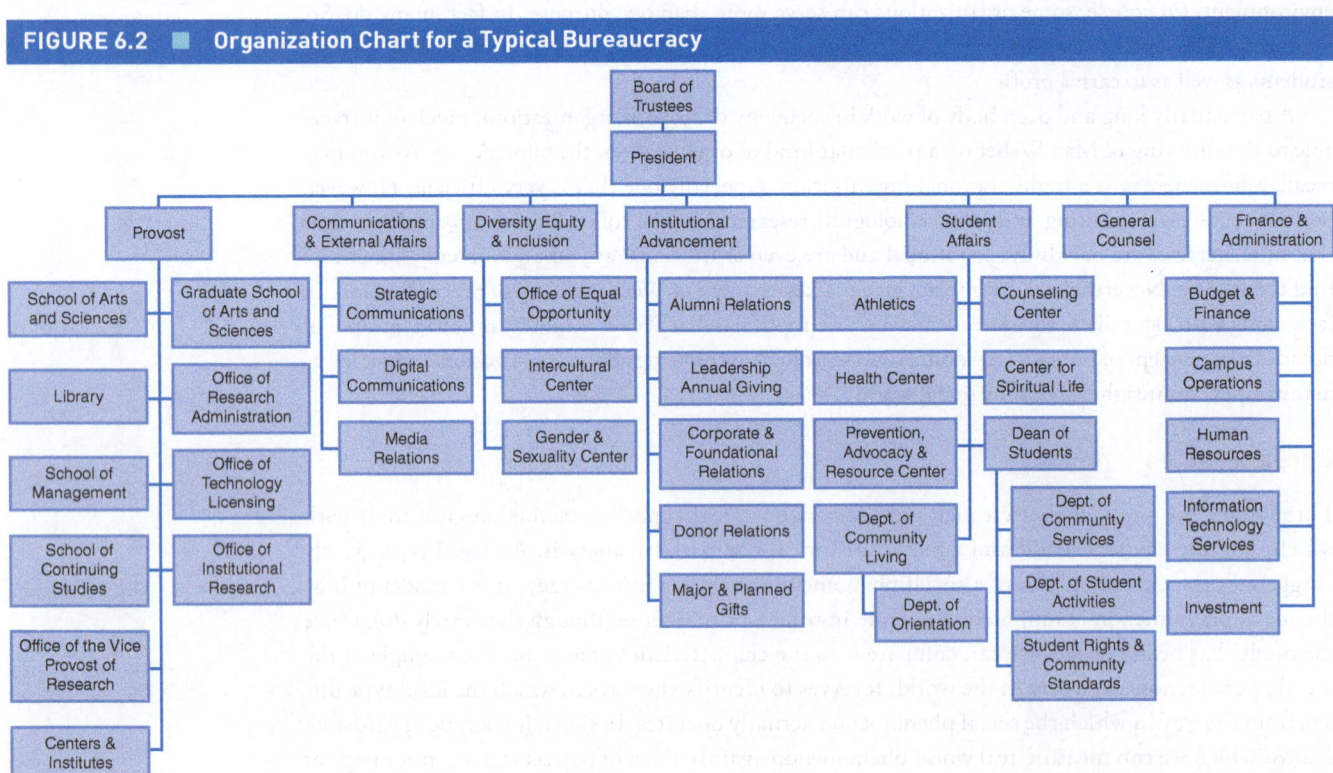

- A continuous series of offices, or positions, exist within the organization. Each office has official functions and is bound by a set of rules.

- Each office has a specified sphere of competence. Those who occupy the positions are responsible for specific tasks and have the authority to handle them. Those in other relevant offices are obligated to help with those tasks.

- The offices exist in a vertical hierarchy.

- The positions have technical requirements, and those who hold those offices must undergo the needed training.
- Those who occupy the positions do not own the things needed to do the job (computers, desks, and so on). The organization provides officeholders with what they need to get the job done.
- Those who occupy particular offices—chief executive officers, for example—cannot take the offices as their own; these remain part of the organization.
- Everything of formal importance—administrative acts, decisions, rules—is documented in writing.

The development of the bureaucracy is one of the defining characteristics of most modern societies. Weber felt that in meeting the needs of large societies for mass administration, there is no better organizational form than, and no alternative to, the bureaucracy.

Authority Structures and Bureaucracy

Weber's work on bureaucracy is related to his thinking on three types of authority structures. Before getting to those types, we need two preliminary definitions. **Domination** is the probability, or likelihood, that commands will be obeyed by subordinates (Weber [1921] 1968). There are degrees of domination. Strong domination involves a high probability that commands will be obeyed; domination is weak when those probabilities are low. **Authority** is a particular type of domination: legitimate domination. The key question, then, is what makes authority legitimate as far as subordinates are concerned.

FIGURE 6.3 ■ Three Types of Authority
The President of the United States has legal-rational authority as a result of national elections every four years.

Getty Images/Win McNamee/Staff

Queen Elizabeth II inherited the throne of the United Kingdom from her father, King George VI, and served as monarch for 70 years until her death in 2022.

Getty Images/DANIEL LEAL

Dr. Martin Luther King, Jr. became the leader of the U.S. Civil Rights movement through his charismatic leadership and oratorical skills.

Getty Images/Michael Ochs Archives

Weber differentiates among three types of authority:

- **Rational-legal authority** is domination legitimated based on legally enacted rules and the right of those with authority under those rules to issue commands. For example, the president of the United States has rational-legal authority to take a variety of actions, such as appointing federal officials, because the president is duly elected in accordance with the country's election laws.

- **Traditional authority** is based on belief in long-running traditions. For example, King Charles is the monarch of the UK and other commonwealth countries because his mother was the queen, and her father was the king before her. In turn, King Charles's eldest son, Prince William, will assume the position of monarch after the King's death. In another example, although the pope is elected by the College of Cardinals, his authority within Catholicism is based primarily on the long traditions associated with his position.

- **Charismatic authority** is based on the devotion of followers to what they define as the exceptional characteristics of a leader. Large numbers of people believed that Martin Luther King Jr. and Mahatma Gandhi had such exceptional characteristics and, as a result, became their devoted followers.

It is important to note that these types of authority are not mutually exclusive and, in fact, rarely are. For example, many members of the Kennedy family in the United States have been elected to positions (starting with President John F. Kennedy) and thus have rational-legal authority. It can be argued that they achieved their positions because they are "Kennedys," thus giving them a type of traditional authority. But in addition, many of them are seen as charismatic (especially John F. Kennedy, as well as his brothers Robert and Ted).

Each type of authority can spawn its own organizational form. However, rational-legal authority is most associated with bureaucracy. In comparison to the bureaucracy, organizations based on traditional and charismatic authority are generally less rational. They are, for example, less efficient than is the highly efficient bureaucracy.

Rationality and Irrationality

Much sociological research on organizations in the twentieth century took Weber's highly rational model of a bureaucracy as a starting point for the study of the ways in which bureaucracies actually worked. However, much of that research found Weber's ideal-typical model to be unrealistic. For one thing, there is no single organizational model. The nature of the organization and its degree of rationality are contingent on such factors as the organization's size and the technologies it employs (Orlikowski 2010; Pugh et al. 1968). For another, researchers found Weber's ideal-typical bureaucracy to be overly rational. This is not surprising because for Weber ([1903–1917] 1949, 47), it was "not a *description* of reality." Weber purposely exaggerated its degree of rationality. The ideal-typical bureaucracy is a fiction designed to serve as a reference point for the study of real-world bureaucracies.

A more limited form of rationality, or what is called **bounded rationality** (Simon [1945] 1976; Williamson 1975, 1985) is rationality that is limited by the instabilities and conflicts that exist in most, if not all, organizations and the domains in which they operate (Scott 2014). It is also restricted by inherent limitations on humans' capacities to think and act in a rational manner. Some members of the organization are capable of acting more rationally than others are. However, none are able to operate in anything approaching the fully rational manner associated with Weber's ideal-typical organization (Cyert and March 1963).

The military is an example of an organization with bounded rationality. One source of instability in the military is the cycling of personnel in and out of it, especially in combat zones. Newcomers to the battle zone rarely know what to do. Their presence in, say, a platoon with experienced combat veterans can reduce the ability of the entire group to function. Another larger source of instability lies in the conflicts that exist between branches of the armed forces, as well as between central command and those in the field. In addition, military actions are often so complex and far-reaching that military personnel cannot fully understand them or rationally decide what actions to take. This phenomenon is sometimes referred to as the "fog of war" (Blight and Lang 2005).

A good deal of sociological research on bureaucracies has dealt with how the rational (that is, what is efficient) often becomes irrational (or inefficient). This is often referred to as the "**irrationality of rationality**"—the irrationality that often accompanies the seemingly rational actions associated with the bureaucracy (Ritzer 2021). For example, Robert Merton ([1949] 1968) and other observers (Gupta 2012) found that instead of operating efficiently, bureaucracies introduce great inefficiency due to, among other things, "red tape." *Red tape* is a colloquial term for the rules a bureaucracy's employees are needlessly required to follow, as well as the unnecessary online and offline questions to be answered and forms to be filled out by the clients of the bureaucracy. Bureaucracies generally demand much more information than they need, often to protect themselves from complaints, bad publicity, and lawsuits. Red tape also includes the telephone time wasted by keeping clients on hold and forcing them to make their way through a maze of prerecorded "customer service" options.

Parkinson's law was conceived as a humorous attempt to point to another source of irrationality in bureaucratic organizations. It was formulated by Cyril Northcote Parkinson (1955), who worked in the British civil service and thus was intimately familiar with the ways in which large bureaucratic organizations functioned. Parkinson's law stated that work expands to fill whatever time is available for it to be completed. Thus, if a bureaucrat is assigned three reports to complete in a month, it will require a month's work to complete all three. If that same employee is assigned two reports during that time, it will take a month to complete two. And the task will still take a month even if the assignment calls for completing only one report.

iStock/SDI Productions

Another source of irrationality is that described by Robert Merton ([1949] 1968) as the **bureaucratic personality**, someone who follows the rules of the organization to such a great extent that the organization's ability to achieve its goals is subverted. For example, an admissions clerk in a hospital emergency department might require incoming patients to fill out so many forms that they do not get needed medical care promptly.

In these and many other ways, the actual functioning of bureaucracies is at variance with Weber's ideal-typical characterization.

The Informal Organization

A great deal of research in the twentieth century focused on the **informal organization**, that is, how the organization actually works as opposed to the way it is supposed to work as depicted, for example, in Weber's ideal-typical formal bureaucracy (Blau 1963). For instance, those who occupy offices lower in the bureaucratic hierarchy often have greater knowledge of and competence in specific issues than do those who rank above them. The secretaries in many organizations often know much more about the day-to-day workings of a place than their bosses. Thus, fellow employees may seek the advice of the lower-level bureaucrat rather than the one who ranks higher in the authority structure. The informal organization can help make up for inadequacies in the formal organization (Gulati and Puranam 2009). It might lead employees to take very useful actions that are ignored by the formal organization. For example, students constitute an informal network that offers advice about which faculty members to seek out if students are looking for undemanding courses or guaranteed high grades. Most generally, it is important *not* to examine informal and formal organizations in isolation from one another. Rather, the focus should be on the many linkages between them (McEvily, Soda, and Tortoriello 2014). Informal organizations often arise to deal with problems and failures in formal organizations, and formal organizations often change to take account of actions in informal organizations.

Employees sometimes do things that exceed what is expected of them by the organization. However, they more often do less, perhaps far less, than they are expected to do. For example, contrary to the dictates of the formal organization, the most important things that take place in an organization may never be put down in writing. Employees may find it simply too time-consuming to fill out every form or document they are supposed to use. Instead, and contrary to the organization's rules, they may handle many tasks orally so that if anything goes wrong, there is no damning evidence that could jeopardize careers and even the organization as a whole.

Although in some bureaucracies, power is meant to be dispersed throughout the offices, it often turns out that an organization becomes an **oligarchy**. That is, a small group of people at the top illegitimately obtain and exercise far more power than they are supposed to have. This can occur in any organization. Interestingly, this undemocratic process was first described by Robert Michels ([1915] 1962) in the most unlikely of organizations—labor unions and socialist parties that supposedly prized democracy. Michels called this "the iron law of oligarchy" (Martin 2015). Those in power manipulate the organization so that the leaders and their supporters can stay in power indefinitely. At the same time, they make it difficult for others to get or to keep power. Although oligarchy certainly develops in some organizations, in reality its occurrence is neither "iron" nor a law. That is, most organizations do not become oligarchical. Nevertheless, the tendency toward oligarchy is another important organizational process not anticipated by Weber's ideal-typical bureaucracy.

The problem for organizations (and individuals) is somewhat different in the digital age. Rather than too little information in writing, the danger is now that too much information is in written, at least typed, form, such as e-mail messages, posts on the internet, tweets, blogs, and the like. Of particular concern are posts that can exist forever and be widely and endlessly circulated. For example, there have been a number of news stories in recent years of high profile individuals being called out for tweets they made, sometimes many years ago. The ability to screenshot images of things online makes it even more difficult to ever erase something once it has been posted.

CONTEMPORARY ORGANIZATIONAL REALITIES

As the social world has changed, so too has sociological thinking about many things, including organizations. New concepts are supplementing the concept of bureaucracy to enrich our understanding of these new realities. These concepts include gendered, racialized, and network organizations and others that help inform our efforts to deal with organizational challenges such as **sexual harassment**, racial injustices, outsourcing of jobs, McDonaldization, and globalization.

Gender Inequalities

Weber's model does not account for discrimination within organizations. In the ideal bureaucracy, any worker with the necessary training can fill any job. However, as a lot of sociological research has shown, bureaucracies do not treat all workers the same. Jobs are often designed for an idealized worker—one who has no obligations except to the organization. Caretakers who carry a responsibility for child-rearing can have difficulty fitting this model. For example, women may face the "competing devotions" of motherhood and work (Wharton and Blair-Loy 2006). Organizations may also discriminate (consciously or unconsciously) in hiring and promotions, with white men (who tend to populate the higher levels of bureaucracies) being promoted over women and minorities. Some women in male-dominated business organizations find that they hit a "**glass ceiling**"—a certain level of authority in a company or organization beyond which they cannot rise (Gorman and Kmec 2009; Wasserman and Frenkel 2015). This is also true in other contexts, such as medicine and higher education (Hart 2016; Zhuge et al. 2011). Women can see the top—hence the "glass"—but cannot reach it. Within other organizations, particularly female-dominated ones, men can find themselves riding the "glass escalator" (Williams 1995). This is an invisible force that propels them past equally competent, or even more competent, women to positions of leadership and authority (Dill, Price-Glynn, and Rakovski 2016).

Although most of these ideas have been developed based on studies of organizations in the United States, they also apply globally. For example, a recent study found that the glass ceiling exists in Ho Chi Minh City, Vietnam (Khuong and Chi 2017). Figure 6.4 shows where women in industrialized nations have the best chance of circumventing the glass ceiling—that is, of being treated equally in the work world. Sweden is best for working women; South Korea is the worst. The United States ranks below the average of other industrialized countries.

FIGURE 6.4 ■ The Glass-Ceiling Index

The Glass-Ceiling Index
Environment for working women, 2020 or latest, 100 = best

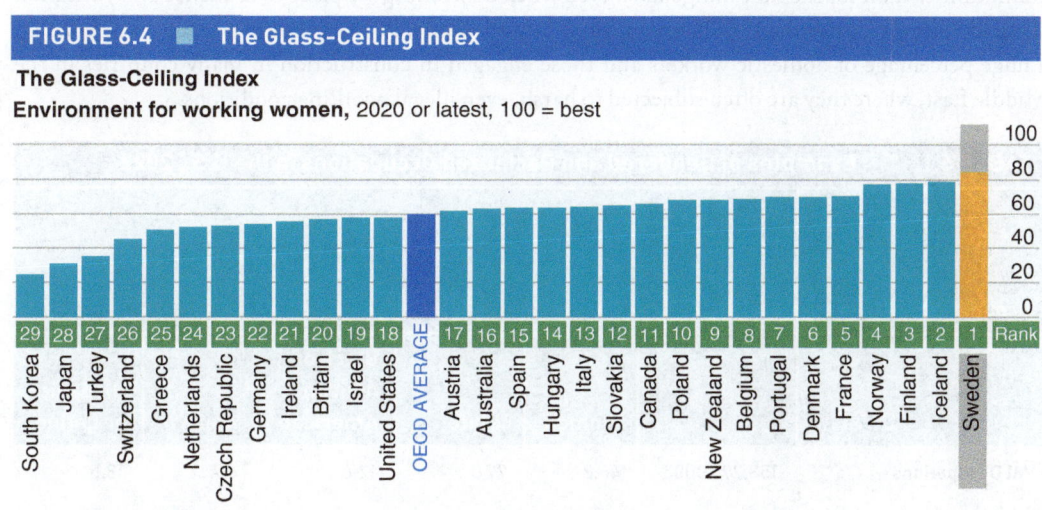

Source: The Economist (2021, March 4). Is the lot of female executives improving? Retrieved January 5, 2022, from https://www.economist.com/graphic-detail/2021/03/04/is-the-lot-of-female-executives-improving

A glass ceiling relates to vertical mobility—and its absence—for women in organizations. The "glass cage" deals with the horizontal segregation of women (and other minorities; Gabriel, Korczynski, and Rieder 2015; Kalev 2009). The idea here is that men and women doing the same or similar jobs operate in separate and segregated parts of the organization. As in the case of the glass ceiling, women can see what is going on in other cages, but, compared with men, they find it more difficult to move between the cages. Although the cage is made of glass, the skills and abilities of women tend to be less visible, and, as a result, stereotypes about them abound. In addition, women have less communication with those outside the cage, are less likely to learn about jobs available there, are not as likely to get high-profile assignments, and are less likely to get needed training. The situation confronting women would improve if there were more collaboration across the boundaries of the glass cage. Of course, the ultimate solution involves the elimination of the glass cage, as well as the glass ceiling.

The concept of the "glass cliff" describes what can happen to women who experience upward mobility when the organization is going through hard times (Peterson 2016; Ryan and Haslam 2005). The implication is that women who rise to high levels at such times end up in highly precarious positions. Of course, the same would be true of men, but Ryan and Haslam found that women are more likely than men to move into positions on boards of directors in organizations that have been performing badly. This means they are more likely than males to find themselves at the edge of that organizational cliff. A disproportionate number of those women (and minorities) are likely to be demoted or fall off that cliff (i.e., lose their jobs) and be replaced by males (Cook and Glass 2014).

Racialized Organizations

Many organizations are also racialized. One way of getting at this is by looking at the racial breakdown of certain professions. For example, in the United States, more than 50 percent of home health aides, security guards and gambling surveillance officers, and cooks identify as Black or African American or Hispanic or Latino (which, it is important to note, is not considered a mutually independent category on U.S. Census forms). Those who identify as Hispanic or Latino also make up more than 48 percent of maids, 49 percent of construction laborers, and 63 percent of roofers. Those who identify as Asian make up nearly 73 percent of manicurists and pedicurists. Meanwhile, more than 90 percent of facilities managers, 90 percent of construction managers, 95 percent of paramedics, and 98 percent of property appraisers and assessors identify as White (U.S. Bureau of Labor Statistics, 2023; see also Table 6.1). These kinds of racial divisions are common in most countries in the world. In Ecuador, for example, the odds of working in a skilled job are more than 70 percent lower for members of indigenous communities than for the non-indigenous, even when controlling for place of residence and education (United Nations Department of Economic and Social Affairs, 2017). Filipino workers also make up a huge percentage of domestic workers and those engaged in construction in many countries in the Middle East, where they are often subjected to harsh, even illegal, working conditions.

TABLE 6.1 ■ **Examples of Gendered and Racialized Occupations in the U.S., 2022**

Occupation	Total Employed, 16 Years and Over	Percentage of Total Employed				
		Women	White	Black or African American	Asian	Hispanic or Latino
All Occupations	158,291,000	46.8	77.0	12.6	6.7	18.5
Chief Executives	1,780,000	29.2	85.9	5.9	6.7	6.8
Human Resources Managers	295,000	72.9	81.5	12.0	4.0	11.6
Computer Programmers	457,000	22.1	69.5	5.5	21.4	8.0
Pharmacists	375,000	59.6	68.1	10.6	18.7	6.9
Dental Hygienists	217,000	96.3	91.4	2.5	5.6	12.7

Occupation	Total Employed, 16 Years and Over	Percentage of Total Employed				
		Women	White	Black or African American	Asian	Hispanic or Latino
Home Health Aides	617,000	86.7	52.5	32.5	11.1	28.9
Elementary and Middle School Teachers	3,336,000	79.7	82.5	11.1	3.9	11.2
Mental Health Counselors	195,000	74.9	82.4	14.9	1.1	10.6
Correctional Officers and Jailers	285,000	29.9	63.7	27.3	4.2	12.8
Police Officers	746,000	12.7	78.3			
Cooks	2,012,000	38.4	69.4	17.7	5.9	36.1
Roofers	208,000	5.0	87.7	6.9	0.0	66.5
Aircraft Pilots and Flight Engineers	187,000	9.2	95.7	2.6	1.6	9.7
Flight Attendants	116,000	69.9	78.4	11.1	6.5	12.5

Source: U.S. Bureau of Labor Statistics, 2023, Current Population Survey. https://www.bls.gov/cps/cpsaat11.htm

Note: Persons whose ethnicity is identified as Hispanic or Latino may be of any race.

Another dimension of racialized organizations can be found in discriminatory hiring practices. An experiment by Kline, Rose, and Walters (2022) sent out more than 83,000 applications to prospective employers in the United States. Among other findings, they found that, "distinctively Black names reduce the probability of employer contact by 2.1 percentage points relative to distinctively white names." Admittance to certain organizations is often limited, blatantly or covertly, by racial preference and discrimination.

Another example of racial profiling in order to gain admittance to an organization can be found in the college admission process. For example, the group Students for Fair Admissions brought a lawsuit against Harvard University claiming that their affirmative action admission policies benefitted Black and Hispanic applicants but, in doing so, disadvantage Asian applicants. They claim that the number of Asian students is being unfairly capped. As of 2022, the courts had upheld Harvard's admission policies; however, the case has since been argued before the Supreme Court and they are expected to issue a ruling on affirmative action by summer 2023.

Victor Ray (2019) has proposed a theory of racialized organizations. Ray's work is an attempt to bridge the gap between organizational scholars, who tend to see organizations as race-neutral bureaucratic structures, and race and ethnicity scholars, who have largely ignored the role of organizations in the social construction of race. To this end, Ray argues that organizations are racial structures and that race is constitutive of organizational foundations, hierarchies, and processes. Racialized organizations involve four tenets:

1. Racialized organizations enhance or diminish the agency of racial groups.
2. Racialized organizations legitimate the unequal distribution of resources.
3. Whiteness is a credential.
4. The decoupling of formal rules from organizational practice is often racialized.

In sum, organizations are not just racialized, they also produce, and reproduce, the social construction of race and various forms of racial inequality.

Other Issues

Beyond the problems associated with gendered and racialized organizations, the ideal-typical bureaucracy makes no provision for an array of other problems in the organization or for problematic organizations. However, in the real world there is no shortage of either. The most heinous example of a problematic (to put it mildly) organization is the Nazi bureaucracy responsible for the murder of more than 12 million people, including 6 million Jews, during the Holocaust (Bauman 1989). The Islamic State, al-Qaeda, the Mafia, and Mexican drug cartels, among many others, would also be considered by most people to be problematic organizations. In addition, many regard global organizations such as the International Monetary Fund and the World Bank as problematic because of the damaging austerity programs and other forms of "structural adjustment" they impose on recipient countries in exchange for monetary assistance and other help. These programs force countries to prioritize debt repayment over expenditure on health, education, and other social services.

Problems also occur in organizations that in themselves are not seen as problematic. For example, until recently the National Football League downplayed the health risks associated with concussions. Players are expected to engage in physical contact and take hard hits as part of their jobs, even if it means risking long-term physical and mental health complications. One of the most troublesome complications suffered by NFL players is chronic traumatic encephalopathy (CTE), a degenerative nerve condition that results from repeated blows to the head.

One of the largest organizations in the world, the Catholic Church, has had to address a global organizational culture that enabled priests and other church officials to perpetuate a system of sexual assaults and abuses against children. This culture has been a huge problem not only because of the behavior of the priests and its impact on children but also because church officials have not done nearly enough to dismiss those responsible and make it more difficult for such assaults to occur in the future. Pope Francis declared "we abandoned them" after a 2018 grand jury in Pennsylvania found that the Church had covered up the abuse perpetuated by some 300 priests on more than 1,000 minors in the past 70 years (Povoledo 2018). This problem and the difficulties involved in uncovering sexual assaults by priests, let alone dealing with them, constitute the central theme of *Spotlight*, the 2016 Academy Award winner for best motion picture.

Disasters (and other unplanned outcomes) are deeply problematic for organizations. Such events often occur as the result of rational organizational processes. For example, in the 1980s, the National Aeronautics and Space Administration (NASA) operated based on what it considered to be a highly reliable and rational plan. As a result, it focused on, among many other things, a variety of quantifiable factors to keep the space shuttle *Challenger* on schedule for its launch. In doing so, the agency cut a number of corners and engaged in various economies. These actions made sense from the perspective of NASA as a rationalized organization. However, they contributed to the disaster on January 28, 1986, in which *Challenger*'s fuel tank broke apart, causing the in-flight destruction of the shuttle and the deaths of seven crew members.

Similarly, initial reports on the crashes of two new Boeing 737 MAX airplanes in 2019 suggested that the underlying cause was a rush to get the plane in the air in order to compete with arch-rival Airbus. Boeing may have cut corners in providing, at no additional cost to the airlines, supplementary safety features. The training of pilots was limited, in part, because the airlines did not have flight simulators, or the pilots were not given access to them. However, the most immediate cause of the crashes appears to have been a malfunctioning automated system (Grondahl, Collins and Glanz, 2019).

Organizations have also faced a myriad of problems over the last several years as a result of the COVID-19 pandemic. As countries went into various periods of lockdown, often more than once, many organizations were brought to a standstill. The sudden shift to online teaching and learning, for example, left many colleges and universities scrambling to figure out how to continue operating (Ryan and Nanda 2022; Smith et. al. 2021). Most experts agree that the COVID-19 pandemic will not be the last global pandemic, so many organizations are now ensuring contingency plans will be in place if, or when, the next pandemic hits.

Tom Williams / Contributor / Getty Images

Contemporary Changes

In the last several decades, bureaucratic organizations have undergone a number of important changes that do not fit well with Weber's view of organizations. Indeed, the very notion, if not reality, of a bureaucracy in Weber's terms is not only changing rapidly but also in some cases disappearing completely. For one thing, contrary to Weber's thinking on the likelihood of the growth and spread of bureaucracy in organizations, many of the largest organizations, especially industrial organizations and labor unions, have been forced to downsize and, in the process, reduce the size of their bureaucracies dramatically (Hyman 2018). The idea that "bigger is better" is no longer the rule in most organizations. Instead of constantly adding new functions, and more employees, organizations are now likely to focus on their "core competencies." For example, the Ford Motor Company is no longer making (among many other things) the steel for the frames of its cars and the rubber for their tires. In addition, in 2018 Ford announced that it was in the process of phasing out, or even dropping, the production of conventional cars and was going to focus in the future on manufacturing the more profitable SUVs and trucks. GM announced a similar cutback a few months later.

In essence, organizations have come to concentrate on being "lean and mean" (Harrison 1994). They have also sought to streamline their systems of production—to develop lean methods of production using more automated and robotized systems and fewer employees (Janoski 2015). Many newer organizations, such as Facebook and even Google, have learned crucial lessons from the problems experienced by organizational giants such as Ford. They are smaller and far less hierarchical; they are increasingly flat structures with the characteristics of social networks discussed in Chapter 5. To adapt to a rapidly changing environment, contemporary organizations have also been forced to become more flexible and agile than the ideal-typical bureaucracy suggests. When today's organizations lack such flexibility, there is a strong likelihood that they will decline or disappear. For instance, the video store chain Blockbuster went bankrupt in 2010 (as of 2022, it had only one remaining store in Bend, Oregon, the subject of the Netflix documentary *The Last Blockbuster*) because it failed to adapt to competition from Netflix, which initially delivered its movies by mail. More important, it failed to anticipate the streaming of movies to one's television or computer (and now to both smart TVs and regular TVs connected through devices such as Roku). Customers are no longer willing to travel to a video store when they can stream movies from the comfort of their homes via a cable provider such as Comcast or online from Netflix, Disney+, Hulu, or Amazon.

Yet another important organizational development is the increasing trend toward **outsourcing**, or the transfer of activities once performed by one organization to another organization in exchange for money (Furneaux 2013; Ritzer and Lair 2007). Since the early 2000s, outsourcing has increased dramatically. For example, in the 1950s U.S. business service firms outsourced only 2 percent of cleaning and janitorial jobs, 3 percent of security jobs, and 4 percent of logistics jobs. By 2015 they outsourced 20 percent of logistics jobs, 25 percent of cleaning and janitorial jobs, and 35 percent of security jobs (Dorn, Schmiede, and Speltzer 2018). Hospitals are increasingly likely to outsource food preparation to outside contractors. Hospitals also often outsource the operation of their emergency rooms to businesses that employ people—including physicians ("hospitalists")—devoted to such work. All of this can adversely affect the functioning of hospitals and the well-being of patients, including an increase in hospital-based infections (Zuberi 2013). Local, state, and federal governments also outsource work to other organizations, especially private businesses.

A very different example of outsourcing that received a lot of negative publicity after the Iraq war was the U.S. government's farming out many military and paramilitary activities in Iraq to a company known as Blackwater. When the news media raised alarms over the company's involvement in unwarranted killings and use of unnecessary force, the company changed its name to Xe Services and later to the more benign-sounding Academi.

Another recent trend in organizations not anticipated by Weber's ideal-typical bureaucracy is that of turning over to clients some of the work formerly performed by officeholders. For example, we are increasingly filling out census forms on our own, thereby doing work that used to be done by census takers. We are scanning checks into our smartphones instead of handing them to tellers, reviewing restaurants and movies online rather than reading reviews by professional critics, and talking about our experiences with products or brands on social networking sites instead of passively accepting advertising messages from producers. More and more, we are scanning our own groceries; the first self-checkout machine was installed in the United States in 1992, and it is estimated that by 2026, more than 1.5 million such machines will be in use around the world. During 2020, and likely as a result of the COVID-19 pandemic, installation of self-checkout machines surged by 25 percent (Troy, 2021). The most recent changes are even eliminating the work performed by customers and clients and turning it over to "smart machines." For example, instead of requiring a person to unload a shopping cart and scan each product at checkout, at Amazon Go convenience stores, a smart machine scans the products in the shopping bag as the customer leaves the store and charges the total to the customer's credit card.

One form of offshore outsourcing that has become familiar to many U.S. consumers is customer service and product support provided by Indian call centers. Why are some employees in such centers encouraged to assume American identities?

Getty Images/GCShutter

Globalization

Most organizations of any significant size have become increasingly global. They are affected by numerous global realities and changes and in many cases have become global forces and players themselves. The global reach of McDonald's is well known. It has more than 39,000 restaurants in 119 countries throughout the world. However, in the fast-food industry, Yum! Brands (corporate parent of Pizza Hut, KFC, and others) is in slightly more countries—155—and has almost 16,000 more restaurants than McDonald's. Walmart is another American global powerhouse, with more than 11,000 stores in 24 countries. Other organizations with a presence in the United States have their roots elsewhere in the world. Examples include IKEA, based in Sweden, with more than 460 stores in 60 countries; H&M, an apparel retailer from Sweden; T-Mobile, a telecommunications company originating in Germany; HSBC, a financial services provider from Hong Kong and Shanghai; and Zara International, a fashion retailer, whose home base is in Spain (Ritzer 2021).

Globalization has also accelerated the transfer of work to organizations in other countries, known as **offshore outsourcing**. See Table 6.2 for a list of the world's top 20 outsourcing destinations. The top destination is India, where a large proportion of the population is fluent in English. This is important because the United States is the world leader in offshore outsourcing. Offshore outsourcing takes many forms, but the one we are probably most familiar with is the outsourcing of call center work. A call center is a centralized office that handles a large volume of telephone calls from people asking an organization for information and help. At first, many U.S. organizations outsourced such work to call centers in the United States. More recently, much of that work has been outsourced offshore because it can be done outside the United States much less expensively.

TABLE 6.2 ■ Most Attractive Locations for Global Outsourcing of Services, 2021

1	India
2	China
3	Malaysia
4	Indonesia
5	Vietnam
6	United States
7	Thailand
8	United Kingdom
9	Brazil
10	Philippines
12	Mexico
13	Estonia
14	Colombia
15	Egypt
16	Germany
17	Lithuania
18	Bulgaria
19	Russia
20	Peru

Source: A.T. Kearney, The 2021 Kearney Global Services Location Index. https://www.prnewswire.com/news-releases/kearney-releases-2021-global-services-location-index-301269526.html

Note: This index measures a country's attractiveness as a destination for outsourcing services based on four factors: financial attractiveness, people skills and availability, business environment, and digital resonance.

India is obviously a particularly attractive location for the outsourcing of call center work once performed in the United States. The pay of call center workers is much lower in India than it is in the United States, and many Indians speak excellent English. In fact, many call center workers outside the United States are expected to "pose as Americans" as part of their employment. In a strategy referred to as "national identity management," they adopt, among other things, American sounding names, accents, and hometowns (Poster 2007).

Recently there has been a backlash against offshore outsourcing. This has occurred in a number of European countries, but it has been especially strong in the United States. Former president Donald Trump railed against the fact that offshore outsourcing has caused loss of companies and the jobs they had provided. In addition, there was already a movement for *backsourcing*, or bringing businesses and jobs back into the countries that were not long ago eager to outsource them (Gylling et al. 2015). However, given the erosion and destruction of plants and equipment in those countries and the seeming paucity of workers willing to take low-wage, low-skill jobs, it remains to be seen how much backsourcing will actually occur in Europe and the United States.

McDonaldization and Bureaucratic Organizations

During the early twenty-first century, the fast-food restaurant can be seen as the best example of the ongoing process of rationalization first described by Weber (Ritzer 2021). Although the fast-food restaurant is a relatively new and important organizational development, it is continuous with the bureaucracy and its basic principles: efficiency, predictability, calculability, control, and the seemingly inevitable irrationalities of rationality. What, then, distinguishes McDonaldized fast-food restaurants from bureaucracies?

Many fast-food restaurants, as well as a variety of other businesses, are franchised (Dicke 1992; Grace and Palmer 2015). In a **franchise system**, a large business (such as McDonald's) sells various rights to franchisees, who control small, legally independent firms. The franchisees invest their own money, and much of the risk of failure falls on them rather than the big business that grants the franchise. In return for their investment, franchisees obtain the right to use, among many other things, the company name, its logo (e.g., the "Golden Arches"), its distinctive products, and its ways of operating. Although each franchise is independent, it "must conform to detailed standards of operation designed and enforced by the parent company" (Dicke 1992, 2–3). Thus, a franchise system combines a small business with a large bureaucratic system in which it exists and functions. Most important, the franchise must operate based on the same rational principles that characterize the large bureaucratic organization.

McDonaldization is therefore applicable to both large organizations and relatively small organizations, most of which are independent operations, not franchises. The principles of bureaucracy have tended to be applied to state governments and giant corporations such as IKEA and Walmart. Such bureaucracies still exist, although in many cases they are much smaller than they once were. The principles of McDonaldization can be applied not only to large corporations such as Starbucks but also to independent restaurants and all sorts of other small enterprises. In short, the model of the McDonaldized fast-food restaurant has much wider applicability than the bureaucratic model does. There are far more small enterprises throughout the world than there are state governments and large corporations.

McDonaldization is applicable to both consumption-oriented and production-oriented organizations. The bureaucratic model is most applicable, outside of government, to large production-oriented corporations. However, many societies, especially the United States and those in Western Europe, have moved away from a society dominated by work and production to one dominated by consumption. As a result, the large corporation involved in goods production has declined in importance, at least in some countries. In its place we have seen the rise of similarly large corporations, such as Walmart, IKEA, and Amazon, devoted to consumption. Although the corporate structures of these organizations remain highly bureaucratized, their real hearts lie in the numerous smaller outlets that constitute the sources of income and profit for the organizations. Thus, of greatest importance now is the McDonaldization of those outlets, not the bureaucratization of the larger organizations in which they exist.

The key point is that bureaucratization involves a kind of highly centralized rationality largely invisible to those who consume the goods and services produced by these organizations. However, McDonaldization is both local and highly visible to those who consume in settings such as fast-food restaurants. People have a lot of direct, person-to-person contact with those who work in McDonaldized settings. This means, among other things, that the fast-food restaurant—and, indeed, almost all McDonaldized systems in the realm of consumption—need to be much more "customer friendly" than does the traditional bureaucracy. Counter people are trained to smile and wish you a "nice day" (Leidner 1993). At Walmart there is even an employee—the greeter—whose sole task is to be warm and friendly to customers when they enter the store. Then there are those "smiley faces" that customers see throughout the store. Similarly, Mac computers maintain their physical presence through aesthetically pleasing Apple stores, which include "genius bars" staffed by friendly and knowledgeable workers who can answer questions in person and fix your laptop. In contrast, tax organizations have no full-time greeters or smiley faces. In fact, it is very difficult even to speak with a governmental tax agent on the phone.

Despite the spread of McDonaldization, some are speculating that it, like bureaucratization, has passed its peak. The online auction site eBay is considered by some to be a new model of organizational development in the contemporary world (Ahuvia and Izberk-Bilgin 2011). Unlike McDonaldization, the basic dimensions of eBayization include variety, unpredictability, and limited control. Millions of products are available on eBay (and Amazon.com) compared to only the few dozen offered at McDonald's. The predictable products of McDonald's are unlike the highly unpredictable products on eBay. Whereas eBay sellers interact directly with buyers of their products with little involvement from the eBay organization, McDonaldized systems exercise more widespread control. McDonald's may be fast, but eBay is vast. However, it is possible to argue that eBay is a highly McDonaldized company. For example, it takes a highly rationalized company and system to offer millions of products for sale.

Network Organizations

The bureaucracy and the fast-food restaurant both continue to be important in the early twenty-first century. However, organizations continue to change and evolve. Further, entirely new organizational forms are coming into existence. One such new form is the network organization. As discussed in more detail next, the **network organization** is defined by its networks, especially those based on and linked together by information (Blaschke, Schoeneborn, and Seidl 2012). The network organization came about in the wake of the revolution in informational technology in the 1970s. Developments included the penetration of television deep into everyday life and the introduction of home computers, smartphones, and the internet (Allan 2007; Van Dijk 2012). The network model is also inextricably entwined with globalization. Most of the important functions and processes in the information age are increasingly dominated by these networks, and many of them are global in scope. This revolution led, in turn, to a fundamental restructuring of the global capitalist system beginning in the 1980s. For example, multinational corporations grew in importance, in part because of great improvements in the ability to communicate globally. Those corporations that were narrowly nation-based experienced serious declines or were themselves transformed into multinationals.

Characteristics of the Network Organization

This new organizational form has several notable characteristics. Of greatest importance is the idea that an organization is composed of several **networks**, or "interconnected nodes" (see the discussion of social networks in Chapter 4). A network organization has the following characteristics:

- *Horizontal structure.* In contrast to the vertical and hierarchical structures that characterize classic bureaucracies, network organizations are flatter, meaning there are fewer positions between the top of the organization and the bottom.

- *Fuzzy boundaries.* Network organizations are *not* seen as distinct entities with clear and definite boundaries, as would be the case with a bureaucracy. Rather, organizations intertwine with one another in many ways. Most obviously, they form strategic alliances with other organizations that have similar or complementary goals.

- *Dispersed decision making.* Many of the differences between network organizations and bureaucracies stem from a number of highly successful Japanese innovations. One such innovation is more collective decision making, or the involvement of many more people in the organization in the decision-making process.

- *Flexible production.* Manufacturing organizations with a network model have moved away from mass production and toward more flexible production methods, such as variable and limited production runs.

An organization with these characteristics is, in comparison with a bureaucracy, more open, more capable of expansion, more dynamic, and better able to innovate without disrupting the system.

In the global information economy, at least in developed nations, the nature of work is being transformed. Workers, including manufacturing employees, are dealing more with information and less with material processes (Caprile and Serrano Pascual 2011). This has reduced the total number of employees needed, even as output increases. In addition, the network organization allows for new kinds of work arrangements because information can flow anywhere, especially anywhere there is a computer or smartphone and a stable internet connection. Thus, for example, more people can work from the comfort of their homes, in transit on airplanes, and in hotels anyplace in the world.

The COVID-19 pandemic further accelerated this transition as it became increasingly apparent, even if not by choice, just how much could be done from remote locations. Studies from the EU have shown that fewer than 5 percent of employees were already teleworking in 2018, and that fewer than 10 percent reported doing so even occasionally. Since the pandemic began, however, the fraction of teleworkable employment increased to an estimated 33–44 percent in all but five EU member countries (Sostero et. al. 2020). Studies of teleworkability in the United States have shown similar numbers: An estimated 37 percent of all jobs can be done at home, with the highest percentages in the categories of "computer and mathematical occupations" (100 percent), "education, training, and library occupations" (98 percent), and "legal occupations" (97 percent). Meanwhile, the sectors of "construction and extraction occupations," "food preparation and serving related occupations," and "building and grounds cleaning and maintenance occupations" all had a rating of 0 percent (Dingle and Neiman 2000). Findings have further shown that the 37 percent of occupations able to be done from home account for 46 percent of all the wages in the United States, and that those who cannot work from home tend to be lower-income, lack a college degree, be non-White, and lack health insurance. There are also significant regional variations. For example, more than 50 percent of jobs in San Jose or Washington, D.C. could be done from home, while fewer than 30 percent of jobs in Las Vegas or Scranton fit that category.

iStock Images/ake1150sb

Informationalism

The processing of knowledge, or what Manuel Castells (1996, 1997, 1998) famously calls **informationalism**, is a key feature of the network organization. Forces of production and consumption, such as factories and shopping malls, are linked through knowledge and information. Thus, for example, the stocking of shelves at Walmart is done nearly automatically. Computerized technology at the local Walmart tracks stock on hand and transmits the information to centralized warehouses. As the stock is being depleted, new shipments are sent out automatically, so that the shelves at the local Walmart will remain well stocked.

Informationalism has five basic characteristics:

- Technologies act on information, such as the depletion of stock at Walmart.
- These technologies have a pervasive effect, as information transmitted to personal computers, tablets, and smartphones increasingly becomes a part of all human activity.
- All organizations, and other systems, using information technologies are defined by a "networking logic" that allows them to affect a wide variety of processes and organizations to which they are linked. For example, Walmart has linkages to its many suppliers throughout the world.
- The new technologies are highly flexible, allowing them to adapt and change constantly.
- The specific technologies associated with information are already merging into a highly integrated system that cuts across many different organizations and areas of the world. Thus, for example, the internet, e-mail, and text messaging link innumerable global organizations.

As a result of informationalism, a new, increasingly profitable global information economy has emerged. The productivity of firms and nations depends on their ability to generate, process, and apply knowledge-based information efficiently. Global communication systems allow those involved in this economy to operate as a unit on a worldwide scale. Although it is a global system, there are regional differences, even among those areas—North America, the European Union, the Asia-Pacific region—at the heart of the new global economy (Matin 2015). Other regions, such as sub-Saharan Africa, have been marginalized or even largely excluded, as are pockets of deprivation in the developed world, including inner cities and small towns in more industrially advanced countries.

The network organization, as well as the informationalism that defines it, is the latest organizational form to draw sociologists' attention, but it will certainly not be the last. As the world begins to (hopefully) recover from the COVID-19 pandemic, sociologists will no doubt turn more of their attention to examining just how much the pandemic, and its associated lockdowns and forced changes to lifestyles, will have lasting effects (Ryan 2022).

SOCIETIES

Sociologists have traditionally defined **society** as a complex pattern of social relationships that persists over time. Although traditionally, societies have had physical geographic boundaries, the digital age has altered that requirement for what it means to be considered a society. All societies, however, have at least two key characteristics: First, they are abstract; second, this abstractness allows them to encompass a wide range of social relationships. Thus, in these terms, a triad (a three-person group) and any larger group would be a kind of society, as would individual countries, as well as global organizations such as the United Nations and the International Monetary Fund.

Ferdinand Tönnies ([1887] 1957) differentiated between two broad types of societies—*gemeinschaft* and *gesellschaft*. He labeled traditional societies **gemeinschaft societies** and defined them as being characterized by face-to-face relations. Tönnies considered families, rural villages, and small towns to be gemeinschaft societies. Such societies tend to be quite small because they are based on intimate interaction. Relationships between people are valued for their intrinsic qualities, such as familiarity and closeness and not, or at least not merely, for their utility. Gemeinschaft societies continue to exist in many parts of the world.

More modern societies are **gesellschaft societies**, characterized by impersonal, distant, and limited social relationships. In such societies, people tend to enter relationships for what they can gain from them rather than for their intrinsic qualities. That is, relationships are often a means to an end. Gesellschaft societies are much more likely to be large-scale societies, or to exist within them.

Of course, gemeinschaft and gesellschaft are ideal types. In the real world, including today's world, aspects of both exist in all societies. The abstract and broad-ranging definition of society mentioned previously encompasses both gemeinschaft and gesellschaft societies and everything in between. Furthermore, both concepts can be applied to every social relationship, from the smallest group, such as a dyad or triad, to the largest society, such as China.

Although the earlier general definition of society has its utility, *society* can be more narrowly and specifically—and usefully—defined as a relatively large population that has a social structure and shares a culture. The United States, China, and Spain would be societies in this macro-level sense of the term; a triad or group or organization would not be a society. This definition also fits the thrust of this chapter, which ends with a discussion of the most macroscopic level of social organization: the global society.

Sociologists who study societies often ask big questions about them and their changing nature. One of the most notable recent efforts to think about the issues facing society as a whole is the work of German sociologist Ulrich Beck. Until recently, it was the norm to think of society as being dominated by industry. In "industrial society," the key issue was wealth and how to distribute it more evenly. This problem continues to concern many sociologists (see Chapter 7). However, Beck ([1986] 1992) argues that we have moved from an industrial society to a **risk society**, where the central issue is risk, especially how to prevent, minimize, and channel it. In addition, although in an industrial society a central concern is equality, in a risk society the focus shifts to how to remain safe in the face of increasing risk. Most important, there is a big difference between the two types of societies in the ways in which solidarity is achieved. In an industrial society, solidarity is achieved by people joining together for the positive goal of creating a more equal society. In a risk society, solidarity is achieved through the largely negative and defensive goal of being spared from danger. The implication is that risk society is weaker, more individualized, and less laudable than industrial society and its humanitarian goal of increased equality.

What accounts for the emergence of risk society? The key is that the risks are far greater in scope today than ever before, and no society is safe from them; risks are increasingly global. The COVID-19 pandemic is the clearest recent example of a global risk. Many societies produce various risks (e.g., climate change, the danger from nuclear plants and weapons, a global economic meltdown such as the one that began in 2007 in the United States, and the Ebola epidemic that exploded in West Africa in 2014 and continues to this day), which threaten not only those societies themselves but others as well. Furthermore, even when risk is exported, consciously or unconsciously, to other societies, it tends to boomerang on the society that is the source of the risk. For example, terrorism is a risk to the United States and other societies. The United States has sought to cope with terrorism by combating it outside its own borders (e.g., in Afghanistan and Iraq). However, those efforts provoked attacks on the United States and its interests elsewhere in the world.

Globalization is the major reason why there are far greater risks to society than ever before. Risks in one society easily flow to many other societies. For example, because of relatively easy and inexpensive air travel, a disease outbreak, like COVID-19, in one society can quickly engulf many other societies. Likewise, plastic waste from numerous countries has collected in the North Pacific Ocean, resulting in a vortex of trash called the Great Pacific Garbage Patch, which threatens marine life and even human health. Thus, modern risks are not easily restricted to one locale or society. A nuclear accident, such as the one that occurred at Chernobyl in Ukraine (then part of the Soviet Union) in 1986, can release radiation that affects surrounding societies and, ultimately, much of the world (see Figure 6.5). Modern risks are also not limited by time. The Chernobyl accident led to genetic defects in Ukrainians and those living in neighboring societies for decades afterward.

Globalization has led some sociologists to call into question the equation of society and the nation-state, arguing that in the contemporary world it is necessary to think about a global society. Debates about the possibility of global citizenship are one example of how the idea of globalization is reshaping how we

FIGURE 6.5 ■ Radiation from Chernobyl Following the 1986 Accident

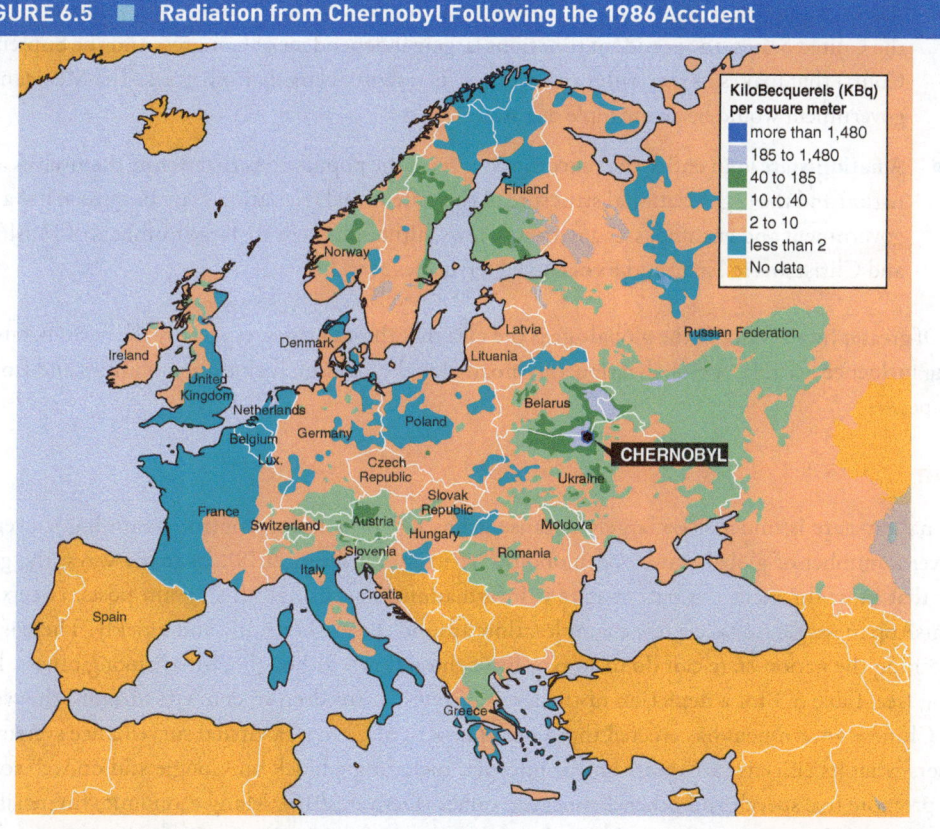

Sources: UNEP/GRID-Arendal, European Environment Agency; AMAP Assessment Report: Arctic Pollution Issues, Arctic Monitoring and Assessment Programme (AMAP), 1998, Oslo; European Monitoring and Evaluation Programme (MEP); Co-operative programme for monitoring and evaluation of the long-range transmission of air pollutants in Europe, 1999. Adapted from Le Monde Diplomatique, July 2000.

think about the boundaries of what we call society (Tully 2014). Other sociologists have suggested that globalization requires an interpretation of society as more fluid and unstable than would be implied by the work of earlier sociologists. Thus, Zygmunt Bauman contends that we live in "liquid times," when structures and institutions no longer "keep their shape for long" (2007, 1). John Urry (2000) has gone further and written about a sociology that goes beyond a focus on societies. He argues that because of all sorts of increased mobilities, we live in a post-societal era. People, objects, and information, among many other things, move too often and too quickly to be encapsulated in societies or, perhaps, anything else.

It is clear from the preceding discussion that sociologists who still analyze societies do not stop at their borders but also examine various mobilities within, among, and between societies. As a result, the focus of such scholarship in recent years has shifted beyond societies and even their interrelationships to the even more macro global level and the mobilities (e.g., migration) that serve to define it.

GLOBAL RELATIONSHIPS

Most sociological work on the global level operates with a different set of concepts from those discussed throughout this chapter. All of these concepts are consistent with the macro sense of society.

- A **nation** is a large group of people linked through common descent, culture, language, or territory. Nations can exist in contiguous geographic areas, regardless of country borders. For example, the Kurds have often been in the news as they have battled the Islamic State in a struggle to survive. In 2017 they were publicly enlisted and armed by the United States in the fight against IS. They live in Kurdistan, a region that overlaps Iraq, Iran, Syria, and Turkey. Nations can also be spread throughout much of the world, such as the Roma people (so-called Gypsies), who live throughout Europe and elsewhere.

- A **state** is a political organizational structure with relatively autonomous officeholders (e.g., in the United States, the president functions largely independent of Congress and the Supreme Court) that makes its own rules and receives its resources largely from taxes. The Mexican government would be an example of a state.

- A **nation-state** is an entity that encompasses both the populations that define themselves as a nation and the organizational structure of the state. Israel is a nation-state because it has a state government and encompasses a nation of Jews (although there are large numbers of Muslims and Christians in Israel and its occupied territories as well).

Of greater importance in the global age is the idea that these entities, especially the nation-state, are losing influence because of globalization and broad global processes, including mobilities and flows of all types.

Controlling Global Flows and Mobilities

The nation-state is under siege largely because it has lost or is losing control (assuming it ever had it) over a number of global flows and mobilities (Ritzer and Dean 2019). In many ways, the global flow that most threatens the nation-state is informationalism. E-mail, Instagram posts, tweets, and WhatsApp messages, to take a few examples, flow around the world readily and quickly. There is little or nothing the nation-state can do to stop or limit those flows, although China, among others, keeps trying (see Table 6.3 for a depiction of the levels of internet freedom in countries around the world). The Chinese government has erected the "Great Firewall of China," a virtual surveillance system that censors what its citizens can access on the internet, including a block on Google and on web sources that promote free speech and other democratic values (Denyer 2016). Many economic, financial, and technological flows around the world involve information of various kinds. Global information flows have the potential to subvert the authority of nation-states because they cover a much larger geographic area than the nation-state. This is especially true of information that would cast a negative light on the nation-state. One example would be the distribution of information throughout Russia about the great inequality that exists there and Russia's human rights abuses, including the invasion of Ukraine.

TABLE 6.3 ■ Freedom on the Internet 2022

Most Internet Freedom: 10 Highest-Ranked Countries			Least Internet Freedom: 10 Lowest-Ranked Countries		
Rank	Country	Score	Rank	Country	Score
1	Iceland	95	61	Ethiopia	27
2	Estonia	93	62	Egypt	27
3	Costa Rica	88	63	Pakistan	26
4	Canada	87	64	Saudi Arabia	24
5	United Kingdom	79	65	Russia	23
6	Taiwan	79	66	Vietnam	22
7	Georgia	78	67	Cuba	20
8	Japan	77	68	Iran	16
9	Germany	77	69	Myanmar	12
10	United States	76	70	China	10

Based on available data for 70 countries. A higher score indicates greater internet freedom. Factors considered include obstacles to access, limits on content, and violation of users' rights.

Source: Freedom House, Freedom on the Net 2022. FOTN_2022_Country_Score_Data.xlsx (live.com)

A more specific example of the decreasing ability of nation-states to isolate themselves from global processes is the health crisis represented by the COVID-19 pandemic. Although the first case of the SARS-CoV-2 virus was reported in China, it quickly spread around the world. Despite the best efforts of countries to isolate themselves, especially island nations, the virus has now been reported in every country (except Turkmenistan, although few global health experts believe the government reports). This rapid spread of the SARS-CoV-2 virus illustrates the importance and power of global flows and demonstrates the inability of the nation-state to do much, if anything, to limit their impact within its borders on its economy and the lives of its citizens.

The flow of diseases is just one of the many global flows that nation-states cannot control. Among the others are flows of undocumented immigrants, new social movements, expertise in various domains, terrorists, criminals, drugs, money (including laundered money and other financial instruments), and human trafficking. Then there are global problems associated with the effects of climate change that flow around the world readily and cannot be handled very well by a nation-state operating on its own.

Thus, the largest unit of analysis in sociology has now become the globe, especially the global flows that best define globalization today. The concept of globalization appears throughout this book in an informal sense, but it is now time for a formal definition of **globalization:** "a transplanetary *process* or set of *processes* involving increasing *liquidity* and the growing multidirectional *flows* of people, objects, places, and information as well as the *structures* they encounter and create that are *barriers* to, or *expedite*, those flows" (Ritzer and Dean 2019, 2 [emphasis in original]; see also Chapter 14). Clearly, this view goes beyond the nation-state and sees it as enmeshed in and subordinated to a global set of flows, mobilities, and structures.

Other Global Flows

Globalization is increasingly characterized by great flows of not just information, ideas, and images but also objects and people. For example, food now flows more quickly and to more people around the world (Inglis 2016). Examples of foods sold in locales far from their sources include fresh fruit from Chile, fresh sushi from Japan, and live lobsters from Maine. Looking at a very different kind of flow, migration within countries and from one country to another has become more common, at least as of now.

Landscapes

Although global flows and globalization contribute to some degree of homogenization of the social experience around the world, they also contribute to greater global cultural diversity and heterogeneity. An important contribution to thinking on the latter aspects of global flows is Arjun Appadurai's (1996) work on what he calls **landscapes**—*scapes* for short. These are fluid, irregular, and variable global flows that produce different results throughout the world. As described next, these scapes can involve the flow of many different things, including people and ideas. At the heart of Appadurai's thinking are five types of landscapes that operate independent of one another to some degree and may even conflict with one another.

- **Ethnoscapes** allow the movement, or fantasies about movement, of various individuals and groups, such as tourists and refugees. The ethnoscape of undocumented immigrants is of particular concern these days. They are often poor people who have in the main been forced to move because of poverty and poor job prospects in their home countries. They have also moved because of the belief, sometimes the fantasy, that economic conditions will be better for them elsewhere in the world, especially in countries like the United States or those in western Europe.

- **Technoscapes** include mechanical technologies such as the containerized ships now used to transport freight, informational technologies such as the internet, and the materials (e.g., refrigerators and e-mail) that move so quickly and freely throughout the world via those technologies.

- **Financescapes** use various financial instruments to allow huge sums of money and other items of economic value (e.g., stocks, bonds, bitcoin, and precious metals, especially gold) to move through nations and around the world at great speed, almost instantaneously. The global economic meltdown as a result of the COVID-19 pandemic demonstrated quite clearly the importance and the power of financescapes in the contemporary world.

- **Mediascapes** include both the electronic capability to produce and transmit information around the world and the images of the world these media create and disseminate. Those who write blogs and download photos (e.g., on Tumblr) and videos (e.g., on YouTube), global filmmakers and film distributors, global TV networks (e.g., CNN, Telemundo, and Al Jazeera), and even old-fashioned newspapers and magazines create a variety of mediascapes.

- **Ideoscapes**, like mediascapes, include images, although they are largely restricted to political images in line with the ideologies of nation-states. Also included here are images and counterideologies produced by social movements oriented toward supplanting those in power or at least gaining a portion of that power.

Further increasing the global heterogeneity that results from the interaction of these landscapes is the fact that the impact of one can be at variance, or even in conflict, with another. In addition, these landscapes are interpreted differently by people and groups in different parts of the world. Interpretations depend on both the cultures in which people live and the people's own subjective perspectives on the scapes. Powerful forces create at least some of these scapes. Nonetheless, those who merely live in or pass through them have the power not only to redefine them in idiosyncratic ways but also ultimately to subvert them in many different ways. For example, those on a guided tour designed to show a given locale in a positive light can break off from the tour and see and hear things that lead to a very different impression of the locale. When the tourists return home, they can portray that locale in a way that contradicts the image presented by the tour creators and guides.

Digital Living: Digital Currency

One relatively recent addition to the global financescape is cryptocurrency, the most popular example of which is Bitcoin (others include Ethereum and Dogecoin). A cryptocurrency is a universal currency that can be used in all countries, so, for example, a Bitcoin user does not need to exchange it for local currencies when they cross national borders (Popper 2015). Bitcoin was created in 2008; since then, more than 85 million Bitcoin accounts ("wallets") have been opened around the world. Unlike national currencies created by central banks and controlled by national governments, Bitcoin is decentralized and overseen by volunteers, who authenticate encrypted electronic signatures on transactions (Kharif 2014; Popper 2015). Bitcoins can be accrued through extensive data mining or purchased on Bitcoin currency exchanges. These online exchanges require consumers to open an account and create a digital wallet. They can then transfer money into the digital wallet, buy and sell bitcoins, and purchase products and services from individuals and companies that accept bitcoins (e.g., PayPal, Whole Foods, Starbucks, or Home Depot). Bitcoin ATMs allow users to deposit cash into their digital wallets at physical locations in their communities. Concern exists, however, over the actual value of a bitcoin and whether this digital currency will crash eventually. In general, cryptocurrencies have been highly volatile, often moving 10 percent or more in value in either direction in a single day.

Libertarians and anarchists were early supporters of Bitcoin because of its decentralized organizational structure and the lack of government regulations for its use (Kharif 2014). Because of the digital nature of bitcoins, they are easy to transfer and difficult to trace, especially their sources and destinations, which remain anonymous. Thus, they are favored by those involved in criminal activities, as well as by those active in the dark web, where cyberpunks challenge the dominance of large global financial institutions (Popper 2015). Criminals appreciate the anonymity of bitcoins because they can use them to buy and sell illegal goods and services on websites on the dark web. The utility of bitcoins for criminals has been manifest most dramatically (so far) in a range of cyberattacks where computers have been attacked by "ransomware" and owners were instructed to pay a ransom in bitcoin.

Steps have been taken to deal with Bitcoin's association with criminality. For example, in 2018 Goldman Sachs, the establishment financial organization, set up the first Bitcoin trading desk on Wall Street (Popper 2018). And some are suggesting the U.S. government create its own Bitcoin, perhaps called "Fedcoin," to rival Bitcoin (Irwin 2018).

In spite of its volatility, Bitcoin has begun to move into the mainstream. Parents are using the digital currency to pay babysitters or distribute allowances to their children (Kharif 2014). It is a quick and convenient way to electronically transfer money to a friend in another country without having to wait for a bank to open or a personal check to clear. Many mass retailers and big-box stores, such as Home Depot, also now accept bitcoins.

Bitcoin ATMs, like this one, allow users to exchange their currency for the digital money.
Ethan Miller/Staff

Global Barriers

The globe and the flows that increasingly pervade it are of central concern to sociology. However, there is another aspect of globalization of growing concern to sociology—the various global barriers to these flows (Bremmer 2018). The world is made up of not just a series of flows but also structures such as trade agreements, regulatory agencies, borders, customs barriers, and standards. Any thoroughgoing account of globalization needs to look at the ways in which structures alter and even block flows as well as how they produce and enhance flows. In other words, there is interplay between flows and structures, especially between flows and the structures created in attempts to inhibit or stop them (Shamir 2005).

As mentioned previously, the most important and obvious barriers to global flows are those constructed by nation-states. There are borders, gates, guards, passport controls, customs agents, health inspectors, trade regulations, and so on in most countries in the world. The wide range of travel restrictions put in place during the COVID-19 pandemic made these barriers to movement particularly well known to many. Although undocumented immigrants, contraband goods, and digitized messages do get through those barriers, some other phenomena that nation-states deem counter to their national interests are successfully blocked or impeded. For example, in 2016 the U.S. government prevented Philips from selling the majority stake of its lighting business, Lumileds, to Asian buyers for "security reasons" (Sterling 2016). Congress also cited U.S. national security as a reason why the federal government should block the acquisition of the Chicago Stock Exchange by a Chinese company (Rogin 2016). Some have noted that as nations focus more on nationalism and militarism, their openness to international trade and other formalized flows across borders decreases (Acemoglu and Yared 2010). This was perhaps nowhere clearer than during Donald Trump's presidency. He adopted nationalistic and militaristic positions to argue for greater barriers to international trade, a ban on immigrants from certain Muslim countries, and the mass deportation of millions of undocumented immigrants, to say nothing of the idea of building a wall between the United States and Mexico (even though this never happened to any real degree).

Are Global Barriers Effective?

Many of the barriers created by nation-states are not effective. For instance, the wall already constructed between Mexico and the United States, combined with the use of cameras, lights, satellites, and drones, has not been able to curtail dramatically the flow of undocumented immigrants into the United States. It has become more difficult, costly, and dangerous to enter the country illegally, but the wall, really more a fence in many places, has not stopped such entry. Moreover, the fence has had the unintended consequence of making it harder for Mexican nationals who are already in the United States illegally to move back to Mexico. The fence between Spain's African enclave—Melilla—and Morocco has not stopped some migrants, who have scaled it to gain entry to Spain and thereby to the EU (Associated Press 2014). Similarly, it is not clear whether the wall between Israel and the West Bank or between Israel and Egypt will stop the flow of individuals into, or out of, Israel. On the positive side, the wall is not stopping Palestinians and Israelis from communicating person to person via digital media.

In the European Union (EU), until recently, barriers to movement between member countries had been greatly reduced, if not eliminated. The EU created a structure that allowed people and products to move much more freely and quickly. However, that has changed recently, as a reaction against what were perceived to be the excesses of such openness (large numbers of refugees entering a country) gained force. For example, a number of EU countries (e.g., Hungary, Bulgaria, Slovenia) began building fences in an effort to keep out refugees (Lyman 2015a, 2015b). The COVID-19 pandemic has put the effectiveness of global barriers squarely into the spotlight. On the one hand, travel restrictions and lockdown measures meant that international travel dropped dramatically. In that sense, the lack of means (airplanes, trains, open borders) and the lack of possibility (tighter controls at entry points) showed one way in which global barriers work in limiting the movement of people. On the other hand, the resulting poor economic conditions as a result of the pandemic meant that in some contexts even more people were trying to cross borders in search of new opportunities. For example, the attempted, and successful, flow of migrants from Africa to Europe increased dramatically, especially those attempting to enter via the Canary Islands, which are a part of Spain but located just over 60 miles off the Western coast of Morocco.

Globalization involves a dialectic of flows and barriers to those flows. Although the barriers seem to be in ascent at the moment, it is likely that the flows will continue and find ways of breaching the new barriers.

Organizational Barriers

There are many kinds of organizations that, though they may expedite flows for some, create all sorts of barriers for others. One example is found in the two-tier system of passport control at international airports, where citizens usually pass through quickly and easily, while foreigners more often wait in long lines. Another example is the protectionist tariff systems that nation-states create to help their own farms send agricultural products (such as wheat) and to help their own manufacturers send goods (such as automobiles) across the borders of other nation-states while inhibiting the inflow of goods from their foreign competition (Bradsher and Russell 2017).

Multinational corporations usually use market competition rather than trade policies to achieve global success. Toyota, for instance, is devoted to optimizing the flow of its automobiles to all possible markets throughout the world. It also seeks to compete with and outperform other multinational corporations in the automobile business. If it is successful, the flow of automobiles from competing corporations is greatly reduced, further advantaging Toyota.

Labor unions are also organizations devoted to promoting the flow of some things while working against the flow of others (Geoghegan 2016). Unions often oppose, for example, the flow of undocumented immigrants because such immigrants are more likely to work for lower pay and fewer benefits (e.g., health insurance) than are indigenous, unionized workers. Similarly, labor unions oppose the flow of goods produced in nonunion shops, in other countries as well as their own. They do so because the success of nonunion shops puts downward pressure on wages and benefits. Unions also tend to oppose free trade agreements such as the now defunct Trans Pacific Partnership (TPP) and the North American Free Trade Agreement (NAFTA). The latter was replaced in late 2018 by the United States-Mexico-Canada Agreement because of the belief that jobs were being lost to Mexico because of its lower wages (Kaufman 2016). Unions have a complex and complicated relationship with global flows and barriers.

More Open Organizations?

Organizations of many types that seek to control global flows are facing increasing competition from organizations that are becoming more fluid and open. The best-known computer operating systems are produced by Microsoft (e.g., Windows 10). They cost a great deal and are closed. Only those who work for the company can, at least legally, work on and modify them. In contrast, IBM, a traditional closed organization, has embraced Linux, a free computer operating system that welcomes changes contributed by anyone in the world with the necessary skills to do so. IBM has also opened up more and more of its own operations to outside inputs. Another example is Apple, which has traditionally kept its Macintosh operating system closed but is now allowing outsiders to produce applications for its iPhone and iPad. Many other manufacturers of smartphones have followed suit. The free online encyclopedia Wikipedia, and wikis more generally, encourage virtually anyone, anywhere in the world, to contribute. In contrast, traditional and costly dictionaries such as *Merriam-Webster's Collegiate Dictionary* and reference works such as *Encyclopedia Britannica* and *The Blackwell Encyclopedia of Sociology* (Ritzer 2007; Ritzer, Rojek, and Ryan forthcoming) are closed to contributions from anyone other than selected and invited experts.

Even with the new open systems, structural realities help some and hinder others. For example, to contribute to Linux or Wikipedia, one must have a computer, computer expertise, and access—preferably high-speed access—to the internet. Clearly, those without economic advantages or access to high speed digital technologies are on the other side of the "digital divide" and do not have access to the tools required for making such contributions. As a result, they are unable to contribute to, or to gain from, open systems to the same degree that those in more advantaged positions can. The fact that women are less likely than men to contribute to Wikipedia suggests additional social factors to be considered here as well (Cohen 2011). Indeed, it is argued that women experience—and need to break through—a glass ceiling (see the previous discussion in this chapter) to contribute to Wikipedia (Jemielniak 2016). Thus, despite the new openness, most organizations and systems remain closed to various flows. These barriers usually benefit some (elites, males) and disadvantage others (the poor, females).

SUMMARY

Much sociological work on organizations is based on Max Weber's model of bureaucracy. However, one criticism of this model is that bureaucracies are not as highly rational as Weber believed them to be. The informal organization refers to how organizations actually work as opposed to how they are intended to function. Although bureaucratic power is supposed to be evenly dispersed, this is not always the case. For example, an oligarchy might develop if a small group of people at the top of an organization illegitimately obtain and exercise more power than they should.

Contemporary organizations face several challenges. Women often encounter a glass ceiling as a result of gender discrimination, which prevents them from achieving vertical mobility. Workers have to contend with outsourcing when corporations transfer their jobs to other countries. A new type of organization, the network organization, is emerging that is based on information and is more open and flexible than bureaucracies are.

Two ideal-typical societies exist—gemeinschaft and gesellschaft societies. Gemeinschaft societies are characterized by face-to-face relationships, while gesellschaft societies are more impersonal and distant. Today, most of us in the Global North live in a risk society, where we are focused on trying to stay safe, as opposed to an industrial society, where individuals are more concerned about wealth distribution.

A key structure in global analysis is the nation-state, which is composed of a population that defines itself as a nation and the organizational structure of a state. The nation-state as a form of social organization is under siege because of global flows over which it has little control. Consequently, sociologists are coming to focus more attention on global relationships and global flows. For example, Arjun Appadurai focuses on five types of fluid global landscapes. Barriers to global flows include nation-states and labor unions.

KEY TERMS

authority
bounded rationality
bureaucracy
bureaucratic personality
charismatic authority
domination
ethnoscapes
financescapes
franchise system
gemeinschaft societies
gesellschaft societies
glass ceiling
globalization
ideal type
ideoscapes
informal organization
informationalism
irrationality of rationality

landscapes (scapes)
mediascapes
nation
nation-state
network organization
networks
offshore outsourcing
oligarchy
organizations
outsourcing
rational-legal authority
risk society
sexual harassment
society
state
technoscapes
traditional authority

REVIEW QUESTIONS

1. What are the characteristics of the ideal-typical bureaucracy? What are some of the ways in which the ideal-typical bureaucracy is unrealistic?

2. Those who occupy offices lower in the bureaucratic hierarchy often have greater knowledge and competence than those who rank above them. What does this suggest about the ideal-typical bureaucracy? Can you think of examples from your own experiences when this has been the case?

3. According to Weber, what are the three types of legitimate authority? How is rational-legal authority related to Weber's concept of bureaucracy?

4. Over the last several decades, what changes have bureaucratic organizations undergone? How are these changes reflective of increasing globalization?

5. What is informationalism, and how has it affected the global economy? How is the emergence of informationalism related to the development of new communication technologies, such as the internet, social networking sites, and smartphones?

6. How has the process of globalization threatened the nation-state? What sorts of barriers have nation-states developed to limit global flows? What sorts of flows have nation-states been unable to limit?

7. In what ways has globalization created a shift from a world dominated by places to one dominated by flows? What have been the benefits and disadvantages of this shift?

8. Discuss each of Appadurai's landscapes, with special focus on the disjunctures among and between them (including examples). What are the implications of these disjunctures for the process of globalization?

9. How are network organizations different from classic bureaucracies? What are the main characteristics of networks?

10. How are open-source technologies reflective of a more fluid and open world? What structural barriers have transnational corporations created to limit these open-source technologies? What do you think is going to be the direction of the future? Why?

PAUL RATJE/AFP/Getty Images

7 DEVIANCE AND CRIME

> **LEARNING OBJECTIVES**
>
> **7.1** Define deviance.
>
> **7.2** Describe explanatory and constructionist approaches to theorizing about deviance.
>
> **7.3** Discuss the criminal justice system and different types of crimes.
>
> **7.4** Summarize the relationship between globalization and crime.

NORMS, LABELS, AND JUDGMENT

When he was first running for president in 2016, Donald Trump labeled immigrants entering the United States from and through Mexico as criminals. He said, "They're bringing drugs. They're bringing crime. They're rapists." As a result, he announced the need to build a wall between Mexico and the United States. Such views and plans contributed much to the support for Trump's campaign and to his eventual victory in the presidential election.

In the early days of Trump's administration, he initiated steps to keep immigrants, especially those who are undocumented, from entering the United States from Mexico. However, by the end of his term in January 2021, the wall had still not been completed. Trump even ceased his oft-repeated claim during the election that Mexico would pay for the wall. (Needless to say, Mexico never agreed to pay for the wall. Taking to Twitter, former Mexican president Vicente Fox responded repeatedly to Trump, stating, "Mexico has spoken; we will never ever pay for the #F******Wall.")

Do the data actually demonstrate the need for a wall and such an enormous expenditure? Are immigrants more likely to commit serious crimes? No. Rather, the data show that immigrants are *less* likely to commit the kinds of crimes that result in a prison sentence. More specifically, census data from 1980 to 2010 show that for men aged 18 to 49, immigrants were only somewhere between one-fifth to one-half as likely to be in prison as those born in the United States. In addition, among those incarcerated in federal and state prisons, a smaller percentage of them are noncitizens than are represented in the population as a whole. Further, although undocumented immigrants had crime rates higher than those of immigrants who had entered the United States legally, even they had lower crime rates than did U.S. citizens. In fact, communities with large numbers of immigrants are safer than most other communities.

This demonstrates a key point in the sociology of crime: Criminalization is not always based on the facts, and it does not occur of its own accord. Some interest group—or an authority figure, in the case of the proposed wall on the U.S.-Mexico border—must seek to have a type of action or a group of people criminalized. This is a political decision, and it is linked to the desire on the part of one powerful group—or its leader—to exert social control over another group.

This chapter deals with two closely related social phenomena: deviance and crime (Atkinson 2014; Downes, Rock, and McLaughlin 2016; Forsyth and Copes 2014; Goode and Thio 2007). Most forms of deviance—for example, having full-face tattoos—are not crimes. However, all crimes—theft, murder, rape—are forms of deviance. To become a crime, a form of deviance must be negatively sanctioned by the legal system, a process known as **criminalization** (Hillyard 2007; Jenness 2004; Muniz 2014).

DEVIANCE

Deviance is any action, belief, or human characteristic that is considered to be a violation of group norms by a large number of members of a society or a social group and for which the violator is likely to be censured or punished (Ben-Yehuda 2019). But what exactly is deviance, and where is the line between deviance and nondeviance? Without giving it much thought, many people would likely express the absolutist view that certain things are deviant in all places, for all groups, and at all times. However, from a sociological perspective, no act, belief, or human characteristic is inherently deviant. Thus, even genocide, although morally reprehensible and indefensible, has not been defined as deviance in some societies and at certain points in time (such as in Nazi Germany). Therefore, to the sociologist, deviance is socially defined.

If a powerful interest group wants to have a form of behavior defined as deviant, it is likely to be so defined. At the same time, powerful interest groups are likely to use their power to resist the efforts of others to define the powerful group's behaviors as deviant (McCaghy et al. 2016). For example, in the wake of the collapse of the home mortgage market in 2008, bankers fought, largely successfully, against being seen as deviant and even as criminal for their fraudulent predatory loan policies (Braithwaite 2010). However, borrowers who lied about their financial situation were less successful in avoiding being seen as deviant, and they suffered far greater negative consequences (Nguyen and Pontell 2011). They were likely to lose their homes, often their jobs, and sometimes even their health. Those interest groups that have social, political, legal, and/or financial power have a great deal of influence over who is (or is not) defined as deviant and who suffers the negative consequences of such a definition.

Shifting Definitions of Deviance

In addition to being influenced by power relationships, what is thought to be deviant varies from one time period to another, from one geographic location to another, from one group to another, and from one context to another. For example, having a tattoo used to be seen as a stigmatizing form of deviance in the United States, but for many it now seems normal, even common, or at least far less stigmatized (Larsen, Patterson, and Markham 2014). Indeed, in 2020, roughly 30 percent of people in the US (roughly 95 million people) have tattoos themselves (up from roughly 21 percent in 2009). In the public realm, we accept the sight of athletes—especially professional basketball players—covered with tattoos. Once associated with the working class and men in the military, tattoos have become much more common today throughout society. Once restricted largely to men, tattoos are more and more popular today with women as well. Some women, such as Kat Von D, have also gained fame as tattoo artists, a historically male dominated occupation. And tattoo parlors, once limited to the marginal areas of town, are now found on Main Street, as well as in the local shopping mall, perhaps next to the maternity shop or the toy store.

Tattoos, once rare and seen a stigmatizing form of deviance, have become common across many groups in society.
MathewHayward/iStockPhoto

As another example of the movement from deviance to normality, consider U.S. attitudes toward premarital sex (Regnerus and Uecker 2011). Just a few decades ago, a leading textbook on the subject of deviance devoted a chapter to "premarital sex" (Bell 1971). Today, premarital sex is so common and widely accepted (or at least tolerated) that it is considered normal in most groups (Barber 2017). In fact, it is now often the case that *not* having premarital sex, or being a "late bloomer" sexually, can be stigmatizing (Wesselmann, Webster, and Garcia 2016).

"Hooking up"—engaging in "something sexual" outside of committed romantic relationships—is common among teens and twentysomethings today, but it was considered deviant behavior by earlier generations (even if they also did it; Gesselman et al. 2018; Reay 2014; Wade 2017). Much the same can be said about cohabitation before marriage (see Chapter 11): It once was defined as "living in sin," but today the pendulum has swung entirely in the other direction, to the point where many people might consider couples who do *not* live together before marriage to be deviant. In other words, cohabitation has become normative, and for some it occurs instead of, or at least before, marriage (Kitchener 2018; Kuo and Raley 2016).

Sexual relations with someone of the same sex is another form of sexual behavior that has changed in the public's perception; many no longer consider it a form of deviance (see Chapter 10). Its normalization is reflected in a host of social changes, such as the inclusion of same-sex partners in family benefits offered by employers, the repeal of the military's "don't ask, don't tell" policy, the 2011 reversal of the federal government's position on the Defense of Marriage Act, and the 2015 U.S. Supreme Court decision legalizing same-sex marriage (see Figure 7.1 for a look at changing attitudes of U.S. adults toward same-sex marriage). Popular actors such as Ian McKellen (Gandalf in the *Lord of the Rings* movies and Magneto in the X-men films), Oscar winner Jodie Foster, and Neil Patrick Harris (Barney on TV's *How I Met Your Mother* and frequent awards show host); talk show hosts like Ellen DeGeneres; musicians such as Adam Lambert, Ricky Martin, and Lance Bass; professional athletes such as Jason Collins (basketball), Michael Sam (football), and Billy Jean King and Martina Navratilova (tennis); and news anchors such as Rachel Maddow and Anderson Cooper publicly identify as gay and are (or were) able to maintain successful careers. Gay and lesbian characters have also featured prominently on television shows such as *Modern Family*, *Orange Is the New Black*, and *Star Trek: Discovery*.

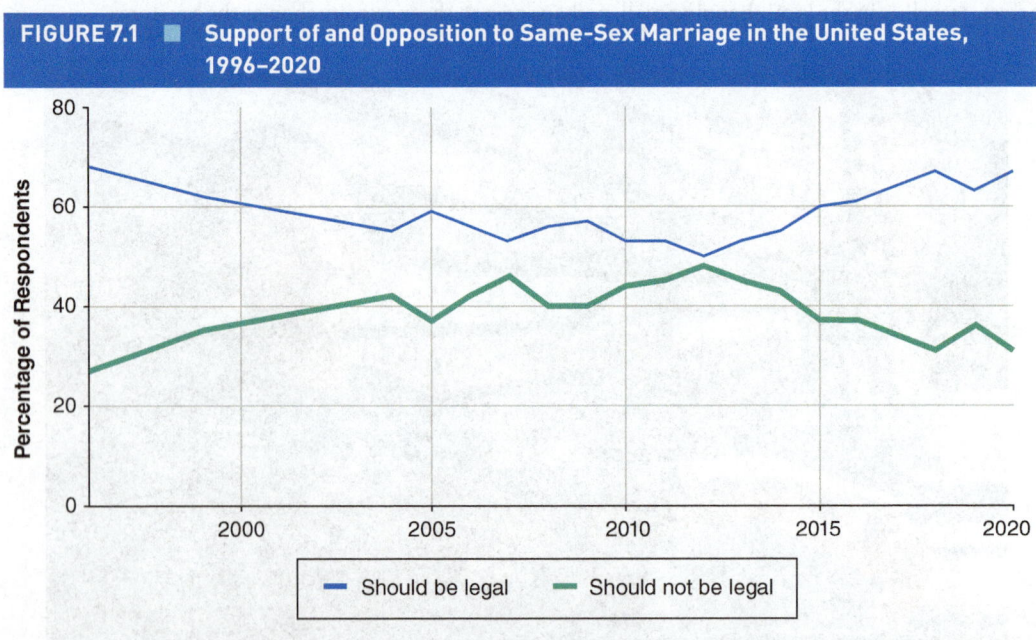

FIGURE 7.1 ■ Support of and Opposition to Same-Sex Marriage in the United States, 1996–2020

Source: Gallup. 2020. "U.S. Support for Same-Sex Marriage Matches Record High." Retrieved January 17, 2022 (https://news.gallup.com/poll/311672/support-sex-marriage-matches-record-high.aspx).

Of course, some members of society cringe at the idea that homosexuality, premarital sex, and cohabitation before marriage are becoming normative. Religious fundamentalists, for example, may believe in an absolute moral standard according to which these behaviors are deviant, no matter how many other people consider them to be normal. Most fundamentalists believe that only married heterosexuals should live together and have sexual intercourse with one another, although even many of those attitudes are changing.

There are great differences from one geographic area to another in the ways in which some behaviors are defined. At one time, smoking cigarettes was an accepted, even admired, form of behavior in the United States. Now, however, smoking is widely considered deviant by many groups in the United States. In Europe, however, it is not viewed as deviant as it is in the U.S. (although that attitude is changing), and it is considered quite normal by many in China.

Two men holding hands is another example of a behavior that is defined differently from one geographic region to another. In many urban centers in the U.S. and Europe, such a behavior hardly raises an eyebrow. In more rural areas, and in many more sexually conservative countries, however, such behavior can invite odd stares, criticism, and sometimes even physical violence. On the other hand, in many countries in the Middle East, two men holding hands is quite normative, although it is viewed as a sign of friendship rather than an indication of sexuality.

Global trends toward normalizing what was defined at one time and in some places as deviant are even clearer and more pronounced. This is particularly the case with changes in the acceptability of various forms of sexuality. Ever greater portions of the world are accepting premarital sex, cohabitation before marriage, and, to a lesser degree, homosexuality. According to the International Lesbian, Gay, Bisexual, Trans and Intersex Association (ILGA), as of December 2020, "deviant" sexuality (consensual same-sex sexual acts) has some form of legal protection in 124 countries. However, same-sex relations are still criminalized in 69 countries. The most common form of punishment is imprisonment, and as many as 11 countries will impose the death penalty on those who are caught engaging in same-sex relations. The barriers to normalizing such forms of sexual behavior remain in place and are quite powerful in many parts of the world, such as in Islamic societies, which tend to be more absolutist on matters relating to sexual deviance. In spite of the barriers, these behaviors occur, often covertly, in all societies, and may well be expanding in the wake of increasing global acceptance.

Context also matters to whether a behavior is defined as deviant or not. For example, during certain festivals, wearing elaborate costumes is seen as the normative behavior and, in some places, not doing so becomes the deviant behavior. As another example, women showing their breasts in public is generally seen as a deviant behavior; however, it is not uncommon to see topless women sunbathing on many beaches in Europe. As an example of in-between acceptance, women exposing their breasts in public in order to breastfeed is becoming normative in some places, with a general trend toward greater acceptance of such behavior.

It is also important to note that some forms of deviant behavior can also be rewarded. For example, breast enlargement is a deviant behavior that is sometimes rewarded with increased attention. Extreme bodybuilding presents a similar example of a deviant physical bodily modification that can be rewarded.

Protesting is a unique example of deviant behavior that tends to elicit strong societal reactions. Namely, those who agree with the cause of the protest tend to view the deviant behavior positively while those who oppose the cause tend to view it as disruptive. Students walking out of class to draw attention to climate change is an example of a form of protest that has found strong support as well as fierce condemnation.

Although there are great differences in what is considered to be deviant, it is important to remember that deviance has existed for all groups, in all parts of the world, and at all times. Virtually all groups define themselves by specifying the limits of acceptable behavior for their members. Such limits, and their violation, help a group sharpen its norms and values. Without limits and at least occasional violations, norms and values might become increasingly unclear and grow weaker over time.

Deviance and Consumption

The most obvious relationship between deviance and consumption is the use of goods and services that are illegal or considered deviant. This form of consumption sometimes also involves committing deviant, or illegal, acts to be able to afford to consume them. For example, many people addicted to drugs commit criminal acts such as prostitution, shoplifting, mugging, and breaking and entering to pay for the high cost of their illegal (and sometimes even legal) drugs.

Poverty drives some to commit illegal and/or deviant acts so that they can afford to consume what is necessary for survival, although not all deviant acts in the realm of consumption are committed by those who are poor. More affluent consumers may shoplift because they feel that they can steal without any detection or that it is compensation for performing (often frustrating) free labor. This is especially the case at self-checkout lanes, where consumers have devised numerous ways to shoplift products. One is the so-called "banana trick," or ringing up expensive items, like lobster tails, with the code for cheap items like bananas. Other self-scanning shoplifting "tricks" involve switching price tags and not scanning some items at all (Chun 2018). A recent study found that a third of U.S. customers regularly steal items when using self-service checkout lanes (Taylor 2014). In 2015, researchers analyzed 1 million self-checkout transactions and discovered that $850,000 worth of goods had been stolen. One reason this type of deviance is so prevalent is that consumers can easily blame the self-checkout scanners for the mis-scanned items (Chun 2018).

As with all sorts of deviance, definitions of what constitutes deviant consumer behavior are frequently in dispute. For instance, deviant consumers often do not see a relationship between deviance and their consumption patterns. For example, most of those who use the services of sex workers or who use marijuana (where it is still illegal) may well see such consumption as justifiable and therefore not as a form of deviance. Their actions are partly due to the fact that the laws prohibiting consumption of the services of sex workers and the use of marijuana are rarely enforced. In the case of sex work, even more rarely are the ones paying the sex worker ever punished at all, making purchasing such services low-risk (though the sex worker themselves are often harshly punished). Purchasing and using marijuana in places where these actions continue to be illegal are treated in a similar fashion, especially for those who are white and middle class.

However, those who consume the "wrong" drugs are more likely to be considered deviant than are those who consume the "right" drugs. Thus, people who consume alcohol, even if they consume it excessively, are far less likely to be considered deviant than people who use marijuana. And the purchase and use of "harder drugs," such as meth, crack cocaine, and heroin, are dealt with more harshly (especially by the law) than is the purchase of marijuana where it continues to be illegal (Chriqui et al. 2002; Jackson-Jacobs 2005).

Deviance and Morality

For a sociologist, just as deviance is socially constructed, so, too, is morality. One could even argue that morality and deviance are two sides of the same coin. That which is deviant is rarely considered moral while that which is moral is rarely considered deviant.

Deviance, almost by definition, implies a moral or ethical judgment on the part of one person or group toward another. People rarely censure something as deviant unless they also find it to offend, or at least not be in line with, their own personal morals. On the other hand, many who engage in deviant behaviors are less likely to view their own behaviors as deviant and, in some cases, may even view the behaviors of the defining majority as the ones who are deviant. For example, as requirements to wear a mask as a public health safety protocol to prevent the spread of COVID-19 have been relaxed, those continuing to wear a mask are sometimes seen as deviant (at least in cultures where wearing a mask was already seen as a deviant behavior before the pandemic). And yet those individuals are likely to find those not wearing a mask to be the deviant group.

Judgment of deviant behaviors also depends on context and symbolism. For example, a person who gets a tear drop tattoo below their eye (a symbol often associated with having murdered someone) is more likely to be seen as deviant than someone who gets a tear drop tattoo on their wrist or ankle in memory of a deceased loved one.

THEORIES OF DEVIANCE

Deviance is a good topic to study if you want to better understand the utility of, and contrasts between, the main types of sociological theories—structural/functional, conflict/critical, and inter/actionist. But before we get to these theories, it is important to make a key distinction between explanatory and constructionist theories of deviance.

- **Explanatory theories** seek to explain why deviance does or does not occur. These theories are also thought of as being scientific, or "positivistic," because they view deviant behavior as objectively real, and they suggest that these forms of real behavior can be studied empirically. Explanatory theories assume that deviant behavior is determined by a wide variety of factors, such as the biological makeup of the person labeled as deviant and the structure of the larger society.

- **Constructionist theories** are concerned with achieving a greater understanding of the process by which people define and classify some behaviors as normal and others as deviant. In other words, these theories focus on how people construct deviance. Whereas explanatory theories focus mainly on people labeled as deviant and what they do or represent (being poor, prone to juvenile delinquency), constructionist theories concentrate on those in power and the actions they take to create and define deviance in the first place. Rather than seeing deviance as "real," this perspective sees it as a social construction.

Of the three types of theories to be discussed next, the structural/functional and conflict/critical theories fall into the explanatory category, while the inter/actionist theories fit within the constructionist approach. However, whatever their theoretical approach, many sociologists use elements of both explanatory and constructionist approaches.

Structural/Functional Theories

Émile Durkheim argued that because deviance and crime have existed in all societies at all times, they must have positive functions for the larger society and its structures. In other words, deviance would not have existed in the past and continue to exist today were it not for the fact that it was, and is, functional; deviance served and continues to serve various purposes.

The most important function of deviance, in Durkheim's view, is that it allows societies, or groups, to define and clarify their collective beliefs—their norms and values. Were it not for deviance, norms and values would not exist. More important, the norms and values that limit or prohibit deviance would grow weak without the need to be exercised on a regular basis in response to deviant acts. The public as a whole, officials, and even potential deviants would grow progressively less aware of, and less sensitive to, the existence of these prohibitions. Thus, in a sense, society needs deviance. If periodic violations of standards of conduct did not occur, those standards would become less clear to all concerned, less strongly held, and less powerful (Dentler and Erikson 1959; Jensen 1988).

Strain

A more contemporary structural/functional approach to deviance is known as **strain theory** (Thaxton and Agnew 2017). According to strain theory, there is a discrepancy between the larger structure and culture of society, especially regarding what is valued, and the structural means available to achieve that which is valued. Strain exists when the culture values something—say, material success—but the structure of society is such that not everyone can achieve or realize that value in a socially acceptable way.

Of greatest interest in this context is the strain placed on some people by the relationship between means and ends. Robert K. Merton identified five possible relationships between means and ends and associated them with five types of adaptation.

- **Conformists** are people who accept both the cultural goals, such as making lots of money, and the traditional means of achieving those goals, including hard work. Conformists are not considered deviant.
- **Innovators** accept the same cultural goals the conformists do, but they reject the conventional means of achieving them. Innovators are deviants in that they choose nonconventional routes to success. Joaquín Guzmán, a.k.a. El Chapo, is a Mexican drug lord who rose swiftly through the ranks to achieve his financial success. By the 2010s, Guzmán had achieved a Robin Hood–like status among some for his provision of much-needed services in Mexico's Sinaloa mountains. Thus, he recognized the need for social services to be provided for the underprivileged (a cultural goal) but used unconventional means of advancing that goal (running a drug cartel).

- **Ritualists** realize that they will not be able to achieve cultural goals, but they nonetheless continue to engage in the conventional behavior associated with such success. Thus, a low-level employee might continue to work diligently even after realizing that such work is not going to lead to much economic success.

- **Retreatists** reject both cultural goals and the traditional routes to their attainment. Retreatists have completely withdrawn from the goal of attaining success as it is defined by the broader social system. One example is the Brown family documented on the Discovery Channel's reality show *Alaskan Bush People*. This family has lived (mostly) off the grid for more than 20 years in the Alaskan bush (although, ironically, their hit television show has put them squarely on the social map).

- **Rebels** are like retreatists in that they reject both traditional means and goals. However, they substitute nontraditional goals and means to achieving those goals. In a sense, that makes them doubly deviant. Revolutionaries such as Ernesto "Che" Guevara can be seen as fitting into the rebel category. Guevara rejected success as it was defined in Cuba during the 1950s. Instead, he chose to assist Fidel Castro in his effort to overthrow the country's dictatorial system. Furthermore, he chose unconventional means—guerrilla warfare waged from the mountains of Cuba and, eventually, Bolivia—to try to attain his nontraditional goal of a Communist society.

Adaptations of means to ends exemplify a structural-functionalist approach because some of the adaptations are highly functional. Conformity certainly has positive consequences in the sense that it allows the social system to continue to exist without disturbance. Innovation is functional because society needs innovations to adapt to new external realities. No society can survive without innovation. Even rebellion can be seen as functional because there are times when society needs more than gradual innovation—it needs to change radically.

True rebels, like Ernesto "Che" Guevara, are doubly deviant in that they reject traditional means and goals—in this case, by engaging in guerilla warfare to overthrow the Cuban dictatorship in the 1950s.

CPA Media - Pictures from History/GRANGER

Structural-functionalism is concerned not only with functions but also with dysfunctions. For example, ritualists and retreatists can be seen as largely dysfunctional for society, or at least as having more dysfunctions than functions. The unchanging behavior of ritualists contributes little or nothing to the requirements of an ever-changing society, and retreatists contribute even less because they are uninvolved in, and have withdrawn from, the larger society.

Conflict/Critical Theories

Proponents of structural/functional theories trace the source of deviance to the larger structures of society and the strains they produce or the fact that they do not exercise adequate social control. Conflict/critical theorists, especially conflict theorists, are also interested in those structures and their effects on people, but they adopt a different orientation toward them. A major focus is the inequality that exists in those structures and the impact it has on individuals. In conflict theorists' view, inequality causes at least some of the less powerful individuals in society to engage in deviant—and criminal—acts because they have few, if any, other ways of succeeding in society. In this way, they are similar to the innovators in Merton's taxonomy of adaptations to strain. Conversely, those in power in executive or managerial positions in organizations are more likely to commit crimes, especially corporate or white-collar crimes (Gottschalk 2016; Simpson 2002, 2013). This is because the nature of their high-level positions in various social structures (business, government) makes it not only possible but also relatively easy for them to do so. Their positions also allow them to better conceal their crimes. White-collar criminals are more likely to use deception in committing their crimes and bribery to conceal them; their crimes are more likely to be clandestine and to remain hidden (Van Slyke, Benson, and Cullen 2016). Further, conflict theorists argue, those in power in society create the laws and rules that define certain things as deviant, or illegal, while others are defined as normal. They do so in a self-serving way that advantages them and disadvantages those who lack power in society.

Deviance and the Poor

Conflict theories can be applied to social inequalities throughout the ages. For instance, they form the basis of research by William Chambliss (1964) on vagrancy laws in medieval England. These laws came into existence as feudalism was falling apart; the first vagrancy law was enacted in England after the Black Plague, around 1348. In the feudal system, serfs were forced to provide labor for landowners, but with the end of feudalism, and therefore of serfdom, a new source of labor was needed. Not coincidentally, the former serfs now lacked permanent homes and sources of income and wandered about the countryside. Those in power saw them as a likely group to provide the needed labor at little cost, so they created vagrancy laws. Under these laws, it was illegal for those without work or a home to loiter in public places, and some of those who violated these laws were arrested. As a result, many people who otherwise might not have worked for the landowners were forced to do so to avoid arrest and imprisonment.

Contemporary conflict theorists, heavily influenced by Marxian theory, have come to see deviance as something created by the capitalist economic system (Edelman 2017). Today's definitions of deviance serve the interests of the capitalists, especially by further enriching them. Conversely, they adversely affect the proletariat, especially the poor, who grow even poorer.

Conflict theorists do not argue that have-nots never commit crimes or deviant acts. Rather, they argue that it is because of the laws created by societal elites that the actions of the have-nots are singled out for notice and for sanctions. Furthermore, the costs to society of elite deviance are much higher than the costs associated with crime and deviance among society's have-nots. Compare, for example, the approximately $65 billion the disgraced and now imprisoned Bernie Madoff cost his clients by engaging in illegal activities to the likely few dollars a mugger takes from his victims.

Deviance and the Elite

Great efforts are made to legitimate elite crimes and acts of elite deviance and, failing that, to pay little or no attention to them. Those who rank high in such hierarchies as business, government, and the military have a much greater ability to commit deviant acts (such as sexually harassing subordinates), to have these acts be seen as legitimate, and to get away with them (Eisinger 2018; Michel, Heide, and Cochran 2016).

However, as is clear in the imprisonment of people like Bernie Madoff and R. Kelly, there are limits to the ability of elites to get away with deviant and criminal behavior. There are times when the acts are so extreme that they can no longer be hidden. They come to light and become great public issues. Once this happens, even the most elite members of society have a difficult time escaping negative judgment and perhaps even punishment and imprisonment.

There is a long list of scandals involving elite public figures of various types who have been found to have committed deviant acts. In the main, their acts were so extreme, or the revelations about them became so public, that they could not be ignored. However, what has often caused difficulties for those involved has been their awkward efforts to lie about, or cover up, their offenses once they first became public. In many cases, especially in this era of the internet, evidence is uncovered or witnesses come forward that make it clear that the public figure has been deceiving the public and the authorities. The following are a few notable examples:

- President Richard Nixon resigned in 1974 (famously stating "I am not a crook") as he faced imminent impeachment for his role in the infamous Watergate break-in and for his efforts to conceal his and his associates' roles in it from the public.

- In 2015, New England Patriots football star Aaron Hernandez was convicted of first-degree murder. He was serving a life sentence in prison without the possibility of parole when he took his own life in April 2017, after being acquitted of murder charges in a second case. Shortly thereafter, a Massachusetts judge vacated Hernandez's murder conviction, although the local district attorney planned to appeal the ruling.

- A number of Ministers in Peru resigned after it was revealed that they had received COVID-19 vaccinations out of turn. Those government officials received early vaccinations even while Peru was experiencing catastrophic death rates as a result of the virus.

- Boris Johnson, former Prime Minister of Great Britain, resigned in July 2022 amidst a number of highly public scandals, including "partygate," which included evidence that he and his associates were having (drunken) parties while the rest of the country was in lockdown and banned from having such gatherings.

- A 2018 exposé by the *New York Times* showed that before he was elected, President Donald Trump had made billions of dollars through questionable, if not illegal, tax schemes (Barstow, Craig, and Buettner 2018). Trump is also facing potential criminal charges for his role in the January 6 attacks on the U.S. Capitol Building, his handling of classified government documents after his term of office ended, and his alleged attempts to interfere with the results of the 2020 presidential election in the state of Georgia (Protess, Feuer, and Hakim 2023).

Former CEO of the Theranos Corporation, Elizabeth Holmes, had an estimated net worth of $4.5 billion. In 2022 she was sentenced to prison for defrauding investors by lying to them about the efficacy of the company's blood-testing technology.

Taylor Hill/FilmMagic/Getty Images

The view of conflict theorists is that, as lengthy as this list of elite deviants and criminals might be, it is merely the tip of the iceberg. Because elites have a wide variety of means at their disposal to conceal their actions, many, many more of their acts of deviance and criminality escape detection and punishment. Such acts by elites can persist for years, decades, or even a lifetime.

Inter/Actionist Theories

Inter/actionism can be used to analyze deviance (Rubington and Weinberg 2016). For example, to the rational choice theorist, a person chooses deviance because it is a rational means to some desired goal. Gang members often join gangs because of the camaraderie and perceived protection offered by the gang, as well as for access to a world in which the member can obtain money and achieve recognition and high status (Howell and Griffiths 2019; Sánchez-Jankowski 2018). Ethnomethodologists are concerned with the ways in which people "do" deviance—that is, the everyday behaviors in which they engage that produce deviance. People need to adopt methods of speech and forms of behavior that make their deviance invisible to most others. However, sometimes those who are deviant want to talk and act in ways that make it clear they are deviant. For example, gang members may use certain phrases, dress in certain ways, and display certain tattoos to make their allegiance clear to other members of the same gang—and to members of opposing gangs (see Chapter 3). However, when they interact with the public or the police, gang members may speak and dress in ways that conceal, or at least attempt to hide, their membership in the gang.

Labeling

Symbolic interactionism is of great utility in analyzing and furthering our understanding of deviance. One variety of symbolic interactionism—labeling theory—is particularly useful in thinking about deviance. From that perspective, at least two things are needed for deviance to occur.

- A **symbol**, or in this case a "label." In the realm of deviance, a number of labels are particularly powerful negative symbols: *alcoholic, drug addict, pedophile, adulterer,* and so on.
- Interaction between the person or group doing the labeling (the labeler) and the person or group to whom the label is applied (the labelee). During this interaction, one or more of these labels is applied to the deviant; a deviant is someone who others say is a deviant. Deviance is a matter of social definition.

Those who do the defining—the labeling—are known as **social control agents**. Some of these agents (police, psychiatrists, judges) are performing official functions, but far more often it is friends or family who label others as, for example, drunks or womanizers. When public figures are labeled as deviant, the media and their representatives are often the ones who do the labeling.

From the perspective of **labeling theory**, a deviant is someone to whom a deviant label has been successfully applied (Becker 1963; Goode 2014; Restivo and Lanier 2015). This stands in contrast to the view of the public and many sociologists, who focus on what an individual does in order to be labeled a deviant. It isn't what someone has done, but rather how others have labeled them that matters. Also of interest in labeling theory is the way in which the person labeled as deviant is affected by the label. The person can accept the label to varying degrees or make efforts to resist, reject, or shed the label. People also vary greatly in how they react to, and feel about, being labeled as deviant. For example, some might be mortified by being labeled sex addicts, but others might take pride in it.

Labeling theory is also concerned about the actions and reactions of social control agents, as well as about their interactions with those being labeled. From the labeling perspective, "deviance is not a consequence of the act the person commits, but rather a consequence of the [creation and] application by others of rules and sanctions to an 'offender'" (Becker 1963, 9). A focus on social control agents, rather than on deviants, leads to the view that deviant labels are not necessarily applied uniformly. Some people and forms of behavior are more likely than others to be labeled as deviant. Thus, murderers and the act of murder are almost uniformly labeled as deviant (and criminal). However, in many other cases, the process is more selective and less clear-cut: "Some men who drink too much are called alcoholics and others are not; some men who act oddly are committed to hospitals and others are not; some men who have no visible means of support are hauled into court and others are not" (Erikson 1964, 11–12). Overall, people are more likely to be socially defined as deviant when they are poor, work in low-status occupations, or are in similarly devalued circumstances (Goffman 1959). A person in a more advantageous social situation often escapes being defined or labeled as deviant, despite manifesting the same forms of behavior. For example, if a woman cheats on her spouse then she is seen as deviant with little exception. However, if a man, especially a rich and powerful one, cheats on his spouse then such behavior is more likely to be written off.

Primary and Secondary Deviance

An important distinction that flows from labeling theory is that between primary and secondary deviance.

- **Primary deviance** consists of early, random acts of deviance, such as an occasional bout of drinking to excess or an isolated act considered strange or out of the ordinary. Virtually all of us commit such acts; we all have engaged in various forms of primary deviance (Lemert [1951] 2012; Wallerstein and Wyle 1947). Isolated acts of primary deviance rarely, if ever, lead to the successful application of a deviant label. Primary deviance consists of acts and behavior, not identities or labels.

- Of far greater interest to labeling theorists is **secondary deviance**, or deviant acts that persist, become more common, and eventually cause people to organize their lives and personal identities around their deviant status (Liberman, Kirk, and Kim 2014). Secondary deviance usually occurs after an individual has been stigmatized and judged for deviant behavior and possibly labeled as deviant. In response, the individual begins to see and define himself or herself as deviant. Although labeling theory tends to focus on others labeling an individual as deviant, it is possible, or even likely, that individuals will label themselves in this way (Thoits 1985, 2011), that they will do so before anyone else does (Norris 2011), and that they will act in accordance with their self-imposed label (Lorber 1967).

Key Ideas in the Labeling Process

Social control is the process by which a group or society enforces conformity to its demands and expectations. One way in which this is accomplished is through the creation and application of rules and labels. This leads to the distinction between rule creators and rule enforcers. **Rule creators** are usually elite members of society who devise its rules, norms, and laws (Ryan 1994). Without rule creators and their rules, there would be no deviance. Rule creators are usually (but not always) distinct from **rule enforcers**, who threaten to or actually do sanction the rule violators (Bryant and Higgins 2010). Another important idea here is that of **moral entrepreneurs**, or those individuals or groups of individuals who come to define an act as a moral outrage and who lead a campaign to have it defined as deviant and to have it made illegal and therefore subject to legal enforcement (Becker 1963; Vuolo, Kadowski, and Kelly 2017). One example of this is Anita Bryant, a well-known celebrity in the 1970s, who began an unfortunately successful campaign called "Save Our Children" to repeal an anti-discrimination ordinance in Florida.

Moral Panics

Moral entrepreneurs can stir up such a fuss that they can cause a **moral panic**, or a widespread and disproportionate reaction to the form of deviance in question (Goode and Ben-Yehuda 2009; Hier 2017; Krinsky 2013). It could be argued that today we are witnessing, especially in Europe and the United States, concern about Muslim immigrants that has morphed into a moral panic (Morgan and Poynting 2012). This moral panic is related, at least in part, to the threat of terrorism posed by radical Islamic groups. In spite of several gruesome and highly publicized attacks by radical Islamic groups, it is important to remember that very few Muslims are Islamist extremists, let alone terrorists.

Moral panics—such as the witch-hunting crazes of Renaissance Europe—rely in part on the use of labels to identify perceived threats. What might help prevent the development of a moral panic?

Granger, NYC — All rights reserved.

A good historical example of a moral panic is the witch craze that occurred in Europe between the fourteenth and sixteenth centuries (Ben-Yehuda 1980, 1985) and, to a lesser extent, also in the United States, made most famous by the Salem Witch Trials. The idea of witches had existed before this time, but it was seen as a more complex phenomenon involving both bad and good witches. In any case, no assumption had been made about a conspiracy between women and Satan to corrupt the world. However, in this era, Dominican friars took the lead in defining witchcraft as such a conspiracy and as a crime subject to corporal punishment, in this case, sometimes even burning at the stake. The friars were the moral entrepreneurs in this example. They played a key role in generating a moral panic that came to involve large numbers of people. Moral panics are, by definition, exaggerated. Thus, the threats posed by witches in the fifteenth century, communists in the 1950s, and immigrants and even terrorists today have been made out by many, especially moral entrepreneurs, to be greater than they really are.

Stigmas

Erving Goffman's *Stigma* (1963) is a very important contribution of symbolic interactionism to our understanding of deviance. A **stigma** is a person's characteristic that others find, define, and often label as unusual, unpleasant, or deviant. Goffman begins his book with analyses of physically stigmatized individuals, such as those missing a nose. He then introduces a wide array of other stigmas, such as being on welfare. In the end, readers come to the realization that they have been reading not only about people who are unlike them, but also about themselves: "The most fortunate of normals is likely to have his half-hidden failing, and for every little failing there is a social occasion when it will loom large, creating a shameful gap" (Goffman 1963, 127). Goffman's idea of stigma has attracted many scholars and has been applied to many forms of deviance, such as prostitution (Benoit et al. 2017), mental illness (Yeh, Jewell, and Thomas 2017), autism (Someki et al. 2018), and tattooing (Dickson et al. 2014).

There are two types of stigmatized individuals. The individual with a **discredited stigma** "assumes his differentness is known about already or is evident on the spot." Those types of stigmas tend to be immediately visible, such as being in a wheelchair or having purple hair. In contrast, those with a **discreditable stigma** assume that their stigma "is neither known about by those present nor immediately perceivable about them" (Goffman 1963, 4). Those types of stigmas can often be hidden and can include things like having a particular STD or having a prison record. Of great importance is the symbolic nature of the stigma and the individual's interaction with others, especially those thought to be normal. Those with a discredited stigma are likely to engage in situation management; that is, because their stigma is already known to those around them, they try to manage the situation. Examples of this are drawing attention to the stigma or even using humor to diffuse social tension. On the other hand, those with a discreditable stigma are likely to engage in knowledge management; that is, because their stigma is likely not known to those around them, they try to manage information so that it does not become known. Hiding information, avoiding subjects or locations, or even lying are examples of knowledge management.

The idea of discreditable stigmas has wide applicability to the contemporary world. For example, the court records of juvenile offenders are often hidden from the public or expunged to avoid stigmatizing otherwise promising young people for a lifetime. People with mental illnesses or substance abuse problems often go to great lengths to hide the real reasons for unscheduled absences from work. Parents of children with mental disabilities, especially those with mild impairments, "mainstream" their children in standard classrooms, in part so that the children's disabilities will be more likely to be discreditable than discredited.

CRIME

As pointed out previously, it is the fact that the law is violated that differentiates crime from other forms of deviance. Criminology is the field devoted to the study of crime. Although many criminologists are now found in university departments and schools devoted to the study of criminology, a large number work in sociology departments. There is a sociology of crime, but the field also includes those from many other disciplines, such as psychologists, economists, biologists, and anthropologists, as well as officials who once worked in the criminal justice system. In fact, the field today has become increasingly multidisciplinary, even interdisciplinary (Wellford 2019).

Although there is growing interdisciplinarity in the study of crime, sociology plays an important role in it. Clearly, a variety of sociological factors are involved in who is likely to commit crimes and which crimes they are likely to commit. The same sociological factors are involved in who gets caught, prosecuted, and incarcerated, as well as how much of their sentences they actually serve. And such factors are also involved in what happens to people after they serve their sentences and whether they are likely to end up back in prison.

The "father of criminology" is Cesare Lombroso, who published *Criminal Man* in 1876. The title of the book reflects the fact that the focus of early criminologists was on criminals and their innate physical or psychological characteristics.

In recent years, criminology has largely shifted away from its focus on criminals and their crimes and toward a concern with the social context of criminal actions and the effects of those actions on the larger society. A key figure in bringing a sociological perspective to criminology was Edwin Sutherland (1883–1950). His work helped shift the focus in criminology from the criminal and their perceived misdeeds to society, especially the societal reaction to those misdeeds, including the labels placed on criminals.

Sutherland's most important contribution to the sociology of crime is differential association theory. The main point of the theory is that people are *not* born criminals; they learn criminal behavior. Therefore, whom a person associates with is crucial. One's family and friends—the primary group—are important sources of attitudes toward crime, knowledge about how to commit crimes, and rationalizations that help one live with being a criminal. Today, we would need to add the fact that criminal behavior can also be learned through television, songs, and especially the internet. Many criticisms were leveled at differential association theory; even Sutherland later came to criticize it on various grounds. For example, it did not explain why some people became criminals while others exposed to the same situations did not. One of Sutherland's own criticisms was the fact that the theory did not give enough attention to the role of opportunity in committing crimes.

Although the previous discussion focuses on the causes of crime, criminology has long had a second focus on the criminal justice system (Siegel and Worrall 2014). This interest is traceable to another early Italian scholar, Cesare Beccaria (1738–1794). Beccaria was a lawyer by training and received a doctorate in law. He is best known for his book *On Crimes and Punishments* ([1764] 1986) and its concern with such issues as the origins of law and the criminal justice system. His work led to an interest not only in this system as a whole but also in whether its major components—law enforcement, courts, and corrections—are fair, effective, and just (Unger, Crete, and Pavlich 2018). In terms of the latter, much work has been done on the (un)fairness, especially as far as race and ethnicity are concerned, of arrest decisions by the police, the length of sentences, and the likelihood of receiving the death penalty.

The Criminal Justice System

The criminal justice system consists of various loosely connected government agencies and the individuals who work in those agencies. It is involved in the apprehension, prosecution, and punishment of those who violate the law. It also seeks to prevent such violations before they occur. Finally, the criminal justice system has much more general responsibilities, such as ensuring public safety and maintaining social order. The major components of the criminal justice system are law enforcement, the courts, and the correctional system.

An enormous number of people are being held in the jail and prison system. In 2021, 1,767,200 adults were incarcerated in U.S. jails and federal and state prisons. The United States has one of the highest rate of incarceration: 531 of every 100,000 individuals is in a federal, state, or local prison. It has 77,000 more prisoners than China and almost 1.3 million more than Russia (see Figure 7.2 for the 20 countries with the highest total prison populations). Although the United States has only about 4 percent of the world's population, it has about 25 percent of the world's prisoners (Cullen, Jonson, and Nagin 2011). This is a very costly system to operate (Bratton 2011). It is estimated that in 2015, local, state, and federal governments spent about $77 billion on corrections, much of it on incarceration (Urban Institute 2017). Further complicating matters is the fact that the economic problems facing the United States in general, and state and local jurisdictions in particular, mean that fewer prisons and jails are being built, while an increasing number of people are being sentenced to them. The growing number of prisoners creates other problems, including overcrowding of the prisons and increased violence among prisoners. Overcrowded prisons have also been particularly difficult places in which to control the spread of COVID-19, with the result that infection and death rates among inmates has tended to be much higher than among the general population. Given the huge numbers involved, prisons have become little more than warehouses for prisoners. The ability of prisons to rehabilitate inmates has declined, and the focus on punishment has strengthened (Howard 2017, Western 2018).

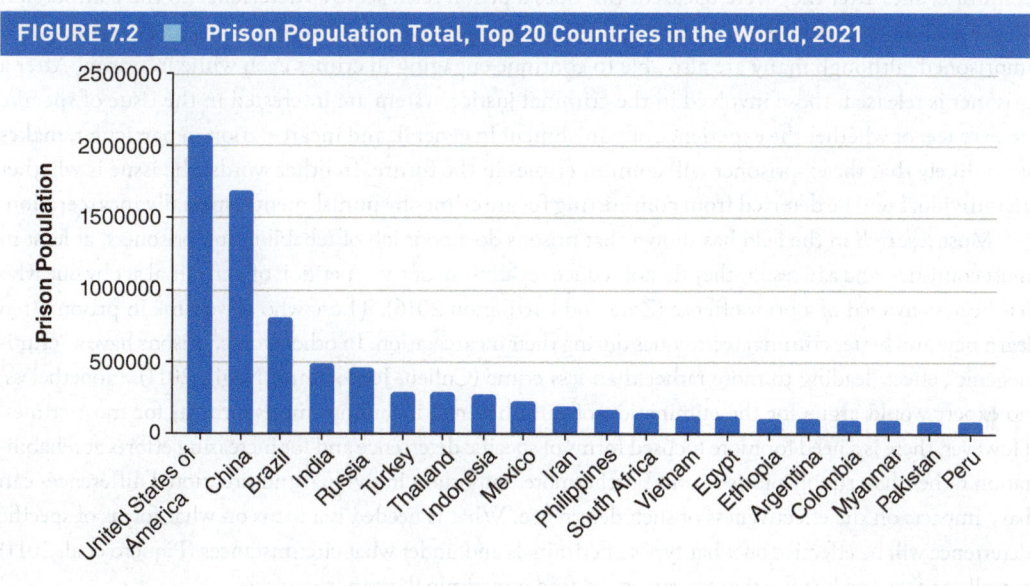

FIGURE 7.2   Prison Population Total, Top 20 Countries in the World, 2021

Source: Institute for Crime and Justice Policy Research

The previous discussion has focused on publicly financed prisons, but there has also been an increase in private prisons in the United States, which as of 2019 housed more than 8 percent of the total prison population. These prisons are staffed by a minimal number of guards with little training whose pay is often pegged to that at Walmart. With a relatively small number of poorly paid and trained guards, these prisons are generally run by the inmates. Private prisons are part of large profit-making corporations with an emphasis on managing prisoners at the lowest possible cost but with the highest possible returns for the corporations (more than $4 billion in revenues in 2019). As poor as public prisons are, private prisons are arguably worse, maybe much worse.

The millions of people in public prisons, and the billions of dollars spent on them, have become hot public issues. In the U.S., more than $80 billion is spent annually on public prisons and jails, with an additional $4 billion being spent on private prisons. Additionally, an estimated $3 billion is spent by prisoners and their families every year on phone calls and (often grossly overpriced) commissary purchases.

Another concern is mandatory minimum sentences for nonviolent offenders, which have helped lead to a sharp increase in the number of nonviolent offenders (often convicted of drug offences) in prison (Williams 2016). Many of those offenders—roughly 200,000—are serving life sentences. This is more than five times the number of those serving such sentences in 1984. Obviously, putting people in prison for life is very costly. In any case, such sentences are highly questionable as punishment for minor, drug-related crimes.

As of the end of 2020, beyond the more than 1.7 million people in prisons and jails in 2020, more than 3.8 million people were under the control of the criminal justice system because they were either on parole (862,100) or on probation (3,053,700). **Parole** is the supervised early release of a prisoner for such efforts as good behavior while in prison. Parole officers work with those on parole to help them adjust to life outside prison and to be sure they are not violating the conditions of their release. If they do violate those conditions, they can have their parole revoked, and they can be sent back to prison. Those who are convicted of less serious crimes may be placed on **probation**, whereby they are released into the community with supervision. They are also released under certain conditions, for example, that they must be enrolled in and complete a substance abuse program. If the offender does not adhere to these conditions, is arrested, or is convicted, probation can be revoked. In that case, a new, more restrictive probation can be imposed, or the offender can be sent to prison. Both parole and probation require the participation of bureaucracies, especially the parole and probation officers employed by them. These systems, like the prison and jail system, are very costly.

It might be argued that the enormous cost of prisons—as well as the parole and probation systems—would be justifiable if incarceration taught people that "crime does not pay." In other words, a case might be made for mass imprisonment if it rehabilitated prisoners so that they were less likely to commit crimes after they were released. But does a prison term serve as deterrence to the commission of crimes after an inmate is released from prison? Some prisoners are deterred from further crime while imprisoned, although many are also able to continue engaging in crimes even while in prison. After a prisoner is released, those involved in the criminal justice system are interested in the issue of **specific deterrence**, or whether the experience of punishment in general, and incarceration in particular, makes it less likely that the ex-prisoner will commit crimes in the future. In other words, the issue is whether an individual will be deterred from committing future crimes by punishment, especially incarceration.

Most research in the field has shown that prisons do a poor job of rehabilitating prisoners, at least in most countries, and as a result, they do not reduce **recidivism**, or the repetition of a criminal act by one who has been convicted of a prior offense (Zara and Farrington 2016). Those who serve time in prison often learn new and better criminal techniques during their incarceration. In other words, prisons have a "criminogenic" effect, leading to more rather than less crime (Cullen, Jonson, and Nagin 2011). Nonetheless, no expert would argue for the elimination of punishments, including imprisonment, for most crimes. However, there is a need for more focused forms of specific deterrence and for increasing efforts at rehabilitation rather than simply punishment. Furthermore, important individual and situational differences can have impacts on the effectiveness of such deterrence. What is needed is a focus on what forms of specific deterrence will be effective on what types of criminals and under what circumstances (Piquero et al. 2011) as well as a focus on helping those incarcerated find noncriminal means to survive.

General deterrence deals with the population as a whole and whether individuals will be less likely to commit crimes because of fear they might be punished or imprisoned for their actions. Although it is not clear how many people do not commit crimes because of fear of punishment, it is clear that such fear constitutes some level of deterrence to some who might otherwise become criminals.

The ultimate example of both forms of deterrence is capital punishment, or the death penalty. Someone who is executed clearly cannot commit another crime. However, there is evidence that even the threat of capital punishment is not a strong general deterrent to crime (Hood and Hoyle 2015; Melusky and Pesto 2017).

Although a number of countries have abolished the death penalty, the United States is one of a handful that continue to employ it. Figure 7.3 shows the legality of the death penalty across U.S. states, as well as data on the number of people on death row per state and the number executed since 1976. The four leading countries in the world, in terms of the number of people executed, are China, Iran, Pakistan, and Saudi Arabia. These are countries the United States would not like to be associated with, especially on this issue.

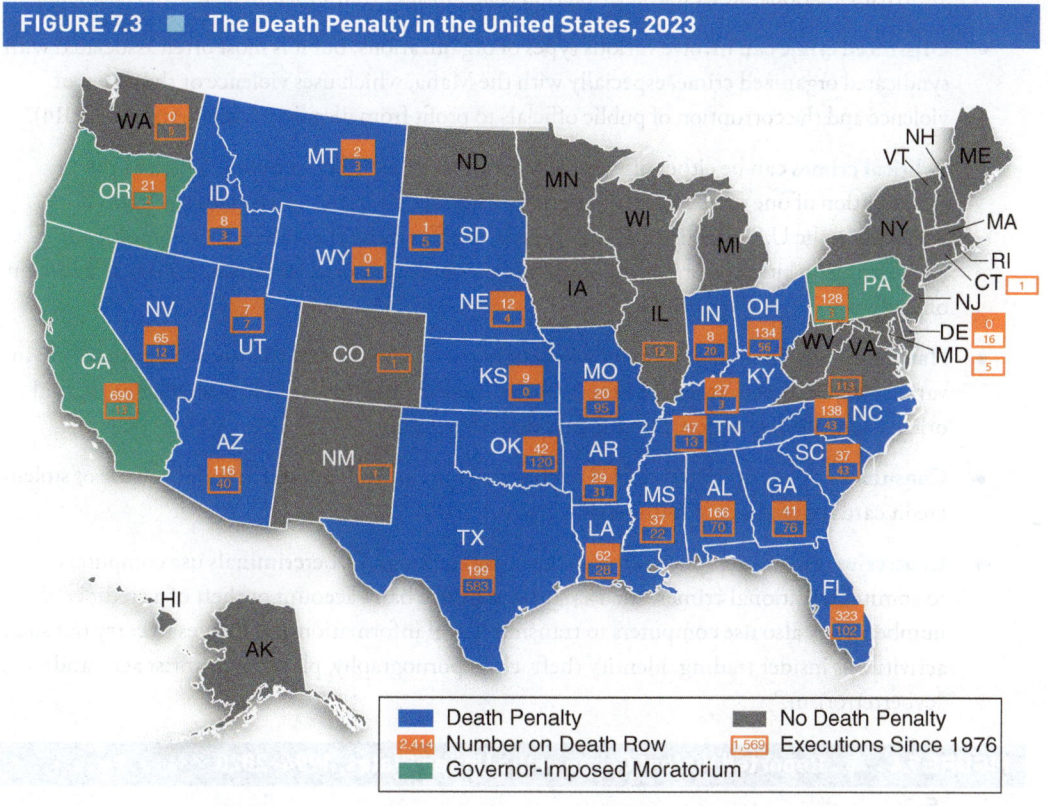

FIGURE 7.3 ■ The Death Penalty in the United States, 2023

Source: Based on data from Death Penalty Information Center, http://www.deathpenaltyinfo.org.

The application of capital punishment continues to be highly controversial. In fact, many death sentences are accompanied by active campaigns against them and vigils protesting executions both before and as they occur. Many feel it is morally wrong for the government to kill anyone. Others are opposed to the death penalty because it is likely that at least some wrongly convicted people are killed in the process (Acker 2017). Finally, there is strong evidence of bias, especially racial bias, in capital punishment. Many studies have shown that Blacks, and nonwhites more generally, convicted of killing Whites are more likely to get the death penalty than are Whites who kill other Whites (Lee, Paternoster, and Rowan 2016).

Types of Crimes

Generally speaking, there are two broad types of crime recognized in many countries. **Violent crime** includes the threat of injury or the threat or actual use of force. Violent crimes include things like murder and nonnegligent manslaughter, forcible rape, robbery, and aggravated assault. Figure 7.4 shows the reported violent crime rates in the United States for 1994 through 2020. In recent years, increasing attention has also been paid to violent crimes related to terrorism, as well as globally to war crimes. **Property** crimes do not involve injury or force but rather are offenses that involve gaining or destroying property. Although there are others (such as shoplifting and forgery), the major property crimes are burglary, larceny-theft, and motor vehicle theft. In the U.S., about three-fourths of all (reported) crime is property crime. Figure 7.5 shows the property crime rates in the United States for 1994 through 2020. Another important way of categorizing crimes is by separating **felonies**, or more serious crimes usually associated with longer jail or prison sentences and larger fines, from **misdemeanors**, or minor offenses punishable by little to no imprisonment and smaller fines. There are also other ways of classifying crimes:

- **White-collar crimes** are those committed "by a person of responsibility and high social status in the course of his [or her] occupation" (Geis 2007b, 850;). These can include things like embezzlement or counterfeiting.

- **Corporate crime** involves legal organizations that violate the law. It includes such illegal acts as antitrust violations, stock market violations (e.g., insider trading), and false advertisements.

- **Organized crime** can involve various types of organizations, but it is most often associated with syndicated organized crime, especially with the Mafia, which uses violence or the threat of violence and the corruption of public officials to profit from illegal activities (Arsovska 2014).

- **Political crimes** can be either offenses against the state to affect its policies, such as the assassination of one of its officials, especially its leader (as in the assassination of John F. Kennedy in the U.S. or Shinzo Abe in Japan), or offenses by the state, either domestically (e.g., spying on citizens) or internationally (e.g., state-sponsored terrorism, bribery of a foreign official).

- **Hate crimes** are those that stem, in whole or in part, from the fact that those victimized are in various ways different from the perpetrators. These differences include race, religion, sexual orientation, gender, national origin, and disability status.

- **Consumer crimes**, or crimes related to consumption, include shoplifting and the use of stolen credit cards or credit card numbers.

- **Cybercrime** targets computers (for instance, by hacking). Cybercriminals use computers to commit traditional crimes, such as stealing from a bank account or theft of a credit card number. They also use computers to transmit illegal information and images to carry out such activities as insider trading, identity theft, child pornography, plans for terrorist acts, and "cyberterrorism."

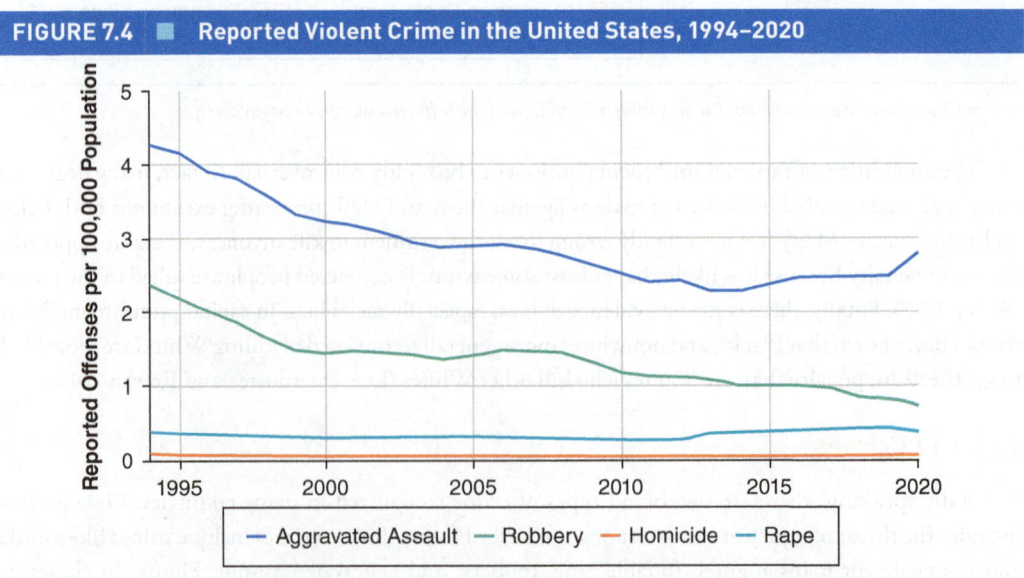

FIGURE 7.4 ■ Reported Violent Crime in the United States, 1994–2020

Source: Data from Federal Bureau of Investigation, Uniform Crime Reports, Table 1: "Crime in the United States by Volume and Rate per 100,000 Inhabitants, 1994–2020," 2021.

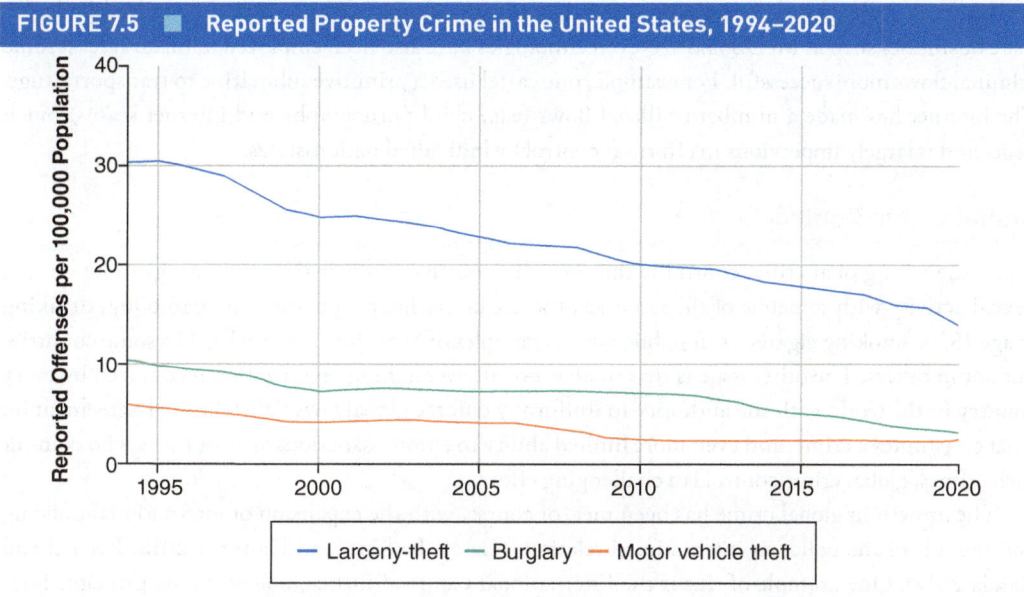

FIGURE 7.5 ■ Reported Property Crime in the United States, 1994–2020

Source: Crime in the United States, 2020. U.S. Department of Justice, Federal Bureau of Investigation.

Although all the offenses described above are classified as crimes, they are not all considered equally abhorrent. In line with the idea that deviance is defined by elites, so are crimes and criminal punishments. Thus, white-collar and corporate crimes are often downplayed, while the crimes usually associated with those in the lower social classes—for example, violent crimes, especially felonies, and property crimes—receive a great deal of attention from the police, the media, and the public.

Nonetheless, violent crime is a major issue in many places. In the United States, this includes murder committed with widely available and readily obtainable guns. In 2020, 45,222 people in the U.S. died as a result of gun-related injuries—more than 123 per day, on average. That number represents a 43 percent increase since 2010. In particular, homicides involving a gun have increased by more than 75 percent since 2010 (Pew Research Center 2023). As a note of comparison, someone has roughly the same chance of dying by gun violence in Japan as they do of being struck by lightning in the U.S. (roughly 1 in 10 million).

GLOBALIZATION AND CRIME

The amount of global, or cross-border, crime has increased with globalization (Roth 2018; Rothe and Friedrichs 2016; also see the journal *Global Crime*). Globalization makes cross-border crime increasingly possible and more likely. International crime has existed for centuries in such forms as piracy on the oceans and war crimes. However, today there seems to be far more of it. This may be due to the fact that, because of the increase in global criminal flows, much more public and government attention is devoted to these crimes.

The apparent growth in global crime is largely traceable to increasing concern about illicit drug use in the United States in the late 1960s and early 1970s, as well as Western Europe's interest in terrorism during roughly the same period. Drugs and terrorism now top the list of concerns about the "global illicit economy" (Andreas 2015), but others include illegal trade in advanced weapon, endangered species, pornography, stolen property (e.g., art and antiquities), counterfeit goods, ivory, toxic waste, and trafficking in human beings (Farr 2005; Weitzer 2015). All of these involve flows of all sorts—drugs, money, waste, weapons, human victims. They also include various illegal content that flows through the internet (e.g., child pornography, laundered funds, computer viruses, calls to commit terroristic acts).

Furthermore, global criminal cartels have come into existence to expedite illegal flows and to increase the profits that can be derived from them. In his book *McMafia* (2008), Misha Glenny attributes much of the cartels' success to increasingly sophisticated organizational methods (including economies of scale, global partnerships, and the opening of new markets) copied from leading legitimate businesses such as McDonald's. New technologies have also been employed to make at least some criminal flows more successful. For example, one cartel used a primitive submarine to transport drugs. The internet has made a number of illegal flows (e.g., child pornography and internet scams) much easier and is largely impervious to efforts at control by individual nation-states.

Global Crime Control

One issue with global crime control is that not all countries consider the same things to be crimes. Sexual activity with someone of the same sex, the use of marijuana, prostitution, gambling, drinking at age 18, or smoking cigarettes in public are all examples of behaviors that are legal in some countries but not in others. The other issue is that there is not an overarching organization recognized by every country in the world with the authority to uniformly enforce global laws. With limited agreement on what constitutes a crime, and even more limited ability to enforce sanctions against those who commit such crimes, global crime control is a challenging effort.

The growth in global crime has been met, of course, with the expansion of international policing and the role of the police in international relations (Casey, Jenkins, and Dammer 2018; Reichel and Randa 2017). One example of this is the International Court of Justice, one of the six principle bodies of the United Nations, and the only recognized body that settles disputes between countries. The court, based in the Netherlands, includes by default all countries which are members of the United Nations. Those countries also agree to comply with decisions made by the court. One flaw, however, is that countries on the UN Security Council have the ability to veto any decision of the court, thereby nullifying its true judicial power. This happened, for example, in 1983 when the United States blocked a decision by the court that found it guilty of supporting insurrection (among many other crimes) in Nicaragua.

Another issue with enforcement of international law has to do with asylum and extradition. **Asylum** is a situation in which an individual fears persecution in their home territory and so looks to find protection in another territory. In other words, it means one jurisdiction protecting someone who has been found, or has the potential to be found, to be criminal in another jurisdiction. Asylum can be granted on multiple grounds, but is most often done for political purposes (a number of outlaw former presidents of countries in Latin America now reside in the United States) or humanitarian purposes (a number of countries offer special programs for LGBTQ+ individuals who are under threat in their home countries).

Extradition is the process whereby one jurisdiction returns a suspected criminal to another jurisdiction. This can be done at multiple levels, for example between individual territories within a single country or between countries themselves. The process is often politically complicated as it requires a request to be made by one jurisdiction to another and it is often the politics between countries, rather than the suspected themselves, that is the determining factor in whether the request is granted.

Since 9/11, there has been a dramatic erosion of distinctions in the world of criminal justice in an effort to forestall further terrorist attacks and to catch or kill people defined as terrorists. For example, the distinction between law enforcement and intelligence operations has eroded as law enforcement authorities seek to gain intelligence on potential terrorists. The distinction between law enforcement and security has also eroded. The USA PATRIOT (Uniting and Strengthening America by Providing Appropriate Tools Required to Intercept and Obstruct Terrorism) Act, signed into law in 2001, has played a key role in this erosion by, for example, extending the concern of law enforcement agencies to domestic terrorism. In addition, surveillance of the border between the United States and Mexico, as well as in immigrant communities in the United States, has increased. In the process, many immigrants have been defined as criminals, apprehended, and then returned to Mexico. It is important to note that far less attention is devoted to surveillance on the much longer border with Canada, and those who do cross that border illegally are much less likely to be defined, or apprehended, as criminals.

Some European countries have recently instituted a similar toughening of border controls and surveillance. However, within the European Union, border law enforcement has become more homogeneous as criminal justice norms and procedures have become more similar and law enforcement contacts and exchanges of information among member states have become more regular. Of great importance has been the formation of Europol, the EU's law enforcement agency, which enables better and increased communication and cooperation among national police agencies.

Although these efforts have improved global crime control, they have a variety of downsides. Democracy and civil rights have been seriously threatened by some of these efforts. Crime control efforts are not always as transparent as they should be, and the officials involved often need to be more accountable. Tougher border and immigration controls have led to more daring and dangerous efforts to cross borders, leading to more deaths in the process. Those who have been denied entry often suffer in poorly constructed and overcrowded border camps. In addition, the global antidrug campaign has generated high levels of crime, violence, corruption, disease, and so on. Efforts to deal with trafficking in women and children have focused more on criminalizing that traffic than on protecting the human rights of the women and children being trafficked. Finally, the attention and money devoted to international crime and its control have tended to distract attention, and to take money away, from efforts to deal with a wide range of fundamental issues within nation-states, including the welfare of large portions of society.

COVID-19, Deviance, and Crime

The COVID-19 pandemic has offered new opportunities to think about the meanings of deviance and crime, especially how they are socially constructed and shift over time and between places and groups. The rapid onset of the pandemic, its impact on the lives of nearly every person on the planet, and the ways in which it has forced us to think about our social connectedness to one another, in both physical and social terms, has also forced individuals and societies around the world to reexamine, and in some cases reinvent, ways of thinking about deviant behavior and criminal activity.

The early years of the pandemic also meant that continuing to participate in many of our everyday activities suddenly was seen as deviant behavior by many. For example, attending large gatherings, including birthday parties and funerals, became an act of deviance. On the other hand, previous acts that had been considered deviant suddenly came to be seen as normal. For example, isolating oneself from others shifted from being an act that would worry loved ones to an act that was applauded as showing concern for others.

Another example is related to face coverings. In the years before COVID-19, many countries, especially in Europe, were pushing legislation to ban face coverings in public. Although many argued that these policies were blatantly Islamophobic, defenders of these proposed laws argued that they were necessary for security reasons. With the onset of the pandemic, however, and the universally advised medical precaution to wear a mask, many had to quickly rethink what it meant to wear a face covering in public. Whereas before the pandemic such behavior was considered a "safety concern" and those doing so were labeled as deviants, that view quickly changed to be the opposite—suddenly those *not* wearing a mask were the safety concern and were labeled as deviants. As the pandemic wears on and mask mandates are lifted, some places are seeing this definition shift yet again, with those wearing masks again sometimes being viewed as deviants, albeit ones whose reasons are now more uniformly understood.

In terms of crime, the pandemic has also brought about several changes, many of which continue to be challenged through the courts and criminal justice system. For example, a number of companies have implemented vaccine mandates—employees must receive a vaccine or their employment will be terminated. A number of universities have done the same (though it is worth noting that vaccine requirements were standard at nearly all universities well before the pandemic). Entire countries have also started requiring citizens to be vaccinated, especially in order to enter public venues. Although the penalties for noncompliance in these examples varied greatly, most simply prevented unvaccinated individuals from participating in a given event or entering a given venue; however, it's possible that more serious criminal sanctions might eventually be implemented against people who do not comply.

In short, the pandemic has shown us the fragility of what it means for something to be deviant or criminal, how quickly such meanings can change, and also how quickly individuals and societies are, in fact, able to adapt to such changes. As the pandemic continues, it will be interesting to see whether what is considered deviant or criminal might also continue to change.

SUMMARY

Deviance is any action, belief, or human characteristic that violates the norms of a group or society. Deviance changes over time—certain actions that were considered norm violations in the past, like cohabitation, are not anymore. Norm violations are an important way in which groups and societies define acceptable behavior and form cohesion.

Explanatory and constructionist theories are two different ways to understand deviance. Explanatory theories attempt to explain why deviance does or does not occur. Constructionist theories are more concerned with the process of how some behaviors are defined and classified as deviant. Structural/functional theories are explanatory. Strain theory, for example, posits that deviance is caused by a discrepancy between the larger structure and culture of society. Conflict/critical theories are also explanatory and focus on how the elite are less likely to be defined as deviant than are the poor. Inter/actionist theories are constructionist, highlighting how social control agents label certain behaviors as deviant. Individuals stigmatized by social control agents organize their lives and identities around their deviant status. Not all deviant actions are necessarily harmful or even objectionable.

Crime is a form of deviance that violates criminal law. The major components of the criminal justice system are law enforcement, the courts, and the correctional system. There are a number of types of crime, but the broadest distinction is between violent crimes that involve the threat or use of force and property crimes that involve gaining or destroying property.

Globalization has been associated with increases in cross-border crime, particularly the international drug trade. Illegal flows are aided by nation-states' declining ability to halt them. International policing has expanded to contend with the growth in global crime.

KEY TERMS

- asylum
- conformists
- constructionist theories
- consumer crimes
- corporate crime
- crime
- criminalization:
- criminology
- cybercrime
- deviance
- differential association
- discreditable stigma
- discredited stigma
- explanatory theories
- extradition
- felonies
- general deterrence
- hate crimes
- innovators
- knowledge management
- labeling theory
- misdemeanors
- moral entrepreneurs
- moral panic
- organized crime
- parole
- political crimes
- primary deviance
- probation
- property crimes
- rebels
- recidivism
- retreatists
- ritualists
- rule creators
- rule enforcers
- secondary deviance
- situation management
- social control
- social control agents
- specific deterrence
- stigma
- strain theory
- symbol
- violent crime
- white-collar crimes

REVIEW QUESTIONS

1. What do sociologists mean when they say that deviance is socially defined? Given a sociological approach, in what ways is tattooing deviant, and in what ways is it not?

2. How can we understand deviance as a global flow? In what ways do countries differ in terms of their interpretations of what is deviant? In an increasingly globalized world, what are the consequences of these differing interpretations?

3. How does consuming the "wrong" products and services make someone a deviant? What does this suggest about the relationships between power and deviance?

4. Adolescents value a certain level of independence from their parents, often wanting more control over their own lives. They want to be able to do what they want to do without needing permission from their parents. Apply Merton's strain theory to explain how adolescents might behave, given this desire for more independence.

5. Why do those who rank high in such hierarchies as business, government, and the military have a much greater ability to commit deviant acts, to have those acts seen as legitimate, and to get away with them? What does this suggest about the "fairness" of deviance?

6. What are the differences between a discredited stigma and a discreditable stigma? What is an example of each?

7. How is crime different from deviance? Why do some forms of deviance become criminalized, whereas others do not?

8. How do you explain the fact that so many people are in prison in the United States? Why is the U.S. incarceration rate the highest in the world?

9. Is the death penalty useful as a form of general deterrence? Are you in favor of the death penalty? If so, for what crimes?

10. What sorts of barriers have countries attempted to implement to limit the global flow of drugs? Why have these been relatively unsuccessful?

MediaNews Group / Orange County Register via Getty Images

8 SOCIAL STRATIFICATION

> **LEARNING OBJECTIVES**
>
> **8.1** Describe the various dimensions of social stratification.
>
> **8.2** Identify factors contributing to economic inequality.
>
> **8.3** Identify different types of social mobility.
>
> **8.4** Discuss theories of social stratification.
>
> **8.5** Discuss the characteristics of global stratification.
>
> **8.6** Outline the different theories of global stratification.
>
> **8.7** Identify the different types of worldwide inequalities.
>
> **8.8** Discuss the changing positions in the global stratification system.

STRATIFICATION AND LIFE SAVING VACCINES

When the WHO first declared the SARS-CoV-2 virus to be a global pandemic in March 2020, a lot of questions were immediately raised (Ryan and Nanda 2023c). What could we do about it? Who was being most impacted? How could we best keep ourselves, and our loved ones, from catching the potentially deadly virus? Although masks and physical distancing were the best solutions we had in the short term, few doubted that the longer-term solution was a cure or, more likely, a vaccine to help prevent the virus. Vaccines have a long history of helping to prevent disease (this is why most people in the world receive literally dozens of them over their lifetimes, including as babies in our first days of life). Vaccines have even helped to virtually wipe out a number of diseases, including smallpox and polio, both diseases responsible for killing, and disabling, millions of people throughout human history. That is why when Margaret Keenan received the first fully approved COVID-19 vaccine in December 2020, the world breathed a small sigh of relief.

But then the realities of the ways in which societies are structured set in. Now there were new questions to be answered. Who were to be the first to receive this life-saving vaccine? How could we get more? Should countries stockpile vaccines for a just-in-case scenario, or should they share them with the rest of the world who was still waiting for a first jab? And, at the center of much of this, who was going to pay, and profit, from it all?

It likely came as a surprise to few who study inequality that the first people to have access to the vaccine were wealthy (mostly White) people living in wealthy (mostly White) countries. Those who already had access to healthcare were also advantaged. But why was this so unsurprising? Why did we *expect* that the world's already privileged would be the first to have access to something that could literally mean the difference between life and death? Why did so few dare to suggest that perhaps the world's most vulnerable should be prioritized—that maybe decisions about who should receive the vaccine should be based on health risk, and on a global scale (this is, after all, a truly global virus), rather than on wealth, privilege, and passports? In many ways, inequality is so deeply embedded in the ways that we live our lives that few of us stop to question it.

That the world is unfair should not be news to anyone. As sociologists, we recognize this reality but also seek to better understand *why* the world is unfair. What social structures are in place that allow, sometimes even encourage, various forms of inequality? Why do some people have more opportunities to succeed than others? How can we better understand structures of inequality and, if we are so inclined, do anything about them? These are just some of the questions this chapter will seek to address.

DIMENSIONS OF SOCIAL STRATIFICATION

We often hear that society is unfair. This is generally taken to mean that a relatively small number of people have way too much, while most of the rest of us have far too little. This unfairness is made abundantly clear when we see news reports about the excesses of the super-rich, such as multimillion-dollar bonuses, private jets, mansions, or condos in New York or London worth tens or hundreds of millions of dollars. At the other extreme, the gap is just as clear when we encounter homeless people seeking assistance on street corners and at turn lanes on heavily traveled roads.

There are many ways in which modern day society is stratified: on the basis of sex and gender, race and ethnicity, religion, nationality, and social economic class, to name just a few. Indeed, most societies, and especially global society, treat people differently based on a seemingly endless array of factors.

What is it that some people have, or are thought to have, and others lack? The most obvious answer is money and what money buys. However, **social stratification** involves hierarchical differences not only in economic positions but also in other important areas, such as status, or social honor, and power. Social stratification has a profound effect on how monetary and nonmonetary resources are distributed in society and around the globe (global stratification is discussed in more detail later in this chapter). Many sociological discussions of stratification draw on an important set of dimensions derived from the work of the social theorist Max Weber ([1921] 1968; Bendix and Lipset 1966). These three dimensions are social class, status, and power.

Social Class

One's economic position in the stratification system, especially one's occupation, and often one's family background, defines one's **social class**. A person's social class position strongly determines and reflects their income and wealth. Those who rank close to one another in wealth and income can be said to be members of the same social class. For example, multibillionaire entrepreneurs such as Mark Zuckerberg, Jeff Bezos, Bill Gates, and Elon Musk belong to one social class; the janitor in your university building and the mechanic who fixes your car at the corner gas station belong to another. Terms often used to describe a person's social class are *upper class* (e.g., large-scale entrepreneurs and many large investors, especially in hedge funds), *middle class* (e.g., nurses, teachers, veterinarians, air traffic controllers, travel agents, and firefighters), *working class* (e.g., manual, clerical, and full-time service workers in industries such as fast food), and *lower class* (e.g., part-time service and other workers and the unemployed). Figure 8.1 illustrates the relationships among occupation, income, and social class in the United States (Gilbert 2018). Its teardrop shape represents the percentage of people in each class; there are substantially more people in the working and lower classes than there are in the upper class. As we will soon see, the United States, and the rest of the world, is even more stratified than Figure 8.1 suggests.

Status

The second dimension of Weber's stratification system, *status*, relates to the prestige attached to a person's positions within society. The existence and importance of this dimension demonstrate the fact that factors other than those associated with money are considered valuable in society. For example, in recent poll, the well-paid doctor was ranked the most prestigious, followed by the less-well-paid scientist, and in third place the comparatively modestly paid firefighter. However, the often exorbitantly paid and rewarded corporate executive was not even in the top 10 occupations in terms of prestige (Harris Interactive 2016).

Power

A third dimension of social stratification is **power**, or the ability to get others to do what you want them to do, even if it is against their will. Those who have a great deal of power rank high in the stratification system, while those with little or no power are arrayed at or near the bottom. This is clearest in the case of politics, when, for example, the president of a country ranks very high in power, while ordinary voters have comparatively little political power. Still lower on the political power scale in many countries are disenfranchised citizens, such as convicted felons, and noncitizens, including undocumented immigrants.

Power, of course, is not restricted to the political system but also exists in many other institutions. Thus, top officials in large corporations have greater power than do workers, religious leaders have

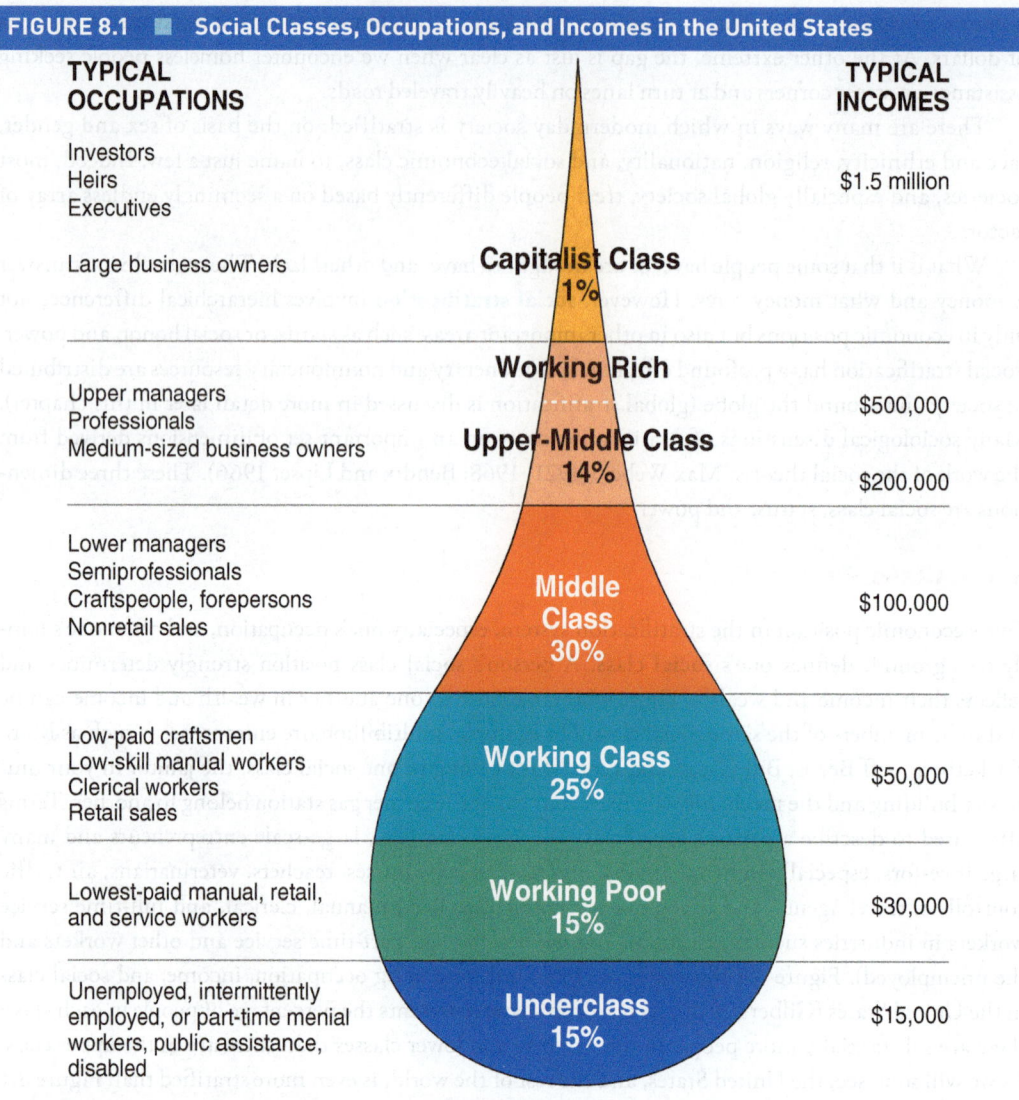

FIGURE 8.1 ■ Social Classes, Occupations, and Incomes in the United States

Source: Adapted from D. L. Gilbert (2021). The American class structure in an age of growing inequality. Thousand Oaks, CA: SAGE.

more power than do parishioners, and those who head households are more powerful than are their spouses or children (Collins 1975).

Greater income is generally associated with more power, but there are exceptions to this rule. In the late 2000s, an increasing number of media stories focused on the phenomenon of "breadwinner wives" and "breadwinner moms," or those wives and moms who are the sole or primary providers of income for their families. Only 11 percent of households with children under 18 had breadwinner moms in 1960, but that had risen to almost 42 percent in 2019. Then there are "alpha wives and moms"—women who earn more than their husbands (Chae 2015). As shown in Figure 8.2, only around 16 percent of wives in 1981 had income greater than that of their husbands, but by 2021, 31 percent of married women were alpha wives. In spite of their greater income, breadwinner wives and moms may not have greater power in the marital relationship, and in many cases, they are compelled to be content with sharing power with their husbands (Cherlin 2010).

Achievement and Ascription

Thus far, we have been describing a system of social stratification defined by status, power, and class—especially economic class. This, however, is but one type of stratification system. A chief characteristic of this system is the idea that social positions are based on **achievement**, or the accomplishments—the

FIGURE 8.2 ■ Percentage of Married Women Who Earn More than Their Husbands, 1981–2021

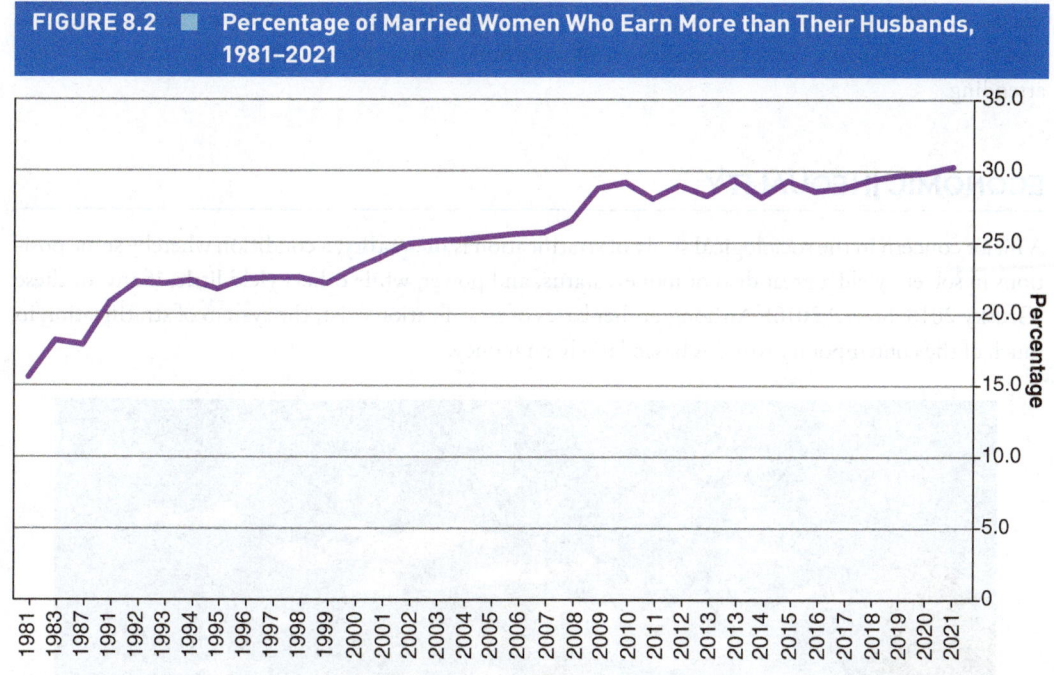

Source: U.S. Census Bureau, Current Population Survey, 1982 to 2022 Annual Social and Economic Supplements (CPS ASEC).

merit—of the individual. For example, a person becomes a physician and thereby attains a high-level position in the stratification system, only after many years of education, hard work, and practical experience. Conversely, some people believe that a person at or near the bottom of the stratification system is there because they lack the accomplishments necessary to achieve a higher level. These people might suggest that a homeless person is homeless because that individual has not worked hard enough to earn a living wage (despite the fact that a great number of homeless people are, in fact, employed). The idea that achievement determines social class is accurate to some extent, but the fact is that where a person ends up in the stratification system may have little or nothing to do with achievement. Instead, it can be explained by external factors over which the individual has little control.

A person's status usually has a great deal to do with **ascription**, or being born with, or inheriting, certain characteristics, such as race, gender, wealth, and high status (or, conversely, poverty and low status; Bond 2012). Thus, a person's position in the social hierarchy may be due to nothing more than the accident of being born a particular sex, or a particular race. Ascribed status has little or nothing to do with a person's accomplishments, skills, or abilities and yet holds great sway over one's position in the social hierarchy.

Distribution of Rewards vs. Distribution of Opportunities for Rewards

What society values (money, big houses, well-paying jobs, college degrees) are distributed unequally throughout society. The **distribution of rewards** refers to how socially valued objects and statuses are found throughout a given society. For example, you are working toward an educational degree, a social reward that is achieved but one that is not distributed equally, or randomly, throughout society. Sociologists are interested in the ways in which rewards are distributed and especially in the ways that those distributions are often not random.

To help better understand how rewards are distributed within a given society, sociologists are especially interested in what opportunities are available for different populations. The **distribution of opportunities for rewards** refers to how the opportunities to attain a certain socially valued object or status are spread throughout society. For example, the children of millionaires have a much greater opportunity to attend college than do the children of those who are working multiple jobs to make ends meet. This does not mean that such children cannot attain the same rewards, but it does mean that they face additional barriers to have the opportunity to be able to do so. In some cases, especially when the law intervenes, people can be barred from opportunities altogether. For example, there is a long history of colleges barring certain populations (Black people, women, undocumented immigrants) from attending.

ECONOMIC INEQUALITY

A major concern in the sociological study of stratification is **inequality**, a condition whereby some positions in society yield a great deal of money, status, and power, while others yield little, if any, of these (Grusky 2018; Sowell 2018). Although other bases of stratification exist, the system of stratification in much of the contemporary world is based largely on money.

Sociologists differentiate between different forms of money. Although income (such as money earned from employment) is important, wealth (such as owning a home or other property) can be more important, because wealth can be inherited or used to generate additional income.

JasonDoiy/iStock Photos

Money can take the form of income or wealth. **Income** is the amount of money a person earns from a job, a business, or returns on various types of assets (e.g., rents on real estate) and investments (e.g., dividends on stocks and bonds). Income is generally measured year by year. For example, you might have an income of $25,000 per year. **Wealth**, on the other hand, is the total amount of a person's financial assets and other properties less the total of various kinds of debts, or liabilities. Assets include, among others, savings, investments, homes, and automobiles, while debts include home mortgages, student loans, car loans, and amounts owed to credit card companies. If all your assets total $100,000 but you owe $25,000, your wealth (or net worth) amounts to $75,000.

Wealth is often thought of as more important in many instances because, unlike income, it can be inherited and passed along to one's children (or other benefactors). You cannot pass your salary on to your children, but you can pass on your home, car, boat, stocks, and other assets. Wealth is also important because it can also generate income. For example, owning a second home that you rent out generates additional income. We will discuss this more later in the chapter.

Income Inequality

Sociologists are interested in inequality in status and power, but they tend to be most concerned about economic inequality. In many parts of the world, incomes became more equitable from the late 1920s until the 1970s. However, since the 1970s, there has been a substantial increase in income inequality in many countries, with a few individuals earning a great deal more and many earning little, if any, more. Even in the United States, which we historically and erroneously regard as an egalitarian society, income inequality has been rising since the 1970s and now rivals levels that existed in the late 1920s (Morduch and Schneider 2017; Stewart 2018b). Sociologists who study income inequality sometimes divide workers into income groups based on their share of total aggregate income earned. In 1970, the U.S. households representing 5 percent of the population with the highest incomes took home 15.6 percent of all income that year; the other 95 percent of households earned 84.4%. By 2021, the disparity between the highest earners and everyone else had increased—the top 5 percent income group kept 22.1 percent of income earned that year, compared to 77.9 percent for everyone else (U.S. Census Bureau, 2022a).

Income inequality today is even greater if we focus not on the top 5 percent but on the elite of the elite, the top 0.1 percent of households. Table 8.1 shows annual income growth for different wage groups in the U.S. In 2021, those in the top 0.1 percent had average incomes of more than $3.3 million. This was more than the total annual incomes of the other 99.9 percent of earners combined. The table also shows how incomes of the top 0.1 percent have increased compared to other wage groups. From 1979 to 2021, the average annual income of these top earners increased by 465 percent, compared to an increase of 206 percent for the top 1 percent of earners and 136 percent for the top 5 percent of earners. Thus, it's a great time to be rich, but it is an even better time to be uber-rich.

Several broad reasons have been put forth to explain recent increases in income inequality.

- *Deindustrialization.* The decline of industry in many developed countries, has led to the loss of many higher-paying industrial jobs (Kollmeyer and Pichler 2013).

- *Decline of labor unions.* Deindustrialization is also related to the decline in the power of labor unions, which had helped many industrial workers obtain higher pay and generous benefits.

- *Technological advances.* The highest-paying new jobs in recent years have been created in high-tech, high-skill areas, such as information technology (IT). Relatively few people have received the training necessary to shift from industrial to high-tech work.

- *Political climate.* One of the many political factors in increasing economic inequality is the fact that the working and lower classes are no longer well-represented in the political system (Edsall 2018b).

Digital Living: Income Inequality in the New Sharing Economy

In the sharing economy, instead of buying or renting in the usual ways, we share goods and services—at low cost or free—with others (Gansky 2010; Stein 2015). Instead of renting a hotel room, we can get a room in a private home, or even an entire home, through the online site Airbnb or Vrbo. Instead of hailing a taxi, we can use Uber or Lyft's smartphone app and get a prepaid ride in a private automobile. Instead of waiting for a table at a "hot" restaurant, we can hire someone online to do so through TaskRabbit.

The sharing economy is clearly the wave of the future. But although some sharing is free of profit making and the exchange of money (Atsushi 2014), big businesses have become deeply engaged, and the sharing economy is growing highly stratified (Schor and Attwood-Charles 2017).

At the top are the founders, executives, and financiers of the most successful companies. Uber is now valued at between $72.23 billion as of 2023, and its founders are likely to be millionaires or even billionaires (Companies Market Cap n.d.-b). But for most of the drivers, the job is part-time and the pay low. Drivers use their own cars, pay their own expenses, and lack benefits and job security. As a result, they are likely to land in or near the lower class. Worse, their success is costing traditional taxi drivers their jobs. Ride-hailing apps capture 85 percent of the market and their cars outnumber the yellow taxis in NYC by nine to one (Schneider, n.d.).

TABLE 8.1 ■ Average Annual Wages and Percent Change Over Time by U.S. Wage Group, 1979–2021.

Average annual wages (2021$)								Long-term change	
Year	1979	1989	2000	2007	2019	2020	2021	1979–2019	1979–2021
Bottom 90%	$28.42	$29,289	$32,770	$33,814	$36,655	$36,660	$36,571	29.0%	28.7%
90th–99th percentile	$93,226	$106,915	$137,93B	$147,705	$164,760	$169,455	$167,639	76.7%	79.8%
90th–95th	$79,140	$86,520	$110,104	$117,084	$129,259	$132,401	$129,724	63.3%	63.9%
95th–99th	$110,833	$132,409	$172,730	$185,981	$209,137	$215,771	$215,032	88.7%	94.0%
Top 5%	$142,159	$194,873	$270,682	$288,048	$308,487	$322,349	$335,891	117.0%	136.3%
Top 1%	$267,464	$444,731	$662,488	$696,316	$705,887	$748,662	$819,324	163.9%	206.3%
99.0th–99.9th	$232,046	$341,410	$444,845	$474,979	$499,389	$521,225	$542,283	115.2%	133.7%
99.9th–100th	$586,222	$1,374,624	$2,621,271	$2,688,346	$2,564,364	$2,795.59	$3,312.69	337.4%	465.1%
Average	$36,639	$40,430	$48,532	$50,689	$54,877	$55,731	$56,195	49.8%	53.4%

Source: Economic Policy Institute analysis of Kopczuk, Saez, and Song, "Uncovering the American Dream: Inequality and Mobility in Social Security Earnings Data Since 1937" (2007) and Social Security Administration wage statistics.

Smartphone apps such as those of Uber and Airbnb create a divide between those who control the sharing economy and those who work in it. Is such increased stratification inevitable?

Russell Hart / Alamy Stock Photo

Airbnb, valued at an estimated $88.27 billion as of 2023, has created a similar stratification system, with founders and executives on top and many who list their apartments and homes nearer the bottom (Companies Market Cap n.d.-a). However, few of those participants are actually individuals sharing space with others. For example, although New York City is attempting to crack down on this, commercial operators there supply more than one-third of Airbnb rental units and earn more than one-third of the profits; 6 percent of the hosts earned 37 percent of the revenue, and one had 272 units, earning revenue of $6.8 million (Inside Airbnb, n.d.). There are now more than a dozen hosts with more than 100 listings each in NYC alone. Some critics argue that, at least in this case, "the very term 'sharing economy' is ridiculous" (Streitfeld 2014, A1).

Belk (2014) argues that in these cases and many others, sharing is being transformed into "pseudo-sharing" by, among others, profit-making organizations that have found this to be a way to grow rich. There is woefully little sharing in the sharing economy. The sharing economy is creating a new stratification system, or at least new positions in the current system. Many people will be at or near the bottom.

Wealth Inequality

As unfair as income inequality may seem, the greatest disparities in society—the largest differences between the haves and the have-nots—are found in the enormous differences in wealth (that is, economic assets) in society. Wealth inequality tends to be much greater than income inequality. The two are linked, however, because wealth tends to produce various sources of income, such as dividends and interest. Those with significant amounts of income from such sources are far more likely to rank toward the top of the stratification system in terms of income than are those who rely mainly on wages and salaries. Thus, wealth itself is important, as is the stream of income that wealth tends to produce.

Growing Wealth Disparities

Like income inequality, wealth inequality has tended to increase in recent years in most countries, and the tax system in most countries has become of *decreasing* utility in reducing that inequality (Looney and Moore 2016; Piketty 2014). In the United States, as of 2021, the country's richest 1 percent own nearly 1/3 of the wealth, even more than the bottom 90 percent combined. They saw their wealth increase by a staggering $6.5 trillion in 2021 alone, and their overall wealth increased by more than 1/3 just during the COVID-19 pandemic.

As with income inequality, the super-rich (the top 0.01 percent in terms of wealth) are growing dramatically better off in terms of wealth. Wealth brings with it a wide range of advantages:

- It can be invested to generate income and ultimately even greater wealth.

- It can be used to purchase material comforts of all sorts: mega-homes, vacation retreats, luxury cars, and custom-tailored clothes, as well as the services of housekeepers, nannies, gardeners, personal trainers, and so forth.

- It can afford far more freedom and autonomy than less wealthy individuals can acquire. An example would be the freedom to leave unsatisfactory employment—or not to work at all—without worrying about how the bills will be paid.

- Most wealth can be passed on to offspring, even generations away, guaranteeing that they will live a similarly privileged lifestyle.

Wealth and the growing disparities in wealth received enormous academic and media attention with the publication of economist Thomas Piketty's *Capital in the Twenty-First Century* (2014; see also Antonio 2014). Piketty sees wealth as being of greater importance than income. Rather than relying on pay or a salary (even though it might be high) for their labor, those with wealth rely much more on the income their wealth produces, such as earned interest, rental from properties, dividends on stocks and bonds, and royalties. Overall returns from such sources have historically outstripped increases in salaries and pay.

Status, Power, and Wealth

Perhaps of greatest importance is the fact that wealth not only accords a high-level position on one dimension of stratification, social class, but it is also an important factor in gaining similar positions on the other dimensions of stratification, status and power. Those who have great wealth tend to rank high in social class because class is, to a considerable degree, defined economically and wealth is a key indicator of it. Those with great wealth are also generally able to buy or to otherwise acquire whatever gives them high status and great power.

In terms of status, the wealthy can afford an increased level and better quality of education. They can, for example, send their children to very expensive and exclusive prep schools and Ivy League universities. In some elite universities, being a "legacy" applicant—the son or daughter of an elite who attended the same school—can increase the chances of gaining admission, perhaps by as much as eight times (Arcidiacono et al. 2021; Barshay 2022). The practice of favoring legacy applicants is sometimes called "affirmative action for the rich" (Kahlenberg 2010). At Princeton, for example, 33 percent of legacy applicants were admitted to the class scheduled to graduate in 2015 compared with 8.5 percent of nonlegacies (Nisen 2013). Likewise, 29 percent of Harvard's incoming class of 2021 was composed of legacy applicants (Blumberg 2017). Since 2000, family legacy determined 15–40 percent of Ivy League admissions, that is, 2–5 times the overall admission rate. For example, in the class of 2019 as many as 36 percent of the applicants accepted at Harvard were legacy students. Based on an 8.5 percent overall acceptance rate, legacy students had a 42 percent advantage of being accepted. At Yale, 20–35 percent of legacy applicants have been accepted since 2000, and 15–33 percent were accepted at Princeton (Ornstein, 2019). A scandal in 2019 revealed that some of the wealthy were even bribing college officials and athletic coaches at elite colleges in order to gain admission for their children.

The wealthy can also purchase more of the trappings of high culture, such as season tickets to the opera or multimillion-dollar paintings by famous artists. The wealthy can also achieve recognition as philanthropists by, for example, attending $1,000-per-ticket charity balls or even donating the money needed to build a new wing of a hospital.

Power over employees is a fact of life for wealthy individuals who own businesses or run other organizations. Their needs for financial, household, and personal services give the wealthy another source of power. They have the ability to direct the activities of many charities and civic groups. And if that weren't enough, the wealthy can buy more power by bribing political officials or making generous campaign contributions to favored politicians. Such contributions often give donors great behind-the-scenes power. In some cases, the wealthy choose to use their money to run for public office themselves; if successful, their families may come to occupy positions that give them great power. These families can even become political dynasties, with two or more generations attaining high political office. For example, Prescott Bush made his money on Wall Street and became a U.S. senator. His son, George H. W. Bush, became president of the United States, as did his grandson, George W. Bush. Another grandson, Jeb Bush, former governor of Florida, was a (failed) candidate for the Republican nomination for president in 2016.

The Perpetuation of Wealth

One of the great advantages of the wealthy is their ability to maintain their social class across generations. Their ability to keep their wealth, if not expand it, often allows the members of the upper class to pass their wealth, and the upper-class position that goes with it, to their children. There is little chance, for example, that the children of Bill Gates, Mark Zuckerberg, or Elon Musk will end up as janitors.

The wealthy are able to perpetuate their wealth in large part because they have been able to use their money and influence to resist taxation systems designed to redistribute at least some of the wealth in society. For example, the wealthy have fought long and hard against the estate tax, which places a high tax on assets worth more than a certain amount that are left behind when an individual dies. Many of the wealthy prefer to refer to the estate tax in more negative terms, as a "death tax." Without government and social mechanisms in place to help promote greater economic equality, the privileged in society are likely to only continue becoming even more privileged.

The Decline of the Middle Class

Much has been written in recent years about the decline, or the hollowing out, of the middle class, especially in the United States (Frank 2013). The major reason for the decline of the middle class is the decline, usually owing to technological change, of middle-income jobs, such as better-paid, often unionized positions in manufacturing. In other cases, those jobs have been lost to successful companies elsewhere in the world. Some displaced workers have been able to get better-paying jobs and thereby move up the stratification hierarchy. However, many more have had to take lower-paying service jobs, such as in the fast-food industry. They have likely dropped into the lower class, as have those who have been unable to find jobs or have been forced to accept poorly paid work.

Another major factor in the decline of the middle class is wage stagnation in the kinds of jobs that members of this class are likely to continue to hold (Greenhouse 2015; Wisman 2013). They may still have the same jobs they had a decade or two ago, but the wages associated with them have tended to increase little and actually have been more likely to decline in real terms over that time. As a result, they are worse off because they are trying to pay for various goods and services whose prices have risen, sometimes dramatically, over time but with wages that have not kept pace with those price rises. As a result, many may still be considered part of the middle class, but they may not feel that way because their expenses have risen faster than their income—they may no longer be able to afford the things usually associated with a middle-class lifestyle.

The Great Recession of 2008–2009 badly hurt the middle class. For example, many lost their homes because they could no longer afford their mortgage payments. Government efforts in the wake of the recession (such as bailing out banks and investment companies) greatly aided the upper class, but they did little or nothing for the middle class (the government bailed out few homeowners in danger of losing their homes; Hacker and Pierson 2010). The COVID-19 pandemic has also had a negative impact on many in the middle class, especially those who were unable to engage in remote work.

The decline of the middle class is of great concern, especially to those who are no longer in it or can no longer aspire to be part of it. From a large-scale perspective, this decline creates a stratification system that splits into the upper and lower classes, with an increasingly massive hole in the middle. This leads to growing inequality and to increasingly less hope for those in the lower classes of finding middle-income positions that will allow them to rise in the stratification system.

How are poverty and social class related? Is poverty inevitable in a stratified society?
AP Photo/Mark Lennihan

Poverty

Poverty, or a lack of necessary resources, is a serious global problem that impacts hundreds of millions of people around the world. Poverty and the many problems associated with it are of great concern both to sociologists and to society as a whole (Desmond 2016; Edin and Schaefer 2015; Iceland 2013).

Poverty is troubling for many reasons, the most important of which is its negative effect on the lives of the poor themselves. The lack of a job, or having one that does not offer a living wage, is likely to be associated with many troubling conditions. Those suffering from poverty are likely to suffer from food insecurity—that is, to have difficulty getting enough to eat. An estimated 1.3 billion people are currently food insecure; that is more than 15 percent of people on the planet (Zereyesus & Cardell, 2022). People living in poverty are also likely to be in poor physical and mental health and, as a result, to have a lower life expectancy. In fact, the poor are falling increasingly behind the rich as the gap between the rich and poor in terms of life span has widened dramatically over the years. For men born in 1920, those in the top 10 percent of earners could expect to live six more years than those in the bottom 10 percent of earners. For men born in 1950, the gap had more than doubled to 14 years. For women over the same time period, the gap had grown from 4.7 years to 13 years (Tavernise 2016).

The great disparity between the rich and the poor is considered by many to be a moral problem, if not a moral crisis, for society as a whole. The poor are often seen as not doing what they should, or could, to raise themselves out of poverty. They are seen as disreputable, which makes them objects of moral censure by those who have succeeded in society (Damer 1974; Matza 1966; Shildrick and MacDonald 2013). They may be blamed for the degradation of society and may even blame themselves for that degradation as well as for their own poverty. However, some see poverty as an entirely different kind of moral problem. They argue that the poor should be seen as the "victims" of a system that impoverishes them. The existence of large numbers of poor people in otherwise affluent societies is a "moral stain" on those societies (Harvey 2007). Something must be amiss in the economic and political systems in societies that perpetuate so much poverty.

Analyzing Poverty

It may be tempting to blame the poor for the existence of poverty, but a sociological perspective notes the larger social forces that create and perpetuate poverty. To the sociologist, poverty persists for at least three basic reasons.

- Poverty is built into the capitalist system, and virtually all societies today—even China—have capitalist economies. Capitalist businesses seek to maximize profits. They do so by keeping wages as low as possible and by hiring as few workers as possible. When business slows, they are likely to fire or lay off people, thrusting many of them into poverty. It is in the interest of the capitalist system to have a large number of unemployed, and therefore poor, people. This population serves as what Marx called the "reserve army of the unemployed." This is a readily available pool of people who can be drawn quickly into the labor force when business booms and more workers are needed. The presence of this reserve army also keeps existing workers in line and reluctant to demand much, if anything, from management.

- Competition among social classes encourages some elite groups of people to seek to enhance their economic position by limiting the ability of other groups to maintain even their lower economic positions. The elites do so by restricting the poor's access to opportunities and resources such as those afforded by various government and social systems.

- Government actions to reduce poverty, or to ameliorate its negative effects on people and society, are generally limited by groups of people who believe that the poor should make it on their own and not be afforded the aid of the government or others in society. They also believe that government aid reduces people's incentive to do what they need to do on their own to rise above the poverty line.

There are two broad types of poverty.

- **Absolute poverty** is a measure of what people need to survive. No matter the standard for measuring poverty, absolute poverty remains constant over time, although its level is revised to take inflation into consideration.

- **Relative poverty** is defined not by some objective standard but rather by the fact that some people, irrespective of income, are, or consider themselves to be, poor, relative to others to whom they relate. Thus, even middle-class people (especially those who have experienced wage stagnation or have lost their jobs) and some upper-class people can see themselves as poor in comparison with some of their even more successful peers.

Poverty in the United States

To measure poverty the U.S. government uses an absolute measure, a **poverty line**, or threshold, in terms of a set income. The formula used involves multiplying the cost of what is deemed to be a nutritionally adequate food plan by three. This is because a family is assumed to spend a third of its budget on food. It is worth noting that many people criticize this calculation for not considering other necessary expenses, such as child care, housing, and transportation. The poverty line in 2023 for a family of four was a pretax income of $30,000; for a single adult it was $14,580 (U.S. Department of Health and Human Services 2023). In 2021, almost 11.6 percent of the U.S. population, or 37.9 million people, lived below the poverty line and were therefore officially categorized as poor (U. S. Census Bureau 2022b).

Of course, millions who exist at or slightly above that line would also be considered poor by many people in society. There have been calls for a stronger focus on the "near poor" (Bruder 2017; Hokayem and Heggeness 2014). Those who have income less than 25 percent above the poverty line would be included in this category. There is no question that poverty is a huge problem in the United States, but it is almost certainly far greater than most of us imagine.

Looking at the longer-term trends shown in Figure 8.3, we can see considerable variation in the numbers of people living in poverty from year to year since 1959. For example, a sharp increase in poverty coincided with the beginning of the Great Recession in 2008, but poverty rates have decreased slightly in the last few years as the economy improved. As you might expect, given their disadvantages in income and wealth, minorities suffer disproportionately from poverty. The poverty rate in 2021 for non-Hispanic Whites was nearly 8.2 percent. The 8.1 percent poverty rate for Asians was down significantly from 16 percent in the mid-1980s. Even more telling, the poverty rate was 19.5 percent for Blacks and 17.1 percent for Hispanics (Statista Research Department 2022b).

FIGURE 8.3 ■ Poverty in the United States, 1959–2020

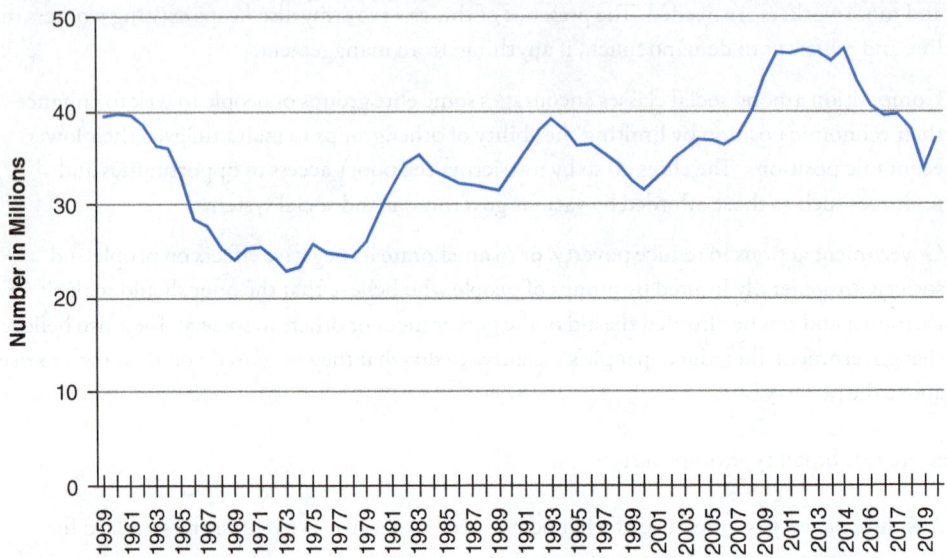

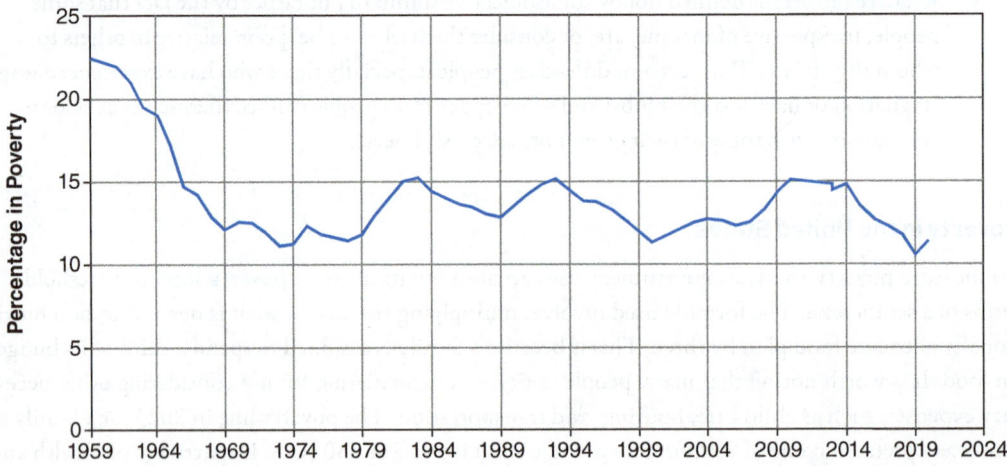

Source: Shrider, Emily, Melisa Kollar, Frances Chen, and Jessica Semega, 2021, *Poverty Status of People by Family Relationship, Race, and Hispanic Origin: 1959 to 2020,* Income and Poverty in the United States: 2020, Report No. P60–273, Table B-4, Washington, D.C: United States Census Bureau.

The Feminization of Poverty

A central issue in the study of poverty is the degree to which women and children are overrepresented among the poor (Abercrombie and Hastings 2016; West et al. 2017). In 2021, 12.5 percent of U.S. women were below the poverty line, whereas only about 10.4 percent of men lived in poverty (Statista Research Department, 2022a). Poverty levels vary by age: Women ages 45 to 74 are less likely to be poor than are those 18 and below and 75 and above (Statista Research Department, 2023). Female poverty levels also vary based on race and ethnicity: Both Black and Latino women are more than twice as likely to be poor as are White women (Bleiweis et al., 2020). Also, as noted previously, female-headed households with no husband present have far higher rates of poverty than do families headed by married couples.

The **feminization of poverty** means that those living in poverty are more likely to be women than men (Goldberg 2010; Pearce 1978). Although in recent years the improved position of women in the work world, as well as increases in women's earnings, would seem to indicate that the poverty gap is narrowing, the gender gap persists. One of the reasons for that persistence is the fact that the trend toward gender wage equalization has been more than offset by the increasing tendency for a greater proportion of men to raise their earnings through "overwork"—that is, by working more than 50 hours per week (Cha and Weeden 2014).

A variety of demographic factors and changes help explain the feminization of poverty:

- Women are more likely than men to live alone (because, for example, single women marry later, and divorced women are less likely to remarry than are divorced men).

- Women have lower average earnings than men do. This is the case even when they do the same work.

- More children are being born to unmarried women, who tend to earn less than married women and who are more likely to be fully responsible for their dependents.

- Women have longer life spans than men do, increasing the likelihood that older women will be living on their own.

Economically, women suffer from a variety of disadvantages. Historically, males were considered to be the main breadwinners, and women, if they worked, were thought of as secondary earners. Women today exist in a sex-segregated labor force in which the best and highest-paying positions go largely to men (or are taken by them). The subordinate economic position of women is reinforced by the systematic wage discrimination practiced against them. They are routinely paid less than men, even for the same work. In regard to income, women are also adversely affected by the fact that they are more likely than men to work part-time, to hold temporary jobs, or to work at home (Presser 2005). Female workers have gained some ground in recent years: They earned about 61 percent of male earnings in 1960 but more than 82 percent in 2020 (Dowell 2022), in part because of stagnation in male earnings. In spite of the improvement, the gender gap in earnings persists to this day (see Figure 8.4).

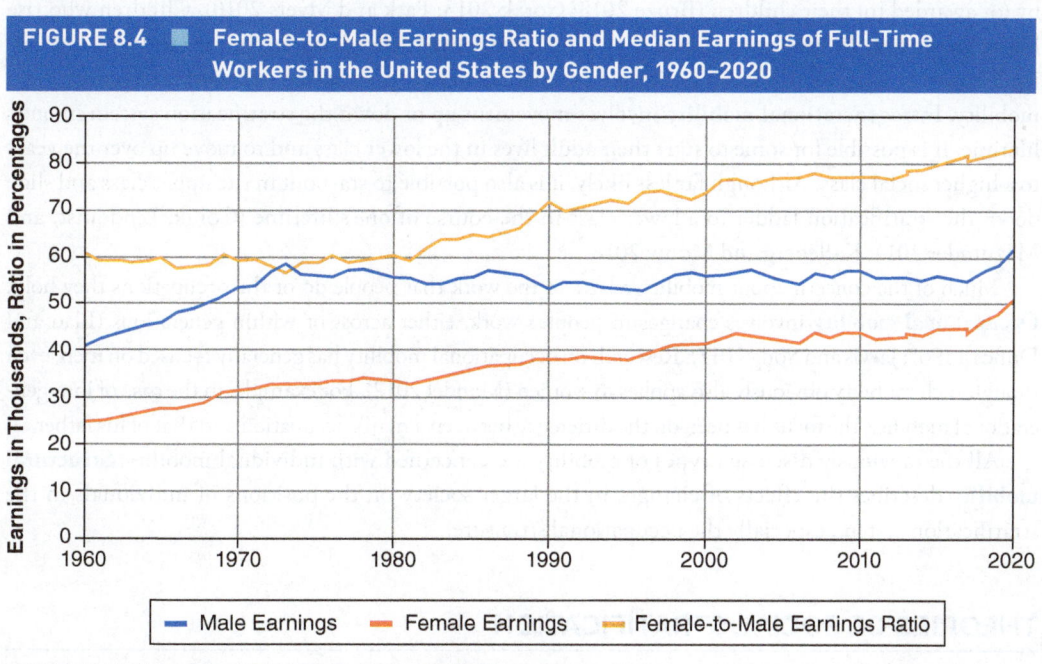

FIGURE 8.4 ■ Female-to-Male Earnings Ratio and Median Earnings of Full-Time Workers in the United States by Gender, 1960–2020

Source: Shrider, Emily, Melisa Kollar, Frances Chen, and Jessica Semega, 2021, *Number and Real Median Earnings of Total Workers and Full-Time, Year-Round Workers by Sex and Female-to-Male Earnings Ratio: 1960 to 2020*, Income and Poverty in the United States: 2020, Report No. P60-273, Table A-7, Washington, D.C.: United States Census Bureau

SOCIAL MOBILITY

Those who live in poverty are understandably eager to improve their lot. However, virtually everyone in a stratified system is concerned about **social mobility**, or the ability or inability to change one's position in the hierarchy (Hout 2015; van Leeuwen and Maas 2010). **Upward mobility**, the ability to move higher, is obviously of great personal concern to many. In addition, the possibility of such mobility for most is what lends legitimacy to the stratification system, indeed the entire economic system (Leventoglu 2014). This is especially the case for those who are poor. Upward mobility is the route out of poverty. However, upward mobility for most poor people is more myth than reality. The poor tend to end up in about the same place in the stratification system as where they started; they have little upward mobility (Alexander, Entwisle, and Olson 2014).

People in all social classes are also concerned about downward mobility (Katz and Kruger 2017). That is, people worry about descending to lower levels within their social class or to lower classes. Downward mobility causes people real hardships, and even its mere possibility is a great cause of concern. Immigrants and refugees who move to a new country almost always experience serious difficulties, such as discrimination and language differences. As a result, they are likely to experience downward mobility during the first generation in their new locale (Guo 2013). This is especially true of those who held high-level occupations in their countries of origin (Gans 2009). Given the current economic problems in the United States and Europe, many people who move there looking for new opportunities will experience downward mobility relative to their parents' status.

Types of Social Mobility

To this point, we have discussed upward and downward mobility, but there are a number of other types of social mobility as well. Upward and downward mobility are the key components of the general process of **vertical mobility**, or movement between social classes. Also of interest is **horizontal mobility**, or movement within one's social class. For example, the chief executive officer (CEO) of a given corporation may experience horizontal mobility by becoming the CEO of a different corporation. At the other end of the spectrum, the taxi driver who becomes an Uber driver also exhibits horizontal mobility.

Sociologists are also concerned about two other types of mobility. One is **intergenerational mobility**, or the difference between parents' position in the stratification system and the positions achieved by (or awarded to) their children (Bruze 2018; Corak 2013; Park and Myers 2010). Children who rise higher in the stratification system than their parents have experienced upward intergenerational mobility. Those who descend to a lower position on the ladder have experienced downward intergenerational mobility. **Intragenerational mobility** involves movement up or down the stratification system in one's lifetime. It is possible for some to start their adult lives in the lower class and to move up over the years to a higher social class. Although far less likely, it is also possible to start out in the upper class and slide down the stratification ladder to a lower class in the course of one's lifetime (Corak, Lindquist, and Mazumder 2014; Kalleberg and Mouw 2018).

Much of the concern about mobility relates to the work that people do or the occupations they hold. **Occupational mobility** involves changes in people's work, either across or within generations (Blau and Duncan 1967; Jarvis and Song 2017). Research on occupational mobility has generally focused on men, even though such mobility obviously also applies to women (Mandel 2012). For example, in the case of intergenerational mobility, the focus has been on the difference between a man's occupation and that of his father.

All the previously discussed types of mobility are concerned with individual mobility. **Structural mobility** describes the effects of changes in the larger society on the positions of individuals in the stratification system, especially the occupational structure.

THEORIES OF SOCIAL STRATIFICATION

Within the sociology of social stratification, the dominant theoretical approaches are structural/functional theory and conflict/critical theory. Also to be discussed here are inter/actionist theories of stratification.

As in all areas of the social world, different theories focus on different aspects of social stratification. Instead of choosing one theory over another, it may make more sense to use all of them. Structural/functional and conflict/critical theories tell us much about the macro structures of stratification, while inter/actionist theories offer great detail about what goes on within those structures at the micro levels.

Structural/Functional Theories

Within structural/functional theory, it is structural-functionalism that offers the most important—and controversial—theory of stratification. It argues that all societies are, and have been, stratified. Further, the theory contends that societies need a system of stratification in order to exist and function properly (Davis and Moore 1945). Stratification is needed, first, to ensure that people are motivated to occupy the less pleasant, more difficult, and more important positions in society. Second, stratification is needed to ensure that people with the right abilities and talents find their way into the appropriate positions. In other words, society needs a good fit between people and the requirements of the positions they occupy.

The structural/functional theory of stratification assumes that higher-level occupations, such as physician and lawyer, are more important to society than are lower-level occupations, such as laborer and janitor. The higher-level positions are also seen as being harder to fill because of the difficulties and unpleasantness associated with them. For example, both physicians and lawyers require many years of rigorous and expensive education. Physicians are required to deal with blood, human organs, and death; lawyers have to defend those who have committed heinous crimes. It is argued that in order to motivate enough people to occupy such positions, greater rewards, such as prestige, sufficient leisure, and especially large amounts of money, need to be associated with them. The implication is that without these high rewards, high-level positions would remain understaffed or unfilled. As a result, structural-functionalists see the stratification system as functional for the larger society. In this case, it provides the physicians and lawyers needed by society.

Conflict/Critical Theories

Conflict/critical theories tend to take a more critical view of stratified social structures because they involve and promote inequality. These theories are especially critical of the structural/functional perspective and its view that stratification is functional for society. Conflict/critical theories take a hard look at who benefits from the existing stratification system and how those benefits are perpetuated.

Social Rewards and Status

Conflict theorists ridicule the idea that higher-level positions in the social structure would go unfilled were it not for the greater rewards they offer. They ask, for example, whether higher-level positions in the stratification system are less pleasant than those at the lower end of the continuum. Is being a surgeon really less pleasant than being a garbage collector? The argument made by structural-functionalists seems preposterous to conflict theorists and many others.

Conflict theorists also wonder whether higher-level positions are always more important. Is a lawyer who engages in shady deals or who defends environmental polluters more important than a garbage collector? In fact, the garbage collector is of great importance to society. Without garbage collectors, diseases that could seriously threaten society would develop and spread.

Conflict theorists also criticize the idea that those at the upper levels of the stratification system require the large rewards offered to them. Many people would be motivated to occupy such positions as CEO of a multinational corporation or hedge fund manager without such extraordinary rewards. Conversely, many people are highly motivated to work in occupations that do not offer the highest levels of economic rewards (like teachers, nurses, and social workers). Fewer economic rewards for those at the top, and more for those at the bottom, would reduce the economic gap and make for a more equal society. Conflict theorists also argue that providing huge sums of money is not the only way to motivate people to pursue an advanced education or whatever else is necessary to occupy high-ranking positions. For example, the status or prestige associated with those positions would be a strong motivator, as would the power that comes with them.

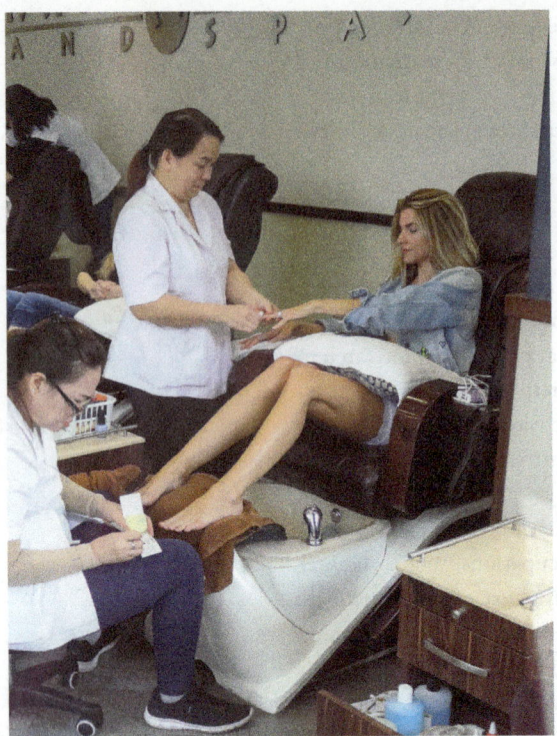

Social stratification is clear in the fact that women tend to be predominant in lower-level, lower-paying, gender-related jobs such as manicurist and pedicurist. Stratification is also clear in the fact that they tend to provide their services to higher-status women.

Gotpap/Bauer-Griffin/GC Images

Women and the Workplace

Operating from another variant of conflict/critical theory, feminist theorists often focus on the issue of stratification in the work world. Because men owned the means of production in the development of capitalism, they gained positions of great power and prestige that yielded major economic rewards (Hartmann 1979). Women, by contrast, were relegated to subordinate positions. Over the years, women's position in the stratification system has improved with the entrance of more women into the workforce and greater legal protections against workplace gender discrimination. There are now many more women in such high-ranking positions as executive, physician, and lawyer. Yet, compared with men overall, women still occupy a subordinate position in the stratification system. They can also find it harder to rise very high in that system.

Further, although males have been advantaged by their ability to engage in overwork and earn extra income (see the previous discussion), females, especially in male-dominated occupations, are likely to be disadvantaged, and even forced to leave the labor force entirely because of excessive work-related demands (Cha 2013). Such factors are far more likely to impede women's career progress.

Although the occupational situation for women has improved in recent years, the occupational world remains segregated based on gender (Gauchat, Kelly, and Wallace 2012). For example, women face a "motherhood penalty" (Bear and Glick 2017; Budig, Misra, and Boeckman 2016) in the workplace that limits upward mobility among women with children. Mothers seeking jobs are less likely to be hired, are offered lower salaries, and are seen by others as less committed to the workplace. Illustrating the pervasiveness of this penalty is the fact that the wage gap between women without children and mothers is greater than the wage gap between men and women (Adda, Dustmann, and Stevens 2017). Even women at the highest levels of the corporate world continue to face barriers unique to their gender. Recent research finds that women tend to boast less about their accomplishments and to give themselves lower self-ratings than do men. This internalized modesty about work performance contributes to lower upward mobility over and above external factors such as the glass ceiling (Smith and Huntoon 2014).

Inter/Actionist Theories

From an inter/actionist theory perspective, social stratification is not a function of macro-level structures but of micro-level individual actions and interactions. Although both structural/functional and conflict/critical theorists see stratification as a hierarchical structure, inter/actionists see it as much more of a process or set of processes. As a process, stratification involves interactions among people in different positions. Those who occupy higher-level positions may try to exert power in their interactions with those below them, but the latter can, and usually do, contest such exertions of power.

To the symbolic interactionist, inequality ultimately depends on face-to-face interaction. It is what happens in face-to-face interaction that leads to inequality. One symbolic interactionist approach identifies four processes that produce and reproduce inequality (Schwalbe et al. 2000). First, the dominant group defines the subordinate group into existence. Second, once in existence, the subordinate group finds ways of adapting to its situation. Third, efforts are made to maintain the boundaries between the two groups. Finally, both groups must manage the emotions associated with their positions in the stratification system. For example, those at the top must not show too much sympathy for those below them, and those at the bottom must not display too much anger toward those above them.

Ethnomethodologists note that people may exist within a stratified structure, but what really matters is what they do within such a structure. As in other aspects of the social world, people use commonsense procedures to operate and make their way in such structures. These procedures are used by elites and the downtrodden alike to "do" their positions in the system. For example, elite members of society are likely to carry themselves with authority and self-importance. In contrast, those at the bottom rungs of the stratification system are more likely to appear overburdened and to slouch throughout the day. In other words, one of the ways in which people do stratification is in their body language.

GLOBAL STRATIFICATION

Stratification on the global level is often seen as a divide between those nation-states, and many of the people within them, located in the so-called Global North, and those located in the so-called Global South (Elizaga 2018; Milanovic 2018). Although an oversimplification (to be discussed below), this phrasing is a popular way of thinking about global stratification and inequalities.

The Global North and Global South

The terms *Global North* and *Global South* are often used to refer countries divided by socioeconomic, and sometimes political, characteristics. Geographically speaking, this divide is largely accurate (most of the countries considered in the Global North are northernmost on a standard globe, and vice versa), but there are exceptions. For example, Australia is often considered as a part of the Global North while China is often considered a part of the Global South. It is important to note that these terms are less based on geography than they are on a shared status of socioeconomic conditions.

For centuries, the North has dominated, controlled, exploited, and oppressed the South. Today the North encompasses the nations that are the wealthiest and most powerful and have the highest status in the world, such as the United States, Germany, France, Great Britain, and Japan. The South, on the other hand, has a disproportionate number of nations that rank at or near the bottom in terms of global wealth and power. Most of the nations of Africa and Latin America are included here, as well as others, especially in Asia.

Immanuel Wallerstein's world-systems theory focuses on the world as the unit of analysis, rather than discrete nations.

Louis MONIER / Contributor

A society's position in the global stratification system greatly affects the stratification within that society. A nation that stands at or near the top of the global stratification system, such as the United States, tends to have a relatively larger proportion of middle- and upper-class positions. In contrast, a low-ranking nation, like Somalia, is dominated by lower-class positions and the poverty associated with them. The problems associated with this stratification system have been recognized by a number of global institutions, including the United Nations.

High-, Middle-, and Low-Income Countries

The wide variation among and between countries is hidden when they are simply categorized as part of either the Global North or the Global South. For example, countries in the same category may have more or less inequality. The United States and France are generally placed in the same category (Global North, high income), but the United States has a greater percentage of people at the bottom of the stratification system living in poverty than France does. Similarly, Vietnam and Nigeria are in the same category (Global South, middle income), but Nigeria has a larger number of wealthy elites than does Vietnam. In other words, the level of income inequality within Nigeria is far greater than that in Vietnam. Argentina has a high standard of living compared with the immense poverty found in many African countries, such as Sudan. However, both countries are considered to be part of the Global South. The Global North–South dichotomy ignores many of the important economic (and political) differences between nations within each category.

A slightly more nuanced category system focuses on low income, lower-middle-income, upper-middle income, and high-income economies (and their countries; see Figure 8.5; Ferrarini and Nelson

2016). As a general rule, low-income countries are concentrated in the Global South, while high-income countries are found in the Global North. Middle-income countries exist in both parts of the world, but a disproportionate number of them are in the Global South.

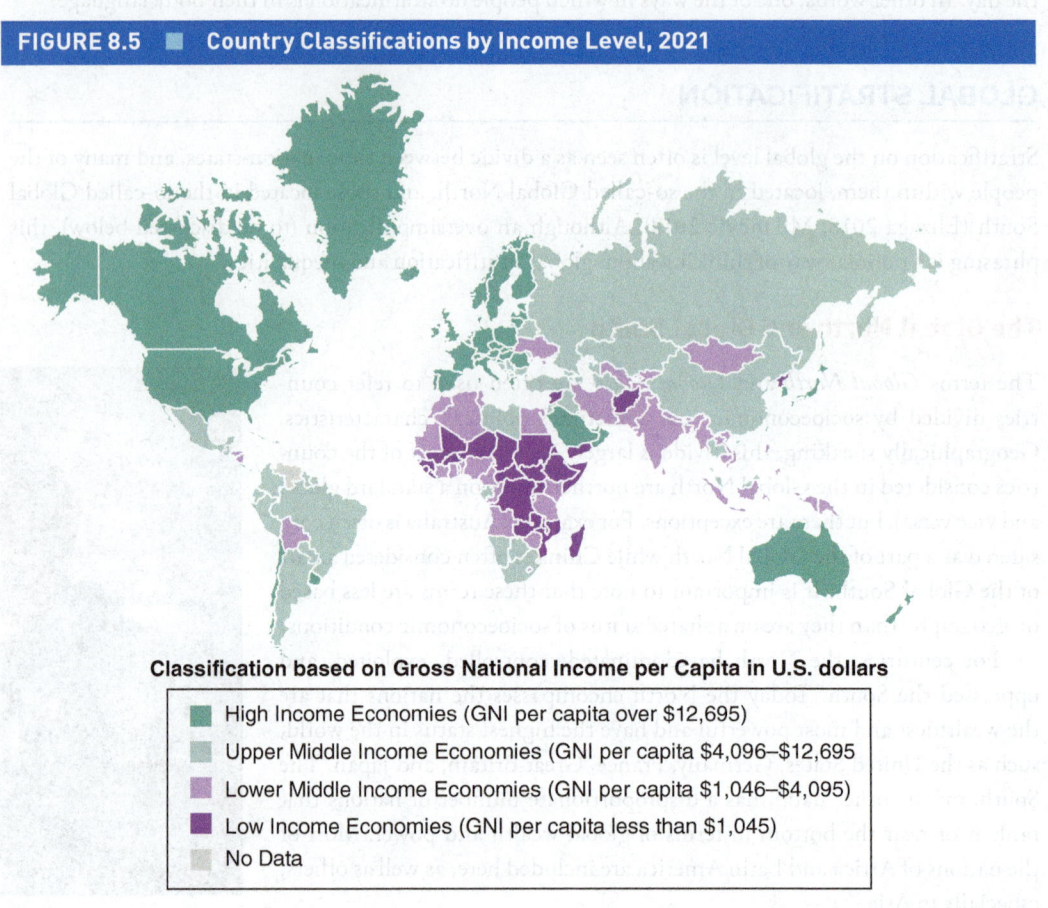

FIGURE 8.5 ■ Country Classifications by Income Level, 2021

Classification based on Gross National Income per Capita in U.S. dollars

- High Income Economies (GNI per capita over $12,695)
- Upper Middle Income Economies (GNI per capita $4,096–$12,695)
- Lower Middle Income Economies (GNI per capita $1,046–$4,095)
- Low Income Economies (GNI per capita less than $1,045)
- No Data

Source: World Bank, Country Classifications by Income Level, 2022. https://blogs.worldbank.org/opendata/new-world-bank-country-classifications-income-level-2022-2023

High-income economies exist in countries with the highest incomes in the world. Countries with gross national income (GNI) per capita of $13,205 are in this category. Currently, 81 countries have GNI that high or higher. As a result, they occupy lofty positions in the global hierarchy. They include countries long considered part of the Global North. However, they also include countries traditionally thought of as part of the Global South, including Chile and Uruguay (Latin America), Equatorial Guinea (Central Africa), and Oman (Middle East). Some of these countries have been considered to have high-income economies since the Industrial Revolution, while others (e.g., Japan) have industrialized—and grown wealthy—more recently. Still other high-income countries are not yet highly industrialized but derive their income from natural resources, such as oil (e.g., Oman). The levels of wealth in the latter countries offer a standard of living unimagined in many other parts of the world.

Middle-income economies are found in countries that have average levels of income on a global level. Countries are placed in this category if they have a GNI per capita between $1,086 and $13,205. This encompasses a significant range that begins at or near the bottom of per capita income, with the Kyrgyz Republic in central Asia (average GNI of $1,180 per capita) and includes Cabo (Cape) Verde and Sudan (Africa), Nicaragua (Central America), and Vietnam (Asia; The World Bank, n.d.-b). Toward the top of this range are upper-middle-income countries including Argentina and Brazil (Latin America), Cuba (Central America), South Africa, and Thailand (Asia). The World Bank considers 108 countries to be in the middle-income category. Many countries in this range, such as China (and most of Asia), began industrializing relatively recently (the 1970s or later). Other middle-income countries were formerly communist countries. They were highly industrialized, but they declined industrially and economically after the collapse of the Soviet Union in the late 1980s.

Low-income economies are in countries that are home to many of the world's poorest people, have very little of the world's wealth, and are largely agrarian societies with low levels of industry. The World Bank counts 34 low-income countries with GNI per capita below $1,085. They include many of the countries in sub-Saharan Africa, North (Democratic Republic of) Korea (East Asia), Afghanistan and Yemen (Asia). People in these countries are much more likely to experience disease, hunger, and malnutrition and have a lower life expectancy.

The Richest People in the World: The Global Concentration of Wealth

There is certainly great inequality between the North and the South, or between high-income and low-income countries, but focus on such relationships tends to obscure the full extent of global inequality. The World Inequality Report 2022 offers a stunning picture of the concentration of wealth in the world: the richest 10 percent of people in the world own 76 percent of the wealth while the bottom 50 percent own just 2 percent of global wealth. A recent Oxfam report found that the richest 1 percent grabbed nearly two-thirds of all new wealth—worth $42 trillion—created since 2020, almost twice as much money as the bottom 99 percent of the world's population (Oxfam International 2023). During the past decade, the richest 1 percent have captured around half of all new wealth.

The bottom line is that the level of global inequality is staggering and will only increase. This prompts the question: Can we (or at least those not in the top 1 percent) really accept living in such a world?

The Poorest People in the World: The Bottom Billion

Also worth considering is the broader category that includes the world's poorest people—the "bottom billion" of global residents (Murphy and Walsh 2014). The vast majority (70 percent) of the people in the bottom billion are in Africa, but countries such as Haiti, Bolivia, and Laos also have significant numbers of people who are part of the bottom billion.

Social stratification refers to the relative positions of people within a society, but global stratification demonstrates that widespread poverty and lack of opportunity can leave an entire nation near the bottom of the global pecking order. This boy is on his way to collect water in an encampment in Madagascar.

STEPHANE DE SAKUTIN/AFP/Getty Images

Wherever they live, the bottom billion have incomes of only about a fifth of those in other countries in the Global South. They also have many other serious problems, such as

- A low life expectancy of about 50 years
- A high infant mortality rate
- A higher likelihood of malnourishment

THEORIES OF GLOBAL STRATIFICATION

As noted previously, the dominant theoretical approaches to social stratification are structural/functional theory and conflict/critical theory.

Structural/Functional Theories

A dominant structural/functional theory of global stratification is **modernization theory**, which explains unequal economic distributions based on the structural (especially technological) and cultural differences between countries. According to this theory, the development of certain structures (especially technologies) and cultural realities (values, norms) is essential for societies to modernize (Jacobsen 2015).

One of the thinkers best known for articulating and promoting modernization theory is Walt Rostow (1960, 1978), an economic theorist who served as an adviser to President John F. Kennedy. In his theory of modernization, which had a major influence on U.S. foreign policy during the Cold War, Rostow argued that low-income countries must abandon their traditional values and ways of life in order to improve their economic standards of living.

Among the critics of modernization theory are those who argue that modernization theory focuses too narrowly on economic production. Edward Tiryakian (1991) argues that technological and cultural differences between countries are important for explaining both economic and social development. He notes that economic modernization can come at a high cost to forms of political and social life. A thriving civic culture, in which people can meaningfully participate in political processes, is also important for a country to be considered modern. The emphasis on cultural values is, therefore, extended beyond ideas such as individualism and competition to include democratization.

Others critique modernization theory for being too "Western" and assuming that the development of rich countries is the best, or only, way to improve the lives of people. It is argued that many countries have been **impoverished**, that is made to be poor through the actions of others. Many of those countries did not have a history of poverty, at least at current levels, until intervention by wealthier nations, especially through the form of imperialism.

Conflict/Critical Theories

At the global level, world-systems theory is one of the most influential conflict/critical theories used in the study of global stratification. **World-systems theory** focuses on the current stratification system by viewing the world as a single economic entity (Wallerstein 1974). It envisions a world divided mainly between the *core* and the *periphery*. The core includes the wealthiest industrialized countries, such as Western European countries, the United States, Australia, and Japan. The nation-states associated with the periphery are dependent on, and exploited by, the core nation-states. The periphery includes most of Africa and parts of Asia (Indonesia, Vietnam, Afghanistan), the Middle East (Iran, Syria), and Latin America (Peru, Bolivia). There are also a number of states in the middle, the *semiperiphery*, including Brazil, Russia, India, China, and South Africa.

The core has been able to benefit from the periphery in a number of ways. Core nation-states have helped keep the countries of the periphery focused on narrow export-oriented economies rather than on developing their industrial capacity. The core benefits from the periphery's cheap labor, and this helps keep profits flowing back to the core. The core can also make loans to peripheral countries, but because of the power imbalance, the core can dictate the terms of the loans, often with significant interest rates. Currently, poor countries owe the United States and other core countries trillions of dollars, leaving them in a weak economic position relative to the core.

World-systems theory argues that we can understand a nation's position in the world system only by examining its current relationship to other countries. Of course, countries in the core, periphery, and semiperiphery can shift positions over time. At one time, Great Britain was the dominant core nation-state in the world, but by the time of World War II, it had been replaced by the United States. Today, the United States is slipping, and China, at one time a peripheral country, shows every sign of moving to the core.

OTHER GLOBAL INEQUALITIES

Although related to economic inequality, the process of globalization is also characterized by numerous other inequalities, including unequal access to information and communication technologies (like the internet). Good health and quality health care are also unequally distributed, a problem made all the more apparent by the COVID-19 pandemic (Ryan 2023). Relatedly, those residing in the Global South often suffer health problems from exposure to hazardous waste, some of it shipped there from the Global North. Gender stratification is a huge problem at the global level, as women, especially in the Global South, frequently perform low-wage work in the informal economy.

The Global Digital Divide

There were about 5.16 billion internet users worldwide at the end of 2023, and that number will certainly continue to increase (Petrosyan, 2023b). It will likely surprise many that it wasn't until 2019 that half of the world's population had access to the internet! At least theoretically, the internet allows for participation by anyone, anywhere in the global digital economy. However, in reality there is a daunting and persistent global digital divide (Pick and Sarkar 2015). The digital divide refers to the gap between those who have access to the internet and associated technologies, and those who do not. According to a recent World Bank report, the percentages of individuals using the internet in 2021 remained very low in many low-income countries in the Global South, such as Uganda (6 percent), South Sudan (7 percent), Chad (10 percent), and Afghanistan (18 percent; The World Bank, n.d.-c). Compare these figures with the Global North, the world's most developed countries, where internet usage is usually above 80 percent. Figure 8.6 shows the difference in internet access between households in different countries.

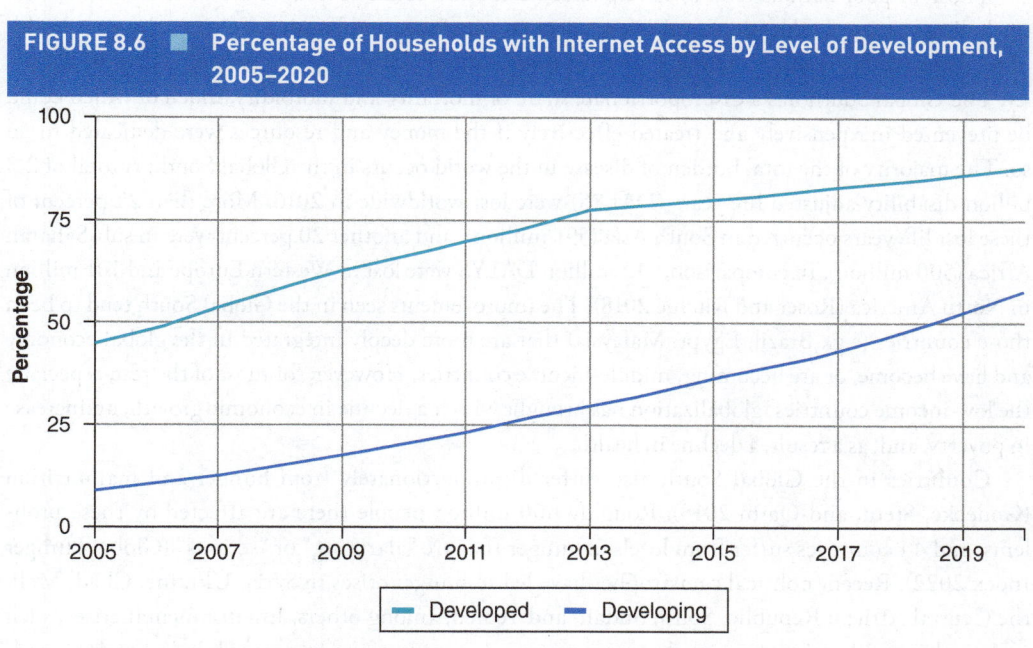

FIGURE 8.6 ■ Percentage of Households with Internet Access by Level of Development, 2005–2020

Source: International Telecommunications Union, 2020, *Measuring Digital Development: Facts and Figures 2020*, World Telecommunication/ICT Indicators Database.

The main barrier to global equality in access to, and use of, the internet, and information and communications technology (ICT) more generally, has until now been the lack of infrastructure within the less-developed countries of the Global South. However, as the infrastructure gap has been reduced in recent years, at least in some locales, a lack of computer skills and differences in usage have increasingly hampered those in the Global South. Also significant are the low incomes in those areas that make complex digital technologies, and therefore access to the internet, prohibitively expensive (Wakefield 2013). Language represents another source of inequality on the internet. Nearly 60 percent of all web content is in English; the next most popular language is Russian, representing about 5 percent of websites (Petrosyan 2023a). Clearly, those who do not speak English—the overwhelming majority of whom live in the Global South—are at a huge disadvantage on the internet.

The digital divide also intersects with other forms of social stratification. For example, in 2019, globally only 48 percent of women used the internet while 58 percent of men did (International Telecommunication Union 2019). There are also significant disparities related to race, with racial minorities having lower rates of access in nearly every country. The divide between those living in urban versus rural areas is also pronounced, especially in terms of speed. Most important, there are clear class divisions, with the world's economically privileged having greater access than those without such privilege.

The COVID-19 pandemic made problems of the digital divide particularly apparent. As physical distancing initiatives were put in place in many countries, those with the ability to work from home, which largely requires access to the internet, fared much better than those who could not do so. This was true whether talking about employment, education, or even entertainment. As Ryan and Nanda (2023c) put it, "the internet has become the rose with many thorns in the pandemic garden" (94).

Global Health Inequality

Although globalization has been associated with increased aggregate life expectancy throughout the world, it also has tended to widen global disparities in life span and health (Lenard and Straehle 2014; Winchester et al. 2016). For example, Johns, Cowling, and Gakidou (2013) found that the widening gap between the world's rich and poor is continuing to increase differences in life expectancy. According to Roser et al. (2019), the average life expectancy of newborns in high-income countries is at least 80 years. In contrast, newborns in sub-Saharan African countries will live less than 60 years on average. Economic inequality accounts for many of these health disparities.

Those in poor nations tend to have poorer health as a result of limited access to health services (including vaccines), education, sanitation, adequate nutrition, and housing. In turn, the poor health of residents tends to limit economic growth in those nations, mainly by adversely affecting productivity. The Global South has a disproportionate share of mortality and morbidity, much of which could be prevented inexpensively and treated effectively if the money and resources were dedicated to do so. The majority of the total burden of disease in the world occurs in the Global South. A total of 2.3 billion disability-adjusted life years (DALYS) were lost worldwide in 2016. More than 25 percent of these lost life years occurred in South Asia (591 million), and another 20 percent were in sub-Saharan Africa (500 million). In comparison, 112 million DALYS were lost in Western Europe and 101 million in North America (Roser and Ritchie 2018). The improvements seen in the Global South tend to be in those countries (e.g., Brazil, Egypt, Malaysia) that are more deeply integrated in the global economy and have become, or are becoming, middle-income countries. However, for most of the rest, especially the low-income countries, globalization has brought with it a decline in economic growth, an increase in poverty, and, as a result, a decline in health.

Countries in the Global South also suffer disproportionately from hunger and malnutrition (Godecke, Stein, and Qaim 2018). Roughly 800 million people there are affected by these problems, and 44 countries suffer from levels of hunger that are "alarming" or "serious" (Global Hunger Index 2022). Recent political catastrophes have led to hunger crises in Syria, Ukraine, Chad, Mali, the Central African Republic, South Sudan, and Yemen, among others. Environmental crises, such as droughts and hurricanes, are other major causes of people going hungry. Hunger involves inadequate or almost totally unavailable food supplies and a lack of assured and continual access to food, as well as poor and unbalanced diets. These problems are especially important for children, who are likely to die young from malnutrition. Poor nutrition causes nearly half of all child deaths in the world (UNICEF 2018). Furthermore, those children who survive even though their growth is stunted because of a lack of food are likely to be less physically and intellectually productive when they become adults and to suffer more chronic illnesses and disabilities. This pattern carries on intergenerationally, as the ability of such adults to provide adequate nutrition for their children is compromised.

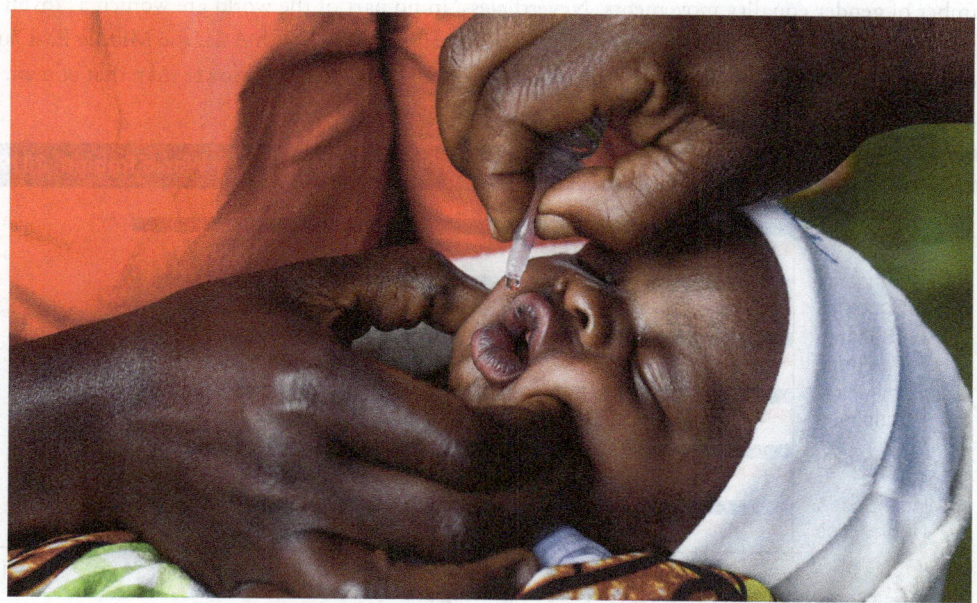

A child in Malawi, Africa, receives a polio vaccine in March, 2022. The extent of inequality in access to health care around the world was made starkly apparent by the COVID-19 pandemic. According to UNICEF, nearly 13 million children missed one or more vaccinations in Africa between 2019 and 2021 because of the disruptive impact of COVID.

Associated Press

Complicating matters is a dramatic increase in obesity among other segments of the poor in the Global South (Global Nutrition Report 2016; McNeil 2016). An estimated 39 million children under five years of age in the world today are overweight, an increase of almost 10 million from 1990 (World Health Organization, 2021). Those in the Global South are therefore now increasingly likely to suffer from a "double nutritional burden"—that is, some do not have enough to eat, and others eat too much, especially of the wrong kinds of foods (e.g., foods high in fat and cholesterol).

Finally, poor countries are less likely to be able to provide adequate health care for their populations. Low-income countries tend to have fewer hospitals, fewer qualified doctors and nurses, and less capacity for research on health and disease. Many countries are taking steps to address these problems. For example, China started to invest heavily in health care more than a decade ago and now provides universal basic health care to 95 percent of its population (Yi, 2021).

It is worth noting that a society's wealth does not always correspond to health coverage or better health outcomes. For example, the United States spends the most in the world on health care, but it ranks significantly lower than other high-income countries (and even several lower-income countries) on a number of public health indicators. Compared with their counterparts in other high-income countries, people in the United States tend to live shorter lives, are more likely to experience violent deaths, are more likely to be obese, and have higher rates of many diseases. Unlike the residents of all other countries in the Global North, many in the United States (particularly those with low incomes) do not have health coverage.

Global Gender Stratification

Globally, individuals face barriers in employment, occupations, and wealth based on gender.

Inequality in Employment, Occupations, and Wealth

Although men's paid labor force participation rates worldwide have decreased slightly over the last several decades, a notable increase has occurred in women's paid labor force participation, particularly in the Americas and Western Europe. There are significant variations within and across regions, but women's paid labor force participation has also risen substantially in sub-Saharan Africa, North Africa, Eastern Europe, Southeast Asia, and East Asia over this period (Elborgh-Woytek et al. 2016; Ndinda and Ndhlovu 2018). This progress in women's employment status is linked at least in part to a growing number of gender equality movements. Nevertheless, in no part of the world are women as involved as men are in the paid labor force (see Figure 8.7). In some areas—South Asia, the Middle East, and North Africa—women's reported paid labor force participation is markedly lower than that of men.

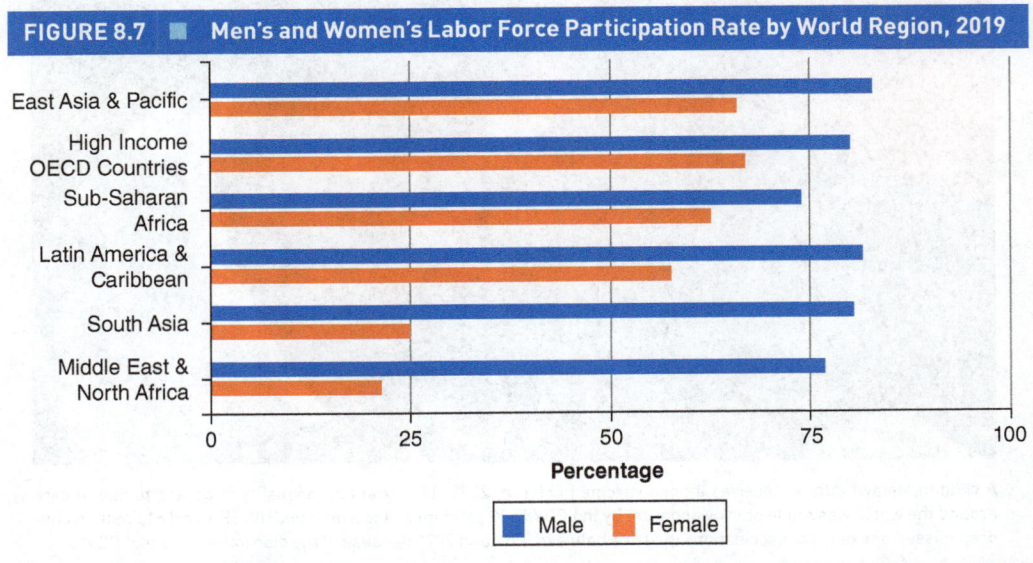

FIGURE 8.7 ■ Men's and Women's Labor Force Participation Rate by World Region, 2019

Source: The World Bank, 2021, *Labor Force Participation Rate, Female (% of female population ages 15–64)*, International Labour Organization, ILOSTAT database.

In much of the Global North, educated middle-class women have made inroads into professional and managerial employment. In the global paid labor market, women predominate as service and clerical workers and in elementary occupations, such as manufacturing. They are likely to work as teachers and university professors, as nurses and doctors in public hospitals, and as workers and administrators in government offices. Women have also made inroads in professional services (Cohn 2017).

However, according to the World Bank, women earn less and participate in the paid labor force less than men do. Globally, Gallup polling finds that men are twice as likely as women to have full-time jobs. The wage gap found in the United States is also a global phenomenon, and the gap is especially large in the Middle East and North Africa. Mothers' wages are lower than fathers' in many countries (Misra and Strader 2013). The historical belief persists that fathers are supporting entire families (and thus need a higher wage), while mothers are not. Despite the gains made by women, high-pay and high-status occupations continue to be dominated by men in both the Global North and the Global South. Even in countries like the United States and those in Western Europe, men still have easier access to, and consequently hold a much larger percentage of, professional and managerial jobs.

Women and Informal Employment

At the same time that some women are finding success in the paid labor force, others are being limited by the nature of their arrangements with employers. Women are more likely than men to have informal jobs (Limoncelli 2016). Informal employment, which has increased in many countries, includes temporary work without fixed employers, paid employment from home, domestic work for households, and industrial work for subcontractors. Informal sectors are characterized by low pay and a lack of secure contracts, worker benefits, and social protections. Workers in the informal economy do not have wage agreements, employment contracts, regular working hours, or health insurance or unemployment benefits (Rogan et al. 2017). They often earn below the legal minimum wage and may not be paid on time (or at all!). Many formal jobs have been replaced by informal ones as lower labor and production costs have increasingly become the major organizing factor in global production.

Although greater informal employment characterizes the entire labor force globally, women and men are concentrated in different types of informal work (Vanek et al. 2014). Men are concentrated mainly in informal wage-based jobs and agricultural employment, while women are typically concentrated in nonagricultural employment, domestic work, and unpaid work in family enterprises. Compared with men's informal employment, women's employment is much more likely to have lower hourly wages and less stability. To reduce labor costs, most multinational corporations establish subcontracting networks with local manufacturers employing low-paid workers, mostly women, who can be laid off quickly and easily. In these production networks, women are more likely to work in small workshops or from home.

Women in Global Care Chains

Another form of global gender inequality occurs within families through caregiving work. As men and women from low-income countries migrate to find better-paying jobs, women especially find employment in domestic work. Arlie Hochschild (2000) argues that the migration of domestic workers creates **global care chains** that involve a series of personal relationships between people across the globe based on the paid or unpaid work of caring (Razavi 2017; Yeates 2012). Care includes social, health, and sexual care services, usually involving household tasks such as cooking, cleaning, and ironing. In global care chains, women supply their own care labor to their employers while consuming other women's care labor, both paid and unpaid. Thus, instead of care chains, it might be better to think of this as "care circulation" (Lutz and Palenga-Mollenbeck 2016). Migrant domestic workers often rely on female relatives, neighbors, and daughters as well as paid domestic workers for the care of their children back in their home countries. For instance, while a mother works as a nanny in a high-income country, her young children may be cared for by an older daughter or by a nanny who migrated from a middle- or low-income country. On one end of the chain is a woman in the North pursuing professional employment. On the other end is a domestic worker's oldest daughter taking over her mother's familial duties. With the increasing use of the internet, mothers (aka "Skype mothers") can play a more active role in their families back home, but such a form of motherhood obviously has great limitations.

CHANGING POSITIONS IN GLOBAL STRATIFICATION

Despite the several forms of global inequality discussed previously, it is possible for countries to change, hopefully improve, their positions within the global stratification system. This section examines the risky strategy of a race to the bottom in offering cheap labor and the controversial use of foreign aid as a means of development.

Race to the Bottom

Those countries that rank lower in the global stratification system often have to engage in a so-called economic race to the bottom in order to have a chance of eventually moving up the global hierarchy. The basic method is to offer lower prices than the competition does—usually other lower-ranking countries. Such nations may lower prices by reducing costs, which they do by offering their citizens lower wages, poorer working conditions, longer hours, ever-escalating pressure and demands, reduced environmental oversights, and dramatic tax benefits (sometimes completely tax-free zones). An especially desperate nation will go further than the others to reduce wages and worsen working conditions in order to lower costs and attract the interest and investments of multinational corporations. However, the "winning" low-income nation remains a favorite of the multinationals only until it is undercut by another low-ranking country eager for jobs. In other words, the countries that get the work are those that "win" the race to the bottom. These, of course, are almost always questionable victories because the work is poorly paid, rarely offers any sustained economic benefit to the country, and subjects workers to horrid circumstances.

In actuality, winning the race to the bottom might mean that a country remains at or near the bottom (or even falls lower). For example, some countries compete in the world economy by focusing on agricultural exports and employing cheap, local labor to plant and harvest crops. As countries battle with one another by paying workers less money, they make their agricultural goods cheaper on the global market. But if these export sectors do not eventually transition to other types of goods and services, with higher wages, the countries might never lift themselves off the bottom.

Foreign Aid and Development

Another way in which global economic inequality can be addressed is through the use of foreign aid to improve a poor country's position within the world economy.[1] **Foreign aid** is defined as economic assistance given by countries or global institutions to a foreign country in order to promote its development and social welfare. In the form that we now know it, foreign aid began following the economic devastation of World War II with the United States' Marshall Plan to help struggling European economies. Foreign aid has continued to expand since that time, totaling $185.9 billion in 2021, according to the Organisation for Economic Co-operation and Development (OECD, n.d.-a).

The OECD states that aid may take the form of grants or subsidized loans and must promote development and welfare. This can include funding or other resources for education, health, debt relief, social or economic infrastructure, humanitarian assistance, or other development projects. To qualify as "aid," loans must be given with interest rates at least 25 percent below market rates. Most aid is bilateral, or given directly from one country to another. Aid can also be multilateral, when resources of many donors are pooled through a third party like the World Bank, which then distributes the aid. This ideally cuts bureaucratic costs and reduces political motivations for giving. The 34 members of the OECD, which include the United States, Western European countries, Canada, Japan, Australia, South Korea, and New Zealand, provide the majority of foreign aid. Other providers of significant aid are China, Brazil, China, India, Kuwait, Qatar, Saudi Arabia, Taiwan, Turkey, and the United Arab Emirates. The United States is one of the largest donors in terms of dollars, giving more than $47.8 billion in foreign aid in 2021 alone (OECD, n.d.-a). However, when measured as a percentage of gross national income (GNI), the United States gives only 0.2 percent, which is considerably short of the

Pascal Saint-Amans, Director of the Center for the Tax Policy at the Organisation for Economic Development, addresses a global audience of policy-makers, business people, and investors, at the annual OECD summit. The OECD plays an important role in the global economy, including overseeing foreign aid to countries in need of economic help for such things as humanitarian assistance and infrastructure improvement.

Horacio Villalobos/Getty Images

target of 0.7 percent set by the United Nations (The World Bank, n.d.-a; OECD, n.d.-b). The countries that typically give the most in foreign aid as a percentage of GNI include several Nordic countries (Norway, Denmark, Finland, and Sweden), Luxembourg, the United Kingdom, and the Netherlands. They tend to meet or surpass the 0.7 percent target. However, in 2017, the United Arab Emirates gave 1.31 percent of GNI as foreign aid, the highest percentage of any country.

There are many criticisms of foreign aid, focusing on issues such as its questionable effectiveness, the political agendas of donors and recipients, and the adverse effects it can have on the countries seeking assistance. Donors often seek to promote the economic growth of nations to enhance their own economic interests, preserve access to natural resources, and benefit their political positions. Foreign aid is also frequently tied to very specific stipulations about how countries may spend it. Donor countries often provide aid for specific purposes, some of the most common of which are education, transportation and communications infrastructure, and the development of government and civil society institutions. Issues can arise concerning such stipulations when the intentions of the donor country are not in line with those of the receiving country. Causes of this can be anything from miscommunication to blatant corruption, and the end result can be the misuse or misdirection of billions of dollars.

SUMMARY

Social stratification results in hierarchical differences and inequalities. Three important dimensions of stratification are social class, status, and power. In the money-based stratification system, wealth and income are the main determinants of social class. Since the 1970s, many countries have experienced increasing income inequality. However, the greatest economic differences in society are due to differences in wealth. People with great wealth often have high class, status, and power and can usually pass most of these advantages to future generations. Those who have little have a difficult time amassing their own wealth. The middle class has declined in recent decades, leaving a large hole in the stratification system between the lower and upper classes. The measure of absolute poverty is the poverty line, the level of income people are thought to need to survive in our society. Members of minority groups, women, and children are overrepresented among the poor.

Sociologists are also concerned about structural mobility, or changes in the occupational structure.

Structural/functional theories of stratification argue that societies need a system of stratification in order to function properly. Conflict theorists challenge this assumption, particularly the idea that positions at the higher end of the stratification system are always more important. Finally, symbolic interactionists view stratification as a process or set of interactions among people in different positions.

Global stratification refers to the hierarchical differences and inequalities among countries and individuals across the world. This stratification is evident in the oppression of the Global South by the Global North; the differences between high-, middle-, and low-income countries; and the differences between the richest and poorest people in the world.

The dominant structural/functional theory of global stratification is modernization theory, which argues that technological and cultural factors explain countries' varying levels of economic and social development. In contrast, conflict theorists, especially world-systems theorists, argue that there is a hierarchy among countries, with rich countries oppressing and exploiting poor countries, thus keeping them poor.

Global economic inequalities take many forms. For example, a large and persistent global digital divide limits the ability of some people from accessing and using the internet. Differences in wealth also lead to global health inequalities, including vastly different life expectancies, levels of nutrition, and disease rates. Though gender stratification exists throughout the world, it is more pronounced in some countries. Typically, men have greater access to high-pay and high-status occupations and wealth, while women are more likely to be found in low-skill jobs that offer less pay and status.

Although global inequalities are highly persistent, it is possible for countries to change their positions within the global stratification system. Some scholars argue that poor countries can compete to offer the lowest wages possible in order to attract further development or focus on industrial upgrading. Foreign aid may also be offered to countries to encourage development and to improve social welfare, although such aid is, at least at times, in the self-interest of the giving nation.

KEY TERMS

- absolute poverty
- achievement
- ascription
- distribution of opportunities for rewards
- distribution of rewards
- feminization of poverty
- foreign aid
- global care chains
- high-income economies
- horizontal mobility
- impoverished
- income
- inequality
- intergenerational mobility
- intragenerational mobility
- low-income economies
- middle-income economies
- modernization theory
- occupational mobility
- poverty
- poverty line
- power
- relative poverty
- social class
- social mobility
- social stratification
- structural mobility
- upward mobility
- vertical mobility
- wealth
- world-systems theory

REVIEW QUESTIONS

1. What is the difference between income and wealth? Which is more important to explaining the differences between the haves and the have-nots? Why?

2. How has inequality in the United States, and elsewhere, changed since the 1970s? In what ways are the explanations for these trends related to globalization?

3. What has happened to the middle class in recent decades? What accounts for the change?

4. What do we mean when we refer to the feminization of poverty? What factors help explain the position of women in the system of social stratification?

5. According to structural/functional theories, how is inequality beneficial to society? How can the income and wealth of celebrities and sports stars be used as a criticism of this model?

6. Compare ways of classifying countries in the global stratification system. What does each classification emphasize?

7. How much health inequality exists in the world? Using the COVID-19 pandemic as an example, explain how differences in wealth affect health outcomes.

8. How are men and women affected differently by the global economy? Do you expect these differences to change significantly in the future? Why or why not?

9. How are families affected by global stratification?

10. Is foreign aid an effective way of addressing global poverty? How might conflict theories explain the role of foreign aid in global stratification?

ENDNOTE

1. Miranda Ames made significant contributions to this section.

Jose Luis Quintana/LatinContent/Getty Images

9 RACE AND ETHNICITY

223

LEARNING OBJECTIVES
9.1 Contrast historical and recent views of racial and ethnic categories and identities.
9.2 Describe majority–minority relations.
9.3 Discuss the foundations of racism, including its measurement.
9.4 Explain race and ethnicity in a global context.

MINORITIES ACQUIRE POLITICAL POWER

In 2005, Evo Morales, a widely popular union leader and political activist, was elected president of Bolivia based on an unorthodox leadership style and a reformist agenda. He was reelected in a landslide in 2009 and again in 2014. A 2016 referendum seemed to prevent him from running for a fourth term, but Bolivia's high court overrode the constitution and scrapped all term limits. Although he later resigned as president in 2019 amid a great deal of political controversy, the importance of his reign, especially as an Aymara, is significant as it marked the first time in nearly 500 years that an indigenous person had been the leader in Bolivia. The Aymara are a racially and ethnically distinct people who have lived in central South America for more than 2,000 years. Conquered first by the Incas and then by Spanish colonists, they lived as an indentured minority group until Bolivia won its independence in 1825. Despite achieving legal freedom, however, the Aymara continued to be stereotyped, discriminated against, and marginalized by the country's Spanish-descended majority.

After nearly two centuries of marginalization, the Aymara rose via a number of social movements to achieve social equality and political power for Bolivia's indigenous populations. Organizations such as the militant Tupac Katari Guerrilla Army and Evo Morales's own Movimiento al Socialismo (MAS) challenged racist norms and championed sweeping reform. Running on a string of successful MAS actions (including the ousting of the previous president) and a populist platform of farmers' rights and antimilitarism, Morales transcended old stereotypes and expectations, rising to his country's highest office.

Like Nelson Mandela before him in South Africa and Barack Obama, his U.S. contemporary, Evo Morales is a living symbol of a particular culture's ongoing struggle with prejudice, racism, and institutional discrimination. His presidency marks an important step in Bolivia's social evolution, but it by no means signifies that the Aymara have achieved social equality. Racism and ethnic discrimination have permeated Bolivia for hundreds—if not thousands—of years. During that time, the country's dominant groups, most often of foreign descent, have accumulated wealth, power, and prestige—assets they have been reluctant to share.

It took roughly eight generations for Bolivia to elect its first indigenous president and slightly longer for the United States to elect its first biracial one. These accomplishments have led some to suggest that we have achieved a postracial, or "color-blind," world. Racism, xenophobia, ethnic conflict, and ethnocentrism are sensitive topics for most people. However, denying that these difficult problems persist will only perpetuate them.

THE CONCEPTS OF RACE AND ETHNICITY

Race is a *socially constructed* definition based on some real or presumed physical, biological characteristic(s), such as skin color or hair texture, as well as on a perceived shared lineage. Although race is often based on real or presumed bodily characteristics, it is more about what people define it to be than about any meaningful physical differences. **Ethnicity** is also socially defined, but on the basis of some real or presumed cultural characteristic, such as language, religion, traditions, or cultural practices. **Ethnic groups** have a sense of shared origins and relatively clear boundaries, and they tend to endure over time. These boundaries may be recognized by both insiders and outsiders (Schaefer 2014).

Race and ethnicity can be defined by oneself, by others, or by societal and governmental institutions. Few of us ask others how they define themselves racially and so most of our social interactions are based on the *perceived* race of others. This issue of the inability of individuals to define their own identities in the face of the perceptions of others will be a recurring theme throughout this book. For example, most acts of discrimination are committed on the perception of race or ethnicity (based on one's name, skin color, or associations). Similarly, information about race or ethnicity on official government censuses in many countries is filled in by the census worker rather than by the individual themselves. In other words, it is how others view our race or ethnicity that most often determines how we will be treated by the larger society.

Although races and ethnicity have been defined separately, the line between them is not always clear (Kivisto and Croll 2012). Races are often considered ethnic groups, and ethnic groups are often considered races. For instance, *White* is a racial category that is frequently subordinated to ethnic categories such as Italian American or White Russian. Similarly, the racial category *Black* has become "ethnicized." For example, Davis (1991) argues that Blacks in the United States are now a self-conscious social group with an "ethnic identity." The creation of Kwanzaa, soul food, and the development of hip-hop all speak to the significance of Black, or *African American*, as a cultural identity—not just a racial one. On the other hand, Jews, most notoriously in Nazi Germany during the Holocaust, have frequently been thought of not simply as an ethnic group but also as a race. However, Jews do not all come from the same genetic background; even if they do tend to have some ethnic characteristics in common, most notably a religion and a shared cultural history. Thus, as you read this chapter, which at times discusses race and ethnicity separately, bear in mind the strong overlap between the two.

Historical Thinking about Race and Ethnicity

The concepts of race and ethnicity have a long history. They have taken many forms over the centuries, but they have always served as a way of differentiating among groups of people and creating hierarchies that empower some and disempower others. Race and ethnicity have also played a key role in most imperial conquests, often with Whites imposing their will on, and then exploiting, other races. During the peak of the British Empire, for example, the British controlled India, the West Indies, and West Africa, all of whose largely darker-skinned populations were subordinated to the British. The rationalizations for this pattern of dominance included both "scientific" and cultural explanations.

"Scientific" Explanations

Following the Enlightenment, and especially in the nineteenth and early twentieth centuries, folk ideas about race and ethnicity were supplemented with "rational" (which today are seen as pseudoscientific) justifications for treating people of other races and ethnicities differently. Although Enlightenment thinkers believed in the unity of humankind, they also believed in classifying people along a continuum from primitive to modern. One result was classification schemes based on race and ethnicity (Sussman 2016).

Another result was the use of allegedly fixed biological characteristics not simply to differentiate among groups of people but also to "scientifically" justify the unequal distribution of wealth, power, prestige, access to resources, and life chances to subordinate racial and ethnic groups, especially to those with lighter skin colors. In 1795, a German naturalist invented the idea of the Caucasian race as the first and most perfect race. In 1800, a French scientist argued that race was involved in social hierarchies and that Whites stood on top of those hierarchies.

Evolutionary thinking spurred interest in racial and ethnic categories. The idea of social Darwinism, associated with sociologist Herbert Spencer (1820–1903), was taken to mean that racial and ethnic differences were the result of evolutionary differences among people. One race or ethnicity was better off, and another was worse off, because of evolution. Further, society was not to try to tamper with, reduce, or eliminate these differences; it was not to interfere with a natural process. Spencer defined this in terms of the "survival of the fittest" (1851, 151).

Also during the nineteenth century, Gregor Mendel's (1822–1884) work on genetics and heredity led to the idea that the races could be distinguished from one another based on their genetic makeup.

This idea played a role in the development of **eugenics**, a movement that became popular in the early twentieth century and that argued that the human population could be genetically improved through scientific manipulation. Especially during the Nazi era, eugenicists defended racial segregation, opposed interracial marriage, and sought the restriction of immigration and the forced sterilization of those considered "unfit." This is still a hot-button issue. In late 2018, there was a movement to remove the name of a University of Vermont scientist from the library because his research in eugenics helped lead to the sterilization of those labeled as "mental defectives" (New York Times 2018).

What is race, and what is ethnicity? This Ethiopian boy, newly arrived in Israel, is a member of an ancient Jewish community.
AP Photo/Ariel Schalit

Contemporary sociologists typically reject single-minded "scientific" explanations of race and ethnicity (Hatch 2016), including the view that genetic differences are responsible for socially significant differences among racial and ethnic groups. Rather, most see the historical, structural, institutional, and oppressive contexts of race and ethnicities as explanations for observable differences among racial and ethnic groups. Sociological research focusing on genetics tends to take the stance that genes matter, but so does environment (Guo, Roettger, and Cai 2008). Conceptualizations by sociologists of race and ethnicity acknowledge that socially constructed racial and ethnic categories overlap with some biological/genetic differences among racial and ethnic groups. However, biological/genetic differences *within* racial and ethnic groups are often as important as those *between* such groups. In other words, there is more in common genetically between different racial and ethnic groups than there is difference.

Cultural Explanations

Even though "scientific" explanations of race and ethnicity continue, explanations based on social and cultural factors such as religion, language, and national origin are more prevalent today. In the second half of the twentieth century, ideas of cultural superiority and inferiority increasingly began to replace those associated with biological superiority and inferiority. For example, Blacks have been described as having a "culture of poverty," which suggests they have a sense of learned helplessness and powerlessness (Lewis 1959). Although this argument has been used against poor people more generally, it has often been racialized to explain the disproportionately high rates of poverty among racial and ethnic minorities.

As is the case with "scientific" explanations, there are often problems with cultural explanations. For instance, the concept of the culture of poverty has been used to legitimate racial and ethnic differences in class position rather than to explain these differences in terms of the structural lack of economic opportunity that racial and ethnic minorities have collectively faced throughout history. Very recently, there has been a revival of interest in serious cultural explanations that avoid the excesses of the culture of poverty argument yet deal critically with aspects of racial and ethnic minority cultures. However, such cultural explanations must not ignore the deeply rooted structural problems facing such communities as well (Ladson-Billings 2017; Patterson and Fosse 2015; Sanneh 2015).

The Fluidity of Racial and Ethnic Categories

Sociologists point to the fact that racial and ethnic categories are often blurred and subject to change by shifting individual and social definitions; race is a dynamic and fluid social concept (see Table 9.1). There are many examples of the fluidity and variability of the race concept in the United States (and globally). For example, former President Barack Obama had a White mother and a Black African father. However, he is referred to as Black or African American, not "half Black" or "half African American" or even as biracial. This is a legacy of the **"one drop" rule** or the "one Black ancestor rule" (Davis 1991). In Virginia, people with as little as one-sixteenth African ancestry were considered by law to be Black; in Florida it was one-eighth, and in Louisiana it was one-thirty-second. That means that in Louisiana if you had even one great-great-great grandparent that was Black, you were legally considered Black as well. In the early twentieth century, several states, including Tennessee and Alabama, adopted the rule that a person with the slightest trace of African ancestry was considered to be Black. Although not as prominent today, the one-drop rule continues to affect how at least some individuals think of themselves (Guo et al. 2014).

TABLE 9.1 ■ Race in the U.S. Census, 1790–Present

Racial Category	Year(s) Used in Census	Description
White or Black	1790–1850	Only White and Black categories were used ("mulatto" was also used if not "fully" Black); Black was divided into "free" and "slave"
Mulatto	1850–1870, 1890, 1910, 1920	Mixed race; one mixed-race parent and one White parent
Quadroon	1890	Mixed race, one-quarter African ancestry
Octoroon	1890	Mixed race, one-eighth African ancestry
Hindu	1910–1940	South Asian Indian
Mexican	1930	Parent or individual was Mexican-born; this was the first and only time this was listed as a race
Hispanic	1980–present	Anyone of Spanish-speaking descent, regardless of race or physical appearance
More than one	2000–present	First time in U.S. history when a person could identify with more than one specific racial category

Source: Race in the U.S. Census, 1790–Present is Reprinted by Permission of Lisa Speicher Muñoz.

The fluidity and variability of the race concept are even clearer when we adopt a global perspective. In South Africa during apartheid (1948–1994), there were three racial categories: White, Black, and Colored. Whites were descended from Europeans and Blacks from Africans. The Colored category was more complex, including both those with mixed racial backgrounds (who might also have been labeled Black) and those descended from Asians. In many Caribbean and Latin American countries, especially

Brazil, race is a matter of gradations between Black and White, with indigenous descent and social status factored in as well. In this case, it is especially clear that the color of an individual's skin does not determine whether that person is "Black" or "White."

It is also true that someone defined as Black in the United States might be considered White in other countries and contexts. Clearly, racial categories embrace far too much variation to claim a scientific basis. As pointed out previously, variation within racial categories is often as great as, or greater than, variation between racial categories.

Because oppression and subordination are often based on race and ethnicity, many individuals from racial and ethnic minorities go to some lengths to identify with the dominant group. They might adopt the cultural values and practices of the dominant culture. For instance, linguistic assimilation—adopting English, perhaps leaving the old language behind—has almost been inevitable among nearly all ethnic minority groups in the United States. Some individuals also opt to change their names to have a more "Anglo" sound; many doing so only when they immigrate to the United States. Some individuals defined as part of a minority racial or ethnic group may physically resemble the dominant race or ethnic group, and they may go so far as to straighten, curl, or color their hair or lighten their skin to increase that resemblance (Campbell 2010). They might even undergo cosmetic surgery (Luo 2013).

At the same time, many members of minority groups have strong and positive attachments to their racial or ethnic identities. They make this evident in various ways, including by supporting racial or ethnic organizations, participating in group-specific celebrations, taking pride in the achievements of highly successful members of their groups, and resisting dominant cultural expectations, such as those regarding beauty (Lloréns 2013).

Table 9.2 shows the racial composition of the U.S. population based on data from the 2010 and 2020 censuses. Of great interest in this table is the strong increase between 2010 and 2020 in various minority populations and the relative decline of the White population.

TABLE 9.2 ■ Racial Composition of the U.S. Population, 2010 and 2020						
	2010		2020		Change, 2010 to 2020	
	Number	Percentage of Population	Number	Percentage of Population	Number	Percentage
Hispanic or Latino	50,477,594	16.3	62,080,044	18.7	11,602,450	23.0
Not Hispanic or Latino	258,267,944	83.7	269,369,237	81.3	11,101,293	4.3
White Alone	196,817,552	63.7	204,277,273	61.6	19,275,992	-8.6
Black or African American	38,929,319	12.6	41,104,200	12.4	2,174,881	5.6
American Indian and Alaska Native	2,932,248	0.9	3,727,135	1.1	794,887	27.1
Asian	14,674,252	4.8	19,886,049	6.0	5,211,797	35.5
Native Hawaiian and Other Pacific Islander	540,013	0.2	689,966	0.2	149,953	27.8
Some Other Race	19,107,368	6.2	27,915,715	8.4	8,808,347	46.1
Two or More Races	9,009,073	2.9	33,848,943	10.2	24,839,870	275.7

Source: United States Census Bureau, 2020, *Race and Ethnicity in the United States: 2010 and 2020 Census.* (https://www.census.gov/library/visualizations/interactive/race-and-ethnicity-in-the-united-state-2010-and-2020-census.html).

Measuring Race and Ethnicity

The United States Census provides one example of the shifting and constructed nature of race that has been well studied. Many have critiqued the U.S. Census's construction of racial categories, including its differentiation of Hispanic or Latino as an "ethnicity" rather than a "race."

An examination of the changing response options available on the United States Census clearly demonstrates how the options given to people to legally define their racial category is dependent upon the historical moment in which the census is being asked as well as the geographic location of the respondent. The first census in the United States was administered in 1790 and was used to count free White males over the age of 16, free White males under the age of 16, free White females, all other free persons detailed by age and "color" (which excluded "Indians not taxed"), and Slaves. The 1850 Census changed the category options to White, Black, and Mulatto. In 1860, the categories of "American Indian" and "Chinese (California only)" were added. By 1870, the distinction of "California only" was dropped from Chinese but added to the new category: Japanese (California only). The 1890 Census became even more complex, especially along the lines of percentage of Black blood offering new options of quadroon and octoroon and with the following instructions and definitions:

> Be particularly careful to distinguish between blacks, mulattoes, quadroons, and octoroons. The word "black" should be used to describe those persons who have three-fourths or more black blood; "mulatto," those persons who have from three-eighths to five-eighths black blood; "quadroon," those persons who have one-fourth black blood; and "octoroon," those persons who have one-eighth or any trace of black blood.

The 1900 Census simplified this complex structure of percentage Black blood to the single category of "Black (Negro or of Negro descent)," and a new category of "Other" was added although no definition or explicit instruction was given on exactly what this category might mean. By 1910, the parenthetical "Negro or of Negro descent" had been dropped to just say "Black." The 1930 Census saw a new wave of racial categories including White, Negro (now used instead of Black), Indian, Japanese, Chinese, Filipino, Hindu, Korean, Mexican, Other. By 1940, Mexican was dropped and "other" was changed to "other race." In 1950, Hindu and Korean were dropped. In 1960, Indian was changed to "American Indian" and four new categories were added for Hawaiian, Part Hawaiian, Aleut, and Eskimo. By 1970, the categories were White, Negro or Black, Indian (Amer.), Japanese, Chinese, Filipino, Hawaiian, Korean, and Other. In 1980, there was another explosion of categories re-adding Eskimo and Aleut as well as new categories of Asian Indian, Samoan, Guamanian, and Vietnamese. In 1990, the category of "Other API" (meaning Asian or Pacific Islander) was added. In 2000, it was changed to White, Black, African American, or Negro, American Indian or Alaska Native, Asian Indian, Chinese, Japanese, Filipino, Korean, Vietnamese, Native Hawaiian, Samoan, Guamanian or Chamorro, Other Asian, Other Pacific Islander, Some other race. Although many people have identified as "mixed race" for generations, it wasn't until the 2000 census that such individuals were allowed to identify officially with two or more races. It is also worth noting that the 1980 Census began asking a question about Hispanic Origin just before the race question.

All of these changes point to the shifting ways by which the United States Census (and no doubt many other aspects of society) constructs racial categories. Interestingly, the only category that has been present in every Census with no evolution is that of "White," a telling indicator or how the majority often sets the standard against which everything else is measured. The category of "Black" has also had an interesting evolution including, at various historical moments, different categories depending on what percentage of Black one was. Other categories, like those of Aleut and Eskimo, have appeared and disappeared, only to reappear again. And still others, like that of Mexican and Hindu, enjoyed only a brief existence as categories on the Census often not appearing more than one or two rounds. All of these changes do not indicate that certain racial categories have not always been in existence, or that they have now become extinct, but rather point to the socially and politically constructed nature of these categories. The political climate, legal standing of persons (especially Blacks and American Indians), and general social attitudes toward categories of people have all influenced the appearance, and disappearance, of certain response options as racial categories. We can imagine someone being born a Slave, attending school as a Mulatto, being married as an Octoroon, and dying a Black (Negro or of Negro descent).

MAJORITY–MINORITY RELATIONS

Race and ethnicity can be understood in the context of a wide range of relationships subsumed under the heading of *majority–minority relations* (Farley 2011; Yetman 1991). The focus in work on such relations is often on the difficulties experienced by minority groups, including racial and ethnic minorities. Many of these problems are traceable to majority group prejudice and discrimination (Jackson 2007) and the unequal ways in which most societies are structured to favor those in the majority.

However, the distinction between *majority* and *minority* raises a number of questions. How can the White race, to take one example, be considered a majority group when it is outnumbered by a wide margin in the world by those of other races? Whites are still numerically dominant in the United States, but the U.S. Census Bureau has projected that by 2045 the non-Hispanic White population in the country will be in the minority when compared with the combined nonwhite population groups, although Whites will still outnumber any single racial/ethnic group (see Edsall 2018a for a more nuanced perspective on this change). We can refer to this situation as a **majority–minority population**, defined as a case "where more than 50 percent of the population is part of a minority group" (U.S. Census Bureau 2011; see also Lichter 2013). Majority–minority racial/ethnic populations already exist in California, Texas, Hawaii, New Mexico, and the District of Columbia. Globally, this situation exists in many countries including, perhaps most famously, South Africa.

As of 2023, there are approximately 166 million men and 169 million women in the United States. How can women be a minority when they outnumber men? The answer to this question lies in the sociological definitions of *majority* and *minority*, which do not rely on the actual number of people who are in a group. Rather, these definitions are based on differences in levels of money, prestige, and power possessed by groups. As the classic social theorist Max Weber defined the terms, a **minority group** is in a subordinate position in terms of wealth, power, and prestige (status), while a **majority group** is in a dominant position on those dimensions. Although these three factors (money, power, prestige) often vary together, a higher ranking in only one or two can be enough to accord a group majority status and, by implication, define another as a minority group. Thus, women can be considered a minority group because although they are in the numerical majority, as a group they have less wealth, power, and prestige than do men.

Stereotypes, Prejudice, and Discrimination

A **stereotype** is a generalization about an entire category of people that is thought to apply to everyone in that category. That Asians are good at math or that all gay guys are stylish are examples of stereotypes. Clearly some Asians are good at math, but not all are, and even for those that are good at math it is not because they are Asian. Similarly, some gay guys are stylish, but many are not. And, again, even if they are stylish, it is not because of their sexual identity.

Stereotypes are frequently manifested in daily social interactions. For example, people might assume that a clean-cut, young, White student-athlete at the elite Stanford University would be highly trustworthy. However, just such a man (and there are a number of others like him), Brock Turner, was convicted in 2016 of felony sexual assault on an intoxicated, unconscious female student. In contrast, stereotypes about racial and ethnic minorities tend to work against them. In department stores, security guards may follow Black and Latinx customers without apparent cause, salespeople may view Black and Latinx shoppers with suspicion, cashiers may avoid physical contact with Black and Latinx customers when giving change, and White customers may exhibit nervousness when joined by a Black or Latinx man in an elevator. This all occurs because of a stereotype relating Black and Latinx people with criminal behavior.

Stereotypes are the basis for prejudice and discrimination. **Prejudice** consists of preconceived attitudes, beliefs, and feelings toward individuals, typically derived from unfounded opinions or stereotypes. For example, believing that Latinx people are all lazy is an example of prejudice. Although we typically think of prejudice as having negative attitudes, beliefs, and feelings toward someone, it can also involve positive ideas. The idea that Asians are smarter or that gay guys make better friends are two examples of positive prejudice. These types of prejudice can be just as harmful, however, as they are still based on unfounded opinions or stereotypes.

Discrimination is different than prejudice in that it implies acting on one's preconceived attitudes, beliefs, and feelings. It is putting one's prejudice into action. Not offering someone a job because of ideas you have about people with their skin color would be an example of discrimination. Like prejudice, discrimination can also be positive. Positive discrimination implies taking actions that benefit someone (or a group) because of a positive prejudice that you have about members of that group. Hiring an Asian math tutor simply because they are Asian would be an example of positive discrimination. Discrimination occurs both formally (e.g., on the job) and informally (e.g., in everyday interactions). It can occur anywhere, including in schools, workplaces, doctor's offices, grocery stores, housing, police stations, prisons, and courtrooms.

It is important to note that prejudice does not always imply discrimination. People can be prejudiced without discriminating; they need not act on their prejudices. However, stereotypes, prejudice, and discrimination often interact with one another. For example, Black women often face stereotypes that identify them as overly sexual and financially irresponsible (Collins 2004; Rosenthal and Lobel 2016). These stereotypes can, and do, have negative real-life consequences. For example, Black women who receive welfare have been compelled to undergo compulsory sterilization at some points in U.S. history. In fact, children as young as 12 were forced to undergo sterilization procedures in some states up until the 1970s (Flavin 2008). The assumption in these cases was that Black women would have too many children and be unable to support them financially.

The stereotype and treatment of Black men as dangerous criminals is one that has had particularly deadly consequences. For example, a number of, most often unarmed, Black men have been killed at the hands of police officers including Michael Brown in Ferguson, Missouri, in 2014; Eric Garner in New York City in 2014; Freddie Gray in Baltimore, Maryland, in 2015; Alton Sterling in Baton Rouge, Louisiana, and Philando Castile in St. Anthony, Minnesota, in 2016; Jordan Edwards in Balch Springs, Texas in 2017; George Floyd in Minneapolis, Minnesota in 2020; and Jayland Walker in Akron, Ohio in 2022. It is important to recognize that a number of Black women have also been unjustly killed at the hands of the police including Breonna Taylor in Louisville, Kentucky in 2020. Most important to recognize is that this list is far longer than space in this textbook allows for, although every victim should be honored with recognition.

Black Lives Matter marchers walk past a mural of George Floyd in Denver, Colorado. Floyd died of cardiopulmonary arrest when he was restrained by a Minneapolis police officer who knelt on his neck for more than eight minutes. Although he had a criminal record and had served time in prison, he was unarmed at the time and was accused of a nonviolent offense. His race and physical size fit a common stereotype of a dangerous criminal.

Helen H. Richardson / MediaNews Group/The Denver Post via Getty Images

Intersectionality

Many groups may be described as minority or majority groups and individuals often belong to both types of groups along different dimensions—for example, gay White men or Native American women who are able bodied. Additionally, people's experiences as one type of minority (or majority) may overlap and intersect with other experiences common to another type of minority (or majority). **Intersectionality** is the idea that members of any given minority (or majority) group are affected by the nature of their position in other systems or other forms of social inequality (Collins and Bilge 2016; Crenshaw 2019). It implies that in order to more fully understand the social experience of an individual we need to account for the multiplicity of their identities. One is not simply Black, for example. They also have a sex, gender, economic standing, citizenship, and so on.

The concept of intersectionality was initially developed to analyze the situation confronting women of color, who face discrimination along both gender and racial lines. It is not enough to simply understand the position of women of color by looking individually at their position as women and separately at their position of people of color. Instead, intersectionality implies that there is something unique about the intersection of those two variables—being a woman and being a person of color—that makes being a woman of color different from either variable independently. Today, intersectionality is used to understand all sorts of unique social locations and gives us a richer understanding of how majority and minority identities interact.

Minority group members can also be seen as being enmeshed in a **matrix of oppression**, an overlapping system of social inequalities that impacts an individual's standing in the social world. This matrix involves not only race and ethnicity but also sex, gender, sexual orientation, age, social class, religion, ability status, and a wide range of other dimensions. Thus, the problems associated with being a member of multiple oppressed minority groups are not simply additive; rather, the disadvantages multiply, as do their effects (Kivisto and Croll 2012).

Female members of a Native American Navajo family representing three generations. Many individuals experience a "matrix of oppression" based on several intersecting statuses or identities, including race or ethnicity, gender, and age.
grandriver/iStockPhoto

The opposite is also true. That is, a person who holds a number of statuses highly valued by society is likely to be extremely advantaged. One of the most esteemed groups consists of people who are male, White, Anglo-Saxon, upper class, heterosexual, and able-bodied,. This could be seen as a "matrix of power and advantage."

Patricia Hill Collins (1986) has argued that members of minority groups can have a particular social location as an "**outsider-within**," that is, a person who has formal membership in a majority group without being given the full informal rights of other members. For example, a Black student who attends a predominantly White high school might be formally a student at that school but without the informal rights and recognition of the White students. As another example, a female president might be formally recognized as the president but some might treat her with less respect than they do male presidents. The position of outsider-within is also a situational knowledge/power relationship, one in which the minority is given access to the majority but without being given the same informal rights and benefits of other members.

Patterns of Interaction

When members of majority and minority groups interact, the outcomes tend to follow one of four patterns: pluralism, assimilation, segregation, or genocide.

Pluralism exists in societies where many groups are able to coexist without any of them losing their individual qualities. In pluralistic societies, there may be multiple races, ethnic groups, and religions and many languages spoken.

Assimilation occurs when a minority group takes on the characteristics of the dominant group in place of their own particular group identities. In the United States, assimilation has occurred when immigrant groups have chosen to give up their native languages for English or when they have adopted mainstream U.S. cultural values and customs. Assimilation is not always voluntary. During the late nineteenth and early twentieth centuries, many Native American children were forced into boarding schools where they were given new names, forced to speak English (and punished for speaking their native languages), and taught Christianity.

The United States has leaned more at times toward pluralism and at other times more toward assimilation. Even when minorities assimilate and feel that their differences are respected, all majority–minority relations are fraught with at least the potential for conflict. Members of the majority group often act to maintain or enhance their positions, and minority group members often struggle to improve theirs, or at least strive to prevent theirs from declining any further. These conflicts, potential or real, are generally resolved in favor of the majority group because it has far greater resources (money, power) than does the minority group.

Segregation is the physical and social separation of majority and minority groups. Historically, segregation was mandated by law in the United States (and elsewhere). As a result, Whites and minorities were not able to attend the same schools, live in the same neighborhoods, or share the same public facilities (such as restrooms, theater seating areas, swimming pools, or courtrooms). The Supreme Court case of *Brown v. Board of Education* (1954) is seen as the beginning of the end of legally mandated segregation in the United States. Although levels of segregation have declined, such history set into motion practices that continue to segregate majority and minority groups. For example, schools are generally still segregated, a reflection of the persistence of residential segregation (Rooks 2017). Further, residential segregation is key to majority–minority, especially racial and ethnic, stratification (D. Massey 2016).

Genocide—an active, systematic attempt at eliminating an entire group of people—is a fourth outcome of majority–minority group relations. A genocidal campaign was conducted against Native Americans from the early days of European settlement in the United States through the 1800s. This was committed even though an official governmental policy of extermination did not exist. In other instances, genocide has been the official government policy, for example, the genocide experienced by Jews, the Roma, and homosexuals during the Holocaust or the Tutsi ethnic group during the genocide in Rwanda.

RACISM

Racism consists of defining a minority group as a race, attributing negative characteristics to that group, and then creating the circumstances that keep that group at a disadvantage relative to the majority (Fluehr-Lobban 2019). In short, racism means treating an individual or group differently because of their race.

Note that the definition of racism used here allows us to discuss negative attitudes and treatment based on either race or ethnicity. Cultural characteristics different from the mainstream, the hallmark of ethnic identity, are almost always associated with racial groups, so cultural discrimination is central to racial discrimination. In short, racism is based on ethnocentrism, or the belief that the norms, values, and customs of one's own group are superior to those of other groups.

If you were to ask most people whether or not they are racist, you would be almost certain to be told that the person is not prejudiced and considers people of all races and ethnicities to be equal. Yet racist and ethnocentric attitudes and behaviors persist. Minority members are likely to have experienced, or to know someone in their group who has experienced, discrimination. A recent Gallup poll of U.S. adults found that Whites are more likely than Blacks to say Black-White relations in our society today are "very or somewhat good": 43 percent of White respondents agreed with this statement in 2021, while only 33 percent of Blacks agreed. However, positive feelings about Black-White relation have declined significantly within both groups over the last decade (see Figure 9.1).

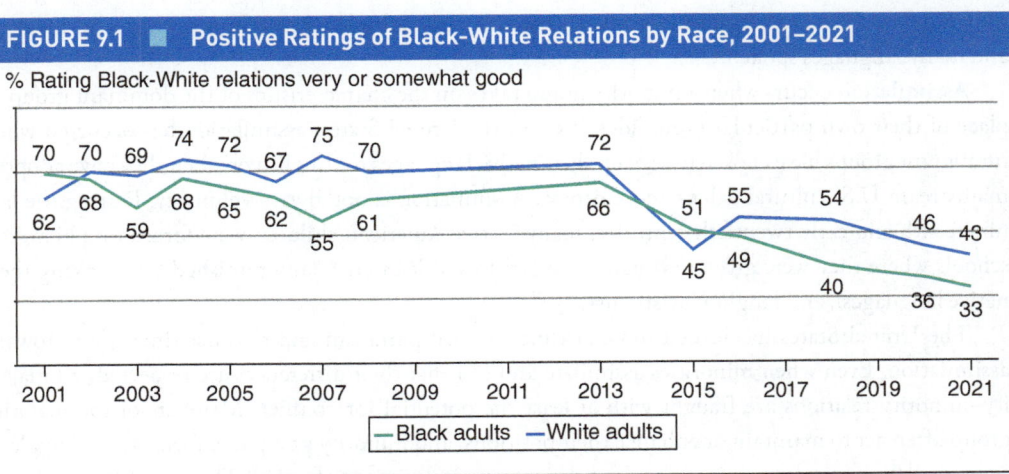

FIGURE 9.1 ■ Positive Ratings of Black-White Relations by Race, 2001–2021

Source: Gallup, "Ratings of Black-White Relations at a New Low," July 21, 2021.

Sometimes acts of racism or ethnic offense are unintentional, although that does not make them any less damaging. Many of these acts take place through language. For example, the use of the term *American* to mean a person from the United States is seen as offensive by many living in the Americas (both North and South America) because in nearly every country on the continent—the United States being the notable exception—the word "American" refers to anyone from the Americas, while those from individual countries are referred to by the name of their country (e.g., Mexicans or Colombians). In Spanish (the most common language in the majority of countries in the Americas), the word for someone from the United States is "estadounidense," roughly translated as "United-Statesian." Thus, many forms of racism and ethnic offense are built directly into our language and are often committed unknowingly; though, again, it is important to note that that does not make them any less damaging.

Although many scholars and citizens have come to believe that racism is on the decline and that the chances for racial integration and a postracial society have improved (Alba 2009; Khanna and Harris 2015), others contend that racism not only continues but also remains highly problematic (Bonilla-Silva 2015; Feagin 2012; Jung, Vargas, and Bonilla-Silva 2011). One way that racism continues to be problematic is, ironically, by people denying they are racist. **Color-blind racism** is the denial that individuals are thought about or treated differently based on their race and the assumption that everyone has equal opportunities. The idea is that in order to end racism, we need to stop seeing race. Unfortunately, such an approach is not so simple because not seeing race denies the historical and ongoing inequalities faced by members of racial and ethnic minorities.

Foundations of Racism

In the United States, and in many other countries around the world, Whites disproportionately occupy higher-level positions, and racial minorities are more likely to be near or at the bottom of the racial hierarchy. However, this is an overly simplistic picture of U.S. and global racial stratification. There are racial and ethnic minorities scattered throughout every level in that hierarchy, even in its highest reaches (see, e.g., the recent presidency of Barack Obama [2009–2017] and that of Evo Morales, mentioned in the opener to this chapter [2006–2019]).

One of the main indicators of racial stratification is the extent to which poverty is linked to race. Figure 9.2 shows the relationship between race/ethnicity and poverty between 1959 and 2020 in the United States. The fact that 19.5 percent of Black people and 17 percent of Hispanic people were below the poverty line in 2020—compared with 8.2 percent of White people and 8.1 percent of Asians—is a strong indicator of economic disadvantage for the first two groups. Also worth noting is the large increase in poverty among Black and Hispanic people beginning in 2008, right after the onset of the Great Recession. The historical influences of segregation and legal discrimination in generations past, coupled with the economic benefits of White privilege, help link economic disadvantage and racism.

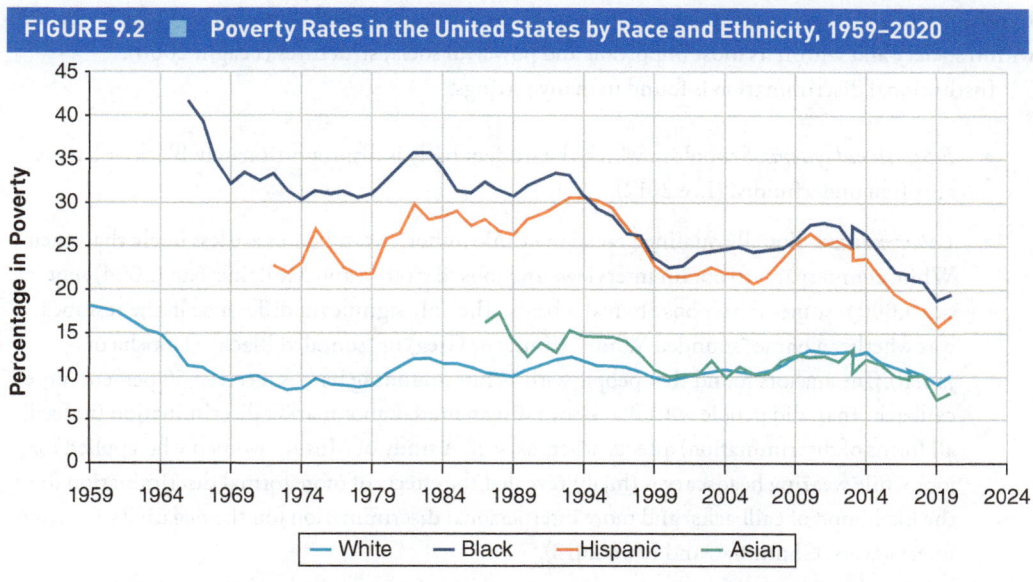

FIGURE 9.2 ■ Poverty Rates in the United States by Race and Ethnicity, 1959–2020

Source: Shrider, Emily, Melisa Kollar, Frances Chen, and Jessica Semega, 2021, *Poverty Status of People by Family Relationship, Race, and Hispanic Origin: 1959 to 2020*, Income and Poverty in the United States: 2020, Report No. P60-273, Table B-4, Washington, D.C.: United States Census Bureau.

Some sociologists argue that a part of the larger culture in many societies involves a "White racial frame" through which Whites, and to some degree racial minorities, view race. The **White racial frame** includes an array of racist ideas, racial stereotypes, racialized stories and tales, racist images, powerful racial emotions, and various inclinations that discriminate against racial minorities. To a certain extent, many racial and ethnic minorities themselves have adopted elements of this frame. This is exemplified in "gangsta" style being identified as part of Black or Latinx culture. It is also found in measures of success—such as graduating from college, gaining a professional job, or living in the suburbs—that are seen by some in minority cultures as selling out, or "acting White." This White racial frame is largely responsible for perpetuating racial stereotypes, as is seen throughout movies, music videos, video games, and television shows.

This set of ideas is pervasive throughout many cultures around the world and is found in and affects many, if not all, of their structures and institutions. These ideas come to "operate as a taken-for-granted, almost unconscious common sense" (Winant 2001, 293) in the minds of the individuals and societies who accept them. Thus, for example, many have the widely held belief that "hard work" underlies educational and occupational success, ignoring the role played by external social factors like race and ethnicity, sex and gender, and sexual orientation. Many firmly believe, often despite evidence to the contrary, that "equal opportunity" and individual habits, like "hard work," are all a person needs to succeed (DiTomaso 2013).

Throughout this discussion, Whiteness as a racial category has either been ignored or, especially in the case of the White racial frame, dealt with negatively as the source of prejudice and discrimination against minority racial and ethnic groups. However, White is also a "racial category," and Whites can also be considered a "racial group" (Hartigan 2014; Smangs 2016). Many Whites are antiracist, and large numbers of them embrace other races. Nevertheless, the relationship of Whites to minorities and the role of Whiteness in prejudice and discrimination need to remain a focus of attention in work on majority–minority relations, as well as in efforts to create a more equitable society.

Institutional Racism

Although there is a general tendency to emphasize individual prejudice and discrimination in discussing racism, from a sociological perspective, institutional discrimination—more specifically, institutional racism (Bobo 2017; Bonilla-Silva 2009; Carmichael and Hamilton 1967; Ward and Rivera 2014)—is also a big problem. **Institutional racism** is race-based discrimination that results from the day-to-day operation of social institutions and social structures and their rules, policies, and practices. In other words, racism is more than attitudes (prejudice) or behavior (discrimination); it is "systemic" within society and within its most important and powerful social structures (Feagin 2006).

Institutional discrimination is found in many settings.

- *Educational systems.* Schools in which the student body is disproportionately Black or Latinx are often underfunded (Lee 2012).

- *Labor markets.* Equally qualified racial or ethnic minority candidates are less likely than their White counterparts to obtain interviews and jobs. Bertrand and Mullainathan (2004) sent out 5,000 résumés in response to real job ads. The only significant difference in the résumés was whether a name "sounded White" (Emily or Greg) or "sounded Black" (Lakisha or Jamal). The authors found that people with White-sounding names received 50 percent more callbacks than did people with Black-sounding names. Labor market discrimination (indeed, all forms of discrimination) affects others as well. A study of Muslim women who applied for jobs while wearing headscarves (hijab) revealed the effects of more formal discrimination (on the likelihood of callbacks) and more interpersonal discrimination (on the negativity felt from interviewers; Ghumman and Ryan 2013).

- *The criminal justice system.* Drug laws and enforcement heavily penalize the selling and possession of the kinds of drugs, especially narcotics, that young Black and Latino men are more likely to use or sell. In contrast, laws against the use of the drugs of preference among affluent Whites—especially cocaine—are less likely to be enforced by the system.

- *The health care system.* Black and Latinx individuals are likely to receive no treatment or poorer-quality treatment in, for example, emergency rooms, rather than in the offices of physicians in private practice (Khazan 2018). They are also less likely to have private medical insurance.

- *The political system.* There has been a lot of publicity in the United States, especially since 2016, about efforts to disenfranchise racial and ethnic minorities by, for example, requiring documentation of various kinds and, in the case of Florida (and a few other states), barring ex-felons from voting. However, a successful ballot initiative in Florida in that year restored voting rights to certain felons after serving their sentence.

The "Invisibility" of Institutional Racism

Individual acts based on racism are often out in the open and easier for all to see than institutional racism, which is often hidden, especially under the guise of the law. In that way, institutional discrimination is far subtler—often even invisible. Individual acts reflective of prejudice (shouting a racial slur) or discrimination (a taxi driver refusing to pick up a Black passenger) are easier to notice. However, the everyday operations of a large organization are often more difficult to see, making institutional discrimination often appear more "natural" and further removed from criticism.

Because their day-to-day operations are largely invisible, institutions that operate in a racist manner are much less likely to be seen as a problem than are individual acts of prejudice or discrimination. This is despite the fact that institutional racism and discrimination arguably represent a far greater problem for racial and ethnic minorities than do individual discrimination and prejudice. In addition, the comparative invisibility of institutional racism makes it far more difficult to find ways of combating it.

Race, Ethnicity, and COVID-19

The COVID-19 pandemic has highlighted many of the structural inequalities associated with race and ethnicity (Navarro and Hernandez 2022; Khan 2023). Racial and ethnic minorities have had higher incidence of infection, hospitalization, and death, while at the same time having lesser access to healthcare and vaccines (Ryan and Nanda 2022). The SARS-CoV-2 virus responsible for causing COVID-19 does not discriminate based on race or ethnicity, but infection and death rates reveal just how much social systems have led to unequal distributions of the disease and its life-long and life-ending implications.

Many governments were slow to track COVID-19 infections and deaths by race and ethnicity. As of June 2022, in the United States, Blacks were 1.1 times more likely than non-Hispanic Whites to have had a confirmed infection, while Hispanics were 1.5 times more likely. Similarly, Blacks were 2.3 times more likely than non-Hispanic Whites to have been hospitalized while Hispanics were 2.2 times more likely. Blacks were also 1.7 times more likely to have died of the virus than non-Hispanic Whites, while Hispanics were 1.8 times more likely. It is important to state again that the virus does not impact people differently just because they are not White; instead, these differences are a result of racist social systems (Ryan and Nanda 2022).

There are several explanations that help us better understand these disparities. For example, racial and ethnic minorities are more likely to live in overcrowded housing, work in frontline jobs, to use public transportation, and to have jobs that do not allow them to work remotely. They are also more likely to have underlying health conditions and to not have health insurance. All of these factors are not because of personal choices (in most cases), but rather the result of a long historical legacy of racist practices and institutions that have placed racial and ethnic minorities at a disadvantage. These disadvantages are being made more apparent with the pandemic.

The pandemic has also led to a dramatic increase in discrimination and racist attacks against people perceived to be of Asian descent, especially Chinese people, in countries around the world, but particularly in the United States (Wong-Padoongpatt and Barrita 2023). These attacks have been spurred, in part, by the unproven theory that the virus was created in a lab in China and the use by former President Trump of terms like "China virus" and "Kung-Flu" to describe the virus. Throughout the pandemic, there have been multiple stories of discrimination and violence against people appearing to be of Asian descent, including the murder of eight people, six of them Asian American women, in Georgia in early 2021.

Social Movements and Race

Hate Groups

Many hate groups in the United States (and elsewhere) are White supremacist movements, with the Ku Klux Klan (KKK) being perhaps the best known. Although the KKK is famous for its racist positions, especially against Blacks, it actually began as a nativist, anti-Catholic, and anti-Semitic group. KKK activity began at a time of high European immigration from places like Ireland, Italy, and other non-WASP (White Anglo-Saxon Protestant) nations. These new arrivals were seen as a threat to national identity.

Other well-known racist hate groups include the neo-Nazis and skinheads. A newer rightwing hate group is the Proud Boys, a neo-fascist, all-male group that glorifies and engages in political violence (Goldmacher 2018). They were made most famous for their leading role in the attacks on the U.S. Capitol Building on January 6, 2021. The Oath Keepers are another far-right hate group who claim to be defending the Constitution of the United States but whose members often engage in extremist acts that are arguably better seen as racist.

In 2021, the Southern Poverty Law Center (SPLC n.d.) identified 733 active hate groups in the United States. The SPLC has cited a rise in ethnic-based hate crimes following the September 11 attacks in the U.S. and again during the COVID-19 pandemic. It reports an increasing number of hate crimes directed toward immigrant populations, thus reflecting continued xenophobia in society. Activities of hate groups include rallies; speeches; marches; leafleting; publishing; maintenance of websites; and criminal activities including vandalism, arson, sexual assaults, and other violence. Figure 9.3 reports the breakdown of hate crimes in 2021 and shows that nearly two thirds of them were motivated by racial and ethnic biases.

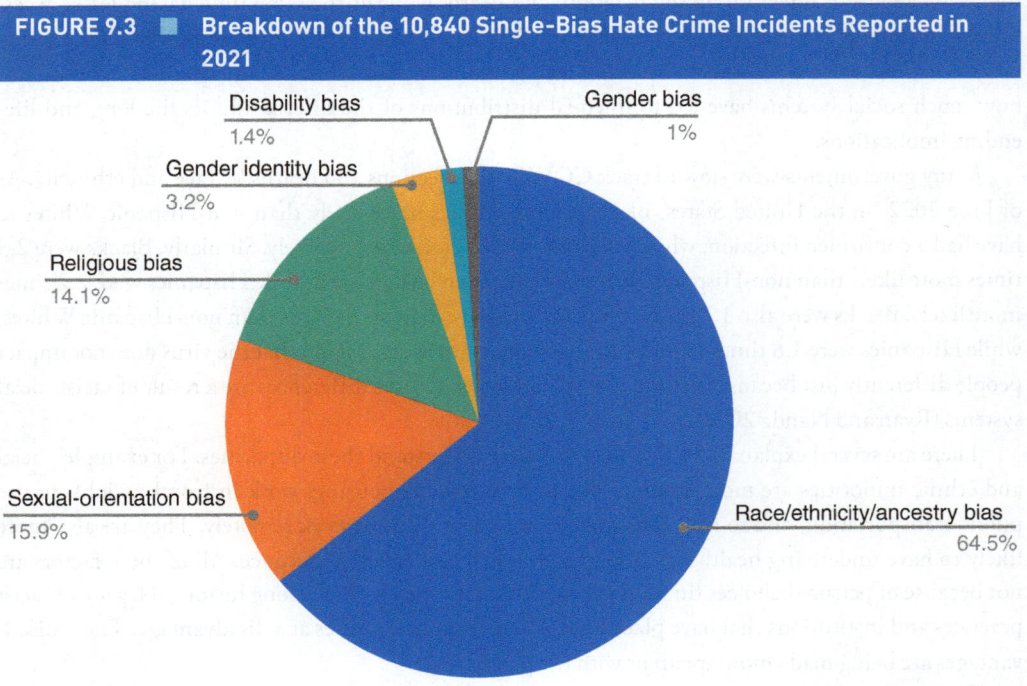

FIGURE 9.3 ■ Breakdown of the 10,840 Single-Bias Hate Crime Incidents Reported in 2021

- Disability bias 1.4%
- Gender bias 1%
- Gender identity bias 3.2%
- Religious bias 14.1%
- Sexual-orientation bias 15.9%
- Race/ethnicity/ancestry bias 64.5%

Source: FBI National Press Office. 2023, March 13. "FBI Releases Supplemental 2021 Hate Crime Statistics." Press release. https://www.fbi.gov/news/press-releases/fbi-releases-supplemental-2021-hate-crime-statistics

Participation in racial hate groups was long considered to be the domain of White men. When White women participated in such movements, they were assumed to have been brought into the movement through husbands and boyfriends. However, sociologist Kathleen Blee (2002), one of the first researchers to study gender in racist hate movements, found that these women have a variety of reasons for joining that do not include the influence of men. She conducted in-depth interviews with women involved in several groups and found that some of them had joined after experiencing life tragedies that they, rightly or wrongly, blamed on another racial group. Others had moved into social circles that supported and propagated racist views, often attributing a variety of social ills to Blacks, Hispanics, and Jews. Blee showed that White women are not just auxiliary members but rather are integrated into positions of power within many of these organizations.

The Civil Rights Movement

Although we have focused here on various forms of oppression of Blacks and other racial and ethnic minority groups, there also has been, and continues to be, resistance to this oppression by many. One major example is the modern civil rights movement, which arose in the mid-1950s and 1960s, to deal with Black oppression maintained by the Jim Crow system (Riches 2017). Under Jim Crow laws, which were instituted after the Civil War and Reconstruction, Blacks were denied political and social rights and were exploited economically.

Blacks and progressive allies had long opposed and fought against this system. However, it was the civil rights movement that brought Jim Crow to an end (although Alexander [2012] argues that there is now a "new" Jim Crow system in, for example, a legal system that discriminates against Blacks, leading to a far higher incarceration rate for Blacks in the United States—five times that of White citizens [Bromwich 2018]). It did so by honing a variety of techniques, such as boycotts, mass marches, and sit-ins. For their part, racist Whites and their representatives (e.g., police) often responded with the use of clubs and other weapons and also with attack dogs. These responses often took place in front of TV news cameras, and the national coverage served to put pressure on the federal government to reform the system.

As a result, from 1955 to 1965, Jim Crow was dismantled. The civil rights movement of that era led to the passage of the Civil Rights Act of 1964 and the Voting Rights Act of 1965, formally striking down legal discrimination in various aspects of public life (although, as implied above, there is a growing concern that many of these gains are in the process of being reversed). Although Blacks today tend to suffer from many of the same problems as they did before the civil rights movement, the problems are now caused more by institutional racism than other forms of more covert racism.

A segregated bus station in Durham, North Carolina, 1940. The civil rights movement eventually brought the Jim Crow era to an end, but racism and discrimination are still with us. Why?

Granger

Collective Identity and "Power" Movements

After the successes of the civil rights movement in the mid-1960s, several social movements arose in the late 1960s and early 1970s that sought to energize racial and ethnic minorities. Winning legal rights was one thing, but many individuals continued to feel belittled and oppressed. The Black Power movement was the best-known attempt to raise a racial minority out of its sense of inferiority. Its slogan was "Black is beautiful."

The visibility of the Black Power movement contributed to racialization among Hispanics. The Brown Berets saw themselves as analogous to the Black Panthers. The Brown Berets adopted the slogan "brown power" (and later "Viva la raza," or "Long live the race"). The 1968 East L.A. Chicano Student Walkout was an important historic event. More than 2,700 students walked out of schools to protest institutional racism that included prohibitions against speaking Spanish in class and guidance counseling that pushed Latinx students to consider menial labor instead of college. Police beat and arrested some students and arrested some of the teachers who helped students mobilize (Global Nonviolent Action Database 2011). More recent politicized racial identities among Latinxs include the *indigena* movement, which elevates South American Indian ancestry to a matter of pride.

Black Lives Matter Movement

The Black Lives Matter movement (sometimes called "BLM" for short) began in 2013 with the use of the #BlackLivesMatter tag on social media following the acquittal of George Zimmerman in the shooting of Trayvon Martin. The movement has since grown to be one of the most recognized and influential social movements operating in the world today. It focuses on dealing with the prejudice and discrimination facing Black people throughout the United States and other parts of the world. More specifically, it is concerned with the phenomenon of Black lives that are "systematically and intentionally targeted for demise." More positively, it involves an "affirmation of Black folks' contributions to this society, our humanity, and our resilience in the face of deadly oppression" (see blacklivesmatter.com). Although it is concerned about violence and many other aspects of Black lives in the United States and internationally, Black Lives Matter is primarily concerned with "state violence," especially extrajudicial violence waged by police officers.

In Paris, protesters march against police violence in May, 2023. Black Lives Matter has become a global social movement.
NurPhoto/Getty Images

The movement gained significant attention after the murder of George Floyd in 2020. An estimated 15 to 25 million people participated in the 2020 BLM protests, making it one of the largest protests in the history of the United States. The movement is largely decentralized, owing in part to its association with social media. It has also gained an international following, making it one of the most truly global social movements of the twenty-first century.

RACE AND ETHNICITY IN A GLOBAL CONTEXT

Historically, ethnic identities (and often also racial ones) have been closely tied to nation-states. For instance, until the modern era, the population of Ireland embraced almost exclusively the Gaelic language and Irish culture. However, nation-based ethnic identity has declined over time. One major factor in this decline is **diaspora**, or the dispersal, typically involuntary, of a racial or ethnic population from its traditional homeland and over a wide geographic area. In recent years, mass migration in an age of globalization has had a powerful impact on ethnic identities and reduced their association with given nation-states.

Such population movement has led to the existence of multiple identities on the global stage. This, in turn, has increased the possibility of people having hybrid ethnic identities. That is, an increasing number of people identify not only with, say, the ethnic group into which they were born but also with other ethnic groups in geographic areas to which they may have migrated. For example, migrants from India to China may see themselves as both Indian and Chinese. Similarly, migrants from Mexico to the United States may seem themselves as both "American" and Mexican.

Ethnic Identity and Globalization

Some see globalization as a threat to ethnic identity; they see globalization as leading toward a world of homogeneous identities. However, others disagree, citing the following reasons.

- Ethnic identities are not nearly as fragile as is often believed. Ethnicity is often taught to us from birth, within the family, and then often in school and by the surrounding culture. Thus, it usually becomes part of a person's core identity.

- Globalization can be a force, maybe the most significant force, in the creation and proliferation of ethnic identity (Tomlinson 2000). Ethnic groups and many aspects of their culture flow around the globe, creating new pockets of ethnic identity and reinforcing that identity in particular locales. Global pressures toward a homogenized identity may also make a person even more committed to maintain ties to their own ethnic culture.

- Ethnic identity and globalization are part of the same modern process. For example, through the development of advanced forms of communication (like the internet or many phone apps), globalization allows ethnic group members to stay in touch with one another which helps to maintain familiar traditions. This more powerful sense of ethnic identity can be exported back to the home country through the same global media.

Global Prejudice and Discrimination

To this point, we have focused on majority–minority relations within specific nation-states, especially within the United States. But we must also examine majority–minority relations in a global context more closely. The North–South distinction is a key factor. The Global North and the Global South are terms used to divide the world along socioeconomic and political characteristics, especially as related to income and standards of living. These terms are not necessarily meant to be geographic references to north and south but are considered less value-laden terms to replace the formerly popular terms of "developed" and "developing" to refer to countries. Many countries in the Global North have engaged in imperialism while many countries in the Global South have been the subject of colonization.

The Global North and its majority groups have long dominated, controlled, exploited, and oppressed the Global South and its minority groups. Historically, imperialism, colonialism, economic development, Westernization, and Americanization have worked in large part to the Global Norths advantage and to the disadvantage of those in the Global South. The system that dominates globalization today—neoliberal economics—helps those in the advantaged categories in the Global North and hurts, often badly, those in the disadvantaged categories in the Global South (Harvey 2005). For example, most of the "bottom billion," or the poorest billion people in the world, are minority group members in the Global South. The richest billion people in the world are largely in the Global North and are mainly members of the majority groups.

Majority groups from the Global North have often "invented" minority groups in the Global South. One example is the creation of "Indians" as an oppressed minority group after the British colonized India. Until that point, Indian society had had its own highly developed system of majority and minority castes. Another example derives from **Orientalism**, a set of ideas and texts produced by the

Global North that served as the basis of systems designed to dominate, control, and exploit the Orient (the Middle East, Asia, and North Africa) and its many minority groups (Said [1979] 1994).

Racism is not exclusive to the West in general, or to the United States in particular, but exists in many societies throughout the world. In Japan, differences in skin color, hair, and even body odor have been used to distinguish among races such as the Ainu and Buraku. Japanese citizens whose ancestry is partly Caucasian or African are also subject to prejudice within their own country. China has 56 officially recognized ethnic groups, totaling about 105 million people; nearly 92 percent (1.2 billion) of all Chinese are in the Han ethnic group. Figure 9.4 shows the geographic distribution of ethnolinguistic groups in China; note the concentration of Han in the heavily populated coastal areas. Uyghurs, a Muslim, Turkic-speaking minority in northwestern China, are particularly heavily discriminated against, with a growing body of evidence showing that they are often imprisoned in reeducation camps and forced into slave labor.

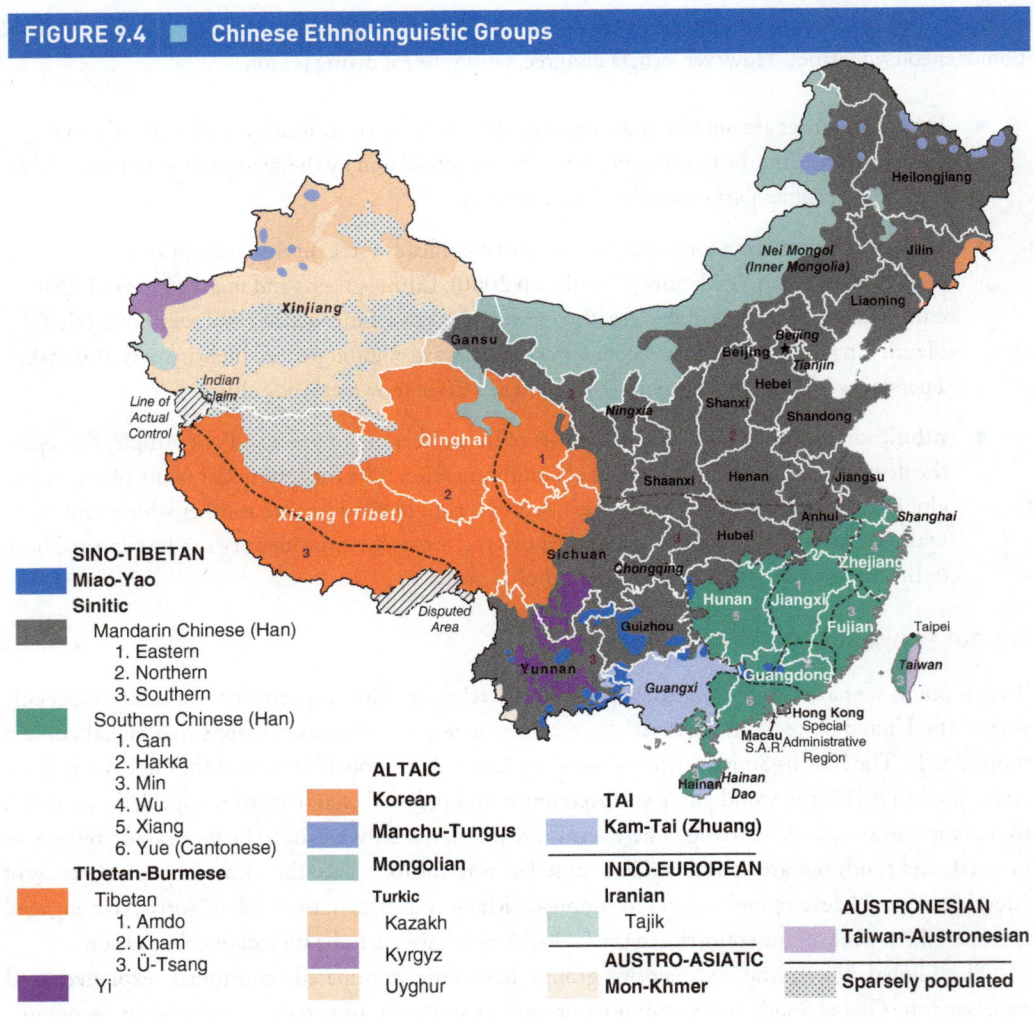

FIGURE 9.4 ■ Chinese Ethnolinguistic Groups

Source: Courtesy of the University of Texas Libraries, The University of Texas at Austin.

Global Flows Based on Race and Ethnicity

One way to think about globalized majority–minority relations is in terms of global flows. Both race and ethnicity can be said to flow around the world. One manifestation is the migration of people of various racial and ethnic groups, who move around the world today with greater ease and rapidity than ever before, although this is changing with renewed nationalism in many parts of the world (Slobodian 2018). People from the North are more likely to be tourists or retirees who visit or take up residence in the nations of the South because of the good weather and low cost of living (Bianchi 2018). In contrast, residents of the South typically migrate to wealthy nations in the North in search of employment, be it in low-skilled or high-skilled positions (Kivisto and Faist 2010), or to escape crime and persecution.

Paul Gilroy's *The Black Atlantic: Modernity and Double Consciousness* (1993) is an important work on majority–minority relations that stresses global flows. Gilroy is particularly interested in the flows that relate to Blacks in the Atlantic region. Figure 9.5 shows those flows, as well as another flow of slaves from Africa to Asia. This image encompasses the flow of slaves from Africa to the eastern coast of the Americas and the later return of some Blacks to Africa. It also encompasses the circulation of activists, ideas, books, works of art, and the like that relate to Blacks and race relations. All are seen as involved in "displacements, migrations, and journeys" (111). Gilroy argues that in trying to understand global flows based on race, we should focus not on national boundaries but rather on the "Black Atlantic," which he portrays as a transnational space.

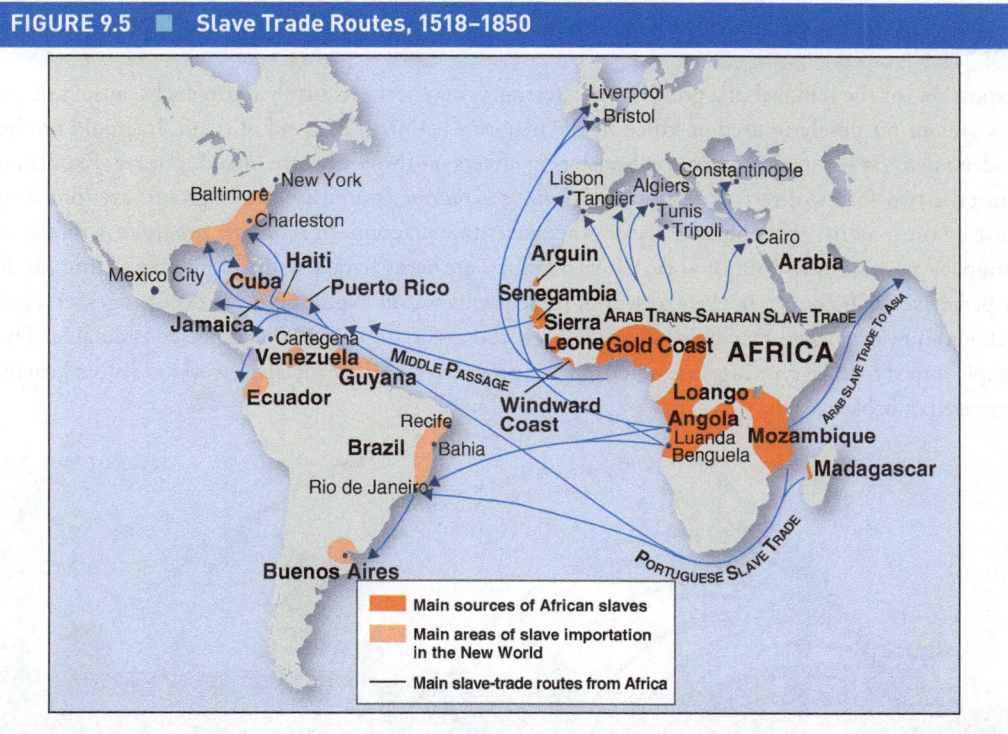

FIGURE 9.5 ■ Slave Trade Routes, 1518–1850

Source: LatinAmericanStudies.org.

Racism itself can be seen as having wide-ranging negative consequences for minority group members as the ideas and practices associated with it flow around the world. This flow of racism around the world has been referred to as the "racialization of the globe" (Dikötter 2008; Treitler 2016). Nevertheless, racist ideas and practices are certainly not the same throughout the world but rather are adapted and modified in each locale. They are affected by local ideas and economic, political, and military realities. As a result, racism as it involves Blacks is not the same in Great Britain as it is in Brazil or the United States. Racism also changes over time, as reflected today in the flow of anti-Asian racism through many parts of the world, especially the United States.

Ethnic Conflict within Nation-States

Greater ethnic diversity and contact between different ethnicities has increased the possibility of ethnic conflict within, and between, many nation-states. Of course, such ethnic conflict is not new. Among the most notable examples in the twentieth and twenty-first centuries have been conflicts between Turks and Armenians in Turkey; between Germans, especially Nazis, and Jews in Germany; between Tamils and the Sinhalese in Sri Lanka; between the Tutsi and Hutu in Burundi and Rwanda; between Arabs and ethnic Africans in Darfur; and between various ethnic groups—Slovenes, Croatians, Serbs, Bosnians, Montenegrins, Macedonians, and Albanians—after the breakup of Yugoslavia in 1991.

However, today, with more members of ethnic groups in more and more countries, there is the potential for a great increase in the number, if not the intensity, of ethnic conflicts.

The possibility of ethnic conflict within nation-states has reached a whole new level in recent years with the vast migration of various peoples from the Middle East and North Africa to Europe (Bhabha 2018), both as a means to seek greater opportunities as well as those fleeing conflict and war. The sheer number of migrants has challenged many countries and locales. Beyond that, migrants often bring with them cultures, religions, and practices that are different from those in their destinations. These migrants are also often seen as competing with local populations for jobs, creating further tension. As a result, there has been a tendency to ghettoize these migrants, thereby increasing polarization between groups and creating greater alienation among both migrants and nationals (Fisher 2016).

The most disturbing examples of ethnic conflict tend to involve the majority group's efforts to "deal" with ethnic minorities through expulsion, ethnic cleansing, or genocide.

Expulsion

Expulsion, or the removal of a group from a territory, may seem relatively harmless because minorities are not purposely injured or killed in the majority's efforts to get rid of them. It should not be understated, however, as it can have devastating effects on those who are forced to leave. Expulsion can take two forms: direct or voluntary. In *direct expulsion,* minority ethnic groups are forced to leave by the majority through military or other government action. In *voluntary expulsion*, a minority group leaves "of its own volition" because its members are being harassed, discriminated against, and/or persecuted. Of course, in the real world, these two forms of expulsion often occur together. And although physical harm may be relatively light, social and economic harm can be considerable. The people forced to leave typically lose much of their property, and their social networks are often heavily damaged or broken.

These people at a UN base in South Sudan are safe, at least momentarily, from the ethnic cleansing associated with rape and other forms of violence aimed at them.

AP Photo/Jason Patinkin, File

Many of the racial and ethnic groups involved in diasporas have experienced both forms of expulsion. This has been particularly true for Jews and the Roma, who have often been forcibly ejected (e.g., Jews were ejected from Jerusalem by the Romans in the second century and from Spain and Portugal in the fifteenth century) or moved voluntarily (e.g., many Jews left Europe after World War II in the wake of continuing anti-Semitism).

Ethnic Cleansing

Ethnic cleansing is the establishment by the dominant group of policies that allow or require the forcible removal, abuse, and even murder of people of another ethnic group (Sekulic 2016). Nazi actions against Jews and Roma fit the definition of ethnic cleansing.

Ethnic cleansing achieved more recent notoriety during the wars associated with the dissolution of Yugoslavia in 1991. The ethnic groups that dominated various regions sought to create ethnically homogeneous areas by expelling and even killing members of other ethnic groups. For example, Croatians were expelled from parts of Croatia inhabited by Serbs. Bosnia, which declared independence in 1992, was composed of three major ethnic groups—Slavic Muslims (the largest single group), Serbs, and Croats. Serbian armed forces created ethnically homogeneous enclaves by forcibly removing and murdering members of the other ethnic groups, especially Muslims.

In situations of ethnic cleansing, women and girls often have been targeted for physical violence and murder, as well as sexual violence in many cases. In Bosnia in the 1990s, Serbian men systematically raped an estimated 50,000 Muslim and Croatian women as part of their campaign of terror. Because the Serbian police were in positions of power, it was difficult, if not impossible, for the women who were victims of rape to get help or to prosecute their attackers.

Mass rape as a weapon of war has also occurred in the region of Darfur within Sudan, with the government-supported Janjaweed militiamen raping Darfuri women and girls held in refugee camps. In 2008, Sudan's then-president, Omar Hassan Ahmed Bashir, was accused (and later indicted) by the prosecutor of the International Criminal Court (ICC) of The Hague of not only mass genocide but also propagating rape as a weapon of war and terror (Scheffer 2008). The accusations and the indictment did not prevent him from being reelected president of Sudan in 2015, with 94 percent of the vote (Kushkush 2015). Sudan only agreed to hand over Bashir in 2021, although as of 2023 he was still in prison in Khartoum. Sudanese armed forces have continued to carry out mass rapes (and killings) in Darfur (Gladstone 2015).

Genocide

The most extreme cases of ethnic conflict involve *genocide*, an active, systematic attempt at eliminating an entire group of people. Genocide was defined in 1948 by the United Nations Convention on the Prevention and Punishment of the Crime of Genocide as "acts committed with the intent to destroy, in whole or in part, a national, ethnic, racial, or religious group." It is seen as one of the principal crimes of the twentieth century, and it shows every sign of continuing to define the twenty-first century. Figure 9.6 shows select genocides of the twentieth and twenty-first centuries. The earliest genocide depicted here dates back to 1914, but there were many other instances of genocide long before that.

The 1948 UN convention on genocide was prompted by the Nazi Holocaust (Karstedt 2016). At first, the Holocaust occurred within the confines of Germany, but it later spread to the European countries allied with, or conquered by, Germany. It was in that sense transnational, and it would have undoubtedly become far more of a global phenomenon had the Nazis achieved their goal of world conquest. For example, had the Nazis succeeded in conquering the United States (see *The Man in the High Castle* on Amazon), we would undoubtedly have seen the genocide of Jews in that country.

A parallel example of large-scale genocide is the mass killings that took place during the rule of Joseph Stalin throughout the then-vast Soviet empire. In the main, however, genocide continues to be practiced within nation-states. Examples include the murder of nearly 2 million people by the Khmer Rouge in Cambodia in the mid- to late 1970s, the killing in 1994 of as many as 1 million people (mostly minority Tutsis) by the majority Hutus in Rwanda, the murder of tens of thousands of Bosnians and Croats in the 1990s by Bosnian Serbs, and the killing of hundreds of thousands of ethnic Africans in Sudan since 2003 by ethnic Arabs.

The global age has brought with it the globalization of genocide, as instances of it have flowed around the world (Karstedt 2016). That is, genocide has become another negative flow making its way from one part of the world to another. Genocide may become more likely in the future because of proliferating and accelerating global flows of ideas, agitators, and weapons. Added to this is the increased inability of nation-states to block many of these flows.

FIGURE 9.6 ■ Select Genocides around the World, 1914–Present

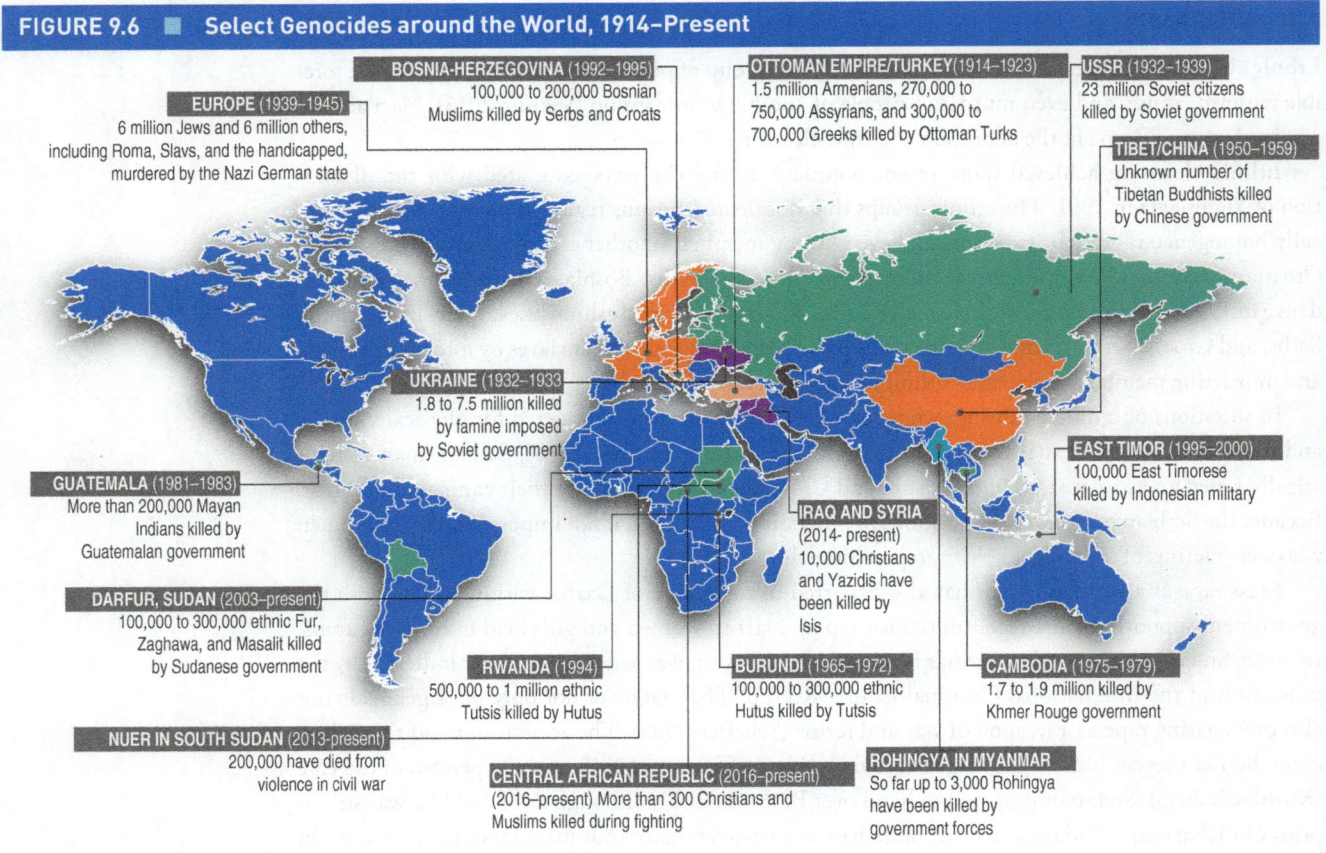

Source: Adapted from Online Resources from The Choices Program, Brown University.

SUMMARY

Race has historically been defined based on a shared lineage and some real or presumed biological characteristic. In the second half of the twentieth century, race began to be defined more as a cultural phenomenon, making it a more fluid than fixed type of identity. Ethnicity is typically defined on the basis of some real or presumed cultural characteristic such as language, religion, traditions, or cultural practices.

Race and ethnicity have long served as a way of stratifying individuals into groups with more or less power. The majority group, even if it has fewer members, has the power to act on its prejudices and discriminate against members of minority groups. Intersectionality, or belonging to more than one type of minority (for example, being Black and female), often compounds disparities. Majority–minority relations devolve into racism when the majority defines a group as a race and attributes negative characteristics to that group. The combination of xenophobia and ethnocentrism makes racism even more impactful. Current racism is also a matter of hegemony, or the majority group foisting its culture on minority groups and the persistence of institutional racism.

Putting majority–minority relations in a global context, the North has more majority group members (at least for the moment) and dominates and oppresses those in the South. Majority groups are better positioned than minority groups to create structures that enhance positive or protective global flows. Greater ethnic diversity within nation-states has opened up more possibilities for internal ethnic conflicts. At the extreme, ethnic conflict leads to expulsion, ethnic cleansing, and genocide of minorities by the majority within a territory.

KEY TERMS

assimilation	majority-minority population
color-blind racism	matrix of oppression
diaspora	minority group
discrimination	"one drop" rule
ethnic cleansing	Orientalism
ethnic groups	outsider-within
ethnicity	pluralism
eugenics	prejudice
expulsion	race
genocide	racism
institutional racism	segregation
intersectionality	stereotype
majority group	white racial frame

REVIEW QUESTIONS

1. What is the difference between race and ethnicity? What are the similarities? How have biological and cultural explanations helped create racial and ethnic differences?

2. Barack Obama is the child of a White mother and a Black African father, but more often than not he is referred to as Black. What does this suggest about the nature of race in the United States? What are the consequences of this perception?

3. What criteria do sociologists use to define a majority group? How do majority groups maintain their positions of privilege?

4. What are the different motivations for racism?

5. What mechanisms have minorities used to resist racism?

6. What is institutional racism, and what are some examples of institutional racism? In what ways is institutional racism more problematic than individual racism?

7. How would you characterize majority–minority relations on a global level?

8. What sorts of advantages do majority groups have on the global level?

9. How is globalization changing the nature of ethnicity on a global scale?

10. In what ways have ethnic groups been able to use advances in communication and media to retain their ethnic identity?

Marmaduke St. John / Alamy Stock Photo

10 GENDERS AND SEXUALITIES

> **LEARNING OBJECTIVES**
>
> **10.1** Discuss the differences between sex, gender, and sexuality.
>
> **10.2** Identify the cultural influences on gender and discuss gendered inequalities.
>
> **10.3** Explain the effects of globalization on gender and sexualities.
>
> **10.4** Examine global flows related to gender and sexuality.
>
> **10.5** Discuss the connection between gender and violence.

CHALLENGING GENDER STEREOTYPES

In a favela (slum) in Rio de Janeiro, Brazil, a thoughtful, handsome man named Marcio talks about his life. "My dream was to be a father," he says, standing with his son and wife. Sending a kite into the gray sky, he continues, "For some people, maybe it's a career, for others, maybe to travel somewhere, but my dream was always to be a father. And to give my son something I never had." Marcio explains that his childhood was marked by constant violence; his father beat his mother, and the community stood by and accepted it. "He had to show he was a man," he says of his father. Marcio learned from his father that manhood meant having many women, drinking, partying, and staying out all night.

As he cries at the memory of his father's absence and lack of attention, Marcio explains how he managed to avoid becoming like his father by finding a group of men who had had similar experiences. As they met, talked, and cried together, Marcio saw how traditional cultural gender stereotypes of masculinity and femininity had been harmful. He became willing to challenge his culture's sex and gender norms to create a better life for himself, his wife, and his son. With the help of Equimundo (formerly Promundo; see equimundo.org), a global organization devoted to gender justice and preventing violence against women, he now works with other men to support their efforts to challenge traditional gender expectations. As Marcio puts it, "The rain doesn't come all at once; it comes a drop at a time. And then it becomes a strong river." Change in the lives of a few can lead to change in the lives of many and, indeed, even in an entire nation or culture.

Beliefs and attitudes about gender and sexuality differ across countries and cultures as well as over time. Globalization, technological advancements in communication, and growing awareness of the consequences of gender inequalities are among the factors changing what we think about gender and sexuality. As the founders of Equimundo listened to accounts of men committing violence against women and children around the world, they saw an opportunity and a need for reform. Equimundo now works with local community stakeholders and agencies such as the World Health Organization in dozens of countries around the world, helping men and boys change themselves and their communities. For the people involved in Brazil—and elsewhere—the ongoing struggle between tradition and freedom is exhilarating and terrifying, joyful and heart-wrenching. For sociologists, it's a testament to the intricate beauty of a living, breathing culture that is always changing. For everyone, it is an opportunity to think about increased social justice.

SEX AND GENDER

Sex and *gender* are terms often used interchangeably and confused with one another. However, it is important that they be distinguished clearly. **Sex** is principally a biological term, usually expressed as *female* or *male* (more on this later). Sex is typically reflected in a person's chromosomes, gonads, genitalia, and hormones. It is also often reflected in their legal documents, including birth certificates, drivers licenses, and passports. **Gender** is a cultural term, connected to societal expectations of certain behaviors, attitudes, and personalities that are often seen as "appropriate" for a given sex; it is usually reflected in terms like *woman* or *man* or *girl* or *boy*. The key difference is that sex is based mainly on biology, whereas gender is based on social distinctions. Conceptualizations of gender assume that there are strong, clear gender differences based on sex. Many people often assume that genitalia are "not only the primary marker of gender identity, but indeed, the underlying *cause* of that identity" (Helliwell 2000, 797; emphasis added). But bodies and biology are socially constructed as the basis for gender. "Gender builds on biological sex, but it exaggerates biological difference, and it carries biological difference into domains in which it is completely irrelevant" (Eckert and McConnell-Ginet 2013, 2). There is nothing in human biology to explain why, for example, we think that only women should wear high heels (which were actually originally designed for men!) or that men should not paint their nails (a practice that is becoming increasingly accepted in many cultures, and subcultures).

Gender and sex are examples—another is race—of a **master status**, a social position that becomes the primary identifying characteristic of an individual. Master statuses dominate all other statuses, including achieved (such as education) and ascribed (such as age) statuses, and are therefore of great consequence. One's master status can vary by setting, but typically includes sex, race, and sexuality. These are parts of one's identity that become the dominant lens through which that person is perceived by others.

Biological sex has long been linked with gender as a social construct, but the two are not as neatly entwined as we have been taught. Furthermore, sex and gender, especially gender, are not simply natural, biological processes. They are both—again, especially gender—strongly affected by social and cultural forces.

Although we tend to think in terms of only two biological sexes, in fact there is a continuum of sex (Homs 2016). **Intersex** is a "general term used for a variety of [medical] conditions in which a person is born with a reproductive or sexual anatomy that doesn't seem to fit the typical definitions of female or male" (Intersex Society of North America 2008). Only a few intersex conditions represent "true medical emergencies," in that the genitalia are a sign of an underlying metabolic medical issue needing immediate treatment. The majority of intersex conditions do not require medical interventions and instead are natural variations in human sex chromosome configurations. Historically, doctors have often surgically altered infants' and children's genitalia to attempt to match more typical male or female anatomy, a process that has been proven to cause great harm. Thanks to intersex advocacy and increased awareness among medical personnel, today this harmful practice is being outlawed in a number of countries and ruled as a form of nonconsensual mutilation of infants.

Most aspects of maleness and femaleness are on a continuum as well. For example, both males and females have the hormones estrogen and testosterone. However, the amounts vary greatly from individual to individual within and between sexes, as well as over time (Liaw and Janssen 2014). Both sexes also have breasts, so although breast cancer is largely a female disease, some males develop it. Facial hair is usually thought of as a male characteristic, but some females grow enough facial hair to need to shave regularly. Biologically, the differences between males and females are few, but much of culture is based on assumptions about sex (and gender) differences. Unfortunately, we rarely encounter "separate but equal" social structures based on notions of such differences. Instead, beliefs about difference are often translated into constructions of superiority and inferiority.

Femininities and Masculinities

Gender identity is a person's internal sense of gender (Wood and Eagly 2015). Individuals may have **gender roles**—the social presentation of gender, which includes clothing, hairstyle, and attitudinal and behavioral traits—that differ from or correspond with the gender identities society has assigned to the sex they were assigned at birth.

Intersex activist Pidgeon Pagonis (right), with SAGE sociology author Georgiann Davis, at the premiere of *National Geographic* magazine's 2016 documentary film, *The Gender Revolution: A Journey with Katie Couric*. National Geographic agreed to reprint a special issue of the magazine, also called *The Gender Revolution*, with corrections after Pagonis and others complained that the first printing referred to intersex as a "disorder."

Desiree Navarro/ Getty Images

As is the case with sex, we often think of gender in binary terms. We think of a *gender binary* involving only two genders, man and woman. But just as sex is not a simple binary, as evidenced in the case of intersexed individuals, gender has multiple aspects, forms, and expressions; it is not a simple, neat binary. As one well-known scholar puts it, "There is no single biological measure that unassailably places each and every human into one of two categories—male and female" (Fausto-Sterling 2018). It is socially constructed and variable across cultures, times, and places. Individuals who might identify themselves as one of the two dominant genders—namely, as a man or a woman—enact a wide range of gender portrayals, roles, and identities.

The terms *femininities* and *masculinities* refer to the cultural definitions of the traits associated with being a "woman" or a "man" acquired during the socialization process. They are plural because there are many forms of both, connected to other characteristics such as race, ethnicity, age, nationality, and social class. Cultural interpretations of femininities and masculinities are subject to change, depending on place and historical era. For example, many male historical figures considered to be quite masculine (e.g. George Washington, Napoleon) wore heels, frilly shirts, wigs, and make-up. These interpretations are also dependent on a variety of other factors, like race, age, and social status. If a male construction worker crosses their legs, we are probably more likely to consider that feminine behavior than if a business executive does so on stage at a conference. In short, masculinity and femininity are social constructs that are not stable across time, place, culture, of even person.

There is a tendency to develop stereotypes about what it means to be a woman and to be feminine (motherly, nurturant, emotional) and to be a man and masculine (dominating, tough, unemotional). However, in reality, these stereotypes are not natural or biological; rather, they are socially constructed. As Simone de Beauvoir famously put it, "One is not born, but rather becomes, a woman" ([1952] 1973, 301). The same is true, of course, for a man. Yet the distinction between men being masculine and women being feminine persists.

Sociologist Raewynn Connell (1997, 2009; Gough 2016) coined the terms *hegemonic masculinity* and *emphasized femininity* and analyzed the roles that these ideas have played in global gender inequalities. *Hegemonic* means dominant. Therefore, **hegemonic masculinity** refers to the dominant form or most idealized vision of masculinity. We take this form for granted as "natural." It is linked to patriarchy, a form of society dominated by men and focused on men and hegemonic masculinity (Miller 2017). Hegemonic masculinity is the vision of masculinity that underlies patriarchal systems.

Raewynn Connell has made important contributions to the study of social stratification and the study of gender, including the idea that gender is a large-scale social structure, not just a matter of personal identity. She frequently uses biographical interviewing in her research and was one of the first people to study the social construction of masculinity.

Photographed by Dianne Reggett. Used with permission of Raewynn Connell.

Emphasized femininity is a set of socially constructed ideas about "model womanhood." These ideas are organized around accommodating the interests of men and the patriarchy. Emphasized femininity focuses on social ability (rather than intellect), male ego stroking, and acceptance of the roles of mother and wife (Spade and Valentine 2016). It represents a subordinate heterosexual femininity. Specific manifestations of femininity and masculinity are measured against these dominant forms.

Hegemonic masculinity and emphasized femininity adversely affect both men and women. Men who do not live up to the stereotype of hegemonic masculinity, especially gay and working-class men, disabled men, and men of color, are negatively affected. Generally, the rigid expectations of hegemonic masculinity mean that many men, even heterosexual, White, middle-class men, will be viewed, and will view themselves, as falling short of the ideal. Many women are also adversely affected because they do not and cannot live up to the ideals associated with emphasized femininity.

Although some men benefit greatly from hegemonic masculinity, their advantages have, at least until recently, been largely invisible to them. Not having to think about masculinity, or what it means to "be a man," has been one of the dividends (or privileges) of gender inequality. In contrast, women often think a great deal about the disadvantages of femininity and the advantages of masculinity. Because they are oppressed by the system of gender inequalities in many different ways, they are more often forced to think about gender stereotypes.

Masculinities and femininities can, and should, be detached from biological sex and the body. Men can act in socially defined "feminine" ways by nurturing others, and women can behave in a socially defined "masculine" manner by competing aggressively. As is true of the continuum of male and female sexes, we should not think in simple either/or terms about gender. There is a continuum of masculinities *and* femininities, resulting in part from the variety of socialization patterns we experience over the life course. People adapt throughout their lives, emphasizing different aspects of gender and interpreting the gender role expectations constructed by society. We merge gendered expectations with those of other intersectional statuses, including race, class, and sexual orientation. Moreover, individuals can be high in both masculinity and femininity, or low in both, and either of these regardless of sex. Gender performance is fluid, not static, and allows room for individuals to choose how to perform gender within socially defined roles (Butler 1994; Goldschmied and Kowalczyk 2016). For example, people who are **agender** may not identify with any gender, while those who are **gender fluid** may feel that their identities change depending on the context. **Genderqueer** is a broad umbrella term that encompasses a range of gendered identities, feelings, and self-determined labels.

Gender Diversity

The term **transgender** is an umbrella term for people whose gender identity and/or gender expression differs from the social expectations associated with the sex they were medically assigned at birth (Ryan 2019). The determination of trans identity is one that is dependent on a variety of social, cultural, historical, and legal factors. These identities could include, but are not limited to, those who identify as transgender, transsexual, genderqueer, third gender, or gender nonbinary, among many other possible identities that would be seen as gender nonconforming by societal standards. For many in the medical profession, the determination of such an identity is a question of biological configurations (i.e., sex). For those working in psychiatry, it is often the diagnosis of a mental condition (i.e., gender identity disorder or gender dysphoria). From a legal perspective, understandings of what it means to be trans are as varied as the countries and, indeed, municipalities, that have laws governing such considerations (Ryan, 2018). And more complex still are the myriad of means by which trans people themselves come to develop and take on such an identity.

In addition, a variety of terms exist that trans individuals use to describe themselves including transsexual, transgender, trans, trans*, fe(male) with a trans history, and gender nonbinary; the list is as expansive as the number of individuals who might use such terms (Ryan 2020). Many of these terms do not hold a consistent definition across time, geography, or cultures. That is, they are often understood in different ways by different peoples to an extent not often seen with other kinds of identity terms. Further, persons with similar gender identities might use different terms to define themselves while persons with different gender identities might use the same term.

Trans individuals do not follow a single path. They may or may not locate themselves somewhere in the broad matrix of gender. They may or may not identify with either of the two culturally dominant genders. They may or may not wish to use hormones or obtain surgeries to change aspects of their physical sex. Trans individuals may choose identities and/or create self-applied labels that do not fit neatly within the gender binary (Ryan 2013).

Not long ago, *Time* magazine ran a cover story, "The Transgender Tipping Point," featuring actor Laverne Cox, a "proud African American transgender woman" (K. Steinmetz 2014b). Kye Allums is a "queer fluid trans artist and athlete" who played Division I college basketball and was the first NCAA player to come out as trans (K. Steinmetz 2014a). Cox and Allums both engage in advocacy work and education; Cox has appeared in many venues, working tirelessly on behalf of trans people, especially trans youth. In 2011, *Dancing with the Stars* featured Chaz Bono, a trans man whose parents are entertainers Sonny and Cher, and in 2015, Olympic gold medalist Caitlyn Jenner (also famous for her association with the Kardashian and Jenner families) came out as transgender.

Although there is greater acceptance of those who identify as transgender in some parts of the world, they still face inordinate amounts of discrimination nearly everyone. For example, in late 2018 former president Trump was considering a proposal to define transgender out of existence by limiting gender to male and female (a clear confusion of sex and gender!). That decision was to be based on external reproductive genitals present at birth and would be unchangeable throughout one's life span (Reuters 2018a). The proposal was met with widespread condemnation, especially by the LGBTQ (lesbian, gay, bisexual, transgender, and queer) community (Associated Press 2018) and failed to become law.

Trans history and context run deeper than suggested by a few years of increased public visibility (Stryker 2017). Sylvia Rivera (1951–2002), a "drag queen [and] bisexual transgender activist," was a "loud and persistent voice for the rights of people of color and low-income queers and trans people" (Sylvia Rivera Law Project 2015). She was among those who clashed with police in the 1969 New York Stonewall bar riot, in which gay, queer, and trans people resisted police harassment. That riot is often seen as the start of the modern U.S., and global, lesbian, gay, bisexual, and trans rights movement

Globally, there are many cultures with various nonbinary understandings of gender. Some North American Native and First Nations tribes include roles for *two-spirit* individuals. They are socially defined as truly distinct, neither man nor woman, nor a combination of the two, and are respected in their tribes (Roscoe 1998). Another kind of gender diversity can be found in some mountain villages in Afghanistan, where a rigidly constructed culture dictates that sons are necessary for families hoping for prestige (Arbabzadah 2011; Nordberg 2014). To gain such prestige, some families without male children present young girls as boys (called *bacha posh*), with the clothing, haircuts, and behavioral shifts common to boys. At puberty, they are "changed" into girls. In some rural areas of Albania, some women become men, adopting men's dress, habits, privileges, and responsibilities (Bilefsky 2008). They are often referred to as "sworn virgins" as they swear off marriage, sex, and children and are accepted by men and respected as if they were men.

In southern Oaxaca State in Mexico, there is a group of people—*muxes*—who do not identify as male or female, although they were born with male bodies. There is a long tradition of a mixed-gender way of life in Mexico. Muxes have historically been widely accepted, and their "embroidery, hairstyling, handicrafts, and cooking" are greatly admired (Burnett 2016, A4). Nevertheless, in recent years protests have arisen about muxes' use of women's restrooms.

The best-known example of a group considered neither male nor female, but a third gender, is the *hijras* of India (Nanda 1999). They normally adopt the dress and mannerisms of women and have historically held very important roles in society, particularly among Hindus. In fact, many still seek the blessings of a hijra before marriage or childbirth.

Gendered Inequalities

As a master status and a primary basis for the persistence of structural, institutional inequalities, gender is a key variable in understanding life chances. Gender is structured into all our social institutions or

A muxe, born with a male body but not identifying as either male or female, takes part in the traditional procession during the Muxes Festival in Juchitán, Mexico. This three-gender system originates in pre-Hispanic indigenous culture.

Jan Sochor/Getty Images

systems—education, families, the economy, the law, and so on. In most cultures throughout the world we socialize people into the binary gender system through our social institutions and then channel them into differently valued activities, attributes, and pursuits. The way in which we gender individuals and social institutions has real consequences for almost everyone.

Gender inequality is a global problem. The World Economic Forum measures gender inequality in terms of gender gaps in health care, education, economy, and politics. Statistics on men's and women's salaries, participation in paid labor, access to education, representation in political bodies, and life expectancy contribute to the score. Scores closer to one indicate that a country has a relatively narrow gap between men and women—that women are doing nearly as well as men. No country in the world has a score of one; no country has full equality between men and women. As you can see in Figure 10.1, Iceland is the most equal country in the world in terms of gender, with a score of 0.908, while Afghanistan is the least equal, with a score of 0.435. The United States, with a score of 0.769, ranks 27th.

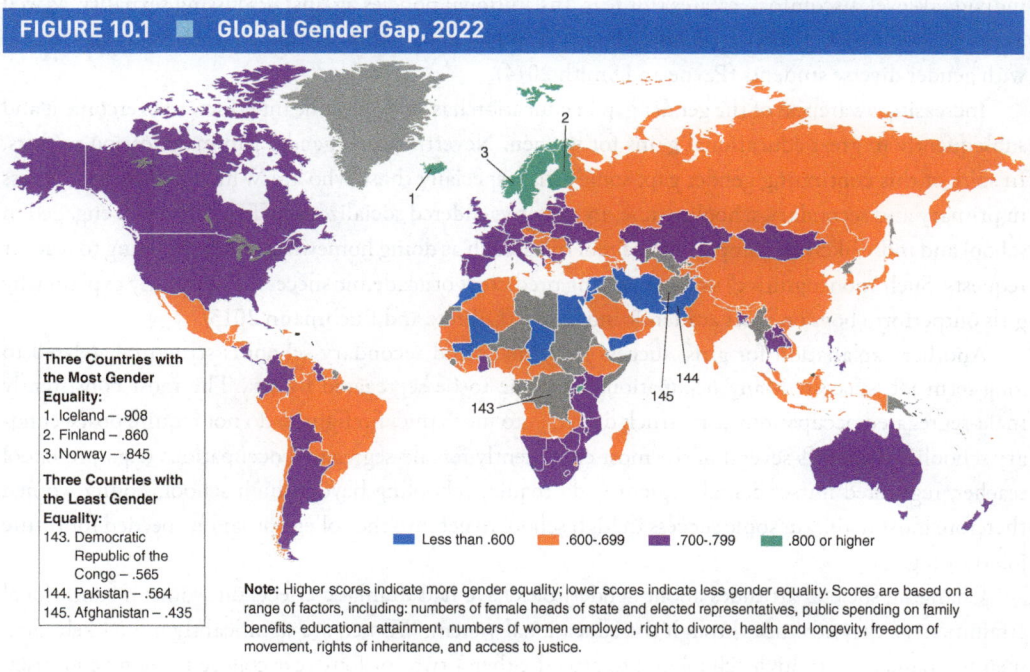

FIGURE 10.1 ■ Global Gender Gap, 2022

Three Countries with the Most Gender Equality:
1. Iceland – .908
2. Finland – .860
3. Norway – .845

Three Countries with the Least Gender Equality:
143. Democratic Republic of the Congo – .565
144. Pakistan – .564
145. Afghanistan – .435

Legend: Less than .600 | .600–.699 | .700–.799 | .800 or higher

Note: Higher scores indicate more gender equality; lower scores indicate less gender equality. Scores are based on a range of factors, including: numbers of female heads of state and elected representatives, public spending on family benefits, educational attainment, numbers of women employed, right to divorce, health and longevity, freedom of movement, rights of inheritance, and access to justice.

Source: World Economic Forum, 2022, Global Gender Gap Report 2022: Insight Report, March 2022, p. 10. (https://www3.weforum.org/docs/WEF_GGGR_2021.pdf).

There are global differences in the ways in which societies deal with gender differences and inequalities. For example, Change.org petitioners in the United Kingdom and Ireland have sought to send a message to toy retailers: Stop labeling some toys for boys (construction sets, cars, and the like) and others for girls (princess outfits, play kitchens). Some Swedes strongly believe that traditional gender norms enhance inequalities. They argue for gender neutral pronouns as a way of promoting equality. Many Swedish preschools and elementary schools have begun to use the gender-neutral pronoun *hen* (Braw 2014).

Gender and Education

Educational systems constitute an important site and source of gender inequality. Historically, families invested relatively little in the education of girls because they were expected to grow up to stay at home as wives and mothers. Women have historically been disadvantaged in the education system for a variety of reasons including greater difficulty in accessing institutions of learning due to economic, cultural, and religious reasons. Thus, there has long been a gender gap in education in many countries.

Clearly the formal educational system, especially at the primary and secondary levels, but even in college and graduate schools, has been a major cause of that gap, and it continues to pose some persistent problems for women. One aspect of that system, and a root cause of the gender gap in education, is often the **hidden curriculum**, or a school's unofficial norms, routines, and structures that transmit dominant cultural norms and values. Schools reproduce unquestioned social norms, such as obedience to authority, hard work, and the value of hierarchy. Most schools foster competitiveness, a push for achievement, and an understanding of the social hierarchy within the school. Because boys are socialized from infancy to enact these preferred values, they are likely to get more attention in class from teachers, to be asked more questions, to get more constructive criticism, and, at least in the early years of school, to monopolize class discussions (Sharp 2012).

There is a deeply hidden curriculum regarding gender conformity and norms. Analyses of elementary teacher training materials and in-depth studies of elementary school classrooms suggest that most teachers are not well trained to deal with gender (or sexuality) issues at school. One exploratory study found that elementary school teachers were afraid of the prospect of having a transgender student (Payne and Smith 2014). Lack of formal training, education, and institutional support, combined with individual-level discomfort, creates this fear. Institutional policies against discussing sexuality, as well as the mistaken perception that gender identity is linked to sexuality, hampered teachers' ability to deal with gender diverse students (Payne and Smith 2014).

Increasing awareness of the gender gap in education has led to significant efforts to overcome it and subsequently to great educational gains for women. Nevertheless, a gender gap in education persists. In spite of this continuing gender gap, some girls, especially those who are White, experience success in primary and secondary schooling due, in part, to gendered socialization. They are more engaged in school and more likely to comply with school rules, such as doing homework and responding to teacher requests. Such "noncognitive" skills are strong predictors of academic success. They partly explain why girls outperform boys on most academic indicators (DiPrete and Buchmann 2013).

Another explanation for girls' success in primary and secondary school is structural, related to long-term job success. Many occupations continue to be segregated by sex. The most consistently male-segregated occupations (e.g., truck driver, auto mechanic, firefighter) do not require postsecondary schooling, whereas several of the most consistently female-segregated occupations (e.g., preschool teacher, registered nurse, dental hygienist) do require schooling beyond high school. Young women therefore must maintain some success in high school to get into the college programs needed for future job training.

Changing societal attitudes about gender roles have had dramatic effects on women's educational attainment as they advance through the educational system. Women are significantly more likely than men to graduate from high school and to attend either a two- or four-year college in many countries. For example, In 1960, women represented less than 40 percent of college undergraduates in the United States; by 2020, 58 percent of students at both two- and four-year colleges were women (National Center for Education Statistics n.d.). Women are more likely than men to receive bachelor's or master's degrees (Bauman and Ryan 2015). Figure 10.2 depicts the dramatic gap between men and women enrolled as undergraduates in the United States, which is expected to remain large. We can also see this trend in the dramatic increases in law and medical degrees earned by women. However, men continue to be more likely to be trained in the most prestigious colleges and universities and to obtain doctoral degrees.

Even with women's gains in higher education, a significant pay gap exists between men and women once they leave school and begin their careers (Merry and Paino 2019). While in college, women are more likely to major in sex/gender segregated academic fields, such as education, English, and psychology, which tend to lead to jobs that do not pay as well as jobs dominated by men. Although there are differences among the fields, women continue to be less likely to major in science, technology, engineering, and math (STEM fields) in college in most countries. Majoring in these fields tends to lead to higher-paying jobs. Figure 10.3 shows that women now earn a majority of degrees in biology, and they had significant gains, especially around the turn of the twenty-first century, in the physical sciences and mathematics/statistics. However, they continue to be less likely than men to earn degrees in STEM fields (at least in the United States and many other countries). Women also lag far behind men in bachelor's degrees in computer science and information science, as well as in engineering. Part of the reason for this underrepresentation is the fact that women continue to be likely to be stereotyped as being less capable scientifically and technically.

Chapter 10 • Genders and Sexualities 257

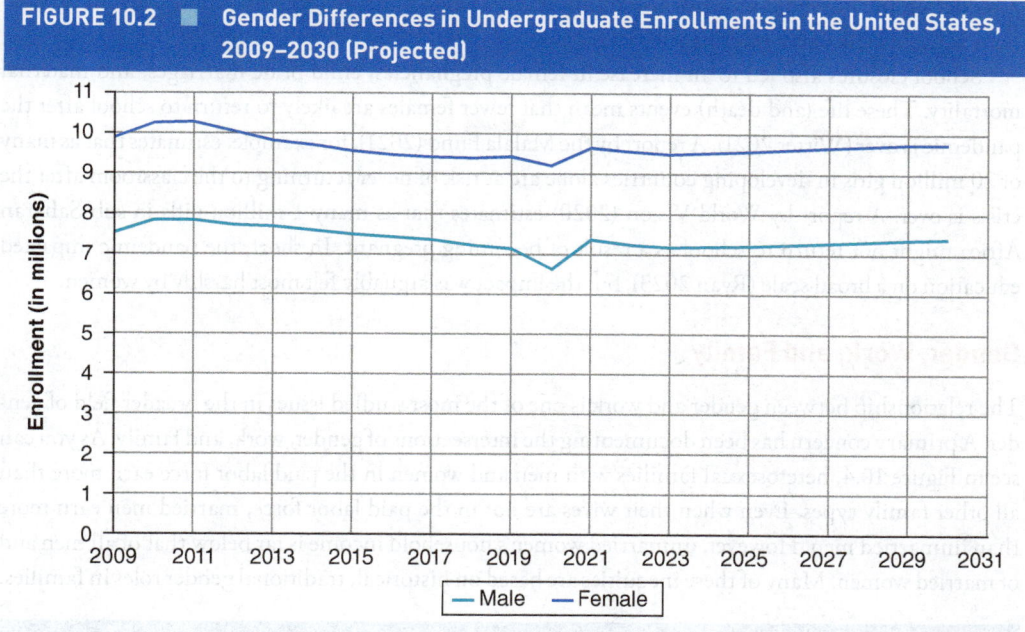

FIGURE 10.2 ■ Gender Differences in Undergraduate Enrollments in the United States, 2009–2030 (Projected)

Source: U.S. Department of Education, National Center for Education Statistics, 2021, "Enrollment in Degree-Granting Institutions Projection Model, through 2030," *Digest of Education Statistics 2021*, Table 303.70. Retrieved August 2, 2022 (https://nces.ed.gov/fastfacts/display.asp?id = 98).

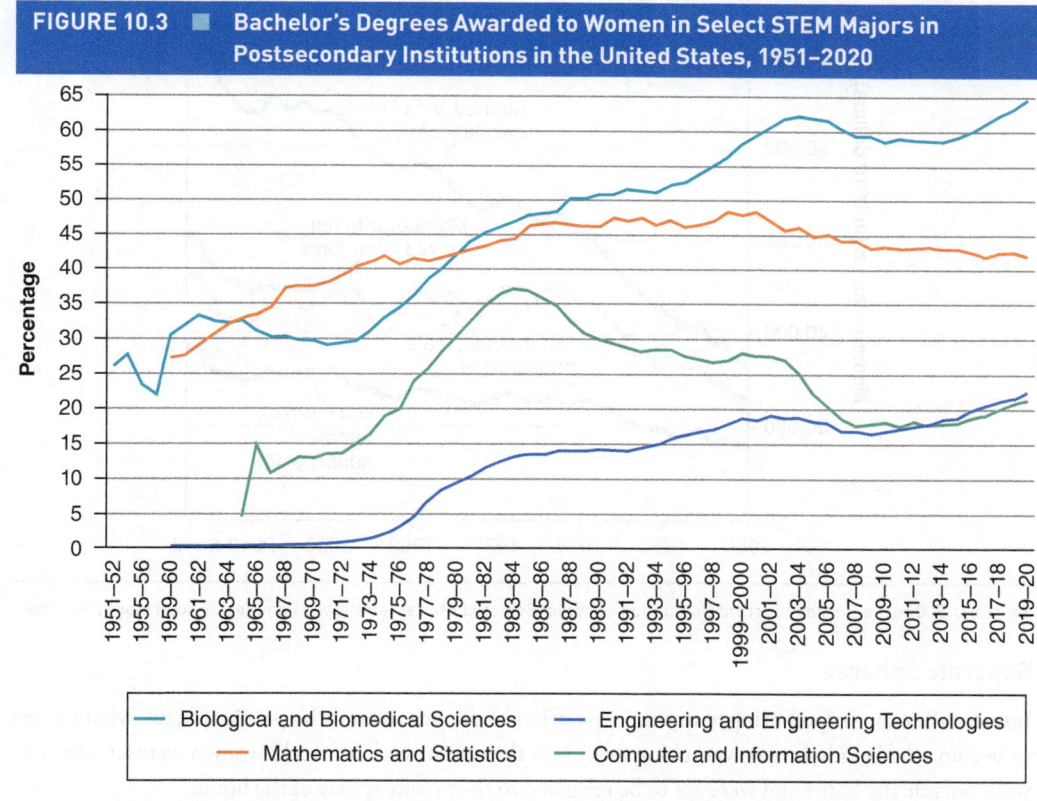

FIGURE 10.3 ■ Bachelor's Degrees Awarded to Women in Select STEM Majors in Postsecondary Institutions in the United States, 1951–2020

Sources: U.S. Department of Education, National Center for Education Statistics, 2021, "Trends in Degrees by Field," *Digest of Education Statistics 2021*, Tables 325.20, 325.35, 325.45, 325.65. Retrieved August 2, 2022 (https://nces.ed.gov/programs/digest/2021menu_tables.asp)

The COVID-19 pandemic has also had an unequal impact on the educational trajectory of women and did a lot to significantly set back many of the gains in recent years (Ryan 2023). School closures led to more women having to take an even larger role in childcare and household responsibilities, which impeded their ability to also stay on top of their roles as students and/or educators (Prior et al 2022).

A reduction in household incomes also meant more women returning to work, most often in occupations at higher risk of contracting the virus.

School closures also led to an increase in female pregnancies, child bride marriages, and maternal mortality. These life (and death) events mean that fewer females are likely to return to school after the pandemic is over (Witter 2021). A report by the Malala Fund (2021), for example, estimates that as many of 20 million girls in developing countries alone are at risk of never returning to the classroom after the crisis is over. A report by World Vision (2020) estimates that as many 1 million girls in sub-Saharan Africa might not return to school as a result of becoming pregnant. In short, the pandemic impacted education on a broad scale (Ryan 2023), but the impact was arguably felt most harshly by women.

Gender, Work, and Family

The relationship between gender and work is one of the most studied issues in the broader field of gender. A primary concern has been documenting the intersections of gender, work, and family. As you can see in Figure 10.4, heterosexual families with men and women in the paid labor force earn more than all other family types. Even when their wives are not in the paid labor force, married men earn more than unmarried men. However, unmarried women's household income is far below that of all men and of married women. Many of these inequities are based on historical, traditional gender roles in families.

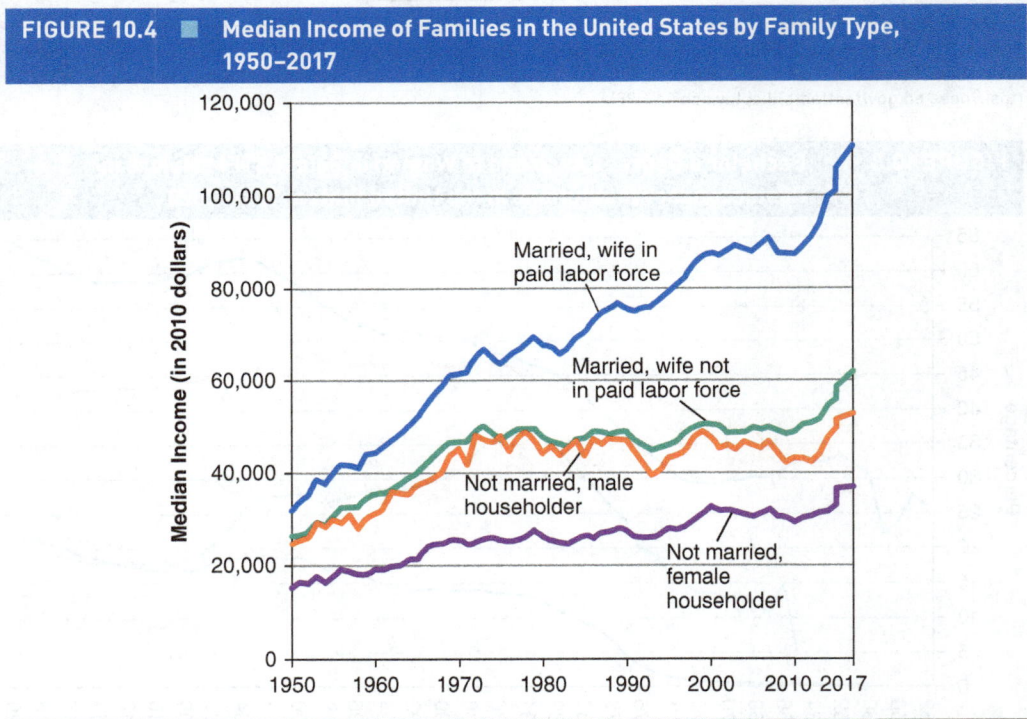

FIGURE 10.4 ■ Median Income of Families in the United States by Family Type, 1950–2017

Source: U.S. Census Bureau, Current Population Surveys, Selected Characteristics of Families by Total Money Income.

Separate Spheres

Industrialization helped bring about the separation of the private and the public spheres. Men tended to become the breadwinners, venturing forth into the public world of work; women were less likely to work outside the home and were apt to be relegated to the private sphere of the home.

The once clear-cut, gender-based differentiation between the public and private spheres has been breaking down in many countries since at least the mid-twentieth century. Now women are more likely not only to be in the work world but also, increasingly, to be the principal—or even the only—wage earner in the family. The heterosexual family characterized by a division between male/breadwinner and female/homemaker has increasingly given way to more blended roles, and even to role reversals, especially in dual-earner families (McClelland, Mok, and Pierce 2014). Figure 10.5 shows the increasing percentage of mothers who earn most of the family income (breadwinners), along with those who are co-breadwinners.

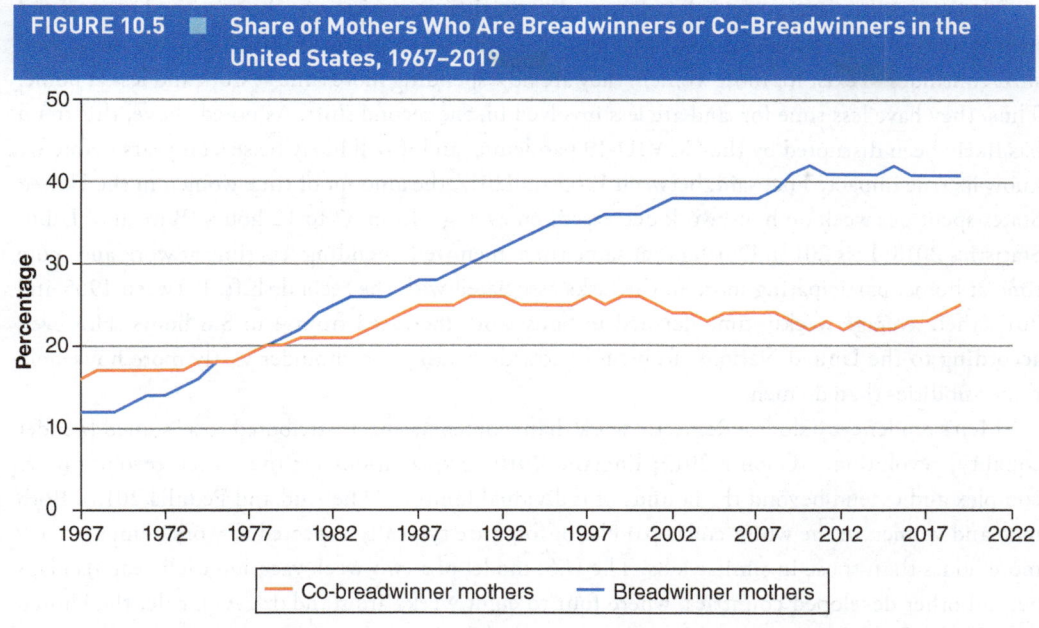

FIGURE 10.5 ■ Share of Mothers Who Are Breadwinners or Co-Breadwinners in the United States, 1967–2019

Source: Glynn, Sarah Jane, 2021, "Breadwinning Mothers are Critical to Families' Economic Security," *Center for American Progress*, March 29. Retrieved August 2, 2022 (https://www.americanprogress.org/article/breadwinning-mothers-critical-familys-economic-security/).

Dual-Earner Households and the Stalled Revolution

A key issue in the study of gender, work, and family is the difference between heterosexual men and women in the ways they use their time in the era of dual-earner families. Arlie Hochschild (1989, 2012) argues that in U.S. dual-earner families with children, wives who work outside the home tend to be saddled with additional labor—the traditionally gendered tasks of childcare and housework—when they get home from their paid work. Such women can be said to be working a **second shift** (Cassano 2017). Figure 10.6 presents 2019 data on gender differences in performing three household tasks: preparing meals, laundry, and, care for children on a daily basis. On an average day, 51 percent of women were more likely to prepare meals, while only 17 percent of men were more likely to do so. More extremely, 58 percent of women were more likely to do laundry on an average day, while only 13 percent of men were more likely to do so. In terms of caring for children on a daily basis, 50 percent of women were more likely to do so, compared to only 7 percent of men more likely to do so.

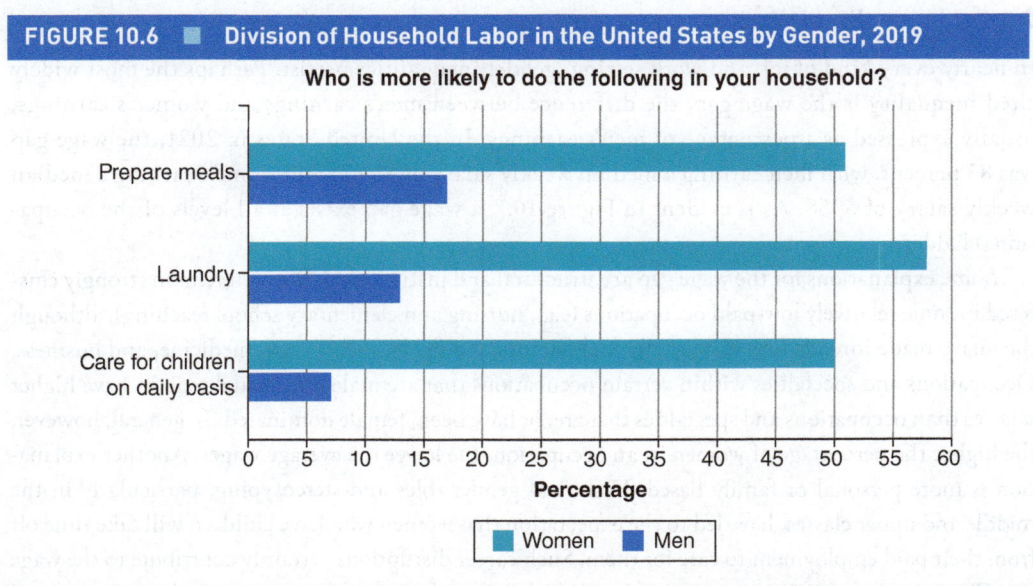

FIGURE 10.6 ■ Division of Household Labor in the United States by Gender, 2019

Source: Brenan, Megan, 2020, "Women Still Handle Main Household Tasks," Gallup, January 29. Retrieved August 2, 2022 (https://news.gallup.com/poll/283979/women-handle-main-household-tasks.aspx).

However, other recent research indicates that the differences between heterosexual women and men in performing household tasks may be narrowing (O. Sullivan 2018). Although the second shift continues to exist for most women, they are now spending more time at work and less at home. Thus, they have less time for, and are less involved in, the second shift. As noted above, this trend has likely been disrupted by the COVID-19 pandemic, and it will likely be several years before we know its true impact. That said, between 1965 and 2017, the amount of time women in the United States spent per week on housework decreased, on average, from 32 to 12 hours (Bureau of Labor Statistics 2018; Liss 2014). During that same time, men were spending less time at work and more time at home, participating more in the tasks associated with the second shift. Between 1965 and 2017, their average weekly time devoted to housework increased from 4 to 8.8 hours. However, according to the United Nations, women worldwide continue to shoulder vastly more household responsibilities than do men.

Men's tendency to do less domestic work than women has been attributed to a "stalled [gender equality] revolution," (Coontz 2013; England 2010). Explanations for the stalled revolution are complex and extend beyond the bounds of individual families (Thébaud and Pedulla 2016). Both men and women in the white-collar paid labor force are typically expected to work comparatively more hours than those in similar jobs. The U.S. model of a two-week vacation each year also lags behind other developed countries, where four to eight weeks are standard. As a rule, the United States is not friendly to parents, whether heterosexual dual earners or single parents, or those creating other family forms. The gender equality revolution has stalled, at least in part, because work–life policies lag behind domestic realities. For example, the United States has no federal maternity leave policies. The Family and Medical Leave Act grants 12 weeks of unpaid maternity leave, but only for full-time employees who have worked 1,250 hours in the year preceding the leave and who work in companies with 50 or more employees. Thus, part-time employees and full-timers in workplaces that employ fewer than 50 people are not covered. Even full-timers may not be able to afford time off without pay for the responsibilities associated with childbirth and beyond. The United States, Papua New Guinea and a few island countries in the Pacific are the only countries that do not have federally supported paid time off for mothers. There is a similar situation with paternity and home care leave. Unlike Austria (which offers full-pay maternity leave for 16 weeks), Canada (which offers partial-pay maternity leave for 15 weeks), and the United Kingdom (which offers 39 weeks maternity leave at partial pay), the United States offers zero paid maternity days (OECD 2017). In fact, the United States ranks at the bottom globally in government-supported time off for new parents.

Gender Inequality at Work

In nearly every kind of job and work setting, gender inequalities persist. Perhaps the most widely cited inequality is the wage gap, the difference between men's earnings and women's earnings, usually expressed as a percentage of men's earnings. In the United States in 2021, the wage gap was 83 percent, with men earning a median weekly salary of $1,154 and women earning a median weekly salary of $958. As is evident in Figure 10.7, a wage gap exists at all levels of the occupational ladder.

Some explanations for the wage gap are structural and institutional. Women remain strongly clustered in some relatively low-paid occupations (e.g., nursing and elementary school teaching), although they have made inroads into historically male-dominated fields, such as law, medicine, and business. Occupations and specialties within certain occupations that are male dominated tend to have higher salaries than occupations and specialties that are, or have been, female dominated. In general, however, the higher the percentage of women in an occupation, the lower the average wages. Another explanation is more personal or family based. Historical gender roles and stereotyping, particularly in the middle and upper classes, have led to the expectation that women who have children will take time off from their paid employment to care for them. Such career disruptions certainly contribute to the wage gap. Women who take time away from the paid labor force lose ground in terms of salaries and rate of advancement into higher-paying positions.

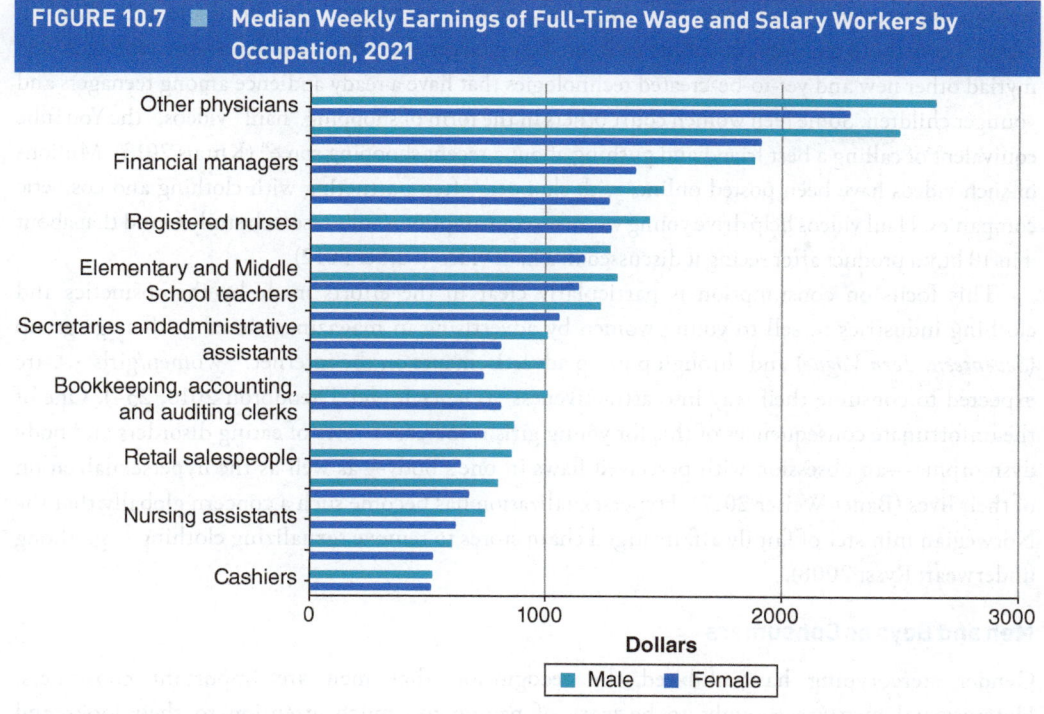

FIGURE 10.7 ■ Median Weekly Earnings of Full-Time Wage and Salary Workers by Occupation, 2021

Source: U.S. Bureau of Labor Statistics, 2021, *Household Data Annual Averages: Median Weekly Earnings of Full-Time Wage and Salary Workers by Detailed Occupation and Sex*, Labor Force Statistics from the Current Population Survey, Washington, DC: United States Department of Labor. Retrieved August 2, 2022 (https://www.bls.gov/cps/cpsaat39.htm).

Gender and Consumer Culture

In consumption, as in many other aspects of the social world, gender matters (Casey 2015; Deutsch 2018). Since the Industrial Revolution, production has been centered outside the household and has primarily been the function of White men. White middle- and upper-class women, largely relegated to the home, were assigned the role of consumers. This is both different and unequal because historically production has been far more highly valued than consumption.

Consumption, Work, and Family

Women were not just defined as the prime consumers—their consumer practices were also closely tied to their domestic practices and roles in the home. Women consumed goods and services to care for, and on behalf of, their families (De Laat and Baumann 2016). Much of women's shopping was related to love, especially their love of family members (Miller 1998); it was an instrumental way of showing caring and love. In one way or another, women generally made purchases for their families and to fulfill their responsibilities in the home and to those who lived there. Women are still thought to constitute a "multiple market"—they purchase things for significant others, family members, and friends. As women have entered the paid work world in increasing numbers, their consumption patterns have changed. They are now more likely to consume an array of subcontracted services, such as cleaning and childcare. Much of this work is done by other women—women are subcontracting work to other women (England 2017). In addition, they are increasingly more likely to consume for themselves than for others. For example, greater involvement in the work world requires the use of a wider variety of clothing: business casual, conservative office work wear, and uniforms, to name a few.

Women and Girls as Consumers

Several historical events mark the development of greater interest in girls, and in children more generally, as consumers (Cook 2007). One was the emergence of the department store in the middle and late 1800s, along with the celebration of Christmas, and its associated gifts, by department stores such as Macy's. Children's consumer culture gained further impetus when department stores began to have separate departments for toys and, more important, separate departments for boys' and girls' clothing. Now, of course, all children, including girls, are being targeted on their computers, smartphones, and myriad other new and yet-to-be-created technologies that have a ready audience among teenagers and younger children. Some teen women court others in the form of shopping "haul" videos, "the YouTube equivalent of calling a best friend and gushing about a recent shopping spree" (Khrais 2013). Millions of such videos have been posted online, with shoppers often partnering with clothing and cosmetic companies. Haul videos help drive young women's consumption—one research study found that about 4 in 10 buy a product after seeing it discussed in a haul video (Parker 2012).

This focus on consumption is particularly clear in the efforts made by the cosmetics and clothing industries to sell to young women by advertising in magazines aimed at this age group (*Seventeen, Teen Vogue*) and through pop-up advertisements on the internet. "Women/girls . . . are expected to consume their way into attractiveness" (Deutsch and Theodorou 2010, 234). One of the unfortunate consequences of this for young girls is increased rates of eating disorders and body dysmorphia—an obsession with perceived flaws in one's body—as well as the hypersexualization of their lives (Banet-Weiser 2012). Hypersexualization has become such a concern globally that the Norwegian minister of family affairs urged chain stores to remove sexualizing clothing (e.g., thong underwear; Rysst 2008).

Men and Boys as Consumers

Gender stereotyping has inhibited the recognition that men are important consumers. Heterosexual men are thought to be wary of paying too much attention to their looks and appearance (Brosdahl and Carpenter 2012). Thus, we develop other labels for them—hipster, metrosexual, lumbersexual (Compton and Bridges 2014)—and define their consumption habits accordingly. Currently, one of the most stereotyped narratives about men's consumption is that of the "man cave," which is a room or space reserved for a man to engage in his hobbies. This area is usually decorated by males who use it, generally, without the influence of females. There are stores designed specifically to cater to men who want to shop for their man caves. Mantiques and More, in Corpus Christi, Texas, is designed as a store for men because "an antique store can be seen as anything but cool, hip, and manly" (Salinas 2014).

Some businesses cater to men by employing the "man cave" narrative—the idea of a room in the house, free from female influence, where men can indulge in suitably "masculine" hobbies.

Derek Trask/Alamy Stock Photo

THE SOCIOLOGY OF SEXUALITIES

Sexuality is a broad term that encompasses one's behaviors, attractions, and identities. Sexuality is often related to both sex and gender and can include sexual attitudes, behaviors, sensuality, values, anatomy, biochemistry, identities, and/or orientations. Sexuality is both individual and personal and collective and public; it is biological and biochemical as well as cultural, social, and historical.

There is a large and growing body of literature on the sociology of sexualities (Plummer 2019). Although bodies and biology are involved, the bulk of this work deals with the social, social psychological, and cultural and social aspects of sexuality (as well as the religious, economic, and other aspects). Sociologists have become increasingly interested in sexuality for a number of reasons.

- The growing number of sexually linked social problems, including sexual violence as well as health issues
- Social changes in attitudes and behaviors related to sexual conduct
- The greater visibility of sexuality-related social movements, especially those associated with women and sexual minorities
- Pharmaceutical changes, such as the exploding popularity of erectile dysfunction (ED) drugs like Viagra and Cialis
- The media's increasing presentation and representations of sexuality in its many forms
- The globalization of sexuality, for example, through sex tourism and human/sex trafficking
- The increase in the use, and manipulation of, expressions of sexuality in consumer culture—not only widespread commerce in sexual activity but also the use of sex to sell virtually everything
- The increasing popularity of the internet's ever more vibrant commercial sex culture

Sexuality is rarely simply a matter of sexual release or satisfaction. It is complex, contradictory, and often confusing (which can be seen as something quite liberating!). For example, we are told that "having sex" is "natural" and that reproduction is the key goal of these activities (despite the widespread use of condoms and other measures to prevent reproduction as a consequence of sexual activity). Similarly, we are told that people "naturally" have hormones, sexual urges, and needs that must be fulfilled. However, we are also told that people should control themselves for religious, social, or cultural reasons. Culture gives us patterns, rules, and codes to manage our sexualities and sexual identities. Laws and formal sanctions, along with informal sanctions, are intended to control, regulate, and sometimes suppress cultural and individual sexualities.

Sexual Selves

Sexual Identities and Orientations

The concept of **sexual identity** refers an understanding of one's sexual self and an association with that understanding, either privately, publicly, or both. The idea that people have sexual orientations and identities is fairly new in human history (although it certainly isn't new that people have such things). Until as recently as 1923, one could still find *heterosexual* defined in the dictionary as a *medical* term (it was not an *identity* term) meaning "morbid sexual passion for one of the opposite sex" (Katz 2004, 44). In the past century, however, we have increasingly begun to classify and label people according to culturally powerful decisions about what is "normal" in terms of sexuality.

Sexual orientation is an umbrella term which encompasses behaviors (with whom we engage in certain activities), attractions (who do we find sexually appealing), and identities (as defined above). These dimensions do not necessarily have to align. For example, one could engage in sexual behaviors with others to whom they are not attracted or one could identify as a particular sexuality without that identity necessarily being associated with their behaviors or attractions (e.g., someone who is in the closet, hiding their sexual attractions and behaviors).

Although there are cultural, social, and historical contexts for our sexualities, sexual expression varies among individuals. For example, someone may define themselves as bisexual, and may be sexual with men and women, but may prefer romantic relationships with women. Another person may define himself as an asexual heteroromantic, someone with no sexual attractions but who is interested in a romantic relationship with someone of the "opposite" sex. Like sex and gender, sexualities and identities are also on continua. In fact, it may be most accurate to conceive of these aspects of ourselves as a matrix. These understandings, interests, fantasies, tastes, and desires may change quite a bit through the life course (DeLamater 2012).

Our attitudes about sexual orientations reflect changes in the larger society. Recently the changes have been profound, as have their effects. The best known example today is the increasing openness many people feel about identifying as gay, lesbian, bisexual, or transgender. In many settings, it is no longer necessary to hide those identities. It is increasingly possible to be very public about having such an identity. However, this does not mean that the LGBTQ community does not suffer from prejudice and discrimination. In fact, sexual minorities are discriminated against in a variety of settings including those related to housing, employment, and family life. The level of acceptance of sexual minorities (including even their ability to openly identify as such) varies tremendously across cultures and countries. Thus, although LGBTQ people are increasingly finding greater acceptance in many cultures and countries, more hate crimes are now aimed at them (per capita) than at African Americans, Jews, and Muslims (at least in the United States, though certainly very likely elsewhere as well; see Figure 10.8).

Homophobia is defined as "the fear of being, appearing, or seeming gay; fear of anyone or 'anything' gay . . . At its most virulent, homophobia inspires hate crimes, murders, assaults (sexual, physical, and emotional), rapes, batteries, and other forms of violence" (Plante 2015, 212). **Heterosexism** is the belief that heterosexuality is superior to other sexual orientations, along with individual and institutional discrimination against those with other orientations. Heterosexism and homophobia combine to drive some of the alienation and aggression experienced by lesbian, gay, bisexual, and trans people.

Sexual Double Standards

One way casual sexual relationships occur is through "hooking up." Hooking up is *not* a clearly socially defined relationship such as dating, seeing someone, having a boyfriend or girlfriend, or being engaged to be married. It *can be* somewhat committed or somewhat casual, emotionally and physically intense or not, sporadic or fairly regular, sober or intoxicated; it can involve friends or strangers. Hooking up involves the occurrence of some sort of sexual event—very broadly defined. It may include only kissing and making out, or it may involve a range of behaviors from touching to oral sex, penile-vaginal sex, and/or anal sex. Hooking up is intended to be an ambiguous concept. Some of our most unquestioned cultural assumptions are that sex "should be" spontaneous, mysterious, even magical. The ambiguity, spontaneity, and apparent lack of rules or expectations for hookups fit these expectations well (Hall, Knox, and Shapiro 2017; Wade 2017).

Researchers have observed that "hooking up" maintains the heterosexual gendered double standard (Hamilton and Armstrong 2009). The **sexual double standard** describes a cultural belief system in which men are expected to desire and seek sex from whomever, whenever, while women are expected to be sexual only within committed, romantic relationships. Those who hold this double standard may also believe that women's sexual behavior is different from men's and should be judged differently. For

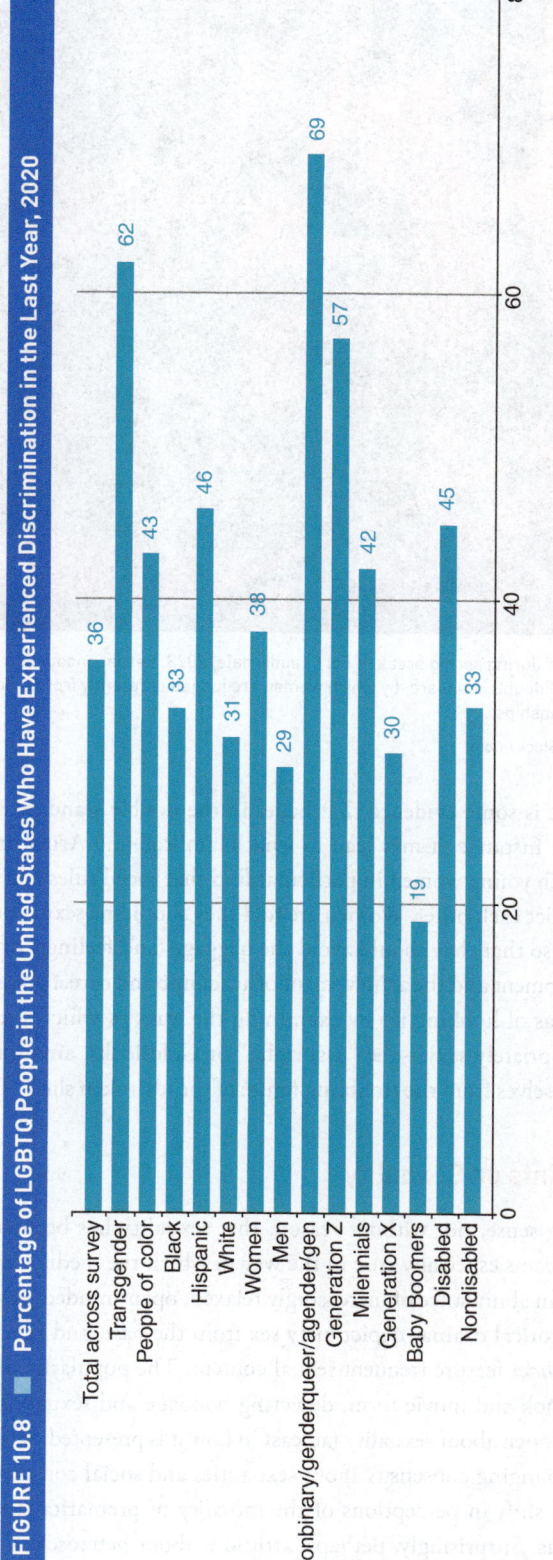

FIGURE 10.8 Percentage of LGBTQ People in the United States Who Have Experienced Discrimination in the Last Year, 2020

Source: Mahowald, Lindsay, Sharita Gruberg, and John Halpin. 2020. *The State of the LGBTQ Community in 2020: A National Public Opinion Study*, Figure 1. Retrieved August 2, 2022 (https://www.americanprogress.org/wp-content/uploads/2020/10/LGBTQpoll-report.pdf).

instance, they may judge women negatively for seeking sex and pleasure outside relationships, while they judge men less harshly, if at all, for the same behavior.

College students gather during spring break in Fort Lauderdale, 2023. Sexual encounters resulting from such an event can invoke the heterosexual double standard, by which women are judged differently from men for being sexual outside of committed, romantic relationships.

ZUMA Press, Inc./Alamy Stock Photo

Although there is some evidence that belief in the double standard is weakening, we still see it in hooking up. For instance, it may lead to what Hamilton and Armstrong (2009, 594) call "sexual dilemmas," in which young women in particular find that social rules and expectations for gender and social class contradict each other. Women are told they should be sexual only in romantic, committed relationships but also that they should avoid the baggage (and feelings) of committed relationships in favor of self-development and the achievement of academic and career goals. Researchers have explored the sexual dilemmas of hooking up by examining the ways in which young women are expected to look and act appropriately sexy—the "just right," or Goldilocks, amount (Plante 2015)—while also "distanc[ing] themselves from the troubling figure of the 'drunken slut'" (Griffin et al. 2012, 187).

Social Constraints on Sexuality

There is a growing sense, not without reason, that sexuality has become increasingly free of social constraints. This seems especially true in the way in which the media treat sexuality. The last several decades have seen an abundance of increasingly relaxed, open-minded portrayals of sexual experiences and attitudes. Historical dramas depict lusty sex from the past, and fantasy dramas such as *Game of Thrones* and *Outlander* feature frequent sexual content. The popularity of *Fifty Shades of Grey* and its sequels, in both book and movie form, depicting bondage and sexual domination, suggests that we have become more open about sexuality (at least in how it is presented publicly).

Examples of changing consensus about sexualities and social constraint are abundant in modern culture. The rapid shift in perceptions of the morality of premarital sex is an excellent example of changing consensus. Surprisingly, perhaps, attitudes about heterosexual marital monogamy remain stable. For decades, Gallup has found that 91 percent of people in the United States believe that "married men and women having an affair" is "morally unacceptable" (Jones 2017). This number is likely even higher in many other cultures.

Although there is much to support the idea of increasing sexual freedom, human sexuality is never totally free from social and cultural constraints and regulatory attempts. For example, a public school in Mississippi canceled its senior prom because a lesbian student wanted to bring her girlfriend as a date (Joyner 2010). The school was afraid of the message it would send if it allowed a same-sex couple to attend. This is not a rare occurrence.

Society's social institutions, such as schools, families, the law, the police, and formal religions, along with cultural customs and mores, constrain our sexualities. But generally speaking, culturally oppressed minorities' relationships and sexualities are more likely to be constrained than those of the hegemonic, or dominant, group. Sodomy laws, which loosely defined acts of sodomy as "crimes against nature" or "unnatural copulations," were intended to punish sexual activities and romantic relationships between homosexual men. People of color have also been subject to numerous dehumanizing laws, customs, and discourses that constrain their sexualities (Garcia 2012; Rousseau 2011).

Culture and Consent

Important to a discussion of social constraints on sexuality are the concepts of consensual sexual activities, sexual assault, and rape. All involve issues of the relative power of the individuals involved, along with complicated sociocultural histories and contexts regarding genders and sexualities. **Consensual sexual activities** are those agreed on by the participants, any of whom have the right to decide to stop at any point and for any reason. **Informed (or "effective") sexual consent** has been in the news recently, as hundreds of college campuses have been investigated for poor enforcement of rape and sexual assault laws. Informed, effective consent can be defined as follows:

- *Informed.* Both parties demonstrate a clear and mutual understanding of exactly what they are consenting to.

- *Freely and actively given.* There is no coercion, force, threats, intimidation, or pressuring.

- *Mutually understandable.* Consent is expressed in words or actions that indicate a clear willingness to do the same thing, at the same time, in the same way, with each other. Silence does not equal consent.

- *Consent is not indefinite.* Furthermore, consent may be withdrawn at any time, and at that time all sexual activity must cease unless and until additional effective consent is given (Reed College 2015).

Under such informed consent, consenting to one behavior does not obligate an individual or imply consent to any other behaviors. Consenting to a person or an act on one occasion also does not obligate an individual or imply consent on any other occasion.

Sexual assault encompasses sexual acts of domination, usually enacted by men against women, other men, and children. Such assaults can occur between strangers, but they usually occur between acquaintances or intimates. **Rape**, also a form of domination, can be defined as "penetration, no matter how slight, of the vagina or anus with any body part or object, or oral penetration by a sex organ of another person, without the consent of the victim" (FBI 2014).

Communities vary in the probability of (reported) sexual assault and the effectiveness of legal, social, and moral constraints on the kinds of behaviors that often lead to such violence. In many religious communities, strong expectations of modesty and expressing sexuality only within marriage often keep reports of sexual violence to a minimum. The nature of residential colleges' sexual climates can promote a **"rape culture"** (Boswell and Spade 1996; Phipps et al. 2018; Plante and Smiler 2014), an environment conducive to sexual assaults and rape. Rape cultures tend to be prevalent in and around, among other places, college campuses because of several factors, including gender imbalances (more women than men enrolled), the routine presence of alcohol and other drugs at social events and parties, the age of the population, and the relatively unsupervised nature of life "at college." Structural aspects of college campuses that can reproduce gender imbalances include party systems controlled by fraternities and social life environments that actively or passively promote settings combining alcohol use with assumptions about sexuality (Corprew and Mitchell 2014; Flack et al. 2007).

Sexual assaults and rapes have, to put it mildly, very serious consequences. Survivors are more likely to suffer from depression and post-traumatic stress disorder, contemplate and attempt suicide, and use illicit drugs than the general public. Sexual violence is endemic in many countries, including the United States, where it has been estimated that every 68 seconds a person is sexually assaulted (RAINN 2023). Most sexual assault victims (54 percent) are aged 18 to 34. Men and women of color are disproportionately likely to be victimized, particularly Native Americans (RAINN, 2023). The mental and physical consequences of assaults combined with systematic racism are profound (Thompson-Miller and Picca, 2017).

Sex and Consumption

Regardless of constraints on sexuality, everyday life has been sexualized to a large degree—the world has been "made sexy" (Rutherford 2007). In our consumer society, sex is used to encourage consumption of all sorts of things not inherently sexual. Advertisements use sexualized images to promote innumerable products, from cars to toothpaste and from clothing to soft drinks. The implication in many of these ads is that use of the products leads to sexual relationships. The well-known media adage that "sex sells" shows no signs of going out of fashion, and it is certainly applied to sexual products, such as Viagra. However, researchers have found that women usually have a strong negative reaction to explicit sexual content in advertising and are less likely to buy merchandise promoted with these types of ads, unless the sexual content is promoting an expensive item (Vohs, Sengupta, and Dahl 2014). In comparison, men tend to feel positively about such ads.

As this oversized billboard in New York City shows, advertisements often focus on—and exaggerate—the female body. The self-esteem of many women suffers because it is difficult for them to measure up to the bodies shown in such advertisements.

Education Images/Universal Images Group via Getty Images

More blatant than the use of sexual images to sell products and services is the way in which human sexualities have been increasingly turned into commodities and marketed (Crewe and Martin 2017). Of course, the consumption of sex is nothing new—after all, prostitution is often referred to as the "world's oldest profession." What is new since the mid-twentieth century is the rise of a huge sex industry, one whose reach and influence span the globe. This sexual marketplace has been described as composed of five interlocking markets (Plummer 2007):

- *Bodies and sexual acts* such as stripping and "real sex" involving "real bodies" available for purchase by those who choose to pay
- *Pornography and erotica*
- *Sexualized objects* such as sex toys and lingerie
- *Sexualized technologies* including contraceptives and genital reconstructive surgery. A new hands-free sex toy for women—Osè—has recently been introduced. It is supposed to produce "blended" orgasms through simultaneous external and internal stimulation (Safronova 2019).
- *Sexualized relationships*. Help for improving a sexualized relationship can be purchased from highly paid sex therapists, from self-help books of all sorts, and now increasingly from a number of internet websites.

SEXUALITY, GENDER, AND GLOBALIZATION

Sex, gender, and sexuality are involved in and affected by a variety of social changes. Today, globalization and global flows of various kinds are especially important in social change in these (and many other) areas.

Social Change and the Globalization of Sexuality

Globalization is one of a number of forces affecting and interacting with sexuality in the twenty-first century (Plummer 2019). The globalization of sexuality is linked to a variety of social changes altering not only sexuality but also much of what transpires in the social world.

- *The globalization of media and technologies*. Sexuality is a growing presence in the global media. The internet—and the social networks it has engendered—is most important. However, photos, movies, music, advertising, and television have also gone global. These media have been sexualized; they can even be said to have undergone a process of "pornographication" (Smith, Atwood, and McNair 2018; Tyler and Quek 2016).
- *Increasing urbanization*. Urbanization is a key trend across the globe, and it has contributed both to increased freedom of sexual expression and to the globalization of sexuality (Bell 2007; Hubbard, Gorman-Murray, and Nash 2015). Cities are at the center of freedoms of all sorts (Simmel [1903] 1971), including sexual freedoms. Sex trafficking and sex tourism take place primarily in the world's cities. The world's major cities, including London, Bangkok, Hong Kong, New York City, and Shanghai, are among the nodes in global "sex-scapes" (Kong 2010; Maginn and Steinmetz 2015).
- *Globalized social movements and social change*. A wide range of global sexualities-related social movements have arisen, as have more specific social change efforts focused on easing or eliminating repressive sex laws. Activists, change agents, and ideas flow, spread, and adapt to their specific contexts (Parker, Garcia, and Buffington 2014).
- *Increased mobility*. It is relatively easier now for people of means to travel to locales far from home. Thus, travel for sex itself is a global and commercial phenomenon, in the form of sex tourism and sex holidays (Altman 2001; Frank 2012).

Global Flows Related to Sex and Sexuality

Sexuality "flows" around the world in many other ways, such as through sex trafficking, sex work, global parties and events, and the sexual diaspora, as members of various sexual subcultures, as well as all sorts of sexual goods and services (especially via the internet), move around the world. Globalization has had a real effect on sexual interactions, identities, and relationships. There are now a number of globally applied sexuality laws, such as those attempting to outlaw the sexual exploitation of children. Organizations like UNICEF monitor these laws and seek to protect the vulnerable from sexual abuse and violence. Laws dealing with sexual crimes, such as rape, have grown increasingly similar. At the cultural level, norms and values about sex have been changing, and those changes have tended to flow around the world.

As a result, some norms and values have grown increasingly similar in many parts of the world. For example, there has been a general movement away from trying to control sexuality and procreation while attempting to maintain the collective order. At the same time, there has been a movement toward viewing sexuality as a series of acts that are mainly about pleasure and self-expression. Premarital (or nonmarital) sex has also become increasingly normative in many (but certainly not all) parts of the world.

Lesbian, Gay, Bisexual, Transgender, and Queer Sexualities in a Global Context

A key issue for many LGBTQ people is the barriers that inhibit their movement around the world or encourage their movement from one place to another (Altman 2001; Carrillo and Fontdevila 2014; Lewis 2014; Mason 2018). Such barriers may be erected within the home country as well as between countries. Barriers at home that might *push* LGBTQ people to migrate include legal prohibitions of consensual sex acts and relationships with same-sex partners, lack of equal opportunity in the workplace, and bans on same-sex marriages. State-sanctioned physical assaults and even murders of LGBTQ people can force them to seek better lives elsewhere in the world. They can also be *pulled* elsewhere in the world by better conditions, such as more opportunities to work, marry, and live more freely with less fear. Urban environments are attractive because large and visible groups of other LGBTQ people often create communities and neighborhoods in cities around the globe (Nash and Gorman-Murray 2014).

Other aspects of globalization, such as increasingly relatively inexpensive air travel and the internet, have made it easier for LGBTQ people to communicate and be together anywhere in the world. Globalization has also contributed to the rise of gay and lesbian global social movements and to the increasing acceptance of same-sex sexual relationships in large parts of the world (Stone and Weinberg 2015; Winter, Forest, and Sénac 2018). Yet while globalization has aided sexual minorities, it has also facilitated the spread of homophobia and other forms of prejudice and discrimination (Binnie 2004; Kaoma 2014). Globalization clearly has not been an unmitigated good as far as LGBTQ people are concerned.

The Global Sex Industry

Industries based on sex have become increasingly important to global capitalism. Bars, dance clubs, massage parlors, pornography, sex work establishments, international hotel chains, airline companies, and the tourist industry create, and help meet, the demand for sexual labor around the globe. It is almost impossible to get accurate numbers on those involved in the global sex industry, and at least some of the data are likely fabricated (Steinfatt 2011). Although sexual labor has a very long history, its current explicitly global quality is a more recent phenomenon.

Sex trafficking, a commercial sex act that includes force, fraud, or coercion and transporting and obtaining a person for sex acts, is truly a global issue (Patterson and Zhou 2018). It is one sector of human trafficking, which the U.S. State Department calls "modern slavery" or forced labor, and includes child soldiers, debt bondage, and domestic servitude. It is estimated that nearly 28 million people are victims of human trafficking around the world (U.S. Department of State n.d.); which generates roughly $100 billion in revenue annually (International Labour Organization 2017).

The flow of people in the global sex industry moves not only from the South to the North but also in the other direction. Over the past several decades, the global sex tourism industry has grown to be a multibillion-dollar enterprise (Weitzer 2012; Wortmann 2007). **Sex tourism** occurs when individuals travel to other countries specifically for the purpose of buying sex from others; sex is the primary or sole purpose of these trips. These encounters can be complicated by the fact that locals and tourists usually do not usually have the same levels of economic privilege. For one thing, tourists have the disposable income to take such trips. Although some sex tourism involves people traveling to the developed countries of the North (e.g., to Amsterdam in the Netherlands), most of it involves customers traveling from the North to the less developed countries of the South. For example, Thailand receives millions of sex tourists every year from many other countries, bringing in billions of dollars to the local economy.

Pattaya, Thailand, is a hub of that country's sex industry and a major sex tourism destination for travelers from many of the world's most developed nations.

Jonas Gratzer/Getty Images

Several factors have contributed to the rise of sex tourism. The internet expedites it, as information about destinations is readily available through websites, chat rooms, e-diaries, blogs, promotional videos, and guidebooks. Websites offer advice on the best tourist sites to visit, the best sex workers at those sites, how to arrange visits, and even how to negotiate with sex workers to get the lowest prices. It is even possible to buy a customized package tour of the best locations in the world for sex tourism, joining other sex tourists. Low-cost travel, at least for those with economic privilege, has permitted more sex tourists to circle the globe in search of sexual relations.

GLOBAL FLOWS RELATED TO GENDER

Global flows are especially important in understanding feminization at the global level. Among other things, migration has been increasingly feminized; more women have entered the labor force globally (mostly in lower-status occupations) and, somewhat paradoxically, women are more likely to be impoverished throughout much of the world. They are also more likely to be noncombatant victims of international violence. Less surprising and more positive is the fact that many women are deeply involved in the global women's movement.

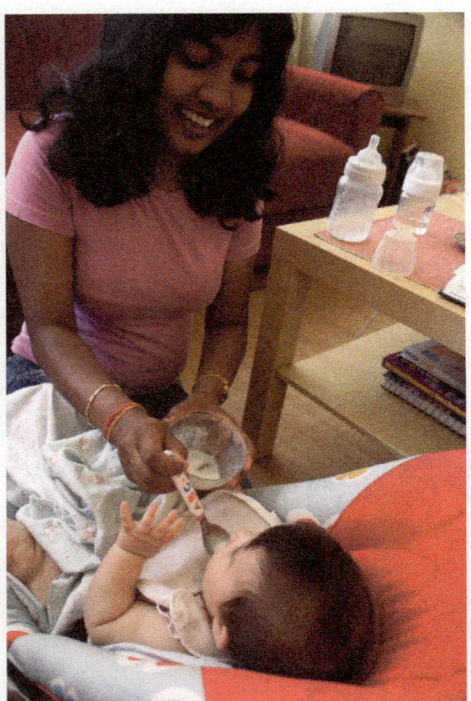

This young woman from Sri Lanka works as a nanny for an affluent family in the United States. Migrants who clean houses and care for children are part of the largest global labor market for women.

Rebecca Erol/Alamy Stock Photo

The Feminization of Migration

The global economy has contributed to an unprecedented increase in women's migration (Ehrenreich and Hochschild 2002, 2). Some have referred to this trend as the "feminization of migration" (Donato and Gabaccia 2015; Parreñas 2015). Much of this flow involves women from the Global South moving to the Global North to handle work historically performed by Northern women (Runyon 2012). Large numbers of women are emigrating from China, India, Indonesia, Myanmar, Pakistan, the Philippines, Sri Lanka, Thailand, and Bangladesh. The migrants often become nannies (Eckenwiler 2014), maids (Ehrenreich 2002; Gündüz 2013), or sex workers (Brennan 2002).

This migrant labor arguably enriches the Global North and enhances its already elevated lifestyle. Domestic work is now considered the largest labor market for women worldwide. Many female labor immigrants clean the homes and care for the children of affluent families while trying to send money (remittances) to their own families in their home countries. The hope for many is that this work will bring with it better pay and improved working conditions, increasing the immigrants' quality of life and that of their families.

Undocumented and informal migration, which is common for women migrating to the North for domestic work, exposes women to the worst forms of discrimination, exploitation, and abuse (Adams and Campbell 2012; Chang 2016). They can be held as debt hostages by recruitment agencies until their transportation and placement fees are paid, imprisoned in the houses of their employers, treated inhumanely, and sometimes murdered. Increasing numbers of migrant women are victims of sexual abuse (including rape), sex trafficking, and prostitution, as discussed previously.

The Feminization of Labor

There has been a notable increase in women's labor force participation rates worldwide, particularly in the Americas and Western Europe. In the United States, 56 percent of women 16 years and older were employed in 2020, compared to 68 percent of men (see Figure 10.9). In 1948, only 31 percent of women were employed, in comparison to 84 percent of men. Even though there are significant variations within and across regions, women's labor force participation has also risen substantially in sub-Saharan Africa,

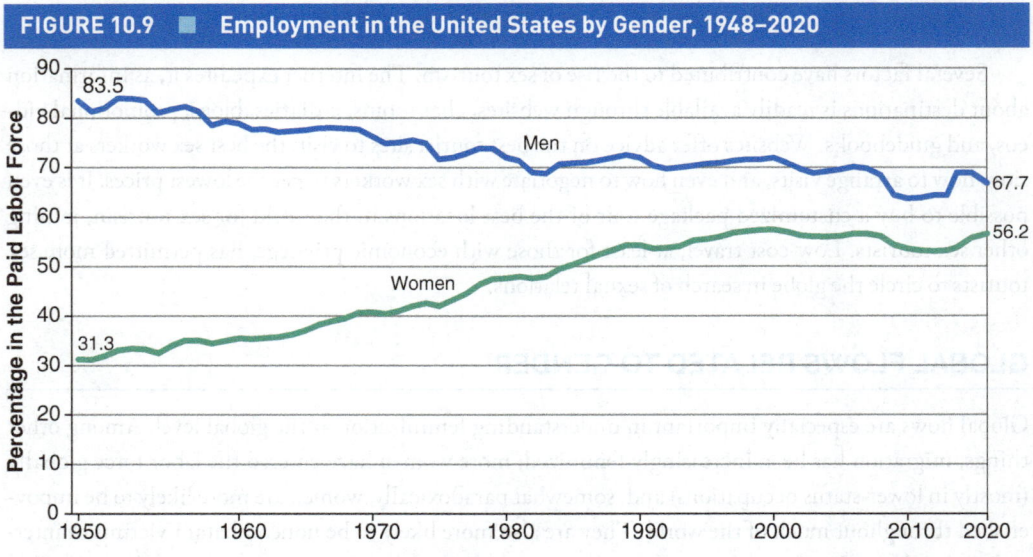

FIGURE 10.9 ■ Employment in the United States by Gender, 1948–2020

Sources: U.S. Bureau of Labor Statistics, 2020, *Women in the Labor Force: a Databook*, Table 2, Washington, DC: United States Department of Labor; U.S. Bureau of Labor Statistics, 2021, *Civilian Labor Force Participation Rate by Age, Sex, Race, and Ethnicity*, Employment Projections, Table 3.3, Washington, DC: United States Department of Labor.

North Africa, Eastern Europe, Southeast Asia, and East Asia over this period (Akorsu 2016). Although the progress in women's employment status is linked, at least in part, to gender equality movements, the key factor in this change has been the better integration of an increasing number of areas into the world economy through trade and production.

The increasing participation of women in the labor force has been termed the **feminization of labor** (Standing 1989). This refers to the rise of female labor participation in all sectors and the movement of women into jobs traditionally held by men. This global trend has occurred in both developing and developed countries (Lechman and Kaur 2015).

The Feminization of Poverty and Female Proletarianization

The feminization of labor, especially in developing economies, is often accompanied by **female proletarianization** as an increasing number of women are channeled into low-status, poorly paid manual work. Female proletarianization is closely related to the feminization of poverty (Brady and Kall 2008). Globally, more women are being drawn into labor-intensive and low-paying industries, such as textiles, apparel, leather products, food processing, and electronics (Brooks 2015; Chen et al. 2013). Jobs in these industries are characterized by the flexible use of labor, high turnover rates, part-time and temporary employment, and a lack of security and benefits. Female employees are preferred in these industries because of the persistence of a number of stereotypes that often have little basis in reality. Such stereotypes include the idea that women will typically work for lower wages and that they are easier for male employers and managers to supervise (English 2013). They are considered not only to be more docile but also to have greater patience and more dexterity than men in performing standardized and repetitive work.

GENDER, WAR, AND VIOLENCE

Men are certainly more likely than women to be killed or wounded in warfare. However, a recent United Nations Security Council report describes the ways in which women bear the brunt of war, violence, and failed peace efforts (United Nations Security Council 2017). More specifically, women are more likely to be the noncombatant victims of wars and other forms of organized collective violence, including being raped and killed (Baumeister 2018). Women are also likely to suffer as a result of local and global terrorism and political violence (Gentry and Sjoberg 2015).

Several changes have made it more likely that women will be the victims of international violence. One is the change in the nature of warfare. For example, "asymmetric warfare," or warfare involving forces of unequal capabilities, often takes the form of shootouts in the streets. Civilians—especially women, children, and the elderly—are more likely to be victims in such cases than they are when conventional ground battles take place. This is evident, for example, in the brutal wars and invasions that have engulfed Ukraine, Syria, Iraq, Libya, and Yemen. Generally, the line between combatants and civilians has blurred, with the result that more civilians, including women, have become the victims of warfare. Finally, women are increasingly likely to participate in the armed forces and in terrorist groups in various countries, and this greatly increases their chances of being the victims of violence. In some cases, terrorist groups use women to carry concealed explosives and to detonate them in or near targets, killing themselves and those in the vicinity (Gentry and Sjoberg 2015).

One unintended consequence of war is that women can sometimes benefit from warfare and its disruption of business as usual. Among other things, they can gain greater economic independence, more freedom to act, and greater mobility. With the norms and values of society disrupted, women can do things they could not do before: acquire a more public role in the community and society, gain greater responsibility for decision-making, and generally acquire more power. Such was the case during World War II, when labor shortages caused by the mobilization of men for military service resulted in more work opportunities for women. The iconic image of Rosie the Riveter working in a factory reflected this new reality, as women entered the blue-collar workforce that had been dominated by males.

Women in the Global South, such as these workers in China, are much more likely than their counterparts in the more industrial Global North to be employed in assembly line work or other low-wage labor. Why does this situation persist?

Cynthia Lee/Alamy Stock Photo

The Global Women's Movement

As you have seen, globalization and the rise of a global economy have created or exacerbated a variety of inequalities faced by women. One response has been expansion of the international women's movement. It has grown dramatically in recent years because of problems created for women by globalization. It has also expanded because of the increased ability of those working on behalf of the movement to travel globally and to communicate with one another. The international women's movement has a long history, traceable to at least the late 1800s. It has focused on issues such as sexual violence, reproductive rights, labor issues, and sexual harassment.

The larger global movement is concerned with a variety of issues: human rights, economic concerns, the environment, health care, and violence against women. The movement has also come to focus on the adverse effects of global capitalism (e.g., increased global trafficking in women), the lack of women's voices in global civil society, the growth of antifeminist fundamentalist movements (the Taliban, IS, Boko Haram), and the HIV/AIDS epidemic. More generally, the international women's movement has focused attention on issues of global justice for women and other minorities. It has had a strong impact on the United Nations and has helped create strong linkages among the United Nations, national governments, and nongovernmental organizations (Baksh and Harcourt 2015).

Women throughout the world not only have been active in the global women's movement but also have responded at local and regional levels to common problems caused by globalization. They also localize global political activities undertaken by the international women's movement and global human rights groups. In addition, they organize against global activities such as militarism and conflict and they use global organizations (such as the United Nations and international nongovernmental organizations) to help in local and regional activities (Fish 2017). However, even the activities that have been primarily or exclusively local in nature have had profound effects globally. Even with all the local variations, the broader women's movement can be seen as a truly global phenomenon.

SUMMARY

Sex is principally a biological concept, while gender is a cultural concept connected to societal expectations of behaviors, attitudes, and personalities. Femininities and masculinities are socially constructed and subject to change and variation. Transgender and intersexed identities help demonstrate how binary understandings of gender and sex are not applicable to lived realities. Gendered inequalities persist in numerous domains, including in education, at home and in families, and at work.

Sexuality is related to behaviors, attractions, and identities and is experienced both individually and collectively. Sexual orientation is more complicated than the few categories we typically use to express it, such as heterosexual, gay, or lesbian. Heterosexism refers to the belief that heterosexuality is superior to other types of sexual orientation. Social constraints shape what types of sexual expressions and activities are considered appropriate (or not). Consensual sexual activities are those agreed on by the participants, in contrast to those that are not, such as sexual harassment and rape.

Globalization reinforces but also destabilizes preexisting gender and sexuality structures on a global scale. The greater flow of people creates more opportunity for traffickers to transport women and children for sexual exploitation and for people to travel for sex tourism. Globalization is linked to the increasing number of women working in the paid labor force, especially those from the Global South, although many are drawn into low-status, poorly paid, and sometimes dangerous work. Women are often victims of international violence, including being raped.

KEY TERMS

agender	intersex
consensual sexual activities	master status
emphasized femininity	rape
female proletarianization	rape culture
feminization of labor	second shift
gender	sex
gender fluid	sex tourism
gender identity	sex trafficking
gender role	sexual assault
genderqueer	sexual double standard:
hegemonic masculinity	sexual identity
heterosexism	sexual orientation
hidden curriculum	sexuality
homophobia	transgender
informed (or effective) sexual consent	

REVIEW QUESTIONS

1. What is the difference between sex and gender?

2. What do sociologists mean when they say gender and sexuality are social constructs?

3. What are the differences in the ways in which men and women experience hegemonic masculinity and emphasized femininity? How do these constructs help create and reinforce gender stratification?

4. How do men and women differ in terms of their educational experiences? In what ways does the hidden curriculum of educational systems reinforce gender stratification?

5. Why are women and men treated differently as consumers? What events in recent decades have changed the way in which women and men are thought of as consumers?

6. What are the differences in the ways in which men and women approach sexuality? How are the differences related to the socialization process? Do you think increasing equality between men and women will affect sexualities?

7. In what ways has the sex industry become increasingly important to global capitalism? How is this sex industry reflective of gender stratification? How is it reflective of inequalities between the Global North and Global South?

8. In what positive and negative ways have lesbians, gays, bisexuals, and trans people been affected by globalization?

9. What do sociologists mean by the "feminization of poverty"? By "female proletarianization"? How are these concepts related to one another and to the more general process of the feminization of labor?

10. What types of violence are women most likely to experience when they live in places experiencing war and other types of armed conflict?

Frazer Harrison/Getty Images

11 FAMILIES

277

LEARNING OBJECTIVES

11.1 Explain basic sociological concepts of the family, marriage, and intimate relationships.

11.2 Describe current social trends changing marriage and the family.

11.3 Apply structural/functional, conflict/critical, and inter/actionist theories to the family.

11.4 Describe current problems associated with the family.

11.5 Identify the effects of globalization on the family.

FICTIONAL FAMILIES GET REAL

The family has been a staple on the screen since the beginning of film and television. Fictional, very traditional families were almost the only ones presented, perhaps most notably on the long-running and top-rated shows *I Love Lucy* (1951–1957) and *The Adventures of Ozzie and Harriet* (1952–1966). Interestingly, although these shows were fictional, in both cases the actors playing husband and wife were married in real life. The best-known early series to deal with a real family in a nonfictional way, and TV's first reality show, was the groundbreaking *An American Family*, which aired on public television in the 1970s. It was intended simply to chronicle the happy, mundane lives of a husband and wife and their five children, but over the course of the series, cracks in the family's calm and stable facade became apparent, exposing events never before seen on U.S. television. The public witnessed the husband and wife's real-life separation and subsequent divorce, for example, and the eldest son's coming out as television's first openly gay person.

Perhaps the most famous fictional family in television history is *The Brady Bunch* (1969–1974). In the show a single father with three sons marries a single mother with three daughters. All are white, the family is clearly upper middle class (their maid Alice was a fan favorite), and most of the "serious problems" they deal with would be considered highly trivial by most people, even then.

Since then, family-based television shows, both fictional and nonfictional, have flourished and become increasingly "real," going far beyond the kinds of problems depicted in *The Brady Bunch*. The fictional *Transparent* (2014–2019) portrays a family with an array of difficulties, most notably drug addiction and issues associated with being trans and a parent. The popular sitcom *Modern Family* (2009–2020) featured several types of families, including a heterosexual couple with three children, a same-sex white couple with an adopted Asian daughter, and a heterosexual couple with an older male married to a much younger woman from Colombia, her son from a previous relationship, and their own son. There are also a number of reality shows that are centered on a particular family—*Braxton Family Values* (2011–2020), *Keeping Up with the Kardashians* (2007–2021)—although most of them are focused on extremely wealthy and famous families.

As television shows indicate, the structure of a family can take a great number of forms. Extended and nuclear families have proven popular in film and television over the last 100 years, but recent social changes have opened a wide variety of other options for viewers. Some couples consist of one man and one woman, but other relationship forms are becoming increasingly recognized (and legal). Some couples, whatever their sex or gender, marry for love, others do so for purely economic reasons, and an increasing number choose not to marry at all. Some have multiple children, while others have only one or even none at all. Some maintain exclusive partnerships until death, others divorce and sometimes remarry, and still others incorporate new members into existing relationships.

Family-based TV shows paint a picture of domestic dynamics and realities that are captivating and intriguing but by no means complete. They largely sidestep issues critical to sociology, such as poverty, gender inequality, and the prevalence of domestic abuse. Also, unlike sociology, most shows in the United States have not adopted a global perspective, choosing instead to focus on U.S. families. That leaves us with much to learn and study.

FAMILY, MARRIAGE, AND INTIMATE RELATIONSHIPS

The U.S. Census Bureau (2019) defines the **family** as "a group of two people or more (one of whom is the householder) related by birth, marriage, or adoption and residing together." Historically, families have been considered especially important in socializing children. Although families do not always succeed in this role, sociologists continue to view the family as an important social institution central to life in most societies. Sociologists are interested in such issues as the relationship between family and marriage, the different forms taken by families, and how families are formed and maintained, expand and contract, and even dissolve. In this section, we will define such basic concepts and ideas as marriage, intimate relationships, and love and explore their roles in the family.

Marriage

Marriage is the legally or formally recognized union of two (or more) individuals in a relationship. Although marriage often has a religious context, most countries do not require a religious recognition of such a union (even though some countries limit the union to between members of particular religions). Instead, marriages in most countries require formal recognition by the law, not necessarily by a religious institution. The number of partners recognized in a marriage also varies by country. Although most countries limit the number to two individuals (with many countries requiring that those members are of the "opposite" sex), several countries also recognize marriage between multiple individuals, most usually one man with many wives.

Monogamy has traditionally been defined as marriage between two individuals. It can also refer to exclusive sexual relationships between two individuals. Other forms of marriage, such as **polygamy**, allow multiple spouses. **Polygyny**, in which a single husband has multiple wives, is a more common form of polygamy than **polyandry**, in which a single wife has multiple husbands.

Historically and around the world, rules, customs, and laws have been created to define and control marriage. Key to understanding marriage (and also many families) is the concept of **endogamy**, or marriage to someone with similar characteristics in terms of race, ethnicity, religion, education level, social class, and so on. In contrast, **exogamy** involves marriage to someone with characteristics dissimilar in these dimensions. Throughout history, families have been defined much more by endogamy than by exogamy. In recent years, though, endogamy has declined in importance, and there is more exogamy. For example, there has been an increasing tendency of people to marry individuals of other races (Vasquez-Tokos 2017). However, as a general rule, families continue to be characterized more by endogamy than by exogamy.

In the last several decades, the nature of family and marriage has undergone a series of rapid changes. The definitions of what constitutes marriage or a family have become less rigid. One thing is clear, however: The close linkage between marriage and the family has been greatly weakened, if not broken. Nevertheless, most people end up being married one or more times during their lifetimes. And those who marry often create families, although they may not stay together as long as families did in the past. Being married and in a family does not mean that the marriage or the family will remain the same for decades, or even years.

Endogamy, or marriage to a partner who is culturally, socially, and racially similar, is still much more common than exogamy, or marriage to someone who is different in these dimensions. Do you think this situation will change in the future?

Westend61/Getty Images

Intimate Relationships

An **intimate relationship** involves partners who have a close, personal relationship with one another. This intimate relationship is often a by-product of courtship rituals in which two people are attracted to each other, develop intimacy, enjoy each other's company, and identify as a couple after a period of dating.

The nature of **intimacy** is not static but changes over time. Fifty or one hundred years ago, couples could be intimate without necessarily sharing very much about themselves with each other, especially their most private thoughts. However, in many cultures today, intimacy increasingly involves disclosing much, if not everything, about oneself to one's partner (Wilding 2018). Levels of disclosure tend to be gendered (Kimmel 2016). Women tend to function as emotional caregivers within heterosexual relationships. One explanation for this is that women are generally socialized to engage in communication in which they express their emotions, whereas men are more often socialized to suppress their emotions and communicate little about them.

Love

Intimacy in many relationships is often associated with love. **Passionate love** has a sudden onset, inspires strong sexual feelings, and tends to include idealizations of the one who is loved. Passionate love brings with it great intimacy, but it is an intimacy very likely to be short-lived. In contrast, **companionate love** develops more gradually, is not necessarily tied to sexual passion, and is based on more rational assessments of the one who is loved. Companionate love is more likely than passionate love to lead to long-lasting intimate relationships. However, these two types of love are not clearly distinguished from one another. This is clearest in the fact that long-term intimate relationships often start out with passionate love, but in those that succeed over time, it tends to be combined with, or even supplanted by, companionate love (Goldscheider, Bernhardt, and Lappegård 2015).

Passionate love, also known as romantic love, has a long and interesting history. For example, some of our more recent senses of love are traceable to 1950s consumer culture (Illouz 2018). It was then that love became closely associated with consumption and travel. The movie, automobile, fashion, and makeup industries capitalized on, and disseminated ideas about, romantic love. Each of these industries, in its own way, glamorized romance and conveyed the message that romance was associated with commodities available for a price.

Zygmunt Bauman sought to get at the essence of love in the contemporary world in his book *Liquid Love* (2003). On the cover of the book is a heart drawn in the sand. However, the sea is nearby, and the implication is that love will soon be washed away by the waves. To Bauman, love, like everything else in today's liquid society, is fleeting. This clearly applies to passionate love, but to Bauman, even companionate love is constantly at risk of erosion and disappearance. This represents a major challenge to all intimate relationships, especially marriage, and to all those involved in them. However, liquid love can also be seen as offering people freedom from lifelong loveless relationships. It also offers the possibility of innumerable experiences with love and the possibility of many different relationships built on love.

It can be argued that our main concerns in this chapter—family and marriage—are also increasingly liquid. Because they are now so liquid, the borders of marriage and the family are increasingly difficult to define. More important, many traditional forms of marriage and the family are confronting the possibility of being changed. As a result, many sociologists have moved away from a focus on the family and marriage and prefer to discuss vaguer phenomena such as "relationships" and "personal life." Nevertheless, most people, including most sociologists, continue to think in terms of marriage and the family. We do the same in this chapter, but with an understanding that both are changing dramatically and refer to phenomena far more liquid than they were in the past.

BROAD CHANGES IN MARRIAGE AND THE FAMILY

Two major changes are discussed in this section: the decline in marriage and changes in the family household.

Decline in Marriage

In 1970, married couples constituted 71 percent of all U.S. households; by 2021, less than 50 percent of all households were married couples (see Figure 11.1). Similarly, the traditional **nuclear family** consisting of two adults and one or more children dropped from 40 percent of all households in 1970 to about 18 percent of all households in 2021 (U.S. Census Bureau 2021b).

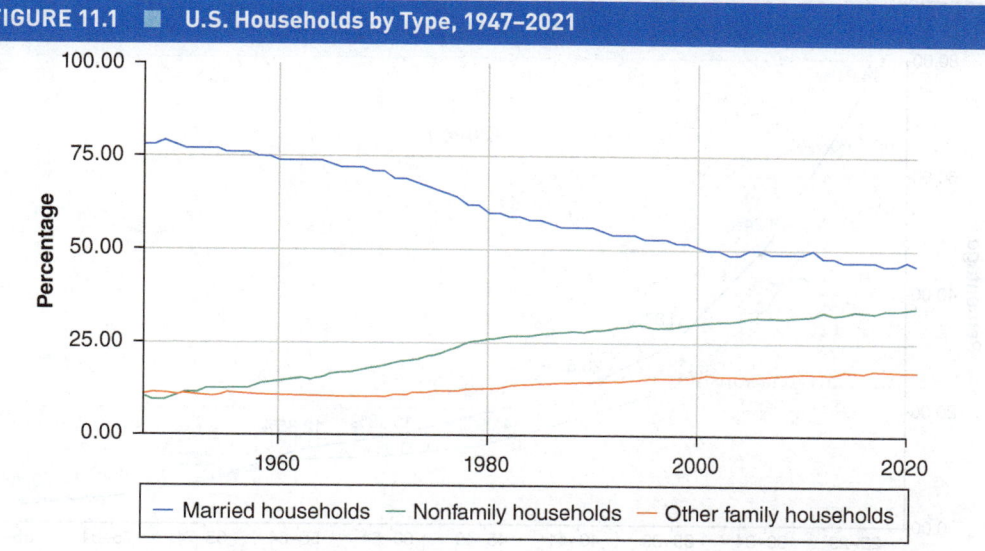

FIGURE 11.1 U.S. Households by Type, 1947–2021

Source: United States Census Bureau, 2021, *Historical Households Tables, Households by Type: 1940 to Present,* Table HH-1, Washington, D.C.: United States Census Bureau. Retrieved August 02, 2022 (https://www.census.gov/data/tables/time-series/demo/families/households.html).

Another way to get a sense of the dramatic change in marriage and the family is to look at the percentage of those who have never been married, which has changed significantly in the past few decades. Figure 11.2 shows that in 2021, 34 percent of men and 31 percent of women in the United States ages 15 and older had never been married, compared to 27 percent of men and 20 percent of women in 1960.

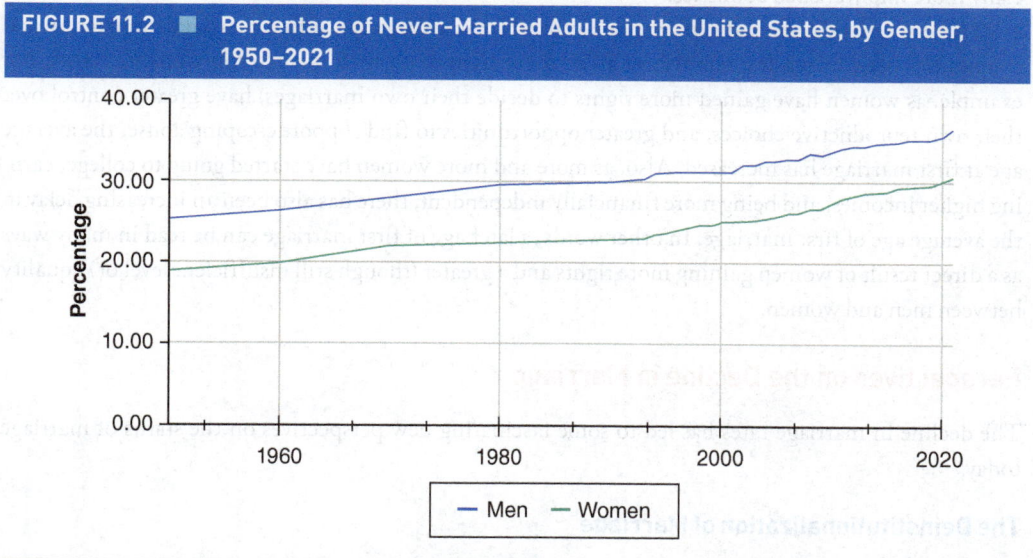

FIGURE 11.2 Percentage of Never-Married Adults in the United States, by Gender, 1950–2021

United States Census Bureau, 2021, *Historical Marital Status Tables, Marital Status of the Population 15 Years Old and Over, by Sex, Race, and Hispanic Origin: 1950 to Present,* Table MS-1, Washington, D.C.: United States Census Bureau. Retrieved August 02, 2022 (https://www.census.gov/data/tables/time-series/demo/families/marital.html).

However, it remains the case that as people age, they are more likely to marry. Figure 11.3 shows that in 2021, 48 percent of men and 36 percent of women had never been married by age 34. But by age 44, 24 percent of men and 19 percent of women had never married, and the percentage of never-married adults continues to decline as men and women reach their 50s, 60s, and 70s.

The average age at first marriage has been steadily increasing in recent decades. For example, the average age of first marriage between heterosexual couples in the United States in the mid-1950s was around 20 for women and 22 for men. By 2018, that number had increased to around 28 for women and 30 for men. In many European countries, those numbers are even higher. For example, in the

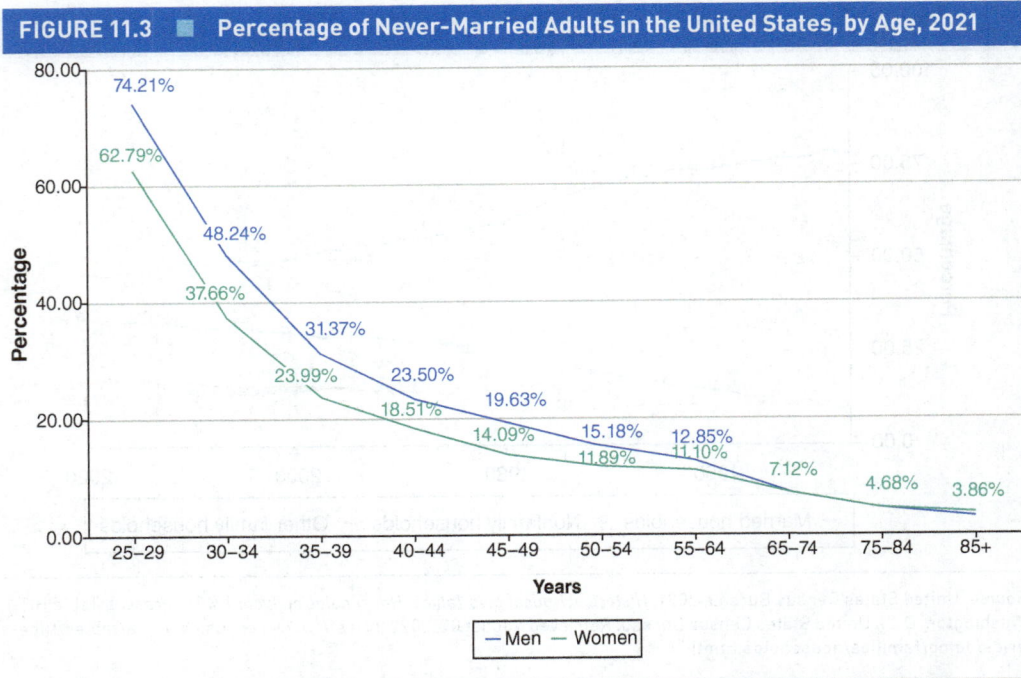

FIGURE 11.3 Percentage of Never-Married Adults in the United States, by Age, 2021

United States Census Bureau, 2021, *Marital Status of People 15 Years and Over, by Age, Sex, and Personal Earnings: 2021*, Table A1, Washington, D.C.: United States Census Bureau. Retrieved August 02, 2022 (https://www.census.gov/newsroom/stories/spouses-day.html).

United Kingdom it is around 31 for women and 33 for men, and in Ireland it is even higher at around 35 for women and 37 for men. On the other hand, the age is much lower in many other countries, especially more impoverished countries.

There are many proposed explanations as to why the average age at first marriage for heterosexual couples has been increasing but almost all of them have to do with increases in women's rights. For example, as women have gained more rights to decide their own marriages, have greater control over their own reproductive choices, and greater opportunities to find support escaping abuse, the average age at first marriage has increased. Also, as more and more women have started going to college, earning higher incomes, and being more financially independent, there has also been an increasing delay in the average age of first marriage. In other words, a later age of first marriage can be read in many ways as a direct result of women gaining more rights and a greater (though still insufficient level of) equality between men and women.

Perspectives on the Decline in Marriage

The decline in marriage rates has led to some fascinating new perspectives on the status of marriage today.

The Deinstitutionalization of Marriage

Andrew Cherlin (2004, 2010) focuses on the "deinstitutionalization of American marriage." By **deinstitutionalization**, he means that the social norms relating to marriage have weakened. As a result, people increasingly question their actions, or those of others, as they relate to marriage. Although Cherlin focuses on this deinstitutionalization in the United States, he recognizes that a similar process is occurring in much of Europe as well as in Canada (and elsewhere, and more generally 21 industrialized countries in various parts of the world; Treas, Lui, and Gubernskays 2014). In the mid-twentieth century, few questioned marriage and the creation of a nuclear family. As a result, most plunged into both, sometimes successfully but more often with dubious or even disastrous results. Now, with marriage and perhaps the nuclear family and the family household deinstitutionalized, it is much easier for people *not* to rush into such arrangements. They are freer to experiment with many other arrangements (Rabin 2018).

In the early twentieth century, institutional marriage was the predominant form. The focus in such a marriage was on the maintenance of the institution of marriage itself. There was less concern that those involved would love or be good companions to one another. Today, many see the time of institutional marriage as past; others, however, see it as alive and well and as having a future, including same-sex marriage (Yulius, Tang, and Offord 2018).

By the middle of the twentieth century, a model of **companionate marriage** (see the previous discussion of companionate love) had become predominant (Burgess and Locke 1945; Simmons 2015). Companionate marriage meshed well with the nuclear family. It involved a clear division of labor between the single-earner breadwinner—almost always the male—and the female homemaker. In spite, or perhaps because, of the strict division of labor, husbands and wives were held together by bonds of sentiment, friendship, and sexuality. They were supposed to be each other's companions, which included being each other's friends, confidants, and lovers. Romantic love was an essential component of companionate marriage.

In the 1960s, a dramatic shift began to take place in the direction of **individualized marriage** (Lindemann 2017). The goal of companionate marriage was the satisfaction of the couple, the family as a whole, and the roles the couple played in the family. However, that focus began to shift increasingly in the direction of the satisfaction of each individual, as well as toward individuals' ability to develop and express themselves. In addition, instead of being as rigid as companionate marriage, individualized marriage became increasingly open and flexible. Furthermore, couples were becoming more open with each other in communicating about and dealing with problems. Many couples, as well as many observers, applauded the greater freedoms and sensitivities associated with individualized marriage, although the changes may not be as clear-cut as was first believed (Yodanis and Lauer 2014).

A major factor in the rise of individualized marriage was the changing place in society of women, especially middle-class women. For example, as more women went to work, they were no longer restricted to the homemaker role and reliance on the male breadwinner. As more women obtained higher education, their occupational prospects were enhanced. This put them in a context in which ideas associated with companionate marriage were increasingly open to question. Greater access to contraception and to abortion enabled more women to plan their reproductive lives, releasing them from some of the constraints of companionate marriage as they related to producing and socializing children.

As a result of all these changes, people today feel freer to never marry, to marry later, to end unhappy marriages, and especially to engage in many other types of intimate relationships. Yet, in spite of these changes, the vast majority of people—as many as 90 percent or more—will eventually marry, although many of their marriages will end long before they reach the "til death do us part" stage. Thus, marriage has not been deinstitutionalized to the degree anticipated by Cherlin (2004, 2010), and it is likely to survive, although it will not be nearly as important as it once was.

Pure Relationships

Because marriage of any kind can be confining and limiting, more people seem to now prefer a **pure relationship** that is entered into for its own sake, or for what each partner can get from it, and those in it remain only as long as each derives enough satisfaction from it. Although pure relationships can exist within marriage, they are more likely to exist outside such relationships. As a result of the increasing predominance of this idea, at least among young people, a relationship is likely to be ended when the couple no longer finds it satisfying. It is also likely that another, different pure relationship (or several) will be formed in relatively short order, perhaps even simultaneously with the existing one. This fits with the increasing individualization of contemporary society as well as the closely related phenomenon of individuals wanting more choices and greater freedom of choice. In whatever type of intimate relationship people find themselves today, the possibility that it will dissolve is often not far from their consciousness. This may be one of the reasons why young adults are putting off developing intimate relationships. They are more likely to consider an intimate, committed relationship as the last stage of adult development, unlike in the 1950s, when such relationships were more likely to develop in early adulthood (Lee 2017; Silva 2015).

Digital Living: Online Dating

In the past, a person was likely to be introduced to a potential partner by family members or friends or to meet them at school, work, or place of worship. Today, one can use an additional intermediary: online dating websites and mobile apps. There are many such dating websites. Match.com began in 1995 and now has websites in more than 50 countries and in 12 languages. It has claimed that one in five relationships begin on online dating sites. eHarmony commercials boast that matches made on its website have resulted in more marriages than other online dating services. There are also a variety of dating websites that cater to specific markets like Jdate, which is aimed at Jewish singles, and FarmersOnly.com, which is aimed at more rural communities and whose commercials claim that "city folks just don't get it."

Unlike traditional intermediaries, online dating sites require us to participate actively in finding and selecting our own partners. eHarmony users, for example, have to complete the site's 29 Dimensions of Compatibility questionnaire, which asks them to provide information about such topics as their family background, personality traits, communication skills, and appearance. After these data have been collected and analyzed via a set of algorithms, compatible users are "matched" to each other. Match.com operates in a similar manner, although it also allows users to state their preferences about their ideal partners.

The use of mobile apps as a way to find potential partners has also increased dramatically in recent years. Tinder users can swipe right on their smartphones to find a potential match. Grindr, which has more than 13 million monthly users, connects gay and bisexual men looking for partners. Though Tinder and Grindr are free, paid subscriptions for premium services on both are available. Paying for dating assistance has been a subject of debate, with critics arguing that it commodifies love. Others wonder whether meeting someone online is as authentic as unexpectedly finding love through a chance encounter in real life. Being "matched" with a potential partner through an online dating service might take the romance out of getting to know someone over time because you can read a profile to discover a person's hobbies or favorite color (Rosewarne 2016). Many people, especially younger people, are not troubled by these concerns.

Nonfamily Households

A **nonfamily household** is one in which a person lives either alone or with nonrelatives. Of greatest interest is the growth of one-person households, or people living alone. As is clear in Figure 11.4, the United States (and many other countries) has witnessed an increase in such households, from 13 percent in 1960 to 29 percent of all households in 2022.

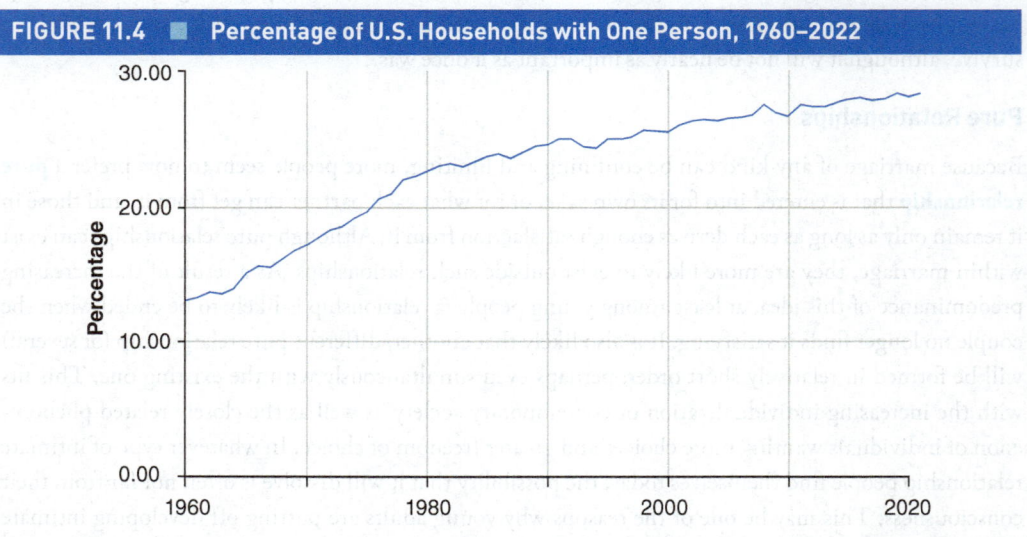

FIGURE 11.4 ■ Percentage of U.S. Households with One Person, 1960–2022

Source: United States Census Bureau, 2021, *Historical Households Tables, Households by Size: 1960 to Present,* Table HH-4, Washington, D.C.: United States Census Bureau. Retrieved August 02, 2022 (https://www.census.gov/data/tables/time-series/demo/families/households.html).

Today, more than 37 million people in the United States live alone (U.S. Census Bureau 2022). The growth of one-person households has been largely due to the increased number of adults aged 65 and older living alone, particularly women.

Other Family Forms and Structures

In this section, we will discuss other forms of family formation and structure including cohabitation, living apart together, arranged marriages, single-parent families, nonresident parents, stepfamilies and blended families, adoption, same-sex families, and families of choice.

Cohabitation

Cohabitation is defined as an arrangement in which a couple shares a living space without being legally married (Kitchener 2018). There are more cohabiting couples today than there were previously, although they still compose only a small proportion (7 percent) of all U.S. households (Stepler 2017). The United States ranks low in cohabitation among developed countries. In fact, cohabitation is much more common in several European countries. For example, 24 percent of adults in Sweden cohabit, and 20 percent of adults in France do as well (Institute for Family Studies 2019).

It is unclear exactly how many people are living in such relationships, because cohabitation is not a formally recognized relationship and it leaves no legal records. Furthermore, it is not clear how many nights, weeks, months, or years a couple must be together to be categorized as cohabiting. It is clear, however, that more young people (especially those ages 25 to 35) are living together outside marriage, even if they are not considered, or do not consider themselves, to be cohabiting couples (Manning and Cohen 2015). Furthermore, there has been a significant increase in cohabitation among older adults (those 50-plus; Stepler 2017).

Living together in this way has come to be considered a refuge for those with failed marriages or for those who never married. It is also a common tryout for, and pathway to, marriage for some people (although few people actually plan to marry when they begin cohabiting). Then again, marriage may never occur or even be discussed, and cohabiting couples may break up and move on to other relationships. A declining number of cohabitating couples end up getting married (Stanley 2018).

Rates of cohabitation vary greatly around the globe. Sweden has a long history of cohabitation, and the process is well institutionalized there. In excess of 90 percent of first partnerships are cohabitations, and more than 40 percent of all first births are to cohabiting couples (Perelli-Harris and Gassen 2012). The legal status, or the rights and privileges, of those who cohabit is virtually the same as that of married couples in terms of such things as social security and taxes. The high rate of cohabitation has led to a decline in the importance of marriage and of the customs, rituals, and ceremonies associated with it. However, during the twenty-first century, there has been evidence of a change in this pattern, as more Swedes are marrying. This reverses a long-term decline in marriage in Sweden between the 1960s and the 1990s (Ohlsson-Wijk, Turunen, and Anderson 2017). Other, mainly Catholic, European countries—Italy and Spain—have much lower rates of cohabitation. There is evidence of the spread of cohabitation throughout much of Europe, including eastern Europe, and elsewhere.

Living Apart Together

Couples who are engaged in a **living apart together** (LAT) relationship have an intimate relationship but do not reside in the same physical residence. These couples might live in houses near to one another, in different cities, or sometimes even in different countries or on different continents. The reasons for this type of relationship can include the employment of one or both of the partners, a desire to live together but not yet being able to do so, or even simply a desire to live alone but still have an intimate relationship.

Although there are no official records for the number of people who are engaged in LAT relationships, there are estimates that somewhere between 6 and 10 percent of couples are in this kind of relationship in the United States, Canada, the UK, and many other countries, especially in Western Europe. There is also agreement that these kinds of relationships are becoming more common.

Arranged Marriages

Arranged marriages are marriages in which the partners were brought together by individuals from outside of the relationship, usually family members. Arranged marriages have been a common form of marriage in many countries, perhaps most famously in India, but also in countries throughout Southeast Asia, the Middle East, North Africa, and elsewhere. Arranged marriages were also common in many European countries until the nineteenth century, especially among royalty and the nobility. Although their prominence has declined in recent decades, arranged marriages are still common, and widely accepted, in many places in the world today.

Many have criticized arranged marriages, arguing that they violate the right of individuals to choose their own partner. These criticisms have grown increasingly louder in a world in which, as we have seen, individualism is becoming a bigger factor in developing relationships. That said, those in arranged marriages are less likely to get divorced and, according to many studies, report higher sustained levels of satisfaction with their relationships, especially in later years of marriage.

Single-Parent Families

Among the developed countries, the United States has the highest rate of single-parent families (27 percent of all households with children), while Japan has the lowest (less than 3 percent; Statistics Japan 2018; U.S. Census Bureau 2016). The percentage of single-parent households in the European Union is about 11 percent; the United Kingdom has one of the highest percentages of single-parent households at nearly 19 percent (Stronger Families 2015–2018).

There are a number of reasons that lead to single-parent families including the death of a parent, divorce, abandonment, or simply a desire to raise a child on one's own (which is made increasingly possible through things like artificial insemination and adoption). Children in single-parent families might face additional difficulties but they might also have distinct advantages. The most important factor is not how many parents there are, but rather the quality of the parenting and the resources available in the household.

Nonresident Parents

Nonresident parents are parents who live apart from their children (Smyth 2007). Most nonresident parents are men, although the number of women in this category is increasing. Historically, there have been many reasons for men to be absent from their families, including work, war, and incarceration. Other reasons include nonmarital childbearing, with the parents never having lived together; the breakdown of cohabiting relationships; and divorce.

Some nonresident parents are in the armed forces. This servicewoman has just returned from assignment. How are the stresses on military families different from those faced by others with nonresident parents?

SDI Productions/iStockPhoto

The issue of nonresident parents is also related to globalization and to the tendency for at least one parent to migrate in search of work. The physical distance created by work migration can makes it more difficult to be physically present, although that is ameliorated by the internet and interaction through e-mail, Skype, Facebook, and text messaging through services such as WhatsApp. Such services have helped create new "cyberparents." Although much of the focus has been on the negative effects of globalization on both nonresident parents *and* their children, it is possible that we are seeing a restructuring of global parenting—and the creation of a new category of transnational parent—with a number of benefits, especially for the children. For example, parents who emigrate for work may end up being better off economically. This is especially true for women who may be empowered and better able to take on the "breadwinner" role. They are likely to be better able to send remittances and "care packages" back to their families (Juozeliūnienė and Budginaitė 2018).

Stepfamilies and Blended Families

A **stepfamily** consists of two adults who are married or cohabiting, at least one of whom has a child or children from a different partner (Ganong and Coleman 2017). A **blended family** includes some combination of children from the partners' previous marriages or relationships, along with one or more children of the currently married or cohabiting couple (Perry-Fraser and Fraser 2018). Stepfamilies and blended families have become common in the United States because about half of all marriages include a partner who was previously married. The U.S. Census Bureau estimates that 50 percent of children under the age of 13 live with one biological parent and that parent's partner (Stepfamily Foundation 2019).

Adoption

Adoption is the process by which an individual assumes a relationship and a responsibility for another, usually a child. Adoption can occur for any number of reasons including that an individual or a couple is unable to give birth or does not want to give birth, to rescue someone from a difficult, even dangerous, situation, or for humanitarian purposes (like children orphaned by the death of a parent by war or disease), among other reasons. The most common form of adoption in the United States is done by foster parents. Other common forms include by family members or step-parents. It is estimated that up to 2 percent of all children in the United States, or 1 in 50, is adopted.

Adoption can be a very complicated, expensive process and, in many places, is restricted to married heterosexual couples. For that reason, and many others, including humanitarian reasons, a number of individuals and couples choose to adopt from foreign countries where adoption processes might be easier, more affordable, or with fewer restrictions.

Same-Sex Families

Same-sex couples have various similarities to, as well as differences from, different-sex couples. One important difference is that same-sex couples tend to be more reflexive and democratic in their family decisions and practices than different-sex couples. This is particularly the case concerning housework and other domestic duties. Some of the reasons for these differences are related to gender socialization.

Same-sex marriage has become increasingly common in the United States and in many other countries (Winter, Forest, and Sénac 2018). As recently as the 1990s, there was no legal recognition of such marriages *anywhere in the world*, and the prospect of such marriages faced considerable hostility and intolerance. A key event occurred in 2001, when the Netherlands extended the right to marry to same-sex couples. As of early 2023, 34 countries now recognize same-sex marriage with many dozens of others recognizing some form of relationship status between two people of the same sex through the form of things like civil unions or domestic partnerships. Arguments that same-sex marriage would lead to a decline in the value of marriage have not turned out to be true, and support for same-sex marriage has been steadily increasing in many countries around the world.

Many same-sex families also include children. It is estimated that as many as 30 percent of same-sex families in the United States have at least one child under the age of 18. Additionally, it is estimated that up to 10 million children in the United States have at least one parent who is LGBTQ+ identified. In addition to children from previous relationships, or through things like artificial insemination, many same-sex couples also choose to adopt.

U.S. Transportation Secretary Pete Buttigieg (right) and his husband Chasten Buttigieg attend the signing ceremony for the Respect for Marriage Act at the White House in December, 2022. The U.S. Congress had recently passed the landmark legislation to protect same-sex marriage under federal law.

BRENDAN SMIALOWSKI / Contributor / Getty Images

Families of Choice

Most definitions of the family involve connections to other members either by blood relations or by legal relationships. **Families of choice** are made up of individuals that are not related either by blood or a legal bond but who still consider themselves to be a family. These kinds of family relationships have been especially important in marginalized communities whose members might have been rejected by their families of blood.

Families of choice have been especially important to many members of the LGBTQ+ community. The 1990 documentary *Paris is Burning*, for example, discusses "houses," which are not physical structure but rather groups of people who consider themselves to be a family (this idea was also featured in the popular Netflix series *Pose*). Members of the same house usually do not live together, but they do often take on a shared last name to show membership in their family of choice.

THEORIZING THE FAMILY

Whatever the family form, the main types of theories outlined in Chapter 2 and used throughout this book—structural/functional, conflict/critical, and inter/actionist theories—can be used to think about and shed light on the family.

Structural/Functional Theories

Writing in the mid-twentieth century, in the heyday of marriage and the nuclear family, Talcott Parsons, the preeminent structural-functionalist, saw the family as a structure with important functions for society as a whole. The nuclear family was especially important in the world of Parsons's day. Its structure freed family members from the obligations of an **extended family**—two or more generations of a family living in the same household or in proximity to one another—and allowed them the mobility needed in the industrial society of the time.

Of greatest concern to Parsons, and to structural-functionalism, was the need for order in society. An important source of that order is the socialization of children into how they are supposed to act, as well as the process by which they learn the norms, values, and morality of society. The family, especially in the heyday of the nuclear family, played a crucial role in socialization. Furthermore, such a family was more likely than any other family form to communicate a coherent sense of society's culture and morality.

This kind of thinking has been picked up by those sociologists who emphasize the functions of the family.

- First, society must at least replace those who die. This is accomplished through childbearing, which traditionally has been preferred to occur within the family.
- Second, the family fulfills the need to provide physical and emotional care to children.
- Third, the family fulfills the socialization function discussed previously.
- Fourth, the family shares resources to meet its economic needs.
- Fifth, the family provides intergenerational support as parents continue to support their adult children economically, emotionally, and in many other ways.
- Sixth, the family has traditionally served to control sexual behavior. That control varies greatly from one society to another; in American society, whatever control the family previously had over sexuality is in decline.
- Finally, the family is a mechanism for helping children find a place in society, especially in its stratification system.

There are many criticisms of the structural/functional theory of marriage and the family, not the least of which is that it applied best to the realities of the 1950s and is increasingly out of touch with today's realities. Most critically, it fails to acknowledge the expanding diversity of family structures in

Structural/functional family theories tend to emphasize nuclear families and the role they play in raising children, socializing them, and providing them with emotional and economic support.

visualspace/iStockPhoto

the world today. Moreover, structural/functional theory has a conservative bias that emphasizes preserving the status quo and downplays conflict, including the array of family-related problems discussed in the following section (see Chapter 2; Cohen 2018; Smith and Hamen 2016).

Conflict/Critical Theories

Unlike structural-functionalists, conflict theorists have never seen the family as a coherent unit or as contributing in an unambiguously positive way to the larger society. For one thing—as pointed out previously and as discussed later in this chapter—the family itself is riddled with stresses, strains, and conflicts that lead to all sorts of problems for the family, its members, and society as a whole (Cohen 2018; Smith and Hamen 2016). The family is an especially rich arena for conflicts based on gender and age (e.g., sibling rivalries, children versus parents). Such conflicts are closely related to the issue of power within the family—who has the most power, how it is used (and abused), and so forth. Above all, conflict can arise when one or more family members seek to wrest power from those who possess it.

In contrast to structural/functionalists' harmonious view of the family, conflict theorists see the family as an arena of gender conflict in which males have historically been the winners, leaving female family members in an inferior position. Similarly, when it comes to age-based conflict within the family, parents are generally victorious and children relatively powerless.

A key issue in looking at inequality and conflict within the family relates to the resources possessed by the various parties involved. In terms of the conflict between adults and children, parents have a variety of resources, including greater size, strength, experience, and ability to satisfy the needs of the young, and as a result, the young are likely to be dominated by the adults. Among the few resources possessed by the young are their socially perceived physical attractiveness and physical prowess. As a result, girls are often socialized to embellish their beauty while boys are more often encouraged to develop athletic skills (Kimmel 2016). However, as children mature, they acquire other resources and are better able to resist adults. The result is more conflict between the generations as children mature.

Feminist Theory

Feminist theory tends to be critical of the dominant family model—male-dominated, white, middle class, heterosexual, with dependent children. Feminist theorists see the family as being internally stratified based on gender: Men and women have different economic and social positions and interests, and they struggle over those differences. Males have been able to create and to impose a gendered division of labor within the family that benefits men and adversely affects women. The family is seen as a patriarchal structure in which males exercise power and oppress women. Male control is enhanced by an ideological mechanism whereby traditional family norms are upheld. According to the staunch feminist Emma Goldman, "The institution of marriage makes a parasite of woman, an absolute dependent" (cited in Shaw and Lee 2009, 387).

Inter/Actionist Theories

The inter/actionist theories discussed in this section, symbolic interactionism and exchange theory, look at the family from a more microscopic perspective than structural/functional or conflict/critical theories do.

Symbolic Interactionism

Symbolic interactionism focuses on the meanings attached to identities, roles, and social relationships, treating meaning as socially constructed. This approach has long been used in family research (Stryker 1959). For example, men may attach different levels of significance to the role of father, and marital partners may redefine their relationship over time. Examples of research carried out from a symbolic interactionism perspective include Johnson, Kelch, and Johnson's (2017) study of how families cope with a family member suffering from dementia, including the stigmas surrounding the disorder. Sensory engagement (such as visual cues from photographs) and using nonverbal communication (like a smile) with a person experiencing dementia are two important ways family members can move beyond the stigma of dementia as a tragedy or "ongoing funeral."

Exchange Theory

Exchange theorists look at the family from the perspective of choices made based on rewards and costs (Landor and Barr 2018). People enter marital relationships because they think the rewards associated with marriage will outweigh the costs. They also tend to think marriage will be more rewarding than the alternatives to it: remaining single or becoming involved in other kinds of intimate relationships. Heterosexual marriage benefits men and women, although men generally benefit the most. However, both married men and married women live longer, have fewer health problems, have more sex, save more money, and have fewer psychological problems, such as depression, than do unmarried men and women (Cohen 2018).

FAMILY ISSUES

There are a wide variety of issues with, and within, families, but we focus on a few of the major ones in this section.

Family Conflict

As in most areas of life and relationships, conflict is also common to family life. Although divorce is usually seen as the major result of family conflict, conflict often exists long before a divorce, and it may not even lead to divorce. Much conflict simmers below the surface in many families, surfacing only now and then. Family conflicts may arise over such issues as the family's objectives, resources, and the need to protect the interests of various family members.

Abuse and Violence within the Family

Heightened conflict within the family can lead to abuse and violence. This can take various forms, but the most common are parental abuse of children and violence by men against their partners. Far less common is women abusing and behaving in a violent manner toward their children or their partners (although this also certainly occurs). Violence within the family can take emotional or psychological forms. It can also involve physical and sexual abuse. Although norms that relate to the acceptability of such behavior have changed in recent years, such abuse and violence are, unfortunately, still common and accepted in some groups and parts of the world.

Child Abuse

Hundreds of millions of children throughout the world are abused, mistreated, and exploited (Whittier 2016). According to the World Health Organization (2018), parents and authority figures are most likely to be the perpetrators of the mistreatment (physical, sexual, and/or emotional abuse and/or neglect) of infants and young children. In addition to mistreatment, adolescents may also be victims of peer violence or intimate partner violence. In the United States alone, reports indicate that several million children (15 percent) are severely mistreated, but this number reflects only official reports—the actual number is certainly much higher. Furthermore, the official number includes only those who have been the victims of severe abuse and who clearly have been injured. The most common forms of child abuse are parents hitting their child with an object (20 percent), kicking or biting their child or hitting their child with their fists (10 percent), or physically beating up their child (5 percent; Kimmel 2016). Fathers and father surrogates are most likely to commit these offenses.

The impact of child abuse is great, especially for the children involved but also for the parents (or other adults) and larger society. Physical and emotional abuse and violence experienced in childhood can lead to an increased likelihood of cognitive impairment, including lower levels of educational attainment, impaired ability to reason morally and a weakly developed conscience, and a greater likelihood of engaging in violence and crime. Children who have been abused or neglected are themselves more likely to be violent toward other children, including siblings, and later in life to abuse or neglect their own children, their spouses, and even elderly parents (Crosson-Tower 2018).

A cycle of violence and abuse toward children often stretches across several generations. Many of the parents who mistreat or neglect their children were themselves victims as children and, as a result, may have developed mental and substance abuse problems that can increase their own likelihood of mistreating or neglecting others. There is also a cost to society traceable to such things as social services provided to families, the lesser contributions of victims to society, and related criminal justice and health care activities.

Although there are things that can be done to deal with the adults involved in terms of intervention and prevention, the structure of society as a whole needs to be addressed in various ways to reduce this problem. Of greatest importance is the need to change a culture in which children are viewed as property that parents and other adults can treat, and abuse, in any way they want. Children also need to be seen as having human rights. In addition, children need to be better protected, helped, and treated by the various agencies involved. More generally, society and the government need to believe in and support a wide range of policies of benefit to children, such as more and better childcare.

Intimate Partner Violence

Intimate partner violence (IPV), or domestic violence, entails the exertion of power over a partner in an intimate relationship through behavior that is intimidating, threatening, harassing, or harmful. The partner can be harmed physically sexually, emotionally, and/or psychologically; the violence can occur multiple times. A debate in this area is whether IPV should be restricted to physical violence or whether abuse in all of these areas qualifies as domestic violence.

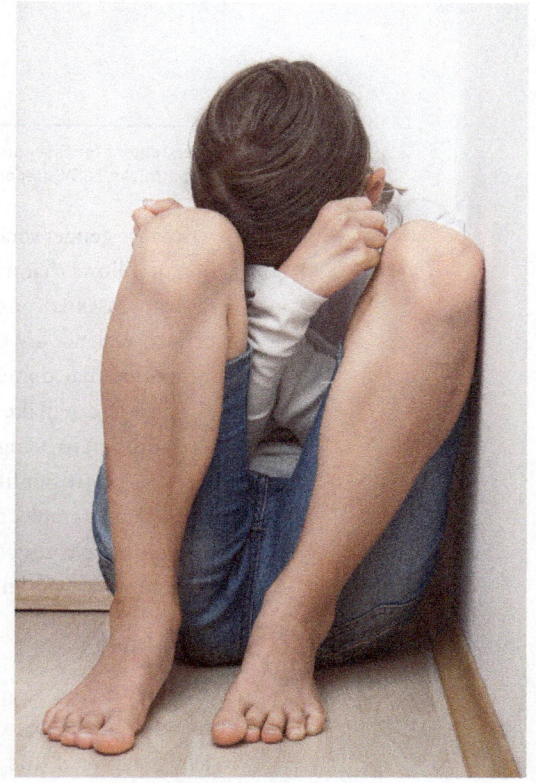

Violence and abuse toward children can be a multigenerational problem. Many parents who mistreat their children were themselves victims as children.

Panther Media GmbH / Alamy Stock Photo

A great deal of research has been done on IPV, including these key findings (National Coalition Against Domestic Violence n.d.):

- Almost 20 people per minute are victims of IPV in the United States, or around 10 million men and women annually.
- 1 in 3 women and 1 in 4 men have been victims of IPV in their lifetime.
- 1 in 7 women and 1 in 18 men have been stalked by an intimate partner in their lifetime.
- IPV accounts for 15 percent of all violent crime.
- Most IPV victims are females 18 to 24 years of age.

Figure 11.5 shows the age at which female victims in the U.S. first experienced contact sexual violence, physical violence, or stalking by an intimate partner. Three quarters of them reported that they were first victimized before age 25, and 1 in 4 were victimized before age 18.

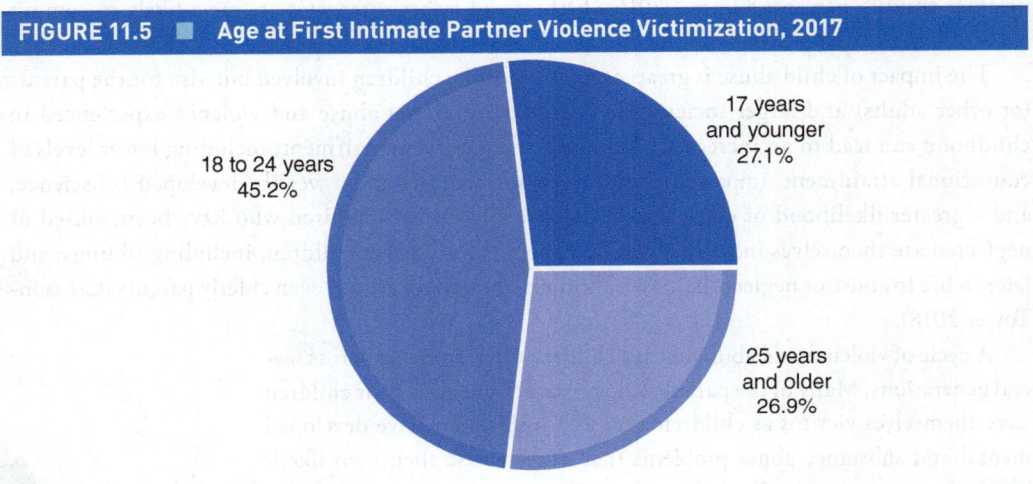

FIGURE 11.5 ■ Age at First Intimate Partner Violence Victimization, 2017

- 17 years and younger 27.1%
- 18 to 24 years 45.2%
- 25 years and older 26.9%

Source: Centers for Disease Control, 2016/2017 Report on Intimate Partner Violence https://www.cdc.gov/violenceprevention/pdf/nisvs/NISVSReportonIPV_2022.pdf

Because gender socialization often leads men to see violence as an appropriate means of communication, it follows that most abusers tend to be men. Heterosexual men and gay men also suffer IPV, as do lesbian, bisexual, and queer people (Cannon and Buttell 2015; Reuter et al. 2017). Men who experience such violence are often discouraged from reporting the crime or seeking social support. Societal assumptions that domestic violence cannot be perpetrated against men, combined with masculine socialization, can make male victims reluctant to report it.

In addition to being very costly to victims and their families, domestic violence is costly to society. Those abused are not likely to be able to function as well in the larger society as those who are not victimized. For example, the abused have higher levels of absenteeism from work. Furthermore, society often needs to pay the costs associated with medical treatment, police involvement, court expenses, and shelters for those victimized.

Elder Abuse

The elderly do not escape abuse merely because of their advanced age. Elder abuse is certainly not new, although it has come to wide-scale public attention in most places only in recent decades (Dong 2017). In a large national study, about 10 percent of elderly respondents reported some type of abuse (Acierno et al. 2010). The elderly are abused in various ways, including physically, psychologically, financially, sexually, and through neglect. Among other things, we know that elderly women are more likely to be abused than elderly men, the very elderly (more than 80 years of age) are most likely to be victims, and adult children and spouses are most likely to perpetrate the abuse. Beyond the elder abuse committed by family members, such abuse also takes place in residential care facilities for the elderly (Reed 2018).

Poverty and the Family

There is a close relationship between family structure and poverty (Cohen 2018). For example, the poverty rate in 2021 in the United States for married-couple families was 5 percent, but for female-headed families it was almost 27 percent—just over five times as much. The likelihood of poverty for female-headed families is much less in many other developed countries, largely because of more generous social welfare programs. The concentration of poverty among female-headed households tends largely to reflect the consequences of gender inequality.

The big debate here is not over the facts but over whether the family structure causes poverty or poverty causes problems within the family. On the one hand, the argument is made that a weak family structure causes poverty. On the other hand, it is contended that poverty causes families to crumble, such as when one parent leaves because they cannot support the family or because a single parent is more likely to qualify for welfare, and the other parent, usually the mother, is left alone to raise the children. The emotional and economic stresses associated with being poor are likely to put intolerable strains on the family.

Being unmarried is likely to be associated with poverty for women with children. Divorce is also likely to drive women, especially those already in a marginal economic situation, into poverty. More generally, divorce is likely to affect almost all women adversely. The only debate in this area concerns how badly women are affected and how much they are hurt economically, as well as in other ways.

Gender Inequalities

Intimate relationships, especially marriages, are often unequal, especially heterosexual relationships between males and females. These inequalities take several forms (Cohen 2018).

The first is inequality in the amount of time devoted to household and childcare tasks (Barnes 2020). Figure 11.6 shows the average number of hours per week mothers and fathers in different-sex households spent on paid work, housework, and childcare in 1965 and 2016. In 2016, mothers on average spent almost twice as much time (18 hours per week) on housework as did fathers (10 hours). Mothers also spent 6 hours more per week on childcare than did fathers. Although the gap has been shrinking since 1965, gender inequalities are still clearly prevalent in the home, even as women's hours

FIGURE 11.6 ■ Average Hours per Week Mothers and Fathers Spend on Paid Work, Housework, and Childcare, 1965 and 2016

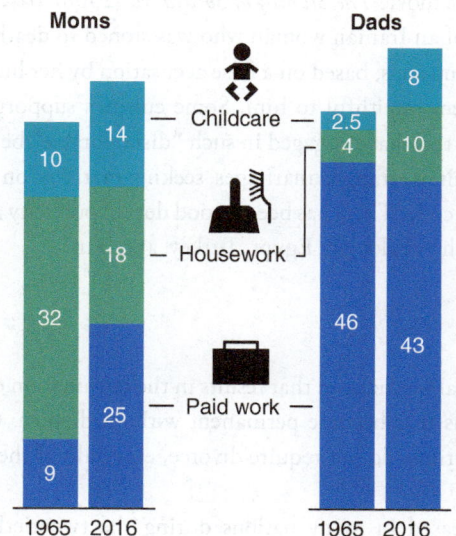

Source: 1965 data from table 5A.1–2, S. M. Bianchi et al., "Changing Rhythms of American Family Life" (2006). 2016 data from Pew Research Center analysis of American Time Use Survey (IPUMS).

of paid work have increased dramatically. In addition, men spend more time on tasks that are discretionary, at least to some degree, while women are more likely to perform regular, repetitive labor. Mothers are more likely to maintain the children, while fathers are more likely to engage in recreational activities with the children. The disparity is even greater when it comes to the care of the ill and the elderly; this is almost always the near-total responsibility of females.

The COVID-19 pandemic powerfully altered parents' time schedules and time pressures as their lives shifted in unique and unprecedented ways. Melissa Milkie (2021) has explored how time spent with children has changed during the ongoing pandemic. She argues that the pandemic changed time *with* children (which increased as they were more likely to be home), *for* children (in terms of paid and unpaid labor), and *toward safeguarding children's futures* (which became more stressful in such uncertain times). In all cases, demands on parents, particularly mothers (when they were present) increased. As one might expect, parents with fewer financial resources suffered worse consequences than those with more resources.

There are often various gender inequalities in power and decision making. As in sociology in general, *power* here is defined as the ability to impose one's will on others despite their opposition. This can involve forcing a spouse to do something or to define a situation in a particular way. In heterosexual marriages, men are often favored in terms of power within the marital relationship, for historical and cultural reasons. They are also likely to earn more money and to dominate conversations, thereby swinging decisions their way. In addition, male power tends to be institutionalized and supported by religious groups and their customs (especially by Evangelical Christians, Hasidic Jews, Muslims, the Amish, and Mormons) as well as by governments and their policies. The latter often assume that husbands are the household heads and are responsible for the support of wives and children, and that wives are supposed to take care of the household and the children.

As we saw previously, women are more likely than men to be the victims of intimate partner violence, even though men are more likely to be victimized by violence in general. In 1993, the United Nations adopted the Declaration on the Elimination of Violence against Women. Within the United Nations, UN Women (previously UNIFEM) is particularly concerned with the violence perpetrated globally against women and girls, especially in the family (see www.unwomen.org/en/about-us). There is a strong preference for male children throughout much of the world, with the result that female embryos are more likely to be aborted, female infants are more likely to be the victims of infanticide, and female children are more likely to be the victims of violence.

Globally, wife beating is the most common form of family violence within the context of heterosexual marriages. In some parts of the world, this is taken to extreme lengths, with wives beaten to death. Brides may be burned to death because of (supposed) infidelity, because the bride's family was unable to pay the dowry in full to the husband, or even because a pregnant 14-year-old bride refused to work in the fields, in one specific case (Mashal 2016). In some parts of the world, women are stoned to death for such offenses. The movie *The Stoning of Soraya M.* (2008), based on a 1994 novel of the same name, tells the true story of an Iranian woman who was stoned to death by members of the community, including her father and sons, based on a false accusation by her husband—who wanted another woman—that she had been unfaithful to him. Some cultures support so-called **honor killings**, or killings of females because they have engaged in such "dishonorable" behaviors as infidelity, same-sex sexual relations, wanting out of arranged marriages, seeking marriage on their own, or even refusing to adhere to a particular dress code. There has been a good deal of publicity about, and public uproar over, honor killings in places such as Pakistan, Egypt, Turkey, and Iran.

Divorce

Divorce is a formal and legal mechanism that results in the termination of legal marriages. Many marriages end with separations that become permanent without divorce. Other intimate relationships, even those that last a long time, do not require divorce, especially if they are not relationships with a legal standing.

Rates of divorce increased in many nations during the twentieth and twenty-first centuries, especially during the COVID-19 pandemic. The United States has one of the highest divorce rates in the world. However, the often-repeated "statistic" that half of all U.S. marriages end in divorce is inaccurate. In 2016, the divorce rate per thousand in the United States was 3.2 (Centers for Disease Control and Prevention 2016b). The once dramatic differences in divorce rates between the United States and Europe have declined, mostly because of increases in divorce across Europe. However, the divorce rate in the United States and several European countries has declined slightly in recent years. For example, 18 OECD countries, including the United States, Belgium, Austria, and Norway, experienced a slight decline of at least 0.5 divorces per 1,000 people between 1995 and 2016 (OECD 2016).

Divorce is often the result of a litany of family problems—for example, violence and abuse—that may have occurred over a long period of time before a divorce was ever contemplated, let alone takes place. Divorce itself can be seen as a problem, as well as one that creates many other problems, but it also can be seen as a solution to many problems. Divorce allows a spouse to get out of a bad, even disastrous, relationship. In fact, to some, it is the relationship, especially a "bad" marriage, that is the problem and not the divorce. Thus, we should not simply assume—as many do—that divorce is in itself a problem.

An important factor in divorce today in the United States, and in the Global North in general, is the increasing emphasis on the self and individualism. This is also linked to the idea of the pure relationship discussed previously. As we have seen, in such a relationship, including a marital relationship, the partners do not necessarily feel they are locked into it for a lifetime or even an extended period of time. Rather, they feel they are in a relationship as long as it continues to work for *them*. Once individuals come to the conclusion that the relationship is no longer working for them, they are free to leave. Indeed, some take the view that they have an obligation to themselves to leave because they should not jeopardize their own need to have a satisfying life.

In the past, there was a tendency to value positively all marriages that remained intact—that did not end in divorce or in other ways. In many ways, a bad marriage can be a far greater problem than one that ends in divorce. For example, children in unhappily married families tend to feel highly neglected and humiliated (Hodgson 2018). As acceptance of divorce has spread, the negative attitudes and social sanctions aimed at those who divorce have declined. Thus, remarried adults are more accepting of divorce and more likely to take steps toward it when experiencing marital distress than are those in first marriages.

As negative attitudes toward divorce have declined, many of the barriers to divorce have eased.
LEE SNIDER / Alamy Stock Photo

Not only have negative attitudes, norms, and values as they relate to divorce declined, but the material circumstances and barriers surrounding divorce have declined as well. Of prime importance is the fact that women today are likely to be better equipped materially to handle divorce than were women in the past. Among other things, they are better educated and more likely to be in the labor force.

Thus, they may be more capable of seeking divorce because they can better afford to be on their own. Changes in the law are another important material factor that has followed from changes in the norms and values that relate to divorce. One important example is no-fault divorce (i.e., when there is no need to show that either party has been guilty of wrongdoing), which not only has made it easier for people to divorce but also seems to be associated with an increase in the divorce rate. No-fault divorce laws have also acted on the larger culture, helping it become even more accepting of divorce.

COVID-19 and the Family

Like everything else in society, the COVID-19 pandemic has had a profound impact on the family. One of the biggest changes, especially during periods of lockdown, was that family members were spending more time physically together. Although some viewed this positively, it was a change for most people to suddenly be spending so much time with other family members. On the other hand, the pandemic meant that people were less able to see other members of their family with whom they did not physically live. This was especially true for those living in retirement homes or those who required long distance travel to visit. Relationships that involved people living in multiple households (e.g., children with parents who do not live together or college students who live both at home and on campus) had to face particular strains in how to negotiate health safety measures.

The pandemic also meant a rapid renegotiation of roles for many families, especially those with children. Children were staying home from school, which meant more time had to be spent caregiving, cleaning, and looking after the child's education. Early studies have shown that a majority of this extra labor was picked up by mothers (when present) in the household, although fathers' participation in childcare also increased during the pandemic.

There has also been a sharp increase in reports of nearly every kind of abuse (child, intimate partner, elder) during the pandemic in nearly every country around the world. Many factors have been used to explain this rise, including increased time spent together in the household, an increase in drug and alcohol abuse, increasing financial strain, and an overall increase in stress and anxiety. These factors also led to a sharp increase in the divorce rate in many countries.

The pandemic will also have long-lasting effects on family structures in a number of ways. For example, it is estimated that up to 10 million children have lost at least one parent or caregiver to the pandemic. Many of these children have been orphaned, entirely without an official caregiver. Many family relationships have been permanently changed, for both worse and better. The economic impacts, most of them more heavily negatively impacting minorities, will also change the ways in which families are structured.

GLOBAL FAMILIES

The meaning of families is changing in an increasingly globalized world, especially accelerated by digital technologies and the COVID-19 pandemic. It is no longer considered unacceptable in many societies for family members to live in different countries, have different passports, be of the same sex, be of different races or ethnicities, or to not share a household in a given locale. Characteristics that used to separate people and made creating global families difficult or impossible are arguably becoming less important in the global age, especially for those with access to digital technologies. National hostilities, religious differences, and even great geographic distances matter less to family formation today than they did in the past (Beck and Beck-Gernsheim 2012).

On the one hand, this clearly makes possible, and even highly likely, a growth of new family types and configurations. For example, it is increasingly possible for family members, even spouses, to live in different countries, even on different continents, and to function quite well as a family (Wilding 2018).

On the other hand, these new realities also create many new possibilities for conflict within the family. That is, family members are now bringing to the family new and far broader stresses and strains of various types; clashes of different languages, cultures, religions, and races create new points of potential conflict and hostility. However, these differences are also likely to enrich the family, as well as the larger society, in various significant ways. As globalization increases, new hybrid forms of the family will almost certainly be created, resulting in innovative and interesting differences within and between families. Families are subject to global flows of all types, and they and their members are increasingly part of those global flows.

Global Flows That Involve the Family

Global flows that involve the family take multiple forms. For example, entire families, even extended families, can move from one part of the globe to another with greater ease than before (assuming they have the resources to do so). They can do so on vacation, in relationship to temporary job changes, or permanently.

Individual family members may also move to a different part of the world. Once they are secure enough economically in their new locations, they are then able to bring over the rest of their family members (if that is even their intention). Of course, it sometimes happens that family members make new lives for themselves in the new locales and leave their families behind in their countries of origin. With increasing economic independence, women are now moving first more often and then bringing the remainder of their families over (or not). However, many women move globally into low-paying, low-status jobs—for example, as care workers—or are moved, by force, into the global sex trade. Such women are unlikely to be in a strong enough economic position to enable other family members to join them.

In terms of children, transnational adoptions generally involve the flow of children from less to more developed countries (Högbacka 2017). The United States is the world leader in the adoption of children from other countries, while very few children from the United States are adopted elsewhere (owing, in large part, to the greater expense and complications of adopting children in/from the United States). Whatever the host and destination countries, adopting a child from another part of the world transforms the family in many ways, including through new complicated questions of culture, language, and issues of rights and citizenship.

This couple from the state of Washington have just arrived in the U.S. with their newly adopted sons from the Democratic Republic of the Congo. In transnational adoptions, children general move from less to more developed countries.

The Washington Post / Contributor / Getty Images

Global Flows That Affect the Family

The global family is affected by, and affects, many other phenomena that make up the global world. We examine just a few of them in this section.

Global Economic Flows

Families are likely to be affected in various ways by global shifts in the economy. For example, a weak economy at home and a boom in another part of the world can lead or even force family members to seek work in the locale that is booming. They are likely to be compelled to leave the rest of the family behind, at least temporarily. This movement of workers can take many forms, such as low-wage male construction workers moving from India or Bangladesh for work in Dubai, female care workers in the Philippines being drawn to Singapore to care for young children or to work as maids in the Middle East, or mostly male workers from many countries drawn to the many low-status, often seasonal jobs available in the cruise line industry. In such cases, families can be broken up for long periods at a time, and the stress of those periods can have permanent negative effects on the marriage, as well as on the children. This has been reduced somewhat in the contemporary world of cell phones, the internet, and social networking, which help maintain family relationships or at least reduce the possibility of them fraying or breaking.

Global Migration

The global family is affected by population flows of various kinds. Of utmost importance is the high rate of global migration, both legal and illegal (see Chapter 15). Among other things, this means that very different people from very different parts of the world are coming together in greater numbers than ever before. Some will settle and marry in diasporic communities composed of people like them; many others will not. Those who do not are likely to create families with people very different from themselves in terms of place of origin, race, ethnicity, religion, and the like.

Global Trafficking

Human trafficking involves selling and buying humans as products. It is likely to affect the family in many ways. Children are sometimes trafficked for the purpose of illegal adoption. As with legal adoption, the children generally flow from poor, weak countries to those that are rich and powerful. Recall from Chapter 9 that women are trafficked for purposes of prostitution and forced marriage, both of which have the potential to disrupt family life.

Global Conflict

Global conflict can affect the family in a number of ways. For one thing, family members, if not entire families, can be forced to flee, sometimes to neighboring countries or even to other parts of the world. For example, after the Vietnam War, more than 2 million people fled Indochina. Many families did not survive intact; in fact, almost 60,000 of the survivors were unaccompanied children. They often were not only traumatized but also suffered from neglect and abuse in the camps in which they found themselves. We are seeing something similar happening with the invasion of Ukraine by Russia. Men between the ages of 18 and 60 (the prime years of being a parent) have been banned from leaving the country while millions of women and children have fled. This will undoubtedly have a long-term impact on many Ukrainian families.

Another impact is the fact that young combatants are the most likely to die in war. This can create a "marriage squeeze," leaving heterosexual women without an equal number of males from which to choose partners (Bethmann and Kvasnicka 2013). Such a squeeze occurred in Vietnam in the 1970s and 1980s. Another has occurred in Lebanon, which has been afflicted with armed conflict for decades. We can assume that such a situation might also occur in Ukraine. Although it is not necessarily true for all wars, it has been discovered that those who served in World War II had higher divorce rates (Pavalko and Elder 1990). Deployment of U.S. troops in more recent wars in Iraq and Afghanistan has also been associated with higher divorce rates (Negrusa, Negrusa, and Hosek 2014). It is also likely that civilians in countries that have experienced armed conflict will have higher rates of divorce.

Then there is the reality of life for military families. Many can become "military nomads," moving from bases throughout the world over the course of their military careers. Although the militaries of many countries have put a lot of supports in place to help families, such perpetual movement can wreak havoc on families, especially in times of deployment during warfare.

The family today is an integral part of globalization, which it is both affecting and being affected by. There is no such thing as a typical global family; at best, there are many global families. More to the point, the people involved in today's families are part, and at the intersection, of innumerable global flows and as a result are enmeshed in constantly changing intimate relationships of all sorts. This may be as good a definition of the family as any in the global age.

SUMMARY

The family is a crucial social institution central to social life. Marriage is a legal union of two people. In an intimate relationship, partners have a close, personal, and domestic relationship with one another. Some relationships are characterized by passionate love with short-lived intimacy, while others involve long-term companionate love based on rational assessment.

Marriage has declined over the years, and so has the traditional nuclear family, which now accounts for only about one-fifth of all households. The social norms associated with marriage have weakened, resulting in a loss of institutional and companionate marriages and the growth of individualized marriages. Many households today are nonfamily households, with a single person who lives alone, or are cohabiting households, composed of couples who are not legally married. Other contemporary households include single-parent families, blended families, and same-sex families.

Structural/functional theorists posit that the family is important to society because of its ability to control adult behavior and socialize children. Conflict/critical theorists see the family primarily as a relationship involving inequality and conflict, particularly between those of different ages and genders. Inter/actionists focus on the meanings and identities associated with the family.

Abuse and domestic violence severely affect many families, as does poverty. Gender inequality in marriages is visible in partners' decision-making and power distribution and in the different amounts of time they devote to household tasks. Some people find their lives enhanced by divorce, whereas others who divorce experience negative effects. For example, divorce tends to have an adverse economic effect on women.

Global flows that affect the family take four major forms: Entire families can move from one part of the globe to another; individual family members can move to a different part of the world and bring the rest of the family later; individuals can immigrate to create new families; and transnational adoptions can bring children from less developed to more developed countries. Global migration, trafficking, economics, and conflict all affect the global family.

KEY TERMS

- adoption
- arranged marriage
- blended family
- cohabitation
- companionate love
- companionate marriage
- deinstitutionalization
- divorce
- endogamy
- exogamy
- extended family
- families of choice
- family
- honor killing
- human trafficking
- individualized marriage
- intimacy
- intimate partner violence (IPV)
- intimate relationship
- living apart together
- marriage
- monogamy
- nonfamily household
- nonresident parents
- nuclear family
- passionate love
- polyandry
- polygamy
- polygyny
- pure relationship
- stepfamily

REVIEW QUESTIONS

1. What is marriage? What are the different types of marriage?
2. What factors account for the deinstitutionalization of marriage over the past few decades?
3. According to structural/functional theorists, why are families so important to society?
4. What criticisms do conflict/critical theorists have of structural/functional theories?
5. What forms can intimate relationships take? Do you think some forms of relationships are valued more highly than others? Do you think these values will change in the future? Why or why not?
6. Explain the growth of nonfamily and cohabiting households. Do you find either of these household arrangements more desirable than a family household? Why or why not?
7. What are the causes and consequences of divorce? What are the benefits and disadvantages of divorce?
8. What are some general conclusions sociologists have made about intimate partner violence? Where is there still debate concerning such violence? What are some other common problems that arise within families?
9. Many sociologists see a close relationship between family structure and poverty. What is this relationship? Does family structure cause poverty, or does poverty cause family problems?
10. In what ways has globalization affected the family?

Michael M. Santiago/Getty Images

12 EDUCATION AND RELIGION

LEARNING OBJECTIVES

12.1 Discuss the purpose of education and its benefits.

12.2 Describe inequality in education, its sources, and its effects.

12.3 Discuss the impact of the COVID-19 pandemic on education.

12.4 Compare the educational systems in different countries around the world.

12.5 Identify the major components of religion.

12.6 Describe the types of religious organizations.

12.7 Describe the relationship between globalization and the world's major religions.

SCIENCE VERSUS RELIGION IN THE PUBLIC SCHOOLS

Proposed by Charles Darwin in 1859 and affirmed by countless twentieth-century biologists, the theory of evolution has achieved consensus as an explanation of the natural origin of humankind over time. In contrast, proponents of the idea of intelligent design see the overwhelming complexity of the universe, including the creation of humankind, as the work of a rational, omnipotent designer, such as a god or other supernatural entity. In the United States, debate has arisen over whether these competing explanations of the origin of humans and the universe should be taught in public schools.

Since 1925, U.S. laws and court cases have challenged the teaching of evolution, creationism (the belief that the biblical God created the universe), and intelligent design in public schools. Advocates of evolution-only science programs cite the First Amendment's Establishment Clause, which supports the separation of church and state and the imperative to teach scientifically valid ideas in the classroom. Many advocates of the teaching of evolution contend that intelligent design has no place in educational courses dedicated to evidence-based knowledge. Intelligent design proponents argue that evolution and intelligent design should be taught equally and that students should be encouraged to decide for themselves which one is valid.

Some religious beliefs are at odds not only with scientific knowledge that is taught in public schools but also with social issues that might be discussed, such as same-sex marriage and abortion. Parents who feel strongly about not exposing their children to ideas and practices that contrast with their religious beliefs often opt to send their children to religious schools or homeschool them. In some U.S. states, parents can use government-issued vouchers, funded by public tax dollars, to pay for their children's tuition at private religious schools. Critics of voucher programs question the constitutionality of this practice, asserting that it violates the separation of church and state. Teaching evolution and other more controversial topics in schools is not a problem exclusive to the United States. For example, the teaching of evolution is banned in Saudi Arabia, Morocco, Oman, and Algeria. In Egypt and Tunisia, evolution is presented as an unproven hypothesis.

EDUCATION

Education is closely related to the process of socialization discussed in Chapter 5 because both involve the learning process. As a general rule, socialization tends to be a more informal process, while education takes place more formally in schools of various types. Much socialization—for example, learning not to eat with one's hands—takes place largely within families in children's early years. Children also usually learn to talk and, in many cases, to read before they begin formal schooling. By the time most children are around five or six years old, the focus has shifted from the highly informal process of socialization in the family to the more formal educational process in schools. Formal educational settings, such as preschools, elementary, middle, and high schools, and colleges and universities, build on and expand the base of knowledge acquired through the early socialization process. In addition, classroom rules teach children about order, respect for authority, and the benefits of conformity. This is often referred to as the **hidden curriculum**, the lessons that are taught informally through the education system. In adulthood, much new learning takes place during socialization processes, such as when starting a new job, but adults also increasingly participate in adult education programs. Overall, some education takes place during socialization processes, and socialization (e.g., orientation when beginning college) occurs in educational settings.

Although five or six years of age is the norm for starting school in many parts of the world, increasingly much younger children are entering preschools. Of course, preschool is only the beginning of the educational process. In most circumstances, education continues for many years, through grade school, middle school, high school, college, graduate school, professional school, and even beyond in formal adult socialization programs. Most people do not progress through all these stages, though the stage at which someone's formal education ends has profound implications for that person's future.

Educational attainment is closely related to employment and earnings. Figure 12.1 shows the correlation between educational attainment and employment and income in 2021. Individuals ages 25 and over with less than a high school diploma were between two and three times more likely to be unemployed than were those with a bachelor's degree; they were more than four times more likely to be unemployed than were those with a professional degree or a doctorate. A person's likelihood of being unemployed in later life decreases as he or she ascends the educational ladder.

Higher levels of education serve as a protection against unemployment, especially in hard economic times. During the Great Recession that began in late 2007, the hardest-hit segment of the population was people with less than a high school diploma. The recession's smallest negative effect was on those with doctoral and advanced professional degrees. The impact of the COVID-19 pandemic was similar with those in more white-collar professions and whose jobs could be done remotely (something that was not a possibility during the Great Depression) faring better than others (Ryan and Nanda 2023b).

Individuals' median weekly earnings increase significantly with level of education, although there is a slight decrease for those with a doctoral degree compared to those who hold a professional degree. Those with a professional degree had the highest median weekly earnings in 2021, at $1,924, nearly four times the earnings of those without a high school degree and almost three times the earnings of individuals with a high school degree. Although there are many other measures of success in life, levels of education and earnings are obviously of great importance (Blau and Duncan 1967). Other individual benefits of having more education include being less likely to commit a crime and being better off in terms of overall health; those with more education are also more open politically (Stewart 2018a).

Those who do not obtain a degree in higher education are sometimes referred to as workers who are Skilled Through Alternative Routes (STARs) and are said to face a **paper ceiling**, an invisible barrier that makes it difficult for those without at least a bachelor's degree to advance in their professional careers. Between 2012 and 2019 in the United States, 69 percent of new jobs that were created required a bachelor's degree or higher for entry. It is important to note that the paper ceiling disproportionately affects minorities, including 61 percent of Black workers, 55 percent of Hispanic workers, 66 percent of rural workers, and 61 percent of veterans (STARS 2022).

Education makes a huge difference not only at the individual level but also at the level of the nation-state. Thus, if we compare nation-states on a global basis, nations with strong educational systems and high levels of education tend to be more economically prosperous.

INEQUALITY IN EDUCATION

A **meritocracy** is a system based on a dominant ideology involving the widely shared belief that all people have an equal chance of succeeding economically based on their hard work and skills. Education is a centrally important institution in a meritocracy because it has the potential to level the playing field and provide equal opportunities for students to learn, work hard, and compete to move up in the social hierarchy.

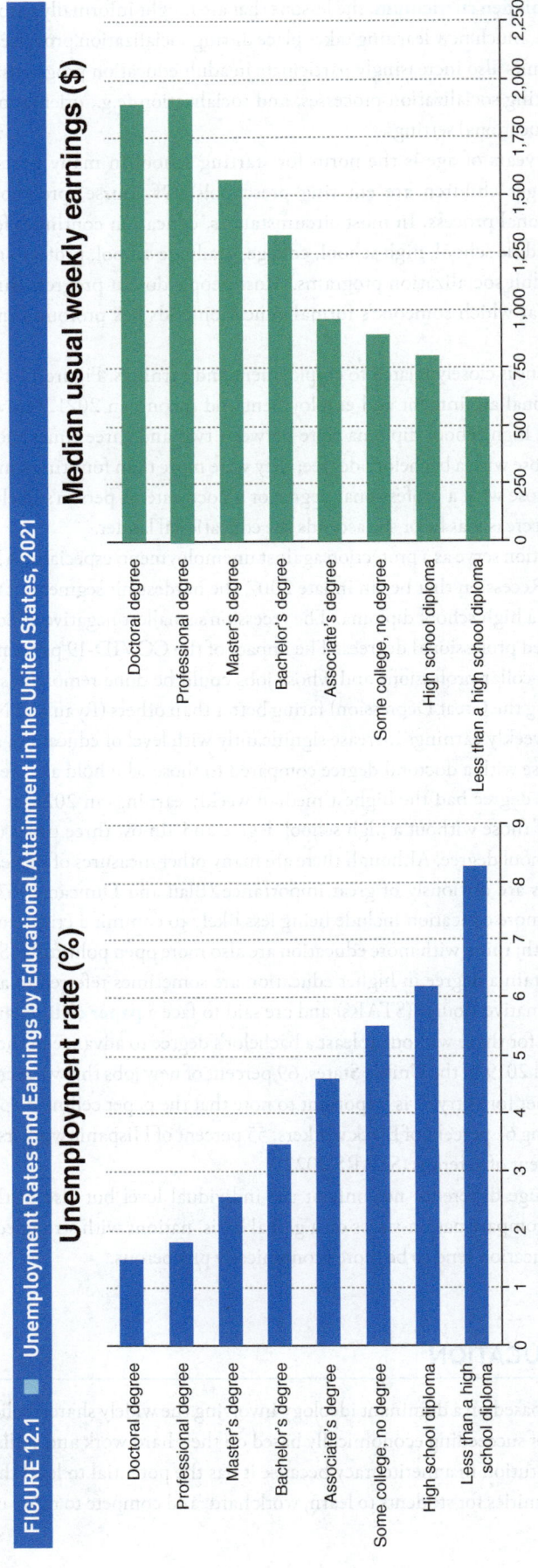

FIGURE 12.1 Unemployment Rates and Earnings by Educational Attainment in the United States, 2021

Source: U.S. Bureau of Labor Statistics, Current Population Survey. https://www.bls.gov/careeroutlook/2022/data-on-display/education-pays.htm

Note: Data are for persons 25 and over. Earnings are for full-time wage and salary workers.

Who Succeeds in School?

In a meritocratic society, we would expect to find that social origin and ascribed status (see Chapter 5) have little effect on how much students learn and how far they go in school.

However, a clear pattern of inequality around the world suggests that most educational systems are not meritocratic. Studies show that students with the highest reading and math scores at the end of high school are those whose parents have the most education. The same pattern is evident if we look at family income and parental occupational status. In terms of race/ethnicity, we see in Figure 12.2 that Asian and White students, both male and female, are more likely than Black or Hispanic students to complete high school and attain a bachelor's or master's degree or higher. Looking at sex differences in the figure, we see that, with the exception of Asians, females generally have better high school completion rates than their male counterparts and are more likely to obtain a bachelor's or master's degree (or higher). Clearly, social origins and ascribed characteristics (race, gender) are strongly related to educational outcomes. To many observers, this suggests that most societies are decidedly unmeritocratic.

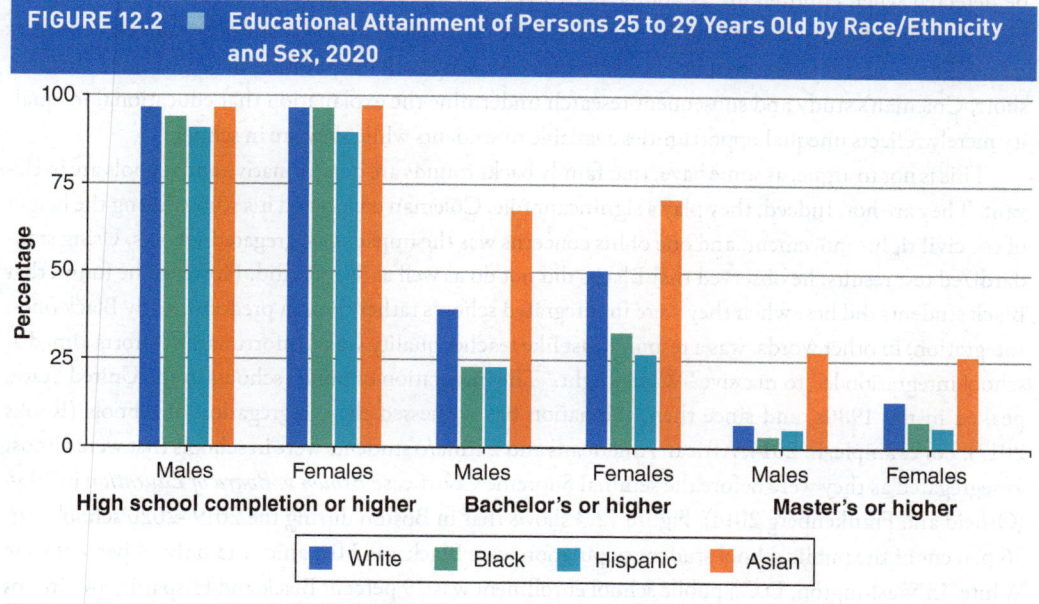

FIGURE 12.2 ■ Educational Attainment of Persons 25 to 29 Years Old by Race/Ethnicity and Sex, 2020

Sources: Data from National Center for Education Statistics, Table 104.20, Percentage of Persons 25 to 29 Years Old with Selected Levels of Educational Attainment, by Race/Ethnicity and Sex: Selected Years, 1920 through 2020.

The Coleman Report: How Much Do Schools Matter?

The first large-scale study of schools in the United States was conducted in the 1960s by James Coleman. Coleman's study was commissioned by the U.S. Congress, and everyone anticipated that the findings would support the conventional wisdom of the time: Differences in student learning reflect inequalities in school quality. Coleman's findings, published in what has become known as the Coleman Report, were a surprise, and they changed the way sociologists understand educational inequality (Downey and Condron 2016; Jackson and Moffitt 2017). Coleman's findings led to a rethinking of the assumption that educational institutions can create equal opportunities that will overcome existing class and racial inequalities in the larger society.

First, Coleman (1966) estimated how much schools differ in "quality." He collected data on teachers' salaries, teacher quality, the number of books in the library, the age of school buildings, the curriculum, and numerous other features of schools. On average, schools were much more similar in these respects than was commonly believed. Subsequent research has supported this finding, and reforms in the past half century have made schools even more similar than they were when Coleman conducted his study.

Second, Coleman found few school characteristics that were related to student learning. School resources, such as per-pupil spending, the books in a library, and so on, did not predict student achievement. In terms of achievement, Coleman found that the most important school characteristics were teacher quality and the family background and racial composition of the students attending the school. Students learned more in schools with better teachers and White, middle-class peers. Finally, Coleman found that the most important predictor of student learning was a student's family background.

Recent research on "school effects" has generally been supportive of Coleman's conclusion that school differences in resources contribute less to educational inequality than has often been assumed. The key point is that schools play a role secondary to that of the different levels of cultural capital students bring to the classroom due to their socioeconomic backgrounds. There have been many studies of the importance of school funding for student learning, and generally the results have been mixed. Numerous studies of public-private differences in student learning have indicated at best only a small advantage in learning for Catholic high school students (Elder and Jepsen 2014), mostly due to more rigorous coursework (see Bryk, Lee, and Holland 1993; Carbonaro and Covay 2010).

Finally, recent large-scale surveys indicate that socioeconomic and racial and ethnic differences in student ability are sizable when children *begin* kindergarten. Furthermore, these differences can be detected when children are as young as two years of age (Hill 2018). Clearly, schools cannot be blamed for producing educational inequalities if the inequalities are present *before students even enter school*. That said, they can often be blamed for exacerbating such inequalities (to be discussed later). In short, Coleman's study and subsequent research undermine the explanation that educational inequality merely reflects unequal opportunities available to students while they are in school.

This is not to argue, as some have, that family backgrounds are determinative and schools are irrelevant. They are not. Indeed, they play a significant role. Coleman conducted his study during the height of the civil rights movement, and one of his concerns was the impact of segregated schools. Using standardized test results, he observed that Blacks did not do as well as Whites did. However, he found that Black students did best when they were in integrated schools rather than in predominantly Black ones. Integration, in other words, was a resource just like teacher quality was. Unfortunately, efforts aimed at school integration led to massive "White flight." The integration of public schools in the United States peaked in the 1980s, and since then, the nation has witnessed the resegregation of schools (Rooks 2017). For example, in 2014, African Americans and Latina/o students were in schools that were almost as segregated as they were before the seminal Supreme Court case *Brown v. Board of Education* in 1954 (Orfield and Frankenberg 2014). Figure 12.3 shows that in Boston during the 2019–2020 school year, 76 percent of the public school student population were Black and Hispanic, and only 14 percent were White. In Washington, D.C., public school enrollment was 79 percent Black and Hispanic, and in Los Angeles, where 65 percent of public school students were Hispanic, only 14 percent were White. The educational achievement gap between Blacks and Whites (Condron et al. 2013) narrowed between the 1960s and 1990s, but since that time, it has remained basically unchanged (Camera 2016; Gamoran and Long 2006; Hansen et al. 2018). There are indications, however, that the COVID-19 pandemic might have again led to a widening of this gap (Ryan 2023).

Although it is certainly not the last word on the debate over the Coleman Report, Downey and Condron (2016) have made the case for a more nuanced and balanced position on the relationship between inequality and schools. That is, some inequalities might be reproduced or even increased by schools, but others (disparities in cognitive skill) may be reduced.

Intelligence and School Success

One possible explanation for Coleman's findings, and those of others, focuses on what are hypothesized as "natural" differences in intelligence. Richard Herrnstein and Charles Murray offered the most widely cited argument in support of this thesis in their controversial book *The Bell Curve* (1994). They argued that educational inequalities are due mostly to "natural" differences in intelligence in human populations rather than systematic differences in educational opportunities. Far more troubling were their claims that Whites had discernibly higher intelligence levels than Blacks and Latinos. However, the consensus of the scientific community is that there are no grounds for contending that there are

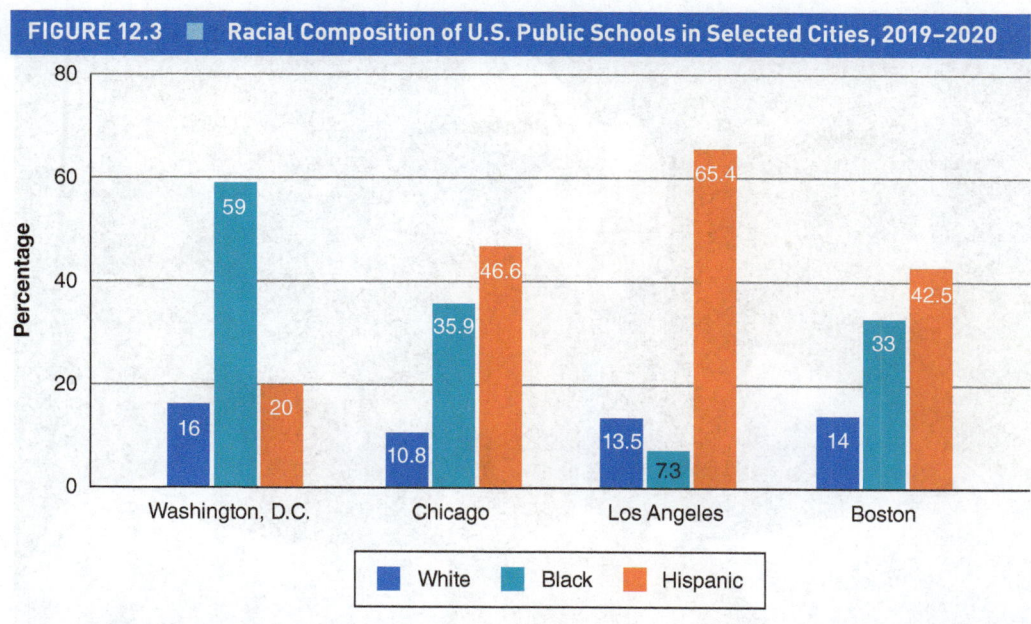

FIGURE 12.3 ■ Racial Composition of U.S. Public Schools in Selected Cities, 2019–2020

Source: District of Columbia Public Schools, 2020, *DCPS Fast Facts 2019–2020*, Washington, D.C.: Government of the District of Columbia. (https://dcps.dc.gov/sites/default/files/dc/sites/dcps/publication/attachments/DCPS-Fast-Facts-2019-20.pdf); Chicago Public Schools, 2020, *Racial/Ethnic Report*, Chicago, IL: Chicago Public Schools. Retrieved August 2, 2022 (https://www.cps.edu/about/district-data/demographics/). Los Angeles Almanac, 2020, *Ethnic Distribution of Pupils by School Districts: Los Angeles County*, Los Angeles, CA: California Department of Education. (https://www.laalmanac.com/education/ed05.php); Boston Public Schools, 2020, *BPS at a Glance: 2019–2020*, Boston, MA: BPS Communications Office. (https://www.bostonpublicschools.org/cms/lib/MA01906464/Centricity/Domain/187/BPS%20at%20a%20Glance%202019–20_FINAL.pdf).

innate intelligence differences along racial lines (Fischer et al. 1996). Angela Duckworth and Martin Seligman (2005; see also Duckworth and Carlson 2013) conducted a study in which students' "self-discipline," such as their work habits and perseverance, was measured and correlated with their grades at the end of the year. The researchers found that a student's self-discipline had a substantially greater impact than intelligence on that student's grades at the end of the year.

Class Differences in Early Childhood

If both school-based and "natural" explanations of educational inequality fail, what remains? Many social scientists have turned their attention to inequalities in children's earliest experiences—the home environment. Betty Hart and Todd Risley (1995) did a fascinating in-depth study of 42 families with children. Each child studied was seven to nine months old when the study began. The researchers visited each family once every month until the children were three years old. For each hour-long visit, Hart and Risley recorded every spoken word and took notes on what happened. They found that the three types of families in their study—professional, working class, and welfare—differed markedly in how they spoke to and interacted with the children. By the time the children were three years of age, there were massive differences in the numbers of words that had been addressed to them among these different families: 35 million words in professional families, 20 million in working-class families, and fewer than 10 million in welfare families. Hart and Risley also found that children in professional families experienced the most encouragement and fewest discouragements by their parents, as well as the greatest diversity in language. In terms of interaction styles, parents in professional families tended to use questions rather than commands to direct children's behavior. They were also more responsive to their children's requests.

Did these differences in home environments matter for early learning outcomes? By age three, children's exposure to differences in parenting practices and styles is highly correlated with vocabulary growth, vocabulary use, and intelligence. These effects persist when intelligence is measured at ages nine and ten. In addition, class differences in early cognitive outcomes are explained almost entirely by differences in parenting. A reanalysis of Hart and Risley's data found that what most mattered in

Students who learn more may have higher IQs, but even more important to their academic success are their solid work habits, self-discipline, and perseverance, as well as mastery of the "hidden curriculum."

Melanie Stetson Freeman/The Christian Science Monitor/Associated Press

children's cognitive development was not social class but the quality of the education given by the parents (Rindermann and Baumeister 2015). However, social class remains important, and the quality of education provided by parents is certainly related to social class.

Annette Lareau (2011) has also examined the impact of differences in the ways that children are raised as one way to help explain different educational outcomes. In her book, *Unequal Childhoods: Class, Race, and Family Life*, Lareau outlines what she argues are two main largely class based strategies of raising children: *natural growth* and *concerted cultivation*.

Natural growth is most common among working classes and is a relatively hands-off approach. Children raised under this style spend more time "hanging out" than in organized educational events, are less likely to question adult authority, and often feel a sense of powerless and constraint. Parents using this style feel that adult life is difficult and that childhood should be a time of play. On the other hand, **concerted cultivation** is a much more engaged parenting style and more common among the upper classes. Children raised under this style spend more time in organized educational opportunities (like piano lessons and sporting events), are more likely to negotiate and question authority, and to experience an emerging sense of entitlement. Parents using this style feel that childhood is a sort of training ground for adult life. In general, schools reward the acquired skills and attributes of those raised under concerted cultivation more than under natural growth.

Preschool

Can we change children's educational outcomes by changing the cognitive culture they experience when very young? Several intensive preschool programs have shown impressive results. From 1962 to 1967, 123 Black children whose families were living in poverty in Ypsilanti, Michigan, participated in a policy experiment (Heckman et al. 2010; Schweinhart, Barnett, and Belfield 2005). Half of the children were assigned to an enriched preschool program (High/Scope Perry Preschool), while the other half—the control group—received no preschooling (Stoolmiller 1999). By the time the program ended, children who had attended the Perry Preschool program for two years were experiencing larger gains in intelligence than the control group. However, this IQ advantage faded only a few years after the program ended. The Perry students performed better in school because they were more motivated to learn. Researchers followed these two groups of students well into adulthood (age 40) and found that the Perry students did substantially better as adults than did members of the control group. The Perry students were more likely to finish high school and college and to hold steady jobs, and they had higher earnings than the control group. Those in the control group were more likely to be arrested and to require public assistance.

James Heckman (2006) has estimated that in the long run, every dollar spent on the Perry Preschool program saved seven dollars in tax revenue. Because the differences in cognitive ability between the two groups were negligible, he attributed the success enjoyed by Perry students as adults to the better social skills they learned in preschool.

Inequality within Schools: Tracking and Student Outcomes

Many studies have examined whether students who attend the same school receive similar learning opportunities. It is common at all levels of schooling in the United States to group students by ability. This is known as **tracking**, which is typically measured by standardized test scores and/or grades. Barr and Dreeben (1983) examined first-grade reading groups in which students were grouped by their reading abilities at the beginning of the year. Students in higher-ability groups learned more new words and improved their reading skills more rapidly than did students in low-ability groups. Better readers were placed in high-ability groups at the beginning of the year. They received more instructional time, were exposed to more new words, and experienced a faster pace of instruction than students placed in low-ability groups. In short, higher-performing students received more learning opportunities than did lower-performing students. Consequently, the gap between high- and low-achieving students grew larger during the year. This process is known as **cumulative advantage**—the most advantaged individuals are awarded the best opportunities, and this increases inequality over time (DiPrete et al. 2006).

As students progress through middle and secondary school, curricular differentiation takes the form of different classes with different content. Traditionally, these curricular tracks are aligned with students' future ambitions: The "high" track entails coursework that prepares students for four-year colleges and professional careers, and the "low" track focuses on basic and/or vocational skills for semiskilled occupations that do not require a college degree. Research consistently finds that high-track classes offer better learning opportunities to students because they are taught by more experienced, higher-quality teachers who have higher expectations of their students (Kelly 2004). Higher-track classes cover more material, and students receive higher-quality instruction (Gamoran et al. 1995). Students in high-track classes are more engaged and exert greater effort in school (Carbonaro 2005), which also helps them learn faster. Research consistently shows that otherwise similar students learn more when placed in a higher-track class because of higher expectations (Karlson 2015), greater effort, and better learning opportunities. Ultimately, high-track students are more likely to attend college than are low-track students.

What determines how students are assigned to different ability groups, tracks, and classes? In a meritocracy, achieved characteristics—hard work and prior academic success—should determine which students have access to high-track classes. Most studies show that prior achievement and grades are indeed the most important predictors of track placement. Because students from high socioeconomic status (SES) families are more likely to be high achievers, they are much more likely than low-SES students to take high-track classes. However, when students with the same test scores and grades are compared, students from higher-SES families are still more likely than their low-SES counterparts to be enrolled in high-track classes (Domina, Penner, and Penner 2017). Thus, high-SES students are doubly advantaged in the track placement process.

Alternatives to Traditional Public Schools

Not everyone attends public schools. For one thing, elite families often send their children to private boarding schools, where they can interact with members of their own upper-class stratum and remain apart from members of other classes (Khan 2011). For another, members of some religious groups opt to send their children to parochial schools to reinforce particular worldviews.

Three major alternatives to public schools have emerged in the past few decades: vouchers, unschooling and homeschooling, and charter schools. Proponents of the various alternatives are highly critical of existing public schools, either for what they claim are shortcomings in educational achievement or for promoting values at odds with their particular beliefs.

Vouchers

School **vouchers** are government-issued certificates that allow students to use public tax dollars to pay tuition at private schools. Parents seeking to remove their children from underperforming public schools find vouchers an attractive alternative. As of 2022, 14 U.S. states and the District of Colombia offered 25 programs relying on vouchers.

Many voucher schools are religious schools. This raises constitutional issues about the separation of church and state and using public money to support religious schools. Moreover, whereas public schools are required by law to accept all students, this does not apply to private schools. Thus, private schools are not required by law to provide special education services if they would have to make major adjustments to do so.

Proponents of school vouchers argue that voucher programs provide parents—particularly poor parents—with options (such as to avoid inadequate public schools) for their children's education that they otherwise would not have. (Betsy DeVos, former secretary of education under Trump, is a major advocate of these vouchers.) In addition, voucher proponents contend that under these programs, the increased competition the local public schools face from private schools stimulates them to enact changes to improve their educational programs. Opponents counter that vouchers encourage the creaming off of the best students from public schools. They question the constitutionality of voucher programs based on the First Amendment. They also express concern that vouchers will reduce funding levels for already underfunded public schools.

Is religious education as relevant today as it was in the past?

Getty Images News/Getty Images

There has been limited research on whether students in voucher schools do better than their counterparts remaining in public schools. However, recent studies conducted in Washington, D.C.; Louisiana; Indiana; and Ohio found that students who used vouchers to attend private schools tended to score lower on tests in mathematics and, in at least one study, in reading (Dynarski and Nichols 2017).

Homeschooling

The popularity of homeschooling has grown, especially in recent years. About 1.5 million children in grades K–12, just under 3 percent of the U.S. school-age population, were homeschooled in 2019 (more current numbers are difficult to obtain, but it is possible that homeschooling rates increased during the height of the COVID-19 pandemic). Roughly 4 percent of White students were homeschooled during that year, compared to 1.2 percent of Black students, 1.9 of Hispanic students, and 2.7 percent of students who identified as some other race/ethnicity (National Center for Education Statistics 2022; U.S. Department of Education 2022). Homeschooling is also growing in many other countries (Donnelly and Huebner 2018), but the United States has the largest percentage of school-age children currently being taught at home (Richardson 2018).

A mother conducts the day's math lesson with her children as part of their homeschooling. Should homeschooling be more heavily regulated by the government, or less?

Harry Lynch/TNS/Newscom

As shown in Figure 12.4, many parents of children who are homeschooled (73 percent) are dissatisfied with the quality of the instruction offered in the public schools and believe their children are not adequately challenged in those schools. Even more parents (80 percent) express concern about environmental factors in schools, such as safety, drugs, and negative peer pressure. However, a large number of parents homeschool their children to ensure they receive religious (59 percent) and moral (75 percent) instruction that the parents do not think can be found outside the home and in traditional schools. Many parents (54 percent) desire a nontraditional approach to their child's education. A smaller number (6 percent) opt for homeschooling because their child has a physical or mental health problem.

As the numbers of homeschooled students have risen, universities have begun to address the need to assess such students as they apply for admission. Based on standardized tests, homeschooled children may, on average, perform slightly better than their public school counterparts, but this is not the case in all regions of the country. Critics point to limitations in much of the research in this area, but more important, they identify two topics that standardized tests do not address. The first has to do with whether homeschooled students have the social skills to function in a diverse society. The second raises concerns about the critical abilities of homeschooled students and whether they look at the world unreflectively, embracing their parents' worldviews.

Charter Schools

Charter schools began in 1992 but have grown dramatically in recent years (Rotberg and Glazer 2018). During the 2020–2021 academic school year there were 7,800 charter schools enrolling 3.7 million students (nearly 7.5 percent of all students in the country; White 2022). Charter schools are a hybrid: They are intended to be alternatives to traditional public schools, but nevertheless they remain part of the public school system. They receive funding from public tax dollars, although they can also

FIGURE 12.4 ■ Percentage of Parents Who Selected Each Reason as One of Their Reasons for Homeschooling Their Child: 2019.

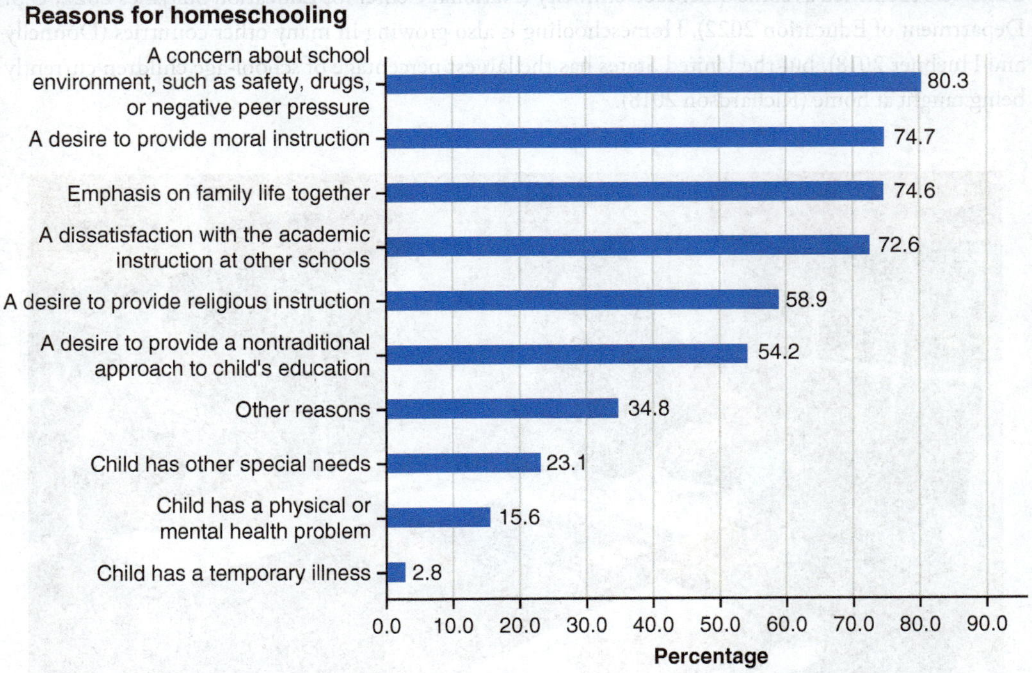

Reasons for homeschooling

Reason	Percentage
A concern about school environment, such as safety, drugs, or negative peer pressure	80.3
A desire to provide moral instruction	74.7
Emphasis on family life together	74.6
A dissatisfaction with the academic instruction at other schools	72.6
A desire to provide religious instruction	58.9
A desire to provide a nontraditional approach to child's education	54.2
Other reasons	34.8
Child has other special needs	23.1
Child has a physical or mental health problem	15.6
Child has a temporary illness	2.8

Source: National Center for Education Statistics, Annual Reports, Preprimary, Elementary, and Secondary Education, 2019.

Note: Homeschooled students are school-age children (ages 5–17) in a grade equivalent to at least kindergarten and not higher than grade 12. Excludes students who were enrolled in public or private school more than 25 hours per week and students who were homeschooled only because of temporary illness.

receive private funding. However, they are not run by the government (although they are accountable to it); they have a separate governance structure that can include parents, teachers, and community and private groups. Charter schools were intended to be schools of choice—alternatives for parents dissatisfied with the local public schools and interested in sending their children to schools over which they had greater control. Unlike private or parochial schools, charter schools do not charge tuition. One thing that distinguishes them from mainstream public schools is that their teachers are not members of teachers' unions. The idea behind charter schools was that they would be more responsive to the concerns of parents and more accountable in terms of ensuring solid student outcomes.

Given the fact that public schools have not managed to provide students in poor communities with the education necessary to become upwardly mobile, a great deal of the interest in charter schools has revolved around assisting the poor—in particular, racial minorities living in neighborhoods characterized by concentrated poverty. These schools are granted greater autonomy than are traditional public schools. They define their own missions and establish criteria for determining whether they achieve their objectives. Charter schools have sponsors, and they are accountable to those sponsors and to the states in which they are located. One of the chief objectives of early proponents of charter schools was to reduce racial segregation in schools by bringing together people who shared a vision of what they wanted for their children's education. At the same time, because the traditional public schools would end up competing with charter schools, proponents argued that the traditional schools would be forced to improve to remain viable.

The results from a quarter century of experience with charter schools are mixed at best (Berends 2015). For one thing, the schools have experienced managerial problems. Somewhere between 10 percent and 15 percent of charter schools have failed and closed. This has led some to propose larger-scale administrative organizations that would overcome some of the shortcomings of existing local charter management (Farrell, Wohlstetter, and Smith 2012). Second, the evidence does not support the idea that racial segregation is being reduced by charter schools. On the contrary, it appears that the self-selection process built into the idea of choice actually increases levels of racial segregation (Glazer 2018). Third, there is no clear evidence supporting the idea that charter school competition results in improved performance of traditional public schools (Silvernail and Johnson 2014).

A 2013 study conducted by the Center for Research on Education Outcomes at Stanford University found that charter schools are improving. But the findings reveal wide differences across states. Table 12.1 shows the performance of independent charter schools relative to that of the traditional public schools in their markets. Students in 29 percent of charter schools demonstrated significantly stronger academic growth than did their public school counterparts in reading, 51 percent were not significantly different, and 20 percent had significantly worse growth than did students in public schools. In math, 30 percent of students in charter schools had stronger academic growth than their public school counterparts, 42 percent had growth that was not significantly different, and 28 percent had growth that was significantly worse. Overall, this is a decidedly mixed picture and does not represent a clear case for or against charter schools. Berends (2015) offers a slightly more positive position. In his view, while the evidence is mixed on student achievement in charter schools, charter school students seem to do better in terms of graduating from high school and attending college.

TABLE 12.1 ■ Academic Performance of Independent Charter Schools Compared to Local Noncharter Schools

	Reading (percentage)	Math (percentage)
Significantly better	29	30
No significant difference	51	42
Significantly worse	20	28

Source: Center for Research on Education Outcomes, Stanford University, "Charter Management Organizations 2017." © 2017 CREDO.

Who Goes to College?

Student learning is an important outcome of schooling, but successfully obtaining educational credentials is critically important for numerous life outcomes, such as income, occupational status, health, and well-being. Figure 12.5 shows that students with more advantaged family backgrounds are more likely to graduate from high school and to enroll in college. Although college enrollment for students from low-income households rose from 31 percent in 1975 to 65 percent in 2016, these students still lagged behind high-income students, who were 17 percent more likely to enroll in college (National Center for Education Statistics 2017).

There are other factors that can play a role in the likelihood of students being able to attend college, including which college they are able to attend. For example, legacy admission is the policy of giving preferential admission treatment to students who have a parent, or another close family member, who attended the same college. Students admitted under these policies are known as **legacy students**. Some studies have found that being a legacy student can raise your chance of admission by almost 20 percent (Golden 2010).

Family background is important not only regarding college enrollment but also graduation from college. Studies from the 1950s through the 1980s found that students from high-income families had a greater likelihood of receiving a college degree. More recent studies, however, suggest that virtually all students—regardless of family background—want and expect to complete a college degree (Schneider and Stevenson 1999). This trend reflects a "college for all" mentality on the part of policy makers, school counselors, and the general public (Martinez and Deil-Amen 2015; Rosenbaum 2001, 2011). This is not only true in the United States; it is a global trend (Marginson 2016).

Students from high-income families are more likely to attend and to graduate from college because they encounter a "college-going habitus" at home and in school; they learn and internalize the "rules of the game," in terms of getting into the right colleges and how to succeed in them

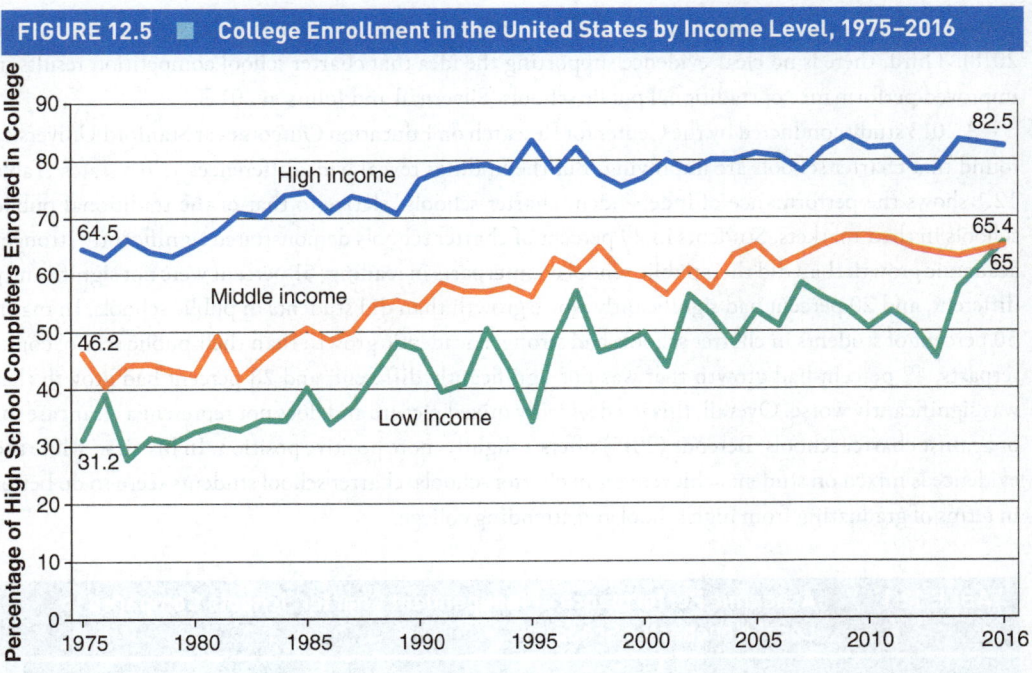

FIGURE 12.5 ■ College Enrollment in the United States by Income Level, 1975–2016

Source: Data from National Center for Education Statistics, Percentage of Recent High School Completers Enrolled in 2-Year and 4-Year Colleges, by Income Level: 1975 through 2016.

(Lareau 2015). A **habitus** is an internalized set of preferences and dispositions learned through experience and social interactions in specific social contexts (Bourdieu and Passeron 1977). For example, children raised in families with highly educated parents may constantly be exposed to justifications of the importance of education in adult life. They may also hear dismissive and derogatory comments that devalue people with less education. It may become clear that education is a critical part of being accepted as a member of the group. Ultimately, children in this situation may not see the pursuit of a college degree as a "choice"; rather, they may see it as an obligation. When minority students enter college, they may come to see the college-for-all ideology as deceptive; as a result, they may not feel ready to take that step (Martinez and Deil-Amen 2015). As students experience different social contexts that do or do not correspond with their family backgrounds, they form different ideas about the importance of college and the role it plays in their lives.

Recently, there have also been a number of high profile cases of celebrities paying (often hundreds of thousands of dollars) to have their children admitted to certain schools. For example, in 2019 Felicity Huffman was convicted of fraud for paying someone to pose as her daughter and take the SAT, and in 2020 Lori Laughlin and her husband were convicted of bribing university officials so that their children could attend prestigious universities.

EDUCATION AND THE COVID-19 PANDEMIC

One of the most important areas in which the COVID-19 pandemic has had a profound impact, and one that is likely to have long-term effects, is education (Ryan 2023). After COVID-19 was declared a pandemic, schools around the world began closing. At the peak, these closings affected more than 1.5 billion learners—more than 90 percent of the student population of the planet—as well as teachers, bus drivers, administrators, and the countless others whose lives depend on institutions of learning (Ryan and Nanda 2023b). In some places, like Kenya, this meant cancelling an entire school year. In other places, like Kazakhstan, it meant several weeks of limbo as institutions tried to figure out what to do (Ryan 2023). In other places, like Tanzania, it meant increasing the use of the radio and television to continue education (Upor 2023). For example, in Ghana, the Ministry of Education partnered with the Ghana Broadcasting Corporation to launch a 24-hour free-to-air channel to provide remote learning opportunities. This channel was available across all of Ghana as well as several other countries across West Africa. Television and radio as means of broadcasting educational initiatives were also used in Nigeria, Uganda, Cuba, Serbia, and several other countries around the world, mostly in low- and middle-income countries. For many students, however, the pandemic led to a turn to emergency remote learning, or online education. The term *pandemic pedagogy* refers to the ways that teaching and learning are modified during a global health crisis.

Learning Outcomes During the Pandemic

Tony Breslin (2021) has suggested that there were at least three types of learners during the pandemic: lockdown thrivers, lockdown survivors, and lockdown strugglers. A **lockdown thriver** is someone with access to good computing technology (most likely at home) as well as stable and sufficient broadband availability. They also tend to be more independently driven learners and to live with someone who has cultural and educational capital. A **lockdown survivor** is someone who is able to get by but who was likely to be ready for a return to face-to-face teaching and learning. Finally, a **lockdown struggler** faced a more difficult time during the sudden switch to online education for a number of reasons, including a lack of access to technology, overcrowded or noisy living conditions, economic struggles, or anxiety. It is important to note, however, that most students moved back and forth between these experiences. As Breslin (2020) notes, "schooling in lockdown did not deliver a single experience to all young people, or a consistent experience to most."

The ability to access the internet was arguably the most important determinant of how students fared during the pandemic. As Corsi and Ryan (2022) noted, "As students and faculty alike experienced a rapid transition to online learning (at least those lucky enough to have digital access; the digital divide has perhaps never been so obvious), there were radical changes in what it meant to be both student and teacher." In short, those who could access the internet did better than those who could not, although it is important to recognize that there were wide variations in terms of access, broadband availability, access to a quiet place to study, and other important factors. Thus, although internet access has not been the only deciding factor (and far from it), it was at least often the most important starting point for continuing education during the pandemic.

A student in Reading, Pennsylvania completes an assignment on her iPad. Ability to access the internet at home was a key factor in how students fared when COVID-19 interrupted in-person learning.

MediaNews Group / Reading Eagle via Getty Images

Pandemic Impact on Minority Students

Although all students were impacted by the COVID-19 pandemic, minority students were hit particularly hard, including females, racial and ethnic minorities, gender and sexual minorities, and students from economically disadvantaged families.

Women have historically been disadvantaged in the education system for a variety of reasons, including historically being denied admission to many institutions and greater difficulty in accessing institutions of learning due to economic, cultural, and religious reasons. The closing of schools and a move to at-home learning also meant that many women had to take on an even larger role in terms of childcare and household responsibilities. A loss of income for many households also meant that many women had to work outside the home, often in jobs that exposed them more to the virus (Ryan 2023).

Even after a return to campus, many women still show increased signs of struggling. A report by the National Survey of Student Engagement (2021) found that 74 percent of first-year female students and 72 percent of female seniors reported mental or emotional exhaustion as compared to 57 percent and 56 percent of male respondents, respectively. There are multiple potential reasons for this including still having increased housework responsibilities, financial pressures, and fallout from an increased burden of emotional labor over the last several years.

There were also significant impacts on racial and ethnic minorities as a result of educational disruption during the pandemic. For one, racial and ethnic households tend to be correlated with lower incomes. Many Black and Hispanic students were also disproportionately affected due to existing racial inequalities in school spending and unequal access to high-quality teachers. A disproportionate number of racial/ethnic minority parents either lost their jobs or were forced to work in jobs where the risk of contracting the virus was higher.

A report by the Black Education Research Collective (Horsford et al. 2021) found that a history of systemic racism, coupled with the impact of the pandemic, had a disproportionate effect on Black students in the United States. Their survey found that 60 percent of respondents had a member of their household who was an essential worker employed in unsafe conditions and that 85 percent indicated their mental health and wellness had been negatively impacted by the pandemic.

The sudden switch to emergency online learning also posed particular challenges for racial and ethnic minorities. For one, racial and ethnic minority students are more likely to be living in households without stable internet access. According to a report by the UCLA Center for Neighborhood Knowledge, limited access to computers and the internet was found in 1.3 to 1.4 times as many Black and Hispanic households in the United States with school-aged children as it was in White households, with more than 40 percent of low-income households having just limited access (Ong 2020).

Gender and sexual minority students have also been particularly hard hit by the pandemic. A report by the Williams Institute (Conron, O'Neill, and Sears 2021) found that during the early years of the pandemic, nearly three times as many LGBTQ-identified students reported that they did not have reliable internet or a quiet place to study as compared to their non-LGBTQ counterparts (9.5 percent vs. 3.3 percent, respectively). That problem was especially pronounced among trans students versus cis-identified students (30.6 percent vs. 4.5 percent, respectively). Another problem for LGBTQ students was housing disruption, with 30.9 percent reporting housing issues (versus 16.9 percent of non-LGBTQ students). For many LGBTQ students, the loss of campus housing more often meant a return to nonsupportive environments, an increased risk of homelessness, and the loss of a supportive community.

Students from low-income households were also particularly hard hit by the pandemic. A study by Kayitsinga (2021) found that "[t]he odds of online learning or distance/other way learning increase significantly by education and household income, whereas the odds of class cancellation decrease by respondent's education and household income." A lack of access to digital technologies, a quiet place to study, and having to share technologies was also more common among students in low-income households. Many students around the world are also dependent on a variety of free and reduced school food programs to meet their nutritional needs. In the United States alone, some 30 million students rely on school lunch programs (Turner and Kamenetz 2020). Although a variety of initiatives were put in place to help those students, many still faced increased hunger.

As interest in the pandemic is waning, many educational institutions are looking for ways to move past, or at least live with, the life-threatening SARS-CoV-2 virus. Even before the pandemic, education was already becoming increasingly politicized, especially in the United States with the shocking number of school shootings that happen every year and the recent attacks on teaching critical race theory (CRT) and topics related to nonheteronormative identities. The future of education is likely to become increasingly politicized, but the best way forward is to find a solution that has the best interests of students and faculty, including their health, in mind.

GLOBALIZATION AND EDUCATION

Education systems around the world vary greatly, including in terms of tracking, expectations, cost, content, and attendance. It is important to better understand how these systems are different and what the consequences of those differences are.

PISA Rankings

The Program for International Student Assessment, or PISA, is a worldwide study of student educational performance. The Organisation for Economic Co-operation and Development (OECD) created the program in 1997. Since 2000, it has measured the proficiency of 15-year-olds in reading, math, and science every three years. Critics have pointed to shortcomings in the assessment, but it remains the best comparative portrait we have today. Figure 12.6 shows the top-performing nations in 2018, when the most recent test was carried out. Students in Asian countries consistently garnered the highest scores in math, reading, and science. Especially worrisome for the United States is the fact that students there ranked well below other countries with similar levels of development—37th in math, 13th in reading, and 18th in science.

Educational experts have been especially fascinated by Finland's consistently high rankings over the years and have pondered whether it may be possible to translate the lessons of the Finnish case to other countries (Sahlberg 2018). What does the Finnish educational system look like? First, teachers are well trained. Gaining acceptance into teacher training programs in universities is competitive. Teachers are not extravagantly paid, but they are paid well, and the teaching profession remains highly respected. Teachers are unionized, a fact that undercuts the argument of conservatives in the United States and elsewhere that teachers' unions have been detrimental to the delivery of quality education. Indeed, there is evidence that teachers in Finland exhibit a high level of accountability, not because of imposed standards but because of their commitment to their profession.

Second, Finland has not embraced any of the policies pursued in recent decades in the United States, including charter schools, vouchers, merit pay for teachers, and evaluation of teachers and schools in terms of how well they perform on standardized tests (Ravitch 2012).

Third, Finnish schools perform at remarkably similar levels. In other words, there is less variation in achievement across the educational system than there is in other countries (Sahlberg 2011). This has led educational reformer Diane Ravitch to conclude that Finland comes "closest to achieving equality of educational opportunity" (2012, 19). This commitment to equal opportunity means, among other things, that school funding is uniform and equitable. The school system reflects the larger national culture, which has been shaped for many decades by a social democratic commitment to equality and a welfare system that promotes it.

German, Japanese, and U.S. Education Systems

As we have seen, the U.S. schooling system does not eliminate inequality in student learning outcomes. Sometimes it compensates for other inequalities, sometimes it reinforces these inequalities, and sometimes it increases educational inequality. Other nations have structured their educational systems differently. These institutional differences have important implications for inequalities in learning among students.

FIGURE 12.6 ■ PISA Scores for Math, Reading, and Science, Top Countries, 2018

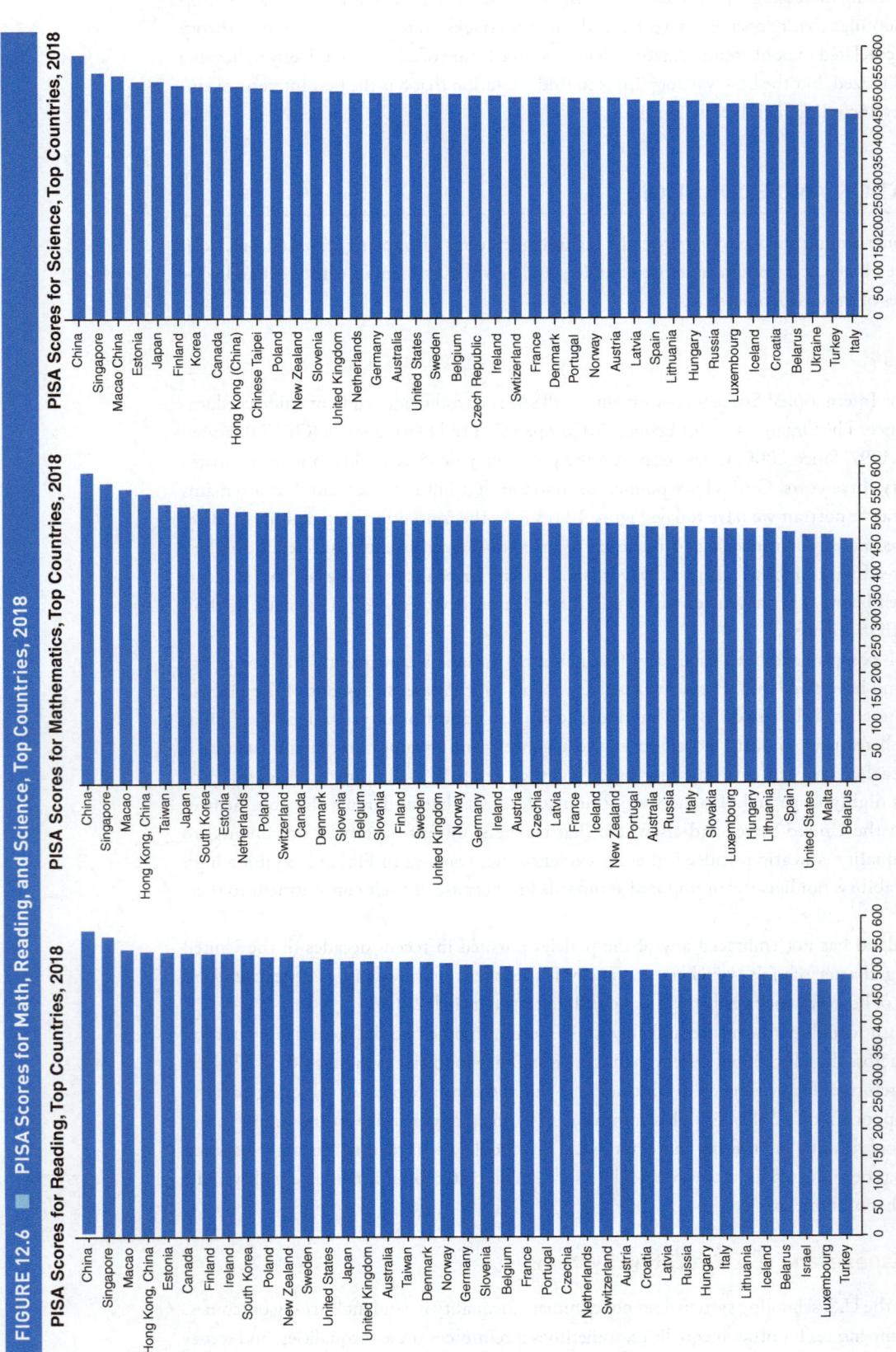

Source: Schleicher, Andreas, 2019, *PISA 2018 Insights and Interpretations*, pp. 6–8, Paris, France: Organisation for Economic Co-operation and Development. Retrieved August 2, 2022 (https://www.oecd.org/pisa/PISA%202018%20Insights%20and%20Interpretations%20FINAL%20PDF.pdf).

Three schooling systems—those in Germany, Japan, and the United States—are compared to illustrate how different nations allocate learning resources to students who will occupy different positions in the social hierarchy.

In Germany, all elementary school students attend *Grundschule*, which does not practice ability grouping; all children are exposed to the same curriculum. At the end of fourth grade, teachers make a recommendation to each child's family regarding the type of secondary school the child should attend, based on his or her test scores and the teachers' subjective assessments of the student's ability. Three types of schools represent academic and vocational tracks: *Gymnasium* (the college track), *Realschule* (the middle track), and *Hauptschule* (the lowest track). Each of these has its own curriculum designed to correspond with the future occupational trajectories of its students. Only 30 percent of students are placed in the *Gymnasium* level. Transferring to a different track is possible, but it is difficult and rare. Between-school tracking continues at the next level of schooling, and only students who attend upper-level *Gymnasium* can proceed to the university system and attain the equivalent of a baccalaureate degree.

Japan has a very different system of educational stratification. From school entry through ninth grade, there is little or no ability grouping among students, either between or within schools. For the first nine years of school, Japanese students are exposed to a remarkably uniform curriculum. At the end of ninth grade, Japanese students take a high-stakes test that determines which type of high school they will attend. About 75 percent of students attend *futsuuka*, which has a college preparatory curriculum. The remaining 25 percent of students attend a variety of technical and vocational schools. Family background still plays an important role in educational success for Japanese students because of a "shadow education" system, in which informal schooling opportunities outside school give more advantaged students better preparation for both high school and college entrance exams.

The German and Japanese systems highlight key features of the U.S. public schooling system. Education in the United States has always been organized around the "common school" ideal: All students in the United States, regardless of their class origins and their future aspirations, attend the same types of schools. Tracking occurs within schools, not between schools. The United States also has more variability in school quality by geographic region. The German and Japanese systems are centralized, while in the United States, each state has a different educational system with different levels of funding and varying curricula. Consequently, the quality and character of a student's education is likely to be affected by where the student's family lives more so than in Japan and Germany.

These differences have implications for achievement outcomes in each nation (Montt 2011). Germany has the highest levels of achievement inequality because of its highly stratified system. Japan has higher average achievement than Germany but much less inequality in outcomes because it does not practice curricular differentiation until very late. The United States has the lowest average achievement and the least variability of these three nations.

Two features of educational systems are significant for student outcomes. First, nations with highly differentiated school systems—with between-school tracking—have more unequal learning outcomes for students, and family background tends to matter more for student outcomes (Van de Werfhorst and Mij 2010). Second, standardization—the degree to which the curriculum and examinations are the same across schools—produces less inequality in student outcomes and a weaker correlation between family background and achievement. Thus, institutions do matter greatly, and the choices nations make have important consequences for how learning is distributed within society.

One additional factor worth noting is the fact that public education in other advanced countries, most notably Germany, is much better funded than in the United States (Dumas 2018). This allows for, among other things, a greatly enriched curriculum, not only in basic areas (such as math and science) but also in optional offerings (e.g., computers, chess, low-cost trips to museums and nearby countries). A *Gymnasium* can have facilities equal to those at top universities. Unlike in the United States, there is no need to hold fundraisers (e.g., bake sales) in order to help finance public education in Germany.

RELIGION

Religion is of great importance to billions of people throughout the world. Similar to education, religion is related to socialization. Religious institutions and organizations teach their members particular beliefs and rituals that shape their identities and influence their behaviors. Some of this religious socialization occurs within educational institutions run by religious groups, such as madrassas (Muslim schools) and parochial schools. Furthermore, as the opening vignette of this chapter illustrates, religious beliefs can influence what is taught even in public schools.

The definition of religion employed here is largely derived from Émile Durkheim's ([1912] 1965) classic statement: **Religion** is a social phenomenon that consists of beliefs about the sacred; the experiences, practices, and rituals that reinforce those beliefs; and the communities that share similar beliefs and practices (Kurtz 2016).

Components of Religion

Three of the major components of religion are beliefs, rituals, and experiences.

Belief

Every religion has a set of interrelated **beliefs,** or ideas that explain the world and identify what should be sacred or held in awe—that is, the religion's ultimate concerns. Many religious beliefs have been shaped over thousands of years; they are embedded in religious traditions and also serve as the "raw material" for new religious beliefs, and even new religions.

Durkheim wrote that religion deals with "things which surpass the limits of our knowledge" ([1912] 1965, 14). The **sacred** is what is extraordinary, set aside, and of ultimate concern and leads to awe and reverence. People can come to *believe* that virtually anything is sacred—a particular god or gods, a place (Jerusalem, Mecca), a particular time or season (Ramadan, Diwali), an idea (freedom), or a thing (an animal, a mountain, a tree, a canyon, a flag, or a rock). The sacred is treated with respect, and one's relation to it is often defined in rituals: For example, you might bow your head when passing in front of an altar or take off your shoes or cover your head when entering a mosque or temple.

The **profane**, in contrast, *is* the ordinary and mundane. People believe that anything not considered sacred is profane. The important distinction here is that what is considered sacred is a question of the value that individuals attribute to it. For example, the Bible is arguably just a book, printed on the same paper, and often on the same press, as other common books. In that way, it could be considered profane. However, many people, especially Christians, consider the Bible to be sacred, and thus treat it with specific reverence (e.g., by never placing anything on top of it or setting it on the floor).

Beliefs are often presented in sacred stories and scriptures. They address questions about the origin and meaning of life, theories about why the world was created, and explanations of suffering and death. They first express a **worldview**, that is, a culture's most comprehensive image of the ways in which life—nature, self, and society—is ordered (Geertz 1973). That worldview, in turn, shapes an *ethos*, which "expresses a culture's and a people's basic attitude about themselves and the world in general" (Geertz 1973, 173). These beliefs are at the same time both models of and models for reality. They provide believers with information and a framework for interpreting the world around them.

One of the most difficult dilemmas for any religion is to explain why good people suffer and bad people sometimes flourish. Although the suffering of the righteous is problematic, most religious explanations suggest that ethical behavior will eventually be rewarded. Most mainstream religions suggest that suffering is just part of the way the universe functions, so everyone is subject to it at one time or another. It is how you deal with suffering that is most important.

Ritual

In most religious traditions, simply believing is never enough; one also has to act. The belief systems of religious traditions are loaded with rituals that reinforce those beliefs, serve as reminders, and help believers enact their beliefs in the world. A **ritual** consists of regularly repeated, prescribed, and traditional behaviors symbolizing a value or belief. Rituals are enacted during ceremonies and festivals, such as funerals, weddings, and baptisms. Rituals are a central part of the **rites of passage** that accompany major transitions in life, such as birth, puberty, marriage, economic crises (O'Loughlin et al. 2016), and death (Hochner 2018; van Gennep 1961). Also included under the heading of rituals are ongoing spiritual practices, such as personal prayer and attending worship services of faith communities, as well as elements of everyday language that serve as religious reminders for many people.

Rituals come in many forms. Some, such as prayer, chanting, singing, and dancing, help people communicate with or show devotion to the gods. Some, such as mantras and meditations, help believers organize their personal and social lives. Some frame daily life, such as those relating to diet, hygiene, and sexual practices, while others celebrate cycles of nature and build community, such as holidays, seasonal festivals, and processionals.

The waters of the Ganges are considered sacred to the pilgrims who bathe there. What do you consider sacred?

Sheeraz Rizvi/Hindustan Times via Getty Images

Rituals solve problems of personal and collective life by providing time-tested actions, words, and sentiments for every occasion. When addressing a serious problem, such as death, violence, natural disaster, or social crisis, people often use rituals to do the following:

1. Identify the source of the problem.
2. Characterize it as evil.
3. Mark boundaries between "us" and "them."
4. Arrive at some means of working toward a solution, or at least the satisfaction that they are doing something about the problem.

In times of crisis, rituals can help people deal with tragedy and offer an opportunity to strengthen social bonds. Consider the ways in which people create and repeatedly visit memorials at the sites of tragedies. Recent examples include memorials at the site of the former World Trade Center in New York City; the site of the 2015 attack on the Bataclan concert venue in Paris, France; the 2016 shooting at the Pulse nightclub in Orlando, Florida; and the 2018 killings at a Pittsburgh synagogue. These memorials often involve prayer candles and services with clergy, similar to what one would find in a house of worship. Such rituals build a sense of solidarity that provides support for the suffering and reinforces the authority of the social order and the institutions that sponsor the rituals, especially when they are being threatened. Rituals can also provide a theory of evil and focus participants' attention on some abstract issue, a personified devil or mythical figure, or a human enemy who needs to be denounced or attacked.

Religious rituals often mark a **liminal period,** or a special time set apart from ordinary reality (Turner 1967). The sacred time during a religious ceremony may involve an inversion of apparent reality, giving hope for the oppressed that they will be liberated, for the sad that they will be comforted, and for the last that they shall be first. In the traditional Catholic Carnival ritual preceding Lent (a period of penitence), the norms of appropriate behavior appear to be suspended as the celebrants sing, dance, and drink to excess.

Family members of victims of the 9/11 terrorist attacks on the World Trade Center leave flowers and American flags at the National 9/11 Memorial on the 20th anniversary of the event. Makeshift memorials are a form of ritual that can provide comfort after a tragedy.

Ed Jones/Getty Images

Experience

The combination of beliefs, rituals, and other practices forms the variety of religious experiences for believers, regardless of which tradition they celebrate. Much of the human community views the world through a religious lens and constructs an identity around religious affiliation and experiences, such as prayer or attendance at religious services. In a survey of 40 countries, large numbers of people, especially in sub-Saharan Africa, the Middle East, and parts of Asia, reported that religion is very important in their lives (see Figure 12.7). Interestingly, a negative relationship exists between wealth and religiosity, with people living in poorer nations being more religious than those in wealthy countries. The major exception is the United States, where 53 percent of respondents report that religion is very important to them. Religion is much more important to people in the United States than it is to people living in other wealthy nations, such as Germany, Britain, and Japan (10 percent), and France (11 percent). In many sub-Saharan countries, no fewer than eight in ten people report religion as very important. Nine in ten of those in the predominantly Muslim countries (such as Indonesia and Pakistan) view religion as very important.

Although religion remains important to most people in the United States, young people do not necessarily accept this view. They—and many others—are increasingly religiously unaffiliated. Well over one-third of those 18 to 29 years of age were unaffiliated in 2020 compared to only 10 percent in 1986. The number of unaffiliated drops steadily with age; only 14 percent of those over age 65 reported being unaffiliated in 2020 (see Figure 12.8). However, according to a recent Pew (2018) survey, 80 percent of all adults say they believe in God.

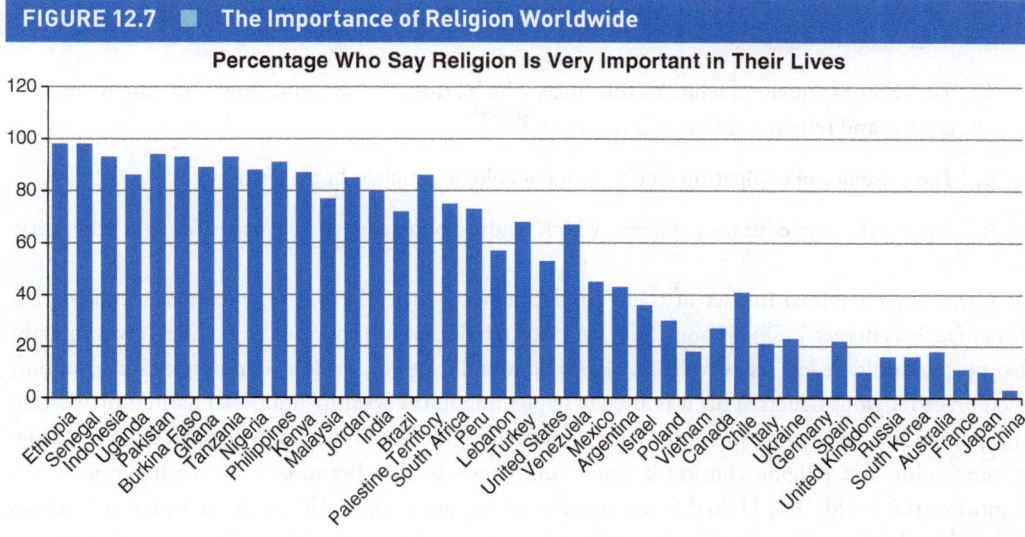

FIGURE 12.7 ■ The Importance of Religion Worldwide

Source: "The Age Gap in Religion Around the World," Pew Research Center, Washington, DC (13 June 2018) http://www.pewforum.org/2018/06/13/the-age-gap-in-religion-around-the-world/

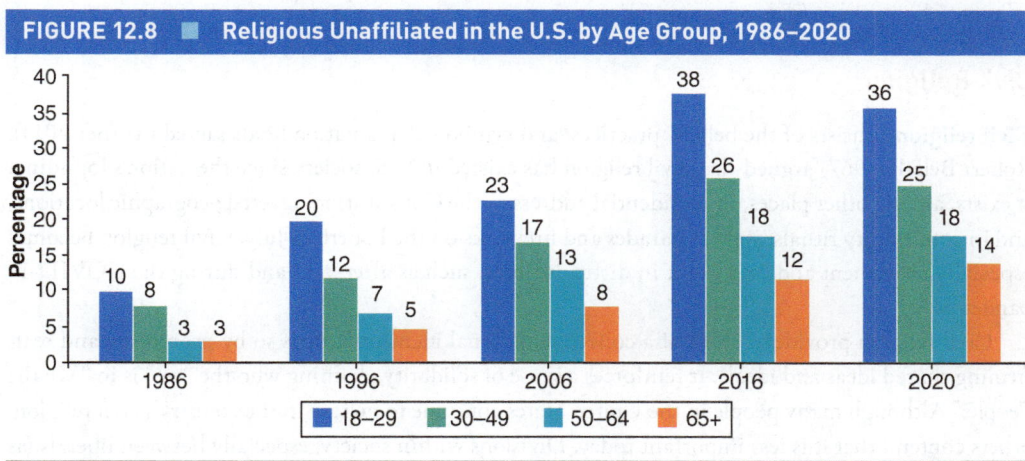

FIGURE 12.8 ■ Religious Unaffiliated in the U.S. by Age Group, 1986–2020

Source: General Social Survey, 1986, 1996, 2006; PRRI American Values Atlas, 2016, 2020. https://www.prri.org/research/2020-census-of-american-religion/

Secularization

Secularization is defined as the declining significance of religion (Voas and Chaves 2016). It occurs at both the societal and individual levels. At the societal level, it can involve the declining power of organized religion as well as the transfer of functions such as education from religion to the state. At the individual level, secularization means that individual experiences with religion are less intense and less important than are other kinds of experiences.

Secularization includes historical developments that have lessened the power and importance of religion. Secularization is often accompanied by an increased respect for science and a move away from faith to relying on scientific evidence. Among the mechanisms seen as contributing to it are the following:

1. The rise of scientific thinking as an alternative way of interpreting the world (the scientific perspective encourages skepticism and doubt, thereby challenging ideas of pure faith and the certainty of religious belief)

2. The development of industrial society, particularly when it results in relative affluence and thus encourages materialism and downplays otherworldly concerns

3. The rise of governments that do not mandate or promote an established religion, or even discourage or outlaw it
4. The encouragement of religious tolerance, which leads to a "watering down" of religion in general and religious differences in particular
5. The existence of competing secular moral ideologies, such as humanism
6. A general rise in educational levels, which tends to be associated with lower levels of religiosity

Given the combined impact of these developments, by the 1960s, proponents of secularization theory (such as Berger 1969; Wilson 1966) assumed religion would continue to decline. It was thought that people would be less likely to believe in God, attend religious services, join religious institutions, or embrace religious beliefs. This was already happening in the wealthy industrial nations of Western Europe, the first to become "modern," and it was believed it would inevitably happen elsewhere, too, at some point. But religion continued—and continues—to be vibrant, even increasingly powerful, in most of the world. The United States remains a religious nation. Although the belief in God has declined in the United States since the 1980s, the fact that 80 percent of people there still believe in God makes it clear that the United States is an exception to the secularization thesis. In fact, given this reality, as well as the rise of Islam in much of the world, it is the more secularized Europe that increasingly looks like the exception. Two examples of secularization are civil religion and the ways in which religion is becoming a form of consumption.

Civil Religion

Civil religion consists of the beliefs, practices, and symbols that a nation holds sacred (Turner 2014). Robert Bellah (1967) argued that civil religion has existed in U.S. society since the nation's founding. It exists, among other places, in presidential addresses, the Constitution, revered geographic locations, and in community rituals, such as parades and fireworks on the Fourth of July. Civil religion becomes especially prominent and important in difficult times, such as after 9/11 and during the COVID-19 pandemic.

Civil religion provides a sense of a collective national identity. It does so by promoting and reaffirming shared ideas and ideals. It reinforces a sense of solidarity, defining who the "we" is in "We the People." Although many people in the United States continue to believe in the country's civil religion, others contend that it is less important today. Divisions within society, especially between liberals (as reflected in the labeled socialism of 2019 presidential candidate Bernie Sanders and his followers) and conservatives (former President Donald Trump and his highly nationalistic conservative policies and followers), indicate that there may no longer be a consensus on the major components of civil religion in the United States. There have been similar conflicts elsewhere, especially in Latin America and many post-Soviet societies.

Religion as a Form of Consumption

An extensive religious, or spiritual, marketplace exists in societies that have a great deal of religious diversity and in which people are free to choose their religion (Moberg and Martikainen 2018). Roger Finke and Rodney Stark (2005) have built on this idea by describing religious institutions in terms of a "religious economy" that operates like commercial economies do. In this context, religious institutions are like business firms seeking to serve a market, and in so doing, they enter into competitive relationships with other "firms" to maintain or expand market share and attract more "consumers" (believers). Not only do religions market themselves; consumers "shop" for religion much as they shop for most other things (Montemaggi 2016). It is in this context that religions must compete against each other and for consumers of religion in much the same way manufacturers and shopping malls compete for customers.

One measure of the degree to which the leaders of religious organizations have become conscious of the need to market their "product" can be seen in the increasing stress placed on treating potential members as customers engaged in a particular form of consumption. Like all other aspects of consumer culture, religions need to respond to the demands of those who consume them and advertise what they have to offer. Among the more obvious examples are efforts to sell all sorts of goods and services linked to religion (Moberg and Martikainen 2018). Many major holidays are associated with one form of consumption or another, including perhaps, most infamously, Christmas (Belk 2013). Christmas, and its associated forms of consumption, has become increasingly globalized. For example, it is even celebrated in tropical locales that have no Christmas tradition (Prideaux and Glover 2014).

We also see the increasing presence of "cathedrals of consumption" (Ryan forthcoming) inside religious structures. For example, a growing number of megachurches have McDonald's and other for-profit food outlets inside their walls. They also often feature stores selling all kinds of merchandise related to the church (sometimes even bits of the church itself). Perhaps most egregiously, there are a number of famous religious structures that charge admission to view certain parts of the structure (e.g. Notre Dame Cathedral in Paris).

How do megachurches like this one exemplify the features of McDonaldization—efficiency, predictability, calculability, and control? What are the advantages for the church? For its congregation? Are there any disadvantages?

AP Photo/Houston Chronicle, Eric Kayne

Digital Living: Practicing Virtual Faith

Instead of being threatened by new technologies like the internet, many religious institutions are finding that their success, even their continued existence, depends on these technologies. Virtual religious services help recruit and sustain members, especially the infirm, those without access to transportation, or students or military personnel who temporarily move away. This trend has increased dramatically as a result of the COVID-19 pandemic. For examples, Catholics can attend a virtual mass officiated by Pope Francis, Buddhists can follow the blog of a Tibetan monk, and Muslims can listen to an imam's prayer service on YouTube. Some churches rely on virtual tithing via PayPal and credit cards for financial support. Facebook pages and internet chat rooms can be a source of spiritual sustenance and a means of building virtual religious communities. One recent study found that evangelical Christians use religious internet chat rooms to expand their sexual knowledge and improve their nonvirtual sex lives within the confines of heterosexual marriage (Burke 2016).

To generate revenue and sustain followers, many religious institutions use the internet to sell traditional religious objects, such as rosaries, yarmulkas (skullcaps), and prayer beads. In addition, they even sell more commercial items, such as religiously themed T-shirts and bumper stickers. The selling of actual religious rituals also occurs and may become more common as religious diasporas grow. For instance, the religious market in India is a multibillion-dollar industry that profits from the sale of online pujas, or religious ceremonies, to Hindus who live in India and abroad. Companies like Shubhpuja.com hire Hindu priests to perform virtual pujas, which customers purchase to pray for a variety of things, like getting a promotion at work, celebrating a wedding, or healing from an illness. Prices for a puja range from $10 to $500 and are typically conducted via Skype (Bengali 2016).

Many religious institutions have increasingly accepted technology, including social networks. Pope Francis joined Instagram in 2016 and tweets regularly. Do you ever use the internet in the practice of religion?

GABRIEL BOUYS/AFP/Getty Images

TYPES OF RELIGIOUS INSTITUTIONS

Various typologies describe the most common religious institutions. Much of this work begins by distinguishing between two basic kinds of religious organizations, the *sect* and the *church*. These two terms are appropriately conceptualized as poles on a continuum, from the sect at one end to the church on the other (Swatos 2007).

Sects

A **sect** is a small group of people who have joined the group consciously and voluntarily to have a personal religious experience. They see themselves as the "true believers" who have privileged access to religious truths, which makes them critical of other religious institutions. The members' religious experiences and general behavior tend to be spontaneous and unregimented. A sect's leadership is usually composed of laypersons rather than those with specialized training. As such, the organizational structure is nonbureaucratic and nonhierarchical. Leaders often arise because they are seen as possessing charisma and thus should be obeyed without question. Sects tend to be antiestablishment, and the members often feel alienated from, and as a result are prone to reject, society and the status quo. In fact, sects can be seen as breakaway, dissident groups that leave established religious institutions. They do so because they think such institutions have compromised too much with "the world" and therefore have polluted the religion's teachings.

Sects tend to set themselves apart from society in terms of such things as how they dress and what they eat. In addition, they might even segregate themselves physically and live in areas largely isolated from the rest of the community.

Numerous sects within the Christian tradition have long histories in the United States, including the Amish, Hutterites, Seventh-Day Adventists, and Jehovah's Witnesses. Sects with twentieth-century origins include the Soldiers of the Cross and Pentecostalism. Some of the latter sometimes handle poisonous snakes during a service. Sunni and Shia are the major sects in Islam. Within Judaism, Hasidic Jews are an example of a sect.

The Puritans were a sect that had enormous influence in the American colonies and in the development of the United States. What other sects are you familiar with? Have you been actively involved in any of them?

Sarin Images/Granger

Churches

A **church** is a large group of religiously oriented people into which members are usually born (instead of joining consciously and voluntarily). The church's leadership is composed of professionals who have highly specialized training. The church as a whole tends to have a highly bureaucratic structure and a complex division of labor (Christiano, Swatos, and Kivisto 2015). Churches tend to draw members from throughout society and across all social classes. While a sect tends to restrict membership to true believers, a church seeks to include as many people as possible. Churches often actively seek out new members, sometimes by employing missionaries. A church's belief systems tend to be highly codified, and rituals are often elaborate and performed in a highly prescribed manner. In comparison with members of sects, church members tend to have a lower level of commitment, and much less is expected of them. While sects tend to reject the status quo, churches accept it.

Although *sect* and *church* are presented here as if they are distinct, in reality there is no clear dividing line between them. In fact, over time there is a tendency for a sect to become transformed into something that takes on the organizational features of a church. As sects become larger, they need, among other things, ever-larger bureaucratic structures with less charismatic leadership and more leadership based on expertise. The behavior of sect members becomes less spontaneous and more formal.

Denominations

A **denomination** is a subgroup within a religion that has slightly different beliefs than other members of that religion. Denominations tend to be hierarchical and bureaucratic and are usually supportive of the social order and of other religious forms. Local organizations are not independent but part of larger regional or national institutional structures. They rely on specialized, professionally trained, full-time clergy. The clergy are generally trained in seminaries run by the denominations to ensure conformity to doctrines.

Among major Christian denominations today are a long list of Protestant groups, including American Baptist, Assemblies of God, Church of Christ, Episcopal, Evangelical Lutheran, Lutheran, Presbyterian, Southern Baptist, United Church of Christ, and United Methodist. Roman Catholics and the Eastern Orthodox Church are also Christian denominations.

Cults and New Religious Movements

A cult resembles a sect in many ways, but it is important to distinguish between the two (Stark and Bainbridge 1979). A sect is a religious group that breaks off from a more established religion as a result of a schism in order to revive itself and rediscover the original beliefs and practices of that organization, but a **cult** is a new, innovative, small, voluntary, and exclusive religious tradition never associated with any religious organization. A cult is often at odds with established religions as well as the larger society. Those who found cults tend to be religious radicals who want to go back to religion's origins, to import ideas from other religions, or to create totally new ideas. Like sects, cults demand high levels of commitment and involvement on the part of members. Because they are new, cults, even more than sects, tend to be led by charismatic figures. Among the better-known cults are Baha'i; the International Society for Krishna Consciousness, commonly known as Hare Krishnas; the Transcendental Meditation movement; Rastafarians; the Peace Mission of Father Divine; and the Rajneesh Movement (made famous by the popular Netflix documentary *Wild, Wild Country*).

The term *cult* has fallen out of favor in sociology because it is has come to be associated in the popular mind and press with such destructive groups as Charles Manson and his "family," which murdered a number of people, including actress Sharon Tate, in 1969. The Manson cult was not actually a religious organization, but a number of religiously based cults have proved to be very destructive. These include Jim Jones's People's Temple, David Koresh's Branch Davidians, and Heaven's Gate. All of these groups ended in tragedy. In the case of the People's Temple, the end involved the 1979 mass suicide and murder of 918 of Jones's followers in their jungle compound in Guyana. In the case of the Branch Davidians, the leader and members died in a controversial confrontation in Waco, Texas, with federal officials from the Bureau of Alcohol, Tobacco, and Firearms. And in the case of Heaven's Gate, a charismatic leader convinced his followers that Comet Hale-Bopp was hiding a mother ship that would take them to a better world. The result was that 39 members committed suicide (famously dressed alike and wearing the same Nike tennis shoes).

Not all cults are religious. A recent example of this is Nxivm (pronounced "Nexium"), a cult founded by Keith Raniere. The purported goals of Nxivm were healing individuals by rewiring their emotional selves and transforming society. However, the cult became infamous for branding women, some quite famous, and using them as "sexual slaves" (Grigoriadis 2018). In the name of empowerment, women (including the actress Allison Mack) recruited other women to the cult. Mack was convicted of racketeering in early 2019, and Raniere was convicted of sex trafficking later in the year.

Bhagwan Shree Rajneesh, right, speaks with his disciples in Rajneeshpuram, a cult movement that started in India but migrated to Oregon in the U.S. during the 1980s. Their conflicts with local residents were the subject of the Netflix documentary *Wild Wild Country*.

Associated Press

Given the negative connotations associated with the term *cult*, many sociologists today have discontinued using it. However, others continue to view cult as a useful sociological concept (Cowan and Bromley 2015). The term *new religious movements* has gained broad acceptance in the sociology of religion. It encompasses sects, cults, and a wide array of other nontraditional, often innovative, religious groups (Lewis and Tollefson 2016). **New religious movements** tend to be typified by their zealous religious converts, their charismatic leaders, their appeal to an atypical portion of the population, their tendency to differentiate between "us" and "them," a distrust of others, and a proneness to rapid fundamental changes. One example is the New Age movement, characterized by a belief in the coming of a global renewal in the "age of Aquarius" as well as an individually oriented, loving spirituality (Cowan and Bromley 2015).

RELIGION AND GLOBALIZATION

Every major religious tradition was originally a local, even tribal, expression of faith that grew out of a specific environment and then diffused across certain regions and eventually the globe. The study of the relationship between religion and globalization is relatively recent, but it is clear that religion globalized before anything else.

Today, as Figure 12.9 shows, Christians make up 31 percent of the world's population, 25 percent are Muslims, 15 percent are Hindus, and smaller proportions are followers of Buddhism (7 percent), folk religions (6 percent), and Judaism (0.2 percent). About 16 percent of the world's population is unaffiliated with any religion.

Two issues are of particular importance in regard to the relationship between globalization and religion. First, transnational migration brings institutional religion to new locales, making those places more multireligious. Migrants also generate in those locales new and different versions of the local religions, even as the migrants' versions are influenced and altered by local religions. This, in turn, can alter religion in the migrants' homeland. Thus, transnational migration globalizes religion spatially and contributes to the further pluralization of religion around the world. Migrants help unify various parts of the world by, for example, making pilgrimages to religious sites like Mecca and the Wailing Wall, posting prayers in cyberspace, and sending money to religious centers in their homelands.

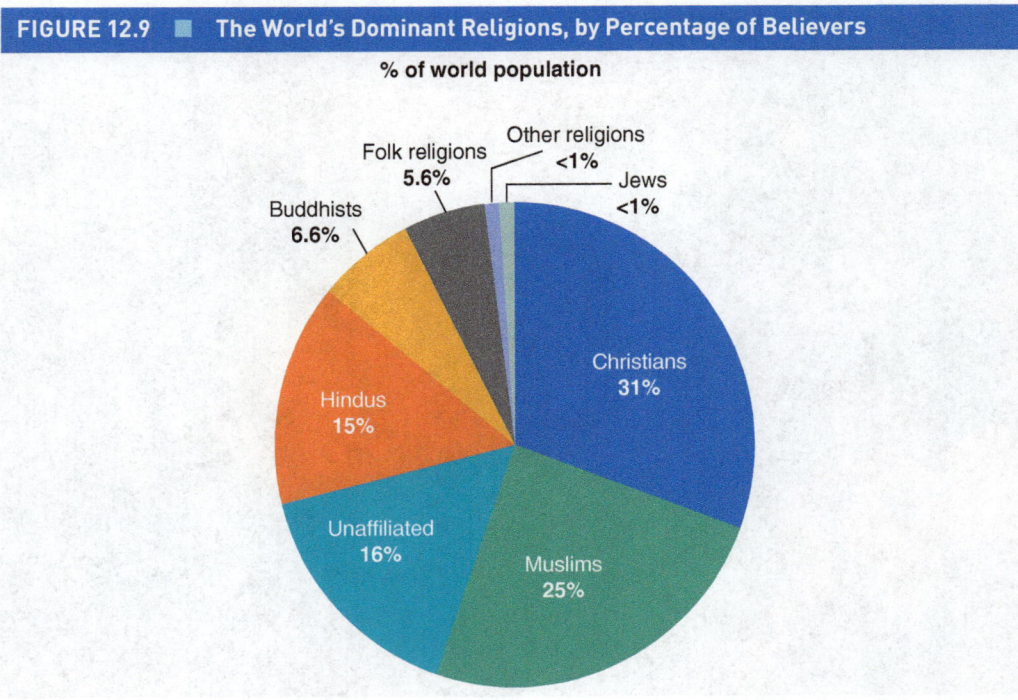

FIGURE 12.9 ■ The World's Dominant Religions, by Percentage of Believers

Source: Pew Research, The Future of World Religions: Population Growth Projections, 2010–2050. https://www.pewresearch.org/religion/interactives/religious-composition-by-country-2010-2050/

Note: 2020 figures are projections based on 2010 baseline estimates.

Second is the spread of religious organizations and movements through independent missions. Here the Christian Church, especially the Roman Catholic Church, has played a central role through its missionaries. In fact, Christianity arguably became the first worldwide religion. Messengers for Islam created the most global system prior to the modern era (see the discussion of Islam that follows).

The Most Prominent Global Religions

This section deals with several globally important religions—Judaism, Hinduism, Buddhism, Islam, and Christianity. Although Mormonism is not a large global religion, and debate continues about whether it should be defined as a Christian denomination or a new religion, we also examine it here because of its contemporary efforts to become a global religion. However, as is clear in Figure 12.10, many of the world's dominant religions, despite their spread, are still to a large extent concentrated in particular parts of the world.

Judaism

Founded more than 3,000 years ago, Judaism is today one of the smallest of the world's religions, with roughly 15 million people in the world defining themselves as Jews, more than half of whom live in the United States. However, for a variety of reasons, Judaism's importance both historically and contemporarily has been far greater than one would think by simply looking at the numbers involved. By the late nineteenth century, there were 12 million Jews in the world, many of whom had migrated from the Middle East and were spread in mostly small enclaves across many countries. There was and continues to be a large concentration of Jews in Europe, but migrations to North America, as well as to Palestine (then under Ottoman control), began during this period. By the onset of World War II, the number of Jews in the world had grown to 16.6 million, but the atrocities of the Nazis led to a reduction in the population to about 11 million. The founding of Israel in 1948 marked an important turning point for Jews, and that nation's Jewish population is now just over 6.5 million people (out of Israel's total population of roughly 9.3 million people). Another large concentration of Jews—more than 8 million—is found in North America, mostly in the United States. The vast majority of the more than 15 million Jews alive today live in either North America or Israel, with fewer than 1 million living elsewhere,

FIGURE 12.10 ■ Distribution of the World's Dominant Religions

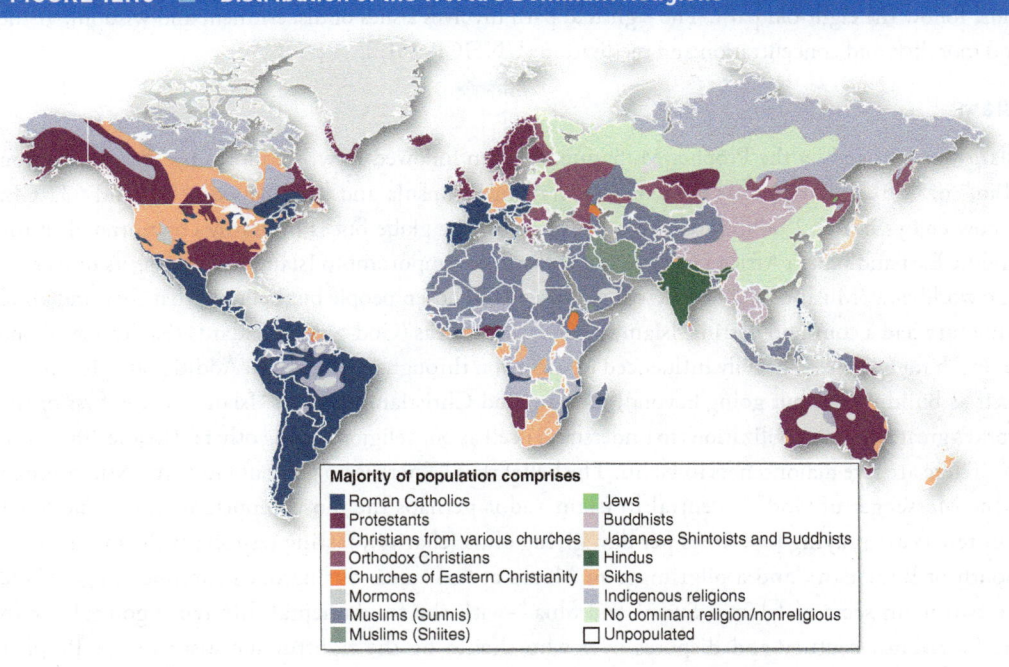

Source: "Faith on the Move—The Religious Affiliation of International Migrants." Pew Research Center, Washington, DC (March 2012). http://www.pewforum.org/2012/03/08/religious-migration-exec/.

mostly in Europe. Just a few of the factors that give Judaism great global significance are the spread of Jews throughout the world, Zionism (which helped lead to the founding of Israel), the Holocaust, anti-Semitism, and the conflict between Israel and its Arab neighbors over Palestine.

Hinduism

Although no precise starting date can be determined, Hinduism began sometime between 800 and 200 BCE (Weightman 2017). Although it has ancient origins, Hinduism became firmly established in India as the country opposed foreign occupation by Muslims (999–1757) and later the British (1757–1947). Today, the vast majority of Hindus (more than 1.1 billion) live in India. Hinduism is strongly defined by the *Vedas*, which are both historical documents and enumerations of incantations needed for successful rituals. Hinduism is also closely associated with India's caste system.

Though it continues to be heavily concentrated in India, Hinduism has also become a global religion. It has been spread by both migrants and traveling religious teachers (Madan 2007). Although it is heavily concentrated geographically, Hinduism has been important as part of the "Easternization of the West" (Campbell 2007) in, for example, the spread of yoga (including, now, "he-man" yoga; Bluestein 2014), Transcendental Meditation, and so on. (And, of course, there has been a parallel, but much stronger, Westernization of the East [Sander and Cavallin 2015].) However, Hinduism has not been nearly as expansionistic as Christianity, Islam, or even Buddhism.

Buddhism

Buddhism arose in the Indus Ganges basin in about the sixth century BCE and began to have a transnational influence about three centuries later (Jerryson 2017). Today there are somewhere around 500 million Buddhists across the globe, although the vast majority are in Asia. China has the largest number of Buddhists, followed by Japan. Other Asian countries with majority Buddhist populations include Thailand, Cambodia, Myanmar, Bhutan, Sri Lanka, Laos, and Vietnam. Thus, although Buddhism moved out from its origins in India, it has remained primarily concentrated on the Asian continent.

There are many forms of Buddhism, although nearly all adhere to the same "three universal truths," "four noble truths," and "noble eightfold path." The three universal truths are that nothing is lost in the universe, everything changes, and the law of cause and effect. The four noble truths are that suffering exists, there is a cause of suffering, there is an end to suffering, and that in order to end suffering you must follow the eightfold path. The eightfold path involves issues of discernment and wisdom, virtue and morality, and concentration and meditation (UNHCR 2012).

Islam

Islam was founded by the Prophet Muhammad (often followed in written form by "Peace Be Upon Him," or "PBUH"), who was born on the Arabian Peninsula and lived between 570 and 632 CE. It now enjoys nearly 2 billion followers spread across the globe but is primarily concentrated in the Middle East and North Africa as well as Southeast Asia. Important to Islam's spread was its universalistic worldview; Muslims did not view themselves as a chosen people but believed that they and all of humanity had a common destiny. Islam's universalistic ideas (God-given standards that lead everyone to search for goodness) heavily influenced its diffusion throughout the world. Additionally, Islam sees itself as building on, but going beyond, Judaism and Christianity. Thus, "Islam was the first of the world's great religious civilizations to understand itself as one religion among others" (Keane 2003, 42).

There are five major tenets in Islam. The belief that "There is no god but God, and Muhammad is the Messenger of God" is central to Islam and is perhaps the most important tenet. The other four tenets are praying five times per day, giving alms (charity), fasting (especially during the holy month of Ramadan), and a pilgrimage to Mecca at least once during one's lifetime (*hajj*). There are two main sects of Islam—Sunni and Shia—with the fundamental difference going back to the fourteenth century and disputes over who should be the rightful successor to the Prophet Muhammad.

Although inaccurately frequently depicted with fundamentalism (discussed below) and especially terrorism, Islam is a generally peaceful religion that encourages acceptance and understanding of (most forms of) diversity and other religions. Unfortunately, as Islam has become increasingly politicized, the tenets of the religion have been overshadowed by the political, and particularly militaristic violent, aspects of the religion. It is important, however, to separate the religion from the political motives of (European formed) nation-states that use the religion as a basis of governance.

Christianity

Christianity and Islam are the two fastest-growing religions in the world today. Christianity spread in the Middle East following the death of Jesus of Nazareth. By 1000 CE, a schism had developed between Roman Catholicism in the West and Orthodoxy in the East, with more Christians living in the East than in the West. A major series of events in the history of globalization was the Crusades, which began in 1095 CE and lasted for centuries. The Crusades were designed to liberate the Holy Land from Muslims and others who had gained control of Jerusalem in 638 CE. This is still a sensitive issue for Muslims, as reflected in protests that erupted when then-president George W. Bush used the word *crusade* in a speech shortly after the 9/11 terrorist attacks.

Christianity today is declining in Europe, but that is more than compensated for by strong growth in the Global South, including parts of Asia, Africa, and Latin America. Growth is so strong in the Global South that it is predicted that by 2050, 80 percent of the world's Christians will be Hispanic. Furthermore, Christianity is different in the Global South—"more . . . morally conservative, and evangelical" (Garrett 2007, 143).

Pentecostalism, a charismatic movement, offers another example of the spread of Christianity around the globe (Anderson 2013). This religion had its origins in revivals attended by poor Blacks and Whites in Los Angeles in 1906. It is now the second-largest and fastest-growing form of Christianity, with about 640 million adherents globally, and has come to exceed in size all forms of Christianity except Catholicism (which has roughly twice as many adherents). Its growth has been especially great in Asia, Africa, and Latin America. In fact, today only 69 percent of adults in Latin America say they are Catholic, compared to 90 percent throughout much of the twentieth century. The growth of Pentecostalism is a major factor in this decline. Pentecostal missionaries from Asia, Africa, and Latin America now often travel to the United States and Europe in search of converts. Many variations and localized forms of Pentecostalism are linked through publications, conferences, electronic media, and travel.

Mormonism

Mormonism, or the Church of Jesus Christ of Latter-Day Saints, has shown substantial growth in the past 60 years (although there are recent signs that its growth is slowing). Founded in the United States in the nineteenth century, Mormonism had fewer than 2 million members in 1960, but today the number has risen to approximately 17 million.

The Church of Jesus Christ of Latter-Day Saints is centrally controlled from its headquarters in Salt Lake City, Utah. Once almost exclusively an American religion, today Mormonism has more members outside the United States and thousands of churches and meetinghouses in most of the world's countries and territories. Ninety thousand missionaries spread Mormonism across the globe. Although the church banned Blacks from becoming priests until 1978, today it is growing rapidly in Africa and has about half a million members there.

In contrast to other globally successful religions, Mormonism has not significantly adapted to local customs and realities. For example, unlike the far more rapidly expanding Pentecostalism, Mormonism has *not* incorporated a variety of indigenous customs (such as drumming and dancing) into its African Sunday services. Through watching Salt Lake City services via satellite, worshippers elsewhere in the world can easily see that the services and the teachings are the same—or at least very similar.

Fundamentalism

Religious **fundamentalism** is a strongly held belief in the fundamental or foundational precepts of any religion. It is also characterized by a rejection of the modern secular world. Fundamentalists see the world in stark terms, dividing it into true believers (the in-group), who are saved, and the rest of the world's population (the out-groups), who are damned. There is often hostility between the in-group and out-groups. Fundamentalists seek to replace doubt and ambiguity with crystal-clear certainty. All of the major world religions have fundamentalist elements, as do many smaller religions.

One example of fundamentalism is strict adherence to *sharia*, or traditional Islamic law. This includes modest dress for women, abstention from alcohol, and public prayers. Sharia law has been seen as the basis of a governmentally enforced legal structure among Islamic fundamentalists, most notably the Taliban in Afghanistan and the now near-defunct terrorist organization the Islamic State (IS) in Iraq and Syria. Moreover, it has been used to justify such inhumane practices as cutting off the hands of thieves, the stoning to death of people convicted of committing adultery, the imprisonment and murder of those suspected in sexual activities with members of the same sex, and the mass murder—most visibly and alarmingly by public beheading—of infidels, especially those who refuse to convert.

Other religions, most notably Christianity, also have a large number of fundamentalist members. Although terrorism is often (wrongly) associated with Islam in the United States (and elsewhere, especially Europe), a large number of terrorist actions have been committed by Christian fundamentalists. For example, the deadliest terrorist attack on United States soil prior to September 11, 2001, was the bombing of a federal building in Oklahoma City carried out by Timothy McVeigh, a Christian fundamentalist.

Fundamentalism can be seen as being involved in globalization in at least two major senses (Wood and Watt 2014). First, it is often expansionistic, seeking to extend its reach into more and more areas of the world and to extend its power in those areas. Second, it is profoundly affected by various globalizations. For example, the globalization of one fundamentalist religion, such as that of Hasidic Jews, is likely to lead to a reaction by another, such as Islamic militants (and vice versa). Another important reaction involves movements against various forces seen as emanating from the contemporary world, including secularism, popular culture, consumerism, rationalization, and the occupation of what is deemed as religious territory by the United States, Israel, and others. Much of the momentum for the recent rise of fundamentalism can be traced to a reaction against such forces. For example, IS reacted against artificial borders in the Middle East drawn and imposed by the West (primarily the French and British) largely after World War I, as well as the West's military involvement and cultural imperialism in that region.

Faith on the Move

The globalization of religion—and the growing diversity of religions around the globe—is also the result of the movement of people. Although the number has probably grown, the United Nations estimates that in 2020, there were 281 million immigrants globally. This figure represents just over 3 percent of the total population of the world. The Pew-Templeton Global Religious Futures Project provides a broad overview of the movement of major world religions. Figure 12.11 summarizes some of its findings. It is perhaps not surprising that the world's two largest religions—Christianity and Islam—contribute the largest numbers of immigrants. Christians account for 2.3 billion adherents worldwide and nearly half of all immigrants. Islam has 1.6 million adherents, and Muslim immigrants amount to 27 percent of all immigrants. Hinduism is the third-largest religion, but only 5 percent of Hindus are migrants. Jews, though the smallest of the world's religious groups, constitute 2 percent of all immigrants. Buddhists constitute 3 percent of all migrants, even though their religion has many more members than does Judaism. This indicates that just as Jews have historically been a diasporic people (i.e., a people scattered around the world), they remain so today.

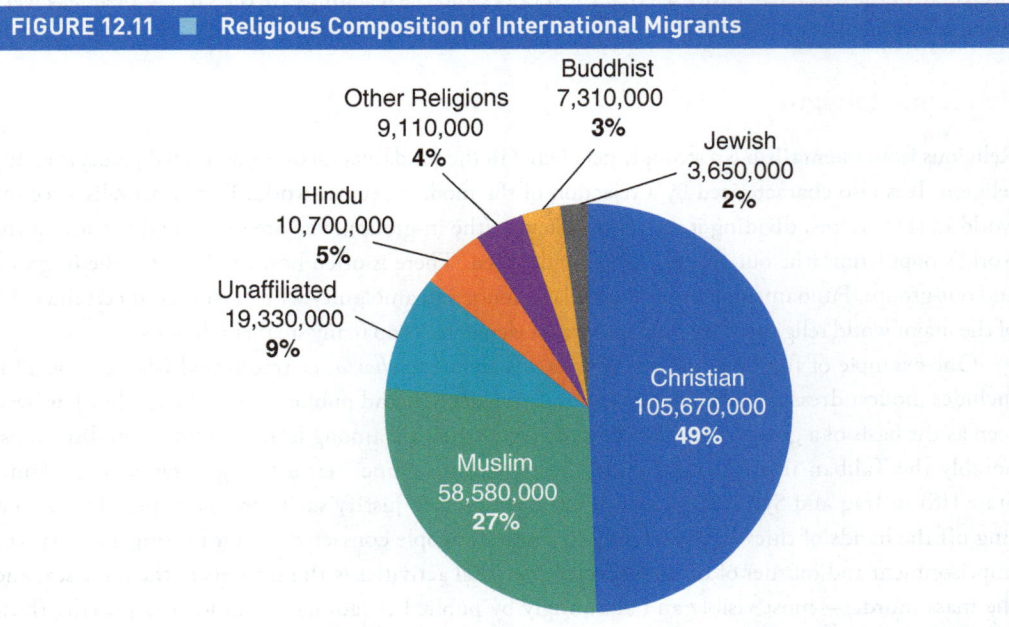

FIGURE 12.11 ■ Religious Composition of International Migrants

- Other Religions 9,110,000 — 4%
- Buddhist 7,310,000 — 3%
- Jewish 3,650,000 — 2%
- Hindu 10,700,000 — 5%
- Unaffiliated 19,330,000 — 9%
- Christian 105,670,000 — 49%
- Muslim 58,580,000 — 27%

Source: "Faith on the Move—The Religious Affiliation of International Migrants." Pew Research Center, Washington, DC (March 2012). http://www.pewforum.org/2012/03/08/religiousmigration-exec/.

The growing Muslim population in Europe has sparked controversy, including over the modest attire of some Muslim women. Some cities have even attempted to ban the "burkini" swimsuit.

FETHI BELAID/AFP/Getty Images

In terms of country of origin, more Christian immigrants are from Mexico than from any other nation. For Muslims, the largest point of origin is Palestine. Most Palestinians are not recent migrants but rather became refugees after the establishment of Israel in 1948. For Jews, the largest point of origin is Russia; for Hindus, it is India; and for Buddhists, it is Vietnam. China, a major country of emigration, is the top country for both "other religions" and the unaffiliated.

Turning to destination countries, the United States is the number one country for Christians, followed by Russia, Germany, Spain, and Canada. The United States is also the number one country for Buddhists, followed by India, Australia, and Canada. Furthermore, the United States is the primary destination for the unaffiliated. Israel is the main destination for Jews; Saudi Arabia is the main destination for Muslims. India is a rather curious case, for it is both the number one country of origin for Hindus and their number one destination. In general, countries with long histories of immigration, like the United States, Australia, and Canada, are especially popular destinations.

SUMMARY

Education is closely related to the process of socialization, although it most often takes place more formally in schools. Research has found that inequalities exist in the educational system that prevent many, especially those from disadvantaged backgrounds, from succeeding. Coleman found that teacher quality, family background, and racial composition of the student body were the most important factors affecting student achievement. In addition, the use of tracking in schools often leads to a cumulative advantage for students placed in higher tracks. Other researchers have discovered that differences in the home environments of very young children and parenting styles also explain differences in educational ability and attainment. Family background also helps determine who is most likely to pursue postsecondary education. Students with more advantaged family backgrounds are more likely to graduate from high school and to enroll in and graduate from college.

The COVID-19 pandemic has had a profound impact on education around the world. Students from minority and disadvantaged backgrounds have been particularly impacted.

Countries vary greatly in their ability to educate students and educate them well. PISA measures the proficiency of 15-year-olds in reading, math, and science every three years. Students in the United States score well below those in other countries with similar levels of development, while students in China and Singapore rank at the top.

Religion is a social phenomenon that consists of shared beliefs, rituals, and experiences. Sociologists study religion not to judge the truth claims of different religions but to understand the social consequences of different beliefs. Beliefs are ideas that explain the world and identify what should be sacred (or extraordinary) and profane (or mundane). Rituals are repeated behaviors that symbolize beliefs and are often a central part of weddings and other rites of passage. Civil religion consists of the beliefs, rituals, and symbols that a nation holds sacred. Secularization refers to the declining importance of religion and the increasing importance of science in making sense of our lives and the world.

Sociologists have identified different types of religious institutions. These include sects, churches, cults, and new religious movements. A sect is a small group of "true believers" who voluntarily join together to have a personal religious experience. A member of a church is typically born into a specific religion instead of voluntarily choosing it. In contrast to a sect, a church is hierarchically organized, with professional leaders. Similar to sects, cults are small, voluntary groups not associated with any religious organization; however, cults are newer and more innovative than sects. Both sects and cults are part of the new religious movements characterized by zealot converts, charismatic leaders, and proneness to rapid fundamental change.

The spread of religion is not new, but it has accelerated with increased globalization. The most prominent global religions are Christianity, Islam, Hinduism, Buddhism, and Judaism. Christianity and Islam are the two largest religions in the world and are growing, while Judaism is the smallest prominent global religion. One factor contributing to growing global religious diversity is global migration.

KEY TERMS

beliefs
church
civil religion
concerted cultivation
cult

cumulative advantage
denomination
fundamentalism
habitus
hidden curriculum

legacy students
liminal period
lockdown struggler
lockdown survivor
lockdown thriver
meritocracy
natural growth
new religious movements
pandemic pedagogy
paper ceiling

profane
religion
rites of passage
rituals
sacred
sect
secularization
tracking
vouchers
worldview

REVIEW QUESTIONS

1. What is a meritocracy, and why is the educational system an important component of a meritocratic society? In what ways is the education system meritocratic, and in what ways is it not meritocratic?

2. According to the Coleman Report, how important is the quality of schools to student achievement? What other factors affect student achievement? What factors have not been found to affect student achievement to any great extent?

3. Describe and evaluate the major alternatives—vouchers, homeschooling, and charter schools—to traditional public schooling.

4. Several Asian countries are at or near the top in the PISA rankings. What aspects of Asian culture might account for these high scores? Can you explain the comparatively low U.S. scores? What are the implications of those scores for the future of the education system in the United States?

5. Compare the German, Japanese, and U.S. educational systems. How do these systems' differences affect achievement outcomes in these countries? How do their attitudes toward grouping reflect the countries' respective cultural norms and values?

6. How has the COVID-19 pandemic impacted education? Which populations were most significantly impacted, and why?

7. How do we define religion? What are the basic elements and components of religious institutions? In what ways have religions changed over time?

8. What are the major religions of the world? How are people distributed among the major religions of the world? In what ways are religions global?

9. What is the difference between a sect and a church? Provide one example of a sect and one of a church. Why has the term *cult* fallen out of favor with sociologists of religion?

10. What is secularization? Which factors that have led to an increase in secularization do you think are most important, and why?

11. What does it mean to speak of a religious or spiritual marketplace? Provide examples that illustrate how religion is marketed to consumers.

MANDEL NGAN/AFP via Getty Images

13 POLITICS AND THE ECONOMY

> **LEARNING OBJECTIVES**
>
> **13.1** Contrast democracy and dictatorship.
>
> **13.2** Outline who rules the world using the perspectives of structural/functional and conflict/critical theories.
>
> **13.3** Explain how global politics affects war and terrorism, geopolitics, and the nation-state.
>
> **13.4** Describe the economic transition from industrial to postindustrial society.
>
> **13.5** Discuss how work, consumption, and leisure shape our understanding of the economy.
>
> **13.6** Describe the effects of globalization on the world economy and consumer culture.

THE COVID-19 PANDEMIC AND POLITICS AND ECONOMIES

The COVID-19 pandemic has radically shaken up both politics and the economy, both within countries and on a global scale. As arguably the most important global event since WWII, and certainly the one with the greatest reach into nearly every nook and cranny of the planet, the pandemic has become a central political and economic concern for nearly everyone. And the impact of that concern is certainly going to stay with us for many years to come.

On a political level, the pandemic served to divide people as responses to the pandemic varied greatly along political lines (Ryan and Nanda 2023a). For example, many conservative political parties and their leaders have downplayed the virus as "a little flu" (as Jair Bolsonaro, former president of Brazil, famously referred to it) or, worse yet, weaponized it (as Donald Trump, former president of the United States, did when referring to it as the "China virus" and "Kung flu"). They have also been more opposed to physical distancing and the use of masks as ways to help prevent the spread of the virus (Meeker 2023). The pandemic has also served as a distraction allowing many questionable statutes to be passed with little attention (Ryan 2022). Victor Orbán in Hungary even passed emergency legislation allowing his government to rule by decree until the pandemic is over, and that only they had the power to decide when that was.

On an economic level, the pandemic has had a truly devastating impact on the lives of billions of individuals and the broader economies of nearly every society. Unemployment soared during the pandemic, especially for those in jobs that were already lower paying, including in the tourism, service and hospitality industries. It has also cost trillions of dollars in funding relief efforts, lost productivity, and medical expenses. All of this money could have been put toward other issues, like hunger, homelessness, education, or finding solutions to the growing environmental catastrophe (whether it actually would have been is, of course, debatable).

At the same time, the pandemic was a windfall for many, especially many of the global elite. Elon Musk, for example, saw his personal wealth increase by more than $250 billion just during the first two years of the pandemic. He was not alone. In fact, the world's 10 richest men saw their wealth double to more than $1.5 trillion during the first years of the pandemic, all while hundreds of millions lost their life savings (if they even had any savings to lose). While conservative members of the United States Congress were arguing that $600 a week was too much for additional unemployment assistance, top executives at Moderna dumped $30 million in stock made after announcing a successful vaccine trial. As sociologists, we should be interested in the economic and political systems that made these kinds of inequalities possible.

The pandemic has also presented many societies with renewed opportunities to think about their priorities, both political and economic (Ryan and Nanda 2023a). This has not always played to the benefit of the world's underprivileged. For example, a number of political leaders took advantage of the pandemic to pass tax cuts that heavily favor the wealthy (as Trump did in the United States). Others have used the pandemic to fuel social divides, for example, by blaming certain populations (e.g. Muslims, immigrants, gay men, and especially Asians) for the spread of the virus. On the other hand, some have seized on this unique moment of shared global grief to propose new solutions to old problems. For example, an increased awareness of, and attention to, issues of loneliness led to a number of organizations focusing on outreach to those who live alone, especially seniors. For some, the pandemic actually led to a renewed sense of connectedness to their neighbors and communities (Bianchi et al. 2023).

In all ways, the pandemic has proven to be not just a serious medical issue, but one that has had far-reaching consequences for politics and economies. It has helped demonstrate the ways in which all parts of our lives are often interconnected and how nearly everything can, and often does, have political and economic consequences.

POLITICS: DEMOCRACY OR DICTATORSHIP

Society can be seen as a collection of groups that compete to determine whose members get what, as well as when and how they get it (Lasswell 2012). When groups operate through established governmental channels to do so, this competition is referred to as **politics**. The **state** is the political body organized for government and civil rule. By putting pressure on the state, a group can advance a given position or promote policies that benefit its members. Therefore, politics is one way of exercising power in society.

Democracy: Citizenship as a Radical Idea

Democracies are political systems in which people within a given state vote to choose their leaders and, in some cases, vote on legislation as well. In modern democracies, people vote to choose their legislators rather than actually managing their own political affairs and directly making decisions about the things that affect their lives. Nevertheless, contemporary theorists of democracy often suggest that the power to rule in democracies comes from the *consent* of the people. Sometimes these systems are called **representative democracies**. The people, as a whole body, do not actually rule themselves but rather have some say in who will best represent them in the state. In **direct democracies**, by contrast, the people have a say in decisions that directly affect them.

Characteristics of Democracies

Democratic states are organized into bureaucracies, with clear hierarchies as well as established and written codes, laws, and rules. The authority legislators have under democracies is based on legal codes that confer this authority on them. Democracies tend to extend rights to **citizens**, the people represented by the state and most often born within its territories. **Citizenship** means that the people of a given state can vote for their representatives and that they have rights and responsibilities as citizens (Sniderman 2017). These rights and responsibilities can vary greatly and can include things like paying taxes, receiving an education, or having access to social services. Under *universal citizenship*, the rights of citizenship are generally conferred on most people residing in a given state's territory. At times, however, citizenship is still denied to groups of immigrants residing within that territory.

Most democratic states guarantee citizens the right to freely express dissent, the right to due process and equality before the law, the rights of freedom of speech and of the press, and the right to privacy. These rights and others are sometimes extended to noncitizens. Even in modern liberal democracies, these "rights" are highly contextual. Consider, for example, how the right to dissent was treated in the United States during the Red Scare of the late 1940s and early 1950s, when the state, led by Senator Joseph McCarthy, saw to it that dissidents were ostracized and harassed. Freedom House, an organization committed to monitoring democratic trends and human rights around the world, publishes an annual survey on 195 countries rating political rights and civil liberties (see Figure 13.1). In 2020, of the 195 countries assessed, 43 percent were rated "free," 29 percent were rated "partly free," and 27 percent were rated "not free." Ratings for the Middle East and North Africa were the worst in the world, followed by Eurasia. Syria, a dictatorship mired in civil war, ethnic division, and uncontrolled terrorism, received the lowest score of any country in more than a decade. The other "worst of the worst" countries are Sudan, Turkmenistan, Eritrea, North Korea, Equatorial Guinea, Tajikistan, and the Central African Republic.

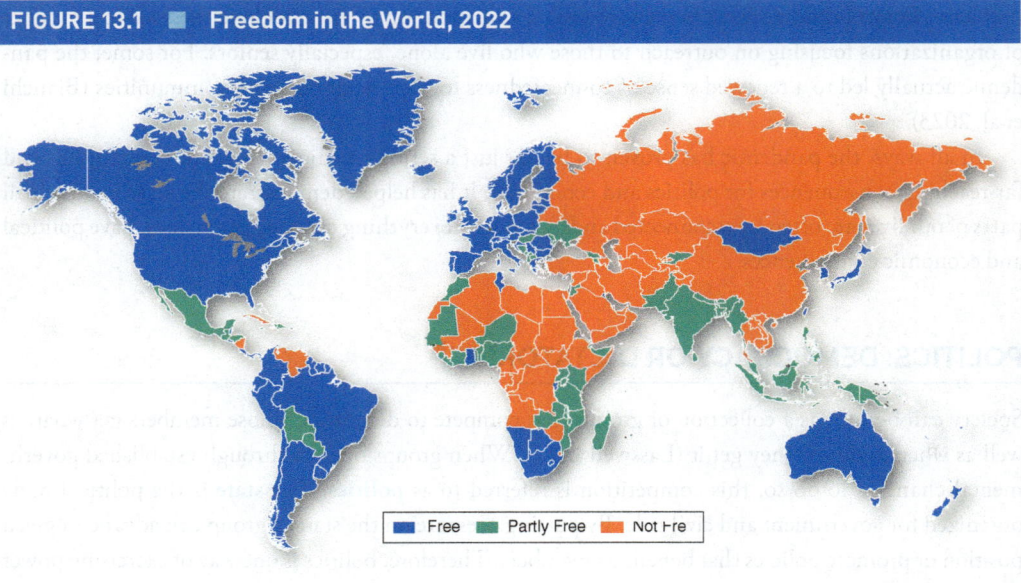

FIGURE 13.1 ■ Freedom in the World, 2022

Source: Data from Freedom House, "Freedom in the World," 2022.

Democracies are not without their critics, even from within. Some have argued that voters are typically uninformed about many political issues. For example, many of those in Great Britain who voted for Brexit were not fully aware of its implications for them. Many working-class voters in the United States did not anticipate that Donald Trump would appoint billionaires and millionaires to his cabinet who would likely be unresponsive to their needs and interests (Duhigg 2017). Also surprising to such voters was a massive 2018 tax cut that greatly helped the rich and large corporations but did little for them. Other critics argue that liberal democracies extend *too many* rights and tend to allow too much diversity of thought and interest, making them unstable.

The Rise of Illiberal Democracy, or Is It Fascism?

The idea of "illiberal democracy" seems to involve a contradiction in terms (Zakaria 1997). After all, aren't democracy (especially free and fair elections and checks and balances) and liberalism (especially rule of law and protection of basic liberties) inevitably linked? It turns out they are not. This is reflected in recent political developments, especially in Europe (e.g., Hungary, Poland) and even in the United States but also, among others, in China, Egypt, Turkey, and the Philippines. Elections exist, but they are structured in such a way that the party in power must inevitably emerge victorious.

Hungary's prime minister, Viktor Orbán, was reelected for the fifth time in 2022. Part of his success stems from the fact that he and his supporters have had the electoral map redrawn to favor them. Orbán has curbed the media and the judiciary; demonized minority immigrants, Jews, and the LGBT community; put his cronies in charge of offices that were supposed to keep the prime minister under control; and dismantled the system of checks and balances. He has also created what is essentially a single-party system. Although there are other parties, they are extremely weak. In part because of the decline in checks and balances, crony capitalism is rampant, with family and associates of Orbán gaining lucrative government contracts (Kingsley 2018a). There is a worrisome drift in many parts of the world, including in Europe and the United States.

Former U.S. secretary of state Madeleine Albright (2018) went beyond the notion of illiberal democracy to discuss whether we have entered a new era of fascism. She sees troubling parallels between the situation in many countries today and those that existed prior to World War II. Among them are chaos in politics, the economy and the social world, divisions among those opposed to fascism, and the fact that conservatives have connived with fascists to bring them to power and keep them there (Berman 2018).

Albright offers a kind of checklist of behaviors that should alert us to the rise of fascism:

1. Catering to our prejudices and not respecting others based on their ethnicity, race, creed, or party affiliation
2. Nurturing our grievances and encouraging revenge against those who are the source of our ire
3. Encouraging contempt for our political system and the electoral process
4. Seeking to weaken or destroy an independent press and the judiciary system
5. Exploiting patriotism and its symbols to turn people against one another
6. Insisting that they won elections in spite of the vote and other evidence indicating they had lost
7. Bragging about themselves and their accomplishments
8. Speaking casually about the use of violence against enemies

Albright worries, as do others, that many politicians in the United States, and elsewhere, are exhibiting these characteristics.

Steven Levitsky and Daniel Ziblatt (2018) make a similar argument in *How Democracies Die*. Based on several historical examples (e.g., Nazi Germany [Hett 2018], Mussolini's Italy, Perón's Argentina), they note four steps in the movement leading to the death of democracy and toward fascism:

- Break political rules or norms
- Delegitimize opponents
- Encourage violence
- Limit opponents' civil liberties

The authors argue that certain political leaders have taken *all* of these steps. They are concerned that without action by counterbalancing forces (e.g., political leaders, parties), many countries, including the United States, could be moving in the direction of fascism.

Dictatorship: The Seizure of Power

Dictatorships are states that are usually totalitarian and ruled either by a single individual or by a small group of people. Dictatorships are governments *without* the consent of the people being governed. In the modern period, dictatorships are often formed in formerly democratic states that have been seized by small groups of political fanatics.

In the years just before and during World War II, the world saw an alliance of dictatorships based on fascist principles. These dictatorships shared some very basic institutional arrangements and principles. They

- were totalitarian in that they attempted to control every facet of social life;
- had a "cult of masculinity" that organized political life and the public sphere around men and punished perceived deficiencies in masculinity, such as homosexuality;
- saw conflict and war as natural states and methods for human betterment; and
- were viciously opposed to liberalism, anarchism, and any form of socialism or communism.

Dictatorships did not end with the defeat of the fascist powers in World War II. Indeed, in the postwar era, the Soviet Union and its satellites in the Eastern Bloc were often organized as dictatorships, with small groups of Communist Party officials controlling society. Latin America has had a number of dictatorships since World War II. Among dictatorships elsewhere in the world today, North Korea is arguably the most dangerous, given its fraught relationship with South Korea and its frequent testing of nuclear weapons. The United States has often sponsored dictatorships and fought against democracy. This has occurred particularly when democratically elected leaders might turn toward political orientations (such as socialism or, as in Turkey today, Islamism) that would make their governments problematic for U.S. political and business interests (Chomsky 1985).

WHO RULES THE WORLD?

Even though many countries are democracies, the issue of who rules them is a source of continuing debate among sociologists (and political scientists).

The Structural/Functional Perspective: Pluralism

Within structural-functionalism, the typical position put forward regarding who rules is **pluralism**. This is the view that a country is characterized by a number of powerful competing interest groups, and no one of them is in control all of the time. In other words, there is a kind of balance of power among these interest groups. In addition, there is a **separation of powers** in the government. That is, the three major branches of government—legislative, executive, and judicial—are separate and counterbalance one another so there is little danger that any one branch of government can wield too much power.

Among pluralists are two major strands of thought. **Group pluralism** focuses on society's many different interest groups and organizations and how they compete for access to political power to attempt to further their interests (Berry and Wilcox 2018). For group pluralists, this jockeying for power by various organizations provides stability for society. They see a *balance of group power,* in which no one group retains power indefinitely and any group can always be challenged by another group. Further, there are *crosscutting group memberships,* with group members belonging to a variety of organizations that see to their needs and interests. This allows people to be political actors in a variety of collective processes. Group pluralists also believe that there tends to be a general *consensus of values* in society. As a result, the state is expected and pressured to legislate according to the common good and the cultural values largely held in common by members of society.

Elite pluralism focuses specifically on how political elites form similar interest groups and organizations that vie for power (Higley and Burton 2006; Lipset 1981; Rose 1967). Although voters may decide which elites represent them, the ultimate decision-making power rests in the hands of those elites. Similar to group pluralists, elite pluralists look at political elites as a diverse social body that organizes into groups to compete with one another for votes. This competition for votes ensures that no one group retains political power indefinitely. Stability is achieved in the system because these political elites must forge agreements with one another to pass legislation. This allows for a diversity of interests to be satisfied through those agreements, which tend to represent the common values of the larger society.

The power elite includes those who occupy powerful positions in the state, the corporate world, and the military. Here, the most powerful person in the political world, the president of the United States, greets William Clay Ford, Jr., executive chairman of the Ford Motor Company, along with United Auto Workers President Ray Curry, at the North American International Auto Show.

MANDEL NGAN/AFP via Getty Images

The Conflict/Critical Perspective: The Power Elite

Pluralism is often juxtaposed to **power elite theory** produced by conflict/critical theorists (Mills 1956). This theory holds that power is not dispersed throughout a stable society—either among citizen groups or among elite groups. Rather, power is concentrated among a small number of people who control the major institutions of the state, the corporate economy, and the military. The powerful people who make up these institutions may have minor disagreements about policy, but for the most part they are unified in their interests and in the business of owning and operating much of society.

These elites develop a common worldview. First, they undergo a process of *cooptation,* whereby they are taught the common ideology of the elite. Further, they forge a shared ideology through their common *class identity.* That is, members of the power elite tend to come from wealthy families, go to similar schools, and belong to similar clubs. These clubs count as their members many of the most powerful people in the world, including corporate leaders, politicians, and top military brass. The clubs provide private spaces where friendships and common policies are forged (Clogher 1981; Domhoff 1974, 2013).

The power elite within the military, state, and corporate world are also often *interchangeable.* That is, the people who hold leadership positions within these three major institutions play a sort of institutional "musical chairs," switching from one powerful institution to another. For example, many former military and business leaders get into politics while many former political leaders take up later careers in business.

GLOBAL POLITICS

Politics has long been global, but it is convenient to trace modern political globalization to 1918 and the end of World War I. After the war, efforts at peace led to the creation of the League of Nations in 1920. Although this organization was weak, in part because the United States never joined, it created an important forum for global political dialogue and relationships. Of course, peace efforts failed, leading to the start of World War II in 1939. The war had disastrous consequences for much of the world, but it did lead to the formation of the United Nations (UN) in 1945 and other global organizations. Although far from an unmitigated success, the UN persists to this day as an important site and source of political globalization. Many other global political organizations have been formed within the UN (e.g., the UN Educational, Scientific, and Cultural Organization, known as UNESCO) or alongside it (e.g., the now-troubled European Union).

However, such organizations have not led to world peace. Since the formation of the UN, there have been several major interstate wars—conflicts fought between different countries—including the Korean War; the war in Vietnam; various wars involving Israel and its Arab neighbors; and conflicts in Iraq, Afghanistan, Syria, Yemen, and Ukraine. However, while the number of interstate wars has decreased significantly since the UN's founding, intrastate conflicts such as civil wars endure, as shown in Figure 13.2.

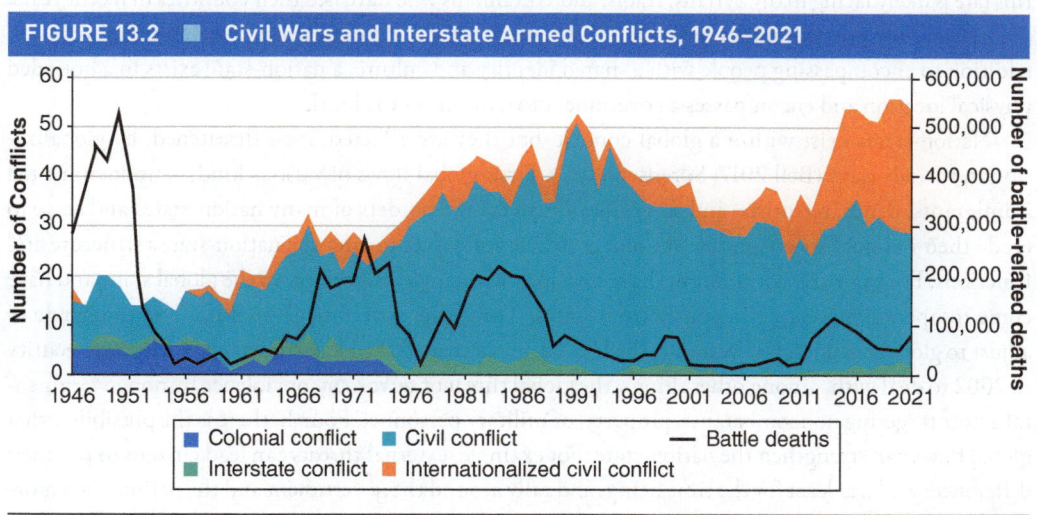

FIGURE 13.2 ■ Civil Wars and Interstate Armed Conflicts, 1946–2021

Source: Palik, Júli, Siri Aas Rustad, and Fredrik Methi, 2020, Conflict Trends: A Global Overview, 1946–2021, Peace Research Institute Oslo. (https://www.prio.org/publications/12442).

Geopolitics

Geopolitics entails political relationships that involve broad geographic areas, including the globe as a whole. On the one hand, geopolitics is concerned with how politics affects geography. One example is the ways in which national borders are redrawn after the end of a war. On the other hand, geopolitics is concerned with the ways in which geography affects politics. One example is the (usually) constant low-level warfare between Israel and its neighbors. After World War II, much of geopolitics focused on the relationship between the United States and the Soviet Union and its allies. There was great concern over the global expansion of communism. The United States and the Soviet Union clashed, usually indirectly, over their political influence in Germany, Korea, Cuba, Vietnam, and elsewhere. For decades, the United States acted based on what was known as the *domino theory:* If one nation was to turn to communism, many neighboring nations would do the same. For example, the United States feared that if Vietnam became communist, neighboring countries like Laos and Cambodia would be next. The United States and its relationships with Russia, China, and the Islamic world are often considered to be at the center of geopolitics today.

The Nation and the Nation-State

Geopolitics relates to core concerns in the global age: the future of the nation and the nation-state. A **nation** is a group of people who share, often over a long period of time, similar cultural, religious, ethnic, and linguistic characteristics (Knott 2017). Jews are a nation by this definition, as are their frequent geopolitical enemies, the Palestinians. Although many Jews and Palestinians live in the Middle East, many others, especially Jews, are spread throughout the world. They are scattered or dispersed; they exist in a diaspora. The wars in Syria and Iraq and the invasion of Ukraine have forced millions to flee, creating a new diaspora that has upended politics in many nations, especially in Europe.

All diasporas share certain characteristics. First, they involve people who have been dispersed from their homelands. Second, the people in the diaspora retain a collective and idealized memory of the homeland that they transmit to their offspring as well as to other members of the diaspora. Third, as a result of this idealization, they are often alienated from their host countries; the realities of the host country cannot measure up to the idealizations associated with the homeland. Fourth, those in the diaspora often take as a political goal the idea and the objective of returning to the homeland (Cohen 1997). Many of those involved in a nation, especially those in the diaspora, may have no direct contact with the homeland or with those who live there. Their linkages to them may be largely or purely imaginary. In other words, they exist in what Benedict Anderson (1991) calls **imagined communities**, or communities socially constructed by those who see themselves as part of them. Thus, Jews who have never been to Israel, or who may never even want to visit there, may still be part of an imagined community rooted in Israel. The same is true of the relationship between Palestine and many Palestinians scattered throughout the world, and this fate is likely facing many Syrians, Iraqis, and Ukrainians who have fled their countries in recent years.

The **nation-state** combines the nation with a geographic and political structure. In other words, in addition to encompassing people with a shared identity and culture, a nation-state exists in a bounded physical location and encompasses a government to administer the locale.

Nation-states exist within a global context, but they are affected, even threatened, by globalization in various ways (Bell 2017; Sørensen 2017). First, global flows of various kinds—undocumented immigrants, drugs, terrorists, and so on—easily pierce the borders of many nation-states and serve to erode their national sovereignties. Second, globalization serves to alter the nation-state's structure and functions. For example, corporations have become increasingly important on the global stage and have come to operate more autonomously from states. Third, the government itself has had to change to adjust to global changes. For example, the United States created the Department of Homeland Security in 2002 to deal with, among other things, the global threat of **terrorism**, or violence by nongovernmental actors targeting noncombatants, property, or military personnel. Fourth, there is the possibility that global flows can strengthen the nation-state. For example, external threats can lead citizens to put their differences aside, at least for the time being, and rally around the government and the nation-state more broadly. There are many serious internal divisions in Ukraine, but the invasion of the country by Russia has led many Ukrainians to put those differences aside and present a united front.

Despite changes such as those described previously, we continue to think of nation-states as being all-powerful. However, not only have states experienced the kinds of problems described here; a number of them have failed, or are on the verge of failing, to fulfill the "basic conditions and responsibilities" of sovereign states (Boas 2012, 633). Among the characteristics of a **failed state** are a "lack of control over own territory, widespread corruption and criminality, huge economic recession and/or hyperinflation, failure to provide basic services, and large flows of refugees and internally displaced persons" (Boas 2012, 633). Failed states also tend to exploit one segment of society (the middle and lower classes, for example) for the benefit of another subset, especially the rich (Acemoglu and Robinson 2012). The Fragile States Index, an annual ranking of 179 nations, highlights weak and failing states around the world based on their levels of stability (see Figure 13.3). In 2022, the countries that received the worst scores were Yemen, Somalia, Syria, South Sudan, and the Central African Republic.

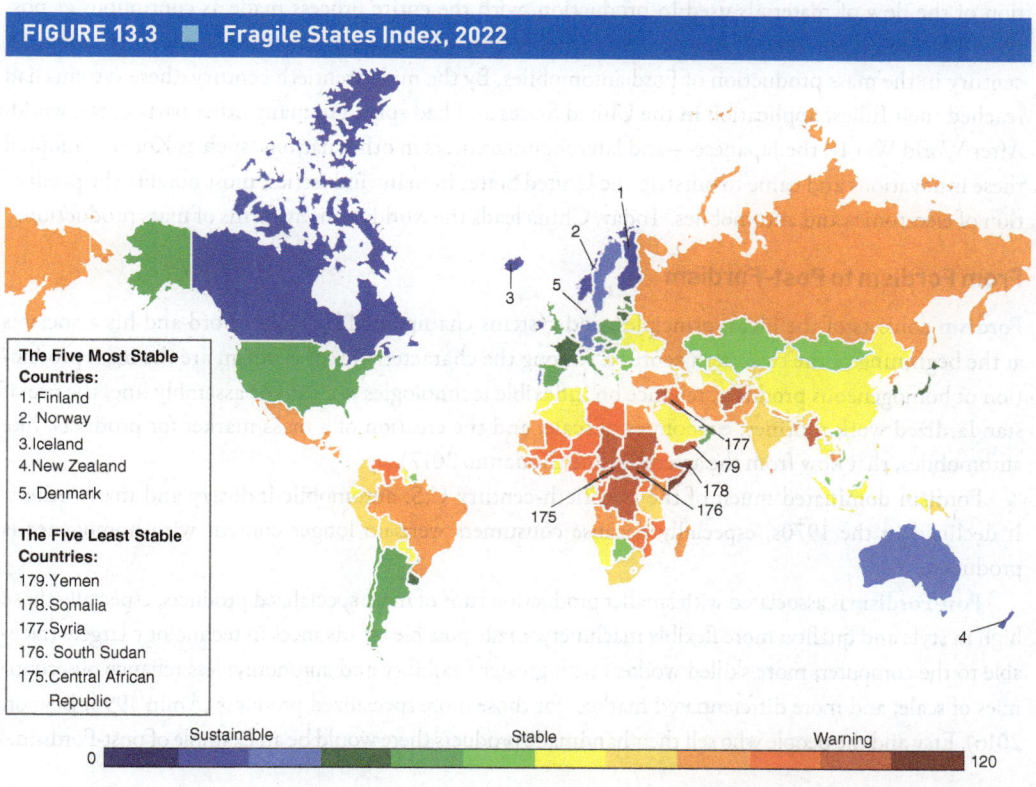

FIGURE 13.3 ■ Fragile States Index, 2022

The Five Most Stable Countries:
1. Finland
2. Norway
3. Iceland
4. New Zealand
5. Denmark

The Five Least Stable Countries:
179. Yemen
178. Somalia
177. Syria
176. South Sudan
175. Central African Republic

Source: Data from Fund for Peace, "Fragile States Index 2022."

THE ECONOMY: FROM INDUSTRIAL TO POSTINDUSTRIAL

The **economy** is the social system involved in the production, consumption, and distribution of goods and services. Over the last 200-plus years, many economies, especially those in the U.S. and the "West," have increasingly moved from reliance on industry and mass production to a postindustrial society characterized by the decline of manufacturing and a corresponding increase in the service and information sectors.

The Industrial Revolution

The key development in the emergence of the modern capitalistic economy was the nineteenth-century Industrial Revolution which introduced the factory system of production (Freeman 2018; Hobsbawm and Wrigley 1999). Instead of making products alone at home or in small groups in workshops, large numbers of workers were brought together in factories. Eventually, manual factory work with hand tools gave way to work in conjunction with machines. In addition, human and animal power were replaced by power supplied by steam and other energy sources. Although there were skilled workers in these early factories, they tended over time to be replaced because skills were increasingly likely to be built into the machinery. This meant that less skilled or even unskilled workers, less well-trained and lower-paid workers, and even children could be—and were—hired to do the work. They tended to work increasingly long hours in harsh working conditions and at ever lower pay. Another defining characteristic of this factory system was an elaborate division of labor by which a single product was produced by a number of workers, each performing a small step in the overall process.

The factories of the early Industrial Revolution were quite primitive, but over time they grew much larger, more efficient, more technologically advanced, and more oriented toward the mass production of a wide variety of goods.

The **mass production** intimately associated with factories has a number of defining characteristics, including large numbers of standardized products, highly specialized workers, interchangeable machine parts, precision tools, a high-volume mechanized production process, and the synchronization of the flow of materials used in production, with the entire process made as continuous as possible. The logical outcome of this was the assembly line, which came to fruition in the early twentieth century in the mass production of Ford automobiles. By the mid-twentieth century, these systems had reached their fullest application in the United States and had spread to many other parts of the world. After World War II, the Japanese—and later manufacturers in other nations, such as Korea—adopted these innovations and came to outstrip the United States in many industries, most notably the production of electronics and automobiles. Today, China leads the world in many forms of mass production.

From Fordism to Post-Fordism

Fordism consists of the ideas, principles, and systems championed by Henry Ford and his associates at the beginning of the twentieth century. Among the characteristics of Fordism are the mass production of homogeneous products, reliance on inflexible technologies such as the assembly line, the use of standardized work routines, economies of scale, and the creation of a mass market for products, like automobiles, that flow from the assembly line (Bonanno 2017).

Fordism dominated much of the twentieth-century U.S. automobile industry and many others. It declined in the 1970s, especially because consumers were no longer content with homogeneous products.

Post-Fordism is associated with smaller production runs of more specialized products, especially those high in style and quality; more flexible machinery, made possible by advances in technology largely traceable to the computer; more skilled workers with greater flexibility and autonomy; less reliance on economies of scale; and more differentiated markets for those more specialized products (Amin 1994; Beynon 2016). Etsy and the people who sell their handmade products there would be an example of post-Fordism.

Other Industrial Revolutions

Although there was certainly a nineteenth-century Industrial Revolution, revolutions in industry did not end with it. This is clear in the preceding discussion of the rise of post-Fordism. However, industrial revolutions continue apace with a combination of new technologies (e.g., digitization, automation, robotization, artificial intelligence), as well as other developments (e.g., globalization), leading to a twenty-first-century industrial revolution that could rival, or even exceed, in impact that of the nineteenth century. As a result of this emerging revolution, there will be an increase in at least short-term unemployment and, more important, a large-scale displacement of workers from middle-class, middle-income jobs (e.g., factory work, truck driving) to those that offer a far lower wage and thrust those who hold them into the lower class (e.g., in food service, care for the elderly). In contrast, those in more upper-class, upper-income occupations will be less affected by these changes, and many will be advantaged by them. The result will be an even more bifurcated work world. In addition, there will likely be an increasingly polarized political system with the winners and losers in this most recent industrial revolution having very different, if not conflicting, economic and political interests (Edsall 2018c).

Socialism, Communism, and Capitalism

From its inception, the Industrial Revolution was capitalist in nature, but it eventually gave rise to the alternative systems of socialism and communism.

Socialism and Communism

The terms *socialism* and *communism* are often used more or less interchangeably. However, it is important to differentiate between them. **Socialism** is an economic system oriented to the collective, rather than the private, ownership of the means of production. The means of production are the tools, machines, and factories that in capitalism are owned by the capitalists and are needed by the workers—the proletariat, in Marx's terms—to produce. Marx hoped that the exploitation of the proletariat would lead them to revolt against the capitalist system. That, in turn, would lead to collective rather than private ownership of the means of production, resulting in a communist economy. Control of the economic base would lead to control of everything else of importance, including the political system.

From a Marxian perspective, **communism** is a historical stage that follows socialism. It involves the effort by society to plan and organize production consciously and rationally so all members of society benefit from it, not just a privileged few. The collective control of the means of production in communism is a first step, but in itself it is not enough to run a society. Once in control of the means of production, the collectivity must set about the task of creating a rational centralized economy (and society) that operates for the good of all and creates social and economic equality.

The ideas associated with communism and socialism are still important in the world today. That said, few countries openly identify themselves as socialist or communist (North Korea, Cuba, and Venezuela are notable exceptions). China continues to see itself as a communist society, even though it is on the cusp of becoming the most powerful capitalist country in the world. In China, a political commitment to communism coexists uncomfortably with a highly capitalistic economic system.

Welfare States

Although there are no fully socialist societies in the world today, many societies have socialistic elements. In fact, nearly all do. The military, public libraries, and the police and fire departments are examples of socialistic elements found in most societies.

Many western European countries have become **welfare states**. They have powerful social welfare programs that are socialistic in nature, in that they are run consciously and rationally by centralized authorities. Welfare states seek both to operate their economic markets efficiently, as capitalism does, and to do so equitably, which capitalism does *not* do (Gamble 2016; Garland 2016). Their goal is to provide for the welfare—the well-being—of their citizens. There are many examples of social welfare programs, including national health plans, old-age plans, childcare and parental leave systems, and social safety nets of various kinds (e.g., unemployment insurance).

Even the United States has social welfare programs, such as unemployment insurance, Social Security, and Medicare. However, the United States lags far behind leaders in Western Europe (and Canada) in these kinds of programs. Powerful forces in the United States aligned with capitalism strongly resist efforts to expand social welfare programs.

While the United States struggles to implement more social welfare programs, the most developed social welfare states in Europe are experiencing something of a crisis and finding it difficult to maintain existing programs (Degen, Kuhn, and van der Brug 2018). In fact, some, especially Great Britain, are retrenching in various ways, such as offering less generous benefits and programs, making it more difficult for people to qualify for them, and making people take greater responsibility for providing for their own welfare. Threats to, and declines in, social welfare programs have spread throughout Europe as a result of the Great Recession and the COVID-19 pandemic (and other reasons). Programs are in danger even in countries such as Sweden, which has long been at the forefront in social welfare programs.

This Russian poster of 1920 depicts Soviet leader Vladimir Lenin sweeping the exploiting classes off the earth.

Granger, NYC—All rights reserved.

Capitalism

Karl Marx lived during the era of **competitive capitalism**, characterized by a large number of relatively small firms. No single firm or small subset of firms could completely dominate and control a given area of the economy. However, in the late nineteenth century and into much of the twentieth century, this situation changed. Huge corporations emerged and, alone or in combination with a few other similarly sized corporations, came to dominate, or monopolize, certain markets. This was **monopoly capitalism** (Baran and Sweezy 1966). Perhaps the best example was the U.S. automobile industry, which for much of the twentieth century was dominated by three huge corporations—General Motors, Ford, and Chrysler.

Although the U.S. automobile companies no longer constitute a monopoly, huge new corporations have emerged that can be considered monopolistic (Posner and Weyl 2018). These include Amazon (Stewart 2018a), Walmart, Facebook, and Alphabet (mainly Google). These new monopolies are being formed despite the continued existence of antimonopoly and antitrust laws in many places. This concentration of economic power is dangerous economically (e.g., by leading to hegemonic companies raising prices with little fear of being undercut by competitors). It is also dangerous politically, with the hegemony of one or a few companies being associated historically with the rise of fascism in Nazi Germany and elsewhere (Wu 2018). Furthermore, we are likely to see the emergence of a global system of monopoly capitalism in which a small number of corporations come to dominate a global, not just national, market.

Whether or not capitalism once again becomes monopolistic, in recent years it has certainly become increasingly global. This can be seen as **transnational capitalism**, in which transnational, rather than national, economic practices predominate (Kauppinen 2013; Sklair 2002). For example, the global flow of automobiles and even money has become far more important than their existence and movement within national boundaries.

It could also be argued that the center of capitalism no longer lies in production but rather in consumption. That is, the focus is on inducing large numbers of people throughout the world to consume at high levels. The capitalism of Marx's day was described as producer capitalism, but we now live more in an era of consumer capitalism. Within the realm of consumption, some of the leading transnational corporations are Amazon, Walmart, IKEA, H&M, and McDonald's.

Ritzer (2015b) has argued that we are living in yet a later stage of capitalism—"prosumer capitalism." The **prosumer** is *both* producer and consumer, often at the same time. Producer and consumer capitalism will continue to exist, but they will gradually be subsumed and supplanted by prosumer capitalism. Prosumption is occurring increasingly in many businesses (e.g., the consumer putting together—"producing"—a bookshelf purchased—"consumed"—at IKEA), but it is most notable on the internet, where there is virtually no distinction between producer and consumer. For example, one must produce the order for what one wants to consume on Amazon.com. With the increasing ubiquity of 3-D printers, prosumers will be able to produce at home (through additive manufacturing) more and more of the things they are now interested in consuming.

An even better example is Facebook (and their many other subsidiaries like Instagram), which will become increasingly profitable on the basis of accumulating—in the form of "Big Data"—all the free information provided to them by prosumers on those Facebook pages (Radford and Lazer 2020). Facebook will sell, and already is selling, that information in anonymous

IKEA exemplifies the idea of prosumer capitalism. Customers are not only consumers but producers, assembling the furniture themselves—often with difficulty!

Iain Masterton / Alamy Stock Photo

batches of Big Data to corporations, which can then use that information to target just the right consumers for their goods and services. If Ford is a model of producer capitalism, and McDonald's is a paradigm of consumer capitalism, then Facebook is likely the model of the coming predominance of prosumer capitalism.

Deindustrialization

Industry and industrial employment were (and are) clearly crucial to economic development in the most countries. However, a number of nations have been undergoing a process of deindustrialization. **Deindustrialization** involves the decline of manufacturing as well as a corresponding increase in various types of services (Goldstein 2017; Koistinen 2016; Linkon 2018).

We tend to think of deindustrialization as a process that has been going on for decades, is now far advanced, and may even be near completion. In the United States, the focus tends to be on the Rust Belt and the demise, beginning in the 1960s, of such steel cities as Pittsburgh and Bethlehem, Pennsylvania; Youngstown and Akron, Ohio; and Gary, Indiana (see Figure 13.4). The steel industries are all but gone, and these cities have suffered greatly, although in a few cases, such as Pittsburgh, they have been able to reinvent themselves. The decline of the auto industry began a bit later, but it, too, has clearly undergone massive deindustrialization. This is reflected in the decline of many cities, most notably in Detroit (Silver 2015). Although Detroit is now slowly being revitalized, it is highly unlikely that its economic woes are over. Deindustrialization has not yet run its course, and other industries, such as the glass industry, are now experiencing this process as well (Uchitelle 2010).

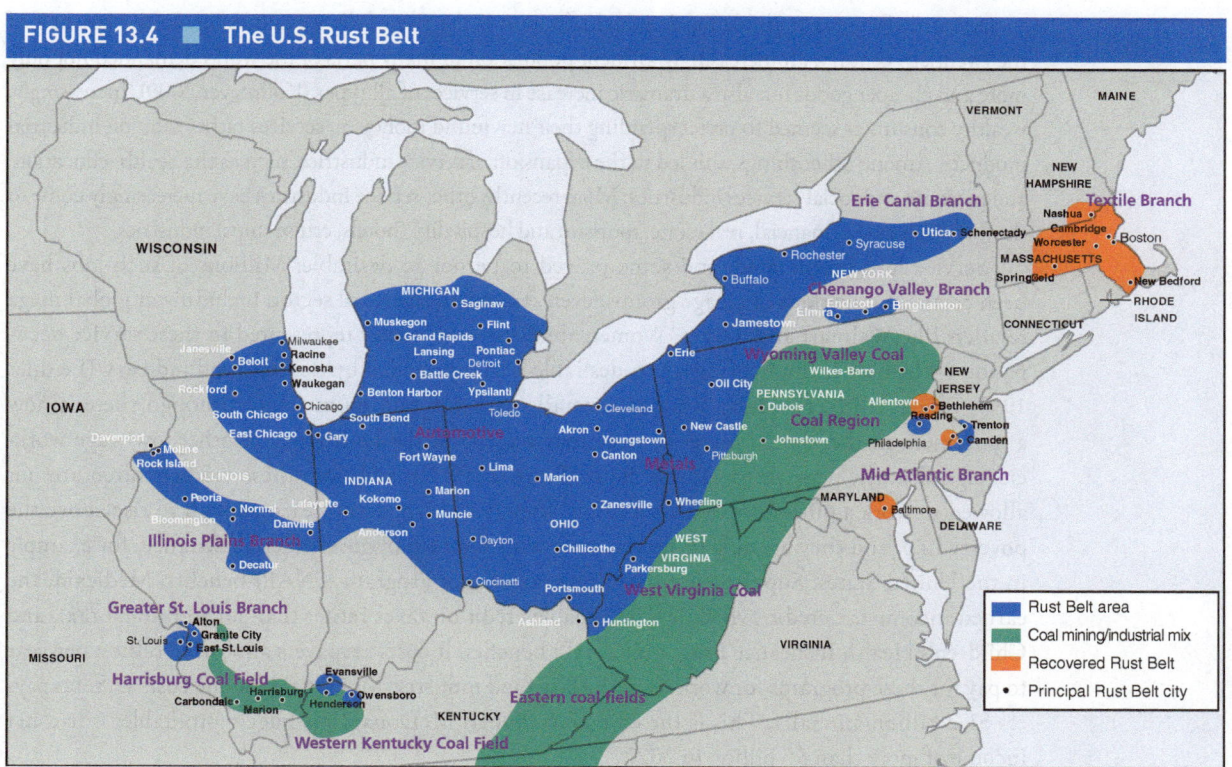

FIGURE 13.4 ■ The U.S. Rust Belt

Factors in Deindustrialization

Several factors were (and are) responsible for deindustrialization. First was the aging technology in many industries. This made them vulnerable to foreign competitors, which were often building new, state-of-the-art factories. Another technological factor was the rise of automation, which greatly reduced the need for many blue-collar workers, and, more recently, robotization, which eliminated the need for many other types of workers (Ford 2016; Ross 2017). Furthermore, the increased efficiency of automated technologies made it possible for corporations to close unnecessary factories, thus cutting many more jobs.

Second was globalization, which brought with it industrial competition from lower-wage workers in other countries. This was especially true in the early years of the emergence of China as an industrial power. Now, of course, China is developing rapidly, but its still relatively low wages and higher population of workers will make it nearly impossible for many foreign industries to compete with Chinese industries. It will take quite some time for Chinese wages—and prices—to rise to a level that approximates those in many other countries, but the trend is in that direction, especially as wages for many workers have risen little in recent years. Another aspect of globalization as it relates to deindustrialization is the closing of factories, especially in the United States, and, in some cases, their movement, or at least the relocation of their jobs, elsewhere in the world (for example, from the United States to Mexico).

A third factor in deindustrialization is the rise of consumer society and the increasing demand for goods of all types. This should have helped some industries, but it led many manufacturers in lower-wage countries to become more eager to sell products to the huge and growing global consumer market. Many industries in higher-wage countries have had great difficulty competing with them. In terms of the demand for goods, there arose, partly as a result of the low prices offered by foreign manufacturers, a mania among consumers for ever lower prices. This worked to the advantage of lower-wage manufacturers because of their much lower cost structures, especially their lower labor costs. Consumer obsession with lower prices for things like fast food and fast fashion has led to the "high cost of low price" (Spotts and Greenwald 2005), or the unfortunate unanticipated consequences of such low prices. Among those consequences are the heightened exploitation of foreign workers, an increasing preference for goods produced by low-cost foreign manufacturers, and a decline in the number of manufacturers in higher-wage countries and the jobs they offer. There have also been untold negative environmental consequences.

A fourth factor responsible for deindustrialization is the rise of the service sector. In the last half of the twentieth century, an increasingly affluent population in many parts of the world demanded not only more and cheaper goods but also a dramatic increase in services of all types (Kollmeyer 2009). Increasingly, wealthy consumers seemed to prefer spending their newfound money on services rather than on industrial products. Among other things, this led to the expansion of service industries, such as the health, education, and personal and social services industries. More recently, other service industries have increasingly come to the fore, such as the financial, real estate, tourism, and hospitality (hotels, cruise ships) industries.

Service jobs proliferated, and some proved to be not so desirable. Millions of such jobs have been created for workers of all age groups, even seniors, in the retail sector, including at global mega retailers like Walmart and Target. Women are disproportionally represented in these service occupations. The best example of less-than-desirable jobs is provided by the fast-food industry (Leidner 1993; Ritzer 2019). Fast-food workers generally earn the minimum wage, although there is now a movement in the United States to raise that wage (and the hourly pay of other low-wage workers) significantly, perhaps to $15 per hour (Barro 2015). In addition, these workers often are not allowed to work a 40-hour week. As a result, they frequently do not earn enough to rise above the poverty line, and they are able to survive only with the help of government assistance, for example in the United States, Supplemental Nutrition Assistance Program (SNAP) benefits, Medicaid, the earned income tax credit (which is a refundable credit on taxes rather than an additional tax), and Children's Health Insurance Program (CHIP) benefits. It costs taxpayers almost $7 billion per year to pay for these programs for workers in the fast-food industry. McDonald's alone costs U.S. taxpayers $1.2 billion annually. This is the case even though McDonald's is hugely profitable; it had net income of more than $6 billion in 2022.

Decline of Labor Unions

Closely related to deindustrialization is the decline of labor unions in the United States (and elsewhere; Dubofsky and McCartin 2017; Hogler 2015; Milkman and Luce 2017). The U.S. labor movement grew from 3 percent of the labor force in 1900 to 23 percent by the close of World War II. A decline began in the 1960s, at about the same time as the onset of deindustrialization and the rise of the service sector. As of 2021, only about 10.3 percent of the U.S. labor force belonged to labor unions (see Figure 13.5). As a result, union power has declined significantly as reflected, for example, in the dramatic decline in recent years in the use of their most powerful weapon—strikes.

FIGURE 13.5 ■ U.S. Union Membership among All Wage and Salary Workers, 1973–2021

Source: Union Membership and Coverage Database, 2021, *Historical Tables: Union Membership, Coverage, Density, and Employment, 1973-2021* (https://unionstats.com/).

A number of reasons explain this decline in unionization, although deindustrialization, the decline of manufacturing, and the loss of blue-collar jobs rank at the top of the list. Many of those jobs either left their home countries or were and are being automated out of existence (and many more will disappear in the coming years). Prosumers are now doing work with little (or no) economic reward. For example, Uber drivers get limited economic rewards. They are part of the growing "**gig economy**" involving generally short-term freelance work usually with and through digital platforms. These are mainly low-paid jobs involving work that many people were paid pretty well to do not too long ago (Prassi 2018). Although Uber is the best-known example of this, there are many others, such as the work to be found on TaskRabbit (Kalleberg and Dunn 2016).

Prosumers also labor for no economic reward (by, for example, serving themselves at fast-food restaurants or doing the work of bank tellers at ATMs). The great increase in service and white-collar work, as well as in the role of prosumers, involves a workforce that is, in the main, uninterested in, or even hostile to, unionization.

Today, the union movement is dramatically smaller, but its membership seems, at least for now, to have stabilized, buttressed by some successes, especially in the public realm. In fact, in 2009, for the first time, a majority of union members in the United States were employed by the government (Greenhouse 2011). One area of success has been teachers and their unions, especially the more than 3-million-member National Education Association (NEA) and the 1.7-million-member American Federation of Teachers (AFT). However, even that outcome has been threatened by movements in some states (Ohio, Wisconsin, and Illinois) to eliminate collective bargaining by teachers, as well as by public-sector employees more generally.

The Postindustrial Society

Clearly, deindustrialization, the decline in industrial jobs and industrial unions, set the stage for the emergence of postindustrialism. An increasing emphasis on consumption and the dramatic growth in service jobs, many of which exist to serve a consumer-oriented society, pushed many countries even further from industrialization and toward a truly postindustrial society (Bell 1973; Hage and Powers 1992; Vogt 2016).

A **postindustrial society** is one that was once industrial, but the focus on the manufacture of goods has been replaced by an increase in service work. The latter is work in which people provide services for one another rather than producing goods. It encompasses a wide range of service-oriented occupations, including lawyer, physician, teacher, financial adviser, computer technician, salesperson, clerk, counter person at a fast-food restaurant, and work performed by those in the gig economy and prosumers. Involvement in such work has increased dramatically in the last century, while there has been a similarly dramatic decline in work relating to goods production. Agricultural work declined earlier and even more steeply.

WORK, CONSUMPTION, AND LEISURE

Much of the preceding discussion has dealt with the economy in terms of general trends and developments. However, most people connect to the economy either through their work or the process of consumption, to be discussed below.

Employment, Unemployment, and Underemployment

The relationship between people and their work is changing rapidly. Not long ago, we tended to think of people as taking jobs, perhaps in large and stable organizations, and embarking on lifelong careers. Those careers entailed at least some upward mobility, sufficient earnings for workers and their families to live on, and retirement with ample pensions when workers reached their early 60s.

However, there are several problems with this romantic scenario. First, even in its heyday from about 1950 to 1990, it applied to only a very small proportion of the population. Employment has ebbed and flowed over time. It has always been true that a number of people have been unable to get a job. **Unemployment** can be defined as being economically active and in the labor force (e.g., not retired), able and willing to work, and seeking employment but unable to find a job. The unemployment rate in the United States has generally run at about 5 percent of the labor force. However, in the midst of the recession in 2009, it reached 10 percent. Many observers believe 10 percent was an underestimate because many people had given up searching for work and were therefore not included in the unemployment statistics (see the discussion of discouraged workers that follows). However, in the midst of a booming economy, in April 2019, the unemployment rate had dropped to 3.6 percent. Unemployment spiked again in spring, 2020, to 14.7 percent as a result of disruptions to the global economy caused by the COVID-19 pandemic; by spring 2023 it had dropped to 3.4 percent (see Figure 13.6).

Unemployment is likely to increase in the future, especially as result of further automation. Machines and artificial intelligence (AI) will be able to do an increasing number of jobs now performed by humans. Although they have already long replaced blue-collar workers, these new technologies will increasingly do some or all of the work now done by more highly paid and skilled workers. For example, fewer clothing buyers or financial advisers will be needed as decisions will increasingly be made by AI (Scheiber 2018).

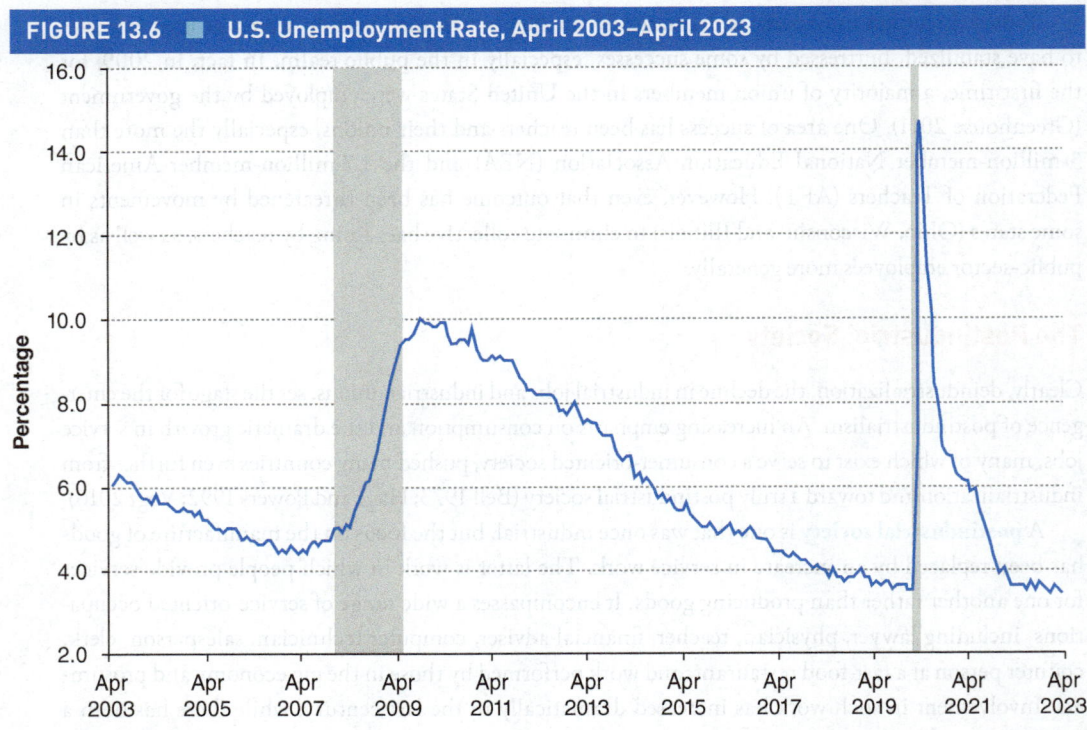

FIGURE 13.6 ■ U.S. Unemployment Rate, April 2003–April 2023

Source: Data from U.S. Department of Labor, Bureau of Labor Statistics, May 2023. U.S. Bureau of Labor Statistics, 2022, *Civilian Unemployment Rate, Seasonally Adjusted,* Washington, DC: United States Department of Labor. Retrieved August 2, 2022 (https://www.bls.gov/charts/employment-situation/civilian-unemployment-rate.htm).

William Julius Wilson has published research on race, social class, and the city and is particularly known for his contributions regarding the reasons for the persistence of poverty and inequality for African Americans. He has received many awards and holds 46 honorary degrees.

Paul Marotta/Getty Images

William Julius Wilson (1997) focuses on long-term unemployment and the problems it creates for Black Americans. Many observers have traced these difficulties (e.g., children without involved fathers, drug abuse) to social structural problems (e.g., institutional racism) that are presumably quite difficult to solve. However, Wilson links them directly to unemployment and thus sees them as solvable through a number of reforms, including the creation of more work for all Black Americans. Black Americans experience not only greater unemployment but also a long list of additional difficulties associated with being unemployed, not the least of which is a higher incidence of poverty. In 2022, the unemployment rate for black Americans was almost double the rate for whites and Asians and 3 percentage points higher than that for Hispanics (see Figure 13.7).

FIGURE 13.7 ■ U.S. Unemployment by Race and Ethnicity, 2022

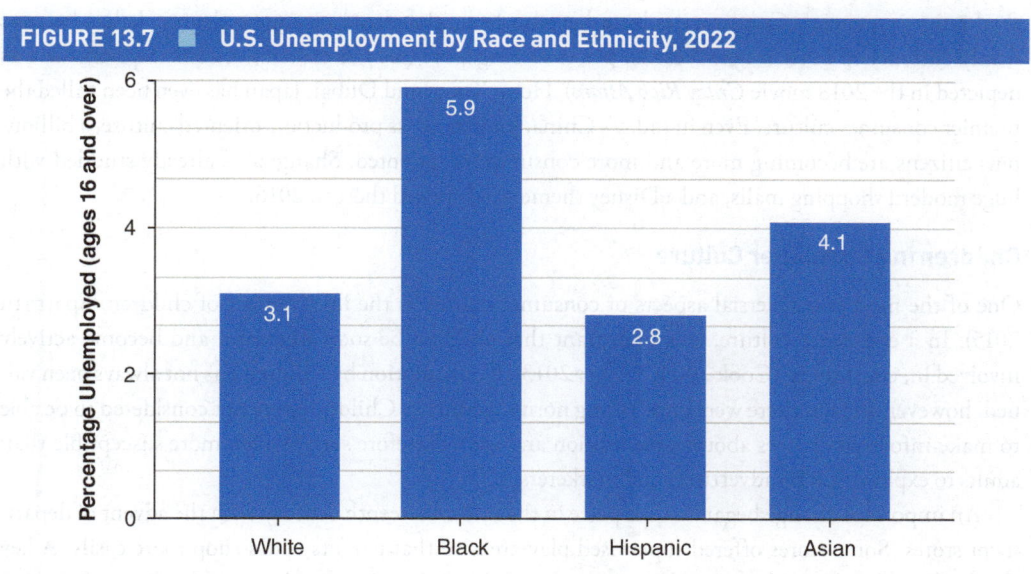

Race/Ethnicity	Percentage Unemployed (ages 16 and over)
White	3.1
Black	5.9
Hispanic	2.8
Asian	4.1

Source: Data from U.S. Department of Labor, Bureau of Labor Statistics, 2022. U.S. Bureau of Labor Statistics, 2022, Unemployment *Rates by Age, Sex, Race, and Hispanic or Latino Ethnicity,* Labor Force Statistics from the Current Population Survey, Washington, DC: United States Department of Labor. Retrieved August 2, 2022 (https://www.bls.gov/web/empsit/cpsee_e16.htm).

The statistics on unemployment understate the problem of lack of work because they deal only with those in the labor force actively seeking work. Another large group of people marginally attached to the workforce includes **discouraged workers**. To be categorized as such, people must have sought work within the last year or since their last job ended, if that was less than a year previous, and must have not sought work in the last four weeks. Other reasons to be considered marginally attached to the labor force include being prevented from working because of family responsibilities or because of a lack of transportation.

A large number of people must also cope with the problem of **underemployment**. This involves (a) being in jobs not up to one's training and ability, such as a college professor driving a taxi at night; (b) being an involuntary part-time worker, that is, working part-time because one cannot find full-time work; or (c) working in jobs that are not fully occupying, such as in a seasonal industry like agriculture, where work slows down dramatically or disappears in the off-season. The latter type of underemployment is also increasingly associated with today's gig economy.

Consumption and Consumer Culture

Consumption is clearly highly valued in many parts of the world (Ryan 2011). Those cultures are increasingly becoming **consumer cultures**, ones in which the core ideas and material objects relate to consumption and in which consumption is a primary source of meaning in life (Berger 2015; Cook and Ryan 2015; Slater 2015; Wiedenhoft Murphy 2017b). In a consumer culture, meaning may be found in the goods and services you buy, in the process of buying them (in shopping malls, cybermalls, and so on), in the social aspects of consumption (shopping with your friends or family), and even in the settings in which consumption takes place (Ritzer, Goodman, and Wiedenhoft 2001; Ryan 2013). There are norms for the consumption process as well. For example, customers should wait patiently in the queue for the cashier, gamblers at a Las Vegas casino should not flaunt their winnings in front of other gamblers and should tip dealers, and so on.

Contemporary consumer culture is unique (Trentman 2016). In the past, culture has generally focused on some other aspect of social life, such as religion, warfare, citizenship, or work. In fact, in the not-too-distant past in many countries, the core ideas and material objects of culture related to work and production. People were thought to derive their greatest meaning from their work. This was true from the Industrial Revolution until approximately 1970, when observers began to realize that some people in some societies were beginning to derive more meaning from consumption (Baudrillard [1970] 1998). Of course, work continues to be important, as do religion, warfare, and citizenship, but many people in the world now live in a culture dominated by consumption.

Today, consumer culture has arguably become *the* culture of many countries and, indeed, of modernity in general. Consumer culture has also been globalized to a great degree. It has become firmly entrenched in such non-Western places as Singapore (see the excesses of consumption there as depicted in the 2018 movie *Crazy Rich Asians*), Hong Kong, and Dubai. Japan has even been called the premier consumer culture. Even in today's China, known for its production-oriented culture, a billion-plus citizens are becoming more and more consumption oriented. Shanghai is already studded with huge modern shopping malls, and a Disney theme park opened there in 2016.

Children in a Consumer Culture

One of the most controversial aspects of consumer culture is the involvement of children (Sparman 2015). In a consumer culture, it is important that children be socialized into, and become actively involved in, consuming (Cook 2004; Pilcher 2013). Consumption by children has not always been valued, however. In fact, there were once strong norms against it. Children were not considered to be able to make informed choices about consumption and were therefore seen as even more susceptible than adults to exploitation by advertisers and marketers.

An important change began to take place in the mid-nineteenth century with the advent of department stores. Some stores offered supervised play areas so that parents could shop more easily. A key development by the mid-twentieth century was children's sections in department stores; they were eventually subdivided into shops for babies, children, and teens. Also during this period, radio programs, movies, and TV shows were increasingly directed at children. Disney was a leader in this trend.

TV shows of the 1950s, such as the Davy Crockett series (*King of the Wild Frontier*), prompted the sale of hundreds of millions of dollars' worth of simulated coonskin caps and other merchandise for children. More recently, children have come to be targeted directly by advertisers on Saturday-morning TV shows and cable channels such as Nickelodeon that specialize in children's programming.

In fact, marketing aimed at children is now pervasive. This is portrayed in detail in the documentary *Consuming Kids* (2008). For example, the Walt Disney Company directly markets baby products, and thus the Disney brand, to new mothers in maternity wards. In schools, branded products are sold at book fairs, and corporate sponsorships adorn everything from sports stadiums to classroom supplies. Brands and logos are woven into textbook problems and examples. Market researchers observe the way in which children use and respond to products and advertising messages not just in focus groups and in the lab but also in natural settings such as school and the home. Marketers have also discovered the importance of the "pester power" of children. This is the ability of children to nag their parents into buying things. It is effective not only for selling children's products but also for getting children to influence their parents' purchases.

Overall, children are much more immersed in consumer culture today than ever before. There is even a growing market for credit cards aimed directly at children! They learn at an early age to value consumer culture as well as the norms involved in participating in it. As adults, then, they will be trained to fit well into a culture with consumption at its core.

Consumer Settings

Consumption occurs in many settings. Outdoor strip malls are traceable to the 1920s, and the first indoor malls were built in the 1950s, but the megamall, which arrived in the 1980s and 1990s (e.g., the Mall of America in Minneapolis in 1992), is the crucial innovation here. What defines the megamall is the combination under one roof of a number of different kinds of consumer settings. The theme park itself is a unique kind of consumption setting—the first landmark development for theme parks was the opening of Disneyland in Southern California in 1955. The modern cruise ship is another example, the first of which set sail in 1966. Yet another example is the hotel-casino, most notably of the type that defines Las Vegas and many other gambling destinations (like Atlantic City or Macau). The first of these in Las Vegas—the Flamingo—was built in 1946. It was the idea of the mobster Bugsy Siegel.

New York, New York, the hotel-casino complex on the Las Vegas strip, is one of the modern cathedrals of consumption.
bluejayphoto/iStockPhoto

Many of these sites can be seen as **cathedrals of consumption** (Ritzer 2010a; Ryan forthcoming). These are the large, sometimes lavish, consumption sites. The use of the term *cathedrals* is meant to indicate the fact that consumption has in many ways become today's religion. We go to the cathedrals of consumption to practice that religion. Thus, for example, many middle-class children make a pilgrimage to Disney World at least once in their lives.

Of course, there are many other important cathedrals of consumption—superstores such as Best Buy and IKEA, huge discounters such as Walmart and Costco, and online retailers and malls such as Amazon and eBay. These cathedrals, along with other consumption sites, especially chain stores such as McDonald's and Starbucks, have come to define not only the sites themselves but also much of consumption as a whole (Ritzer, Ryan, and Stepnisky 2005).

In the past we had to travel, sometimes long distances, to cathedrals of consumption such as department stores (Howard 2015), but now many of them are available via the internet on our home computers or the smartphones in our pockets or bags. As a result, brick-and-mortar cathedrals of consumption, such as department stores, shopping malls, and casinos, are in decline. However, innovative new brick-and mortar cathedrals of consumption continue to be created, especially in Asia (Friedman 2018). These include sites that emphasize experiences that build brand equity rather than simply increase sales. Consumption continues to grow, but in spite of innovations in Asia, much of it has shifted from offline to online cathedrals.

Other Types of Consumer Settings

An interesting aspect of consumer culture is the way in which it has spread beyond the economy to other aspects of society. For example, higher education is increasingly characterized by consumer culture. Students and their parents shop around for the best colleges and the most conspicuous degrees or for the best values in a college education. College rankings, such as those published by *Kiplinger* and *U.S. News & World Report*, are a big business. In spite of a great deal of criticism (and some recent failures) for-profit colleges have become a booming industry. Enterprises such as the University of Phoenix and Kaplan University enroll hundreds of thousands of students who pay for the opportunity to earn their degrees on a flexible schedule.

Not long ago, students were largely passive recipients of what educational systems had to offer, but now they are more active consumers of education. For example, college students shop for the best classes, or the best class times, and regularly rate their professors and choose classes on the basis of the professors' ratings. They are also much more likely to make demands for up-to-date "products" and attentive service from their professors and colleges, as they do from shopping malls and salespeople.

A key site of consumption is now the internet. A good portion of the time people spend online is related to consumption, either directly (by purchasing items on sites such as Etsy or Amazon) or indirectly (by buying things on game sites such as Farmville or CastleVille Legends with real dollars). The growing importance of online consumption is reflected in the increasing amount spent each year on "Cyber Monday" (the Monday after Thanksgiving). Cyber Monday 2022 saw shoppers in the United States alone spend $11.3 billion. Similarly, "Single's Day" is celebrated in China every year on November 11 (or 11-11; the ones, or singles, give the day its name). In 2021, Single's Day saw record-breaking sales of more than $139 billion, despite the ongoing COVID-19 pandemic. In addition, in a process known as "contextual advertising," advertisements are often woven seamlessly into the content of internet sites—even into games designed for children. Beyond that, many websites carry pop-up ads for goods and services targeted to the interests of the individuals viewing the sites. More specifically, if you use Google to shop for shoes or Amazon for books, ads for shoes and books will pop up for days, or even months, later on many of the sites you visit.

It could be argued that people in general, and especially children and teens, are becoming more immersed in consumer culture as they become more deeply enmeshed with the internet. This is even more the case now because we increasingly carry the internet—and the ability to shop there—with us all the time on our smartphones. As a result, consumer culture has become an even more inescapable part of our daily lives. Furthermore, consumption on the internet is increasingly wedded to the material world. You can pay for parking and rental cars using smartphone apps. An app allows a driver to open the doors of their rented Zipcar with their phone and honk its horn to locate it. The Hunt app brings into play a community of fashion-minded people to help us hunt down desired fashion items.

A Postconsumer Culture?

Many people are now doing something that would have been unthinkable only a few years ago: saving money. There are also a growing number of social movements, especially those connected to growing environmental concerns, that encourage people to consume less. These changes in the behavior of consumers and their attitudes speak to a change in the larger value system. Consuming less is a sure indication of at least a temporary decline of consumer culture. It may even be the beginning of a **postconsumer culture**. Among the characteristics of such a culture, beyond buying less and saving more, are sharing more things in the "sharing economy" (Belk 2014; Sundararajan 2016), renting consumer items (such as dresses on sites like Rent the Runway), taking pride in buying less expensive or even recycled items, buying less showy brands (a Kia rather than a BMW), dining at home more often than eating at restaurants, and showing a greater concern for the environment in terms of what we buy and, more important, do not buy. It is not clear that we are in a postconsumer culture, and if we are, it is uncertain how long it will last. However, just as we entered what is best described as a consumer culture in the last half of the twentieth century, it is at least possible that we are entering a postconsumer culture in the first half of the twenty-first century.

Another dent in consumer culture has been created by organized groups actively seeking to subvert aspects of both consumer culture and the larger culture. The success of Burning Man is one indication of such subversion. Begun in 1986, this annual weeklong event in Nevada's Black Rock Desert drew nearly 80,000 participants in 2019 who commit themselves during their stay to self-expression, decommodification (e.g., cash transactions between participants are banned), and community building (Chen 2009; Jones 2011).

Leisure

One of the dominant trends of our time is that more and more of our leisure time is devoted to consumption. For example, in golf, consumption includes acquisition of the equipment and proper clothing, payment of greens fees, and perhaps even the purchase of membership in a country club. Leisure time also takes place in settings entirely devoted to consumption, such as cruise ships or online casinos. Furthermore, for many people, consumption *is* leisure. Going to the shopping mall, online and offline, and making a variety of purchases can be very relaxing for some.

Leisure is defined as a means of escape from the obligations associated with work and daily obligations. It involves social activities that are not coerced. They are relaxing, perhaps informative, and set apart in time and often in space (Rojek 2005, 2007). People engaging in leisure are not just free from their usual obligations; they are also free to think differently and to do different things. It is presumed that when people are at leisure, they have much more freedom of choice than when they are at work.

However, much leisure activity takes place in settings designed to control and limit the thoughts and actions of those at leisure. The best example is Disney World, where all sorts of conveyances are provided to lead people to move around the park and its attractions quickly, efficiently, and in given directions. Even during the times when visitors seem to be wandering around the park on their own, subtle kinds of controls are exercised over them. Examples include preset paths, directional arrows, and signs. Most interesting from this perspective is what Walt Disney called "weenies," or highly visible attractions—mountains, castles, and the like—to which virtually all visitors will be drawn. Thus, they move in the direction of the weenies, the way that Disney management wants them to move. They do so without anyone telling them where they should go and how they should get there. This allows for the efficient movement of large numbers of visitors. On the way, they are led past many kiosks, shops, restaurants, and the like, where they can spend even more money.

Leisure time is strongly affected by social class. Many leisure activities (e.g., cruises, golf) are very expensive. Those in the lower rungs of the stratification system are largely excluded from them. Of course, there are many inexpensive and even free forms of leisure available to virtually everyone, but these are not generally deemed the most desirable forms in today's world. Furthermore, the demands of work, and even survival, make it difficult for the have-nots of the world to have much time for leisure-time activities.

Crowds at Walt Disney World, a global destination for leisure and consumption.
Joe Burbank/Orlando Sentinel/Tribune News Service via Getty Images

Women's leisure, in comparison with men's, has also tended to be more constrained by economic factors (Holland 2013). That is changing somewhat, as women in the middle classes are increasingly likely to have substantial incomes associated with occupations of their own. These occupations also tend to give them more demarcated time for leisure (e.g., vacation time), something that historically has been the province of men. Yet, because women still spend more hours per week on childcare and household maintenance than men do, a gendered leisure divide remains.

GLOBALIZATION AND THE ECONOMY

Globalization is associated with many changes in the economy. One of the most remarkable changes has been in **macrofinance**, or globalization as it relates to money and finance. Not long ago, money and finance were closely tied to the nation-state that issued the money and to the financial transactions that took place therein. Moving money and financial instruments—for example, stocks and bonds,—from one part of the world to another was difficult and cumbersome. Travelers needed to change their own country's currency into the currency of the country to which they were traveling. And if they were going to many different countries, they needed to repeat this transaction for each one. Now, however, all a traveler needs is a credit or debit card, which can be used in many places in most nations in the world to rapidly and efficiently pay for goods and services with the currency of each of the nations visited. As Dodd (2012, 1446) puts it, "We are witnessing the end of money's geography."

As a result, money is increasingly liquid, and it flows around the world readily. This is clearly true for tourists and businesspeople, but it is true in other ways as well: Substantial flows of money are associated with the informal economy, criminal networks, the international drug trade, and money laundering. For example, a 2016 scandal involved Panamanian law firm Mosseck Fonseca, which, among other things, was involved in the proliferation of shell companies and tax havens for the very rich that allowed them to evade taxation in their home country (Semple, Ahmed, and Lipton 2016). This became a global scandal that even resulted in the resignation of Iceland's prime minister and involved a number of celebrities being named including Lionel Messi, Tiger Woods, Simon Cowell, and Daddy Yankee.

To take another, more mundane example of the fluidity of money globally, much money flows in the form of remittances, largely from migrants in the Global North to family and friends back home in the Global South. In fact, in 2022, recorded remittances totaled $794 billion—though much more probably went unreported. Although this sounds like a great deal of money, it pales in comparison with other types of global financial transactions. For example, in only one aspect of the global financial market, the market for the world's currencies, just over $5 trillion changes hands *every day*.

The largest amounts of money by far flow easily and quickly through electronic transmissions associated with global financial markets (Knorr Cetina 2012). People and businesses increasingly depend on electronic transfers for the credit they need, or think they need, in today's world. Individuals usually need credit to purchase such things as homes and automobiles. Credit is also central to the growth and investments of corporations and governments.

Even more important is global trade in a series of obscure financial instruments. Questionable banking practices and speculative financial instruments tied to the U.S. housing market set off a global chain reaction in 2007–2008 that devastated international economic flows and triggered a global recession. Central to these problems was the fact that financial markets in both the United States and much of the rest of the world were deregulated to a great degree. Without governmental oversight, many of these markets were allowed to run wild. For example, rampant speculation in exotic financial instruments produced an economic bubble that burst violently, causing the recession to develop and gather momentum.

Cryptocurrencies are a growing way that money is moved around the world. Cryptocurrencies are a form of exchange that circulate without the oversight of a single authority, such as a central government. In 2022, there were more than 9000 cryptocurrencies in circulation, more than 70 of which were worth more than $1 billion each. As these currencies are often untraceable, including in who owns, and spends, them, they can be used for illegal purchases. Advocates argue that it allows for more privacy in terms of how we spend our money while critics worry that their rise will lead to an increase of the black market for things like weapons and drugs.

Globalization and Consumption

There has been a tendency to associate consumption with the United States and, as far as the globe is concerned, with Americanization (Ritzer and Ryan 2004). This is largely traceable to the affluence of the United States after the close of World War II and the economic difficulties encountered by most other societies in the world during that period. Thus, the United States developed an unprecedented and unmatched consumer society for several decades after the end of the war. At the same time, it began exporting consumer society—and its various elements—to much of the rest of the world. Much of U.S. consumer society has come to be adopted elsewhere in the world.

Stillerman (2015) argues that, in fact, the major areas for the expansion of consumer society are not in the Global North (mainly the United States and Europe) but in the lesser developed Global South. Although much about consumption there is the same or similar, there are also distinctive patterns of consuming an array of unique products and services. Beyond its sources in the United States and the Global North, consumption has roots in many other places in the world. Consumption as a central life interest is now a truly global phenomenon; we have increasingly become "a world of consumers" (Trentmann 2016).

The latter point brings us to the issue of globalization and consumption. The emphasis in the global economy is on greatly increasing flows of everything related to consumption and greatly decreasing any barriers to those flows. Especially important is expediting global flows of consumer goods and services of all types and of the financial processes and instruments that facilitate those flows. Thus, for example, the relatively small number of credit (and debit) card brands with origins in the United States, especially Visa and MasterCard, are increasingly accepted and used throughout the world (Ritzer 1995). They are usable at ATMs and checkout counters at businesses throughout the world. Especially notable in this regard are online consumption sites, some of them global in reach, that allow people to consume many of the same products using their credit cards. Credit cards serve to expedite not only global consumption but also the flow of global consumers, including tourists.

Local and Regional Differences

There was, and continues to be, a significant U.S. component to the globalization of consumption (Ritzer and Ryan 2003). However, it is important to recognize that the heyday of the United States in this area is long past. In any case, there has always been much more to the globalization of consumption than Americanization (Stillerman 2015). That is, local areas have certainly not always, or perhaps ever, been overwhelmed by U.S. imports but have integrated them into local cultural and economic realities. Furthermore, other nations and regions have been significant exporters of important aspects of consumer society, such as Mercedes-Benz and BMW automobiles from Germany and a seemingly endless stream of exports of consumer products from China. Finally, much of consumption remains largely, if not totally, local in character. One example is the growing consumption of a mild stimulant, khat, or *qat*, in Kenya, where it is defined in a highly positive way locally. In addition, there is active resistance to external definitions of it, especially the U.S. definition of khat as a dangerous drug (Anderson and Carrier 2006).

Although many consumer objects and services remain highly local (e.g., khat, mentioned previously), an increasing number have been globalized. On the one hand are the global objects, such as automobiles from the United States, Germany, Korea, and Japan. On the other hand are global services, such as those offered by accounting firms like KPMG International, as well as package delivery services like DHL.

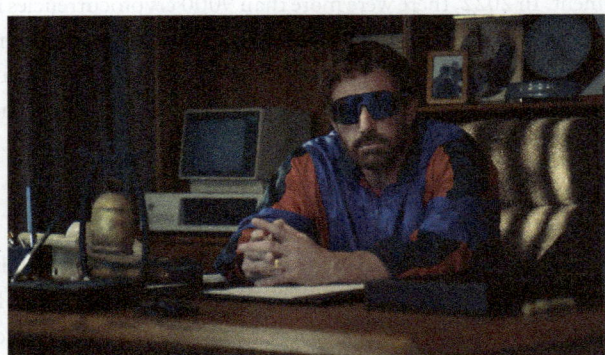

The movie *Air*, starring Ben Affleck as Nike founder and CEO Phil Knight, tells the story of how Nike turned their Air Jordan basketball shoes into a global brand.

stockelements/iStockPhoto; FlixPix / Alamy Stock Photo

Global Brands

A **brand** is a symbol that serves to identify and differentiate one product or service from others. A brand can be contrasted with, and seeks to differentiate itself from, generic commodities such as no-name flour and soap (Brown 2016). The process of branding a product or service is undertaken because, if successful, not only is the brand distinguished from the basic commodity, but more of it can be sold and at a higher price. We are all familiar with the most successful brands in the world (Apple, Coca-Cola, McDonald's, Walmart, Nike, Mercedes, and so on), and much consumption is oriented toward the purchase of brand-name products and services. Furthermore, even people come to be brand names (Lady Gaga, LeBron James, Cristiano Ronaldo) and as such are "consumed" globally to a large degree. As brands themselves, they come to be closely associated with various brand-name products, some of the best-known examples being the association of LeBron James with Nike and Sofia Vergara with Head & Shoulders.

Nike is one of those brands that has made itself so important it can be said to have created a culture, and, to some degree, we live in Nike culture (Goldman and Papson 1998; Hollister 2008). However, that culture is but a part of the larger *brand culture* in which we live. That is, brands are a key part of the larger culture: They infuse it with meaning, and contemporary society as a whole is profoundly affected by brands.

Brands are of great importance globally. Indeed, much money and effort is invested in creating brand names that are recognized and trusted throughout the world. Klein ([2000] 2010) details the importance of brands in the contemporary world and the degree to which they are globalized—corporate logos are virtually an international language—and have global impacts.

SUMMARY

Politics is one way to advance a given position or policy through the use of, or by putting pressure on, the state. Democracy is a political system in which people within a given state vote to choose their leaders, and in some cases, to approve legislation. This is in contrast to dictatorships, which are usually totalitarian governments operating without the consent of the governed.

The question of who rules the world is a source of continuing debate. In analyzing politics, structural-functionalists emphasize pluralism, while conflict theorists focus on power elite theory. One way of dealing with political disagreements is through war.

Sociologists define the economy as the social system that ensures the production and distribution of goods and services. In the last 200 years, many capitalist economies have transitioned from industrial to postindustrial society. There have been dramatic changes in many nation's labor force as a result of this transition. The number of unemployed, discouraged, and underemployed workers rose during the Great Recession. Although that number has declined more recently, employment problems remain. Deindustrialization is associated with the decline of labor unions, the growth of service jobs, the increasingly important gig economy, and a growing focus on consumption. All of this set the stage for, and is part of, the postindustrial society. One of the dominant trends of the last several decades is the increasing amount of leisure time devoted to consumption and the increasing growth of global consumer culture.

KEY TERMS

- brand
- cathedrals of consumption
- citizens
- citizenship
- communism
- competitive capitalism
- consumer cultures
- cryptocurrencies
- deindustrialization
- democracies
- dictatorships
- direct democracies
- discouraged workers
- economy
- elite pluralism
- failed state
- Fordism
- geopolitics
- gig economy
- group pluralism
- imagined communities
- leisure
- macrofinance
- mass production
- monopoly capitalism
- nation
- nation-state
- pluralism
- politics
- postconsumer culture
- post-Fordism
- postindustrial society
- power elite theory
- prosumer
- representative democracies
- separation of powers
- socialism
- state
- terrorism
- transnational capitalism
- underemployment
- unemployment
- welfare states

REVIEW QUESTIONS

1. What factors help explain the emergence of democratic political systems? How is democracy related to bureaucracy and rational-legal concepts that you learned about in previous chapters?

2. In what ways is citizenship an important component of a democratic political system?

3. The question of who rules the world is still being debated. In what ways does a pluralist understanding of power and politics differ from the power elite perspective? Do you think globalization has an effect on who rules the world? Why or why not?

4. In what ways are socialism and communism alternatives to capitalism? What elements of welfare states are socialistic, and what forces are resistant to social welfare programs?

5. What factors help explain deindustrialization, and how does deindustrialization relate to the decline of labor unions?

6. In what ways has the internet changed the nature of work? What are some examples of the ways you use the internet as a producer, consumer, and prosumer?

7. Is our society characterized by rampant and insatiable consumerism? How do we use consumption to satisfy our needs in the world today? Do you agree that we tend to consume beyond our needs?

8. In what ways might consumption today be described as the new religion?

9. How do leisure activities create distinctions between groups of people? In what ways are these distinctions reflective of the system of social stratification?

10. What has helped lead to the growth of a global consumer culture? How have brands played a role in this growth?

Kevin Dietsch-Pool/Getty Images

14 THE BODY, MEDICINE, HEALTH, AND HEALTH CARE

LEARNING OBJECTIVES
14.1 Explain the sociology of health.
14.2 Discuss sociological concepts that relate to the body.
14.3 Outline medical sociology's approach to health issues.
14.4 Describe the relationship between globalization and current major health problems.

THE OPIOID CRISIS

Health problems, even crises, have occurred and continue to occur throughout the world. However, in recent years the opioid crisis has attracted increasing attention and great concern, especially in the United States. Opioids include drugs derived from opium (especially heroin and morphine), as well as synthetic or semisynthetic drugs (especially fentanyl, which is 50 times more potent than heroin). In 2019, more than 10 million people in the United States over the age of 12 reported they had misused opioids during the past year (Health and Human Services 2022). More than 80,000 people in the U.S. died from opioid overdose in 2021 (National Institute on Drug Abuse 2023). The use of fentanyl has skyrocketed and accounted for nearly half of those deaths. Because millions of people are now addicted to opioids, the annual number of deaths from them can be expected to grow in the coming years. Some estimates (Beyer 2022) now indicate that the opioid crisis is taking a $1.5 trillion toll on the national economy. Opioids and addiction to them have a long history in the United States, going back to the aftermath of the Civil War and the increasing use of hypodermically injected morphine. The current crisis can be traced to the 1980s, when physicians' fears about prescribing opioids for pain relief eased, in part because of self-serving reassurances from the pharmaceutical industry. The 1990s saw the aggressive marketing of a synthetic opioid, oxycodone, by pharmaceutical companies. The proliferation of synthetic forms of the drug, especially fentanyl, has continued and expanded.

Even though they are highly addictive, opioids have been traditionally prescribed, and often overprescribed, to relieve pain. Consequently, many people have become addicted through prescriptions for the drug, although many others have become addicted through its illegal acquisition or have moved on to heroin. Many of those who take, and die from, either the synthetic fentanyl (or counterfeit versions of it) or heroin are in their 20s and 30s. Fentanyl is often used as a surgical anesthetic, but it is also manufactured illegally and sold on the streets and on the dark web. The opioid problem exists throughout the United States (and elsewhere); however, it is especially prevalent in the rural areas of Appalachia, the Rust Belt, and New England. Although suburban middle- and upper-income White Americans (and others) are addicted to opioids, rural lower-income White people are more likely to be stigmatized, even criminalized, for their addiction.

Dealing with the opioid crisis is vexing because there is huge legal and illegal demand for opioids. Making it too difficult to obtain opiates can make it hard for those in severe pain to obtain them and can increase the illegal use of the drug. However, making acquisition too easy—even for those who legitimately need opioids—can exacerbate the problem. Better education is needed across the board for physicians, legitimate patients, casual users, and the addicted. In March 2023, the U.S. Food and Drug Administration approved over-the-counter sales of the overdose treatment drug Naloxone (more commonly known as Narcan), which could help ease the problem. Still, better treatment options are needed.

THE SOCIOLOGY OF HEALTH

The central concerns of this chapter—the body, medicine, health (including mental health), and health care—are at the top of many individuals' personal agenda. This is, no doubt, even more the case since the onset of the COVID-19 pandemic. Globally, there is much concern not only about COVID-19, but also about other epidemics such as HIV/AIDS, malaria, the flu, Ebola, and Zika, as well as the great inequalities in health and health care throughout the world. As we read in the opening vignette, the United States is currently embroiled in, among other things, a furor over the overprescription of addictive drugs, especially opioids. More generally, many countries have been—and may well continue to be—wracked by heated debates over reforming health care. Among other things, reformers have sought to address flagrant inequalities and increasing costs in health care. Some changes in health care (to be discussed later in this chapter) have been instituted, although they have been far less significant than many had hoped and often provided unequally. For example, tens of millions of Americans still do not have health care, even though government-mandated reforms took effect in 2014. These global and societal issues affect the health and health care of individuals. Among those most concerned about such issues are those who are, or will be, patients—that is, virtually everyone—as well as the large and growing number of people who work in health care.

Ultimately, much of the interest in health comes down to a growing focus on, and concern about, the state of our bodies. However, interest in the body manifests in different ways for various social groups. If you are young, your main concerns, and those of your friends, are likely to be how to remain good looking, healthy, and fit through diet, exercise, and perhaps even a nip or a tuck here or there. These are likely to be lifelong concerns. However, as you age, your focus will shift to the increasing likelihood that you will develop various diseases, especially breast cancer for women and prostate cancer for men, as well as heart disease for both men and women. You will also become increasingly concerned about how to avoid those diseases, if possible. If you are diagnosed with one, your focus will be on how to deal with it—*if* it can be dealt with. Gender affects the types of health-protective behaviors you employ. Women tend to be more active participants in their health maintenance than men. Health-protective behaviors include screenings, self-examinations, and regular checkups.

Some of you will fall ill, be hospitalized, and perhaps die in middle age (or even earlier). However, most of you will face health-related issues with increasing frequency and intensity as you move into old age. New health-related concerns will then emerge, such as the possibility of developing Alzheimer's disease. As shown in Figure 14.1, it is estimated that the number of people age 65 and older with Alzheimer's disease will grow from 6.1 million to 13.8 million between 2020 and 2060. As you age, you may wonder whether you are going to have the funds, or the insurance, needed to pay the often astronomical health care costs associated with the inevitable illnesses of your last years, and you may worry about how you will die and whether you will be able to do so with dignity.

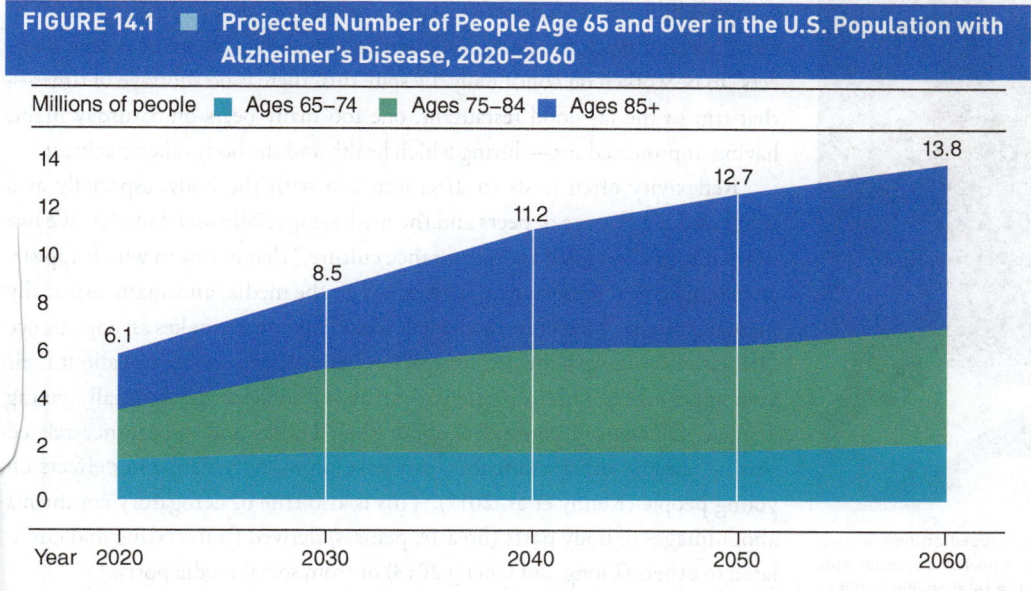

FIGURE 14.1 ■ Projected Number of People Age 65 and Over in the U.S. Population with Alzheimer's Disease, 2020–2060

Source: Alzheimer's Association, Alzheimer's Disease Facts and Figures, 2023. Reprinted with permission from the Alzheimer's Association. https://www.alz.org/alzheimers-dementia/facts-figures

For these reasons and others, the body has emerged in recent years as a major concern in sociology (Adelman and Ruggi 2016; Shilling 2018; B. Turner 2008). However, before we turn to a discussion of the body, it is important to remember that the mind and mental processes have long been of concern and interest to many sociologists (e.g., see the discussion of Mead's work on these topics in Chapter 4). Although this chapter focuses on physical illnesses, mental illnesses such as depression, schizophrenia, and the mental problems associated with Alzheimer's disease are also major concerns at the global, national, and individual levels (Cockerham 2019). There is no clear line between the mind and the body. The brain, which houses the mind, is, after all, a body part. Mental processes affect the body (such as in psychosomatic illnesses), and the body affects the mind. One example of the latter is postpartum depression, which is caused, at least in part, by hormonal imbalances (Stanescu et al. 2018). Another is depression that develops following a diagnosis of breast or prostate cancer or heart disease (Bronner et al. 2018). However, it is important to remember that mental processes can also have positive effects on the body and its well-being. A strong sense of self-efficacy can be helpful to someone trying to quit smoking, lose weight, or recover from a heart attack, among other things.

THE BODY

Sociology has always had some interest in the body, but there has been a recent explosion of interest in that topic. This scholarly interest reflects the growing concern, even obsession, of many people with their bodies' well-being.

The Healthy Body: Lifestyle, Beauty, and Fitness

We live in an increasingly reflexive society. In the context of health, **reflexivity,** or the habit of self-examination and reflection, creates a heightened awareness of the body and of ourselves more generally. Nevertheless, many of us engage in risky behaviors (e.g., basking for hours in the summer sun; having unprotected sex with an acquaintance; smoking) that endanger our health as well as the way we look and our physical fitness. However, reflexivity can lead us to be more likely to avoid risky situations, protect ourselves when we are in those situations (e.g., by using sunblock or condoms), and seek more beneficial ones. More generally, many of us focus on creating lifestyles we hope will make us fit, attractive, and healthy. We may feel a responsibility to take care of ourselves, especially to do everything possible to avoid becoming sick and dying. Our bodies, and our health, have become "projects" to be worked on continually. Despite this, there is no shortage of times—that trip to the fast-food restaurant, one too many beers on Saturday night, having unprotected sex—during which health and the body take a backseat.

Reflexivity often leads to dissatisfaction with the body, especially as a result of the influence of peers and the media, especially social media. We live in what might be called an "appearance culture," that is, one in which appearance is of central importance to peers and in the media, and again, especially on social media. That culture includes ideas about what makes an appearance "attractive," and such ideas can negatively affect people's feelings about their own appearance. This is particularly true for adolescents, especially young women. Derogatory comments about their bodies and appearance-related teasing, among other influences, can have profoundly damaging effects on young people (Kenny et al. 2017). This is also true of derogatory comments about images of body parts (breasts, penises) derived from sexting and circulated to others (Liong and Cheng 2018) or from social media posts.

More generally, everyone has concerns about their bodies, although the nature of those concerns is often different. For example, little boys tend to

Frenchman Michel Foucault's work focused on how knowledge leads to power and how those in power are better able to gain knowledge. He also studied the relationship between knowledge of, and power over, the body.

AP Photo/Alexis Duclos

want strong bodies in order to engage in sports, while little girls are apt to want bodies that "look good" (Tatangelo and Ricciardelli 2013). Boys who do not have strong bodies and girls who do not "look good" are likely to feel dissatisfied with their bodies. However, beliefs about the body are socially contextualized and socially constructed, and they vary by, among other things, race. For example, Black female students report less dissatisfaction with their bodies than do their White and Latina counterparts (Ordaz et al. 2018). Even desired skin tone and complexion have cultural and social determinants. However, one recent study found that a preference for lighter skin exists in nearly all cultures. This is driving the global growth of skin bleaching (Dixon and Teller 2017).

Beauty: Cultural Contexts

The social construction of beauty made it onto more people's radar after the publication of Naomi Wolf's book *The Beauty Myth* ([1991] 2002). Wolf argues that the media present the vast majority of people with an unattainable standard of beauty. The "objectifying gaze," rooted in patriarchal and Eurocentric ideals of beauty and attractiveness and expressed through media, includes a narrow standard for beauty and desirability (Dixon and Teller 2017). Heterosexual men and women report feeling more positive toward women who meet that standard—for example, women who have a typical hourglass shape (small waist, curvy chest and hips).

U.S. model Ashley Graham walks the runway at a fashion show in Melbourne, Australia. Plus-size models are challenging standards of beauty and attractiveness in the fashion world that might seem unattainable to most.

Naomi Rahim/Getty Images

We often use beauty, as measured by physical appearance, as a means of determining who is attractive and as a way to distribute socially valuable resources. Economist Daniel Hamermesh (2011) has studied the economic effects of beauty, finding that those deemed beautiful earn more and are more successful at work. It even matters in choices made among candidates for the House of Representatives. Those who are less informed politically are more likely to choose candidates who are physically attractive (Stockemer and Praino 2015). We often are not even consciously aware of the ways in which stereotypical beauty matters in the decisions we—and others—make (Kwan and Trautner 2011).

Race, ethnicity, and class are implicated in stereotypical conceptualizations of beauty. One study compared satisfaction with body shape and skin tone, finding that biracial women were most satisfied with their skin tone, while Afro-Caribbean and African women were more satisfied with their body shapes compared to African American women (Mucherah and Frazier 2013).

Efforts to attain a high standard of stereotypical beauty may include excessive dieting, bingeing, and purging. Women are particularly susceptible to these actions. However, such actions often lead to failure, negative self-image, and low self-esteem (Rodgers et al. 2017; Rosenberg 1979). Some gay men feel compelled to diet excessively to fit the "twink" body type, a very slender physique deemed particularly attractive by some in the gay male community (Jones 2015). Similarly, increased media attention to men's bodies leads to a preoccupation with ideas about the ideal male form. Internalization of ideals about the superiority of muscular bodies influences some men's drive to develop muscular physiques (Flave-Novak and Coleman 2018). However, male desire for a muscular body is not universal. For example, research reveals that college-age men in China are just as likely to idealize thin bodies as muscular ones (Wang et al. 2018).

The Quest for the Ideal, the Consumption of Beauty, and the Fit Body

The rewards for being beautiful are so great that many try to at least approximate the mythic ideal. In consumer culture, beauty has become a commodity that can be bought (or at least it is thought so) through great effort, often pain, and almost always expenditures of large sums of money. This is clear, for example, in the hundreds of billions of dollars spent around the world on cosmetics, fitness, and clothing. Most of the global consumers of beauty products are women. Rachel Berryman and Misha Kavka (2017) found that consumption related to beauty and appearance pervades vlogs (video blogs) mostly viewed by young women on YouTube.

The most extreme efforts to become beautiful involve cosmetic surgeries of all sorts. Beauty is deemed so important in Brazil (and elsewhere) that cosmetic surgeries are offered to all who can pay for the anesthesia. Poor and rich Brazilians alike can thus buy procedures to create the culturally ideal physique. For women, that physique features small breasts, a small waist with a large buttocks, and a slim nose and lips (Edmonds 2010).

About 90 percent of cosmetic surgical procedures in the United States (and the United Kingdom) are undergone by women (Tranter and Hanson 2015). As Table 14.1 shows, the most popular modifications are breast augmentation, liposuction, nose reshaping, eyelid surgery, and tummy tuck. Far less common are procedures that illustrate just how many aspects of the human body can be changed. For example, there are reports of some fantasy fiction fans having their ears modified to a pointed "elfin" shape. Some people have genital cosmetic surgeries intended to enhance sexual response (clitoral hood reduction, vaginal tightening) or to improve the size, shape, and even color of their genitals. These procedures are not to be confused with surgeries linked to gender or sex reassignment, which some trans people may elect to have (e.g., mastectomy or vaginal construction).

TABLE 14.1 ■ The Five Most Popular Cosmetic Procedures in the United States, 2020	
Procedure	Number
Nose reshaping	352,555
Eyelid surgery	325,112
Facelift	234,374
Liposuction	211,067
Breast augmentation	193,073

Source: American Society of Plastic Surgeons, 2020, Plastic Surgery Statistics Report, p.5, Arlington Heights, IL: ASPS National Clearinghouse of Plastic Surgery Procedural Statistics. Retrieved August 2, 2022 (https://www.plasticsurgery.org/documents/News/Statistics/2020/plastic-surgery-statistics-full-report-2020.pdf).

Looks-related stress affects many people, although young women are particularly susceptible. The greater likelihood of such stress among young women can be found in many places around the world including Sweden, South Korea, and New Zealand (Jose, Kramar, and Hou 2014; Landstedt and Gådin 2012; Lee 2012).

Interest in the way we look, although not new, has grown dramatically in the current era of increasing reflexivity. We are more aware of how we (and others) look. One reason for this is social media and the increasing time many people, especially younger people, spend looking at pictures of themselves (and others) online. Before social media, most of us only saw ourselves when we looked in a mirror. Now, however, those with a social media presence are often looking at themselves, or at least pictures of themselves. The "reward" of likes and positive comments online helps to feed this concern with appearance.

We are also more conscious not only of the steps we can take to improve our appearance but also of the many means available to us for doing so. The increase in pure relationships (see Chapter 11) may add greater importance to this focus on appearance because others are more likely to leave relationships with us if they are dissatisfied with the way we look (and vice versa). Our good looks are seen as a resource, or a form of capital, that can positively shape our social networks (O'Connor and Gladstone 2018).

Fitness and the Healthy Body

Closely related to the emphasis on beauty is the focus among many people on physical activity, physical fitness, sports, and bodybuilding (Fernández-Balboa and González-Calvo 2017). All these are seen, at least in part, as ways of creating a body that is not only more beautiful but also healthier—or at least appears that way. Hutson (2016) discussed the results of such efforts under the heading of **bodily capital**. That is, the work involved in becoming fitter, more muscular, healthier, and more beautiful can all be seen as efforts to accrue more bodily capital. People invest much time, energy, and money in order to acquire—and to retain—bodily capital. More bodily capital can, in turn, be used to increase people's status and enable them to be on a more equal footing with those who have more of other kinds of capital. Thus, for example, female trainers in fitness centers can use their fitness to develop higher status than (and power over) their male clients, occupy higher status positions in the fitness world, or both.

There is an array of methods employed to acquire bodily capital. Walking, cycling, jogging, and at-home or gym-based workouts typically do not include competition and are clearly good for most people. Through those activities, people can hone their bodies and in the process acquire bodily capital. However, the increasingly competitive nature of many sports may actually have adverse effects on health and appearance. Such sports require great exertion and are often violent. They can be damaging, even dangerous, to the body and reduce, or even eliminate, bodily capital. Consider the increasing alarm over the effect of concussions and other brain traumas on those involved in various sports, especially professional football. Attention is now also focused on those risks in youth football.

Joining a gym and hiring a personal fitness trainer are just some of the ways to acquire bodily capital.
Natalie Kolb/MediaNews Group/Reading Eagle via Getty Images

Some contact sports, such as wrestling and boxing, require competitors to qualify for, and remain in, very restrictive weight classes. This requirement can lead participants to engage in bouts of starvation and dehydration to "make the weight." Such practices, in turn, can evolve into "manorexia," a male analogue of the mainly female disorder of anorexia, by which women strive to attain slimmer bodies (Kershaw 2008). A phenomenon known as "bigorexia," or the Adonis complex (Kimmel 2016; Mosley 2009), may affect men who have grown up with photos of bodybuilders and who aspire to have similar physiques. Such men are likely to feel that their biceps, to take one example, are inadequate compared to those of such idealized models. They might be led to lift weights obsessively and to consume mainly, or only, proteins. Such practices are especially rampant among competitive bodybuilders. Some sports, taken to extremes, can have a variety of deleterious effects on the body in both the short and long term and thereby reduce bodily capital.

Exercise, sports, and physical activity often take as their goal the improvement of the body and of health more generally. They are increasingly oriented toward outcomes, such as losing weight and strengthening muscles. In other words, the focus is on acquiring bodily capital. However, such a focus means people often overlook the enjoyment associated with exercise and, more generally, the process involved in acquiring such capital (Wellard 2012).

Body Modifications

Body modification practices have been nearly universal across societies and throughout history (Faulkner and Bailey 2019). However, in recent years, there has been something of a boom in such practices around the world. There are several major forms of body modification, including tattooing, scarification (scarring or cutting of the skin), piercing, and various surgical procedures. At one time, body modification was associated with deviants of various types, including gang members, prisoners, and sex workers. It was also associated with certain conventional groups, such as those in the military, particularly the navy.

Although tattoos are most associated with performers and athletes, they have become increasingly popular among the general public, especially young people.
Elena Aquila/Pacific Press/LightRocket via Getty Images

Today, some body modifications, especially tattoos, have become so widespread and common that they are now mainstream (Barron 2017; Hill 2016). The media are full of images of movie stars and especially star athletes adorned, if not covered, with tattoos. Consider, for example, former soccer player

David Beckham, football player Chris Andersen, and basketball players Kevin Durant, LeBron James, and J. R. Smith. Historically associated with men, body modifications are also increasingly common among women (Thompson 2015), including star professional basketball player Brittney Griner and actress Angelina Jolie. Parents seem less likely to reject the idea of tattoos on their children. They may even have tattoos themselves. Body modification is now in fashion and is itself a fashion statement. Figure 14.2 shows that more than 1 in 4 people living in the United States report having one or more tattoos (Statista 2021).

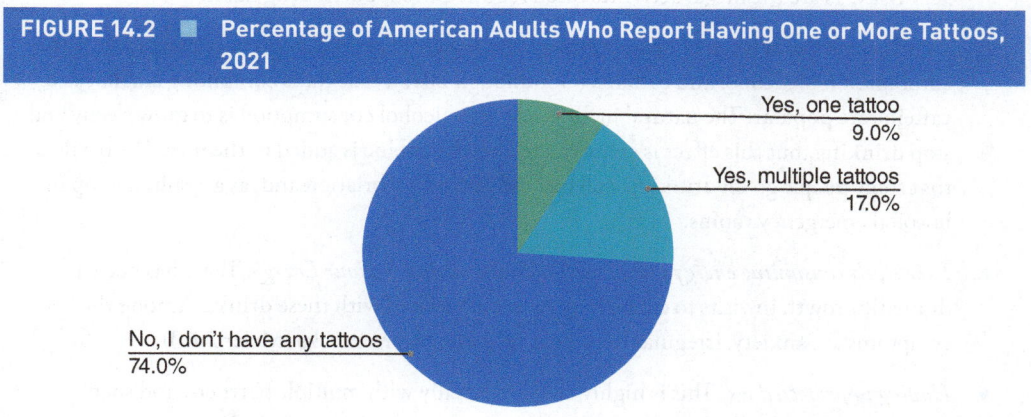

FIGURE 14.2 ■ Percentage of American Adults Who Report Having One or More Tattoos, 2021

- Yes, one tattoo: 9.0%
- Yes, multiple tattoos: 17.0%
- No, I don't have any tattoos: 74.0%

Source: Statista, "Share of Americans with One or More Tattoos as of 2021, by Generation and Number of Tattoos." Retrieved August 2, 2022 (https://www.statista.com/statistics/1261721/americans-with-at-least-one-tattoo-by-number-and-generation/).

Body modification reflects the increase in reflexivity. Ever-greater reflexivity is required with each succeeding decision about which new form or style of body modification to have. Among the issues to be decided are whether the modification—say, a new tattoo—should be visible to others, where it should be placed, and how traditional or creative and unique it should be. Furthermore, a variety of different tastes in tattooing have emerged, many of which are gendered (Thompson 2015), raced, and classed (Tranter and Grant 2018).

As tattoos have grown more mainstream and even common among some groups, the people originally drawn to them have sought other ways of distinguishing their bodies from those of others. Many have been drawn to piercings of various types (Romanienk 2011). Most popular are earlobe and tongue piercings. However, as those, too, have become more common, more people are looking for new ways to creatively express themselves through body modification, such as ear gauging (stretching the pierced holes in earlobes).

Risky Behavior

Risky behavior has become a central concern in many areas of sociology, and one of those is the way in which it relates to the body and health.

People take a wide range of risks that have the potential to jeopardize their health. On the one hand are the things people do *not* do, such as see their physicians, have regular medical checkups, and take prescribed medicines. Another example is the failure, or refusal, to be vaccinated against various diseases. This has become an especially relevant topic in recent years as millions of people are refusing to get the COVID-19 vaccine, a decision which has not only endangered their own health, but also the health of others.

As tattoos become more common, some people are drawn to body piercing as a way to distinguish themselves from others.

axelbueckert/iStockPhotos

On the other hand, people engage in many behaviors they know pose health risks:

- *Cigarette smoking (and vaping) is at, or near, the top of the list.* Smoking itself can be considered a disease, but it is also a major risk factor in a number of diseases, including lung cancer and many other cancers, chronic obstructive pulmonary disease (COPD), stroke, high blood pressure, and heart disease (Brody 2016).

- *Taking illegal drugs of various sorts, especially those, like opioids, that are addictive.* This is clearly very risky, as are the illegal activities often required to support a drug habit.

- *Drinking alcohol to excess or driving under the influence of alcohol.* Especially dangerous is the combination of alcohol and caffeine (Goodnough 2010). Cocktails combining alcohol and caffeine are popular. The natural inclination with alcohol consumption is to grow sleepy and stop drinking, but this effect is counteracted when caffeine is added to the mix. The result is that some people go on drinking well beyond normal inebriation and, as a result, end up in hospital emergency rooms.

- *Excessively consuming energy drinks such as Red Bull and 5-Hour Energy.* There has been a dramatic growth in visits to emergency rooms associated with these drinks. Among the symptoms are anxiety, irregular heartbeat, and even heart attacks (Meier 2013).

- *Having unprotected sex.* This is highly risky, especially with multiple partners, and such behavior has been linked to other risky behaviors, such as drug and alcohol abuse.

- *Overeating, allowing oneself to become obese, and staying that way.* The overwhelming evidence linking obesity to various illnesses makes it clear that this is a risky behavior.

- *Talking on cell phones and texting while driving.* People engage in these behaviors even though they are illegal in many states, and the increased risk of having an accident associated with them has received a great deal of publicity (see, e.g., Caird et al. 2014).

In some cases, the nature of work is risky. One example is the exposure to radiation risked by nuclear weapons workers, which can make them ill and perhaps kill them (Boice 2017). Of course, many occupations, such as coal mining (Chen and Zorigt 2013), carry with them a variety of health risks. Figure 14.3 shows the total number of fatal work injuries and the fatal work injury rate by industry. In 2021, construction workers accounted for the most fatalities (986), with transportation and warehousing second, with 976 fatalities. The agriculture, forestry, fishing, and hunting industries had the highest injury rate, at 19.5 fatalities per 100,000 full-time workers.

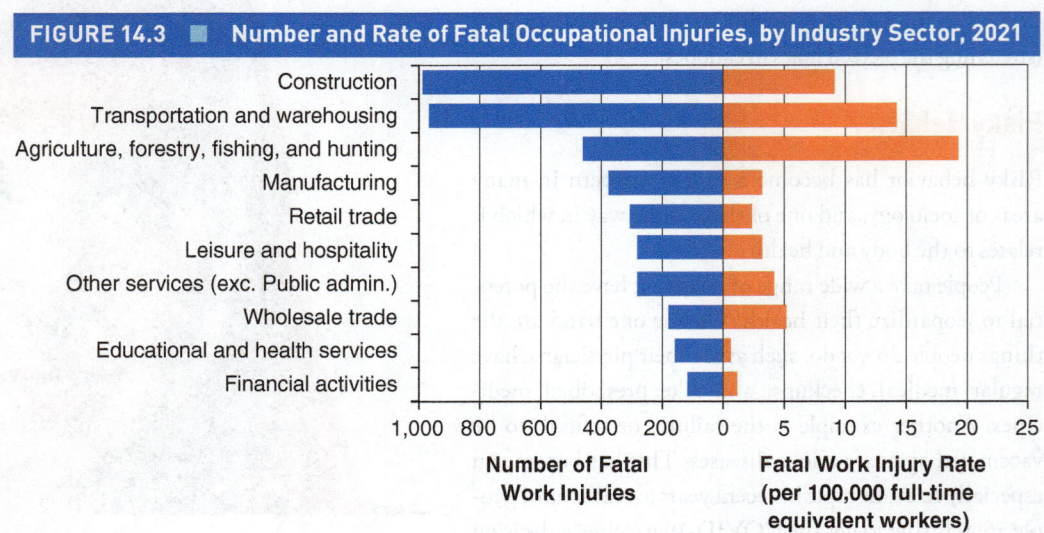

FIGURE 14.3 ■ Number and Rate of Fatal Occupational Injuries, by Industry Sector, 2021

Source: U.S. Bureau of Labor Statistics, 2021, Number and Rate of Fatal Work Injuries, by Industry Sector, Washington, DC: United States Department of Labor. https://www.bls.gov/charts/census-of-fatal-occupational-injuries/number-and-rate-of-fatal-work-injuries-by-industry.htm

There is, however, another side to engaging in risky behavior. It may well be that taking some risks makes some people happier and mentally, and perhaps even physically, healthier. This connection may help account for the growing interest in extreme sports, such as surfing and snowboarding. Also, many smokers report that having a cigarette helps lower their stress levels. Of course, these positive outcomes do not negate the fact that such activities pose extraordinary physical and health risks.

THE SOCIOLOGY OF MEDICINE

Medical sociology is one of the largest specialty areas within sociology. It is concerned with the social causes and consequences of health and illness (Cockerham 2019). Social factors are also deeply involved in the delivery of health care. This has become an increasingly important issue during the COVID-19 pandemic. Medical sociology addresses a wide variety of specific issues, including the following:

- The basic causes of health inequalities in terms of social class, gender, race/ethnicity, and sexuality
- The linkage between stress and health
- The relationships between patients and health care providers
- The increasing use of advanced medical technology
- The astronomical and spiraling cost of medical care
- The changing nature of the medical profession
- Changes in medical education

Among the changes taking place in the medical profession are its declining status, the trials and tribulations of obtaining reimbursement from insurance companies and government agencies for medical services rendered, the more active role of patients as prosumers of their own health care, the more complicated relationships between patients and health care providers, and the fact that those relationships are likely to last longer because people are living longer and suffering from more chronic ailments.

The Medical Profession

In the mid-twentieth century, a great deal of power was accorded to the health care system and especially to the medical profession, the key player in that system. Physicians exercised significant power over virtually everyone else involved in the health care system—nurses, hospital administrators, and so on. They also gained and retained great power over birth and death. This was an era in which the professions of medicine, law, and other fields not only exercised great power but also acquired great autonomy. In fact, a profession is distinguished from other occupations mainly by its high level of power and considerable autonomy. Other characteristics often associated with the professions are advanced education, mastery of knowledge and skills, the need to be licensed or accredited, high prestige, and typically higher incomes.

Although many men have entered the nursing profession in recent years, nursing is still seen as a female occupation. Why?

Hero Images Inc. / Alamy Stock Photo

Historically, physicians have been disproportionately male (and White in the United States and much of Europe). However, that profile has changed dramatically, at least in some ways, in the last half century. For example, in the United States, only 1 in 4 medical school graduates in the U.S. were women in 1980. By 2006 women and men were becoming physicians at virtually the same rate, and that pattern has continued since then (see Figure 14.4; Association of American Medical Colleges 2019). However, White male physicians' historical power continues to be evident in their starting salaries, which are consistently higher than those of their female counterparts. In fact, a salary gap exists even for physicians who teach at medical schools. On average, with the exception of radiology, female academic physicians at medical schools earn 80 percent ($206,600) of the earnings of their male counterparts ($258,000; acknowledging that both salaries are significantly higher than nearly every other profession). Women earn less than men in every medical specialty, including those they dominate, such as pediatrics, where they earn only 76 percent of what male pediatricians earn (Frintner et al 2019).

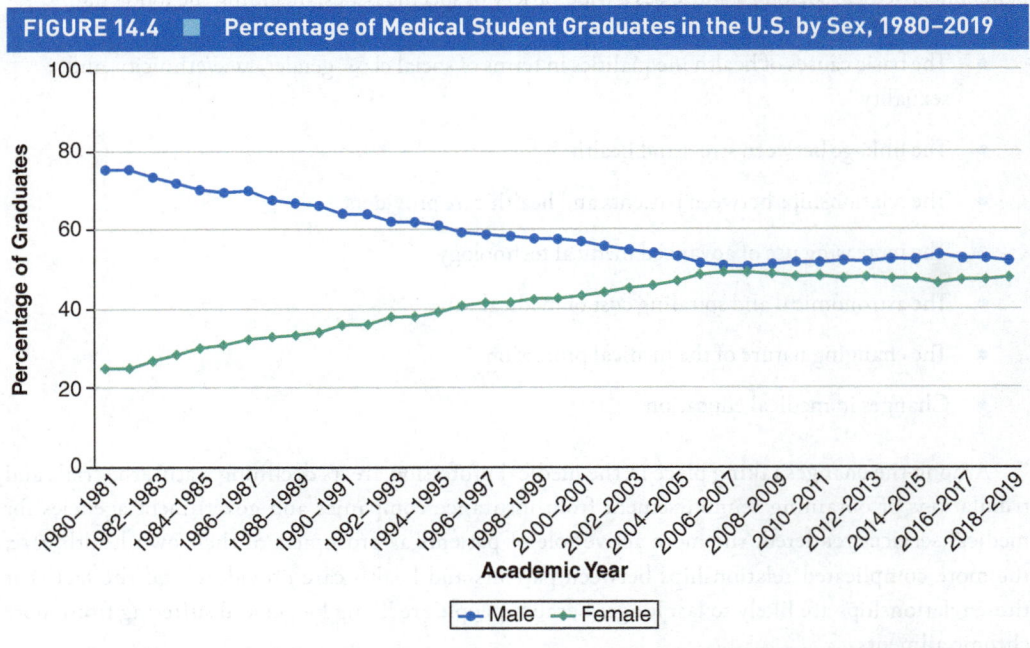

Source: Association of American Medical Colleges, 2019, Percentage of U.S. Medical School Graduates by Sex, Academic Years 1980–1981 through 2018–2019, Diversity in Medicine: Facts and Figures 2019, Figure 12, Washington, D.C.: Association of American Medical Colleges. (https://www.aamc.org/data-reports/workforce/interactive-data/figure-12-percentage-us-medical-school-graduates-sex-academic-years-1980-1981-through-2018-2019).

The professions generally, and the medical profession in particular, continue to enjoy considerable power, autonomy, and high status. However, there has been a marked decline in all of those dimensions in the last half century. In fact, in the last several decades, the professions have been characterized by a process of **deprofessionalization**. That is, their power and autonomy, as well as their high status and associated wealth, have declined, at least relative to the exalted position they once held (Siebert et al. 2018). A variety of factors are involved in the declining power of the medical profession, including the increasing power of patients, especially their ability to use the internet to try and inform themselves about their medical problems and options; third-party payers, such as the government through Medicare and Medicaid; and the pharmaceutical industry. However, although the medical profession is weaker than it once was, it remains a powerful force in the practice of medicine and in the larger society. In other words, the medical profession has proven itself resilient.

How do we account for the deprofessionalization of physicians? First, they arguably had acquired too much power to sustain it at that level for long. Second, the public, which granted (or at least ceded to) the medical profession that power and autonomy, came to question the medical profession. One basis of this increasing doubt was a growing awareness of the extraordinary wealth and power acquired by many physicians. Another was the revelation of medical malpractice, which demonstrated that physicians did not always adhere to their own code of ethics (Parks-Savage et al. 2018). The growth in malpractice suits was aided, if not instigated, by the other major profession, law, which reaped great economic rewards from medical malpractice lawsuits. Third, the government came to exert more power over the medical profession through, for example, Medicare and Medicaid. Fourth, as discussed in the coming pages, patients became much more active and aggressive consumers (really prosumers) of physician services as well as of other aspects of the medical system. Fifth, and perhaps most important, private health insurance companies like UnitedHealthcare became the most powerful players in the medical care system (and political lobbying).

Of course, there are many other kinds of workers in the health care system—physician's assistants (PAs) and hospitalists (doctors who work only in hospitals) are increasingly ubiquitous (Cockerham and Hinote 2015); however, the most notable and important are nurses (Hunt 2017). Historically, nurses were unable to achieve full professional status. Nursing was often thought of as a semiprofession (Etzioni 1969). It lacked anything approaching the power, status, income, and autonomy of the medical profession. Much of this failure had to do with the enormous power wielded by physicians and their desire to keep occupations that had the potential to compete with theirs in a subordinate position (Hunt 2017). However, a more important factor was the fact that nursing is an occupation that was—and still is—dominated by females. Males in powerful positions, not only as physicians but also as high-level executives such as hospital administrators, were generally opposed to according professional status to occupations dominated by women. (Schoolteachers and social workers suffered much the same fate as nurses.)

As a result, team-based, collaborative care involving both physicians and nurses has been adopted only to a limited degree (Bell, Michalec, and Arenson 2014). A major factor in this relative failure is the continuation of gender discrimination in medicine and the fact that physicians are predominantly men and nurses continue to be overwhelmingly women. Nevertheless, doctors, adhering to traditional definitions of the roles of women and nurses, have come to rely heavily on nurses because they engage in, among many other things, "emotion work," or the emotional maintenance of patients (Chapman 2018). The result has been that although physicians have almost all of the formal power and often do not deal with nurses as equals, nurses often have a great deal of informal power over the day-to-day decisions and operation of hospitals and doctors' offices.

Weaknesses in the U.S. Health Care System

There has been a broad consensus that the U.S. system of health care (as well as those elsewhere) is badly flawed. One major problem is the astronomically high cost of medical care. In 2020, health care spending in the United States reached $4.1 trillion, about $12,530 per person (Centers for Medicare and Medicaid Services 2021). The cost per person dramatically dwarfs that of other countries around the world, although the health outcomes are often better in other places.

The United States spent 17.8 percent of its gross domestic product (GDP) on health care in 2021—the highest percentage among Organization for Economic Co-operation and Development (OECD) countries by a considerable margin (see Figure 14.5). In fact, the United States spends a higher percentage of its GDP on health care than any other country in the world (World Bank 2019).

Costs of health insurance are rising rapidly. Among the reasons for the high cost of medicine and medical care in the United States are the following:

- The increased use of expensive advanced medical technologies, such as magnetic resonance imaging (MRI)
- The profit motive at the base of decisions by health insurance companies, for-profit hospitals, large medical equipment and pharmaceutical manufacturers, and physicians in private practice
- The use of lobbyists by the health care industry in Washington to resist efforts to cut costs and reduce profits
- An aging population that spends more proportionately on health care than other age groups

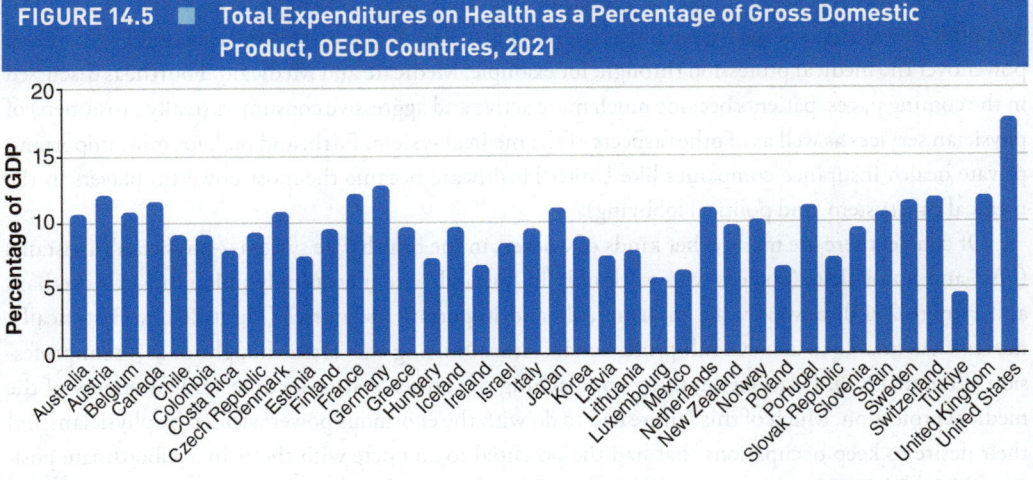

FIGURE 14.5 Total Expenditures on Health as a Percentage of Gross Domestic Product, OECD Countries, 2021

Source: Organisation for Economic Co-operation and Development, 2021, Health Expenditures and Financing: Health Expenditure Indicators, Health Spending Report, Paris, France: Organisation for Economic Co-operation and Development. Retrieved August 2, 2022 (https://data.oecd.org/healthres/health-spending.htm).

- The fact that healthcare is not considered a fundamental human right and is treated more like a consumer product, available only to those who can afford to pay
- The growing anti-vaccination movement which is resulting in increasing public expenditures taking care of those who are suffering from illnesses that could have been prevented

Despite spending more than almost any other country absolutely and per capita, the U.S. health care system fares poorly in comparison to the health care systems in many other countries. The United States ranks 58th in the world in life expectancy at 79.7 years. In 2023, life expectancy in Monaco was the highest in the world at 87 years, and the lowest was in Chad at 53.7 years (World Population Review 2023). Infant mortality is higher in the United States than in most other industrialized countries. Although there is hope for improvement, more than 45,000 people in the United States still die each year because of a lack of medical care (Wilper et al. 2009).

Inequalities in U.S. Health Care

The well-off in the United States (and around the world) can afford any medical care they wish (including that offered by private and concierge medical practices). They are also able to purchase "Cadillac" health insurance policies that pay a large proportion of medical costs. In contrast, even with the Affordable Care Act, more than 30 million people in the United States (more than 9 percent of the population) have no health insurance, and tens of millions of others are underinsured.

The inequalities in health and health care in the United States—and everywhere else in the social world—are unjust, artificial, undesirable, and almost certainly avoidable. Among the major inequalities are those based on social class, race, gender, and sexuality.

Social Class and Health. There is a largely constant relationship between social class and health. That is, the lower one's social class, the poorer one's health is likely to be (Khazan 2018). This relationship holds across countries (although there are variations from country to country) and over time (Pascoe et al. 2016). In fact, inequalities based on social class have generally increased over the years, especially during the COVID-19 pandemic (Ryan and Nanda 2023c).

There are a number of causes of social class differences in health. First, the conditions in which children live matter a great deal because early differences may have long-lasting health consequences. Thus, living in poverty can contribute to ill health in childhood and therefore later in life (Green et al. 2018). Second, conditions in the adult years also affect health. Contributors to poor physical and mental health among adults include poor living conditions, especially those associated with living in unhealthy urban neighborhoods; working lives that are unrewarding economically and psychologically; and high levels of stress. Third, a variety of health-related behaviors contribute to inequalities in health. These include the greater likelihood that those in the lower classes will use illegal drugs, smoke, drink to excess, and be obese as a result of poor eating habits and a lack of sufficient exercise. Finally, the presence or absence of health care in general, and high-quality health care in particular, can play a huge role in health inequalities. Those who see physicians in high-priced concierge practices are likely to have better health than those who get no health care or get it sporadically from hospital emergency rooms.

A good example of the relationship between social class and health is the adverse health consequences associated with smoking (Marron 2017; Scambler 2018). In the 1950s, those in the upper social classes were more likely than those in the lower classes to be smokers. This difference was due, in part, to the influence of the movies, which glamorized smoking, associating it with travel and romance (Kimmel 2016). However, by the 1960s, those in the lower social classes were more likely to smoke. During this period, medical knowledge about the adverse health effects of smoking became better known and publicized. Although that knowledge was disseminated quickly in the upper classes, it had a much harder time working its way to and through the lower classes (Phelan et al. 2004; Phelan, Link, and Tehranifar 2010). A key factor here was the lower educational level among members of the lower classes, who thus had less ability to access and understand the research and data available on the negative effects of smoking (Layte and Whelan 2009). In any case, to this day, the lower classes suffer much more from the ill effects of smoking than do the upper classes.

Race and Health. The relationship between race and health is closely related to that between social class and health. In the United States, for example, White people are more likely to be in the middle and upper classes, while Black and Hispanic people are disproportionately in the lower classes. Overall, White people tend to have better health than Black people (and Hispanic people). As a result, in 2019, White Americans had a life expectancy of 78.9 years while Black Americans had a life expectancy of 75.3 years. On other hand, Asian Americans had a life expectancy of 85.7 years (National Institutes of Health 2022). Why do Black people have poorer health than White people? Racism, both today and as a legacy of the past, plays a major role. Given the history of experiments on Black women's bodies during slavery, as well as notoriously unethical clinical trials such as the Tuskegee experiments (see Chapter 3), many Black women and men have great distrust of the medical system because of what they see as its practice of medical racism (Khazan 2018).

Black people continue to have great difficulty getting the education they need to gain higher-status occupations and the higher incomes associated with them. Even with such education, they may still be unable to obtain those jobs. As a result, they are more likely to remain in the working class and are less likely to have the best health insurance, or they may have none at all. They are also less likely to have the money to visit health care professionals, at least regularly. The health care they do get from hospital emergency rooms, public hospitals, or more marginal physicians is likely to be inferior. Even if they can afford better care, offices and centers that offer such health care may be far from their homes, often in White middle- and upper-class neighborhoods.

Black people are also more likely to be poorly treated, or even mistreated, by the health care system, even if they are suffering from life-threatening diseases such as cancer (Khazan 2018; Matthew 2018). As a result, they are likely to underuse that system, to not use it at all, or to use alternative medicines (such as folk and faith healers). They are also likely to be put off by the underrepresentation of Black Americans in high-status health care positions and occupations—only about 6 percent of physicians are Black (Williams 2018).

Working-class and lower-middle-class Black Americans are more likely to be relegated to neighborhoods and conditions that adversely affect their health. Examples include living near waste dumps where the land, air, and water are contaminated and in apartments or houses with lead-based paint that poses a health risk, especially to young children (Taylor 2014). And stress associated with racism throughout the life course increases the mortality rates of Black adults and infants (Krieger 2017).

Gender and Health. On the surface, inequality in health does not appear to be a problem that afflicts women because their life expectancy throughout the Western world exceeds that of men by a significant margin. However, although women live longer, there is a widespread, although not fully accepted, view that they have poorer health than men during their lifetimes.

A good example of an area in which women *are* disadvantaged compared to men is coronary heart disease. Men are more likely to have this disease than women, but the gap is narrowing. Heart disease is the leading killer of *both* men and women. Medical care helps prevent and treat coronary heart disease, but it has reduced the disease more for men than women. Doctors are less likely to give women with coronary symptoms close attention and the needed diagnostic tests (Doshi 2015). Women are more likely not to get treatment until the disease is well advanced. They are also more likely to have emergency surgery for it. Less is known about heart disease in women because in the past, epidemiological studies and clinical trials tended not to include them as subjects. Even though the disease is somewhat different in women and men, the medical profession has simply treated women based on the findings from research on men.

Coronary heart disease is related to stress, and women appear to experience more stress than men (Wiegner et al. 2015). This is in part because they are less likely than men to be in control of the settings in which they find themselves. At work, they are more likely to be in lower-status jobs that give them less control over what they do as well as offer less security and fewer financial rewards. Many women who work outside the home have the additional stress of having to continue to handle household responsibilities, including childrearing.

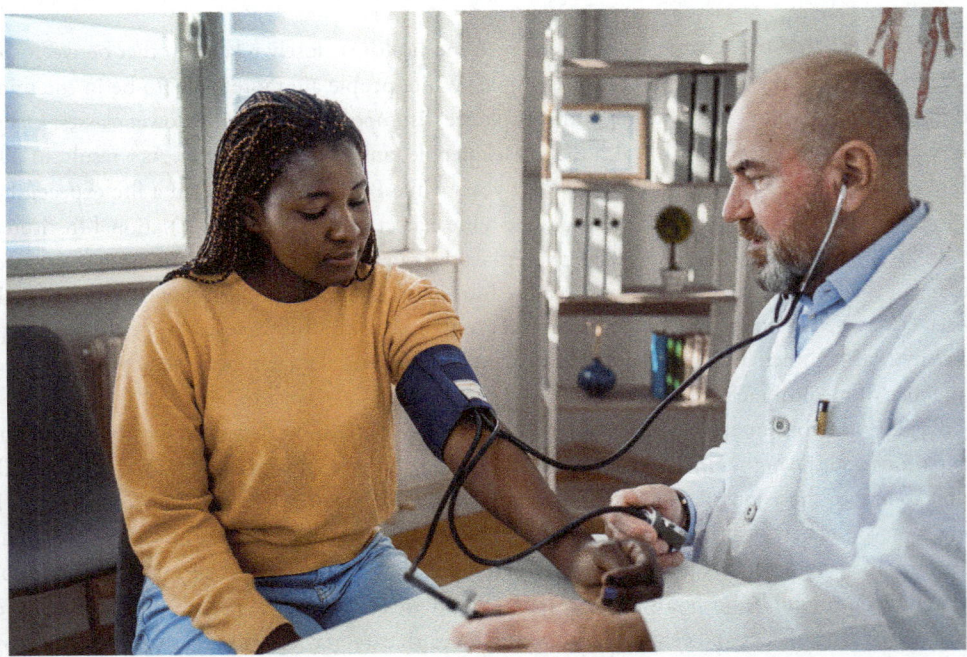

The race or sex of both patient and physician can have significant effect on the quality of care for many serious health problems, such as heart disease.

nortonrsx/iStockPhoto

Both women and men have experienced the medicalization of everyday aspects of their lives. **Medicalization** is the process of labeling and defining aspects of life as medical problems that were not previously so labeled and defined. Medicalization also involves overdiagnosing problems (e.g., many cases of prostate cancer, especially among older men), often using expensive advanced technologies, which would never have caused difficulties for the patient. This can lead to additional health problems stemming from unnecessary treatment. Furthermore, medicalization involves a tendency to exaggerate the ability of medicine to deal with certain phenomena or syndromes (Conrad and Waggoner 2017).

Medicalization is particularly clear in the case of childbirth, a natural process now defined as a "medical problem" that can be dealt with only by physicians in hospital settings. Perhaps the most infamous example of an aspect of life that was once medicalized is the female orgasm. This was long seen not as a natural aspect of female sexuality but rather as an element of "hysterical" disease that required medical attention (Maines 2001). Many other aspects of women's health have been medicalized in recent years, including premenstrual syndrome (PMS), which has been renamed premenstrual dysphoric disorder (PMDD) and is argued to affect potentially as many as 85 million menstruating women in the United States alone. Part of the medicalization of PMDD has included renaming the antidepressant Prozac as the more supposedly friendly sounding (to women) Sarafem and marketing it as treatment for PMDD symptoms (Gehlert et al. 2009). Infertility and menopause have also been medicalized.

Sexuality and Health. Sexual minorities face a number of unique health and health care related concerns. Various studies have indicated that sexual minorities experience higher rates of depression, anxiety, and suicide, as well as increased rates of smoking and alcohol and drug abuse, as compared to heterosexual individuals. There are, however, important caveats to make when considering these studies. The first is that due to a long history of discrimination, there has been comparatively little representative research done on the health of sexual minorities. Researchers and activists are still advocating for improved data collection methods so that we can even have a better idea of how many people identify as a sexual minority (Ryan 2013).

More important is the consideration that few, if any, of the decreased health outcomes among sexual minorities are due to their sexual identities. Instead, they are an outcome of the stigma and discrimination that many sexual minorities face. For example, many sexual minorities report putting off health care because they are afraid of facing homophobia or transphobia from medical professionals. Social stigma and discrimination are also the primary contributing factors to poor health choices like smoking and alcohol abuse. In short, there is nothing inherent about being a sexual minority that results in poorer health outcomes; instead, it is the continued discrimination against sexual minorities, including by many medical professionals, that leads to these outcomes.

Health Care Reform in the United States

In the wake of the kinds of problems discussed previously, especially those that relate to social class differences, the Affordable Care Act (ACA) was enacted into law. The law came fully into effect in 2014 and as of 2022, some 35 million people in the United States use this form of health insurance. Although highly imperfect and far from providing universal coverage, at least one of the desired goals of ACA was achieved as more of the have-nots—especially immigrants and minorities—experienced the sharpest rise in health care coverage under the law (Tavernise and Gebeloff 2016), as did those with preexisting conditions who could not previously receive coverage.

An array of problems with the ACA have become clear. Premiums have been rising, making insurance less affordable for many who need it (though whether or not these rising prices are directly tied to ACA is debatable). Major health insurance companies (e.g., Aetna, UnitedHealthcare) have exited—or threatened to exit—the program in some states because they argue it has reduced their profits. This was due, in part, to the fact that too many of the "wrong" kind of people (the elderly and those among the poor who were more likely to become sick and therefore were most costly to the system) were signing up. Conversely, not enough younger, healthier, and therefore less costly people were enrolling.

Consumerism and Health Care

Historically, thinking about health care involved a tendency to focus on the "producers" of health care, especially physicians, nurses, other health care workers, hospitals, and government agencies. Also included here are the insurance companies, Medicare, and Medicaid. Although much attention continues to be paid to all of those producers of health care, the focus began to shift several decades ago in the direction of the consumers of that care. Larger numbers of patients began to realize they did not simply have to accept what was offered to them by physicians, hospitals, and others. They recognized that they were consumers of those services in much the same way they were consumers of many other services (and goods).

This was due, in part, to the deprofessionalization of physicians. As physicians came to be seen as less powerful professionals, it was increasingly easy for patients to question them. At the same time, the increasing questioning furthered physicians' decline in status and power. The entry of consumerism into medicine meant that more patients began to shop around for physicians and to question doctors' diagnoses and treatment recommendations (at least those who had the economic and other resources necessary to do so).

The best example of increasing consumerism in contemporary medicine is associated with pharmaceutical companies' decision to improve sales of prescription drugs through direct appeals to consumers, using catchy advertisements in newspapers and magazines, online, and on television. The avalanche started in 1997 when the U.S. Food and Drug Administration began to relax restrictions on direct-to-consumer prescription drug advertisements. Since that time, pharmaceutical companies have increasingly used direct-to-consumer advertising to supplement their marketing to physicians through advertisements in medical journals, salespeople, and free samples. Direct marketing also increasingly targets the ultimate consumer of pharmaceuticals: the patient (Lazarus 2017). This is nowhere clearer than in the ubiquitous TV advertisements for pharmaceuticals of various kinds, especially on national newscasts because they are watched disproportionately by older people who are more likely to have health problems. The irony is that, in general, patients cannot go out and obtain the advertised drugs on their own; they need prescriptions from their physicians. Thus, the idea is to motivate patients to ask their doctors for, and in some cases demand, the desired prescriptions. The evidence is that this works, and as a result, the pharmaceutical companies are increasing presences in the media. We are all now familiar with endless advertisements for the leading and most profitable prescription drugs, such as Neulasta for use after chemotherapy, and especially the seemingly ubiquitous advertisements for drugs that treat erectile dysfunction, especially Viagra and Cialis. All of these ads suggest, either directly or indirectly, that viewers should ask their physicians to prescribe these medications for them.

The Internet and the Consumption of Health Care

The internet has become deeply implicated in the consumption of health care (e-health) in various ways. The first and most obvious way is by allowing people (at least those with access and know-how) to find health care providers of all sorts more easily. The internet is a vast resource for finding providers by specialty on the local, national, and even global levels.

Not only is it possible to find the names and addresses of providers on the internet; in addition, and more important, lots of information about them is available there. For example, one can get rankings of health care providers as well as information from previous patients about their experiences and recommendations. There is also a wealth of information and evaluation available on pharmaceuticals, medical technologies, and alternative treatments.

The increasing amount of health care–related data of all sorts on the internet allows people to become much more knowledgeable consumers (prosumers) of health care services and products. At the moment, most of the information is scattered, widely and unsystematically, across the internet. Another problem is that it is not linked to individuals, their diseases, and their specific needs. Increasingly, however, consumer-patients can comparison shop for medical care on the internet in much the same way they shop for hotels and airfares. For example, on sites such as Health in Reach and Healthcare Bluebook, people can compare prices on everything from flu vaccines and annual physicals to mastectomies and bowel surgeries. Health insurance companies are also increasingly providing information online about benefits, stating, for example, what they pay out for office visits and various medical procedures. However, it is often difficult for consumer-patients to compare medical procedures because there are no standard terminological codes, available information is highly jargonistic, and the same procedure may have a dozen different prices at the same hospital because of separate negotiations with different health insurers.

A patient who uses online resources can become a much more sophisticated, knowledgeable, and independent consumer of medical services and products. For example, consumers can obtain many products and services legally or illegally—and often more inexpensively—through the internet without going through intermediaries associated with the health care system (Benner and Frenkel 2018; Vida et al. 2017). Also available online are a variety of tests that can be done at home, such as a DNA test that can be had for as little as $59 from companies like 23andMe and

AncestryDNA. Individuals and couples can use such tests to discover on their own whether they are carriers of life-threatening diseases, such as cystic fibrosis, that could show up in their children. However, there are concerns that these tests may not be reliable, that they may give test takers a false sense of assurance, that the costs are too high, that the privacy of the test results may not be ensured, and that those who rely on these tests will not get the expert advice of trained medical professionals (Kolata 2018).

Two serious problems with using the internet for self-diagnosis are that a lot of the information on the internet is false and that the general public often lacks the sophisticated medical knowledge to properly diagnose themselves. Many of us have probably looked to the internet to find remedies for a common ailment, like a headache or a hangover, only to end up concerned that we might have a brain tumor. Although it can be a useful starting point, the internet should not replace medical experts as a means of diagnosing health.

Other problems associated with using the internet for health-related consumption include the possibility of getting counterfeit, and perhaps ineffective, medications, as well as bogus services and information (Lavorgna 2015). During the COVID-19 pandemic, the internet, and especially social media, were rife with a number of unproven, and often dangerous, "cures." Political leaders and celebrities frequently posted false medical information and suggested ineffective or even harmful remedies. Although the internet has expanded the ability of some individuals to have their voices heard, it should be medical education, not number of followers, that determines who we listen to when seeking medical advice.

Telemedicine

Most people spend countless hours every year visiting their doctors and seeking health care. Most of this time is not actually spent with doctors, however, but on travel and in waiting rooms. A patient who has to take time off from work for a medical appointment can lose wages. As a student, your grade in a course might drop if you have to miss class to visit a doctor. **Telemedicine**, that is, using technology to consult with doctors rather than going to their office, has the potential to save us time and make health care more convenient, especially for people who live in rural areas. E-mails and video chats are popular ways to communicate with health care providers without having to leave the comfort of our homes, workplaces, or schools. Some workplaces and schools have even installed telemedicine kiosks for their employees and students. One review of telemedicine research found no health care outcome differences between video conferencing and face-to-face delivery for patients experiencing mental health issues, substance abuse problems, and dermatological conditions (Flodgren et al. 2015). This same review also found that telemedicine helped diabetics control their blood sugar levels better than did traditional doctor visits.

The COVID-19 pandemic led to a sharp increase in the use of telemedicine. For example, in the United States, there was a 50 percent rise in the use of telehealth services in the first quarter of 2020 as compared to the same period in 2019. The last week in March 2020 alone saw a 154 percent increase in virtual medical visits (Koonin et al. 2020). Of interest is that only 7 percent of these virtual visits were classified as COVID-19 related, indicating that although the pandemic lockdown was a driving factor behind the sharp increase in the use of telehealth services, concerns over infection with COVID-19 were not the motive for the increase.

Telemedicine is not without obstacles. Although video chatting with our therapist when we are experiencing anxiety or e-mailing our dermatologist a photo of a bug bite that looks infected might seem like reasonable issues to manage with telemedicine, not all health care problems can be

The COVID-19 pandemic drove demand for telehealth providers, such as this physician who is consulting with a patient online.

Yaroslav Olieinikov/iStockPhoto

handled by distance health care delivery. Telemedicine may prove more beneficial in helping us manage chronic health conditions than in diagnosing initial symptoms. Also, the digital divide prevents those without internet access from taking advantage of telemedicine, and not all insurers cover e-visits. In addition, telemedicine requires our active participation. We are required to inspect, monitor, and care for our bodies more closely than required for face-to-face medical visits. This increases our own responsibility over the state of our health—and perhaps self-blame if we fail to monitor it adequately.

In addition to consultations with medical professions, the internet also provides a means of contacting nonprofessionals for medical help and advice. A number of crowdsourcing groups exist where individuals share their personal experiences and can help others track down medications or other medical supplies. In Kazakhstan, for example, an online group was formed during the early days of the COVID-19 pandemic to help locals find medicines they might need that were either unavailable or in short supply. Members of the group exchanged and donated medicines to one another and also coordinated requests for vigilantes who went to other countries (i.e., Russia) to acquire supplies. Although such practices were illegal, they also provided many with life-saving medications and other medical necessities that were either absent from or in short supply in local markets (Ryan and Nanda 2023c).

GLOBALIZATION AND HEALTH

There is a nearly endless array of issues that could be discussed under the heading of globalization and health. We will focus on a few of them here.

Growing Global Inequality

Although globalization has been associated with increased aggregate life expectancy, it also has tended to widen global disparities in health (Marmot 2015). Women and children tend to be the most vulnerable populations globally, due to such things as economic inequality and poor access to health care (Boyd-Judson and James 2015; Subrahmanian and Swamy 2018). Often, people in poor nations (and especially the poor in poor nations) tend to have poorer health as a result of limited access to health care services, poor education, inadequate sanitation, and inadequate nutrition and housing. In turn, poor health tends to limit economic growth in those nations, mainly by adversely affecting productivity. Developing countries have a disproportionate share of mortality and **morbidity** (rates of illness and disease within a population), much of which could be prevented inexpensively and treated effectively if the money and resources were available to do so.

For the reasons mentioned previously, and others, there is a significant gap in life expectancy between developed and less developed, or high- and low-income, countries. Figure 14.6 shows life expectancy at birth for select countries around the world. Note the 33-year age difference in life expectancy between highly developed Singapore at the top of the list and the far less developed Afghanistan at the bottom. The greatest increases in life expectancy have occurred in developing countries such as Brazil, Egypt, and Malaysia, which have tended to be increasingly and successfully involved in economic globalization. However, for most of the rest, especially the least developed, low-income countries in the Global South (such as Chad, the Central African Republic, and Afghanistan), globalization has been accompanied by a decline in economic growth, an increase in poverty, and, as a result, a decline in health.

Disease

The vast majority of not only acute (or temporary) but also chronic (or longer-lasting) diseases occur at younger ages and in low- and middle-income countries. The rising cost of dealing with chronic diseases in developing countries will likely adversely affect the countries' ability to deal with acute infectious diseases. Of special importance from the point of view of globalization is the increasing global marketing of tobacco, alcohol, sugar, and fat—the latter two especially aimed at children—and the consequent global spread of the diseases (lung cancer, cirrhosis of the liver, diabetes, heart disease) associated with these products.

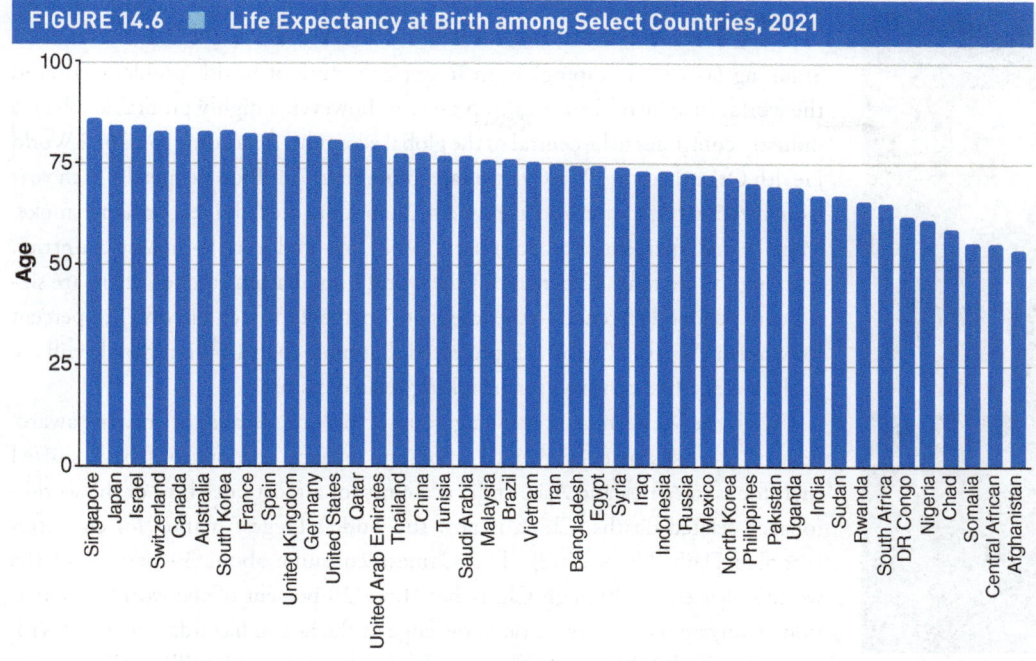

FIGURE 14.6 Life Expectancy at Birth among Select Countries, 2021

Source: Central Intelligence Agency, 2021, The World Factbook: Life Expectancy at Birth, Washington, D.C: Central Intelligence Agency. Retrieved August 2, 2022 (https://www.cia.gov/the-world-factbook/field/life-expectancy-at-birth/).

Malnutrition

Countries in the Global South suffer disproportionately from hunger and malnutrition (Webb et al. 2018). In 2021, more than 828 million people were facing issues of hunger and malnutrition, a number that increased more than 150 million just since the 2019 onset of COVID-19 (World Health Organization 2022a). Dealing with hunger and malnutrition is especially important for children because those who are underweight are, as adults, likely to be less physically and intellectually productive and to experience more chronic illnesses and disabilities. This carries on across generations as the ability of such adults to provide adequate nutrition for their children is compromised.

Undernutrition is a form of malnutrition involving an inadequate intake of nutrients, including calories, vitamins, and minerals. The other form of malnutrition involves **obesity**, which is caused by an excessive intake of nutrients, especially calories. Developing countries now increasingly suffer from a "double nutritional burden," with some people not having enough to eat and others eating too much, especially the wrong kinds of food (e.g., food high in fat and cholesterol; Webb et al. 2018). Although obesity is increasing in the less-developed world, undernutrition remains the greatest problem there, particularly for mothers and children. Undernutrition creates difficulties that continue throughout the life cycle and is responsible for stunted growth, lower levels of schooling, lower productivity, and chronic diseases; undernourished women also give birth to low-birthweight infants. Undernutrition has also been linked to rapid weight gain and obesity among formerly underweight children.

Undernutrition is related to problems not only for individuals but also for societies as a whole. It leads to underdevelopment and tends to perpetuate poverty. Without adequate nutrition, the human capital needed for economic development is more difficult to develop.

Food insecurity is a major cause of undernutrition in less-developed countries, and it is also an important issue in developed countries like the United States and the United Kingdom (Purdam, Garratt, and Esmail 2015). Such insecurity exists when people do not have sufficient access to safe and nutritious food—a condition necessary for leading a healthy and productive life. There are many causes of food insecurity. Poverty is the central cause of food insecurity nearly everywhere, although a lack of access to nutritional foods is also an issue. A number of global programs have been undertaken to help deal with this problem through the creation of agricultural diversification programs, community gardens, farmers markets, and the like.

Smoking

Although China has become the world's biggest market for cigarettes, only one in five people there are aware of smoking's dangers. What would it take for this situation to change? Who would benefit, and who would be harmed?

GOH CHAI HIN/AFP via Getty Images

Smoking (as well as vaping) is an important cause of health problems around the world. In spite of those health problems, however, a highly profitable tobacco industry continues to be central to the global economy. According to a 2022 World Health Organization (WHO) estimate, more than 7 million people die each year from direct tobacco use, and almost a million more die from secondhand smoke. More than 80 percent of tobacco users live in low- and middle-income countries. Although more than 22 percent of the world's population smokes, there are significant gender differences—the rate is 36.7 percent for men but only 7.8 percent for women (WHO 2022b). It is projected that more than 1 billion people will die in the twenty-first century from smoking-related diseases.

With the Western market for cigarettes shrinking because of growing awareness of the risks associated with smoking, tobacco corporations have shifted their focus to Africa and Asia. India accounts for almost one-third of the world's tobacco-related deaths. China is now the world's biggest market for cigarettes (People's Daily News 2018). The Chinese consume about 30 percent of the world's cigarettes, although China has about 20 percent of the world's population. Many appear to have little knowledge of the health hazards associated with smoking (WHO 2010a). As a result, the deaths of about 1 million Chinese are traceable to smoking cigarettes. By 2050 the number of smoking-related deaths in China could increase to 3 million people if no action is taken to reduce smoking rates (WHO 2010a). For their part, Western powers are the major exporters of cigarettes to the rest of the world. The United States is the single largest exporter of cigarettes as well as of globally recognized cigarette advertisements and brands.

Borderless Diseases

Another negative aspect of globalization as far as health is concerned is the flow of borderless diseases (Wirth 2018). Although borderless diseases have become much more common in recent years, most notably COVID-19, they are not a new phenomenon. Tuberculosis (TB) was known in ancient times. Today the WHO (2023) estimates that more than one-third of the world's population is infected with the cause of the disease—the TB bacillus. Almost 10 million people in the world have the disease, and an estimated 1.6 million of them died from it in 2021. Sexually transmitted infections (STIs) of various types have long diffused globally. A specific example is syphilis, which has spread globally and continues to circulate, especially throughout a number of less-developed countries. However, the roots of the disease were probably in Europe, and it was originally spread by European colonialism and military exploits. In fact, for many in the less-developed world, the disease was closely associated with French soldiers, and it came to be known in some parts of the world as the "French disease."

Then there is the increasing prevalence of other borderless diseases, many of them relatively new. Examples include COVID-19; monkeypox; bovine spongiform encephalopathy (BSE, or "mad cow disease"), which is often found in cattle and can cause a brain disease in humans; avian flu; Ebola; Zika; and HIV/AIDS. The nature of these diseases and their spread—either actually (COVID-19, HIV/AIDS, Ebola) or merely, at least so far, a frightening possibility (avian flu)—tells us a great deal about the nature and reality of globalization in the twenty-first century. The pathogens that cause these diseases flow, or have the potential to flow, readily throughout the globe.

Several factors help explain the great and increasing global mobility of borderless diseases (Zhou and Coleman 2016):

- The increase in global travel and the increasing rapidity of that travel. Tourists both carry borderless diseases and can be infected by them in tourist destinations throughout the world (monkeypox, for example, has been traced to a tourist center).

- The growing human migration and the ease with which (at least some) people can cross borders. As a result, people often bring with them diseases not detected at national borders.

- The expansion of massive urban areas, such as New York City; Cairo, Egypt; and Lagos, Nigeria, has created vast mixing bowls where large numbers of people in close and frequent proximity can easily infect one another.

- The increasing human presence in previously untouched natural habitats. There, people can have contact with pathogens for which they have no immunity that can spread rapidly throughout the world. It is believed that humans initially caught Ebola (and other diseases, including COVID-19) from wild animals.

- Mechanisms to combat disease—including vaccines, medications, and personal protective equipment—have not been made available equally around the world. Inequality in access to preventative and curative measures, including through vaccine hoarding, has resulted in a continued spread of disease.

The flow of efforts to deal with these diseases must be equally global (Ryan and Nanda 2023c). That is, there is a need for global responses to the increasing likelihood of the spread of various diseases. However, some nations have proven unable or unwilling to respond to this global need.

HIV/AIDS

HIV/AIDS was first recognized in the United States in 1981 (although it was initially called GRID—Gay-Related Immuno-Deficiency—a term that highlights its original, and ongoing, false association with sexual identity) and has since been acknowledged as a scourge throughout not only the United States but also much of the world. By 2021, an estimated 40 million people worldwide had died from AIDS since the first diagnosis. More than 38 million, many of whom might eventually die from the disease, were living with HIV in 2021. The numbers of people infected with HIV and living with AIDS vary widely around the globe. Table 14.2 shows that Africa has been hit hardest, with nearly 70 percent (20.6 million) of the world's HIV population living on this continent. Of the 1.5 million people newly infected in 2021 around the world, 670,000 live in eastern and southern Africa. Just over 2.5 million people live with HIV in Latin America and the Caribbean combined, including 124,000 newly infected in 2021. Some groups in these areas, such as the indigenous Warao of Venezuela, are especially hard hit because, in part, of cutbacks in AIDS programs due to Venezuela's catastrophic economic situation (Semple 2018). An estimated 6 million people are living with HIV in Asia and the Pacific. The huge population of this region means that even relatively low prevalence rates translate into large numbers of people infected with HIV. In contrast, people in the Middle East and North Africa have the lowest rate of HIV, at 0.1 percent, or fewer than 189,000 HIV-infected persons. It should be noted that these numbers are estimates. A lack of testing, stigma associated with the disease, and misdiagnosis all contribute to underestimates.

TABLE 14.2 ■ HIV Prevalence and Incidence by Region, 2021

Region	Total Number Living with HIV	Newly Infected	Adult Prevalence (Percentage)
Africa, Eastern & Southern	20,600,000	670,000	6.2
Africa, West & Central	5,000,000	190,000	1.3
Asia & Pacific	6,000,000	260,000	0.2
Caribbean	330,000	14,000	1.2
Eastern Europe & Central Asia	1,800,000	160,000	1.1
Latin America	2,200,000	110,000	0.5
Middle East & North Africa	180,000	14,000	< 0.1
Western & Central Europe & North America	2,300,000	63,000	0.3

Source: The Global HIV/AIDS Epidemic January 19, 2018; Kaiser Foundation. UNAIDS, 2022, *Regional Data-2021*, Fact Sheet 2022, p.5, Geneva, Switzerland: UNAIDS Secretariat. Retrieved August 2, 2022 (https://www.unaids.org/sites/default/files/media_asset/UNAIDS_FactSheet_en.pdf).

HIV/AIDS cannot be contracted through casual contact with people who have the disease. The disease spreads only through intimate human contact with body fluids, especially through unprotected sex and intravenous drug use. Thus, in spite of the large numbers of people with HIV/AIDS, it is *not* an easy disease to contract. For instance, fellow passengers on an international flight will not contract HIV/AIDS simply because they sit next to, or talk with, a fellow passenger with the disease.

The spread of HIV/AIDS is linked to globalization, especially the increased global mobility associated with tourism (notably, sex tourism), the greater migration rates of workers, increased legal and illegal immigration, much higher rates of commercial and business travel, the movement (sometimes on a mass basis) of refugees, military interventions and the movement of military personnel, and so on.

People who have the disease can travel great distances over a period of years without knowing they have been infected. They therefore have the ability to transmit the disease unknowingly to many others in widely scattered locales. When people with HIV/AIDS travel to other countries and have sexual contact with people there, they are likely to transmit the disease to at least some of them. Similarly, those without the disease can travel to nations where HIV/AIDS is prevalent, contract it, and then bring it back to their home country. In either case, the disease moves from region to region, country to country, and ultimately globally, carried by human vectors.

Superbugs

There is growing concern around the world about superbugs, which are bacteria resistant to all known drugs. These are garden-variety germs rather than the more exotic ones like Ebola. Superbugs (e.g., C. difficile) are often picked up during hospitalizations and have been cured easily in the past with antibiotics. Bacteria that are resistant to certain drugs can pass that resistance on to other germs that may already be resistant to other drugs. Over the years, bacteria—for example, the one associated with TB—have grown resistant to an increased number of overused drugs (e.g., penicillin). For example, we are down to the last drug, Colistin, that can treat carbapenem-resistant bacteria (CRE). When bacteria become resistant to that drug, CRE bacteria will be unstoppable, at least until a new cure can be found. According to the director of the Centers for Disease Control and Prevention, this is one of many indicators that we are entering a "post-antibiotic world" (cited in Tavernise and Grady 2016). Just as diseases of all sorts can move readily around the world, so, too, can bacteria and their associated diseases that are resistant to all known drugs.

COVID-19

The SARS-CoV-2 virus, more commonly referred to as COVID-19, has been one of the most impactful global events in living memory (Ryan 2021a; Ryan 2021b). The first case of a "pneumonia with an unknown cause" was reported to the World Health Organization (WHO) by the Chinese authorities on December 31, 2019. The WHO declared COVID-19 to be a global pandemic not quite three months later on March 11, 2020 (they had already labeled it a "public health emergency of international concern" as early as January 30). Today, there are few, if any, people on the planet who have not in some way been impacted, either directly by the virus itself, or by the various social measures put in place to try to control it, or by the economic impact of the pandemic.

As of June 2023, there have been more than 765 million confirmed cases of the virus and more than 6.9 million confirmed deaths as a result of it (see Figure 14.7). We know, however, that these numbers are quite conservative and that the actual counts are much higher (Ryan 2021b). The pandemic has also resulted in countless other deaths through the impact on hunger and starvation, routine vaccinations (not just those for COVID-19), job loss, and a reduction in routine medical care, to name just a few secondary effects.

We should take careful note of the differences between the SARS-CoV-2 virus and the COVID-19 pandemic. A virus is an entity (whether it is alive or not is still highly debated; see Astorino and Nicola 2021) that infects living organisms. The term *pandemic*, on the other hand, has a more social connotation and refers to the outbreak, occurrence, and spread of a particular disease. There is a clear overlap but there are also important distinctions. Medical professionals, for example, are primarily responding to the SARS-CoV-2 virus, while politicians, economists, and social scientists are primarily responding to the COVID-19 pandemic.

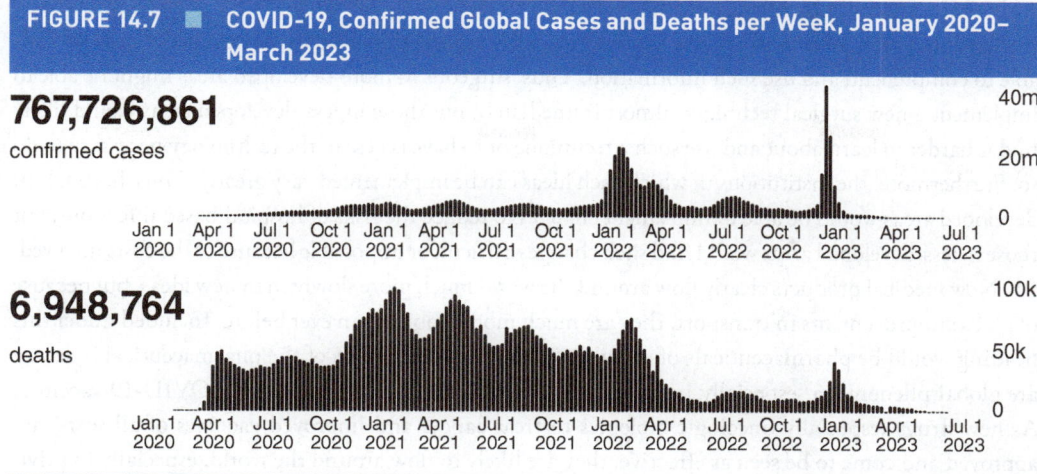

FIGURE 14.7 ■ COVID-19, Confirmed Global Cases and Deaths per Week, January 2020–March 2023

Source: World Health Organization, COVID-19 Dashboard, April 2023.

Viruses impact societies, but societies also impact viruses. The rapid spread of the virus and the various mechanisms put in place (or not) to try to control its spread have had profound social implications. On the other side, social issues—like crowded housing conditions, poorly funded medical systems, the spread of misinformation, and politicizing disease—have also allowed the virus to spread more easily. The impact of the virus, then, has spread well beyond just medical issues, also impacting the social, cultural, economic, political, and the everyday lives of nearly everyone all over the world. The virus, like other diseases, is a medical issue, but the pandemic has also had profound impacts on issues of education, housing, employment, discrimination, food security, and religion, to name just a few.

We can think about the difference between more medical and more social issues by thinking about the difference between contagion issues and systemic issues. **Contagion** refers to how easily something spreads, how likely it is to spread, and how quickly it spreads. The SARS-CoV-2 virus is contagious. **Systemic issues**, on the other hand, refer to things that are underlying factors in the ways in which societies operate. They are widespread and often parts of broader social and political systems. Discrimination against racial minorities is a systemic issue. It is important to note that contagion issues and systemic issues are often interdependent. As discussed above, the medical and the social are heavily intertwined and the ways in which diseases are able to spread (contagion) is dependent, to a large degree, on broad systemic issues.

The COVID-19 pandemic, like other global catastrophes, has called attention to the many deep-rooted and far-reaching inequalities throughout the world (Ryan and Nanda 2022). We know that the pandemic has not affected everyone equally. Women, racial minorities, sexual minorities, the disabled, the elderly, the poor, and those living in impoverished conditions and countries have all been impacted more heavily. Thus, although the virus itself does not discriminate, the health outcomes from the virus show just how much human societies do.

Globalization and Improvements in Health and Health Care

We have focused in the last few sections on the negative effects of globalization on health. It is clear, however, that globalization has also brought with it an array of developments that have improved, or at least have the potential to improve, the quality of health throughout the world. One example is the growth of global health-related organizations, such as the WHO, the Red Cross, and Médecins sans Frontières (Doctors without Borders). Of course, as with much else about globalization, the effects have been uneven and affected by a variety of local circumstances

Increasing interpersonal relations among and between various regions throughout the world means that positive developments in one part of the world are increasingly able to find their way to most other parts of the world, and quite rapidly (whether or not they actually do so is largely a question of politics and issues of global inequality). In addition, there is a ready flow of new ideas associated with health and health care. In the era of the internet and online journals—in this case, medical journals—information about new medical developments flashes around the world virtually instantaneously, at least for those with internet access. Of course, how those ideas are received and whether, and how quickly, they can be implemented vary enormously. There is great variability around the world in the number of professionals able to comprehend and use such information. Thus, surgeons in more-developed areas might be able to implement a new surgical technique almost immediately, but those in less-developed areas would likely find it harder to learn about and use such a technique or to have access to the technology necessary to do so. Furthermore, the institutions in which such ideas can be implemented vary greatly. Thus, hospitals in developed areas would be able to implement changes to reduce the risks of hospital-based infections, but those in less-developed areas would find such changes difficult or impossible because of the costs involved.

New medical products clearly flow around the world much more slowly than new ideas, but because of global improvements in transport, they are much more mobile than ever before. Included under this heading would be pharmaceuticals of all types. Clearly, the superstars of the pharmaceutical industry are global phenomena, especially in recent years those associated with various COVID-19 vaccines. As new drugs (especially oncologic biologics to treat cancer and improved vaccines of all sorts) are approved and come to be seen as effective, they are likely to flow around the world, especially to privileged countries and to elites everywhere.

Unfortunately, the drugs most likely to be produced and distributed globally are those considered likely to be most profitable, not necessarily those that would have the biggest impact on saving lives. More profitable drugs tend to address the health problems of the wealthier members of global society, such as hypertension, high cholesterol, impotence, and hair loss. Because they produce the greatest earnings for pharmaceutical companies, these drugs are most likely to achieve global distribution.

Conversely, drugs that might save many lives are not apt to be produced (Moran et al. 2009). Few, if any, of the pharmaceutical companies surveyed in the United States, Europe, and Japan devote research and development money to creating drugs that would help those in less-developed countries who suffer from diseases such as sleeping sickness and malaria (Moderna's research into a potential malaria vaccine is a notable exception). Such drugs are unlikely to yield great profits because those who need them are mainly the poor who would be unable to afford them, even if they were available. Thus, as we have seen, Africa is a hotbed of many diseases, such as malaria, some of which kill millions of people each year. However, these are largely poor people in impoverished countries, and the major drug companies based primarily in the West and wealthy developed countries are little interested in doing the research and paying the start-up and production costs necessary to produce drugs that are not likely to be profitable and may even lose money. To be fair, we are beginning to see new drugs that treat sleeping sickness (Maxmen 2017) and prevent and treat malaria, but they are a long way from mass production and distribution. In the meantime, tens of millions continue to die from these diseases.

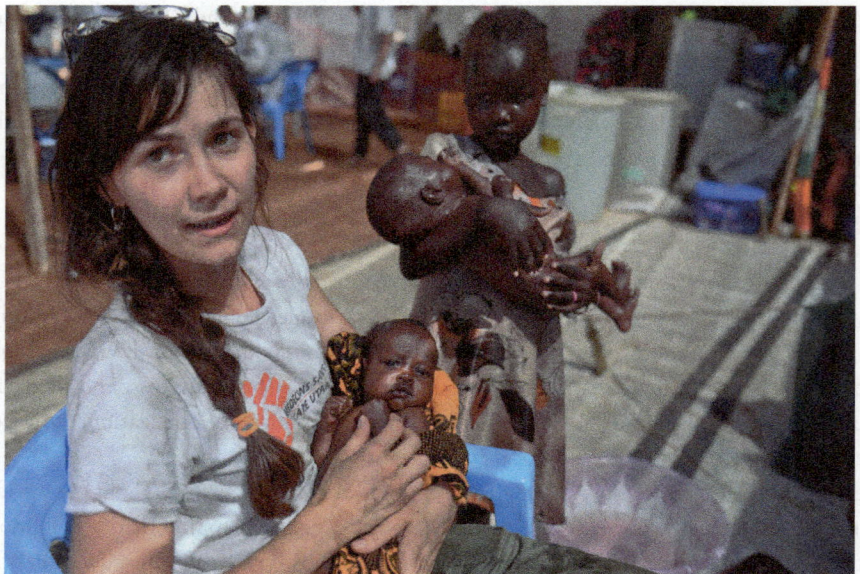

A worker for Doctors without Borders helps children in South Sudan, where the World Health Organization hopes to carry out a massive vaccination campaign against cholera. What challenges does this effort face, given that unrest in that country has displaced almost one million people?

EMILI_VISION/Getty

Similar points can be made about the flow of advanced medical technologies, including MRIs and CAT scans, throughout the world. These are extraordinarily expensive technologies found largely in the wealthy developed countries of the Global North. The machines are not only more likely to exist in these developed countries but also more likely to be used extensively there because patients, either on their own or because of health insurance, can afford the very expensive scans and tests associated with them. Also concentrated in developed countries are the highly trained personnel needed to administer and interpret the results of, say, an MRI. In contrast, relatively few of these technologies flow to less-developed countries in the Global South; they are used there less extensively, and there are relatively few trained people there capable of conducting the tests and interpreting the results (Debas 2010; WHO 2010a).

In terms of networks of people, much the same picture emerges. Medical and health-related personnel in the Global North are tightly linked through an array of professional networks. As a result, personnel can more easily move about within those networks. More important, the latest findings and developments in health and medicine are rapidly disseminated through those networks (especially in English). The problem in the Global South is not only that fewer professionals are involved in these networks but also that the flow of new information to them is more limited (Shiffman 2017). More important, even if they are able to get the information, they generally lack the resources and infrastructure to use it, or to use it adequately.

SUMMARY

The sociology of the body encompasses a wide range of concerns, such as sexuality, bodily pain, body modifications, as well as health and illness.

The medical profession has gone through a process of deprofessionalization, characterized by a decline in power and autonomy as well as in status and wealth among members. Challenges to the authority of physicians include the threat of medical malpractice, the creation of government medical programs and policies, and the rise of private health insurance programs. Patients have become more active prosumers in the health care system, too, using the internet to shop for the lowest prices for medical procedures and reading fellow patients' reviews.

Disparities in health and health care have often been tied to globalization. Individuals in the Global South suffer disproportionately from hunger, malnutrition, and food insecurity. The spread of diseases such as COVID-19, HIV/AIDS, and Ebola are linked to increased global mobility and urbanization in the Global South. The ability to implement new medical technologies and afford new treatments varies by region, with the Global South lagging far behind the Global North, but the rise of antibiotic-resistant superbugs poses a danger to the treatment of some diseases in all parts of the world.

KEY TERMS

bodily capital
contagion
deprofessionalization
food insecurity
medicalization
medical sociology
morbidity

obesity
profession
reflexivity
systemic issues
telemedicine
undernutrition

REVIEW QUESTIONS

1. We live in an increasingly reflexive society with a heightened awareness of our bodies. How does the "beauty myth" perpetuate such reflexivity?

2. What satisfaction do people get from risk-taking behavior?

3. What are the pros and cons of our obsession with our appearance and the fitness of our bodies?

4. What are the characteristics of a profession? What factors can help explain why physicians have become increasingly deprofessionalized?

5. What are the weaknesses of the health care system in the United States? How are these weaknesses related to systems of stratification?

6. Explain the increasing medicalization of society. How has it affected women in particular?

7. How have the internet, new social media technologies, and telemedicine affected the consumption of health care? What are some of the disadvantages of having access to more information about health care?

8. In what ways are patients increasingly knowledgeable and empowered consumers (prosumers) of health care? How has this change affected the power of physicians?

9. How has globalization tended to widen global disparities in health care? What kinds of health problems are you most likely to find in the Global South? What could be done to prevent some of these problems?

10. What are the major borderless diseases? In what ways are they made worse by globalization? Can globalization also play a role in curing them, or at least in reducing their prevalence?

11. How did the COVID-19 pandemic impact how we think about health and health care? What kinds of global inequalities has it revealed?

UCG/Getty Images

15 POPULATION, URBANIZATION, AND THE ENVIRONMENT

> **LEARNING OBJECTIVES**
>
> **15.1** Explain the causes and effects of population growth and decline.
>
> **15.2** Discuss the implications of the growing urbanization of the world's population.
>
> **15.3** Explain global cities and discuss their role in globalization.
>
> **15.4** Discuss major environmental problems and efforts to solve them.

THE PARIS AGREEMENT

Efforts to deal with climate change seemed to succeed, at least to some degree, with the Paris Agreement of the United Nations Climate Change Conference. Negotiated at the end of 2015, the agreement was signed by 174 countries on Earth Day, April 22, 2016 (as of 2023, 194 countries plus the European Union had signed on). Most notably, the countries involved agreed to limit carbon emissions—largely from the burning of fossil fuels and forest destruction—as soon as possible. Each country was to set a target to reduce or limit its emissions, but the "nationally determined contribution" was to be voluntary. There are no enforcement mechanisms or penalties for failure to meet the targets. Each country also agreed to do its best to keep the temperature increase globally to well below 2 degrees centigrade (3.6 degrees Fahrenheit). Virtually all countries involved realized that these steps were not sufficient, or strong enough, to slow down, let alone stop, the increase in ecological problems. As a result, they set up a system to regularly monitor and review the global ecological situation. As Gillis (2015) put it, even with this agreement, the "great ice sheets remain imperiled, the oceans are still rising, people are dying by tens of thousands in heat waves and floods, and the agriculture system that feeds seven billion human beings is still at risk." Even though it is a weak agreement, in mid-2017, President Trump announced that the United States would withdraw from it in 2020. Under President Biden, however, the United States rejoined in 2021.

The Paris Agreement is one of many environmental agreements that have been negotiated in recent years (although it is arguably the most important one). A growing body of scientific evidence is showing the multiple ways in which human beings are destroying, sometimes irrevocably, our planet and such agreements are one way that governments are attempting to limit such damage. Although there are many worthwhile criticisms of such agreements (mostly that they do not go far enough to truly save the planet), they are at least a step forward toward limiting the damage caused to our environment by the human population and our increasingly energy-dependent and consumer-based lifestyles. The Supreme Federal Court of Brazil even went so far as to recognize the Paris Agreement as a human rights treaty in July of 2022.

Problems with the natural environment are closely tied to the other key issues discussed in this chapter: population and urbanization. Although each is important in its own right, they are covered here together because of the many ways in which they are interrelated. For example, population growth tends to lead to more densely populated, or at least geographically larger, cities, and an increased population, and its associated needs, is likely to wreak even more havoc on the environment.

POPULATION

Demography is the scientific study of population, especially its growth and decline, as well as the movement of people. Those who study these population dynamics are **demographers**. Demography is both a distinct field of study and a subfield within sociology.

Basic Population Processes

Three basic processes are of concern to demographers. The first is **fertility**, or people's reproductive behavior, especially the number of births. Key to understanding fertility is the **birthrate**—the number of childbirths per 1,000 people per year. Second is **mortality**, or deaths and death rates within a population. Finally, there is **migration**, or the movements of people, or *migrants*, and the impact of these movements on both the sending and the receiving locales. Although these are dynamic processes, demographers are also concerned about more structural issues such as population composition, especially the age and sex characteristics of a population.

Fertility

In 2021, the global **fertility rate**, or the average number of live births per woman, was 2.3 (World Population Review 2023). However, fertility levels vary widely around the globe. In 2021, they ranged from 1 birth per woman in South Korea to 6.9 births per woman in Niger (World Population Review 2023). In this section, we deal with the economic and social factors affecting fertility, regional differences in fertility, and fertility trends in the United States.

Economic Factors. Fertility is affected by a variety of economic factors. For example, record lows in population growth were associated with the Great Depression. Low points were also recorded in the 1970s, when an oil crisis led to a dramatic jump in oil prices and rampant inflation. In general, there tend to be fewer babies born when times are rough.

Social Factors. Fertility is also affected by a variety of social factors. For instance, there is the obvious impact of age on fertility. Most childbearing involves women between the ages of 15 and 45. Especially important in the context of age is the fertility and childbearing of adolescents (less than 20 years old). The rate is as high as 101 per 1,000 births in Sub-Saharan Africa (World Health Organization 2022). The United States has the highest rate of births to teenage mothers of all industrial nations; it is more than four times the rate of many western European countries (World Health Organization 2018). However, the teenage birthrate in the United States has been declining dramatically in recent years. The peak year was 1957, with a birthrate of 96.3 per 1,000 teenage women ages 15 to 19. By 2019, the birthrate for such women had reached a record low of 16.7 (Centers for Disease Control and Prevention [CDC] 2021; see Figure 15.1). The overall adolescent birth rate has also been declining globally, from 64.5 births per 1,000 females in 2000 to a rate of 42.5 in 2021 (World Health Organization 2022).

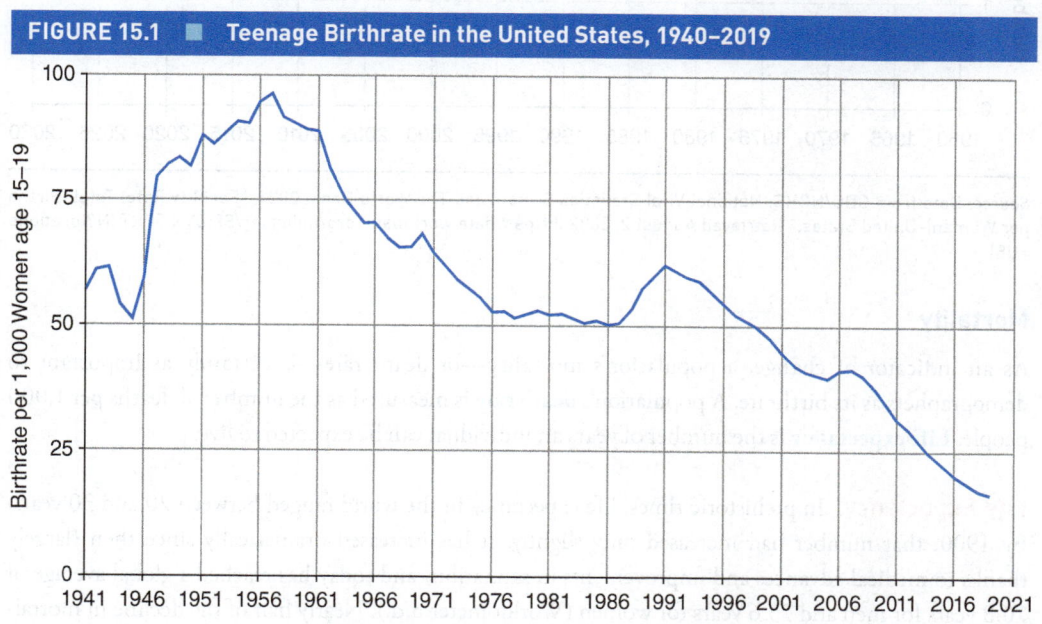

FIGURE 15.1 ■ Teenage Birthrate in the United States, 1940–2019

Source: Data from U.S. Centers for Disease Control and Prevention, 2001, "Births to Teenagers in the United States, 1940–2000," *National Vital Statistics Reports* 49(10): 2. Retrieved August 2, 2022 (https://www.cdc.gov/nchs/data/nvsr/nvsr49/nvsr49_10.pdf).

U.S. Centers for Disease Control and Prevention, "U.S. and State Trends on Teen Births, 1990–2019," National Center for Health Statistics Data Visualization Gallery, Washington, D.C.: Centers for Disease Control and Prevention. Retrieved August 2, 2022 (https://www.cdc.gov/nchs/data-visualization/teen-births/index.htm).

A second, and related, issue involves the broader category of nonmarital fertility; not all such fertility is accounted for by adolescents (Fletcher and Polos 2018). Nonmarital fertility has increased dramatically in the United States, rising from only 5 percent of all births in 1960 to one-third in 2000; it now accounts for roughly 40 percent of all births (CDC 2023). The United States is not unique among Western industrialized countries in this: Its rate of nonmarital fertility is higher than some, such as Germany's and Ireland's; on par with others, such as Austria, Spain, and Finland; and lower than others, such as Mexico and Iceland, where almost two-thirds of children are born outside marriage (Chamie 2017).

U.S. Fertility Trends. When the United States was founded in 1776, the average fertility rate was slightly less than 8 births per woman (although many of those died before reaching the age of 5); that rate declined throughout the nineteenth century and most of the first half of the twentieth century. Then World War II led to an increase in the birthrate, and it remained high throughout the 1950s. The rise in the birthrate between 1946 and 1960 is referred to as the *baby boom*. The peak in fertility in the United States was reached in 1957, after which the fertility rate has generally tended to decline. Today the fertility rate is around 1.66 (see Figure 15.2; CDC 2022a). In other words, fertility in the United States is below the 2.1 **replacement-level fertility**—the number needed to replace the population.

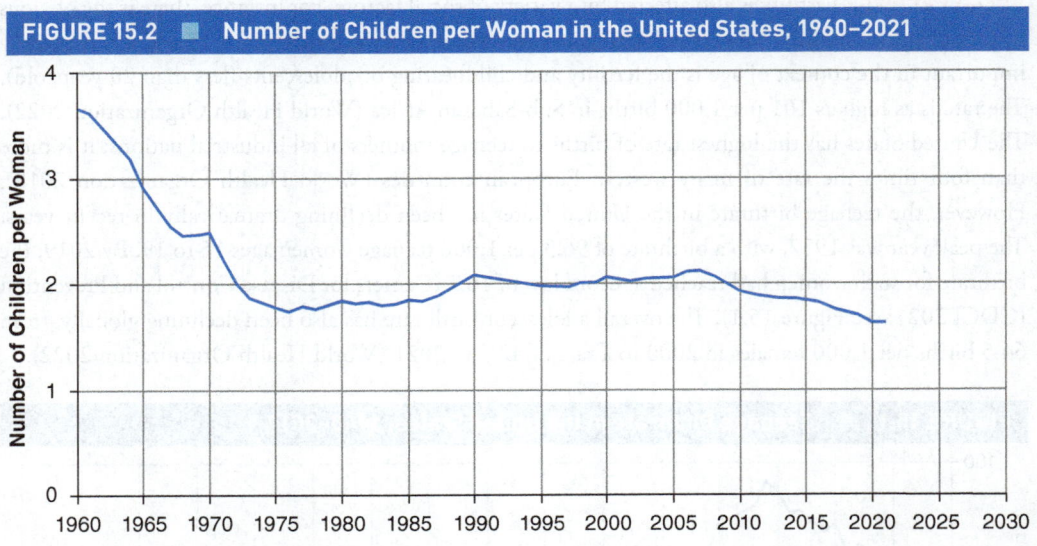

FIGURE 15.2 ■ Number of Children per Woman in the United States, 1960–2021

Source: Data from CDC/NCHS, National Vital Statistics System and The World Bank, 2021, "Fertility Rate, Total (Births per Woman)-United States." Retrieved August 2, 2022 (https://data.worldbank.org/indicator/SP.DYN.TFRT.IN?locations=US).

Mortality

As an indicator of change, a population's mortality—or death rate—is certainly as important to demographers as its birthrate. A population's **death rate** is measured as the number of deaths per 1,000 people. **Life expectancy** is the number of years an individual can be expected to live.

Life Expectancy. In prehistoric times, life expectancy in the world ranged between 20 and 30 years. By 1900, that number had increased only slightly. It has increased dramatically since then (largely thanks to medical advances and improvements in sanitation) and today has reached a global average of 70.8 years for men and 75.6 years for women (Worldometer n.d.). Nearly half of the decline in mortality in developed countries took place in the twentieth century. Life expectancy for those born in 2022 is 75 years for men and 82 years for women in more developed countries, 69 years for men and 73 years for women in less developed countries, and 62 years for men and 67 years for women in the least developed countries (Statista 2023). Hong Kong has the highest life expectancy in the world at 85.3 years while the Central African Republic has the shortest at just 54.3 years (Worldometer n.d.). Life expectancy in the United States was 79.1 years in 2022. Broken down by gender, the life expectancy for women in the United States is about 81.7 years; for men it is 76.6 years (Worldometer n.d.).

Macro-Social Factors. Although death is, of course, a biological inevitability, increased life expectancy and lower death rates in a population can be affected by a variety of macro-social factors. Major factors in the decline in mortality (with a few examples) include the following:

- A general improvement in standards of living (better housing quality, improved nutrition)
- Better public health (improved sanitation, cleaner drinking water), and improved access to health services
- Cultural and behavioral factors (stronger norms regarding healthy lifestyles, including reductions in rates of smoking)
- Advances in medicine and medical technologies (new and improved vaccines, antibiotics and newer drugs, immunizations, improved surgical techniques), which not only led to an aging population but also reduced infant mortality rates
- Government actions (better control of the causes of diseases such as malaria), including increased funding for health research

Of course, important factors that keep death rates high continue to exist (including infectious diseases such as pneumonia, malaria, Ebola, and HIV/AIDS), and other factors that could increase the death rate, including global epidemics like the ongoing COVID-19 pandemic, loom on the horizon.

Mortality is greatly affected by one's position in the system of social stratification (see Chapter 8). In general, those in the lower classes are likely to have shorter life spans than those who rank higher in the stratification system. In the United States, the life expectancy for the wealthiest 1 percent of men is 14.6 years longer than the poorest 1 percent of men. The wealthiest 1 percent of women live 10.1 years longer than the poorest 1 percent of women (Dizikes 2016). As for race, although the mortality rate for racial minorities tends to be higher than that for Whites in most places. Morality rates also tend to be higher for those with lower levels of education. In general, socially and economically privileged categories tend to enjoy long life spans. In terms of gender, women have a longer life expectancy than men despite the various disadvantages they confront that stem from the system of gender stratification (see Chapter 8). This difference is due, in part, to the fact that women tend to engage in more health-protective behaviors than men, such as visiting physicians more often and smoking less. Gender roles also tend to protect women from fatal disease and injury. For example, women are less likely than men to engage in potentially disabling or deadly activities, such as using illegal drugs, driving dangerously, and engaging in violent behavior. In general, "women now live longer than men not because their biology has changed, but because their social position and access to resources have changed" (Weitz 2017). Nevertheless, in some parts of the world, such as Swaziland and Botswana, females have a lower life expectancy than males. This is traceable, at least in part, to the fact that females in some regions are more likely to die in infancy, perhaps because of parental neglect or female infanticide, or when giving birth to their own children.

Micro-Social Factors. Mortality is also affected by a number of micro-social factors, especially those associated with poor lifestyle choices, including smoking, drug addiction (especially to opioids; see Chapter 14), lack of exercise, overeating, and eating unhealthy foods. Obesity has long been related to higher death rates from heart disease and stroke. A more recent discovery is the linkage between obesity and death from various forms of cancer, including breast, kidney, and pancreatic cancer. The American Cancer Society (2018) estimates that about 7 percent of all cancer deaths are a result of obesity. Conversely, healthy lifestyle choices can lead to longer lives. For example, religious groups (such as Mormons) that restrict the use of tobacco products, alcohol, coffee, and addictive drugs tend to have longer life expectancies. Globally, the lifestyle of the Japanese, which includes eating more fish and less red meat, is closely related to their greater longevity.

The Demographic Transition

The issues of fertility and mortality are central to demographic transition theory. According to this theory, population changes are related to the shift from an agricultural society to a more industrialized and urbanized society (Davis 1945). Four stages are associated with the **demographic transition**, that is, population changes that are related to the shift from an agricultural society to a more industrialized and urbanized society (see Figure 15.3). In the first, or preindustrial stage, there is a rough balance between high death rates (mortality) and high birthrates (fertility). As a result, the population growth rate, although high, is fairly stable.

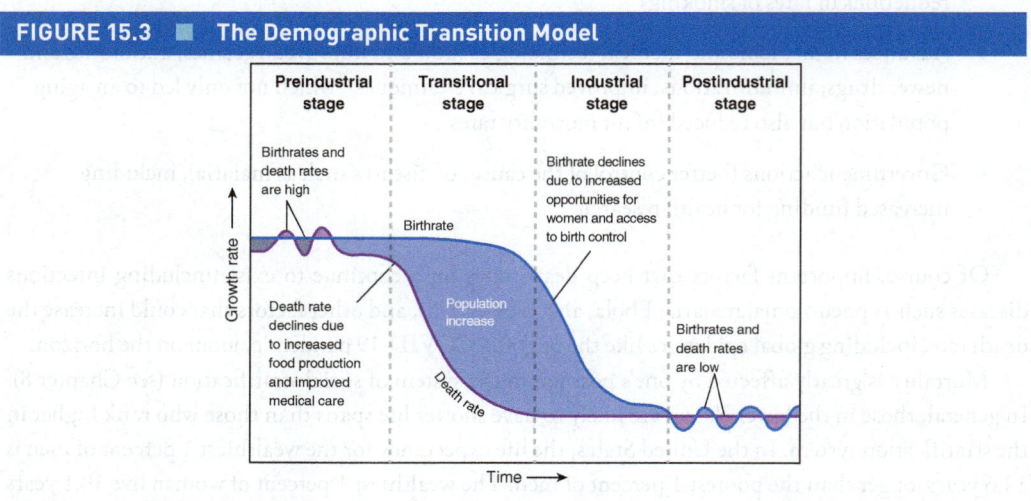

FIGURE 15.3 ■ The Demographic Transition Model

Source: Adapted from *A Dictionary of Geography*, 2nd edition, by Susan Mayhew (1997). Figure 20, p. 122. By permission of Oxford University Press.

In the second, or transitional stage, the death rate declines dramatically while the birthrate remains high (although it begins to decline slowly toward the end of this stage). The total population grows rapidly under these circumstances. In this stage, death rates decline first in developed countries for various reasons, including improvement in food production, a higher standard of living, a better-informed population, improved hygiene, and better health care. This was the situation in most of the developed countries of Europe beginning in the eighteenth century.

In the industrial stage, the death rate drops more slowly over time, to its lowest level. The deep decline in the death rate leads to more children in the family and community. As a result, people begin thinking about limiting the number of children. Women begin to have greater access to, and are more likely to use, birth control. In addition, fewer children are required because not as many workers are needed on the family farms. Many family members move into the cities and take jobs in industries and other organizations. Thus, another main cause of the decline of the birthrate in the industrial age is the fact that women have increased work-related opportunities. For these and other reasons, it is to the family's advantage to limit family size. Eventually, the birthrate drops to a level roughly equal to the low level of the death rate.

In the postindustrial stage, although there is some variation over time, birthrates and death rates remain low. As a result, in the postindustrial stage, as in the latter part of the industrial stage, population growth remains slow or stabilizes.

In western Europe, the entire demographic transition took about 200 years, from the mid-1800s until the mid-twentieth century. The process continues today in much of the rest of the world. However, in recent years, in less-developed countries, the transition process has taken significantly less time. This is traceable to the much more rapid decline in the death rate because of the importation of advanced, especially medical, technologies and improved access to immunizations and vaccines. Because birthrates have remained high while death rates have declined, population growth in less developed countries has remained high.

Given this recent rapid population growth in less developed countries, the issue has become what can be done about it, especially in the areas of the world where fertility remains high. In other words, how can the birthrate be reduced in those areas?

Reducing Fertility. Adopting the view that development is the best contraceptive, one approach to reducing fertility is to stress economic development, especially for women. This follows from what has been learned from the demographic transition in Europe and the United States, where economic development did lead to lower fertility. A second approach is voluntary family planning. This includes providing people with information about reproductive physiology and the use of contraceptive techniques, actually providing such things as birth control pills and condoms, and developing societal or local informational programs to support the use of contraception and the ideal of small(er) families. A third approach involves a change in the society as a whole, especially in places where large numbers of children have been considered both advantageous and desirable. In many societies, children are still needed to work to help the family survive and to provide for the parents in their old age. Changes such as compulsory childhood education and child labor laws can counter the fact that these realities lead families to have large numbers of children. They serve to make children less valuable economically because they cannot work when they are in school and are kept out of the labor force for years by child labor laws. As a result, at least some parents have fewer children. Another important step is to be sure that women acquire public roles beyond the family realm. When women have greater educational and occupational opportunities, their fertility declines, and families have fewer children (Bongaarts, Mensch, and Blanc 2017). However, solutions that require changing cultural ideas about women and reproduction can be difficult and slow to achieve.

The practice of infanticide, or the murder of a child less than one year old, is an unfortunate reality in some parts of the world, and the selection of females for infanticide is especially problematic for various reasons, including its impact on fertility. The selective killing of female fetuses (female infanticide) subsequently affects fertility because males end up outnumbering females in a population and there are fewer potential mothers. Infanticide is most common in South and East Asia, although it is also found in other areas of the world, including North Africa and the Middle East (Szczepanski 2018).

A Second Demographic Transition. In the 1980s, some scholars began thinking in terms of a second demographic transition to describe the general decline in the fertility rate and of population growth, especially in developed countries (Zaidi and Morgan 2017). This decline is linked to parents coming to focus more on the quality of life of one child, or a few children, as well as on the quality of their own lives. Better occupational prospects, and therefore a more affluent lifestyle, especially for females, have come to be associated with having fewer children.

The second demographic transition involves three stages. The first stage, between 1955 and 1970, is of greatest importance. The key factor during this period was the end of the baby boom, aided by the revolution in contraception that made it less likely that people would have unwanted children. Also beginning at this time was the gender revolution, which meant, among other things, that women began to marry later, have improved access to education, and to divorce more. They also entered the work world in greater numbers. This tended to reduce the birthrate, as did the fact that there were fewer women at home to care for children. These and other factors can be said to be associated with a second demographic transition involving subreplacement fertility, lower birthrates, and a declining rate of population growth.

Migration

Although migration certainly takes place within national borders, our primary concern here—and in the world today—is cross-border, international, or global migration. Such migration is considered a central aspect of globalization (Mavroudi and Nagel 2016). The focus in the United States in recent years has been on illegal migration, especially through and from Mexico. This is largely because Donald Trump made the stopping of illegal migration the centerpiece of his presidential campaign, as well as of his presidency. He sought to do this by, among other things, promising to build a much larger and stronger wall between Mexico and the United States (and claiming, unsuccessfully, he could force Mexico to pay for it). He made this a major goal of his administration despite the fact that the flow of illegal immigration through Mexico and to the United States has slowed dramatically, largely because of improved economic conditions in Mexico (Porter 2016). In late 2018, without agreement from Congress to build such a wall, Trump ordered thousands of troops to the Mexican border to help contain what is, at best, a trickle of illegal immigrants. The impasse over the wall led to the longest government shutdown in history in late 2018 and early 2019.

Concern about Migration. Globally, concern about migration reached a crescendo in 2015–2016 as massive numbers of people fled their home countries because of warfare, failed states, and hostility to minority groups. Syria, Iraq, Libya, and Yemen were sites of catastrophic warfare and can be considered failed, or at least failing, states. Minority groups such as the Yazidi in Syria and Iraq fled as a result of persecution and even genocide at the hands of the Islamic State (Cumming-Bruce 2015). In Myanmar (and Bangladesh), many Rohingya, a Muslim minority, fled to escape violence perpetrated by the Hindu majority in that country (Fuller and Cochran 2015). In the seas around Europe and Southeast Asia, many rickety boats (some of which sank) carried people to what they thought would be safe havens in other countries. However, most countries did not welcome these people and even (sometimes violently) rejected them. These countries feared, among other things, terrorism and the cost of maintaining the immigrants until they could be integrated economically into society. Governments, especially in Germany, have come under severe attack because of their open-door policies toward migrants (Bennhold 2018).

Although concern in Europe about migrants has reached crisis proportions (Fisher and Bennhold 2018), the number of migrants arriving in Europe had actually dropped dramatically by 2018 due to greater border controls in Europe. Beyond that, the European Union (EU) and/or specific nations in Europe paid or induced countries such as Morocco, Turkey, Sudan, and Libya to stanch the flow of migrants long before they reached the shores of Europe. In recent years, there has been increased media attention in Europe to the flight of migrants, including the many thousands who die, especially by drowning, trying to enter.

Controlling Migration. Prior to the beginning of the fifteenth century, people moved across borders rather freely, although they were greatly hampered by limitations in transportation. However, with the rise of the nation-state in the fifteenth century, much more notice was taken of such movement, and many more barriers were erected to limit and control it (Hollifield and Jacobson 2012). Nevertheless, as late as the end of the nineteenth century, there was still much freedom of movement, most notably in the great Atlantic migration to the United States from Europe. An estimated 50 million people left Europe for the United States between 1820 and the end of the nineteenth century. Prior to 1880, entry into the United States was largely unregulated—virtually anyone who wanted to could get in. World War I changed attitudes and the situation dramatically; nation-states began to impose drastic restrictions on the global movement of people. Today, although there is variation among nation-states, "there is not a single state that allows free access to all immigrants" (Moses 2006, 54). With legal migration restricted in various ways and border controls more stringent, one unintended consequence has been an increase in illegal immigration, often involving human smugglers.

These migrants from Northern Africa are being assisted by a humanitarian organization off the coast of Spain. Large numbers of migrants have attempted this perilous journey across the Mediterranean to southern Europe in recent years, resulting in thousands of deaths at sea.

Aris Messinis/Getty Images

A great deal of migration is associated with globalization (Hoskin 2017). In 2022, about 281 million people, or roughly 3.6 percent of the global population, lived outside their countries of origin (UNHCR 2023). To some observers, this represents a large and growing number (although the rate of increase has declined dramatically in recent years). However, to other observers, the sense that we live in a global era of unprecedented international migration is exaggerated because the actual rate was higher in the late nineteenth and early twentieth centuries (Guhathakurta, Jacobson, and DelSordi 2007).

Migration Today. Several interesting and important changes have affected the nature of today's international migrants. Unlike much else in the modern world (trade, finance, investment), legal restrictions on the migration of people, especially labor migration, have *not* been liberalized (Polakow-Suransky 2017) and are now being tightened significantly. The major exception has been within the EU, and only for the citizens of member nations. Former U.S. President Trump notoriously imposed severe restrictions on immigration from Mexico and several predominantly Muslim countries.

Elsewhere in the world, restrictions on migration remain in place, as they do in the EU for non-EU citizens. In some places, and for some less welcome migrants, restrictions have not only been increased but in some cases also militarized (Schuster 2012). Some European borders have been sealed (e.g., between Hungary and Croatia [Lyman 2015b]; between Greece and Macedonia; around the entrance in France through the Chunnel). Walls and fences have been constructed in various places in Europe (e.g., Austria, Bulgaria, Greece, Hungary, and Macedonia) to stem, if not totally block, the flow of unwanted migrants. Beyond the physical barriers, the former president of the European Council, among others, issued a stark warning to illegal migrants: "Do not come to Europe" (Kanter and Chan 2016). In mid-2018, Hungary went so far as to enact a law making it a *crime* to help undocumented migrants (Kingsley 2018b).

However, there are daunting problems involved in attempting to control global human migration. For one thing, the sheer numbers of such people involved make control extremely difficult. According to one estimate, "Tens of millions of people cross borders on a daily basis" (Hollifield and Jacobson 2012, 1390). The greatest pressure is on the United States and Europe, which are often considered (rightly or wrongly) the most desirable destinations for many migrants, both legal and illegal. For another thing, controls are very costly, and few nations can afford to engage in much more than token efforts. Then there is the fact that attempts to control migration inevitably lead to heightened and more sophisticated efforts to evade those controls. A lucrative market opens up for those, such as smugglers, in the business of transporting people across borders illegally (Alderman 2016). Finally, the increased efforts at control lead to increasingly desperate efforts to evade them. This, in turn, leads to more deaths and injuries.

Explaining Migration. Migration is influenced by a combination of push and pull factors. Among the *push* factors are the desire of migrants for better or safer lives; problems in the home country, such as unemployment and low pay, making it difficult or impossible for migrants to achieve their goals; and major disruptions, such as war, famine, political and religious persecution, and economic depression. *Pull* factors include features of the host country, such as its being a liberal nation at peace and having a favorable immigration policy, a prosperous economy, higher pay and lower unemployment, a strong social welfare program, available food, a good educational system, formal and informal networks that cater to immigrants, labor shortages, more equitable civil and human rights, and language and culture similar to those of the home country.

Types of Migrants. **Refugees** are migrants forced to leave their homeland or who leave involuntarily because they fear for their safety (Collier and Betts 2017). The Office of the UN High Commissioner for Refugees is charged with determining whether migrants are defined as refugees.

Asylum seekers flee their home country, usually to escape political oppression, religious persecution, or issues related to personal identity (such as identifying as a member of the LGBTQ+ community). They seek to remain in the country to which they flee and are in a state of limbo until a decision is made on their request for asylum (Schuster 2012). If and when that claim is accepted, the asylum seeker is considered a refugee. If the claim is rejected, it is likely that asylum seekers will be returned to their home country. In mid-2018, in an effort to reduce the number of immigrants entering the country, especially from Central America, the United States sought to limit or end the practice of allowing those escaping gang violence or domestic violence to claim asylum (Romero and Jordan 2018).

Labor migrants are those who move from their home country to another country due to push and pull factors (Basaran and Guild 2018). The major pull factor is the existence of jobs paying higher wages than those back home. Examples are millions of women who immigrate globally (especially to the United States or the Middle East) to find employment as domestic workers. Among the push factors for such women are civil wars and economic crises in their home countries.

People fleeing violence, like these members of the minority Yazidi sect in a camp near the Iraq-Turkey border, are usually considered refugees rather than simply migrants. War and fighting in the Middle East and Africa have forced millions of people from their homelands in the last few years. What obligation toward them do the rest of the world's people have?

Anadolu Agency/Getty Images

Undocumented immigrants are those residing in a receiving country without valid authorization (Wides-Muñoz 2019). This category overlaps with some of the previously discussed types of migrants; both asylum seekers and labor migrants may be undocumented immigrants. There are three broad types of undocumented immigrants. The first are those who manage to gain entry without passing through a checkpoint or without undergoing the required inspection. The second type comprises those who gain entry legally but then stay beyond the period permitted by their visas. Third are those who immigrate based on false documents. As shown in Figure 15.4, the number of undocumented immigrants to the United States increased from about 3.5 million in 1990 to a high of 12.2 million in 2007, before declining to about 10.5 million in 2017. Immigrants from Mexico account for the majority of undocumented immigrants. Of the 10.5 million undocumented immigrants in 2016, 5 million were of Mexican descent (Krogstad, Passel, and Cohn 2018).

As of 2021, an estimated 10.7 million immigrants from Mexico are living in the United States. Despite anti-immigration political rhetoric, this actually represents a decline of more than 1 million (roughly 9 percent) since 2010 (Migration Policy Institute 2022). Many of these individuals migrate because although they may be paid poverty wages by U.S. standards, that may be more than they could earn in Mexico (and often for doing the same job). Many Mexican immigrants work on U.S. and Canadian farms picking fruits and vegetables and are paid low wages, work long hours, and live in substandard housing (Dias-Abey 2018).

Many immigrants also enter the United States to pursue educational opportunities not available in their home countries. Because the U.S. Supreme Court holds that states cannot deny undocumented students access to primary and secondary education, education plays a central role in social mobility for these students (and their families).

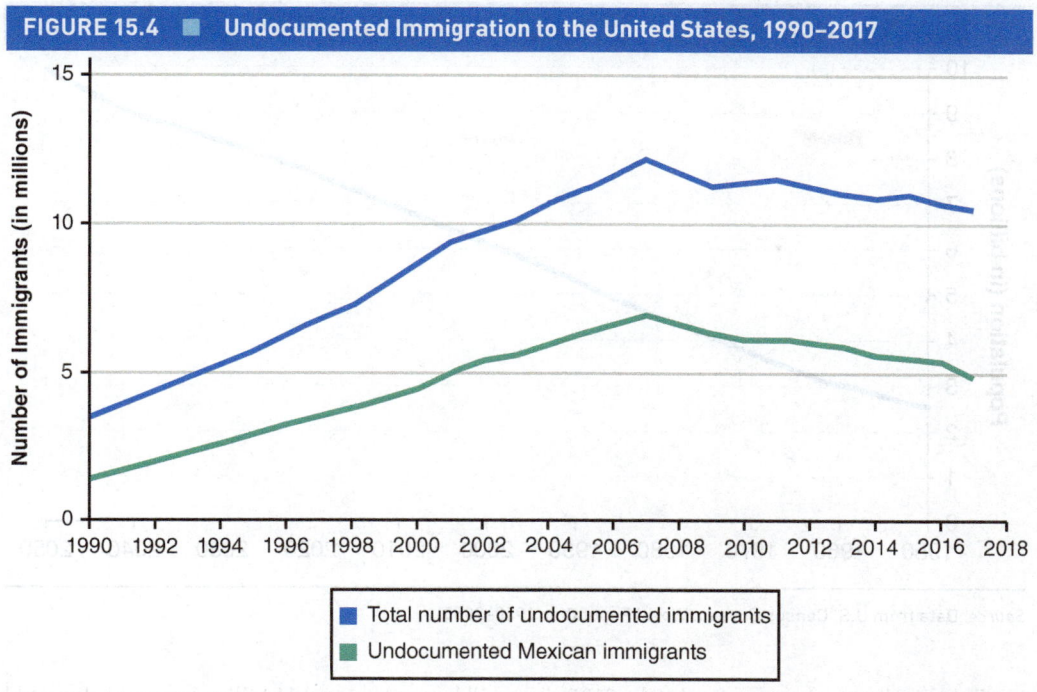

FIGURE 15.4 ■ Undocumented Immigration to the United States, 1990–2017

Sources: Hugo Lopez, Mark, Jeffrey Passel, and D'vera Cohn, 2021, "Key Facts About the Changing U.S. Unauthorized Immigrant Population," *Pew Research Center*, April 13. Retrieved August 2, 2022 (https://www.pewresearch.org/fact-tank/2021/04/13/key-facts-about-the-changing-u-s-unauthorized-immigrant-population/); Passel, Jeffrey, and D'vera Cohn, 2019, "Mexicans Decline to Less Than Half the U.S. Unauthorized Immigrant Population for the First Time," *Pew Research Center*, June 12. Retrieved August 2, 2022 (https://www.pewresearch.org/fact-tank/2019/06/12/us-unauthorized-immigrant-population-2017/).

Population Growth

A great deal of attention has been devoted to population growth and the idea of a population explosion, or the "population bomb" (Ehrlich 1968). Some of that fear has dissipated in recent years. This has happened, at least in part, because of the ability of the world's second most populous country (after India, and the most populous until 2023), China, to slow its population growth through, among other things, its one-child policy. Although that policy was discontinued at the beginning of 2016, China's population is already huge and will continue to grow. Population increases are important and of interest not only in themselves but also because of the need for greater resources to support a growing population. Also of concern is the strain such increases place on national and city services, as well as on the environment.

Overall fertility rates are dropping globally, but the world's population continues to increase, although at a declining rate. It was not until the early 1800s that the global population exceeded 1 billion people; it reached 2 billion in just one century (by 1930), then 3 billion in 30 more years (by 1960). In the next 14 years, it reached 4 billion (1974); 13 years later, it was 5 billion (1987); and in another 12 years, it reached 6 billion (1999; Roberts 2009). In 12 more years (October 2011) the world's population exceeded 7 billion people and in November 2022, it topped 8 billion people (more than 1/3 of which live in China and India alone). Despite these staggering numbers, there has been a slowdown in population growth in recent decades. It is now estimated that *only* about 9.9 billion people will be in the world by 2050 (see Figure 15.5; Population Reference Bureau 2018). Although this is a dramatic reduction in future estimates, it still represents a major increase in the world's population. This growth is occurring, and will continue to occur, despite high death rates in many parts of the world due to high infant mortality, war, starvation, disease (including COVID-19), and natural disasters. The death rate—the number of deaths per 1,000 people—may increase dramatically in the twenty-first century if, as many expect, the disastrous effects of climate change accelerate, although that increase is unlikely to have much of an impact on overall population projections. Nevertheless, although there is less talk these days about a population explosion, there is little doubt that the world's population is increasing, perhaps at an unsustainable rate.

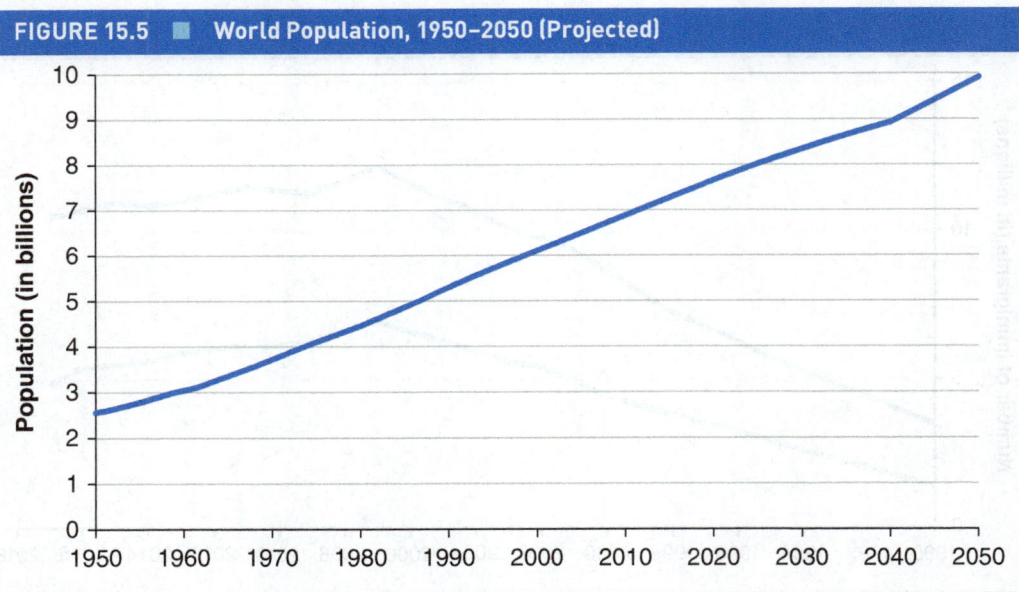

FIGURE 15.5 ■ World Population, 1950–2050 (Projected)

Source: Data from U.S. Census Bureau, World Population 1950–2050.

Taking a longer time perspective, by 2100 there will be an estimated 11 billion people in the world (United Nations Department of Economic and Social Affairs 2019). The reason for the significant increase is largely that in many countries (such as Ethiopia and Niger), rapid population growth continues. In fact, despite the ravages of warfare and diseases such as COVID-19, malaria, HIV/AIDS, and Ebola, the population of Africa as a whole is expected to double by 2050 and constitute about half of the world's population by 2100 (United Nations Department of Economic and Social Affairs 2019).

Population Decline

Historically, population decline has not been considered as important as growth, but it has recently come to the fore in various parts of the world, especially in a number of European countries (Italy, Germany, Spain) and Japan (Coale and Watkins 2017). By 2050, the population of Germany is projected to *drop* from 82.3 million to 78.6 million, while Japan's population is projected to decline from 126.8 million to 102.1 million. Also of concern is the decline expected to occur in Russia, from 144.5 million to 135.1 million in 2050 (Population Reference Bureau 2018), numbers that do not even account for the losses as a result of the invasion of Ukraine. A variety of problems, such as high alcoholism rates and greatly unequal development across the country, as well as those fleeing military inscription and discriminatory policies, have led to predictions of the "depopulation" of Russia. Similar declines, and problems, are expected in a number of former Soviet Bloc countries, such as Bulgaria, and Latvia. The Russian invasion and widespread destruction in Ukraine is also having a dramatic impact on the population of that country.

Population decline can be caused by a low birthrate. It can also be caused by a high death rate, more emigration than immigration, or some combination of the three. In countries with aging populations, birthrates are often below the level needed to maintain the population.

Of interest here are not only the various causes of such declines but also their impact on society as a whole. For one thing, population decline can weaken nations in various ways, including militarily (Yoshihara and Sylva 2011). This is because the power of nations is often associated with having large populations; a smaller population generally translates into a smaller military (Israel is an exception). For another, population decline (not just a smaller population) can weaken a nation's economy because the total number of productive, especially younger, workers decreases. Third, the fact that population decline is generally accompanied by an aging population brings with it various problems, including a "financial time bomb." This is because of the high costs associated with caring for the elderly—especially government pensions and health-related expenses. A parallel decline in the number of younger people in the labor force means fewer people to help pay those costs through taxes (LeVine and Stevens 2018; Singer 2010).

It would be wrong to conclude that population decline brings with it only a series of problems. Among the gains would be a potential reduction of the ecological problems caused by a growing population. For example, a smaller population would arguably produce fewer automobile emissions and create less pollution. In addition, the pressure on the world's diminishing supplies of oil and clean drinking water would arguably be reduced.

Although some nations will be hurt by an aging population, others, especially developing countries, will get a "demographic dividend" (Pace and Ham-Chande 2016) because they have a favorable ratio between those who are able to work and those who are dependents, such as the aged and children. The dividend results, in part, from the presence of a large younger population able to work and earn money. At the same time, there are relatively few in need of their support. A significant part of the dividend is traceable to education and the greater productivity associated with a better-educated younger generation (Allison 2018).

URBANIZATION

The world has, until very recently, been predominantly rural; even in 1800, there were only a handful of large urban areas in the world. As late as 1850, only about 2 percent of the world's population lived in cities of more than 100,000 residents. Urban areas have grown rapidly since then. In the first decade of the present century, more people around the world lived in urban, rather than rural, areas (Gotham and King 2019). Today, some 56 percent of people live in urban areas (World Bank 2023). However, there are great differences among the nations of the world in terms of their degrees of urban development: In the United Kingdom, 83 percent of the population is urban; in the United States, 82 percent is; but only 17 percent of Rwanda's population is urban (World Bank 2018). It is projected that by 2050, 68 percent of the world's population will live in urban areas (World Bank 2018). The greatest growth will be in developing areas, where 90 percent of urban growth will occur in Asia and Africa (United Nations Department of Economic and Social Affairs 2018).

The importance of **cities**, or large, permanent, and spatially concentrated human settlements, has progressively increased. The city became increasingly central, and it has become much more important in the context of today's "global" cities (discussed later in this chapter).

The term *urban* generally refers to city dwelling, but it also has more specific and technical meanings (what is considered urban varies from society to society). To be considered **urban** (an "urbanized" or "metropolitan statistical" area) in the United States, an area must have more than 50,000 inhabitants, while in Iceland, an area need have only 200 residents to be considered urban. **Urbanization** is the process by which an increasing percentage of a society's population comes to be located in relatively densely populated urban areas (Gotham and King 2019). It is clear that urbanization occurred even in ancient times; however, it has accelerated greatly in the modern era (although the COVID-19 pandemic has [perhaps] temporarily reversed that trend to some degree in many areas). **Urbanism** is the way of life that emerges in, and is closely associated with, urban areas. That way of life includes distinctive lifestyles, attitudes, and social relationships. In terms of the last, one example is the greater likelihood in cities of interacting with strangers (Simmel [1903] 1971) and generally higher levels of anonymity.

Ever-Larger Urban Areas

Cities have grown considerably larger in recent decades (see Figure 15.6). (We discuss the world's largest cities—megacities—shortly when we turn to the issue of globalization.) However, cities have become part of even larger spatial forms. The **metropolis** is a large, powerful, and culturally influential urban area that contains a central city and its surrounding communities, known as **suburbs**, which are economically and socially linked to the center but located outside the city's political boundaries (Lacy 2016). Suburbs often create band-like structures around cities. Although suburbs in the United States have tended, at least until recently, to be populated by the middle class, suburbs in other societies, such as France and many of those in South America, are more likely to be dominated by the lower class, including many recent immigrants. As we will see, suburbs in the United States are coming to resemble those other suburbs to an increasing degree.

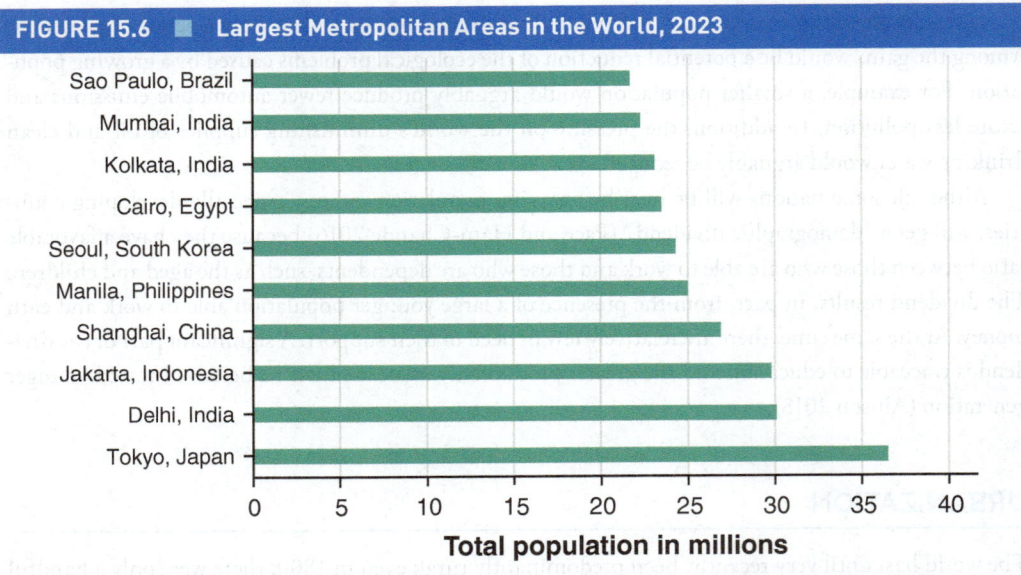

FIGURE 15.6 Largest Metropolitan Areas in the World, 2023

Source: World Population Review, 2023. https://worldpopulationreview.com/world-city-rankings/largest-metro-areas-in-the-world

A **megalopolis** is a cluster of highly populated cities that can stretch over great distances (Gotham and King 2019). There are currently 20 megalopolises in the United States, with "BosWash," the area between Boston and Washington, D.C. (including northern Virginia), being the classic example. Another now stretches from San Diego to San Francisco and ultimately may extend as far as Seattle and even Vancouver. The cities that surround the Great Lakes constitute another megalopolis.

Suburbanization

The process of **suburbanization** has traditionally occurred when large numbers of people move out of the city and into nearby, less densely populated environs. They are often impelled by urban problems such as crime, pollution, poverty, homelessness, and poor schools. The "American dream" of the last half of the twentieth century of an affordable one-family home was more likely to be found in the suburbs than in the city.

Construction of a new suburb of Sacramento, California. Although suburbs in the United States have often attracted the middle and upper classes, that is changing as more of them move even farther away from the city or back to the gentrifying city. As a result, more poor people are moving to at least some suburbs where housing prices have declined and, in many cases, are much lower than in the city.

halbergman/iStockPhoto

Various criticisms have been directed at suburbanization. One is that it led to the creation of vast areas characterized by a seemingly endless sprawl of tract houses and the businesses, especially strip malls, created to serve them (Duany, Plater-Zyberk, and Speck 2010). More recently, many have noted the problem of suburban sprawl promoting high levels of traffic congestion and environmental degradation.

Suburban development has seen the emergence of **gated communities**. Although usually associated with the United States, gated communities have developed globally in many places, including Brazil (Ayoobi 2018) and China (Webster, Ruan, and Sun 2018). In gated communities, gates, surveillance cameras, and guards provide residents with a feeling of security from the dangers they think, sometimes wrongly, they have left behind in the city (Atkinson and Blandy 2017). For example, there are fewer burglaries in such communities, although some gated communities offer better protection than others (Addington and Rennison 2015; Breetzke, Landman, and Cohn 2014). Nevertheless, no matter the reality, such communities tend to produce a heightened sense of fear and insecurity among residents (Low 2003).

Although suburbanization was first associated with the United States, it long ago became a global phenomenon. However, there is considerable variation around the world in this process and the nature of suburbs. It would be a mistake to assume that the U.S. model fits suburbs elsewhere in the world (Harris 2019).

The Changing Nature of Major Cities

Although there has been much talk about the decline of major cities, and much of that decline continues, at least some cities (e.g., New York, Cairo, Paris, Atlanta, San Francisco, Seattle) have been booming in recent years.

In the United States, many major cities (e.g., Detroit, Pittsburgh, Akron) that developed with the industrialization of the nation underwent substantial deterioration as a result of deindustrialization, or the decline in the manufacturing sector. This decline was accompanied by "White flight"—the exodus of White people from cities—which led not only to highly segregated urban areas but also to areas that had declining tax bases and deteriorating infrastructure (roads, water and sewage systems, public transportation, and especially the subway systems in the northeastern cities of New York, Boston, and Washington, D.C. [Fitzsimmons 2016]) and thus a declining ability to provide basic services for residents (Kye 2018).

For example, in some cities, the water supply has been compromised in various ways. One notable recent example was the contamination of the water in Flint, Michigan. This is a city with a predominantly Black population, and many residents are poor (see the classic documentary *Roger & Me* for insights into inequality in Flint, Michigan and elsewhere). The contamination occurred in early 2014 when, in a cost-saving measure, the city switched from a satisfactorily treated water supply drawn from Lake Huron to water it was supposed to treat itself from the Flint River. The city's treatment was inadequate (due mainly to lead leaching from ancient pipes), and the water was eventually deemed undrinkable, even dangerous to the health of those who drank it. Although the governor of Michigan declared in 2018 that the water was safe, many residents continue to think of it as undrinkable and believe it remains a health hazard. The contamination of Flint's water can be seen as an example of **environmental racism**, or the disproportionate exposure of racial minorities to polluted air, water and soil.

Detroit's return to prosperity may be a long and slow process. Vacant homes like this one have become a common sight after years of declining tax revenues and population flight. What are some possible effects of blight on those who remain behind?

Visions of America/UIG via Getty Images

In some cases, cities have rebuilt at least some of their infrastructure in a process of urban renewal. A related process is **gentrification**, in which real estate capital is reinvested in blighted inner-city areas to refurbish housing for the upwardly mobile middle class (Schlichtman, Patch, and Hill 2017). A recent instance is the change that has taken place in the Shaw neighborhood in Washington, D.C. (Gringlas 2017). Another prominent example is the borough of Brooklyn, which in the 1940s and 1950s was largely shunned by New Yorkers because of its industrial-era slums. Today, much of Brooklyn, with its famous brownstones, has been transformed into a model postindustrial landscape. Town houses and condominiums have been renovated, and many are ultra-expensive. Brooklyn has become one of the least affordable home ownership markets in the United States (Leefeldt 2018). Restaurants, bars, and other businesses catering to the new residents have sprung up all over the borough. Pioneers in the process of gentrification are often young professionals, hipsters, younger gay men, and artists (Zukin 1982). Gentrification allows the wealthier residents (the "gentry") who grew up in the suburbs to return to the city. The expectation is that they will rebuild its depressed areas not only physically but also economically, socially, and culturally. In the process, working-class and poor residents are often forced out.

Beyond gentrification, the ultra-rich have been increasingly drawn to major global cities. As a result, there has been a boom in expensive high-rises in the downtown areas of cities like New York, where penthouses can cost $100 million or more. A similar trend is seen in global cities such as London and Singapore (Brass 2015).

CITIES AND GLOBALIZATION

From the beginning, cities have been central to both scholarly and popular work on globalization (Sassen 2019). Cities are seen as being **cosmopolitan**, or open to a variety of external and global influences (Pogge 2017). In contrast, small towns and rural areas are more likely to be viewed as **local**, or inward rather than outward looking. Cities therefore came to be seen as inherently global, and they grew more so as they came to encompass a range of populations, cultures, ethnicities, languages, and consumer products from around the world. Cities also exerted a powerful influence over surrounding areas.

Cities today are a key part of global flows of people, products, information, and more (McCann and Ward 2011). Urban policies and ideas on how to improve the city flow easily throughout the world's urban areas. The many city-based organizations are linked through elaborate networks to organizations in other cities throughout the home country and world. Furthermore, people in those cities are themselves involved in a wide range of global networks and are linked to people throughout the world.

Global Cities

At the top of the world's hierarchy of cities are the global cities, including New York City, London, and Tokyo. Saskia Sassen (1991) embeds the concept of global cities in the process of economic (capitalistic) globalization. In this context, she accords priority to the three cities already mentioned based on their place in the world economy. Specifically, they are **global cities** because they are the

- key locations for leading industries and marketplaces and the high-level management and specialized services they require;
- centers of the production and creation of innovative, cutting-edge financial services;
- homes of new financial, legal, and accountancy products; and
- settings from which businesses and organizations exercise global command and control.

Much of what global cities achieve is made possible by a wide range of new electronic technologies. These cities have great financial centers, but they are also likely to be at the epicenter of monumental collapses (as well as renaissances) in the global economy

Global cities are central nodes in a new international division of labor. Of great importance are the linkages among and between these global cities and the flows, both positive and negative, among and between them. In many ways, the global cities have more in common with one another than with the smaller cities and the hinterlands within their own countries. They are also more integrated into the global economy than those hinterlands. The direct linkages between global cities point to the fact that nation-states are less important in the global age than they were previously. They are unable to control the flows between global cities. As Sassen (2012, 189) puts it, the global city "engages the global directly, often bypassing the national." In addition, the nation-state is unable to stem such global flows as undocumented immigrants and illegal drugs.

Megacities (and Beyond)

Megacities are defined as cities with populations greater than 10 million. Of course, the global cities discussed previously meet that criterion, but what is striking is the large and growing number of cities in the less-developed world that can be defined as megacities (Kleer and Nawrot 2018). In 2023, there were 40 urban areas qualifying as megacities (up from 10 in 1990), led by Tokyo, with 37 million people. Eight additional megacities are expected to develop by 2030 (see Figure 15.7). China alone has six megacities and India has five (United Nations Department of Economic and Social Affairs 2018). Such population concentrations bring with them enormous problems associated with the large numbers of very poor people living in these cities, especially those in less developed countries.

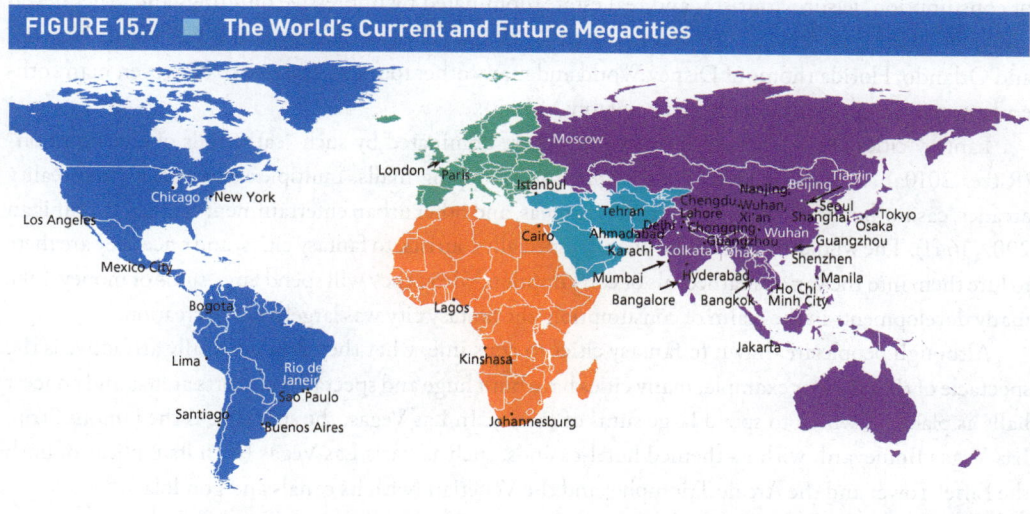

FIGURE 15.7 ■ The World's Current and Future Megacities

*Projected to be megacities by 2030: Santiago, Chengdu, Xi'an, Wuhan, Nanjing, Ahmedabad, Surat, Kuala Lumpur.

Source: UNESCO, 2020, "Megacities Worldwide: Current and Future Megacities in the World." https://en.unesco.org/events/eaumega2021/megacities

These megacities, even the most blighted of them, have wealthy residents as well. Thus, they are sites of some of the most profound inequalities in the world. A stunning example of this inequality is found in Mumbai, where Mukesh Ambani, the richest person in India, with a reported net worth of more than $100 billion, built a 27-story, single-family home that may be valued at more than $1 billion. Among other things, it has nine elevators, a six-level garage, helipads, "airborne swimming pools," a spa, hanging gardens, a 50-person theater, and a grand ballroom. To function, the structure requires hundreds of servants and staff. All this is found in a city noted for its poverty, where about 60 percent of the population lives in slums (Yardley 2010). In 2018, Ambani hosted a wedding for his daughter that cost between $15 and $100 million and had a guest list that included Beyoncé and Hillary Clinton (Ives and Goel 2018).

The Center of Culture and Consumption

Cities have arguably played a highly positive role in the development of societies throughout the world. Compared with rural areas, cities tend to have better-educated residents, promote more tolerance, are more likely to generate new ideas, tend to have the best hospitals, offer more jobs, and so on. Much of what we think of as culture, especially "high culture," has its origins, and has become centered, in the city. Thus, a large number of the world's great universities, museums, symphony orchestras, opera companies, theaters, and restaurants are found in the world's great cities. Much of pop culture—such as hip-hop and rap music—also emanates from the city.

The city is also the source of many developments in the world of consumption. For example, shopping arcades (Benjamin 1999), world's fairs, and department stores had their origins in nineteenth-century Paris and other European cities (Williams [1982] 1991). In the twentieth century, U.S. cities became the world leaders in such consumption sites, most notably New York City, with its world-famous department stores (Macy's and Gimbels) as well as the 1939 and 1964 World's Fairs. When those who lived outside the city could afford to travel and wanted to consume, they often made regular treks to the city to shop, go to the theater, and so on. Cities like Paris and New York also played other key roles in consumption, such as being national and global centers of fashion (Lipovetsky [1987] 2002; Simmel [1904] 1971). Furthermore, cities, especially New York and its famed Madison Avenue, became centers for the advertising industry, which functions to drive consumption (Schudson 1987). A number of cities have become more specialized centers of consumption, the most notable examples being gambling centers such as Las Vegas and Macau. Dubai has undergone a massive building boom in an effort to become the commercial and consumption center for a good part of the world, stretching from Cairo to Tokyo.

A **fantasy city** is one in which great emphasis is placed on creating a spectacle, especially in the areas of consumption, leisure, tourism, and real estate, dominated by impressive buildings and other developments. Hannigan (1998, 2007) sees only two cities as full-scale fantasy cities: Las Vegas, Nevada, and Orlando, Florida (home of Disney World and many other tourist attractions). However, many others have moved in that direction (most notably Macau).

Fantasy cities are characterized by infrastructure dominated by such "cathedrals of consumption" (Ritzer 2010a) as "themed restaurants, nightclubs, shopping malls, multiplex cinemas, virtual reality arcades, casino-hotels . . . sports stadiums and arenas, and other urban entertainment centers" (Hannigan 2007, 1641). The whole idea is to draw people, especially tourists, to fantasy cities, and once they are there to lure them into the various cathedrals of consumption, where they will spend large sums of money. Like many developments in the realm of consumption, the fantasy city was largely a U.S. creation.

Although people are drawn to fantasy cities to consume, what they find especially attractive is the spectacle of the city. For example, many cities have built huge and spectacular sports arenas and concert halls as places in which to spend large sums of money. In Las Vegas, the spectacle is the famous Strip, Las Vegas Boulevard, with its themed hotel-casinos, such as Paris Las Vegas (with its replicas of both the Eiffel Tower and the Arc de Triomphe) and the Venetian (with its canals and gondolas).

Digital Living: Smart Cities

Smart cities use digital technology in their attempts to achieve environmental sustainability, quality public services, and an efficient infrastructure for their residents. In addition to bridging the digital divide and ensuring that everyone has access to digital data through wireless networks and web-enabled devices, smart cities are focusing on three key sectors to help residents improve their quality of life: energy, transportation, and security. For example, a smart city might use high-tech sensors to measure how full waste containers are, to gauge how many seats are available on the next bus or subway, or to turn streetlights on and off (Etezadazdeh 2016). Daily air pollution reports and one-time emergency alerts can be delivered to residents via smartphones. Police and fire departments in smart cities can use digital networks and real-time information to help them respond to emergencies faster. Interactive digital kiosks in these cities can help tourists reserve a table at a popular restaurant or buy a dress at a local shop that can be delivered to their hotel room.

Given that nearly 70 percent of the world's population will be living in cities by 2050 and that cities currently consume 75 percent of the world's energy, the growth of smart cities is imperative (United Nations Department of Economic and Social Affairs 2018). Digital technologies can help meet future population demands for energy and transportation in an environmentally sustainable and efficient manner. For example, Zurich, Switzerland has smart streetlights that only illuminate when absolutely necessary, supply power to electric cars, collect environmental data, measure the flow of traffic, and act as a public WiFi antenna (Lai 2023). In downtown San Jose, California, sensors detect when parking spaces are empty and send the information to a digital display so drivers can easily find available parking (Cheung 2021). The top three smart cities in the world are Singapore; Helsinki, Finland; and Zurich, Switzerland (Lai 2023). To increase the number of smart cities around the world, partnerships between private technology firms and municipal governments need to be encouraged.

THE ENVIRONMENT

In recent years, there has been an explosive growth of a wide range of environmental problems (e.g., extreme temperatures, flooding, brush and forest fires, powerful storms) leading to greatly increased attention to them. Because of concern over, and even fear of, those problems, many sociologists have been drawn to, and even led, the study of the environment, especially of environmental problems (York and Dunlap 2019). There is now even a journal titled *Environmental Sociology*. The field was inspired, as was public interest as a whole, by such highly influential books as Rachel Carson's *Silent Spring* (1962), which focused on poisons such as insecticides and weed killers and the threats they posed to the food supply. This interest has expanded exponentially, and for many it has grown to alarm, as the public has been exposed to, and made aware of, the multiple threats posed by environmental problems.

Environmental problems, as well as sociological attention to them, are likely to increase dramatically in the coming years, especially as those problems grow worse and become increasingly global in scope (Kütting and Herman 2018).

Perspectives on the Environment and Its Problems

Sociological approaches to the environment differ depending on the theoretical perspective employed (Antonio and Clark 2015). Structural/functional theories tend to focus on large-scale structures and systems and their impact on environmental problems, as well as on their ability to deal with them. For example, because large-scale structures are differentiated functionally (politically, economically, legally), they have difficulty coming together to deal with environmental problems. The conflict/critical perspective focuses on free-market capitalism and the need for corporations to grow and to show ever-increasing profits. In other words, capitalism creates a "treadmill of production" whereby everyone in the system depends on continuous productive growth and increasing profits (Curran 2017). This often leads to the exploitation of nonrenewable natural resources and other negative effects on the environment. One recent study showed that the capitalist treadmill of production has an adverse effect not only on the habitat but also on the survival strategies of indigenous people in developing countries (Lynch, Stretesky, and Long 2018).

Among the inter/actionists, symbolic interactionists focus on the ways in which we come to define various environmental issues as problems. We also define ourselves in relationship to environmental issues. This can include our views of ourselves if we engage in sustainable ("green") consumption, as well as how others view such consumption (Bedard and Tolmie 2018).

Rational choice theorists focus on the fact that there have been great rewards, such as high profits and pay, for those who adversely affect the environment. Conversely, there have been weak, or nonexistent, rewards and even high costs (lower profits, lower wages, higher prices for environmentally friendly products) for those interested in being more environmentally responsible by, for example, consuming fewer natural resources. Clearly, from this perspective, the reward and cost structures need to be changed if we hope to induce people (and organizations) to change their behavior and to take actions that help, rather than hurt, the environment. We need to see, for example, that we can live better by consuming less and, at the same time, have the rewards associated with being more responsible as far as the environment is concerned (Jackson 2014).

This energy plant in Beveren, Belgium, is nuclear powered. Sociologists study the way we define and grapple with the environmental consequences of our actions.

Arterra Picture Library / Alamy Stock Photo

Globalization and the Environment

The environment performs three general functions for humans and other species. First, the environment is a kind of "supply depot" that provides us with the natural resources needed for life to exist. Among the renewable and nonrenewable resources provided are air, water, food, shelter, and the materials (e.g., oil and other fossil fuels) needed for industries to operate. However, overuse of such renewable resources as water and such nonrenewable resources as fossil fuels can deplete, if not empty, the supply depot.

Second, in consuming those resources, humans produce wastes of various kinds. The environment serves as a "sink" to absorb or dispose of the waste. However, it is possible to produce so much waste that the environment cannot absorb it all. For example, too much sewage can lead to water pollution. There are ongoing efforts to find various uses for the waste we produce. For example, human excrement is being converted into fuel for everything from buses to rockets.

Third, the environment provides us with living space, or a "habitat—where we live, work, play, and travel" (Dunlap and Jorgenson 2012, 530). However, having too many people in a living space (e.g., a megacity) creates numerous problems associated with overcrowding and overpopulation. In terms of all three functions, it could be argued that humans are beginning to exceed the "carrying capacity" of Earth.

There is great global inequality in these three functions. Basically, developed nations adversely affect the ability of less developed nations to perform these functions. For example, they use less developed nations as supply depots for natural resources for which they have historically underpaid. In the process, they often adversely affect the ability of the less developed nations to continue to produce these resources. Developed nations also often ship waste, including toxic waste, to developing countries, polluting them and their people with the minerals and chemicals in this dangerous debris. As just one, of many, examples, the Bhalswa landfill in Delhi, India is now more than 200 feet high. This, in turn, despoils the living spaces and the ecosystems of those developing countries.

China has been the major destination for a lot of the world's dangerous debris. However, it recently announced that it will no longer function as the world's garbage dump. It has begun to refuse many types of solid, recyclable waste, especially plastics, because of the danger they pose to its own environment. As other counties also develop policies refusing to be the garbage dump for others, we can expect similar actions seeking to protect their own populations from the toxic effects of waste imported from the world's more privileged countries.

Although many environmental problems *are* global issues, this view has been challenged in various ways:

- Not everyone or every part of the world is equally to blame for the most pressing global environmental problems. Those from the most developed countries, especially the privileged within those countries, are disproportionately responsible for them, although those in developing countries are starting to play a more significant role (Sweet 2016).

- Such problems do not, and will not, affect everyone and all areas of the world in the same way. For example, the rise of the level of the seas as a result of climate change will mostly affect those who live in coastal areas or on islands (it is estimated that up to 80 percent of the Maldives could be under water by 2050). Such areas will also be most affected by the expected increase in the number and severity of hurricanes and cyclones. Tornadoes are also expected to increase, although they are likely to affect some geographic areas, such as the American Midwest, more than others. In addition, the global elite will be better able than the globally disadvantaged to find ways of avoiding or dealing with all but the most catastrophic of the problems caused by climate change.

- There are global differences in the importance accorded to, and the dangers associated with, these problems. Politics plays a huge role here, with more conservative leaders tending to focus less on environmental issues.

- The main sources of environmental problems change. For example, the center of manufacturing, with its associated pollutants, has been moving from the United States to China.

The Leading Environmental Problems

There are many important environmental problems, and we have touched on several in the preceding sections. In this section, we cover a few in more depth: the destruction of natural habitats, adverse effects of human activity on marine life, the decline in freshwater, and global warming.

Destruction of Natural Habitats

Natural habitats such as forests and wetlands (e.g., the vast Everglades in Florida or the Amazon rain forest spread across South America) are being destroyed across the globe, often as the result of population growth and the conversion of some of those natural habitats into human habitats (Scanes 2018). Many areas are also being destroyed to allow for cattle grazing to meet the world's growing demand for beef. Forests not yet destroyed are being divided into smaller and more isolated, less self-sufficient fragments surrounded by human environments. Both their smaller size and their human surroundings threaten their continued existence.

The most notable deforestation in the world has been taking place in the Amazon rain forest (mostly in Brazil), where more than half of the tree species are under threat, but other parts of the world are also destroying or losing their forests (most notably, Indonesia). The Amazon forest is being decimated to allow the area to be "developed"—to create farms and areas for livestock to graze—and for the creation of more human settlements. Brazil's forests are so huge, and they play such a large role in the global ecology, that their destruction will have negative effects on the world as a whole. For example, the burning of all those felled trees releases huge amounts of carbon dioxide, which drifts into the atmosphere and flows around the globe, contributing to climate change. The loss of the forest leads to other problems for humans, including a diminished supply of timber and other raw materials. This is of great concern also because, especially in the areas undergoing deforestation, forests protect against soil erosion, are essential to the water cycle and prevention of drought, and provide habitats for many plants and animals.

Overfishing is one of the many problems facing the ocean today. A major culprit is industrialized fishing that is dramatically reducing fish stocks in many places in the world. Given that lots of money is still to be made from it, what can be done to at least limit overfishing, to say nothing of other threats to marine life?

Jeff Rotman/Alamy Stock Photo

Adverse Effects on Marine Life

A large portion of the protein consumed by humans comes from fish. Marine life in the world's oceans has been greatly diminished by overfishing. Nearly 90 percent of the world's marine fish stocks are considered either "fully exploited," "overexploited," or "depleted" (Kituyi and Thomson 2018). A major culprit in the decimation of marine life is industrial fishing involving the use of huge nets that catch large numbers of fish. A recent study found that industrial fishing is to blame for the decline in "big fish" populations due to the practice of discarding fish that are too small or unwanted because they are the wrong species. In fact, even though fish stocks are declining, approximately 10 million tons of fish are discarded every year by industrial fishers (Zeller et al. 2018). As the amount of sea life declines, the fishing industry compensates by using much more industrialized and intensive techniques. Modern industrial fishing is also characterized by the use of factory ships that process the fish on board rather than waiting until the ships return to port. These technologies contribute to overfishing and, in the process, destroy complex ecosystems. Aquaculture, which involves growing seafood under controlled conditions such as fish farms, is not an adequate replacement for the loss of natural fishing areas. It also causes a whole series of ecological and other problems (Stickney 2017).

The Decline in Fresh Water

Water is becoming an increasingly critical global issue. Many observers have expressed concern about the "water crisis" in some parts of the world, including California and Nevada in the United States (Newton 2016; Schmidt 2017). However, the less-developed countries in the world are most likely to be negatively affected by a water crisis as water-dependent manufacturing industries locate themselves within their borders. In addition, they are the least likely to have environmental regulations to prevent problems or to be able to do very much about problems once they begin. Among the concerns about water are the following:

- *Water inequality.* The United States has a water footprint double that of the world average and four times that of China. Even though many in the world have little access to clean drinking water, people in the United States use approximately 9 billion gallons of water a day just to irrigate lawns and gardens (EPA 2017).

- *Water pollution.* Humans contribute to the pollution of water through manufacturing processes, mining, agriculture, and inadequate treatment and management of waste (especially fecal matter). One result of this pollution is an increase in waterborne diseases, especially those that affect children.

- *Marine pollution.* This involves human activity that disrupts marine ecosystems, especially oceans. These disruptions include acidification from burning fossil fuels and noise from offshore drilling. Among the most important causes of marine pollution is the dumping into the oceans of the herbicides, pesticides, and fertilizers used in modern industrial agriculture.

- *Flooding.* Experts contend that because warmer air holds more moisture, heavy precipitation is expected to increase in some regions as a result of climate change.

- *Increasing Scarcity of Water.* There is the possibility that the flow of water could slow or stop completely, at least in some locales. In 2018, India faced its greatest water shortage ever. An estimated 200,000 people a year are dying there because they do not have adequate access to clean water. There is a multitude of causes of the water shortage, including global warming, rising temperatures, and declining rain and snowfall (Abi-Habib and Kumar 2018).

Some nations are forced to choose among essential uses of water, such as between drinking and irrigating crops. There are tensions within nations and between nations—and even the possibility of war—over increasingly scarce water supplies (Chellaney 2015).

Desertification is the decline in the water supply as a result of the degradation and deterioration of soil and vegetation (Reed and Stringer 2016). Water, once considered a public good, is increasingly becoming a valuable and privatized commodity as many places run low on clean drinking water. Another preventable decline in water supply is caused by the wasting of those supplies; for example, nearly two-thirds of all water used for irrigation, in addition to as much as half of city water supplies, is wasted due to leaky pipes.

Although we usually think of water as abundant and readily accessible, more than 2 billion people do not have reliable sources of safe drinking water at home, and more than 3.6 billion do not have adequate sanitation systems (CDC 2022b). The poorest areas of the globe and the poorest people within those areas experience a disproportionate share of water-related problems. The situation is apt to grow worse in coming years; it is possible that half the world's population will be faced with water related problems by the 2030s.

A less visible water problem involves international trade, especially in agricultural and industrial products. For example, when China and Japan buy crops (which are water-intensive to produce) from the United States, pressure is put on that country's water supplies. People throughout the world are using water from elsewhere on the globe. This is called "virtual water" because almost all the water has been used in production of some commodity (Vos and Hinojosa 2016). If people do not realize they are using or abusing water, how can they do anything about it?

Global Warming

Global warming is a concept often used interchangeably with climate change, but here we treat it as the most significant aspect of climate change. New long-term (since 1880; Gillis 2015) global heat records have been set. All 10 of the hottest years on record have occurred just since 2010.

We are only in the early stages of global warming, with the coming years projected to bring still hotter temperatures. Temperatures are now predicted to rise 3 to 5 degrees Celsius by the end of the twenty-first century. This is far more than had been hoped and likely will have far more disastrous consequences for much of the world (Reuters 2018c).

As the planet heats up even more, some parts of the world will become wetter, but others will grow drier. As a general rule, already wet areas will grow wetter and already dry areas drier; both floods and droughts will grow more common and intensify (Schwartz 2018). To deal with more droughts, we are likely to see increasingly desperate and expensive efforts to find water by, for example, drilling ever deeper for underground water supplies (Ferguson et al. 2018). Among the areas likely to grow drier are southern Europe, the Middle East, South Australia, Patagonia, and the southwestern United States. In May 2008, Barcelona became the first major city in the world to begin importing large amounts of water by ship to help deal with a long-term drought and a precipitous drop in water resources. There are predictions of Dust Bowl–like conditions in the American Southwest and the resulting possibility of mass migrations. In Mexico, similar conditions may lead to mass migrations to Mexican cities and to the United States. Such increases threaten to create even greater problems and animosities than those that already exist in the United States as a result of both legal and, especially, undocumented immigration from Mexico. In more general terms, we are increasingly likely to see the emergence of an entirely new group of people in the world: climate refugees (Wennersten and Robbins 2017). The United States is planning to resettle its first climate refugees from a waterlogged area, Isle de Jean Charles, in Louisiana; they won't be the last. Estimates are that worldwide as many as 250 million people will be displaced by rising water this century (Phelan 2022).

Another problem traceable to global warming is the melting of mountaintop glaciers that are important sources of drinking water for many people in the world. As those glaciers melt and fail to re-form fully, they will produce less and less water for those who need the water to survive. The affected populations, too, are likely to become climate refugees and are apt to come into conflict with residents of the still water-rich areas to which they are likely to move.

Humans have produced greenhouse gases that have damaged the atmosphere and, in the view of most experts, are leading to a dramatic rise in the temperature of Earth. During the twentieth century, Earth's temperature rose by about 0.74 degrees centigrade; projections for the end of the twenty-first century are for a rise of at least four times that much. Because of the accumulation of greenhouse gases, heat generated by the sun that would ordinarily be reflected back into the atmosphere is trapped and radiated back to the Earth at a greater rate than before. Great concern these

As mountaintop glaciers melt as a result of global warming, people who depend on them as sources of fresh water are likely to become climate refugees.

Tatiana Dyuvbanova / Alamy Stock Photo

days is focused on the burning of fossil fuels (hydrocarbons such as coal, gas, oil), the resulting emission of carbon dioxide, and the role this plays in the accumulation of greenhouse gases and global warming. Rates of carbon dioxide emissions, mainly from industrialized countries, increased from 380 parts per million in 2006 to more than 424 parts per million in 2023 (National Oceanic and Atmospheric Administration 2023). Figure 15.8 shows the relationship between global temperature and carbon dioxide concentration.

Despite efforts to politicize the issue, all of the objective scientific evidence indicates that global warming and, more generally, climate change are real phenomena that have been significantly impacted by human causes. Furthermore, the predominant view is that global warming is already well advanced and is progressing rapidly. Many scientists have further added that some negative effects of global warming, such as the thawing of permafrost (soil that has been at or below the freezing point of water for more than two years), will be irreversible once they start. Global warming is expected to affect humans adversely in a number of ways. It will bring with it more, and more intense, heat waves, and excessive heat can be deadly. The year 2022 saw the worst heat waves on record in many parts of the world, resulting in hundreds of thousands of deaths from heat-related illnesses. The aging of the population throughout much of the developed world makes more people vulnerable to being made ill and dying due to excessive heat. Urbanization also increases the likelihood of death because cities can become **heat islands**, or urbanized areas that experience higher temperatures than surrounding areas. Other factors that make death from excessive heat more likely are being very young, ill, or poor, or lacking the ability to move away from superheated areas. Things can be done to mitigate the dangers of heat stress, such as greater use of air-conditioning, but many people in the world have no access to air-conditioning or cannot afford it. Further, the use of air-conditioning causes other problems, such as a huge demand on energy resources.

Sea levels are projected to rise dramatically, especially as the glaciers melt. A conservative estimate is that sea levels will rise about 1 meter during the twenty-first century. More than 100 million people in the world, mostly in Asia and in island nations, live within a meter of sea level, and their homes would be washed away by such a rise. However, this estimate does not take into account the melting of the Greenland and Antarctic ice sheets, which could add 10 or more meters to the rising seas. In such a case, much larger areas of the world would be inundated.

FIGURE 15.8 ■ Historical Global Temperature and Carbon Dioxide Concentration

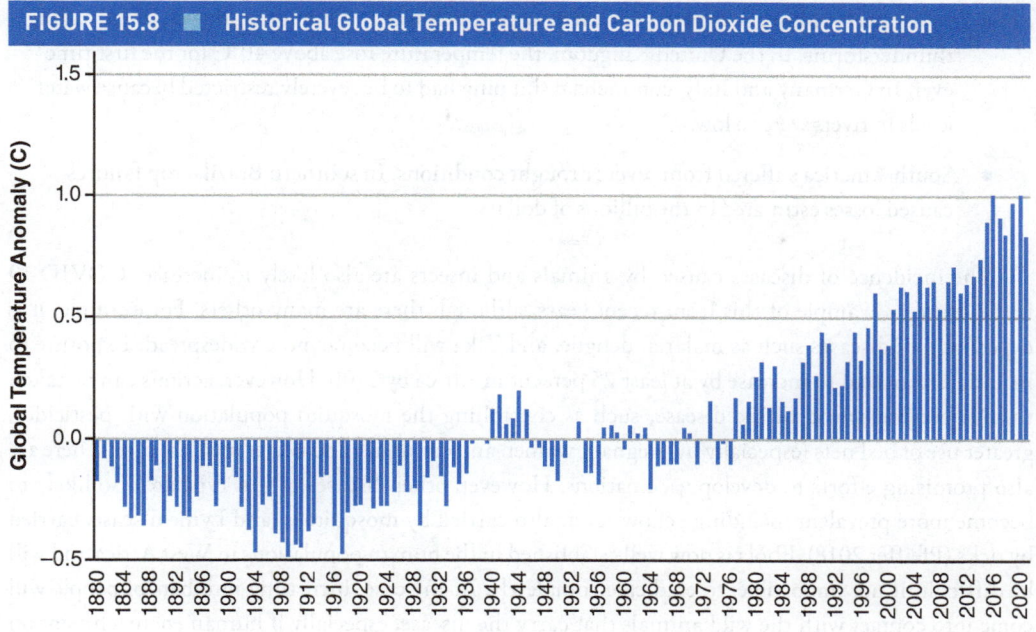

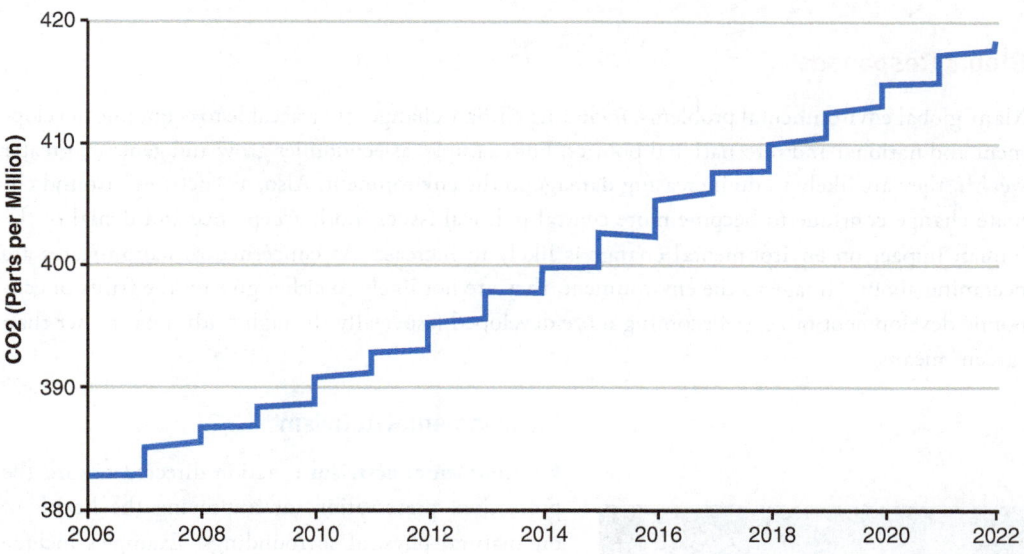

Source: NASA's Goddard Institute for Space Studies, 2022, "Global Land-Ocean Temperature Index," *Global Climate Change*. Retrieved August 2, 2022 (https://climate.nasa.gov/).

Source: NASA's Goddard Institute for Space Studies, 2022, "Carbon Dioxide Direct Measurements: 2005-Present," *Global Climate Change*. Retrieved August 2, 2022 (https://climate.nasa.gov/).

Global warming, and climate change more generally, will lead to a wide range of problems, many of which are already upon us. Figure 15.9 shows all the natural catastrophes around the world in 2022, including extreme weather events. A very small sample of such events is included here:

- Hurricane Ian caused an estimated $100 billion in damage to Florida and other parts of the Southeast United States. Only four other storms in recorded history have been stronger when making landfall in the United States.

- Severe flooding in Pakistan, caused by record monsoon rains and high temperatures that accelerated glacial melting, killed at least 1700 people.

- In Australia, extreme rainfall the states of Queensland and New South Wales led to flash floods and severe river flooding. Many residents had to be rescued from their homes by boat or helicopter, and major cities were affected.

- Many parts of Europe experienced extreme summer heat and drought followed by damaging thunderstorms. In the United Kingdom, the temperature rose above 40°C for the first time ever. In Germany and Italy, commercial shipping had to be severely restricted because water levels in rivers were so low.

- South America suffered from severe drought conditions. In southern Brazil, crop failures caused losses estimated in the billions of dollars.

The incidence of diseases caused by animals and insects are also likely to increase. COVID-19 is the primary example of this from recent years, although there are many others. For example, it is expected that diseases such as malaria, dengue, and Zika will become more widespread. Exposure to malaria is expected to increase by at least 25 percent in Africa by 2100. However, actions can be taken to mitigate the spread of the disease, such as controlling the mosquito population with pesticides, greater use of bed nets (especially by pregnant women and children), and better medical care. There are also promising efforts to develop vaccinations. However, other diseases of this type are also likely to become more prevalent including yellow fever, also carried by mosquitoes, and Lyme disease, carried by ticks (Pfeiffer 2018). Ebola is now well established in the human populations in West Africa and will be difficult, if not impossible, to eradicate completely. In any case, increasing numbers of people will come into contact with the wild animals that carry the disease, especially if human encroachment on natural environments continues.

Global Responses

Many global environmental problems, including climate change, are traceable to economic development and national and international politics. For example, as economies grow and generate greater wealth, they are likely to do increasing damage to the environment. Also, as "debates" around climate change continue to become more central political issues, both acceptance and denial of the human impact on environmental change is likely to increase. As concerned as nation-states are becoming about damage to the environment, they are not likely to either give up the fruits of economic development or cease becoming more developed (especially through traditional rather than "green" means).

Environmental Activism

Environmental activism is action directed toward the protection, preservation, or improving the health of our natural physical surroundings. Examples include marches, walkouts, lobbying, directed consumer action, and education. Such forms of activism can be carried out by individuals, organizations, or even governments and international agencies.

Greta Thunberg is a Swedish environmental activist who has become a spokesperson not just for environmental activism but for youth activism as well. At only 15 years old, she began striking outside of the Swedish parliament with a sign that read "school strike for climate." Soon the movement caught on and by 2019, there were more than a million students striking on a weekly basis to call attention to the impact of climate change and the need for world leaders and governments to take more serious action. Her actions have not only brought great attention to environmental issues but also to the power of younger people to effect social change.

Police officers detain climate activist Greta Thunberg at a demonstration against the expansion of the Garzweiler coal mine near the village of Luetzerath, Germany, in 2023 in Erkelenz.

Hesham Elsherif / Getty Images

Chapter 15 • Population, Urbanization, and the Environment   417

FIGURE 15.9 ■ Natural Catastrophes Worldwide, 2022

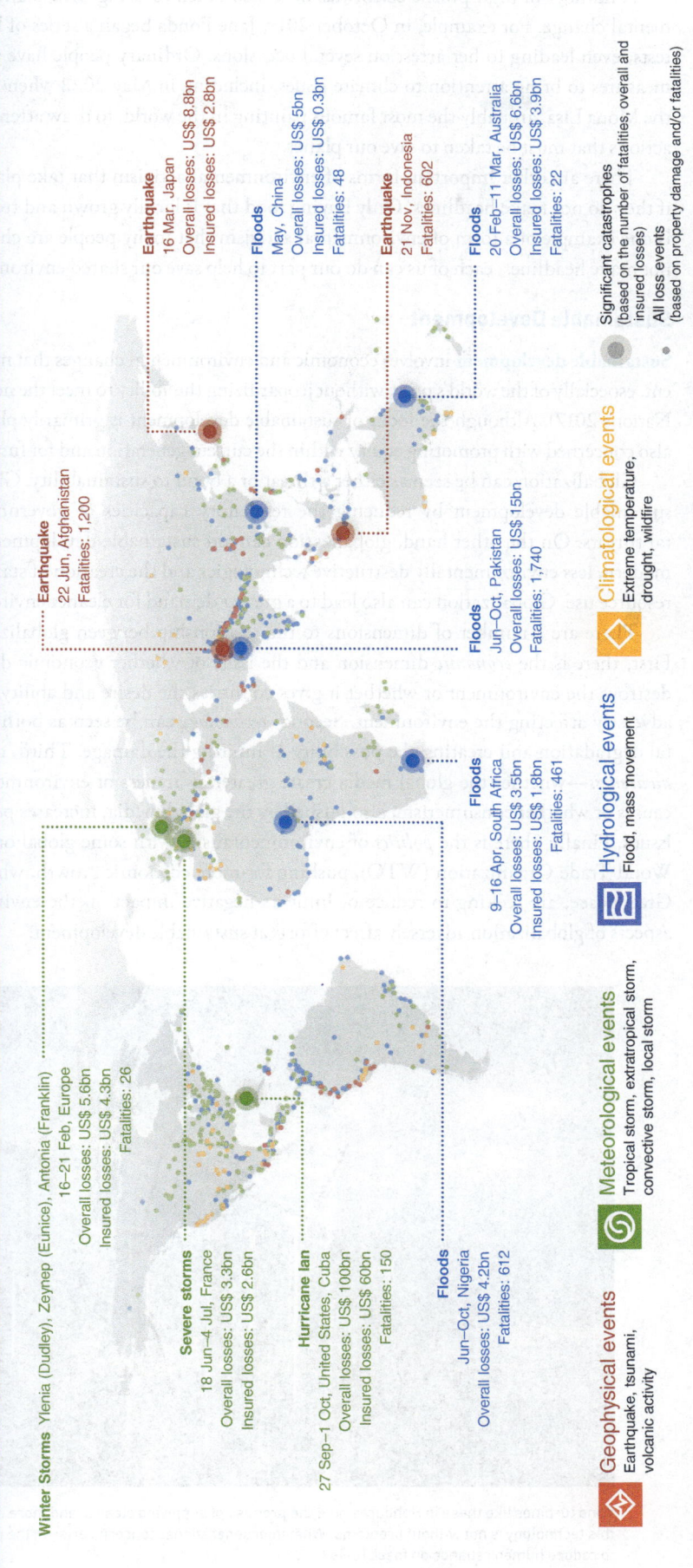

Source: Munich RE, NatCatSERVICE, 2022. "Relevant Natural Catastrophe Loss Events Worldwide 2022." https://www.munichre.com/en/company/media-relations/media-information-and-corporate-news/media-information/2023/natural-disaster-figures-2022.html

A number of high-profile celebrities have also taken to using their platforms to call for environmental change. For example, in October 2019, Jane Fonda began a series of high-profile climate protests, even leading to her arrest on several occasions. Ordinary people have also taken extraordinary measures to bring attention to climate issues, including in May 2022 when an activist threw cake at the Mona Lisa, arguably the most famous painting in the world, to draw attention to the much-needed actions that must be taken to save our planet.

There are other important forms of environmental activism that take place on a daily basis, even if they do not make headlines. Only buying food that is locally grown and free-range or chemical free is one example of a form of environmental activism that many people are choosing. Although it may not make headlines, each of us can do our part to help save our shared environment before it is too late.

Sustainable Development

Sustainable development involves economic and environmental changes that meet the needs of the present, especially of the world's poor, without jeopardizing the ability to meet the needs of the future (United Nations 2017). Although the focus of sustainable development is primarily physical sustainability, it is also concerned with promoting equity within the current generation and for future generations.

Globalization can be seen as either a threat or a boon to sustainability. Globalization can threaten sustainable development by reducing the regulatory capacities of governments over environmental threats. On the other hand, globalization can aid sustainable development through the spread of modern, less environmentally destructive technologies and the creation of standards for more efficient resource use. Globalization can also lead to a greater demand for cleaner environments.

There are a number of dimensions to the relationship between globalization and sustainability. First, there is the *economic* dimension and the issue of whether economic development irretrievably destroys the environment or whether it gives countries the desire and ability to better control factors adversely affecting the environment. Second, *technology* can be seen as both producing environmental degradation and creating the possibility of limiting the damage. Third, there is the dimension of *awareness*—whether the global media create greater awareness of environmental problems and their causes or whether consumerism, also pushed by the global media, increases people's blindness to these issues. Finally, there is the *politics* of environmentalism, with some global organizations, such as the World Trade Organization (WTO), pushing for more economic growth, while many others, such as Greenpeace, are seeking to reduce or limit its negative impact on the environment. Overall, many aspects of globalization adversely affect efforts at sustainable development.

Wind turbines like these in Honduras hold the promise of supplying cleaner and more affordable energy, but this technology is not without problems. What intergenerational concerns arise in the process of attempting to reduce human reliance on fossil fuels?

ORLANDO SIERRA/AFP/Getty Images

Technological Fixes

There is growing interest in finding technological fixes for at least some global environmental problems, especially those related to climate change. This is part of a long-standing desire to find technological solutions to all social problems (Johnson 2018). To many, creating new technologies seems far easier and less painful than the much harder task of getting large numbers of people to change their behavior. That is, people tend to be reluctant to change their consumption patterns and thus prefer the hope of technological fixes for any resultant ecological problems. Furthermore, many industries have a vested interest in the continuation of high levels of consumption. Thus, even though the burning of fossil fuels is a major cause of global warming, innumerable industries and people are wedded to it. Automobile culture, which exists in both the developed and developing worlds, is one consequential example. The growing interest in, and market for, electric and hybrid vehicles is one sign of hope in this area.

Enter "geoengineering" and a series of relatively new and controversial proposals for dealing with global ecological problems, especially global warming, while leaving untouched and unaddressed the underlying and growing causes of climate change (Asayama 2015). For example, there are proposals to capture and store harmful carbon dioxide emissions in order to permit the Earth's atmosphere to retain less heat. Another set of proposals involves reflecting sunlight and its heat away from the Earth (Fountain 2015). Scientific support for these and other, sometimes outlandish, possibilities has generally been less than enthusiastic.

Undertaking such projects would require truly global efforts and a massively funded global governance structure. The hope is that already functioning global governance, such as that which organizes air traffic control, will be a model for what is needed to deal with global climate problems (Bruckmeier 2018). However, it seems unlikely that geoengineering, or any other technological fix, will solve a set of problems that are, at their base, caused by human actions. Although technology can help, the only real solution lies in dramatically changing those behaviors.

COVID-19 and the Environment

In the early days of the COVID-19 pandemic, there were positive signs that although the human population was suffering, the natural environment was improving. In many places around the world, air and water pollution reached their lowest recorded levels. Distant landmarks became visible for the first time in decades as air cleared up and people were, despite the virus, breathing easier in many polluted cities. There were also reports of positive changes in sea color in places such as Cox's Bazar, located in Bangladesh and reputedly the longest natural unbroken sea beach in the world. There were also reports of dolphins returning to the Bay of Bengal in Bangladesh and to the canals and waterways of Venice. The white rhino population in Nepal also reached its highest levels in more than a decade amidst a drop in tourism. The natural environment seemed to be recovering amidst a drop in human pollution and interference.

As the world opened up, however, all of those gains were reversed. Even by the fall of 2020, less than a year after the pandemic was declared, CO_2 emissions in many of the world's largest economies, including China, India, and the United States, were already higher than they had been just one year before. There was also a new form of pollution: pandemic waste, including a dramatic increase in the improper disposal of things like masks and toxic clinical waste. According to OceanAsia (Bondaroff and Cooke 2020), "From a global production projection of 52 billion masks for 2020, we estimate that 1.56 billion masks will enter our oceans in 2020, amounting to between 4,680 and 6,240 metric tonnes of plastic pollution" (3). Contaminated masks became an increasing form of pollution in our waterways, on our sidewalks, and in our trash cans.

Although thought of by many as "too little, too late," several countries did announce improved plans to reach zero emissions during the pandemic years. For example, China, responsible for some 28 percent of the world's carbon emissions, announced that it plans to be carbon neutral by 2060. Several other countries, including South Africa, Japan, South Korea, the United States, and Canada, have all set carbon neutral targets for 2050. Most environmentalists agree that these targets are still insufficient and point out that they all still allow for an increase in environmental damage (albeit more limited), rather than true efforts to stop, much less reduce, the impact of human beings on the environment.

SUMMARY

Overall fertility rates are dropping globally, but the world's population continues to increase, although at a declining rate. Demographers focus on three main processes of population change: fertility, or people's reproductive behavior; mortality, or death and death rates; and migration, the movements of people.

Demographic transition theory posits that over time, both fertility and mortality rates will decrease, resulting in stabilizing population growth.

Urbanization is the process by which an increasing percentage of a society's population comes to be located in relatively densely populated urban areas. Suburbs are communities adjacent to but outside the political boundaries of central cities. Looking for cheaper land and housing, people have pushed even farther out into areas between the suburbs and rural areas.

Global cities are the most important of the world's cities and are key locations for leading industries in innovation and financial services. Some global cities are megacities that have populations of greater than 10 million. Global cities are cosmopolitan in regard to cultural influences and often attract large numbers of immigrants.

Increasing environmental problems have led sociologists to examine the environment more closely. Most environmental problems are global in nature and scope. The relationship between globalization and sustainability has a number of dimensions, including economic, technological, and political, as well as media awareness. Cooperation between nations is crucial for achieving sustainability, particularly in terms of reducing carbon emissions from burning fossil fuels.

KEY TERMS

asylum seekers	infanticide
birthrate	labor migrants
cities	life expectancy
cosmopolitan	local
death rate	megacities
demographers	megalopolis
demographic transition	metropolis
demography	migration
desertification	mortality
environmental activism	refugees
environmental racism	replacement-level fertility
fantasy city	suburbanization
fertility	suburbs
fertility rate	sustainable development
gated communities	undocumented immigrants
gentrification	urban
global cities	urbanism
heat islands	urbanization

REVIEW QUESTIONS

1. How does the "demographic dividend" differ from the "financial time bomb"? Overall, is the United States in a period of a demographic dividend or a financial time bomb? Why?

2. According to demographic transition theory, what role do technological advances play in changing demographics? Why is "development the best contraceptive"?

3. How does the nature of today's migrants differ from the nature of migrants in the past? Are today's barriers to migration consistent with the situation in the past? How have the "push" and "pull" factors associated with migration changed in the global age?

4. Distinguish between refugees, asylum seekers, labor migrants, and undocumented immigrants.

5. What are the arguments in favor of international migration? How do these fit into today's popular and political dialogue regarding immigration in the United States?

6. What makes cities cultural and consumption centers? How is a "fantasy city" different from a traditional urban area? In what ways are fantasy cities related to processes of Americanization?

7. This chapter cites environmental problems arising in cities yet points to the possibility of new forms of urban development (e.g., smart cities) that could be less ecologically destructive. How can sustainable development create a more ecologically friendly city? How would this development differ from those of the last 200 years?

8. What are the world's major environmental problems? Are there technological fixes that can deal with our environmental problems? If so, what are they?

9. Do you think globalization is ultimately a threat or a boon to sustainability? What current evidence would you cite to support your position?

10. How has the COVID-19 pandemic impacted our natural environment?

vdbvsl / Alamy Stock Photo

16 SOCIAL CHANGE, SOCIAL MOVEMENTS, AND COLLECTIVE ACTION

> **LEARNING OBJECTIVES**
>
> **16.1** Discuss the significance of social movements.
>
> **16.2** Explain how social movements emerge.
>
> **16.3** Identify different types of collective action.
>
> **16.4** Provide contemporary examples of the "liquids" and "flows" associated with globalization.

WORKERS' RIGHTS, CONSUMER ACTIVISM, AND SOCIAL CHANGE

The fruits and vegetables you purchase in the grocery store were most likely harvested by undocumented workers from Mexico or Central America. These workers pay smugglers thousands of dollars to help them cross the border illegally into the United States. The lucky ones find work on farms for meager pay and substandard working conditions. Hundreds die each year from dehydration, heat stroke, or direct violence as they attempt to cross the border; others are caught by Border Patrol agents and deported. Some become trapped in a debt bondage system referred to as modern slavery; they are forced to work on farms to repay the cost of their border crossing. Typically, these undocumented farmworkers are not paid by the hour but by the weight of the produce they harvest. Being paid by weight compels many of them to work 10 hours or more per day with few breaks. Those in debt bondage rarely earn enough to pay off their debt and remain enslaved. This was the scenario for undocumented workers who picked tomatoes in Immokalee, Florida, until the Coalition of Immokalee Workers (CIW) launched a boycott against Taco Bell in 2001.

CIW issued three demands to Taco Bell: (1) that it establish a program to stop human rights violations in its supply chain; (2) that it pay one penny more per pound of tomatoes, which would go to the workers; and (3) that it encourage other major retailers to follow its lead. With pressure from consumer activists, particularly college students and members of religious organizations, Taco Bell agreed to these demands in 2005. More recently, McDonald's, Burger King, Trader Joe's, and Whole Foods have also agreed to these demands. Currently, CIW is boycotting Wendy's, Kroger, and Publix, three large purchasers of tomatoes who refuse to join its Fair Food Program. In March 2023, CIW and its allies marched from Pahokee to Palm Beach, Florida (a five-day trek of nearly 50 miles) to celebrate a decade of success for the Fair Food Program.

A Juneteenth celebration in Black Lives Matter Plaza, Washington, D.C. The area has become a gathering place for activists fighting for racial equality.

Caroline Brehman/CQ-Roll Call, Inc via Getty Images

CIW boycotts could not succeed without consumers using their purchasing power as a tactic to persuade corporations to change their unjust business practices. Boycotts, or the threat of withholding consumer spending from unethical companies, have a long history in the United States. Consumer activism can also take the form of "buycotts"—that is, using purchasing power to support ethical business practices. For example, the Fair Trade movement encourages consumers to buy products produced by workers who receive living wages. As corporations come to hold increasing amounts of wealth and power around the world and social media allows for widespread and rapid communication and organization, consumer activism can be a critical and effective way to hold corporations accountable for their actions.

SOCIAL MOVEMENTS

Social change involves variations over time in every aspect of the social world, ranging from changes affecting individuals to transformations having global impacts. Sociologists are concerned with social change itself, as well as with the ways in which social changes affect individuals, the structures of society, global economic and political systems, and much more. A social movement is a sustained and intentional collective effort, usually operating outside established institutional channels, either to bring about, speed up, slow down, or stop social change. A social movement is characterized by the following:

- It is a collective effort involving a significant number of people.
- It is sustained for a long period of time.
- It is brought into existence intentionally.
- It operates outside official institutional channels.
- It attempts to bring about substantial change.

Social movements range in scope from those focused on relatively local issues to those focusing on broader global concerns. Those participating in social movements can also come from a wide range of backgrounds. In the following sections, we will look at some of the more prominent social movements of our day.

The Civil Rights Movement

One of the most influential social movements in the United States was, and may still be, the civil rights movement. Perhaps the key event in the history of the civil rights movement was the successful 1955 boycott of segregated city buses in Montgomery, Alabama. At the time, Black people had to ride in the back of public buses. Although the movement was organized locally, it was led by the Reverend Martin Luther King, Jr. His success there catapulted him into the position of leader of the national civil rights movement. The Montgomery boycott served as a model for future civil rights action and many other subsequent social movements. It emphasized nonviolent action, made it clear that the Black community could overcome internal divisions to become an effective force for change, showed the central role the Black church could play in such a social movement, and demonstrated that the Black community was able to finance these actions with little or no outside help.

The success of the Montgomery bus boycott led existing Black organizations to become more involved in civil rights activities. These included the National Association for the Advancement of Colored People (NAACP, formed in 1910) and the Congress of Racial Equality (CORE, organized in 1942). It also led to the formation of new organizations, especially the Southern Christian Leadership Conference (SCLC), and to the creation and active involvement of innumerable local groups. The actions spurred on by these groups and organizations encountered significant opposition from White people, sometimes leading to violence. A key development in 1960 was the large-scale involvement of Black college students in sit-ins at segregated lunch counters throughout the South. These students were crucial to the formation of another new organization, the Student Nonviolent Coordinating Committee (SNCC), in 1960. SNCC, in turn, drew many White students into the movement.

In the 1960s, the civil rights movement became a significant force through boycotts, sit-ins, freedom rides, mass marches, and mass arrests. Black people and their White allies participated. In some cases, media coverage of vicious attacks against Black activists gave the movement great visibility and elicited much sympathy from those not initially inclined to support it.

Perhaps no one symbolizes the civil rights movement as well as Martin Luther King, Jr. Here King waves to supporters from the steps of the Lincoln Memorial during the 1963 March on Washington.

Dom Slike/Alamy Stock Photo

Many of the "invisible leaders" of the civil rights movement were Black women, such as Fannie Lou Hamer, Septima Poinsette Clark, and Ella Baker. Their invisibility in leadership positions was an unfortunate by-product of the gender hierarchy as it existed in the 1950s. When women spearheaded successful civil rights campaigns, more "visible" men in the movement took the credit and usurped women's leadership positions. The many women who participated in the movement served as volunteers, and their numbers far surpassed those of their male counterparts.

The movement had great success, manifest especially in the Civil Rights Act of 1964, which banned discrimination on the basis not only of race but also of sex, religion, and national identity. Of course, the larger goal of eliminating racism eluded the civil rights movement and continues to elude it to this day (Riches 2017).

The global nature of the civil rights movement is especially clear in the antiapartheid movement led by Nelson Mandela in South Africa. Apartheid was a system of racial separation made legal in 1948. Soon thereafter a social movement against it emerged, led by the African National Congress. It garnered great international support and succeeded in achieving its goals in less than half a century (Waldmeir [1997] 2001). By 1994, both apartheid and White hegemony in South Africa had ended (Clark and Worger 2016).

Feminist Movements

The movements of concern in this section are based on **feminism**, or the belief that women are equal to men, especially socially, politically, and economically (see Chapter 10). They have all the characteristics of a social movement outlined previously. The people involved intended to bring the movements into being and to maintain them. Feminist movements—often called women's movements—have, at least until recently, had to work outside established institutional channels. Historically, women were likely to be denied access to these channels by the men in control of the institutions. The movements have demonstrated durability in many countries around the world. And they are oriented toward dramatically improving the position of women throughout the world (Morris and Withers 2018).

The Women's Movement in the United States

Although the Equal Rights Amendment was not ratified, the women's movement in the United States remains a potent force both in the United States and globally.

Ann E. Zelle/Getty Images

One key moment in the women's movement can be traced back to England and Mary Wollstonecraft's 1792 book *A Vindication of the Rights of Women*, which was one of the first influential books to make the case for women's equality. The first wave of the women's movement in the United States is traditionally traced to the 1840s. It focused largely on the issue of suffrage, or gaining the right to vote for women. It had its roots in the early involvement of women in the anti-alcohol (temperance) movement and especially the antislavery movement. However, women were largely subordinated and ignored in these movements. Anger about such treatment led to the 1848 Seneca Falls Convention, which focused on such issues as restrictions on women's roles within the family, women's rights in terms of education and property, and, especially, women's suffrage. Decades of meetings, protests, marches, and social activism followed, including the arrest of prominent suffrage leaders (for attempting to vote). Several national organizations were formed to push forward women's right to vote. The movement included battles between Black and White women, with prominent White suffragist Susan B. Anthony saying, "I will cut off this right arm of mine before I will ever work or demand the ballot for the Negro and not the [White] woman" (quoted in Wilson and Russell 1996, 30). Black suffragists, including Ida B. Wells and Anna Julia Cooper, were routinely excluded from the White women's marches and protests. Although the Nineteenth Amendment gave women voting rights as early as 1848, it did not become law until August 26, 1920. Table 16.1 shows when women won the right to vote in select countries in the twentieth century. By the 1930s, Black women's voting rights had become severely circumscribed; their political disenfranchisement lasted until the civil rights movement of the 1960s.

The second wave of the women's movement began in the 1950s and 1960s. It drew from the first

Jose Jordan/Getty Images

TABLE 16.1 ■ When Women Won the Right to Vote in Selected Countries, Twentieth Century

Country	Year
Finland	1906
Norway	1913
Netherlands	1917
Russia	1917
Canada	1918
Germany	1918
Czechoslovakia	1919
Sweden	1919
United States	1920
Spain	1931
Brazil	1932
Indonesia	1941
Italy	1945
France	1945
Japan	1945
Vietnam	1945
Mexico	1953
Paraguay	1961
Iran	1963
Switzerland	1971
Jordan	1974

wave but went beyond it in various ways. Several key books, including Simone de Beauvoir's *The Second Sex* ([1952] 1973) and Betty Friedan's *The Feminine Mystique* (1963), had a strong effect on the movement and articulated a number of its key ideas. More practically, the second wave, like the first, grew out of the dissatisfaction of activists with their involvement in other social movements, especially the New Left and civil rights movements (Maxwell and Shields 2018), and their failure to deal with gender issues. Activists were also angered by the fact that these movements themselves were patriarchal. An important event in the midst of the second wave was the founding of the National Organization for Women (NOW) in 1966. The founders were women in government dissatisfied with the government's failure to deal with sex discrimination against females in the workplace. NOW eventually came to focus on a much wider range of issues, such as discrimination against women in education, the rights of women within the family, and the problems of poor women.

The second wave reached its peak during the 1970s and early 1980s. A number of developments occurred during this period, including the founding of *Ms.* magazine; the appearance of women's studies programs on college campuses; the passage of Title IX of the U.S. Education Amendments, ending discrimination on the basis of sex in publicly funded education; and the 1973 Supreme Court decision in the case of *Roe v. Wade*, legalizing abortion (which was overturned by the U.S. Supreme Court in 2022). However, the second wave was soon wracked by internal conflicts. Some women— women of color, lesbians, working-class women—protested that their interests were not being adequately reflected in or addressed by the more publicly visible women's movement (Aikau, Erikson, and Pierce 2018). These internal conflicts resulted in a polarization of feminism. More conservative feminists, the reformists, were primarily concerned about gender equality in the workplace (hooks 2000). Revolutionary feminists criticized the limited goals of the reformists, who focused primarily on the concerns of White middle-class women. They also emphasized the ways in which conservative feminists often acted in a patriarchal and sexist manner toward other women.

By the early 1990s, it was clear that feminism was once again alive and well as a third wave of the women's movement emerged (Davies 2018). The defining characteristics of the third wave are greater racial and ethnic inclusivity and more focus on problems such as racism, classism, transphobia, and homophobia. The movement also addresses the place of women in the larger culture and a variety of specific issues, such as the wage gap between men and women, sexual harassment, violence against women, and sexual assault and rape.

Cyberfeminism and activism on the internet can be seen as part of the third wave, although some see these developments as marking the dawning of a fourth wave (Ray 2018). Feminists discuss, debate, and mobilize on a variety of websites, including the Crunk Feminist Collective and Feministing. They use social media and write blogs to raise awareness about the right to bodily autonomy and other issues. The emerging fourth wave of feminism is centered on the idea that gender and sexuality are fluid and aims to challenge the binary bias of these identities (Sollee 2015). Reproductive justice is also a key issue in fourth wave feminism, as is the struggle for women to achieve full human rights. These rights include not just gender equality in social institutions, like the workplace and school, but also the physical and emotional well-being of women and girls.

Among the contemporary issues faced by the women's movement is the fact that many online video games (such as *Grand Theft Auto V*), among many other aspects of contemporary society, are sexist and misogynistic, to say nothing of being racist and classist. Men who play these games are more likely than those who do not to develop sexist attitudes (LaCroix, Burrows, and Blanton 2018). Given the internet's booming importance, online abuses and other negative effects of internet use take on special importance for many interest groups, including the women's movement. "Gamergate" is a label for the problems posed by the internet, particularly concerning video games, for women (in particular those who have the audacity to criticize the sexism of the video game industry; Wingfield 2014a). Because sexism remains a problem on the internet—and in many other contexts—new and future developments will continue to reflect negative feelings toward women and become new targets for a continuingly evolving women's movement.

Women's marches have attracted millions of participants in recent years. What should be the goals of today's women's movement? Have they changed over time?

B Christopher / Alamy Stock Photo

The Global Women's Movement

Organizing women on a transnational basis took off between the 1830s and 1860s (Berkovitch 1999). At first, this was highly informal, but formal organizations did emerge, such as the World Women's Christian Temperance Union (WWCTU), founded in 1874. Although the WWCTU focused on the problem of alcohol, it was concerned about other issues as well, such as political equality for women. By the time of its first international convention in 1891, the WWCTU had branches in 26 countries. Members adopted the view that "universal sisterhood" existed and that women throughout the world experienced a common fate. Suffrage became an increasingly important issue globally, and led to the founding of the International Woman Suffrage Alliance (IWSA) in 1904.

One of the most striking events in the early twentieth century was the gathering of more than a thousand women in the Netherlands in 1915 at the International Congress of Women. This meeting took place despite the fact that World War I raged around the attendees, which made it very difficult to pass through national borders. The main goal of the meeting was to find ways to resolve conflicts and prevent future wars. After World War I, the founding of the League of Nations and the International Labour Organization (ILO) created new opportunities for global action by women (and others). However, women's activities in and through these organizations achieved few tangible results, in part because many women within these groups supported colonialism despite the presence of fellow members who suffered under colonial rule (Roth 2017). Moreover, the reproduction of colonial relationships within the movement was yet another facet of the contentious beginnings of an international women's movement. In reaction to this, Black women from Africa and the United States formed the International Council of Women of the Darker Races in 1920. They called for support in their struggle not only for personal independence but also national independence from colonial domination (Umoren 2018).

Much greater strides were made as a result of the founding of the United Nations (UN) after World War II. Instrumental in this progress was the UN Commission on the Status of Women. Its initiative led to a world conference on women in 1975 and to the declaration of that year as the UN International Women's Year. Yet men dominated the speeches and leadership positions at the 1975 conference; they tended to represent the interests of their respective governments rather than those of women's organizations. Women continued to press for equality, however, and were eventually granted more leadership roles to foster discussions about the gaps between male and female opportunities. This was followed by the UN Decade for Women (1976–1985), conferences during that decade, and a number of follow-up conferences. Because of such meetings, women from all over the world could interact face-to-face and develop transnational interpersonal ties. As a result of these associations, many local and transnational women's organizations emerged (Moghadam 2015).

In addition to these formal organizations, many transnational feminist networks have developed in recent years (Moghadam 2015). These are more fluid organizational forms, lacking formal membership and bureaucratic structures. They have been aided in their formation and interaction by new communication technologies, especially the internet and social media. However, rather than these developments leading to a single global sisterhood, divisions have emerged in the global women's movement. For example, there is growing recognition that women in the Global South often have different interests and face different degrees of oppression than women in the Global North (Hughes and Dubrow 2018). Despite these divisions, the women's movement today is far more global than ever. It is having an impact on the position of women throughout the world and shaping, and being shaped by, globalization (Basu 2016). This can be seen, for example, in the millions of women around the world who participated in the Women's March on January 21, 2017 and those involved in the #MeToo movement.

Digital Living: #MeToo Movement

Although the "Me Too" movement was founded in 2007 by Black feminist activist Tarana Burke, it did not gain momentum until after the *New York Times* reported allegations of sexual harassment made against film producer Harvey Weinstein in October 2017. The movement went viral after actress Alyssa Milano posted on Twitter: "If you've been sexually harassed or assaulted write 'me too' as a reply to this tweet." Two months later, 1.7 million tweets that included the hashtag #MeToo had been posted on Twitter by followers in 85 countries (Park 2017). Social media have encouraged thousands of survivors of sexual violence to share their stories and make a public stand against their perpetrators. Sexual misconduct in the workplace, in particular, became a central focus of #MeToo. Many prominent men, including television host Bill O'Reilly, politician Al Franken, and comedian Louis C. K., lost their jobs after allegations of sexual misconduct. In total, 201 men in powerful positions had lost their jobs one year after #MeToo went viral (see Figure 16.1).

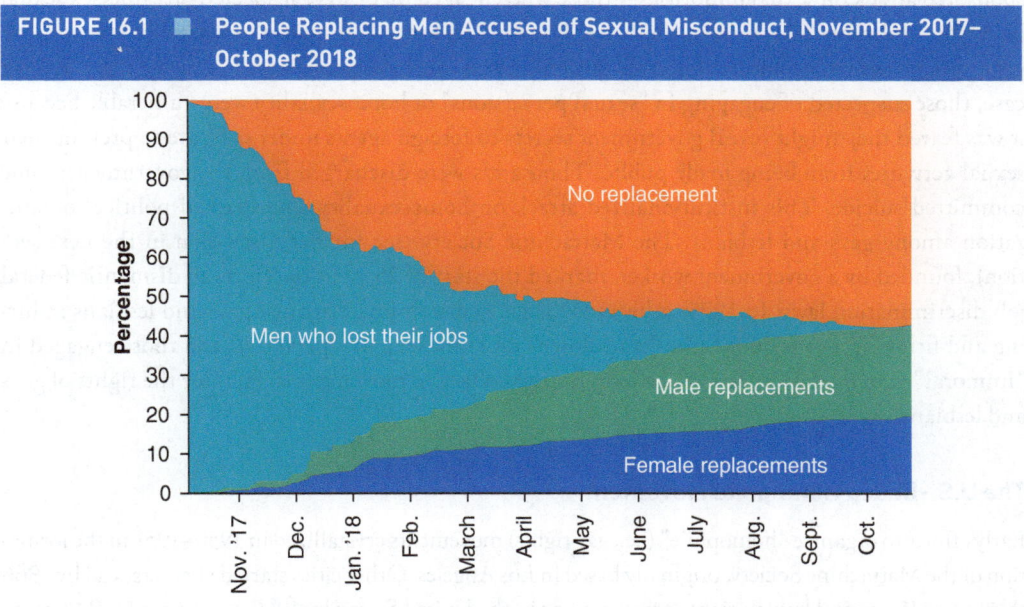

FIGURE 16.1 ■ People Replacing Men Accused of Sexual Misconduct, November 2017–October 2018

Source: Adapted from Audrey Carlsen et al., "#MeToo Brought Down 201 Powerful Men. Nearly Half of Their Replacements Are Women." 29 October 2018, *The New York Times.*

The #MeToo movement is not without its detractors and has faced something of a backlash. This is due, in part, to the controversy surrounding Brett Kavanaugh's (successful) Supreme Court nomination in 2018 and accusations of sexual assault while he was in high school. The percentage of men and women who believe that false allegations are a bigger problem than unreported sexual assaults has increased. The percentage of men and women who think a man who sexually harassed a woman more than 20 years ago should not lose his job has also increased ("Measuring the #MeToo" 2018). However, this backlash does not appear to be weakening the #MeToo movement as new allegations continue to be made and substantiated.

LGBTQ Movements

The origins of the U.S.-based lesbian, gay, bisexual, transgender, and queer (LGBTQ) movement can be traced back to the 1890s.[1] There were earlier LGBTQ movements in other places, such as Germany, and there are, of course, LGBTQ movements throughout the world today (Peterson, Wahlström, and Wennerhag 2018; Stulberg 2018). These movements still have much work to do. For example, same-sex acts remain illegal in more than 70 countries.

The focus here is mainly on LGBTQ movements in the United States, although the importance of such movements is growing around the world. The LGBTQ movement is discussed as the successor to such previous movements as gay liberation, lesbian feminism, and queer activism. It encompasses those earlier movements but goes beyond them to "embrace bisexuality and transgender issues" (Ghaziani, Taylor, and Stone 2016, 171).

World War II and the Lavender Scare

Some problems for gays and lesbians (such as mobilization against them in the military) developed during the World War II era (Bérubé 2010). Men and women engaged in new experiences as they left home, settled in new living situations, and found themselves in same-sex milieus in the military or civilian workplaces. This period has been described as "somewhat of a nationwide coming out experience" (Bérubé, quoted in Johnson

2004, 51). The war years allowed for increased possibilities and opportunities for sexual encounters, as well as an "anything goes" mentality. However, beginning in 1948, the United States entered a period of mounting public criticism of the "moral decay" of homosexuality, as well as of communism.

What came to be known as the "Lavender Scare" signaled a turning point for the history of gay and lesbian movements in the United States. Starting in 1950, the Lavender Scare was a government-sponsored attack on sexual minorities—those who engaged in, or were suspected of, same-sex sexual behaviors (Johnson 2004). As in the better-known Red Scare (a response to fears of communism), government agents attempted to ferret out employees who were considered security risks. In this case, those suspected of engaging in "sexual perversions" or homosexuality were vulnerable because it was feared they might reveal government secrets to foreign agents under pressure to prevent their sexual activities from being made public. Thousands were discharged from the government; some committed suicide. This institutionalized attack on homosexuality also sparked political organization among gays and lesbians. The Mattachine Society (see further discussion in the next section), founded by a government worker, marked the start of 25 years of efforts to dismantle federal job discrimination laws. In 1975, it became illegal to discriminate against gays and lesbians in hiring and firing decisions. Thus, the "crackdown" on homosexuals, "perverts," and those engaged in "immoral" sexual relations fostered a long-lasting collective movement to fight for the rights of gays and lesbians.

The U.S.-Based Homophile Movement

Early efforts to organize "homophile" (i.e., gay rights) movements crystallized in 1950–1951 in the formation of the Mattachine Society, originally based in Los Angeles. Other cities started chapters, and by 1966 there were 15 gay and lesbian rights organizations in the United States; by 1969, there were 50 (D'Emilio 1983; Hay 2012). The Daughters of Bilitis (DOB), an offshoot of the Mattachine Society focusing on the rights of gay women, was founded in 1955 (Enke 2018). These organizations emphasized education and largely embraced assimilationist strategies to gain mainstream acceptance. Although gay and lesbian activists worked alongside each other, gender privilege (particularly male) remained and was a source of dissatisfaction for lesbians active in the homophile movement. As one lesbian activist stated, "There wasn't a Women's Movement yet.... We knew our place—we were always the coffee makers.... There was a clear set of chores for women" (Shroedel and Fiber 2000, 99).

Patrons of the Stonewall Inn in Greenwich Village fought back when police raided the gay enclave in 1969, in what proved to be a watershed moment. Do you agree with those who feel the civil rights, antiwar, and feminist movements had an impact on the struggle for gay rights? If so, what was that impact?

New York Daily News Archive / Contributor / Getty Images

Stonewall

The 1969 uprisings at Greenwich Village's Mafia-owned gay bar, the Stonewall Inn, are regarded by many as pivotal in the twentieth-century struggle for gay rights and as denoting the beginning of the modern gay rights movement (Faderman 2016). On June 27, 1969, the patrons of the Stonewall Inn—"Puerto Rican drag queens, lesbians, effeminate men, and young street people" (Nardi, Sanders, and Marmor 1994, 14)—reacted violently to a police raid. Law enforcement officials and members of the gay community alike credited this event with inspiring gays and lesbians to more aggressively demand equality and freedom from abuse. Within a few years, there were hundreds of gay and lesbian groups all over the United States. Today, gay pride days and marches continue to commemorate the assertion of collective queer identity and entitlement to rights that emerged as a result of Stonewall. However, some question LGBTQ history's emphasis on the Stonewall uprisings. They remind us that new forms of the gay and lesbian movement owe much to the foundational work of homophile groups, as well as to twentieth-century civil rights, antiwar, and feminist organizations.

Lesbian Herstory

Given the underlying male privilege embodied in groups such as the Mattachine Society, many lesbians were dissatisfied with their organizing experiences alongside gay men. And although lesbians found a respite from sexism in the mainstream second-wave women's movement, the heterosexism and sometimes overt hostility encountered by lesbians in feminist groups made these organizing spaces less than hospitable. Consequently, many lesbians split off from the mainstream gay and feminist movements. Numerous lesbian separatist groups emerged, such as the Furies, who framed lesbianism as a political choice in opposition to male supremacy.

Not all lesbians politicized their sexual identities in this way. For women who desired other women in butch/femme (traditionally male/traditionally female) space, a masculine–feminine relationship continued. But lesbian separatists argued that to truly be feminists, women had to remove themselves completely from the male sphere. In practice, this resulted in the formation of women-only communities or "women's lands" and lesbian-driven, woman-centered activism. These women "wanted to create entirely new institutions and to shape a women's culture that would embody all of the best values that were not male" (Faderman 1991, 216).

HIV/AIDS, ACT UP, and Queer Nation

The recognition of HIV/AIDS in 1981 by the Centers for Disease Control and Prevention (CDC) had a tremendous impact on gay and lesbian politics and communities. The activism that emerged from this period was embodied in the early efforts of the AIDS Coalition to Unleash Power (ACT UP; Roth 2017). In 1989, ACT UP pressured pharmaceutical company Burroughs Wellcome to make its new antiretroviral drug, AZT, more affordable for HIV-positive patients. ACT UP embodied a new kind of LGBTQ activism that included civil disobedience, activist art, and other forms of creative activities and representations. ACT UP chapters opened throughout the nation. In 1990, some ACT UP activists formed a new group, Queer Nation, which, although short-lived, served as the beginning of a public and direct representation of LGBTQ issues. Out of HIV/AIDS activism and via the efforts of Queer Nation, the gay and lesbian movement shifted into a politics of queer spaces and identities.

The Ongoing Fight for Marriage Equality

Almost from the inception of the LGBTQ movement, marriage equality was a part of its national agenda. That effort really took off when the movement legally challenged the 1996 Defense of Marriage Act (Frank 2017). That act restricted marriage to "one man and one woman" and barred federal recognition of same-sex marriages. The efforts of the LGBTQ movement—and others—met with considerable success, and in 2011, the act was determined to be unconstitutional and the Justice Department stopped defending the law in court. In 2013, the U.S. Supreme Court struck down the section of the act that defined marriage as involving one man and one woman. It also declared unconstitutional the barring of federal recognition of same-sex marriages. As a result of the 2013 Supreme Court decision, same-sex couples gained many federal and state benefits that were formerly denied to them and automatically conferred on heterosexual couples. By mid-2015, the Supreme Court legalized same-sex marriage for the nation as a whole. Globally, same-sex couples also enjoy the legal right to marry in (as of this writing) 33 other countries, including Argentina, Belgium, Brazil, Canada, Colombia, Denmark, Finland, France, Iceland, Ireland, Luxembourg, the Netherlands, New Zealand, Norway, Portugal, Spain, South Africa, Sweden, Taiwan, the United Kingdom, and Uruguay. Despite these gains, same-sex couples continue to struggle for marriage equality in most countries around the world.

Resistance to gay marriage continues to come from both outside and inside the gay rights movement. Many religious conservatives continue to oppose same-sex marriage, arguing that it threatens the sanctity of marriage and the traditional family. Many queer-identified groups have also criticized gay marriage. For example, an emphasis on the central importance of securing legal marriage is criticized for failing to address the inequalities inherent in the institution of marriage itself (Bernstein, Harvey, and Naples 2018).

The level of support for same-sex marriage has increased in the United States over time (see Figure 16.2). In 2001, 57 percent of all adults opposed same-sex marriage while 35 percent were in favor of it. However, by 2021, more than 70 percent of people in the United States supported same-sex marriage. Younger generations support same-sex marriage more than older generations. More than 84 percent of those aged 18–34 support same-sex marriage while 60 percent of those over age 55 do. Different levels of support also exist between Democrats (83 percent) and Republicans (55 percent).

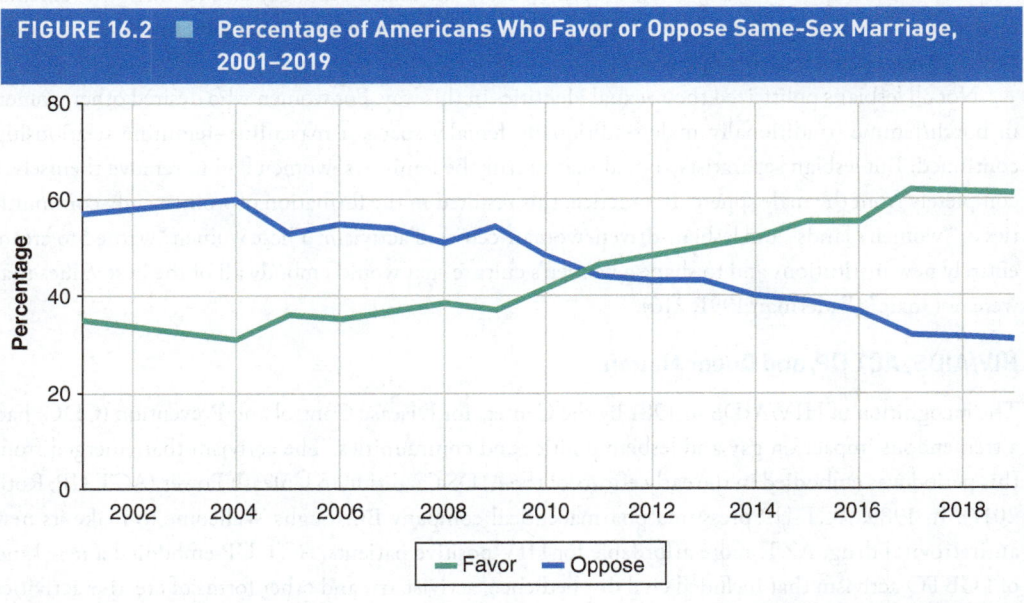

FIGURE 16.2 ■ Percentage of Americans Who Favor or Oppose Same-Sex Marriage, 2001–2019

Source: Pew Research Center, 2019, "Attitudes on Same-Sex Marriage: Public Opinion on Same-Sex Marriage," May 14. Retrieved August 2, 2022.

Trans Rights

Although social movements related to trans equality have existed for a long time, the size, scope, and attention paid to such movements has arguably increased significantly over the last decade. There are many reasons for this, including the overall greater attention being paid to broader social and gender equality movements, the increased attacks against the social and civil rights of trans individuals, and also the greater gains being made toward equality for trans individuals. The prominence of trans celebrities (like Caitlyn Jenner or Laverne Cox) has also played a role (Ryan 2021).

It also worth noting the particularly important role that trans individuals have played in broader social movements for gender and sexual equality (and others). For example, trans individuals (especially Martha P. Johnson and Sylvia Rivera) were at the center of the Stonewall Riots. Sylvia Rivera also founded Street Transvestite Action Revolutionaries (STAR), which is widely considered to be one of the first successful organizations of the queer liberation movement.

COVID-19 and Social Movements

The COVID-19 pandemic has sparked a number of social movements. As legal and social regulations related to public health safety increased at the beginning of the pandemic (especially those related to wearing masks and stay-at-home orders), people began organizing both for and against such measures. The availability of vaccines, and associated mandates by some entities (including healthcare facilities and colleges and universities), has also sparked a new wave of social movements, again, both for and against such measures.

One area that has sparked a lot of protest is the policies enacted by educational institutions (most likely even the one you are studying at now). Many universities around the world have begun to mandate that students, faculty, and staff have the COVID-19 vaccine as a requirement of employment or attendance.

Those who are against this requirement argue that forcing people to have a vaccine is unconstitutional and should not be a requirement to get an education (or have a job). A crucial element overlooked by this argument, however, is that nearly all educational institutions already require students and employees to have a large number of vaccines (e.g., against measles, mumps, rubella, and other infectious diseases), so although specifically requiring a COVID-19 vaccine is new, requiring vaccinations is not (Ryan 2023).

Stay-at-home measures (often referred to as "lockdowns") have also led to the growth of a number of protests. Such protests have happened around the world, perhaps most notably in the United States, UK, Germany, the Netherlands, and China. The specific reasons that individuals have engaged in these protests have varied and include a denial that the virus exists, a belief that the virus is part of a larger conspiracy by someone (i.e., Bill Gates) or some country (i.e., China) that manufactured the virus, and a belief that any form of restricting movement is a direct violation of individual rights. Aside from individual rationales, most of the participants in these protests hold more general perspectives that are anti-science and anti-government (Ryan and Nanda 2023a).

An irony of these protests has been that by holding large mass events—ones at which very few people, if any, were wearing masks or vaccinated—the protesters themselves have contributed to a further spread of the virus. In that way, these protests have helped to further necessitate the very condition (lockdowns, mask requirements) against which they were fighting. It is also worth noting that although these protests have received a large amount of media attention, they have actually been relatively rare. Most people have followed health protocols.

EMERGENCE, MOBILIZATION, AND IMPACT OF SOCIAL MOVEMENTS

A variety of conditions determine whether a social movement will emerge. To start, there must be grievances, or matters that large numbers of people find troublesome (Simmons 2018). Grievances about the unfair treatment of women, gays and lesbians, and Black people, as well as against new government measures, animated the social movements discussed previously. However, grievances alone are not sufficient for a social movement to arise. Individuals and organizations must be mobilized to do something about them. All of the movements discussed previously were successful in mobilizing people to act.

Factors in the Emergence of a Social Movement

Assuming a set of grievances and efforts at mobilization, certain other conditions must exist for a social movement to emerge. First, there must be openings or opportunities within the political system. For example, many movements use their organizational networks in Washington, D.C. to gain access to federal political institutions and to influence members of Congress.

A second factor involves various spatial arrangements, such as the physical proximity of those involved. Clearly, social movements develop more easily when those who at least have the potential to become involved come into contact with one another fairly easily or regularly (although the internet and the use of social media has increasingly challenged this, as discussed below). Another spatial factor is whether there are "free spaces" where those involved can meet. It is in such spaces that a movement can develop, out of the limelight and free of external surveillance and control. Women on college campuses existed in close proximity to one another, and this helped in the formation of the women's movement, while free spaces such as churches were especially important to the development of the civil rights movement.

A third factor is the availability of resources. This is the concern of **resource mobilization theory**, one of the most popular approaches to understanding social movements. The focus is on what groups need to do to mobilize effectively to bring about social change. This theory assumes some strain within the larger society and that groups have grievances that result from those strains. One of the most important works in this tradition is that of Jack Goldstone (1991) on **revolutions**. These are social movements in which the strains produced by state breakdown (e.g., failure of the government to function properly, fiscal distress) play a key role in the development of revolutionary movements. Major examples of revolutions include the French, American, and Russian Revolutions. Once a strain exists, the issue, then, is the resources needed for these groups to become social movements, perhaps even successful social movements.

Resources and Mobilization of Social Movements

Five types of resources have been identified as important to the mobilization of social movements:

- First are *material resources* such as money, property, and equipment. It is often very costly to mount a successful social movement, and money and other material resources are often needed.

- Second are *social-organizational resources,* which include infrastructure (internet access is especially important today), social networks (insiders with access to important groups and organizations), and the organizations formed by the social movement (e.g., NAACP, ACT UP).

- Third are *human resources*, such as the leadership, expertise, skills, and day-to-day labor of those in the organization. More specific resources might be dynamic public speakers (such as Martin Luther King, Jr.) and spokespersons, skilled web designers, or people skilled in organizational dynamics.

- Fourth are *moral resources*, such as the degree to which the larger public regards the movement as legitimate. Other moral resources include a sense of a high level of integrity among the leaders as well as in the membership as a whole (Jasper 1997).

- Finally, *cultural resources* are important—such as bodies of knowledge or skills tacitly shared by at least some members of the movement. These might include knowledge of how to organize a protest, hold a news conference, create and run a website, or run a meeting.

Another important issue is the source of such resources. One source is simply having members who are themselves able to produce the resources by, for example, raising money, developing networks, or socializing their children to become part of the movement as adults. Another is aggregating external resources, such as soliciting donations from a wide range of donors. Also of importance is the need to locate patrons who can be relied on to support the group monetarily and in many other ways (e.g., by providing staff members). Finally, a social movement can co-opt the resources of other organizations. For example, the civil rights movement in the United States co-opted the resources of churches by, for example, using their buildings, their staff, and their moral authority.

Participation

Once a social movement is under way, methods must be found to ensure member participation. First, people need to be asked to participate. For that to occur, they need to be embedded in social networks involving other movement members. Second, a variety of social psychological factors are involved. These include personally identifying with the movement and its causes, being aroused emotionally by the issues involved and becoming committed to dealing with them, and being at a point in life—retired, unemployed, in college—when one is available to participate in the movement. Third, incentives need to be offered so that the gains to members for their involvement outweigh the risks and costs. For example, for participants in the civil rights movement, the achievement of greater rights for Black people outweighed the risk of being beaten or murdered and the cost of lost time and income. Although material incentives are important, of far greater importance are the social incentives associated with joining with others as part of the movement, as well as the moral incentive of being involved in something one believes in strongly (Fominaya 2019).

Goals, Strategies, and Tactics

Once formed, a social movement needs to have goals, a strategy, and a variety of tactics to succeed. *Goals* relate to what the movement seeks to do, such as cut taxes, make society more equal, or even impeach a president. *Strategy* involves the movement's long-term plan for achieving its goals. Once a strategy is in place, tactics become important. *Tactics* are more short-term. They need to be fluid and able to adapt quickly in light of changes taking place in the immediate or larger environment. In the case of the civil rights movement, the strategy was to create situations that brought the plight of Black Americans, especially those who lived in the South, to the attention of the media, the public, and political leaders. Tactics, in this case, involved engaging in *civil disobedience*, or nonviolent public acts that are against the law and aimed at changing the law or government policies (Wanis-St. John and Rosen 2017). For example, Black people attempted to order food at segregated lunch counters. The acts of civil disobedience produced reactions (e.g., White protests, police action) that attracted media and public attention and eventually public outrage. Of particular importance are the actions of countermovements and government officials. For example, the civil rights movement had to adapt to the hostile actions of both White supremacists and many local government officials.

Climate activists in London, opposed to the expansion of Heathrow airport, created this massive traffic jam by blocking a tunnel that provides access to the airport.

Mark Kerrison / Alamy Stock Photo

Factors in Success

A variety of factors help determine whether a social movement will succeed (Snow et al. 2019). One is its sheer *size*. All social movements start small, but those that succeed are likely to have recruited large numbers of activists and supporters. Another is *novelty*, or the uniqueness of the movement and its goals. Uniqueness and size are important because they lead to a great deal of media attention, which, in turn, is likely to generate additional supporters and funds. The latter are two of the many *resources* social movements need to succeed (see the previous discussion). *Violence* can also sometimes be useful in achieving results. However, it also can be counterproductive by turning off potential supporters and members. Perhaps more important, it can lead to violent reactions that can end in the suppression of the movement. *Militancy* can also be double-edged because a highly militant social movement might be able to achieve its goals quickly, but militancy, like violence, can lead to counterreactions and suppression. *Nonviolence* has been a successful method for social movements because it avoids the powerful counterreactions engendered by violent and militant social movements. The nonviolent approach is traceable largely to Mahatma Gandhi and his use of such means as noncooperation with the British-controlled government to gain Indian independence in 1947. Today, a large number of social movements, including the women's and LGBTQ movements, have largely adopted a nonviolent approach. Globally, many organizations associated with the environmental movement, as well as those associated with the World Social Forum and operating in opposition to at least some aspects of globalization, rely almost exclusively on nonviolent methods. More generally, the ability of social movements to network—with individuals involved, as well as with other movements nationally and internationally—is increasingly a key to success. Part of that, and important in itself, is the ability of the movement and its members to use the internet and social media to create, ramp up, and maintain broad support.

Although various aspects of social movements themselves strongly affect whether they will be successful, many other factors are in play. Of great importance is the ability of individuals, groups, or the state (especially the police, the military, and the state more generally) to suppress a social movement (Chen and Gallagher 2018). Efforts at suppressing social movements can be covert, such as the FBI's wiretapping of the phones of members of dissident groups, especially suspected communist and civil rights groups, in the United States in the mid-1950s through the early 1970s. They can also be overt, a major example being the violent suppression in 1989 of antigovernment protests in Tiananmen Square by the Chinese government and the military.

The Impact of Social Movements

Whether or not they are successful, social movements often leave their imprint, sometimes a powerful one. A government might suppress a social movement, but it is likely that aspects of the government and the way it operates will be affected by the movement as well as by its efforts to suppress it. For example, in the 1940s and 1950s, the U.S. government was able to suppress efforts to increase the influence of communism throughout the country. However, although it was successful in those efforts, it engaged in a variety of highly questionable actions. Major examples include the activities of the House UnAmerican Activities Committee (HUAC) and especially those of the infamous senator Joseph McCarthy. McCarthy and his associates often made wild public accusations without presenting any supporting evidence. Long-lasting changes were brought about in the government as a result of the public's revulsion over the reprehensible tactics used by McCarthy and his supporters. Since that time, government actions that even hint at the kind taken during the 1940s and 1950s are labeled "McCarthyism" and, as a result, are unlikely to succeed.

Nevertheless, the government retains, at least to some degree, the ability to suppress social movements, and in many ways that ability and its extent have increased. This is a result, in part, of the fact that distinctions among activism, terrorism, and extremism are being eroded by government agencies, especially those concerned with law enforcement (Kaldor 2018). The danger here is that many activist social movements with positive goals and legal methods may end up being suppressed along with terroristic and extremist movements that pose a genuine threat.

Social movements, especially those that achieve some success, often leave strong legacies for, and have powerful impacts on, later movements. For example, the civil rights movement was an inspiration and a model for many later movements, such as the student, antiwar, environmental, gay and lesbian, and disability movements. Social movements outside the United States—for example, South Africa's antiapartheid movement, the Solidarity movement in Poland, and the democracy movement in China—have also been strongly affected by the civil rights movement.

The Internet, Globalization, and Social Movements

Two of the most important recent developments as far as social movements are concerned relate to globalization and the internet, as well as other media technologies, such as smartphones (Carty 2018; Vanden, Funke, and Prevost 2018).

The internet has proven to be an important means of involving and organizing large numbers of people, sometimes millions of them, who are widely separated from one another, perhaps even in different parts of the world. In other words, people no longer need to be in close physical proximity to be involved in social movements. People can also now communicate more easily through the use of smartphones, and especially social media, even from the sites of events. This communication offers new possibilities for mobilizing those engaged in social movements. It is possible for participants in a movement not only to communicate verbally with others in the movement but also to snap pictures or shoot videos with their smartphones and send them instantaneously via YouTube, Facebook, or Twitter to large numbers of interested parties. This allows people to see for themselves what is transpiring in the social movement. For example, the Islamic State (IS) was effective in using the internet to recruit supporters, many of whom trekked to Syria to participate in conflict there and in the region. IS was particularly successful at using Facebook to attract female adherents from the West (Erlanger 2014). Now online activists (e-activists) are creating electronic social movements (e-movements; Dolata and Schrape 2016; O'Brien, Selhoe, and Hayward 2018). At least some e-movements have the possibility of becoming social movements in the nonvirtual world.

The internet and other technologies enable social movements to cover wide geographic areas and even to become global in scope. Like much else in the world today, social movements are less constrained than ever before by national borders. It seems likely that the future will bring an increasing number of global social movements. We discuss the internet and globalization further later in this chapter.

COLLECTIVE ACTION

Collective action is generated, or engaged in, by a group of people to encourage or prevent social change (Brooker and Meyer 2019). Social movements are one kind of collective action; others include crowds, riots, and disasters. Like social movements, forms of collective action usually occur outside established institutional channels. However, forms of collection action are different from social movements in at least two ways. First, most forms of collective action are short-lived compared to social movements. Thus, a crowd, for example, can come together and disperse within hours, but a social movement can be sustained for years or decades. Second, a social movement is intentional; other forms of collective action are not. For instance, a community that comes together immediately after a disaster such as an earthquake or a flood does not do so intentionally. It has been brought together and springs into action because of some unanticipated external event. After Hurricane Maria devastated Puerto Rico in 2017, communities across the island came together to help each other. They are continuing to work on sustainable solutions to minimize damage from future natural disasters. Killings of Black males by White police officers across the United States—in Ferguson, Missouri; Cleveland, Ohio; Staten Island, New York; Charlotte, North Carolina; and Baltimore, Maryland—brought together Black people (and others) in those communities, as well as multiracial groups throughout the country, in an effort to deal with the problem and its roots. More recently, the wildfire that destroyed many properties in Paradise, California, saw collective efforts to raise funds to help those communities recover, including celebrities like Ellen DeGeneres donating $100,000 to the Los Angeles Fire Department.

Although social movements have been theorized separately and somewhat differently (resource mobilization theory), the dominant approach to thinking about other forms of collective action is **emergent norm theory** (Tierney 2018; Turner and Killian 1987). This theory is based on the idea that new norms emerge in light of some precipitating event. These norms guide the often nontraditional actions that characterize collective behavior. Implicit in this theory is the idea that in collective behavior, conventional norms cease to be as effective or as important, at least to some degree. Contrary to popular opinion, however, collective behavior is not irrational, random, or out of control. It is rational and guided by the new norms that develop in the situation.

Crowds

The clearest application of emergent norm theory to collective action involves the case of a **crowd**, a temporary gathering of a relatively large number of people in a common geographic location at a given time (Mele 2018;

A rash of widely publicized violence by White police officers against Black males in several states led to many instances of collective action, including this rally in Charlotte, North Carolina, to protest the deaths of Michael Brown, Eric Garner, and others.

Sean Rayford/Getty Images

Springer 2018). We are all familiar with all sorts of crowds, such as those that gather at the sites of celebrations or catastrophes. There are also online crowds, such as flash crowds that develop on the internet to cause disruptions, such as denial-of-service attacks whereby a system is flooded with meaningless requests, making it unavailable to legitimate users.

Today, virtual crowds are becoming the new norm on, for example, crowdfunding sites such as Kickstarter and GoFundMe. People come together online from all over the world, to offer financial support for a common cause. Examples of crowdfunding include efforts to fund medical bills or travel fees, to raise money that will buy land to protect the environment, and even to support authors in publishing independent stories or artists and musicians. Through crowdfunding, people can choose to support charities, businesses, education, and other endeavors. Together, all kinds of people achieve the same goal and represent the interconnectedness of the world through the internet.

One concern in the literature on crowds is the degree to which individuals behave differently in crowds than they do in other social contexts. Emergent norm theory suggests that they do behave differently, but that is because they are conforming to a different set of norms than exist elsewhere in the social world. That is more comforting than the alternative view, which sees people in crowds as losing control of their cognitive processes, complying blindly with the suggestions of crowd leaders, copying mindlessly what is done by those around them in the crowd, and acting selfishly. A large body of research has failed to find any support for the latter view (Junger 2016).

Social media (e.g., Facebook, Twitter) help spread the word about crowdfunding opportunities, and people can also go directly to sites like GoFundMe and Kickstarter to look for opportunities to support causes. This is the opposite of the all-too-common social media phenomenon of trolling, when people whose names and faces are hidden by the anonymity of the internet will argue, disparage, and even threaten violence against others.

Riots

A riot is temporary unruly collective action that causes damage to persons or property (Morgner 2018). There have been a number of relatively recent riots in the United States, including race riots in the 1960s in Los Angeles, Detroit, and Washington, D.C. One notable set of race riots occurred in Los Angeles in 1992 following the acquittal of four police officers charged with the beating of motorist Rodney King. An even more recent, if less violent, riot occurred after the 2014 shooting death of an unarmed Black man, Michael Brown, by a White police officer in Ferguson, Missouri. Riots, of course, have happened elsewhere in the world; they are a global phenomenon.

Negative Views of Riots

We are likely to have negative views of riots and rioters. However, riots may not be irrational outbursts. Rather, they may be motivated by frustrations over various kinds of abuses and the inability to do much about them under normal circumstances (Useem 2018). It is hard to generalize about rioters, but there is little support in the research for the idea that rioters are more likely to be criminals, unemployed, or uneducated. A few things seem clear about those who participate in riots. They are more likely to be men, to be young, to have been physically close to where the riots occur, and to feel that their actions can make a difference.

It is also worth noting that the mass media can contribute to rioting through the ways in which they treat riots. For one thing, live coverage of riots can inflame them by drawing in additional participants. Live, immediate media reports on rioting are also more likely to be inaccurate and to involve inflammatory reporting. For another thing, media reports of riots can suggest that this is a form of action to be emulated at other places and times. Social media can also quickly draw large numbers of people to riot sites.

Disasters

Disasters are events that suddenly, unexpectedly, and severely disrupt and harm the environment, the social structure, people, and property (Tierney 2018). They are distinguished from accidents (e.g., automobile and airplane crashes) by their far greater impact. Many disasters have resulted in billions of dollars' worth of damage, and the numbers of such huge disasters have increased in recent years (see Figure 16.3). For example, an earthquake in Haiti in 2010 decimated a significant portion of that Caribbean nation. No one knows the exact numbers, but it is estimated that more than 200,000 people were killed and another 300,000 were injured. Innumerable poorly constructed homes, schools, and other buildings were destroyed. The government virtually ceased functioning as its offices collapsed, literally and figuratively, and many officials were killed or injured (Bhatty 2010). Some progress has been made, but Haiti continues to suffer the ill effects of the 2010 earthquake even more than a decade later. Although it is a stark example, the disaster in Haiti represents just one of the many natural disasters that have occurred in recent years.

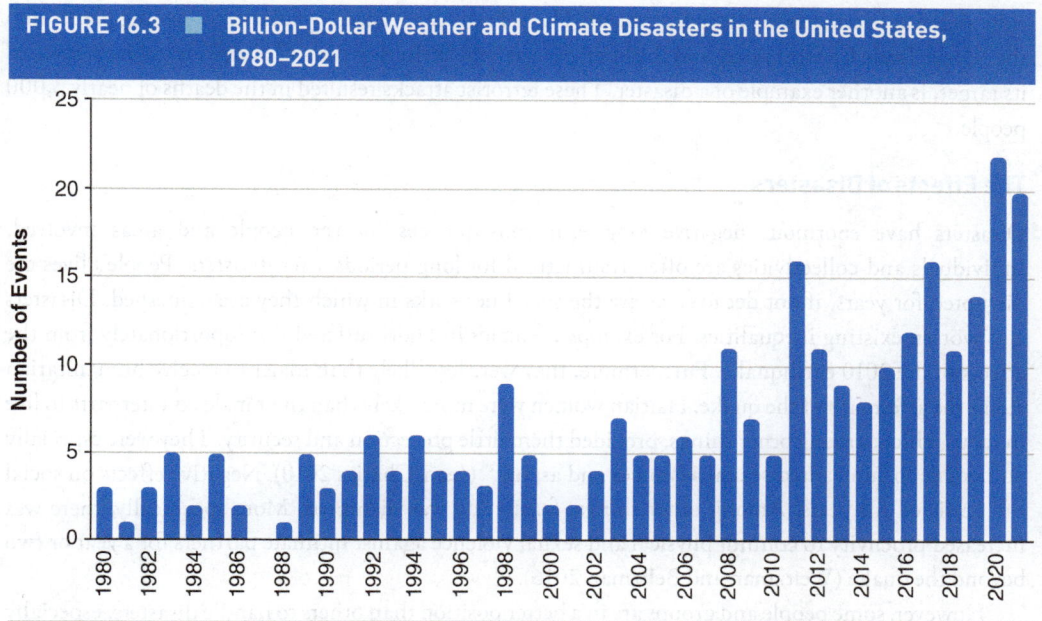

FIGURE 16.3 ■ Billion-Dollar Weather and Climate Disasters in the United States, 1980–2021

Source: NOAA National Centers for Environmental Information, 2022, "Billion Dollar Weather and Climate Disasters." Retrieved August 2, 2022 (https://www.ncei.noaa.gov/access/monitoring/billions/).

Human Involvement in Disasters

Disasters such as earthquakes and hurricanes are natural phenomena, but humans often play a role in bringing disasters about and exacerbating the consequences of natural disasters. People frequently build in areas—for example, on geological fault lines, on the coast, or on floodplains—where there should be no significant building. Furthermore, what they build is often flimsy and likely to be destroyed in a natural disaster. Building stronger structures can be very costly, and impoverished nations such as Haiti simply cannot afford it (Interlandi 2010). Responses to disasters are often inadequate, leading to unnecessary human suffering and delayed efforts at helping those affected. Rebuilding affected communities often takes much too long, and in impoverished areas it may not occur at all.

There are, of course, disasters that result from human error or corruption. On April 20, 2010, a huge explosion on the BP *Deepwater Horizon* oil rig in the Gulf of Mexico killed 11 workers and left oil gushing into the gulf for three months ("Louisiana Oil Rig" 2010). During that period, 206 million gallons of oil flowed into the water, affecting nearly 1,000 miles of coastline (Morris et al. 2013). There had been warnings for decades about the dangers associated with deep-sea drilling and oil wells. However, such drilling was pushed forward by the desire for ever-escalating profits on the part of corporations like BP and the voracious need for oil, especially in the United States and other developed nations. Once the *Deepwater Horizon* oil gusher occurred, it became clear that no one knew how to go about stopping it; the well was not finally capped until July 15. The spilled oil caused great damage to the gulf's marine life, its beaches, and the businesses that depend on tourists drawn to the area.

Recall from Chapter 5 that the space shuttle *Challenger* disintegrated a little over a minute into its flight on January 28, 1986, killing all seven crew members. To get needed funds and to launch space shuttles in a timely manner, NASA had ignored warnings, taken risks, and tolerated mistakes and deception. Although Vaughan (1996) views this disaster as a unique occurrence, Charles Perrow (1999) sees such accidents as "normal." That is, highly complex systems such as those associated with NASA and the space shuttle will inevitably have such disasters, although they happen only rarely.

The most recent example of this are the crashes with hundreds of fatalities involving two of Boeing's new 737 MAX planes in late 2018 and early 2019. After the second crash, the plane was grounded to deal with technical difficulties that played a key role in the crashes. In both cases, the pilots were not able to wrest control of the planes from the automated flight control system and prevent them from crashing.

Human-made disasters also can be political in nature, and they are associated with revolutions, riots, and acts of terrorism. For example, in mid-2010, the center of Bangkok, Thailand, was ravaged by riots aimed at overthrowing the government. The 9/11 disaster caused by hijackers crashing planes into the World Trade Center towers and the Pentagon, as well as the downing of one plane before it reached its target, is another example of a disaster. These terrorist attacks resulted in the deaths of nearly 3,000 people.

The Effects of Disasters

Disasters have enormous negative long-term consequences for the people and areas involved. Individuals and collectivities are often traumatized for long periods after disasters. People's lives are disrupted for years, if not decades, as are the social networks in which they are enmeshed. Disasters also worsen existing inequalities. For example, females in Haiti suffered disproportionately from the effects of the 2010 earthquake. Furthermore, they were less likely than males to receive humanitarian aid in the aftermath of the quake. Haitian women were more likely than their male counterparts to live in tents, which, among other things, provided them little protection and security. They were especially vulnerable to "unwanted sexual advances and assault" (Jean-Charles 2010). Negative effects on social life persisted for years. Among other things, family life was disrupted. More specifically, there was increased proclivity to commit physical and sexual violence against intimate partners for a year or two beyond the quake (Weitzman and Behrman 2016).

However, some people and groups are in a better position than others to handle disasters, especially those with greater access to resources. Disasters can also bring people and communities together in unprecedented ways to deal with the aftereffects. The heroism of many of those involved in helping after the 9/11 disaster—firefighters, police officers, and citizens—is one example of this (Fritsch 2001; Rozdeba 2011; Saxon 2003). Within Haiti, a number of aid agencies worked for years to provide aid to women and girls, including the UN Population Fund, the World Food Programme, and World Vision. In addition, "cash for work" programs, instituted by the Haitian Ministry of Women's Affairs, helped 100,000 women displaced by the earthquake survive (Jean-Charles 2010). Moreover, in response to the increased vulnerability of women and girls, Femmes Citoyennes Haiti Solidaire, or Women Citizens Haiti United, formed an alliance of activists to continue addressing gender inequality and injustices in Haiti.

SOCIAL CHANGE: GLOBALIZATION AND THE INTERNET

Social change is intimately connected to the topics discussed in the first part of this chapter. Social movements, especially those that are successful, often lead to major social changes. For example, the women's, LGBTQ, and civil rights movements have all led, and continue to lead, to such social changes. Collective action is less likely to lead to social change, but there have certainly been many examples of crowd behavior, riots, and disasters that have led to change. For example, the Los Angeles race riots of 1992 and the more recent demonstrations related to the Black Lives Matter movement, led to changes not only in police behavior but also in efforts to deal with the underlying causes of the riots.

Although social change occurs on local levels, it is increasingly taking on more global dimensions. Increasing global interconnectedness is changing the world in which we live and is likely to lead to a variety of even more dramatic changes in the future. For example, the changing nature of the global economy, especially the arguable shift of its center away from the United States and in the direction of China and Asia more generally, means that the job prospects of Americans are changing and apt to change even more in the future. Some economic prospects have declined, especially those that relate to the production of goods and the jobs associated with it. However, others have improved. New jobs have arisen—especially those that involve computers and the internet. Clearly, the internet is important not only in this sense but also because it is an arena in which great and extremely rapid change has taken place in recent years. The internet will certainly continue to change and affect our lives in innumerable ways.

Globalization as Social Change

Prior to the current epoch of globalization, one of the things that characterized people, things, information, places, and much else was their greater solidity. That is, all of them tended to (figuratively) harden over time and, therefore, among other things, to remain largely in place. As a result, people did not venture very far from where they were born and raised. Their social relationships were limited to those nearby. Much the same could be said of most objects (tools, food), which tended to be used where they were produced. The solidity of most material manifestations of information (stone tablets, books) also made them at least somewhat difficult to move very far. Furthermore, because people didn't move very far, neither did information. Places, too, were not only solid and immovable but tended to be surrounded by solid barriers (mountains, oceans, walls, borders) that made it difficult for people and things to exit or enter.

Global "Liquids"

Increasingly over the last few centuries, and especially the last several decades, what once seemed so solid has tended to "melt." Instead of thinking of people, objects, information, and places as being like solid blocks of ice, we need to see them as tending to melt and become increasingly liquid (Beilharz 2012). Needless to say, it is far more difficult to move blocks of ice than it is to move the water produced when those blocks melt. Of course, to extend the metaphor, there continue to exist blocks of ice, even glaciers, in the contemporary world that have not melted, at least not completely. Solid material realities, such as people, cargo, and newspapers, continue to exist, but because of a wide range of technological developments in transportation, communication, and the internet, they can move across the globe far more readily. Also of note are recent efforts around the world to erect new solid barriers (e.g., walls) to movement, especially of immigrants. However, although some such efforts will succeed, at least for a time, they will not do much to stem most of the flows associated with globalization.

Thus, following the work of Zygmunt Bauman (1925–2017; 2000, 2003, 2005, 2006), the perspective on globalization presented here involves increasing liquidity (Ritzer and Dean 2019). There is a constant interplay between liquidity and solidity, with increases in what is liquid (e.g., terrorist attacks launched against Palestine) leading to counterreactions and the erection of new solid forms (e.g., fences and walls between Israel and the West Bank). However, at the moment and for the foreseeable future, the momentum lies with increasing and proliferating global liquidity.

Global "Flows"

Closely related to the idea of liquidity, and integral to it, is another key concept in thinking about globalization, the idea of "flows" (Appadurai 1996; Inda 2012). After all, liquids flow easily, far more easily than solids. Because so much of the world has "melted," or is in the process of "melting," globalization is increasingly characterized by great flows of increasingly liquid phenomena of all types, including people, objects, information, decisions, and places. In many cases, the flows have become raging floods that are increasingly less likely to be impeded by place-based barriers of any kind, including the oceans, mountains, and especially the borders of nation-states. For example, the financial impact of the COVID-19 pandemic is one that has flowed around the world.

Zygmunt Bauman first studied sociology while he served in the Polish military and went on to teach at universities in Europe and Israel. Among his notable contributions to the field are his work on the problems associated with the rationalized modern world and the increasing liquidity associated with late modernity and globalization.

Agence Opale / Alamy Stock Photo

Looking at a very different kind of flow, people in many parts of the world believe they are being swamped by migrants, especially poor undocumented migrants (Triandafyllidou 2018). This is especially true of concerns in the United States about migrants from Latin America and in Europe about Muslim immigrants. Whether or not these are actually floods, they have come to be seen as such by many people, often aided by politicians (most notably former President Donald Trump) and media personalities who have established their reputations and acquired their positions by portraying migrants in that way. Places, too, can be said to be flowing around the world, as immigrants re-create the places (and cultures) from which they come in new locales.

Ideas, images, and information, both legal (blogs) and illegal (child pornography), flow everywhere, undoubtedly because of their immateriality. They do so through interpersonal contact and the media, especially now via the internet. Much of what would have been considered the height of global liquidity only a few years ago now seems increasingly sludgelike. This is especially the case when we focus on the impact of the computer and the internet on the global flow of all sorts of things. For example, instead of scouring an import VHS catalog and waiting weeks for an anime movie to ship from Japan, a person can simply open the Netflix app on their console and stream any number of anime movies instantly.

Globalization and the Internet

Since its onset in the 1990s, the internet has profoundly affected almost every aspect of life for a growing number of people around the world. The internet has expedited the globalization of many different things and is itself a profound form and aspect of globalization. The internet is global in several senses, but the most important is that although its users are not equally divided between North and South, rich and poor, and so on, they *do* exist virtually everywhere in the world. It is also global in the sense that it was produced and is maintained by a number of global and transnational corporations and organizations, including multinational corporations (such as Intel), intergovernmental organizations, and international nongovernmental organizations. For instance, the World Intellectual Property Organization regulates intellectual property rights, the Internet Corporation for Assigned Names and Numbers coordinates domain names, and the UN Educational, Scientific, and Cultural Organization promotes computer and internet use in schools throughout the world.

Cyberactivism

For those who have internet access, the opportunity to connect with like-minded individuals across the country and around the world has contributed to the rise of **cyberactivism**, or using social media and other internet-based communication methods to create, promote, or manage activism. Recent examples of cyberactivism include R.I.P. Medical Debt, which raises money to pay off the medical debt of those who cannot afford it; Greenpeace's Greenwire, which digitally connects volunteers with environmental campaigns; and the Women's March on Washington, which was organized online and generated global demonstrations involving millions of women and men. Another recent notable example is the wide-ranging impacts of the so-called Arab Spring, which was largely orchestrated, at least initially, through social media.

The relationship between globalization and cyberactivism has been demonstrated more recently in a wide range of e-activism, including hashtag activism (most notably #BlackLivesMatter and #MeToo; see above). The latter terms are derived from the use of hashtags (#) on Twitter to spread the word about a particular cause. Those involved are not required to take any action; they merely indicate their support by, for example, liking a tweet or retweeting something they approve of.

WikiLeaks is one of the most notable and controversial examples of cyberactivism. A global audience for its release of private documents has developed. The release of such documents often exposes behavior and planning hidden from the public. Although WikiLeaks's home was originally in Sweden, it is now hosted by a number of servers around the world.

In 2010, WikiLeaks began releasing classified diplomatic cables between Washington and many of its consulates around the world. Later that year, documents were released—some classified as confidential or secret—relating to the Afghanistan and Iraq wars. The documents implicated numerous officials around the world in questionable, if not illegal, acts. Many lost their positions or suffered other adverse consequences as a result of the documents' release. In addition, revelations from leaked cables from the U.S. Embassy played a key role in launching the revolution in Tunisia and thereby ultimately in the aforementioned wider rebellion known as the Arab Spring.

Edward Snowden is a computer specialist and whistle-blower who was employed by a contractor associated with the National Security Agency (NSA; see the Oscar-winning 2014 documentary *Citizenfour* and the 2016 movie *Snowden*). Claiming he was disturbed by the misuse of U.S. surveillance programs, Snowden copied and eventually released through the conventional news media (e.g., the *New York Times*, the *Guardian*) classified NSA information. Early on, he was helped by WikiLeaks personnel when he fled first to Hong Kong and then to Moscow, where he has been ever since. However, Snowden has been critical of WikiLeaks for insufficient oversight over the information it released. It did not edit and remove sensitive information, especially about the identity of people mentioned in the leaks (Chokshi 2016). As a result, Snowden chose to release further information through the more traditional news media because he felt that he could exercise greater control over what information was—and was not—released. Although the initial news releases appeared in the United States, Great Britain, and Germany, the information was quickly disseminated globally.

The information released by Snowden revealed that the NSA, in cooperation with similar agencies in Australia, Canada, and the United Kingdom, had been operating a global surveillance system. Among other things, these agencies derived user data from online service providers (e.g., Google), read e-mails, tracked peoples' browsing patterns and histories as well as their social media activities, and so on. These revelations were explosive, particularly when it was revealed that the NSA was spying on leaders of allied nations, such as Germany.

From the point of view of globalization, the key points are, first, that the NSA's surveillance program involved global power alignments among secret government agencies (Lyon 2015a). Second, the revelations about the program and its excesses were publicized globally. Finally, the implications of, and reactions to, the program were similarly global in scope. To some degree, at least, reforms also took place globally.

Although some people see Snowden as a hero for revealing some of the government's dirty secrets, others see him as committing treason in revealing classified information that adversely affected what the U.S. government (and others) considered to be important surveillance operations. The U.S.

government continues to threaten to arrest Snowden if he leaves Russia. Nevertheless, human rights groups continue to seek a pardon for Snowden, seeing it as important in preventing abuses of power, protecting whistle-blowers, and, more generally, in maintaining a free society (Naheem 2015; Savage 2016).

SUMMARY

Social change creates variations over time in every aspect of the social world. Social movements are sustained and intentional collective efforts, usually operating outside established institutional channels, either to bring about social change or to prevent it. Prominent social movements include the feminist, LGBTQ, and civil rights movements as well as more recent ones related to the COVID-19 pandemic.

The emergence of a social movement requires a set of grievances, efforts at mobilization, opportunities within the political system, the proximity of people or access to digital technologies, the availability of free space to meet, and the availability of resources. Factors that affect the success of a social movement include its size and uniqueness, as well as other groups' ability to suppress the movement. When successful, a social movement can leave a lasting legacy. Unlike social movements, some collective action is short-lived and spontaneous. For example, crowds are temporary gatherings of a large number of people in a common geographic location. Riots, responses to disasters, and cyberactivism are other types of collective action that lack the organizational structure, resources, and leadership of social movements.

Globalization is arguably the most important change in human history and is characterized by great flows of liquid phenomena across the globe. The internet is both a form and an aspect of globalization and has expedited globalization. Barriers are being erected to at least some of these flows, but in most cases, they are not likely to succeed, or to succeed for very long.

KEY TERMS

collective action
crowd
crowdfunding
cyberactivism
disasters
emergent norm theory

feminism
resource mobilization theory
revolution
riot
social change
social movement

REVIEW QUESTIONS

1. Can digital movements be considered true social movements? What, if anything, do they lack?
2. What have been the three waves of the women's movement? How did the goals and strategies of the women's movement change during each of these three waves?
3. In what ways has the COVID-19 pandemic impacted social movements and collective action?
4. How have communication technologies like the internet and social networking sites (e.g., Facebook and Twitter) aided global social movements? What types of resources move more easily because of these new technologies?
5. According to resource mobilization theory, what do groups of people need in order to mobilize effectively? How can we apply this theory to the discussion of the civil rights movement in this chapter?

6. What mechanisms do social movements use to ensure member participation? How are these mechanisms related to the LGBTQ movements discussed in this chapter?

7. What factors are used to determine whether a social movement is successful? In what ways has the women's movement been successful? What forms has resistance to the movement taken? What has given it renewed impetus? How might these things affect the movement's future success?

8. According to emergent norm theory, are individuals likely to behave rationally when in crowds? Using emergent norm theory, how can we explain at least some irrational behavior in crowds?

9. The earthquakes in Haiti (2010) and Nepal (2015) and the 2017 hurricane in Puerto Rico are examples of disasters. In what ways did humans exacerbate the consequences of these natural disasters? What sorts of negative long-term consequences can be expected from disasters like these?

10. In what ways is globalization the "ultimate social change"? How has the world become more liquid because of globalization? What role have new communication technologies played in making the world more liquid?

ENDNOTE

1. An earlier version of this section was written by Tracy Royce and Danielle Antoinette Hidalgo. It is reprinted with their permission.

GLOSSARY

absolute poverty: An absolute measure—such as the U.S. poverty line—that makes it clear what level of income people need in order to survive.

acculturation: The process whereby minority groups take on aspects of the dominant culture but still retain distinctive elements of their own culture.

achieved status: A position acquired by people on the basis of what they accomplish or the nature of their capacities.

achievement: The accomplishments, or the merit, of the individual.

adoption: The process by which an individual assumes a relationship with and a responsibility for another, usually a child.

agender: An individual who may not identify with any particular gender.

agents of socialization: Those who socialize others.

alienation: In a capitalist system, being unconnected to one's work, products, fellow workers, and human nature.

Americanization: The importation by other countries of products, images, technologies, practices, norms, values, and behaviors that are closely associated with the United States.

anomie: The feeling of not knowing what is expected of oneself in society or of being adrift in society without any clear, secure moorings.

anti-Americanism: An aversion to the United States in general, as well as to the influence of its culture abroad.

anticipatory socialization: The teaching (and learning) of what will be expected of one in the future.

arranged marriage: Marriage in which the members involved were brought together by individuals from outside of the relationship, usually family members.

ascribed status: A position in which individuals are placed, or to which they move, that has nothing to do with what they have done or their capacities or accomplishments.

ascription: Being born with or inheriting certain characteristics (wealth, high status, etc.).

assimilation: The process by which a minority group takes on the characteristics of the dominant group in place of their own particular group identities.

asylum: A situation in which an individual fears persecution in their home territory and seeks protection in another territory.

asylum seekers: People who flee their home country, usually to escape political oppression or religious persecution.

authority: A particular type of domination: legitimate domination.

back stage: The part of the social world where people feel free to express themselves in ways that are suppressed in the front stage.

beliefs: Ideas that explain the world and identify what should be sacred or held in awe—that is, a religion's ultimate concerns.

birthrate: The number of births per 1,000 people per year.

blended family: A family that includes some combination of children from the partners' previous marriages or relationships, along with one or more children of the currently married or cohabiting couple.

bodily capital: Increased social status that comes from being healthier and more physically attractive.

bounded rationality: Rationality limited by, among other things, instabilities and conflicts within most, if not all, organizations, as well as by the limited human capacity to think and act in a rational manner.

brand: A symbol that serves to identify and differentiate one product or service from others.

breaching experiment: The purposeful violation of a social norm to see how others will react.

bureaucracy: A highly rational organization, especially one that is highly efficient.

bureaucratic personality: A type of bureaucrat who slavishly follows the rules of the organization, to such an extent that the ability to achieve organizational goals is subverted.

butterfly effect: The far-ranging or even global impact of a small change in a specific location, over both time and distance.

capitalism: In Marx's view, an economic system based on one group of people (the capitalists, or owners) owning what is needed for production and a second group (the proletariat, or workers) owning little but their capacity for work.

capitalists: Those who own what is needed for production—factories, machines, tools—in a capitalist system.

cathedrals of consumption: Large and lavish consumption sites, created mostly in the United States in the last half of the twentieth century and into the early twenty-first century.

charismatic authority: Authority based on the devotion of the followers to what they define as the exceptional characteristics, such as heroism, of the leaders.

church: A large group of religiously oriented people into which members are usually born (instead of joining consciously and voluntarily).

cities: Large, permanent, and spatially concentrated human settlements.

citizens: The people represented by a given state, most often born within its territories.

citizenship: The idea that people of a given state can vote for their representatives within the state but also that they have access to rights and responsibilities as citizens.

civil religion: The beliefs, practices, and symbols a nation holds sacred.

class consciousness: According to Marx, a mental state in which the workers (proletariat) come to truly understand capitalism, their collective role in it, and their relationship to one another, as well as to the capitalists.

cohabitation: An arrangement in which a couple share a home and a bed without being legally married.

collective action: Action generated, or engaged in, by a group of people to encourage or retard social change.

collective conscience: The set of beliefs shared by people throughout society.

collectivist culture: A culture that prioritizes the well-being of the larger group.

color-blind racism: The denial that individuals are thought about or treated differently based on their race and the assumption that everyone has equal opportunities.

communism: To Marx, a historical stage that follows socialism involving the effort by society to plan and organize production consciously and rationally so all members of society benefit from it.

companionate love: A kind of love typified by gradual onset and not necessarily tied to sexual passion but based on more rational assessments of the one loved.

companionate marriage: A marriage emphasizing a clear division of labor between a breadwinner and a homemaker and held together by sentiment, friendship, and sexuality. The predominant model of marriage in the mid-twentieth century. See also companionate love.

competitive capitalism: A form of capitalism in which there is a large number of relatively small firms, with the result that no one or small subset of them can completely dominate and control a given area of the economy.

concerted cultivation: A child-rearing approach in which children spend more time in parent-guided educational opportunities.

conflict theory: A theory that sees society as held together by coercion and focuses on its negative aspects.

conformists: People who accept both cultural goals and the traditional means of achieving those goals.

consensual sexual activities: Sexual activities agreed upon by the participants, any of whom have the right to decide to stop at any point and for any reason.

constructionist theories: Theories of deviance that seek a greater understanding of the process by which people define and classify some behaviors as normal and others as deviant.

consumer crimes: Crimes related to consumption, including shoplifting and using stolen credit cards or credit card numbers.

consumer culture: A culture in which the core ideas and material objects relate to consumption and in which consumption is a primary source of meaning in life.

consumer cultures: Cultures in which the core ideas and material objects relate to consumption and in which consumption is a primary source of meaning in life.

consumption: The process by which people obtain and use goods and services.

contagion: The spreading of something (such as a virus) from one person to another.

content analysis: Systematic and objective analysis of the content of cultural artifacts in print, visual, audio, and digital media, using both qualitative and quantitative analysis.

convenience samples: Readily available groups of people who fit the criteria for participating in a research project.

conversation analysis: The analysis of how people accomplish conversations.

conversation of gestures: Communication that involves few, if any, conscious thought processes.

corporate crime: Violation of the law by legal organizations, including antitrust violations and stock market violations.

cosmopolitan: Open to a variety of external and global influences.

countercultures: Groups that adhere to norms and values that may be incompatible with those of the dominant culture. They may, in fact, consciously and overtly act in opposition to the dominant culture.

crime: A violation of the criminal law.

criminalization: The process by which the legal system negatively sanctions some form of deviant behavior.

criminology: The study of all aspects of crime.

critical theories of race and racism: A set of ideas arguing that race continues to matter and that racism continues to exist and adversely affect people of color.

critical theory: A set of critical ideas derived from Marxian theory but focusing on culture rather than the economy.

crowd: A temporary gathering of a relatively large number of people in a common geographic location at a given time.

crowdfunding: Collective action in which people come together online from all across the country, or even the world, to financially support a common cause.

cryptocurrencies: A form of economic exchange that circulates without the oversight of a single authority, such as a central government.

cult: A new, innovative, small, voluntary, and exclusive religious tradition that was never associated with any religious organization.

cultural imperialism: The imposition of one culture, more or less consciously, on other cultures.

cultural relativism: The idea that aspects of culture, such as norms and values, need to be understood within the context of a person's own culture and that there are no universally accepted norms and values.

culture: A collection of ideas, values, practices, and material objects that mean a great deal to a group of people, even an entire society, and allow them to carry out their collective lives in relative order and harmony.

culture industry: The rationalized and bureaucratized structures that control modern culture.

culture jamming: The radical transformation of an intended message in popular culture, especially one associated with the mass media, to protest underlying realities of which consumers may be unaware.

culture war: A conflict that pits subcultures and countercultures against the dominant culture or that pits dominant groups within society against each other.

cumulative advantage: The process by which the most advantaged individuals are awarded the best opportunities, which increases inequality over time.

cyberactivism: Using social media and other internet-based communication methods to create, promote, or manage activism.

cyberbullying: The willful and repeated harm inflicted through the use of computers, cell phones, and other electronic devices.

cybercrime: Crime that targets computers, uses computers to commit traditional crimes, or uses computers to transmit illegal information and images.

cyberculture: An emerging online culture that has the characteristics of all cultures, including distinctive values and norms.

dangerous giants: Entities that have agency and the potential to disrupt and destroy the structures in which they find themselves.

death rate: The number of deaths per 1,000 people.

debunking: The task of the sociologist to look beneath and beyond social facades.

deindustrialization: The decline of manufacturing as well as a corresponding increase in various types of services.

deinstitutionalization: Weakened social norms, especially regarding the institution of marriage.

democracies: Political systems in which people within a given state vote to choose their leaders and, in some cases, vote on legislation.

demographers: Those who study population dynamics.

demographic transition: Population changes that are related to the shift from an agricultural society to a more industrialized and urbanized society.

demography: The scientific study of population, especially its growth and decline, as well as the movement of people.

denomination: A subgroup within a religion that has slightly different beliefs than other members of that religion.

dependent variable: A characteristic or measurement that is the result of manipulating an independent variable.

deprofessionalization: The process whereby a profession's power and autonomy, as well as high status and great wealth, decline, at least relative to the exalted position the profession once held.

descriptive statistics: Numerical data that allow researchers to see trends over time or compare differences between groups in order to describe some findings based on a phenomenon in the real world.

descriptive survey: A questionnaire or interview used to gather accurate information about those in a group, people in a given geographic area, or members of organizations.

desertification: A decline in the water supply as a result of the degradation and deterioration of soil and vegetation.

deviance: Any action, belief, or human characteristic that a large number of people who are members of a society or a social group consider to be a violation of group norms and for which the violator is likely to be censured or punished.

diaspora: The dispersal, typically involuntarily, of a racial or ethnic population from its traditional homeland over a wide geographic area.

dictatorships: States that are usually totalitarian and are ruled either by a single individual or by a small group of people.

differential association: A theory that focuses on the fact that people learn criminal behavior; therefore, it is crucial whom a person associates with.

direct democracies: Political systems in which people directly affected by a given decision have a say in that decision.

disasters: Events that suddenly, unexpectedly, and severely disrupt and harm the environment, the social structure, people, and their property.

discouraged workers: Those who have sought work within the last year or since their last job ended, if that was less than a year ago, and have not sought work in the last four weeks (and are therefore not in the labor force).

discreditable stigma: A stigma that the affected individual assumes is neither known about nor immediately perceivable.

discredited stigma: A stigma that the affected individual assumes is already known about or readily apparent.

discrimination: The unfavorable treatment of Black Americans and other minorities, either formally or informally, simply because of their race or some other such characteristic.

distribution of opportunities for rewards: How the opportunities to attain a certain socially valued object or status are spread throughout society.

distribution of rewards: How socially valued objects and statuses are spread throughout a given society.

divorce: A formal and legal mechanism that results in the termination of legal marriages.

domination: The probability or likelihood that commands will be obeyed by subordinates.

double consciousness: Among Black Americans, the sense of "two-ness," that is, of being both Black and American.

dramaturgy: The view that social life is a series of dramatic performances akin to those that take place in a theater and on a stage.

dyad: A two-person group.

dysfunctions: Observable consequences that negatively affect the ability of a given system to survive, adapt, or adjust.

economy: The social system involved in the production and distribution of a wide range of goods and services.

elite pluralism: The formation by political elites of similar interest groups and organizations that vie for power.

emergent norm theory: A theory arguing that, in light of some precipitating event, new norms emerge that guide the often nontraditional actions that characterize collective behavior.

emphasized femininity: A set of socially constructed ideas about "model womanhood" organized around accommodating the interests of men and the patriarchy.

empiricism: The gathering of information and evidence using one's senses, especially one's eyes and ears, to experience the social world.

endogamy: Marriage to someone with similar characteristics in terms of race, ethnicity, religion, education level, social class, and so on.

environmental activism: Action directed toward the protection, preservation, or improving the health of our natural physical surroundings.

environmental racism: The disproportionate exposure of racial minorities to polluted air, water, and soil.

ethics: A set of beliefs concerning right and wrong in the choices that people make and the ways in which those choices are justified.

ethnic cleansing: The establishment by the dominant group of policies that allow or require the forcible removal of people of another ethnic group.

ethnic groups: Groups typically defined based on some cultural characteristic, such as language, religion, traditions, or cultural practices.

ethnicity: A sense, shared by members of a group, of belonging to and identifying with a given ethnic group.

ethnocentrism: The belief that one's own group or culture—including its norms, values, customs, and so on—is superior to, or better than, others.

ethnography: Observational (sometimes participatory) research, usually intensive and conducted over lengthy periods, that leads to an account of what people do and how they live.

ethnomethodology: An inter/actionist theory focusing on what people do rather than on what they think.

ethnoscapes: Landscapes that allow the movement, or fantasies about movement, of various individuals and groups.

eugenics: A movement that became popular in the early twentieth century and that argued that the human population could be genetically improved through scientific manipulation.

exchange relationships: Stable and persistent bonds between individuals who interact, generally formed because their interactions are rewarding.

exchange theory: A set of ideas related to the rewards and costs associated with human behavior.

exogamy: Marriage to someone with characteristics that are dissimilar in terms of race, ethnicity, religion, education level, social class, and so on.

experiment: The manipulation of a characteristic under study (an independent variable) to examine its effect on another characteristic (the dependent variable).

explanatory survey: A questionnaire or interview used to uncover potential causes for some observation.

explanatory theories: Theories of deviance (or some other social phenomenon) that try to explain why it occurs.

exploitation: A feature of capitalism in which the workers (proletariat) produce virtually everything but get few rewards, while the capitalists, who do little, reap the vast majority of the rewards.

expulsion: Removal of a minority group from a territory, either by forcible ejection through military and other government action or by "voluntary" emigration due to the majority's harassment, discrimination, and persecution.

extended family: Two or more generations of a family living in the same household or in proximity to one another.

extradition: The process whereby one jurisdiction returns a suspected criminal to another jurisdiction.

fact: A piece of knowledge about the world that can be proven by scientific methods.

failed state: A state experiencing extreme problems such as lack of control over its own territory, widespread corruption and criminality, economic recession and/or hyperinflation, failure to provide basic services, and large flows of refugees and internally displaced persons.

false consciousness: In capitalism, the proletariat's lack of understanding of capitalism's nature and the erroneous belief that capitalism operates to workers' benefit.

families of choice: Families made up of individuals who are not related either by blood or a legal bond but who still consider themselves to be a family.

family: A group of two people or more (one of whom is the householder) related by birth, marriage, or adoption and residing together.

fantasy city: A city in which great emphasis is placed on creating a spectacle, especially in the areas of consumption, leisure, tourism, and impressive buildings and other real estate developments.

felonies: Serious crimes punishable by a year or more in prison.

female proletarianization: The channeling of an increasing number of women into low-status, poorly paid manual work.

feminism: The belief that women are equal to men, especially socially, politically, and economically.

feminist theory: A set of ideas critical of the social situation confronting women and offering solutions for improving, if not revolutionizing, their situation.

feminization of labor: The rise of female labor participation in all sectors and the movement of women into jobs traditionally held by men.

feminization of poverty: The rise in the number of women falling below the poverty line.

fertility: People's reproductive behavior, especially the number of births.

fertility rate: The average number of live births per woman.

field experiments: Research that occurs in natural situations but allows researchers to exert at least some control over who participates and what happens during the experiment.

financescapes: Landscapes that use various financial instruments to allow huge sums of money and other things of economic value to move into and across nations and around the world at great speed, almost instantaneously.

folkways: Norms that are relatively unimportant and, if violated, carry few, if any, sanctions.

food insecurity: Lack of sufficient access to safe and nutritious food.

Fordism: The ideas, principles, and systems created by Henry Ford (who is credited with the development of the modern mass production system) and his associates at the beginning of the twentieth century.

foreign aid: Economic assistance given by countries or global institutions to a foreign country in order to promote its development and social welfare.

franchise system: A method of distributing goods and services in which a large company grants trademark and branding rights to many smaller entities that operate as legally independent businesses.

front stage: The part of the social world where the social performance is idealized and designed to define the situation for those who observe it.

functions: Observable, positive consequences that help a system survive, adapt, or adjust.

fundamentalism: A strongly held belief in the fundamental or foundational precepts of any religion, or a rejection of the modern secular world.

game stage: Mead's second stage in the socialization process, in which a child develops a self in the full sense of the term because it is then that the child begins to take on the role of a group of people simultaneously rather than the roles of discrete individuals.

gated communities: Communities in which gates, surveillance cameras, and guards provide the residents with a feeling of security from the problems (crime, panhandling) they think they left behind in the city.

gemeinschaft societies: Traditional societies characterized by face-to-face relations.

gender: The physical, behavioral, and personality characteristics that are socially defined as appropriate for one's sex.

gender fluid: An individual who may feel that their gender identities change depending on the context

gender identity: A person's internal sense of gender.

genderqueer: A broad umbrella term that encompasses a range of gendered identities, feelings, and self-determined labels.

gender role: The social presentation of gender, which includes clothing, hairstyle, and attitudinal and behavioral traits.

general deterrence: The deterrence of the population as a whole from committing crimes, for fear they will be punished or imprisoned for their actions.

generalized other: The attitude of the entire group or community taken by individuals in the process of developing their own behaviors and attitudes.

genocide: An active, systematic attempt to eliminate an entire group of people.

gentrification: The reinvestment of real estate capital in blighted inner-city areas to rebuild residences and create a new infrastructure for the well-to-do.

geopolitics: Political relationships that involve large geographic areas or the globe as a whole.

gesellschaft societies: Modern societies characterized by impersonal, distant, and limited social relationships.

gestures: Movements of one animal or human that elicit a mindless, automatic, and appropriate response from another animal or human.

gig economy: Short-term freelance work, usually with and through digital platforms.

glass ceiling: A certain level of authority in a male-dominated company or organization beyond which women are unable to rise.

global care chains: Series of personal relationships between people across the globe based on the paid or unpaid work of caring.

global cities: The cities, especially New York City, London, and Tokyo, with the world's leading industries and marketplaces.

global ethnography: A type of ethnography that is "grounded" in various parts of the world and that seeks to understand globalization as it exists in people's social lives.

globalization: The increasing fluidity of global flows and the structures that expedite and impede those flows.

group: A relatively small number of people who over time develop a patterned relationship based on interaction with one another.

group pluralism: The competition of society's various interest groups and organizations for access to political power in an attempt to further their interests.

habitus: An internalized set of preferences and dispositions learned through experience and social interactions in specific social contexts.

hate crimes: Crimes that stem from the fact that the victims are in various ways different from, and disesteemed by, the perpetrators.

Hawthorne Effect: The degree to which individuals change their behaviors when they know they are being observed.

heat islands: Urbanized areas that experience higher temperatures than surrounding areas.

hegemonic masculinity: The dominant form or most idealized vision of masculinity; taken for granted as natural and linked to the patriarchy.

heterosexism: The belief that heterosexuality is superior to other sexual orientations; individual and institutional discrimination against those with other orientations.

hidden curriculum: A school's unofficial norms, routines, and structures that transmit dominant cultural norms and values.

hidden curriculum: Lessons about order, authority, and conformity that are taught informally to students through the education system.

high culture: Cultural elements typically associated with elites.

high-income economies: Economies in countries with the highest wealth and income in the world.

historical-comparative research: A research methodology that contrasts how different historical events and conditions in various societies (or components of societies) lead to different societal outcomes.

homophobia: The fear of being, appearing, or seeming gay; fear of anyone or "anything" gay.

honor killing: The sanctioned killing of a female because she has engaged in such "dishonorable" behaviors as infidelity, same-sex sexual relations, wanting out of arranged marriages, seeking marriage on her own, or refusing to adhere to a particular dress code.

horizontal mobility: Movement within one's social class.

human trafficking: The selling and buying of humans as products.

hyperconsumption: Consumption of more than one needs, really wants, and can afford.

"I": The immediate response of an individual to others; the part of the self that is incalculable, unpredictable, and creative.

ideal culture: Norms and values indicating what members of a society should believe in and do.

ideal type: An exaggeratedly rational model that is used to study real-world phenomena.

identity politics: The use of a minority group's power to strengthen the position of the cultural group with which it identifies.

ideology: A set of shared beliefs that explains the social world and guides people's actions.

ideoscapes: Landscapes that include images, largely political images, often in line with the ideologies of nation-states.

imagined communities: Communities socially constructed by those who see themselves as part of them.

impoverished: Made to be poor through the actions of others.

impression management: People's use of a variety of techniques to control the images of themselves that they want to project during their social performances.

income: The amount of money a person earns in a given year from a job, a business, or various types of assets and investments.

independent variable: In an experiment, a condition that can be independently manipulated by the researcher with the goal of producing a change in some other variable.

individualist culture: A culture that prioritizes the rights and freedoms of individuals over the larger group.

individualized marriage: A model of marriage emphasizing the satisfaction of the individuals involved.

inequality: The condition whereby some positions in society yield a great deal of money, status, and power while others yield little, if any, of these.

infanticide: The murder of a child less than 1 year old.

inferential statistics: Numerical data that allow researchers to use data from a small group to speculate with some level of certainty about a larger group.

informal organization: How an organization actually works, as opposed to the way it is supposed to work.

informationalism: The processing of knowledge.

informed (or effective) sexual consent: Participants' understanding of and free consent to specific sexual activities in a mutually understandable way.

informed consent: Consent given by a participant to be studied, with knowledge of the potential harms and benefits they might experience in the course of the research.

in-group: A group to which people belong and with which they identify, perhaps strongly.

innovators: Individuals who accept cultural goals but reject conventional means of achieving success.

institutional racism: Race-based discrimination that results from the day-to-day operation of social institutions and social structures and their rules, policies, and practices.

interaction: A social engagement that involves two or more individuals who perceive, and orient their actions to, one another.

interaction order: An area of interaction that is organized and orderly but in which the order is created informally by those involved in the interaction rather than by some formal structure.

intergenerational mobility: The difference between the parents' social class position and the position achieved by their child(ren).

intersectionality: The idea that members of any given minority (or majority) group are affected by the nature of their position in other systems or other forms of social inequality. It implies that in order to more fully understand the social experience of an individual we need to account for the multiplicity of their identities.

intersex: A general term used for a variety of medical conditions in which a person is born with reproductive or sexual anatomy that does not seem to fit the typical definitions of male or female.

interviews: A research method in which information is sought from participants (respondents) who are asked a series of questions that have been formulated, at least to some degree, before the research is conducted.

intimacy: A close and personal relationship built over time.

intimate partner violence (IPV): Also known as domestic violence, it entails the exertion of power over a partner in an intimate relationship through behavior that is intimidating, threatening, harassing, or harmful.

intimate relationship: A close, personal, and domestic relationship between partners.

intragenerational mobility: Movement up or down the stratification system in one's lifetime.

irrationality of rationality: irrational practices (such as "red tape" or extreme rule-following) that sometimes accompany the seemingly rational actions of an organization.

key informant: A person who has intimate knowledge of the group being studied.

knowledge management: A strategy for hiding a discreditable stigma by withholding information, avoiding certain situations, or lying.

labeling theory: A theory contending that a deviant is someone to whom a deviant label has been successfully applied.

laboratory experiments: Research that occurs in a laboratory, giving the researcher great control over both the selection of the participants to be studied and the conditions to which they are exposed.

labor migrants: Those who migrate because they are driven by either "push" factors (a lack of work, low pay) in their homeland or "pull" factors (jobs and higher pay available elsewhere).

landscapes (scapes): Fluid, irregular, and variable global flows that produce different results throughout the world.

language: A set of meaningful symbols that makes possible the communication of culture as well as communication more generally within a given culture.

latent functions: Unintended positive consequences.

laws: Norms that have been codified, or written down, and are formally enforced through institutions such as the state.

legacy students: Students given preferential admission to an educational institution because a parent or other family member attended that same institution.

leisure: A means of escape from the obligations associated with work and family, involving social activities that are uncoerced, relaxing, and perhaps informative and that are set apart from work in time and often in space.

life expectancy: The average number of years an individual can be expected to live in a population.

liminal period: A special time set apart from ordinary reality.

living apart together: A committed intimate relationship in which a couple do not reside in the same physical residence.

local: Inward looking rather than outward looking.

lockdown struggler: A student during the COVID-19 pandemic whose academic performance suffered significantly because of lack of access to technology, overcrowded or noisy living conditions, economic struggles, or anxiety.

lockdown survivor: A student during the COVID-19 pandemic who adjusted to virtual learning adequately but needed to return to in-person learning in order to regain their prior level of academic performance.

lockdown thriver: A student during the COVID-19 pandemic who was adept at independent learning and living in a household with quality computer technology and significant cultural capital.

looking-glass self: The self-image that reflects how others respond to a person, particularly as a child.

low-income economies: Economies in countries with the lowest levels of income in the world, defined by the World Bank as a gross national income per capita below $1,046.

macro: Macroscopic; used to describe large-scale social phenomena, such as groups, organizations, cultures, society, and the globe.

macrofinance: The globalization of money and finance.

majority group: A group in a dominant position along the dimensions of wealth, power, and prestige.

majority-minority population: A population in which more than 50 percent of the members are part of a minority group.

manifest functions: Positive consequences that are brought about consciously and purposely.

marriage: The legally or formally recognized union of two (or more) individuals in a relationship.

mass culture: Cultural elements that are administered by large organizations, lack spontaneity, and are phony.

mass production: Production characterized by large numbers of standardized products, highly specialized workers, interchangeable machine parts, precision tools, a high-volume mechanized production process, and the synchronization of the flow of materials used in production, with the entire process made as continuous as possible.

master status: A position that is more important than any others, both for the person in the position and for all others involved.

material culture: All the material objects that are reflections or manifestations of a culture.

matrix of oppression: An overlapping system of social inequalities that impacts an individual's standing in the social world.

McDonaldization: The process by which the rational principles of the fast-food restaurant are coming to dominate more and more sectors of society and more societies throughout the world.

"me": The organized set of others' attitudes assumed by the individual; involves the adoption by the individual of the generalized other.

mechanical solidarity: Cohesion among a group of people based on the fact that they all do essentially the same things.

mediascapes: Landscapes that include the electronic capability to produce and transmit information and images around the world.

mediated interaction: Social interaction in which technological devices come between the participants, unlike in face-to-face interaction.

medicalization: The process of labeling and defining aspects of life as medical problems that were not previously so labeled and defined.

medical sociology: A field concerned with the social causes and consequences of health and illness.

megacities: Cities with populations greater than 10 million.

megalopolis: A cluster of highly populated cities that can stretch over great distances.

meritocracy: A system based on a dominant ideology involving the widely shared belief that all people have an equal chance of succeeding economically based on their hard work and skills.

meso: Mesoscopic; used to describe middle or intermediate social phenomena, such as individuals' relationships to specific networks or organizations.

metropolis: A large, powerful, and culturally influential urban area that contains a central city and surrounding communities that are economically and socially linked to the center.

micro: Microscopic; used to describe small-scale social phenomena, such as individuals and their thoughts and actions.

micro–macro continuum: The range of social entities from the individual, even the mind and self, to the interaction among individuals, the groups often formed by that interaction, formally structured organizations, societies, and increasingly, the global domain.

middle-income economies: Economies in countries with income that is average for the world.

migration: The movements of people and their impact on the sending and receiving locales.

mind: An internal conversation that arises in relation to, and is continuous with, interactions, especially conversations that one has with others in the social world.

minority group: A group in a subordinate position in terms of wealth, power, and prestige.

misdemeanors: Minor offenses punishable by imprisonment of less than a year.

mixed methods research: Combining qualitative and quantitative methods in a single study.

modernization theory: A structural-functionalist theory that explains unequal economic distributions based on the structural (especially technological) and cultural differences between countries.

monogamy: Marriage or exclusive sexual relationships between two individuals.

monopoly capitalism: A form of capitalism in which huge corporations monopolize the market.

moral entrepreneurs: Individuals or groups who come to define an act as a moral outrage and who lead a campaign to have it defined as deviant and to have it made illegal and therefore subject to legal enforcement.

moral panic: A widespread and disproportionate reaction to a form of deviance.

morbidity: Illness and disease, and the rates at which they occur within a population.

mores: Important norms whose violation is likely to be met with severe sanctions.

mortality: Deaths and death rates within a population.

multiculturalism: The encouragement of cultural differences within a given environment, both by the state and by the majority group.

nation: A group of people who share, often over a long period of time, similar cultural, religious, ethnic, and linguistic characteristics.

nation-state: The combination of a nation with a geographic and political structure; encompasses both the populations that define themselves as a nation with various shared characteristics and the organizational structure of the state.

natural experiments: Experiments that occur when researchers take advantage of a naturally occurring event to study its effect on one or more dependent variables.

natural growth: A child-raising approach in which children spend more time in self-directed play than in organized educational opportunities.

netnography: An ethnographic method in which the internet becomes the research site and what transpires there is the sociologist's research interest.

network organization: A new organizational form that is flat and horizontal, is intertwined with other organizations, is run and managed in very different ways from traditional organizations, uses more flexible production methods, and is composed of a series of interconnected nodes.

networks: Interconnected nodes that are open, capable of unlimited expansion, dynamic, and able to innovate without disrupting the system in which they exist.

new religious movements: Movements that attract zealous religious converts, follow charismatic leaders, appeal to an atypical portion of the population, have a tendency to differentiate between "us" and "them," are characterized by distrust of others, and are prone to rapid fundamental changes.

nonfamily household: A household consisting of a person who lives either alone or with nonrelatives.

nonmaterial culture: Elements of culture that we can not necessarily see or touch, such as ideas and beliefs.

nonparticipant observation: A research method in which the sociologist plays little or no role in what is being observed.

nonresident parents: Fathers and mothers who live apart from their children.

norms: Informal rules that guide what members of a culture do in given situations and how they live.

nuclear family: A family with two married adults and one or more children.

obesity: A form of malnutrition caused by excessive intake of nutrients, especially calories.

observation: A research method that involves systematically watching, listening to, and recording what takes place in a natural social setting over some (extended) period of time.

occupational mobility: Changes in people's work, either across or within generations.

offshore outsourcing: The transfer of work to organizations in other countries.

oligarchy: An organization with a small group of people at the top obtaining, and exercising, far more power than they are supposed to have.

"one drop" rule: The notion that a person with the slightest trace of African ancestry is considered to be Black. (Also known as the "one Black ancestor" rule.)

opinion: A perspective of a particular individual or group that is based on feelings or beliefs with or without any scientific evidence to support it.

organic solidarity: Cohesion among a group of people based on their need for what others do and produce in order to survive.

organizations: Collectives purposely constructed to achieve particular ends.

organized crime: Crime that may involve various types of organizations but is most often associated with syndicated organized crime that uses violence (or its threat) and the corruption of public officials to profit from illegal activities.

Orientalism: A set of ideas and texts produced in the West that served as the basis for dominating, controlling, and exploiting the Orient (the East) and its many minority groups.

out-group: A group to which outsiders (at least from the perspective of the in-group) belong.

outsider-within: A person who has formal membership in a majority group without being given the full informal rights of other members.

outsourcing: The transfer of activities once performed by one organization to another organization in exchange for money.

pandemic pedagogy: Ways in which teaching and learning are realized during a global health crisis.

paper ceiling: An invisible barrier that makes it difficult for those without at least a bachelor's degree to advance in their professional careers.

paradigm: A general model of the world accepted by most practitioners in the field.

parole: The supervised early release of a prisoner for such things as good behavior while in prison.

participant observation: A research method in which the researcher actually plays a role, even a minor one, in the group or setting being observed.

passionate love: A kind of love typified by sudden onset, strong sexual feelings, and idealization of the one who is loved.

play stage: Mead's first stage in the socialization process, in which children learn to take on the attitudes of specific others toward themselves.

pluralism: The coexistence of many groups without any of them losing their individual qualities.

pluralism: A political system in which there is a balance of power among many competing interests, none of which has complete control.

political crimes: Crimes involving either illegal offenses against the state to affect its policies or offenses by the state, whether domestically or internationally.

politics: Societal competition through established governmental channels to determine which group's members get what, as well as when and how they get it.

polyandry: Marriage (of a wife) to multiple husbands.

polygamy: Marriage to multiple spouses.

polygyny: Marriage (of a husband) to multiple wives.

popular culture: Cultural elements that typically have broader appeal to the masses.

postconsumer culture: A culture characterized by less consumption in general, less conspicuous consumption, more saving and sharing, and more concern for the environment in terms of what is consumed.

post-Fordism: A production environment associated with smaller production runs of more specialized products, especially those high in style and quality; more flexible machinery made possible by advances in technology largely traceable to the computer; more skilled workers with greater flexibility and autonomy; less reliance on economies of scale; and more differentiated markets for those more specialized products.

postindustrial society: A society that was at one time industrial but the focus on the manufacture of goods has been replaced by an increase, at least initially, in service work—that is, work in which people are involved in providing services for one another rather than producing goods.

postmodernism: The emergence of new and different cultural forms in music, movies, art, architecture, and the like.

postmodernity: The state of having moved beyond the modern era analyzed by the classic social theorists and into a new postmodern epoch characterized by less rationality and more eclecticism.

postmodern theory: A set of ideas oriented in opposition to modern theory by, for example, rejecting or deconstructing the grand narratives of modern social theory.

poverty: Lack of resources to meet basic human needs.

poverty line: The threshold, in terms of income, below which a household is considered poor.

power: The ability to get others to do what you want them to do, even if it is against their will.

power elite theory: A theory holding that power is not dispersed throughout a stable society but is concentrated in a small number of people who control the major institutions of the state, the corporate economy, and the military.

prejudice: Negative attitudes, beliefs, and feelings toward individuals.

primary deviance: Early, nonpatterned acts of deviance, or an act here or there that is considered to be strange or out of the ordinary.

primary groups: Groups that are small, are close-knit, and have intimate face-to-face interaction.

primary socialization: The acquisition of language, identities, gender roles, cultural routines, norms, and values from parents and other family members at the earliest stages of an individual's life.

probation: A system by which those who are convicted of less serious crimes may be released into the community but under supervision and under certain conditions, such as being involved in and completing a substance abuse program.

profane: To Durkheim, what has not been defined as sacred, or what is ordinary and mundane.

profession: An occupation distinguished from other occupations mainly by its power and considerable autonomy.

professional sociologist: A person who has a deep body of knowledge about the social world and a refined skill set to better analyze that world.

proletariat: Workers as a group, or those in the capitalist system who own little or nothing except for their capacity for work (labor), which they must sell to the capitalists in order to survive.

property crimes: Crimes that do not involve injury or force but rather the theft or destruction of property.

prosumer: A consumer who produces value in the process of consumption; one who combines the acts of consumption and production.

Protestant ethic: A belief in hard work, frugality, and good work as means to achieve both economic success and heavenly salvation.

pure relationship: A relationship that is entered into for what each partner can get from it and in which those involved remain only as long as each derives enough satisfaction from it.

qualitative research: Research methods employed in natural settings that produce in-depth, descriptive information (e.g., in respondents' own words) about the social world.

quantitative research: Research methods that involve the analysis of numerical data, usually derived from surveys and experiments.

queer theory: A theory based on the idea that there are no fixed and stable identities (such as "heterosexual" or "homosexual") that determine who we are; a diverse group of ideas about how cultures develop gender and sexuality norms, notions of conformity, and power relations.

questionnaires: Usually self-administered, written sets of questions.

race: A social definition based on some real or presumed physical or biological characteristic of a person, such as skin color or hair texture, as well as a shared lineage.

racism: The act of defining a group as a race and attributing negative characteristics to that group.

random sample: A subset of a population in which every member of the group has an equal chance of being included.

rape: Penetration, no matter how slight, of the vagina or anus with any body part or object, or oral penetration with a sex organ of another person, without the consent of the victim.

rape culture: An environment conducive to sexual assaults and rape.

rational choice theory: A set of ideas that sees people as rational and as acting purposively to achieve their goals.

rationalization: The process by which social structures are increasingly characterized by the most direct and efficient means to their ends.

rational-legal authority: Authority that is legitimated on the basis of legally enacted rules and the right of those with authority under those rules to issue commands.

real culture: What people actually think and do in their everyday lives.

rebels: Individuals who reject both traditional means and goals and instead substitute nontraditional goals and means to achieve those goals.

recidivism: The repetition of a criminal act by one convicted of a prior offense.

reciprocity: The expectation that those involved in an interaction will give and receive rewards of roughly equal value.

reference groups: Groups that people take into consideration when evaluating themselves.

reflexivity: The habit of self-examination and reflection.

refugees: Migrants who are forced to leave their homeland or who leave involuntarily because they fear for their safety.

relative poverty: The state of being or feeling poor relative to others, irrespective of income.

reliability: The degree to which a given question (or another kind of measure) produces the same results time after time.

religion: A social phenomenon that consists of beliefs about the sacred; the experiences, practices, and rituals that reinforce those beliefs; and the communities that share similar beliefs and practices.

replacement-level fertility: The number of live births needed to replace the population.

representative democracies: Political systems in which people, as a whole body, do not actually rule themselves but rather have some say in who will best represent them in the state.

resocialization: The unlearning of old behaviors, norms, and values and the learning of new ones.

resource mobilization theory: An approach to understanding social movements that focuses on what groups of people need to do to mobilize to bring about social change.

retreatists: Individuals who reject both cultural goals and the traditional routes to their attainment; they have completely given up on attaining success within the system.

reverse socialization: The socialization of those who normally do the socializing—for example, children socializing their parents.

revolution: a social movement in which the strains caused by breakdown of the state lead to mass mobilization and a new social/political order.

riot: A temporary unruly collective behavior that causes damage to persons or property.

risk society: A society in which central issues involve risks and ways to protect oneself from them.

rites of passage: Events, usually rituals, that surround major transitions in life, such as birth, puberty, marriage, and death.

ritualists: Individuals who realize that they will not be able to achieve cultural goals but who nonetheless continue to engage in the conventional behavior associated with such success.

rituals: Sets of regularly repeated, prescribed, and traditional behaviors that serve to symbolize some value or belief.

role: What is generally expected of a person who occupies a given status.

role conflict: Conflicting expectations associated with a given position or multiple positions.

role making: The ability of people to modify their roles, at least to some degree.

role overload: Confrontation with more expectations than a person can possibly handle.

rule creators: Individuals who devise society's rules, norms, and laws.

rule enforcers: Individuals who threaten to or actually enforce the rules.

sacred: To Durkheim, what is extraordinary, set aside, and of ultimate concern and leads to awe and reverence.

sample: A representative portion of the overall population.

sanctions: The application of rewards (positive sanctions) or punishments (negative sanctions) when norms are accepted or violated.

Sapir-Whorf hypothesis: The idea that our ability to understand and experience the world around us is shaped by our knowledge of language.

scientific method: A structured way to find answers to questions about the world.

secondary data analysis: Reanalysis of data, often survey data, collected by others, including other sociologists.

secondary deviance: Deviant acts that persist, become more common, and eventually cause people to organize their lives and personal identities around their deviant status.

secondary groups: Generally large, impersonal groups in which ties are relatively weak and members do not know one another very well, and whose impact on members is typically not very powerful.

second shift: the household chores, such as cleaning, cooking, or child care, required of working people (usually women) in addition to their paid employment

sect: A small group of people who have joined a group consciously and voluntarily to have a personal religious experience.

secularization: The declining significance of religion.

segregation: The physical and social separation of majority and minority groups.

self: The sense of oneself as an object.

separation of powers: The separation and counterbalancing of different branches of government so that no one branch of government can wield too much power.

sex: A biological term, expressed as *female* or *male*; typically reflected in chromosomes, gonads, genitalia, and hormones.

sex tourism: Activity that occurs when individuals travel to other countries for the purpose of buying sex from men, women, and children in those locations; sex is the primary or sole purpose of these trips.

sex trafficking: A commercial sex act that includes force, fraud, or coercion and transporting and obtaining a person for sex acts.

sexual assault: Sexual acts of domination, usually enacted by men against women, other men, and children.

sexual double standard: A cultural belief system in which men are expected to desire and seek sex from whomever, whenever they wish, while women are expected to be sexual only within committed, romantic relationships.

sexual harassment: Unwanted sexual attention that takes place in the workplace or other settings.

sexual identity: An internal sense of one's sexual self.

sexuality: The ways in which people think about, and behave toward, themselves and others as sexual beings.

sexual orientation: Involves whom one desires (fantasies), with whom one wants to have sexual relations (behavior), and with whom one has a sense of connectedness (feelings).

significant symbol: A gesture that arouses in the individual making it a response of the same kind as the one it is supposed to elicit from those to whom it is addressed.

simulation: An inauthentic or fake version of something.

situation management: A strategy for minimizing a discredited stigma, such as deliberately drawing attention to it or using humor to diffuse social tension.

social change: Variations over time in every aspect of the social world, ranging from changes affecting individuals to transformations having an impact on the globe as a whole.

social class: One's economic position in the stratification system, especially one's occupation, which strongly determines and reflects one's income and wealth.

social construction of reality: The continuous process of individual creation of structural realities and the constraint and coercion exercised by those structures.

social control: The process by which a group or society enforces conformity to its demands and expectations.

social control agents: Those who label a person as deviant.

social facts: Macro-level phenomena—social structures and cultural norms and values—that stand apart from and impose themselves on people.

socialism: A historical stage following communism involving the effort by society to plan and organize production consciously and rationally so that all members of society benefit from it.

socialization: The process through which a person learns and generally comes to accept the ways of a group or of society as a whole.

social mobility: The ability or inability to change one's position in the social hierarchy.

social movement: A sustained and intentional collective effort, usually operating outside established institutional channels, either to bring about or to retard social change.

social processes: The dynamic and ever-changing aspects of the social world.

social sciences: The various scholarly fields that study various aspects of human society and social relationships.

social stratification: Hierarchical differences and inequalities in economic positions, as well as in other important areas, especially political power and status or social honor.

social structures: Enduring and regular social arrangements, such as the family and the state.

society: A complex pattern of social relationships that is bounded in space and persists over time.

sociological imagination: A unique perspective that gives sociologists a distinctive way of looking at data and reflecting on the world around them.

sociology: The systematic study of the ways in which people are affected by and affect the social structures and social processes associated with the groups, organizations, cultures, societies, and world in which they exist.

specific deterrence: Deterrence from criminal behavior based on the concept that the experience of punishment in general, and incarceration in particular, makes it less likely that an individual will commit crimes in the future.

state: the political body organized for government and civil rule.

statistics: The mathematical method used to analyze numerical data.

status: A dimension of the social stratification system that relates to the prestige attached to people's positions within society.

stepfamily: A family in which two adults are married or cohabiting and at least one of them has a child or children from a previous marriage or cohabitation living with him or her.

stereotype: An exaggerated generalization about an entire category of people that is thought to apply to everyone in that category.

stigma: A person's characteristic that others find, define, and often label as unusual, unpleasant, or deviant.

strain theory: A theory based on the idea that the discrepancy between the larger structure of society and the means available to people to achieve what the society considers to be of value produces strain that may cause an individual to undertake deviant acts.

stratified sample: A sample created when a larger group is divided into a series of subgroups and then random samples are taken within each of these groups.

strength of weak ties: The idea that mere acquaintances within a group can provide important linkages.

structural-functionalism: A set of ideas focused on social structures as well as the functions and dysfunctions that such structures perform.

structuralism: A social theory interested in the social impact of hidden or underlying structures.

structural mobility: The effect of changes in the larger society on the position of individuals in the stratification system, especially the occupational structure.

subcultures: Groups of people who accept much of the dominant culture but are set apart from it by one or more culturally significant characteristics.

suburbanization: The process whereby large numbers of people move out of the city and into nearby, less densely populated environs.

suburbs: Communities adjacent to, but outside the political boundaries of, large central cities.

survey research: A research methodology that involves the collection of information from a population, or more usually a representative portion of a population, through the use of interviews and, more important, questionnaires.

sustainable development: Economic and environmental changes that meet the needs of the present, especially of the world's poor, without jeopardizing the ability to meet the needs of the future.

symbol: A word, gesture, or object that stands in for something or someone (a "label").

symbolic culture: Various symbols that we use to represent cultural norms and values.

symbolic interaction: Interaction on the basis of not only gestures but also significant symbols.

symbolic interactionism: A sociological perspective focusing on the role of symbols and how their meanings are shared and understood by those involved in human interaction.

systemic issues: Underlying factors that help explain the way society operates.

technology: The interplay of machines, tools, skills, and procedures for the accomplishment of tasks.

technoscapes: Landscapes that use mechanical and informational technologies as well as the material that moves quickly and freely through them.

telemedicine: Using technology to consult with doctors, such as an online video call, rather than going to a physical office.

terrorism: Acts of violence by nongovernmental actors that target noncombatants, property, or military personnel to influence politics.

theories: Sets of interrelated ideas that have a wide range of application, deal with centrally important issues, and have stood the test of time.

total institution: A closed, all-encompassing place of residence and work set off from the rest of society that meets all of the needs of those enclosed within it.

tracking: Grouping students by ability, which is typically measured by standardized test scores and/or grades.

traditional authority: Authority based on a belief in long-running traditions.

transgender: An umbrella term for people whose gender identity and/or gender presentation differs from the gender assigned at birth or in infancy.

transnational capitalism: An economic system in which transnational economic practices predominate.

triad: A three-person group.

unanticipated consequences: Unexpected social effects, especially negative effects.

underemployment: Employment in jobs that are not consonant with one's training and ability, such as part-time work when one is capable and desirous of full-time work, or in jobs that are not fully occupying.

undernutrition: A form of malnutrition involving an inadequate intake of nutrients, including calories, vitamins, and minerals.

undocumented immigrants: Immigrants residing in a receiving country without valid authorization.

unemployment: The state of being economically active and in the labor force, being able and willing to work, and seeking employment but being unable to find a job.

upward mobility: The ability to change one's position in the social hierarchy by moving higher.

urban: City dwelling; in the United States, to be considered urban, an area must have more than 50,000 inhabitants.

urbanism: The distinctive way of life (lifestyles, attitudes, social relationships) that emerges in, and is closely associated with, urban areas.

urbanization: The process by which an increasing percentage of a society's population comes to be located in relatively densely populated urban areas.

validity: The degree to which a question (or another kind of measure) gets an accurate response or measures what it is supposed to measure.

values: General and abstract standards defining what a group or society as a whole considers good, desirable, right, or important—in short, its ideals.

vertical mobility: Both upward and downward mobility.

violent crime: Crime that involves the threat of injury or the threat or actual use of force, including murder, rape, robbery, and aggravated assault, as well as terrorism and, globally, war crimes.

vouchers: Government-issued certificates that allow students to use public tax dollars to pay tuition at private schools.

wealth: The total amount of a person's assets less the total of various kinds of debts.

welfare states: States that seek both to run their economic markets efficiently, as capitalism does, and to do so equitably, which capitalism does not do.

white-collar crimes: Crimes committed by responsible and (usually) high-social-status people in the course of their work.

white racial frame: An array of racist ideas, racial stereotypes, racialized stories and tales, racist images, powerful racial emotions, and various inclinations to discriminate against minority races, especially Black people.

world-systems theory: A system of thought that focuses on the stratification of nation-states on a global scale.

worldview: A culture's most comprehensive image of the ways in which life—nature, self, and society—is ordered.

REFERENCES

Abdill, Aasha. 2018. *Fathering from the Margins*. New York: Columbia University Press.

Abercrombie, Sarah H., and Sarah L. Hastings. 2016. "Feminization of Poverty." In *Wiley-Blackwell Encyclopedia of Gender and Sexuality Studies*, edited by Nancy Naples. Malden, MA: Wiley-Blackwell (published online first).

Abi-Habib, Maria, and Hari Kumar. 2018. "Deadly Tensions Rise as India's Water Supply Runs Dangerously Low." *New York Times*, June 17.

Acemoglu, Daron, and James A. Robinson. 2012. *Why Nations Fail: The Origins of Power, Prosperity, and Poverty*. New York: Crown Business.

Acemoglu, Daron, and Pierre Yared. 2010. "Political Limits to Globalization." Working Paper 15694, National Bureau of Economic Research, Cambridge, MA. Accessed March 28, 2012. http://www.nber.org/papers/w15694.

Acierno, Ron, Melba A. Hernandez, Ananda B. Amstadter, Heidi S. Resnick, Kenneth Steve, Wendy Muzzy, and Dean G. Kilpatrick. 2010. "Prevalence and Correlates of Emotional, Physical, Sexual, and Financial Abuse and Potential Neglect in the United States: The National Elder Mistreatment Study." *American Journal of Public Health* 100: 292–297.

Acker, James. 2017. "Taking Stock of Innocence: Movements, Mountains, and Wrongful Convictions." *Journal of Contemporary Criminal Justice* 33(1): 8–25.

Acquittal in Hoax Call That Led to Sex Assault. 2006. NBC News, October 31. Accessed April 24, 2015. http://www.nbcnews.com/id/15504125/#.VTqGqiFVhBd

Adams, Margaret E., and Jacquelyn Campbell. 2012. "Being Undocumented and Intimate Partner Violence (IPV): Multiple Vulnerabilities through the Lens of Feminist Intersectionality." *Women's Health and Urban Life* 11(1): 15–34.

Adda, Jérôme, Christian Dustmann, and Katrien Stevens. 2017. "The Career Costs of Children." *Journal of Political Economy* 125(2): 293–337.

Addington, Lynn A., and Callie Marie Rennison. 2015. "Keeping the Barbarians Outside the Gate? Comparing Burglary Victimization in Gated and Non-gated Communities." *Justice Quarterly* 32(1): 168–192.

Adelman, M., and L. Ruggi. 2016. "The Sociology of the Body." *Current Sociology* 64(6): 907–930.

Adichie, Chimamanda Ngozi. 2015. *We Should All Be Feminists*. New York: Anchor Books.

Ahuvia, Aaron, and Elif Izberk-Bilgin. 2011. "Limits of the McDonaldization Thesis: EBayization and Ascendant Trends in Postindustrial Consumer Culture." *Consumption, Markets and Culture* 14: 361–364.

Aikau, Hokulani K., Karla Erickson, and Jennifer L. Pierce. 2018. "Feminism, First-, Second-, and Third-Wave." In *The International Encyclopedia of Anthropology*, edited by H. Callan. Oxford, UK: Wiley-Blackwell. doi:10.1002/9781118924396.wbiea1587

Akorsu, A. D. 2016. "Feminization of Labor." In *The Wiley Blackwell Encyclopedia of Gender and Sexuality Studies*, edited by A. Wong, M. Wickramasinghe, R. Hoogland, and N. A. Naples. Chicester, UK: Wiley.

Alatas, Syed Farid. 2011. "Ibn Khaldun." In *The Wiley-Blackwell Companion to Major Social Theorists*, Vol. 1, *Classical Theorists*, edited by George Ritzer and Jeffrey Stepnisky, 12–29. Malden, MA: Wiley-Blackwell.

Alatas, Syed Farid. 2013. *Ibn Khaldun*. New York: Oxford University Press.

Alatas, Syed Farid. 2014. *Applying Ibn Khaldun: The Recovery of a Lost Tradition in Sociology*. New York: Routledge.

Alba, Richard. 2009. *Blurring the Color Line: The New Chance for a More Integrated America*. Cambridge, MA: Harvard University Press.

Albright, Madeleine. 2018. *Fascism: A Warning*. New York: Harper.

Albrow, Martin. 1996. *The Global Age*. Cambridge, MA: Polity Press.

Alderman, Liz. 2016. "Smugglers Sense Opportunity as Borders Shut." *New York Times*, March 12.

Aldrich, Howard E., and Stephen Lippmann, 2018. "The McDonaldization of Everything: Teaching Weber to Undergraduates." *Entrepreneur and Innovation Exchange*, January 8.

Aleman, Ana M., and Katherine Link Wartman. 2008. *Online Social Networking on Campus: Understanding What Matters in Student Culture*. New York: Routledge.

Alexander, Karl, Doris Entwisle, and Linda Olson. 2014. *The Long Shadow: Family Background, Disadvantaged Urban Youth, and the Transition to Adulthood*. New York: Russell Sage Foundation.

Alexander, Michelle. 2012. *The New Jim Crow: Mass Incarceration in the Age of Colorblindness*. New York: Free Press.

Alger, Janet M., and Steven F. Alger. 1997. "Beyond Mead: Symbolic Interaction between Humans and Felines." *Society and Animals* 5(1): 65–81.

Allan, Stuart. 2007. "Network Society." In *The Blackwell Encyclopedia of Sociology*, edited by George Ritzer, 3180–3182. Malden, MA: Blackwell.

Alleyne, Brian. 2018. "Computer Hacking as a Social Problem." In *Cambridge Handbook of Social Problems*, edited by A. Javier Treviño, 127–142. Cambridge, UK: Cambridge University Press.

Allison, Christine Lynn. 2018. "Youth Entrepreneurship Education and Training (EET) Programmes: Realizing the Demographic Dividend." In *Youth Entrepreneurship and Africa's Sustainable Industrialization*, edited by Farai Kapfudzaruwa, Masafumi Nagao, and Emmanuel Mutisya. Denver, CO: Spears Media Press.

Altman, Dennis. 2001. *Global Sex*. Chicago: University of Chicago Press. Alvarez, Lizette. 2011. "Pull of Family Reshapes U.S.–Cuban Relations." *New York Times*, November 22.

American Cancer Society. 2018. "Does Body Weight Affect Cancer Risk?" Accessed April 24, 2019. https://www.cancer.org/cancer/cancer-causes/diet-physical-activity/body-weight-and-cancerrisk/effects.html

Amin, Ash, ed. 1994. *Post-Fordism*. Oxford, UK: Blackwell.

Anderson, Allan Heaton. 2013. *An Introduction to Pentecostalism: Global Charismatic Christianity*. Cambridge, UK: Cambridge University Press.

Anderson, Benedict. 1991. *Imagined Communities: Reflections on the Origin and*

Spread of Nationalism. 2nd ed. London: Verso Books.

Anderson, Chris. 2009. *Free: The Future of a Radical Price.* New York: Hyperion.

Anderson, David M., and Neil Carrier. 2006. "'Flower of Paradise' or 'Polluting the Nation': Contested Narratives of Khat Consumption." In *Consuming Cultures, Global Perspectives: Historical Trajectories, Transnational Exchanges,* edited by J. Brewer and F. Trentmann, 145–166. Oxford, UK: Berg.

Andreas, Peter. 2015. "International Politics and the Illicit Global Economy." *Perspectives on Politics* 13: 782–788.

Anspach, Renee, and Nissim Mizrachi. 2006. "The Field Worker's Fields: Ethics, Ethnography, and Medical Sociology." *Sociology of Health and Illness* 28(6): 713–731.

Antonio, Robert J. 2011. "Karl Marx." In *The Wiley-Blackwell Companion to Major Social Theorists,* Vol. 1, *Classical Theorists,* edited by George Ritzer and Jeffrey Stepnisky, 115–164. Malden, MA: Wiley-Blackwell.

Antonio, Robert J. 2014. "Piketty's Nightmare Capitalism: The Return of Rentier Society and De-democratization." *Contemporary Sociology* 43: 783–790.

Antonio, Robert J., and Brett Clark. 2015. "The Climate Change Divide in Social Theory." In *Climate Change and Society: Sociological Perspectives,* edited by Riley Dunlap and Robert J. Brulle, 333–368. Oxford, UK: Oxford University Press.

Appadurai, Arjun. 1996. *Modernity at Large: Cultural Dimensions of Globalization.* Minneapolis: University of Minnesota Press.

Arbabzadah, Nushin. 2011. "Girls Will Be Boys in Afghanistan." *The Guardian,* November 30. Accessed April 18, 2015.

Archibold, Randal C. 2014. "As Child Migrants Flood to the Border, U.S. Presses Latin America to Act." *New York Times,* June 20.

Arcidiacono, P., Kinsler, J., & Ransom, T. 2021. Legacy and Athlete Preferences at Harvard. *Journal of Labor Economics, 40*(1). https://doi.org/10.1086/713744

Arsovska, Jane. 2014. "Organized Crime." In *The Encyclopedia of Criminology and Criminal Justice,* edited by Jay Albanese. Oxford, UK: Wiley Blackwell.

Asayama, Shinichiro. 2015. "Catastrophism toward 'Opening Up' or 'Closing Down'? Going beyond the Apocalyptic Future and Geoengineering." *Current Sociology* 63(1): 89–93.

Asch, Solomon E. 1952. *Social Psychology.* New York: Prentice Hall.

Associated Press. 2014. "10 Injured as Migrants Storm Spanish Border Fence." *New York Times,* October 15.

Associated Press. 2018. "Fury Reported over Federal Plan Targeting Transgender People." *New York Times,* October 22.

Association of American Medical Colleges. 2019. "Percentage of U.S. Medical School Graduates by Sex, Academic Years 1980–1981 through 2018–2019." *Diversity in Medicine: Facts and Figures 2019.* Washington, D.C.: Association of American Medical Colleges.

Astorino, Joseph A. and Anthony V. Nicola. 2021. "Making the Invisible Visible: Viral Cloud Moments in the SARS-CoV-2 Pandemic." In *COVID-19: Global Pandemic, Societal Responses, Ideological Solutions,* edited by J. Michael Ryan, 184–196. London: Routledge.

Atkinson, Rowland. 2014. *Shades of Deviance: A Primer on Crime, Deviance, and Social Harm.* New York: Routledge.

Atkinson, Rowland, and Sarah Blandy. 2017. *Domestic Fortress: Fear and the New Home Front.* Manchester, UK: Manchester University Press.

Atsushi, Miura. 2014. *The Rise of Sharing: Fourth-Stage Consumer Society in Japan.* Tokyo: International House of Japan.

Auster, Carol J. 2016. "Gender Neutral." In *The Wiley Blackwell Encyclopedia of Gender and Sexuality Studies,* edited by Nancy Naples, Renee Hoogland, Maithree Wickramasinghe, and Wai Ching Angela Wong. West Sussex, UK: Wiley-Blackwell (Published online).

Avishai, Orit. 2007. "Managing the Lactating Body: The Breast-Feeding Project and the Privileged Mother." *Qualitative Sociology* 30: 135–142.

Ayoobi, Thayana. 2018. "A Tale of Modern Segregation in High-end Brazilian Gated Communities." *The Globe Post,* May 25.

Ayres, Tammy C., and James Treadwell. 2012. "Bars, Drugs, and Football Thugs: Alcohol, Cocaine Use, and Violence in the Night Time Economy among English Football Firms." *Criminology and Criminal Justice* 12: 83–100.

Baehr, Peter, and Daniel Gordon. 2012. "Unmasking and Disclosure as Sociological Practices: Contrasting Modes for Understanding Religious and Other Beliefs." *Journal of Sociology* 48: 380–396.

Baksh, Rawwida, and Wendy Harcourt, eds. 2015. *The Oxford Handbook of Transnational Feminist Movements.* Oxford, UK: Oxford University Press.

Banet-Weiser, Sarah. 2012. "Free Self-Esteem Tools?" In *Commodity Activism,* edited by Roopali Mukherjee and Sarah Banet-Weiser, 39–56. New York: New York University Press.

Baran, Paul A., and Paul M. Sweezy. 1966. *Monopoly Capital: An Essay on American Economic and Social Order.* New York: Modern Reader.

Barber, Nigel. 2017. "Cross-National Variation in Attitudes to Premarital Sex: Economic Development, Disease Risk, and Marriage Strength." *Cross-Cultural Research* 52(3): 259–273.

Barmaki, Reza. 2016. "On the Origin of the Concept of Deviant Subculture in Criminology: W. I. Thomas and the Chicago School of Sociology." *Deviant Behavior* 37: 795–810.

Barnes, Medora. 2020. *Wiley-Blackwell Companion to Sociology,* 2nd ed. Edited by George Ritzer and Wendy Wiedenhoft Murphy. Chichester, UK: John Wiley & Sons.

Barr, Rebecca, and Robert Dreeben. 1983. *How Schools Work.* Chicago: University of Chicago Press.

Barro, Josh. 2015. "A $15 Minimum Wage: But Why Just for Fast-Food Workers?" *New York Times,* July 28.

Barron, Lee. 2017. *Tattoo Culture: Theory and Contemporary Contexts.* London and New York: Rowman & Littlefield.

Barshay, J. 2022, October 25. *PROOF POINTS: Why elite colleges won't give up legacy admissions.* Retrieved May 18, 2023, from https://hechingerreport.org/proof-points-why-elite-colleges-cant-give-up-legacy-admission

Barstow, David, Susanne Craig, and Russ Buettner. 2018. "Behind the Myth of a Self-Made Billionaire, a Vast Inherited Fortune." *New York Times,* October 7.

Basaran, Tugba, and Elspeth Guild. 2018. *Global Labor and the Migrant Premium: The Cost of Working Abroad.* New York: Routledge.

Basu, Amrita. 2016. *Women's Movements in the Global Era: The Power of Local Feminisms,* 2nd ed. London: Routledge.

Baudrillard, Jean. [1970] 1998. *The Consumer Society.* London: SAGE.

Baudrillard, Jean. [1983] 1990. *Fatal Strategies.* New York: Semiotext(e).

Bauman, Kurt, and Camille Ryan. 2015. "Women Now at the Head of the Class, Lead Men in College Attainment." *Random Samplings: The Official Blog of the U.S. Census Bureau,* October 7. Accessed February 1, 2017. http://blogs.census.gov/2015/10

/07/women-now-at-the-head-of-the-class-lead-men-in-collegeattainment/?cid=RS23.

Bauman, Zygmunt. 1989. *Modernity and the Holocaust*. Ithaca, NY: Cornell University Press.

Bauman, Zygmunt. 2000. *Liquid Modernity*. Cambridge, MA: Polity Press.

Bauman, Zygmunt. 2003. *Liquid Love*. Cambridge, MA: Polity Press.

Bauman, Zygmunt. 2005. *Liquid Life*. Cambridge, MA: Polity Press.

Bauman, Zygmunt. 2006. *Liquid Fear*. Cambridge, MA: Polity Press.

Bauman, Zygmunt. 2007. *Liquid Times: Living in an Age of Uncertainty*. Cambridge, MA: Polity Press.

Baumeister, H. 2018. *Sexualised Crimes, Armed Conflict and the Law*. London: Routledge.

Bear, Julia, and Peter Glick. 2017. "Breadwinner Bonus and Caregiver Penalty in Workplace Rewards for Men and Women." *Social Psychological and Personality Science* 8(7): 780–788.

Bearak, 2014. "The New Bazaar: In India, Online Stores Catch on with Buyers." *New York Times*, July 29.

Beccaria, Cesare. [1764] 1986. *On Crimes and Punishments*. Indianapolis, IN: Hackett.

Beck, Ulrich. [1986] 1992. *Risk Society: Towards a New Modernity*. London: Sage.

Beck, Ulrich, and Elisabeth Beck-Gernsheim. 2012. "Families." In *The Wiley-Blackwell Encyclopedia of Globalization*, edited by George Ritzer, 637–639. Malden, MA: Wiley-Blackwell.

Becker, Howard S. 1963. *Outsiders: Studies in the Sociology of Deviance*. New York: Free Press.

Becker, Howard S., and Blanche Geer. 1958. "The Fate of Idealism in Medical School." *American Sociological Review* 23: 50–56.

Bedard, Stephanie Anne Nicole, and Carri Reisdorf Tolmie. 2018. "Millennials' Green Consumption Behaviour: Exploring the Role of Social Media." *Corporate Social Responsibility and Environmental Management* 25(6): 1388–1396.

Beilharz, Peter. 2012. "Liquidity." In *The Wiley-Blackwell Encyclopedia of Globalization*, edited by George Ritzer, 1299–1230. Malden, MA: Wiley-Blackwell.

Belk, Russell. 2013. "The Sacred in Consumer Culture." In *Consumption and Spirituality*, edited by D. Rinallo, L. Scott, and P. Maclaren, 69–80. New York: Routledge.

Belk, Russell. 2014. "Sharing vs. Pseudo-Sharing in Web 2.0." *Anthropologist* 18: 7–23.

Bell, Ann V., Barret Michalec, and Christine Arenson. 2014. "The (Stalled) Progress of Interprofessional Collaboration: The Role of Gender." *Journal of Interprofessional Care* 28: 98–102.

Bell, Daniel. 1973. *The Coming of Post-industrial Society: A Venture in Social Forecasting*. New York: Basic Books.

Bell, David. 2007. "Sexualities, Cities and." In *The Blackwell Encyclopedia of Sociology*, edited by George Ritzer, 4254–4256. Malden, MA: Blackwell.

Bell, Matthew. 2017. "The Biggest Megachurch on Earth and South Korea's Crisis of Evangelicalism." PRI. Accessed April 24, 2019. https://www.pri.org/stories/2017-05-01/biggest-megachurchearth-facing-crisis-evangelism.

Bell, Robert R. 1971. *Social Deviance: A Substantive Analysis*. Homewood, IL: Dorsey.

Bellah, Robert N. 1967. "Civil Religion in America." *Daedalus*, Winter.

Ben-Yehuda, Nachman. 1980. "The European Witch Craze of the 14th to 17th Centuries: A Sociologist's Perspective." *American Journal of Sociology* 86(1): 1–31.

Ben-Yehuda, Nachman. 1985. *Deviance and Moral Boundaries*. Chicago: University of Chicago Press.

Ben-Yehuda, Nachman. 2019. "Deviance: A Sociology of Unconventionalities." In the Wiley-Blackwell Companion to Sociology. Edited by George Ritzer and Wendy Wiedenhoft Murphy. Chichester: John Wiley & Sons.

Benaim, Michael. 2018. "From Symbolic Values to Symbolic Innovation: Internet-Memes and Innovation." *Research Policy* 47: 901–910.

Bendix, Reinhard, and Seymour Martin Lipset, eds. 1966. *Class, Status, and Power: Social Stratification in Comparative Perspective*, 2nd rev. ed. New York: Free Press.

Bengali, Shashank. 2016. "For Hindus Far from Home, Online Religious Services Can Be a Valued Connection." *Los Angeles Times*, May 1.

Benjamin, Walter. 1999. *The Arcades Project*. Cambridge, MA: Belknap.

Benner, Katie, and Sheera Frenkel. 2018. "Drug Dealers Targeted in Sweep of Illicit Online Marketplaces." *New York Times*, June 26.

Bennett, M. D., and M. W. Fraser. 2000. "Urban Violence among African American Males: Integrating Family, Neighborhood, and Peer Perspectives." *Journal of Sociology and Social Welfare* 27: 93–117.

Bennhold, Kartrin. 2018. "'Already an Exception': Merkel's Legacy Is Shaped by Migration and Austerity." *New York Times*, December 15.

Benoit, Cecilia, S. Mikael Jansson, Michaela Smith, and Jackson Flagg. 2017. "Prostitution Stigma and Its Effect on the Working Conditions, Personal Lives, and Health of Sex Workers." *The Journal of Sex Research* 55(4–5): 457–471.

Benzaquen, Adriana. 2006. *Encounters with Wild Children: Temptation and Disappointment in the Study of Human Nature*. Montreal: McGill-Queen's University Press.

Berends, Mark. 2015. "Sociology and School Choice: What We Know after Two Decades of School Choice." *Annual Review of Sociology* 41: 159–180.

Berger, Arthur Asa. 2015. *Ads, Fads, & Consumer Culture*. Lanham, MD: Rowman & Littlefield.

Berger, Peter L. 1963. *Invitation to Sociology*. New York: Doubleday.

Berger, Peter L. 1969. *The Sacred Canopy: Elements of a Sociological Theory of Religion*. New York: Doubleday.

Berger, Peter L., and Thomas Luckmann. 1967. *The Social Construction of Reality: A Treatise in the Sociology of Knowledge*. New York: Anchor Books.

Bergquist, Magnus. 2003. "Open-Source Software Development as Gift Culture: Work and Identity Formation in an Internet Community." In *New Technologies at Work: People, Screens, and Social Virtuality*, edited by C. Garsten and H. Wulff. New York: Berg.

Berkovitch, Nitza. 1999. *From Motherhood to Citizenship: Women's Rights and International Organizations*. Baltimore: Johns Hopkins University Press.

Berman, Sheri. 2018. "Can It Happen Here? Madeleine Albright Examines Fascism Then and Now." *New York Times*, April 20.

Bernhardt, Annette, Martina Morris, Mark S. Handcock, and Marc A. Scott. 2001. *Divergent Paths: Economic Mobility in the New American Labor Market*. New York: Russell Sage Foundation.

Bernstein, Mary, Brenna Harvey, and Nancy Naples. 2018. "Marriage, the Final Frontier? Same-Sex Marriage and the

Future of the Lesbian and Gay Movement." *Sociological Forum* 33(1): 30–52.

Berry, Jeffrey, and Clyde Wilcox. 2018. *The Interest Group Society*. 6th ed. New York: Routledge.

Berryman, Rachel, and Misha Kavka. 2017. "'I Guess a Lot of People See Me as a Big Sister or a Friend': The Role of Intimacy in the Celebrification of Beauty Vloggers." *Journal of Gender Studies* 26(3): 307–320.

Bertrand, Marianne, and Sendhil Mullainathan. 2004. "Are Emily and Greg More Employable than Lakisha and Jamal? A Field Experiment on Labor Market Discrimination." *American Economic Review* 94(4): 991–1013.

Bérubé, Allan. 2010. *Coming Out under Fire: The History of Gay Men and Women in World War II*. Chapel Hill: University of North Carolina Press.

Bethmann, Dirk, and Michael Kvasnicka. 2013. "World War II, Missing Men, and Out of Wedlock Childbearing." *Economic Journal* 123: 162–194.

Beyer, Don. (2022, September 28). *JEC Analysis Finds Opioid Epidemic Cost U.S. Nearly $1.5 Trillion in 2020*. Retrieved April 29, 2023, from https://beyer.house.gov/news/documentsingle.aspx?DocumentID=5684#

Beynon, Huw. 2016. "Beyond Fordism." In *The Sage Handbook of the Sociology of Work and Employment*, edited by Stephen Edgell, Heidi Gottfried, and Edward Granter, 306–328. London: Sage.

Bhabha, Jacqueline. 2018. *Can We Solve the Migration Crisis?* Cambridge, UK: Polity Press.

Bhatty, Ayesha. 2010. "Haiti Devastation Exposes Shoddy Construction." *BBC News*, January 15. Accessed March 31, 2012. http://news.bbc.co.uk/2/hi/8460042.stm.

Bianchi, Francesca, Stella Milani, and Marika Rullo. 2023. "Neighborhood Solidarity as a Local Response to the Emergency of the Pandemic: An Explorative Study of Informal Support in Italy." In *COVID-19: Individual Rights and Community Responsibilities*, edited by J. Michael Ryan, 167–184. London: Routledge.

Bianchi, Raoul. 2018. "The Political Economy of Tourism Development: A Critical Review." *Annals of Tourism Research* 70: 88–102.

Bilefsky, Dan. 2008. "Albanian Custom Fades: Woman as Family Man." *New York Times*, June 25. Accessed April 18, 2015. http://www.nytimes.com/2008/06/25/world/europe/25virgins.html.

Bills, David B. 2013. "Comments from the Editor: The Sociology of Failure and Rejection." *Sociology of Education* 86: 270–271.

Binnie, Jon. 2004. *The Globalization of Sexuality*. London: SAGE.

Black, Donald. 2013. "On the Almost Inconceivable Misunderstandings Concerning the Subject of Value-Free Social Science." *British Journal of Sociology* 64: 763–780.

Blaschke, Steffen, Dennis Schoeneborn, and David Seidl. 2012. "Organizations as Networks of Communication Episodes: Turning the Network Perspective Inside Out." *Organization Studies* 33: 879–906.

Blau, Peter. 1963. *The Dynamics of Bureaucracy*. Chicago: University of Chicago Press.

Blau, Peter, and Otis Dudley Duncan. 1967. *The American Occupational Structure*. New York: Wiley.

Blee, Kathleen. 2002. *Inside Organized Racism*. Berkeley: University of California Press.

Bleiweis, R., Boesch, D., & Gaines, A. C. 2020, August 3. *The Basic Facts About Women in Poverty*. Retrieved May 18, 2023, from https://www.americanprogress.org/article/basic-facts-women-poverty/

Blight, James G., and Janet M. Lang. 2005. *The Fog of War: Lessons from the Life of Robert S. McNamara*. Lanham, MD: Rowman & Littlefield.

Blommaert, Lieselotte, and Marcel Coenders. 2014. "Discrimination of Arabic-Named Applicants in the Netherlands: An Internet-Based Field Experiment Examining Different Phases in Online Recruitment Procedures." *Social Forces* 92: 957–982.

Bluestein, Adam. 2014. "DDP Yoga Is Everywhere, but Does It Deliver?" *Men's Journal*, June. Accessed April 18, 2015. http://www.mensjournal.com/health-fitness/exercise/ddp-yoga-iseverywhere-but-does-it-deliver-20140609.

Blum, Dinur, Stacy L. Smith and Adam G. Sanford. 2021. "Toxic Wild West Syndrome: Individual Rights vs. Community Needs." In *COVID-19: Social Consequences and Cultural Adaptations*, edited by J. Michael Ryan, 122–133. London: Routledge.

Blumberg, Yoni. 2017. "Harvard's Incoming Freshman Class Is One-Third Legacy—Here's Why That's a Problem." CNBC, September 6. Accessed April 24, 2019. https://www.cnbc.com/2017/09/06/harvards-incoming-class-is-one-third-legacy.html.

Boas, Morten. 2012. "Failed States." In *The Wiley-Blackwell Encyclopedia of Globalization*, edited by George Ritzer, 633–635. Malden, MA: Wiley-Blackwell.

Bobo, Lawrence D. 2017. "Racism in Trump's America: Reflections on Culture, Sociology, and the 2016 Presidential Election." *British Journal of Sociology* 68: S85–S104.

Boice, John. 2017. "Epidemiological Study of One Million U.S. Radiation Workers and Veterans." USDOE: Office of Science. Accessed April 24, 2019. https://www.osti.gov/biblio/1413399.

Bonanno, Alessandro. 2017. "Fordism post Fordism." In *The Wiley-Blackwell Encyclopedia of Globalization*, edited by George Ritzer, 680–682. Malden, MA: Wiley-Blackwell.

Bond, Matthew. 2012. "The Bases of Elite Social Behaviour: Patterns of Club Affiliation among Members of the House of Lords." *Sociology* 46: 613–632.

Bondaroff, Teale Phelps, and Sam Cooke. 2020. "Masks on the Beach: The Impact of COVID-19 on Marine Plastic Pollution." OceansAsia. https://oceansasia.org/wp-content/uploads/202/12/Marine-Plastic-Pollution-FINAL-1.pdf.

Bongaarts, John, Barbara S. Mensch, and Ann K. Blanc. 2017. "Trends in the Age at Reproductive Transitions in the Developing World: The Role of Education." *Population Studies* 71(2): 139–154.

Bonilla-Silva, Eduardo. 2009. *Racism without Racists: Color-Blind Racism and the Persistence of Racial Inequality in the United States*. Lanham, MD: Rowman & Littlefield.

Bonilla-Silva, Eduardo. 2015. "The Structure of Racism in Color-Blind, 'Post-Racial' America." *American Behavioral Scientist* 59: 1358–1376.

Boswell, A. Ayres, and Joan Z. Spade. 1996. "Fraternities and Collegiate Rape Culture: Why Are Some Fraternities More Dangerous Places for Women?" *Gender & Society* 10(2): 133–147.

Bourdieu, Pierre. 1992. *The Logic of Practice*. Palo Alto, CA: Stanford University Press.

Bourdieu, Pierre, and Jean-Claude Passeron. 1977. *Reproduction in Education, Society, and Culture*. Beverly Hills, CA: Sage.

Bowring, Finn. 2016. "The Individual and Society in Durkheim: Unpicking the Contradictions." *European Journal of Social Theory* 19: 21–38.

Boyd-Judson, Lyn, and Patrick James, eds. 2015. *Women's Global Health: Norms and State Policies*. Lanham, MD: Lexington Books.

Bradsher, Keith, and Karl Russell. 2017. "Building Trade Walls." *New York Times*, March 7.

Brady, David, and Denise Kall. 2008. "Nearly Universal, but Somewhat Distinct: The Feminization of Poverty in Affluent Western Democracies, 1969–2000." *Social Science Research* 37(3): 976–1007.

Braithwaite, John. 2010. "Diagnostics of White-Collar Crime Prevention." *Criminology and Public Policy* 9: 621–626.

Brass, Kevin. 2015. "House Hunting in Singapore." *New York Times*, December 30.

Bratton, William J. 2011. "Reducing Crime through Prevention Not Incarceration." *Criminology and Public Policy* 10: 63–68.

Braw, Elisabeth. 2014. "The Three Letter Word Driving a Gender Revolution." *Newsweek*, September 29. Accessed April 17, 2015. http://www.newsweek.com/2014/10/03/three-letter-worddriving-gender-revolution-272654.html.

Breetzke, Gregory D., Karina Landman, and Ellen G. Cohn. 2014. "Is It Safer behind the Gates? Crime and Gated Communities in South Africa." *Journal of Housing and the Built Environment* 29: 123–139.

Bremmer, Ian. 2018. *Us vs Them: The Failure of Globalization*. New York: Portfolio/Penguin.

Brems, Cara, Martina Temmerman, Todd Graham, and Marcel Broersma. 2017. "Personal Branding on Twitter." *Digital Journalism* 5(4): 443–459.

Brennan, Denise. 2002. "Selling Sex for Visas: Sex Tourism as a Stepping-Stone to International Migration." In *Global Woman: Nannies, Maids, and Sex Workers in the New Economy*, edited by B. Ehrenreich and A. R. Hochschild. New York: Henry Holt.

Breslin, Tony. 2020. *Capturing the Lessons of Lockdown*. Collins. https://freedomtoteach.collins.co.uk/capturing-the-lessons-of-lockdown/.

Breslin, Tony. 2021. *Lessons from Lockdown: The Educational Legacy of COVID-19*. London: Routledge.

Brim, Orville. 1968. "Adult Socialization." In *Socialization and Society*, edited by J. A. Clausen, 182–226. Boston: Little, Brown.

Brimeyer, T. M., J. Miller, and R. Perrucci. 2006. "Social Class Sentiments in Formation: Influence of Class Socialization, College Socialization, and Class Aspirations." *Sociological Quarterly* 47: 471–495.

Brody, Jane E. 2016. "No Such Thing as a Healthy Smoker." *New York Times*, June 20.

Bromley, Victoria. 2012. *Feminisms Matter: Debates, Theories, Activism*. Toronto: University of Toronto Press.

Bromwich, Jonah Engel. 2018. "Why Are American Prisons So Afraid of This Book?" *New York Times*, January 18.

Bronner, Ethan. 2011. "Virtual Bridge Allows Strangers in Mideast to Seem Less Strange." *New York Times*, July 10. Accessed March 29, 2012. http://www.nytimes.com/2011/07/10/world/middleeast/10mideast.html.

Bronner, Madelon, Mihn Hao Nguyen, Ellen Smets, Anthony VandeVen, and Julia van Weert. 2018. "Anxiety during Cancer Diagnosis." *Psycho-Oncology* 27(2): 661–667.

Brooker, Megan, and David Meyer. 2019. "Coalitions and the Organization of Collective Action." In *The Wiley-Blackwell Companion to Social Movements*, edited by David Snow, Sarah Soule, Hanspeter Kries, and Holly McCammon, 252–260. Chichester, UK: John Wiley & Sons.

Brooks, Andrew. 2015. *Clothing Poverty: The Hidden World of Fast Fashion and Second-Hand Clothes*. London: Zed Books.

Brosdahl, Deborah J. C., and Jason M. Carpenter. 2012. "U.S. Male Generational Cohorts: Retail Format Preferences, Desired Retail Attributes, Satisfaction, and Loyalty." *Journal of Retailing & Consumer Services* 19(6): 545–552.

Brown, Stephen. 2016. *Brands and Branding*. Los Angeles: SAGE.

Brubaker, Ralph, Robert W. Lawless, and Charles J. Tabb. 2012. *A Debtor World: Interdisciplinary Perspectives on Debt*. Oxford, UK: Oxford University Press.

Bruckmeier, Karl. 2018. *Global Environmental Governance: Social-Ecological Perspectives*. Cham, Switzerland: Palgrave Macmillan.

Bruder, Jessica. 2017. *Nomadland: Surviving America in the Twenty-First Century*. New York: W. W. Norton.

Bruze, Gustaf. 2018. "Intergenerational Mobility: New Evidence from Consumption Data." *Journal of Applied Econometrics* 33(4): 580–593.

Bryant, Melanie, and Vaughan Higgins. 2010. "Self-Confessed Troublemakers: An Interactionist View of Deviance during Organizational Change." *Human Relations* 63: 249–277.

Bryk, Anthony, Valerie Lee, and Peter Holland. 1993. *Catholic Schools and the Common Good*. Cambridge, MA: Harvard University Press.

Bryman, A. 2004. *The Disneyization of Society*. London: SAGE.

Budig, Michelle J., Joya Misra, and Irene Boeckman. 2016. "Work-Family Policy Tradeoffs for Mothers? Unpacking the Cross-National Variations in Motherhood Earnings Penalties." *Work and Occupations* 43: 119–177.

Bukowski, William M., Melisa Castellanos, Frank Vitaro, and Mara Brendgen. 2015. "Socialization and Experiences with Peers." In *Handbook of Socialization: Theory and Research*, 2nd ed., edited by Joan E. Grusec and Paul D. Hastings, 228–250. New York: Guilford Press.

Bulut, Elif. 2016. "Pride and Prejudice: The Context for Reception of Muslims in the United States." *Contemporary Social Science*, May 16 (published online).

Burawoy, Michael. 2000. "Introduction: Reaching for the Global." In *Global Ethnography: Forces, Connections, and Imaginations in a Postmodern World*, edited by M. Burawoy, J. A. Blum, S. George, Z. Gille, T. Gowan, L. Haney, M. Klawiter, S. H. Lopez, S. Ó Riain, and M. Thayer, 1–40. Berkeley: University of California Press.

Bureau of Labor Statistics. 2018. "American Time Use Survey—2017 Results." Accessed April 24, 2019. https://www.bls.gov/news.release/pdf/atus.pdf.

Burgess, Ernest W., and Harvey J. Locke. 1945. *The Family: From Institution to Companionship*. New York: American Book.

Burke, Kelsey. 2016. *Christians Under Covers: Evangelicals and Sexual Pleasure on the Internet*. Berkeley: University of California Press.

Burnett, Victoria. 2016. "Bathroom Debate Complicates a Town's Acceptance of a Third Gender." *New York Times*, June 22.

Bursell, Moa. 2014. "The Multiple Burdens of Foreign-Named Men: Evidence from a Field Experiment on Gendered Ethnic Hiring Discrimination in Sweden." *European Sociological Review* 30(3): 399–409.

Butler, Judith. 1990. *Gender Trouble: Feminism and the Subversion of Identity*. New York: Routledge.

Butler, Judith. 1994. *Undoing Gender*. New York: Routledge.

Cahill, Spencer E., William Distler, Cynthia Lachowetz, Andrea Meaney, Robyn Tarallo, and Teena Willard. 1985. "Meanwhile Backstage: Public Bathrooms and the Interaction Order." *Journal of Contemporary Ethnography* 14: 33–58.

Caird, Jeff K., Kate A. Johnston, Chelsea R. Willness, Mark Asbridge, and Piers Steel. 2014. "A Meta-analysis of the Effects of Texting on Driving." *Accident Analysis & Prevention* 71: 311–318.

Camera, Lauren. 2016. "Achievement Gap Between White and Black Students Still Gaping." *U.S. News & World Report*, January 13. Accessed April 24, 2019. www.usnews.com/news/blogs/datamine/2016/01/13/achievement-gap-between-white-and-black-students-still-gaping.

Cameron, Abigail. 2015. "How I Learned to Stop Worrying and Love the IRB." *Contexts* 14: 72–74.

Campbell, Colin. 2007. *The Easternization of the West: A Thematic Account of Cultural Change in the Modern Era*. Boulder, CO: Paradigm Press.

Campbell, Nnenia M. 2010. "Coil Conscious: African American Women's Development of Internet-Based Alternative Hair Communities." Paper presented at the annual meeting of the American Sociological Association, Atlanta, GA.

Cannon, Claire, and Fredrick Buttell. 2015. "Illusion of Inclusion: The Failure of the Gender Paradigm to Account for IPV in LGBT Relationships." *Partner Abuse* 6(1): 65–77.

Caprile, Maria, and Amparo Serrano Pascual. 2011. "The Move Towards the Knowledge-Based Society: A Gender Approach." *Work and Organization* 18: 48–72.

Carbonaro, William. 2005. "Tracking, Student Effort, and Academic Achievement." *Sociology of Education* 78: 27–49.

Carbonaro, William, and Elizabeth Covay. 2010. "Tracking Student Effort and Academic Achievement in the Era of Standards Based Reforms." *Sociology of Education* 83: 160–182.

Carey, Stephen. 2011. *A Beginner's Guide to Scientific Method*. Boston: Wadsworth.

Carmichael, Stokely, and Charles V. Hamilton. 1967. *Black Power: The Politics of Liberation*. New York: Vintage Books.

Carrillo, Héctor, and Jorge Fontdevila. 2014. "Border Crossings and Shifting Sexualities among Mexican Gay Immigrant Men: Beyond Monolithic Conceptions." *Sexualities* 17(8): 919–938.

Carson, Rachel. 1962. *Silent Spring*. New York: Houghton Mifflin.

Carty, Victoria. 2018. *Social Movements and New Technology*. London: Routledge.

Carver, Terrell. 2018. *Marx*. Cambridge, UK: Polity Press.

Casey, Emma. 2015. "Gender and Consumer Culture." In *The Wiley Blackwell Encyclopedia of Consumption and Consumer Studies*, edited by Daniel Thomas Cook and J. Michael Ryan, 316–321. Malden, MA: Wiley-Blackwell.

Casey, John, Michael Jenkins, and Harry Dammer. 2018. *Policing the World: The Practice of International and Transnational Policing*, 2nd ed. Durham, NC: Carolina Academic.

Cassano, Graham. 2017. "Second Shift." In Bryan S. Turner et al., eds., *The Wiley-Blackwell Encyclopedia of Social Theory*. Malden, MA: Wiley-Blackwell.

Castells, Manuel. 1996. *The Information Age: Economy, Society, and Culture*, Vol. 1, *The Rise of the Network Society*. Oxford, UK: Blackwell.

Castells, Manuel. 1997. *The Information Age: Economy, Society, and Culture*, Vol. 2, *The Power of Identity*. Oxford, UK: Blackwell.

Castells, Manuel. 1998. *The Information Age: Economy, Society, and Culture*, Vol. 3, *End of Millennium*. Oxford, UK: Blackwell.

Castells, Manuel. 2010. *The Rise of the Network Society. The Information Age: Economy, Society, and Culture*, Vol. 1. Malden, MA: Wiley-Blackwell.

CDC. 2021. *About Teen Pregnancy*. Retrieved May 12, 2023, from https://www.cdc.gov/teenpregnancy/about/index.htm

CDC. 2022a. *Births: Provisional Data for 2021*. Retrieved May 12, 2023, from https://www.cdc.gov/nchs/data/vsrr/vsrr020.pdf

CDC. 2022b. *Global WASH Fast Facts*. Retrieved May 12, 2023, from https://www.cdc.gov/healthywater/global/wash_statistics.html

CDC. 2023. *Unmarried Childbearing*. Retrieved May 12, 2023, from https://www.cdc.gov/nchs/fastats/unmarried-childbearing.htm

Centers for Disease Control and Prevention. 2016b. "Marriage and Divorce." Accessed April 12, 2019. https://www.cdc.gov/nchs/fastats/marriage-divorce.htm.

Centers for Disease Control and Prevention. (2022, August 9). *Data and Statistics About ADHD*. Retrieved May 18, 2023, from https://www.cdc.gov/ncbddd/adhd/data.html

Centers for Disease Control and Prevention. 2023. *Screen Time vs. Lean Time*. https://www.cdc.gov/nccdphp/dnpao/multimedia/infographics/getmoving.html

Centers for Medicare & Medicaid Services (2021, December 1). *National Health Expenditure Data*. CMS.gov. Retrieved April 29, 2023, from https://www.cms.gov/Research-Statistics-Data-and-Systems/Statistics-Trends-and-Reports/NationalHealthExpendData/NationalHealthAccountsHistorical

Cha, Youngjoo. 2013. "Overwork and the Persistence of Gender Segregation in Occupations." *Gender & Society* 27: 158–184.

Cha, Youngjoo, and Kim A. Weeden. 2014. "Overwork and the Slow Convergence in the Gender Gap in Wages." *American Sociological Review* 79: 457–484.

Chae, Haesook. 2014. "Marx on the Family and Class Consciousness." *Rethinking Marxism* 26: 262–277.

Chae, Jiyoung. 2015. "Am I a Better Mother than You?" *Communication Research* 42: 503–525.

Chakravarti, Arjun, Tanya Menon, and Christopher Winship. 2014. "Contact and Group Structure: A Natural Experiment of Interracial College Roommate Groups." *Organization Science* 25(4): 1216–1233.

Chambers, Erve. 2010. *Native Tours: The Anthropology of Travel and Tourism*. Prospect Heights, IL: Waveland Press.

Chambliss, William J. 1964. "A Sociological Analysis of the Law of Vagrancy." *Social Problems* 12: 67–77.

Chamie, Joseph. 2017. "YaleGlobal Online." Yale University. Accessed April 24, 2019. https://yaleglobal.yale.edu/content/out-wedlockbirths-rise-worldwide.

Chang, Grace. 2016. *Disposable Domestics: Immigrant Women Workers in the Global Economy*, 2nd ed. Chicago: Haymarket Books.

Chapman, Jamie. 2018. "How Do Nurses Perceive Role-Taking and Emotional Labor Processes to Influence Work–Family Spillover?" In *The Work-Family Interface: Spillover, Complications, and Challenges*, edited by Lee Blair Sampson and Josip Obradović, 245–264. Bingley, UK: Emerald.

Chatzky, Jean. 2018. "Job-hopping Is on the Rise." Accessed April 24, 2019. https://www.nbcnews.com/better/business/jobhopping-rise-should-you-consider-switching-roles-make-morencna868641.

Chellaney, Brahma. 2015. *Water, Peace, and War: Confronting the Global Water Crisis*. New York: Rowman & Littlefield.

Chen, James K. C., and Dulamjav Zorigt. 2013. "Managing Occupational Health and

Safety in the Mining Industry." *Journal of Business Research* 66: 2321–2331.

Chen, Katherine. 2009. *Enabling Creative Chaos: The Organization behind the Burning Man Event*. Chicago: University of Chicago Press.

Chen, Patricia, and Mary Gallagher. 2018. "Mobilization without Movement: How the Chinese State 'Fixed' Labor Insurgency." *IRL Review* 71(5): 1029–1052.

Chen, Zihong, Ying Ge, Huiwen Lai, and Chi Wan. 2013. "Globalization and Gender Wage Inequality in China." *World Development* 44: 256–266.

Cherlin, Andrew J. 2004. "The Deinstitutionalization of American Marriage." *Journal of Marriage and Family* 66: 848–861.

Cherlin, Andrew J. 2010. "The Housewife Anomaly." *New York Times*, January 24.

Cheung, Jordan. 2021. "Top 10 Smart Cities in the U.S." Earth.Org. https://earth.org/top-10-smart-cities-in-the-us/

Chokshi, Niraj. 2016. "Snowden and Wikileaks Clash over How to Disclose Secrets." *New York Times*, July 29.

Chomsky, Noam. 1985. *Turning the Tide: U.S. Intervention in Central America and the Struggle for Peace*. Boston: South End Press.

Chriqui, James F., Rosalie Liccardo Pacula, Duane C. McBride, Deborah A. Reichmann, Curtis J. Vanderwaal, and Yvonne Terry-McElrath. 2002. *Illicit Drug Policies: Selected Laws from the 50 States*. Princeton, NJ: Robert Wood Johnson Foundation.

Christiano, Kevin J., William H. Swatos, and Peter Kivisto. 2016. *Sociology of Religion: Contemporary Developments*, 3rd ed. Lanham, MD: Rowman & Littlefield.

Chun, Rene. 2018. "The Banana Trick and Other Acts of Self-Checkout Thievery." *Atlantic*, March.

Clark, Nancy, and William Worger. 2016. *South Africa: The Rise and Fall of Apartheid*, 3rd ed. New York: Routledge.

Clegg, Stewart, and Michael Lounsbury. 2009. "Sintering the Iron Cage: Translation, Domination, and Rationalization." In *The Oxford Handbook of Sociology and Organization Studies: Classical Foundations*, edited by P. S. Adler, 118–145. Oxford, UK: Oxford University Press.

Clogher, R. 1981. "Weaving Spiders Come Not Here: Bohemian Grove: Inside the Secret Retreat of the Power Elite." *Mother Jones*, August 28–35.

Coakley, Jay. 2007. "Socialization and Sport." In *The Blackwell Encyclopedia of Sociology*, edited by George Ritzer, 4576–4579. Malden, MA: Blackwell.

Coale, Ansley, and Susan Watkins, eds. 2017. *The Decline of Fertility in Europe*. Princeton, NJ: Princeton University Press.

Cockerham, William. 2019. "Medicine and Health." In *The Wiley-Blackwell Companion to Sociology*, 2nd ed., edited by George Ritzer and Wendy Wiedenhoft Murphy. Chichester, UK: John Wiley & Sons.

Cockerham, William C., and Brian P. Hinote. 2015. "PAs in a Changing Society: A Sociologic Perspective." *Journal of the American Academy of Physicians Assistants* 28: 18–20.

Cohen, Noam. 2011. "Define Gender Gap? Look Up Wikipedia's Contributor List." *New York Times*, January 30. Accessed December 3, 2011. http://www.nytimes.com/2011/01/31/business/media/311ink.html.

Cohen, Philip. 2018. *The Family: Diversity, Inequality, and Social Change*, 2nd ed. New York: Norton.

Cohen, Robin. 1997. *Global Diasporas: An Introduction*. London: Routledge.

Cohn, Samuel. 2017. "The Determinants of the Division of Labor between Men and Women in Paid Employment in the Global North and South: How Occupational Sex-Typing Informs the Study of Gender and Development." *Sociology of Development* 3(1): 1–23.

Cole, Ellen, and Jessica Henderson Daniel. 2005. *Featuring Females: Feminist Analyses of Media*. Washington, DC: American Psychological Association.

Coleman, James. 1966. *Equality of Educational Opportunity*. Washington, DC: U.S. Department of Health, Education, and Welfare.

Coleman, James. 1990. *Foundations of Social Theory*. Cambridge, MA: Belknap Press.

Collier, Paul, and Alexander Betts. 2017. *Refuge: Rethinking Refugee Policy in a Changing World*. Oxford, UK: Oxford University Press.

Collins, Patricia Hill. 1986. "Learning from the Outsider Within: The Sociological Significance of Black Feminist Thought." *Social Problems* 33(6): s14–s32.

Collins, Patricia Hill. 2000. *Black Feminist Thought: Knowledge, Consciousness, and the Politics of Empowerment*, 2nd ed. New York: Routledge.

Collins, Patricia Hill. 2004. *Black Sexual Politics: African Americans, Gender, and the New Racism*. New York: Routledge.

Collins, Patricia Hill, and Sirma Bilge. 2016. *Intersectionality*. Cambridge, UK: Polity Press.

Collins, Randall. 1975. *Conflict Society: Toward an Explanatory Science*. New York: Academic Press.

Collins, Randall. 2008. *Violence: A Micro-Sociological Theory*. Princeton, NJ: Princeton University Press.

Collins, Randall. 2009. "Micro and Macro Causes of Violence." *International Journal of Conflict and Violence* 3: 9–22.

Colosi, Rachel. 2010. *Dirty Dancing? An Ethnography of Lap-Dancing*. Abingdon, UK: William.

Common Sense Media. 2017a. "Zero to Eight: Children's Media Use in America 2017." Fall. Accessed January 28, 2019. https://www.commonsensemedia.org/research/the-common-sense-censusmedia-use-by-kids-age-zero-to-eight-2017.

Companies Market Cap. n.d.-a. *Airbnb*. Retrieved May 18, 2023, from https://companiesmarketcap.com/airbnb/marketcap/

Companies Market Cap. n.d.-b. *Uber*. Retrieved May 18, 2023, from https://companiesmarketcap.com/uber/marketcap/

Compton, D'Lane, and Tristan Bridges. 2014. "Power, Pomp, and Plaid: Lumbersexuals and White, Heteromasculine Pageantry." *Society Pages*, December 25. Accessed April 18, 2015. http://thesocietypages.org/feminist/2014/12/25/power-pomp-andplaid-lumbersexuals-and-white-heteromasculine-pageantry.

Condron, Dennis J., Daniel Tope, Christina R. Steidl, and Kendralin J. Freeman. 2013. "Racial Segregation and the Black/White Achievement Gap, 1992 to 2009." *Sociological Quarterly* 54(1): 130–157.

Conley, Dalton, and Brian J. McCabe. 2011. "Body Mass Index and Physical Attractiveness: Evidence from a Combination of Image-Alteration/List Experiment." *Sociological Methods and Research* 40: 6–31.

Connell, Raewyn. 2009. *Gender*. Cambridge, UK: Polity Press.

Connell, Robert W. 1997. "Hegemonic Masculinity and Emphasized Femininity." In *Feminist Frontiers IV*, edited by L. Richardson, V. Taylor, and N. Whittier, 22–25. New York: McGraw-Hill.

Conrad, Peter, and Miranda Waggoner. 2017. "Anticipatory Medicalization." In *Medical Ethics, Prediction, and Prognosis*, edited by Mariacarla Gadebusch Bondio, Francesca Spöring, and John-Stewart Gordon. London: Routledge.

Conron, Keith J., Kathryn O'Neill, and Brad Sears. 2021. "COVID-19 and Students in Higher Education." https://williamsinstitute.law.ucla.edu/wp-content/uploads/LGBTQ-College-Student-COVID-May-2021.pdf

Contreras, Randol. 2017. *The Stickup Kids: Race, Drugs, Violence, and the American Dream*. Berkeley: University of California Press.

Cook, Alison, and Christy Glass. 2014. "Women and Top Leadership Positions: Towards an Institutional Analysis." *Gender, Work & Organization* 21(1): 91–103.

Cook, Daniel Thomas. 2004. *The Commodification of Childhood: The Children's Clothing Industry and the Rise of the Child Consumer*. Durham, NC: Duke University Press.

Cook, Daniel Thomas. 2007. "Consumer Culture, Children's." In *The Blackwell Encyclopedia of Sociology*, edited by George Ritzer, 693–697. Malden, MA: Blackwell.

Cook, Daniel Thomas, and J. Michael Ryan, eds. 2015. *The Wiley-Blackwell Encyclopedia of Consumption and Consumer Studies*. Malden, MA: Wiley-Blackwell.

Cook, Karen S., Richard M. Emerson, Mary B. Gilmore, and Toshio Yamagishi. 1983. "The Distribution of Power in Exchange Networks: Theory and Experimental Results." *American Journal of Sociology* 89: 275–305.

Cooley, Charles Horton. 1909. *Social Organization: A Study of the Larger Mind*. New York: Scribner.

Coontz, Stephanie. 2013. "Why Gender Equality Stalled." *New York Times Sunday Review*, February 17, SR1.

Corak, Miles. 2013. "Income Inequality, Equality of Opportunity, and Intergenerational Mobility." *Journal of Economic Perspectives* 27: 79–102.

Corak, Miles, Matthew J. Lindquist, and Bhashkar Mazumder. 2014. "A Comparison of Upward and Downward Intergenerational Mobility in Canada, Sweden, and the United States." *Labour Economics* 30: 185–200.

Corprew, Charles S., III, and Avery D. Mitchell. 2014. "Keeping It Frat: Exploring the Interaction among Fraternity Membership, Disinhibition, and Hypermasculinity on Sexually Aggressive Attitudes in College-Aged Males." *Journal of College Student Development* 55(6): 548–562.

Corsaro, William. 2018. *The Sociology of Childhood*, 5th ed. Thousand Oaks, CA: SAGE.

Corsi, Marcella, and J. Michael Ryan. 2022. "The Impact of COVID-19 on the Social Sciences." *International Review of Sociology* 32(1): 1–9.

Coser, Lewis. 1956. *The Functions of Social Conflict*. New York: Free Press.

Costello, Barbara, and Trina Hope. 2016. *Peer Pressure, Peer Prevention: The Role of Friends in Crime and Conformity*. New York: Routledge.

Cowan, Douglas, and David Bromley. 2015. *Cults and New Religions: A Brief History*. Chichester, UK: Wiley-Blackwell.

Crenshaw, Kimberlé 2019. *On Sectionality: Essential Writings of Kimberlé Crenshaw*. New York: Free Press

Creswell, John W., and J. David Creswell. 2018. *Research Design: Qualitative, Quantitative, and Mixed Methods Approaches*, 5th ed. Thousand Oaks, CA: SAGE.

Crewe, Louise, and Amber Martin. 2017. "Sex and the City: Branding, Gender, and the Commodification of Sex Consumption in Contemporary Retailing." *Urban Studies* 54(3): 582–599.

Crosson-Tower, Cynthia. 2018. *Exploring Child Welfare*, 7th ed. London: Pearson.

Crothers, Lane. 2018. *Globalization and American Popular Culture*, 4th ed. Lanham, MD: Rowman & Littlefield.

Cullen, Francis T., Cheryl Lero Jonson, and Daniel S. Nagin. 2011. "Prisons Do Not Reduce Recidivism: The High Cost of Ignoring Science." *Prison Journal* 91: 48S–65S.

Cumming-Bruce, Nick. 2015. "United Nations Investigators Accuse ISIS of Genocide over Attacks on Yazidis." *New York Times*, March 19.

Curran, Dean. 2017. "The Treadmill of Production and the Positional Economy of Consumption." *Canadian Review of Sociology* 54(1): 28–47.

CursedByTheDiceGods. n.d. "Wal-Mart." Imgflip. Accessed February 27, 2017. https://i.imgflip.com/4vm17.jpg

Curtiss, Susan. 1977. *Genie: A Psycholinguistic Study of a Modern-Day "Wild Child."* New York: Academic Press.

Cyert, Richard Michael, and James G. March. 1963. *A Behavioral Theory of the Firm*. Englewood Cliffs, NJ: Prentice Hall.

Dahlberg, Lincoln. 2010. "Cyber-Libertarianism 2.0: A Discourse Theory/Critical Political Economy Examination." *Cultural Politics* 6: 331–356.

Dahrendorf, Ralf. 1959. *Class and Class Conflict in Industrial Society*. Stanford, CA: Stanford University Press.

Damer, Sean. 1974. "Wine Alley: The Sociology of a Dreadful Enclosure." *Sociological Review* 22: 221–248.

Davies, Edward Burlton. 2018. *Third Wave Feminism and Transgender*. New York: Routledge.

Davis, F. James. 1991. *Who Is Black? One Nation's Definition*. Philadelphia: Penn State University Press. Accessed January 27, 2012.

Davis, Kingsley. 1940. "Extreme Social Isolation of a Child." *American Journal of Sociology* 45(4): 554–565.

Davis, Kingsley. 1945. "The World Demographic Transition." *Annals of the American Academy of Political and Social Science* 237: 1–110.

Davis, Kingsley. 1947. "Final Note on a Case of Extreme Isolation." *American Journal of Sociology* 50: 432–437.

Davis, Kingsley, and Wilbert E. Moore. 1945. "Some Principles of Stratification." *American Sociological Review* 10(2): 242–249.

De Laat, Kim, and Shyon Baumann. 2016. "Caring Consumption as Marketing Schema: Representations of Motherhood in an Era of Hyperconsumption." *Journal of Gender Studies* 25: 183–199.

De Silva, Dakshina G., Robert P. McComb, Young-Kyu Moh, Anita R. Schiller, and Andres J. Vargas. 2010. "The Effect of Migration on Wages: Evidence from a Natural Experiment." *American Economic Review: Papers and Proceedings* 100(May): 321–326.

Debas, Haile T. 2010. "Global Health: Priority Agenda for the 21st Century." *UN Chronicle* 47(2). Accessed March 29, 2012. https://www.un-ilibrary.org/content/journals/15643913/47/2/2.

de Beauvoir, Simone. [1952] 1973. *The Second Sex*, translated by H. M. Parshley. New York: Vintage Books.

Deeming, Chris, and David Hayes. 2012. "Worlds of Welfare Capitalism and Wellbeing: A Multilevel Analysis." *Journal of Social Policy* 41(4): 811–829.

Degen, D., T. Kuhn, and W. van der Brug. 2018. "Granting Immigrants Access to Social Benefits? How Self-Interest Influences Support for Welfare State Restrictiveness." *Journal of European Social Policy*. doi:10.1177/0958928718781293

DeLamater, John. 2012. "Sexual Expression in Later Life: A Review and Synthesis." *Journal of Sex Research* 49(2–3): 125–141.

Delgado, Richard, and Jean Stefancic. 2017. *Critical Race Theory: An Introduction*. 3rd ed. New York: New York University Press.

D'Emilio, John. 1983. *Sexual Politics, Sexual Communities*. Chicago: University of Chicago Press.

Denegri-Knott, Janice, and Detlev Zwick. 2012. "Tracking Prosumption Work on eBay: Reproduction of Desire and the Challenge of Slow Re-McDonaldization." *American Behavioral Scientist* 56: 439–458.

Dentler, Robert A., and Kai T. Erikson. 1959. "The Function of Deviance in Small Groups." *Social Problems* 7: 98–107.

Denyer, Simon. 2016. "China's Scary Lesson to the World: Censoring the Internet Works." *The Washington Post*, March 23.

Denzin, Norman, ed. 2018. *Qualitative Inquiry in the Public Sphere*. New York: Routledge.

Desmond, Matthew. 2016. *Evicted: Poverty and Profit in the American City*. New York: Crown.

Deutsch, Nancy L., and Eleni Theodorou. 2010. "Aspiring, Consuming, Becoming: Youth Identity in a Culture of Consumption." *Youth & Society* 42(2): 229–254.

Deutsch, Tracey. 2018. "Gender and Consumption in the Modern United States." In *The Oxford Handbook of American Women's and Gender History*, edited by Ellen Hartigan-O'Connor and Lisa G. Materson, 355–374. Oxford, UK: Oxford University Press.

Dey, Eric L. 1997. "Undergraduate Political Attitudes: Peer Influence in Changing Social Contexts." *Journal of Higher Education* 68: 398–416.

Dias-Abey, Manoj. 2018. "Justice on Our Fields." *Harvard Civil Rights-Civil Liberties Law Review* 53: 167–211.

Dicke, Thomas S. 1992. *Franchising in America: The Development of a Business Method, 1840–1980*. Chapel Hill: University of North Carolina Press.

Dickson, Lynda, Richard Dukes, Hilary Smith, and Noel Strapko. 2014. "Stigma of Ink: Tattoo Attitudes among College Students." *Social Science Journal*, 51(2): 268–276.

Dikùtter, Frank. 2008. "The Racialization of the Globe: An Interactive Interpretation." *Ethnic and Racial Studies* 31(8): 1478–1496.

Dill, Janette S., Kim Price-Glynn, and Carter Rakovski. 2016. "Does the 'Glass Escalator' Compensate for the Devaluation of Care Work Occupations? The Careers of Men in Low- and Middle-Skill Health Care Jobs," *Gender & Society* 30(2): 334–360.

Dingel, Jonathan I., and Brent Neiman. 2020. "How Many Jobs Can Be Done at Home?" *Journal of Public Economics* 189 (2020): 104235. https://doi.org/10.1016/j.jpubec0.2020.104235

DiPrete, Thomas A., and Claudia Buchmann. 2013. *The Rise of Women: The Growing Gender Gap in Education and What It Means for American Schools*. New York: Russell Sage Foundation.

DiPrete, Thomas A., Gregory M. Eirich, Karen S. Cook, and Douglas S. Massey. 2006. "Cumulative Advantage as a Mechanism for Inequality: A Review of Theoretical and Empirical Developments." *Annual Review of Sociology* 32: 271–297.

DiTomaso, Nancy. 2013. *The American Non-dilemma: Racial Inequality without Racism*. New York: Russell Sage Foundation.

Dixon, Angela, and Edward Teller. 2017. "Skin Color and Colorism: Global Research, Concepts, and Measurement." *Annual Review of Sociology* 43: 405–424.

Dizikes, Peter. 2016. "New Study Shows Rich, Poor, Have Hugh Mortality Gaps in U.S." Accessed April 26, 2019. http://news.mit.edu/2016/study-rich-poor-huge-mortality-gap-us-0411.

Dodd, Nigel. 2012. "Money." In *The Wiley-Blackwell Encyclopedia of Globalization*, edited by George Ritzer, 1444–1448. Malden, MA: Wiley-Blackwell.

Dolata, Ulrich, and Jan-Felix Schrape. 2016. "Masses, Crowds, Communities, Movement: Collective Action in the Internet Age." *Social Movement Studies* 15: 1–18.

Dombrowski, Stefan C., Karen L. Gischlar, and Martin Mrazik. 2011. "Feral Children." In *Assessing and Treating Low Incidence/High Severity Psychological Disorders of Childhood*, 81–93. New York: Springer.

Domhoff, G. William. 1974. *The Bohemian Grove and Other Retreats: A Study in Ruling-Class Cohesiveness*. New York: Harper & Row.

Domhoff, G. William. 2013. *Who Rules America? The Triumph of Corporate Rich*. New York: McGraw-Hill.

Domina, Thurston, Andrew Penner, and Emily Penner. 2017. "Categorical Inequality: Schools as Sorting Machines." *Annual Review of Sociology* 43: 311–330.

Donato, Katharine, and Donna Gabaccia. 2015. *Gender and International Migration*. New York: Russell Sage Foundation.

Dong, X. 2017. *Elder Abuse: Research, Practice, and Policy*. Cham, Switzerland: Springer Science and Business.

Donnelly, Michael, and Gerald Huebner. 2018. "As Homeschooling Grows Globally, Challenges Grow with It." HSLDA. Accessed April 26, 2019. https://hslda.org/content/hs/international/20180412-ashomeschooling-grows-globally-challenges-grow-with-it.aspx

Dorn, David, Johannes Schmieder, and James Speltzer. 2018. *Domestic Outsourcing in the United States*. Washington, DC: Department of Labor.

Doshi, Vidhi. 2015. "Why Doctors Still Misunderstand Heart Disease in Women." *The Atlantic*, October 26.

Dowell, E. K. 2022, January 27. *Women Consistently Earn Less Than Men*. Census.gov. Retrieved May 18, 2023, from https://www.census.gov/library/stories/2022/01/gender-pay-gap-widens-as-women-age.html

Downes, David, Paul Rock, and Eugene McLaughlin. 2016. *Understanding Deviance: A Guide to the Sociology of Crime and Rule-Breaking*. Oxford, UK: Oxford University Press.

Downey, Douglas B., and Dennis J. Condron. 2016. "Fifty Years Since the Coleman Report: Rethinking the Relationship between Schools and Inequality." *Sociology of Education* 89: 207–220.

Dowson, Thomas A. (2009). "Queer Theory Meets Archaeology: Disrupting Epistemological Privilege and Heteronormativity in Constructing the Past." In *The Ashgate Research Companion to Queer Theory*, edited by Noreen Giffney and Michael O'Rourke, 277–294. New York: Routledge.

Doyle, Alison. 2018. "How Often Do People Change Jobs?" Accessed April 26, 2019. https://www.thebalancecareers.com/how-oftendo-people-change-jobs-2060467.

Drane, John. 2008. *After McDonaldization: Mission, Ministry, and Christian Discipleship in an Age of Uncertainty*. Grand Rapids, MI: Baker.

Du Bois, W. E. B. [1899] 1996. *The Philadelphia Negro: A Social Study*. Philadelphia: University of Pennsylvania Press.

Du Bois, W. E. B. [1903] 1966. *The Souls of Black Folk*. New York: Modern Library.

Duany, Andrés, Elizabeth Plater-Zyberk, and Jeff Speck. 2010. *Suburban Nation: The*

Rise of Sprawl and the Decline of the American Dream. 10th anniversary ed. New York: North Point Press.

Dubofsky, Melvyn, and Joseph McCartin. 2017. *Labor in America*, 9th ed. Wiley-Blackwell.

Duckworth, Angela L., and Martin E. P. Seligman. 2005. "Self-Discipline Outdoes IQ in Predicting Academic Performance of Adolescents." *Psychological Science* 16: 939–944.

Duckworth, Angela L., and Stephanie M. Carlson. 2013. "Self-Regulation and School Success." In *Self-Regulation and Autonomy: Social and Developmental Dimensions of Human Conduct*, edited by B. W. Sokol, F. M. E. Grouzet, and U. Müller, 208–230. New York: Cambridge University Press.

Duhigg, Charles. 2017. "Business Government." *New York Times*, January 19.

Dumas, Firoozeh. 2018. "Why I Dread Returning to an American Public School." *New York Times*, November 10.

Duneier, Mitchell. 1999. *Sidewalk*. New York: Farrar, Straus and Giroux.

Dunlap, Riley E., and Andrew K. Jorgenson. 2012. "Environmental Problems." In *The Wiley-Blackwell Companion to Sociology*, edited by George Ritzer, 529–536. Malden, MA: Wiley-Blackwell.

Dunning, Eric, Patrick Murphy, and John Williams. 1988. *The Roots of Football Hooliganism*. London: Routledge & Kegan Paul.

Durkheim, Émile. [1893] 1964. *The Division of Labor in Society*. New York: Free Press.

Durkheim, Émile. [1897] 1951. *Suicide*. New York: Free Press.

Durkheim, Émile. [1912] 1965. *The Elementary Forms of the Religious Life*. New York: Free Press.

Dusi, Davide. 2017. "Investigating the Exploitative and Empowering Potential of the Prosumption Phenomenon." *Sociology Compass* 11(6): 1–11.

Dustin, Donna. 2007. *The McDonaldization of Social Work*. Burlington, VT: Ashgate.

Dynarski, Mark, and Austin Nichols. 2017. "More Findings about School Vouchers and Test Scores, and They Are Still Negative." *Brookings Institute Evidence Speaks Report* 2(18): 1–9.

Eckenwiler, Lisa. 2014. "Care Worker Migration, Global Health Equity, and Ethical Place-Making." *Women's Studies International Forum* 47: 213–222.

Eckert, Penelope, and Sally McConnell-Ginet. 2013. *Language and Gender*, 2nd ed. New York: Cambridge University Press.

Edelman, Peter. 2017. *Not a Crime to Be Poor: The Criminalization of Poverty in America*. New York: The New Press.

Edin, Kathryn J., and H. Luke Schaefer. 2015. *$2 a Day: Living on Almost Nothing in America*. New York: Houghton, Mifflin, Harcourt.

Edmonds, Alex. 2010. *Pretty Modern: Beauty, Sex, and Plastic Surgery in Brazil*. Durham, NC: Duke University Press.

Edsall, Thomas B. 2018a. "Who's Afraid of a White Minority? *New York Times*, August 30.

Edsall, Thomas B. 2018b. "Why Is It So Hard for Democracy to Deal with Inequality?" *New York Times*, February 15.

Edsall, Thomas B. 2018c. "The Industrial Revolutions Are Political Wrecking Balls." *New York Times*, May 3.

Ehrenreich, Barbara. 2001. *Nickel and Dimed: On (Not) Getting by in America*. New York: Henry Holt.

Ehrenreich, Barbara. 2002. "Maid to Order." In *Global Woman: Nannies, Maids, and Sex Workers in the New Economy*, edited by B. Ehrenreich and A. R. Hochschild. New York: Henry Holt.

Ehrenreich, Barbara, and Arlie Russell Hochschild. 2002. "Introduction." In *Global Woman: Nannies, Maids, and Sex Workers in the New Economy*, edited by B. Ehrenreich and A. R. Hochschild, 1–14. New York: Henry Holt.

Ehrlich, Paul. 1968. *The Population Bomb*. New York: Ballantine. Eisenhower, Dwight D. 1961. "Farewell Address by President Dwight D.

Eisinger, Jesse. 2018. *The Chickenshit Club: Why the Justice Department Fails to Prosecute Executives*. New York: Simon & Schuster.

Elborgh-Woytek, Katrina, Monique Newiak, Kalpana Kochhar, Stefania Fabrizo, Kangi Kpodar, Philippe Wingender, Benedict Clements, and Gerd Schwartz. 2016. *Women, Work, and the Economy: Macroeconomic Gains from Gender Equity*. Washington, DC: International Monetary Fund.

Elder, Todd, and Christopher Jepsen. 2014. "Are Catholic Primary Schools More Effective than Public Primary Schools?" *Journal of Urban Economics* 80: 28–38.

Elgin, Duane. 2010. *Voluntary Simplicity: Toward a Way of Life That Is Outwardly Simple, Inwardly Rich*, 2nd ed. New York: Quill.

Elizaga, Raquel Sosa, ed. 2018. *Facing an Unequal World: Challenges for Global Sociology*. London: Sage.

Ellis, Allison M., Talya N. Bauer, and Berrin Erdogan. 2015. "New-Employee Organizational Socialization: Adjusting to New Roles, Colleagues, and Organizations." In *Handbook of Socialization: Theory and Research*, 2nd ed., edited by Joan E. Grusec and Paul D. Hastings, 301–324. New York: Guilford Press.

Emerson, Robert M., ed. 2001. *Contemporary Field Research: Perspectives and Formulations*, 2nd ed. Long Grove, IL: Waveland Press.

Engels, Friedrich. [1884] 1970. *The Origins of the Family, Private Property, and the State*. New York: International Publishers.

England, Paula. 2010. "The Gender Revolution: Uneven and Stalled." *Gender & Society* 24(2): 149–166.

England, Paula. 2017. *Comparable Worth: Theories and Evidence*. New York: Routledge.

English, Beth. 2013. "Global Women's Work: Historical Perspectives on the Textile and Garment Industries." *Journal of International Affairs* 67(1): 67–82.

Enke, Finn. 2018. "Collective Memory and the Transfeminist 1970s: Toward a Less Plausible History." *TSQ* 5(1): 9–29.

Entwistle, Joanne. 2015. *The Aesthetic Economy of Fashion: Markets and Value in Clothing and Modelling*. New York: Berg.

EPA. 2017. "Outdoor Water Use in the United States." Accessed April 26, 2019. https://19january2017snapshot.epa.gov/www3/watersense/pubs/outdoor.html.

Erikson, Emily, and Nicholas Occhiuto. 2017. "Social Networks and Macrosocial Change." *Annual Review of Sociology* 43(1): 229–248.

Erikson, Kai T. 1964. "Notes on the Sociology of Deviance." In *The Other Side: Perspectives on Deviance*, edited by H. S. Becker. New York: Free Press.

Erlanger, Steven. 2014. "In West ISIS Finds Women Eager to Enlist." *New York Times*, October 23.

Etezadzadeh, Chirine. 2016. *Smart City—Future City? Smart City 2.0 as a Livable City and Future Market*. Neu-Isenburg, Germany: Springer.

Etzioni, Amitai, ed. 1969. *The Semi-professions and Their Organization: Teachers, Nurses, and Social Workers*. New York: Free Press.

Faderman, Lillian. 1991. *Odd Girls and Twilight Lovers: A History of Lesbian Life in Twentieth-Century America*. New York: Penguin.

Faderman, Lillian. 2016. *The Gay Revolution*. New York: Simon & Schuster.

Farley, John E. 2011. *Majority–Minority Relations*. 6th ed., Census Update. Upper Saddle River, NJ: Prentice Hall.

Farr, Kathryn. 2005. *Sex Trafficking: The Global Market in Women and Children*. New York: Worth.

Farrell, Caitlin, Priscilla Wolhstetter, and Joanna Smith. 2012. "Charter Management Organizations: An Emerging Approach to Scaling Up What Works." *Educational Policy* 26(4): 499–532.

Fassmann, Heinz, and Rainer Munz. 1992. "Patterns and Trends of International Migration in Western Europe." *Population and Development Review* 18: 457–480.

Faulkner, Nicholas, and Diane Bailey. 2019. *The History of Tattoos and Body Modification*. New York: Rosen.

Fausto-Sterling, Anne. 2018. "Why Sex Is Not Binary." *New York Times*, October 25.

Feagin, Joe R. 2006. *Systemic Racism: A Theory of Oppression*. New York: Routledge.

Feagin, Joe R. 2012. *White Party, White Government: Race, Class, and U.S. Politics*. New York: Routledge.

Federal Bureau of Investigation. 2014. "Frequently Asked Questions about the Change in the UCR Definition of Rape." December 11. Accessed April 19, 2015. http://www.fbi.gov/about-us/cjis/ucr/recent-program-updates/new-rape-definition-frequently-askedquestions.

Ferguson, Grant, Jennifer C. McIntosh, Debra Perrone, and Scott Jasechko. 2018. "Competition for Shrinking Window of Low Salinity Groundwater." *Environmental Research Letters* 13(11).

Fernández-Balboa, Juan Miguel, and Gustavo González-Calvo. 2017. "A Critical Narrative Analysis of the Perspectives of Physical Trainers and Fitness Instructors in Relation to Their Body Image, Professional Practice, and the Consumer Culture." *Sport, Education, and Society* 23: 866–878.

Ferrarini, Tommy, and Kenneth Nelson. 2016. "Social Transfers and Poverty in Middle- and High-Income Countries—A Global Perspective." *Global Social Policy* 16: 22–46.

Ferret, Jerome, and Randall Collins. 2018. "On the Internal Dynamics of the Conflict/Violence Process: A Discussion with Randall Collins." *American Sociologist* 49: 5–15.

Fetscherin, Marc, and Renee-Marie Stephano. 2016. "The Medical Tourism Index: Scale Development and Validation." *Tourism Management* 52: 539–556.

Field, Kelly. 2018. "Why Are Women Still Choosing the Lowest Paying Jobs?" *Atlantic*, January 25.

Fielding, A. J. 1989. "Migration and Urbanization in Western Europe since 1950." *Geographical Journal* 155: 60–69.

Fikry, Noha, Nada M. Ahmed, Malin E. Almeland-Grøhn, Laila El Koussy, Mostafa A. El Sharkawy, Farah Seifeldin, and Ahmed Ashraf Younis. 2021. "COVID-19, the Pand(m)emic : Social Media Explorations from the Arab World." In *COVID-19: Global Pandemic, Societal Responses, Ideological Solutions*, edited by J. Michael Ryan, 234–247. London: Routledge.

Fikry, Noha and J. Michael Ryan. 2015. "Queer Theory." In *The Wiley Blackwell Encyclopedia of Gender and Sexuality Studies*, London: Wiley.

Fine, Gary Alan. 1987. *With the Boys: Little League Baseball and Preadolescent Culture*. Chicago: University of Chicago.

Fine, Gary Alan. 2008. *Kitchens: The Culture of Restaurant Work*. Berkeley: University of California Press.

Fine, Gary Alan. 2010. *Authors of the Storm: Meteorologists and the Culture of Prediction*. Chicago: University of Chicago Press.

Fine, Gary Alan. 2012. "Group Culture and the Interaction Order: Local Sociology on the Meso-Level." *Annual Review of Sociology* 38: 159–179.

Fine, Gary Alan. 2015. *Players and Pawns: How Chess Builds Community and Culture*. Chicago: University of Chicago Press.

Finke, Roger, and Rodney Stark. 2005. *The Churching of America, 1776–2005: Winners and Losers in Our Religious Economy*. New Brunswick, NJ: Rutgers University Press.

Fischer, Claude S., Michael Hout, Martin Sanchez Jankowski, and Samuel R. Lucas, eds. 1996. *Inequality by Design: Cracking the Bell Curve Myth*. Princeton, NJ: Princeton University Press.

Fish, Jennifer. 2017. *Domestic Workers of the World Unite! A Global Movement for Dignity and Human Rights*. New York: New York University Press.

Fisher, Max. 2016. "Attack in Nice, France, Represents Terrorism's New Reality." *New York Times*, July 15.

Fisher, Max, and Katrin Bennhold. 2018. "Germany's Europe-Shaking Political Crisis over Migrants, Explained." *New York Times*, July 3.

Fitzsimmons, Emma G. 2016. "Subways in Northeast Showing Their Age. That Isn't the Only Problem." *New York Times*, May 27.

Flack, William F., Jr., Kimberly A. Daubman, Marcia L. Caron, Jenica A. Asadorian, Nicole R. D'Aureli, Shannon N. Gigliotti, A. T. Hall, S. Kiser, and E. R. Stine. 2007. "Risk Factors and Consequences of Unwanted Sex among University Students: Hooking Up, Alcohol, and Stress Response." *Journal of Interpersonal Violence* 22(2): 139–157.

Flave-Novak, Daniel, and Jill Coleman. 2018. "Pluralistic Ignorance of Physical Attractiveness in the Gay Male Community. *Journal of Homosexuality*. https://doi.org/10.1080/00918369.2018.1522811

Flavin, Jeanne. 2008. *Our Bodies, Our Crimes*. New York: New York University Press.

Fletcher, Jason, and Jessica Polos. 2018. "Nonmarital and Teen Fertility." In *The Oxford Handbook of Women and the Economy*, edited by Susan Averett, Laura Argys, and Saul Hoffman, 195–217. Oxford, UK: Oxford University Press.

Flodgren, Gerd, Antoine Rachas, Andrew Farmer, Marco Inzitiari, and Sasha Shepperd. 2015. "Interactive Telemedicine: Effects on Professional Practice and Healthcare Outcomes." *Cochrane Database of Systemic Reviews* 9.

Fluehr-Lobban, Carolyn. 2019. *Race and Racism: An Introduction*. Lanham, MD: Rowman & Littlefield.

Fominaya, Cristina Flesher. 2019. "Collective Identity in Social Movements: Assessing the Limits of a Theoretical Framework." In *The Wiley-Blackwell Companion to Social Movements*, edited by David Snow, Sarah Soule, Hanspeter Kries, and Holly McCammon, 429–446. Chichester, UK: John Wiley & Sons.

Ford, Martin. 2016. *Rise of the Robots: Technology and the Threat of a Jobless Future*. New York: Basic Books.

Forsyth, Craig J., and Heath Copes, eds. 2014. *Encyclopedia of Social Deviance*. Thousand Oaks, CA: Sage.

Foucault, Michel. [1975] 1979. *Discipline and Punish: The Birth of the Prison*. New York: Vintage Books.

Foucault, Michel. 1978. *The History of Sexuality*, Vol. 1, *An Introduction*. New York: Vintage Books.

Fountain, Henry. 2015. "Panel Urges Research on Geoengineering as a Tool against Climate Change." *New York Times*, February 10.

Fournier, Marcel. 2013. *Émile Durkheim: A Biography*. Cambridge: Polity Press.

Francis, Mark. 2011. "Herbert Spencer." In *The Wiley-Blackwell Companion to Major Social Theorists*, Vol. 1, *Classical Theorists*, edited by George Ritzer and Jeffrey Stepnisky, 165–184. Malden, MA: Wiley-Blackwell.

Frank, David John. 2012. "Global Sex." In *The Wiley-Blackwell Encyclopedia of Globalization*, edited by George Ritzer. Malden, MA: Wiley-Blackwell.

Frank, Nathaniel. 2017. *Awakening: How Gays and Lesbians Brought Marriage Equality to America*. Cambridge, MA: Harvard University Press.

Frank, Robert H. 2013. *Falling Behind: How Rising Inequality Harms the Middle Class*. Berkeley: University of California Press.

Freedman, Samuel G. 2016. "North Dakota Mosque a Symbol of Muslims' Long Ties in America." *New York Times*, May 27.

Freeman, Joshua B. 2018. *BEHEMOTH: A History of the Factory and the Making of the Modern World*. New York: W. W. Norton.

Friedan, Betty. 1963. *The Feminine Mystique*. New York: Dell.

Friedkin, N. E. 2001. "Norm Formation in Social Influence Networks." *Social Networks* 23(3): 167–189.

Friedman, Debra, and Michael Hechter. 1988. "The Contribution of Rational Choice Theory to Macrosociological Research." *Sociological Theory* 6: 201–218.

Friedman, Vanessa. 2018. "Selling in the Experience Economy." *New York Times*, November 25.

Friedmann, Naama, and Dana Rusou. 2015. "Critical Period for First Language: The Crucial Role of Language Input During the First Year of Life." *Current Opinion in Neurobiology* 35: 27–34.

Friedrichs, Robert. 1970. *A Sociology of Sociology*. New York: Free Press.

Frintner, M. P., Sisk, B., Byrne, B. J., Freed, G. L., Starmer, A. J., & Olson, L. M. (2019, October 1). *Gender Differences in Earnings of Early- and Midcareer Pediatricians*. AAP.org. Retrieved April 29, 2023, from https://publications.aap.org/pediatrics/article/144/4/e20183955/76967/Gender-Differences-in-Earnings-of-Early-and?

Fritsch, Jane. 2001. "A Day of Terror: The Response; Rescue Workers Rush In, and Many Do Not Return." *New York Times*, September 12. Accessed March 29, 2012. http://www.nytimes.com/2001/09/12/us/a-day-of-terror-the-response-rescue-workers-rush-in-andmany-do-not-return.html.

Fuller, Thomas, and Joe Cochran. 2015. "Rohingya Migrants from Myanmar, Shunned by Malaysia, Are Spotted Adrift in Andaman Sea." *New York Times*, May 14.

Furneaux, Craig. 2013. "Outsourcing and Subcontracting." In *Sociology of Work: An Encyclopedia*, edited by V. Smith, 669–673. Thousand Oaks, CA: Sage.

Gabriel, Yiannis, Marek Korczynski, and Kirsten Rieder. 2015. "Organizations and Their Consumers: Bridging Work and Consumers." *Organization* 22: 629–643.

Gambino, Matthew. 2013. "Erving Goffman's Asylums and Institutional Culture in the Mid-Twentieth-Century United States." *Harvard Review of Psychiatry* 21: 52–57.

Gamble, Andrew. 2016. *Can the Welfare State Survive?* Cambridge, UK: Polity Press.

Gamoran, Adam, Martin Nystrand, Mark Berends, and Paul C. LePore. 1995. "An Organizational Analysis of the Effects of Ability Grouping." *American Educational Research Journal* 32: 687–715.

Gamoran, Adam, and Daniel A. Long. 2006. "Equality of Educational Opportunity: A 40-Year Retrospective." WCER Working Paper 2006–9, Wisconsin Center for Education Research, Madison. Accessed July 13, 2013. http://www.wcer.wisc.edu.

Ganong, Lawrence, and Marilyn Coleman. 2017. *Stepfamily Relationships: Development, Dynamics, and Intervention*, 2nd ed. New York: Springer.

Gans, Herbert J. 1979. *Deciding What's News*. New York: Pantheon.

Gans, Herbert J. 2009. "First Generation Decline: Downward Mobility among Refugees and Immigrants." *Ethnic and Racial Studies* 32: 1658–1670.

Gansky, Lisa. 2010. *The Mesh: Why the Future of Business Is Sharing*. New York: Penguin.

Garcia, Lorena. 2012. *Respect Yourself, Protect Yourself: Latina Girls and Sexual Identity*. New York: New York University Press.

Gardner, Margo, and Laurence Steinberg. 2005. "Peer Influence on Risk Taking, Risk Preference, and Risky Decision Making in Adolescence and Adulthood: An Experimental Study." *Developmental Psychology* 41: 625–635.

Garland, David. 2016. *The Welfare State: A Very Short Introduction*. Oxford, UK: Oxford University Press.

Garrett, William. 2007. "Christianity." In *Encyclopedia of Globalization*, edited by J. A. Scholte and R. Robertson, 139–144. New York: MTM.

Gauchat, Gordon, Maura Kelly, and Michael Wallace. 2012. "Occupational Gender Segregation, Globalization, and Gender Earnings Inequality in U.S. Metropolitan Areas." *Gender & Society* 26: 718–747.

Gautier, Pieter A., Michael Svarer, and Coen N. Teulings. 2010. "Marriage and the City: Search Frictions and Sorting of Singles." *Journal of Urban Economics* 67: 206–218.

Geertz, Clifford. 1973. *The Interpretation of Cultures*. New York: Basic Books.

Gehlert, S., I. H. Song, C. H. Chang, and S. A. Hartlage. 2009. "The Prevalence of Premenstrual Dysphoric Disorder in a Randomly Selected Group of Urban and Rural Women." *Psychological Medicine* 39: 129–136.

Geis, Gilbert. 2007b. "Crime, White-Collar." In *The Blackwell Encyclopedia of Sociology*, edited by George Ritzer, 850–851. Malden, MA: Blackwell.

Gentina, Elodie, and Isabelle Muratore. 2012. "Environmentalism at Home: The Process of Ecological Resocialization by Teenagers." *Journal of Consumer Behaviour* 11: 162–169.

Gentry, Caron, and Laura Sjoberg. 2015. "Terrorism and Political Violence." In *Gender Matters in Global Politics: A Feminist Introduction to International Relations*, 2nd ed., edited by L. J. Shepherd, 120–130. New York: Routledge.

Geoghegan, Thomas. 2016. *Only One Thing Can Save Us: Why America Needs a New Kind of Labor Movement*. New York: The New Press.

George, Sheba. 2000. "'Dirty Nurses' and 'Men Who Play': Gender and Class in Transnational Migration." In *Global Ethnography: Forces, Connections, and Imaginations in a Postmodern World*, edited by M. Burawoy, J. A. Blum, S. George, Z. Gille, T. Gowan, L. Haney, M. Klawiter, S. H. Lopez, S. Ó Riain, and M. Thayer, 144–174. Berkeley: University of California Press.

Gerhardt, H. Carl, and Franz Huber. 2002. *Acoustic Communication in Insects and Anurans: Common Problems and Diverse Solutions*. Chicago: University of Chicago Press.

Gesselman, Amanda N., Gregory D. Webster, and Justin R. Garcia. 2016. "Has Virginity Lost Its Virtue? Relationship Stigma Associated with Being a Sexually Inexperienced Adult." *Journal of Sex Research*, March 2016 (published online).

Ghaziani, Amin, Verta Taylor, and Amy Stone. 2016. "Cycles of Sameness and Difference in LGBT Social Movements." *Annual Review of Sociology* 42: 165–183.

Ghumman, Sonia, and Ann Marie Ryan. 2013. "Not Welcome Here: Discrimination towards Women Who Wear the Muslim Headscarf." *Human Relations* 66: 671–698.

Giddens, Anthony. 1984. *The Constitution of Society: Outline of the Theory of Structuration*. Berkeley: University of California Press.

Gilbert, Dennis L. 2018. *The American Class Structure in an Age of Growing Inequality*. 10th ed. Thousand Oaks, CA: SAGE.

Gillespie-Lynch, Kristen, Patricia M. Greenfield, Yunping Feng, Sue Savage-Rumbaugh, and Heidi Lyn. 2013. "A Cross-Species Study of Gesture and Its Role in Symbolic Development: Implications for the Gestural Theory of Language Development." *Frontiers in Psychology* 4: 160.

Gillis, Justin. 2015. "Climate Accord Is a Healing Step, If Not a Cure." *New York Times*, December 12.

Gilman, Nils, Jesse Goldhammer, and Steven Weber, eds. 2011. *Deviant Globalization: Black Market Economy in the 21st Century*. London: Continuum.

Gilroy, Paul. 1993. *The Black Atlantic: Modernity and Double Consciousness*. London: Verso Books.

Giordano, Peggy C., Angela M. Kaufman, Wendy D. Manning, and Monica A. Longmore. 2015. "Teen Dating Violence: The Influence of Friendships and School Context." *Sociological Focus* 48: 150–171.

Gitlin, Todd. 1993. *The Sixties: Years of Hope, Days of Rage*. New York: Bantam.

Gladstone, Rick. 2015. "Report Details New Atrocities in Darfur by Sudanese Forces." *New York Times*, September 9.

Glazer, Joshua, ed. 2018. *Choosing Charters: Better Schools or More Segregation?* New York: Teachers College Press.

Glenny, Misha. 2008. *McMafia: A Journey through the Global Criminal Underworld*. New York: Knopf.

Global Hunger Index. 2022. *Food Systems Transformation and Local Governance*. Retrieved May 18, 2023, from https://www.globalhungerindex.org/

Global Nonviolent Action Database, Swarthmore College. 2011. "East Los Angeles Students Walkout for Educational Reform (East L.A. Blowouts), 1968." Accessed May 8, 2015. http://nvdatabase.swarthmore.edu/content/east-los-angeles-students-walkouteducational-reform-east-la-blowouts-1968.

Global Nutrition Report. 2016. *From Promise to Impact: Ending Malnutrition by 2030*. Washington, DC: International Food Policy Research Institute.

Gloor, Peter, and Scott Cooper. 2007. *Coolhunting: Chasing Down the Next Big Thing*. New York: AMACOM.

Gmelch, Sharon Bohn, ed. 2010. *Tourists and Tourism: A Reader*. Prospect Heights, IL: Waveland Press.

Godecke, Theda, Alexander Stein, and Matin Qaim. 2018. "The Global Burden of Chronic and Hidden Hunger: Trends and Determinants." *Global Food Security* 17: 21–29.

Goffman, Erving. 1959. *The Presentation of Self in Everyday Life*. Garden City, NY: Anchor Books.

Goffman, Erving. 1961a. *Asylums: Essays on the Social Situation of Mental Patients and Other Inmates*. Garden City, NY: Anchor Books.

Goffman, Erving. 1961b. *Encounters*. Indianapolis, IN: Bobbs-Merrill.

Goffman, Erving. 1963. *Stigma: Notes on the Management of Spoiled Identity*. Englewood Cliffs, NJ: Prentice Hall/Spectrum.

Goffman, Erving. 2000. *Exploring the Interaction Order*. Cambridge, UK: Polity Press.

Goldberg, Gertrude Schaffner, ed. 2010. *Poor Women in Rich Countries: The Feminization of Poverty over the Life Course*. New York: Oxford University Press.

Golden, Daniel (2010). "An Analytic Survey of Legacy Preferences." In *Affirmative-Action for the Rich: Legacy Preferences in College Admissions*, edited by Richard D. Kahlenberg, 73. New York: The Century Foundation Press.

Goldmacher, Shane. 2018. "Fight Breaks out Near Republican Club after Visit by Gavin McInnes, Police Say." *New York Times*, October 12.

Goldman, Robert, and Stephen Papson. 1998. *Nike Culture*. London: SAGE.

Goldscheider, Frances, Eva Bernhardt, and Trude Lappegård. 2015. "The Gender Revolution: A Framework for Understanding Changing Family and Demographic Behavior." *Population and Development Review* 41(2): 207–239.

Goldschmied, Nadav, and Jason Kowalczyk. 2016. "Gender Performance in the NCAA Rifle Championship: Where Is the Gap?" *Sex Roles* 74: 310–322.

Goldstein, Amy. 2017. *Janesville: An American Story*. New York: Simon & Schuster.

Goldstone, Jack. 1991. *Revolution and Rebellion in the Early Modern World*. Berkeley: University of California Press.

Goode, Erich. 2002. "Sexual Involvement and Social Research in a Fat Civil Rights Organization." *Qualitative Sociology* 25(4): 501–534.

Goode, Erich. 2014. "Labeling Theory." In *Encyclopedia of Criminology and Criminal Justice*, edited by G. Bruinsma and D. Weisburd, 2807–2814. New York: Springer.

Goode, Erich, and Alex Thio. 2007. "Deviance, Crime and." In *The Blackwell Encyclopedia of Sociology*, edited by George Ritzer, 1092–1095. Malden, MA: Blackwell.

Goode, Erich, and Nachman Ben-Yehuda. 2009. *Moral Panics: The Social Construction of Deviance*. 2nd edition. Malden, MA: Blackwell.

Goodman, David M. 2016. "The McDonaldization of Psychotherapy: Processed Foods, Processed Therapies, and Economic Class." *Theory and Psychology* 26: 77–95.

Goodnough, Abby. 2010. "Doctors Point to Caffeinated Alcoholic Drinks' Dangers." *New York Times*, October 27.

Gorman, Elizabeth H., and Julie A. Kmec. 2009. "Hierarchical Rank and Women's Organizational Mobility: Glass Ceilings in Corporate Law Firms." *American Journal of Sociology* 114: 1428–1474.

Gotham, Kevin Fox, and Arianna King. 2019. "Urbanization." In *The Wiley-Blackwell Companion to Sociology*, 2nd ed., edited by George Ritzer and Wendy Wiedenhoft Murphy. Chichester, UK: John Wiley & Sons.

Gottschalk, Peter. 2016. "Convenience in White-Collar Crime: Introducing a Core Concept." *Deviant Behavior* 38(5): 605–619.

Gottschalk, Simon. 2010. "The Presentation of Avatars in Second Life: Self and Interaction in Social Virtual Spaces." *Symbolic Interaction* 33(4): 501–525.

Gough, Brendan. 2016. "Hegemonic Masculinity." In *The Wiley Blackwell Encyclopedia of Gender and Sexuality Studies*, edited by A. Wong, M. Wickramasinghe, R. Hoogland, and N. A. Naples. Chicester, UK: Wiley. doi:10.1002/9781118663219.wbegss585

Gould, Stephen Jay. 1981. *The Mismeasure of Man*. New York: Norton.

Gouldner, Alvin W. 1960. "The Norm of Reciprocity: A Preliminary Statement." *American Sociological Review* 25(2): 161–178.

Gouldner, Alvin W. 1962. "Anti-Minotaur: The Myth of a Value-Free Sociology." *Social Problems* 9(3): 199–213.

Gove, Walter R., and Michael Hughes. 1979. "Possible Causes of the Apparent Sex Differences in Physical Health: An Empirical Investigation." *American Sociological Review* 44: 126–146.

Gozdecka, Dorota A., Slen A. Ercan, and Magdalena Kmak. 2014. "From Multiculturalism to Post-multiculturalism: Trends and Paradoxes." *Journal of Sociology* 50: 51–64.

Grace, Anthony R., and Janet E. Palmer. 2015. "The Homogeneity of Society: The Role of Franchising in the Health and Food Sectors." *Sociology and Anthropology* 3: 661–664.

Granfield, Robert. 1992. *Making Elite Lawyers: Visions of Law at Harvard and Beyond*. New York: Routledge, Chapman and Hall.

Granovetter, Mark. 1973. "The Strength of Weak Ties." *American Journal of Sociology* 78(6): 1360–1380.

Green, Michael, Haley Stritzel, Chelsea Smith, Frank Popham, and Robert Crosnoe. 2018. "Timing Poverty in Childhood and Adolescent Health: Evidence from the U.S. and the U.K." *Social Science & Medicine* 197: 136–143.

Greenebaum, Jessica, and Clinton R. Sanders. 2015. "Human-Animal Interaction." In *The Wiley-Blackwell Encyclopedia of Sociology*, 2nd ed., edited by George Ritzer. Malden, MA: Wiley-Blackwell.

Greenhouse, Steven. 2011. "Union Membership in U.S. Fell to a 70-Year Low Last Year." *New York Times*, January 21.

Greenhouse, Steven. 2015. "The Mystery of the Vanishing Pay Raise." *New York Times*, October 31.

Grice, Elizabeth. 2006. "Cry of an Enfant Sauvage." *Daily Telegraph*, July 17.

Griffin, Christine, Isabelle Szmigin, Andrew Bengry-Howell, Chris Hackley, and Willm Mistral. 2012. "Inhabiting the Contradictions: Hypersexual Femininity and the Culture of Intoxication among Young Women in the UK." *Feminism & Psychology* 23(2): 184–206.

Grigoriadis, Vanessa. 2018. "The Empowerment Cult." *New York Times Magazine*, June 3: 28ff.

Gringlas, Sam. 2017. "Old Confronts New in a Gentrifying D.C. Neighborhood." NPR, January 16. Accessed April 26, 2019. https://www.npr.org/2017/01/16/505606317/d-c-s-gentrifyingneighborhoods-a-careful-mix-of-newcomers-and-old-timers.

Griswold, Alison. 2014. "Are Smartphones Ruining the Restaurant Experience?" *Slate*, July 16. Accessed April 22, 2015. http://www.slate.com/articles/business/moneybox/2014/07viral_craigslist_post_on_smartphones_in_restaurants_is_tech_ruining_the.html.

Grondahl, Mika, Keith Collins, and James Glanz, 2019. "The Dangerous Flaws in Boeing's Automated System." *New York Times*, April 4.

Grusee, Joan, and Paul Hastings, eds. 2015. *Handbook of Socialization*. New York: Guilford Press.

Grusky, David, ed. 2018. *Inequality in the 21st Century*. New York: Routledge.

Gubrium, Jaber F., James A. Holstein, Amir B. Marvasti, and Karyn D. McKinney, eds. 2012. *The SAGE Handbook of Interview Research: The Complexity of the Craft*, 2nd ed. Thousand Oaks, CA: SAGE.

Guhathakurta, Subhrajit, David Kanter, James, and Sewell Chan. 2016. "Europe, Reeling from Strain, Tells Economic Migrants: Don't Bother." *New York Times*, March 3.

Gulati, Ranjay, and Phanish Puranam. 2009. "Renewal through Reorganization: The Value of Inconsistencies between Formal and Informal Organization." *Organization Science* 20: 422–440.

Gündüz, Zuhal Yesilyurt. 2013. "The Feminization of Migration: Care and the New Emotional Imperialism." *Monthly Review* 65(7): 32–43.

Guo, Guang, Michael E. Roettger, and Tianji Cai. 2008. "The Integration of Genetic Propensities into Social-Control Models of Delinquency and Violence among Male Youths." *American Sociological Review* 73(4): 543–568.

Guo, Guang, Yilan Fu, Hedwig Lee, Tianji Cai, Kathleen Mullan Harris, and Yi Li. 2014. "Genetic Bio-Ancestry and Social Construction of Racial Classification in Social Surveys in the Contemporary United States." *Demography* 51: 141–172.

Guo, Shibao. 2013. "Economic Integration of Recent Chinese Immigrants in Canada's Second-Tier Cities: The Triple Glass Effect and Immigrants' Downward Social Mobility." *Canadian Ethnic Studies* 45: 95–115.

Gupta, Akhil. 2012. *Red Tape: Bureaucracy, Structural Violence, and Poverty in India*. Durham, NC: Duke University Press.

Gylling, Michael, Jussi Heikkilä, Kari Jussila, and Markku Saarinen. 2015. "Making Decisions on Offshore Outsourcing and Backsourcing: A Case Study in the Bicycle Industry." *International Journal of Production Economics* 162: 92–100

Hacker, Jacob S., and Paul Pierson. 2010. *Winner-Take-All Politics: How Washington Made the Rich Richer—and Turned Its Back on the Middle Class*. New York: Simon & Schuster.

Hafferty, Frederic W. 2009. "Professionalism and the Socialization of Medical Students." In *Teaching Medical Professionalism*, edited by R. L. Cruess, S. R. Cruess, and Y. Steinert, 53–69. New York: Cambridge University Press.

Hage, Jerald, and Charles H. Powers. 1992. *Post-Industrial Lives: Roles and Relationships in the 21st Century*. Newbury Park, CA: SAGE.

Hall, Scott S., David Knox, and Kelsey Shapiro. 2017. "'I Have,' 'I Would,' 'I Won't': Hooking up among Sexually Diverse Groups of College Students." *Psychology of Sexual Orientation and Gender Diversity* 4(2): 233–240.

Hamermesh, Daniel. 2011. *Beauty Pays: Why Attractive People Are More Successful*. Princeton, NJ: Princeton University Press.

Hamilton, Laura, and Elizabeth A. Armstrong. 2009. "Gendered Sexuality in Young Adulthood: Double Binds and Flawed Options." *Gender & Society* 23(5): 589–616.

Handelman, Jay M., and Robert V. Kozinets. 2007. "Culture Jamming." In *The Blackwell Encyclopedia of Sociology*, edited by George Ritzer, 945–946. Malden, MA: Blackwell.

Hannigan, John. 1998. *Fantasy City: Pleasure and Profit in the Postmodern Metropolis*. London: Routledge.

Hannigan, John. 2007. "Fantasy City." In *The Blackwell Encyclopedia of Sociology*, edited by George Ritzer, 1641–1644. Malden, MA: Blackwell.

Hansen, Michael, Elizabeth Mann Levesque, Diana Quintero, and Jon Valant. 2018. "Have We Made Progress on Educational Achievement Gaps? Looking at

Evidence from the NAEP Results." https://www.brookings.edu/blog/brown-center-chalkboard/2018/04/17/havewe-made-progress-on-achievement-gaps-looking-at-evidencefrom-the-new-naep-results/.

Hanson, Andrew, and Zackary Hawley. 2010. "Do Landlords Discriminate in the Rental Housing Market? Evidence from an Internet Field Experiment in US Cities." *Journal of Urban Economics* 70: 99–14.

Harris, Richard. 2019. "Suburban Stereotypes." In *The Routledge Handbook of the Suburbs*, edited by Bernadette Hanlon and Thomas Vicino, 29–38. New York: Routledge.

Harris Interactive. 2016. "Doctor Tops List of Prestigious Occupations." *Press release*, March 29. Accessed January 23, 2016. http://media.theharrispoll.com/documentsPrestigious+Occupations_ Data+Tables.pdf.

Harrison, Bennett. 1994. *Lean and Mean: The Changing Landscape of Corporate Power in the Age of Flexibility*. New York: Basic Books.

Hart, Betty, and Todd Risley. 1995. *Meaningful Differences in the Everyday Experience of Young American Children*. Baltimore: Paul H. Brookes.

Hart, Jeni. 2016. "Dissecting a Gendered Organization: Implications for Career Trajectories for Mid-Career Faculty Women in STEM." *Journal of Higher Education* 87(5): 605–634.

Hartigan, John. 2014. "Whiteness, Class, and the Legacies of Empire: On Home Ground." *Ethnic and Racial Studies* 37(10): 1941–1944.

Hartmann, Heidi. 1979. "Capitalism, Patriarchy, and Job Segregation by Sex." In *Capitalist Patriarchy and the Case for Socialist Feminism*, edited by Z. Eisenstein, 206–247. New York: Monthly Review Press.

Harvey, David. 2005. *A Brief History of Neoliberalism*. Oxford, UK: Oxford University Press.

Harvey, David. 2007. "Poverty and Disrepute." In *The Blackwell Encyclopedia of Sociology*, edited by George Ritzer, 3589–3594. Malden, MA: Blackwell.

Hatch, Anthony. 2016. *Blood Sugar: Racial Pharmacology and Food Justice in Black America*. Minneapolis: University of Minnesota Press.

Hatton, Erin, and Mary Nell Trautner. 2011. "Equal Opportunity Objectification? The Sexualization of Men and Women on the Cover of Rolling Stone." *Sexuality & Culture* 15: 256–278.

Hay, Harry. 2012. "Birth of a Consciousness." *Gay & Lesbian Review Worldwide* 19: 15–18.

Hayes, Dennis, ed. 2017. *Beyond McDonaldization: Visions of Higher Education*. London: Routledge.

Hayes, Dennis, and Robin Wynyard, eds. 2002. *The McDonaldization of Higher Education*. Westport, CT: Bergin and Garvey.

Haynie, L. 2001. "Delinquent Peers Revisited: Does Network Structure Matter?" *American Journal of Sociology* 106: 1013–1057.

Hays, Sharon. 1998. *The Cultural Contradictions of Motherhood*. New Haven, CT: Yale University Press.

Health and Human Services (2022, December 16). *Opioid Facts and Statistics*. HHS.gov. Retrieved April 29, 2023, from https://www.hhs.gov/opioids/statistics/index.html

Heckman, James. 2006. "Skill Formation and the Economics of Investing in Disadvantaged Children." *Science* 312: 1900–1902.

Heckman, James J., Seong Hyeok Moon, Rodrigo Pinto, Peter A. Savelyev, and Adam Yavitz. 2010. "The Rate of Return to the HighScope Perry Preschool Program." *Journal of Public Economics* 94: 114–128.

Hedgecoe, Adam. 2016. "Reputational Risk, Academic Freedom, and Research Ethics Review." *Sociology* 50: 486–501.

Helle, Horst. 2015. *The Social Thought of Georg Simmel*. Thousand Oaks, CA: SAGE.

Helliwell, Christine. 2000. "'It's Only a Penis': Rape, Feminism, and Difference." *Signs* 25(3): 789–816.

Heritage, John, and Tanya Stivers. 2012. "Conversation Analysis and Sociology." In *The Handbook of Conversation Analysis*, edited by J. Sidnell and T. Stivers, 659–673. Malden, MA: Wiley Blackwell.

Herrnstein, Richard J., and Charles Murray. 1994. *The Bell Curve: Intelligence and Class Structure in American Life*. New York: Free Press.

Hett, Benjamin Carter. 2018. *The Death of Democracy: Hitler's Rise to Power and the Downfall of the Weimar Republic*. New York: Henry Holt.

Hier, Sean. 2017. "Good Moral Panics? Normative Ambivalence, Social Reaction, and Coexisting Responsibilities in Everyday Life." *Current Sociology* 65(6): 867–885.

Higley, John, and Michael Burton. 2006. *Elite Foundations of Liberal Democracy*. Lanham, MD: Rowman & Littlefield.

Hill, Brittany Marie. "Body Modifications: Perceptions of Tattoos and the Examination of Gender, Tattoo Location, and Tattoo Size." MA thesis, Texas State University, 2016.

Hill, Heather. 2018. "Cradle to Kindergarten: A New Plan to Combat Inequality." *Social Service Review* 92(2): 304–307.

Hillyard, Daniel. 2007. "Deviance, Criminalization of." In *The Blackwell Encyclopedia of Sociology*, edited by George Ritzer, 1095–1100. Malden, MA: Blackwell.

Himanen, Pekka. 2001. *The Hacker Ethic, and the Spirit of the Information Age*. New York: Random House.

Hoang, Kimberly Kay. 2015. *Dealing in Desire: Asian Ascendancy, Western Decline, and the Hidden Currencies of Global Sex Work*. Berkeley: University of California Press.

Hobsbawm, E. J., and Chris Wrigley. 1999. *Industry and Empire: The Birth of the Industrial Revolution*. New York: New Press.

Hochner, Nicole. 2018. "On Social Rhythm: A Renewed Assessment of Van Gennep's Rites of Passage." *Journal of Classical Sociology* 18(4): 299–312.

Hochschild, Arlie Russell (with Anne Machung). 1989. *The Second Shift*. New York: Viking.

Hochschild, Arlie Russell (with Anne Machung). 2012. *The Second Shift*. Updated ed. New York: Penguin.

Hochschild, Arlie Russell. 2000. "Global Care Chains and Emotional Surplus Value." In *On the Edge: Living with Global Capitalism*, edited by W. Hutton and A. Giddens. London: Jonathan Cape.

Hodgson, Nichi. 2018. "If You're in a Bad Marriage, Don't Try to Mend It – End It." Accessed April 27, 2019. https://www.theguardian.com/commentisfree/2018/jul/19/bad-marriage-unhappy-marriageshealth.

Hodkinson, Paul. 2015. "Bedrooms and Beyond: Youth, Identity and Privacy on Social Network Sites." *New Media and Society* 10.

Hoecker-Drysdale, Susan. 2011. "Harriet Martineau." In *The Wiley-Blackwell Companion to Major Social Theorists*, Vol. 1, *Classical Theorists*, edited by George Ritzer and Jeffrey Stepnisky, 61–95. Malden, MA: Wiley-Blackwell.

Hoffman, Steve. 2013. "Who Needs a General Theory of Social Reality?" *Contemporary Sociology* 42: 51–55.

Högbacka, Riitta. 2017. *Global Families, Inequality, and Transnational Adoption: The* de-Kinning of First Mothers. London: Palgrave Macmillan.

Hogler, Raymond. 2015. *The End of American Labor Unions: The Right-to-Work Movement and the Erosion of Collective Bargaining*. Santa Barbara, CA: Praeger.

Hokayem, Charles, and Misty L. Heggeness. 2014. *Living in Near Poverty in the United States: 1966–2012*. Current Population Reports P60-248. Washington, DC: U.S. Census Bureau, May. Accessed April 19, 2015. https://www.census.gov/prod/2014pubs/p60-248.pdf.

Holcomb, Jeanne. 2017. "Resisting Guilt: Mothers' Breastfeeding Intentions and Formula Use." *Sociological Focus* 50(4): 361–374.

Holland, Samantha. 2013. "Three Generations of Women's Leisure: Changes, Challenges, and Continuities." *Journal of Gender Studies* 22: 309–319.

Hollifield, James E., and David Jacobson. 2012. "Migration and the State." In *The Wiley-Blackwell Encyclopedia of Globalization*, edited by George Ritzer, 1390–1400. Malden, MA: Wiley-Blackwell.

Hollister, Geoff. 2008. *Out of Nowhere: The Inside Story of How Nike Marketed the Culture of Running*. Maidenhead, UK: Meyer and Meyer Sport.

Holt, Justin. 2015. *The Social Thought of Karl Marx*. Thousand Oaks, CA: SAGE.

Homans, George. 1961. *Social Behavior: Its Elementary Forms*. New York: Harcourt, Brace, and World.

Homs, Morgan, ed. 2016. *Critical Intersex*. London: Routledge.

Hood, Roger, and Carolyn Hoyle. 2015. *The Death Penalty: A Worldwide Perspective*, 5th ed. Oxford, UK: Oxford University Press.

hooks, bell. 2000. *Feminist Thought: From Margin to Center*. Cambridge, MA: South End Press.

Horsford, S. D., Cabral, L., Touloukian, C., Parks, S., Smith, P. A., McGhee, C., Qadir, F., Lester, D., & Jacobs, J. 2021. *Black Education in the Wake of COVID-19 and Systemic Racism: Toward a Theory of Change and Action*. Black Education Research Collective. Teachers College, New York, Columbia University

Hoskin, Marilyn. 2017. *Understanding Immigration: Issues and Challenges in the Era of Mass Population Movement*. Albany: SUNY Press.

Hout, Michael. 2015. "A Summary of What We Know about Social Mobility." *The Annals* 657: 27–36.

Howard, Marc Morjé. 2017. *Prison, Punishment, and Real American Exceptionalism*. Oxford, UK: Oxford University Press.

Howard, Vicki. 2015. *From Main Street to Mall: The Rise and Fall of the American Department Store*. Philadelphia: University of Pennsylvania Press.

Howell, James, and Elizabeth Griffiths. 2019. *Gangs in America's Communities*, 3rd ed. Thousand Oaks: SAGE.

Hubbard, Phil, Andrew Gormley-Murray, and Catherine J. Nash. 2015. "Cities and Sexualities." In *Handbook of the Sociology of Sexualities*, edited by John DeLemater and Rebecca F. Plante, 287–303. New York: Springer.

Huddleston, Gabriel S., Julie C. Garlen, and Jennifer A. Sandlin. 2016. "The New Dimension of Disney Magic." In *Disney, Culture and Curriculum*, edited by Jennifer A. Sandlin and Julie C. Garlen, 220–232. New York: Routledge.

Hughes, Melanie, and Kjerulf Joshua Dubrow. 2018. "Intersectionality and Women's Political Empowerment Worldwide." In *Measuring Women's Political Empowerment across the Globe. Gender and Politics*, edited by Alexander Amy, Catherine Bolzendahl, and Farida Jalalzai, 77–96. Cham, Switzerland: Palgrave Macmillan.

Humphreys, Laud. 1970. *Tearoom Trade: A Study of Homosexual Encounters in Public Places*. Chicago: Aldine.

Hunt, Deborah Dolan. 2017. *Fast Facts about the Nursing Profession: Historical Perspectives*. New York: Springer.

Hunter, James Davison. 1992. *Culture Wars: The Struggle to Control the Family, Art, Education, Law, and Politics in America*. New York: Basic Books.

Huntington, Samuel P. 1996. *The Clash of Civilizations and the Remaking of the World Order*. New York: Simon & Schuster.

Hurdle, Jon. 2014. "A Casino Shuts Down amid Tears and Questions about a City's Direction." *New York Times*, September 1.

Hutson, David J. 2016. "Training Bodies, Building Status: Negotiating Age and Gender Differences in the U.S. Fitness Industry." *Qualitative Sociology* 39: 49–70.

Hyman, Louis. 2018. *Temp: How American Work, American Business, and the American Dream Became Temporary*. New York: Viking.

Ibáñz-Cubillas, Pilar, Cristina Díaz-Martín, and Ana-Belen Pérez-Torregrosa. 2017. "Social Networks and Childhood. New Agents of Socialization." *Procedia Social and Behavioral Sciences* 237(11): 64–69.

Iceland, John. 2013. *Poverty in America: A Handbook*. Updated ed. Berkeley: University of California Press.

Illouz, Eva. 2018. "Is Love Still Part of the Good Life?" In *The Good Life and Beyond*, edited by Hartmut Rosa and Christoph Henning. New York: Routledge.

Inda, Jonathan Xavier. 2012. "Flows." In *The Wiley-Blackwell Encyclopedia of Globalization*, edited by George Ritzer, 668–670. Malden, MA: Wiley-Blackwell.

Inglehart, Ronald, Roberto Foa, Christopher Peterson, and Christian Welzel. 2008. "Development, Freedom, and Rising Happiness: A Global Perspective (1981–2007)." *Perspectives on Psychological Science* 3(4): 264–285.

Inglis, David. 2016. "Globalization and Food." In *The Routledge International Handbook of Global Studies*, 2nd ed., edited by Bryan S. Turner and Robert S. Holton, 469–489. New York: Routledge.

Inglis, David. 2017. "Cultural Imperialism." Wiley Online Library. Accessed May 2, 2019. https://onlinelibrary.wiley.com/doi/abs/10.1002/9781118430873.est0798.

Inside Airbnb. n.d. *New York City*. Retrieved May 18, 2023, from http://insideairbnb.com/new-york-city

Institute for Family Studies. 2019. World Family Map 2019. Accessed October 29, 2019. https://ifstudies.org/ifs-admin/resources/reports/worldfamilymap-2019-051819final.pdf

Intergovernmental Panel on Climate Change. 2007. "Summary for Policymakers." In *Climate Change 2007: The Physical Science Basis*, edited by S. Solomon, D. Qin, M. Manning, Z. Chen, M. Marquis, K. B. Averyt, M. Tignor, and H. L. Miller. *Contribution of Working Group I to the Fourth Assessment Report of the Intergovernmental Panel on Climate Change*. Cambridge, UK: Cambridge University Press.

Interlandi, Jeneen. 2010. "Why the Palace Fell: Lessons Learned from the Destruction of Haiti's Presidential Home." *Newsweek*, January 20. Accessed March 31, 2012. http://www.thedailybeast.com/newsweek/2010/01/20/why-the-palace-fell.html.

International Labour Organization. 2017. "Forced Labour, Modern Slavery, and Human Trafficking." Accessed April 27, 2019. https://www.ilo.org/global/topics/forced-labour/lang-en/index.htm.

International Telecommunication Union. 2019, November 5. "New ITU Data Reveal Growing Internet Uptake but a Widening Digital Gender Divide." https://www.itu.int/en/mediacentre/Pages/2019-PR19.aspx

Intersex Society of North America. 2008. "FAQ: What Is Intersex?" Accessed May 15, 2015. http://www.isna.org/faq/what_is_intersex.

Irvine, Leslie. 2004. "A Model of Animal Selfhood: Expanding Interactionist Possibilities." *Symbolic Interaction* 27: 3–21.

Irwin, Neil. 2018. "Should the Fed Create 'Fedcoin' to Rival Bitcoin? A Former Top Official Says 'Maybe.'" *New York Times*, May 4.

Ives, Mike, and Vindu Goel. 2018. "Beyonce, Bhangra, and a Bill in the Millions: The Wedding That Has India Obsessed." *New York Times*, December 11.

Jackson, Margot I., and Susan L. Moffitt. 2017. "The State of Unequal Educational Opportunity: Introduction to the Special Issue on the Coleman Report 50 Years Later." *The ANNALS of the American Academy of Political and Social Science* 674(1): 6–8.

Jackson, Michelle, and D. R. Cox. 2013. "Principles of Experiment al Design and Their Application to Sociology." *Annual Review of Sociology* 39: 27–49.

Jackson, Shirley A. 2007. "Majorities." In *The Blackwell Encyclopedia of Sociology*, edited by George Ritzer, 2701–2702. Malden, MA: Blackwell.

Jackson, Tim. 2014. "Sustainable Consumption." In *Handbook of Sustainable Development*, 2nd ed., edited by Giles Atkinson, Simon Dietz, Eric Neumayer, and Matthew Agarwala, 279–290. Northampton, MA: Edward Elgar.

Jackson-Jacobs, Curtis. 2005. "Hard Drugs in a Soft Context: Managing Trouble and Crack Use on a College Campus." *Sociological Quarterly* 45(4): 835–856.

Jacobsen, Joannes. 2015. "Revisiting the Modernization Hypothesis: Longevity and Democracy." *World Development* 67: 174–185.

Jacobsen, Michael Hviid, and Soren Kristiansen. 2015. *The Social Thought of Erving Goffman*. Thousand Oaks, CA: SAGE.

James, Nalita. 2016. "Using Email Interviews in Qualitative Research: Creating Space to Think and Time to Talk." *International Journal of Qualitative Studies in Education* 29: 150–163.

Janoski, Thomas. 2015. "The New Division of Labor as Lean Production." *International Journal of Sociology* 45: 85–94.

Jarvis, Benjamin, and Xi Song. 2017. "Rising Intragenerational Occupational Mobility in the United States, 1969–2011." *American Sociological Review* 82(3): 568–599.

Jasper, James. 1997. *The Art of Moral Protest*. Chicago: University of Chicago Press.

Jean-Charles, Régine Michelle. 2010. "Cracks of Gender Inequality: Haitian Women after the Earthquake." Social Science Research Council. Accessed March 30, 2012. http://www.ssrc.org/features/pages/haiti-now-and-next/1338/1428.

Jemielniak, Dariusz. 2016. "Breaking the Glass Ceiling on Wikipedia." *Feminist Review* 1: 103–108.

Jenness, Valerie. 2004. "Explaining Criminalization: From Demography and Status Politics to Globalization and Modernization." *Annual Review of Sociology* 30: 141–171.

Jensen, Gary F. 1988. "Functional Perspectives on Deviance: A Critical Assessment and Guide for the Future." *Deviant Behavior* 9: 1–17.

Jerolmack, Colin. 2009. "Humans, Animals, and Play: Theorizing Interaction When Intersubjectivity Is Problematic." *Sociological Theory* 27(4): 371–389.

Jerolmack, Colin. 2013. *The Global Pigeon*. Chicago: University of Chicago Press.

Jerryson, Michael, ed. 2017. *The Oxford Handbook of Contemporary Buddhism*. New York: Oxford University Press.

Johns, Nicole, Krycia Cowling, and Emmanuela Gakidou. 2013. "The Wealth (and Health) of Nations: A Cross-Country Analysis of the Relation between Wealth and Inequality in Disease Burden Estimation." *The Lancet* 381: S66.

Johnson, C., R. Ford, and J. Kaufman. 2000. "Emotional Reactions to Conflict: Do Dependence and Legitimacy Matter?" *Social Forces* 79(1): 107–137.

Johnson, Christopher, Jordan Kelch, and Roxanna Johnson. 2017. "Dementia at the End of Life and Family Partners: A Symbolic Interactionist Perspective on Communication." *Behavioral Sciences* 7(3): 1–10.

Johnson, David K. 2004. *The Lavender Scare: The Cold War Persecution of Gays and Lesbians in the Federal Government*. Chicago: University of Chicago Press.

Johnson, Sean F. 2018. "The Technological Fix as Cure-All: Origins and Implication." *IEEE Technology and Society Magazine* 37: 47–54.

Jones, Jeffery. 2017. "Americans Hold Record Liberal Views on Most Moral Issues." Gallup. Accessed April 27, 2019. https://news.gallup.com/poll/210542/americans-hold-record-liberal-views-moral-issues.aspx

Jones, Richard G. 2015. "Queering the Body Politic: Intersectional Reflexivity in the Body Narratives of Queer Men." *Qualitative Inquiry* 21: 766–775.

Jones, Steven T. 2011. *The Tribes of Burning Man: How an Experiment in the Desert Is Shaping the New American Counterculture*. San Francisco: Consortium of Collective Consciousness.

Jose, Paul E., Kerstin Kramar, and Yubo Hou. 2014. "Does Brooding Rumination Moderate the Stress to Depression Relationship Similarly for Chinese and New Zealand Adolescents?" *Journal of Educational and Developmental Psychology* 4(1): 114–127.

Joyner, Chris. 2010. "Miss. Prom Canceled after Lesbian's Date Request." *USA Today*, March 11. Accessed March 30, 2012. http://www.usatoday.com/news/nation/2010-03-10-noprom_N.htm.

Jung, Moon-Kie, João H. Costa Vargas, and Eduardo Bonilla-Silva, eds. 2011. *State of White Supremacy: Racism, Governance, and the United States*. Stanford CA: Stanford University Press.

Junger, Sebastian. 2016. *Tribe: On Homecoming and Belonging*. New York: 12 Books.

Juozeliūnienė, Irena, and Irma Budginaitė. 2018. "How Transnational Mothering Is Seen to Be 'Troubling': Contesting and Reframing Mothering." *Sociological Research Online* 23(1): 262–281.

Jurgenson, Nathan. 2012. "When Atoms Meet Bits: Social Media, the Mobile Web, and Augmented Revolution." *Future Internet* 4: 83–91.

Kahlenberg, Richard D., ed. 2010. *Affirmative Action for the Rich: Legacy Preferences in College Admissions*. Washington, DC: Brookings Institution Press.

Kahn, Richard, and Douglas Kellner. 2007. "Resisting Globalization." In *The Blackwell Companion to Globalization*, edited by George Ritzer, 662–674. Malden, MA: Blackwell.

Kalberg, Stephen. 1980. "Max Weber's Types of Rationality: Cornerstones for the Analysis of Rationalization Processes in History." *American Journal of Sociology* 85(5): 1145–1179.

Kalberg, Stephen. 2011. "Max Weber." In *The Wiley-Blackwell Companion to Major Social Theorists*, Vol. 1, *Classical Theorists*, edited by George Ritzer and Jeffrey Stepnisky, 305–372. Malden, MA: Wiley-Blackwell.

Kalberg, Stephen. 2017. *The Social Thought of Max Weber*. Thousand Oaks, CA: SAGE.

Kaldor, Mary. 2018. *Global Security Cultures*. Cambridge, UK: Polity Press.

Kalev, Alexandra. 2009. "Cracking the Glass Cages? Restructuring and Ascriptive Inequality at Work." *American Journal of Sociology* 114: 1591–1643.

Kalleberg, Arne L., and Michael Dunn, 2016. "Good Jobs, Bad Jobs in the Gig Economy." *Perspectives on Work* 10–14.

Kalleberg, Arne L., and Ted Mouw. 2018. "Occupations, Organizations, and Intragenerational Career Mobility." *Annual Review of Sociology* 44: 283–303.

Kane, Emily W. 2006. "'No Way My Boys Are Going to Be Like That!' Parents' Responses to Children's Gender Nonconformity." *Gender & Society* 20(2): 149–176.

Kane, Emily W. 2012. *The Gender Trap: Parents and the Pitfalls of Raising Boys and Girls*. New York: New York University Press.

Kane, Emily W. 2018. "Parenting and Gender." In *Handbook of Sociology of Gender*, 2nd ed., edited by Barbara Risman, Carissa M. Froyum, and William J. Scarborough. Cham, Switzerland: Springer.

Kanter, James, and Sewell Chan. 2016. "Europe, Reeling from Strain, Tells Economic Migrants: Don't Bother." *New York Times*, March 3.

Kaoma, Kapya. 2014. "The Paradox and Tension of Moral Claims: Evangelical Christianity, the Politicization and Globalization of Sexual Politics in Sub-Saharan Africa." *Critical Research on Religion* 2(3): 227–245.

Karlson, Kristian Berndt. 2015. "Expectations on Track? High School Tracking and Adolescent Educational Expectations." *Social Forces* 94: 115–141.

Karstedt, Suzanne. 2016. "Genocide." In *The Wiley-Blackwell Encyclopedia of Race, Ethnicity, and Nationalism*, edited by John Stone, Rutledge M. Dennis, Polly Rizova, Anthony D. Smith, and Xiaoshuo Hou. Malden, MA: Wiley-Blackwell.

Kasarda, John D. 2016. "Welcome to Aerotropolis, the City of the Future." *The World Post*, May 1. Accessed March 13, 2017. http://www.huffingtonpost.com/john-d-kasard aaerotropolis-cityfuture_b_7269152.html.

Kasarda, John D., and Greg Lindsay. 2011. *Aerotropolis: The Way We'll Live Next*. New York: Farrar, Straus and Giroux.

Katz, Jonathan Ned. 2004. "'Homosexual' and 'Heterosexual': Questioning the Terms." In *Sexualities: Identities, Behaviors, and Society*, edited by M. S. Kimmel and R. F. Plante, 44–46. New York: Oxford University Press.

Katz, Lawrence, and Alan Krueger. 2017. "Documenting Decline in U.S. Economic Mobility." *Science* 356(6336): 382–383.

Kaufman, Dan. 2016. "Which Side Are You On, Hillary?" *New York Times*, March 12.

Kauppinen, Ilkka. 2013. "Academic Capitalism and the Informational Fraction of the Transnational Capitalist Class." *Globalisation, Societies and Education* 11: 1–22.

Kayitsinga, Jean. 2021. "Racial/Ethnic Differences in Education Disruptions During the COVID-19 Pandemic," Julian Samora Research Institution. Michigan State University. Available at https://jsri.msu.edu/publications/nexo/vol/no-2-spring-2021/racial-ethnic-differences-in-education-disruptions-during-the-covid-19-pandemic

Keane, John. 2003. *Global Civil Society*. Cambridge, UK: Cambridge University Press.

Keller, Jared. 2018. "How Celebrity Deaths Reveal the Hidden Threat of Suicide Contagion." *Pacific Standard*, January 12.

Kellner, Douglas. 2011. "Jean Baudrillard." In *The Wiley-Blackwell Companion to Major Social Theorists*, Vol. 1, *Classical Theorists*, edited by George Ritzer and Jeffrey Stepnisky, 310–339. Malden, MA: Wiley-Blackwell.

Kelly, Erin, Phyllis Moen, J. Michael Oakes, Wen Fan, Cassandra Okechukwu, Kelly D. Davis, Leslie B. Hammer, Ellen Ernst Kossek, Rosalind Berkowitz King, Ginger C. Hanson, Frank Mierzwa, and Lynne M. Casper. 2014. "Changing Work and Work-Family Conflict Evidence from the Work, Family, and Health Network." *American Review of Sociology* 79(3): 485–516.

Kelly, Sean. 2004. "Are Teachers Tracked? On What Basis and with What Consequences?" *Social Psychology of Education* 7: 55–72.

Kenny, Ursula, Mary-Pat O'Malley-Keighran, Michal Molcho, and Colette Kelly. 2017. "Peer Influence on Adolescent Body Image: Friends or Foes?" *Journal of Adolescent Research* 32(6): 768–799.

Kenway, Jane, and Cameron McCarthy, eds. 2016. *Elite Schools in Globalizing Circumstance*. New York: Routledge.

Kershaw, Sarah. 2008. "Starving Themselves, Cocktail in Hand." *New York Times*, March 2. Accessed January 1, 2012. http://www.nytimes.com/2008/03/02/fashion/02drunk.html.

Khan, Nazneen. 2023. "Pandemic Eugenics: The Delta Variant, Child Mortality, and the New Racism," In *COVID-19: Surviving a Pandemic*, edited by J. Michael Ryan, 57–66. London: Routledge.

Khan, Shamus Rahman. 2011. *Privilege: The Making of an Adolescent Elite at St. Paul's School*. Princeton, NJ: Princeton University Press.

Khanna, Nikki, and Cherise A. Harris. 2015. "Discovering Race in a 'Post-racial' World: Teaching Race through Primetime Television." *Teaching Sociology* 43: 39–45.

Kharif, Olga. 2014. "Not Just for Libertarians and Anarchists Anymore." *Bloomberg*, October 9.

Khazan, Olga. 2018. "Being Black in America Can Be Hazardous to Your Health." *The Atlantic*, July/August.

Khrais, Reema. 2013. "Showing Off Shopping Sprees, Fashion 'Haulers' Cash in Online." NPR, March 14. Accessed April 19, 2015. http://www.npr.org/2013/03/14/174305909showing-off-shoppingsprees-fashion-haulers-cash-in-online.

Khuong, Mai Ngoc, and Nguyen Thi Lan Chi. 2017. "Effects of the Corporate Glass Ceiling Factors on Female Employees Organizational Commitment: An Empirical of Ho Chi Minh City, Vietnam." *Journal of Advanced Management Science* 5(4): 255–263.

Kidder, Jeffrey L. 2012. "Parkour, the Affective Appropriation of Urban Space, and the RealVirtual Dialectic." *City and Community* 11: 229–253.

Kim, Mingyung, Jeeyeon Kim, Jeonghye Choi, and Minakshi Trivedi. 2017. "Mobile Shopping Through Applications: Understanding Application Possession and Mobile Purchase." *Journal of Interactive Marketing* 39: 55–68.

Kimmel, Michael S. 2016. *The Gendered Society*, 6th ed. New York: Oxford University Press.

King, Anthony. 2004. *The Structure of Social Theory*. London: Routledge.

Kingsley, Patrick. 2018a. "As West Fears the Rise of Autocrats, Hungary Shows What's Possible." *New York Times*, February 10.

Kingsley, Patrick. 2018b. "Hungary Criminalizes Aiding Illegal Immigrants" *New York Times*, June 20.

Kirk, Roger E. 2007. "Experimental Design." In *The Blackwell Encyclopedia of Sociology*, edited by George Ritzer, 1533–1537. Malden, MA: Blackwell.

Kitchener, Caroline. 2018. "The Age of 'Shotgun Cohabitation.'" *The Atlantic*, April 25.

Kituyi, Mukhisa, and Peter Thomson. 2018. "90 percent of Fish Stocks Are Used Up." https://unctad.org/en/pages/newsdetails.aspx?OriginalVersionID=1812

Kivisto, Peter, and Paul R. Croll. 2012. *Race and Ethnicity: The Basics*. New York: Routledge.

Kivisto, Peter, and Thomas Faist. 2010. *Beyond the Border: The Causes and Consequences of Contemporary Immigration*. Thousand Oaks, CA: Pine Forge Press.

Kleer, Jerzy, and Katarzyna Anna Nawrot, eds. 2018. *The Rise of Megacities: Challenges, Opportunities, and Unique Characteristics*. London: World Scientific Europe.

Klein, Naomi. [2000] 2010. *No Logo: Taking Aim at the Brand Bullies*. Toronto: Vintage.

Kline, Patrick M., Evan K. Rose, and Christopher R. Walters. 2022. "Systemic Discrimination Among Large U.S. Employers." *The Quarterly Journal of Economics*, 137(4), 1963–2036. https://www.nber.org/papers/w29053

Kline, Ronald R. 2015. *The Cybernetics Moment: or Why We Call Our Age the Information Age*. Baltimore: Johns Hopkins University Press.

Klinenberg, Eric. 2015. *Heat Wave: A Social Autopsy of Disaster in Chicago*. Chicago: University of Chicago Press.

Knoblauch, Hubert, and Rene Wilke. 2016. "The Common Denominator: The Reception and Impact of Berger and Luckman's *The Social Construction of Reality*." *Human Studies* 39: 51–69.

Knorr Cetina, Karin. 2012. "Financial Markets." In *The Encyclopedia of Globalization*, edited by George Ritzer, 653–664. Malden, MA: Wiley-Blackwell.

Knott, Eleanor. 2017. "Nationalism and Belonging: Introduction." *Nations and Nationalism* 23(2): 220–226.

Koistinen, David. 2016. *Confronting Decline: The Political Economy of Deindustrialization in Twentieth Century New England*. Gainesville: University of Florida Press.

Kolata, Gina. 2018. "When Reporting on Mail-In Genetic Testing Comes Home." *New York Times*, July 3.

Kollmeyer, Christopher. 2009. "Explaining Deindustrialization: How Affluence, Productivity Growth, and Globalization Diminish Manufacturing Employment." *American Journal of Sociology* 114: 1644–1674.

Kollmeyer, Christopher, and Florian Pichler. 2013. "Is Deindustrialization Causing High Unemployment in Affluent Countries? Evidence from 16 OECD Countries, 1970–2003." *Social Forces* 91: 785–812.

Kong, Travis. 2010. *Chinese Male Homosexualities*. London: Routledge.

Koonin L. M., Hoots B., Tsang C. A., et al. "Trends in the Use of Telehealth During the Emergence of the COVID-19 Pandemic — United States, January–March 2020." Centers for Disease Control and Prevention. *MMWR Morbidity and Mortality Weekly Report* 69, October 30, 2020: 1595–1599. doi: http://dx.doi.org/10.15585/mmwr.mm6943a3

Korda, Andrew. 2006. "The Nazi Medical Experiments." *ADF Health* 7(April): 33–37.

Kosic, Ankica, Arie W. Kruglanski, Antonio Pierro, and Lucia Mannetti. 2004. "The Social Cognition of Immigrants' Acculturation: Effects of the Need for Closure and the Reference Group at Entry." *Journal of Personality and Social Psychology* 86: 796–813.

Kozinets, Robert. 2015. *Netnography Redefined*. London: SAGE.

Kreager, Derek. 2007. "Unnecessary Roughness? School Sports, Peer Networks, and Male Adolescent Violence." *American Sociological Review* 72(5): 705–724.

Krieger, Nancy. 2017. "What's Killing Black Infants?" *The Nation*, February.

Krinsky, Charles, ed. 2013. *The Ashgate Research Companion to Moral Panics*. Burlington, VT: Ashgate.

Krogstad, Jens Manuel, Jeffrey S. Passel, and D'Vera Cohn. 2018. "5 Facts about Illegal Immigrants in the U.S." Accessed April 27, 2019. http://www.pewresearch.org/fact-tank/2018/11/28/5-factsabout-illegal-immigration-in-the-u-s/

Kroneberg, Clemens, and Frank Kalter. 2012. "Rational Choice Theory and Empirical Research: Methodological and Theoretical Contributions in Europe." *Annual Review of Sociology* 38: 73–92.

Kuehn, Kathleen. 2015. "Culture Jamming." In *Encyclopedia of Consumption and Consumer Studies*, edited by Daniel Thomas Cook and Michael Ryan, 236–238. Malden, MA: Wiley-Blackwell.

Kuhn, Thomas. [1962] 1970. *The Structure of Scientific Revolutions*, 2nd ed. Chicago: University of Chicago Press.

Kuisel, Richard. 1993. *Seducing the French: The Dilemma of Americanization*. Berkeley: University of California Press.

Kuo, Janet Chen-Lan, and R. Kelly Raley. 2016. "Diverging Patterns of Union Transition Among Cohabitors by Race/Ethnicity and Education: Trends and Marital Intentions in the United States." *Demography*, June 15 (published online first).

Kuperberg, Arielle, and Joseph E. Padgett. 2015. "The Role of Culture in Explaining College Students' Selection into Hookups, Dates, and Long-Term Romantic Relationships." *Journal of Social and Personal Relationships* 33(8): 1–27.

Kurtz, Annalyn. 2014. "Americans Still Hesitant to Spend More." CNN Money, June 26. Accessed April 22, 2015. http://money.cnn.com/2014/06/26/news/economy/americans-not-spend.

Kurtz, Lester R. 2016. *Gods in the Global Village*, 4th ed. Thousand Oaks, CA: SAGE.

Kurzban. 2006. "Post-Sept. 11, 2001." In *Immigration Law Sourcebook*, 10th ed., xxi–xxiii. Washington, DC: American Immigration Law Foundation.

Kushkush, Isma'il. 2015. "President of Sudan Is Re-elected with 94 Percent of Vote." *New York Times*, April 27.

Kütting, Gabriela, and Kyle Herman. 2018. *Global Environmental Politics*, 2nd ed. New York: Routledge.

Kwan, Samantha, and Mary Nell Trautner. 2011. "Judging Books by Their Covers: Teaching about Physical Attractiveness Biases." *Teaching Sociology* 39: 16–26.

Kye, Samuel. 2018. "The Persistence of White Flight in Middle-Class Suburbia." *Social Science Research* 72: 38–52.

LaCroix, Jessica M., Christopher N. Burrows, and Hart Blanton. 2018. "Effects of Immersive, Sexually Objectifying, and Violent Video Games on Hostile Sexism in Males." *Communication Research Reviews* 35(5): 413–423.

Lacy, Karyn. 2016. "The Sociology of Suburbs: A Research Agenda for Analysis of

Emerging Trends." *Annual Review of Sociology* 42(1): 369–384.

Ladson-Billings, Gloria. 2017. "Makes Me Wanna Holler: Refuting the 'Culture of Poverty' Discourse in Urban Schooling." *The ANNALS of the American Academy of Political and Social Science* 673: 80–90.

Lai, Olivia. 2023. "Top 7 Smart Cities in the World in 2023." Earth.Org. https://earth.org/top-7-smart-cities-in-the-world/

Laible, Deborah, Ross A. Thompson, and Jill Froimson. 2015. "Early Socialization: The Influence of Close Relationships." In *Handbook of Socialization: Theory and Research*, 2nd ed., edited by Joan E. Grusec and Paul D. Hastings, 35–59. New York: Guilford Press.

Lakoff, George. 2016. *Moral Politics: How Liberals and Conservatives Think*. Chicago: University of Chicago Press.

Landor, Antoinette, and Ashley Barr. 2018. "Politics of Respectability, Colorism, and the Terms of Social Exchange in Family Research." *Journal of Family Theory and Review* 10: 330–347.

Landstedt, Evelina, and Katja Gillander Gådin. 2012. "Seventeen and Stressed: Do Gender and Class Matter?" *Health Sociology Review* 21: 82–98.

Lareau, Annette. 2011. "Unequal Childhoods." In *Unequal Childhoods*. Los Angeles: University of California Press.

Lareau, Annette. 2015. "Cultural Knowledge and Social Inequality." *American Sociological Review* 80: 1–27.

Larsen, Gretchen, Maurice Patterson, and Lucy Markham. 2014. "A Deviant Art: Tattoo-Related Stigma in an Era of Commodification." *Psychology & Marketing* 31: 670–681.

Lash, Scott, and Celia Lury. 2007. *Global Culture Industry*. Cambridge, UK: Polity Press.

Lasn, Kalle. 2000. *Culture Jam: How to Reverse America's Suicidal Consumer Binge—and Why We Must*. New York: Quill.

Lasn, Kalle. 2012. *Meme Wars*. New York: Seven Stories Press.

Lasswell, Harold D. 2012. *Politics: Who Gets What, When, How*. Whitefish, MT: Literary Licensing.

Lavorgna, Anita. 2015. "The Online Trade in Counterfeit Pharmaceuticals: New Criminal Opportunities, Trends, and Challenges." *European Journal of Criminology* 12(2): 226–241.

Layte, Richard, and Christopher T. Whelan. 2009. "Explaining Social Class Inequalities in Smoking: The Role of Education, Self-Efficacy, and Deprivation." *European Sociological Review* 25: 399–410.

Lazarus, David. 2017. "Direct-to-Consumer Drug Ads: A Bad Idea That's about to Get Worse." *Los Angeles Times*, February 15.

Leaper, Campbell, and Timeas Farkas. 2015. "The Socialization of Gender During Childhood and Adolescence." In *Handbook of Socialization: Theory and Research*, 2nd ed., edited by Joan E. Grusec and Paul D. Hastings, 541–565. New York: Guilford Press.

Lechman, Ewa, and Harleen Kaur. 2015. "Economic Growth and Female Labor Force Participation—Verifying the U-Feminization Hypothesis. New Evidence for 162 Countries over the Period 1990–2012." Available at SSRN: https://ssrn.com/abstract=2551476.

Ledbetter, James. 2011. *Unwarranted Influence: Dwight D. Eisenhower and the Military-Industrial Complex*. New Haven, CT: Yale University Press.

Lee, Gary. 2017. *The Limits of Marriage*. New York: Rowman & Littlefield.

Lee, Jacqueline G. C., Ray Paternoster, and Zachary Rowan. 2016. "Death Penalty and Race." In *The Wiley Encyclopedia of Race, Ethnicity, and Nationalism*, edited by John Stone, Rutledge M. Dennis, Polly Rizova, Anthony D. Smith, and Xiaoshuo Hou. Malden, MA: Wiley Blackwell.

Lee, Jaekyung. 2012. "Educational Equity and Adequacy for Disadvantaged Minority Students: School and Teacher Resource Gaps toward National Mathematics Proficiency Standard." *Journal of Educational Research* 105: 64–75.

Lee, Julie. 2012. "The Relationship between Appearance-Related Stress and Internalizing Problems in South Korean Adolescent Girls." *Women's Studies International Journal* 40: 903–918.

Leefeldt, Ed. 2018. "Where Gentrification Is Having the Biggest Impact on Cities." *CBS Moneywatch*, March 5.

Leicht, Kevin, and Scott Fitzgerald. 2006. *Postindustrial Peasants: The Illusion of Middle-Class Prosperity*. New York: Worth.

Leidner, Robin. 1993. *Fast Food, Fast Talk*. Berkeley: University of California Press.

Lekakis, Eleftheria. 2017. "Culture Jamming and Brandalism for the Environment: The Logic of Appropriation." *Popular Communication* 15(4): 311–327.

Lemert, Charles, and Anthony Elliott. 2006. *Deadly Worlds: The Emotional Costs of Globalization*. Lanham, MD: Rowman & Littlefield.

Lemert, Edwin. [1951] 2012. *Social Pathology: A Systematic Approach to the Theory of Sociopathic Behavior*. Whitefish, MT: Literary Licensing.

Lenard, Patti Tamara, and Christine Straehle, eds. 2014. *Health Inequalities and Global Justice*. Edinburgh, UK: Edinburgh University Press.

Lengermann, Patricia Madoo, and Gillian Niebrugge-Brantley. 2014. "Feminist Theory." In *Sociological Theory*, 9th ed., edited by George Ritzer and Jeffrey Stepnisky, 440–485. New York: McGraw-Hill.

Leventoglu, Bahar. 2014. "Social Mobility, Middle Class, and Political Transitions." *Journal of Conflict Resolution* 58: 825–864.

LeVine, Steve, and Harry Stevens. 2018. "Special Report: The Aging, Childless Future." *Axios*, July 21.

Levitsky, Steven, and Daniel Ziblatt. 2018. *How Democracies Die*. New York: Crown.

Lewis, James R., and Inga B. Tollefson, eds. 2016. *New Religious Social Movements*, Vol. 2. New York: Oxford University Press.

Lewis, Nathaniel. 2014. "Moving 'Out,' Moving On: Gay Men's Migrations through the Life Course." *Annals of the Association of American Geographers* 104(2): 225–233.

Lewis, Oscar. 1959. *Five Families: Mexican Case Studies in the Culture of Poverty*. New York: New American Library.

Liaw, Karen Ron-Li, and Aron Janssen. 2014. "Not by Convention: Working with People on the Sexual and Gender Continuum." In *Massachusetts General Hospital Textbook on Diversity and Cultural Sensitivity in Mental Health*, edited by R. Parekh, 89–117. New York: Springer.

Liberman, Akiva M., David S. Kirk, and Kideuk Kim. 2014. "Labeling Effects of First Juvenile Arrest: Secondary Deviance and Secondary Sanctioning." *Criminology* 52: 345–370.

Lichter, Daniel T. 2013. "Integration or Fragmentation: Racial Diversity and the American Future." *Demography* 50: 359–391.

Limoncelli, S. A. 2016. "Informal Economy." In *The Wiley Blackwell Encyclopedia of Gender and Sexuality Studies*, edited by A. Wong, M. Wickramasinghe, R. Hoogland, and N. A. Naples. Chichester, UK: John Wiley & Sons. doi:10.1002/9781118663219.wbegss243

Lin, Nan. 1999. "Social Networks and Status Attainment." *Annual Review of Sociology* 25: 467–487.

Lindemann, Danielle. 2017. "Going the Distance: Individualism and Interdependence in the Commuter Marriage." *Journal of Marriage and Family* 79(5): 1419–1434.

Linkon, Sherry. 2018. *The Half-Life of Deindustrialization*. Ann Arbor: University of Michigan Press.

Liong, Mario, and Grand Cheng. 2018. "Objectifying or Liberating? Investigation of the Effects of Sexting on Body Image." *The Journal of Sex Research*. https://doi.org/10.1080/00224499.2018.1438576.

Lipovetsky, Gilles. [1987] 2002. *The Empire of Fashion: Dressing Modern Democracy*. Princeton, NJ: Princeton University Press.

Lipset, Seymour M. 1981. *Political Man*. Expanded ed. Baltimore: Johns Hopkins University Press.

Liss, Miriam. 2014. "Inequality in the Division of Household Labor and Childcare." In *Women, Work, and Family: How Companies Thrive with a 21st-Century Multicultural Workforce*, edited by M. A. Paludi, 23–40. Santa Barbara, CA: ABC-CLIO.

Liu, Yu Cheng. 2012. "Ethnomethodology Reconsidered: The Practical Logic of Social Systems Theory." *Current Sociology* 60: 581–598.

Lloréns, Hilda. 2013. "Latina Bodies in the Era of Elective Aesthetic Surgery." *Latino Studies* 11(4): 547–569.

Looney, Adam, and Kevin B. Moore. 2016. "Changes in the Distribution of After-Tax Wealth in the U.S.: Has Income Policy Increased Wealth Inequality?" *Fiscal Studies* 37: 77–104.

Lopez-Aguado, Patrick. 2016. "The Collateral Consequences of Prisonization: Racial Sorting, Carceral Identity, and Community Criminalization." *Sociology Compass* 10(1): 12–23.

Lorber, Judith. 1967. "Deviance as Performance: The Case of Illness." *Social Problems* 14: 302–310.

Lorber, Judith. 2000. "Using Gender to Undo Gender: A Feminist Degendering Movement." *Feminist Theory* 1(1): 79–95.

Lorenz, Edward. 1995. *The Essence of Chaos*. Seattle: University of Washington Press.

"Louisiana Oil Rig Explosion: Underwater Machines Attempt to Plug Leak." 2010. *Telegraph*, April 26. Accessed March 31, 2012. https://www.telegraph.co.uk/finance/newsbysector/energy/oilandgas/7633286/Louisiana-oil-rig-explosion-Underwatermachines-attempt-to-plug-leak.html.

Low, Setha. 2003. *Behind the Gates: Life, Security, and the Pursuit of Happiness in Fortress America*. New York: Routledge.

Lucas, Jeffrey W., Corina Graif, and Michael J. Lovaglia. 2008. "Prosecutorial Misconduct in Serious Cases: Theory and Design of a Laboratory Experiment: Can You Study a Legal System in a Laboratory?" In *Experiments in Criminology and Law: A Research Revolution*, edited by C. Horne and M. J. Lovaglia, 119–136. Lanham, MD: Rowman & Littlefield.

Luker, Kristin. 1984. *Abortion and the Politics of Motherhood*. Berkeley: University of California Press.

Lunneborg, Clifford E. 2007. "Convenience Sample." In *The Blackwell Encyclopedia of Sociology*, edited by George Ritzer, 788–790. Malden, MA: Blackwell.

Luo, Wei. 2013. "Aching for the Altered Body: Beauty Economy and Chinese Women's Consumption of Cosmetic Surgery." *Women's Studies International Forum* 38: 1–10.

Lutfey, K., and J. Mortimer. 2006. "Development and Socialization through the Adult Life Course." In *Handbook of Social Psychology*, edited by J. DeLamater. New York: Kluwer Academic/Plenum.

Lutz, Helma, and Ewa Palenga-Mollenbeck. 2016. "Global Care Chains." In *Routledge Handbook of Immigration and Refugee Studies*, edited by Anna Triandafillidou. New York: Routledge.

Luxton, David D., Jennifer D. June, and Julie T. Kinn. 2011. "Technology-Based Suicide Prevention: Current Applications and Future Directions." *Telemedicine and e-Health* 17(1): 50–54.

Lyman, Rick. 2015a. "Bulgaria Puts up a New Wall, but this One Keeps People Out." *New York Times*, April 5.

Lyman, Rick. 2015b. "Hungary Seals Border with Croatia in Migrant Crackdown." *New York Times*, October 16.

Lynch, Michael Patrick. 2016. *The Internet of Us: Knowing More and Understanding Less in the Age of Big Data*. New York: Liveright.

Lynch, Michael, Paul Stretesky, and Michael Long. 2018. "Green Criminology and Native Peoples: The Treadmill of Production and the Killing of Indigenous Environmental Activists." *Theoretical Criminology* 3(22): 318–341.

Lyon, David. 2015a. "The Snowden Stakes: Challenges for Understanding Surveillance Today." *Surveillance and Society* 13: 139–152.

Lyotard, Jean-François. [1979] 1984. *The Postmodern Condition: A Report on Knowledge*. Minneapolis: University of Minnesota Press.

Madan, T. N. 2007. "Hinduism." In *Encyclopedia of Globalization*, edited by J. A. Scholte and R. Robertson, 571–573. New York: MTM.

Madden, Stephanie, Melissa Janoske, Rowena Briones Winkler, and Zach Harpole. 2018. "Who Loves Consent? Social Media and the Culture Jamming of Victoria's Secret." *Public Relations Inquiry* 7(2): 171–186.

Maginn, Paul J., and Christine Steinmetz. 2015. "Spatial and Regulatory Contours of the (Sub)Urban Sexscape." In *(Sub)Urban Sexscapes: Geographies and Regulation of the Sex Industry*, edited by P. J. Maginn and C. Steinmetz, 1–17. London: Routledge.

Maines, Rachel. 2001. *The Technology of Orgasm: "Hysteria," the Vibrator, and Women's Sexual Satisfaction*. Baltimore: Johns Hopkins University Press.

Mair, Carolyn. 2018. *The Psychology of Fashion*. London: Routledge. Majora Carter Group. 2009. "Majora Carter Group." Accessed February 28, 2012. http://www.majoracartergroup.com.

Mak, Athena H. N., Margaret Lumbers, and Anita Eves. 2012. "Globalisation and Food Consumption in Tourism." *Annals of Tourism Research* 39: 171–196.

Malala Fund. 2021. "Girls' Education and COVID-19," Available at https://downloads.ctfassets.net/00an5gk9rgbh/6TMYLYAcUpjhQpXLDgmdIa/3e1c12d8d827985ef2b4e815a3a6da1f/COVID19_GirlsEducation_corrected_071420.pdf

Malik, Anand. 2014. "Thomas Kuhn and Changing Paradigm in Geography: Critical Review." *Asian Journal of Multiple Disciplinary Studies* 4: 41–46.

Mandel, Hadas. 2012. "Occupational Mobility of American Women: Compositional and Structural Changes, 1980–2007." *Research in Social Stratification and Mobility* 30: 5–16.

Manning, Peter. 2005. "Impression Management." In *The Encyclopedia of Social Theory*, edited by George Ritzer, 397–399. Thousand Oaks, CA: SAGE.

Manning, Peter. 2007. "Dramaturgy." In *The Blackwell Encyclopedia of Sociology*, edited by George Ritzer, 1226–1229. Malden, MA: Blackwell.

Manning, Robert D. 2001. *Credit Card Nation: The Consequences of America's Addiction to Debt*. New York: Basic Books.

Manzo, John. 2010. "Coffee, Connoisseurship, and an Ethnomethodologically Informed Sociology of Taste." *Human Studies* 33(2): 141–155.

Marginson, Simon. 2016. "The Worldwide Trend to High Participation Higher Education: Dynamics of Social Stratification in Inclusive Systems." *Higher Education* (published online first).

Marmo, Marinella, and Chazel, Narida. 2016. *Transnational Crime and Criminal Justice*. Los Angeles: Sage.

Marmot, Michael. 2015. *The Health Gap: The Challenge of an Unequal World*. New York: Bloomsbury Press.

Marron, Donncha. 2009. *Consumer Credit in the United States: A Sociological Perspective from the 19th Century to the Present*. New York: Palgrave Macmillan.

Marron, Donncha. 2017. "Smoke Gets in Your Eyes: What Is Sociological about Cigarettes?" *Sociological Review* 65: 882–897.

Marsden, Peter V., and Elizabeth H. Gorman. 2001. "Social Networks, Job Changes, and Recruitment." In *Sourcebook on Labor Markets: Evolving Structures and Processes*, edited by I. Berg and A. L. Kalleberg, 467–502. New York: Kluwer Academic/Plenum.

Marshall, Catherine, and Gretchen Rossman. 2010. *Designing Qualitative Research*. Thousand Oaks, CA: SAGE.

Martin, Edward J. 2015. "Oligarchy, Anarchy, and Social Justice." *Contemporary Justice Review* 18.

Martin, Karin A. 2005. "William Wants a Doll. Can He Have One? Feminists, Child Care Advisors, and Gender-Neutral Child Rearing." *Gender & Society* 19: 456–479.

Martinez, Guadalupe F., and Regina Deil-Amen. 2015. "College for All Latinos? The Role of High School Messages in Facing College Challenges." *Teachers College Record* 117(3): 1–50.

Marx, Karl. [1843] 1970. "A Contribution to the Critique of Hegel's Philosophy of Right." In *Marx/Engels Collected Works*, Vol. 3, 3–129. New York: International Publishers.

Marx, Karl. [1857–1858] 1964. *Pre-capitalist Economic Formations*. New York: International Publishers.

Marx, Karl, and Friedrich Engels. 1848. *The Communist Manifesto*. London: Communist League.

Mashal, Mujib. 2016. "Clash of Values Emerges after Afghan Child Bride Burns to Death." *New York Times*, July 18.

Mason, Brandon, and Martha Smithey. 2012. "The Effects of Academic and Interpersonal Stress on Dating Violence among College Students." *Journal of Interpersonal Violence* 27: 974–986.

Mason, Corrine, ed. 2018. *Routledge Handbook of Queer Development Studies*. London: Routledge.

Massey, Douglas. 2003. *Beyond Smoke and Mirrors: Mexican Immigration in an Era of Economic Integration*. New York: Russell Sage Foundation.

Massey, Douglas. 2016. "Residential Segregation Is the Linchpin of Racial Stratification." *City and Community* 15: 4–7.

Mather, Mark. 2009. *Reports on America: Children in Immigrant Families Chart New Path*. Washington, DC: Population Reference Bureau.

Mathews, Russell A., Doan E. Winkel, and Julie Holiday Wayne. 2014. "A Longitudinal Examination of Role Overload and Work-Family Conflict: The Mediating Role of Interdomain Transfers." *Journal of Organizational Behavior* 35: 72–91.

Matin, Abdul. 2015. "Relevance of Social Exclusion in Castellian Theory of Informationalism for South Asia." *Journal of Exclusion Studies* 5: 103–112.

Matthew, Dayna Bowen. 2018. *Just Medicine: A Cure for Racial Inequality in American Health Care*. New York: New York University Press.

Matza, David. 1966. "The Disreputable Poor." In *Class, Status, and Power: Social Stratification in Comparative Perspective*, 2nd rev. ed., edited by R. Bendix and S. M. Lipset, 289–302. New York: Free Press.

Mavroudi, Elizabeth, and Caroline Nagel. 2016. *Global Migration: Patterns, Processes, and Politics*. London: Routledge.

Maxmen, Amy. 2017. "Sleeping Sickness Can Now Be Cured with Pills" *Nature*, October.

Maxwell, Angie, and Todd Shields, eds. 2018. *Legacy of Second-Wave Feminism in American Politics*. Palgrave Macmillan.

Mazelis, Joan Maya. 2015. "'I Got to Try to Give Back': How Reciprocity Norms in a Poor Peoples' Organization Influence Members' Social Capital." *Journal of Poverty* 19: 109–131.

McCaghy, Charles H., Timothy A. Capron, J. D. Jamieson, and Sandra Harley H. Carey. 2016. *Deviant Behavior: Crime, Conflict and Interest Groups*, 8th ed. New York: Routledge.

McCann, Eugene, and Kevin Ward, eds. 2011. *Mobile Urbanism: Cities and Policymaking in the Global Age*. Minneapolis: University of Minnesota Press.

McCann, Hannah. 2016. "Epistemology of the Subject: Queer Theory's Challenge to Feminist Theory." *Women's Quarterly Studies* 44(3&4): 224–243.

McClelland, Robert, Shannon Mok, and Kevin Pierce. 2014. "Labor Force Participation Elasticities of Women and Secondary Earners within Married Couples." Working Paper 2014-06, Congressional Budget Office, September. Accessed April 20, 2015. https://www.cbo.gov/sites/default/files/cbofilesattachments/49433-LaborForce.pdf.

McCormick, Ken. 2011. "Thorstein Veblen." In *The Wiley-Blackwell Companion to Major Social Theorists*, Vol. 1, *Classical Theorists*, edited by George Ritzer and Jeffrey Stepnisky, 185–204. Malden, MA: Wiley-Blackwell.

McEvily, Bill, Giuseppe Soda, and Marco Tortoriello. 2014. "More Formally: Rediscovering the Missing Link between Formal Organization and Informal Social Structure." *The Academy of Management Annals* 8: 299–345.

McHale, Susan, Ann C. Crouter, and Shawn D. Whiteman. 2003. "The Family Contexts of Gender Development in Childhood and Adolescence Social Development." *Social Development* 12: 125–148.

McLanahan, Sara S. 1999. "Father Absence and the Welfare of Children." In *Coping with Divorce, Single Parenting, and Remarriage: A Risk and Resiliency Perspective*, edited by E. M. Hetherington, 117–146. Mahwah, NJ: Lawrence Erlbaum.

McLaughlin, Caitlin, and Jessica Vitak. 2011. "Norm Evolution and Violation on Facebook." *New Media & Society* 14(2) 299–315.

McNeil, Donald G., Jr. 2016. "Malnutrition and Obesity Coexist in Many Countries, Report Finds." *New York Times*, June 13.

McPhate, Mike. 2016. "Ashley Madison Faces F.T.C. Inquiry Amid Rebranding." *New York Times*, July 6.

Mead, George Herbert. [1934] 1962. *Mind, Self, and Society: From the Standpoint of a Social Behaviorist*. Chicago: University of Chicago Press.

"Measuring the #MeToo Backlash." 2018. *The Economist*. Accessed April 26, 2019. https://www.economist.com/unitedstates/2018/10/20/measuring-the-metoo-backlash.

Meeker, James. 2023. "Spreading the Disease: Risk Management in the Age of COVID-19." In *COVID-19: Individual Rights and Community Responsibilities*, edited by J. Michael Ryan, 124–138. London: Routledge.

Meier, Barry. 2013. "More Emergency Visits Linked to Energy Drinks." *New York Times*, January 11.

Mele, Vincenzo. 2018. "Before and Beyond the Masses: Simmel, Benjamin and the Sociology of Crowds." *The Tocqueville Review* 39(1): 119–140.

Melnick, Merrill L., and Daniel L. Wann. 2011. "An Examination of Sport Fandom in Australia: Socialization, Team Identification, and Fan Behavior." *International Review for the Sociology of Sport* 46: 456–470.

Melusky, Joseph, and Keith Pesto. 2017. *The Death Penalty: A Reference Handbook*. Santa Barbara, CA: ABC-CLIO.

Merry, Joseph and Maria Paino. 2019. "Sociology of Education." In *The Wiley-Blackwell Companion to Sociology*, 2nd ed., edited by George Ritzer and Wendy Wiedenhoft Murphy. Chichester, UK: John Wiley & Sons.

Merton, Robert K. [1949] 1968. *Social Theory and Social Structure*, 3rd ed. New York: Free Press.

Merton, Robert K. 1957. *Social Theory and Social Structure*. Rev. ed. Glencoe, IL: Free Press.

Merton, Robert, and Alice S. Kitt. 1950. "Contributions to the Theory of Reference Group Behavior." In *Continuities in Social Research*, edited by R. K. Merton and P. F. Lazarsfeld, 40–105. Glencoe, IL: Free Press.

Mészáros, István. 2006. *Marx's Theory of Alienation*, 5th ed. London: Merlin Press.

Meuleman, Roza, and Marcel Lubbers. 2016. "Parental Socialization and the Consumption of Domestic Films, Books, and Music. *Journal of Consumer Culture*. May 16 (published online).

Michel, C., K. M. Heide, and J. K. Cochran. 2016. "The Consequences and Knowledge about Elite Deviance." *American Journal of Criminal Justice* 41(2): 359–382.

Michels, Robert. [1915] 1962. *Political Parties*. New York: Collier Books.

Migration Policy Institute. 2022, October 13. *Mexican Immigrants in the United States*. Retrieved May 12, 2023, from https://www.migrationpolicy.org/article/mexican-immigrants-united-states

Milanovic, Branko. 2018. *Global Inequality: A New Approach for the Age of Globalization*. Cambridge, MA: Harvard University Press.

Milgram, Stanley. 1974. *Obedience to Authority: An Experimental View*. New York: Harper & Row.

Milibrandt, Tara, and Frank Pearce. 2011. "émile Durkheim." In *The Wiley-Blackwell Companion to Major Social Theorists*, Vol. 1., *Classical Theorists*, edited by George Ritzer and Jeffrey Stepnisky, 236–282. Malden, MA: Wiley-Blackwell.

Milkie, Melissa. 2021. "Changing Times: New Sources of Parenting Stress and the Shifting Meanings of Time with and for Children." In *COVID-19: Social Consequences and Cultural Adaptations*, edited by J. Michael Ryan, 152-164. London: Routledge.

Milkie, Melissa A. 1999. "Social Comparisons, Reflected Appraisals, and Mass Media: The Impact of Pervasive Beauty Images on Black and White Girls' Self-Concepts." *Social Psychology Quarterly* 62: 190–210.

Milkman, Ruth, and Stephanie Luce. 2017. "Labor Unions and the Great Recession." *The Russell Sage Foundation Journal of the Social Sciences* 3(3): 145–165.

Miller, Daniel. 1998. *A Theory of Shopping*. Ithaca, NY: Cornell University Press.

Miller, Pavia. 2017. *Patriarchy*. London: Routledge.

Mills, C. Wright. 1951. *White Collar*. New York: Oxford University Press.

Mills, C. Wright. 1956. *The Power Elite*. New York: Oxford University Press.

Minnotte, Krista Lynn, and Michael Minnotte. 2018. "Work-Family Conflict among Dual-Earners: Are Partner, Family, and Friends Resources or Liabilities?" *Journal of Family and Economic Issues* 39(2): 258–276.

Misra, Joya, and Eiko Strader. 2013. "Gender Pay Equity in Advanced Countries: The Role of Parenthood and Policies." *Journal of International Affairs* 67(1): 27–41.

Moberg, Marcus, and Tuomas Martikainen. 2018. "Religious Change in Market and Consumer Society: The Current State of the Field and New Ways Forward." *Religion* 48(3): 418–435.

Moghadam, Valentine. 2015. "Transnational Feminist Activism and Movement-Building." In *The Oxford Handbook of Transnational Feminist Movements*, edited by Rawwida Baksh and Wendy Harcourt, 53–81. Oxford, UK: Oxford University Press.

Molm, Linda D. 2007. "Power-Dependence Theory." In *The Blackwell Encyclopedia of Sociology*, edited by George Ritzer, 3598–3602. Oxford, UK: Blackwell.

Molm, Linda D. 2010. "The Structure of Reciprocity." *Social Psychology Quarterly* 73: 119–131.

Molm, Linda D., Monica M. Whithama, and David Melameda. 2012. "Forms of Exchange and Integrative Bonds: Effects of History and Embeddedness." *American Sociological Review* 77: 141–165.

Molm, Linda D., and Karen S. Cook. 1995. "Social Exchange and Exchange Networks." In *Sociological Perspective on Social Psychology*, edited by K. S. Cook, G. A. Fine, and J. S. House, 209–235. Boston: Allyn & Bacon.

Montemaggi, Francesca. 2016. "Shopping for a Church." In *Religion in Consumer Society*, edited by Francois Gauthier and Tuomas Martikainen, 109–124. New York: Routledge.

Montoya, I. D. 2005. "Effect of Peers on Employment and Implications for Drug Treatment." *American Journal of Drug and Alcohol Abuse* 31: 657–668.

Montt, Guillermo. 2011. "Cross-National Differences in Educational Inequality." *Sociology of Education* 84: 49–68.

Moore, Dahlia. 1995. "Role Conflict: Not Only for Women? A Comparative Analysis of 5 Nations." *International Journal of Comparative Sociology* 36 (1–2): 17–35.

Moraga, Cherrie, and Gloria Anzaldua, eds. 2015. *This Bridge Called My Back: Writings by Radical Women of Color*, 4th ed. Albany: SUNY Press.

Moran, Mary, Javier Guzman, Anne-Laure Ropars, Alina McDonald, Nicole Jameson, Brenda Omune, Sam Ryan, and Lindsey Wu. 2009. "Neglected Disease Research and Development: How Much Are We Really Spending?" *PLoS Med* 6(2): e1000030.

Morduch, Jonathan, and Rachel Schneider. 2017. *The Financial Diaries: How American Families Cope in a World of Uncertainty*. Princeton, NJ: Princeton University Press.

Morgan, George, and Scott Poynting, eds. 2012. *Global Islamophobia: Muslims* and the Moral Panic in the West. New York: Routledge.

Morgner, Christian. 2018. "The Relational Meaning-Making of Riots: Narrative Logic and Network Performance of the London 'Riots.'" In The Palgrave Handbook of Relational Sociology, edited by François Dépelteau, 579–600. Cham, Switzerland: Palgrave Macmillan.

Morris, Bonnie, and D. M. Withers. 2018. The Feminist Revolution: The Struggle for Women's Liberation. Washington, DC: Smithsonian Books.

Morris, J. Glenn, Lynn M. Grattan, Brian M. Mayer, and Jason K. Blackburn. 2013. "Psychological Responses and Resilience of People and Communities Impacted by the Deepwater Horizon Oil Spill." Transactions of the American Clinical and Climatological Association 124: 191–201.

Moses, Jonathon. 2006. International Migration: Globalization's Last Frontier. London: Zed Books.

Mosley, Philip E. 2009. "Bigorexia: Bodybuilding and Muscle Dysmorphia." European Eating Disorders Review 17: 191–198.

Mount, Ian. 2014. "Shopping in Europe: The New 'Grand Tour.'" Fortune, July 2. Accessed April 22, 2015. http://fortune.com/2014/07/02europe-global-shopping-tourism.

Mucherah, Winnie, and Andrea Dawn Frazier. 2013. "How Deep Is Skin-Deep? The Relationship between Skin Color Satisfaction, Estimation of Body Image, and Self-Esteem among Women of African Descent." Journal of Applied Social Psychology 43: 1177–1184.

Mukherjee, Ashesh. 2018. The Internet Trap: 5 Costs of Living Online. Toronto: University of Toronto Press.

Muniz, Ana. 2014. "Maintaining Racial Boundaries: Criminalization, Neighborhood Context, and the Origins of Gang Injunctions." Social Problems 61(2): 216–236.

Murphy, Susan, and Patrick Paul Walsh. 2014. "Social Protection beyond the Bottom Billion." Economic and Social Review 45(2): 261–284.

Naheem, Mohammed Ahmad. 2015. "AML Compliance—A Banking Nightmare? The HSBC Case Study." International Journal of Disclosure and Governance 12: 300–310.

Nanda, Serena. 1999. Neither Man nor Woman: The Hijras of India, 2nd ed. Belmont, CA: Wadsworth.

Naquin, Charles E., Terri R. Kurtzberg, and Liuba Y. Belkin. 2008. "E-mail Communication and Group Cooperation in Mixed Motive Contexts." Social Justice Research 21: 470–489.

Nardi, Peter M., David Sanders, and Judd Marmor. 1994. Growing Up before Stonewall: Life Stories of Some Gay Men. London: Routledge.

Nash, Catherine J., and Andrew Gorman-Murray. 2014. "LGBT Neighbourhoods and 'New Mobilities': Towards Understanding Transformations in Sexual and Gendered Urban Landscapes." International Journal of Urban & Regional Research 38(3): 756–772.

National Center for Education Statistics. 2017. "Percentage of Recent High School Completers." Accessed April 29, 2019. https://nces.ed.gov/programs/digest/d16/tables/dt16_302.30.asp

National Center for Education Statistics. 2022. "Table 206.10. Number and Percentage of Homeschooled Students Ages 5 through 17 with a Grade Equivalent of Kindergarten through 12th Grade, by Selected Child, Parent, and Household Characteristics: Selected Years, 1999 through 2019." https://nces.ed.gov/programs/digest/d21/tables/dt21_206.10.asp

National Center for Education Statistics. n.d. Enrollment. Retrieved May 16, 2023, from https://nces.ed.gov/fastfacts/display.asp?id=98

National Coalition Against Domestic Violence. n.d. "Statistics." Accessed June 17, 2023. https://ncadv.org/statistics

National Institute on Drug Abuse (2023, February 9). Drug Overdose Death Rates. NIDA.NIH.gov. Retrieved April 29, 2023, from https://nida.nih.gov/research-topics/trends-statistics/overdose-death-rates

National Institutes of Health (2022, June 16). Life expectancy in the U.S. Increased between 2000-2019, but widespread gaps among racial and ethnic groups exist. NIH.gov. Retrieved April 29, 2023, from https://www.nih.gov/news-events/news-releases/life-expectancy-us-increased-between-2000-2019-widespread-gaps-among-racial-ethnic-groups-exist

National Oceanic and Atmospheric Administration. 2023. "Broken Record: Atmospheric Carbon Dioxide Levels Jump Again." Accessed from https://www.noaa.gov/news-release/broken-record-atmospheric-carbon-dioxide-levels-jump-again

National Survey of Student Engagement. 2021. https://nsse.indiana.edu/research/annual-results/2021/index.html.

Navarro, Sharon S. and Samantha L. Hernandez. Eds. 2022. The Color of COVID-19: The racial inequality of marginalized communities. London: Routledge.

Ndinda, C., and T. P. Ndhlovu. 2018. "Gender, Poverty, and Inequality: Explorations from a Transformative Perspective." Journal of International Women's Studies 19(5): 1–12.

Nederveen Pieterse, Jan. 2015. Globalization and Culture: Global Melange, 2nd ed. Lanham, MD: Rowman & Littlefield.

Negrusa, Sebastian, Brighita Negrusa, and James Hosek. 2014. "Gone to War: Have Deployments Increased Divorces?" Journal of Population Economics 27: 473–496.

Neslihan, James, Eliza Weitbrecht, Trenel Francis, and Sarah Whitton. 2018. "Hooking Up and Emerging Adults' Relationship Attitudes and Expectations." Sexuality and Culture 19(72): 1–18.

Neuendorf, Kimberly A., Thomas D. Gore, Amy Dalessandro, Patricie Janstova, and Sharon Snyder-Suh. 2009. "Shaken and Stirred: A Content Analysis of Women's Portrayals in James Bond Films." Sex Roles 62: 747–776.

Newton, Davide. 2016. The Global Water Crisis: A Reference Handbook. Santa Barbara, CA: ABC-CLIO.

Newton, Isaac (with Stephen Hawking). [1687] 2005. Principia (On the Shoulders of Giants). Philadelphia: Running Press.

Newton, Michael. 2002. Savage Girls and Wild Boys: A History of Feral Children. London: Faber and Faber.

New York Times. 2018. "Eugenics' Backer's Name May Be Dropped from College Library." October 18.

Nguyen, Tomson H., and Henry N. Pontell. 2011. "Fraud and Inequality in the Subprime Mortgage Crisis." In Economic Crisis and Crime, edited by M. Deflem, 3–24. Bingley, UK: Emerald.

Nisen, Max. 2013. "Legacies Still Get a Staggeringly Unfair College Admissions Advantage." Business Insider, June 5. Accessed April 29, 2019. https://www.businessinsider.com/legacy-kids-have-anadmissions-advantage-2013-6.

Nordberg, Jenny. 2014. The Underground Girls of Kabul: In Search of a Hidden Resistance in Afghanistan. New York: Crown Group.

Norris, Dawn. 2011. "Interactions That Trigger Self-Labeling: The Case of Older Undergraduates." Symbolic Interaction 34: 173–197.

Obara-Minnitt, Mika. 2014. "Alternative Globalizations: An Integrative Approach to Studying Dissident Knowledge in the Global Justice Movement." *Journal of Contemporary European Studies* 22: 222–223.

O'Brien, Jodi. 2016. "Seeing Agnes: Notes on a Transgender Biocultural Ethnomethodology." *Symbolic Interaction* 39: 306–329.

O'Brien, Karen, Elin Selhoe, and Bronwyn M. Hayward. 2018. "Exploring Youth Activism on Climate Change: Dutiful, Disruptive, and Dangerous Dissent." *Ecology and Society* 23.

O'Connor, Brendan, and Martin Griffiths. 2005. *The Rise of Anti-Americanism*. London: Routledge.

O'Connor, Kathleen, and Eric Gladstone. 2018. "Beauty and Social Capital: Being Attractive Shapes Social Networks." *Social Networks* 52: 42–47.

OECD. 2016. "Marriage and Divorce Rates." Accessed April 29, 2019. https://www.oecd.org/els/family/SF_3_1_Marriage_and_divorce_rates.pdf.

OECD. 2017. "Key Characteristics of Parental Leave Systems." Accessed April 29, 2019. https://www.oecd.org/els/soc/PF2_1_Parental_leave_systems.pdf.

OECD. n.d.-b. *The 0.7% ODA/GNI Target: A History*. Retrieved May 18, 2023, from https://www.oecd.org/dac/financing-sustainable-development/development-finance-standards/the070dagnitarget-ahistory.htm

OECD. n.d.-a. *Official Development Assistance (ODA)*. Retrieved May 18, 2023, from https://www.oecd.org/dac/financing-sustainable-development/development-finance-standards/official-development-assistance.htm

Ohlsson-Wijk, Sofi, Jani Turunen, and Gunnar Anderson. 2017. "Family Forerunner? An Overview of Family Demographic Change in Sweden." *Working Paper* 2017 3: 1–25.

O'Loughlin, Deirdre M., Isabelle Szmigin, Morven G. McEachern, Belem Barbosa, Kalipso Karantinou, and María Eugenia Fernández-Moya. 2016. "Man Thou Art Dust: Rites of Passage in Austere Times." *Sociology* March 15 (published online).

Ong, Paul M. 2020. *COVID-19 and the Digital Divide in Virtual Learning, Fall 2020*. UCLA Center for Neighborhood Knowledge.

Ordaz, Luis, Lauren Schaeffer, Emily Choquette, Jordan Schueler, Lisa Wallace, and Kevin Thompson. 2018. "Thinness Pressure in Ethically Diverse College Women in the United States." *Body Image* 24: 1–4.

Orfield, Gary, and Erica Frankenberg. 2014. "Brown at 60: Great Progress, a Long Retreat and an Uncertain Future." The Civil Rights Project. Accessed April 29, 2019. https://civilrightsproject.ucla.edu/research/k-12-education/integration-and-diversity/brown-at-60-great-progress-a-long-retreat-and-an-uncertain-future.

Orlikowski, Wanda J. 2010. "Technology and Organization: Contingency All the Way Down." In *Technology and Organization: Essays in Honour of Joan Woodward*, edited by N. Phillips, G. Sewell, and D. Griffiths, 239–246. Bingley, UK: Emerald.

Ornstein, A. 2019. Wealth, Legacy and College Admission. *Society, 56*, 335–339. https://doi.org/10.1007/s12115-019-00377-2

Ortmeyer, David L., and Michael A. Quinn. 2012. "Coyotes, Migration Duration, and Remittances." *Journal of Developing Areas* 46: 185–203.

Orwell, George. 1949. *Nineteen Eighty-Four*. London: Secker and Warburg.

Ovaska, Tomi, and Ryo Takashima. 2010. "Does a Rising Tide Lift All the Boats? Explaining the National Inequality of Happiness." *Journal of Economic Issues* 44(1): 205–223.

Oxfam International. 2023, January 16. *Richest 1% bag nearly twice as much wealth as the rest of the world put together over the past two years*. Retrieved May 18, 2023, from https://www.oxfam.org/en/press-releases/richest-1-bag-nearly-twice-much-wealth-rest-world-put-together-over-past-two-years

Pace, Roberta, and Roberto Ham-Chande, eds. 2016. *Demographic Dividends: Emerging Challenges and Policy Implications*. Cham, Switzerland: Springer International.

Pager, Devah. 2009. *Marked: Race, Crime, and Finding Work in an Era of Mass Incarceration*. Chicago: University of Chicago.

Pager, Devah, and Bruce Western. 2012. "Identifying Discrimination at Work: The Use of Field Experiments." *Journal of Social Issues* 68: 221–237.

Pakulski, Jan. 2014. "Confusions about Multiculturalism." *Journal of Sociology* 50: 23–36.

Pantzar, Mike, and Elizabeth Shove. 2010. "Understanding Innovation in Practice: A Discussion of the Production and Reproduction of Nordic Walking." *Technology Analysis and Strategic Management* 22: 447–461.

Parigi, Paolo, Jessica J. Santana, and Karen S. Cook. 2017. "Online Field Experiments: Studying Social Interactions in Context." *Social Psychology Quarterly* 80: 1–19.

Park, Andrea. 2017. "#MeToo Reaches 85 Countries with 1.7M Tweets." Accessed April 29, 2019. https://www.cbsnews.com/news/metooreaches-85-countries-with-1-7-million-tweets/.

Park, Julie, and Hout Myers. 2010. "Intergenerational Mobility in the Post-1965 Immigration Era: Estimates by an Immigrant Generation Cohort Method." *Demography* 47: 369–392.

Parker, Pamela. 2012. "Study: Mobile and Video Are Key Drivers of Apparel Purchases." Marketing Land, August 14. Accessed April 20, 2015. http://marketingland.com/study-mobile-and-video-are-key-drivers-of-apparel-purchases-18927.

Parker, Richard, Jonathan Garcia, and Robert M. Buffington. 2014. "Sexuality and the Contemporary World: Globalization and Sexual Rights." In *A Global History of Sexuality: The Modern Era*, edited by R. M. Buffington, E. Luibhéid, and D. J. Guy, 221–260. Chichester, UK: Wiley.

Parkinson, Cyril Northcote. 1955. "Parkinson's Law." *Economist*, November 19.

Parks-Savage, Agatha, Linda Archer, Heather Newton, Elizabeth Wheeler, and Shaun Hubbard. 2018. "Prevention of Medical Errors and Malpractice: Is Creating Resilience in Physicians Part of the Answer?" *International Journal of Law and Psychiatry* 60: 35–39.

Parreñas, Rhacel Salazar. 2015. *Servants of Globalization: Migration and Domestic Labor*. Stanford, CA: Stanford University Press.

Pascoe, John M., David L. Wood, James H. Duffee, and Alice Kuo. 2016. "Mediators and Adverse Effects of Child Poverty in the United States." *Pediatrics* 37: e1–e17.

Pasquali, M. (2023, February 27). *E-commerce worldwide—statistics & facts*. Retrieved May 18, 2023, from https://www.statista.com/topics/871/online-shopping/

Patchin, Justin W., and Sameer Hinduja. 2010. "Trends in Online Social Networking: Adolescent Use of MySpace over Time." *New Media and Society* 12: 197–216.

Patterson, Charlotte J., Rachel H. Farr, and Paul D. Hastings. 2015. "Socialization in the Context of Family Diversity." In *Handbook of Socialization: Theory and Research*, 2nd ed., edited by Joan E. Grusec and Paul D. Hastings, 202–227. New York: Guilford Press.

Patterson, Orlando, and Ethan Fosse, eds. 2015. *The Cultural Matrix: Understanding*

Black Youth. Cambridge, MA: Harvard University Press.

Patterson, Orlando, and Xiaolin Zhou. 2018. "Modern Trafficking, Slavery, and Other Forms of Servitude." *Annual Review of Sociology* 44: 407–439.

Pavalko, Eliza K., and Glen H. Elder Jr. 1990. "World War II and Divorce: A Life-Course Perspective." *American Journal of Sociology* 95: 1213–1234.

Payne, Elizabeth, and Melissa Smith. 2014. "The Big Freak Out: Educator Fear in Response to the Presence of Transgender Elementary School Students." *Journal of Homosexuality* 61(3): 399–418.

PBS. 2010. *Frontline: Digital Nation*. Accessed May 25, 2011. http://www.pbs.org/wgbh/pagesfrontline/digitalnation/view.

Pearce, Diane. 1978. "The Feminization of Poverty: Women, Work, and Welfare." *Urban and Social Change Review* 11: 28–36.

Pearlin, Leonard I. 1989. "The Sociological Study of Stress." *Journal of Health and Social Behavior* 30: 241–256.

Pelikán, Vojtech, Lucie Galcanova, and Lukas Kala. 2017. "Ecological Habitus Intergenerationally Reproduced: The Children of Czech 'Voluntary Simplifiers' and Their Lifestyle." *Journal of Consumer Culture*. https://doi.org/10.1177/1469540517736560

People's Daily News. 2018. "China Has Become the World's Fastest Growing Tobacco Consumer Market: Report." Accessed April 29, 2019. http://en.people.cn/n3/2018/0102/c90000-9310770.html.

Perelli-Harris, Brienna, and Nora Sanchez Gassen. 2012. "How Similar Are Cohabitation and Marriage? Legal Approaches to Cohabitation across Western Europe." *Population and Development Review* 38: 435–467.

Perez, Sarah. 2017. "Target Rolls out Bluetooth Beacon Technology in Stores to Power New Indoor Map in its App." Accessed April 29, 2019. https://techcrunch.com/2017/09/20/target-rolls-outbluetooth-beacon-technology-in-stores-to-power-new-indoormaps-in-its-app/.

Perrow, Charles. 1999. *Normal Accidents*. Princeton, NJ: Princeton University Press.

Perry-Fraser, Charity, and Rick Fraser. 2018. "A Qualitative Analysis of the Stepparent Role on Transition Days in Blended Families." *Open Journal of Social Sciences* 6(8): 240–251.

Peterson, Abby, Mattias Wahlström, and Magnus Wennerhag. 2018. *Pride Parades and LGBT Movements*. New York: Routledge.

Peterson, Helen. 2016. "Is Managing Academics 'Women's Work'? Exploring the Glass Cliff in Higher Education Management." *Educational Management Administration and Leadership* 44: 112–127.

Petrosyan, Ani. 2023a. *Common Languages Used for Web Content 2023, by Share of Websites*. https://www.statista.com/statistics/262946/most-common-languages-on-the-internet/

Petrosyan, Ani. 2023b, April 3. *Number of Internet and Social Media Users Worldwide as of January 2023 (in billions)*. Retrieved May 18, 2023, from https://www.statista.com/statistics/617136/digital-population-worldwide/

Pew Research Center. 2018. "When Americans Say They Believe in God, What Do They Mean?" April 25. Accessed April 29, 2019. https://www.pewforum.org/2018/04/25/when-americans-saythey-believe-in-god-what-do-they-mean/.

Pew Research Center. 2023. "What the Data Says about Gun Deaths in the U.S." Available at https://www.pewresearch.org/short-reads/2023/04/26/what-the-data-says-about-gun-deaths-in-the-u-s/ft_23-04-20_gundeathsupdate_2/

Pfeffer, Max J., and Pilar A. Parra. 2009. "Strong Ties, Weak Ties, and Human Capital: Latino Immigrant Employment Outside the Enclave." *Rural Sociology* 74(2): 241–269.

Pfeffer, Naomi. 2011. "Eggs-ploiting Women: A Critical Feminist Analysis of the Different Principles in Transplant and Fertility Tourism." *Reproductive Biomedicine Online* 23: 634–641. doi:10.1016/j.rbm0.2011.08.005

Pfeiffer, Mary Beth. 2018. *Lyme: The First Epidemic of Climate Change*. Washington, DC: Island Press.

Phelan, Jo C., Bruce G. Link, Ana Diez-Roux, Ichiro Kawachi, and Bruce Levin. 2004. "'Fundamental Causes' of Social Inequalities in Mortality: A Test of the Theory." *Journal of Health and Social Behavior* 45: 265–285.

Phelan, Jo C., Bruce G. Link, and Parisa Tehranifar. 2010. "Social Conditions as Fundamental Causes of Health Inequalities: Theory, Evidence, and Policy Implications." *Journal of Health and Social Behavior* 51: S28–S40.

Phelan, Joe. 2022, March 27. *What countries and cities will disappear due to rising sea levels*? Live Science. Retrieved May 12, 2023, from https://www.livescience.com/what-places-disappear-rising-sea-levels

Phipps, Alison, Jessica Ringrose, Emma Renold, and Carolyn Jackson. 2018. "Rape Culture, Lad Culture, and Everyday Sexism: Researching, Conceptualizing, and Politicizing New Mediations of Gender and Sexual Violence." *Journal of Gender Studies* 27(1): 1–8.

Pick, James B., and Aviit Sarkar. 2015. *The Global Digital Divides: Explaining Change*. Dordrecht, The Netherlands: Springer.

Pickering, Mary. 2011. "Auguste Comte." In *The Wiley-Blackwell Companion to Major Social Theorists*, Vol. 1, *Classical Theorists*, edited by George Ritzer and Jeffrey Stepnisky, 30–60. Malden, MA: Wiley-Blackwell.

Piketty, Thomas. 2014. *Capital in the Twenty-First Century*. Cambridge, MA: Belknap Press.

Pilcher, Jane. 2013. "'Small but Very Determined': A Novel Theorization of Children's Consumption of Culture." *Cultural Sociology* 7: 86–100.

Pilkington, Pamela D., and Holly Rominov. 2017. "Fathers' Worries During Pregnancy: A Qualitative Content Analysis of Redditt." *The Journal of Perinatal Education* 26(4): 208–218.

Piquero, Alex R., Raymond Paternoster, Greg Pogarsky, and Thomas Loughran. 2011. "Elaborating the Individual Difference Component in Deterrence Theory." *Annual Review of Law and Social Science* 7: 335–360.

Plante, Rebecca F. 2015. *Sexualities in Context: A Social Perspective*, 2nd ed. New York: Routledge.

Plante, Rebecca F., and Andrew P. Smiler. 2014. "Time for a Sexual-Climate Change." *Chronicle of Higher Education*, November 26. Accessed April 17, 2015. http://chronicle.com/blogs/conversation/2014/11/26/time-for-a-sexual-climate-change.

Pleyers, Geoffrey. 2010. *Alter-Globalization: Becoming Actors in the Global Age*. Cambridge, UK: Polity Press.

Plummer, Ken. 2007. "Sexual Markets, Commodification, and Consumption." In *The Blackwell Encyclopedia of Sociology*, edited by George Ritzer, 4242–4244. Malden, MA: Blackwell.

Plummer, Ken. 2019. "Critical Sexuality Studies." In *The Wiley-Blackwell Companion to Sociology*, 2nd ed., edited by George Ritzer and Wendy Wiedenhoft Murphy, 243–268. Chichester, UK: John Wiley & Sons.

Pogge, T. 2017. "Cosmopolitanism." In *A Companion to Contemporary Political Philosophy*, edited by R. E. Goodin, P. Pettit, and T. Pogge, 312–331. Chichester, UK: John Wiley & Sons.

Polakow-Suransky, Sasha. 2017. *Go Back to Where You Came From: The Backlash against Immigration and the Fate of Western Democracy.* New York: Nation Books.

Polgreen, Linnea A., and Nicole B. Simpson. 2011. "Happiness and International Migration." *Journal of Happiness Studies* 12(3): 819–840.

"Police Discover Five Children 'Hidden from Society in Squalid Home and Raised without Schooling or Healthcare.'" 2010. *Daily Mail*, November 30. Accessed May 25, 2015. http://www.dailymail.co.uk/news/article-1334132/Police-discover-5-children-hidden-society-squalid-home.html.

Popenoe, David. 1993. "American Family Decline, 1960–1990: A Review and Appraisal." *Journal of Marriage and the Family* 55: 527–542.

Popper, Nathaniel. 2015. *Digital Gold*. New York: Harper.

Popper, Nathaniel. 2018. "Goldman Sachs to Open a Bitcoin Trading Operation." *New York Times*, May 2.

Population Reference Bureau. 2018. "2018 World Population Data Sheet with Focus on Changing Age Structures." Accessed April 29, 2019. https://www.prb.org/2018-world-population-data-sheet-withfocus-on-changing-age-structures/.

Porter, Eduardo. 2016. "The Crumbling Case for a Mexican Border Wall." *New York Times*, September 6.

Posner, Eric, and Glen Weyl. 2018. "The Real Villain Behind Our New Gilded Age." *New York Times*, May 1.

Poster, Winnifred. 2007. "Who's on the Line? Indian Call Center Agents Pose as Americans for U.S.-Outsourced Firms." *Industrial Relations* 46(2): 271–304.

Povoledo, Elisabetta. 2018. "'We Abandoned Them': Pope Francis Condemns Sex Abuse Cover-Up." *New York Times*, August 20.

Prassi, Jeremais. 2018. *Humans as a Service: The Promise and Perils of Work in the Gig Economy*. New York: Oxford University Press.

Presser, Harriet B. 2005. *Working in a 24/7 Economy*. New York: Russell Sage Foundation.

Prideaux, Bruce, and Petra Glover. 2014. "'Santa Claus Is Coming to Town': Christmas Holidays in a Tropical Destination." *Asia Pacific Journal of Tourism Research*, September 29 (published online). doi:1 0.1080/10941665.2014.951061

Prior, Sarah, Brooke de Heer, and Megan Maas. 2022. "Navigating Structural Inequalities of Mothering in the Academy during COVID-19." In *Pandemic Pedagogies: Teaching and Learning during the COVID-19 Pandemic*, edited by J. Michael Ryan. London: Routledge.

Prot, Sara, Craig A. Anderson, Douglas A. Gentile, Wayne Warburton, Muniba Saleem, Christopher L. Groves, and Stephanie C. Brown. 2015. "Media as Agents of Socialization." In *Handbook of Socialization: Theory and Research*, 2nd ed., edited by Joan E. Grusec and Paul D. Hastings, 276–300. New York: Guilford Press.

Protess, Ben, Alan Feuer, and Danny Hakim. 2023. "Donald Trump Faces Several Investigations. Here's Where They Stand." *New York Times*, June 16. Available at https://www.nytimes.com/article/trump-investigations-civil-criminal.html

Pugh, Allison. 2015. *The Tumbleweed Society: Working and Caring in an Age of Insecurity*. New York: Oxford University Press.

Pugh, Derek S., David Hickson, C. R. Hinings, and C. Turner. 1968. "The Context of Organizational Structures." *Administrative Science Quarterly* 14: 91–114.

Purdam, Kingsley, Elisabeth A. Garratt, and Aneez Esmail. 2015. "Hungry? Food Insecurity, Social Stigma, and Embarrassment in the UK." *Sociology* 50: 1072–1088.

Putnam, Robert. 2001. *Bowling Alone: The Collapse and Revival of American Community*. New York: Simon & Schuster.

Quinton, Sarah. 2018. *Understanding Research in the Digital Age*. London: SAGE.

Quist-Adade, Charles. 2018. *Symbolic Interactionism: The Basics*. Wilmington, NC: Vernon Press.

Rabin, Roni Caryn. 2018. "Put a Ring on It? Millennial Couples Are in No Hurry." *New York Times*, May 29.

Radesky, Jenny S., Caroline J. Kistin, Barry Zuckerman, Katie Nitzberg, Jamie Gross, Margot Kaplan-Sanoff, Marilyn Augustyn, and Michael Silverstein. 2014. "Patterns of Mobile Device Use by Caregivers and Children during Meals in Fast Food Restaurants." *Pediatrics*, March 10 (published online). doi:10.1542/peds.2013–3703

Radford, Jason, and David Lazer. 2020. "Big Data for Sociological Research." In *The Wiley-Blackwell Companion to Sociology*, 2nd ed., edited by George Ritzer and Wendy Wiedenhoft Murphy. Malden, MA: Wiley-Blackwell.

RAINN. 2023. "About Sexual Assault." Accessed June 24, 2023. https://www.rainn.org/about-sexual-assault.

Ram, Uri. 2007. *The Globalization of Israel: McWorld in Tel Aviv, Jihad in Jerusalem*. London: Routledge.

Ravitch, Diane. 2012. "Schools We Can Envy." *New York Review of Books*, March 8, 19–20.

Rawls, Anne. 2015. "Interaction Order: The Making of Social Facts." In *Order on the Edge of Chaos*, edited by Edward J. Lawler, Shane R. Thye, and Jeongkoo Yoon, 227–247. New York: Cambridge University Press.

Ray, Paula. 2018. "Surfing the Fourth Wave of the Feminist Movement via SNS." In *Orienting Feminism*, edited by Catherine Dale and Rosemary Overell, 113–133. Cham, Switzerland: Palgrave Macmillan.

Ray, V. (2019). A Theory of Racialized Organizations. *American Sociological Review*, 84(1), 26–53. https://doi.org/10.1177/0003122418822335

Razavi, Shahra. 2017. "Care Going Global? Afterword." In *Gender, Migration, and the Work of Care*, edited by S. Michel and I. Peng, 295–304. Cham, Switzerland: Palgrave Macmillan.

Reay, Barry. 2014. "Promiscuous Intimacies: Rethinking the History of American Casual Sex." *Journal of Historical Sociology* 27: 1–24.

Reed College. 2015. "Sexual Assault Prevention and Response at Reed." Accessed March 28, 2015. http://www.reed.edu/sexual_assault/definitions/consent.html.

Reed, Mark S., and Lindsay C. Stringer. 2016. *Land Degradation, Desertification and Climate Change: Anticipating, Assessing and Adapting to Future Change*. New York: Routledge.

Reed, Shayla. 2018. "Protecting Our Elders: Potential Signs of Nursing Home Abuse and Neglect." *Nebraska Lawyer Magazine* 21(3): 11.

Regnerus, Mark, and Jeremy Uecker. 2011. *Premarital Sex in America: How Young Americans Meet, Mate, and Think about Marrying*. Oxford, UK: Oxford University Press.

Reich, Adam, and Peter Bearman. 2018. *Working for Respect: Community and Conflict at Walmart*. New York: Columbia University Press.

Reichel, Philip, and Ryan Randa, eds. 2017. *Transnational Crime and Global Security.* Santa Barbara, CA: Praeger.

Reid, Colleen. 2004. "Advancing Women's Social Justice Agendas: A Feminist Action Research Framework." *International Journal of Qualitative Methods* 3(3): 1–15.

Restivo, Emily, and Mark M. Lanier. 2015. "Measuring the Contextual Effects and Mitigating Factors of Labeling Theory." *Justice Quarterly* 32(1): 116–141.

Reuter, T. R., M. E. Newcomb, S. W. Whitton, and B. Mustanski. 2017. "Intimate Partner Violence Victimization in LGBT Young Adults: Demographic Differences and Associations with Health Behaviors." *Psychology of Violence* 7(1): 101–109.

Reuters. 2018a. "Cuba Says United States Pursues 'Path of Confrontation.'" *New York Times*, October 24.

Reuters. 2018c. "Villagers Fear for Survival on India's Disappearing Island." *New York Times*, November 28.

Reverby, Susan. 2009. *Examining Tuskegee: The Infamous Syphilis Study and Its Legacy.* Chapel Hill: University of North Carolina Press.

Richardson, Valerie. 2018. "Educational Decline: Homeschooling Surges as Parents Seek Safe Option for Children." *Washington Post*, May 30.

Riches, William Martin. 2017. *The Civil Rights Movement*, 4th ed. London: Palgrave.

Rieger, Jon H. 2007. "Key Informant." In *The Blackwell Encyclopedia of Sociology*, edited by George Ritzer, 2457–2458. Malden, MA: Blackwell.

Rindermann, Heiner, and Antonia E. E. Baumeister. 2015. "Parents' SES vs. Parental Educational Behavior and Children's Development: A Reanalysis of the Hart and Risley Study." *Learning and Individual Differences* 37: 133–138.

Rippeyoug, Phyllis L. F., and Mary C. Noonan. 2012. "Is Breastfeeding Truly Cost Free? Income Consequences of Breastfeeding for Women." *American Sociological Review* 77: 244–267.

Ritzer, George. 1975. *Sociology: A Multiple Paradigm Science.* Boston: Allyn & Bacon.

Ritzer, George. 1995. *Expressing America: A Critique of the Global Credit Card Society.* Thousand Oaks, CA: Pine Forge Press.

Ritzer, George. 2010a. "Cathedrals of Consumption: Rationalization, Enchantment, and Disenchantment." In *McDonaldization: The Reader*, 3rd ed., edited by George Ritzer, 234–239. Thousand Oaks, CA: Pine Forge Press.

Ritzer, George. 2010b. *Enchanting a Disenchanted World: Continuity and Change in the Cathedrals of Consumption.* Thousand Oaks, CA: Sage.

Ritzer, George. 2012a. "'Hyperconsumption' and 'Hyperdebt': A 'Hypercritical' Analysis." In *A Debtor World: Interdisciplinary Perspective on Debt*, edited by Ralph Brubaker, Robert W. Lawless, and Charles J. Tabb, 60–80. New York: Oxford University Press.

Ritzer, George. 2013. "The 'New' Prosumer: Collaboration on the Digital and Material 'New Means of Prosumption.'" Paper presented at the annual meeting of the Eastern Sociological Society, Boston, March.

Ritzer, George. 2015b. "Prosumer Capitalism." *Sociological Quarterly* 56: 413–443.

Ritzer, George. 2016. "Deglobalization? Not a Chance." November 24. Accessed March 13, 2017. https://georgeritzer.wordpress.com/2016/11/24/deglobalization-not-a-chance.

Ritzer, George. 2019. *The McDonaldization of Society: Into the Digital Age*, 9th ed. Thousand Oaks, CA: SAGE.

Ritzer, George. 2021. *The McDonaldization of Society: Into the Digital Age*, 10th ed. Thousand Oaks, CA: Sage.

Ritzer, George. 2021. The McDonaldization of Society, 10th ed. Thousand Oaks, CA: Sage.

Ritzer, George, Chris Rojek, and J. Michael Ryan. Forthcoming. *Blackwell Encyclopedia of Sociology*, 2nd ed. London: Wiley-Blackwell.

Ritzer, George, Douglas Goodman, and Wendy Wiedenhoft. 2001. "Theories of Consumption." In *Handbook of Social Theory*, edited by George Ritzer and B. Smart, 410–427. London: SAGE.

Ritzer, George, ed. 2007. *The Blackwell Encyclopedia of Sociology.* Malden, MA: Blackwell.

Ritzer, George, ed. 2010c. *The McDonaldization of Society: The Reader*, 3rd ed. Thousand Oaks, CA: Pine Forge Press.

Ritzer, George, ed. 2012b. *The Wiley-Blackwell Encyclopedia of Globalization.* Malden, MA: Wiley-Blackwell.

Ritzer, George, J. Michael Ryan, and Jeff Stepnisky. 2005. "Transformations in Consumer Settings: Landscapes and Beyond." In *Inside Consumption*, edited by R. Ratneshwar and D. Mick, 292–308. New York: Routledge.

Ritzer, George, and Craig Lair. 2007. "Outsourcing: Globalization and Beyond." In *The Blackwell Companion to Globalization*, edited by George Ritzer, 307–329. Malden, MA: Blackwell.

Ritzer, George and J. Michael Ryan. 2003. "Toward a Richer Understanding of Global Commodification: Glocalization and Grobalization," *The Hedgehog Review*, 5 (2): 66–76.

Ritzer, George and J. Michael Ryan. 2004. "Americanisation, McDonaldisation, and Globalisation." In *Issues in Americanisation and Culture*, edited by Neil Campbell, Jude Davies, and George McKay, 41–60. Edinburgh, Scotland: Edinburgh University Press.

Ritzer, George, and Jeffrey Stepnisky, eds. 2018. *Sociological Theory*, 10th ed. Thousand Oaks, CA: SAGE.

Ritzer, George and Michael Ryan. 2004. "Americanisation, McDonaldisation, and Globalisation." In *Issues in Americanisation and Culture*, edited by Neil Campbell, Jude Davies, and George McKay, 41–60. Edinburgh, Scotland: Edinburgh University Press.

Ritzer, George, and Nathan Jurgenson. 2010. "Production, Consumption, Prosumption: The Nature of Capitalism in the Age of the Digital 'Prosumer.'" *Journal of Consumer Culture* 10(1): 13–36.

Ritzer, George, and Paul Dean. 2019. *Globalization: The Essentials*, 2nd ed. Malden, MA: Wiley-Blackwell.

Ritzer, George, and Paul Dean. 2021. *Globalization: A Basic Text*. 3rd ed. London: Wiley.

Ritzer, George, and Steve Miles. 2019. "The Changing Nature of Consumption and the Intensification of McDonaldization in the Digital Age." *Journal of Consumer Culture* 19: 3–20.

Rizvi, Fazal. 2012. "Bollywood." In *The Wiley-Blackwell Encyclopedia of Globalization*, edited by George Ritzer, 120–121. Malden, MA: Wiley-Blackwell.

Roberts, Sam. 2009. "In 2025, India to Pass China in Population, U.S. Estimates." *New York Times*, December 16.

Rodgers, R. F., S. R. Damiano, E. H. Wertheim, and S. J. Paxton. 2017. "Media Exposure in Very Young Girls: Prospective and Cross-Sectional Relationships with BMIz, Self-Esteem, and Body Size Stereotypes." *Developmental Psychology* 53(12): 2356–2363.

Rodriguez-Franco, Diana. 2016. "Internal Wars, Taxation, and State Building." *American Sociological Review* 81(1): 190–213.

Roehling, Patricia, Loma Hernandez Jarvis, and Heather Swope. 2005. "Variations in Negative Work–Family Spillover among White, Black, and Hispanic American Men and Women." *Journal of Family Issues* 26(6): 840–865.

Rogan, Michael, Sally Roever, Martha Alter Chen, and Françoise Carré. 2017. "Informal Employment in the Global South: Globalization, Production Relations, and 'Precarity.'" In *Precarious Work (Research in the Sociology of Work)*, Vol. 31, edited by Arne L. Kalleberg and Steven P. Vallas, 307–333. Bingley, UK: Emerald.

Rogin, Josh. 2016. "Congress Wary of National Security Implications of Chinese Deal for Chicago Stock Exchange," *Chicago Tribune*, February 17. Accessed March 8, 2017. http://www.chicagotribune.com/business/ct-congress-chicago-stock-exchange-sale-20160217-story.html.

Rojek, Chris. 2005. *Leisure Theory: Principles and Practice*. New York: Palgrave Macmillan.

Rojek, Chris. 2007. *The Labour of Leisure: The Culture of Free Time*. London: SAGE.

Romanienk, Lisiunia. 2011. *Body Piercing and Identity Construction: A Comparative Perspective*. New York: Palgrave.

Romero, Simon, and Miriam Jordan. 2018. "On the Border; a Discouraging New Message for Asylum Seekers: Wait." *New York Times*, June 12.

Rooks, Noliwe. 2017. *Cutting School: Privatization, Segregation, and the End of Public Education*. New York: New Press.

Roscoe, Will. 1998. *Changing Ones: Third and Fourth Genders in Native North America*. New York: Palgrave/St. Martin's Press.

Rose, Arnold. 1967. *The Power Structure*. New York: Oxford University Press.

Rose, Claire. 2010. *Making, Selling, and Wearing Boys' Clothes in Late-Victorian England*. Burlington, VT: Ashgate.

Rosenbaum, James. 2001. *Beyond College for All: Career Paths for the Forgotten Half*. New York: Russell Sage Foundation.

Rosenbaum, James. 2011. "The Complexities of College for All: Beyond Fairy-Tale Dreams." *Sociology of Education* 84: 113–117.

Rosenberg, Morris. 1979. *Conceiving the Self*. New York: Basic Books.

Rosenstein, Judith E. 2008. "Individual Threat, Group Threat, and Racial Policy: Exploring the Relationship between Threat and Racial Attitudes." *Social Science Research* 37: 1130–1146.

Rosenthal, Lisa, and Marci Lobel. 2016. "Stereotypes of Black American Women Related to Sexuality and Motherhood." *Psychology of Women Quarterly* 40: 414–427.

Roser, Max, Ortiz-Ospina, E., & Ritchie, H. 2019, October. *Life Expectancy*. Retrieved May 18, 2023, from https://ourworldindata.org/life-expectancy

Roser, Max, and Hannah Ritchie. 2018. "Burden of Disease." Accessed April 30, 2019. https://ourworldindata.org/burden-of-disease.

Rosewarne, Laruen. 2016. *Intimacy on the Internet*. New York: Routledge.

Ross, Alec. 2017. *The Industries of the Future*. New York: Simon & Schuster.

Rossi, Alice. 1983. "Gender and Parenthood." *American Sociological Review* 49: 1–19.

Rostow, Walt. 1960. *The Stages of Economic Growth: A Non-Communist Manifesto*. Cambridge, UK: Cambridge University Press.

Rostow, Walt. 1978. *The World Economy: History and Prospect*. Austin: University of Texas Press.

Roszak, Theodore. [1968] 1995. *The Making of a Counter Culture: Reflections on the Technocratic Society and Its Youthful Opposition*. Berkeley: University of California Press.

Rotberg, Iris C., and Joshua L. Glazer. 2018. *Choosing Charters: Better Schools or More Segregation?* New York: Teachers College.

Roth, Benita. 2017. *The Life and Death of ACT UP/LA: Anti-AIDS Activism in Los Angeles from the 1980s to the 2000s*. Cambridge, UK: Cambridge University Press.

Roth, Julius A. 1963. *Timetables: Structuring the Passage of Time in Hospital Treatment and Other Careers*. Indianapolis, IN: Bobbs-Merrill.

Roth, Mitchell. 2018. *Global Organized Crime*, 2nd ed. New York: Routledge.

Rothe, Dawn, and David O. Friedrichs. 2016. "The State of Criminology of Crimes of the State." In *Recent Developments in Criminology Theory: Toward Disciplinary Diversity and Theoretical Integration*, edited by Stuart Henry and Scott A. Lucas, 147–161. New York: Routledge.

Rousseau, Nicole. 2011. *Black Women's Burden: Commodifying Black Reproduction*. New York: Palgrave Macmillan.

Roxburgh, S. 2004. "There Just Aren't Enough Hours in the Day: The Mental Health Consequences of Time Pressures." *Journal of Health and Social Behavior* 45: 115–131.

Rozdeba, Suzanne. 2011. "Firefighters Recall Spirit of 9/11 Hero." *New York Times, East Village Local*, January 10. Accessed March 31, 2012. http://localeastvillage.com/2011/01/10/firefighters-recall-spirit-of-911-hero/.

Rubington, Earl, and Martin Weinberg, eds. 2016. *Deviance: The Interactionist Approach*, 10th ed. New York: Routledge.

Rumens, Nick. 2016. "Sexualities and accounting: A queer theory perspective." *Critical Perspectives on Accounting* 35: 111–120.

Runyon, Anne Sisson. 2012. "Gender." In *The Wiley-Blackwell Encyclopedia of Globalization*, edited by George Ritzer, 725–734. Malden, MA: Wiley-Blackwell.

Rutherford, Paul. 2007. *The World Made Sexy: Freud to Madonna*. Toronto: University of Toronto Press.

Ryan, J. Michael. 2011. "Globalizing Consumption and Consuming Globalization: Exploring Theories of Global Consumer Culture." In *Inequality in a Globalizing World: Perspectives, Processes, and Experiences*, edited by Sangeeta Parashar and Yong Wang, 347–356. Dubuque, IA: Kendall Hunt.

Ryan, J. Michael. 2013. *Easton: A 21st Century (R)evolution in Consumption, Community, Urbanism, and Space*. Ann Arbor, MI: ProQuest.

Ryan, J. Michael. 2013. "Improving Survey Measurement Questions for Sexual Minorities and the Trans Population: Toward an Understanding of the Socially Constructed Nature of the Trans Life." PhD diss., University of Maryland.

Ryan, J. Michael. "Postmodern Social Theory." In *The Wiley-Blackwell Encyclopedia of Sociology*, 7 December, 2017. https://doi.org/10.1002/9781405165518.wbeosp070.pub2

Ryan, J. Michael. 2018. "Gender Identity Laws: The Legal Status of Global Sex/Gender Identity Recognition." *LGBTQ Policy Journal* VIII: 3–16.

Ryan, J. Michael. 2019. "Communicating Trans Identity: Toward an Understanding of the Selection and Significance of Gender Identity–Based Terminology," *Journal of Language and Sexuality* 8(2): 221–241. doi: 10.1075/jls.19001.rya

Ryan, J. Michael. 2020. "Expressing Identity: Toward an Understanding of How Trans Individuals Navigate the Barriers and Opportunities of Official Identity." *Journal of Gender Studies* 29(3): 349–360. doi:10.1080/09589236.2019.1570841

Ryan, J. Michael. 2020. "Queer Theory." In *The Wiley Companion to Sexuality Studies*, edited by Nancy Naples, 79–95. London: Wiley-Blackwell.

Ryan, J. Michael. 2021. "Trans Celebrity: An Examination of the Pros and Cons of the Trans Spokesperson." In *Beyond Binaries: Trans Identities in Contemporary Culture*, edited by John Lamonthe. Washington, D.C.: Lexington.

Ryan, J. Michael. 2021. "The SARS Cov-2 Virus and the COVID-19 Pandemic," In *COVID-19: Global Pandemic, Societal Responses, Ideological Solutions*, edited by J. Michael Ryan, 9–19. London: Routledge.

Ryan, J. Michael. 2022. "Global Consciousness of COVID-19: Where Can We Go from Here?" In *Creative Resilience and COVID-19: Figuring the Everyday in a Pandemic*, edited by Irene Gammel and Jason Wang. London: Routledge.

Ryan, J. Michael. 2022. "The Blessings of COVID-19 for Nationalism, Neoliberalism, and Neoconservative Ideologies." In *COVID-19: Global Pandemic, Societal Responses, Ideological Solutions*, edited by J. Michael Ryan, 80–93. London: Routledge.

Ryan, J. Michael. 2023. "Pandemic Pedagogies: Teaching and Learning During the COVID-19 Pandemic." In *Pandemic Pedagogies: Teaching and Learning during the COVID-19 Pandemic*, edited by J. Michael Ryan, 14–30. London: Routledge.

Ryan, J. Michael, ed. 2021a. *COVID-19: Volume II: Social Consequences and Cultural Adaptations*. London: Routledge.

Ryan, J. Michael., ed. 2023. *COVID-19: Individual rights and community responsibilities*. London: Routledge.

Ryan, J. Michael, ed. 2023. *COVID-19: Surviving a Pandemic*. London: Routledge.

Ryan, J. Michael, ed. 2023. *Pandemic Pedagogies: Teaching and Learning during the COVID-19 Pandemic*. London: Routledge.

Ryan, J. Michael. Forthcoming. "Cathedrals of Consumption." In *The Wiley-Blackwell Encyclopedia of Sociology*, 2nd ed., edited by George Ritzer, Chris Rojek, and J. Michael Ryan. London: Wiley.

Ryan, J. Michael and Serena Nanda. 2022. *COVID-19: Social Inequalities and Human Possibilities*. London: Routledge.

Ryan, J. Michael, and Serena Nanda. 2023. "The Importance of Culture in Understanding the COVID-19 Pandemic." In *COVID-19: Cultural Change and Institutional Adaptations*, edited by J. Michael Ryan. London: Routledge.

Ryan, J. Michael and Serena Nanda. 2023a. "Pandemic Politics and the Politics of the Pandemic." In *COVID-19: Individual Rights and Community Responsibilities*, edited by J. Michael Ryan, 105–123. London: Routledge.

Ryan, J. Michael and Serena Nanda. 2023b. "School Closures during the COVID-19 Pandemic: Diverse Strategies, Unequal Impacts." In *Pandemic Pedagogies: Teaching and Learning during the COVID-19 Pandemic*, edited by J. Michael Ryan, 58–72. London: Routledge.

Ryan, J. Michael and Serena Nanda. 2023c. "Vaccines: Are We Really All in This Together?," In *COVID-19: Surviving a Pandemic*, edited by J. Michael Ryan, 170–190. London: Routledge.

Ryan, Kevin. 1994. "Technicians and Interpreters in Moral Crusades: The Case of the Drug Courier Profile." *Deviant Behavior* 15: 217–240.

Ryan, M. K., and S. A. Haslam. 2005. "The Glass Cliff: Evidence That Women Are Over-represented in Precarious Leadership Positions." *British Journal of Management* 16: 81–90.

Ryave, A. Lincoln, and James N. Schenkein. 1974. "Notes on the Art of Walking." In *Ethnomethodology: Selected Readings*, edited by R. Turner, 265–275. Harmondsworth, UK: Penguin.

Rysst, Mari. "I Want to Be Me. I Want to Be Kul": An Anthropological Study of Norwegian Preteen Girls in the Light of a Presumed "Disappearance" of Childhood." PhD diss., 2008. University of Oslo.

Safronova, Valeriya. 2019. "What's So 'Indecent' About Female Pleasure?" *New York Times*, January 18.

Sahlberg, Pasi. 2011. *Finnish Lessons: What Can the World Learn from Educational Change in Finland*? New York: Teachers College Press.

Sahlberg, Pasi. 2018. "PISA in Finland: An Education Miracle or an Obstacle to Change." *Center for Educational Policy Studies Journal* 1(3): 119–140.

Said, Edward W. [1979] 1994. *Orientalism*. New York: Knopf.

Salinas, Rebecca. 2014. "Corpus Christi 'Mantique' Store Equips the Man Cave." *San Antonio Express-News, My San Antonio* Blog, July 28. Accessed April 21, 2015. http://www.mysanantonio.com/news/local/article/Corpus-Christi-man-opens-mantiquestore-5651705.php.

Sánchez-Jankowski, Martin. 2018. "Gangs, Culture, and Society in the United States." In *Outlaw Motorcycle Clubs and Street Gangs*, edited by Tereza Kuldova and Martin Sánchez-Jankowski, 25–43. New York: Palgrave Macmillan.

Sander, Ake, and Clemen Cavallin. 2015. "Hinduism Meets the Global Order: The 'Easternization of the West'" In *The Changing World Religion Map*, edited by Stanley D. Brunn, 1743–1763. New York: Springer.

Sanneh, Kelefa. 2015. "Don't Be Like That: Does Black Culture Need to Be Reformed?" *New Yorker*, February 9, 62–69.

Sassen, Saskia. 1991. *The Global City: New York, London, Tokyo*. Princeton, NJ: Princeton University Press.

Sassen, Saskia. 2012. "Cities." In *The Wiley-Blackwell Encyclopedia of Globalization*, edited by George Ritzer, 187–202. Malden, MA: Wiley-Blackwell.

Sassen, Saskia. 2019. *Cities in a World Economy*, 5th ed. Thousand Oaks: Sage.

Saussure, Ferdinand de. [1916] 1966. *Course in General Linguistics*. New York: McGraw-Hill.

Savage, Charlie. 2016. "Rights Groups, Riding Films Publicity, Urge Pardon for Edward Snowden." *New York Times*, September 14.

Saxon, Wolfgang. 2003. "Adm. Richard E. Bennis, a Hero of 9/11, Dies at 52." *New York Times*, August 9. Accessed March 31, 2012. http://www.nytimes.com/2003/08/09/nyregion/adm-richard-e-bennisa-hero-of-9-11-dies-at-52.html.

Scaff, Lawrence A. 2011. "Georg Simmel." In *The Wiley-Blackwell Companion to Major Social Theorists*, Vol. 1, *Classical Theorists*, edited by George Ritzer and Jeffrey Stepnisky, 205–235. Malden, MA: Wiley-Blackwell.

Scambler, Graham. 2018. "Social Class and Health Inequalities." In *Sociology as Applied to Health and Medicine*, edited by Graham Scambler. New York: Bloomsbury.

Scanes, Colin. 2018. "Human Activity and Habitat Loss: Destruction, Fragmentation, and Degradation." In *Animals and Human Society*, edited by Colin Scanes and Samia Toukhsati, 451–482. Amsterdam, The Netherlands: Elsevier.

Schaefer, Richard. 2014. *Racial and Ethnic Groups*, 14th ed. London: Pearson.

Scheffer, David. 2008. "Rape as Genocide in Darfur." *Los Angeles Times*, November 13.

Scheiber, Noam. 2018. "High-Skilled White Collar Work? Machines Can Do That, Too." *New York Times*, July 7.

Schlichtman, John, Jason Patch, and Marc Lamont Hill. 2017. *Gentrifier*. Toronto: University of Toronto Press.

Schlueter, E., and P. Scheepers. 2010. "The Relationship between Outgroup Size and Anti-outgroup Attitudes: A Theoretical Synthesis and Empirical Test of Group Threat and Intergroup Contact Theory." *Social Science Research* 39(2): 285–295.

Schmidt, Jeremy. 2017. *Water: Abundance, Scarcity, and Security in the Age of Humanity*. New York: New York University Press.

Schmidt, Susanne, Ulrike Roesler, Talin Kusserow, and Renate Rau. 2014. "Uncertainty in the Workplace: Examining Role Ambiguity and Role Conflict, and Their Link to Depression—A Meta-analysis." *European Journal of Work and Organizational Psychology* 23(1): 91–106.

Schneider, Barbara, and David Stevenson. 1999. *The Ambitious Generation: America's Teenagers, Motivated but Directionless*. New Haven, CT: Yale University Press.

Schneider, S. L. 2008. "Anti-Immigrant Attitudes in Europe: Outgroup Size and Perceived Ethnic Threat." *European Sociological Review* 24(1): 53–67.

Schneider, Todd W. n.d. *Taxi and Ridehailing Usage in New York City*. Retrieved May 18, 2023, from https://toddwschneider.com/dashboards/nyc-taxi-ridehailing-uber-lyft-data/

Scholz, Trebor, ed. 2013. *Digital Labor: The Internet as Playground and Factory*. New York: Routledge.

Schor, Juliet. 1993. *The Overworked American: The Unexpected Decline of Leisure*. New York: Basic Books.

Schor, Juliet. 1998. *The Overspent American: Why We Want What We Don't Need*. New York: Basic Books.

Schor, Juliet. 2005. *Born to Buy: The Commercialized Child and the New Consumer Culture*. New York: Scribner.

Schor, Juliet B., and William Attwood-Charles. 2017. "The Sharing Economy, Labor, Inequality, and Social Connection on For-Profit Platforms." *Sociology Compass*, July 13.

Schudson, Michael. 1987. *Advertising, the Uneasy Persuasion: Its Dubious Impact on American Society*. New York: Basic Books.

Schuster, Liza. 2012. "Asylum-Seekers." In *The Wiley-Blackwell Encyclopedia of Globalization*, edited by George Ritzer, 89–92. Malden, MA: Wiley-Blackwell.

Schutt, Russell. 2019. "Quantitative Methods." In *The Wiley-Blackwell Companion to Sociology*, 2nd ed., edited by George Ritzer and Wendy Wiedenhoft Murphy. Chichester, UK: John Wiley & Sons.

Schwalbe, Michael, Sandra Godwin, Daphne Holden, Douglas Schrock, Shealy Thompson, and Michele Wolkomir. 2000. "Generic Processes in the Reproduction of Inequality: An Interactionist Analysis." *Social Forces* 79: 419–452.

Schwartz, John. 2018. "More Floods and More Droughts: Climate Change Delivers Both." *New York Times*, December 12.

Schweinhart, Lawrence J. W., Steven Barnett, and Clive R. Belfield. 2005. *Lifetime Effects: The High/Scope Perry Preschool Study through Age 40*. Ypsilanti, MI: High/Scope Press.

Scott, James. 2014. *Two Cheers for Anarchism*. Princeton, NJ: Princeton University Press.

Sekulic, Dusko. 2016. "Ethnic Cleansing and Ethnic Swamping." In *The Wiley-Blackwell Encyclopedia of Race, Ethnicity, and Nationalism*, edited by John Stone, Rutledge M. Dennis, Polly Rizova, Anthony D. Smith, and Xiaoshuo Hou. Malden, MA: Wiley-Blackwell.

Selwyn, Neil. 2015. "Education, Technology, and the Sociological Imagination—Lessons to Be Learned from C. Wright Mills." *Learning, Media and Technology* 42(2): 230–245.

Semple, Kirk. 2018. "AIDS Runs Rampant in Venezuela, Putting an Ancient Culture at Risk." *New York Times*, May 7.

Semple, Kirk, Azam Ahmed, and Eric Lipton. 2016. "Panama Papers Leak Casts Light on a Law Firm Founded on Secrecy." *New York Times*, April 6.

Shamir, Ronen. 2005. "Without Borders? Notes on Globalization as a Mobility Regime." *Sociological Theory* 23(2): 197–217.

Sharp, Gwen. 2012. "Gender in the Hidden Curriculum (Update)." *Society Pages*, November 16. Accessed April 11, 2013. http://www.thesocietypages.org/socimages/2012/11/16/gender-in-thehidden-curriculum.

Shaw, Susan, and Janet Lee. 2009. *Women's Voices, Feminist Visions*. New York: McGraw-Hill.

Sherif, Muzafer, O. J. Harvey, William R. Hood, Carolyn W. Sherif, and Jack White. [1954] 1961. *Intergroup Conflict and Cooperation: The Robbers Cave Experiment*. Norman: University of Oklahoma Book Exchange.

Shiffman, Jeremy. 2017. "Four Challenges That Global Health Networks Face." *International Journal of Health Policy and Management* 6(4): 183–189.

Shildrick, Tracy, and Robert MacDonald. 2013. "Poverty Talk: How People Experiencing Poverty Deny Their Poverty and Why They Blame the Poor." *Sociological Review* 61: 285–303.

Shilling, Chris. 2018. "Embodying Culture: Body Pedagogics, Situated Encounters, and Empirical Research." *The Sociological Review* 66(1): 75–90.

Shroedel, Jean Reith, and Pamela Fiber. 2000. "Lesbian and Gay Policy Priorities: Commonality and Difference." In *The Politics of Gay Rights*, edited by C. A. Rimmerman, K. D. Wald, and C. Wilcox, 97–118. Chicago: University of Chicago Press.

Siebert, Sabina, Stacey Bushfield, Graeme Martin, and Brian Howieson. 2018. "Eroding 'Respectability': Deprofessionalization through Organizational Spaces." *Work, Employment, and Society* 32(2): 330–347.

Siegel, Larry J., and John L. Worrall. 2014. *Essentials of Criminal Justice*, 9th ed. Stamford, CT: Cengage.

Silva, Jenn. 2015. *Coming Up Short*. Oxford, UK: Oxford University Press.

Silver, Hilary. 2015. "Editorial: The Urban Sociology of Detroit." *City and Community* 14: 97–101.

Silverman, David, ed. 2016. *Qualitative Research*, 4th ed. London: SAGE.

Silvernail, David L., and Amy F. Johnson. 2014. "The Impacts of Public Charter Schools on Students and Traditional Public Schools: What Does the Empirical Evidence Tell Us?" Maine Education Policy Research Institute, *University of Southern Maine*, January. Accessed April 17, 2015.

Simmel, Georg. [1903] 1971. "The Metropolis and Mental Life." In *Georg Simmel: On Individuality and Social Forms*, edited by D. Levine. Chicago: University of Chicago Press.

Simmel, Georg. [1904] 1971. "Fashion." In *Georg Simmel: On Individuality and Social Forms*, edited by D. Levine, 294–323. Chicago: University of Chicago Press.

Simmel, Georg. [1906] 1950. "The Secret and the Secret Society." In *The Sociology* of *Georg Simmel*, edited by K. H. Wolff, 307–376. New York: Free Press.

Simmel, Georg. [1908] 1971a. "Domination." In *Georg Simmel: On Individuality and Social Forms*, edited by D. Levine, 96–120. Chicago: University of Chicago Press.

Simmons, C. 2015. "Companionate Marriage." In *The International Encyclopedia of Human Sexuality*, edited by A. Bolin and P. Whelehan. Oxford, UK: Wiley. doi:10.1002/9781118896877.wbiehs096

Simmons, E. S. 2018. "Targets, Grievances, and Social Movement Trajectories." *Comparative Political Studies*. doi:10.1177/0010414018806532

Simmons, Rachel. 2011. *Odd Girl Out*. New York: Mariner Books.

Simon, Herbert A. [1945] 1976. *Administrative Behavior*. New York: Macmillan.

Simone, Alina. 2015. "How My Mom Got Hacked." *New York Times*, January 2. Accessed April 27, 2015. http://www.nytimes.com/2015/01/04/opinion/sunday/how-my-mom-got-hacked.html

Simpson, Sally S. 2002. *Corporate Crime, Law, and Social Control*. New York: Cambridge University Press.

Simpson, Sally S. 2013. "White-Collar Crime: A Review of Recent Developments and Promising Directions for Future Research." *Annual Review of Sociology* 39: 309–331.

Singer, Natasha. 2010. "The Financial Time Bomb of Longer Lives." *New York Times*, October 16.

Sink, Alexander, and Dana Mastro. 2016. "Depictions of Gender on Primetime Television: A Quantitative Content Analysis." *Mass Communication and Society* 20(1): 3–22.

Sirkin, Monroe G., Rosemarie Hirsch, William Mosher, Chris Moriarty, and Nancy Sonnenfeld. 2011. "Changing Methods of NCHS Surveys: 1960–2010 and Beyond." *Morbidity and Mortality Weekly Report*, suppl. 60(7): 42–48.

Sitton, John F., ed. 2010. *Marx Today: Selected Works and Recent Debates*. New York: Palgrave Macmillan.

Skinner, Quentin, ed. 1985. *The Return of Grand Theories in the Human Sciences*. Cambridge, UK: Cambridge University Press.

Sklair, Leslie. 2002. *Globalization: Capitalism and Its Alternatives*. Oxford, UK: Oxford University Press.

Skloot, Rebecca. 2011. *The Immortal Life of Henrietta Lacks*. New York: Crown.

Skocpol, Theda. 1979. *States and Social Revolutions*. Cambridge, UK: Cambridge University Press.

Skrovan, Sandy. 2017. "How Shoppers Use Their Smartphones in Stores." *Retail Dive*, June 7.

Slater, Don. 2015. "Consumer Culture." In *Encyclopedia of Consumption and Consumer Studies*, edited by Daniel Thomas Cook and Michael Ryan, 112–118. Malden, MA: Wiley-Blackwell.

Slatton, Brittany Chevon, and Joe Feagin. 2019. "Racial and Ethnic Issues: Critical Race Approaches in the United States." In *The Wiley-Blackwell Companion to Sociology*, 2nd ed., edited by George Ritzer and Wendy Wiedenhoft Murphy. Chichester, UK: John Wiley & Sons.

Slobodian, Quinn. 2018. *Globalists: The End of Empire and the Birth of Neoliberalism*. Cambridge, MA: Harvard University Press.

Smangs, Mattias. 2016. "Doing Violence, Making Race: Southern Lynching and White Racial Group Formation." *American Journal of Sociology* 121: 1329–1374.

Smith, Aaron, and Monica Anderson. 2018. "Social Media Use in 2018." Pew Research Center. Accessed April 30, 2019. http://www.pewinternet.org/2018/03/01/social-media-use-in-2018/.

Smith, Clarissa, Feona Atwood, and Brian McNair, eds. 2018. *The Routledge Companion to Media, Sex, and Sexuality*. London: Routledge.

Smith, Jessi L., and Meghan Huntoon. 2014. "Women's Bragging Rights: Overcoming Modesty Norms to Facilitate Women's Self-Promotion." *Psychology of Women Quarterly* 38: 447–459.

Smith, Stacy L., Adam G. Sanford, and Dinur Blum. 2021. "Spotlighting Hidden Inequalities: Post-Secondary Education in a Pandemic," In *COVID-19: Global Pandemic, Societal Responses, Ideological Solutions*, edited by J. Michael Ryan, 124–138. London: Routledge.

Smith, Suzanne, and Raeann Hamen. 2016. *Exploring Family Theories*, 4th ed. Oxford, UK: Oxford University Press.

Smyth, Bruce. 2007. "Non-resident Parents." In *The Blackwell Encyclopedia of Sociology*, edited by George Ritzer, 3223–3227. Malden, MA: Blackwell.

Sniderman, Paul. 2017. *The Democratic Faith*. New Haven, CT: Yale University Press.

Snow, David, Sarah Soule, Hanspeter Kries, and Holly McCammon, eds. 2019. *The Wiley-Blackwell Companion to Social Movements*. Chichester, UK: John Wiley & Sons.

Sollee, Kristen. 2015. "6 Things to Know About 4th Wave Feminism." *Bustle*, October 30. Accessed March 9, 2017. https://www.bustle.com/articles/119524-6-things-to-know-about-4th-wave-feminism.

Someki, Fumio, Miyuki Torii, Patricia J. Brooks, Tatsuya Koeda, and Kristen Gillespie-Lynch. 2018. "Stigma Associated with Autism among College Students in Japan and the United States: An Online Training Study." *Research in Developmental Disabilities* 76: 88–98.

Sørensen, Georg. 2017. "Globalization and the Nation-State." In *Comparative Politics*, edited by Daniele Caramani, 422–436. Oxford, UK: Oxford University Press.

Sostero, Matteo, Santo Milasi, John Hurley, Enrique Fernandez-Maciías and Martina Bisello. 2020. *Teleworkability and the COVID-19 crisis: A New Digital Divide?* JRC121193. https://ec.europa.eu/jrc/sites/jrcsh/files/jrc121193.pdf

Sowell, Thomas. 2018. *Discrimination and Disparities*. New York: Basic Books.

Spade, Joan Z., and Catherine G. Valentine. 2016. *The Kaleidoscope of Gender: Prisms, Patterns, and Possibilities*. Thousand Oaks, CA: Pine Forge Press.

Sparman, Anna. 2015. "Children's Consumer Culture." In *Encyclopedia of Consumption and Consumer Studies*, edited by Daniel Thomas Cook and Michael Ryan, 75–77. Malden, MA: Wiley-Blackwell.

Speer, Jamin. 2017. "The Gender Gap in College Major: Revisiting the Role of Pre-College Factors." *Labour Economics* 44: 69–88.

Spencer, Herbert. 1851. *Social Statics*. London: Chapman.

Spitz, Vivien. 2005. *Doctors from Hell: The Horrific Account of Nazi Experiments on Humans*. Boulder, CO: Sentient.

SPLC. n.d. *In 2021, We Tracked 733 Hate Groups across the U.S.* Retrieved May 16, 2023, from https://www.splcenter.org/hate-map

Spotts, Greg, and Robert Greenwald. 2005. *Walmart: The High Cost of Low Price*. New York: Disinformation Press.

Springer, Nikki. 2018. *James Surowiecki's The Wisdom of Crowds*. London: Macat Library.

Spurlock, Morgan. 2005. *Don't Eat This Book: Fast Food and the Supersizing of America*. New York: Putnam.

Stacey, Clare L., and Lindsey L. Ayers. 2012. "Caught between Love and Money: The Experiences of Paid Family Caregivers." *Qualitative Sociology* 35: 47–64.

Standing, Guy. 1989. "Global Feminization through Flexible Labor: A Theme Revisited." *World Development* 27(3): 583–602.

Stanescu, Anca, Denisa Balalau, Liana Ples, Stauna Paunica, and Christian Balalau. 2018. "Postpartum Depression: Prevention and Multi Modal Therapy." *Journal of Mind and Medical Sciences* 5(2): 163–168.

Stanley, Scott. 2018. "The Risks for Couples Moving in Together." *Psychology Today*. Accessed April 30, 2019. https://www.psychologytoday.com/us/blog/sliding-vs-deciding/201807/whymoving-in-together-is-so-risky.

Stark, Rodney, and William Sims Bainbridge. 1979. "Of Churches, Sects, and Cults: Preliminary Concepts for a Theory of Religious Movements." *Journal for the Scientific Study of Religion* 18(2): 117–131.

STARS. 2022. "The Paper Ceiling." https://www.tearthepaperceiling.org/the-paper-ceiling

Statista. 2021. "Share of Americans with One or More Tattoos as of 2021, by Generation and Number of Tattoos." Retrieved August 2, 2022. https://www.statista.com/statistics/1261721/americans-with-at-least-one-tattoo-by-number-and-generation/.

Statista. 2023. "Average Life Expectancy at Birth in 2022, by Continent and Gender (in Years)." https://www.statista.com/statistics/270861/life-expectancy-by-continent/.

Statista Research Department. 2022a, October 11. *Number of People Living below the Poverty Line in the United States from 1990 to 2021, by Gender (in Millions)*. Statista. Retrieved May 18, 2023, from https://www.statista.com/statistics/233145/number-of-people-living-below-the-poverty-in-the-us-by-gender/

Statista Research Department. 2022b, September 30. *Poverty Rate in the United States in 2021, by Ethnic Group*. Statista. Retrieved May 18, 2023, from https://www.statista.com/statistics/200476/us-poverty-rate-by-ethnic-group/

Statista Research Department. 2023, April 24. *Poverty Rate in the United States in 2021, by Age and Gender*. Statista. Retrieved May 18, 2023, from https://www.statista.com/statistics/233154/us-poverty-rate-by-gender/

Statistics Japan. 2018. "Rate of Single-Parent Households." Accessed April 30, 2019. https://stats-japan.com/t/kiji/11954.

Stearns, Cindy A. 2009. "The Work of Breastfeeding." *Women's Studies Quarterly* 37: 63–80.

Steger, Manfred. 2017. *Globalization: A Very Short Introduction*, 4th ed. Oxford, UK: Oxford University Press.

Stein, Joel. 2015. "Baby, You Can Drive My Car, and Do My Errands, and Rent My Stuff . . ." *Time*, February 9, 34–40.

Steinfatt, Thomas. 2011. "Sex Trafficking in Cambodia: Fabricated Numbers versus Empirical Evidence." *Crime, Law and Social Change* 56: 443–462.

Steinmetz, Katy. 2014a. "Meet the First Openly Transgender NCAA Division I Athlete." *Time*, October 28. https://time.com/3537849/meet-the-first-openly-transgender-ncaa-athlete/.

Steinmetz, Katy. 2014b. "The Transgender Tipping Point." *Time*, May 29. Accessed April 21, 2015. http://time.com/135480/transgendertipping-point.

Stepfamily Foundation. 2019. "Stepfamily Statistics." Accessed April 30, 2019. www.stepfamily.org/stepfamily-statistics.Html.

Stepler, Renee. 2017. "Number of U.S. Adults Cohabiting with a Partner Continues to Rise, Especially Among Those 50 and Older." FACTTANK Pew Research Center, April 6. Accessed April 30, 2019. http://www.pewresearch.org/fact-tank/2017/04/06/number-of-us-adults-cohabiting-with-a-partner-continues-to-rise-especially-among-those-50-and-older/.

Sterling, Toby. 2016. "U.S. Blocks Philips' $3.3 Billion Sale of Lumileds to Asian Buyers." Reuters, January 22. Accessed March 8, 2017. http://www.reuters.com/article/us-philips-lumileds-sale-idUSKCN0V02D4.

Stewart, Matthew. 2018a. "The Birth of a New Aristocracy." *The Atlantic*, June.

Stewart, Matthew. 2018b. "The 9.9 Percent is the New American Aristocracy." *The Atlantic* June.

Stickney, Robert. 2017. *Aquaculture*, 3rd ed. Boston: CABI.

Stillerman, Joel. 2015. *The Sociology of Consumption: A Global Approach*. London: Polity Press.

Stockemer, Daniel, and Rodrigo Praino. 2015. "Blinded by Beauty? Physical Attractiveness and Candidate Selection in the U.S. House of Representatives." *Social Science Quarterly* 96: 430–443.

Stokoe, Elizabeth. 2006. "On Ethnomethodology, Feminism, and the Analysis of Categorical Reference to Gender in Talk-in-Interaction." *Sociological Review* 54(3): 467–494.

Stone, Amy, and Jill Weinberg. 2015. "Sexualities and Social Movements: Three Decades of Sex and Social Change." In *Handbook of the Sociology of Sexualities*, edited by J. DeLamater and R. F. Plante, 453–485. Dordrecht, Netherlands: Springer.

Stoolmiller, Michael. 1999. "Implications of the Restricted Range of Family Environments for Estimates of Heritability and Nonshared Environments in Behavior-Genetic Adoption Studies." *Psychological Bulletin* 125: 392–409.

Stouffer, S. A., E. A. Suchman, L. C. DeVinney, S. A. Star, and R. M. Williams. 1949. *The American Soldier: Adjustment during Army Life*, Vol. 1. Princeton, NJ: Princeton University Press.

Streitfeld, David. 2014. "Airbnb Listings Mostly Illegal, State Contends." *New York Times*, October 16.

Stronger Families. 2015–2018. "One Parent Families in Europe." Accessed April 30, 2019. http://strongerfamilies.eu/about-us-2/one-parent-families-in-europe/.

Stryker, Sheldon. 1959. "Symbolic Interaction as an Approach to Family Research." *Marriage and Family Living* 21(2): 111–119.

Stryker, Susan. 2017. Transgender History. New York: Seal Press.

Stulberg, Lisa. 2018. *LGBTQ Movements*. Cambridge, UK: Polity Press.

Subrahmanian, Krishnan, and Padma Swamy. 2018. *Global Child Health: A Toolkit to Address Health Disparities*. New York: Springer.

Sullivan, Oriel. 2018. "The Gendered Division of Household Labor." In *Handbook of the Sociology of Gender*, edited by Barbara J. Risman, Carrisa M. Froyum, and William J. Scarborough, 377–392. Cham, Switzerland: Springer.

Sumner, Colin. 1994. *The Sociology of Deviance: An Obituary*. New York: Continuum.

Sumner, William Graham. [1906] 1940. *Folkways: A Study of the Sociological Implications of Usages, Manners, Customs, Mores, and Morals*. Boston: Ginn.

Sundararajan, Arun. 2016. *The Sharing Economy: The End of Employment and the

Rise of Crowd-Based Capitalism. Cambridge, MA: MIT Press.

Surk, Barbara. 2015. "Slovenia Builds Border Fence to Stem Flow of Migrants." *New York Times*, November 11.

Sussman, Robert Wald. 2016. *The Myth of Race: The Troubling Persistence of an Unscientific Idea*. Cambridge, MA: Harvard University Press.

Swatos, William H., Jr. 2007. "Sect." In *The Blackwell Encyclopedia of Sociology*, edited by George Ritzer, 4135–4140. Malden, MA: Blackwell.

Sweet, William. 2016. *Climate Diplomacy from Rio to Paris*. New Haven, CT: Yale University Press.

Sykes, Gresham. [1958] 2007. *The Society of Captives: A Study of a Maximum Security Prison*. Princeton, NJ: Princeton University Press. Sylvia Rivera Law Project. 2015. "Who Was Sylvia Rivera?" Accessed March 17, 2015. http://srlp.org/about/who-was-sylvia-rivera.

Sylvia Rivera Law Project. 2015. "Who Was Sylvia Rivera?" Accessed March 17, 2015. http://srlp.org/about/who-was-sylvia-rivera.

Szczepanski, Kallie. 2018. "Female Infanticide in Asia." ThoughtCo, June 14. Accessed April 30, 2019. www.thoughtco.com/femaleinfanticide-in-asia-195450.

Tansey, Oisín. 2006. "Process Tracing and Elite Interviewing." Paper presented at the annual meeting of the American Political Science Association, Philadelphia, August 31.

Tatangelo, Gemma L., and Lina A. Ricciardelli. 2013. "A Qualitative Study of Preadolescent Boys' and Girls' Body Image: Gendered Ideals and Sociocultural Influences." *Body Image* 10: 591–598.

Tavernise, Sabrina. 2016. "Life Spans of the Rich Leave the Poor Behind." *New York Times*, February 13.

Tavernise, Sabrina, and Denise Grady. 2016. "An Infection Raises the Specter of Superbugs Resistant to All Antibiotics." *New York Times*, A12, A15.

Tavernise, Sabrina, and Robert Gebeloff. 2016. "Immigrants and Minorities Gain Insurance." *New York Times*, April 18.

Taylor, Dorceta. 2014. *Toxic Communities*. New York: New York University Press.

Taylor, Paul C. 2011. "William Edward Burghardt Du Bois." In *The Wiley-Blackwell Companion to Major Social Theorists*, Vol. 1, *Classical Theorists*, edited by George Ritzer and Jeffrey Stepnisky, 426–447. Malden, MA: Wiley-Blackwell.

Thaxton, Sherod, and Robert Agnew. 2017. "When Criminal Coping Is Likely: An Examination of Conditioning Effects in General Strain Theory." *Journal of Quantitative Criminology* 34: 1–34.

Thébaud, Sarah, and David S. Pedulla. 2016. "Masculinity and the Stalled Revolution: How Gender Ideologies and Norms Shape Young Men's Responses to Work-Family Policies." *Gender & Society* 30: 590–617.

Thoits, Peggy A. 1985. "Self-Labeling Processes in Mental Illness: The Role of Emotional Deviance." *American Journal of Sociology* 91(2): 221–249.

Thoits, Peggy A. 2011. "Perceived Social Support and the Voluntary, Mixed, or Pressured Use of Mental Health Services." *Society and Mental Health* 1: 4–19.

Thompson, Beverly Yuen. 2015. *Covered in Ink: Tattoos, Women, and the Politics of the Body*. New York: New York University Press.

Thompson-Miller, Ruth, and Leslie Picca. 2017. "'There Were Rapes!': Sexual Assaults of African American Women and Children in Jim Crow." *Violence Against Women* 23(8): 934–950.

Thorne, Barrie. 1993. *Gender Play: Girls and Boys in School*. New Brunswick, NJ: Rutgers University Press.

Thorpe, Holly, and Nida Ahmad. 2015. "Youth Action Sports and Political Agency in the Middle East: Lessons from a Grassroots Parkour Group in Gaza." *International Review for the Sociology of Sport* 50: 678–704.

Tierney, Kathleen. 2018. "Disasters as Social Problem and Social Construct." In *Cambridge Handbook of Social Problems*, edited by A. Javier Treviño, 79–94. Cambridge, UK: Cambridge University Press.

Tiryakian, Edward. 1991. "Modernization: Exhumateur in Pace (Rethinking Macrosociology in the 1990s)." *International Sociology* 6(2): 165–180.

Tocqueville, Alexis de. [1835–1840] 1969. *Democracy in America*. Garden City, NY: Doubleday.

Todd, Breanna, and Catherine Armstrong Soule. 2018. "Delineating between Fandom, Brand Communities, and Brand Publics." In *Exploring the Rise of Fandom in Contemporary Culture*, edited by Cheng Lu Wang, 18–34. Hershey, PA: IGI Global.

Tomlinson, John. 1999. *Globalization and Culture*. Chicago: University of Chicago Press.

Tomlinson, John. 2000. "Globalization and Cultural Identity." In *The Global Transformations Reader*, edited by D. Held and A. McGrew, 269–277. Cambridge, UK: Polity Press.

Trading Economics. (May 2023). *United States Imports from China*. Retrieved May 18, 2023, from https://tradingeconomics.com/united-states/imports/china.

Tranter, Bruce, and Dallas Hanson. 2015. "The Social Bases of Cosmetic Surgery in Australia." *Journal of Sociology* 51: 189–206.

Tranter, Bruce, and Ruby Grant. 2018. "A Class Act? Social Background and Body Modification in Australia." *Journal of Sociology* 54(3): 412–428.

Treas, Judith, Jonathan Lui, and Zoya Gubernskays. 2014. "Attitudes on Marriage and New Relationships: Cross-National Evidence on the Deinstitutionalization of Marriage." *Demographic Research* 30: 1495–1526.

Treitler, Vilna Bashi. 2016. "Racialization and Its Paradigms: From Ireland to North America." *Current Sociology* 64: 213–227.

Trentmann, Frank. 2016. *Empire of Things: How We Became a World of Consumers, from the Fifteenth Century to the Twenty-First*. New York: Harper.

Triandafyllidou, Anna, ed. 2018. *Handbook of Migration and Globalisation*. Cheltenham, UK: Edward Elgar.

Troy, M. 2021. Self-Checkout Installations Surged 25% in 2020. *Progressive Grocer*. https://progressivegrocer.com/self-checkout-installations-surged-25-2020

Tsuda, Takeyuki, Maria Tapias, and Xavier Escandell. 2014. "Locating the Global in Transnational Ethnography." *Journal of Contemporary Ethnography* 43: 123–147.

Tùennies, Ferdinand. [1887] 1957. *Community and Society*. New York: Harper Torchbooks.

Tully, James. 2014. *On Global Citizenship: James Tully in Dialogue*. London: Bloomsbury Academic.

Turner, Bryan S. 2008. *The Body and Society: Explorations in Social Theory*. 3rd ed. London: SAGE.

Turner, Bryan S. 2014. "Religion and Contemporary Sociological Theories." *Current Sociology* 62: 771–788.

Turner, Cory, and Anya Kamenetz. 2020. "Schools Race to Feed Students Amid

Coronavirus Closures." *NPR*, March 20, 2020. www.npr.org/2020/03/20/818300504/schools-race-to-feed-students-amid-coronavirus-closures

Turner, Fred. 2008. *From Counterculture to Cyberculture: Stewart Brand, the Whole Earth Network, and the Rise of Digital Utopianism*. Chicago: University of Chicago Press.

Turner, Ralph H. 1978. "The Role and the Person." *American Journal of Sociology* 84: 1–23.

Turner, Ralph H., and Lewis M. Killian. 1987. *Collective Behavior*, 3rd ed. Englewood Cliffs, NJ: Prentice Hall.

Turner, Victor. 1967. *The Forest of Symbols: Aspects of Ndembu Ritual*. Ithaca, NY: Cornell University Press.

Tyler, Meagan, and Kaye Quek. 2016. "Conceptualizing Pornographication: A Lack of Clarity and Problems for Feminist Analysis." *Sexualization, Media & Society* 2(2): 1–14.

Uchitelle, Louis. 2010. "Another Shifting Industry." *New York Times*, January 19.

Umoren, Imaobong. 2018. *Race Women Internationalists*. Berkeley: University of California Press.

Unger, Matthew, Jean-Phillippe Crete, and George Pavlich. 2018. "Criminal Entryways in the Writing of Cesare Beccaria." In *The Handbook of the History and Philosophy of Criminology*, edited by Ruth Ann Triplett, 17–31. Oxford, UK: Wiley Blackwell.

UNHCR. (2012, December 12). *The Buddhist Core Values And Perspectives For Protection Challenges: Faith And Protection*. Retrieved May 16, 2023, from https://www.unhcr.org/media/buddhist-core-values-and-perspectives-protection-challenges-faith-and-protection

UNHCR. 2023. *OHCHR and Migration*. Retrieved May 12, 2023, from https://www.ohchr.org/en/migration

UNICEF. 2018. "Malnutrition." Accessed May 1, 2019. https://data.unicef.org/topic/nutrition/malnutrition/.

United Nations. 2017. "International Migration Report." Accessed May 1, 2019. http://www.un.org/en/development/desa/population/migration/publications/migrationreport/docs/MigrationReport2017_Highlights.pdf.

United Nations Department of Economic and Social Affairs. 2017. *Employment Opportunities: Do Race and Ethnicity Matter?* Social Development Brief #3. https://www.un.org/development/desa/socialperspectiveondevelopment/wp-content/uploads/sites/27/2017/07/RWSSPolicyBrief3.pdf

United Nations Department of Economic and Social Affairs. 2018. "2018 Revision of World Urbanization Prospects." https://www.un.org/development/desa/en/news/population/2018-revision-of-world-urbanization-prospects.html

United Nations Department of Economic and Social Affairs. 2019. *World Population Prospects 2019: Highlights* (ST/ESA/SER.A/423). https://population.un.org/wpp/publications/files/wpp2019_highlights.pdf

United Nations Security Council. 2017. "8234th Meeting." Accessed May 1, 2019. https://www.un.org/sexualviolenceinconflict/wp-content/uploads/sg-factsheets/N1810885_Meeting-Record.pdf.

Upor, Rose Acen. 2023. "Adapting Technology in Language Teaching and Learning in Sub-Saharan Africa: Lessons from the COVID-19 Pandemic in Tanzania." In *Pandemic Pedagogies: Teaching and Learning during the COVID-19 Pandemic*, edited by J. Michael Ryan. London: Routledge.

Urban Institute. 2017. "Police and Corrections Expenditures." Accessed May 1, 2019. https://www.urban.org/policy-centers/crosscenter-initiatives/state-local-finance-initiative/state-and-localbackgrounders/police-and-corrections-expenditures.

Urry, John. 2000. *Sociology beyond Societies: Mobilities for the Twenty-first Century*. London: Routledge.

U.S. Department of Health and Human Services. 2023. *HHS Poverty Guidelines for 2023*. ASPE Office of the Assistant Secretary for Planning and Evaluation. Retrieved May 18, 2023, from https://aspe.hhs.gov/topics/poverty-economic-mobility/poverty-guidelines

U.S. Bureau of Labor Statistics. 2023. Employed Persons by Detailed Occupation, Sex, Race, and Hispanic or Latino Ethnicity. *Current Population Survey*, 2022. https://www.bls.gov/cps/cpsaat11.htm

U.S. Census Bureau. 2011. "2010 Census Shows America's Diversity." Accessed May 1, 2019. https://www.census.gov/newsroom/releases/archives/2010_census/cb11-cn125.html.

U.S. Census Bureau. 2016. "The Majority of Children Live with Two Parents, Census Bureau Reports." Accessed May 1, 2019. https://www.census.gov/newsroom/press-releases/2016/cb16-192.html.

U.S. Census Bureau. 2019. "Subject Definitions." Accessed July 29 2019. https://www.census.gov/programs-surveys/cps/technical-documentation/subject-definitions.html.

U.S. Census Bureau. 2020. "Table H3. Mean Household Income Received by Each Fifth and Top 5 Percent." https://www.census.gov/data/tables/time-series/demo/income-poverty/historical-income-households.html

U.S. Census Bureau. 2021b. *Historical Households Tables, Households by Type: 1940 to Present*, Table HH-1, Washington, DC: United States Census Bureau. Accessed August 02, 2022. https://www.census.gov/data/tables/time-series/demo/families/households.html

U.S. Census Bureau. 2022, November 1. "Historical Households Tables." Accessed April 29, 2023. https://www.census.gov/data/tables/time-series/demo/families/households.html

U.S. Census Bureau. 2022a. "Historical Income Tables: Income Inequality." Table F-2. Share of Aggregate Income Received by Each Fifth and Top 5 Percent of All Families: 1947 to 2021. https://www.census.gov/data/tables/time-series/demo/income-poverty/historical-income-inequality.html

U.S. Census Bureau. 2022b, December 20. *National Poverty in America Awareness Month: January 2023*. Retrieved May 18, 2023, from https://www.census.gov/newsroom/stories/poverty-awareness-month.html

U.S. Department of Education. 2017. "Fast Facts: Homeschooling." Accessed May 1, 2019. http://nces.ed.gov/fastfacts/display.asp?id=91.

U.S. Department of State. n.d. *About Human Trafficking*. Retrieved May 16, 2023, from https://www.state.gov/humantrafficking-about-human-trafficking.

Useem, Bert. 2018. "Prison Riots." In *The Oxford Handbook of Prisons and Imprisonment*. Edited by John Wooldredge and Paula Smith. Oxford University Press.

Vaidhyanathan, Siva. 2011. *The Googlization of Everything (and Why We Should Worry)*. Berkeley: University of California Press.

van der Lippe, Tanja, Vincent Frey, and Milena Tsvetkova. 2012. "Outsourcing of Domestic Tasks: A Matter of Preferences?" *Journal of Family Issues* 34(12): 1574–1597.

Van de Werfhorst, Herman G., and Jonathan J. B. Mij. 2010. "Achievement Inequality and the Institutional Structure of Educational Systems: A Comparative Perspective." *Annual Review of Sociology* 36: 407–428.

Van Dijk, Jan A. G. M. 2012. *The Network Society*, 3rd ed. Thousand Oaks, CA: Sage.

van Gennep, Arnold. 1961. *The Rites of Passage*. Chicago: University of Chicago Press.

van Leeuwen, Marco H. D., and Ineke Maas. 2010. "Historical Studies of Social Mobility and Stratification." *Annual Review of Sociology* 36: 429–451.

Van Maanen, John. 1983. "The Moral Fix: On the Ethics of Field Work." In *Contemporary Field Research: Perspectives and Formulations*, edited by R. M. Emerson. Longrove, IL: Waveland Press.

Van Slyke, Shanna R., Michael L. Benson, and Francis T. Cullen, eds. 2016. *The Oxford Handbook of White-Collar Crime*. New York: Oxford University Press.

Van Valen, L. 1974. "Brain Size and Intelligence in Man." *American Journal of Physical Anthropology* 40: 417–423.

Vanden, Harry, Peter Funke, and Gary Prevost, eds. 2018. *The New Global Politics: Global Social Movements in the Twenty-First Century*. London: Routledge.

Vanek, Joann, Martha Chen, Ralf Hussmanns, and Francoise Carre. 2014. *Women and Men in the Informal Economy: A Statistical Picture*, 2nd ed. Geneva: International Labour Organization.

Vasquez-Tokos, Jessica. 2017. *Marriage Vows and Racial Choices*. New York: Russell Sage Foundation.

Vaughan, Diane. 1996. *The Challenger Launch Decision: Risky Technology, Culture, and Deviance at NASA*. Chicago: University of Chicago Press.

Veblen, Thorstein. [1899] 1994. *The Theory of the Leisure Class*. New York: Penguin.

Venkatesh, Sudhir. 1994. "Learnin' the Trade: Conversations with a Gangsta." *Public Culture* 6: 319–341.

Venkatesh, Sudhir. 2008. *Gang Leader for a Day: A Rogue Sociologist Takes to the Streets*. New York: Penguin.

Vida, Róbert György, András Fittler, Ivett Mikulka, Eszter Ábrahám, Viktor Sándor, F. Kilár, and Lajos Botz. 2017. "Availability and Quality of Illegitimate Somatotrin Products Obtained from the Internet." *International Journal of Clinical Pharmacy* 39(1): 78–87.

Vidal, Matt, Paul Adler, and Rick Delbridge. 2015. "When Organization Studies Turns to Societal Problems: The Contribution of Marxist Grand Theory." *Organization Studies* 36: 405–422.

Voas, David, and Fenella Fleischmann. 2012. "Islam Moves West: Religious Change in the First and Second Generations." *Annual Review of Sociology* 38: 525–545.

Voas, David, and Mark Chaves. 2016. "Is the United States a Counterexample to the Secularization Thesis." *American Journal of Sociology* 121(5): 1517–1556.

Vogt, Kristoffer Chelsom. 2016. "The Post-Industrial Society: From Utopia to Ideology." *Work, Employment and Society* 30: 366–376.

Vohs, Kathleen D., Jaideep Sengupta, and Darren W. Dahl. 2014. "The Price Had Better Be Right: Women's Reactions to Sexual Stimuli Vary with Market Factors." *Psychological Science* 25(1): 278–283.

Vos, Jeroen, and Leonith Hinojosa. 2016. "Virtual Water Trade and the Contestation of Hydrosocial Territories." *Water International* 41: 37–53.

Vuolo, Mike, Joy Kadowaki, and Brian Kelly. 2017. "Marijuana's Moral Entrepreneurs, Then and Now." *Contexts* 16(4): 20–25.

Wade, Lisa. 2017. *American Hookup: The New Culture of Sex on Campus*. New York: Norton.

Wakefield, Kelly. 2013. "Global Digital Divide: Inequality and Internet Access." *Geography Review* 26: 10–13.

Waldmeir, Patti. [1997] 2001. *Anatomy of a Miracle: The End of Apartheid and the Birth of a New South Africa*. New Brunswick, NJ: Rutgers University Press.

Walker, Henry A., and David Willer. 2007. "Experimental Methods." In *The Blackwell Encyclopedia of Sociology*, edited by George Ritzer, 1537–1541. Malden. MA: Blackwell.

Wallerstein, Immanuel. 1974. *The Modern World-System*. New York: Academic Press.

Wallerstein, James S., and Clement J. Wyle. 1947. "Our Law-Abiding Law-Breakers." *Federal Probation* 25: 107–112.

Wang, Kui, Rui Liang, Zhen-Ling Ma, Eric Cheung, David Roalt, Ruben Gur, and Raymond Chan. 2018. "Body Image Attitude Among Chinese College Students." *Psych Journal* 7(1): 31–40.

Wang, Shanshan, and Eric Pfanner. 2013. "China's One-Day Shopping Spree Sets Record in Online Sales." *New York Times*, November 11.

Wanis-St. John, Anthony, and Noah Rosen. 2017. *Negotiating Civil Resistance*. Washington, DC: United States Institute of Peace.

Ward, James D., and Mario A. Rivera. 2014. *Institutional Racism, Organizations, & Public Policy*. New York: Peter Lang.

Ward, Thomas W. 2012. *Gangs without Borders*. Oxford, UK: Oxford University Press.

Warde, Alan. 2017. *Consumption: A Sociological Analysis*. London: Palgrave Macmillan.

Wasserman, Varda, and Michal Frenkel. 2015. "Spatial Work in between Glass Ceiling and Glass Walls: Gender-Class Intersectionality and Organizational Aesthetics." *Organization Studies* 36: 1485–1505.

Webb, Patrick, Ramoni Wijesinha-Bettoni, Prakash Shetty, Anna Lartey, and Gunhild Anker Stordalen. 2018. "Hunger and Malnutrition in the 21st Century." *British Journal of Medicine* 361: K2238.

Weber, Max. [1904–1905] 1958. *The Protestant Ethic and the Spirit of Capitalism*. New York: Scribner.

Weber, Max. [1919] 1958. "Politics as a Vocation." In *From Max Weber: Essays in Sociology*, edited by H. Gerth and C. Wright Mills, 77–128. New York: Oxford University Press.

Weber, Max. [1921] 1968. *Economy and Society: An Outline of Interpretative Sociology*, edited by G. Roth and C. Wittich. Totowa, NJ: Bedminster Press.

Weber, Max. [1903–1917] 1949. *The Methodology of the Social Sciences*. New York: Free Press.

Webster, Chris, Jingjing Ruan, and Guibo Sun. 2018. "Private Gains and Social Costs of China's Gated Communities." In *Handbook of Cultural Security*, edited by Yasushi Watanabe. Cheltenham, UK: Edward Elgar.

Weigel, Moira. 2016. *Labor of Love: The Invention of Dating*. New York: Farrar, Straus and Giroux.

Weightman, S. 2017. "Hinduism." In *A New Handbook of Living Religions*, edited by J. R. Hinnells. Wiley Online Library. doi:10.1002/9781405166614.ch5

Weitz, Rose. 2017. *The Sociology of Health, Illness, and Health Care: A Critical Approach*, 7th ed. Boston: Wadsworth Cengage.

Weitzer, Ronald. 2012. *Legalizing Prostitution: From Illicit Vice to Lawful Business*. New York: New York University Press.

Weitzer, Ronald. 2015. "Human Trafficking and Contemporary Slavery." *Annual Review of Sociology* 41: 223–242.

Weitzman, Abigail, and Julia Andrea Behrman. 2016. "Disaster, Disruption to

Family Life, and Intimate Partner Violence: The Case of the 2010 Earthquake in Haiti." *Sociological Science* 3: 167–189.

Wellard, Ian. 2012. "Body-Reflexive Pleasures: Exploring Bodily Experiences within the Context of Sport and Physical Activity." *Sport, Education and Society* 17: 21–33.

Wellford, Charles. 2019. "Criminology." In the Wiley-Blackwell Companion to Sociology. Edited by George Ritzer and Wendy Wiedenhoft Murphy. Chichester: John Wiley & Sons.

Wennersten, John, and Denise Robbins. 2017. *Rising Tides: Climate Refugees in the Twenty-First Century*. Bloomington: Indiana University Press.

West, Candace, and Don Zimmerman. 1987. "Doing Gender." *Gender & Society* 1: 125–151.

West, S., M. Banerjee, B. Phipps, and T. Friedline. 2017. "Coming up Short: Family Composition, Income, and Household Savings." *Journal of the Society for Social Work and Research* 8(3): 355–377.

Western, Bruce. 2018. *Homeward: Life in the Year after Prison*. New York: Russell Sage Foundation.

Wharton, Amy S., and Mary Blair-Loy. 2006. "Long Work Hours and Family Life: A Cross-National Study of Employees' Concerns." *Journal of Family Issues* 27(3): 415–436.

White, J. (2022, December 6). *How Many Charter Schools and Students Are There?* Retrieved May 16, 2023, from https://data.publiccharters.org/digest/charter-school-data-digest/how-many-charter-schools-and-students-are-there/

Whittier, Nancy. 2016. "Where Are the Children? Theorizing the Missing Piece in Gendered Sexual Violence." *Gender & Society* 30: 95–108.

Whyte, William Foote. 1943. *Street Corner Society: The Social Structure of an Italian Slum*. Chicago: University of Chicago.

Wides-Muñoz, Laura. 2019. *The Making of a Dream*. New York: Harper.

Wiedenhoft Murphy, Wendy. 2017a. "Boycotts, Buycotts, and Legislation: Tactical Lessons from Workers and Consumers during the Progressive Era." In *Shopping for Social Change: Consumer Activism and the Possibilities of Purchasing Power*, edited by Louis Hyman and Joseph Tohill, 29–40. Ithaca, NY: Cornell University Press.

Wiedenhoft Murphy, Wendy. 2017b. *Consumer Culture and Society*. Thousand Oaks, CA: SAGE.

Wiegner, Lilian, Dominique Hange Cecilia Björkelund, and Gunnar Ahlborg Jr. 2015. "Prevalence of Perceived Stress and Associations to Symptoms of Exhaustion, Depression, and Anxiety in a Working Age Population Seeking Primary Care—An Observational Study." *BMC Family Practice* 16.

Wilding, Raelene. 2018. *Families, Intimacy, and Globalization*. London: Palgrave.

Williams, Christine L. 1995. *Still a Man's World*. Berkeley: University of California Press.

Williams, Conor P. 2018. "Betsy DeVos Loves Charter Schools. That's Bad for Charter Schools." *New York Times*, June 2.

Williams, Rosalind. [1982] 1991. *Dream Worlds: Mass Consumption in Late Nineteenth-Century France*. Berkeley: University of California Press.

Williams, Timothy. 2016. "One Robber's 3 Life Sentences: '90s Legacy Fills Prisons Today." *New York Times*, July 4.

Williamson, Oliver E. 1975. *Markets and Hierarchies: Analysis and Antitrust Implications*. New York: Free Press.

Williamson, Oliver E. 1985. *The Economic Institutions of Capitalism*. New York: Free Press.

Wilper, Andrew P., Steffie Woolhandler, Karen E. Lasser, Danny McCormick, David H. Bor, and David U. Himmelstein. 2009. "Health Insurance and Mortality in US Adults." *American Journal of Public Health* 99(12): 2289–2295.

Wilson, Bryan R. 1966. *Religion and Secular Society*. London: Watts.

Wilson, Midge, and Kathy Russell. 1996. *Divided Sisters: Bridging the Gap between Black and White Women*. New York: Anchor Books.

Wilson, Stephen R. 1984. "Becoming a Yogi: Resocialization and Deconditioning as Conversion Processes." *Sociological Analysis* 45(4): 301–314.

Wilson, William Julius. 1997. *When Work Disappears: The World of the New Urban Poor*. New York: Vintage.

Winant, Howard. 2001. *The World Is a Ghetto: Race and Democracy since World War II*. New York: Basic Books.

Winchester, M. S., R. BeLue, T. Oni, U. Wittwer-Backofen, D. Deobagkar, H. Onya, T. A. Samuels, S. A. Matthews, C. Stone, and C. Airhihenbuwa. 2016. "The Pan-University Network for Global Health: Framework for Collaboration and Review of Global Health Needs." *Globalization and Health* 12. Accessed February 7, 2017. https://globalizationandhealth.biomedcentral.com/articles/10.1186/s12992-016-0151-2.

Wines, Michael. 2011. "Picking Brand Names in China Is a Business Itself." *New York Times*, November 11. Accessed April 1, 2012. http://www.nytimes.com/2011/11/12/world/asia/picking-brand-namesin-china-is-a-business-itself.html.

Wingfield, Nick. 2014a. "Feminist Critics of Video Games Facing Threats in 'Gamergate.'" *New York Times*, October 15.

Wingfield, Nick. 2014b. "In Games Like Minecraft, Tech Giants See More than Fun." *New York Times*, September 11.

Wingfield, Nick. 2014c. "Virtual Games Draw Real Crowds and Big Money." *New York Times*, August 31.

Winter, Browyn, Maxine Forest, and Réjane Sénac, eds. 2018. *Global Perspectives on Same-Sex Marriage*. New York: Palgrave.

Wirth, Thierry. 2018. "Globalization and Infectious Diseases." In *Biodiversity and Evolution*, edited by Philippe Grandcolas and Marie-Christine Maurel, 123–113. Amsterdam, Netherlands: Elsevier.

Wisman, Jon D. 2013. "Wage Stagnation, Rising Inequality, and the Financial Crisis of 2008." *Cambridge Journal of Economics* 37: 921–945.

Witter, Arielle. 2021. "How COVID-19 is threatening girls' education," *One*. March 5, 2021. Available at: https://www.one.org/international/blog/girls-education-crisis-covid-19/

Wolf, Naomi. [1991] 2002. *The Beauty Myth: How Images of Beauty Are Used Against Women*. New York: Harper Perennial.

Wong-Padoongpatt, Gloria and Aldo M. Barrita. 2023. "The Fast and Slow Violence of the COVID-19 Pandemic on Asians in the USA," In *COVID-19: Cultural Change and Institutional Adaptations*, edited by J. Michael Ryan, 147–158. London: Routledge.

Wood, Simon, and David Harrington Watt, eds. 2014. *Fundamentalism: Perspectives on a Contested History*. Columbia: University of South Carolina Press.

Wood, Wendy, and Alice H. Eagly. 2015. "Two Traditions on Research on Gender Identity." *Sex Roles* 73: 461–473.

World Bank. 2018. "Record High Remittances to Low- and Middle- Income Countries in 2017." Accessed May 1, 2019. https://www.worldbank.org/en/news/press-release/2018/04/23/record-highremittan

ces-to-low-and-middle-income-countries-in-2017.

World Bank. 2019. *Urban Population*. Accessed October 21, 2019. http://data.worldbank.org/indicator/sp.urb.totl.in.zs

World Bank. 2023, April 3. *Overview*. Retrieved May 12, 2023, from https://www.worldbank.org/en/topic/urbandevelopment/overview

The World Bank. n.d.-a. *GNI (Current US$)—United States*. Retrieved May 18, 2023, from https://data.worldbank.org/indicator/NY.GNP.MKTP.CD?locations=US

The World Bank. n.d.-b. *GNI per Capita, Atlas Method (Current US$)—Kyrgyz Republic*. Retrieved May 18, 2023, from https://data.worldbank.org/indicator/NY.GNP.PCAP.CD?locations=KG

The World Bank. n.d.-c. *Individuals Using the Internet (% of Population)*. Retrieved May 18, 2023, from https://data.worldbank.org/indicator/IT.NET.USER.ZS

World Health Organization. 2010a. "Tobacco Free Initiative: China Releases Its Global Adult Tobacco Survey Data." Accessed April 1, 2012. http://www.who.int/tobacco/surveillance/gats_china/en/index.html.

World Health Organization. 2018. "Violence against Children." Accessed May 1, 2019. http://www.who.int/violence_injury_prevention/violence/violence-against-children/en/.

World Health Organization. 2021, June 9. *Obesity and Overweight*. Retrieved May 18, 2023, from https://www.who.int/news-room/fact-sheets/detail/obesity-and-overweight

World Health Organization. 2022, September 15. *Adolescent Pregnancy*. Retrieved May 12, 2023, from https://www.who.int/news-room/fact-sheets/detail/adolescent-pregnancy

World Health Organization (2022a, July 6). N Report: Global hunger numbers rose to as many as 828 million in 2021. WHO. Retrieved April 29, 2023, from https://www.who.int/news/item/06-07-2022-un-report--global-hunger-numbers-rose-to-as-many-as-828-million-in-2021

World Health Organization (2022b, May 24). Tobacco. WHO. Retrieved April 29, 2023, from https://www.who.int/news-room/fact-sheets/detail/tobacco

World Health Organization. (2023, April 21). Tuberculosis. WHO. Retrieved April 29, 2023, from https://www.who.int/news-room/fact-sheets/detail/tuberculosis

World Inequality Report. 2022. *Executive Summary*. Retrieved May 18, 2023, from https://wir2022.wid.world/executive-summary

Worldometer. n.d. *Life Expectancy of the World Population*. Retrieved May 12, 2023, from https://www.worldometers.info/demographics/life-expectancy/

World Population Review. 2023. *Total Fertility Rate 2023*. Retrieved May 12, 2023, from https://worldpopulationreview.com/country-rankings/total-fertility-rate

World Vision. 2020. "COVID-19 Aftershocks: Access Denied: Teenage Pregnancy Threatens to Block a Million Girls Across Sub-Saharan Africa from Returning to School." August 21, 2022. https://reliefweb.int/report/world/covid-19-aftershocks-access-denied-teenage-pregnancy-threatens-block-million-girls

Wortmann, Susan L. 2007. "Sex Tourism." In *The Blackwell Encyclopedia of Sociology*, edited by George Ritzer, 4200–4203. Malden, MA: Blackwell.

Wu, Tim. 2018. "Be Afraid of Economic 'Bigness.' Be Very Afraid." *New York Times*, November 10.

Wuthnow, Robert. 2018. *The Left Behind: Decline and Rage in Rural America*. Princeton, NJ: Princeton University Press.

Wysocki, Diane Kholos, and Cheryl D. Childers. 2011. "'Let My Fingers Do the Talking': Sexting and Infidelity in Cyberspace." *Sexuality & Culture* 15: 217–239.

Yardley, Jim. 2010. "Soaring above India's Poverty, a 27-Story Single-Family Home." *New York Times*, October 29.

Yeates, Nicola. 2009. *Globalizing Care Economies and Migrant Workers: Explorations in Global Care Chains*. New York: Palgrave Macmillan.

Yeates, Nicola. 2012. "Global Care Chains: A State-of-the-Art Review and Future Directions in Care Transnational Research." *Global Networks* 12(2): 135–154.

Yeginsu, Ceylan, and Anemona Hartocollis. 2015. "Amid Perilous Mediterranean Crossings, Migrants Find a Relatively Easy Path to Greece." *New York Times*, August 16.

Yeh, Marie, Robert D. Jewell, and Veronica L. Thomas. 2017. "The Stigma of Mental Illness: Using Segmentation for Social Change." *Journal of Public Policy & Marketing* 36(1): 97–116.

Yetman, Norman R., ed. 1991. *Majority and Minority: The Dynamics of Race and Ethnicity in American Life*, 5th ed. Boston: Allyn & Bacon.

Yi, B. 2021. An Overview of the Chinese Healthcare System. *Hepatobiliary Surgery and Nutrition, 10*(1), 93–95. https://doi.org/10.21037/hbsn-2021-3

Yodanis, Carrie, and Sean Lauer. 2014. "Is Marriage Individualized? What Couples Actually Do." *Journal of Family Theory and Review* 6: 184–197.

York, Richard, and Riley Dunlap. 2019. "Environmental Sociology." In *The Wiley-Blackwell Companion to Sociology*, 2nd ed., edited by George Ritzer and Wendy Wiedenhoft Murphy. Chichester, UK: John Wiley & Sons.

Yoshihara, Susan, and Douglas A. Sylva, eds. 2011. *Population Decline and the Remaking of Great Power Politics*. Washington, DC: Potomac Books.

Yulius H., S. Tang, and B. Offord. 2018. "The Globalization of LGBT Identity and Same-Sex Marriage as a Catalyst of Neo-institutional Values: Singapore and Indonesia." In *Global Perspectives on Same-Sex Marriage*, edited by B. Winter, M. Forest and R. Sénac, 171–196. Cham, Switzerland: Palgrave Macmillan.

Zafirovski, Milan. 2013. "Beneath Rational Choice: Elements of 'Irrational Choice Theory.'" *Current Sociology* 61: 3–21.

Zaidi, Batool, and S. Philip Morgan. 2017. "The Second Demographic Transition Theory: A Review and Appraisal." *Annual Review of Sociology* 43(1): 473–492.

Zakaria, Farid. 1997. "The Rise of Illiberal Democracy." *Foreign Affairs* November–December. Accessed May 1, 2019. https://www.foreignaffairs.com/articles/1997-11-01/rise-illiberal-democracy.

Zara, Georgia, and David Farrington. 2016. *Criminal Recidivism: Explanation, Prediction, and Prevention*. New York: Routledge.

Zeller, Dirk, Tim Cashion, Maria Palomares, and Daniel Pauly. 2018. "Global Marine Fisheries Discards: A Synthesis of Reconstructed Data." *Fish and Fisheries* 19(1): 30–39.

Zereyesus, Y. A., & Cardell, L. 2022, November 28. *Global Food Insecurity Grows in 2022 Amid Backdrop of Higher Prices, Black Sea Conflict*. USDA Economic Research Service. Retrieved May 18, 2023, from https://www.ers.usda.gov/amber-waves/2022/november/global-food-insecurity-grows-in-2022-amid-backdrop-of-higher-prices-black-sea-conflict/

Zhang, Yang, and Michael John Hitchcock. 2014. "The Chinese Female Tourist Gaze: A Netnography of Young Women's Blogs on Macao." *Current Issues in Tourism*, June 9 (published online). doi:10.1080/13683500.2014.904845

Zhou, Yanqui Rachel, and William D. Coleman. 2016. "Accelerated Contagion and Response: Understanding the Relationship among Globalization, Time, and Disease." *Globalizations* 13: 285–299.

Zhuge, Ying, Joyce Kaufman, Diane M. Simeone, Herbert Chen, and Omaida C. Velazquez. 2011. "Is There Still a Glass Ceiling for Women in Academic Surgery?" *Annals of Surgery* 253: 637–643.

Zimbardo, Philip. 1973. "On the Ethics of Intervention in Human Psychological Research: With Special Reference to the Stanford Prison Experiment." *Cognition* 2: 243–256.

Zimmerman, Don H. 1988. "On Conversation: The Conversation Analytic Perspective." In *Communication Yearbook 11*, edited by James A. Anderson, 406–432. Newbury Park, CA: Sage.

Zinn, Maxine Baca. 2012. "Patricia Hill Collins: Past and Future Innovations." *Gender & Society* 26: 28–32.

Zuberi, An. 2013. *Cleaning Up: How Hospital Outsourcing Is Hurting Workers and Endangering Patients*. Ithaca, NY: Cornell University Press.

Zukin, Sharon. 1982. *Loft Living: Culture and Capital in Urban Change*. Baltimore: Johns Hopkins University Press.

INDEX

#MeToo movement, 430

Abdill, Aasha, 68
Abortion, 103, 428
Absolute poverty, 205
Abu Dhabi, 17
Abuse and violence within families, 290–94
Achieved status, 131
Achievement, 196–97
Adbusters, 102
Adolescent childbearing, 393
Adonis complex, 370
Adoption, 297
Advertising
 of drugs, 380
 sex and, 268
Afghanistan, 213, 254, 333, 382, 445
African Americans
 body satisfaction, 367
 civil rights movement, 238, 426
 consumer culture and, "culture of poverty," 226
 double consciousness, 41
 Du Bois's sociology, 40–41
 health-related issues, 377
 identity, 225
 school segregation, 233, 306
 single-parent families, 286
 unemployment and, 353
 See also Race, Race and ethnicity
Age and fertility, 392
Agency, 12
Agents of socialization, 122
Aging-related changes, 129
AIDS. See HIV/AIDS
AIDS Coalition, 433
Ainu, 242
Airbnb, 4, 199
Albania, 254
Albright, Madeline, 340
Alienation, 35
Allums, Kye, 253
Alzheimer's disease, 365
Amazon.com, 22, 141, 348, 356
Ambani, Mukesh, 407
American Federation of Teachers (AFT), 351
Americanization, 108. See also McDonaldization
American Sociology Association, 28
Anderson, Benedict, 344
Animal interactions and behavior, 117
Anomie, 39, 62
Anthony, Susan B., 427

Anthropology, 15
Anti-Americanism, 108
Anticipatory socialization, 122
Apartheid, 227, 426
Appadurai, Arjun, 161
Appearance culture, 366
Apple, 141, 165
Apple stores, 155
Aquaculture, 412
Arab Spring, 445
Argentina, 211–12, 433
Aristotle, 34
Armenians, 243
Artificial intelligence (AI), 352
Asch, Solomon, 135
Ascribed status, 131
Ascription, 197
Assembly line, 25, 37
Assimilation, 228, 233
Asylum seekers, 399
Atlantic City, New Jersey, 23
Attention-deficit/hyperactivity disorder (ADHD), 10
Australia, 334, 445
Austria, 260, 394, 399
Authority, 143
Avatars, 130
Avian flu, 384
Ayers, Lindsay L., 68

Baby boom, 394
Backsourcing, 154
Back stage, 120
Baker, Ella, 426
Bangladesh, 398
Bashir, Omar Hassan Ahmed, 245
Baudrillard, Jean, 51
Bauman, Zygmunt, 280, 443
Beauty, 367–68
Beccaria, Cesare, 182
Beck, Ulrich, 158
Belgium, 433
Beliefs, 320
The Bell Curve (Herrnstein & Murray), 306
Berryman, Rachel, 368
Bezos, Jeff, 195
Bhutan, 331
Big Brother, 69
Bigorexia, 370
Bird flu (avian flu), 384
Birthrate, 392, 396, 402. See also Fertility
Black Americans. See African Americans
Black Panthers, 239
Black Power movement, 239

Blackwater, 152
Blee, Kathleen, 238
Blended families, 287
Blockbuster, 151
Blogging about sociology, 6
Bodily capital, 369
Body, 365–71
 appearance, 366
 beauty, 367–68
 fitness, 368–69
Body mass index (BMI), 77
Body modification, 368, 371
Bolivia, 213, 224
Bollywood, 108
Bono, Chaz, 254
Borderless diseases, 384
Border walls or fences, 19, 163, 170, 188, 398
Bosnians, 243
Botswana, 395
Bounded rationality, 145
Brain, 63, 366
Branch Davidians, 328
Brandalism, 102
Brand communities, 100
Brand culture, 360
Brand names, 98
Brands, 360
Brazil, 212, 250, 368, 382, 411, 433
Breadwinner wives, 196
Breastfeeding, 99
Brexit, 17, 340
Brown Berets, 239
Brown v. Board of Education of Topeka (1954), 233, 306
Buddhism, 331
Bulgaria, 164, 399
Buraku, 242
Burawoy, Michael, 28
Bureaucracies, 141–46. See also Organizations
Bureaucratic personality, 146
Burning Man, 357
Burundi, 243
Bush, George H. W., 203
Bush, George W., 203
Bush, Jeb, 203
Bush, Prescott, 203
Butterfly effect, 3

Call centers, 153
Calvinism, 37
Cambodia, 245, 331, 344
Canada, 334, 433, 445
Cancer, 395
Cape Verde, 212

501

Capitalism
    environmental issues, 409
    female oppression and, 45
    illiberal democracy, 340
    Industrial Revolution, 345
    Marxist theory, 35–36, 44, 61
    poverty and, 204
    prosumer, 349
    as rational, 37
    See also Marx, Karl
Capitalists, 35
Capital punishment, 185
Carbon dioxide emissions, 414
Caregiving work, 219
Casinos, 23
Castells, Manuel, 157
Cathedrals of consumption, 356, 408
Catholic Church, 150, 332
Caucasian race, 225
Cellphones. See Smartphones
Censorship, 140
Census data, 77, 79
Central African Republic, 216, 382
Chad, 216, 382
Challenger disaster, 441
Chambliss, William, 177
Charismatic authority, 144
Charter schools, 313
Cherlin, Andrew, 282–83
Chernobyl disaster, 158
Child abuse, 291
Childcare tasks, 293
Child development
    development of the self, 118–19
    socialization, 122
Children in consumer culture, 354
Chile, 212
China
    avian flu and, 384
    body ideals, 368
    Buddhism, 331
    capitalist economy, 205
    capital punishment, 185
    censorship, 140
    elections in, 340
    environmental issues, 410
    foreign aid and development, 220
    Global North, 211
    health care system, 217
    imports from, 21
    internet surveillance, 160
    mass production, 346
    megacities, 407
    middle-income economy, 212
    poverty and, 213
    racism and, 242
    social mobility in, 208
    Tiananmen Square, 438
    U.S. deindustrialization and, 350
    U.S. relationship, 344
    U.S. tariffs and, 44
Christian fundamentalists, 333
Christianity, 332
Christian sects, 327

Chronic illnesses, 383
Churches, 327
Church of Jesus Christ of the Latter-Day
    Saints, 333
Cigarette smoking. See Smoking
Cities, 403
    culture and consumption, 407
    smart, 408
    See also Urbanization
Citizenship, 339
Civil disobedience, 437
Civil liberties, 339
Civil rights movement, 238, 426
Clark, Septima Poinsette, 426
Class. See Social class
Class consciousness, 36
Climate change, 16, 60, 63, 413–15, 419
Coalition of Immokalee Workers (CIW), 424
Cohen, Philip, 27
Coleman Report, 305–6
Collective action, 439
    crowds, 439
    riots, 440
Collective conscience, 38
Collins, Randall, 11, 32
Colombia, 433
Common sense, 16
Communication studies, 15
Companionate love, 280
Companionate marriage, 283
Competitive capitalism, 348
Computer hackers, 101
Comte, Auguste, 14, 34
Conflict/critical theories, 45
    deviance and, 179
    environmental issues, 409
    families, 290
    feminist, 47
    global stratification, 214
    power elite theory, 342
    queer theory, 48
    social stratification, 210
    See also Critical theory, Feminist theory
Conflict groups, 46
Conflict theory, 45–46. See also Conflict/
    critical theories
Conformists, 175
Conformity to the group, 135
Consensual sexual activities, 267
Conservative-liberal culture war, 103
Conspicuous leisure, 42
Consumer activism, 424
Consumer capitalism, 348–49
Consumer culture, 103
    beauty and fitness, 368, 370
    brand culture, 360
    gender and, 261
    socialization and, 125
Consumption, 22
    capitalism and, 348
    cathedrals of, 356, 408
    cities and, 407
    credit card debt, 20, 51
    critical study of, 22

    gender and, 261
    globalization and, 359
    health care and, 379–81
    hyperconsumption, 51
    internet and, 356
    leisure and, 357
    McDonaldization, 23
    religion and, 324, 356
    sex and, 268, 270
    smartphones and, 26
    socialization and, 125
    subcultures, 100
    Veblen's theory, 41
    work and family intersections, 261
    See also Consumer culture
Contact sports. See Sports
Content analysis, 79–80
Contreras, Randol, 83
Convenience samples, 74
Conversation analysis, 131
Conversations, 53
Conversations of gestures, 116
Cooley, Charles Horton, 116
Cooper, Anna Julia, 427
Coronary heart disease, 378
Corporate crime, 186
Corrections system, 183
Cosmetic surgery, 368
Cosmopolitan areas, 406
The Cosmopolitan Canopy
Costello, Barbara, 123
Cost of medical care, 375
Countercultures, 101
Cox, Laverne, 253
Credit card debt, 21, 51
Credit card globalization, 445
Crime
    DNA analysis, 186
    elites and, 177, 179
    global crime control, 189
    globalization and, 187
    racial/ethnic prejudice and discrimination, 230
    recidivism, 184
    research ethics considerations, 84–85
    types, 185–86
    undocumented immigrants and, 170
    white-collar, 177, 186
    See also Illegal drug use or trafficking
Criminalization, 170
Criminal justice system, 183
Criminology, 182–83
Critical theory, 46, 48
    race and racism, 49–50
    See also Conflict/critical theories, Feminist theory
Croatians, 243, 399
Crony capitalism, 340
Crowdfunding, 440
Crowds, 439
Cuba, 176, 212
Cults, 328
Cultural definitions of femininities/masculinities, 251

Cultural differences, 99
  countercultures, 101
  ideal and real culture, 99
  ideology, 99
  multiculturalism, 104
  subcultures, 100
Cultural discrimination, 234
Cultural explanations of race, 226–27
Cultural imperialism, 108
Cultural relativism, 107
Culture
  assimilation, 104
  body appearance and, 367
  cities and, 407
  consumer culture, 103, 126
  critical theory and, 46, 48
  global, 108
  ideal and real, 99
  interviewing considerations, 72
  postmodernism, 50
  sexual consent and, 267
  symbolic, 97
  values, 94, 101, 103
  work and, 354
  See also Consumer culture
Culture industry, 46
Culture of poverty, 226–27
Culture wars, 103
Cumulative advantage, 309
Curricular tracks, 309, 319
Cyberactivism, 445
Cyberculture, 109
Cyber Monday, 356
Cyberparents, 286

Dahrendorf, Ralf, 46
Darfur, 243, 245
Data analysis, 62, 77–80
Dating, 33
Daughters of Bilitis (DOB), 432
Death penalty, 185
Death rate. *See* Mortality
de Beauvoir, Simone, 252, 428
Debunking, 45
Deception and social research, 81
Deepwater Horizon disaster, 441
Defense of Marriage Act, 172, 433
Deficit model of family conflict, 290
Deforestation, 411
Deindustrialization, 350
Democracies, 339–40
Democracy and national values, 94
Demographic transition theory, 396–97
Demography and demographers, 392
Denmark, 433
Department of Homeland Security, 344
Dependent variable, 76
Depression, 366
Deprofessionalization, 374, 379
Descriptive statistics, 66
Descriptive surveys, 73
Desertification, 412
Desmond, Matthew, 28

Deterrence, 184
Deviance, 170
  body modification and tattooing, 170
  conflict/critical theory, 177–79
  consumption and, 173
  definition, 171
  drug use and, 173
  inter/actionist theories, 179
  labeling theory, 179–80
  primary and secondary, 180
  sexuality and, 173
  social control theory, 180
  stigma, 181
  strain theory, 175
  structural/functional theories, 43, 175–77
  theories of, 174
  See also Crime
DeVos, Betsy, 310
Diasporas, 241, 244, 344
Dictatorships, 341
Differential association theory, 182
Digital currency, 162
Digital divide, 215
Digital technology, 23. *See also* Social media
Direct democracies, 339
Disasters, 441
Discouraged workers, 354
Discreditable stigma, 181
Discredited stigma, 181
Discrimination, 230. *See also* Racism
Disney World, 357
Divorce, 290, 293–95, 298
DNA tests, 380
Dog whistles, 49
"Doing" interaction, 130
Domestic labor, 260, 287
Domestic violence, 291–92
Domination, 143
Domino theory, 344
"Don't ask, don't tell policy," 172
Double consciousness, 41
Downward mobility, 208
Dramaturgy, 120
Drug use. *See* Illegal drug use
  Marijuana use
Dubai, 354
Du Bois, W. E. B., 40–41, 49, 71
Duckworth, Angela, 307
Duke, David, 50
Durkheim, Émile, 34, 38–39, 62–63
  on religion, 320
  structural-functionalism, 43
Dyads, 133
Dysfunctions, 43

eBay, 155
Ebola, 384
Economic factors affecting fertility, 393
Economic inequality, 198
  decline of the middle class, 203
  health care, 375–77
  megacities and, 407

  social mobility, 208
  wealth, 201
  See also Poverty, Social class, Wealth
economics, 15
Economy
  capitalism, 348–49
  credit card debt, 20
  decline of labor unions, 350–51
  deindustrialization, 350
  digital currency, 162
  employment, unemployment, and underemployment, 354
  financescapes, 162
  globalization and, 358
  informationalism, 157
  outsourcing, 152
  postindustrial society, 351
  religion and, 37
  sharing economy, 4, 199, 357
  socialism and communism, 347
  tariffs and, 44
  technology and, 4
  transnational corporations, 348
  welfare states, 347
  See also Capitalism, Consumption, Globalization, Global stratification, Great Recession, Social stratification, Work
Education
  charter schools, 313
  comparing U.S. and other systems, 319
  consumer culture and, 356
  gender and, 255
  inequality in, 303
  preschool programs, 308
  race and ethnicity and, 236, 306
  segregation, 233, 306
  unschooling and homeschooling, 309
  See also Higher education
Educational attainment
  class differences, 307
  Coleman Report, 305
  employment and income relationship, 303–4
  families and, 305
  inequality in, 303
  intelligence and, 306
  international student assessment rankings, 317
  school differences, 306
  tracking, 309, 319
Egypt, 19, 294, 340, 382
eHarmony, 284
Ehrenreich, Barbara, 68
El Chapo, 175
Elder abuse, 292
Elite pluralism, 342
Emergent norm theory, 439
Emotion work, 375
Emphasized femininity, 252
Empiricism, 60
Endogamy, 279
Engels, Friedrich, 45

Environmental issues, 392, 409
   climate change, 16, 60, 63, 413–15
   Flint water crisis, 405
   freshwater, 405, 417
   globalization, 410
   global responses, 416–19
   habitat destruction, 412
   marine life, 412
   theoretical perspectives, 409
Environmental racism, 405
Estrogen, 251
Ethical codes, 85
Ethics in social research, 80–87
Ethiopia, 402
Ethnic cleansing, 244
Ethnic conflicts, 243–46
Ethnic groups, 224
Ethnocentrism, 107
Ethnography, 69
Ethnomethodology, 53, 130
   deviance and, 179
Ethnoscapes, 161
Euro, 19
European Union (EU), 19
   Brexit, 17, 340
Europol, 189
Exchange relationships, 54, 130
Exchange theory, 54, 290
Exogamy, 279
Experiments, 66, 75, 77
   ethical considerations, 81–82
Explanatory surveys, 73
Exploitation, 35
Expulsion, 244
Extended families, 288

Facebook, 25
   mass culture outlet, 46
   prosumer capitalism, 348–49
   social movements and, 438
   social network theory and research, 134
   See also Social media
Failed states, 345, 398
Fake news, 47
False consciousness, 36
Families
   abuse and violence within, 290–94
   adolescent motherhood, 393
   blended, 287
   child socialization and, 122
   conflict/critical theories, 289–90
   conflict within, 290
   decline in marriage, 280
   educational attainment and, 305
   extended, 288
   gender and work intersections, 258
   gender inequalities, 293–94
   globalization and, 286
   higher education enrollment and, 313–14
   inter/actionist theories, 290
   nonfamily households, 284
   nonresident parents, 286
   nuclear family ideal, 122, 280
   poverty and, 293
   single-parent, 286
   stepfamilies, 287
   structural/functional theories, 288
   television depictions, 278
   See also Marriage
Family and Medical Leave Act, 260
Family conflict, 290
Fantasy cities, 408
Fashion, 13
Fast-food employees, 23, 350
Fast-food restaurants, McDonaldization. See McDonaldization
Felonies, 186
Female orgasm, 378
Female proletarianization, 273
Femininities, 251
Feminism, 426–29
Feminist culture jamming, 102
Feminist movements, 274, 426, 433
Feminist theory, 47
   families, 290
   postmodern, 50
   scientific sociology and, 15
   social stratification, 210
   women of color and, 48
Feminization of labor, 272–73
Feminization of poverty, 206–7, 273
Fentanyl, 364
Ferguson, Missouri, 231
Fertility, 392–97
Field experiments, 76
Film industries, 108
Financescapes, 162
Fine, Gary, 69
Finke, Roger, 324
Finland, 317, 394, 433
Fishing, 412
Fitness, 368–69
Flint, Michigan, 405
Folkways, 96
Food insecurity, 383
FORCE, 102
Fordism, 346
Ford Motor Company, 151
Foreign aid and development, 220–21
Foucault, Michel, 51
Fox, Vicente, 170
Fox News, Fragile States Index, 345
France
   foreign aid and development, 220
   Global North, 211
   same-sex marriage, 433
Franchise system, 154
Freedom House, 339
Friedan, Betty, 428
"Friends with benefits," 54
Front and back stage, 120
Functions in structural-functionalism, 43

Game stage, 118
Gandhi, Mahatma, 144
Gans, Herbert, 79–80
Gated communities, 404
Gates, Bill, 195

Gay rights movements, 432
Gemeinschaft societies, 157
Gender, 250
   consumer culture and, 261
   ethnomethodological approach, 53
   femininities and masculinities, 251, 253
   feminization of poverty, 206–7
   global glows related to, 271
   intersectionality, 50, 232
   nonbinary, 254
   racist hate movements and, 238
   scientific sociology and, 15
   sex and, 250
   socialization, 123
   social mobility and, 208
   social stratification, 210
   symbolic interactionist theory, 52
   See also Feminist theory
Gender differences
   body satisfaction, 367
   brain and intelligence, 63
   feminist theory, 47
   life expectancy, 394–95
   medical professionals, 373–75
Gendered leisure divide, 358
Gender identity, 253
Gender inequality, 254–55
   #MeToo movement, 430
   capitalism and, 45
   civil rights movement and, 426
   feminist theory, 47
   feminization of poverty, 206, 272
   health-related issues, 377
   household and childcare tasks, 293
   medicalization, 378
   wage gap, 218, 373
   women's movements, 274, 426–30
   work and organizations, 147, 260
   See also Feminist theory
Genderqueer, 253
Gender roles, 253
Gender socialization, 124
Gender stereotypes, 250
General deterrence, 184
Generalized other, 118
Genetics and race, 225
Genocide, 233, 245
Gentrification, 406
Geoengineering, 419
Geography, 16
Germany
   educational system, 317
   as emigration destination, 334
   foreign aid and development, 220
   Global North, 211
   immigration policy, 398–99
   importance of religion in, 322
   Jews and, 244, 246
   nonmarital fertility, 393
   NSA spying, 445
   population decline, 402
   violent crime in, 185
Gesellschaft societies, 158
Gestures, 116

Gig economy, 4
Gilroy, Paul, 243
Glass ceiling, 147
Glenny, Misha, 187
Global brands, 360
Global cities, 406
Global crime control, 189
Global culture, 108
Global digital divide, 215
Global economy, 358
Global ethnography, 69
Global families, 299
Global information economy, 157
Globalization, 20
    barriers to flows, 163
    borderless diseases, 384
    cities and, 406
    controlling flows and mobilities, 160–63
    countercultures and, 102
    crime and, 187–89
    definition, 161
    deviance and, 173
    drugs and vaccines, 387, 389
    the economy and, 358
    education and, 26
    environmental issues, 410
    families and, 286, 299
    flows, 17
    flows and liquidity, 443
    gender-related flows, 274
    health-related issues, 215–389
    internet and, 445
    McDonaldization, 154
    migration and, 397–98
    nation-states and, 344
    new words related to, 98
    nonresident parents, 286
    organizations and, 151–55
    outsourcing, 152–53
    race/ethnicity and, 241–45
    religion and, 329, 333–34
    sex and sexuality, 270
    social change and, 442–45
    social movements and, 438
    social sciences and, 15–16
    society and, 158
    structural/functional theories, 43
    sustainability and, 418
    transnational corporations, 348
    U.S. deindustrialization, 350
    of values, 107
    World Values Survey, 77
    See also Migration and immigration
Global "liquids," 443
Global North and South, 211
Global religions, 333
Global responses to environmental problems, 416–19
Global sex industry, 270–71
Global stratification
    concentration of wealth, 213
    conflict/critical theories, 214
    digital divide, 215
    foreign aid and development, 220
    poverty and, 213
    race to the bottom, 219
    structural/functional theories, 214
Global surveillance, 445
Global warming, 16, 63, 413–15, 419. See also Climate change
Global women's movement, 274, 430
GM, 151
Goffman, Erving, 12, 120, 131, 181
GoFundMe, 440
Goldman, Emma, 290
Goldstone, Jack, 435
Google, 141
Gouldner, Alvin, 87
Granovetter, Mark, 133
Great Britain. See United Kingdom
Great Recession, 22
    decline of the middle class, 203
    global trade and, 359
Greece, 399
Greenhouse gases, 413
Gross national income (GNI) per capita, 212
Group conformity, 135
Group pluralism, 342
Groups, 134. See also Organizations
Guevara, Ernesto "Che," 176
Guinea, 212
Guzmán, Joaquín, 175
Gypsies (Roma), 159, 244

Habitat destruction, 411–12
Hackers, 101
Haiti, 442
Hamer, Fannie, 426
Hamermesh, Daniel, 367
Hart, Betty, 307
Harvard, 202
Hate crimes, 186
Hate groups, 237–38
Haul videos, 262
Health care consumerism, 379
Health care inequality, 217
Health care reform, 379. See also Affordable Care Act
Health insurance companies, 375
Health insurance costs, 375
Health-related issues, 365, 371
    ADHD, 10
    the body, 371
    borderless diseases, 384
    breastfeeding, 99
    contact sports, 150, 370
    fitness, 368–69
    gender, 377
    global concerns, 215, 364, 379, 381–89
    lifestyle, 366
    medical care cost, 375–76
    medicalization, 378
    medical profession, 373
    medical sociology, 373
    medical technologies, 389
    opioid crisis, 364
    race, 376–77
    risky behavior, 373
    social class, 376
    texting while driving, 372
    U.S. inequalities, 375–77
    war and, 387
Heart disease, 378
Heaven's Gate, 328
Hegemonic masculinity, 252
Herrnstein, Richard, 306
Heterosexism, 264
Hidden curriculum, 256
Higher education
    consumer culture and, 356
    factors affecting enrollment, 313–14
    social stratification, 195
Hinduism, 331, 334
Hippocratic oath, 85
Hispanic collective identity movements, 239
Historical-comparative research, 79
HIV/AIDS, 384–85, 433
H&M, 348
Hochschild, Arlie, 259
Hohmans, George, 54
Holidays, 325
Home care workers, 69
Homophobia, 264
Homosexuality
    the Lavender Scare, 431
    queer theory, 48
    research ethics problems, 84
    See also Lesbian, gay, bisexual, queer and transgender (LGBQT) people, Sexual orientation
Hong Kong, 354
Honor killings, 294
"Hooking up," 54
Hope, Trina, 123
Horizontal mobility, 208
Household labor, 259–60, 287, 293
HSBC, 153
Human-animal interactions, 116
Human trafficking, 270, 298
Hungary, 164, 340, 399
Hunger crises, 216
Hurricane Maria, 439
Hyperconsumption, 51
Hypotheses, 61

"I,," 119
IBM, 165
ICANN, 19
Iceland, 255, 394, 433
Ideal culture, 99
Ideological differences, 99
Ideoscapes, 162
IKEA, 153, 348
Illegal drug use or trafficking
    deviance and, 173
    global drug trade, 187
    marijuana, 73
    Mexican gangs, 189
    opioid crisis, 364
Imagined communities, 344

Immigrants, 17
    assimilation, 104
    families and child socialization, 123
    fertility, 393
    global ethnography, 69
    multiculturalism and, 104–7
    president Trump and, 105, 170
    reference groups, 135
    religious faiths, 334
    spaces of global flows, 161
    types of migrants, 399
    See also Migration and immigration, Undocumented immigrants
Immigration detention facilities, 19
Impression management, 120
Incarceration, 183–84. *See also* Prisons
Income inequality
    decline of the middle class, 203
    educational attainment and, 303–4
    as emigration destination, 334
    foreign aid and development, 220
    megacities, 407
    poverty and, 213
    See also Economic inequality, Social class
Indian immigrants, 161
Individualized marriage, 283
Individuals, 114
Industrial Revolution, 3, 345
Industrial society, 158
Inequality, 27, 198
    See also Economic inequality
Infant mortality, 376
Informal employment, 218
Informal organizations, 146
Information age, 4
Informationalism, 157
Information flows, 18
Informed (or "effective") sexual consent, 267
In-groups, 135
Innovators, 175
Institutional marriage, 283
Institutional racism, 236
Institutional review board (IRB), 85
Intelligence
    brain size and, 63
Interaction
    "doing," 130
    reciprocity and exchange, 129
    status and role, 131
    superior-subordinate, 40
    symbolic, 117
    See also Symbolic interactionism
Inter/actionist theories, 52–54
    deviance and, 179
    exchange, 54
    families, 290
    rational choice, 54
    social stratification, 210
    See also Ethnomethodology, Symbolic interactionism
Intergenerational mobility, 208
International crime, 187–89
International Monetary Fund (IMF), 141, 150

Internet
    access to, 25
    censorship, 140
    Chinese surveillance system, 160
    consumer culture and, 356
    cyberculture, 109
    education and, 26
    free information flow, 18
    global digital divide, 215
    globalization and, 359, 444
    health care consumption and, 380
    open-source advocates, 104
    religion and, 324
    sex tourism, 271
    social movements and, 438
    social network theory and research, 134
    sociological experiments and, 77
    women and video games, 429
    See also Social media
Internet commerce, 21
Intersectionality, 50, 232
Intersex, 251
Interviews, 65, 73
Intimate partner violence (IPV), 291, 293–94
Intimate relationships
    online dating, 284
    See also Marriage, Sexuality
Intragenerational mobility, 208
iPhone, 21
iPod, 97
Iran, 140, 159, 185, 294
Iraq, 18, 152, 159, 273, 333, 344, 398, 445
Ireland, 255, 394, 433
ISIS. *See* Islamic State
Islam, 331
Islamic fundamentalism, 333
Islamic State (IS), 11, 18, 333, 398, 438
Israel, 19, 330, 344
    as emigration destination, 334
    McDonaldization, 61
    nation-state, 160
    West Bank border wall, 164
Italy, 105, 107, 285, 402

Jails and prisons, 183. *See also* Prisons
Japan
    cult in, 328
    foreign aid and development, 220
    Global North, 211
    high-income economy, 211
    importance of religion in, 322
    industrial technology, 346
    population decline, 402
    racism and, 242
Japanese life expectancy, 383, 395–96
Jewish people
    Holocaust, 245
    as imagined community, 344
    immigrants, 334
    as a race or ethnicity, 225
    religion (Judaism), 330
Judaism, 330

Kavka, Misha, 368
Kenya, 360
Key informants, 72
Khaldun, Ibn Abdel Rahman, 3, 34
Khat, 360
Khmer Rouge, 245
Kickstarter, 440
King, Martin Luther, Jr., 144
King, Rodney, 440
Kuhn, Thomas, 63–64
Ku Klux Klan (KKK), 50, 237
Kurdistan, 159
Kurds, 159
Kyrgyz Republic, 212

Labeling theory, 179–80
Laboratory experiments, 76
Labor migrants, 400
Labor movement, 350
Labor unions, 146, 164, 199, 350
Lacks, Henrietta, 81
Landscapes, 161
Language
    global digital divide, 216
    interviewing considerations, 72
    linguistic assimilation, 228
    significant symbols, 117
    symbolic culture, 97
Laos, 213, 331
Las Vegas, Nevada, 355, 408
Latent functions, 44
Lavender Scare, 431
Laws, 95
Lebanon, 298
Leisure, conspicuous, 42
Leisure class, 41
Lesbian, gay, bisexual, queer and transgender (LGBQT) people
    deviance and, 173
    globalized context, 269–70
    prejudice and discrimination, 264
    queer theory, 48
    religion and, 331
    same-sex marriage, 172–73, 433–34
    sexual orientation, 264
    Stonewall uprising, 254
    See also Homosexuality, Sexual orientation, Transgender
Levitsky, Steven, 341
Liberal-conservative culture war, 103
Liberalism, 340
Libya, 18, 107, 273, 398
Life expectancy, 214, 216, 376, 382, 394–95
Lifestyles, 366
    fitness, 368–69
    mortality and, 396
    risky behavior, 373
Liminal period, 322
Linux, 165
Liquidity, 443
Local areas, 406
Lombroso, Cesare, 182
Looking-glass self, 116

Love, 280
Lower class, 195
Lower Ed
Luxembourg, 433
Lyft, 4

Macedonia, 399
Macrofinance, 358
Macro social phenomena, 11
Madoff, Bernie, 177
Majority-minority relations, 233
    global context, 240
    social movements and, 237
    See also Immigrants
        Race and ethnicity
        Racism
Malaysia, 382
Mali, 216
Malls. *See* Shopping malls
Malnutrition, 216–17
Malpractice, 374
Man cave, 262
Manifest functions, 44
Manorexia, 370
Manson, Charles, 328
Marijuana use, 73
Marine life, 412
Marriage
    blended families, 287
    decline in, 280
    deinstitutionalization of, 282–83
    divorce, 290, 293–95, 298
    Engels' theory, 45
    types of, 280, 283
    See also Intimate relationships
Marriage equality (same-sex marriage), 172, 433–34
Martineau, Harriet, 34, 47
Marx, Karl (and Marxist theory), 34, 36, 61
    conflict theory and, 45
    on micro-macro relationships, 11
    secondary data analysis, 77
    social reform and, 15
Masculinities, 251
Mass culture, 46
Mass media and socialization, 125
Mass production, 346
Master status, 132
Maternity leave, 260
Matrix of oppression, 232
Mattachine Society, 432
McCarthy, Joe, 339, 438
McDonaldization, 23, 61, 154
The McDonaldization of Society. See also McDonaldization
McDonald's, 153, 348, 350, 356
"Me," 119
Mead, George Herbert, 116–18
Mechanical solidarity, 39
Mediascapes, 162
Mediated interaction, 26
Medical care costs, 375
Medicalization, 378

Medical malpractice, 374
Medical profession, 373–75
Medical tourism, 21
Megacities, 407
Megalopolis, 404
Megamalls, 355
Melilla, 164
Men and boys as consumers, 262
Mendel, Gregor, 225
Meritocracy, 100, 303
Merton, Robert, 43–44, 146
Metropolis, 403
Mexico, 17, 334
    climate change and, 413
    infant mortality, 376
    muxes gender group, 254
    nonmarital fertility, 393
    same-sex marriage, 433
    U.S. border controls and migration, 19, 164, 170, 188, 397, 399–400
    U.S. deindustrialization and, 350
Michels, Robert, 146
Micro-level social structures, 132–36
Micro-macro relationship, 114
Micro social phenomena, 11
Microsoft Bing, 99, 165
Middle class, 195, 203
Migration and immigration, 17
    borderless diseases, 384
    border walls or fences, 19, 170, 189, 398
    diasporas, 344
    families and, 298
    feminization of, 272
    flows based on race/ethnicity, 242–43
    global flows, 161, 444
    population considerations, 397
    push and pull factors, 399
    religion and, 329, 335
    types of migrants, 399
    See also Immigrants, Undocumented immigrants
Milgram experiment (1974), 81–82
Militancy, 437
Military as total institution, 128
Military conflict. *See* War
Mills, C. Wright, 9, 15
Mind and self, 117
Minorities. *See* Gender inequality
    Immigrants
        Lesbian, gay, bisexual, queer and transgender (LGBQT) people
        Race and ethnicity
Minority group, defined, 228
Misdemeanors, 186
Modernity, 50
Modernization theory, 214
Monogamy, 279
Monopoly capitalism, 348
Moral entrepreneur, 180–81
Morales, Evo, 224
Moral panics, 180–81
Mores, 96
Mormonism, 333
Morocco, 164

Morris, Robert Tappan, 101
Mortality, 214, 376, 395, 401. *See also* Health-related issues
Movimiento Socialismo (MAS), 224
Ms. Magazine, 428
Multiculturalism, 104
Multinational corporations, 164
Multitasking, 26
Murray, Charles, 306
Muslim immigrants, 105, 180–81
Muslim religious experience, 320, 322
Myanmar, 331, 398

Nanjiani, Kumail, 98
National Aeronautics and Space Administration (NASA), 150
National Education Association (NEA), 351
National Football League (NFL), 150
National Organization for Women (NOW), 428
National Security Agency (NSA), 445
Nations, 159, 344
Nation-states, 160, 344
Natural disasters, 441
Natural experiments, 76
Natural habitat destruction, 411–12
Nature and nurture, 115
Nazi Holocaust, 245
Netherlands, 105, 287, 430, 433
Netiquette, 109
Netnography, 70
Network organizations, 155–56
Network theory, 133
New racism, 49
New religious movements, 329
New Songdo, South Korea, 18
Newton, Isaac, 34
New Zealand, 368, 433
Nicaragua, 212
Niger, 393, 402
Nigeria, 211, 385
Nike, 360
Nineteenth Amendment, 427
Nonfamily households, 284
Nonparticipant observation, 68–69
Nonresident parents, 286
Nonviolence, 437
North American Free Trade Agreement (NAFTA), 165
North Korea, 45, 68, 211, 342
Norway, 433
Nuclear accidents, 158
Nuclear family, 122, 280
Nuremberg Code, 85
Nurses, 375
Nutrition problems, 216–17
Nxivm, 328

Obama, Barack, 235
Obesity, 217, 372, 383, 395
Objectivity in social research, 87
Observational research, 65, 67–71
Occupational gender stratification, 210

Occupational health risks, 372
Occupational mobility, 208
Offshore outsourcing, 153
Oligarchies, 146
Oman, 212
One-drop rule, 227
Online dating, 284
Online shopping, 21, 127. See also Amazon.com
OPEC, 17
Open-ended interviews, 72
Open-source advocates, 104
Opioid crisis, 364
Orban, Viktor, 340
Organic solidarity, 39
Organisation for Economic Cooperation and Development (OECD), 220
Organizations, 140
　authority structures, 143
　bureaucracies, 141–46
　contemporary changes, 151
　global flows and, 165
　globalization and, 151
　informal, 146
　informationalism, 157
　institutional racism, 236
　networks, 155–56
　oligarchies, 146
　Peter principle and Parkinson's law, 144
　rationality and irrationality, 144
Organized crime, 186
Orientalism, 241
Orlando, Florida, 42, 321, 408
Out-groups, 135
Outsourcing, 98, 152–53
Overeating, 372

Pager, Devah, 75
Pakistan, 185, 294
Pakistani immigrants, 161
Palestinians, 164, 344
Paradigms, 63–64
Parental abuse of children, 290–91
Paris Agreement, 392
Parkour, 101
Parochial schools, 309
Parole, 184
Parsons, Talcott, 288
Participant observation, 68–69
Partisanship, 32
Passionate love, 280
Patriarchy, 47, 252. See also Feminist theory
Peers and socialization, 123
People for the Ethical Treatment of Animals (PETA), 102
People's Temple, 328
Performances of the self, 120
Pharmaceutical industry, 380, 388
Philippines, 340
Piketty, Thomas, 202
Plato, 34
Play stage, 118

Pluralism, 233, 342
Poland, 340, 438
Political crimes, 186
Politics
　democracy, 339–40
　dictatorship, 341
　global, 343
　nations and nation-states, 160
　pluralism and power elite theory, 342
Polyandry, 279
Polygamy, 279
Population
　demographic transition theory, 396–97
　demography, 392
　fertility, 392–93
　growth, 402
　migration and, 397
　mortality and life expectancy, 395
Portugal, 433
Post-Fordism, 346
Postindustrial age, 4
Postindustrial society, 351
Postmodernism, 50
Postmodern theory, 50–51
Postpartum depression, 366
Poverty
　"culture of poverty," 226–27
　families and, 293
　feminization of, 206
　racial stratification, 235
Poverty line, 205
Power, 195–96
　wealth inequality and, 202
Prejudice and discrimination, 230, 241. See also Racism
Premenstrual dysphoric disorder (PMDD), 379
Premenstrual syndrome (PMS), 379
Preschool programs, 302, 308
Prestige, 195
Prestructured interviews, 71–72
Primary deviance, 180
Primary groups, 134
Primary socialization, 122
Princeton, 202
Prisons, 184
　private, 184
　simulation experiment, 83
　total institutions, 128
Private prisons, 184
Procedural objectivity, 87
Profession, 373
Program for International Student Assessment (PISA), 317–18
Proletariat, 35
Prosumer capitalism, 348–49
Prosumers, 351
Protestant ethic, 37
Prozac, 379
Psychology, 16
Puerto Rico, 439
Pugh, Allison, 127
Pure relationships, 369
Putnam, Robert, 62

Al-Qaeda, 11
Qualitative methods, 61, 66
Quantitative methods, 61, 67
Queer theory, 48
Questionnaires, 65, 73

Race
　cultural explanations, 226–27
　fluidity of categories, 227
　"scientific" explanations, 226
　whiteness and, 235–36
　See also Race and ethnicity
Race and ethnicity
　capital punishment and, 185
　civil rights movement, 238
　critical theory and, 49–50
　double consciousness, 41
　Du Bois's sociology, 40–41
　feminist theory and, 47
　global context, 240
　health-related issues, 377
　intelligence and, 306
　intersectionality, 50, 232
　majority-minority relations, 228
　mortality and, 396
　poverty and, 235
　social movements and, 237
　U.S. census data, 79
Race to the bottom, 219
Racial and ethnic identities, 225, 229
Racial/ethnic prejudice and discrimination, 230
Racial/ethnic stereotypes, 230
Racial segregation, 233, 306, 312
Racism, 224
　back stage, 120
　critical theory, 49–50
　definition, 234
　environmental, 405
　European, 49
　global flows, 243
　health and, 376
　institutional, 236
　social structure and, 235
Racist hate groups, 237–38
Ram, Uri, 61
Random sampling, 74
Raniere, Keith, 328
Rape, 245, 267
Rape cultures, 267
Rational choice theory, 54–55, 179
Rationality, 144
　bounded, 145
　bureaucracies and, 144
　modernity and, 50
Rationalization, 37
Rational-legal authority, 144
Real culture, 99
Rebels, 176
Recession crisis of 2007. See Great Recession
Recidivism, 184
Reciprocity, 129

Red Scare, 339
Reference groups, 135
Reflexivity, 366, 371
Refugees, 399
Relative poverty, 205
Reliability, 80
Religion
 consumption and, 356
 economy and, 37
 globalization and, 333
 global religions, 333
 secularization, 323
 types of institutions, 328
Religious fundamentalism, 333
Religious schools, 310
Representative democracies, 339
Research ethics, 80–87
Research methods. *See* Sociological research
Resocialization, 127
Resource mobilization theory, 435
Retreatists, 176
Reverse socialization, 123
Rights, 339
Riots, 440
Risk society, 158
Risky behavior, 373
Risley, Todd, 307
Rites of passage, 321
Ritualists, 176
Rituals, 320–21
Ritzer, George, 27, 61, 348
Rivera, Sylvia, 254
"Robbers Cave" experiment, 75, 77, 81
Roe v. Wade (1973), 428
Rohingya, 398
Role conflict, 132
Role making, 132
Role overload, 132
Roles, 132
Roma, 159, 244
Roman Catholic Church, 150, 332
Romantic love, 280
Romantic relationships and behaviors. *See* Marriage, Sexuality
Rostow, Walt, 214
Roszak, Theodore, 101
Rule creators, 180
Rule enforcers, 180
Russia
 as emigration destination, 334
 population decline, 402
 U.S. relationship, 344
Rwanda, 243, 245

Sacred, 320
Same-sex households, 287
Same-sex marriage, 172
Sampling, 74
Sanctions, 95
Sarafem, 379
Sassen, Saskia, 406
Saudi Arabia, 17, 185, 334
School funding, 306

School vouchers, 310
Science, technology, engineering, and math (STEM) fields, 256
"Scientific" explanations of race, 225–26
Scientific knowledge, 63
Scientific method, 60
Sea level rise, 414
Secondary data analysis, 77
Secondary deviance, 180
Secondary groups, 134
Sects, 327
Secularization, 323
Segregation, 233, 306
Self
 development of the, 115
 performances of the, 120
Seligman, Martin, 307
Service sector, 350
Sex, 250
Sex change, 54. *See also* Transgender
Sex hormones, 251
Sexting, 73
Sex tourism, 271
Sex trafficking, 270
Sexual assaults, 267–68
Sexual harassment, 430
Sexuality, 263
 culture and consent, 267
 deviance and, 173, 263
 ethnomethodological approach, 53
 exchange relationships, 54
 globalization of, 269
 "hooking up," 54
 observational research, 67
 risky behavior, 372
 social constraints and, 266–67
 See also Intimate relationships
Sexually transmitted infections (STIs), 384
Sexual orientation, 264
 prejudice and discrimination, 264
 queer theory, 48
 See also Homosexuality, Lesbian, gay, bisexual, queer and transgender (LGBQT) people
Sexual violence, 245
Sex work, 270–71
Sharia, 333
Sharing economy, 4, 199, 357
Shoedazzle, 22
Shopping haul videos, 261
Shopping malls, 22, 261
Significant symbols, 117
Simmel, George, 40, 132
Simulation, 51
Single-parent families, 286
Skateboarder subculture, 101
Skocpol, Theda, 79
Slovenia, 164
Smart cities, 408
Smartphones, 21, 25
 consumption and, 26
 socialization and, 125
 social movements and, 438
 widespread availability, 26

Smoking
 class and, 376
 deviance and, 173
 health risks, 372, 384
Snowden, Edward, 140, 445
Social change, 2, 424, 442
 collective action, 439
 disasters and, 442
 globalization and, 359
 internet and, 359, 442, 445
 workers' rights, 424
 See also Social movements
Social class
 conspicuous leisure and consumption, 42
 higher education enrollment and, 313–14
 intersectionality, 50
 leisure and, 42, 357
 Marxist theory, 35
 mortality and, 396
 power elite theory, 342
 social mobility, 204, 208
 taste and, 221
 wealth and, 202
 See also Economic inequality
Social constraints on sexuality, 266–67
Social construction of reality, 12
 gender differences, 48
 racial/ethnic difference, 230
Social control agents, 179
Social control theory, 180
Social Darwinism, 225
Social facts, 38
Socialization, 122
 adults, 128
 agents of, 122
 childhood, 122
 education and, 302
 families and, 122
 gender and, 123, 254
 mass media and, 124–25
 peers and, 123
 primary and anticipatory, 122
 resocialization, 127
 reverse, 123
Social media, 22, 438
 beauty and appearance related consumption, 368
 censorship, 140
 consumption and, 102
 crime and, 189
 critical theory and, 46
 crowdfunding and, 440
 impression management and, 120
 netiquette, 109
 netnography, 70
 prosumer capitalism, 348–49
 sharing economy, 4
 socialization and, 125
 social movements and, 438
 sociology and, 6
 suicide and, 62
 See also Facebook, Twitter, YouTube
Social mobility, 208

Social movements, 424
- civil rights, 238, 426
- collective action, 439
- factors in emergence of, 435
- factors in success of, 437
- globalization and, 438
- global women's movement, 274
- impact of, 438
- the internet and, 438
- LGBTQ, 431
- race/ethnicity and, 237
- resources and mobilization of, 436
- suppression of, 437–38
- women and, 426

Social networks, 132
Social performances, 120
Social processes, 14
Social reform, 15
Social sciences, 15
Social stratification, 195
- achievement, 196–97
- ascription, 197
- economic inequality, 198
- health care inequalities, 375–77
- mortality, 395
- social class, 195
- social mobility, 208
- status and power, 195
- status consistency, 195
- theories of, 208
- See also Economic inequality, Global stratification, Race and ethnicity, Social class

Social structures
- groups, 134
- interpersonal relationships, 132
- micro-level, 132–36
- networks, 132
- societies, 17
- See also Economy, Organizations, Societies

Social welfare programs, 347
Societies, 17, 157–59
Sociological imagination, 9–20
Sociological research, 65–66
- ethics, 80
- ethnography, 69
- experiments, 66, 75, 77
- historical-comparative, 79
- interviews, 65, 73
- netnography, 70
- objectivity and value-free sociology, 87
- observation, 65, 67–71
- qualitative, 61, 66
- quantitative, 61, 66–67
- sampling, 74
- scientific knowledge, 63–65
- scientific method, 60
- secondary data analysis, 77
- surveys, 65, 73
- validity and reliability, 80

Sociological theories, 32, 34
- conflict/critical, 45
- early theorists, 34
- emergence of, 34
- feminist, 47
- inter/actionist, 52–54
- postmodern, 50–51
- queer, 48
- structural/functional, 43–44
- See also Conflict/critical theories, Ethnomethodology, Feminist theory, Inter/actionist theories, Specific theorists, Structural/functional theory, Symbolic interactionism

Sociology
- blogging and tweeting about, 6
- common sense versus, 16
- historical roots, 3–4, 21
- as science, 54
- science versus reform, 21
- social sciences, 15, 23

Solidarity, 39
Solidarity movement of Poland, 438
Somalia, 211
South Africa, 212, 227, 426, 433, 438
Southern Poverty Law Center (SPLC), 238
South Korea, 18, 147, 368
South Sudan, 216
Spain, 105, 107, 285, 394, 433
Specific deterrence, 184
Spencer, Herbert, 34, 225
Sports
- health-related issues, 369
- health risks, 150
- socialization and, 123

Sri Lanka, 243, 331
Stacey, Clare L., 68
Starbucks, 356
Stark, Rodney, 324
States, 159
Statistics, 66
Status, 131, 195
Status consistency, 195
Stepfamilies, 287
Stereotypes
- gender, 250
- racial/ethnic, 230

Sterilization, 231
Stigmas, 181
Stonewall uprising, 254, 432
Strain theory, 175
Stratification. See Social stratification
Stratified samples, 74
Stress response, 378
Structural-functionalism, 43. See also Structural/functional theory
Structural/functional theory, 43–44
- deviance and, 175
- environmental issues, 409
- families, 288
- functions and dysfunctions, 43
- modernization, 214
- pluralism, 342
- religion, 328

Structuralism, 44–45. See also Structural/functional theory
Structural mobility, 208
Subcultures, 100

Suburbanization, 406
Suburbs, 403
Sudan, 211, 245, 398
Suicide
- Durkheim's research, 38–39, 62

Superior-subordinate interactions, 40
Survey research, 64, 73–74
- World Values Survey, 77

Sustainable development, 418
Sutherland, Edwin, 182
Swaziland, 395
Sweden, 147, 285, 368, 433
Symbolic interaction, 117
Symbolic interactionism, 52
- development of the self, 115–20
- families and, 290

Symbols as labels, 179
Syphilis, 384
Syria, 18, 140, 159, 216, 273, 333, 339, 344, 398, 439

Taliban, 333
Tariffs, 44, 164
Tattoos, 170, 371
Technology, 23–26
- education and, 26
- environmental issues and, 419
- global digital divide, 215
- informationalism, 157
- McDonaldization, 23
- medical, 389
- postindustrial age, 4
- religion and, 324
- sexualized, 268
- smart cities, 408
- See also Internet, Smartphones

Technoscapes, 161
Teenage birthrate, 393
Television
- socialization and, 125

Terrorism, international crime, 187
Testosterone, 251
Texting
- sexting, 73
- while driving, 372

Thailand, 212, 271, 331
Theories, 32. See also Sociological theories
Tiryakian, Edward, 214
T-Mobile, 153
Tobacco use. See Smoking
Tocqueville, Alexis de, 94
Tokyo, Japan, 406
Total institutions, 128
Tracking, 309, 319
Traditional authority, 144
Transgender, 254
- education and, 256
- history and context, 254
- president Trump and, 254

Transnational adoptions, 297
Transnational capitalism, 348
Transnational corporations, 348
Travel, 21

Triads, 133
Trump, Donald, 178
    globalization and, 17
    health care policy, 217, 377–79
    immigration policy, 19, 105, 398
    international trade policies, 163, 165
    news media and, 47
    North Korea and, 45
    offshore outsourcing and, 154
    opioid crisis and, 364
    the press and, 339
    racial perspective, 49
    transgender policy, 254
    use of authority, 143
    use of tweeting, 27
Trust of research subjects, 72
Tuberculosis, 384
Tufekci, Zeynep, 28
Tunisia, 445
Turkey, 159, 243, 294, 340, 398
Tuskegee study, 81, 85, 377
Twitter, 25
    critical theory and, 46, 48
    impression management and, 120
    president Trump and, 27
    social movements and, 438
    sociology and, 6
    See also Social media

Uber, 4, 199, 351
Ukraine, 216
Unanticipated consequences, 44
UN Decade for Women, 430
Underemployment, 354
Undernutrition, 383
Undocumented immigrants, 400, 424
    crime rates, 170
    global policies, 399
    labor unions and, 164
    population considerations, 397
    student support for, 12
    See also Immigrants, Migration and immigration
Unemployment, 303
UNICEF, 270
Unions, 146, 164, 199, 350
United Arab Emirates, 220
United Kingdom (Great Britain)
    Brexit, 17, 340
    as emigration destination, 334
    foreign aid and development, 220
    gender roles and, 255
    Global North, 211
    global surveillance system, 445
    immigrants and, 161, 398
    importance of religion in, 322
    same-sex marriage, 433
    single-parent families, 286
    social welfare programs, 347
United Nations, 343
United States and the Global North, 211
United States as a religious nation, 322–23
United States as emigration destination, 334

United States deindustrialization, 350
United States educational system, comparing with other systems, 317–19
United States health care inequalities, 376–77
United States-Mexico-Canada Agreement, 165
Universal citizenship, 339
Unschooling, 309
Unstructured interviews, 72
Upper class, 195
Upward mobility, 208
Urbanism, 403
Urbanization
    sexuality and, 269
    suburbanization, 406
    See also Cities
Uruguay, 212
USA Patriot Act, 188
U.S. Department of Homeland Security, 344
U.S. military
    divorce rates, 298
    don't ask, don't tell policy, 172
Uyghurs, 242

Validity, 80
Value-free sociology, 87
Values, 94, 101, 103
    globalization of, 107
    in social research, 87
    World Values Survey, 77
Veblen, Thorstein, 41
Venkatesh, Sudhir, 28, 72–73
Vertical mobility, 208
Video games, 5, 125, 429
Vietnam, 68, 211–12, 298, 331, 344
Vietnamese immigrants, 147
Violence
    and abuse within families, 290–94
    homicides, 186
    theories of, 32, 34
    See also Sexual assaults, War
Violent crime, 185
Virtual reality, 130
Vocal gestures, 117
Voucher systems, 309

Wage inequality, 373. See also Income inequality
Wage stagnation, 203
Walmart, 103, 141, 153, 155, 157, 348, 356
War, 343
    families and, 298–99
    health-related issues, 387
    sexual violence and, 245
Water, 405, 412
Wealth, 201
    global cities and, 406
    global concentration of, 213
    mortality and, 396
    See also Social class

Weber, Max, 34, 37, 61
    on bureaucracy, 141, 143, 145, 151
    on cities, 403
    historical-comparative research, 79
    on minority and minority groups, 228
    on Protestant ethic, 37
    value-free sociology, 87
Weinstein, Harvey, 430
Welfare programs, 347
Welfare states, 347
Wells, Ida B., 427
Whistle-blowers, 140
White-collar crime, 177, 186
White flight, 405
White racial frame, 235
Whyte, William F., 72
WikiLeaks, 445
Wikipedia, 104, 165
Wilson, William Julius, 353
Witch craze, 181
Wollstonecraft, Mary, 427
Women and girls as consumers, 261
Women in jails or prisons, 183
Women in organizations, 146
Women of color, 48, 232
Women's health, 379
Women's leisure, 358
Women's movements, 274, 426–30
Women's social mobility, 208
Work
    caregiving, 219
    educational attainment and, 303–4
    employment, unemployment, and underemployment, 354
    fast-food employees, 23
    gender and family intersections, 261
    gender inequalities, 147–219, 256, 260–61
    gig economy, 4
    health risks, 372
    labor migrants, 400
    mechanical and organic solidarity, 39
    occupational mobility, 208
    services, 350
    social stratification, 210
    See also Economy
Workers' rights, 424
World Bank, 150
World Social Forum (WSF), 102
World Values Survey (WVS), 77
World Women's Christian Temperance Union (WWCTU), 430
Wuthnow, Robert, 71

Yemen, 216, 273, 398
YouTube, 5, 368, 438. See also Social media
Yugoslavia, 243
Yum! Brands, 153

Ziblatt, Daniel, 341
Zika, 384
Zimbardo, Philip, 83
Zuckerberg, Mark, 195

S Sage College Publishing

Teaching isn't easy. | **Learning** never ends.
We are here for you.

 Learn more about Sage teaching and learning solutions for your course at **sagepub.com/collegepublishing**.

About Sage

Founded in 1965, Sage is a leading independent academic and professional publisher of innovative, high-quality content. Known for our commitment to quality and innovation, Sage has helped inform and educate a global community of scholars, practitioners, researchers, and students across a broad range of subject areas.

Cover Image: iStock.com/grinvalds

S **Sage**
www.sagepublications.com

ISBN 978-1-0718-7517-9